FUNDAMENTALS OF INVESTING

EIGHTH EDITION

LAWRENCE J. GITMAN
SAN DIEGO STATE UNIVERSITY

MICHAEL D. JOEHNK
ARIZONA STATE UNIVERSITY

Addison
Wesley

Boston San Francisco New York
London Toronto Sydney Tokyo Singapore Madrid
Mexico City Munich Paris Cape Town Hong Kong Montreal

**Dedicated to
Robin . . . 30 great years and counting . . .
and to
Colwyn Thomas Joehnk**

Editor-in-Chief: Denise Clinton
Acquisitions Editor: Donna Battista
Senior Project Manager: Mary Clare McEwing
Development Editor: Ann Torbert
Senior Production Supervisor: Nancy Fenton
Marketing Manager: Adrienne D'Ambrosio
Design Manager: Regina Hagen
Cover Designer: Leslie Haimes
Media Producer: Jennifer Pelland
Senior Manufacturing Buyer: Hugh Crawford
Project Coordination, Text Design, Art Studio, and Electronic Page Makeup:
    Thompson Steele, Inc.

For permission to use copyrighted material, grateful acknowledgment is made to the copyright holders
on pp. C-1–C-2, which are hereby made part of this copyright page.

Library of Congress Cataloging-in-Publication Data

Gitman, Lawrence J.
    Fundamentals of investing / Lawrence J. Gitman, Michael D. Joehnk. — 8th ed.
        p.   cm.
    Includes bibliographical references and index.
    ISBN 0-321-08808-5 (alk. paper)
        1. Investments.   2. Investments--Problems, exercises, etc.   I. Joehnk, Michael D.   II.
Title.

HG4521.G547   2001
332.6--dc21   2001024933

Please visit our Web site at http://www.awl.com

2 3 4 5 6 7 8 9 10—QWT—05 04 03 02

BRIEF CONTENTS

CONTENTS

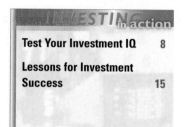
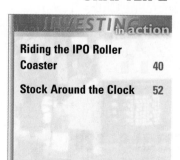

CHAPTER 3

ONLINE INVESTING, INFORMATION, AND TRADING 71

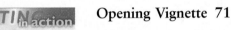

PART TWO

IMPORTANT CONCEPTUAL TOOLS 129

CHAPTER 4

INVESTMENT RETURN AND RISK 130

Opening Vignette 130

MODERN PORTFOLIO CONCEPTS 175

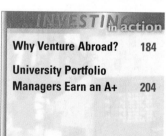

PART THREE — INVESTING IN COMMON STOCK 221

CHAPTER 6 — COMMON STOCK INVESTMENTS 222

INVESTING in action

CHAPTER 7 — ANALYTICAL DIMENSIONS OF STOCK SELECTION 272

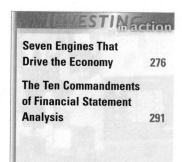

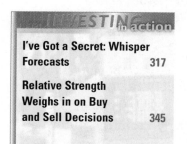

PART FOUR   INVESTING IN FIXED-INCOME SECURITIES 369

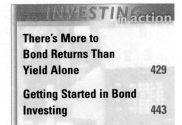

CHAPTER 11

PREFERRED STOCKS
AND CONVERTIBLE SECURITIES 453

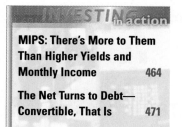

PART FIVE

PORTFOLIO MANAGEMENT 489

CHAPTER 12

MUTUAL FUNDS: PROFESSIONALLY MANAGED
INVESTMENT PORTFOLIOS 490

**Adding ETFs to your
Investment Portfolio   502**

**Knowing Where to Look Is
Half the Battle   526**

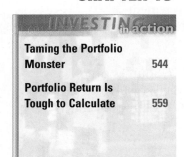

**Taming the Portfolio
Monster   544**

**Portfolio Return Is
Tough to Calculate   559**

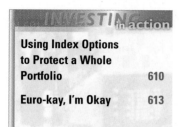
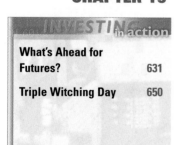

PREFACE

"It was the best of times. It was the worst of times." No, you haven't stumbled into an English course. But that opening line from *A Tale of Two Cities* really does describe the behavior of the stock market over the past couple of years. It applies especially to the Nasdaq market, which is home to most of the technology stocks—of both large and small technology companies. Consider, for example, that between January 1999 and March 2000, the Nasdaq Composite Index, a popular measure of market performance, rose an eye-popping 130%. But in the next twelve months, from March 2000 to March 2001, the index fell 57%. During that decline, four out of every ten stocks listed on the Nasdaq—about 1,700 stocks—lost 50% or more of their value. Among the losers were a number of well-known technology companies, including Sun Microsystems, Oracle Corporation, Cisco Systems, and Yahoo!

After nearly two decades of unprecedented growth in the stock market, the events of 1999 and 2000 are a reminder that economic recessions and falling markets really aren't a thing of the past after all. They do happen every now and then, and investors have to be prepared to deal with them. Fortunately, far more often than not, the investor is faced with the pleasant task of trying to make the most of a good ("bull") market. In the midst of market euphoria on one hand and the prospect of serious market decline on the other, stands the individual investor, wondering what to do with his or her investment capital. This book offers guidance in today's investment environment.

This eighth edition of *Fundamentals of Investing* serves investors who wish to actively develop and monitor their own investment portfolios. It meets the needs of professors and students in the first course in investments offered at colleges and universities, junior and community colleges, professional certification programs, and continuing education courses. Focusing on both individual securities and portfolios, *Fundamentals of Investing* explains how to implement investment goals in light of risk-return tradeoffs. A conversational tone and liberal use of examples guide students through the material and demonstrate important points.

Key Features of the Eighth Edition

Using information gathered from both academicians and practicing investment professionals, plus feedback from adopters, the eighth edition reflects the realities of today's investment environment. At the same time, it provides a structured framework for successful teaching and learning.

Clear Focus on the Individual Investor

Today, about half of all U.S. households own stock either directly or indirectly [through mutual funds or participation in 401(k)s]. The focus of

Fundamentals of Investing has always been on the individual investor. This focus gives students the information they need to plan, implement, and manage a successful investment program. It also provides students with a solid foundation of basic concepts, tools, and techniques. Subsequent courses can build on that foundation by presenting the advanced concepts, tools, and techniques used by institutional investors and money managers.

Comprehensive yet Flexible Organization

The text provides a firm foundation for learning by first describing the overall investment environment, including online investing. Next it presents conceptual tools needed by investors—the concepts of risk and return and the basics of portfolio construction. It then examines each of the popular investment vehicles—common stocks, bonds, preferred stocks, convertible securities, and mutual funds. Following this series of chapters on investment vehicles comes a chapter on how to administer one's own portfolio. The final section of the book focuses on derivative securities—options and futures—which require more expertise. Although the first two parts of the textbook are best covered at the start of the course, instructors can cover particular investment vehicles in just about any sequence. The comprehensive yet flexible nature of the book enables instructors to customize it to their own course structure and teaching objectives.

We organized each chapter according to a decision-making perspective, and we have been careful always to point out the pros and cons of the various vehicles and strategies that we present. With this information, individual investors can select the investment actions that are most consistent with their objectives. In addition, we've illustrated investment vehicles and strategies in such a way that students learn the decision-making implications and consequences of each investment action they contemplate.

Timely Topics

Various issues and developments constantly reshape financial markets and investment vehicles. Virtually all topics in this book take into account changes in the investment environment. For example, sources of online investment information, as well as the process of online investing, are covered in Chapter 3. Similarly, coverage of tech stocks (in Chapters 6 and 8) presents timely information needed for a thorough understanding of today's investment opportunities.

Globalization

One issue that is reshaping investing is the growing globalization of securities markets. As a result, *Fundamentals of Investing* continues to stress the global aspects of investing. We initially look at the growing importance of international markets, investing in foreign securities (indirectly or directly), international investment performance, and the risks of investing internationally. In later chapters, popular international investment opportunities and strategies are described as part of the coverage of each specific type of investment vehicle. This integration of international topics helps students understand the importance of maintaining a global focus when planning, building, and managing an investment portfolio. Global topics are highlighted by inclusion of a globe icon.

Comprehensive and Integrated Learning System

Another feature of the eighth edition is its comprehensive and integrated learning system. Learning Goals at the beginning of each chapter are the central feature of this proven teaching/learning system. Each Learning Goal is tied by a special icon to the associated first-level head in the text, and these goals are restated and reviewed, point by point, at the chapter's end. To support these Learning Goals, Concepts in Review questions appear at the end of each section of the chapter. These review questions allow students to test their understanding of each section before moving on to the next section of the chapter. In addition, each goal is keyed to the end-of-chapter discussion questions, problems, cases, and selected supplements.

By focusing on the Learning Goals, students will know what material they need to learn, where they can find it in the chapter, and whether they've mastered it by the end of the chapter. In addition, instructors can build lectures and assignments around the Learning Goals.

Enriched Web Site

This edition of *Fundamentals of Investing* features a Web site that is enriched with additional information that should be of interest to students and professors. Visitors will find links to the sites mentioned in the Hot Links boxes in each chapter; links to sites mentioned in the Web Exercises at the end of chapters; interviews with investors, who share their investing philosophies and their successes or failures; information on more investors' resources; a calculator keystrokes manual; and the *Fundamentals of Investing* software. The Hot Links to other sites will be updated regularly, to minimize the problem of "dead" links. Tax laws will also be regularly updated at this Web site. Also available at the Web site are additional *Investing in Action* essays on various topics and additional material that is beyond the normal scope of the first-level investments course. These enrichment materials are referenced in the Hot Links boxes in the textbook.

Also at the book's Web site are two complete chapters that appeared in the book in earlier editions: "Real Estate and Other Tangible Investments" and "Tax-Advantaged Investments." These highly informative chapters were updated and moved to the Web site in response to user, reviewer, and our own preference that the text focus solely on securities investing. In addition to its improved focus, moving these chapters to the Web site allows us both to tighten and improve a number of text discussions and to shorten the text's overall length. We feel this change improves the text's effectiveness in terms of both content and length.

Specific Content Changes

Our many adopters are interested first and foremost in how the content has changed from the seventh to the eighth edition. We hope that this same information will interest potential new adopters also, because it indicates our desire to stay current with the field of investments and to shape a book that will truly meet the classroom needs of professors and students.

Organizational Changes

Before we list the chapter-by-chapter content changes, we should first describe some organizational changes in the chapter sequence, along with the rationale for such changes. Many of these changes were made after careful consideration of suggestions made by users of the book and by reviewers.

The key changes are these:

- *Portfolio concepts now are included as Chapter 5 in the new Part Two.* Chapter 16 ("Portfolio Construction") from the seventh edition has been revised, restructured, retitled ("Modern Portfolio Concepts"), and moved to appear as Chapter 5, following the chapter on investment return and risk. Together these chapters make up Part Two, "Important Conceptual Tools." These changes allow students to gain a solid grasp of important return, risk, and portfolio concepts before they learn about specific investment securities and strategies. This revision is a major factor in improving the text's focus.

- *The mutual fund and portfolio administration chapters are included in the new Part Five.* In the seventh edition, these topics were covered in Chapter 13 ("Mutual Funds") and Chapter 17 ("Portfolio Management and Control"). Revised versions of these two chapters now make up Part Five, "Portfolio Management." Chapter 12, "Mutual Funds: Professionally Managed Investment Portfolios," focuses on the key aspects of mutual funds and their use as professionally managed portfolios; Chapter 13, "Administering Your Own Portfolio," emphasizes the basics of portfolio administration—monitoring and managing a portfolio—from the perspective of an individual investor. The placement of Part Five immediately after the chapters covering traditional investment securities allows professors who do not choose to cover derivative securities (now in Part Six) to bring convenient and logical closure to the investment process.

- *The revised derivatives chapters have been moved to the end of the book.* The two derivatives chapters have been moved from Part Four (Chapters 11 and 12) in the seventh edition to appear now as Part Six (Chapters 14 and 15), at the end of the book. As noted above, this revision was made to improve the text's focus and to allow those professors who cover only the traditional investment securities presented in Parts Three and Four (Chapters 6 through 11) to cover Part Five on portfolio management (Chapters 12 and 13) in sequence. The new organization was requested by both users and reviewers in order to improve the structure and length of the text.

- *Two chapters have been moved out of the book and onto the book's Web site.* As mentioned above, Chapter 14 ("Real Estate and Other Tangible Investments") and Chapter 15 ("Tax-Advantaged Investments"), which appeared together with the mutual fund chapter in Part Five of the seventh edition, have been revised, updated, and moved to the book's Web site. This revision was driven by both the desire to keep the text's focus on securities investing and to reduce the book's length to better align with one-semester or one-quarter courses. For those professors wishing to cover real estate, other tangible investments, or tax-advantaged investments, the Web-based chapters are readily available.

Chapter-by-Chapter Content Changes

- *Chapter 1*, on the role and scope of investments, now includes a brief restructured discussion of making investment plans based on the presentation of investment planning that was included in Chapter 3 of the seventh edition. Also moved into this chapter (from Chapter 3 of the seventh edition) is a discussion of meeting liquidity needs by investing in short-term vehicles. This discussion has been revised to be more descriptive; also, the formulas for bond equivalent yield (BEY) and Treasury-bill yield have been moved to our Web site. In addition, the discussions of real estate, other tangible investments, and tax-advantaged investments have been shortened, consistent with the removal of these topics from the text to our Web site. Updates on tax changes have been added to our Web site.

- *Chapter 2*, on investment markets and transactions, includes an expanded discussion of the primary market, including going public (the IPO process) and the investment banker's role. A discussion of alternative trading systems, including electronic communications networks (ECNs), is now included in the coverage of the over-the-counter market. The discussion of globalization of securities markets has been updated and streamlined. Additionally, coverage of trading hours and regulation of securities markets has been revised and expanded and now appears as a separate section. The discussions of the basic types of securities transactions have also been revised and streamlined.

- *Chapter 3*, on online investing, information, and trading, begins with a new section on online investing and using the Internet wisely. The coverage of investment planning and short-term vehicles has been moved from this chapter to Chapter 1. Revised and expanded references to online sources have been integrated throughout the chapter. A discussion and table of the investment information sources have been added to the chapter. Coverage of making securities transactions (moved from Chapter 2 of the seventh edition) includes separate subsections on online trading of stocks, bonds, and mutual funds. Also included in the section on online stock trading are discussions of day trading, technical and service problems, and tips for successful online trades. The discussion of investment decisions has been expanded to include coverage of and reference to sources of online investment advice.

- *Chapter 4*, on investment return and risk, now includes text explanations of financial table and calculator use in the time value of money discussions and in the discussions of yield and growth-rate calculations. In addition, marginal calculator displays showing keystrokes accompany these new text explanations. These computational improvements make this chapter more useful to students in applying the important concepts that are presented.

- *Chapter 5*, on modern portfolio concepts, has been moved up from Chapter 16 in the seventh edition and coupled with Chapter 4, to convey the key conceptual tools to readers early in the course. The chapter has been restructured to provide a more conceptual focus. It includes the basic CAPM coverage from Chapter 4 of the seventh edition, which is now integrated into the discussion of portfolio risk and diversification. In addition, the discussion of the benefits of international diversification has been expanded.

- *Chapter 6,* on common stock investments, contains updated information on market performance through the third quarter of 2000, including the remarkable behavior of the Nasdaq during 1999 and 2000. Also new to this edition is discussion of the comparative performance of the Dow, the S&P, and the Nasdaq, as well as an entire new section on the active tech-stock segment of the market, plus some interesting discussion of several popular investment styles, like growth, value, income, sector rotation, and momentum investing.

- *Chapter 7,* on analytical dimensions of stock selection, has undergone major modifications with the introduction of a new company being used as the basis of analysis and valuation. The new firm is a growth-oriented company that straddles both the old economy and the ever-expanding world of technology. Such a company offers the student the opportunity to deal with both the challenges and the rewards of valuing and investing in seasoned but rapidly growing companies.

- *Chapter 8,* on stock valuation and investment decisions, has also undergone some major revisions, particularly with respect to the valuation of different types of companies. This new edition emphasizes the valuation not only of mature, dividend-paying stocks, but also of rapidly growing stocks that pay little or nothing in dividends. Also new is a section on the valuation of tech stocks, where we look at companies that may not even have much in the way of earnings, let alone dividends.

- *Chapter 9,* on bond investments, includes updated information on market performance through mid-2000. New to this edition is a section dealing with comparative returns on stocks and bonds during the 1990s, along with discussion of the effects that the budget surplus is having on the market for U.S. Treasury securities.

- *Chapter 10,* on bond valuation and analysis, continues its focus on the various valuation procedures employed in the bond market, including different yield measures, bond pricing, and bond price volatility (duration). In this edition, we've added coverage of yield-to-call, and at several points in the chapter, we show how financial calculators can be used to determine prices and measure yields.

- *Chapter 11,* on preferred stocks and convertible securities, has been thoroughly updated to reflect the latest market trends, including the use of convertible securities to help finance the growing need for capital in the high-tech sector of the market. Calculator solutions have been added to this chapter, showing how financial calculators can be used to compute the expected return on a convertible bond.

- *Chapter 12,* on mutual funds, has been revised and updated throughout and now includes some valuable statistical information on the growth of the mutual fund industry. Also new to this chapter is an entire section on one of the hottest new products in the mutual fund arena, exchange-traded funds (ETFs).

- *Chapter 13,* on administering your own portfolio, has been developed from Chapter 17 in the seventh edition. The chapter's focus was improved by including in it the discussion of portfolio planning in action from

Chapter 16 of the seventh edition. The discussions that focus on evaluating the performance of individual investments have been revised, updated, and streamlined for consistency with the text's improved focus on traditional securities investments. The new chapter features improved balance between the practical and quantitative aspects of portfolio administration.

- *Chapter 14,* on options (puts, calls, and warrants), presents added coverage of stock options contracts and now provides expanded discussion of the valuation of stock-index options. The chapter continues the theme of showing how these investment vehicles can be used both to enhance yields and modify risks.

- *Chapter 15,* on commodities and financial futures, provides up-to-date coverage of financial futures products. Also added in this edition is expanded coverage of the use of futures contracts as hedging vehicles.

Pedagogical Features

This textbook has long been recognized for its numerous pedagogical features, designed to help students focus their study of investments. Among the useful features it includes are Learning Goals, *Investing in Action* boxed essays, Investor Facts, Internet linkages, Concepts in Review questions, a marginal glossary, and varied end-of-chapter materials. New in this edition are calculator keystrokes and the CFA exam questions.

LG 1 ### Learning Goals

Each chapter begins with Learning Goals, labeled with numbered icons (noted at left of head), that clearly state the concepts and materials to be covered. The Learning Goal icons are tied to first-level headings, are reviewed point by point at the chapter's end, and are keyed to end-of-chapter discussion questions, problems, and cases.

Alongside the chapter's Learning Goals at the beginning of each chapter is a brief story (opening vignette). It features an investment situation involving a real company or event and ties it to the chapter topics, to help motivate student interest in the chapter.

Investing in Action

Each chapter features two boxed essays, called *Investing in Action,* that also describe real-life investing situations or events. Although we have revised and retained a few of the most popular boxes from the previous edition, the majority are new. These high-interest boxes, which have been written specifically for this textbook, demonstrate concepts introduced in the text and enliven the students' reading at a level consistent with their abilities.

Investor Facts

Each chapter also contains two to three Investor Facts—brief sidebar items that give an interesting statistic or cite an unusual investment experience. The facts and figures in these boxes are intended to stimulate student interest and motivate further thought. For example, the Investor Facts box on page 223 (Chapter 6) discusses the differences between a routine market decline, a market correction, and a bear market. The Investor Facts on page 281 (Chapter 7) compares GDP rates of various countries. And an Investor Facts on page 553 (Chapter 13) suggests what you can do if you need to calculate a capital gain for tax purposes but have kept bad records.

Internet Linkages

The growth of the Internet and its increasing use in college coursework has impelled us to add several types of Internet linkages in the eighth edition. The first is *Hot Links* boxes, which are interspersed throughout. These inserts refer students to Web sites related to the topic being covered in the text.

The second Internet linkage is to the textbook's home page (at www.awl .com/gitman_joehnk). As described earlier, this resource offers a wide variety of informational resources for students and instructors including tax law updates.

Finally, each chapter ends with Web Exercises, which are described under the heading "End-of-Chapter Materials" later in the Preface.

We feel certain that the inclusion of these rich Internet linkages in the eighth edition of the textbook adds further realism and a timely source of useful information for both students and instructors.

Concepts in Review

Included in each chapter are several Concepts in Review elements, each of which contains a series of questions dealing with the topics that have just been discussed. These Concepts in Review questions appear at the end of each section of the chapter (positioned before the next first-level heading) and are marked with a special design element. As students progress through the chapter, they can test their understanding of each concept, tool, or technique before moving on to the next section. Included are Concepts in Review questions related to the *Investing in Action* boxes. These questions help to integrate the key concepts in the boxes with the text material. Answers to these questions can be found on the book's Web site (at www.awl.com/gitman_joehnk).

Marginal Glossary

New terms are set in boldface type and defined when first introduced in the text. In addition, each term appears with its definition in the text margin, to facilitate student learning and review. The page numbers on which these entries appear within the text are noted in boldface in the book's index, to make it easy to find these definitions.

Calculator Keystrokes

At appropriate places in the book, we have added sections on use of financial tables and financial calculators. Chapter 4, for example, shows how a variety of time value calculations can readily be made with the aid of financial tables and a handheld financial calculator. It also demonstrates the use of a financial calculator to make yield and growth-rate calculations. In Chapter 10 we illustrate the use of a calculator in computing various bond yield and pricing measures. Also, in Chapters 11 and 14 we show how the calculator can be used to find the expected return on a convertible bond and a warrant, respectively. These brief new sections are accompanied by new marginal calculator graphics that show the inputs and functions to be used. (See page 141 for an example.)

End-of-Chapter Materials

A number of important elements at the end of each chapter reinforce the concepts, tools, and techniques described in the chapter and help students review and integrate chapter content.

Summary Each summary lists the chapter's key concepts and ideas, which correspond directly to the numbered Learning Goals presented at the beginning of the chapter. The Learning Goal icons precede each summary item, which begins with a boldfaced restatement of the learning goal.

Discussion Questions A handful of thought-provoking Discussion Questions, keyed to the Learning Goals, are included. They guide students to integrate, investigate, and analyze the key concepts presented in the chapter. Many questions require that students apply the tools and techniques presented in the chapter to investment information they have obtained, and then make a recommendation with regard to a specific investment strategy or vehicle. These project-type questions are far broader than the Concepts in Review questions included within the chapter.

 Problems A set of 8 to 15 Problems is included at the end of each chapter. Keyed to the Learning Goals, the problems vary in complexity and scope and thus ensure professors a wide choice of assignable materials. An icon appears next to those Problems that can be solved using the *Fundamentals of Investing* software described below.

Case Problems Two Case Problems, keyed to the Learning Goals, encourage students to use higher-level critical thinking skills: to apply techniques presented in the chapter, to evaluate alternatives, and to recommend how an investor might solve a specific problem.

Web Exercises The Web Exercises—fully revised in the eighth edition—require students to obtain data, information, or computational assistance from particular Web sites in order to answer questions or solve simple problems. These Web sites are linked through our book's home page at www.awl.com/gitman _joehnk. S. P. Umamaheswar Rao of the University of Louisiana revised and updated these Web exercises, as well as the *Hot Links* boxes, described earlier.

CFA Exam Questions

New in the eighth edition, CFA Exam Questions appear at the end of five of the book's six parts. (Due to the nature of the material in some of the early chapters, the CFA questions for Parts One and Two are combined, and appear at the end of Part Two.) A series of 8 to 12 questions per part offer students an opportunity to test their investment knowledge against that required for the CFA Level I exam. These questions have been taken from old CFA Level I exams and from the study material provided by AIMR (the Association for Investment Management and Research). Answers to the questions are provided at the end of each set of CFA Exam Questions.

Supplemental Materials

We recognize the key role of a complete and creative package of materials to supplement a basic textbook. We believe that the following materials, offered with the eighth edition, will enrich the investments course for both students and instructors.

Fundamentals of Investing Software

The *Fundamentals of Investing* software can be downloaded from this text's Web site. It was revised and improved for this edition by Kathryn E. Coates and David Geis of KDC Software Solutions to include a calculator tutorial and graphing capabilities for selected problems. The purpose of the software is to perform the calculations of virtually all of the formulas, ratios, and valuation procedures presented in the book. The software is very user-friendly and fully interactive. More than a problem solver, it also enhances the student's understanding of the investment process. The software is keyed to all applicable text discussions and end-of-chapter and ancillary materials with the icon shown to the left of the heading above. Detailed instruction for using the software can be found on this text's Web site: www.awl.com/gitman_joehnk.

Fundamentals of Investing Homepage

As described earlier, the book's homepage offers students and professors a rich, dynamic, and up-to-date source of supplemental materials. This resource is located at www.awl.com/gitman_joehnk. Visitors to the site will find links to the sites mentioned in the text, including updates whenever a site moves or disappears, additional material not found in the text, a downloadable copy of "Using Financial and Business Calculators," a link to our online career center, the downloadable software mentioned above, and more. Instructors will also receive access to the instructions for the *Student Investment Management (SIM) Game,* described below.

Study Guide

The Study Guide to accompany *Fundamentals of Investing,* Eighth Edition, prepared by Karin B. Bonding, CFA, of the McIntire School at the University of Virginia and President of Capital Markets Institute, Inc., Ivy, Virginia, has been completely revised. Each chapter of the *Study Guide* contains a chapter summary, a chapter outline, and a programmed self-test that consists of true-false and multiple-choice questions. Following the self-test are problems with detailed solutions and, where appropriate, calculator key strokes showing use of the calculator to solve certain problems. All elements are similar in form and content to those found in the book.

Instructor's Manual

Written by the text authors, with the assistance of Joseph Greco of California State University, Fullerton, the *Instructor's Manual* contains chapter outlines; a list of major topics discussed in each chapter; detailed chapter reviews; answers/suggested answers to all Concepts in Review questions, Discussion Questions, and Problems; solutions to the Case Problems; and ideas for outside projects. Instructions for outside projects are printed on separate sheets, for ease in duplicating them for classroom distribution.

Test Bank

Revised for the eighth edition by Kay Johnson of Pennsylvania State University, Erie, the *Test Bank* now includes a substantial number of new questions. Each chapter now contains approximately 15 to 35 true-false questions, 40 to 60 multiple-choice questions, and several problems and short-essay questions. The *Test Bank* is also available in Test Generator Software (TestGen-EQ with QuizMaster-EQ for Windows). Fully networkable, this software is available for Windows and Macintosh. TestGen-EQ's friendly graphical interface enables instructors to easily view, edit, and add questions; export questions to create tests; and print tests in a variety of fonts and forms. Search and sort features let the instructor quickly locate questions and arrange them in a preferred order. QuizMaster-EQ automatically grades the exams, stores results on disk, and allows the instructor to view or print a variety of reports.

PowerPoint Transparency Slides

To facilitate classroom presentations, PowerPoint slides of key text images are available for Windows and Macintosh. A PowerPoint viewer is provided for use by those who do not have the full software program.

The Student Investment Management (SIM) Game

Written by S. P. Umamaheswar Rao of the University of Louisiana, *The Student Investment Management (SIM) Game* is designed to teach students about investing and trading in the stock market, using the Internet for information processing and online research, and applying the theory and analytical tools they have learned from this text to real-world situations. Students learn to think and act like professionals as they make choices about the stocks in their portfolios. As game participants, they discover the risks and rewards involved in decision making, and they can see how some of their stock selection techniques stack up against those of other traders. By frequently checking and rebalancing their portfolios, game participants make educated guesses about the direction of the stock market, interest rates, and the overall economy. The game lasts for up to 10 weeks; by its end students will have a new sense of the markets—how they function and what they mean.

Internet Guide for Finance

Written by Chip Wiggins and Patrick Gregory of Bentley College, this booklet showcases the many ways in which technology in general and the Internet in particular have influenced the ways in which students study finance today. The authors address such issues as how technology has affected the infrastructure of finance courses, how the Internet can be used to enrich the study of finance, what kinds of eCareers are open in finance, and how technology affects students' lives more generally as they find themselves more and more part of an eCampus.

Acknowledgments

Many people gave their generous assistance during the initial development and revisions of *Fundamentals of Investing*. The expertise, classroom experience, and general advice of both colleagues and practitioners have been invaluable. Reactions and suggestions from students throughout the country—comments we especially enjoy receiving—sustained our belief in the need for a fresh, informative, and teachable investments text.

A few individuals provided significant subject matter expertise in the initial development of the book. They are Terry S. Maness of Baylor University, Arthur L. Schwartz, Jr., of the University of South Florida at St. Petersburg, and Gary W. Eldred. Their contributions are greatly appreciated. In addition, Addison-Wesley obtained the advice of a large group of experienced reviewers. We appreciate their many suggestions and criticisms, which have had a strong influence on various aspects of this volume. Our special thanks go to the following people, who reviewed all or part of the manuscript for the previous seven editions of the book.

M. Fall Ainina
Gary Baker
Harisha Batra
Richard B. Bellinfante
Cecil C. Bigelow
Paul Bolster
A. David Brummett
Gary P. Cain
Gary Carman
Daniel J. Cartell
P. R. Chandy
David M. Cordell
Timothy Cowling
Robert M. Crowe
Richard F. DeMong
Clifford A. Diebold
James Dunn
Betty Marie Dyatt
Steven J. Elbert
Thomas Eyssell

Frank J. Fabozzi
Robert A. Ford
Albert J. Fredman
Chaim Ginsberg
Joel Gold
Frank Griggs
Brian Grinder
Harry P. Guenther
Mahboubul Hassan
Gay Hatfield
Robert D. Hollinger
Sue Beck Howard
Roland Hudson, Jr.
Donald W. Johnson
Ravindra R. Kamath
Bill Kane
Daniel J. Kaufmann, Jr.
Nancy Kegelman
Phillip T. Kolbe
Sheri Kole

Christopher M. Korth
Thomas M. Krueger
George Kutner
Robert T. LeClair
Chun I. Lee
Larry A. Lynch
Weston A. McCormac
David J. McLaughlin
Keith Manko
Timothy Manuel
Kathy Milligan
Warren E. Moeller
Homer Mohr
Majed R. Muhtaseb
Joseph Newhouse
Joseph F. Ollivier
John Park
Thomas Patrick
Ronald S. Pretekin
Stephen W. Pruitt

William A. Richard
Linda R. Richardson
William A. Rini
Roy A. Roberson
Edward Rozalewicz
William J. Ruckstuhl
David Russo
Keith V. Smith
Pat R. Stout
Nancy E. Strickler
Glenn T. Sweeney
Amir Tavakkol
Phillip D. Taylor
Wenyuh Tsay
Robert C. Tueting
Howard E. Van Auken
John R. Weigel
Peter M. Wichert
John C. Woods
Richard H. Yanow

The following people provided extremely useful reviews and input to the eighth edition:

Ping Hsiao, *San Francisco State University*

Larry Lynch, *Roanoke College*

John Palffy, *Wayne State University*

Michael Polakoff, *University of Maryland at College Park*

Barbara Poole, *Central Connecticut State University*

S. P. Umamaheswar Rao, *University of Louisiana at Lafayette*

Arthur L. Schwartz, Jr., *University of South Florida at St. Petersburg*

Howard Van Auken, *Iowa State University*

Because of the wide variety of topics covered in the book, we called upon many experts for advice. We thank them and their firms for allowing us to draw on their insights and awareness of recent developments, to ensure that the text is as current as possible. In particular, we want to mention Jeff Buetow, CFA, BFRC Services, Charlottesville, VA; John Markese, President, American Association of Individual Investors, Chicago, IL; George Ebenhack, Oppenheimer & Co., Los Angeles, CA; Mark D. Erwin, Northwestern Mutual Financial Network, San Diego, CA; Richard Esposito, Prana Investments, Inc., New York; Dennis P. Hickman, La Jolla, CA; Andrew Temte, CFA, Schweser Study Program, La Crosse, WI; Martin P. Klitzer, Sunrise Capital Partners, Del Mar, CA; David M. Love, C.P. Eaton and Associates, Rancho Santa Fe, CA; David H. McLaughlin, Chase Investment Counsel Corp., Charlottesville, VA; Michael R. Murphy, Sceptre Investment Counsel, Toronto, Ontario, Canada; Mark S. Nussbaum, PaineWebber, La Jolla, CA; John Richardson, Northern Trust Bank of Arizona, Phoenix, AZ; Pat Rupp, IDS, Inc., Dayton, OH; Richard Russell, Dow Theory Letters, La Jolla, CA; Mike Smith, Economic Analysis Corporation, Los Angeles, CA; Fred Weaver, Washington Mutual, Phoenix, AZ; and Lynn Yturri, BancOne Arizona, Phoenix, AZ.

We greatly appreciate the support of our colleagues at San Diego State University and Arizona State University. Special thanks to attorney Robert J. Wright of Wright & Wrights, CPAs, San Diego, for his help in revising and updating the many tax discussions, and to Professor Edward Nelling of Drexel University for his help in preparing the material on tech stocks and tech-stock valuation. We also thank S. P. Umamaheswar Rao ("Spuma") of the University of Louisiana for his work on the Hot Links and Web exercises of the eighth edition and for his creation of *The Student Investment Management (SIM) Game;* Karin Bonding of the University of Virginia for her useful feedback and for revising the *Study Guide;* Kay Johnson of Pennsylvania State University, Erie, for revising and updating the *Test Bank;* Joseph Greco of California State University, Fullerton, for revising and updating the *Instructor's Manual;* Tom Krueger and Dianne Morrison of the University of Wisconsin, La Crosse, for their careful reviews of the *Study Guide, Test Bank,* and *Instructor's Manual;* and Chip Wiggins and Patrick Gregory of Bentley College for creating the extremely useful *Internet Guide for Finance,* which accompanies this book.

Special thanks to Marlene Bellamy of Writeline Associates, La Jolla, California, for her work in updating certain chapters and preparing chapter vignettes, *Investing in Action* boxes, and *Investor Facts*. Our thanks also go to Kaye Coates and David Geis of KDC Software Solutions for developing the *Fundamentals of Investing* software.

The staff at Addison-Wesley, particularly Donna Battista and Denise Clinton, contributed their creativity, enthusiasm, and commitment to this text-book. Freelance development editor Ann Torbert, senior project manager Mary Clare McEwing of Addison-Wesley, Nancy Freihofer of Thompson Steele Production Services, senior production supervisor Nancy Fenton of Addison-Wesley, senior designer Regina Hagen of Addison-Wesley, and media producer Jennifer Pelland of Addison-Wesley warrant special thanks for shep-herding the project through the development, production, and Web site con-struction stages. Without their care and concern, this text would not have evolved into the teachable and interesting text we believe it to be.

Finally, our wives, Robin and Charlene, and our children, Jessica and Zachary, and Chris and Terry and his wife, Sara, played important roles by providing support and understanding during the book's development, revision, and production. We are forever grateful to them, and we hope that this edition will justify the sacrifices required during the many hours we were away from them working on this book.

Lawrence J. Gitman

Michael D. Joehnk

CHAPTER 1

THE ROLE AND SCOPE OF INVESTMENTS

LEARNING GOALS

After studying this chapter, you should be able to:

LG 1 Understand the meaning of the term *investment* and the factors commonly used to differentiate among types of investments.

LG 2 Describe the investment process and types of investors.

LG 3 Discuss the principal types of investment vehicles.

LG 4 Describe the steps in investing, particularly establishing investment goals, and cite fundamental personal tax considerations.

LG 5 Discuss investing over the life cycle and investing in different economic environments.

LG 6 Understand the popular types of short-term investment vehicles.

I n just a few years, the world of investments has moved to center stage in American life. Twenty years ago, most people's only exposure to investment news was a 10-second announcement on the evening news about the change in the Dow Jones Industrial Average that day.

Today, about half of all Americans own stocks, and 20% of them only began investing after 1996. Cable TV stations such as CNNfn and CNBC specialize in business and financial news. You can't pass a newsstand without seeing headlines that scream, "Ten Stocks to Buy Now!" or "The Hottest Mutual Funds." Besides the *Wall Street Journal*, you can subscribe to *Investor's Business Daily, Financial Times, Barron's, Kiplinger's Personal Finance Magazine, Money, Smart Money,* and dozens more publications that focus on investing.

The Internet has played a large role in opening the world of investing to individual investors. By giving them access to tools formerly restricted to investment professionals, it creates a more level playing field. The Internet also places enormous amounts of information and a means of trading securities just a few mouse clicks away. In short, technology makes investing much easier, but it can also increase the risks for inexperienced investors.

Regardless of whether you make transactions online or use a traditional broker, the same investment fundamentals presented in this textbook apply. The first chapter introduces you to the types of investments, the investment process, key investment vehicles, the role of investment plans, and the importance of meeting liquidity needs. Becoming familiar with investment alternatives and developing realistic investment plans should greatly increase your chance of financial success.

Investments and the Investment Process

LG 1　LG 2

Note: The Learning Goals shown at the beginning of the chapter are keyed to text discussions using these icons.

investment
any vehicle into which funds can be placed with the expectation that it will generate positive income and/or preserve or increase its value.

returns
the rewards from investing, received as current income and/or increased value.

securities
investments that represent evidence of debt or ownership or the legal right to acquire or sell an ownership interest.

property
investments in real property or in tangible personal property.

direct investment
investment in which an investor directly acquires a claim on a security or property.

indirect investment
investment made in a *portfolio,* or collection of securities or properties.

portfolio
collection of securities or properties, typically constructed to meet one or more investment goals.

debt
funds lent in exchange for interest income and the promised repayment of the loan at a given future date.

If you have money in a savings account, you already have at least one investment to your name. An **investment** is simply any vehicle into which funds can be placed with the expectation that it will generate positive income and/or that its value will be preserved or increased. The rewards, or **returns,** from investing are received in two basic forms: current income and increased value. For example, money invested in a savings account provides current income in the form of periodic interest payments. A share of common stock purchased as an investment is expected to increase in value between the time it is purchased and the time it is sold.

Is cash placed in a simple (no-interest) checking account an investment? No, because it fails both tests of the definition. It does not provide added income, nor does its value increase. (In fact, the value of the cash in a checking account is likely to decrease, because it is eroded over time by inflation.)

We begin our study of investments by looking at types of investments and at the structure of the investment process.

Types of Investments

When you invest, the organization in which you invest—whether it is a company or a government entity—offers you an expected future benefit in exchange for the current use of your funds. Organizations compete for the use of your funds. The one that will get your investment dollars is the one that offers a benefit you judge to be better than any competitor offers. But, different investors judge benefits differently. As a result, investments of every type are available, from "sure things" such as earning 3% interest on your bank savings account, to the possibility of tripling your money fast by investing in a newly issued dot-com stock. The investments you choose will depend on your resources, your goals, and your personality. We can differentiate types of investments on the basis of a number of factors.

Securities or Property Investments that represent debt or ownership or the legal right to acquire or sell an ownership interest are called **securities.** The most common types of securities are stocks, bonds, and options. The focus of this book is primarily on securities.

Property, on the other hand, consists of investments in real property or tangible personal property. *Real property* is land, buildings, and that which is permanently affixed to the land. *Tangible personal property* includes items such as gold, artwork, antiques, and other collectibles.

Direct or Indirect A **direct investment** is one in which an investor directly acquires a claim on a security or property. If you buy a stock or bond in order to earn income or preserve value, you have made a direct investment.

An **indirect investment** is an investment made in a **portfolio,** or collection of securities or properties, typically constructed to meet one or more investment goals. For example, you may purchase a share of a *mutual fund.* This share gives you a claim on a fraction of the entire portfolio rather than on the security of a single firm.

Debt, Equity, or Derivative Securities Usually, an investment represents either a debt or an equity interest. **Debt** represents funds lent in exchange for interest income and the promised repayment of the loan at a given future date.

When you buy a debt instrument like a *bond,* in effect you lend money to the issuer. The issuer agrees to pay you a stated rate of interest over a specified period of time, at the end of which the original sum will be returned.

equity
ongoing ownership in a business or property.

Equity represents ongoing ownership in a business or property. An equity investment may be held as a security or by title to a specific property. The most popular type of equity security is *common stock.*

derivative securities
securities that are structured to exhibit characteristics similar to those of an underlying security or asset and that derive their value from the underlying security or asset.

Derivative securities are neither debt nor equity. They derive their value from, and have characteristics similar to those of, an underlying security or asset. *Options* are an example: An investor essentially buys the opportunity to sell or buy another security or asset at a specified price during a given period of time. Options and other derivative security investments, though not so common as debt and equity investments, have grown rapidly in popularity in recent years.

Low- or High-Risk Investments are sometimes differentiated on the basis of risk. As used in finance, **risk** is the chance that actual investment returns will differ from those expected. The broader the range of possible values or returns associated with an investment, the greater its risk.

risk
the chance that actual investment returns will differ from those expected.

Investors are confronted with a continuum of investments that range from low to high risk. Although each type of investment vehicle has a basic risk characteristic, the actual level of risk depends on the specific vehicle. For example, stocks are generally believed to be more risky than bonds. However, it is not difficult to find high-risk bonds that are more risky than the stock of a financially sound firm such as IBM or McDonald's.

speculation
the purchase of high-risk investment vehicles that offer highly uncertain returns and future value.

Low-risk investments are those considered safe with regard to the receipt of a positive return. *High-risk investments* are considered speculative: Their levels of return are highly uncertain. **Speculation** offers highly uncertain returns and future value, so it is high-risk investment. Because of this greater risk, the returns associated with speculation are expected to be greater. Both investment and speculation differ from gambling, which involves playing games of chance. In this book we will use the term *investment* for both investment and speculation.

short-term investments
investments that typically mature within one year.

long-term investments
investments with maturities of longer than a year or with no maturity at all.

Short- or Long-Term The life of an investment can be described as either short- or long-term. **Short-term investments** typically mature within one year. **Long-term investments** are those with longer maturities or, like common stock, with no maturity at all. It is not unusual to find investors matching the maturity of an investment to the period of time over which they wish to invest their funds.

Note: Discussions of international investing are highlighted by this icon.

Domestic or Foreign As recently as 10 to 15 years ago, individuals invested almost exclusively in purely **domestic investments**: the debt, equity, and derivative securities of U.S.-based companies. Today, these same investors routinely also look for **foreign investments** (both direct and indirect) that might offer more attractive returns or lower risk than purely domestic investments. Information on foreign companies is now readily available, and it is now relatively easy to make foreign investments. As a result, many individuals now actively invest in foreign securities. All aspects of foreign investing are therefore routinely considered throughout this book.

domestic investments
debt, equity, and derivative securities of U.S.-based companies.

foreign investments
debt, equity, and derivative securities of foreign-based companies.

The Structure of the Investment Process

The investment process brings together *suppliers* of extra funds with *demanders* who need funds. Suppliers and demanders of funds are most often brought together through a financial institution or a financial market. (Occasionally, especially in property transactions, buyers and sellers deal directly with one another.) **Financial institutions** are organizations that channel the savings of governments, businesses, and individuals into loans or investments. Banks and insurance companies are financial institutions. **Financial markets** are forums in which suppliers and demanders of funds make financial transactions, often through intermediaries. They include securities, commodities, and foreign exchange markets.

> **financial institutions**
> organizations that channel the savings of governments, businesses, and individuals into loans or investments.

> **financial markets**
> forums in which suppliers and demanders of funds make financial transactions.

The dominant financial market in the United States is the *securities market.* It includes stock markets, bond markets, and options markets. Similar markets exist in most major economies throughout the world. Their common feature is that the price of an investment vehicle at any point in time results from an equilibrium between the forces of supply and demand. As new information about returns and risk becomes available, the changes in supply and demand may result in a new equilibrium or *market price.* Financial markets streamline the process of bringing together suppliers and demanders of funds, and they allow transactions to be made quickly and at a fair price. They also publicize security prices.

Figure 1.1 diagrams the investment process. Note that the suppliers of funds may transfer their resources to the demanders through financial institutions, through financial markets, or in direct transactions. As the broken lines show, financial institutions can participate in financial markets as either suppliers or demanders of funds.

Participants in the Investment Process Government, business, and individuals are the three key participants in the investment process. Each may act as a supplier and a demander of funds. For the economy to grow and prosper, funds must be available to qualified individuals and to government and business. If

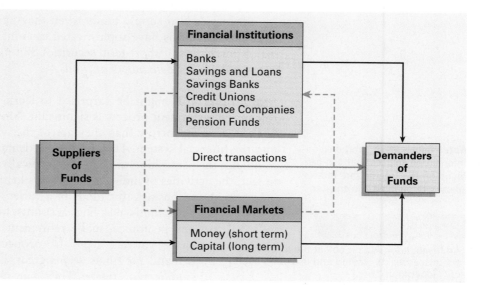

FIGURE 1.1

The Investment Process

Note that financial institutions participate in the financial markets as well as transfer funds between suppliers and demanders. Although the arrows go only from suppliers to demanders, for some transactions (e.g., the sale of a bond), the principal amount borrowed by the demander from the supplier (the lender) is eventually returned.

Note: Investor Facts offer interesting or entertaining tidbits of information.

INVESTOR FACTS

AMERICANS LOVE STOCKS—
A recent survey showed that 48% of Americans now own stocks or stock mutual funds, compared to just 19% in 1983. Stocks and stock mutual funds account for about 36% of total household financial assets, up from 28% in 1995. As the rising equity markets made stocks more popular, holdings of other financial assets—particularly checking, savings, and money market accounts; money market mutual funds; and bonds— declined.

Source: Arthur B. Kennickell, Martha Starr-McCluer, and Brian J. Surette, "Recent Changes in U.S. Family Finances: Results from the 1998 Survey of Consumer Finances," *Federal Reserve Bulletin,* Board of Governors of the Federal Reserve System, Washington, DC, January 2000, pp. 8–9.

Note: Addresses of additional information sources that can be found on the Internet are interspersed throughout the chapter.

HOT LINKS

An Investing in Action box at the text's Web site discusses the saving and investing habits of "Generation Xers."

www.awl.com/gitman_joehnk

individuals began suddenly hiding their excess funds under floorboards rather than putting them in financial institutions or investing them in the financial markets, then government, business, and individuals in need of funds would have difficulty obtaining them. As a result, government spending, business expansion, and consumer purchases would decline, and economic activity would slow.

Government All levels of government—federal, state, and local—require vast sums of money. Some goes to finance *capital expenditures:* long-term projects related to the construction of public facilities such as schools, hospitals, public housing, and highways. Usually the financing for such projects is obtained by issuing various types of long-term debt securities. Another demand for funds comes from *operating needs*—the money required to keep the government running. At the federal level, for example, these funds are used to pay employee and other costs associated with national defense, education, public works, welfare, Social Security, Medicare, and so on, as well as interest on the national debt. These operating costs are usually paid from tax revenue and fee collections. However, when operating expenditures exceed government revenues or when there is a timing mismatch between government receipts and payments, the government borrows funds—typically by issuing short-term debt securities.

Occasionally, governments are also suppliers of funds. If a state has temporarily idle cash, it may make a short-term investment to earn a positive return. In general, though, government is a *net demander of funds.* That is, it demands more funds than it supplies. The financial activities of governments, both as demanders and suppliers of funds, significantly affect the behavior of financial institutions and financial markets.

Business Most business firms require large sums of money to support operations. Like government, business has both long- and short-term financial needs. On the long-term side, businesses seek funds to build plants, acquire equipment and facilities, and develop products. Their short-term needs center on obtaining funds to finance inventory and accounts receivable and to meet other operating costs. Businesses issue a wide variety of debt and equity securities to finance these needs.

Businesses also supply funds when they have excess cash. In fact, many large business firms have sophisticated cash-management operations and are major purchasers of short-term securities. But like government, business firms in general are *net demanders of funds.*

Individuals You might be surprised to learn that the individual investor's role in the investment process is significant. Most individuals are more aware of their need to borrow than they are of the ways in which they put money into the financial system. They frequently demand funds in the form of loans to finance the acquisition of property—typically automobiles and houses. Yet, in fact, the activities of individual investors help to satisfy the net demands of government and business for funds in a variety of ways: Individual investors place funds in savings accounts, buy debt or equity instruments, buy insurance, make retirement plan contributions, and purchase various types of property. Although the individual demand for funds seems great, individuals as a group are *net suppliers of funds:* They put more funds into the financial system than they take out.

HOTLINKS

Getting investment information is now only a few "mouse clicks" away. Everything from stock quotations, to news articles, to Wall Street research is available on the Web. There are many Web sites that provide tutorials on financial information.

CyberInvest.com contains contains free investing guides. Check out [Guides]. Guides compare resources and features at hundreds of the best investing sites on the Web. The guides can save you time—and thus money— by revealing at a glance how investing Web sites stack up against each other. Then you can jump to the site of your choice by clicking on its name. Especially check the *Investing 101* guide under [Education Center].

www.cyberinvest.com

Note: Two *Investing in Action* boxes per chapter describe real-life investing situations or elaborate on innovative investment vehicles. These high-interest boxes have been written for this textbook, with student readers in mind. Some of the concept review questions in the chapter are related to material in these boxes.

individual investors
investors who manage their own funds.

institutional investors
investment professionals paid to manage other people's money.

Note: The concepts in review questions at the end of each text section encourage you, before you move on, to test your understanding of the material you've just read.

Types of Investors When we refer to individuals in the investment process, we do so to differentiate households from government and business. We can further characterize the participation of individuals in the investment process in terms of who manages the funds. **Individual investors** manage their personal funds in order to achieve their financial goals. The individual investor usually concentrates on earning a return on idle funds, building a source of retirement income, and providing security for his or her family. The accompanying *Investing in Action* box on page 8 offers a quiz to determine a baseline on your investing "know-how."

Individuals who lack the time or expertise to make investment decisions often employ **institutional investors**—investment professionals who are paid to manage other people's money. These professionals trade large volumes of securities for individuals, businesses, and governments. Institutional investors include financial institutions (banks, life insurance companies, mutual funds, and pension funds). Financial institutions invest large sums in order to earn a significant return for their customers. For example, a life insurance company invests its premium receipts to earn returns that will permit payments to policyholders or beneficiaries.

Both individual and institutional investors apply similar fundamental principles. However, institutional investors generally invest larger sums of money on behalf of others and therefore are often more sophisticated in investment knowledge and methods. The information presented in this textbook is aimed primarily at individual investors; it represents only the first step toward developing the expertise needed to qualify as an institutional investor.

IN REVIEW

CONCEPTS

1.1 Define the term *investment,* and explain why individuals invest.

1.2 Differentiate among the following types of investments, and cite an example of each: (a) securities and property investments; (b) direct and indirect investments; (c) debt, equity, and derivative securities; and (d) short-term and long-term investments.

1.3 Define the term *risk,* and explain how risk is used to differentiate among investments.

1.4 What are *foreign investments*, and what role do they play today for the individual investor?

1.5 Describe the structure of the overall investment process. Explain the role played by *financial institutions* and *financial markets.*

1.6 Classify the role of (a) government, (b) business, and (c) individuals as net suppliers or net demanders of funds.

1.7 Differentiate between *individual investors* and *institutional investors.*

1.8 How high is your investment IQ, as measured by the quiz in the *Investing in Action* box on page 8? Make a note of your score so that you can impress yourself at the end of the course with how much you've learned.

INVESTING in action

Test Your Investment IQ

How much do you know about investing? Take this investor literacy quiz, developed by *Money* magazine and the Vanguard Group to test the investment savvy of 1,500 mutual fund investors.

The average score (for the full 20-question quiz) was only 37%. But don't despair if you, too, don't score well. You'll learn the answers to these and many other questions from this book.

1. Which type of investment has offered the best protection against inflation over long periods of time?
   a. Money market funds and bank accounts.
   b. Government National Mortgage Association securities (also known as Ginnie Maes or GNMAs).
   c. Stocks.
   d. Corporate bonds.

2. Common stocks always provide higher returns than bonds or money market investments.
   a. True.
   b. False.

3. As an individual, the most you can contribute to an IRA each year is:
   a. $1,000.
   b. $2,000.
   c. $5,000.
   d. $10,000.

4. Interest earned by municipal bonds is exempt from federal income tax.
   a. True.
   b. False.

5. If interest rates declined, the price of a bond or bond fund generally would:
   a. Increase.
   b. Decrease.
   c. Stay about the same.
   d. It is impossible to predict.

6. If you own only U.S. stocks in your investment portfolio, you will reduce your overall risk by adding international stocks.
   a. True.
   b. False.

7. Which market benchmark or stock exchange is the best gauge of the performance of the entire U.S. stock market?
   a. S&P 500 Index.
   b. Wilshire 5000 Total Market Index.
   c. Dow Jones Industrial Average.
   d. Nasdaq Composite Index.

8. If you invest in a 401(k) plan at work, you are not eligible to contribute to an IRA.
   a. True.
   b. False.

9. From 1926 to 1999, the return on U.S. stocks has averaged:
   a. 5% per year.
   b. 11% per year.
   c. 19% per year.
   d. 28% per year.

10. Which of the following is not an attribute of mutual funds?
    a. Diversification.
    b. Professional management.
    c. Guaranteed return.
    d. None of the above.

11. If your investment returned 10% last year and inflation was 3%, your "real" (i.e., adjusted for inflation) return was:
    a. 3.3%.
    b. 7%.
    c. 13%.
    d. 30%.

12. A mutual fund that invests in government securities is guaranteed not to lose money.
    a. True.
    b. False.

Answers: 1 (c); 2 (b); 3 (b); 4 (a); 5 (a); 6 (a); 7 (b); 8 (b); 9 (b); 10 (c); 11 (b); 12 (b).

Sources: Laura Lallos, "What's Your Investing IQ?" *Money*, August 2000, pp. 91–92; quiz downloaded from cgi.money.com/cgi-bin/money/polls/vanguard/vanguard.plx

Investment Vehicles

LG 3

A wide variety of investment vehicles are available to individual investors. Vehicles differ in terms of maturities or lives, costs, return and risk characteristics, and tax considerations. We devote the bulk of this book—Chapters 6 through 15—to describing the characteristics, special features, returns and risks, and possible investment strategies that can be used with vehicles available to the individual investor. Here we will introduce these investment vehicles. Table 1.1 summarizes the information presented in this section.

Short-Term Vehicles

short-term vehicles
savings instruments that usually have lives of 1 year or less.

liquidity
the ability of an investment to be converted into cash quickly and with little or no loss in value.

Short-term vehicles include savings instruments that usually have lives of 1 year or less. Short-term vehicles generally carry little or no risk. Often such instruments are used to "warehouse" idle funds and earn a return while long-term vehicles are being evaluated. They are also popular among conservative investors, who may use short-term vehicles as a primary investment outlet. Short-term vehicles also provide **liquidity**. That is, they can be converted into cash quickly and with little or no loss in value. Provision for liquidity is an important part of any financial plan. The role of short-term vehicles in financial planning and the key features of the most popular short-term vehicles are discussed later in this chapter.

TABLE 1.1   Overview of Investment Vehicles

Type	Description	Examples	Where Covered in This Book
Short-term vehicles	Savings instruments with lives of 1 year or less. Used to warehouse idle funds and to provide liquidity.	Deposit accounts Series EE savings bonds U.S. Treasury bills (T-bills) Certificates of deposit (CDs) Commercial paper Banker's acceptances Money market mutual funds	Ch. 1 Ch. 1 Ch. 1 Ch. 1 Ch. 1 Ch. 1 Ch. 1
Common stock	Equity investment vehicles that represent ownership in a corporation.		Chs. 6–8
Fixed-income securities	Investment vehicles that offer a fixed periodic return.	Bonds Preferred stock Convertible securities	Chs. 9, 10 Ch. 11 Ch. 11
Mutual funds	Companies that raise money from sale of shares and invest in and professionally manage a diversified portfolio of securities.		Ch. 12
Derivative securities	Securities that are neither debt nor equity but are structured to exhibit the characteristics of the underlying securities or assets from which they derive their value.	Options Futures	Ch. 14 Ch. 15
Other popular investment vehicles	Various other investment vehicles that are widely used by investors.	Real estate Tangibles Tax-advantaged investments	On text's Web site, www.awl.com/gitman_joehnk

Common Stock

common stock
equity investment that represents ownership in a corporation; each share represents a fractional ownership interest in the firm.

Common stock is an equity investment that represents ownership in a corporation. Each share of common stock represents a fractional ownership interest in the firm. For example, one share of common stock in a corporation that has 10,000 shares outstanding would represent 1/10,000 ownership interest. Next to short-term vehicles and home ownership, common stock is the most popular form of investment vehicle.

The return on investment in common stock comes from either of two sources: dividends or capital gains. **Dividends** are periodic payments made by the corporation to its shareholders from its current and past earnings. **Capital gains** result from selling the stock (or any asset) at a price that *exceeds* its original purchase price. For example, say you purchased a single share of One Tech Industries common stock for $40 per share. During the first year you owned it, you received $2.50 per share in cash dividends. At the end of the year, you sold the stock for $44 per share. If we ignore the costs associated with buying and selling the stock, you earned $2.50 in dividends and $4 in capital gains ($44 sale price—$40 purchase price).

dividends
periodic payments made by firms to their shareholders.

capital gains
the amount by which the sale price of an asset *exceeds* its original purchase price.

Fixed-Income Securities

fixed-income securities
investment vehicles that offer a fixed periodic return.

Fixed-income securities are investment vehicles that offer a fixed periodic return. Some forms offer contractually guaranteed returns. Others have specified, but not guaranteed, returns. Because of their fixed returns, fixed-income securities tend to be popular during periods of high interest rates, when investors seek to "lock in" high returns. The key forms of fixed-income securities are bonds, preferred stock, and convertible securities.

bonds
long-term debt instruments (IOUs), issued by corporations and governments, that offer a known interest return plus return of the bond's *face value* at maturity.

Bonds **Bonds** are the long-term debt instruments (IOUs) issued by corporations and governments. A bondholder has a contractual right to receive a known interest return, plus return of the bond's *face value* (the stated value given on the certificate) at maturity (typically 20 to 40 years). If you purchased a $1,000 bond paying 9% interest in semiannual installments, you would expect to be paid $45 (9% × ½ year × $1,000) every 6 months. At maturity you would receive the $1,000 face value of the bond. An investor may be able to buy or sell a bond prior to maturity.

preferred stock
ownership interest in a corporation; has a stated dividend rate, payment of which is given preference over common stock dividends of the same firm.

Preferred Stock Like common stock, **preferred stock** represents an ownership interest in a corporation. Unlike common stock, preferred stock has a stated dividend rate. Payment of this dividend is given preference over common stock dividends of the same firm. Preferred stock has no maturity date. Investors typically purchase it for the dividends it pays, but it may also provide capital gains.

convertible security
a fixed-income obligation (bond or preferred stock) with a feature permitting conversion into a specified number of shares of common stock.

Convertible Securities A **convertible security** is a special type of fixed-income obligation (bond or preferred stock). It has a feature permitting the investor to convert it into a specified number of shares of common stock. Convertible bonds and convertible preferreds provide the fixed-income benefit of a bond (interest) or preferred stock (dividends) while offering the price-appreciation (capital gain) potential of common stock.

Mutual Funds

A company that raises money from sale of its shares and invests in and professionally manages a diversified portfolio of securities is called a **mutual fund.** Investors in the fund own an interest in the fund's portfolio of securities. All mutual funds issue and repurchase shares of the fund at a price that reflects the value of the portfolio at the time the transaction is made. **Money market mutual funds** are mutual funds that invest solely in short-term investment vehicles.

Derivative Securities

As noted earlier, *derivative securities* derive their value from that of an underlying security or asset. They typically possess high levels of risk, because they usually have uncertain returns or unstable market values. But, because of their above-average risk, these vehicles also have high levels of expected return. The key derivative securities are options and futures.

Options **Options** are securities that give the investor an opportunity to sell or buy another security at a specified price over a given period of time. Most often, options are purchased in order to take advantage of an anticipated change in the price of common stock. However, the purchaser of an option is not guaranteed any return and could even lose the entire amount invested because the option does not become attractive enough to use. Aside from their speculative use, options are sometimes used to protect existing investment positions against losses. Three common types of options are *puts, calls,* and *warrants,* which we will discuss in detail in Chapter 14.

Futures **Futures** are legally binding obligations stipulating that the sellers of such contracts will make delivery and the buyers of the contracts will take delivery of a specified commodity or financial instrument at some specific date, at a price agreed on at the time the contract is sold. Examples of commodities sold by contract include soybeans, pork bellies, platinum, and cocoa. Examples of financial futures are contracts for Japanese yen, U.S. Treasury securities, interest rates, and stock indexes. Trading in commodity and financial futures is generally a highly specialized, high-risk proposition.

Other Popular Investment Vehicles

Various other investment vehicles are also used by investors. The most common are real estate, tangibles, and tax-advantaged investments.

   Real estate consists of entities such as residential homes, raw land, and a variety of forms of income property, including warehouses, office and apartment buildings, and condominiums. The appeal of real estate investment is the potential returns in the form of rental income, tax write-offs, and capital gains. **Tangibles** are investment assets, other than real estate, that can be seen

mutual fund
a company that raises money
from sale of its shares and invests
in and professionally manages a
diversified portfolio of securities.

money market mutual funds
mutual funds that invest solely in
short-term investment vehicles.

options
securities that give the investor
an opportunity to sell or buy
another security at a specified
price over a given period of time.

futures
legally binding obligations stipulating that the sellers of such
contracts will make delivery and
the buyers of the contracts will
take delivery of a specified commodity or financial instrument at
some specific date, at a price
agreed on at the time the contract is sold.

real estate
entities such as residential
homes, raw land, and income
property.

tangibles
investment assets, other than real
estate, that can be seen or
touched.

tax-advantaged investments
investment vehicles and strategies for legally reducing one's tax liability.

or touched. They include gold and other precious metals, gemstones, and collectibles such as coins, stamps, artwork, and antiques. These assets are purchased as investments in anticipation of price increases. Because the federal income tax rate for an individual can be as high as 39.6%, many investors look for **tax-advantaged investments.** These are investment vehicles and strategies for legally reducing one's tax liability. With them, investors find that their after-tax rates of return can be far higher than with conventional investments.

IN REVIEW

CONCEPTS

1.9 What are *short-term vehicles?* How do they provide *liquidity?*

1.10 What is *common stock* and what are its two sources of potential return?

1.11 Briefly define and differentiate among the following investment vehicles. Which offer fixed returns? Which are derivative securities? Which offer professional investment management?
a. Bonds
b. Preferred stock
c. Convertible securities
d. Mutual funds
e. Options
f. Futures

Making Investment Plans

The process of investing can be carried out by following a logical progression of steps. It is important that your investment plans take into account the impact of taxes. Your plans also should be responsive to your stage in the life cycle and to the changing economic environment.

LG 4   LG 5

Steps in Investing

Investing can be conducted on a strictly intuitive basis or on the basis of plans carefully developed to achieve specific goals. Evidence favors the more logical approach that begins with establishing a set of overall financial goals and then developing and executing an investment program consistent with those goals. The following brief overview of the steps in investing provides a framework for discussion of the concepts, tools, and techniques presented throughout the book.

Step 1: Meeting Investment Prerequisites Before investing, you must make certain that the *necessities of life* are adequately provided for. This category includes funds for housing, food, transportation, taxes, and clothing. In addition, a pool of easily accessible funds should be established for meeting emergency cash needs. (Meeting liquidity needs is discussed later in this chapter.)

Another prerequisite is adequate protection against the losses that could result from death, illness or disability, damage to property, or a negligent act. Protection against such risks can be acquired through life, health, property, and liability insurance.

investment goals
the financial objectives that one wishes to achieve by investing.

Step 2: Establishing Investment Goals Once you have satisfied the prerequisites and set clearly defined financial goals, the next step is to establish *investment goals*. **Investment goals** are the financial objectives you wish to achieve by investing. Clearly, your investment goals will determine the types of investments you will make. Common investment goals include:

1. *Accumulating Retirement Funds.* Accumulating funds for retirement is the *single most important reason for investing.* Too often, people tend to rely heavily on Social Security and employers for retirement funds. It is of the utmost importance to review the amounts that can realistically be expected from these sources. You can then decide, on the basis of your retirement goals, *whether they will be adequate to meet your needs.* If they are not, they must be supplemented through your own investment program. The earlier in life you assess your retirement needs, the greater your chance of accumulating sufficient funds to meet them.

2. *Enhancing Current Income.* Investments enhance current income by earning dividends or interest. Retirees frequently choose investments offering *high current income at low risk.* The idea of a retired person "clipping coupons"—collecting interest—from high-grade bonds is a fair description of what most senior citizens should be doing at that point in their lives.

HOTLINKS

Tax-advantaged investments are discussed on the text's Web site. Click on the Web chapter titled Tax-Advantaged Investments.

www.awl.com/gitman_joehnk

3. *Saving for Major Expenditures.* Families often put aside money over the years to accumulate the funds needed to make major expenditures. The most common of these are the down payment on a home, education, vacation travel, and capital to start a business. The appropriate types of investment vehicles depend on the purpose and the amount of money needed. For purposes such as the down payment on a home or a child's education, for example, much less risk should be tolerated than for other goals. The attainment of such basic goals should not, if possible, be placed in jeopardy.

4. *Sheltering Income from Taxes.* Federal income tax law allows certain noncash charges to be deducted from specified sources of income. Such deductions reduce the amount of final taxable income. Obviously, if a person can avoid (or defer) paying taxes on the income from an investment, he or she will have more funds left for reinvestment.

investment plan
a written document describing how funds will be invested and specifying the target date for achieving each investment goal and the amount of tolerable risk.

Step 3: Adopting an Investment Plan Once your general goals have been established, you should adopt an **investment plan**—a written document describing how funds will be invested. A series of supporting investment goals can be developed for each long-term goal. For each goal, specify the target date for achieving it and the amount of tolerable risk.

Generally, the more important the financial objective, the lower the risk that should be assumed. Suppose, for example, one long-run goal is to accumulate $80,000 in cash by the end of 10 years. That goal could be spelled out as a plan to accumulate $80,000 in cash by investing in a portfolio evenly divided between low-risk and speculative stocks providing a total return of 10% per year. The more specific you can be in your statement of investment goals, the easier it will be to establish an investment plan consistent with your goals.

diversification
the inclusion of a number of different investment vehicles in a portfolio to increase returns or reduce risk.

Step 4: Evaluating Investment Vehicles Once you have your investment goals and plan laid out, you will want to evaluate investment vehicles by assessing each vehicle's potential return and risk. This process typically involves *valuation,* the use of measures of return and risk to estimate the worth of an investment vehicle. (Chapter 4 offers a general discussion of the procedures for measuring these key dimensions of potential investments. Subsequent chapters focus on the valuation of specific vehicles.)

Step 5: Selecting Suitable Investments You now gather additional information and use it to select specific investment vehicles consistent with your goals. The best investments may not be those that simply maximize return. Other factors, such as risk and tax considerations, may also be crucial. For example, to receive maximum annual dividends, you might purchase the common stock of a firm expected to pay high dividends. However, if the firm whose stock you purchased goes bankrupt, you could lose the money. The stock of a firm that pays lower dividends but with less risk of bankruptcy might have been a better choice. Careful selection of investment vehicles is essential to successful investing. Vehicles should be consistent with established goals and offer acceptable levels of return, risk, and value.

Step 6: Constructing a Diversified Portfolio Selecting suitable investments involves choosing vehicles that enable you to achieve investment goals and that optimize return, risk, and investment values. To do this, you will assemble an investment *portfolio* that meets one or more investment goals. For example, your portfolio might contain common stock, government bonds, and short-term investments. **Diversification** is the inclusion of a number of different investment vehicles in a portfolio to increase returns or reduce risk. By *diversifying* in this way, investors are able to earn higher returns or be exposed to less risk than if they limit their investments to just one or two vehicles. Diversification is the financial term for the age-old advice "Don't put all your eggs in one basket." (Chapter 5 includes discussions of diversification and other modern portfolio concepts.)

Step 7: Managing the Portfolio Once you have constructed your portfolio, you should measure its actual behavior in relation to expected performance. If the investment results are not consistent with your objectives, you may need to take corrective action. Such action usually involves selling certain investments and using the proceeds to acquire other vehicles for the portfolio. *Portfolio management* involves monitoring the portfolio and restructuring it as dictated by the actual behavior of the investments. (Portfolio management is discussed in detail in Chapters 12 and 13.)

The *Investing in Action* box on page 15 summarizes some general tips for successful investing.

Considering Personal Taxes

Besides developing plans for achieving your specific investment goals, it's also important to consider the tax consequences associated with various investments. A knowledge of the tax laws can help you reduce taxes. By doing so, you increase the amount

INVESTING in action

Lessons for Investment Success

The stock market has taken investors on a roller coaster ride in recent years. Even in such volatile times, however, some basic rules still apply. Becoming a successful investor takes time and effort; there are no sure-fire schemes for beating the market. Here are some tips to help you get started on the road to financial security.

- **Harness the power of compounding.** With compounding, time is your biggest ally. The longer you invest your money, the faster it will grow. If you earn a 9% annual return on your investment and reinvest your yearly earnings at the same rate for a 20-year period, your overall return is 460%, an average annual return of 23% (460%/20). Start now; waiting will cost you money. If you invest $2,000 a year for 10 years ($20,000 total) at 8% per year, in 35 years you'll have $198,422. But wait 10 years and invest $2,000 a year for 25 years at 8% per year, and your (considerably greater) $50,000 investment will be only $146,212 at the end of that same 35-year period. You can start small. Invest just $200 at 10% and you'll have almost $20,000 in 25 years. Make investing a habit now.

- **Don't wait for the "right" time to invest.** There isn't one! The "best" time to invest is now. You can always find a reason to put off taking the plunge: It's an election year, the market is too high, there's a crisis somewhere in the world. Studies show that it's more important to invest than to pick the right time. In the short run, market activity is unpredictable, even for the experts. Don't make excuses, like you are too busy, investing is too hard, or you can't possibly save enough for college or retirement. Investing is one of the best uses of your time. Rethink your priorities: Is it more important to go to the movies

or to plan for your financial future? And don't be intimidated by the investment process. Set realistic goals, learn the basics, and start with simple investments that you understand. Once you gain control of your finances, your confidence will increase.

- **Diversify your portfolio.** Spreading your money among different types of investments is less risky than putting all your eggs in one investment basket. If some of your holdings go down, others go up, and vice versa. Diversify your portfolio by investing in several types of securities: short-term vehicles such as money market funds, intermediate-term bonds or bond funds, and, for the long-term, growth stocks or growth mutual funds. You should also have some international stocks or mutual funds. Don't concentrate too heavily in one industry or buy just one or two stocks. No one knows which sector will be hot tomorrow.

- **Monitor your investments.** Don't just buy securities and hold them forever. Review your portfolio monthly to check your progress against your goals. Weed out your poor performers and evaluate current holdings relative to other investment opportunities. Don't be too quick to unload a stock or mutual fund or to chase after that hot stock tip, though. Do your homework and be sure you have a good reason to buy or sell.

Sources: Jonathan Clements, "Don't Ignore Luck's Role in Stock Picks," *Wall Street Journal,* September 26, 2000, p. C1; Jonathan Clements, "Lessons from the School of Hard Knocks, *Wall Street Journal,* March 14, 2000, p. C1; "Money 101: Basics of Investing," *Money.com,* downloaded from www.money.com/money/101; Peter Psaras, "Ten Tips for Successful Investing," *The Motley Fool,* September 13, 2000, downloaded from fool.com

of after-tax dollars available for achieving your investment goals. Because tax laws are complicated and subject to frequent revision, we present only the key concepts and how they apply to popular investment transactions.

Basic Sources of Taxation The two major types of taxes are those levied by the federal government and those levied by state and local governments. The federal *income tax* is the major form of personal taxation. Federal rates currently range from 15 to 39.6% of taxable income.

State and local taxes vary from area to area. Some states have income taxes that range as high as 15% or more of income. Some cities, especially large East Coast cities, also have local income taxes that typically range between 1% and 5% of income. In addition to income taxes, state and local governments rely heavily on sales and property taxes, which vary from community to community, as a source of revenue.

Income taxes at the federal, state, and local levels have the greatest impact on security investments, whose returns are in the form of dividends, interest, and increases in value. Property taxes can have a sizable impact on real estate and other forms of property investment.

Types of Income The income of individuals is classified into one of *three basic categories* defined below.

1. *Active income* consists of everything from wages and salaries to bonuses, tips, pension income, and alimony. Active income is made up of income earned on the job as well as most other forms of *noninvestment* income.
2. *Portfolio income* is earnings generated from various types of investment holdings. This category of income covers most (but not all) types of investments, from savings accounts, stocks, bonds, and mutual funds to options and futures. For the most part, portfolio income consists of interest, dividends, and capital gains (the profit on the sale of an investment).
3. *Passive income* is a special category of income, composed chiefly of income derived from real estate, limited partnerships, and other forms of tax-advantaged investments.

The key feature of these categories is that they limit the amount of deductions (write-offs) that can be taken, particularly for portfolio and passive income. The amount of allowable deductions for portfolio and passive income is *limited to the amount of income derived from these two sources.* For example, if you had a total of $380 in portfolio income for the year, you could deduct no more than $380 in investment-related interest expense. For deduction purposes, the portfolio and passive income categories cannot be mixed or combined with each other or with active income. *Investment-related expenses can be used only to offset portfolio income,* and (with a few exceptions) *passive investment expenses can be used only to offset the income from passive investments.*

 Ordinary Income Regardless of whether it's classified as active, portfolio, or passive, ordinary income is taxed at one of five rates: 15, 28, 31, 36, or 39.6%. There is one structure of tax rates for taxpayers who file *individual* returns and another for those who file *joint* returns with a spouse. Table 1.2 shows the tax rates and income brackets for these two categories. Note that the rates are *progressive.* That is, taxpayers with taxable income above a specified amount are taxed at a higher rate.

An example will demonstrate how ordinary income is taxed. Consider the Ellis sisters, Joni and Cara. Both are single. Joni's taxable income is $18,000. Cara's is $36,000. Using Table 1.2, we can calculate their taxes as follows:

TABLE 1.2	Tax Rates and Income Brackets for Individual and Joint Returns (2000)	
	Taxable Income	
Tax Rates	Individual Returns	Joint Returns
15%	$0 to $26,250	$0 to $43,850
28%	$26,251 to $63,550	$43,851 to $105,950
31%	$63,551 to $132,600	$105,951 to $161,450
36%	$132,601 to $288,350	$161,451 to $288,350
39.6%	Over $288,350	Over $288,350

Joni:

$(0.15 \times \$18,000) = \underline{\$2,700}$

Cara:

$(0.15 \times \$26,250) + [0.28 \times (\$36,000 - \$26,250)]$
$= \$3,938 + \$2,730 = \underline{\$6,668}$

The progressive nature of the federal income tax structure can be seen by the fact that although Cara's taxable income is twice that of Joni, her income tax is about 2.5 times Joni's.

Capital Gains and Losses A *capital asset* is property owned and used by the taxpayer for personal reasons, pleasure, or investment. The most common types are securities and real estate, including one's home. A *capital gain* represents the amount by which the proceeds from the sale of a capital asset *exceed* its original purchase price. Capital gains are taxed at two different rates depending on the holding period.

The capital gains tax rate is 20% if the asset is held for more than 12 months. This 20% capital gains tax rate assumes that you're in the 28%, 31%, 36%, or 39.6% tax bracket. If you're in the 15% tax bracket, then the capital gains tax rate on an asset held for more than 12 months is just 10%. If the asset is held for less than 12 months, then the amount of any capital gain realized is added to other sources of income, and the total is taxed at the rates given in Table 1.2.

For example, imagine that James McFail, a single person who has other taxable income totaling $45,000, sold 500 shares of stock at $12 per share. He originally purchased this stock at $10 per share. The total capital gain on this transaction was $1,000 [500 shares $\times$ ($12/share $-$ $10/share)]. Thus James's taxable income would total $46,000, which puts him in the 28% tax bracket (see Table 1.2).

If the $1,000 capital gain resulted from an asset that was held for more than 12 months, and because James is in the 28% tax bracket, the capital gain would be taxed at the maximum rate of 20%. His total tax would be calculated as follows:

Ordinary income ($45,000)
$(0.15 \times \$26,250) + (0.28 \times [\$45,000 - \$26,250]) = \$9,187.50$

Capital gain ($1,000)
$(0.20 \times \$1,000) =$ 200.00
                                    Total tax $\underline{\$9,387.50}$

James's total tax would be $9,387.50. Had his other taxable income been below $26,251 (i.e., in the 15% bracket), the $1,000 capital gain would have been taxed at 10% rather than 20%. Had James held the asset for less than 12 months, his $1,000 capital gain would have been taxed as ordinary income, which in James's case would result in a 28% rate.

Capital gains are appealing to investors because they are not taxed until actually realized. For example, if you own a stock originally purchased for $50 per share that at the end of the tax year has a market price of $60 per share, you have a "paper gain" of $10 per share. This *paper (unrealized) gain* is not taxable, because you still own the stock. *Only realized gains are taxed.* If you sold the stock for $60 per share during the tax year, you would have a realized—and therefore taxable—gain of $10 per share.

capital loss
the amount by which the proceeds from the sale of a capital asset are *less than* its original purchase price.

A **capital loss** results when a capital asset is sold for *less than* its original purchase price. Before taxes are calculated, all gains and losses must be netted out. Up to $3,000 of **net losses** can be applied against ordinary income in any year. Losses that cannot be applied in the current year may be carried forward and used to offset future income, subject to certain conditions.

net losses
the amount by which capital losses exceed capital gains; up to $3,000 of net losses can be applied against ordinary income in any year.

Investments and Taxes   The opportunities created by the tax laws make tax planning important in the investment process. **Tax planning** involves looking at your earnings, both current and projected, and developing strategies that will defer and minimize the level of taxes. The tax plan should guide your investment activities so that over the long run you will achieve maximum after-tax returns for an acceptable level of risk. For example, the fact that capital gains are not taxed until actually realized allows you to defer tax payments on them as well as control the timing of these payments. However, investments that are likely to lead to capital gains income generally have higher risk than those that provide only current investment income. Therefore, the choice of investment vehicles cannot be made solely on the basis of the possible reduction of tax payments. The levels of both return and risk need to be viewed in light of their tax effects. *It is the after-tax return and associated risk that matter.*

tax planning
the development of strategies that will defer and minimize an individual's level of taxes over the long run.

Tax plans should also reflect the (1) form of returns—current income, capital gains, or tax-advantaged income—and (2) the timing of loss recognition and profit taking. One common strategy is to claim losses as soon as they occur and to delay profit taking. Such an approach allows you to benefit from the tax deductibility of a loss and to delay having to claim income from gains. Tax planning, which is usually done in coordination with an accountant, tax expert, or tax attorney, is most common among individuals with high levels of income ($200,000 or more annually). Yet sizable savings can result for investors with lower incomes as well.

HOTLINKS

The material on tax strategies and tax-advantaged investments available on this text's Web site provides more detailed information on this topic. Click on Chapter 17.

www.awl.com/gitman_joehnk

Investing Over the Life Cycle

Investors tend to follow different investment philosophies as they move through different stages of the life cycle. Generally speaking, most investors tend to be more aggressive when they're young and more conservative as they grow older. Typically, investors move through the following investment stages.

TAX BITE—If you invest just $2,000 a year in taxable accounts and investments for the next 30 years and earn an 8% average compounded annual rate of return, you'll accumulate about $227,000—until you pay Uncle Sam his share. Then you will have only $175,230, assuming that an average federal income tax rate of 31% is applied to your earnings above the total investment of $60,000 ($2,000 × 30 years). Taxes will reduce your earnings from the investment by nearly one-third!

Growth-oriented youth (age: 20 to 45)	→	Middle-age consolidation (age: 45 to 60)	→	Income-oriented retirement years (age: 60 to ?)

Most young investors, in their twenties and thirties, tend to prefer growth-oriented investments that stress *capital gains* rather than current income. Often young investors don't have much in the way of investable funds, so capital gains are viewed as the quickest (if not necessarily the surest) way to build capital. Young investors tend to favor growth-oriented and speculative vehicles, particularly high-risk common stocks, options, and futures.

As investors approach the middle-age consolidation stage of life (the mid-forties), family demands and responsibilities such as educational expenses and retirement contributions become more important. The whole portfolio goes through a transition to *higher-quality securities*. Low-risk growth and income stocks, preferred stocks, convertibles, high-grade bonds, and mutual funds are all widely used at this stage.

Finally, investors approach their retirement years. Preservation of capital and current income become the principal concerns. A secure, high level of income is paramount. Capital gains are viewed as merely a pleasant, occasional by-product of investing. The investment portfolio now becomes *highly conservative*. It now consists of low-risk income stocks, high-yielding government bonds, quality corporate bonds, bank certificates of deposit (CDs), and other short-term vehicles. At this stage, investors reap the rewards of a lifetime of saving and investing.

Investing in Different Economic Environments

Despite the government's arsenal of weapons for moderating economic swings, numerous changes are sure to occur in the economy during your lifetime of investing. At all stages of the life cycle, your investment program must be flexible enough to allow you to recognize and react to changing economic conditions. The first rule of investing is to know *where* to put your money. The second is to know *when* to make your moves.

The first question is easier to deal with, because it involves matching the risk and return objectives of your investment plan with the available investment alternatives. For example, if you're a seasoned investor who can tolerate the risk, then speculative stocks may be right for you. If you're a novice who wants a fair return on your capital, perhaps you should consider a good growth-oriented mutual fund. Unfortunately, although stocks and growth funds may do well when the economy is expanding, they can turn out to be disasters at other times. This leads to the second, and more difficult, question: What effect do economic and market conditions have on investment returns?

The question of when to invest is difficult because it deals with *market timing*. The fact is that most economists and most professional money managers—not to mention most investors—cannot consistently predict the peaks and troughs in the economy or stock market. It's a lot easier to get a handle on the *current state* of the economy/market. That is, knowing whether the economy/market is in a state of expansion or decline is considerably different from being able to pinpoint when it's about to change course. Thus, for our purposes, we can define **market timing** as the process of identifying the current

market timing
the process of identifying the current state of the economy/market and assessing the likelihood of its continuing on its present course.

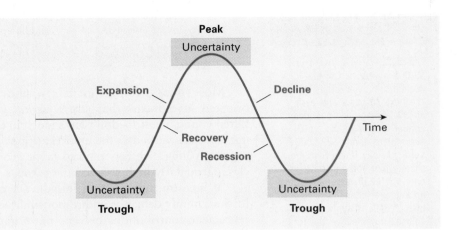

FIGURE 1.2

Different Stages of an Economic/Market Cycle

The economic/market cycle shows three different conditions: (1) a state of recovery/expansion, (2) a state of decline/recession, and (3) uncertainty as to the direction in which the economy/market is going to move (shown by the shaded areas).

state of the economy/market and assessing the likelihood of its continuing on its present course.

As an investor, it's best to confine your assessment of the economy to three distinct conditions: (1) a state of recovery or expansion, (2) a state of decline or recession, or (3) uncertainty as to the direction of its movement. These different stages are illustrated in Figure 1.2. It's easy to see when things are moving up (recovery/expansion) and when they're moving down (decline/recession). The difficulty comes with the peaks and troughs. At those points, you don't know whether the economy will continue in its current direction, up or down, or whether it will change direction. That is why these areas in the figure are shaded, depicting *uncertainty*. How you will respond to these conditions depends on the types of investment vehicles you hold (for example, stocks or bonds).

Stocks and the Business Cycle Common stocks and other equity-related securities (convertible securities, stock mutual funds, stock options, and stock index futures) are highly responsive to conditions in the economy. Economic conditions are described generically as the *business cycle*. The business cycle reflects the current status of a variety of economic variables, including GDP (gross domestic product), industrial production, personal disposable income, the unemployment rate, and more.

A strong economy is reflected in an expanding business cycle. When business is good and profits are up, stocks react by increasing in value and return. Growth-oriented and speculative stocks tend to do especially well in strong markets. To a lesser extent, so do low-risk and income-oriented stocks. In contrast, when economic activity is declining, the values and returns on common stocks tend to be off as well.

Bonds and Interest Rates Bonds and other forms of fixed-income securities (preferred stocks and bond funds) are highly sensitive to movements in interest rates. In fact, interest rates are the single most important variable in determining bond price behavior and returns to investors. Interest rates and bond prices move in opposite directions (as will be explained in Chapters 9 and 10).

Therefore, rising interest rates are unfavorable for bonds already held in an investor's portfolio. Of course, high interest rates enhance the attractiveness of new bonds because these bonds must offer high returns to attract investors.

IN REVIEW

CONCEPTS

1.12 What should an investor first establish before developing and executing an investment program? Briefly describe each of the seven steps involved in investing.

1.13 What are four common investment goals?

1.14 According to the *Investing in Action* box on page 15, why is it important to start investing now? Why is it a good idea to diversify?

1.15 Define and differentiate among the following. Explain how each is related to federal income taxes.
a. Active income
b. Portfolio and passive income
c. Capital gain
d. Capital loss
e. Tax planning

1.16 Describe the differing investment philosophies typically applied during each of the following stages of an investor's life cycle.
a. Youth (ages 20 to 45)
b. Middle age (ages 45 to 60)
c. Retirement years (age 60 on)

1.17 Describe the four stages of the economic/market cycle, and discuss the impact of this cycle on stock and bond investments.

Meeting Liquidity Needs: Investing in Short-Term Vehicles

LG 6

As discussed earlier, you should ensure that you have adequate liquidity. This provision is a prerequisite to implementing long-term investment goals. *Liquidity* is the ability to convert an investment into cash quickly and with little or no loss in value. A checking account is highly liquid. Stocks and bonds are not liquid, because there is no definite assurance that you will be able to quickly sell them at a price equal to or greater than their purchase price.

The Role of Short-Term Vehicles

Short-term vehicles are an important part of most savings and investment programs. They generate income—which can be quite high during periods of high interest rates. However, their primary function is to provide a pool of reserves that can be used for emergencies or simply to accumulate funds for some specific purpose. As a rule of thumb, financial planners often suggest that anywhere from 3 to 6 months' worth of after-tax income should be held in short-term vehicles to meet unexpected needs or to take advantage of attractive opportunities.

Investors usually hold short-term vehicles in their investment portfolios as a *temporary*, highly liquid investment until something better comes along. Some individuals choose to hold short-term vehicles because they simply are more comfortable with them. In fact, this approach has considerable merit during periods of economic and investment instability. Regardless of your motives for holding short-term vehicles, you should evaluate them in terms of their risk and return, just as you would longer-term investments.

Interest on Short-Term Investments Short-term investments earn interest in one of two ways. Some investments, such as savings accounts, pay a *stated rate of interest*. In this case, you can easily find the interest rate—it's the stated rate on the account.

Alternatively, interest is earned on short-term investments on a **discount basis**. This means that the security is purchased at a price below its redemption value, and the difference is the interest earned. U.S. Treasury bills (T-bills), for example, are issued on a discount basis.

discount basis
a method of earning interest on a security by purchasing it at a price below its redemption value; the difference is the interest earned.

Risk Characteristics Short-term investments are generally considered low in risk. Their primary risk results from the *loss of potential purchasing power* that occurs when the rate of return on these investments falls short of the inflation rate. This has often been the case with such vehicles as *passbook savings accounts*, the traditional bank savings accounts that generally pay a low rate of interest and have no minimum balance. Over long periods of time most other short-term investments have rates of return that are about equal to, or maybe slightly higher than, the average inflation rate.

The *risk of default*—nonpayment—is virtually nonexistent with short-term investment vehicles. The principal reason is that the primary issuers of most short-term vehicles are highly reputable institutions, such as the U.S. Treasury, large banks, and major corporations. Deposits in commercial banks, savings and loans, savings banks, and credit unions also are insured for up to $100,000 per account by government agencies. Finally, because the value of short-term investments does not change much in response to changing interest rates, exposure to capital loss is correspondingly low.

HOT LINKS

A relatively simple formula can be applied when interest is earned on a discount basis in order to compare returns with vehicles earning a stated rate of interest. See this text's Web site for discussion of the formula.

www.awl.com/gitman_joehnk

Advantages and Disadvantages of Short-Term Investments As noted, the major advantages of short-term investments are their high liquidity and low risk. Most are available from local financial institutions and can be readily converted to cash with minimal inconvenience. Finally, because the returns on most short-term investments vary with inflation and market interest rates, investors can readily capture higher returns as rates move up. On the negative side, when interest rates go down, returns drop as well.

Although a decline in market rates has undesirable effects on most short-term vehicles, perhaps their biggest disadvantage is their relatively low return. Because these securities are generally so low in risk, you can expect the returns on short-term investments to average less than the returns on long-term investments.

Popular Short-Term Investment Vehicles

Over the past 25 years or so, the number of short-term investment vehicles being offered has greatly expanded. Investing in short-term securities is no longer the easy task it once was, when the decision for most people amounted to whether to place funds in a passbook savings account or in U.S. savings bonds. Today, even some checking accounts pay interest on idle balances. Along with the increase in investment alternatives has come greater sophistication in short-term investment management. Investors now know they can use short-term vehicles as secure investment outlets for the long haul or as a place to hold cash until they find a longer-term outlet for the funds.

In the material that follows, we will first examine the best-known short-term investment vehicles—deposit accounts, Series EE savings bonds, and U.S. Treasury bills. Next we will describe some of the most popular nongovernment short-term securities. Finally, we will look at several ways to use these deposits/securities in an investment portfolio.

Deposit Accounts Banks offer investors several forms of deposit accounts that pay interest on account balances. (*Note:* We use the term *bank* to refer to commerical banks, savings and loans (S&Ls), savings banks, and credit unions—all of which issue deposit accounts.) Four such accounts are **passbook savings accounts, NOW (negotiated order of withdrawal) accounts, money market deposit accounts (MMDAs), and asset management accounts.** The distinguishing features of these accounts are summarized in Table 1.3. The first two—passbook savings accounts and NOW accounts—are primarily used as savings vehicles. They provide the individual investor with a highly liquid pool of funds that can be accessed easily to meet scheduled as well as unexpected expenditures. The second two—MMDAs and asset management accounts—are more likely to be used for investment purposes. For this use, they earn a reasonably competitive short-term return while maintaining sufficient liquidity to meet unexpected needs and seize attractive investment opportunities.

Series EE Savings Bonds **Series EE savings bonds** are the well-known savings bonds that have been available for decades. You may have been given some by thrifty or patriotic relatives on birthdays or other special occasions. (First issued in 1941, these savings bonds used to be called Series E bonds.)

Series EE bonds are **accrual-type securities.** This means that interest is paid when the bond is cashed, on or before maturity, rather than periodically over the life of the bond. They are sold at a discount—the purchase price of all denominations is 50% of the face value. Thus a $100 bond costs $50 and will be worth $100 at maturity. Series EE bonds are backed by the full faith and credit of the U.S. government. They can be replaced without charge in case of loss, theft, or destruction. They can be purchased at banks or other thrift institutions or through payroll deduction plans. They are issued in denominations of $50 through $10,000. A person is limited to maximum annual Series EE bond purchases of $15,000 (i.e., $30,000 face value).

The actual maturity date on EE bonds is unspecified because they pay a variable rate of interest. The higher the rate of interest being paid, the shorter the period of time it takes for the bond to *accrue* from its discounted purchase price to its face value. The rate of interest paid on EE bonds is 90% of the average 5-year Treasury security market yields for the preceding 6 months. Bonds can be redeemed any time after the first 6 months. All EE bonds held from 6 months to 5 years are penalized by forfeiting the last 3 months of interest earned. The U.S. Treasury calculates interest rates every 6 months (in May and November). Interest rates change in accordance with prevailing Treasury

---

passbook savings account
a savings account, offered by banks, that generally pays a low rate of interest and has no minimum balance.

NOW (negotiated order of withdrawal) account
a bank checking account that pays interest; has no legal minimum balance, but many banks impose their own.

money market deposit accounts (MMDAs)
a bank deposit account with limited check-writing privileges; has no legal minimum balance, but many banks impose their own.

asset management account
a comprehensive deposit account that combines checking, investing, and borrowing activities; it automatically "sweeps" excess balances into short-term investments and borrows to meet shortages.

Series EE savings bonds
savings bonds issued by the U.S. Treasury and sold at banks and through payroll deduction plans, in varying denominations, at 50% of face value; pay a variable rate of interest tied to U.S. Treasury security market yields and calculated every six months in May and November.

accrual-type securities
securities for which interest is paid when the bond is cashed, on or before maturity, rather than periodically over the life of the bond.

TABLE 1.3	Distinguishing Features of Interest-Paying Deposit Accounts			
Type of Account	Brief Description	Minimum Balance	Interest Rate	Federal Insurance
Passbook savings account	Savings accounts offered by banks.* Used primarily for convenience or if investors lack sufficient funds for other short-term vehicles.	Typically none	2%–6% depending on economy	Yes, up to $100,000 per deposit.
NOW (negotiated order of withdrawal) account	Bank checking account that pays interest on balances.	No legal minimum, but often set at $500 to $1,000	At or near passbook rates	Yes, up to $100,000 per deposit.
Money market deposit account (MMDA)	Bank deposit account with limited check-writing privileges.	No legal minimum, but often set at about $2,500	Typically about 1% above passbook rate	Yes, up to $100,000 per deposit.
Asset management account	Deposit account at bank, brokerage house, mutual fund, or insurance company that combines checking, investing, and borrowing. Auto- matically "sweeps" excess balances into short-term investments and borrows to meet shortages.	Typically $5,000 to $20,000	Similar to MMDAs	Yes, up to $100,000 per deposit in banks. Varies in other institutions.

*The term *bank* refers to commercial banks, savings and loans (S&Ls), savings banks, and credit unions.

security market yields. You can obtain current rates on Series EE bonds from your bank or simply by calling 800-487-2663. (*Note:* For bonds purchased after May 1, 1997, the rate for the 6-month period ending October 31, 2001, was 4.50%.) Interest is credited every 6 months and compounds semiannually.

In addition to being exempt from state and local taxes, Series EE bonds provide an appealing tax twist: *Investors need not report the interest earned on their federal tax returns until the bonds are redeemed.* Interest *can* be reported annually. This might be done, for example, if the bonds are held in the name of a child who has limited interest income. But most investors choose to defer reporting the interest. In effect, this means the funds are being reinvested at an after-tax rate equal to the bond's current interest rate. Another attractive tax feature allows partial or complete tax avoidance of EE bond earnings when proceeds are used to pay education expenses (such as col- lege tuition) for the bond purchaser, a spouse, or other IRS-defined depen- dent. To qualify the purchaser must be age 24 or older and must, after December 31, 1999, have adjusted gross income below $54,100 for single filers and $81,100 for married couples. (The maximum income levels are adjusted annually.)

The U.S. government also issues Series HH and Series I savings bonds. Both are issued at face value. The HH bonds pay interest twice a year. The I bonds, which are inflation-indexed, pay accrued interest at the bond's matu- rity, which is 30 years.

U.S. Treasury bills (T-bills)
obligations of the U.S. Treasury, sold on a discount basis, and having varying short-term maturi- ties; regarded as the safest of all investments.

U.S. Treasury Bills U.S. **Treasury bills (T-bills)** are obligations of the U.S. Treasury issued as part of its ongoing process of funding the national debt. T-bills are sold on a discount basis in minimum denominations of $1,000 and are issued with 3-month and 6-month maturities. The U.S. Treasury auctions off the 3- and 6-month bills every Monday.

Purchasing T-Bills You can purchase T-bills *directly*, through participation in the weekly Treasury auctions. Or you can purchase them *indirectly*, through local commercial banks, securities dealers, or brokers who buy bills for investors on a commission basis. You can directly purchase T-bills over the Internet (www.publicdebt.treas.gov) or by using a touch-tone phone (call Treasury Direct Electronic Services at 800-722-2678 and follow the interactive menu to complete transactions). You also can purchase outstanding Treasury bills in the resale market through banks or brokers. The biggest advantage of the resale market is that you have a much wider selection of maturities to choose from, ranging from less than a week to as long as 6 months.

It is relatively simple to buy T-bills directly. All you need to do is submit a tender offer to the nearest Federal Reserve Bank or branch, specifying both the amount and the maturity of T-bills desired. (Tender forms can be obtained by writing the Bureau of the Public Debt, Department N, Washington, DC 20239-1500, or by calling 202-622-2000.) The Treasury tries to accommodate individual investors through its noncompetitive bidding system, which most people use because of its simplicity. In essence, all noncompetitive tender offers (by mail, over the Internet, and by phone) are awarded T-bills at a price equal to the average of all the accepted competitive bids. Thus you are assured of buying bills in the quantity desired, while obtaining the benefits of an open auction system—all without going through the hassle of a competitive bid. Note, though, that T-bills bought directly through noncompetitive bidding are meant to be held to maturity. You should not purchase T-bills by noncompetitive bid if you want to trade them. It is difficult and time-consuming to sell these T-bills in the aftermarket.

Evaluating T-Bills A particularly attractive feature of T-bills is that they are *exempt from state and local income taxes*, which in some areas can be as high as 20%. Federal taxes are not due until the interest is actually received at maturity. Also, because they are issued by the U.S. Treasury, T-bills are regarded as the safest, though generally the lowest-yielding, of all investments. Furthermore, there is a highly active secondary market for Treasury bills (other than those bought through noncompetitive bidding), so you can easily sell them if you need the cash.

Nongovernment Short-Term Securities We have seen that you can use deposit accounts, Series EE savings bonds, and U.S. Treasury bills to meet liquidity needs. You can also meet liquidity needs by using *nongovernment short-term securities*. These securities generally tend to have higher yields than deposit accounts, EE bonds, and T-bills with similar maturities due to the slightly higher risk associated with them. The principal nongovernment marketable securities include certificates of deposit, commercial paper, banker's acceptances, and money market mutual funds. Each is briefly described below.

Certificates of Deposit **Certificates of deposit (CDs)** differ from the deposit accounts discussed above in that funds must remain on deposit for a specified period. This period can range from 7 days to a year or more. Although it is

certificates of deposit (CDs) savings instruments in which funds must remain on deposit for a specified period; withdrawals prior to maturity incur interest penalties.

possible to withdraw funds prior to maturity, an interest penalty (equal to 31 to 90 days of interest) usually makes withdrawal costly. Banks today are free to offer any rate and maturity on these securities. The interest rate on CDs is fixed over their stated maturity.

CDs are convenient to buy and hold, and all offer attractive and highly competitive returns plus federal insurance protection (up to $100,000 per deposit). The decision whether to invest in a CD or in a more liquid short-term investment vehicle (such as a MMDA or a T-bill) generally depends on the length of the holding period and interest rate expectations. Uncertain holding periods and expected interest rate increases would favor MMDAs and T-bills; certain holding periods and expected interest rate declines would favor CDs.

brokered CDs
certificates of deposit sold by stockbrokers; offer slightly higher yields than other CDs and typically can be sold prior to maturity without incurring a penalty.

CDs can also be purchased from stockbrokers, in the form of **brokered CDs**. The brokerage house looks around the country for the highest yield it can get, buys these CDs, and then resells them to its clients. In essence, a bank issues the CDs, and the brokerage house places them with the investing public. There's usually no commission to pay, because the broker earns its commission from the issuing bank. The minimum denomination is usually $1,000. Brokered CDs are attractive for two reasons: (1) They can be sold prior to maturity without incurring a penalty. (2) They may provide higher yields—frequently ¼ to ¾ of a percent higher—than those available from a local bank.

commercial paper
short-term, unsecured promissory notes (IOUs) issued by corporations with very high credit standings.

Commercial Paper **Commercial paper** is short-term, unsecured promissory notes (IOUs) issued by corporations with very high credit standings. Most commercial paper is initially sold in multiples of $100,000. Typical maturities range from a few days up to 270 days, the maximum maturity that does not require registration with the Securities and Exchange Commission (SEC). Because the resale market for commercial paper is limited, most investors hold commercial paper to maturity. Its yield is comparable to the rate of return earned on large-denomination CDs. Most individual investors who obtain commercial paper do so from a bank or broker, who will "break down" the paper and sell the investor a small portion. However, returns on commercial paper are generally comparable to returns on CDs, which have a fixed maturity like commercial paper but in addition also have federal insurance protection.

banker's acceptances
short-term, low-risk investment vehicles arising from bank guarantees of business transactions; are sold at a discount from their face value and generally provide yields slightly below those of CDs and commercial paper.

Banker's Acceptances **Banker's acceptances** arise from short-term credit arrangements used by business firms to finance transactions. Most often these involve firms in foreign countries or with unknown credit capacities. Typically, an importer's bank agrees to pay its foreign supplier on behalf of the importer, who is contractually obligated to repay the bank within the 3 to 6 months it takes to receive and sell the merchandise involved in the transaction. The importer's bank may either hold the acceptance to maturity or sell it at a discount to obtain immediate cash. An investor who buys a banker's acceptance is therefore promised payment of its face value by the importer at the specified future date. As a result of its sale, the banker's acceptance becomes a marketable security.

The initial maturities of banker's acceptances are typically between 30 and 180 days, 90 days being most common. If the importer fails to pay the amount due at maturity, the bank is liable for the payment. Because of this, banker's acceptances, which typically have a minimum denomination of $100,000, are low-risk securities with good resale markets. The yields on banker's acceptances are generally slightly below those of CDs and commercial paper; they can usually be purchased through a bank or stockbroker.

money market mutual fund (MMMF)
a mutual fund that pools the capital of a large number of investors and uses it to invest exclusively in high-yielding, short-term securities.

Money Market Mutual Funds A **money market mutual fund (MMMF)** is a mutual fund that pools the capital of a large number of investors and uses it to invest exclusively in high-yielding, short-term securities, such as Treasury bills, large certificates of deposit, and commercial paper. Because such securities are sold in denominations of $1,000 to $1 million (or more), most small investors cannot purchase them individually. The MMMF makes these vehicles, which very often offer the highest short-term returns, available to even small investors. Shares of MMMFs can be purchased through brokers or directly from the fund in initial amounts as small as $500 to $1,000. MMMFs provide easy access to funds through check-writing privileges. You continue to earn interest while the check is being cleared through the banking system. Almost every major brokerage firm has a money fund of its own; hundreds more are unaffiliated with a specific brokerage firm.

The returns on money funds amount to what fund managers are able to earn from their investment activity in various short-term securities. Thus, the returns rise and fall with money market interest rates. Though they are not federally insured, MMMFs have very low risk because the securities they hold are very low in risk and diversification by the funds lowers risk even more. (More information about the features and types of MMMFs is included as part of the discussion of mutual funds in Chapter 12.)

Investment Suitability

Individual investors use short-term vehicles for both savings and investment. They use short-term vehicles to maintain a desired level of savings that will be readily available if the need arises—in essence, to provide *safety and security*. For this purpose, high yield is less important than safety, liquidity, and convenience. Passbook savings accounts, NOW accounts, and Series EE savings bonds are the most popular savings vehicles.

When short-term vehicles are used for *investment purposes*, yield is often just as important as liquidity. However, because the objective is different, the short-term vehicles tend to be used much more aggressively. Most investors will hold at least a part of their portfolio in short-term, highly liquid securities, if for no other reason than to be able to act on unanticipated investment opportunities. Some investors, in fact, devote all or most of their portfolios to such securities.

One of the most common uses of short-term securities as investment vehicles is as temporary outlets. In that use, investors buy short-term vehicles either to warehouse funds until an attractive permanent investment can be found or to sit on the sidelines in times of unsettled or undesirable market conditions. For example, if you have just sold some stock but do not have a suitable long-term investment alternative, you might place the proceeds in a money fund until you find a longer-term use for them. Or if you feel that interest rates are about to rise sharply, you might sell your long-term bonds and use the proceeds to buy T-bills. The high-yielding securities—like MMDAs, CDs, commercial paper, banker's acceptances, and money funds—are generally preferred for use as part of an investment program, as are asset management accounts at major brokerage firms.

To decide which securities are most appropriate for a particular situation, you need to consider such issue characteristics as availability, safety, liquidity, and yield. Though all the investments we have discussed satisfy the basic liquidity demand, they do so to varying degrees. A NOW account is

TABLE 1.4   A Scorecard for Short-Term Accounts and Securities

Savings or Investment Vehicle	Availability	Safety	Liquidity	Yield (Average Rate)*
Passbook savings account	A+	A+	A	D (1.0%)
NOW account	A–	A+	A+	F (0.5%)
Money market deposit account (MMDA)	B	A+	A	B– (4.0%)
Asset management account	B–	A	A+	B (5.0%)
Series EE savings bond	A+	A++	C–	B+ (5.7%)
U.S. Treasury bill (91-day)	B–	A++	A–	A– (6.0%)
Certificate of deposit (3-month, large denomination)	B	A+	C	A (6.6%)
Commercial paper (90-day)	B–	A–	C	A– (6.5%)
Banker's acceptance (90-day)	B–	A	B	A– (6.5%)
Money market mutual fund (MMMF)	B	A/A+	B+	A– (6.0%)

*The average rates reflect representative or typical rates that existed in late 2000.

unquestionably the most liquid of all. You can write as many checks on the account as you wish and for any amount. A certificate of deposit, on the other hand, is not so liquid, because early redemption involves an interest penalty. Table 1.4 summarizes the key characteristics for most of the short-term investments discussed here. The letter grade assigned for each characteristic reflects an estimate of the investment's quality in that area. For example, MMMFs rate only a B+ on liquidity, because withdrawals must usually be made in a minimum amount of $250 to $500. NOW accounts are somewhat better in this respect, because a withdrawal can be for any amount. Yields are self-explanatory. You should note, though, that if an investment scores lower on availability, safety, or liquidity, it will generally offer a higher yield.

IN REVIEW

CONCEPTS

1.18 What makes an asset liquid? Why hold liquid assets? Would 100 shares of IBM stock be considered a liquid investment? Explain.

1.19 Explain the characteristics of short-term investments with respect to purchasing power and default risk.

1.20 Briefly describe the key features and differences among the following deposit accounts.
a. Passbook savings account
b. NOW account
c. Money market deposit account
d. Asset management account

1.21 Define, compare, and contrast the following short-term investments.
a. Series EE savings bonds
b. U.S. Treasury bills
c. Certificates of deposit
d. Commercial paper
e. Banker's acceptances
f. Money market mutual funds

Summary

LG 1

Note: The end-of-chapter Summaries restate the chapter's Learning Goals and review the key points of information related to each goal.

Understand the meaning of the term *investment* and the factors commonly used to differentiate among types of investments. An investment is any vehicle into which funds can be placed with the expectation that they will generate positive income and/or that their value will be preserved or will increase. The returns from investing are received either as current income or as increased value.

Some investment vehicles are securities; others are forms of property. Some investments are made directly, others indirectly. An investment can be a debt, an equity, or a derivative security such as an option. It can possess risk ranging from very low to extremely high. An individual can invest in either short-term or long-term vehicles. Today, individual investors have ready access to both domestic and foreign investments.

LG 2

Describe the investment process and types of investors. The investment process is structured around financial institutions and financial markets that bring together suppliers and demanders of funds. The dominant financial market in the United States is the securities markets for stocks, bonds, and options. The participants in the investment process are government, business, and individuals. Of these groups, only individuals are net suppliers of funds. Investors can be either individual investors or institutional investors.

LG 3

Discuss the principal types of investment vehicles. A broad range of investment vehicles is available. Short-term vehicles have low risk. They are used to earn a return on temporarily idle funds, to serve as a primary investment outlet of conservative investors, and to provide liquidity. Common stocks offer dividends and capital gains. Fixed-income securities—bonds, preferred stock, and convertible securities—offer fixed periodic returns with some potential for gain in value. Mutual funds allow investors conveniently to buy or sell interests in a professionally managed, diversified portfolio of securities.

Derivative securities are high-risk, high-expected-return vehicles. The key derivatives are options and futures. Options offer the investor an opportunity to buy or sell another security at a specified price over a given period of time. Futures are contracts between a seller and a buyer for delivery of a specified commodity or financial instrument, at a specified future date, at an agreed-on price. Other popular investment vehicles include real estate, tangibles, and tax-advantaged investments.

LG 4

Describe the steps in investing, particularly establishing investment goals, and cite fundamental personal tax considerations. Investing is a process that should be driven by well-developed plans established to achieve specific goals. It involves a logical set of steps: meeting investment prerequisites, establishing investment goals, adopting an investment plan, evaluating investment vehicles, selecting suitable investments, constructing a diversified portfolio, and managing the portfolio. Investment goals determine the types of investments made. Common investment goals include accumulating retirement funds, enhancing current income, saving for major expenditures, and sheltering income from taxes.

The tax consequences associated with various investment vehicles and strategies must also be considered. The key dimensions are ordinary income, capital gains and losses, and tax planning.

LG 5

Discuss investing over the life cycle and investing in different economic environments. The investment vehicles selected are affected by the investor's stage in the life cycle and by economic cycles. Younger investors tend to prefer growth-oriented investments that stress capital gains. As they age investors move to higher-quality securities. As they approach retirement they become even more conservative. The stage of the economy— (1) recovery or expansion, (2) decline or recession, or (3) uncertainty as to direction of movement—both current and expected, also affects investment choice.

LG 6   **Understand the popular types of short-term investment vehicles.** Investment plans must ensure adequate liquidity. Liquidity needs can be met by investing in various short-term vehicles, which can earn interest at a stated rate or on a discount basis. They typically have low risk. Numerous short-term investment vehicles are available from banks, the government, and brokerage firms. Their suitability depends on the investor's attitude toward availability, safety, liquidity, and yield.

Discussion Questions

LG 4

LG 5

Note: The Discussion Questions at the end of the chapter ask you to analyze and synthesize information presented in the chapter. These questions, like all other end-of-chapter assignment materials, are keyed to the chapter's learning goals.

LG 6

Q1.1 Assume that you are 35 years old, are married with two young children, are renting a condo, and have an annual income of $90,000. Use the following questions to guide your preparation of a rough investment plan consistent with these facts.

a. What are your key investment goals?
b. How might personal taxes affect your investment plans? Use current tax rates to assess their impact.
c. How might your stage in the life cycle affect the types of risk you might take?
d. What impact might the current economic environment have on the investment vehicles you choose?
e. Can you realistically expect to achieve the goals you specified in part (a)?

Q1.2 What role, if any, will short-term vehicles play in your portfolio? Why? Complete the following table for the short-term investments listed. Find their yields in a current issue of the *Wall Street Journal*, and explain which, if any, you would include in your investment portfolio.

Savings or Investment Vehicle	Minimum Balance	Yield	Federal Insurance	Method and Ease of Withdrawing Funds
a. Passbook savings account	None		Yes	In person or through teller machines; very easy
b. NOW account				Unlimited check-writing privileges
c. Money market deposit account (MMDA)				
d. Asset management account				
e. Series EE savings bond	Virtually none			
f. U.S. Treasury bill				
g. Certificate of deposit (CD)				
h. Commercial paper				
i. Banker's acceptance				
j. Money market mutual fund (MMMF)				

Problems

LG 4

LG 5

P1.1 Sonia Gomez, a 45-year-old widow, wishes to accumulate $250,000 over the next 15 years to supplement the retirement programs that are being funded by the federal government and her employer. She expects to earn an average annual return of about 8% by investing in a low-risk portfolio containing about 20% short-term securities, 30% common stock, and 50% bonds.

Note: The Problems at the end of the chapter offer opportunities to perform calculations using the tools and techniques learned in the chapter. A Web icon appears next to problems that can be solved using the text's software accessible at its Web site: www.awl.com/gitman_joehnk

Sonia currently has $31,500 that at an 8% annual rate of return will grow to about $100,000 at the end of 15 years (found using time-value techniques that will be described in Chapter 4). Her financial adviser indicated that for every $1,000 Sonia wishes to accumulate at the end of 15 years, she will have to make an annual investment of $36.83. (This amount is also calculated on the basis of an 8% annual rate of return using the time-value techniques that are described in Chapter 4.) Sonia plans to accumulate needed funds by making equal, annual, end-of-year investments over the next 15 years.

   a. How much money does Sonia need to accumulate by making equal, annual, end-of-year investments to reach her goal of $250,000?
   b. How much must Sonia deposit annually to accumulate at the end of year 15 the sum calculated in part (a)?

LG 4

P1.2 During 2000, the Allens and the Zells both filed joint tax returns. The Allens' taxable income was $130,000, and the Zells had total taxable income of $65,000 for the tax year ended December 31, 2000.

   a. Using the federal tax rates given in Table 1.2, calculate the taxes for both the Allens and the Zells.
   b. Calculate and compare the ratio of the Allens' to the Zells' taxable income and the ratio of the Allens' to the Zells' taxes. What does this demonstrate about the federal income tax structure?

Case Problem 1.1

LG 1   LG 2   LG 3

Note: Two Case Problems appear at the end of every chapter. They ask you to apply what you have learned in the chapter to a hypothetical investment situation.

Investments or Golf?

Judd Read and Judi Todd, senior accounting majors at a large midwestern university, have been good friends since high school. Each has already found a job that will begin after graduation. Judd has accepted a position as an internal auditor in a medium-sized manufacturing firm. Judi will be working for one of the major public accounting firms. Each is looking forward to the challenge of a new career and to the prospect of achieving success both professionally and financially.

Judd and Judi are preparing to register for their final semester. Each has one free elective to select. Judd is considering taking a golf course offered by the physical education department, which he says will help him socialize in his business career. Judi is planning to take a basic investments course. Judi has been trying to convince Judd to take investments instead of golf. Judd believes he doesn't need to take investments, because he already knows what common stock is. He believes that whenever he has accumulated excess funds, he can invest in the stock of a company that is doing well. Judi argues that there is much more to it than simply choosing common stock. She feels that exposure to the field of investments would be more beneficial than learning how to play golf.

Questions

a.   Explain to Judd the structure of the investment process and the economic importance of investing.

b.   List and discuss the other types of investment vehicles with which Judd is apparently unfamiliar.

c.   Assuming that Judd already gets plenty of exercise, what arguments would you give to convince Judd to take investments rather than golf?

Case Problem 1.2

LG 4   LG 5   LG 6

Preparing Carolyn Bowen's Investment Plan

Carolyn Bowen, who just turned 55, is a widow currently employed as a receptionist for the Xcon Corporation, where she has worked for the past 20 years. She is in good health, lives alone, and has two grown children. A few months ago, her husband died. Carolyn's husband left her with only their home and the proceeds from a $75,000 life insurance policy. After she paid medical and funeral expenses, $60,000 of the life insurance proceeds remained. In addition to the life insurance proceeds, Carolyn has $37,500 in a savings account, which she had secretly built over the past 10 years. Recognizing that she is within 10 years of retirement, Carolyn wishes to use her limited resources to develop an investment program that will allow her to live comfortably once she retires.

Carolyn is quite superstitious. After consulting with a number of psychics and studying her family tree, she feels certain she will not live past 80. She plans to retire at either 62 or 65, whichever will better allow her to meet her long-run financial goals. After talking with a number of knowledgeable individuals—including, of course, the psychics—Carolyn estimates that to live comfortably, she will need $45,000 per year, before taxes, once she retires. This amount will be required annually for each of 18 years if she retires at 62 or for each of 15 years if she retires at 65. As part of her financial plans, Carolyn intends to sell her home at retirement and rent an apartment. She has estimated that she will net $112,500 if she sells the house at 62 and $127,500 if she sells it at 65. Carolyn has no financial dependents and is not concerned about leaving a sizable estate to her heirs.

If Carolyn retires at age 62, she will receive from Social Security and an employer-sponsored pension plan a total of $1,359 per month ($16,308 annually); if she waits until age 65 to retire, her total retirement income will be $1,688 per month ($20,256 annually). For convenience, Carolyn has already decided that to convert all her assets at the time of retirement into a stream of annual income, she will at that time purchase an annuity by paying a single premium. The annuity will have a life just equal to the number of years remaining until her 80th birthday. Because Carolyn is uncertain as to the actual age at which she will retire, she obtained the following interest factors from her insurance agent in order to estimate the annual annuity benefit provided for a given purchase price.

Life of Annuity	Interest Factor
15 years	11.118
18 years	12.659

The yearly annuity benefit can be calculated by dividing the factors into the purchase price. Carolyn plans to place any funds currently available into a savings account paying 6% compounded annually until retirement. She does not expect to be able to save or invest any additional funds between now and retirement. To calculate the future value of her savings, she will need to multiply the amount of money currently available to her by one of the following factors, depending on the retirement age being considered.

Retirement Age	Time to Retirement	Future-Value Interest Factor
62	7 years	1.504
65	10 years	1.791

Questions

a.   Assume that Carolyn places currently available funds in the savings account. Determine the amount of money Carolyn will have available at retirement once she sells her house if she retires at (1) age 62 and (2) age 65.

b.   Using the results from question (a) and the interest factors given above, determine the level of annual income that will be provided to Carolyn through purchase of an annuity at (1) age 62 and (2) age 65.

c.   With the results found in the preceding questions, determine the total annual retirement income Carolyn will have if she retires at (1) age 62 and (2) age 65.

d.   From your findings, do you think Carolyn will be able to achieve her long-run financial goal by retiring at (1) age 62 or (2) age 65? Explain.

e.   Evaluate Carolyn's investment plan in terms of her use of a savings account and an annuity rather than some other investment vehicles. Comment on the risk and return characteristics of her plan. What recommendations might you offer Carolyn? Be specific.

Web Exercises

A revolutionary aspect of "Web investing" is the wealth of information and resources online. You can use the Web to transform your investment world in some very amazing ways. Web "portal" sites, such as Yahoo! Finance (finance.yahoo.com), Excite (excite.com), Lycos (lycos.com), America Online (www.aol.com), and Microsoft's MSN (moneycentral.msn.com), serve as gateways to the Web. These sites vie with each other to be your one-stop financial portal. Visit these sites. Many of them have a personal finance, money, or investing section. Online portals can help steer you in the right direction on the Web and offer abundant links.

Also check other popular Web sites such as Netscape Net Center (netscape.com), Quicken.com, and CBS Market Watch (CBS.marketwatch.com). All of them do a good job of assembling information and presenting it clearly, and each has special strengths. For example, Yahoo! focuses on data, MoneyCentral is big on tools, and Quicken.com excels at broad coverage and consistency.

Of course, no single site can do it all, and each of these sites has features that will appeal to some users more than to others. We recommend that you give all of them a test drive. Bookmark those sites that are of interest to you. The Web is a great place to learn, thanks to many sites maintained by reputable organizations. But it is also filled with erroneous and fraudulent information, so you should be careful as you surf the Web.

The following exercises guide you to specific sites and ask you to search out certain information.

W1.1   This chapter introduces many of the different types of assets that are available for individual investors. The following sites provide information on certain investment assets. Go to each of the sites, and write a brief description of the type of asset or assets on which information can be found at that site. You may want to keep this list as the start of an index of useful investing sites and add to it, for your own use, throughout the course.
a. www.cme.com
b. www.frbsf.org
c. www.realestate.com
d. www.quote.com
e. www.publicdebt.treas.gov

W1.2   Investors avoid risk and demand a reward for engaging in risky investments. A risk tolerance quiz can help you assess your tolerance for investment risk. Take this quiz at the MSN MoneyCentral site (moneycentral.msn.com/investor/calcs/n_riskq/main.asp). Another risk tolerance quiz is offered by Vanguard (http://victory.vanguard.com/educ/newsstnd/moneywhys/1998Winter/riskquiz.html). Take one (or both) of the two quizzes. Are you a conservative, moderate, or aggressive investor?

For additional practice with concepts from this chapter, visit

| www.awl.com/gitman_joehnk |

CHAPTER 2

INVESTMENT MARKETS AND TRANSACTIONS

The Paris, Amsterdam, and Brussels stock exchanges merge to form Euronext, a larger cross-border stock exchange. The Scandinavian exchanges do the same, creating Norex. Competitive pressures bombard the venerable New York Stock Exchange (NYSE), whose cumbersome auction system has lost significant market share to Nasdaq's electronic trading system, home to most technology stocks. Upstart electronic communications networks (ECNs) that match buyers and sellers grab trades away from Nasdaq.

Welcome to the changing world of securities markets, where national boundaries are losing importance. Thanks to advances in telecommunications, networks of electronic screens replace the traditional stock exchange trading floor. Some industry observers envision the creation of a centralized "World Stock Exchange," an electronic marketplace that follows the sun, trading in issues listed on any recognized stock exchange. Others predict that three or four world markets will emerge. Opponents of such immense multinational exchanges call them unnecessary. Investors can already buy in London and sell in Hong Kong through online or traditional brokers. They worry that fewer securities markets will reduce competition. They also cite the very different national regulations as a major stumbling block to successful market consolidation.

In this chapter, we will study the markets, the exchanges, the regulations, and the transactions that enable companies to raise money in the capital markets and enable institutions and individuals to invest in these companies.

Learning Goals

After studying this chapter, you should be able to:

LG 1   Identify the basic types of securities markets and describe the IPO process.

LG 2   Explain the characteristics of organized securities exchanges.

LG 3   Understand the over-the-counter markets, including Nasdaq and alternative trading systems, and the general conditions of securities markets.

LG 4   Review the importance of global securities markets, their performance, and the investment procedures and risks associated with foreign investments.

LG 5   Discuss trading hours and the regulation of securities markets.

LG 6   Explain long purchases and the motives, procedures, and calculations involved in making margin transactions and short sales.

Securities Markets

LG 1   LG 2   LG 3

securities markets
forums that allow suppliers and demanders of *securities* to make financial transactions; they include both the *money market* and the *capital market.*

money market
market in which *short-term* securities are bought and sold.

capital market
market in which *long-term* securities such as stocks and bonds are bought and sold.

primary market
the market in which *new issues* of securities are sold to the public.

initial public offering (IPO)
the first public sale of a company's stock.

Securities and Exchange Commission (SEC)
federal agency that regulates securities offerings and markets.

public offering
the sale of a firm's securities to the general public.

rights offering
an offer of new shares of stock to existing stockholders on a pro rata basis.

private placement
the sale of new securities directly to selected groups of investors, without SEC registration.

Securities markets are forums that allow suppliers and demanders of *securities* to make financial transactions. They permit such transactions to be made quickly and at a fair price. In this section we will look at the various types of markets, their organization, and their general behavior.

Types of Securities Markets

Securities markets may be classified as either money markets or capital markets. The **money market** focuses on the purchase and sale of *short-term* securities. Investors turn to the **capital market** for transactions involving *long-term* securities such as stocks and bonds. In this book we will devote most of our attention to the capital market. There, investors can make stock, bond, mutual fund, options, and futures transactions. Capital markets can be classified as either *primary* or *secondary,* depending on whether securities are being sold initially by their issuing company or by intervening owners.

The Primary Market   The market in which *new issues* of securities are sold to the public is the **primary market**. In the primary market, the issuer of the equity or debt securities receives the proceeds of sales. In 2000, 452 companies offered their stock for sale in the primary market. The main vehicle in the primary market is the **initial public offering (IPO)**, the first public sale of a company's stock. The primary markets also sell new securities, called s*easoned new issues,* for companies that are already public.

Before offering its securities for public sale, the issuer must register them with and obtain approval from the **Securities and Exchange Commission (SEC)**. This federal regulatory agency must confirm both the adequacy and the accuracy of the information provided to potential investors before a security is publicly offered for sale. In addition, the SEC regulates the securities markets.

To market its securities in the primary market, a firm has three choices. It may make (1) a **public offering**, in which the firm offers its securities for sale to the general public; (2) a **rights offering**, in which the firm offers new shares to existing stockholders on a pro rata basis; or (3) a **private placement**, in which the firm sells new securities directly, without SEC registration, to selected groups of investors such as insurance companies and pension funds.

Going Public: The IPO Process   Most companies that go public are small, fast-growing companies that require additional capital to continue expanding. For example, biotechnology company Orchid Biosciences raised almost $48 million when it went public in May 2000 at $8 per share. In addition, large companies may decide to spin off a unit into a separate public corporation. AT&T did this when it spun off its wireless operations into AT&T Wireless in April 2000, raising over $10 billion at $29.50 per share.

When a company decides to go public, it first must obtain the approval of its current shareholders, the investors who own its privately issued stock. Next, the company's auditors and lawyers must certify that all documents for the company are legitimate. The company then finds an investment bank willing to *underwrite* the offering. This underwriter is responsible for promoting the stock and facilitating the sale of the company's IPO shares. The underwriter often brings in other investment banking firms as participants. We'll discuss the role of the investment banker in more detail in the next section.

prospectus
a portion of a security registration statement that describes the key aspects of the issue, the issuer, and its management and financial position.

red herring
a preliminary prospectus made available to prospective investors during the waiting period between the registration statement's filing with the SEC and its approval.

INVESTOR FACTS

HOT IPO MARKETS—IPO markets have been really hot in recent years. In 2000, 452 newly public U.S. companies raised a record $80.6 billion through new equity offerings. In the last quarter of 2000, new issues tapered off to just 63 IPOs valued at $8.8 billion.

investment banker
financial intermediary that specializes in selling new security issues and advising firms with regard to major financial transactions.

The company files a registration statement with the SEC. One portion of the registration statement is called the **prospectus.** It describes the key aspects of the issue, the issuer, and its management and financial position. During the waiting period between the statement's filing and its approval, prospective investors can receive a preliminary prospectus. This preliminary version is called a **red herring,** because a notice printed in red on the front cover indicates the tentative nature of the offer. The cover of the preliminary prospectus describing the 2001 stock issue of Reliant Resources, Inc. is shown in Figure 2.1. Note the red herring printed vertically on its left edge.

After the SEC approves the registration statement, the investment community can begin analyzing the company's prospects. However, from the time it files until at least one month after the IPO is complete, the company must observe a *quiet period,* during which there are restrictions on what company officials may say about the company. The purpose of the quiet period is to make sure that all potential investors have access to the same information about the company—that which is presented in the preliminary prospectus—and not to any unpublished data that might give them an unfair advantage.

The investment bankers and company executives promote the company's stock offering through a *road show,* a series of presentations to potential investors around the country and sometimes overseas. In addition to providing investors with information about the new issue, road show sessions help the investment bankers gauge the demand for the offering and set an expected pricing range. After the underwriter sets terms and prices the issue, the SEC must approve the offering.

Table 2.1 shows the offering date and price, first-day gain, and return based on the price on August 31, 2000, for selected IPOs. Nuance Communications' offering price doubled on the first day and continued to rise. Often the investment banker adjusts the IPO offering price if demand seems very high or low. For example, the preliminary offering price range for the America Online Latin America IPO was $15–$17. Because of lukewarm investor reaction, the investment banker dropped the offering price to $8. The opposite may also be true. In recent years many IPO deals have been *underpriced,* resulting in huge first-day gains. Some industry experts question whether the underwriters misjudge demand for the issue or set the price artificially low to please their institutional clients, who buy at the offering price and then resell the shares. Sometimes companies themselves support undervaluation so that their stock will generate excitement and additional investor interest when the price zooms upward on opening day.

The IPO markets have been particularly active in recent years. Such activity has been a direct result of the strength of the public equity markets. However, investing in IPOs is risky business, particularly for individual investors who can't easily acquire shares at the offering price. Most of those shares go to institutional investors and brokerage firms' best clients. Although many news stories chronicle huge first-day gains, the stocks may not be good long-term investments. In the *Investing in Action* box on page 40 you will learn more about the perils and rewards of IPO investments.

The Investment Banker's Role Most public offerings are made with the assistance of an **investment banker.** The investment banker is a financial

FIGURE 2.1

Cover of a Preliminary Prospectus for a Stock Issue

Some of the key factors related to the 2001 common stock issue by Reliant Resources, Inc. are summarized on the cover of the prospectus. The type printed vertically on the left edge is normally red, which explains its name "red herring."
(*Source:* Reliant Resources, Inc., April 16, 2001, p. 1.)

The information in this preliminary prospectus is not complete and may be changed. These securities may not be sold until the registration statement filed with the Securities and Exchange Commission is effective. This preliminary prospectus is not an offer to sell nor does it seek an offer to buy these securities in any jurisdiction where the offer or sale is not permitted.

Subject to Completion. Dated April 16, 2001.

52,000,000 Shares

 Reliant Resources™

Reliant Resources, Inc.

Common Stock

This is an initial public offering of shares of common stock of Reliant Resources, Inc. All of the 52,000,000 shares of common stock are being sold by Reliant Resources.

Prior to this offering, there has been no public market for the common stock. It is currently estimated that the initial public offering price per share will be between $26.00 and $28.00. Our common stock has been approved for listing on the New York Stock Exchange under the trading symbol "RRI," subject to official notice of issuance.

See "Risk Factors" on page 11 to read about factors you should consider before buying shares of common stock.

Neither the Securities and Exchange Commission nor any other regulatory body has approved or disapproved of these securities or passed upon the accuracy or adequacy of this prospectus. Any representation to the contrary is a criminal offense.

	Per Share	Total
Initial public offering price	$	$
Underwriting discount...	$	$
Proceeds, before expenses, to Reliant Resources.....................	$	$

To the extent that the underwriters sell more than 52,000,000 shares of common stock, the underwriters have the option to purchase up to an additional 7,800,000 shares from Reliant Resources at the initial public offering price less the underwriting discount.

The underwriters expect to deliver the shares in New York, New York on   , 2001.

Goldman, Sachs & Co.   **Credit Suisse First Boston**
   ABN AMRO Rothschild LLC
           Banc of America Securities LLC
               Deutsche Banc Alex. Brown
                  Merrill Lynch & Co.
                      UBS Warburg

Prospectus dated   , 2001.

TABLE 2.1   Performance of Selected IPOs

Company Name	IPO Offering Date	IPO Offering Price	First-Day Gain	Current Price (8/31/00)	Return (IPO price to current price)
Vignette	2/18/99	$19.00	124.7%	$38.13	100.7%
FlashNet Communications	3/16/99	17.00	156.6	3.75	−77.9
Skechers USA	6/9/99	11.00	−3.4	17.81	61.9
Arriba	6/22/99	23.00	291.3	157.38	584.3
7/24 Solutions	1/27/00	26.00	176.2	46.88	80.3
Antigenics	2/3/00	18.00	241.0	15.56	−13.5
Buy.com	2/7/00	13.00	93.3	2.69	−79.3
Homegrocer.com	3/9/00	12.00	17.8	4.06	−66.2
Nuance Communications	4/12/00	17.00	99.6	131.63	674.3
Orchid Biosciences	5/4/00	8.00	36.8	43.00	437.5

Source: "Initial Public Offerings, Top to Bottom," *Wall Street Journal*, January 3, 2000, p. R4; and IPOhome www.TheIPOsite.com

FIGURE 2.2

The Selling Process for a Large Security Issue

The investment banker hired by the issuing corporation may form an underwriting syndicate. The underwriting syndicate buys the entire security issue from the issuing corporation at an agreed-on price. The underwriter then has the opportunity (and bears the risk) of reselling the issue to the public at a profit. Both the originating investment banker and the other syndicate members put together a selling group to sell the issue on a commission basis to investors.

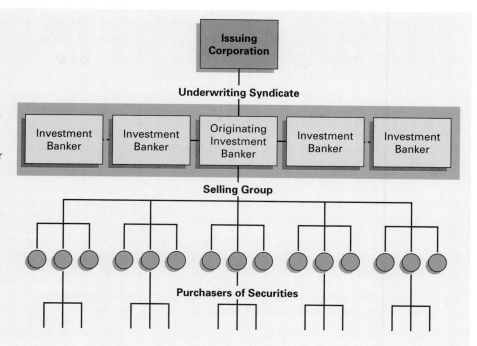

underwriting
the role of the *investment banker* in bearing the risk of reselling, at a profit, the securities purchased from an issuing corporation at an agreed-on price.

underwriting syndicate
a group formed by an investment banker to share the financial risk associated with *underwriting* new securities.

selling group
a large number of brokerage firms that join the originating investment banker(s); each accepts responsibility for selling a certain portion of a new security issue.

intermediary (such as Salomon Brothers or Goldman Sachs) that specializes in selling new security issues and advising firms with regard to major financial transactions. The main activity of the investment banker is **underwriting**. This process involves purchasing the security issue from the issuing corporation at an agreed-on price and bearing the risk of reselling it to the public at a profit. The investment banker also provides the issuer with advice about pricing and other important aspects of the issue.

In the case of very large security issues, the investment banker brings in other bankers as partners to form an **underwriting syndicate**. The syndicate shares the financial risk associated with buying the entire issue from the issuer and reselling the new securities to the public. The originating investment banker and the syndicate members put together a **selling group**, normally made up of themselves and a large number of brokerage firms. Each member of the selling group accepts the responsibility for selling a certain portion of the issue and is paid a commission on the securities it sells. The selling process for a large security issue is depicted in Figure 2.2.

The relationships among the participants in this process can also be seen in the so-called *tombstone* for the June 27, 2000, common stock offering for Community Health Systems, Inc. shown in Figure 6.4 (on page 233). This layout of the announcement indicates the roles of the various participating firms. Isolated firm names or a larger typeface differentiates the underwriter and the underwriting syndicate from the selling group. (In the figure, the key participants in the offering are labeled in the margin at the right.)

Compensation for underwriting and selling services typically comes in the form of a discount on the sale price of the securities. For example, an investment banker may pay the issuing firm $24 per share for stock that will be sold for $26 per share. The investment banker may then sell the shares to members of the selling group for $25.25 per share. In this case, the

INVESTING in action

Riding the IPO Roller Coaster

eToys comes to market at $20 and quadruples to $80 on its first day. Palm Inc., offered at $38, jumps to $95 on its first day and eventually reaches $160. Once reserved for institutional investors and high-net-worth individuals, IPO offerings like these are now available to average investors as well.

Start by visiting Web sites like IPOhome (www.ipohome.com), IPO.com (www.ipo .com), and IPO Central (www.hoovers.com /ipo) to find announcements of upcoming IPOs, market information, and research. (Also check www.iporesources.org, maintained by UCLA faculty members.) Then open an account with one of the online brokerage firms that deals in IPOs, such as DLJdirect, E*Trade/E*Offering, Charles Schwab, or Fidelity. Track IPO allocations on the broker's Web site or register for email alerts.

Once you find an interesting IPO, you have only a few days to review its preliminary prospectus and submit a conditional offer for a certain number of shares at a specified price. Because demand for IPO shares outstrips supply, your broker may not get shares. Even if it does, not all orders will be filled. If you are one of the lucky investors, you'll have only a very short time to confirm your purchase.

Brokers discourage investors from selling their shares quickly to profit from early price gains (this is called "flipping"). They request that you hold shares bought at the offering price for 15 to 60 days, depending on the broker's policy, after the IPO. This is not a binding rule, but don't expect to get more IPO shares from that broker if you don't comply.

Should you play the IPO game? Just as with other stock investments, do your homework. Understand the industry and its prospects. Study the prospectus and analyze the financial statements. You may have to trust your instincts and use some "guesstimates," too. "In a lot of ways, IPO investing is a shot in the dark or a leap of faith," says Tom Taulli, an analyst for EDGAR Online who specializes in IPOs. Not only is the company young and without a trading history, but its industry also may be new, as is the case with Internet firms. Market analysis becomes very important in IPO selection.

Taulli advises individuals not to buy an IPO on the first day of trading, however. "There is typically a tremendous amount of hype, and in some cases hysteria, that surrounds that first day," he says. You can often pick up good stocks at prices at or near their IPO price in the aftermarket, once things have settled down and you can gauge market acceptance of the issue. Besides, many of the best first-day performers turn out to be the worst over the longer term.

Sources: Cassell Bryan-Low, "Small Investors Wait Online for Hot IPOs," *Wall Street Journal*, July 28, 2000, pp. C1, C16; Dan McCarthy, "The Basics: How to Get in on IPOs," *IPO.com*, August 31, 2000, downloaded from www.ipo.com; Tom Taulli's IPO Tips and Tactics, *Business Week Online Daily Briefing*, May 17, 1999, downloaded from www.businessweek.com

original investment banker earns $1.25 per share ($25.25 sale price − $24 purchase price). The members of the selling group earn 75 cents for each share they sell ($26 sale price − $25.25 purchase price). Although some primary security offerings are directly placed by the issuer, the majority of new issues are sold through public offering via the mechanism just described.

secondary market
the market in which securities are traded *after they have been issued*.

Secondary Markets The market in which securities are traded *after they have been issued* is the **secondary market,** or the *aftermarket*. The secondary market provides a way for owners of securities that are already issued to sell them to others. In the secondary market, unlike the primary market, the transaction does not involve the corporation that issued the securities. Instead, money and securities are exchanged between investors; the seller exchanges securities for cash paid by the buyer. The secondary market gives security purchasers *liquidity*. It

organized securities exchanges
centralized institutions in which transactions are made in already outstanding securities.

over-the-counter (OTC) market
widely scattered telecommunications network through which transactions are made in both *initial public offerings (IPOs)* and already outstanding securities.

also provides a mechanism for continuous pricing of securities to reflect their value at each point in time, on the basis of the best information then available.

The secondary markets include the various organized securities exchanges and the over-the-counter market. **Organized securities exchanges** are centralized institutions that bring together the forces of supply and demand for securities that are already outstanding. These exchanges are *auction markets* in which the flow of buy and sell orders determines the price. The **over-the-counter (OTC) market**, on the other hand, is a widely scattered telecommunications network through which transactions are made in both *initial public offerings (IPOs)* and securities that are already outstanding. The OTC markets use a quote system in which negotiation and dealer quotes determine the price. Because popular investment vehicles trade on the organized exchanges and in the over-the-counter market, individual investors are likely to make transactions in both of these markets.

Organized Securities Exchanges

Securities that trade on *organized securities exchanges* account for about 46% of the total *dollar volume* of domestic shares traded. Persons who are members of a given exchange (for example, the New York Stock Exchange on Wall Street) conduct all trading for that exchange in one place, under a broad set of rules. The best-known exchanges for stock and bond transactions are the New York Stock Exchange (NYSE) and the American Stock Exchange (AMEX), both located in New York City. They account for approximately 93% and 3%, respectively, of the total annual dollar volume of shares traded on *organized* U.S. exchanges. Other domestic exchanges include *regional exchanges*, such as the Chicago Stock Exchange and the Pacific Stock Exchange. Regional exchanges deal primarily in securities with regional or local appeal. Together, the regional exchanges account for about 4% of the annual dollar volume of shares traded on organized U.S. exchanges. In addition, foreign stock exchanges list and trade shares of firms in their own foreign markets. Separate domestic exchanges exist for options trading and for trading in futures. Here we will consider the basic structure, rules, and operations of each of these organized domestic securities exchanges. (We'll discuss foreign exchanges later.)

HOT LINKS

Go to the NYSE site and click on [Glossary] to find out the definition of a "growth stock," "American Depositary Receipt, ADR," and "S&P 500."

www.nyse.com

The New York Stock Exchange Most organized securities exchanges are modeled after the New York Stock Exchange (NYSE). It is the dominant organized exchange, often referred to as the "Big Board." To be a member, an individual or firm must own or lease a "seat" on the exchange. The word seat is used only figuratively, because its members trade securities standing up. The majority of seat holders are brokerage firms, and each typically owns more than one seat. The largest brokerage firm, Merrill Lynch Pierce Fenner & Smith, Inc., owns over 20 of the 1,366 seats on the NYSE.

Firms such as Merrill Lynch designate officers to occupy seats. Only such designated individuals can make transactions on the floor of the exchange. Although the majority of members make purchase and sale transactions on behalf of their customers, some members specialize in making transactions for other members or for their own account. For example, *commission brokers* are paid commissions by brokerage firms for executing their orders, and *floor brokers* are brokerage firm employees who execute orders for their firm.

Trading Activity Exchange members make all trades on the floor of the organized exchanges. The largest—the floor of the NYSE—is an area about the size of a football field. Its operation is typical of the various exchanges (though details vary). The NYSE floor has 18 trading posts. Certain stocks trade at each post. (Bonds and less active stocks are traded in an annex.) Around the perimeter are telephones and electronic equipment that transmit buy and sell orders from brokers' offices to the exchange floor and back again after members execute the orders.

All transactions on the floor of the exchange occur through an auction process. The goal is to fill all buy orders at the lowest price and to fill all sell orders at the highest price, with supply and demand determining the price. The actual auction takes place at the post where the particular security trades. Members interested in purchasing a given security publicly negotiate a transaction with members interested in selling that security. The job of the **specialist**—an exchange member who specializes in making transactions in one or more stocks—is to manage the auction process. The specialist buys or sells (at specified prices) to provide a continuous, fair, and orderly market in those securities assigned to her or him.

specialist
stock exchange member who specializes in making transactions in one or more stocks.

Listing Policies To list its shares on an organized stock exchange, a firm must file an application and meet certain listing requirements. Currently, over 3,025 firms list their securities on the NYSE; they account for about 3,300 stocks (common and preferred) and 1,750 bond issues. Of these firms, almost 400 are non-U.S. corporations. Some firms have **dual listing**, or listings on more than one exchange.

dual listing
listing of a firm's shares on more than one exchange.

The New York Stock Exchange has the strictest listing requirements. To be listed on the NYSE, a firm must have at least 2,000 stockholders owning 100 or more shares and a minimum of 1.1 million shares of publicly held stock; pretax earnings of at least $6.5 million over the previous 3 years, with no loss in the previous 2 years; and a minimum of $100 million in stockholders' equity. A foreign company must have pretax earnings of at least $100 million over the previous 3 years, with at least $25 million in each of the previous 2 years. The firm also must pay a listing fee. Once the NYSE accepts a firm's securities for listing, the company must continue to meet SEC requirements for exchange-listed securities. Listed firms that fail to meet specified requirements may be *de-listed* from the exchange.

The American Stock Exchange The American Stock Exchange (AMEX) is the second largest organized U.S. securities exchange in terms of number of listed companies. In terms of dollar volume of trading, the AMEX is actually smaller than the two largest regional exchanges—the Chicago and the Pacific. Its organization and its procedures are similar to those of the NYSE. Because its listing requirements are less stringent, many smaller and younger firms choose to list on the AMEX. In mid-1998 the AMEX merged with the National Association of Securities Dealers (NASD)—the backbone of the over-the-counter market—and, like the OTC, became a subsidiary of the NASD Market Holding Company. The AMEX has approximately 660 seats and about 770 listed stocks.

In recent years the AMEX has reinvented itself to focus on more specialized market instruments. Today about two-thirds of its daily volume comes from tradable index mutual funds, a security developed at the AMEX about 10 years ago. These funds track a published stock market benchmark. Trading in stock options accounts for another large segment of the AMEX's business.

Regional Stock Exchanges Each of the regional exchanges typically lists the securities of 100–500 companies. As a group, these exchanges handle about 4% of the dollar volume of all shares traded on organized U.S. exchanges. The best-known regional exchanges are the Chicago, Pacific (co-located in Los Angeles and San Francisco), Philadelphia, Boston, and Cincinnati exchanges. During 2001 the Pacific Exchange closed its Los Angeles and San Francisco trading floors and moved its equity trading operations to the Archipelago Exchange, the first fully electronic national stock market in the United States. At this writing the success of the Archipelago Exchange is unknown. Most other regional exchanges are modeled after the NYSE, but their membership and listing requirements are considerably more lenient. Trading costs are also lower.

The majority of securities listed on regional exchanges are also listed on the NYSE or the AMEX. About 100 million NYSE shares pass through one of the regional exchanges on a typical trading day. This dual listing may enhance a security's trading activity. In addition, the *Intermarket Trading System (ITS)* links nine markets—five regional exchanges, the NYSE, the AMEX, the over-the-counter market, and the Chicago Board Options Exchange—through an electronic communications network that allows brokers and other traders to make transactions at the best prices.

Like the AMEX, the regional exchanges are looking for ways to differentiate themselves to survive. In October 1999, the Chicago Stock Exchange became the first to offer extended floor-trading hours. The Pacific and Philadelphia exchanges trade heavily in stock options.

Options Exchanges *Options* allow their holders to sell or to buy another security at a specified price over a given period of time. The dominant options exchange is the Chicago Board Options Exchange (CBOE). Options are also traded on the AMEX, the NYSE, the Pacific Stock Exchange, and the Philadelphia Stock Exchange. Usually, an option to sell or buy a given security is listed on only one of the options exchanges, although dual listing sometimes occurs. Options exchanges deal only in security options. Other types of options (not discussed in this text) result from private transactions made directly between sellers and buyers.

Futures Exchanges *Futures* are contracts that guarantee the delivery of a specified commodity or financial instrument at a specific future date at an agreed-on price. The dominant exchange for trading commodity and financial futures is the Chicago Board of Trade (CBT). There are a number of other futures exchanges, some of which specialize in certain commodities and financial instruments rather than handling the broad spectrum listed on the CBT. The largest of these exchanges are the New York Mercantile Exchange, the Chicago Mercantile Exchange, the Deutsche Terminboerse, the London International Financial Futures Exchange, the New York Coffee, Sugar & Cocoa Exchange, the New York Cotton Exchange, the Kansas City Board of Trade, and the Minneapolis Grain Exchange.

The Over-the-Counter Market

The *over-the-counter (OTC) market* is not a specific institution. It represents another way of trading securities. The OTC market is the result of an intangible relationship among sellers and purchasers of securities, who are linked by a telecommunications network. Nasdaq, the leading OTC market, accounts for about 54% of the total dollar volume of domestic shares traded, compared to appproximately 43% for the NYSE, 1% for the AMEX, and 2% for regional exchanges. Instead of an auction system, the OTC market uses a quote system. This system relies on negotiation and dealer quotes to determine the prices at which securities trade in the OTC market. The actual process, which is described later, depends on the general activity of the security. Securities traded in this market are sometimes called *unlisted securities*.

About 35,000 stocks trade over the counter, as do most government and corporate bonds. The OTC market has three tiers. About 6,400 stocks have an active market in which transactions take place frequently, and another 5,000 trade on the OTC Bulletin Board. The rest are stocks of small, thinly traded companies. A majority of all corporate bonds, some of which are also listed on the NYSE, trade in the OTC market.

New Issues and Secondary Distributions

secondary distributions
the public sales of large blocks of previously issued securities held by large investors.

New Issues and Secondary Distributions To create a continuous market for unlisted securities, the OTC market also serves as a forum in which to sell both listed and unlisted *initial public offerings (IPOs)*. Subsequent transactions for listed securities then shift to the appropriate organized securities exchange; unlisted securities continue to trade in the OTC market. **Secondary distributions**—the public sales of large blocks of previously issued securities held by large investors—are also made in the OTC market to minimize the potentially negative effects of such transactions on the price of listed securities. These transactions are forms of third- or fourth-market trades, which we will describe in a moment.

dealers
traders who "make markets" by offering to buy or sell certain over-the-counter securities at stated prices.

The Role of Dealers The market price of OTC securities results from a matching of supply and demand for securities by traders known as **dealers**. Each dealer "makes markets" in certain securities by offering to buy or sell them at stated prices. Unlike the organized exchanges, where a *broker* brings together the buyer and seller of a security, the OTC market links a buyer or seller with a *dealer*. That is, the second party to an OTC transaction is always a dealer.

bid price
the highest price offered by a dealer to purchase a given security.

ask price
the lowest price at which a dealer is willing to sell a given security.

For example, a dealer making a market in Raco Enterprises might offer to buy shares from investors at $29.50 and sell shares to other investors at $31. The **bid price** is the highest price the dealer offers to purchase a given security. The **ask price** is the lowest price at which the dealer is willing to sell a given security. Because more than one dealer frequently makes a market in a given security, dealers compete. Buyers and sellers attempt to find and negotiate the best price—lowest buy price or highest sell price—when making OTC market transactions. The dealer makes a profit from the spread between the bid price and the ask price.

Nasdaq (National Association of Securities Dealers Automated Quotation) system
an automated system that provides up-to-date bid and ask prices on certain selected, highly active OTC securities.

Nasdaq OTC dealers connect with the sellers and purchasers of securities through the **Nasdaq (National Association of Securities Dealers Automated Quotation) system**. Nasdaq is the first electronic communications network for securities trading. Its automated system provides up-to-date bid and ask prices on about 5,000 selected, highly active OTC securities. It enables buyers and sellers to locate one another easily. Not all OTC securities are listed on Nasdaq, however. To trade in securities not quoted on Nasdaq, buyers and sellers must find each other through references or through known dealers in the securities involved.

H O T L I N K S

Go to the Nasdaq site and scroll down the
page and take a site tour by clicking [Tour].

www.nasdaq.com

Nasdaq National Market
a list of national or international
Nasdaq stocks that meet certain
qualification standards of
financial size, performance, and
trading activity.

third market
over-the-counter transactions
made in securities listed on the
NYSE, the AMEX, or one of the
other organized exchanges.

fourth market
transactions made directly
between large institutional buyers
and sellers of securities.

**electronic communications
networks (ECNs)**
privately owned electronic trading
networks that automatically
match buy and sell orders that
customers place electronically.

The Nasdaq Stock Market includes about 6,400 stocks divided into two groups. Included in the **Nasdaq National Market** are about 5,000 companies with a national or international shareholder base. These stocks meet certain qualification standards of financial size, performance, and trading activity. To list initially, companies must have significant net tangible assets or operating income, a minimum public float of 1,100,000 shares, at least 400 shareholders, and a bid price of at least $5. Another 1,400 companies are part of the *Nasdaq SmallCap Market*. These companies too must also meet specified (but less stringent) requirements to list and trade their securities through Nasdaq's sophisticated electronic trading and surveillance system. Transactions in these two groups of stocks are reported quickly (immediately) and in detail similar to NYSE and AMEX trades in the financial press.

Alternative Trading Systems

Some individual and institutional traders now make direct transactions, without using brokers, securities exchanges, or Nasdaq, in the *third* and *fourth markets*. The **third market** consists of over-the-counter transactions made in securities listed on the NYSE, the AMEX, or one of the other organized exchanges. It allows large institutional investors, such as mutual funds, pension funds, and life insurance companies, to make large transactions at a reduced cost. These transactions are typically handled by firms or dealers that are not members of an organized securities exchange. Dealers charge lower commissions than the organized exchanges or Nasdaq would to bring together large buyers and sellers. Institutional investors are thus often able to realize sizable savings in brokerage commissions and to have minimal impact on the price of the transaction. Nasdaq also has third-market operations, called the Nasdaq InterMarket.

The **fourth market** consists of transactions made directly between large institutional buyers and sellers of securities. Unlike third-market transactions, fourth-market transactions bypass the dealer. The fourth market is a direct outgrowth of advanced computer technology. **Electronic communications networks (ECNs)** are at the heart of the fourth market. These privately owned electronic trading networks were formed in response to institutional investor frustration with the way organized exchanges handled large blocks of securities. Archipelago, Datek's Island, Reuter's Instinet, MarketXT, and Redibook are a few of the many ECNs that handle these trades.

The ECNs' trading volume already accounts for about a third of all Nasdaq transactions, as well as for an increasing share of New York Stock Exchange volume. They are most effective for high-volume, actively traded securities, and they play a key role in after-hours trading, discussed later in this chapter. They automatically match buy and sell orders that customers place electronically. If there is no immediate match, the ECN acts like a broker and posts its request on the Nasdaq under its own name. The trade will be executed if another trader is interested in making the transaction at the posted price.

ECNs can save customers money because they take only a transaction fee, either per share or based on order size. Money managers and institutions such as pension funds and mutual funds with large amounts of money to invest like ECNs for this reason. Many also use ECNs or trade directly with each other to find the best prices for their clients.

General Market Conditions: Bull or Bear

bull markets
favorable markets normally associated with rising prices, investor optimism, economic recovery, and government stimulus.

bear markets
unfavorable markets normally associated with falling prices, investor pessimism, economic slowdown, and government restraint.

Conditions in the securities markets are commonly classified as "bull" or "bear," depending on whether securities prices are rising or falling over time. Changing market conditions generally stem from changes in investor attitudes, changes in economic activity, and government actions aimed at stimulating or slowing down economic activity. **Bull markets** are favorable markets normally associated with rising prices, investor optimism, economic recovery, and government stimulus. **Bear markets** are unfavorable markets normally associated with falling prices, investor pessimism, economic slowdown, and government restraint. Since late 1990, the stock market has been bullish primarily as a result of low inflation, improving trade balances, shrinking budget deficits, and economic recovery.

In general, investors experience higher (or positive) returns on common stock investments during a bull market. However, some securities are bullish in a bear market or bearish in a bull market. During bear markets, many investors invest in vehicles other than securities to obtain higher and less risky returns. Market conditions are difficult to predict and usually can be identified only after they exist. Sources of information that can be used to assess market conditions are described in Chapter 3 and are applied to the analysis and valuation of common stock in Chapters 7 and 8.

IN REVIEW

CONCEPTS

2.1 Differentiate between each of the following pairs of words:
  a. *Money market* and *capital market*
  b. *Primary market* and *secondary market*
  c. *Organized securities exchanges* and *over-the-counter (OTC) market*

2.2 Briefly describe the IPO process and the role of the investment banker in underwriting a public offering. Differentiate among the terms *public offering*, *rights offering*, and *private placement*.

2.3 According to the *Investing in Action* box on page 40, how can individual investors buy IPO shares? Describe some ways to minimize the risks of buying these new shares.

2.4 For each of the items in the left-hand column, select the most appropriate item in the right-hand column. Explain the relationship between the items matched.
  a. AMEX
  b. CBT
  c. NYSE
  d. Boston Stock Exchange
  e. CBOE

  f. OTC

  1. Trades unlisted securities
  2. Futures exchange
  3. Options exchange
  4. Regional stock exchange
  5. Second largest organized U.S. exchange
  6. Has the most stringent listing requirements

2.5 Explain how the *over-the-counter market* works. Be sure to mention dealers, bid and ask prices, Nasdaq, and the Nasdaq National Market. What role does this market play in initial public offerings (IPOs) and secondary distributions? What are the *third* and *fourth markets*?

2.6 Differentiate between a *bull market* and a *bear market*.

Globalization of Securities Markets

diversification
the inclusion of a number of different investment vehicles in a portfolio to increase returns or reduce risk.

Today investors, issuers of securities, and securities firms look beyond the markets of their home countries to find the best returns, lowest costs, and best international business opportunities. The basic goal of most investors is to earn the highest return with the lowest risk. This outcome is achieved through **diversification**—the inclusion of a number of different investment vehicles in a portfolio to increase returns or reduce risk. The investor who includes foreign investments in a portfolio can greatly increase the potential for diversification by holding (1) a wider range of industries and securities, (2) securities traded in a larger number of markets, and (3) securities denominated in different currencies. The smaller and less diversified an investor's home market is, the greater the potential benefit from prudent international diversification. However, even investors from the United States and other highly developed markets can benefit from global diversification.

Advances in technology and communications, together with the elimination of many political and regulatory barriers, allow investors to make cross-border securities transactions with relative ease. More and more financial markets are opening up and becoming integrated with the rest of the world's markets. Both investors and seekers of funds can view the world's markets as available to them. In short, globalization of the securities markets enables investors to seek out opportunities to profit from rapidly expanding economies throughout the world. Here we consider the growing importance of international markets, international investment performance, ways to invest in foreign securities, and the risks of investing internationally.

Growing Importance of International Markets

Securities exchanges now operate in over 100 countries worldwide. Both large (Tokyo) and small (Fiji), they are located not only in the major industrialized nations such as Japan, Great Britain, Canada, and Germany but also in emerging economies such as Brazil, Chile, India, South Korea, Malaysia, Mexico, Poland, Russia, and Thailand. The top four securities markets worldwide (based on dollar volume) are the Nasdaq, New York, London, and Tokyo stock exchanges. Other important foreign exchanges include Paris, Osaka, Toronto, Montreal, Sydney, Hong Kong, Zurich, and Taiwan.

The economic integration of the European Union (EU), along with pressure from financial institutions that want an efficient process for trading shares across borders, is changing the European securities market environment. Instead of many small national exchanges, countries are banding together to create cross-border markets and compete more effectively in the pan-European equity-trading markets. The Paris, Amsterdam, and Brussels exchanges merged to form Euronext, and the Scandinavian markets formed Norex. Other stock exchanges are forming cooperative agreements—for example, Tokyo and Australia. The New York, Tokyo, Hong Kong, Australia, Mexico, Toronto, São Paulo, and Euronext exchanges are discussing the formation of a Global Equity Market (GEM). The exchanges would not merge but would form a 24-hour global market alliance, trading the stocks of selected large international companies via an electronic order-matching system. Nasdaq, with joint ventures in Japan, Hong Kong, Canada, and Australia, plans to expand into Latin America and the

Middle East. As noted at the beginning of the chapter, these mergers and cooperative arrangements could be the first step toward a worldwide stock exchange.

Bond markets, too, have become global, and more investors than ever before regularly purchase government and corporate fixed-income securities in foreign markets. The United States dominates the international government bond market, followed by Japan, Germany, and Great Britain.

International Investment Performance

A primary motive for investing overseas is the lure of high returns. In fact, only once since 1980 did the United States finish first among the major stock markets of the world in terms of the rate of increase in its stock price index. For example, in 2000, a generally bad year, investors would have earned higher returns in some markets. During that year the stock price index in U.S. dollars for Denmark increased 22%; for France decreased 8%; for Germany decreased 16%; for Israel increased 2%; for Japan decreased 31%; for Mexico decreased 22%; for Russia decreased 33%; and for Thailand decreased 51%. By comparison, the U.S. stock price index decreased 10%. Of course, foreign securities markets tend to be more risky than U.S. markets. A market with high returns in one year may not do so well in the next.

Investors can compare activity on U.S. and foreign exchanges by following market indexes that track the performance of those exchanges. For instance, the Dow Jones averages and the Standard & Poor's indexes are popular measures of the U.S. markets, and indexes for more than 20 different stock markets are available. (We'll discuss indexes in more detail in Chapter 3.) The *Wall Street Journal* publishes daily reports on most major indexes, trading activity in selected stocks on major foreign exchanges, and currency exchange rates. Other financial publications also include regular reports. Also, the *Wall Street Journal*'s "World Stock Markets" in Section C frequently compares the performance of the U.S. exchanges with that of selected foreign markets.

Ways to Invest in Foreign Securities

Investors can make foreign security transactions either indirectly or directly. One form of *indirect* investment is purchasing shares of a U.S.-based multinational with substantial foreign operations. Many U.S.-based multinational firms, such as Exxon, IBM, Citicorp, Dow Chemical, Coca-Cola, Colgate-Palmolive, and Hewlett-Packard, receive more than 50% of their revenues from overseas operations. By investing in the securities of such firms, an investor can achieve a degree of international diversification. Purchasing shares in a mutual fund that invests primarily in foreign securities is another way to invest indirectly. Investors can make both of these indirect foreign securities investment transactions in a conventional fashion through a stockbroker, as explained in Chapter 3 and in Chapter 12 (which is devoted to mutual funds).

To make *direct* investments in foreign companies, investors have three options: They can purchase securities on foreign exchanges, buy securities of

For a ranking of ADRs, see:

www.worldlyinvestor.com

Yankee bonds
dollar-denominated debt securities issued by foreign governments or corporations and traded in U.S. securities markets.

American depositary receipts (ADRs)
dollar-denominated negotiable receipts for the stocks of foreign companies that are held in the vaults of banks in the companies' home countries.

foreign companies that trade on U.S. exchanges, or buy *American depositary receipts (ADRs)*. The first way—purchasing securities on foreign exchanges—involves additional risks because the securities do not trade in U.S. dollars. This approach is not for the timid or inexperienced investor.

Because each country's exchange has its own regulations and procedures, investors must cope with currency exchange (dollars to pesos, for example). They also must cope with different securities exchange rules, transaction procedures, accounting standards, tax laws, and with language barriers. Direct transactions are best handled either through brokers at major Wall Street firms with large international operations or through major banks, such as Chase Manhattan and Citicorp, that have special units to handle foreign securities transactions. Alternatively, investors can deal with foreign broker-dealers, but such an approach is more complicated and more risky.

The second form of direct investment is to buy the securities of foreign companies that trade on both organized and over-the-counter U.S. exchanges. Transactions in foreign securities that trade on U.S. exchanges are handled in the same way as exchange-traded domestic securities. These securities are issued by large, well-known foreign companies. Stocks of companies such as Alcan (Canada), Gucci (Netherlands), National Westminster Bank (U.K.), and Unilever (Netherlands) trade directly on U.S. exchanges. In addition, **Yankee bonds**, dollar-denominated debt securities issued by foreign governments or corporations and traded in U.S. securities markets, trade on organized exchanges and in the over-the-counter market in the United States.

Finally, foreign stocks also trade on U.S. exchanges in the form of **American depositary receipts (ADRs)**. These are dollar-denominated negotiable receipts for the stocks of foreign companies that are held in the vaults of banks in the companies' home countries. Today, nearly 1,200 ADRs representing about 40 different home countries are traded on U.S. exchanges. About one-fourth of them are actively traded. Included are ADRs of well-known companies such as Nippon, Nokia, Sony, Toyota, and Volvo. ADRs, which trade in the same way as standard domestic securities, are further discussed in Chapter 6.

Risks of Investing Internationally

Investing abroad is not without pitfalls. In addition to the usual risks involved in making any security transaction, investors must consider the risks associated with doing business in a particular foreign country. Changes in trade policies, labor laws, and taxation may affect operating conditions for the country's firms. The government itself may not be stable. When making investments in foreign markets, you must track similar environmental factors in each foreign country. This is clearly more difficult than following your home market, because you are less familiar with the foreign economic and political environments and may be following several countries.

U.S. securities markets are generally viewed as highly regulated and reliable. Foreign markets, on the other hand, may lag substantially behind the United States in both operations and regulation. Some countries place various restrictions on foreign investment. In Korea and Taiwan, for example, mutual funds are the only way for foreigners to invest. Mexico has a two-tier market, with some securities restricted to foreigners. Some countries make it difficult for foreigners to get their funds out, and many impose taxes on dividends. For example, Swiss taxes are about 20% on dividends paid to foreigners. In addition, accounting standards vary from country to country. Differences in accounting practices can affect a company's apparent profitability, conceal other attractive assets (such as the hidden reserves and undervalued assets that are permitted in many countries), and fail to disclose other risks. As a result, it is difficult to compare the financial performances and positions of firms operating in different foreign countries. Other difficulties include illiquid markets and an inability to obtain reliable investment information because of a lack of reporting requirements.

Furthermore, international investing involves securities denominated in foreign currencies. Trading profits and losses are affected not only by a security's price changes but also by changes in currency exchange rates. The values of the world's major currencies fluctuate with respect to each other on a daily basis. The relationship between two currencies at a specified date is called the **currency exchange rate**. On May 31, 2000, the currency exchange rate for the French franc (Ff) and the U.S. dollar (US$) was expressed as follows:

currency exchange rate
the relationship between two currencies on a specified date.

US$ 1.00 = Ff 6.99   Ff 1.00 = US$ 0.143

On that day, you would have received 6.99 French francs for every $1. Conversely, each French franc was worth $0.143.

Changes in the value of a particular foreign currency with respect to the U.S. dollar—or any other currency—are called *appreciation* and *depreciation*. For example, on August 29, 2000, the Ff/US$ exchange rate was 7.28. In the 3 months since May 31, 2000, the French franc had *depreciated* relative to the dollar (and the dollar had appreciated relative to the franc). On August 29, it took more francs to buy $1 (7.28 versus 6.99), so each franc was worth less in dollar terms ($0.137 versus $0.143). Had the French franc instead *appreciated* (and the dollar depreciated relative to the franc), each franc would have been worth more in dollar terms.

currency exchange risk
the risk caused by the varying exchange rates between the currencies of two countries.

Currency exchange risk is the risk caused by the varying exchange rates between the currencies of two countries. For example, assume that on May 31, 2000, you bought 100 shares of a French stock at 100 Ff per share, held it for about 3 months, and then sold it for its original purchase price of 100 French francs. The following table summarizes these transactions:

Date	Transaction	Number of Shares	Price in Ff	Value of Transaction Ff	Exchange Rate Ff/US$	Value in US$
5/31/00	Purchase	100	100	10,000	6.99	$1,430.62
8/29/00	Sell	100	100	10,000	7.28	$1,373.63

Although you realized the original purchase price in French francs, in dollar terms the transaction resulted in a loss of $56.99 ($1,430.62 − $1,373.63). The value of the stock in dollars decreased because the French franc was worth less—had depreciated—relative to the dollar. Investors in foreign securities must be aware that the value of the foreign currency in relation to the dollar can have a profound effect on returns from foreign security transactions.

CONCEPTS

IN REVIEW

2.7 Why is globalization of securities markets an important issue today? How have international investments performed in recent years?

2.8 Describe how foreign security investments can be made, both indirectly and directly.

2.9 Describe the risks of investing internationally, particularly *currency exchange risk.*

Trading Hours and Regulation of Securities Markets

LG 5

Understanding the structure of domestic and international securities markets is an important foundation for developing a sound investment program. Now let's look at market trading hours and the regulation of U.S. securities markets.

Trading Hours of Securities Markets

The regular trading session for organized U.S. exchanges and Nasdaq runs from 9:30 A.M. to 4:00 P.M. Eastern time. However, trading is no longer limited to these hours. The exchanges, Nasdaq, and ECNs offer extended trading sessions before and after regular hours. These allow U.S. securities markets to compete more effectively with foreign securities markets, in which investors can execute trades when U.S. markets are closed. In mid-1991, the NYSE added two short electronic-trading sessions that begin after the 4:00 P.M. closing bell. One session, from 4:15 to 5:00 P.M., trades stocks at that day's closing prices via a computer matching system. Transactions occur only if a match can be made and are handled on a first-come, first-served basis. The other session lasts from 4:00 to 5:15 P.M. and allows institutional investors to trade large blocks of stock valued at $1 million or more. Since their inception, the NYSE has experienced growing interest in both sessions. From 1997 to 1999, both the average daily number and the dollar volume of shares traded in these two sessions more than doubled.

Nasdaq began its own extended-hours electronic-trading session in January 1992. Its Nasdaq International Market Session runs from 3:30 A.M. (when the London Exchange opens) to 9:00 A.M. Eastern Time, half an hour before the start of regular trading sessions in U.S. markets. Because it lists NYSE stocks as well as other U.S. equities and has less stringent disclosure requirements than other markets, Nasdaq International attracts traders from both the New York and the London exchanges. In addition, Nasdaq has an extended-hours session from 4:00 to 6:30 P.M. Eastern time, as well as two SelectNet trading sessions for large blocks of stock, from 8:00 to 9:30 A.M. Eastern time and from 4:00 to 5:15 P.M. Eastern time. Regional exchanges have also moved to after-hours trading sessions.

Until 1999, only large institutional investors could trade after hours. Most of this trading was through ECNs like Instinet, which facilitated fourth-market transactions in about 10,000 U.S. and European stocks. Now individual investors, too, can participate in after-hours trading activity. Many

INVESTING in action

Stock Around the Clock

Trading 24/7—the idea sounds great. Pick up the phone or go to your computer at any hour and buy or sell stocks and mutual funds. Such round-the-clock trading is not yet a reality, but individual investors can trade securities for several hours before and after the close of regular trading sessions.

What's the appeal of extended trading hours? Some investors don't have time to reflect on market news during the day. Investors in the Pacific time zone (3 hours behind New York) want a longer trading day; their regular trading day ends at 1 P.M. Pacific time. Others want to act on company news that is released after the markets close. For example, on January 19, 2000, IBM announced favorable year-end earnings about an hour after the New York Stock Exchange closed. After-hours traders were able to buy the stock at a discount from the next morning's opening price of $123.

But jumping in quickly may not be the right move. One day in February 2000, telephone equipment maker Lucent Technologies Inc. stock closed normal trading at $69.06 a share, down slightly. Sales by institutional night traders pushed the stock down to $51.75 by the opening bell, so that waiting to buy would have been a better strategy.

As these examples illustrate, after-hours investing brings greater risks for most individual investors. After-hours markets—especially the early-morning sessions—are very fragmented.

Electronic communications networks (ECNs) handle after-hours trading. Each ECN serves only its client brokerages, and prices and volumes can differ from ECN to ECN. Currently there is no consolidated price reporting that lets investors compare prices, although some ECNs are working on agreements to share trading information. These sessions are also volatile and less liquid than regular trading sessions. Although interest is growing, fewer than a dozen stocks trade actively during most sessions. There are no market makers to create volume, so huge price swings are typical. Average bid-ask spreads on Nasdaq are often twice as high as during regular trading. Many in the investment community worry that knee-jerk reactions to earnings reports and other news will create havoc with market supply and demand.

To protect investors, most brokerages require limit orders (discussed further in Chapter 3) for after-hours trades. This type of order prevents investors from paying more than they intended or selling for less than they wished.

Sources: Bill Deener, "Timing the Market," *The Dallas Morning News,* April 13, 2000, p. 1D; James McNair, "Happy-Hours Trading," *The San Diego Union-Tribune,* July 2, 2000, pp. I-1, I-6; and Ruth Simon, "After-Hours Trading Carries Sizable Costs for Investors," *Wall Street Journal,* February 9, 2000, pp. C1, C17. For an index of articles about after-hours trading, see www.thestreet.com/basics/nightowl/777198.html

large brokerage firms, both traditional and online, offer after-hours trading services for their individual clients. For example, PaineWebber's extended-hours trading program runs from 8:00 to 9:00 A.M. and from 4:30 to 6:30 P.M. Eastern time. Charles Schwab's extended-hours trading sessions run from 7:45 to 9:15 A.M. and from 4:30 to 7:00 P.M. Eastern time.

ECNs handle after-hours trades for various brokerage firms, with each ECN executing transactions for its specific brokerage clients. Charles Schwab, Fidelity, and DLJ Direct use Redibook, for example. Most ECNs offer after-hours trading between 4 and 6:30 P.M. Eastern time. Is the increase in after-hours trading a positive trend? The *Investing in Action* box above discusses the pros and cons of extended trading hours.

Regulation of Securities Markets

Securities laws protect investors and participants in the financial marketplace. A number of state and federal laws require that investors receive adequate and accurate disclosure of information. Such laws also regulate the activities of participants in the securities markets. State laws that control the sale of securities within state borders are commonly called *blue sky laws* because they are intended to prevent investors from being sold nothing but "blue sky." These laws typically establish procedures for regulating both security issues and sellers of securities doing business within the state. Most states have a regulatory body, such as a state securities commission, that is charged with enforcing the related state statutes. However, the most important securities laws, briefly summarized below, are those enacted by the federal government.

Securities Act of 1933 Congress passed the *Securities Act of 1933* to ensure full disclosure of information about new security issues and to prevent a stock market collapse similar to that of 1929–1932. The act requires the issuer of a new security to file with the Securities and Exchange Commission (SEC) a registration statement containing information about the new issue. As discussed in the earlier section on IPOs, the firm cannot sell the security until the SEC approves the registration statement, which usually takes about 20 days. If the SEC approves the statement, the issuer can offer the new security issue for sale. If it determines that the registration statement is fraudulent, the SEC will reject the issue and may also sue the directors and others responsible for the misrepresentation.

As an investor, you should realize that approval of the registration statement by the SEC does not mean that the security is a good investment. It merely indicates that the facts presented in the statement appear to reflect the firm's true position.

Securities Exchange Act of 1934 The *Securities Exchange Act of 1934* formally established the SEC as the agency in charge of administering federal securities laws. The act gave the SEC the power to regulate the organized securities exchanges and the over-the-counter market by extending disclosure requirements to outstanding securities. It required the stock exchanges as well as the stocks traded on them to be registered with the SEC.

As a result of this act, the SEC covers the organized exchanges and the OTC market; their members, brokers, and dealers; and the securities traded in these markets. Each of these participants must file reports with the SEC and periodically update them. The act has been instrumental in providing adequate disclosure on issues that are traded in the secondary markets. The 1934 act has been amended several times over the years. It remains a key piece of legislation that protects participants in the securities markets.

Maloney Act of 1938 The *Maloney Act of 1938,* an amendment to the Securities Exchange Act of 1934, provided for the establishment of trade associations to self-regulate the securities industry. Since its passage, only one such trade association, the National Association of Securities Dealers (NASD), has been formed. NASD members include nearly all of the nation's securities firms that do business with the public. The NASD, operating under SEC supervision, establishes standardized procedures for securities trading and ethical behavior, monitors and enforces compliance with these procedures, and serves as the industry spokesperson. Membership in the NASD allows member firms to make transactions with other member firms at rates below those charged to nonmembers. Today, any securities firms that are not members of the NASD must agree to direct SEC supervision. Because the SEC can revoke the NASD's registration, it has the same power over this organization as over the exchanges. In addition to its self-regulatory role, the NASD greatly streamlined the functioning of the over-the-counter market by creating Nasdaq.

Investment Company Act of 1940 The *Investment Company Act of 1940* protects purchasers of investment company shares. An *investment company* is one that obtains funds by selling its shares to numerous investors and uses the proceeds to purchase securities. The dominant type of investment company is the *mutual fund* (discussed in detail in Chapter 12). The Investment Company Act of 1940 established rules and regulations for investment companies and formally authorized the SEC to regulate their practices and procedures. It required the investment companies to register with the SEC and to fulfill certain disclosure requirements. A 1970 amendment prohibits investment companies from paying excessive fees to their advisers and from charging excessive commissions to purchasers of company shares.

Investment Advisers Act of 1940 The *Investment Advisers Act of 1940* was passed to protect investors against potential abuses by *investment advisers*—persons hired by investors to advise them about security investments. It requires that advisers disclose all relevant information about their backgrounds, conflicts of interest, and so on, as well as about any investments they recommend. Advisers must register and file periodic reports with the SEC. A 1960 amendment extended the SEC's powers to permit inspection of the records of investment advisers and to revoke the registration of advisers who violate the act's provisions. *This act does not provide any guarantee of competence on the part of advisers.* It merely helps to protect the investor against *fraudulent and unethical practices by the adviser.*

Securities Acts Amendments of 1975 In 1975 Congress amended the securities acts to require the SEC and the securities industry to develop a competitive national system for trading securities. As a first step, the SEC abolished fixed-commission schedules, thereby providing for negotiated commissions. (Commissions are discussed in more detail in Chapter 3.) A second action was to establish of the *Intermarket Trading System (ITS),* an electronic communications network linking nine markets and trading over 4,000 eligible issues. This system allows trades to be made across these markets wherever the network shows a better price for a given issue.

Insider Trading and Fraud Act of 1988 The 1980s were a decade of general economic prosperity and rapidly rising stock prices. As typically happens during such periods in the financial markets, the decade also witnessed a takeover and buyout mania that spawned a host of speculators intent on profit. Many times these speculators operated without regard for the legality of their actions. Although the tactics varied, many of the illegal gains were achieved through insider-trading practices. **Insider trading** involves using nonpublic information to make profitable securities transactions. It is both illegal and unethical.

insider trading
the illegal use of *nonpublic* information about a company to make profitable securities transactions.

The *Insider Trading and Fraud Act of 1988* defined an insider as one who possesses material *nonpublic* information, and it established penalties for insider trading. Insiders are typically a company's directors, officers, major shareholders, bankers, investment bankers, accountants, or attorneys. Of course, insiders are not legally prohibited from trading the firm's shares once private information becomes public. To allow it to monitor insider trades, the SEC requires corporate insiders to file monthly reports detailing all transactions made in the company's stock. These reports are typically available at its Edgar Web site, www.sec.gov/edgarhp.htm, and large trades are frequently summarized and reported in various news media, including the *Wall Street Journal*.

The prosecution and conviction of a number of high-profile insiders during the 1980s and early 1990s created a body of case law that more clearly defines illegal and unethical acts. The definition of the term *insider*, which originally referred only to a company's employees, directors, and their relatives, was expanded to include anyone who obtains nonpublic information about a company. Recent legislation substantially increased the penalties for insider trading and gave the SEC greater power to investigate and prosecute claims of illegal insider-trading activity.

ethics
standards of conduct or moral judgment.

Clearly, the many insider-trading cases of the 1980s and early 1990s heightened the public's awareness of **ethics**—standards of conduct or moral judgment—in business. The financial community is continuing to develop and enforce ethical standards that will motivate market participants to adhere to laws and regulations. Although it is difficult to enforce ethical standards, it appears that opportunities for abuses in the financial markets are being reduced, thereby providing a more level playing field for all investors.

IN REVIEW

CONCEPTS

2.10 What role do ECNs play in after-hours trading?

2.11 According to the *Investing in Action* box on page 52, what risks should individual investors consider before engaging in after-hours trading?

2.12 Briefly describe the key rules and regulations that resulted from each of the following securities acts:
a. Securities Act of 1933.
b. Securities Exchange Act of 1934.
c. Maloney Act of 1938.
d. Investment Company Act of 1940.
e. Investment Advisers Act of 1940.
f. Securities Acts Amendments of 1975.
g. Insider Trading and Fraud Act of 1988.

Basic Types of Securities Transactions

LG 6

An investor can make a number of basic types of security transactions. Each type is available to those who meet certain requirements established by various government agencies as well as by brokerage firms. Although investors can use the various types of transactions in a number of ways to meet investment objectives, we describe only the most popular use of each transaction here, as we consider the long purchase, margin trading, and short selling.

Long Purchase

long purchase
a transaction in which investors buy securities in the hope that they will increase in value and can be sold at a later date for profit.

The **long purchase** is a transaction in which investors buy securities in the hope that they will increase in value and can be sold at a later date for profit. The object, then, is to *buy low and sell high*. A long purchase is the most common type of transaction. Because investors generally expect the price of a security to rise over the period of time they plan to hold it, their return comes from any dividends or interest received during the ownership period, *plus* the difference (capital gain) between the price at which they sell the security and the price they paid to purchase it. This return, of course, is reduced by the transaction costs.

Ignoring any dividends (or interest) and transaction costs, we can illustrate the long purchase by a simple example. After studying various aspects of Varner Industries, you are convinced that its common stock, which currently sells for $20 per share, will increase in value over the next few years. On the basis of your analysis, you expect the stock price to rise to $30 per share within 2 years. You place an order and buy 100 shares of Varner for $20 per share. If the stock price rises to, say, $40 per share, you will profit from your long purchase. If it drops below $20 per share, you will experience a loss on the transaction. Obviously, one of the major motivating factors in making a long transaction is an expected rise in the price of the security.

Margin Trading

margin trading
the use of borrowed funds to purchase securities; magnifies returns by reducing the amount of equity that the investor must put up.

Security purchases do not have to be made on a cash basis; investors can use borrowed funds instead. This activity is referred to as **margin trading**. It is used for one basic reason: to magnify returns. As peculiar as it may sound, the term *margin* refers to the amount of equity (stated as a percentage) in an investment, or the amount that is *not* borrowed. If an investor uses 75% margin, for example, it means that 75% of the investment position is being financed with the person's own funds and the balance (25%) with borrowed money. Brokers must approve margin purchases. The brokerage firm then lends the purchaser the needed funds and retains the purchased securities as collateral. It is important to recognize that margin purchasers must pay a specified rate of interest on the amount they borrow.

margin requirement
the minimum amount of equity that must be a margin investor's own funds; set by the Federal Reserve Board (the "Fed").

The Federal Reserve Board (the "Fed"), which governs our banking system, sets the **margin requirement**, specifying the minimum amount of equity that must be the margin investor's own funds. The margin requirement for stocks has been at 50% for some time. By raising and lowering the margin requirement, the Fed can depress or stimulate activity in the securities markets.

A simple example will help to clarify the basic margin transaction. Assume that you wish to purchase 70 shares of common stock, which is currently selling for $63.50 per share. With the prevailing margin requirement of 50%, you need put up only $2,222.50 in cash ($63.50 per share × 70 shares × 0.50). The remaining $2,222.50 will be lent to you by your brokerage firm. You will, of course, have to pay interest on the amount you borrow, plus the applicable brokerage fees. With the use of margin, investors can purchase more securities than they could afford on a strictly cash basis. In this way, investors can magnify their returns (as demonstrated in a later section).

financial leverage
the use of debt financing to magnify investment returns.

Although margin trading can lead to increased returns, it also presents substantial risks. One of the biggest is that the issue may not perform as expected. If this occurs, no amount of margin trading can correct matters. Margin trading can only magnify returns, not produce them. And if the security's return is negative, margin trading magnifies the loss. Because the security being margined is always the ultimate source of return, choosing the right securities is critical to this trading strategy.

Essentials of Margin Trading Investors can use margin trading with most kinds of securities. It is regularly used, for example, with both common and preferred stocks, most types of bonds, mutual funds, options, warrants, and futures. It is not normally used with tax-exempt municipal bonds, because the interest paid on such margin loans is not deductible for income tax purposes. Since mid-1990, it has been possible to use margin on certain foreign stocks and bonds that meet prescribed criteria and appear on the Fed's "New List of Foreign Margin Stocks." For simplicity, we will use common stock as the vehicle in our discussion of margin trading.

Magnified Profits and Losses With an investor's equity serving as a base, the idea of margin trading is to employ **financial leverage**—the use of debt financing to magnify investment returns. Here's is how it works: Suppose you have $5,000 to invest and are considering the purchase of 100 shares of stock at $50 per share. If you do not margin, you can buy outright 100 shares of the stock (ignoring brokerage commissions). If you margin the transaction—for example, at 50%—you can acquire the same $5,000 position with only $2,500 of your own money. This leaves you with $2,500 to use for other investments or to buy on margin another 100 shares of the same stock. Either way, by margining you will reap greater benefits from the stock's price appreciation.

The concept of margin trading is more fully illustrated in Table 2.2. It shows an unmargined (100% equity) transaction, along with the same transaction using various margins. Remember that the margin rates (e.g., 65%) indicate the investor's equity in the investment. When the investment is unmargined and the price of the stock goes up by $30 per share (see Table 2.2, part A), the investor enjoys a very respectable 60% rate of return. However, observe what happens when margin is used: The rate of return shoots up as high as 120%, depending on the amount of equity in the investment. This occurs because the gain is the same ($3,000) *regardless of how the investor finances the transaction.* Clearly, as the investor's equity in the investment *declines* (with lower margins), the rate of return *increases* accordingly.

Three facets of margin trading become obvious from the table: (1) The price of the stock will move in whatever way it is going to, regardless of how the position is financed. (2) The lower the amount of the investor's equity in the position, the *greater the rate of return* the investor will enjoy when the price of the security rises. (3) The *loss is also magnified* (by the same rate) when the price of the security falls (see Table 2.2, part B).

Advantages and Disadvantages of Margin Trading A magnified return is the major advantage of margin trading. The size of the magnified return depends on both the price behavior of the security that is margined and the

TABLE 2.2   The Effect of Margin Trading on Security Returns

	Without Margin (100% Equity)	With Margins of		
		80%	65%	50%
Number of $50 shares purchased	100	100	100	100
Cost of investment	$5,000	$5,000	$5,000	$5,000
Less: borrowed money	0	1,000	1,750	2,500
Equity in investment	$5,000	$4,000	$3,250	$2,500
A. Investor's position if price rises by $30 to $80/share				
Value of stock	$8,000	$8,000	$8,000	$8,000
Less: cost of investment	5,000	5,000	5,000	5,000
Capital gain	$3,000	$3,000	$3,000	$3,000
Return on investor's equity (capital gain/ equity in investment)	60%	75%	92.3%	120%
B. Investor's position if price falls by $30 to $20/share				
Value of stock	$2,000	$2,000	$2,000	$2,000
Less: cost of investment	5,000	5,000	5,000	5,000
Capital loss	$3,000	$3,000	$3,000	$3,000
Return on investor's equity (capital loss/ equity in investment)*	(60%)	(75%)	(92.3%)	(120%)

*With a capital loss, return on investor's equity is *negative*.

amount of margin used. Another, more modest benefit of margin trading is that it allows for greater diversification of security holdings, because investors can spread their capital over a greater number of investments.

The major disadvantage of margin trading, of course, is the potential for magnified losses if the price of the security falls. Another disadvantage is the cost of the margin loans themselves. A **margin loan** is the official vehicle through which the borrowed funds are made available in a margin transaction. All margin loans are made at a stated interest rate, which depends on prevailing market rates and the amount of money being borrowed. This rate is usually 1% to 3% above the **prime rate**—the lowest interest rate charged the best business borrowers. For large accounts, it may be at the prime rate. The loan cost, which investors pay, will increase daily, reducing the level of profits (or increasing losses) accordingly.

Making Margin Transactions To execute a margin transaction, an investor must establish a **margin account** with a minimum of $2,000 in equity, in the form of either cash or securities. The broker will retain any securities purchased on margin as collateral for the loan.

The margin requirement established by the Federal Reserve Board sets the minimum amount of equity for margin transactions. Investors need not execute all margin transactions by using exactly the minimum amount of margin; they can use more than the minimum if they wish. Moreover, it is not unusual for brokerage firms and the major exchanges to establish their own margin requirements, which are more restrictive than those of the Federal Reserve. In

margin loan
vehicle through which borrowed funds are made available, at a stated interest rate, in a margin transaction.

prime rate
the lowest interest rate charged the best business borrowers.

margin account
a brokerage account for which margin trading is authorized.

TABLE 2.3   **Initial Margin Requirements for Various Types of Securities**

Security	Minimum Initial Margin (Equity) Required
Listed common and preferred stock	50%
OTC stocks traded on Nasdaq National Market	50%
Convertible bonds	50%
Corporate bonds	30%
U.S. Treasury bills, notes, and bonds	8% of principal
Other federal government issues	10% of principal
Federal-government-guaranteed issues	15% of principal
Options	Option premium plus 20% of market value of underlying stock
Futures	2% to 10% of the value of the contract

addition, brokerage firms may have their own lists of especially volatile stocks for which the margin requirements are higher. There are basically two types of margin requirements: initial margin and maintenance margin.

initial margin
the minimum amount of equity that must be provided by a margin investor *at the time of purchase.*

Initial Margin   The minimum amount of equity that must be provided by the investor *at the time of purchase* is the **initial margin**. It prevents overtrading and excessive speculation. Generally, this is the margin requirement to which investors refer when discussing margin trading. All securities that can be margined have specific initial requirements, which the governing authorities can change at their discretion. Table 2.3 shows initial margin requirements for various types of securities. The more stable investment vehicles, such as U.S. Treasury issues, generally have substantially lower margin requirements and therefore offer greater opportunities to magnify returns. OTC stocks traded on the Nasdaq National Market can be margined like listed securities; all other OTC stocks are considered to have no collateral value and therefore cannot be margined.

restricted account
a margin account whose equity is less than the initial margin requirement; the investor may not make further margin purchases and must bring the margin back to the initial level when securities are sold.

As long as the margin in an account remains at a level equal to or greater than prevailing initial requirements, the investor may use the account in any way he or she wants. However, if the value of the investor's holdings declines, the margin in his or her account will also drop. In this case, the investor will have what is known as a **restricted account**, one whose equity is less than the initial margin requirement. It does not mean that the investor must put up additional cash or equity. But as long as the account is restricted, the investor may not make further margin purchases and must bring the margin back to the initial level when securities are sold.

maintenance margin
the absolute minimum amount of margin (equity) that an investor must maintain in the margin account at all times.

Maintenance Margin   The absolute minimum amount of margin (equity) that an investor must maintain in the margin account at all times is the **maintenance margin**. When an insufficient amount of maintenance margin exists, an investor will receive a **margin call**. This call gives the investor a short period of time (perhaps 72 hours) to bring the equity up to the initial margin. If this doesn't happen, the broker is authorized to sell enough of the investor's margined holdings to bring the equity in the account up to this standard.

margin call
notification of the need to bring the equity of an account whose margin is below the maintenance level up to the initial margin level or to have enough margined holdings sold to reach this standard.

Margin investors can be in for a surprise if markets are volatile. When the Nasdaq stock market fell 14% in one day in early April 2000, brokerages made many more margin calls than usual. Investors rushed to sell shares, often at a loss, to cover their margin calls—only to watch the market bounce back a few days later.

The maintenance margin protects both the brokerage house and investors: Brokers avoid having to absorb excessive investor losses, and investors avoid being wiped out. The maintenance margin on equity securities is currently 25%. It rarely changes, although it is often set slightly higher by brokerage firms for the added protection of brokers and customers. For straight debt securities such as Treasury bonds, there is no official maintenance margin except that set by the brokerage firms themselves.

The Basic Margin Formula The amount of margin is always measured in terms of its relative amount of equity, which is considered the investor's collateral. A simple formula can be used with all types of long purchases to determine the amount of margin in the transaction at any given point. Basically, only two pieces of information are required: (1) the prevailing market value of the securities being margined and (2) the **debit balance,** which is the amount of money being borrowed in the margin loan. Given this information, we can compute margin according to Equation 2.1.

Note: Key financial topics offer opportunities for additional study to enhance learning. A Web icon appears next to topics covered in the tutorials that are featured at the book's Web site.

debit balance
the amount of money being borrowed in a margin loan.

Equation 2.1

Equation 2.1a

$$\text{Margin} = \frac{\text{Value of securities} - \text{Debit balance}}{\text{Value of securities}}$$

$$= \frac{V - D}{V}$$

To illustrate the use of this formula, consider the following example. Assume you want to purchase 100 shares of stock at $40 per share at a time when the initial margin requirement is 70%. Because 70% of the transaction must be financed with equity, the (30%) balance can be financed with a margin loan. Therefore, you will borrow $0.30 \times \$4,000$, or $1,200. This amount, of course, is the *debit balance.* The remainder ($4,000 − $1,200 = $2,800) represents your equity in the transaction. In other words, equity is represented by the numerator $(V - D)$ in the margin formula.

What happens to the margin as the value of the security changes? If over time the price of the stock moves to $65, the margin is then:

$$\text{Margin} = \frac{V - D}{V} = \frac{\$6,500 - \$1,200}{\$6,500} = 0.815 = \underline{81.5\%}$$

Note that the margin (equity) in this investment position has risen from 70% to 81.5%. *When the price of the security goes up, the investor's margin also increases.*

On the other hand, *when the price of the security goes down, so does the amount of margin.* For instance, if the price of the stock in our illustration drops to $30 per share, the new margin is only 60% [($3,000 − $1,200) ÷ $3,000]. In that case, we would be dealing with a *restricted account,* because the margin level would have dropped below the prevailing initial margin of 70%.

Finally, note that although our discussion has been couched largely in terms of individual transactions, the same margin formula applies to margin accounts. The only difference is that we would be dealing with input that applies to the account as a whole—the value of all securities held in the account and the total amount of margin loans.

 Return on Invested Capital When assessing the return on margin transactions, you must take into account the fact that you put up only part of the funds. Therefore, you are concerned with the *rate of return* earned on only the portion of the funds that you provided. Using both current income received from dividends or interest and total interest paid on the margin loan, we can apply Equation 2.2 to determine the return on invested capital from a margin transaction.

Equation 2.2

$$\text{Return on invested capital from a margin transaction} = \frac{\substack{\text{Total} \\ \text{current} \\ \text{income} \\ \text{received}} - \substack{\text{Total} \\ \text{interest} \\ \text{paid on} \\ \text{margin loan}} + \substack{\text{Market} \\ \text{value of} \\ \text{securities} \\ \text{at sale}} - \substack{\text{Market} \\ \text{value of} \\ \text{securities} \\ \text{at purchase}}}{\text{Amount of equity at purchase}}$$

This equation can be used to compute either the expected or the actual return from a margin transaction. To illustrate: Assume you want to buy 100 shares of stock at $50 per share because you feel it will rise to $75 within 6 months. The stock pays $2 per share in annual dividends, and during your 6-month holding period you will be entitled to receive half of that amount, or $1 per share. You are going to buy the stock with 50% margin and will pay 10% interest on the margin loan. Therefore, you are going to put up $2,500 equity to buy $5,000 worth of stock that you hope will increase to $7,500 in 6 months. Because you will have a $2,500 margin loan outstanding at 10% for 6 months, you will pay $125 in total interest costs ($2,500 × 0.10 × 6/12 = $125). We can substitute this information into Equation 2.2 to find the expected return on invested capital from this margin transaction:

$$\text{Return on invested capital from a margin transaction} = \frac{\$100 - \$125 + \$7,500 - \$5,000}{\$2,500} = \frac{\$2,475}{\$2,500} = 0.99 = \underline{\underline{99\%}}$$

Keep in mind that the 99% figure represents the rate of return earned over a 6-month holding period. If you wanted to compare this rate of return to other investment opportunities, you could determine the transaction's annualized rate of return by multiplying by 2 (the number of 6-month periods in a year). This would amount to 198% (99% × 2 = 198%).

pyramiding
the technique of using paper profits in margin accounts to partly or fully finance the acquisition of additional securities.

 Uses of Margin Trading Investors most often use margin trading in one of two ways. As we have seen, one of its uses is to magnify transaction returns. The other major margin tactic is called pyramiding, which takes the concept of magnified returns to its limits. **Pyramiding** uses the paper profits in margin accounts to partly or fully finance the acquisition of additional securities. This allows

excess margin
more equity than is required in a margin account.

investors to make such transactions at margins below prevailing initial margin levels, and sometimes substantially so. In fact, with this technique it is even possible to buy securities with no new cash at all. Rather, they can all be financed entirely with margin loans. The reason is that the paper profits in the account lead to **excess margin**—more equity in the account than required. For instance, if a margin account holds $60,000 worth of securities and has a debit balance of $20,000, it is at a margin level of 66⅔% [($60,000 − $20,000) ÷ $60,000]. This account would hold a substantial amount of excess margin if the prevailing initial margin requirement were only 50%.

The principle of pyramiding is to use the excess margin in the account to purchase additional securities. The only constraint—and the key to pyramiding—is that when the additional securities are purchased, the investor's margin account must be at or above the prevailing required initial margin level. Remember that it is the *account,* not the individual transactions, that must meet the minimum standards. If the account has excess margin, the investor can use it to build up security holdings. Pyramiding can continue as long as there are additional paper profits in the margin account and as long as the margin level exceeds the initial requirement that prevails when purchases are made. The tactic is somewhat complex but is also profitable, especially because it minimizes the amount of new capital required in the investor's account.

In general, margin trading is simple, but it is also risky. Risk is primarily associated with potential price declines in the margined securities. A decline in prices can result in a *restricted account.* If prices fall enough to cause the actual margin to drop below the maintenance margin, the resulting margin call will force the investor to deposit additional equity into the account almost immediately. In addition, losses (resulting from the price decline) are magnified in a fashion similar to that demonstrated in Table 2.2, part B. Clearly, the chance of a margin call and the magnification of losses make margin trading more risky than nonmargined transactions. Margin should be used only by investors who fully understand its operation and appreciate its pitfalls.

Short Selling

In most cases, investors buy stock hoping that the price will rise. What if an investor expects the price of a particular security to fall? By using short selling, the investor may be able to profit from falling security prices. (Until 1997 investors could use short selling to *protect* themselves from falling security prices, a strategy called *shorting-against-the-box.*) Almost any type of security can be "shorted": common and preferred stocks, all types of bonds, convertible securities, listed mutual funds, options, and warrants. In practice, though, the short-selling activities of most investors are limited almost exclusively to common stocks and to options.

short selling
the sale of borrowed securities, their eventual repurchase by the short seller, and their return to the lender.

Essentials of Short Selling **Short selling** is generally defined as the practice of selling borrowed securities. Unusual as it may sound, selling borrowed securities is (in most cases) legal and quite common. Short sales start when securities that have been borrowed from a broker are sold in the marketplace. Later, when the price of the issue has declined, the short seller buys back the securities, which are then returned to the lender. A short seller must make an initial

TABLE 2.4	The Mechanics of a Short Sale	
Step 1—Short sale initiated:		
100 shares of borrowed stock are *sold* at $50/share: Proceeds from sale to investor		$5,000
Step 2—Short sale covered:		
Later, 100 shares of the stock are *purchased* at $30/share and returned to broker from whom stock was borrowed:		
Cost to investor		3,000
Net profit		$2,000

equity deposit with the broker, subject to rules similar to those for margin trading. The deposit plus the proceeds from sale of the borrowed shares assure the broker that sufficient funds are available to buy back the shorted securities at a later date, even if their price increases. Short sales, like margin transactions, require investors to work through a broker.

Making Money When Prices Fall Making money when security prices fall is what short selling is all about. Like their colleagues in the rest of the investment world, short sellers are trying to make money by *buying low and selling high*. The only difference is that they reverse the investment process: *They start the transaction with a sale and end it with a purchase.*

Table 2.4 shows how a short sale works and how investors can profit from such transactions. (For simplicity, we ignore transaction costs.) The transaction results in a net profit of $2,000 as a result of an initial sale of 100 shares of stock at $50 per share (step 1) and subsequent covering (purchase) of the 100 shares for $30 per share (step 2). The amount of profit or loss generated in a short sale depends on the price at which the short seller can buy back the stock. Short sellers earn profit only when the proceeds from the sale of the stock are greater than the cost of buying it back.

Who Lends the Securities? Acting through their brokers, short sellers obtain securities from the brokerage firm or from other investors (brokers are the principal source of borrowed securities). As a service to their customers, they lend securities held in the brokers' portfolios or in *street name* accounts. It is important to recognize that when the brokerage firm lends street name securities, it is lending the short seller the securities of other investors. Individual investors typically do not pay fees to the broker for the privilege of borrowing the shares and, as a result, do not earn interest on the funds they leave on deposit with the broker.

Advantages and Disadvantages The major advantage of selling short is, of course, the chance to profit from a price decline. The key disadvantage of many short-sale transactions is that the investor faces limited return opportunities, along with high risk exposure. The price of a security can fall only so far (to a value of or near zero), yet there is really no limit to how far such securities can rise in price. (Remember, a short seller is hoping for a price decline; when a security goes up in price, a short seller loses.) For example, note in

Table 2.4 that the stock in question cannot possibly fall by more than $50, yet who is to say how high its price can go?

A less serious disadvantage is that short sellers never earn dividend (or interest) income. In fact, short sellers owe the lender of the shorted security any dividends (or interest) paid while the transaction is outstanding. That is, if a dividend is paid during the course of a short-sale transaction, the short seller must pay an equal amount to the lender of the stock. (The mechanics of these payments are taken care of automatically by the short seller's broker.)

Uses of Short Selling Investors short sell primarily to seek speculative profits when they expect the price of a security to drop. Because the short seller is betting against the market, this approach is subject to a considerable amount of risk. The actual procedure works as demonstrated in Table 2.4. Note that had you been able to sell the stock at $50 per share and later repurchase it at $30 per share, you would have generated a profit of $2,000 (ignoring dividends and brokerage commissions). However, if the market had instead moved against you, all or most of your $5,000 investment could have been lost.

IN REVIEW

2.13 What is a *long purchase?* What expectation underlies such a purchase? What is *margin trading,* and what is the key reason why it is sometimes used as part of a long purchase?

2.14 How does margin trading magnify profits and losses? What are the key advantages and disadvantages of margin trading?

2.15 Describe the procedures and regulations associated with margin trading. Be sure to explain *restricted accounts,* the *maintenance margin,* and the *margin call.* Define the term *debit balance,* and describe the common uses of margin trading.

2.16 What is the primary motive for *short selling?* Describe the basic short-sale procedure. Why must the short seller make an initial equity deposit?

2.17 Describe the key advantages and disadvantages of short selling. How are short sales used to earn speculative profits?

Summary

LG 1 **Identify the basic types of securities markets and describe the IPO process.** Short-term investment vehicles trade in the money market; longer-term securities, such as stocks and bonds, trade in the capital market. New security issues are sold in the primary market. Once securities are outstanding, investors buy and sell them in the secondary markets. The first public issue of a company's common stock is called an initial public offering (IPO). The company selects an investment banker to advise it and sell the securities. The lead investment banker may form a selling syndicate with other investment bankers to sell the issue. The IPO process includes filing a registration statement with the Securities and Exchange Commission (SEC), getting SEC approval, promoting the offering to investors, pricing the issue, and selling the shares.

LG 2 **Explain the characteristics of organized securities exchanges.** The organized securities exchanges are auction markets. They include the New York Stock Exchange (NYSE), the American Stock Exchange (AMEX), regional stock exchanges, options exchanges, and futures exchanges. In these centralized markets, the forces of supply and demand determine prices. The organized exchanges act as secondary markets where existing securities trade.

LG 3 **Understand the over-the-counter markets, including Nasdaq and alternative trading systems, and the general conditions of securities markets.** The over-the-counter (OTC) market acts as a primary market in which initial public offerings are made. It also handles secondary trading in unlisted securities. It is a dealer market in which negotiation and dealer quotes, often obtained through its automated system, Nasdaq, determine price. Over-the-counter transactions in listed securities are made in the third market. Transactions directly between buyers and sellers are made in the fourth market. Electronic communications networks (ECNs) now offer an alternative to organized exchanges and Nasdaq. Market conditions are commonly classified as "bull" or "bear," depending on whether securities prices are generally rising or falling.

LG 4 **Review the importance of global securities markets, their performance, and the investment procedures and risks associated with foreign investments.** Today securities markets must be viewed globally. Securities exchanges operate in over 100 countries—both large and small. Foreign security investments can be made indirectly by buying shares of a U.S.-based multinational with substantial foreign operations or by purchasing shares of a mutual fund that invests primarily in foreign securities. Direct foreign investment can be achieved by purchasing securities on foreign exchanges, by buying securities of foreign companies that are traded on U.S. exchanges, or by buying American Depositary Receipts (ADRs). International investments can enhance returns, but they entail added risk, particularly currency exchange risk.

LG 5 **Discuss trading hours and the regulation of securities markets.** No longer are investors limited to trading securities during regular market hours (9:30 A.M. to 4:00 P.M., Eastern time). Pre- and post-market trading sessions are available to both individual and institutional investors. Trading activity during these sessions can be quite risky because of greater volatility and lack of centralized pricing data. The securities markets are regulated by the federal Securities and Exchange Commission (SEC) and by state commissions. The key federal laws regulating the securities industry are the Securities Act of 1933, the Securities Exchange Act of 1934, the Maloney Act of 1938, the Investment Company Act of 1940, the Investment Advisers Act of 1940, the Securities Acts Amendments of 1975, and the Insider Trading and Fraud Act of 1988.

LG 6 **Explain long purchases and the motives, procedures, and calculations involved in making margin transactions and short sales.** Most investors make long purchases—buy low, sell high—in expectation of price increases. Many investors establish margin accounts to use borrowed funds to enhance their buying power. The Federal Reserve Board establishes the margin requirement—the minimum investor equity in a margin transaction, both initially and during the margin transaction. The return on invested capital in a margin transaction is magnified; positive returns *and* negative returns are larger than in a comparable unmargined transaction. Paper profits can be used to pyramid a margin account by investing its excess margin. The risks of margin trading are the chance of a restricted account or margin call and the consequences of magnification of losses due to price declines.

Short selling is used when a decline in security prices is anticipated. It involves selling borrowed securities with the expectation of earning a profit by repurchasing them at a lower price in the future. To execute a short sale, the investor must make an initial equity deposit with the broker. The investor borrows the shares from the broker. The major advantage of selling short is the chance to profit from a price decline. The disadvantages of selling short are that the return opportunities are limited in spite of the unlimited potential for loss, and that short sellers never earn dividend (or interest) income. Short selling is used primarily to seek speculative profits from an anticipated decline in share price.

Discussion Questions

LG 1

Q2.1 From 1990 to 1998 the average IPO rose 14% in its first day of trading. In 1999 over 110 deals doubled on the first day, compared to 39 in the previous 24 years combined. What factors might contribute to the huge price runup on the first day of recent issues? Some critics of the current IPO system say underwriters may knowingly underprice an issue. Why might they do this? Why might companies accept lower IPO prices, and what impact do institutional investors have on IPO pricing?

LG 2 **LG 3**

Q2.2 Why do you think some large, well-known companies such as Apple Computer, Intel, and Microsoft prefer to trade on the Nasdaq National Market rather than on a major organized exchange such as the NYSE (for which they easily meet the listing requirements)? Discuss the pros and cons of listing on a major organized exchange.

LG 2 **LG 3** **LG 4**

Q2.3 On the basis of the current structure of the world's financial markets and your knowledge of the NYSE and OTC, describe the key features, functions, and problems that would be faced by a single global market (exchange) on which transactions can be made in all securities of all of the world's major companies. Discuss the likelihood of such a market developing.

LG 5

Q2.4 Critics of longer trading hours believe that expanded trading sessions turn the stock market into a casino and place the emphasis more on short-term gains than on long-term investment. Do you agree? Why or why not? Is it important to have a "breathing period" to reflect on the day's market activity? Why are smaller brokerages and ECNs, more than the NYSE and Nasdaq, pushing for longer trading hours?

LG 6

Q2.5 Describe how, if at all, conservative and aggressive investors might use each of the following types of transactions as part of their investment programs. Contrast these two types of investors in view of these preferences.
a. Long purchase.
b. Margin trading.
c. Short selling.

Problems

LG 4

P2.1 In each of the following cases, calculate the price of one share of the foreign stock measured in United States dollars (US$).
a. A Belgian stock priced at 9,000 Belgian francs (Bf) when the exchange rate is 43.4 Bf/US$.
b. A French stock priced at 700 French francs (Ff) when the exchange rate is 7.2 Ff/US$.
c. A Japanese stock priced at 1,350 yen (¥) when the exchange rate is 110 ¥/US$.

LG 4

P2.2 Lola Paretti purchased 50 shares of BMW, a German stock traded on the Frankfurt Exchange, for 500 Deutsche marks (DM) per share exactly 1 year ago, when the exchange rate was 1.90 DM/US$. Today the stock is trading at 530 DM per share, and the exchange rate is 2.09 DM/US$.

a. Did the DM *depreciate* or *appreciate* relative to the US$ during the past year? Explain.

b. How much in US$ did Lola pay for her 50 shares of BMW when she purchased them a year ago?

c. For how much in US$ can Lola sell her BMW shares today?

d. Ignoring brokerage fees and taxes, how much profit (or loss) in US$ will Lola realize on her BMW stock if she sells it today?

Note: A Web icon appears next to problems and case questions that can be solved using the computation routines available at the book's Web site.

LG 6

P2.3 Elmo Inc.'s stock is currently selling at $60 per share. For each of the following situations (ignoring brokerage commissions), calculate the gain or loss that Maureen Katz realizes if she makes a 100-share transaction.

a. She sells short and repurchases the borrowed shares at $70 per share.

b. She takes a long position and sells the stock at $75 per share.

c. She sells short and repurchases the borrowed shares at $45 per share.

d. She takes a long position and sells the stock at $60 per share.

 LG 6

P2.4 Assume that an investor buys 100 shares of stock at $50 per share, putting up a 70% margin.

a. What is the *debit balance* in this transaction?

b. How much equity funds must the investor provide to make this margin transaction?

c. If the stock rises to $80 per share, what is the investor's new margin position?

 LG 6

P2.5 Jerri Kingston bought 100 shares of stock at $80 per share, using an *initial margin* of 60%. Given a *maintenance margin* of 25%, how far does the stock have to drop before Ms. Kingston faces a *margin call*? (Assume that there are no other securities in the margin account.)

 LG 6

P2.6 An investor buys 200 shares of stock selling at $80 per share, using a margin of 60%. The stock pays annual dividends of $1 per share. A margin loan can be obtained at an annual interest cost of 8%. Determine what return on invested capital the investor will realize if the price of the stock increases to $104 within 6 months. What is the annualized rate of return on this transaction?

LG 6

P2.7 Marlene Bellamy purchased 300 shares of Writeline Communications stock at $55 per share, using the prevailing minimum *initial margin* requirement of 50%. She held the stock for exactly 4 months and sold it without any brokerage costs at the end of that period. During the 4-month holding period, the stock paid $1.50 per share in cash dividends. Marlene was charged 9% annual interest on the margin loan. The minimum *maintenance margin* was 25%.

a. Calculate the initial value of the transaction, the *debit balance,* and the equity position on Marlene's transaction.

b. For each of the following share prices, calculate the actual margin percentage, and indicate whether Marlene's margin account would have excess equity, would be restricted, or would be subject to a margin call.
(1) $45.
(2) $70.
(3) $35.

c. Calculate the dollar amount of (1) dividends received and (2) interest paid on the margin loan during the 4-month holding period.

d. Use each of the following sale prices at the end of the 4-month holding period to calculate Marlene's annualized rate of return on the Writeline Communications stock transaction.
(1) $50.
(2) $60.
(3) $70.

LG 6   **P2.8**   Not long ago, Dave Edwards bought 200 shares of Almost Anything Inc. at $45 per share; he bought the stock on margin of 60%. The stock is now trading at $60 per share, and the Federal Reserve has recently lowered *initial margin* requirements to 50%. Dave now wants to do a little *pyramiding* and buy another 300 shares of the stock. What is the minimum amount of equity that he'll have to put up in this transaction?

LG 6   **P2.9**   Calculate the profit or loss per share realized on each of the following short-sale transactions.

Transaction	Stock Sold Short at Price/Share	Stock Purchased to Cover Short at Price/Share
A	$75	$83
B	30	24
C	18	15
D	27	32
E	53	45

LG 6   **P2.10**   Charlene Hickman expected the price of Bio International shares to drop in the near future in response to the expected failure of its new drug to pass FDA tests. As a result, she sold short 200 shares of Bio International at $27.50. How much would Charlene earn or lose on this transaction if she repurchased the 200 shares 4 months later at each of the following prices per share?
   a. $24.75.   b. $25.13.
   c. $31.25.   d. $27.00.

Case Problem 2.1   *Dara's Dilemma: What to Buy?*

LG 6   Dara Simmons, a 40-year-old financial analyst and divorced mother of two teenage children, considers herself a savvy investor. She has increased her investment portfolio considerably over the past 5 years. Although she has been fairly conservative with her investments, she now feels more confident in her investment knowledge and would like to branch out into some new areas that could bring higher returns. She has between $20,000 and $25,000 to invest.

Attracted to the hot market for technology stocks, Dara was interested in purchasing a tech IPO stock and identified "NewestHighTech.com," a company that makes sophisticated computer chips for wireless Internet connections, as a likely prospect. The 1-year-old company had received some favorable press when it got early-stage financing and again when its chip was accepted by a major cell phone manufacturer.

Dara also was considering an investment in 400 shares of Casinos International common stock, currently selling for $54 per share. After a discussion with a friend who is an economist with a major commercial bank, Dara believes that the long-running bull market is due to cool off and that economic activity will slow down. With the aid of her stockbroker, Dara researchs Casinos International's current financial situation and finds that the future success of the company may hinge on the outcome of pending court proceedings on the firm's application to open a new floating casino on a nearby river. If the permit is granted, it seems likely that the firm's stock will experience a rapid increase in value, regardless of economic conditions. On the other hand, if the company fails to get the permit, the falling stock price will make it a good candidate for a short sale.

Dara felt that the following alternatives were open to her:

Alternative 1: Invest $20,000 in NewestHighTech.com when it goes public.

Alternative 2: Buy Casinos International now at $54 per share and follow the company closely.

Alternative 3: Sell Casinos short at $54 in anticipation that the company's fortunes will change for the worse.

Alternative 4: Wait to see what happens with the casino permit and then decide whether to buy or short the Casinos International stock.

Questions

a. Evaluate each of these alternatives. On the basis of the limited information presented, recommend the one you feel is best.

b. If Casinos International's stock price rises to $60, what will happen under alternatives 2 and 3? Evaluate the pros and cons of these outcomes.

c. If the stock price drops to $45, what will happen under alternatives 2 and 3? Evaluate the pros and cons of these outcomes.

Case Problem 2.2   *Ravi Dumar's High-Flying Margin Account*

LG 6

Ravi Dumar is a stockbroker who lives with his wife, Sasha, and their five children in Milwaukee, Wisconsin. Ravi firmly believes that the only way to make money in the market is to follow an aggressive investment posture—for example, to use margin trading. In fact, Ravi himself has built a substantial margin account over the years. He currently holds $75,000 worth of stock in his margin account, though the *debit balance* in the account amounts to only $30,000. Recently, Ravi uncovered a stock that, on the basis of extensive analysis, he feels is about to take off. The stock, Running Shoes (RS), currently trades at $20 per share. Ravi feels it should soar to at least $50 within a year. RS pays no dividends, the prevailing *initial margin* requirement is 50%, and margin loans are now carrying an annual interest charge of 10%. Because Ravi feels so strongly about RS, he wants to do some *pyramiding* by using his margin account to purchase 1,000 shares of the stock.

Questions

 a. Discuss the concept of pyramiding as it applies to this investment situation.

b. What is the present margin position (in percent) of Ravi's account?

 c. Ravi buys the 1,000 shares of RS through his margin account (bear in mind that this is a $20,000 transaction).

    (1) What will the margin position of the account be after the RS transaction if Ravi follows the prevailing initial margin (50%) and uses $10,000 of his money to buy the stock?

    (2) What if he uses only $2,500 equity and obtains a margin loan for the balance ($17,500)?

    (3) How do you explain the fact that the stock can be purchased with only 12.5% margin when the prevailing initial margin requirement is 50%?

 d. Assume that Ravi buys 1,000 shares of RS stock at $20 per share with a minimum cash investment of $2,500 and that the stock does take off and its price rises to $40 per share in a year.

(1) What is the *return on invested capital* for this transaction?

(2) What return would Ravi have earned if he had bought the stock without margin—that is, if he had used all his own money?

e. What do you think of Ravi's idea to pyramid? What are the risks and rewards of this strategy?

Web Exercises

W2.1 Check the Morgan Stanley Internet Index (www.morganstanley.com/mox). Morgan Stanley uses the "equal dollar-weighting" methodology to calculate its index. Explain the methodology and why it is used.

W2.2 Credit ratings for various countries are presented at www.iimagazine.com/premium /rr/ [Site requires free registration before you can view content]. The scale goes from 0 to 100, with 100 representing the least chance of default. What is the global average rating for the latest period? What is the rating of the United States? What are the ratings of China, India, Singapore, Mexico, and Switzerland?

W2.3 Go to the Vanguard site (www.vanguard.com/vbs/services/margins.html). What are margin and maintenance requirements for:
a. U.S. government bonds with less than one year to maturity?
b. Municipal bonds?

W2.4 Go to the Nasdaq site (www.nasdaq.com). Scroll down and click [Index Shares] on the menu bar. What are the currently available broad-based index shares?

W2.5 Again at the Nasdaq site, go to the screen that shows index shares (www.nasdaq.com/indexshares/index_shares_faq.stm). Index shares (iShares) based on Morgan Stanley Capital International (MSCI) indexes track companies in a foreign country and are termed international-based.
a. What iShares are available on MSCI Index Funds?
b. Why invest in index shares?
c. What are the benefits of index shares trading as stocks?
d. Can index shares be sold short?
e. Can index shares be purchased on margin?

For additional practice with concepts from this chapter, visit

www.awl.com/gitman_joehnk

In Elizabethan days, the motley fool was the court jester who wore multicolored garb. Fools were the only people who could get away with telling the king or queen the truth. The Motley Fool Web site (www.fool.com) was created by two English majors who studied more Shakespeare than investments when in college but are now in the business of offering investment advice. David and Tom Gardner talk to their readers in a straightforward yet humorous manner, referring to readers as "fools" in search of the truth about investing. They ask investors to think for themselves— and give them the tools to do so. The Motley Fool's strategy for beginners is (1) learn the rudiments of investment research, (2) pay down debt before beginning, (3) start with mutual funds that mimic the major stock indexes, and (4) invest in stocks you expect to hold for a long time. Meanwhile, their Motley Fool Rule Breaker and Rule Maker Portfolios consistently stack up well against market professionals. Through year-end 1999, these portfolios significantly outperformed the Standard & Poor's 500 Index.

Fool.com is one of many Web sites where investors can learn about, choose, and buy and sell securities. The Internet has revolutionized the financial services industry, empowering individual investors and simplifying the investing process. In this chapter, you'll learn how to use online investment resources wisely and find the information to make and monitor investment decisions. We'll discuss the basics of making securities transactions through a traditional broker or online, as well as whether to hire an investment adviser or join an investment club. Most of this material is serious and straightforward. But as the Motley Fool has shown, some aspects of investing can also be fun.

CHAPTER 3

ONLINE INVESTING, INFORMATION, AND TRADING

Learning Goals

After studying this chapter, you should be able to:

LG 1 Discuss the growth in online investing, including educational sites and investment tools, and the effective use of the Internet.

LG 2 Identify the major types and sources of traditional and online investment information.

LG 3 Explain the characteristics, interpretation, and uses of the commonly cited stock and bond market averages and indexes.

LG 4 Review the roles of traditional and online stockbrokers, including the services they provide, selection of a stockbroker, opening an account, and transaction basics.

LG 5 Describe the basic types of orders (market, limit, and stop-loss), online transactions, transaction costs, and the legal aspects of investor protection.

LG 6 Discuss the roles of investment advisers and investment clubs.

Online Investing

LG 1

Only a few years ago, online investing focused on finding the lowest transaction costs at one of a few discount brokers that offered cheap electronic trades. Today the Internet is a major force in the investing environment. It has opened the world of investing to individual investors, creating a more level playing field and providing access to tools formerly restricted to professionals. You can trade many types of securities online and also find a wealth of information. This information ranges from real-time stock price quotes to securities analysts' research reports and tools for investment analysis. The savings from online investing in terms of time and money are huge. Instead of wading through mounds of paper, investors can quickly sort through vast databases to find appropriate investments, monitor their current investments, and make securities transactions—all without leaving their computers.

This chapter introduces you to online investing, types and sources of investment information, and the basics of making securities transactions. We will continue discussing online investing in subsequent chapters focused on analysis and selection of various types of securities. In addition, throughout the book you will find descriptions of useful investing Web sites that will help you become a more proficient and confident investor.

Because new Web sites appear every day and existing ones change constantly, it's impossible to describe all the good ones. Our intent is to give you a sampling of Web sites that will introduce you to the wealth of investing information available on the Internet. You'll find plenty of good sources to help you stay current. Many business and personal finance magazines include online investing departments and periodically publish "best of the Web" sections. Magazines such as *Online Investing* are devoted just to finding and evaluating Web sites relevant to investing.

The Growth of Online Investing

Online investing's popularity has grown almost as fast as stock market valuations. In just one year, from 1998 to 1999, the percentage of retail securities trades executed online jumped from 27% to more than 50%. Investors have opened over 16 million online accounts at the 170 brokerage firms that offer online services. About 4 million households manage over $550 billion in assets online. It's easy to see why online investing attracts thousands of new investors daily: The Internet makes buying and selling securities convenient, relatively simple, inexpensive, and fast. In today's rapidly changing stock markets, it provides the most current information, updated continuously. Even if you prefer to use a human broker, the Internet provides an abundance of resources to help you become a more informed investor.

How can you successfully navigate the cyberinvesting universe? You probably already have the technology you need: a computer, modem, and Internet service provider (ISP) to connect you to the Internet. Open your Web browser, and you are ready to explore the multitude of investing sites. These sites typically include a combination of resources for novice and sophisticated investors alike. For example, look at brokerage firm Charles Schwab's homepage (www.schwab.com), shown in Figure 3.1. With a few mouse clicks you can learn about Schwab's services, open an account, and place orders. In addition, you will find the day's and week's market activity, price quotes, and analysts' research reports. You can use screening tools to select stocks and mutual

FIGURE 3.1

Investment Resources at the Charles Schwab & Co., Inc. Web Site

Charles Schwab's Web site presents a wealth of investment resources. You can check the day's market news, get company research, look up the current price of a stock, find stocks and mutual funds that meet specific investment objectives, and more. (*Source:* Charles Schwab, & Co., Inc., San Francisco, California, **www.schwab.com**)

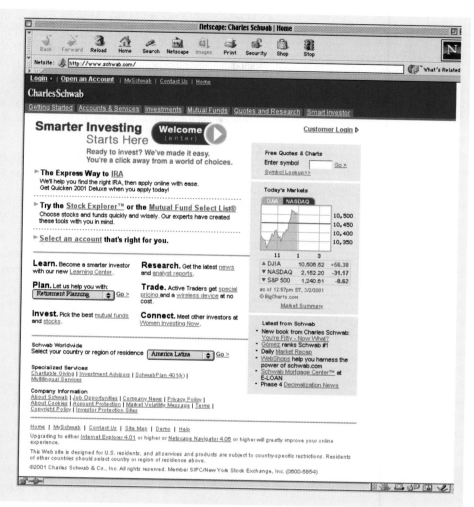

funds, register for an online course at the Learning Center, get advice on retirement planning, and even set up a customized page that delivers the news and stock quotes you request.

All this information can be overwhelming and intimidating. It takes time and effort to use the Internet wisely. But the Internet itself helps you sort through the maze. Educational sites are a good place to start. Then you can check out the many investment tools. In the following section, we'll discuss how to use the Internet wisely to become a smarter investor.

Investment Education Sites The Internet offers many tutorials, online classes, and articles to educate the novice investor. Even experienced investors will find sites that expand their investing knowledge. Although most investing-oriented Web sites and financial portals (described later) include many educational resources, here are a few good sites that feature investing fundamentals.

- *The Motley Fool Fool's School* (www.fool.com) has sections on investing basics, mutual fund investing, choosing a broker, and investment strategies and styles, as well as lively discussion boards and more.

- America Online's (AOL) *Money Basics*, developed with *Smart Money* magazine and for subscribers only, offers Investing 101, which covers basic investment theory, risk management, asset categories, and taxes. Other departments include building and managing your portfolio, investment strategies, and personal finance topics.

- Investopedia (www.investopedia.com) is an educational site featuring Investopedia University, articles on basic investing and personal finance topics, and a glossary of investing terms.

- Zacks Investment Research (www.zacks.com) offers a comprehensive "Investing 101" tutorial and a glossary of financial terms.

- *WSJ.com Online Investing* (www.investing.wsj.com), a free site from the *Wall Street Journal*, is an excellent starting place to learn what the Internet can offer investors.

- Nasdaq (www.nasdaq.com) has an Investor Resources section that helps with financial planning and choosing a broker.

Other good educational sites include leading personal finance magazines such as *Money* (www.money.com), *Kiplinger's Personal Finance Magazine* (www.kiplinger.com), and *Smart Money* (www.smartmoney.com).

Investment Tools Once you are familiar with investing basics, you can use the Internet to develop financial plans and set investment goals, find securities that meet your objectives, analyze potential investments, and organize your portfolio. Many of these tools, once used only by professional investment advisers, are free online. You'll find financial calculators and worksheets, screening and charting tools, and stock quotes and portfolio trackers at general financial sites (described in the later section on financial portals) and at the Web sites of larger brokerage firms. You can even set up a personal calendar that notifies you of forthcoming earnings announcements and can receive alerts when one of your stocks has hit a predetermined price target.

HOTLINKS

See NAIC, a not-for-profit organization site for investment education of individuals and investment clubs.

www.better-investing.org

Planning Online calculators and worksheets help you find answers to your financial planning and investing questions. With them you can figure out how much to save each month for a particular goal, such as the down payment for your first home, a college education for your children, or retiring when you are 60. For example, the brokerage firm Fidelity (www.Fidelity.com) has a wide selection of planning tools: investment growth, college planning, retirement planning—even a "spend or save" calculator. (Because not all calculators give the same answer, you may want to try out those at several sites.)

One of the best sites for financial calculators is FinanCenter.com (www.financenter.com). It includes over 100 calculators for financial planning, insurance, auto and home buying, and investing. Figure 3.2 shows a calculator that answers the following question about stock: "What selling price provides my desired return?" Other investment-related calculators show the difference between selling a stock before or after one year, your current yield from dividends, how exchange rates affect foreign stock transactions, how fees and costs affect your mutual fund purchases, bond yield to maturity, whether a taxable or a tax-exempt bond provides a better return, and more.

FIGURE 3.2 **Financial Calculator: What selling price provides my desired return?**

At sites like FinanCenter.com, you'll find many calculators similar to the one shown here to help with investment planning. Input the variables for your situation, and the calculator will show you the selling price at which you will earn the desired return on your stock investment. (*Source:* FinanCenter.com, **www.financenter.com/products/analyzers/ stock.fcs**)

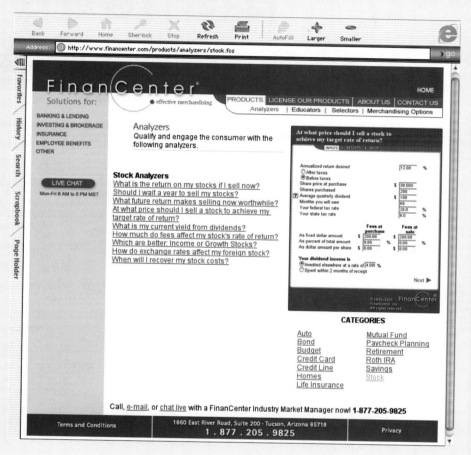

Screening With screening tools, you can quickly sort through huge databases of stocks, bonds, and mutual funds to find those that have specific characteristics. For stocks, you can specify low or high price/earnings ratios, small market value, high dividend return, specific revenue growth, and/or a low debt-to-equity ratio. For bonds, you can specify a given industry, maturity date, or yield. For mutual funds, you might specify low minimum investment, a particular industry or geographical sector, and low fees. Each screening tool uses a different method to sort. You answer a series of questions to specify the type of stock or fund, performance criteria, cost parameters, and so on. Then you can do more research on the stocks, bonds, or mutual funds that meet your requirements.

Quicken.com (www.quicken.com) has some of the best free tools. Figure 3.3 shows the opening page for Quicken's "EasyStep Search" stock screen, which walks you through a customized search and explains each variable. Other steps let you select valuation, growth rates, financial strength, and similar qualities. Morningstar (www.morningstar.com) offers some free tools but charges $9.95 a month or $99 a year for its premium tools. Wall Street City

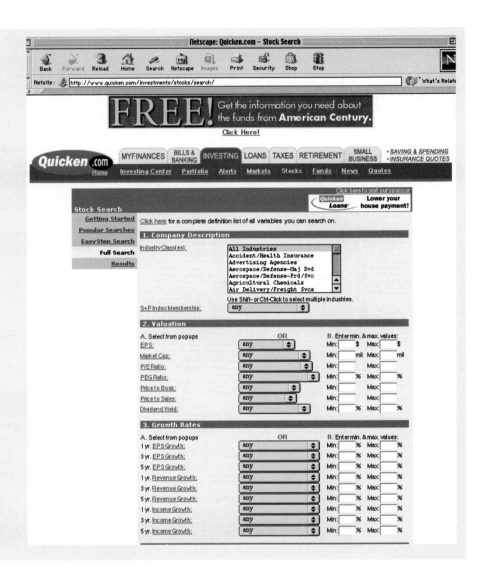

FIGURE 3.3

Quicken's Stock Screening Tool

Select from a list of variables, such as industry, valuation criteria, growth rates, and financial strength, and Quicken's stock screening tool will give you a list of stocks that meet your specifications. (*Source:* Quicken.com, **www.quicken.com /investments/stocks/search**. © Intuit Inc. Quicken.com is a unit of Intuit Inc., 2535 Garcia Avenue, Mountain View, California. Phone: 650-944-6000.)

(www.wallstreetcity.com) offers some of the best screening tools. You can check out the site's "standard" screens free—for example, "high insider buying" and "weak stocks recovering." More experienced investors can subscribe to its ProSearch screening tool for $9.95 a month and customize stock screens with up to 40 of 700 criteria.

Charting *Charting* is a technique that plots the performance of stocks over a specified time period, from months to decades and beyond. Looking at the 1-year stock chart for Qualcomm (QCOM) in Figure 3.4, it's obvious that charting can be tedious and expensive. But by going online, today you can see the chart for a selected stock in just seconds. With another click you can compare one company's price performance to that of other stocks, industries, sectors, or market indexes, choosing the type of chart, time frame, and indicators. Several good sites are Barchart.com (**www.barchart.com**), BigCharts (**www.bigcharts.com**), and Stock Charts (**www.stockcharts.com**). All have free charting features; Barchart.com charges a monthly fee for advanced capabilities.

FIGURE 3.4

Stock Chart for Qualcomm

Specify the company's time frame and frequency (daily, weekly, etc.), and BigCharts will in seconds perform the tedious process of charting the selected stock's price (in this case, the price of Qualcomm) over the specified time frame (in this case, the year ended February 2001). (*Source:* BigCharts Inc. is a service of CBS MarketWatch.com, Inc., 123 North 3rd Street, Minneapolis, MN 55401. www.bigcharts.com /intchart/frames/frames .asp?symb=&time=&freq=)

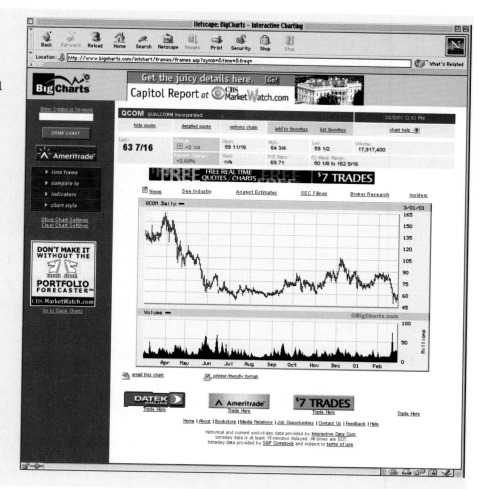

Stock Quotes and Portfolio Tracking Almost every investment-oriented Web site includes stock quotation and portfolio tracking tools. Simply enter the stock symbol to get the price, either in real-time or delayed several minutes. Once you create a portfolio of stocks in a portfolio tracker, the tracker automatically updates your portfolio's value every time you check. You can usually link to more detailed information about each stock. Many sites let you set up multiple portfolios. The features, quality, and ease of use of stock trackers varies, so check several to find the one that best meets your needs. Quicken.com, MSN MoneyCentral Investor (www.investor.msn.com), and E*Trade (www.etrade.com) have portfolio trackers that are easy to set up and customize. Quicken's tracker, also available on Excite and AOL, alerts you whenever an analyst changes the rating on one of your stocks, and it tells you how well you are diversified among the major asset classes or sectors you hold.

Using the Internet Effectively

The power of the Internet as an investing tool is alluring. "Do-it-yourself" investing is now possible for the average investor, even novices who have never before bought stock. However, online investing also carries risks. Trading on the Internet requires that investors exercise the same—and possibly more—caution than they would if they were getting information from and placing orders with a human broker. You don't have the safety net of a live broker suggesting that you rethink your trade. The ease of point-and-click investing can be the financial downfall of inexperienced investors. Drawn by stories of others who have made lots of money, many novice investors take the plunge before they acquire the necessary skills and knowledge—often with disastrous results.

Online or off, the basic rules for smart investing are the same. Know what you are buying, from whom, and at what level of risk. Be skeptical. If it sounds too good to be true, it probably is! Always do your own research; don't accept someone else's word that a security is a good buy. Perform your own analysis before you buy, using the skills you will develop in later chapters of this book.

Here is some additional advice:

- Don't let the speed and ease of making transactions blind you to the realities of online trading. More frequent trades mean high total transaction costs. Although some brokers advertise per-trade costs as low as $8, the average online transaction fee is higher (about $20 in March 2001). If you trade often, it will take longer to recoup your costs. Studies reveal that the more often you trade, the harder it is to beat the market. In addition, on short-term trades of less than one year, you'll pay taxes on profits at the higher, ordinary income rates, not the lower capital gains rate.

- Don't believe everything you read on the Internet. It's easy to be impressed with a screen full of data touting a stock's prospects or to act on a hot tip you find on a discussion board or in an online chat (more on these later). But what do you know about the person who posts the information? He or she could be a shill for a dealer, posing as an enthusiastic investor to push a stock. Stick to the sites of major brokerage firms, mutual funds, academic institutions, and well-known business and finance publications.

- If you get bitten by the online buying bug, don't be tempted to use margin debt to increase your stock holdings. You may instead be magnifying your losses, as noted in Chapter 2.

We will return to the subject of online investment fraud and scams and will discuss guidelines for online transactions in subsequent sections of this chapter.

IN REVIEW

CONCEPTS

3.1 Discuss the impact of the Internet on the individual investor, and summarize the types of resources it provides.

3.2 Identify the four main types of online investment tools. How can they help you become a better investor?

3.3 What are some of the pros and cons of using the Internet to choose and manage your investments?

Types and Sources of Investment Information

LG 2

descriptive information
factual data on the past behavior of the economy, the market, the industry, the company, or a given investment vehicle.

analytical information
available current data in conjunction with projections and recommendations about potential investments.

As you learned in Chapter 1, becoming a successful investor starts with developing investment plans and meeting your liquidity needs. Once you have done this, you can search for the right investments to implement your investment plan and monitor your progress toward achieving your goals. Whether you use the Internet or print sources, you should examine various kinds of investment information to formulate expectations of the risk-return behaviors of potential investments and to monitor them once they are acquired. This section describes the key types and sources of investment information; the following section focuses on market averages and indexes.

Investment information can be either descriptive or analytical. **Descriptive information** presents factual data on the past behavior of the economy, the market, the industry, the company, or a given investment vehicle. **Analytical information** presents available current data in conjunction with projections and recommendations about potential investments. The sample page from *Value Line* included in Figure 3.5 provides both descriptive and analytical information on PepsiCo, Inc. Items that are primarily descriptive are marked with a D, analytical items with an A. Examples of descriptive information are the company's capital structure (7D) and monthly stock price ranges for the past 13 years (13D). Examples of analytical information are rank for timeliness (1A) and projected price range and associated annual total returns for the next 3 years (4A).

Some forms of investment information are free; others must be purchased individually or by annual subscription. You'll find free information on the Internet; in newspapers, magazines, and at brokerage firms; and at public, university, and brokerage firm libraries. Alternatively, you can subscribe to free and paid services that provide periodic reports summarizing the investment outlook and recommending certain actions. Many Internet sites now offer free e-mail newsletters and alerts. You can even set up your own personalized homepage at many financial Web sites so that stock quotes, portfolio tracking, current business news, and other information on stocks of interest to you appear whenever you visit the site. Other sites charge for premium content, such as brokerage research reports, whether in print or online form.

Although the Internet has increased the amount of free information, it may still make sense to pay for services that save you time and money by gathering material you need. But first consider the value of potential information: For example, paying $40 for information that increases your return by $27 would not be economically sound. The larger your investment portfolio, the easier it is to justify information purchases, because they are usually applicable to a number of investments.

Types of Information

Investment information can be divided into five types, each concerned with an important aspect of the investment process.

1. *Economic and current event information* includes background as well as forecast data related to economic, political, and social trends on a domestic as well as a global scale. Such information provides a basis for assessing the environment in which decisions are made.
2. *Industry and company information* includes background as well as forecast data on specific industries and companies. Investors use such information to assess the outlook in a given industry or a specific company.

FIGURE 3.5   A Report Containing Descriptive and Analytical Information

Value Line's full-page report on PepsiCo, Inc. from February 9, 2001, contains both descriptive (marked D) and analytical (marked A) information. (*Source:* Adapted from *The Value Line Investment Survey,* Ratings and Reports, Edition 10, February 9, 2001, p. 1542. © Value Line Publishing, Inc.)

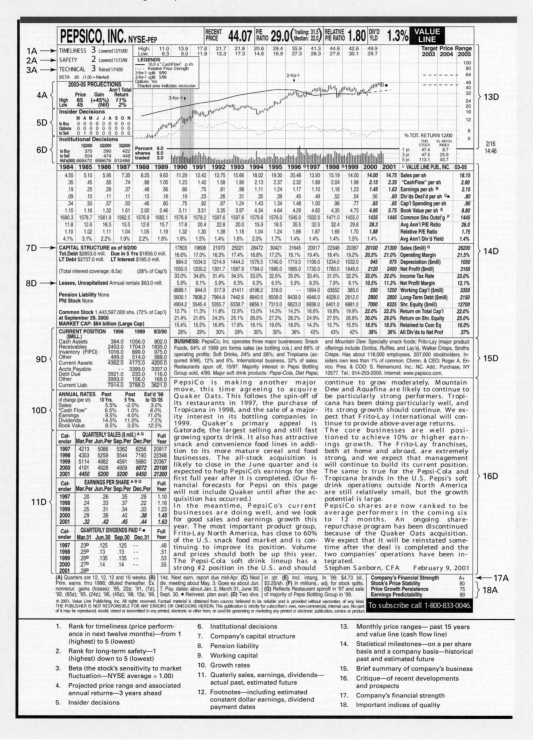

1. Rank for timeliness (price performance in next twelve months)—from 1 (highest) to 5 (lowest)
2. Rank for long-term safety—1 (highest) down to 5 (lowest)
3. Beta (the stock's sensitivity to market fluctuation—NYSE average = 1.00)
4. Projected price range and associated annual returns—3 years ahead
5. Insider decisions
6. Institutional decisions
7. Company's capital structure
8. Pension liability
9. Working capital
10. Growth rates
11. Quarterly sales, earnings, dividends—actual past, estimated future
12. Footnotes—including estimated constant dollar earnings, dividend payment dates
13. Monthly price ranges—past 15 years and value line (cash flow line)
14. Statistical milestones—on a per share basis and a company basis—historical past and estimated future
15. Brief summary of company's business
16. Critique—of recent developments and prospects
17. Company's financial strength
18. Important indices of quality

Because of its company orientation, it is most relevant to stock, bond, or options investments.

3. *Information on alternative investment vehicles* includes background and predictive data for securities other than stocks, bonds, and options, such as mutual funds and futures.

4. *Price information* includes current price quotations on certain investment vehicles, particularly securities. These quotations are commonly accompanied by statistics on the recent price behavior of the vehicle.

5. *Information on personal investment strategies* includes recommendations on investment strategies or specific purchase or sale actions. In general, this information tends to be educational or analytical rather than descriptive.

Sources of Information

A complete listing of the sources of each type of investment information is beyond the scope of this book. Our discussion focuses on the most common online and traditional sources of information on economic and current events, industries and companies, and prices, as well as other online sources.

Economic and Current Event Information Investors who are aware of current economic, political, and business events tend to make better investment decisions. Popular sources of economic and current event information include financial journals, general newspapers, institutional news, business periodicals, government publications, and special subscription services. These are available in print and online versions; often the online versions are free but may have limited content. Most offer free searchable article archives and charge a nominal fee for each article downloaded.

Wall Street Journal
a daily business newspaper, published regionally; the most popular source of financial news.

Financial Journals The **Wall Street Journal** is the most popular source of financial news. Published daily Monday through Friday in regional, European, and Asian editions, the *Journal* also has an online version called the *WSJ Interactive Edition* (www.wsj.com), which is updated frequently throughout the day and on the weekends. In addition to giving daily price quotations on thousands of investment vehicles, it reports world, national, regional, and corporate news. The first page of the third section of the *Journal* usually contains a column called "Heard on the Street" that focuses on specific market and company events. In addition, articles that address personal finance issues and topics are often included on that page. A print subscription to the *Wall Street Journal* costs $175 annually, compared to $59 per year for the online version; print subscribers pay $29 to add the online edition. *WSJ Interactive* includes features such as Briefing Books on individual companies and mutual funds; article searches; special online-only articles; and access to the Dow Jones Publications Library, a comprehensive database of articles from major general and business periodicals.

HOTLINKS

Federal Reserve Economic Data (FRED) has a historical database of economic and financial statistics.

www.stls.frb.org/fred

Barron's
a weekly business newspaper; a popular source of financial news.

A second popular source of financial news is **Barron's,** which is published weekly. *Barron's* generally offers lengthier articles on a variety of topics of interest to individual investors. Probably the most popular column in *Barron's* is Alan Abelson's "Up & Down Wall Street," which provides a critical and often humorous assessment of major developments affecting the stock market and business. *Barron's* also includes current price quotations and a summary of statistics on a range of investment vehicles. Subscribers to *WSJ Interactive* also have access to *Barron's* online edition (www.barrons.com) because both are published by Dow Jones & Co.

Investor's Business Daily is a third national business newspaper published Monday through Friday. It is similar to the *Wall Street Journal* but contains more detailed price and market data. Its Web site (www.investors.com) has limited free content. Another source of financial news is the *Financial Times* (www.ft.com), with U.S., United Kingdom, and global editions.

General Newspapers Major metropolitan newspapers such as the *New York Times*, the *Washington Post*, and the *Los Angeles Times* provide investors with a wealth of financial information in their print and online editions. Most major newspapers contain stock price quotations for major exchanges, price quotations on stocks of local interest, and a summary of the major stock market averages and indexes. Local newspapers are another convenient source of financial news. In most large cities, the daily newspaper devotes at least a few pages to financial and business news. Another popular source of financial news is *USA Today*, the national newspaper published daily Monday through Friday. Each issue contains a "Money" section (Section B) devoted to business and personal financial news and to current security price quotations and summary statistics.

Institutional News The monthly economic letters of the nation's leading banks, such as Bank of America (based in Charlotte, North Carolina), Northern Trust (Chicago), and Wells Fargo (San Francisco), provide useful economic information. Wire services such as Dow Jones, Bloomberg Financial Services, AP (Associated Press), and UPI (United Press International) provide economic and business news feeds to brokerages, other financial institutions, and Web sites that subscribe to them. Bloomberg has its own comprehensive site (www.bloomberg.com). Business.com (www.business.com) offers industry-by-industry news, targeted business searches, and market coverage. Web sites specializing in financial news include CNNfn (money.cnn.com) and CBS MarketWatch (cbs.marketwatch.com).

Business Periodicals Business periodicals vary in scope. Some present general business and economic articles, others cover securities markets and related topics, and still others focus solely on specific industries. Regardless of the subject matter, most business periodicals present descriptive information, and some also include analytical information. They rarely offer recommendations.

The business sections of general-interest periodicals such as *Newsweek*, *Time*, and *U.S. News & World Report* cover business and economic news. Strictly business- and finance-oriented periodicals, including *Business Week*, *Fortune*, *Business Month*, and *Nation's Business*, provide more in-depth articles. These magazines also have investing and personal finance articles.

Some financial periodicals specialize in securities and marketplace articles. The most basic, commonsense articles appear in *Forbes*, *Kiplinger's Personal Finance Magazine*, *Money*, *Smart Money*, and *Worth*. *Forbes*, published every two weeks, is the most investment-oriented. Each January it publishes an

"Annual Report on American Industry" that compares the growth and performance of key industries over the past five years. In August of each year, *Forbes* also publishes a comparative evaluation of mutual funds. *Kiplinger's Personal Finance Magazine, Money, Smart Money,* and *Worth* are published monthly and contain articles on managing personal finances and on investments.

All these business and personal finance magazines have Web sites with free access to recent, if not all, content. Most include a number of other features. For example, *Smart Money* has interactive investment tools, including a color-coded "Map of the Market" that shows the current hot sectors.

Government Publications A number of government agencies publish economic data and reports useful to investors. The annual *Economic Report of the President* provides a broad view of the current and expected state of the economy. This document reviews and summarizes economic policy and conditions and includes data on important aspects of the economy. The *Federal Reserve Bulletin,* published monthly by the Board of Governors of the Federal Reserve System, and periodic reports published by each of the 12 Federal Reserve District Banks provide articles and data on various aspects of economic and business activity. (Visit www.federalreserve.gov to read many of these publications.) A useful Department of Commerce publication is the *Survey of Current Business.* Published monthly, it includes indicators and data related to economic and business conditions. A good source of financial statement information on all manufacturers, broken down by industry and asset size, is the *Quarterly Financial Report for Manufacturing Corporations,* published jointly by the Federal Trade Commission and the Securities and Exchange Commission. Most of these reports are now available at the Web sites of the issuing government agency; a good search engine such as Google (www.google.com) will quickly locate them for you.

Special Subscription Services Investors who want additional insights into business and economic conditions can subscribe to special services. These reports include business and economic forecasts and give notice of new government policies, union plans and tactics, taxes, prices, wages, and so on. One popular service is the *Kiplinger Washington Letter,* a weekly publication that provides a wealth of economic information and analyses.

Industry and Company Information Of special interest to investors is information on particular industries and companies. Often, after choosing an industry in which to invest, an investor will want to analyze specific companies. A recent change in disclosure rules, discussed below, gives individual investors access to more company information than before. General business periodicals such as *Business Week, Forbes,* the *Wall Street Journal,* and *Fortune* carry articles on the activities of specific industries and individual companies. Trade publications such as *Chemical Week, American Banker, Computerworld, Industry Week, Oil and Gas Journal,* and *Public Utilities Fortnightly* provide more focused industry and company information. *Red Herring, The Industry Standard, Business 2.0, Fast Company,* and *Upside* are magazines that can help you keep up with the high-tech world; all have good Web sites. Other specific popular sources are discussed in Table 3.1 on the next page.

TABLE 3.1	Online Sources for Industry and Company Information	
Web Site	Description	Cost
Hoover's Online (www.hoovers.com)	Reports and news on public and private companies as well as 300 industries grouped into 28 sectors.	Considerable free information; $125 per year for in-depth reports and financial statements, advanced search, and stock screen.
CNET (www.news.com)	One of the best sites for high-tech news, analysis, breaking news, great search capabilities, links.	Free.
Company Sleuth (www.companysleuth.com)	Gathers "the inside scoop" on companies from around the Web: stock quotes, news, insider trades, and trademark and patent registrations; message boards; personalized daily e-mail reports.	Free; registration required.
News Alert (www.newsalert.com)	Latest company news from various wire services. Searchable by industry or company. Good for earnings announcements and tech news.	Free.

The Internet makes it easy to research specific industries and companies at the company's Web site, a publication's archive search, or database services such as the Dow Jones Publications Library. Table 3.1 presents several free and subscription resources that emphasize industry and company information.

Fair Disclosure Rules Until recently, executives at public companies could disclose market-moving information privately to investment professionals—analysts, money managers, and large institutional investors—before releasing it to the general public. This selective disclosure gave broker-dealers and their clients an unfair advantage. They could act on the information before the average investor could act. In August 2000, the SEC passed the **fair disclosure rule,** known as **Regulation FD,** a new rule requiring senior executives to disclose critical information such as earnings forecasts and news of mergers and new products simultaneously to investment professionals and the public via press releases or SEC filings. However, it does not apply to communications with journalists and securities ratings firms like Moody's Investor Services and Standard & Poor's. Violations of the rule carry injunctions and fines but are not considered fraud.

The new regulations are not without controversy. The Securities Industry Association expressed concern that executives would be afraid to talk to anyone outside their companies, and that the rule would therefore curtail rather than increase the flow of information. Companies may limit contact with analysts if they are unsure whether the information requires a press release.

Stockholders' Reports An excellent source of data on an individual firm is the **stockholders' report,** or **annual report,** published yearly by publicly held corporations. These reports contain a wide range of information, including financial statements for the most recent period of operation, along with summarized statements for several prior years. These reports are free and may be obtained from the companies themselves or from brokers. A sample page from PepsiCo, Inc.'s 2000 stockholders' report is shown in Figure 3.6. Most

fair disclosure rule (Regulation FD)
rule requiring senior executives to disclose critical information simultaneously to investment professionals and the public via press releases or SEC filings.

stockholders' (annual) report
a report published yearly by a publicly held corporation; contains a wide range of information, including financial statements for the most recent period of operation.

FIGURE 3.6 **A Page from a Stockholders' Report**

This page of the 2000 Annual Report of PepsiCo, Inc. quickly acquaints the investor with the key information on the firm's operations over the past year, in tabular and graphical form. The contents of the Annual Report are also shown on this page. (*Source:* PepsiCo, Inc. 2000 Annual Report; available at PepsiCo's Web site www.pepsico.com; PepsiCo, Inc. Investor Relations, 914-253-3055; PepsiCo, Inc., Purchase, NY 10577.)

Financial Highlights

PepsiCo, Inc. and Subsidiaries
($ in millions except per share amounts; all per share amounts assume dilution)

	As Reported			Pro Forma[b]		
	2000	1999	% Chg[a]	2000	1999	% Chg[a]
Summary of Operations						
Net sales	$20,438	$20,367	–	$20,144	$18,666	8
Segment operating profit	$ 3,550	$ 3,068	16	$ 3,482	$ 3,080	13
Net income	$ 2,183	$ 2,050	6	$ 2,139	$ 1,850	16
Net income per share	$ 1.48	$ 1.37	8	$ 1.45	$ 1.24	17
Other Data						
Net cash provided by operating activities	$ 3,911	$ 3,027	29			
Share repurchases	$ 1,430	$ 1,285	11			
Dividends paid	$ 796	$ 778	2			
Long-term debt	$ 2,346	$ 2,812	(17)			
Capital spending	$ 1,067	$ 1,118	(5)			

(a) Percentage changes are based on unrounded amounts.

(b) PepsiCo's fiscal year ends on the last Saturday in December and, as a result, a fifty-third week is added every 5 or 6 years. The fiscal year ended December 30, 2000 consisted of fifty-three weeks. For comparative purposes, the pro forma information for 2000 excludes the impact of the fifty-third week. The pro forma information for 1999 also gives effect to the bottling transactions described in Note 2 to the financial statements as if the transactions occurred at the beginning of PepsiCo's 1998 fiscal year. In addition, the 1999 pro forma results exclude the Frito-Lay impairment and restructuring pre-tax charge of $65 million ($40 million after-tax), the pre-tax gain on the sale of a chocolate business in Poland of $28 million ($25 million after-tax), the pre-tax net gain on the PBG and Whitman bottling transactions of $1 billion ($270 million after-tax) and the income tax provision of $25 million related to the PepCom transaction. The pro forma information does not purport to represent what PepsiCo's results of operations would have been had such transactions been completed as of the dates indicated nor does it give effect to any other events.

Pro Forma PepsiCo Net Sales
Total: $20,144
$ In Millions

- Frito-Lay $12,656 63%
- Pepsi-Cola $5,095 25%
- Tropicana $2,393 12%

Pro Forma Segment Operating Profit
Total: $3,482
$ In Millions

- Frito-Lay $2,294 66%
- Pepsi-Cola $968 28%
- Tropicana $220 6%

Contents

Michael Thomas
Shareholder since 2001.

To help us toast a great year, we invited several PepsiCo shareholders to pose for a few pictures eating, drinking and being merry. As you'll see, they very kindly obliged.

Form 10-K
a statement that must be filed annually with the SEC by all firms having securities listed on an organized exchange or traded in the Nasdaq market.

companies now place their annual reports on their Web sites. Annual Report Gallery (www.reportgallery.com) provides links to many company reports.

In addition to the stockholders' report, many serious investors review a company's **Form 10-K**. This is a statement that firms with securities listed on an organized exchange or traded in the Nasdaq market must file annually with the SEC. Finding 10-K and other SEC filings is now a simple task, thanks to SEC/Edgar (Electronic Data Gathering and Analysis Retrieval), which has reports filed by any company traded on a major exchange. You can read them free at EDGAR Online's FreeEdgar site (www.freeedgar.com).

Comparative Data Sources Sources of comparative data, typically broken down by industry and firm size, are a good tool for analyzing the financial condition of companies. Among these sources are Dun & Bradstreet's *Key Business Ratios,* Robert Morris and Associates' *Annual Statement Studies,* the *Quarterly Financial Report for Manufacturing Corporations* (cited above), and the *Almanac of Business and Industrial Financial Ratios.* These sources, which are typically available in public and university libraries, are a useful benchmark for evaluating a company's financial condition.

Subscription Services A variety of subscription services provide data on specific industries and companies. Today, many of these services are available on the Internet. (See the Investor's Resources section on the book's Web site.) Generally, a subscriber pays a basic fee to access the service's information and can purchase premium services for greater depth or range. The major subscription services provide both descriptive and analytical information, but they generally do not make recommendations. Most investors, rather than subscribing to these services, access them through their stockbrokers or a large public or university library. The Web sites for most services offer some free information and charge for the rest.

Standard & Poor's Corporation (S&P)
publisher of a large number of financial reports and services, including *Corporation Records* and *Stock Reports.*

Moody's Investor Services
publisher of a variety of financial material, including *Moody's Manuals.*

Value Line Investment Survey
one of the most popular subscription services used by individual investors; subscribers receive three basic reports weekly.

The dominant subscription services are those offered by Standard & Poor's Corporation, Moody's Investor Services, and Value Line. Table 3.2 summarizes the most popular services of these companies. **Standard & Poor's Corporation (S&P)** offers a large number of different financial reports and services. Its Personal Wealth Web site, owned by *Business Week* (www.businessweek.com/investor) is geared toward individual investors. Although basic news and market commentary is free, for just $100 a year subscribers get access to S&P stock reports on 4,600 companies and screening tools. **Moody's Investor Services** also publishes a variety of material, including its securities ratings, corporate research, and well-known reference manuals on eight industries. The *Value Line Investment Survey* is one of the most popular subscription services used by individual investors; it is available at most libraries and online (www.valueline.com).

back-office research reports
a brokerage firm's analyses of and recommendations on investment prospects; available on request at no cost to existing and potential clients or for purchase at some Web sites.

Brokerage Reports Brokerage firms often make available to their clients reports from the various subscription services and research reports from their own securities analysts. They also provide clients with prospectuses for new security issues and *back-office research reports.* As noted in Chapter 2, a *prospectus* is a document that describes in detail the key aspects of the issue, the issuer, and its management and financial position. The cover of the prospectus describing the 2001 stock issue of Reliant Resources, Inc. was shown in Figure 2.1. **Back-office research reports** include the brokerage firm's analyses of and recommendations on prospects for the securities markets, specific industries, or

TABLE 3.2 Popular Offerings of the Major Subscription Services

Subscription Service/ Offerings	Coverage	Frequency of Publication
Standard & Poor's Corporation		
Corporation Records	Detailed descriptions of publicly traded securities of over 10,000 public corporations.	Annually with updates throughout the year.
Stock Reports (sample shown in Figure 7.1, page 299)	Summary of financial history, current finances, and future prospects for thousands of companies.	Annually with updates throughout the year.
Stock Guide	Statistical data and analytical rankings of investment desirability for major stocks.	Monthly.
Bond Guide	Statistical data and analytical rankings of investment desirability for major bonds.	Monthly.
The Outlook	Analytical articles with investment advice on the market, industries, and securities.	Weekly magazine.
Moody's Investor Services		
Moody's Manuals	Eight reference manuals—*Bank and Finance, Industrial, International, Municipal and Government, OTC Industrial, OTC Unlisted, Public Utility,* and *Transportation*—with historical and current financial, organizational, and operational data on major firms.	Annually with biweekly updates.
Handbook of Common Stocks	Common stock data.	Quarterly.
Dividend Record	Recent dividend announcements and payments.	Twice weekly, with annual summary.
Bond Survey	Bond market conditions and new offerings.	Weekly.
Bond Record	Price and interest rate behavior of thousands of bonds.	Monthly.
Value Line Investment Survey		
Includes three reports: 1. *Summary and Index* 2. *Ratings and Reports* (sample shown in Figure 3.5) 3. *Selection and Opinion*	Covers 1,700 of the most widely held stocks. Current ratings for each stock. Full-page report including financial data, descriptions, analysis, and ratings for each of about 130 stocks. Selected investment, business, and stock market prospects, and advice on investment strategy.	Weekly.

specific securities. Usually a brokerage firm publishes lists of securities classified by its research staff as either "buy," "hold," or "sell." Brokerage research reports are available on request at no cost to existing and potential clients.

Securities analyst's reports are now available on the Web, either from brokerage sites or from sites that consolidate research from many brokerages. At Multex Investor (www.multexinvestor.com), a leading research site, reports from 500 brokerage and research firms cost from $4 to $150 each. Investors can use Zacks's (www.zacks.com) Brokerage Research Engine to find and purchase reports from 3,200 analysts on 7,500 companies for $10 to $150 per report or to read free brokerage report abstracts with earnings revisions and recommendations.

investment letters
newsletters that provide, on a subscription basis, the analyses, conclusions, and recommendations of experts in securities investment.

Investment Letters Investment letters provide, on a subscription basis, the analyses, conclusions, and recommendations of experts in securities investment. Some letters concentrate on specific types of securities; others are concerned solely with assessing the economy or securities markets. Among the more popular investment letters are *Bob Nurock's Advisory,* the *Dick Davis Digest, Dines Letter, Dow Theory Letters,* the *Growth Stock Outlook,*

Professional Tape Reader, the *Prudent Speculator,* and *Street Smart Investing.* Most newsletters come out weekly or monthly and cost from $75 to $400 a year. Advertisements for many of these investment letters can be found in *Barron's* and in various business periodicals.

The *Hulbert Financial Digest* (www.hulbertdigest.com) monitors the performance of investment letters. It is an excellent source of objective information on investment letters and a good place to check out those that interest you. Many newsletters now offer online subscriptions. Use a general search engine or the Newsletter Access (www.newsletteraccess.com), a searchable database of newsletters that lists over 1,600 stock-investing newsletters!

quotations
price information about various types of securities, including current price data and statistics on recent price behavior.

Price Information Price information about various types of securities is contained in their **quotations,** which include current price data and statistics on recent price behavior. The Web makes it easy to find price quotes for actively traded securities, and many financially oriented sites include a stock price look-up feature or a stock ticker running across the screen, much like the ones that used to be found only in brokerage offices. The ticker consolidates and reports stock transactions made on the NYSE, AMEX, regional exchanges, and Nasdaq National Market as they occur. Cable TV subscribers in many areas can watch the ticker at the bottom of the screen on certain channels, including CNNfn, CNN Headline News, and MSNBC. The ticker symbols for some well-known companies are listed in Table 3.3.

Investors can easily find the prior day's security price quotations in the published news media, both nonfinancial and financial. They also can find delayed or real-time quotations at numerous Web sites, including *financial portals* (described below), most business periodical Web sites, and brokerage sites. The Web sites for CNNfn and CNBC-TV have real-time stock quotes, as do sites that subscribe to their news feed. Stock quotes are usually free, but investors may have to pay for bond quotes. For example, Quote.com (www.quote.com) charges $9.95 a month for prices on Treasury securities.

TABLE 3.3	Symbols for Some Well-Known Companies		
Company	Symbol	Company	Symbol
Amazon.com	AMZN	McDonald's Corp.	MCD
America Online	AOL	Microsoft	MSFT
Apple Computer	AAPL	Merrill Lynch	MER
AT&T	T	Nike	NKE
Cisco	CSCO	Oracle	ORCL
Dell Computer	DELL	PepsiCo, Inc.	PEP
Eastman Kodak	EK	Reebok	RBK
ExxonMobil	XOM	Sears, Roebuck	S
Genentech	DNA	Starbucks	SBUX
General Electric	GE	Sun Microsystems	SUNW
Hewlett-Packard	HWP	Texas Instruments	TXN
Intel	INTC	United Airlines	UAL
Int'l. Business Machines	IBM	Xerox Corporation	XRX
Lucent Technologies	LU	Yahoo!	YHOO

financial portals
supersites on the Web that bring together many investing features, including real-time quotes, stock and mutual fund screens, portfolio trackers, news, research, and transaction capabilities, along with other personal finance features.

The major published source of security price quotations is the *Wall Street Journal*, which presents quotations for each previous business day's activities in all major markets. (We'll explain how to read and interpret actual price quotations in later chapters.)

Prior to April 2000, stock prices were quoted in fractional form: eighths and, more recently, sixteenths. Starting in August 2000, some stocks began trading in decimals instead of this awkward pricing—⅛ of a point equals 12.5¢, ¹⁄₁₆ equals 6.25¢. Today all stocks are priced in decimals, a format that is much easier to read and understand.

Other Online Investment Information Sources Many other excellent Web sites provide information of all sorts to increase your investment skills and knowledge. Let's now look at financial portals, sites for bonds and mutual funds, international sites, and investment discussion forums. Table 3.4 lists some of the most popular financial portals, bond sites, and mutual fund sites. We'll look at online brokerage and investment adviser sites later in the chapter, and you'll find more specialized Web links in all chapters.

Financial Portals **Financial portals** are supersites that bring together a wide range of investing features, such as real-time quotes, stock and mutual fund screens, portfolio trackers, news, research, and transaction capabilities, along with other personal finance features. These sites want to be your investing homepage. Some portals are general sites such as Yahoo! and Excite that offer a full range of investing features along with their other services, or they may be investing-oriented sites. You should check out several to see which best suits your needs, because their strengths and features vary greatly. *Investorama*, for example, is primarily a collection of links to other financial Web sites. Other portals want you to stay at their site and offer customization options so that your start page includes the data you want. Although finding one site where you can manage your investments is indeed appealing, you may not be able to find the best of what you need at one portal. You'll want to explore several sites to find the ones that meet your needs. Table 3.4 includes a summary of the features of several popular financial portals.

Although you can personalize financial portals, you generally have to visit several sites to manage your financial affairs. A new breed of financial portal aggregates all your financial information on one Web page: bank accounts, credit cards, brokerage and mutual fund accounts, retirement funds, and even frequent-flyer mileage! You provide the passwords, and the software gathers the financial information from other sites. With one click you can view summaries of all your personal accounts—finances, shopping, travel, e-mail, and more. You can even access your data from Web-enabled wireless devices. Figure 3.7 shows a sample of Yodlee's summary page. Although these sites can save you a lot of time, many consumers are hesitant to submit account numbers and passwords to one site. To counter these concerns, aggregators use multiple encryption techniques and limit employee access to client data. Banks and brokerage firms, already very security-conscious, are among the companies that offer these sites. Independent aggregation services include Yodlee (www.yodlee.com) and 1View Network (www.1viewnetwork.com).

TABLE 3.4   **Popular Investment Web Sites**

The following Web sites are just a few of the thousands of sites that provide investing information. Unless otherwise mentioned, all are free.

Web Site	Description
Financial Portals	
America Online (www.aol.com)	Offers free Quicken analysis tools. Its Personal Finance channel for subscribers has 14 areas, including market and business news, research, education, tools, message boards, and a stock-trading simulation game. Ease of use is a big plus.
Investorama (www.investorama.com)	Links to 14,000 financial sites; personal homepage; stock power-search feature.
MSN MoneyCentral Investor (www.moneycentral.msn.com)	More editorial content than many sites; good research and interactive tools like Research Wizard; can consolidate accounts in portfolio tracker. (Many tools don't run on Macintosh.)
Motley Fool (www.fool.com)	Comprehensive and entertaining site with educational features, research, news, and message boards. Model portfolios cover a variety of investment strategies. Free but offers premium services such as Portfolio Trade Alerts for $25 a year.
Wall Street City (www.wallstreetcity.com)	For more experienced investors, with live Webcasts of company presentations and analysts' reports; advanced market analysis and stock-screening tools. ProSearch custom screening tool costs $9.95 per month.
Yahoo! Finance (finance.yahoo.com)	Simple design, content-rich; easy to find information quickly. Includes financial news, price quotes, portfolio trackers, bill paying, personalized homepage, and a directory of other major sites.
Yodlee (www.yodlee.com)	Aggregation site that collects financial account data from banking, credit card, brokerage, mutual fund, mileage, and other sites. One-click access saves time; offers e-mail accounts; easy to set up and track finances. Security issues concern potential users; few analytical tools.
Bond Sites	
Investing in Bonds (www.investinginbonds.com)	The Bond Market Association's Web site; good for novice investors. Investing guides, research reports, historical data, and links to other sites. Searchable database.
BondsOnline (www.bondsonline.com)	Comprehensive site for news, education, free research, ratings, and other bond information; strong emphasis on municipal bonds. Searchable database; Some charges for research.
CNNfn Bond Center (www.cnnfn.com/markets/bondcenter)	Individual investors can search for bond-related news, market data, and bond offerings.
Bureau of the Public Debt Online (www.publicdebt.treas.gov)	Run by U.S. Treasury Department; information about U.S. savings bonds and Treasury securities; can also buy Treasury securities online through Treasury Direct program.
Mutual Fund Sites	
Morningstar (www.morningstar.com)	Profiles of over 6,500 funds with ratings; screening tools, portfolio analysis and management; fund manager interviews, e-mail newsletters; educational sections. Advanced screening and analysis tools are $9.95 a month or $99 per year.
Mutual Fund Investor's Center (www.mfea.com)	Not-for-profit, easy-to-navigate site from the Mutual Fund Education Alliance with investor education, search feature, and links to profiles of funds, calculators for retirement, asset allocation, and college planning.
Fund Alarm (www.fundalarm.com)	Takes a different approach and identifies underperforming funds to help investors decide when to sell; alerts investors to fund manager changes. Lively commentary from the site founder, a CPA.
Findafund (www.maxfunds.com)	In addition to the basics, has a tool to compare funds based on stocks they own to build a diversified portfolio.
IndexFunds.com (www.indexfunds.com)	Comprehensive site covering only index funds.
Personal Fund (www.personalfund.com)	Especially popular for its fund expense calculator that shows the true cost of ownership, after fees, brokerage commissions, and taxes. Suggests lower-cost alternatives with similar investment objectives.

FIGURE 3.7

An Aggregation Site: Bringing It All Together

Yodlee offers users summaries and one-click access to personal account information—including bank balances, credit card balances, investments, travel reservations, e-commerce sites, e-mail, news, and more—from thousands of leading Web sites. (*Source:* **www.yodlee.com /demo/demo.html** Yodlee Inc., Redwood Shores, California; 650-980-3600; info@yodlee.com)

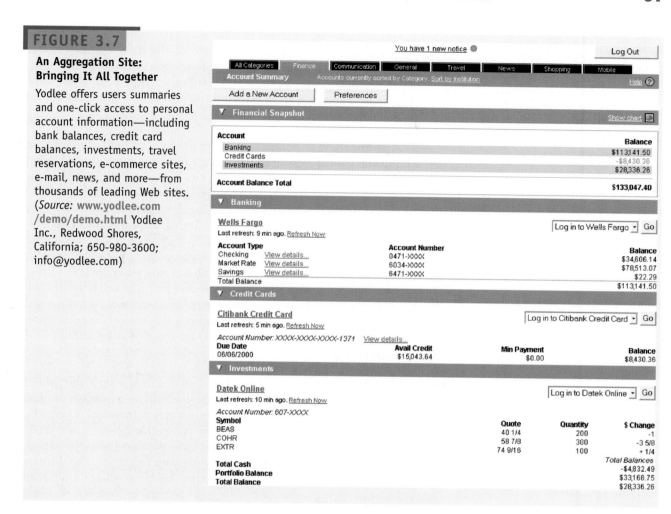

Bond Sites Although many general investment sites include bond and mutual fund information, you can also visit sites that specialize in these investments. Because Internet bond-trading activity is fairly limited at the present time, there are fewer online resources for individuals. Some brokerage firms are starting to allow clients access to bond information that formerly was restricted to investment professionals. In addition to the sites listed in Table 3.4, other good sites for bond and interest rate information include Briefing.com (www.briefing.com), TheStreet.com (www.thestreet.com), and WSJ.com (wsj.com).

The sites of the major bond ratings agencies—Moody's Investor Services (www.moodys.com), Standard & Poor's (www.standardpoor.com), and Fitch IBCA (www.fitchibca.com)—provide ratings lists, recent ratings changes, and information about how they determine ratings. Moody's free services also include a daily summary of the bond markets and some research reports.

Mutual Fund Sites With thousands of mutual funds, how do you find the ones that match your investment goals? The Internet makes this task much easier, offering many sites with screening tools and worksheets. Almost every major mutual fund family has its own Web site as well. Some allow visitors to hear interviews or participate in chats with fund managers. Fidelity (www.fidelity.com) is one of the most comprehensive sites, with educational articles, fund selection tools, fund profiles, and more. Portals and brokerage sites also offer these tools. Table 3.4 includes some independent mutual fund sites that are worth checking out.

International Sites The international reach of the Internet makes it a natural resource to help investors sort out the complexity of global investing, from country research to foreign currency exchange. WorldlyInvestor (www.worldlyinvestor.com) is a comprehensive portal just for international investing. Free newsletters, articles, economic insights, and screening tools for mutual funds and ADRs are among this site's features. For more localized coverage, check out European Investor (www.europeaninvestor.com), UK-Invest (www.uk-invest.com), LatinFocus (www.latin-focus.com), and similar sites for other countries and regions. J.P. Morgan's ADR site (www.adr.com) is a good place to research American depositary receipts and includes analysts' recommendations. For global business news, the *Financial Times* site (www.ft.com) gets high marks. CBS Marketwatch (cbs.marketwatch.com) has good technology and telecommunications news, as well as coverage of international markets and an ADR report.

Investment Discussion Forums Investors can exchange opinions about their favorite stocks and investing strategies at the *online discussion forums* (message boards and chat rooms) found at most major financial Web sites. However, remember that the key word here is opinion. You don't really know much about the qualifications of the person posting the information. *Always do your own research before acting on any hot tips!* The Motley Fool's (www.fool.com) boards are among the most popular, and Fool employees monitor the discussions. Message boards at Yahoo! Finance (finance.yahoo .com) are among the largest online, although many feel that the quality is not so good as at other sites. The Raging Bull (www.ragingbull .com) includes commentary, news, and analysis along with its discussion groups. Technology investors flock to Silicon Investor (www.siliconinvestor .com), a portal site whose high-tech boards are considered among the best. You can read messages free, but to post you'll pay $120 a year or $200 for a lifetime membership.

If you want to check what people are saying about a stock on several different message boards, megasite Cnet (www.cnet.com) makes this easy. It compiles postings from six sites, including Motley Fool, Yahoo!, and Raging Bull. You'll get unlimited messages if you register at Eprobity; otherwise, you only get three per board.

Avoiding Online Scams Just as the Internet increases the amount of information available to all investors, it also makes it easier for scam artists and others to spread false news and manipulate information. Anyone can sound like an investment expert online, posting stock tips with no underlying substance. As mentioned earlier, you may not know the identity of the person touting or panning a stock on the message boards. The person panning a stock could be a disgruntled former employee or a short seller. For example, the ousted former chief executive of San Diego's Avanir Pharmaceuticals posted

INVESTING in action

Have I Got a Tip for You!

On the morning of Friday, August 25, 2000, a Web-based wire service called Internet Wire sent out a press release about Emulex, a Costa Mesa, California, fiber-optics company. The news was not good: The company was restating earnings, the CEO had resigned, and the SEC was launching an accounting investigation. This came as a shock to investors, because just three weeks earlier, Emulex had reported a doubling of revenues and 150% earnings increase. As the news spread to other news services such as Bloomberg, Dow Jones, and CNBC-TV, the company's stock plunged as much as 60% in Nasdaq trading.

Soon after, however, Emulex sent its own press releases to the major newswires, calling the prior news report a hoax and refuting its allegations. By the end of the trading day, Emulex had regained most of the losses.

A few days later the SEC and FBI cracked the case, arresting on securities-fraud charges a 23-year-old former community college student and ex-Internet Wire employee who sent the phony press release. His intent? To get out of a short sale of Emulex stock. He then repurchased the shares while they were down and profited as the price rebounded after the company proved the report false.

Emulex and its investors joined many other victims of phony press releases and false or overhyped message board postings. On Yahoo's boards the most outrageous posters are nick-named "Yahooligans." Acting on a hot tip without researching a company leads to disaster, as investors who snapped up shares of Uniprime Capital learned. The company they thought was developing a successful cure for AIDS wasn't even a health-care company but a Las Vegas car dealership. Sometimes postings that appear to be from a company insider aren't. Callaway Golf brought court action against a man with 27 aliases who had posted 163 negative messages about Callaway. He turned out to be the chief executive of another golf club manufacturer.

Stock scams like these have increased because the Internet makes it easy to disseminate information rapidly. Fortunately, the SEC has stepped up the speed and level of its enforcement activities. To keep from being a victim yourself, follow the rules of good investing and *always* do your own research.

Sources: "E-Mail Trail Leads to Emulex Hoax Suspect," *Wall Street Journal,* September 21, 2000, pp. C1, C2; Amy Feldman, "The Seedy World of Online Stock Scams," *Money,* February 2000, pp. 143–148; Mike Freeman, "No-Name Critics Give Companies Chat-Room Fits," *San Diego Union Tribune,* April 2, 2000, pp. I-1, I-7; Michael Schroeder and John R. Ehmshwiller, "SEC Acts at Cyberspeed to Halt Suspect Trades," *Wall Street Journal,* August 7, 2000, pp. C1, C15.

negative remarks on stock message boards, adversely affecting share price. The company sued and won a court order prohibiting him from ever posting derogatory statements about the company on any Internet message boards.

In the fast-paced online environment, two types of scams turn up frequently: "pump-and-dump" schemes and get-rich-quick scams. In pump-and-dump schemes, promoters hype stocks, quickly send the prices sky-high, and then dump them at inflated prices. In get-rich-quick scams, promoters sell worthless investments to naïve buyers. One well-publicized pump-and-dump scheme demonstrates how easy it is to use the Internet to promote stocks. In September 2000, the SEC caught a 15-year-old boy who had made over $270,000 by promoting small-company stocks. The self-taught young investor would buy a block of a company's shares and then send out a barrage of false and/or misleading e-mail messages and message board postings singing the praises of that stock and the company's prospects. Once this misinformation pushed up the stock price, he sold and moved on to a new target company. His postings were so articulate that others at Silicon Investor's message boards thought he was a 40-year-old. The *Investing in Action* box on page 93 describes other online hoaxes and how they were shut down.

To crack down on cyber-fraud, the SEC created the Office of Internet Enforcement. The agency now has 15 staff members and several regional offices that quickly investigate reports of suspected hoaxes and prosecute the offenders. Former SEC Chairman Arthur Levitt cautions investors to remember that the Internet is basically another way to send and receive information, one that has no controls for accuracy or truthfulness. The SEC Web site (www.sec.gov/investor/online/scams.htm) includes tips to avoid investment scams. Three key questions that investors should ask are:

- *Is the stock registered?* Check the SEC's EDGAR database (www.sec.gov/edgar.shtml) and with your state securities regulator (www.nasaa.org).

- *Who is making the sales pitch?* Make sure the seller is licensed in your state. Check with the NASD for any record of complaints or fraud.

- *Is it too good to be true?* Then it probably is. Just being on the Web doesn't mean it's legitimate.

Another place to check on possible frauds is Stock Detective, a section of the Financial Web portal site (www.financialweb.com/skdindex.asp) that investigates suspicious stocks and reports on SEC activities against investment fraud.

IN REVIEW

CONCEPTS

3.4 Differentiate between *descriptive information* and *analytical information*. How might one logically assess whether the acquisition of investment information or advice is economically justified?

3.5 What popular financial business periodicals would you use to follow the financial news? General news? Business news? Would you prefer to get your news from print sources or online, and why?

3.6 Briefly describe the types of information that the following resources provide.
a. Stockholders' report.　　b. Comparative data sources.
c. Standard & Poor's Corporation. d. Moody's Investor Services.
e. *Value Line Investment Survey.*

3.7 How would you access each of the following types of information, and how would the content help you make investment decisions?
a. Prospectuses.　　b. Back-office research reports.
c. Investment letters.　　d. Price quotations.

3.8 Briefly describe several types of information that are especially well-suited to being made available on the Internet. What are the differences between the online and print versions, and when would you use each?

3.9 Using information in the text and the *Investing in Action* box on page 93, describe some common types of online investment scams and hoaxes. How can you protect yourself from them?

Understanding Market Averages and Indexes

LG 3

The investment information we have discussed in this chapter helps investors understand when the economy is moving up or down and how individual investments have performed. Investors can use this and other information to formulate expectations about future investment performance. It is also important to know whether market behavior is favorable or unfavorable. The ability to interpret various market measures should help you to select and time investment actions.

A widely used way to assess the behavior of securities markets is to study the performance of market averages and indexes. These measures allow you conveniently to (1) gauge general market conditions, (2) compare your portfolio's performance to that of a large, diversified (market) portfolio, and (3) study market cycles, trends, and behaviors in order to forecast future market behavior. Here we discuss key measures of stock and bond market activity. In later chapters, we will discuss averages and indexes associated with other investment vehicles. Like price quotations, these measures of market performance are available at many Web sites.

Stock Market Averages and Indexes

Stock market averages and indexes measure the general behavior of stock prices over time. Although the terms *average* and *index* tend to be used interchangeably when people discuss market behavior, technically they are different types of measures. **Averages** reflect the arithmetic average price behavior of a representative group of stocks at a given point in time. **Indexes** measure the current price behavior of a representative group of stocks in relation to a base value set at an earlier point in time.

Averages and indexes provide a convenient method of capturing the general mood of the market. They also can be compared at different points in time to assess the relative strength or weakness of the market. Current and recent values of the key averages and indexes are quoted daily in the financial news, in most local newspapers, and on many radio and television news programs. Figure 3.8, a version of which is published daily in the *Wall Street Journal*, provides a summary and statistics on the major stock market averages and indexes. Let's look at the key averages and indexes listed there.

The Dow Jones Averages Dow Jones & Company, publisher of the *Wall Street Journal*, prepares five stock averages. The most popular is the **Dow Jones Industrial Average (DJIA)**. This average is made up of 30 stocks selected for total market value and broad public ownership. The group consists of high-quality stocks whose behaviors are believed to reflect overall market activity. The box within Figure 3.9 lists the stocks currently included in the DJIA.

Occasionally, a merger, bankruptcy, or extreme lack of activity causes a change in the makeup of the average. Citicorp's merger with Travelers moved it (Citigroup) to the DJIA. Changes to the 30 stocks also occur when Dow Jones believes that the average does not reflect the broader market. For example, in recent years technology companies such as Microsoft and Intel and financial services companies such as American Express replaced Allied Signal, Goodyear, and Union Carbide; Home Depot replaced Sears. When a

averages
numbers used to measure the general behavior of stock prices by reflecting the arithmetic average price behavior of a representative group of stocks at a given point in time.

indexes
numbers used to measure the general behavior of stock prices by measuring the current price behavior of a representative group of stocks in relation to a base value set at an earlier point in time.

Dow Jones Industrial Average (DJIA)
a stock market average made up of 30 high-quality stocks selected for total market value and broad public ownership and believed to reflect overall market activity.

FIGURE 3.8

Major Stock Market Averages and Indexes

The "Stock Market Data Bank" summarizes the key stock market averages and indexes. It includes statistics showing the change from the previous day, the annual change, and the year-to-date change. (*Source: Wall Street Journal,* September 29, 2000, p. C2. Reprinted by permission of the *Wall Street Journal.* © Dow Jones & Company, Inc. All rights reserved.)

STOCK MARKET DATA BANK — 9/28/00

MAJOR INDEXES

†12-MO HIGH	†12-MO LOW		DAILY HIGH	DAILY LOW	CLOSE	NET CHG	% CHG	†12-MO CHG	% CHG	FROM 12/31	% CHG
DOW JONES AVERAGES											
11722.98	9796.03	30 Industrials	10856.25	10623.18	10824.06	+ 195.70	+ 1.84	+ 487.11	+ 4.71	− 673.06	− 5.85
3099.67	2263.59	20 Transportation	2577.73	2513.63	2572.32	+ 57.79	+ 2.30	− 336.84	− 11.58	− 404.88	−13.60
397.04	269.20	15 Utilities	398.65	391.67	396.37	+ 5.24	+ 1.34	+ 98.11	+ 32.89	+ 113.01	+ 39.88
3305.46	2751.55	65 Composite	3216.10	3155.10	3211.63	+ 56.79	+ 1.80	+ 198.62	+ 6.59	− 2.75	− 0.09
364.71	285.95	DJ US Total Mkt	345.15	335.80	344.69	+ 7.88	+ 2.34	+ 53.14	+ 18.22	+ 3.13	+ 0.91
NEW YORK STOCK EXCHANGE											
677.58	576.17	Composite	669.08	655.94	667.75	+ 11.70	+ 1.78	+ 74.96	+ 12.65	+ 17.45	+ 2.68
851.94	728.87	Industrials	828.46	815.18	826.38	+ 10.73	+ 1.32	+ 80.07	+ 10.73	− 1.83	− 0.22
519.96	443.98	Utilities	467.73	451.61	467.34	+ 15.26	+ 3.38	− 14.64	− 3.04	− 43.81	− 8.57
493.03	353.51	Transportation	411.74	401.58	410.84	+ 8.47	+ 2.11	− 37.78	− 8.42	− 55.86	−11.97
634.16	442.71	Finance	628.25	611.13	626.56	+ 15.43	+ 2.52	+ 147.62	+ 30.82	+ 109.95	+ 21.28
STANDARD & POOR'S INDEXES											
1527.46	1247.41	500 Index	1461.65	1425.79	1458.29	+ 31.72	+ 2.22	+ 175.58	+ 13.69	− 10.96	− 0.75
1917.64	1544.13	Industrials	1746.52	1704.33	1742.62	+ 36.96	+ 2.17	+ 161.31	+ 10.20	− 99.30	− 5.39
338.42	215.62	Utilities	337.30	333.51	336.99	+ 3.48	+ 1.04	+ 94.22	+ 38.81	+ 109.77	+ 48.31
548.60	369.50	400 MidCap	542.98	528.23	542.35	+ 13.31	+ 2.52	+ 161.76	+ 42.50	+ 97.68	+ 21.97
225.12	168.96	600 SmallCap	219.15	212.04	219.03	+ 6.86	+ 3.23	+ 42.83	+ 24.31	+ 21.24	+ 10.74
324.40	262.26	1500 Index	312.42	304.75	311.85	+ 6.92	+ 2.27	+ 42.40	+ 15.74	+ 2.96	+ 0.96
NASDAQ STOCK MARKET											
5048.62	2688.18	Composite	3778.38	3626.55	3778.32	+ 122.02	+ 3.34	+1032.16	+ 37.59	− 290.99	− 7.15
4704.73	2362.11	Nasdaq 100	3725.75	3556.34	3725.15	+ 153.25	+ 4.29	+1317.25	+ 54.71	+ 17.32	+ 0.47
2841.00	1549.93	Industrials	2084.53	2005.66	2084.53	+ 68.64	+ 3.40	+ 475.14	+ 29.52	− 154.44	− 6.90
2075.12	1602.08	Insurance	1881.65	1863.75	1879.85	+ 4.85	+ 0.26	− 153.15	− 7.53	− 16.43	− 0.87
1837.10	1340.36	Banks	1784.44	1739.05	1783.47	+ 41.88	+ 2.40	+ 100.32	+ 5.96	+ 92.18	+ 5.45
2964.66	1448.32	Computer	2217.78	2121.76	2217.38	+ 70.40	+ 3.28	+ 713.59	+ 47.45	− 108.02	− 4.65
1230.06	616.80	Telecommunications	731.80	689.85	731.73	+ 27.51	+ 3.91	+ 106.94	+ 17.12	− 283.67	−27.94
OTHERS											
1036.40	774.49	Amex Composite	940.19	926.18	939.80	+ 11.37	+ 1.22	+ 151.57	+ 19.23	+ 62.83	+ 7.16
813.71	646.79	Russell 1000	785.46	765.38	784.09	+ 17.68	+ 2.31	+ 120.26	+ 18.12	+ 16.12	+ 2.10
606.12	408.90	Russell 2000	524.09	507.62	523.81	+ 15.68	+ 3.09	+ 96.51	+ 22.59	+ 19.06	+ 3.78
844.78	667.03	Russell 3000	811.99	791.30	811.03	+ 18.70	+ 2.36	+ 126.23	+ 18.43	+ 17.72	+ 2.23
439.78	394.35	Value-Line (geom.)	422.95	413.81	422.54	+ 8.51	+ 2.06	+ 4.89	+ 1.17	− 8.50	− 1.97
14751.64	11446.60	Wilshire 5000	....	....	13786.28	+ 321.01	+ 2.38	+2072.48	+ 17.69	− 26.39	− 0.19

†-Based on comparable trading day in preceding year.

new stock is added, the average is readjusted so that it continues to behave in a manner consistent with the immediate past.

The value of the DJIA is calculated each business day by substituting the *closing share prices* of each of the 30 stocks in the average into the following equation:

Equation 3.1

$$\text{DJIA} = \frac{\begin{array}{c}\text{Closing share price} \\ \text{of stock 1}\end{array} + \begin{array}{c}\text{Closing share price} \\ \text{of stock 2}\end{array} + \cdots + \begin{array}{c}\text{Closing share price} \\ \text{of stock 30}\end{array}}{\text{DJIA divisor}}$$

The value of the DJIA is merely the sum of the closing share prices of the 30 stocks included in it, divided by a "divisor." The purpose of the divisor is to adjust for any stock splits, company changes, or other events that have occurred over time. Without the divisor, whose calculation is very complex, the DJIA value would be totally distorted. The divisor makes it possible to use the DJIA to make time-series comparisons. On September 28, 2000, the sum of the closing prices of the 30 industrials was 1829.27, which, when divided by the divisor of 0.169, resulted in a DJIA value of 10824.06. The current

The DJIA from March 31, 2000, to September 28, 2000

During this 6-month period, the stock market remained generally bullish but experienced two significant dips—one in April and one in September. (*Source: Wall Street Journal,* September 29, 2000, p. C3. Reprinted by permission of the *Wall Street Journal.* © Dow Jones & Company, Inc. All rights reserved.)

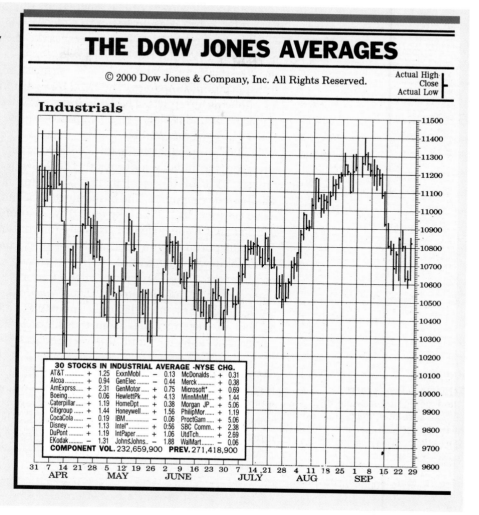

THE DOW JONES AVERAGES

© 2000 Dow Jones & Company, Inc. All Rights Reserved.

Industrials

divisor is included in the *Wall Street Journal* table "Dow Jones Averages Hour by Hour," which is printed on the same page as the chart with the averages.

Because the DJIA results from summing the prices of the 30 stocks, higher-priced stocks tend to affect the index more than do lower-priced stocks. For example, a 5% change in the price of a $50 stock (i.e., $2.50) has less impact on the index than a 5% change in a $100 stock (i.e., $5.00). In spite of this and other criticisms leveled at the DJIA, it remains the most widely cited stock market indicator.

The actual value of the DJIA is meaningful only when compared to earlier values. For example, the DJIA on September 28, 2000, closed at 10824. This value is meaningful only when compared to the previous day's closing value of 10629, a change of 1.84%. Many people mistakenly believe that one DJIA "point" equals $1 in the value of an average share. Actually, one point currently translates into about 0.56 cents in average share value. Figure 3.9 shows the DJIA over the 6-month period March 31, 2000, to September 29, 2000. During this 6-month period, the stock market remained generally bullish, although it experienced two significant dips. It started at 11200 and dropped to 10300 in mid-April. During the following 90 days, the market was somewhat sideways until it increased steadily from late July to early September, when it again began to slide.

The four other Dow Jones averages are the transportation, utilities, composite, and U.S. total market The *Dow Jones Transportation Average* is based on 20 stocks, including railroads, airlines, freight forwarders, and mixed transportation companies. The *Dow Jones Utilities Average* is computed using 15 public utility stocks. The *Dow Jones 65 Stocks Composite Average* is made up of the 30 industrials, the 20 transportations, and the 15 utilities. The *Dow Jones U.S. Total Market Index* is a market-weighted index. "Market-weighted" means that companies with large total market values have the most effect on the index's movement. The Dow Jones U.S. Total Market Index reflects 95% of the total market value for large-sized, medium-sized, and small-sized companies. The base value of the index is 100, which represents its value on June 30, 1997. Like the DJIA, each of the other Dow Jones averages is calculated using a divisor to allow for continuity of the average over time. The transportation, utilities, and 65-stocks composite are often cited in the financial news along with the DJIA, as shown in Figure 3.8.

In early 1999, Dow Jones introduced a new measure to monitor performance of U.S. Internet stocks. The *Dow Jones Internet Index (DJII),* a 40-stock benchmark, includes only companies that generate a minimum of 50 percent of their revenues from the Internet. It has two component indexes, "Internet Commerce" and "Internet Services."

Standard & Poor's indexes
true indexes that measure the current price of a group of stocks relative to a base (set in the 1941–1943 period) having an index value of 10.

Standard & Poor's Indexes Standard & Poor's Corporation, another leading financial publisher, publishes six major common stock indexes. One oft-cited S&P index is the 500-stock composite index. Unlike the Dow Jones averages, **Standard & Poor's indexes** are true indexes. They are calculated each business day by substituting the *closing market value of each stock* (closing price × number of shares outstanding) into the following equation:

Equation 3.2

$$\text{S\&P Index} = \frac{\begin{array}{c}\text{Current closing} \\ \text{market value} \\ \text{of stock 1}\end{array} + \begin{array}{c}\text{Current closing} \\ \text{market value} \\ \text{of stock 2}\end{array} + \cdots + \begin{array}{c}\text{Current closing} \\ \text{market value} \\ \text{of last stock}\end{array}}{\begin{array}{c}\text{Base period} \\ \text{closing market} \\ \text{value of stock 1}\end{array} + \begin{array}{c}\text{Base period} \\ \text{closing market} \\ \text{value of stock 2}\end{array} + \cdots + \begin{array}{c}\text{Base period} \\ \text{closing market} \\ \text{value of last stock}\end{array}} \times 10$$

The value of the S&P index is found by dividing the sum of the market values of all stocks included in the index by the market value of the stocks in the base period and then multiplying the resulting quotient by 10, the base value of the S&P indexes. Most S&P indexes are calculated in a similar fashion. The main differences lie in the stocks included in the index, the base period, and the base value of the index. For example, on September 28, 2000, the ratio of the closing market values of the S&P 500 composite stocks to the 1941–1943 base-period closing market values was 145.829, which, when multiplied by the base value of the S&P index of 10, results in an index value of 1458.29 (as shown in Figure 3.8).

Certain of the S&P indexes contain many more shares than the Dow averages do, and all of them are based on *market*

INVESTOR FACTS

ELECTION RETURNS—During election years, the stock market tends to rise substantially more than the average annual increase. Look at the market returns for U.S. presidential elections since 1976: In every year except 2000—a unique election in every way!—the market rose substantially more than the average.

Year and Election Winner	S&P 500 Return for the Year
2000–George W. Bush	−10.1%
1996–Bill Clinton	+16.0%
1992–Bill Clinton	+17.7%
1988–George H. Bush	+12.4%
1984–Ronald Reagan	+25.8%
1980–Ronald Reagan	+19.1%
1976–Jimmy Carter	+15.6%

values rather than *share prices*. Therefore, many investors feel that the S&P indexes provide a more broad-based and representative measure of general market conditions than do the Dow averages. Although some technical computational problems exist with these indexes, they are widely used—frequently as a basis for estimating the "market return," an important concept that will be introduced in Chapter 4.

Like the Dow averages, the S&P indexes are meaningful only when compared to values in other time periods or to the 1941–1943 base-period value of 10. For example, the September 28, 2000, value of the S&P 500 Stock Composite Index of 1458.29 means that the market values of the stocks in the index increased by a factor of 145.829 (1458.29 ÷ 10) since the 1941–1943 period. The September 28, 2000, market value of the stocks in the index was 1.17 times the lowest index value of 1247.41 in the preceding 365-day period (1458.29 ÷ 1247.41), and hence represented an increase of 17%.

The eight major common stock indexes published by Standard & Poor's are

- The *industrials index*, made up of the common stock of 400 industrial firms.

- The *transportation index*, which includes the stock of 20 transportation companies.

- The *utilities index*, made up of 40 public utility stocks.

- The *financials index*, which contains 40 financial stocks.

- The *composite index* (described above), which consists of the total of 500 stocks that make up the industrials, transportation, utilities, and financials indexes.

- The *midcap index*, made up of the stocks of 400 medium-sized companies.

- The *smallcap index*, made up of 600 small-sized companies.

- The *1500 index*, which includes all stocks in the composite, midcap, and smallcap indexes.

The S&P midcap, smallcap, and 1500 indexes are the newest. Their popularity results from strong investor interest in the stocks of medium-sized and small companies. Like the Dow averages, many of the S&P indexes are frequently quoted in the financial news, as shown in Figure 3.8.

Although the Dow Jones averages and S&P indexes tend to behave in a similar fashion over time, their day-to-day magnitude and even direction (up or down) can differ significantly because the Dows are averages and the S&Ps are indexes.

NYSE, AMEX, and Nasdaq Indexes   Three indexes measure the daily results of the New York Stock Exchange (NYSE), the American Stock Exchange (AMEX), and the National Association of Securities Dealers Automated Quotation (Nasdaq) system. Each reflects the movement of stocks listed on its exchange. The **NYSE composite index** includes all of the 3,000 or so stocks listed on the "Big Board." The index's base of 50 reflects the December 31, 1965, value of stocks listed on the NYSE. In addition to the composite index,

NYSE composite index
measure of the current price behavior of the stocks listed on the NYSE, relative to a base of 50 set at December 31, 1965.

AMEX composite index
measure of the current price behavior of the stocks listed on the AMEX, relative to a base of 100 set at August 31, 1973.

Nasdaq indexes
measures of current price behavior of securities sold OTC, relative to a base of 100 set at February 5, 1971.

the NYSE publishes indexes for industrials, utilities, transportation, and finance subgroups. The behavior of the NYSE industrial index is normally similar to that of the DJIA and the S&P 500 indexes.

The **AMEX composite index** reflects the price of all shares traded on the American Stock Exchange, relative to a base of 100 set at August 31, 1973. Although it does not always closely follow the S&P and NYSE indexes, the AMEX index tends to move in the general direction they do.

The **Nasdaq indexes** reflect over-the-counter market activity. They are based on a value of 100 set at February 5, 1971. The most comprehensive of the Nasdaq indexes is the OTC *composite index,* which is calculated using the 6,400 or so domestic common stocks traded on the Nasdaq system. Also important is the *Nasdaq 100,* which includes the top 100 nonfinancial companies listed on Nasdaq. The other five commonly quoted Nasdaq indexes are the *industrials,* the *insurance,* the *banks,* the *computer,* and the *telecommunications indexes.* Although their degrees of responsiveness may vary, the Nasdaq indexes tend to move in the same direction at the same time as the other major indexes.

Value Line composite index
stock index that reflects the percentage changes in share price of about 1,700 stocks, relative to a base of 100 set at June 30, 1961.

Value Line Indexes Value Line publishes a number of stock indexes constructed by equally weighting the price of each stock included. This is accomplished by considering only the percentage changes in stock prices. This approach eliminates the effects of differing market price and total market value on the relative importance of each stock in the index. The **Value Line composite index** includes the approximately 1,700 stocks in the *Value Line Investment Survey* that are traded on the NYSE, AMEX, and OTC markets. The base of 100 reflects the stock prices on June 30, 1961. In addition to its composite index, Value Line publishes indexes for *industrials, rails,* and *utilities.*

Wilshire 5000 index
measure of the total dollar value (in billions of dollars) of 5,000 actively traded stocks, including all those on the NYSE and the AMEX in addition to active OTC stocks.

Other Averages and Indexes A number of other indexes are available. The **Wilshire 5000 index,** published by Wilshire Associates, Inc., is reported daily in the *Wall Street Journal.* It represents the total dollar value (in billions of dollars) of 5,000 actively traded stocks, including all those on the NYSE and the AMEX in addition to active OTC stocks. Frank Russell Company, a pension advisory firm, publishes three primary indexes. The *Russell 1000* includes the 1,000 largest companies, the *Russell 2000* includes 2,000 small companies, and the *Russell 3000* includes the 3,000 largest U.S. companies. *Barron's* publishes a 50-stock average. The *New York Times* publishes its own average, which is similar to the Dow Jones averages. Moody's Investor Services prepares market indicators for a variety of groupings of common stock.

In addition, the *Wall Street Journal* publishes a number of global and foreign stock market indexes in Section C. These indexes are summarized in the "International Stocks" section on the first page and are listed in greater detail in "World Stock Markets." Included are Dow Jones indexes for countries in the Americas, Latin America, Europe, South Africa, and the Asia-Pacific region that are based on a value of 100 set at December 31, 1991. More than 20 foreign stock market indexes and the Morgan Stanley Indexes are also given for major countries, including a *World Index* and the *Europe/Australia/ Far East (EAFE) Index.* Each of the Morgan Stanley Indexes is calculated in local currencies and based on a value of 100 set at December 31, 1969. Like the purely domestic averages and indexes, these international averages and indexes measure the general price behavior of the stocks that are listed and traded in the given market. Useful comparisons of the market averages and indexes over time and across markets are often made to assess both trends and relative strengths of foreign markets throughout the world.

Bond Market Indicators

A number of indicators are available for assessing the general behavior of the bond markets. A "Bond Market Data Bank" that includes a wealth of return and price index data for various types of bonds and various domestic and foreign markets is published daily in the *Wall Street Journal.* However, there are fewer indicators of overall bond market behavior than of stock market behavior. The key measures of overall U.S. bond market behavior are bond yields, the Dow Jones bond averages, and the New York Stock Exchange bond diary.

bond yield
summary measure of the total return an investor would receive on a bond if it were purchased at its current price and held to maturity; reported as an annual rate of return.

Bond Yields A **bond yield** is a summary measure of the total return an investor would receive on a bond if it were purchased at its current price and held to maturity. Bond yields are reported as annual rates of return. For example, a bond with a yield of 8.50% would provide its owner with a total return from periodic interest and capital gain (or loss) that would be equivalent to an 8.50% annual rate of earnings on the amount invested, if the bond were purchased at its current price and held to maturity.

Typically, bond yields are quoted for a group of bonds that are similar with respect to type and quality. For example, *Barron's* quotes the yields on the Dow Jones bond averages of 10 utilities, 10 industrials, and 20 bond composites, as well as for specified grades of corporate bonds. In addition, like the *Wall Street Journal,* it quotes numerous other bond indexes and yields, including those for Treasury and municipal bonds. Similar bond yield data are available from S&P, Moody's, and the Federal Reserve. Like stock market averages and indexes, bond yield data are especially useful when viewed over time.

Dow Jones bond averages
mathematical averages of the *closing prices* for groups of utility, industrial, and composite bonds.

Dow Jones Bond Averages The **Dow Jones bond averages** include a utility, an industrial, and a composite bond average. Each average reflects the simple mathematical average of the *closing prices,* rather than yields, for each group of bonds included. The utility bond average is based on the closing prices of 10 utility bonds; the industrial bond average is based on the closing prices of 10 industrial bonds; and the composite bond average is based on the closing prices of 10 utility and 10 industrial bonds.

Like bond price quotations, the bond averages are presented in terms of the percentage of face value at which the bond sells. For example, the September 28, 2000, Dow Jones 20-bond composite average of 95.97 indicated that, on average, bonds were on the day reported selling for 95.97 percent of their par or face value. For a $1,000 bond, the average price of an issue would equal about $959.70. The Dow Jones bond averages are published daily in the *Wall Street Journal* and summarized weekly in *Barron's.* Similar bond market indexes, prepared primarily by leading investment bankers such as Lehman Brothers and Merrill Lynch, are also published daily in the *Wall Street Journal* and summarized weekly in *Barron's.*

NYSE Bond Diary The New York Stock Exchange is the dominant organized exchange on which bonds are traded. Thus certain summary statistics on daily bond-trading activity on the NYSE provide useful insight into the behavior of the bond markets in general. These statistics include the number of issues traded and the number that advanced, declined, or remained unchanged. On September 28, 2000, 136 domestic issues were traded; 64 advanced, 53 declined, and 19 remained unchanged. Of the issues traded, 6 achieved a new price high for the year, and 4 fell to new price lows. Total sales volume was $7,489,000. The NYSE bond diary is published daily in the *Wall Street Journal* and summarized weekly in *Barron's*.

IN REVIEW

CONCEPTS

3.10 Describe the basic philosophy and use of stock market averages and indexes. Explain how the behavior of an average or index can be used to classify general market conditions as bull or bear.

3.11 List each of the major averages or indexes prepared by (a) Dow Jones & Company and (b) Standard & Poor's Corporation. Indicate the number and source of the securities used in calculating each average or index.

3.12 Briefly describe the composition and general thrust of each of the following indexes.
  a. NYSE composite index.
  b. AMEX composite index.
  c. Nasdaq indexes.
  d. Value Line composite index.
  e. Wilshire 5000 index.

3.13 Discuss each of the following as they are related to assessing bond market behavior.
  a. Bond yields.
  b. Dow Jones bond averages.
  c. NYSE bond diary.

Making Securities Transactions

Now that you know how to find information to help you locate attractive security investments, you should understand how to make securities transactions. Whether you decide to start a self-directed online investment program or to use a traditional stockbroker, you must first open an account with a stockbroker to buy and sell securities. In this section we will look at the role stockbrokers play and how that role has changed with the growth in online investing. We will also explain the basic types of orders you can place, the procedures required to make regular and online securities transactions, the costs of investment transactions, and investor protection.

The Role of Stockbrokers

stockbrokers
individuals licensed by both the SEC and the securities exchanges to facilitate transactions between buyers and sellers of securities.

Stockbrokers—also called *account executives, investment executives,* and *financial consultants*—act as intermediaries between buyers and sellers of securities. They typically charge a commission to facilitate these securities transactions. Stockbrokers must be licensed by both the SEC and the securities exchanges on which they place orders and must follow the ethical guidelines of those bodies.

TOO MUCH PAPERWORK—
Wasn't the computer supposed to cut down on paperwork? Tell that to the stock brokerage firms and mutual fund companies that send you monthly and year-end statements, confirmations of buy and sell orders, newsletters, and so on. What can you throw away? Keep your most recent brokerage statements and the year-end documents (which you'll need to prepare your tax returns). Check over the monthly statements to make sure they're correct—and then toss them when the next month's statements arrive.

street name
stock certificates issued in the brokerage firm's name but held in trust for its client, who actually owns them.

Although the procedure for executing orders on organized exchanges may differ from that in the OTC market, it starts the same way: An investor places an order with his or her stockbroker. The broker works for a brokerage firm that owns seats on the organized securities exchanges, and members of the securities exchange execute orders that the brokers in the firm's various sales offices transmit to them. For example, the largest U.S. brokerage firm, Merrill Lynch, transmits orders for listed securities from its offices in most major cities throughout the country to the main office of Merrill Lynch and then to the floor of the stock exchanges (NYSE and AMEX), where Merrill Lynch exchange members execute them. Confirmation of the order goes back to the broker placing the order, who relays it to the customer. This process can take a matter of seconds with the use of sophisticated telecommunications networks and Internet trading.

For an over-the-counter securities transaction, brokerage firms transmit orders to market makers, who are dealers in the OTC market specializing in that security. As we learned in Chapter 2, the Nasdaq system, along with the available information on who makes markets in certain securities, enables brokers to execute orders in OTC securities. Normally, OTC transactions are executed rapidly, because market makers maintain inventories of the securities in which they deal.

Brokerage Services The primary activity of stockbrokers is to execute clients' purchase and sale transactions at the best possible price. Brokerage firms will hold the client's security certificates for safekeeping; the stocks kept by the firm in this manner are said to be held in **street name**. Because the brokerage house issues the securities in its own name and holds them in trust for the client (rather than issuing them in the client's name), the firm can transfer the securities at the time of sale without the client's signature. Street name is actually a common way of buying securities, because many investors do not want to be bothered with the handling and safekeeping of stock certificates. In such cases, the brokerage firm records the details of the client's transaction and keeps track of his or her investments through a series of bookkeeping entries. Dividends and notices received by the broker are forwarded to the client who owns the securities.

Stockbrokers also offer clients a variety of other services. For example, the brokerage firm normally provides free information about investments. Quite often, the firm has a research staff that periodically issues analyses of economic, market, industry, or company behavior and makes recommendations to buy or sell certain securities. As a client of a large brokerage firm, you can expect to receive regular bulletins on market activity and possibly a recommended investment list. You will also receive a statement describing your transactions for the month and showing commission and interest charges, dividends and interest received, and detailed listings of your current holdings.

Today, most brokerage firms will invest surplus cash left in a customer's account in a money market mutual fund, allowing the customer to earn a reasonable rate of interest on these balances. Such arrangements help the investor earn as much as possible on temporarily idle funds.

Types of Brokerage Firms Just a few years ago, there were three distinct types of brokerage firms: full-service, discount, and online. No longer are the lines between these categories clear-cut. Most brokerage firms, even the most

full-service broker
broker who, in addition to executing clients' transactions, provides them with a full array of brokerage services.

discount broker
broker who charges low commissions to make transactions for customers but provides little or no free research information or investment advice.

online broker
typically a deep-discount broker through which investors can execute trades electronically online via a commercial service or on the Internet.

traditional ones, now offer online services to compete with the increasingly popular online firms. And many discount brokers now offer services, like research reports for clients, that were once available only from a full-service broker.

The traditional broker, or so-called **full-service broker**, in addition to executing clients' transactions, offers investors a full array of brokerage services: providing investment advice and information, holding securities in street name, offering online brokerage services, and extending margin loans. Investors who wish merely to make transactions and are not interested in taking advantage of other services should consider either a discount broker or an online broker.

Discount brokers focus primarily on making transactions for customers. They charge low commissions and provide little or no free research information or investment advice. The investor calls a toll-free number or visits the broker's Web site to initiate a transaction, and the discount broker confirms the transaction by phone, e-mail, or regular mail. Discount brokers that charge the lowest commissions and provide virtually no services are commonly referred to as *deep discounters*. However, brokers like Charles Schwab, the first discount broker, now offer many of the same services that you'd find at a full-commission broker. Other discounters still focus on transactions.

Online brokers, also called *Internet brokers* and *electronic brokers,* are typically deep-discount brokers through which investors can execute trades electronically online via a commercial service or on the Internet. The investor accesses the online broker's Web site to open an account, review the commission schedule, or see a demonstration of the available transactional services and procedures. Confirmation of electronic trades can take as little as 10 seconds, and most trades occur within 1 minute. Some firms, such as Ameritrade, E*Trade, and Datek Online, operate only online. In response to the rapid growth of online investors, particularly among affluent young investors who enjoy surfing the Web, most brokerage firms now offer online trading.

The rapidly growing volume of business done by discount and online brokers attests to their success. Today, many banks and savings institutions are making discount and online brokerage services available to their depositors who wish to buy stocks, bonds, mutual funds, and other investment vehicles. Some of the major full-service, discount, and online brokers are listed in Table 3.5.

Selecting a Stockbroker If you decide to start your investing activities with the assistance of either a full-service or discount stockbroker, select the person you believe best understands your investment goals. Choosing a broker whose disposition toward investing is similar to yours is the best way to establish a solid working relationship. Your broker should also make you aware of investment possibilities that are consistent with your objectives and attitude toward risk.

You should also consider the cost and types of services available from the firm with which the broker is affiliated, to receive the best service at the lowest possible cost to you. The basic discount brokerage service is primarily transactional, and the online brokerage service is *purely* transactional. Contact with a broker, advice, and research assistance generally are available only at a higher price. Investors must weigh the added commissions they pay a full-service broker against the value of the advice they receive, because the amount of available advice is the only major difference among online, discount, and full-service brokers.

TABLE 3.5	Major Full-Service, Discount, and Online Brokers

Type of Broker		
Full-Service	Discount	Online-Only
Charles Schwab	Fidelity Brokerage Services	Ameritrade
Merrill Lynch	Jack White & Company	Datek Online
Morgan Stanley Dean Witter	Kennedy, Cabot & Co.	DLJ Direct
Prudential Securities	Muriel Siebert & Co.	E* Trade
Salomon Smith Barney	Quick & Reilly	National Discount Brokers
UBS PaineWebber	TD Waterhouse	Scottrade

Referrals from friends or business associates are a good way to begin your search for a stockbroker. Don't forget to consider the investing style and goals of the person making the recommendation. However, it is not important—and often not even advisable—to know your stockbroker personally. And in this age of online brokers, you may never meet your broker face to face! A strictly business relationship eliminates the possibility that social concerns will interfere with the achievement of your investment goals. This does not mean that your broker's sole interest should be commissions. Responsible brokers do not engage in **churning**—that is, causing excessive trading of their clients' accounts to increase commissions. Churning is both illegal and unethical under SEC and exchange rules. However, it is often difficult to prove.

churning
an illegal and unethical practice engaged in by a broker to increase commissions by causing excessive trading of clients' accounts.

Opening an Account To open an account, the customer fills out various documents that establish a legal relationship between the customer and the brokerage firm. A signature card and a personal data card provide the information needed to identify the client's account. The stockbroker must also have a reasonable understanding of a client's personal financial situation to assess his or her investment goals—and to be sure that the client can pay for the securities purchased. The client also provides the broker with instructions regarding the transfer and custody of securities. Customers who wish to borrow money to make transactions must establish a margin account (described below). If the customer is acting as a custodian, trustee, or executor or is a corporation, the brokerage firm will require additional documents.

Investors may have accounts with more than one stockbroker. Many investors establish accounts at different types of firms to obtain the benefit and opinions of a diverse group of brokers and to reduce their overall cost of making purchase and sale transactions. You can even open an account online at some brokerage firms.

Next you must select the type of account best suited to your needs. We will briefly consider several of the more popular types.

Single or Joint A brokerage account may be either single or joint. Joint accounts are most common between husband and wife or parent and child. The account of a minor (a person less than 18 years of age) is a **custodial account**, in which a parent or guardian must be part of all transactions. Regardless of the form of the account, the name(s) of the account holder(s) and an account number are used to identify it.

custodial account
the brokerage account of a minor; requires a parent or guardian to be part of all transactions.

cash account
a brokerage account in which a customer can make only cash transactions.

margin account
a brokerage account in which the customer has been extended borrowing privileges by the brokerage firm.

wrap account
a brokerage account in which customers with large portfolios pay a flat annual fee that covers the cost of a money manager's services and the commissions on all trades.

odd lot
less than 100 shares of stock.

round lot
100-share units of stock or multiples thereof.

market order
an order to buy or sell stock at the best price available when the order is placed.

Cash or Margin A **cash account**, the more common type, is one in which the customer can make only cash transactions. Customers can initiate cash transactions via phone or online and are given 3 business days in which to transmit the cash to the brokerage firm. The firm is likewise given 3 business days in which to deposit the proceeds from the sale of securities in the customer's cash account.

A **margin account** is an account in which the brokerage firm extends borrowing privileges to a creditworthy customer. By leaving securities with the firm as collateral, the customer can borrow a prespecified proportion of the securities' purchase price. The brokerage firm will, of course, charge the customer a stated rate of interest on borrowings. (The mechanics of margin trading are covered in Chapter 2.)

Wrap The **wrap account** allows brokerage customers with large portfolios (generally $100,000 or more) to shift stock selection decisions conveniently to a professional money manager, either in-house or independent. In return for a flat annual fee equal to between 1% and 3% of the portfolio's total asset value, the brokerage firm helps the investor select a money manager, pays the manager's fee, and executes the money manager's trades. Initially the investor and manager discuss the client's overall goals. Wrap accounts are appealing for a number of reasons other than convenience. The annual fee in most cases covers commissions on all trades, virtually eliminating the chance of the broker churning the account. In addition, the broker monitors the manager's performance and provides the investor with detailed reports, typically quarterly.

Odd-Lot or Round-Lot Transactions Investors can buy stock in either odd or round lots. An **odd lot** consists of less than 100 shares of a stock. A **round lot** is a 100-share unit or a multiple thereof. You would be dealing in an odd lot if you bought, say, 25 shares of stock but in a round lot if you bought 200 shares. A trade of 225 shares would be a combination of an odd lot and two round lots.

Transactions in odd lots require either additional processing by the brokerage firm or the assistance of a specialist. For odd lots, an added fee—known as an *odd-lot differential*—is tacked on to the normal commission charge, driving up the costs of these small trades. Small investors in the early stages of their investment programs are primarily responsible for odd-lot transactions.

Basic Types of Orders

Investors can use different types of orders to make security transactions. The type placed normally depends on the investor's goals and expectations. The three basic types of orders are the market order, the limit order, and the stop-loss order.

Market Order An order to buy or sell stock at the best price available when the investor places the order is a **market order**. It is generally the quickest way to fill orders, because market orders are usually executed as soon as they reach the exchange floor or are received by the dealer. Because of the speed with which market orders are executed, the buyer or seller of a security can be sure that the price at which the order is transacted will be very close to the market price prevailing at the time the order was placed.

Limit Order A **limit order** is an order to buy at or below a specified price or to sell at or above a specified price. When the investor places a limit order, the broker transmits it to a specialist dealing in the security. The specialist notes the number of shares and price of the limit order in his or her book and executes the order as soon as the specified market price (or better) exists. The specialist must first satisfy all other orders with precedence—similar orders received earlier, buy orders at a higher specified price, or sell orders at a lower specified price. Investors can place the limit order in one of the following forms:

limit order
an order to buy at or below a specified price or to sell at or above a specified price.

1. A *fill-or-kill order*, which is canceled if not immediately executed.
2. A *day order*, which if not executed is automatically canceled at the end of the day.
3. A *good-'til-canceled (GTC) order*, which generally remains in effect for 6 months unless executed, canceled, or renewed.

Assume, for example, that you place a limit order to buy, at a limit price of $30, 100 shares of a stock currently selling at $30.50. Once the specialist clears all similar orders received before yours, and once the market price of the stock falls to $30 or less, he or she executes your order. It is possible, of course, that your order might expire (if it is not a GTC order) before the stock price drops to $30.

Although a limit order can be quite effective, it can also keep you from making a transaction. If, for instance, you wish to buy at $30 or less and the stock price moves from its current $30.50 price to $42 while you are waiting, you have missed the opportunity to make a profit of $11.50 per share ($42 − $30.50). If you had placed a *market order* to buy at the best available price ($30.50), the profit of $11.50 would have been yours. Limit orders for the sale of a stock are also disadvantageous when the stock price closely approaches, but does not attain, the minimum sale price limit before dropping substantially. Generally speaking, limit orders are most effective when the price of a stock fluctuates greatly, because there is then a better chance that the order will be executed.

stop-loss (stop) order
an order to sell a stock when its market price reaches or drops below a specified level; can also be used to buy stock when its market price reaches or rises above a specified level.

Stop-Loss Order When an investor places a **stop-loss order** or **stop order**, the broker tells the specialist to sell a stock when its market price reaches or drops below a specified level. Stop-loss orders are *suspended orders* placed on stocks; they are activated when and if the stock reaches a certain price. The stop-loss order is placed on the specialist's book and becomes active once the stock reaches the stop price. Like limit orders, stop-loss orders are typically day or GTC orders. When activated, the stop order becomes a *market order* to sell the security at the best price available. Thus it is possible for the actual price at which the sale is made to be well below the price at which the stop was initiated. Investors use these orders to protect themselves against the adverse effects of a rapid decline in share price.

For example, assume you own 100 shares of Ballard Industries, which is currently selling for $35 per share. Because you believe the stock price could decline rapidly at any time, you place a stop order to sell at $30. If the stock price does in fact drop to $30, the specialist will sell the 100 shares at the best price available at that time. If the market price declines to $28 by the time your stop-loss order comes up, you will receive less than $30 per share. Of course, if the market price stays above $30 per share, you will have lost nothing as a result of placing the order, because the stop order will never be initiated. Often investors raise the level of the stop as the price of the stock rises. Such action helps to lock in a higher profit when the price is increasing.

Investors can also place stop orders to buy a stock, although buy orders are far less common than sell orders. For example, an investor may place a stop order to buy 100 shares of MJ Enterprises, currently selling for $70 per share, once its price rises to, say, $75 (the stop price). These orders are commonly used either to limit losses on short sales (discussed in Chapter 2) or to buy a stock just as its price begins to rise.

To avoid the risk of the market moving against you when your stop order becomes a market order, you can place a *stop-limit order,* rather than a plain stop order. This is an order to buy or sell stock at a given price, or better, once a stipulated stop price has been met. For example, in the Ballard Industries example, had a stop-limit order been in effect, then when the market price of Ballard dropped to $30, the broker would have entered a limit order to sell your 100 shares at $30 a share or *better*. Thus you would have run no risk of getting less than $30 a share for your stock—unless the price of the stock kept right on falling. In that case, as is true for any limit order, you might miss the market altogether and end up with stock worth much less than $30. Even though the stop order to sell was triggered (at $30), the stock will *not* be sold, with a stop-limit order, if it keeps falling in price.

Online Transactions

The competition for your online business increases daily as more players enter an already crowded arena. Brokerage firms are encouraging customers to trade online and offering a variety of incentives to get their business, including free trades! However, low cost is not the only reason to choose a brokerage firm. As with any financial decision, you must consider your needs and find the firm that best matches them. One investor may want timely information, research, and quick, reliable trades from a firm like Fidelity or Merrill Lynch. Another, who is an active trader, will focus on cost and fast trades rather than research and so will sign up with Ameritrade or Datek. Ease of site navigation is a major factor in finding an online broker. Table 3.6 compares the costs and services of a number of leading brokerage firms, all of which offer online trading of stocks. Some also offer online trading of bonds and mutual funds as well. A good site for objective, in-depth reviews of firms with online brokerage divisions is Gómez Advisors (www.gomez.com). It rates brokers on numerous factors, including response time, ease of use, online resources, and availability of 24-hour customer service.

Stocks If you decide that do-it-yourself investing is for you, choose an online broker and open an account. In most cases, you can fill out the application forms online, print and sign them, and mail them with a check to fund your account initially. As soon as you receive confirmation that the funds are in your account, you can start trading. You can place the same types of orders as with a traditional broker.

TABLE 3.6 Comparison of Costs and Services: Leading Brokerage Firms Offering Online Trading

Firm/Web Site	Online Products	Minimum Balance[1]	Base Stock Commission[2]	Other Services
Ameritrade (ameritrade.com)	Stocks, mutual funds, options, bonds (phone only)	$2,000	Online, $8 for market orders, $13 for limit orders; more for phone and broker trades	ATM/debit card, check writing; after-hours trading; alerts; fee for real-time quotes
Charles Schwab (www.schwab.com)	Stocks, mutual funds, options, bonds (phone only)	$5,000	$29.95 per online trade, less for active traders; minimum of $39.95 for broker trades	Check writing, ATM/debit card, electronic bill paying; access to stockbrokers; referrals to 3rd-party investment adviser
Datek (datek.com)	Stocks, mutual funds	none	Online, $9.99; Broker-assisted, $25	Check writing; 60-second execution guarantee
E*Trade (www.etrade.com)	Stocks, mutual funds, options, bonds (phone only)	$1,000	$14.95 for market orders, $19.95 for Nasdaq stocks, limit orders; more for phone and broker trades	Internet banking, online bill paying, ATM/debit cards; partnership with DirectAdvice.com
Fidelity (www.fidelity.com)	Stocks, mutual funds, options, bonds	$2,500	$25 per online trade, less for active traders; considerably more for phone and broker trades	Check writing, charge/debit card, electronic bill paying; free real-time quotes; access to stockbrokers and Fidelity consultants
Merrill Lynch (www.ml.com)	Stocks, mutual funds, options (phone only), bonds (phone only)	$2,000	Online, $29.95 per trade; also offers unlimited trades for a flat annual fee	Check writing, ATM/credit/debit card, electronic bill paying; access to stockbrokers and Merrill Lynch consultants
National Discount Brokers (www.ndb.com)	Stocks, mutual funds, options, bonds (phone only)	none	$14.75 for market orders, $19.75 for limit orders for multiple same-day same side (buy or sell) trades on same stock; more for phone and broker trades	Check writing, debit card, credit card
TD Waterhouse (www.tdwaterhouse.com)	Stocks, mutual funds, options, bonds (phone only)	$1,000	$12 for market orders, $15 for limit orders	Check writing, ATM/debit card, electronic bill paying and account transfers; Advisor Direct referral service for large accounts

[1]For cash account; may be different for retirement account and higher for margin account. These commissions are, of course, subject to change; also, some brokers/dealers may charge more than the indicated commission, others less.
[2]Some firms add a per-share surcharge after the first 1,000 or 5,000 shares.

Sources: Brokerage firm Web sites and "Discount Brokerage Comparison Table," *The Motley Fool,* downloaded from www.fool.com/dbc/tables/compare, October 1, 2000; "Full Service on the Net," *Business Week,* May 22, 2000, p. 152; "The Online Lineup," *Wall Street Journal,* June 12, 2000, p. 10.

Order Ticket for an Online Broker

Ameritrade's advanced order ticket makes it easy to place a long or short order and to specify the order type (market, limit, stop, or stop-limit). (*Source:* Trading demo, Ameritrade.com, downloaded from **https://wwws.ameritrade.com/cgi-bin/logins.cgi.** Ameritrade Holding Corporation, 4211 S. 102nd St. Omaha, Nebraska 68127. Phone: 800-237-8692.)

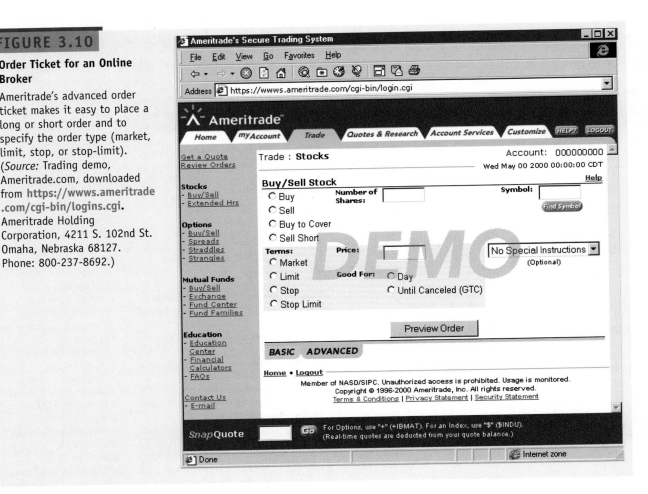

Here are the steps in making an online stock purchase transaction at Ameritrade's Web site. The specifics may vary slightly at other brokerage sites but will follow a similar pattern.

1. Go to your brokerage firm's Web site and log in with your account number and personal identification number (PIN) to access your account. This takes you to your personal trading homepage.
2. At your personal trading page, you'll have access to your account information, trade screens, market news, daily market summaries, stock quotes, research, and more. If you have already done your research and know what stock you wish to buy, you move on to the order page.
3. Using the brokerage site's order form, place your order. Ameritrade has two order tickets: a basic ticket for market, limit, and stop orders and an advanced stock order ticket, shown in Figure 3.10. The advanced order ticket also includes selling short, stop-limit orders, and a place to enter special instructions to set the terms of your trade.
4. After placing your securities order, click to see a preview or confirmation page to review your order before submitting it. If everything is correct, click "Place Order." Otherwise click "Do Not Place Order" to delete the order information.

5. Clicking on the "Place Order" button takes you to the order-sent page that confirms Ameritrade's receipt of your order. You can check the status of your order at the "Review Orders" link.

Now you can even invest in non-U.S. stocks online at global trading sites Globeshare.com (www.globeshare.com) and IntlTrader.com (www.intltrader .com). IntlTrader.com charges $29.99 per trade; Globeshare commissions vary depending on the country.

See how easy it is? In fact, the ease of Internet investing has created a new type of investor: the compulsive investor, who can't get enough of investing. The *Investing in Action* box on page 112 describes the dilemmas of these investment addicts.

day trader
an investor who buys and sells stocks quickly throughout the day in hopes of making quick profits.

Day Trading For some investors, online stock trading is so compelling that they become day traders. The opposite of buy-and-hold investors with a long-term perspective, **day traders** buy and sell stocks quickly throughout the day. They hope that their stocks will continue to rise in value for the very short time they own them—sometimes just seconds or minutes—so they can make quick profits. Some also sell short, looking for small price decreases. True day traders do not own any stocks overnight—hence the term "day trader"—because they believe that the extreme risk of prices changing radically from day to day will lead to large losses. Day trading is not illegal or unethical, but it is highly risky. To compound their risk, day traders usually buy on margin to use leverage to earn higher profits. But as we saw in Chapter 2, margin trading also increases the risk of large losses.

Until recently, day trading was a little-known activity. Now that the Internet makes investment information and transactions accessible to the masses, it is a dangerously popular one. Day traders watch their computer screens continuously, trying to track numerous ticker quotes and price data to identify market trends. It's a very difficult task—essentially a very stressful, full-time job. Yet pitches for day trading make it seem like an easy route to quick riches. Quite the reverse is true. Day traders typically incur major financial losses when they start trading. Some never achieve profitability. Day traders also have high expenses for brokerage commissions, training, and computer equipment. By some estimates, they must make a 56% profit annually to break even on fees and commissions alone.

Technical and Service Problems As the number of online investors increases, so do the problems that beset brokerage firms and their customers. The number of complaints about online brokerage services doubled from 1998 to 1999, with technical difficulties the biggest category. Investors who report trading problems are also upset about the lack of response from brokers. And they claim that brokers do not get the best prices for stock orders.

Many online brokerage firms were not prepared for the heavy volume at their Web sites. Victims of their own successful marketing campaigns, the firms had inadequate computer systems and capacity. Software problems have also been to blame in some service outages. The resulting online traffic jams have left customers locked out of brokerage Web sites, unable to view their account information or place trades. Most firms have upgraded their systems to reduce the number of service outages.

The problems go beyond the brokerage sites, though. Once an investor places a trade at a firm's Web site, it goes through several other parties to be

INVESTING in action

Investing as Gambling

It's a common story: Howard, a young investor, watched his friends strike it rich and stepped gingerly into the waters of online investing. He made $4,000 in a matter of minutes on his first trade, and soon he was deep into *day trading*—buying and selling stocks very quickly to make a profit of a few cents per share. He sat, eyes glued to his computer screen, all day in search of a quick profit. As he met with some success, he opened a margin account to leverage his profits. Before long he was a confirmed "investaholic." Not until the market tanked and he was deep in debt did reality hit. "It all happened so unbelievably fast. I got sucked into believing," he laments.

Howard is not alone. The number of people who are addicted to investing is growing at an alarming rate. As long as the markets were up and paper profits climbed, naive investors rode the wave to profits. When the market became more volatile, investors began losing money. "As the markets get more treacherous, these people begin to see that they really were gambling," says Paul Good, a San Francisco psychologist specializing in stock market addiction.

Investing as gambling? Hard to accept, but at some Gamblers Anonymous meetings, stock traders now account for about half the participants. Investment addicts get a rush from watching stock prices move across the computer screen and quick satisfaction from point-and-click stock trading. Although the speed and simplicity of online investing are beneficial to many investors, for addicts they lead to increased impulse buying—as well as the chance to do it secretly. David G. admits that there are parallels between trading and gambling. "All the thrills are there when you make the right trade. There is absolutely no difference."

Nasdaq's spring 2000 plunge was a wake-up call for many investors, including 24-year-old Ryan G. He was making as many as 50 trades a day. "Fortunately, as the market went down, I lost my addiction," he says. Most of his funds are now in money market accounts, which he calls his "nicotine patch."

Sources: Ruth Simon and E. S. Browning, "Some Online Investors Can't Say No to Playing the Market," *Wall Street Journal*, August 4, 2000, pp. A1, A4; and Paul Sloan, "Can't Stop Checking Your Quotes?" *U.S. News & World Report*, July 10, 2000, p. 40.

executed. Most online brokers don't have their own trading desks and have agreements with other trading firms to execute their orders on the *New York Stock Exchange* or *Nasdaq Stock Market.* Slowdowns at any point in the process can create problems confirming trades. Investors, thinking that their trades had not gone through, might place the order again—only to discover later that they have bought the same stock twice. Online investors who don't get immediate trade execution and confirmation use the telephone when they can't get through online or to solve other problems with their accounts, and they often face long waiting times on hold.

Tips for Successful Online Trades Successful online investors take additional precautions before submitting their orders. Here are some tips to protect yourself from common problems:

- *Know how to place and confirm your order before you begin trading.* This simple step can keep you from having problems later.

- *Verify the stock symbol of the security you wish to buy.* Two very different companies can have similar symbols. Some investors have bought the wrong stock because they didn't check before placing their order.

- *Use limit orders.* The order you see on your computer screen may not be the one you get. With a limit order, you avoid getting burned in fast-moving markets. Although limit orders cost more, they can save you thousands of dollars. For example, customers eager to get shares of a hot IPO stock placed market orders. Instead of buying the stock near the offering price of $9, some were shocked to find that their orders were filled at prices as high as $90 during the stock's first trading day. Investors who were aware of the price run-up tried to cancel orders but couldn't get through to brokers. Charles Schwab and E*Trade accept only limit orders for online IPO purchases on the first day of trading.

- *Don't ignore the online reminders that ask you to check and recheck.* It's easy to make a typo that adds an extra digit to a purchase amount.

- *Don't get carried away.* It's easy to churn your own account. In fact, new online investors trade about twice as much as they did before they went online. To control impulse trading, have a strategy and stick to it.

- *Open accounts with two brokers.* This protects you if your online brokerage's computer system crashes. It also gives you an alternative if one brokerage is blocked with heavy trading volume.

- *Double-check orders for accuracy.* Make sure each trade was completed according to your instructions. It's very easy to make typos or use the wrong stock symbol, so review the confirmation notice to verify that the right number of shares was bought or sold and that the price and commissions or fees are as quoted. Check your account for "unauthorized" trades.

Bonds Electronic bond trading accounts for about 6% of the overall trading volume, and only 1% is from individual investors. Few fully automated online bond transactions systems are available to individual investors. Typically, you must find the information at Web sites like the ones mentioned earlier in the chapter and then phone your broker to fill the order. At E*Trade's Bond Center, investors can research various types of bonds to learn the price, yield, and maturity dates, although they must still place their orders by telephone. Some firms let customers place e-mail orders but then execute the order in the traditional way. TradeWeb (www.tradeweb .com) is one site where individuals can trade U.S. government securities.

HOTLINKS

Also check two popular sites that are used: The Bond Market Association and Bonds Online at:

www.investinginbonds.com
www.bonds-online.com

It won't be long, however, before individual investors can trade bonds online much as they do stocks. Many firms are developing online bond-trading capabilities in response to customer demand for full-service online investing. W.R. Hambrecht's OpenBook (www.openbook.com) offers online auctions of corporate bonds to investors. Dow Chemical and Ford Motor Credit have already auctioned bonds through OpenBook. A group of leading international investment banks established Market Axess (www.marketaxess.com) to offer institutional investors trading in investment grade corporate, Eurobond, high yield, emerging market, and convertible bonds.

Mutual Funds As we noted earlier in this chapter, the Internet is a big time-saver when it comes to sorting through thousands of mutual funds. Many sites offer descriptions of funds, what they invest in, and their track records, as well as screening tools to find funds that meet specific needs or goals.

You can buy and sell funds online at fund company or brokerage firm Web sites. You can also transfer your investment from one fund to another. As with stocks, you must first open an account and have a signature on file. You may be able to download and print a sign-up form and mail in a check either to the fund itself for direct transactions or to the brokerage firm. Once you fund your account, making online transactions is fairly easy.

Brokerage sites like Charles Schwab offer fund supermarkets where investors can buy funds from many different fund companies, instead of having to go from fund family site to fund family site to compare and then purchase them. However, some brokerage firms charge commissions on purchases of funds that you can buy without an initial sales charge if you purchase them directly from the fund family. Availability and commissions differ from one brokerage firm to another, so be sure you understand the fee structure before executing an order. Fund transactions are made through a major stock exchange or Nasdaq; there is no open public market for traditional mutual funds although, as explained in Chapter 12, *exchange-traded funds* are a new type of publicly traded fund.

Transaction Costs

Making transactions through brokers or dealers is considerably easier for investors than it would be to negotiate directly, trying to find someone who wants to buy that which they want to sell (or vice versa). To compensate the broker for executing the transaction, investors pay transaction costs, which are usually levied on both the purchase and the sale of securities. When making investment decisions, you must consider the structure and magnitude of transaction costs, because they affect returns.

fixed-commission schedules fixed brokerage commissions that typically apply to the small transactions usually made by individual investors.

negotiated commissions brokerage commissions agreed to by the client and the broker as a result of their negotiations; typically apply on large institutional transactions and to individual investors who maintain large accounts.

Since the passage of the Securities Acts Amendments of 1975, brokers have been permitted to charge whatever brokerage commissions they deem appropriate. Most firms have established **fixed-commission schedules** that apply to small transactions, the ones most often made by individual investors. On large institutional transactions, the client and broker may arrange a **negotiated commission**—commissions to which both parties agree. Negotiated commissions are also available to individual investors who maintain large accounts, typically above $50,000.

The commission structure varies with the type of security and the type of broker. We'll describe the basic commission structures for various types of securities in subsequent chapters. Because of the way brokerage firms charge commissions on stock trades, it is difficult to compare prices precisely. Traditional brokers generally charge on the basis of number of shares and the price of the stock at the time of the transaction. Internet brokers usually charge flat rates, often for transactions up to 1,000 shares, with additional fees for larger or more complicated orders. However, many traditional brokerage firms have reduced their commissions on broker-assisted trades and have instituted annual flat fees set as a specified percentage of the value of the assets in the account. Unless you are a very active trader, you will probably be better off paying commissions on a per-transaction basis.

Obviously, discount and online brokers charge substantially less than full-service brokers for the same transaction. However, most discounters charge a minimum fee to discourage small orders. For example, Charles Schwab, the largest online broker, charges a minimum fee of about $40 for a broker-assisted order and $30 for an online stock transaction. The savings from the discounter are substantial: Depending on the size and type of transaction, discount and online brokers can typically save investors between 30% and 80% of the commission charged by the full-service broker.

Investor Protection: SIPC and Arbitration

Although most investment transactions take place safely, it is important for you to know what protection you have if things *don't* go smoothly. As a client, you are protected against the loss of the securities or cash held by your broker. The **Securities Investor Protection Corporation (SIPC)**, a nonprofit membership corporation, was authorized by the *Securities Investor Protection Act of 1970* to protect customer accounts against the consequences of financial failure of the brokerage firm. The SIPC currently insures each customer's account for up to $500,000, with claims for cash limited to $100,000 per customer. Note that SIPC insurance does not guarantee that the investor will recover the dollar value of the securities; it guarantees only that the securities themselves will be returned. Some brokerage firms also insure certain customer accounts for amounts in excess of $500,000. Certainly, in light of the diversity and quality of services available among brokerage firms, this may be an additional service you should consider when you select a firm and an individual broker.

The SIPC provides protection in case your brokerage firm fails. But what happens if your broker gave you bad advice and, as a result, you lost a lot of money on an investment? Or what if you feel your broker is *churning* your account, the illegal but difficult-to-prove practice of causing excessive trading to increase commissions? In either case, the SIPC won't help. It's not intended to insure you against bad investment advice or churning. Instead, if you have a dispute with your broker, the first thing you should do is discuss the situation with the managing officer at the branch where you do business. If that doesn't do any good, then contact the firm's compliance officer and the securities regulator in your home state.

If you still don't get any satisfaction, you can use litigation (judicial methods in the courts) to resolve the dispute. Alternative dispute resolution processes that may avoid litigation include *mediation* and *arbitration*. **Mediation** is an informal, voluntary approach in which you and the broker agree to a mediator, who facilitates negotiations between the two of you to resolve the case. The mediator does not impose a solution on you and the broker. The NASD and securities-related organizations encourage investors to mediate disputes rather than arbitrate them, because mediation can reduce costs and time for both investors and brokers.

If mediation is not pursued or if it fails, you may have no choice but to take the case to **arbitration**, a formal process whereby you and your broker present the two sides of the argument before an arbitration panel. The panel then decides the case. Many brokerage firms require you to resolve disputes by *binding arbitration;* in this case, you don't have the option to sue. You must accept the arbitrator's decision, and in most cases you cannot go to court to review your case. Before you open an account, check whether the brokerage agreement contains a binding-arbitration clause.

Securities Investor Protection Corporation (SIPC)
a nonprofit membership corporation, authorized by the federal government, that insures each brokerage customer's account for up to $500,000, with claims for cash limited to $100,000 per customer.

HOTLINKS
The Securities Investor Protection Corporation (SIPC) protects customers of broker-dealers registered with the U.S. Securities and Exchange Commission.
www.sipc.org

mediation
an informal, voluntary dispute resolution process in which a customer and a broker agree to a mediator, who facilitates negotiations between them to resolve the case.

arbitration
a formal dispute resolution process in which a customer and a broker present their argument before a panel, which then decides the case.

Settling securities disputes through mediation or arbitration rather than litigation has advantages and disadvantages. Mediation and arbitration proceedings typically cost less and are resolved more quickly than litigation. Recent legislation has given many investors the option of using either securities industry panels or independent arbitration panels such as those sponsored by the American Arbitration Association (AAA). Independent panels are considered more sympathetic toward investors. In addition, only one of the three arbitrators on a panel can be connected with the securities industry. However, the average arbitration award is about 60% of the original investment, before deducting any fees.

Probably the best thing you can do to avoid the need to mediate, arbitrate, or litigate with your broker is to select him or her carefully, understand the financial risks involved in the broker's recommendations, thoroughly evaluate the advice he or she offers, and continuously monitor the volume of transactions that he or she recommends and executes. Clearly, it is much less costly to choose the right broker initially than to incur later the financial and emotional costs of having chosen a bad one.

If you have a problem with an online trade, immediately file a written—not e-mail—complaint with the broker. Cite dates, times, and amounts of trades, and include all supporting documentation. File a copy with the NASD regulatory arm Web site (www.nasdr.com) and with your state securities regulator. If you can't resolve the problems with the broker, you can try mediation and then resort to arbitration, litigation being the last resort.

IN REVIEW

CONCEPTS

3.14 Describe the types of services offered by brokerage firms, and discuss the criteria for selecting a suitable stockbroker.

3.15 Briefly differentiate among the following types of brokerage accounts:
a. Single or joint.   b. Custodial.
c. Cash.   d. Margin.
e. Wrap.

3.16 Differentiate among market orders, limit orders, and stop-loss orders. What is the rationale for using a stop-loss order rather than a limit order?

3.17 In what two ways, based on the number of shares transacted, do brokers typically charge for executing their clients' transactions? Differentiate between the services and costs associated with full-service, discount, and online brokers.

3.18 Summarize the steps you would take to make an online stock transaction. What is *day trading*, and why is it risky?

3.19 Based on the *Investing in Action* box on page 112, do you believe that compulsive investing is the same as gambling? What steps can an investor take to keep his or her trading habits under control?

3.20 How can you avoid problems as an online trader?

3.21 What capabilities currently exist for buying bonds and mutual funds online?

3.22 What protection does the Securities Investor Protection Corporation (SIPC) provide securities investors? How are mediation and arbitration procedures used to settle disputes between investors and their brokers?

Investment Advisers and Investment Clubs

investment advisers
individuals or firms that provide investment advice, typically for a fee.

Although financial information is available from numerous sources, many investors have neither the time nor the expertise to analyze it and make decisions on their own. Instead, they turn to an **investment adviser,** which is an individual or firm that provides investment advice, typically for a fee. Alternatively, some small investors join investment clubs. Here we will discuss using an investment adviser and then briefly cover the key aspects of investment clubs.

Using an Investment Adviser

The "product" provided by an investment adviser ranges from broad, general advice to detailed, specific analyses and recommendations. The most general form of advice is a newsletter published by the adviser. These letters comment on the economy, current events, market behavior, and specific securities. Investment advisers also provide complete individualized investment evaluation, recommendation, and management services.

Regulation of Advisers As we noted in Chapter 2, the Investment Advisers Act of 1940 ensures that investment advisers make full disclosure of information about their backgrounds, about conflicts of interest, and so on. The act requires professional advisers to register and file periodic reports with the SEC. A 1960 amendment permits the SEC to inspect the records of investment advisers and to revoke the registration of those who violate the act's provisions. However, financial planners, stockbrokers, bankers, lawyers, and accountants who provide investment advice in addition to their main professional activity are not regulated by the act. Many states have also passed similar legislation, requiring investment advisers to register and to abide by the guidelines established by the state law.

Be aware that the federal and state laws regulating the activities of professional investment advisers do not guarantee competence. Rather, they are intended to protect the investor against fraudulent and unethical practices. It is important to recognize that, at present, no law or regulatory body controls entrance into the field. Therefore, investment advisers range from highly informed professionals to totally incompetent amateurs. Advisers who possess a professional designation are usually preferred because they have completed academic courses in areas directly or peripherally related to the investment process. Such designations include CFA (Chartered Financial Analyst), CIC (Chartered Investment Counselor), CFP (Certified Financial Planner), ChFC (Chartered Financial Consultant), CLU (Chartered Life Underwriter), and CPA (Certified Public Accountant).

Online Investment Advice You can also find financial advice online. Whether it's a retirement planning tool or advice on how to diversify your assets, automated financial advisers may be able to help you. If your needs are specific rather than comprehensive, you can find good advice at other sites. For example, T. Rowe Price has an excellent college planning section (www.troweprice.com/college). Financial Engines (www.financialengines.com), AdviceAmerica.com (www.adviceamerica.com), and DirectAdvice.com (www.directadvice.com) are among several independent advice sites that offer

TABLE 3.7	Online Investment Advisers	
Web Site	Description	Fees
AdviceAmerica (www.adviceamerica.com)	Comprehensive Web-based financial planning advice on mutual funds; evaluates outcomes of various investment choices; makes asset allocation recommendations.	$29 per quarter; $99 per year
DirectAdvice (www.directadvice.com)	Develops investment strategy based on goals; recommends specific stock, bond, and money market mutual funds for maximum diversification. Online interview to assess goals, income, and investments. Fast data entry; easy to navigate and run "what-if" scenarios. College savings, retirement, and investing plans.	$75 per year
Financial Engines (www.financialengines.com)	Independent site. Retirement planning focus. Data input is easy. Powerful forecasting tools run hundreds of possible economic scenarios to analyze current portfolio performance and show probability of achieving goals. Subscription service offers specific buy and sell suggestions for mutual funds for tax-deferred accounts keyed to retirement date, expected income in retirement, savings rate, return assumptions, and risk tolerance.	Forecast free; portfolio recommendations $55 a year ($150 for multiple accounts)
Vanguard Funds (www.vanguard.com)	Vanguard Online Planner offers advice on allocating assets among stock, bond, and cash investments. Suggests appropriate Vanguard funds based on risk tolerance and personal financial situation. Helps choose investments for a total financial plan or just for college, retirement, investment, or estate planning.	Free; must be customer to save data

broader planning capabilities. Many mutual fund family Web sites have online financial advisers. For example, Vanguard (www.vanguard.com) has a financial planning section that helps you choose funds for specific investment objectives, such as retirement or financing a college education. Table 3.7 compares the features and capabilities of several investment advice sites.

The Cost and Use of Investment Advice Professional investment advice typically costs, annually, between 0.25% and 3% of the dollar amount of money being managed. For large portfolios, the fee is typically in the range of 0.25% to 0.75%. For small portfolios (less than $100,000), an annual fee ranging from 2% to 3% of the dollar amount of funds managed would not be unusual. These fees generally cover complete management of a client's money, excluding any purchase or sale commissions. The cost of periodic investment advice not provided as part of a subscription service could be based on a fixed-fee schedule or quoted as an hourly charge for consultation. Online advisers are much less expensive; they either are free or charge an annual fee.

Whether you choose a traditional investment advisory service or decide to try an online service, some are better than others. More expensive services do not necessarily provide better advice. It is best to study carefully the track record and overall reputation of an investment adviser before purchasing his or her services. Not only should the adviser have a good performance record, but he or she also should be responsive to the investor's personal goals.

How good is the advice from online advisers? It's very hard to judge. Their suggested plans are only as good as the input. Beginning investors may not have sufficient knowledge to make wise assumptions on future savings, tax, or inflation rates or to analyze results thoroughly. A good personal financial planner will ask lots of questions to assess your investing expertise and explain what you don't know. These early-stage automated tools may take too narrow a focus and not consider other parts of your investment portfolio. For many investors, online advisers lack what leads them to get help in the first place—the human touch. They want hand-holding, reassurance, and gentle nudging to follow through on their plans.

Investment Clubs

Another way to obtain investment advice and experience is to join an investment club. This route can be especially useful for those of moderate means who do not want to incur the cost of an investment adviser. An **investment club** is a legal partnership binding a group of investors (partners) to a specified organizational structure, operating procedures, and purpose. The goal of most clubs is to earn favorable long-term returns by making investments in vehicles of moderate risk.

Individuals with similar goals usually form investment clubs to pool their knowledge and money to create a jointly owned and managed portfolio. Certain members are responsible for obtaining and analyzing data on a specific investment vehicle or strategy. At periodic meetings, the members present their findings and recommendations for discussion and further analysis by the membership. The group decides whether to pursue the proposed vehicle or strategy. Most clubs require members to make scheduled contributions to the club's treasury, thereby regularly increasing the pool of investable funds. Although most clubs concentrate on investments in stocks and bonds, some may concentrate on specialized investments such as options or futures.

Membership in an investment club provides an excellent way for the novice investor to learn the key aspects of portfolio construction and investment management, while (one hopes) earning a favorable return on his or her funds. In fact, many investment clubs regularly earn returns above the market and even above professional money managers. The reason? Investment clubs typically buy stocks for the long term, rather that trying to make the quick buck.

As you might expect, investment clubs have also joined the online investing movement. By tapping into the Internet, clubs are freed from geographical restrictions. Now investors around the world, many who have never met, can form a club and discuss investing strategies and stock picks just as easily as if they gathered in person. Finding a time or place to meet is no longer an issue. Some clubs are formed by friends; others are strangers who have similar investing philosophies and may have met online. Online clubs conduct business via e-mail or set up a private Web site. Members of the *National Association of Investors Corporation (NAIC)*, a not-for-profit organization, qualify for a site at Yahoo! that includes meeting rooms, investment tools, and other investment features. Other portals offer sites for nonmembers.

NAIC, which has over 730,000 individual and club investors and 37,000 regular and online investment clubs, publishes a variety of useful materials and also sponsors regional and national meetings. (To learn how to start an investment club, visit the NAIC Web site at www.better-investing.org. Or order an

investment club
a legal partnership through which a group of investors are bound to a specified organizational structure, operating procedures, and purpose, which is typically to earn favorable long-term returns from moderate-risk investments.

HOTLINKS
Frequently asked questions about investment clubs are answered at:
www.better-investing.org/faq/2.html

information package by calling the toll-free number 877-ASK-NAIC (877-275-6242) or writing NAIC, P.O. Box 220, Royal Oak, MI 48068.)

IN REVIEW

CONCEPTS

3.23 Describe the services that professional investment advisers perform, how they are regulated, online investment advisers, and the cost of investment advice.

3.24 What benefits does an *investment club* offer the small investor? Why do investment clubs regularly outperform the market and the pros? Would you prefer to join a regular or an online club, and why?

Summary

LG 1 **Discuss the growth in online investing, including educational sites and investment tools, and the effective use of the Internet.** The Internet has empowered individual investors by providing information and tools formerly available only to investing professionals and by simplifying the investing process. The savings it provides in time and money are huge. Investors get the most current information, including real-time stock price quotes, market activity data, research reports, educational articles, and discussion forums. Tools such as financial planning calculators, stock-screening programs, charting, and stock quotes and portfolio tracking are free at many sites. Buying and selling securities online is convenient, relatively simple, inexpensive, and fast.

LG 2 **Identify the major types and sources of traditional and online investment information.** Investment information, descriptive or analytical, includes information about the economy and current events, industries and companies, and alternative investment vehicles, as well as price information and personal investment strategies. It can be obtained from financial journals, general newspapers, institutional news, business periodicals, government publications, special subscription services, stockholders' reports, comparative data sources, subscription services, brokerage reports, investment letters, price quotations, and electronic and online sources. Most print publications also have Web sites with access to all or part of their content. Financial portals bring together a variety of financial information online. Investors will also find specialized sites for bond, mutual fund, and international information, as well as message boards that discuss individual securities and investment strategies. Because it is hard to know the qualifications of those who make postings on message boards, participants must do their own homework before acting on an online tip.

LG 3 **Explain the characteristics, interpretation, and uses of the commonly cited stock and bond market averages and indexes.** Investors commonly rely on stock market averages and indexes to stay abreast of market behavior. The most often cited are the Dow Jones averages, which include the Dow Jones Industrial Average (DJIA). Also widely followed are the Standard & Poor's indexes, the NYSE composite index, the AMEX composite index, the Nasdaq indexes, and the Value Line indexes. Numerous other averages and indexes, including a number of global and foreign market indexes, are regularly reported in financial publications.

Bond market indicators are most often reported in terms of average bond yields and average prices. The Dow Jones bond averages are among the most popular. A wealth of return and price index data is also available for various types of bonds and various domestic and foreign markets. Both stock and bond market statistics are published daily in the *Wall Street Journal* and summarized weekly in *Barron's*.

LG 4 **Review the roles of traditional and online stockbrokers, including the services they provide, selection of a stockbroker, opening an account, and transaction basics.** Stockbrokers facilitate transactions among buyers and sellers of securities, and they provide a variety of other client services. An investor should select a stockbroker who has a compatible disposition toward investing and whose firm offers the desired services at competitive costs. Today the distinctions among traditional, discount, and online brokers is blurring. Most brokers now offer online trading capabilities, and many no-frills brokers are expanding their services to include research and advice. Investors can open a variety of types of brokerage accounts, such as single, joint, custodial, cash, margin, and wrap. An investor can make odd-lot transactions (less than 100 shares) or round-lot transactions (100 shares or multiples thereof). An added fee is typically charged on odd-lot transactions.

LG 5 **Describe the basic types of orders (market, limit, and stop-loss), online transactions, transaction costs, and the legal aspects of investor protection.** A market order is an order to buy or sell stock at the best price available. A limit order is an order to buy at a specified price or below or to sell at a specified price or above. Stop-loss orders become market orders as soon as the minimum sell price or the maximum buy price is hit. Limit and stop-loss orders can be placed as fill-or-kill orders, day orders, or good-'til-canceled (GTC) orders.

On small transactions, most brokers have fixed-commission schedules; on larger transactions, they will negotiate commissions. Commissions also vary by type of security and type of broker: full-service, discount, or online broker. The Securities Investor Protection Corporation (SIPC) insures customers' accounts against the brokerage firm's failure. To avoid litigation, mediation and arbitration procedures are frequently employed to resolve disputes between investor and broker. These disputes typically concern the investor's belief that the broker either gave bad advice or churned the account.

LG 6 **Discuss the roles of investment advisers and investment clubs.** There are a variety of different types of investment advisers, who charge an annual fee ranging from 0.25% to 3% of the dollar amount being managed and are often regulated by federal and state law. Web sites that provide investment advice such as retirement planning, asset diversification, and stock and mutual fund selection, are now available as well. Investment clubs provide individual investors with investment advice and help them gain investing experience. Online clubs have members in various geographical areas and conduct business via e-mail or at a private Web site.

Discussion Questions

LG 2 Q3.1 Thomas Weisel, chief executive of a securities firm that bears his name, believes that individual investors already have too much information. "Many lose money by trading excessively on stray data," he says. Other industry professionals oppose the SEC's fair disclosure rule for the same reason. The Securities Industry Association's general counsel expressed concern that the rule will restrict rather than encourage the flow of information. Other securities professionals argue that individual investors aren't really capable of interpreting much of the information now available to them. Explain why you agree or disagree with these opinions.

LG 2   **Q3.2** Innovative Internet-based bookseller Amazon.com has now expanded into other retail categories. Gather appropriate information from relevant sources to assess the following with an eye toward investing in Amazon.com.
   a. Economic conditions and the key current events during the past 12 months.
   b. Information on the status and growth (past and future) of the bookselling industry and specific information on Amazon.com and its major competitors.
   c. Brokerage reports and analysts' recommendations with respect to Amazon.com.
   d. A history of the past and recent dividends and price behavior of Amazon.com, which is traded on the Nasdaq National Market.
   e. A recommendation with regard to the advisability of investing in Amazon.com.

LG 2   LG 6   **Q3.3** Visit four financial portals or other financial information Web sites listed in Table 3.4. Compare them in terms of ease of use, investment information, investment tools, advisory services, and links to other services. Also catalog the costs, if any, of obtaining these services. Which would you recommend, and why?

LG 3   **Q3.4** Gather and evaluate relevant market averages and indexes over the past 6 months to assess recent stock and bond market conditions. Describe the conditions in each of these markets. Using recent history, coupled with relevant economic and current event data, forecast near-term market conditions. On the basis of your assessment of market conditions, would you recommend investing in stocks, in bonds, or in neither at this time? Explain the reasoning underlying your recommendation.

LG 4   **Q3.5** Prepare a checklist of questions and issues you would use when shopping for a stockbroker. Describe both the ideal broker and the ideal brokerage firm, given your investment goals and disposition. Discuss the pros and cons of using a full-service rather than a discount or online broker. If you plan to trade online, what additional questions would you ask?

LG 4   **Q3.6** Visit the sites of two brokerages listed in Table 3.6 or any others you know. After exploring the sites, compare them for ease of use, quality of information, availability of investing tools, reliability, other services, and any other criteria important to you. Summarize your findings and explain which you would choose if you were to open an account, and why.

LG 5   **Q3.7** Describe how, if at all, a conservative and an aggressive investor might use each of the following types of orders as part of their investment programs. Contrast these two types of investors in view of these preferences.
   a. Market.
   b. Limit.
   c. Stop-loss.

LG 5   **Q3.8** Learn more about day trading at sites such as Edgetrade.com (www.edgetrade.com), Daytrading Stocks (www.daytradingstocks.com), Intelligent Speculator (www.intelligentspeculator.com), and Rookie Day trader (www.rookiedaytrader.com). On the basis of your research, summarize how day trading works, some strategies for day traders, the risks, and the rewards. What type of person would make a good day trader?

LG 6   **Q3.9** Differentiate between the financial advice you would receive from a traditional investment adviser and one of the new online planning and advice sites. Which would you personally prefer to use, and why? How could membership in an investment club serve as an alternative to a paid investment adviser?

Problems

LG 2

P3.1 Bill Shaffer estimates that if he does 10 hours of research using data that will cost $75, there is a good chance that he can improve his expected return on a $10,000, 1-year investment from 8% to 10%. Bill feels that he must earn at least $10 per hour on the time he devotes to his research.
   a. Find the cost of Bill's research.
   b. By how much (in dollars) will Bill's return increase as a result of the research?
   c. On a strict economic basis, should Bill perform the proposed research?

LG 3

P3.2 Imagine that the Mini-Dow Average (MDA) is based on the closing prices of five stocks. The divisor used in the calculation of the MDA is currently 0.765. The closing prices for each of the five stocks in the MDA today and exactly a year ago, when the divisor was 0.790, are given in the accompanying table.

	Closing Stock Price	
Stock	Today	One Year Ago
Ace Computers	$ 65	$74
Coburn Motor Company	37	34
National Soap & Cosmetics	110	96
Ronto Foods	73	72
Wings Aircraft	96	87

   a. Calculate the MDA today and that of a year ago.
   b. Compare the values of the MDA calculated in part (a) and describe the apparent market behavior over the last year. Was it a bull or a bear market?

LG 3

P3.3 The SP-6 index (a fictitious index) is used by many investors to monitor the general behavior of the stock market. It has a base value set equal to 100 at January 1, 1970. In the acompanying table, the closing market values for each of the six stocks included in the index are given for three dates.

	Closing Market Value of Stock		
Stock	June 30, 2002 (Thousands)	January 1, 2002 (Thousands)	January 1, 1970 (Thousands)
1	$ 430	$ 460	$240
2	1,150	1,120	630
3	980	990	450
4	360	420	150
5	650	700	320
6	290	320	80

   a. Calculate the value of the SP-6 index on both January 1, 2002, and June 30, 2002, using the data presented here.
   b. Compare the values of the SP-6 index calculated in part (a) and relate them to the base index value. Would you describe the general market condition during the 6-month period January 1 to June 30, 2002, as a bull or a bear market?

LG 3

P3.4 Carla Sanchez wishes to develop an average or index that can be used to measure the general behavior of stock prices over time. She has decided to include six closely followed, high-quality stocks in the average or index. She plans to use August 15, 1978, her birthday, as the base and is interested in measuring the value of the average or index on August 15, 1999, and August 15, 2002. She has found the closing prices for each of the six stocks, A through F, at each of the three dates and has calculated a divisor that can be used to adjust for any stock splits, company changes, and so on that have occurred since the base year, which has a divisor equal to 1.00.

Stock	Closing Stock Price		
	August 15, 2002	August 15, 1999	August 15, 1978
A	$46	$40	$50
B	37	36	10
C	20	23	7
D	59	61	26
E	82	70	45
F	32	30	32
Divisor	0.70	0.72	1.00

Note: The number of shares of each stock outstanding has remained unchanged at each of the three dates. Therefore, the closing stock prices will behave identically to the closing market values.

a. Using the data given in the table, calculate the market average, using the same methodology used to calculate the Dow averages, at each of the three dates—the 15th of August 1978, 1999, and 2002.

b. Using the data given in the table and assuming a base index value of 10 on August 15, 1978, calculate the market index, using the same methodology used to calculate the S&P indexes, at each of the three dates.

c. Use your findings in parts (a) and (b) to describe the general market condition—bull or bear—that existed between August 15, 1999, and August 15, 2002.

d. Calculate the percentage changes in the average and index values between August 15, 1999, and August 15, 2002. Why do they differ?

LG 5

P3.5   Al Cromwell places a *market order* to buy a round lot of Thomas, Inc., common stock, which is traded on the NYSE and is currently quoted at $50 per share. Ignoring brokerage commissions, how much money would Cromwell probably have to pay? If he had placed a market order to sell, how much money will he probably receive? Explain.

LG 5

P3.6   Imagine that you have placed a *limit order* to buy 100 shares of Sallisaw Tool at a price of $38, though the stock is currently selling for $41. Discuss the consequences, if any, of each of the following.

a. The stock price drops to $39 per share 2 months before cancellation of the limit order.

b. The stock price drops to $38 per share.

c. The minimum stock price achieved before cancellation of the limit order was $38.50. When the limit order was canceled, the stock was selling for $47.50 per share.

LG 5

P3.7   If you place a *stop-loss order* to sell at $23 on a stock currently selling for $26.50 per share, what is likely to be the minimum loss you will experience on 50 shares if the stock price rapidly declines to $20.50 per share? Explain. What if you had placed a *stop-limit order* to sell at $23, and the stock price tumbled to $20.50?

Case Problem 3.1   *The Perezes' Good Fortune*

LG 2   LG 4   LG 6

Angel and Marie Perez own a small pool hall located in southern New Jersey. They enjoy running the business, which they have owned for nearly 3 years. Angel, a retired professional pool shooter, saved for nearly 10 years to buy this business, which he and his wife own free and clear. The income from the pool hall is adequate to allow Angel, Marie, and their two children, Mary (age 10) and José (age 4), to live comfortably. Although he lacks formal education beyond the tenth grade, Angel has become an avid reader. He enjoys reading about current events and personal finance, particularly investing. He especially likes *Money* magazine, from which he has gained numerous ideas for better managing the family's finances. Because of the long hours required to run the business, Angel can devote 3 to 4 hours a day (on the job) to reading.

Recently, Angel and Marie were notified that Marie's uncle had died and left them a portfolio of stocks and bonds with a current market value of $300,000. They were elated to learn of their good fortune but decided it would be best not to change their lifestyle as a result of this inheritance. Instead, they want their newfound wealth to provide for their children's college education as well as their own retirement. They decided that, like their uncle, they would keep these funds invested in stocks and bonds. Angel felt that in view of this, he needed to acquaint himself with the securities currently in the portfolio. He knew that to manage the portfolio himself, he would have to stay abreast of the securities markets as well as the economy in general. He also realized that he would need to follow each security in the portfolio and continuously evaluate possible alternative securities that could be substituted as conditions warranted. Because Angel had plenty of time in which to follow the market, he strongly believed that with proper information, he could manage the portfolio. Given the amount of money involved, Angel was not too concerned with the information costs; rather, he wanted the best information he could get at a reasonable price.

Questions

a. Explain what role the *Wall Street Journal* and/or *Barron's* might play in meeting Angel's needs. What other general sources of economic and current event information would you recommend to Angel? Explain.

b. How might Angel be able to use the services of Standard & Poor's Corporation, Moody's Investor Services, and the *Value Line Investment Survey* to learn about the securities in the portfolio? Indicate which, if any, of these services you would recommend, and why.

c. Recommend some specific online investment information sources and tools to help Angel and Marie manage their investments.

d. Explain to Angel the need to find a good stockbroker and the role the stockbroker could play in providing information and advice. Should he consider hiring a financial adviser to manage the portfolio?

e. Give Angel a summary prescription for obtaining information and advice that will help to ensure the preservation and growth of the family's newfound wealth.

Case Problem 3.2

Peter and Deborah's Choices of Brokers and Advisers

Peter Chang and Deborah Barry, friends who work for a large software company, decided to leave the relative security of their employer and join the staff of OnlineSpeed Inc., a 2-year-old company working on new broadband technology for fast Internet access. Peter will be a vice president for new-product development; Deborah will be treasurer. Although they are excited about the potential their new jobs offer, they recognize the need to consider the financial implications of the move. Of immediate concern are their 401(k) retirement plans. On leaving their current employer, each of them will receive a lump-sum settlement of about $75,000 that they must roll over into self-directed, tax-deferred retirement accounts. The friends met over lunch to discuss their options for investing these funds.

Peter is 30 years old and single, with a bachelor's degree in computer science. He rents an apartment and would like to buy a condominium fairly soon but is in no rush. For now, he is happy using his money on the luxuries of life. He considers himself a bit of a risk taker and has dabbled in the stock market from time to time, using his technology expertise to invest in software and Internet companies. Deborah's undergraduate degree was in English, followed by an M.B.A. in finance. She is 32, is married, and hopes to start a family very soon. Her husband is a physician in private practice.

Peter is very computer-savvy and likes to pick stocks on the basis of his own Internet research. Although Deborah's finance background gives her a solid understanding of investing fundamentals, she is more conservative and has thus far stayed with blue chip stocks and mutual funds. Among the topics that come up during their lunchtime conversation are stockbrokers and financial planners. Peter is leaning toward a bare-bones online broker with low cost per trade that is offering free trades for a limited time. Deborah is also cost-conscious but warns Peter that the low costs can be deceptive if you have to pay for other services or find yourself trading more often. She also thinks Peter is too focused on the technology sector and encourages him to seek financial advice to balance his portfolio. They agree to research a number of brokerage firms and investment advisers and meet again to compare notes.

Questions

a.   Research at least four different full-service, discount, and online stock brokerage firms, and compare the services and costs. What brokers would suit Peter's needs best, and why? What brokers would suit Deborah's needs best, and why? What are some key questions each should ask when interviewing potential brokers?

b.   What factors should Peter and Deborah consider before deciding to use a particular broker? Compare the pros and cons of getting the personal attention of a full-service broker with the services provided by an online broker.

c.   Do you think that a broker that offers *no* online trading but focuses on personal attention would be a good choice for either Peter or Deborah?

d.   Peter mentioned to Deborah that he had read an article about *day trading* and wanted to try it. What would you advise Peter about the risks and rewards of this strategy?

e.   Prepare a brief overview of the traditional and online sources of investment advice that could help Peter and Deborah create suitable portfolios. Which type of adviser would you recommend for Peter? For Deborah? Explain your reasoning.

Web Exercises

W3.1 S&P indexes are available at www.spglobal.com. The S&P 500 is used by 97% of U.S. money managers and pension plan sponsors. More than $1 trillion is indexed to the S&P 500. Click on [S&P Global 1200] and then [Description].
a. List the six regional indexes.
b. Now click on [Sector Indices]. Identify the first three sectors.
c. Go back to the main page and check out the descriptions of a few international indexes.

W3.2 From the main page at www.spglobal.com, click on [U.S. indices], [Supercomp 1500].
a. Describe the portfolio characteristics of the S&P SuperComposite 1500.
b. Now click on [S&P 500]. Describe its portfolio characteristics.
c. What are the differences between the S&P 500 and the SuperComposite 1500?

W3.3 The economy at a glance is shown at www.bls.gov/eag/. Check [U.S. Economy at a Glance.] and later [Industry at a Glance]. At the Economy at a Glance site (stats.bls.gov/eag/eag.us.htm), you can see 6 months of data on key economic figures: the unemployment rate, change in payroll employment, consumer price index, producer price index, U.S. import price index, employment cost index, and productivity.
a. At the Economy at a Glance site, for each economic indicator (such as the unemployment rate), under History you can access both the 10-year historical data and a graph of the data for over a decade. Access either data or graph for Unemployment rate, and describe what happened over the last decade
b. Click on your home state to see how the economy is there.
c. Industry at a Glance contains profiles of the nine major industry groups. Which are the top four industries from the standpoint of employment?

W3.4 Visit the Wall Street Research Net at www.wsrn.com. Go to [Calendars], [Earning Announcements].
a. List the earnings announcement information (date, time of day, quarter) for any three companies. What impact did the announcement have on the price of the company's stock on that date? Offer an explanation of why the stock price reacted as it did.
b. At the same site, go to [Economic Calendar]. What is on the calendar for the latest date?
c. This site has nice links to the Department of Commerce, Economic Research (has several domestic-economics-related links, such as Conference Board Consumer and Business Confidence, Economic Statistics Briefing Room, StatUSA, and Yardeni's site) and International Research (has links such as Oxford Economic Forecasting, United Nations System of Organizations, and World Bank Group). Check out some links that interest you. Write a brief description of what you found (be sure to include the address of the site) to share with your class.

W3.5 Go to www.quicken.com/investments/charts. This site lets you compare as many as nine stocks and/or indexes on the same chart. Enter the following ticker symbols:

MRK INTU INTC SLE IBM ADM MSFT AOL F

a. What companies do these nine ticker symbols stand for?
b. Compare their 3-year closing prices.

For additional practice with concepts from this chapter, visit

www.awl.com/gitman_joehnk

CHAPTER 4

INVESTMENT RETURN AND RISK

When you go shopping for a computer, stereo system, or clothes, you go to a store, a catalog, or a Web site to examine the merchandise. When you invest in the stock of a company, what can you sample? For one thing, you can visit the company's Web site to find corporate information and financial data. Let's say you did that for Microsoft by going to www.microsoft.com. You would learn that the company was in great financial shape at September 30, 2000, the end of its fiscal year. Revenue was up 16% and net income 21%, compared to 1999, and earnings per share rose almost 20%. Microsoft also had substantial cash on hand and no long-term debt.

It is harder to discover the risks associated with owning the stock. Searching the business press and online investment sites for articles and investment research about Microsoft would provide insight into the various risks the company faces. In the case of Microsoft, your research would reveal that Microsoft is appealing a U.S. Justice Department ruling that the firm had violated U.S. antitrust laws and must be broken up. In addition, you would learn that Microsoft continues to look for ways to expand its technological base beyond personal computer software, where it has a dominant position, into television, games, wireless, and personal information appliances, where it faces greater competition. The stock is trading at about $69 per share, about 40 times earnings. Although this is high for the general market, it is not out of line for technology stocks. Microsoft exceeded analysts' earnings estimates in fiscal-year 1999, and most analysts have the stock on their "strong buy" or "moderate buy" lists. Its 25% return on equity is about five times the software industry average.

To use this information wisely, you need to understand the concepts of return and risk, which are at the heart of any investment decision. In this chapter we'll explain what factors affect the level of investment return and how to assess the different types of risk.

The Concept of Return

LG 1

return
the level of profit from an investment—that is, the reward for investing.

Investors are motivated to invest in a given vehicle by its expected return. The **return** is the level of profit from an investment—that is, the reward for investing. Suppose you have $1,000 in an insured savings account paying 5% annual interest, and a business associate asks you to lend her that much money. If you lend her the money for 1 year, at the end of which she pays you back, your return will depend on the amount of interest you charge. If you make an interest-free loan, your return will be zero. If you charge 5% interest, your return will be $50 (0.05 × $1,000). Because you are already earning a safe 5% on the $1,000, it seems clear that to equal that return you should charge your associate a minimum of 5% interest.

Some investment vehicles guarantee a return; others do not. The $1,000 deposited in an insured savings account at a large bank can be viewed as a certain return. The $1,000 loan to your business associate might be less certain. What is your return if she runs into financial difficulty? If she can repay you only $850, your return will be minus $150 ($850 − $1,000), or minus 15% (−$150 ÷ $1,000). Thus the size of the expected return is one important factor in choosing a suitable investment.

Components of Return

The return on an investment may come from more than one source. The most common source is periodic payments, such as dividends or interest. The other source of return is appreciation in value, the gain from selling an investment vehicle for more than its original purchase price. We call these two sources of return *current income* and *capital gains* (or *capital losses*), respectively.

current income
usually cash or near-cash that is periodically received as a result of owning an investment.

Current Income Current income may take the form of dividends from stocks, interest received on bonds, or dividends received from mutual funds. To be considered income, it must be in the form of cash or be readily convertible into cash. For our purposes, **current income** is usually cash or near-cash that is periodically received as a result of owning an investment.

Using the data in Table 4.1, we can calculate the current income from investments A and B, both purchased for $1,000, over a 1-year period of ownership. Investment A would provide current income of $80, investment B $120. Solely on the basis of the current income received over the 1-year period, investment B seems preferable.

Capital Gains (or Losses) The second dimension of return is concerned with the change, if any, in the market value of an investment. As noted in Chapter 1, the amount by which the proceeds from the sale of an investment exceed its original purchase price is called a *capital gain*. If an investment is sold for less than its original purchase price, a *capital loss* results.

total return
the sum of the current income and the capital gain (or loss) earned on an investment over a specified period of time.

We can calculate the capital gain or loss of the investments as shown in Table 4.1. For investment A, a capital gain of $100 ($1,100 sale price − $1,000 purchase price) is realized over the 1-year period. For investment B, a $40 capital loss results ($960 sale price − $1,000 purchase price).

Combining the capital gain (or loss) with the current income (calculated in the preceding section) gives the **total return** on each investment shown in

TABLE 4.1   **Profiles of Two Investments**

	Investment	
	A	B
Purchase price (beginning of year)	$1,000	$1,000
Cash received		
1st quarter	$ 10	$ 0
2nd quarter	20	0
3rd quarter	20	0
4th quarter	30	120
Total current income (for year)	$ 80	$ 120
Sale price (end of year)	$1,100	$ 960

TABLE 4.2   **Total Returns of Two Investments**

	Investment	
Return	A	B
Current income	$ 80	$120
Capital gain (loss)	100	(40)
Total return	$180	$ 80

Table 4.2. In terms of the total return earned on the $1,000 investment over the 1-year period, investment A is superior to investment B.

The use of *percentage returns* is generally preferred to the use of dollar returns. Percentages allow direct comparison of different sizes and types of investments. Investment A earned an 18% return ($180 ÷ $1,000), whereas B yielded only an 8% return ($80 ÷ $1,000). At this point investment A appears preferable, but differences in risk might cause some investors to prefer B. (We will see why later in this chapter.)

Why Return Is Important

Return is a key variable in the investment decision: It allows us to compare the actual or expected gains of various investments with the levels of return we need. For example, you would be satisfied with an investment that earns 12% if you needed it to earn only 10%. You would not be satisfied with a 10% return if you needed a 14% return. Return can be measured historically, or it can be used to formulate future expectations.

Historical Performance Although most people recognize that future performance is not guaranteed by past performance, they would agree that past data often provide a meaningful basis for future expectations. A common practice in the investment world is to look closely at the historical performance of a given vehicle when formulating expectations about its future.

Interest rates and other measures of financial return are most often cited on an annual basis. Evaluation of past investment returns is typically done on the same basis. Consider the data for a hypothetical investment presented in Table 4.3. Two aspects of these data are important. First, we can determine the

TABLE 4.3	Historical Investment Data for a Hypothetical Investment					
		Market Value (Price)			Total Return	
Year	(1) Income	(2) Beginning of Year	(3) End of Year	(4) (3) − (2) Capital Gain	(5) (1) + (4) ($)	(6) (5) ÷ (2) (%)*
1993	$4.00	$100	$ 95	−$ 5.00	−$ 1.00	− 1.00%
1994	3.00	95	99	4.00	7.00	7.37
1995	4.00	99	105	6.00	10.00	10.10
1996	5.00	105	115	10.00	15.00	14.29
1997	5.00	115	125	10.00	15.00	12.00
1998	3.00	125	120	− 5.00	− 2.00	− 1.60
1999	3.00	120	122	2.00	5.00	4.17
2000	4.00	122	130	8.00	12.00	9.84
2001	5.00	130	140	10.00	15.00	11.54
2002	5.00	140	155	15.00	20.00	14.29
Average	$4.10			$ 5.50	$ 9.60	8.10%

*Percent return on beginning-of-year market value of investment.

average level of return generated by this investment over the past 10 years. Second, we can analyze the trend in this return. As a percentage, the average total return (column 6) over the past 10 years was 8.10%. Looking at the yearly returns, we can see that after the negative return in 1993, 4 years of positive and generally increasing returns occurred before the negative return was repeated in 1998. From 1999 through 2002, positive and increasing returns were again realized.

expected return
the return an investor thinks an investment will earn in the future.

Expected Return In the final analysis, it's the future that matters when we make investment decisions. Therefore, **expected return** is a vital measure of performance. It's what you think the investment will earn in the future that determines what you should be willing to pay for it.

To see how, let's return to the data in Table 4.3. Looking at the historical return figures in the table, an investor would note the increasing trend in returns from 1999 through 2002. But to project future returns, we need insights into the investment's prospects. If the trend in returns seems likely to continue, an expected return in the range of 12% to 15% for 2003 or 2004 would seem reasonable. On the other hand, if future prospects seem poor, or if the investment is subject to cycles, an expected return of 8% to 9% may be a more reasonable estimate. Over the past 10 years, the investment's returns have cycled from a poor year (1993 and 1998) to 4 years of increasing returns (1994–1997 and 1999–2002). We might therefore expect low returns in 2003 to be followed by increasing returns in the 2004–2007 period.

Level of Return

The level of return achieved or expected from an investment will depend on a variety of factors. The key factors are internal characteristics and external forces.

Internal Characteristics Certain characteristics of an investment affect its level of return. Examples include the type of investment vehicle, the quality of management, how the investment is financed, and the customer base of the issuer. For example, the common stock of a large, well-managed, completely equity-financed plastics manufacturer whose major customer is IBM would be expected to provide a level of return different from that of a small, poorly managed, largely debt-financed clothing manufacturer whose customers are small specialty stores. As we will see in later chapters, assessing internal factors and their impact on return is one important step in analyzing potential investments.

HOT LINKS

An *Investing in Action* box on the book's Web site demonstrates that moderate deflation positively affects consumers and investors, but greater deflation poses some threat to them.

www.awl.com/gitman_joehnk

External Forces External forces such as Federal Reserve actions, shortages, war, price controls, and political events may also affect the level of return. None of these are under the control of the issuer of the investment vehicle. Investment vehicles are affected differently by these forces. It is not unusual to find two vehicles with similar internal characteristics offering significantly different returns. As a result of the same external force, the expected return from one vehicle may increase, while that of another decreases. Likewise, the economies of various countries respond to external forces in different ways.

Another external force is the *general level of price changes,* either up—**inflation**—or down—**deflation**. Inflation tends to have a positive impact on investment vehicles such as real estate, and a negative impact on vehicles such as stocks and fixed-income securities. Rising interest rates, which normally accompany increasing rates of inflation, can significantly affect returns. The actions, if any, the federal government takes to control inflation can increase, decrease, or have no effect on investment returns. Furthermore, the return on each type of investment vehicle exhibits its own unique response to inflation. The *Investing in Action* box on page 135 looks at the returns in the stock market in recent years, and considers whether such returns are likely to continue and what to do if they do not.

inflation
a period of generally rising prices.

deflation
a period of generally declining prices.

IN REVIEW

CONCEPTS

4.1 Explain what is meant by the *return* on an investment. Differentiate between the two components of return—current income and capital gains (or losses).

4.2 What role do historical performance data play in estimating the expected return from a given investment? Discuss the key factors affecting investment returns—internal characteristics and external forces.

4.3 What has history taught us about the stock market, according to the *Investing in Action* box on page 135? What should you do to ride out the market's twists and turns?

INVESTING in action

Many Happy Returns . . . Maybe

In recent years it's been fairly easy to make money in the stock market. From April 1991 through December 2000, the economy had been expanding—a record 117 months, compared to an average expansion of 35 months. Even novice investors enjoyed stellar returns. From 1990 through 1999, the average annual return on the S&P 500 stocks was 18.2%, and it climbed to a whopping 28.6% from 1995 to 1999. That annual return is considerably above the 1926–1999 average annual return of 11.4% on large-company stocks and 12.6% for small companies reported by market researcher Ibbotson Associates.

This seems like great news for today's investors, many of whom started buying stocks only in the past few years. These newcomers now *expect* average returns of 15% to 30%. Many of them ignore the market's brief bear-like periods, saying, "It's just a minor correction. Stocks will bounce back." And they did in the late 1990s on through the middle of 2000. But the recent stock market pattern of sudden crashes and quick "corrections" is not the norm. More often the recovery is extremely slow.

"We laugh about this, but it's really getting scary," says California financial planner Judith Martindale. "More and more investors think they are competent rather than lucky. When their luck runs out, they'll lose their money."

There's another hidden danger in expecting high returns: poor financial decisions. Investors who expect to earn 20% or more on their portfolio may spend more and allocate less to saving, counting on high returns to increase their nest eggs. Novice investors, many of whom have never experienced a bear market, may invest too heavily in equities or focus on the current hot sector. They won't be so happy when that industry falls from favor and normal return levels are restored.

When this will happen is anyone's guess. Market pundits have been predicting the end of the bull market for years, only to be proved wrong as the market repeatedly stumbles and then recovers. Even though uncertainty is a given in both the economy and the securities markets, economists and financial experts agree that the situation in mid-2000 was unlike any other. Both unemployment and inflation were low. No one was quite sure why the economy continued to grow or why stocks with no earnings traded at 100 times revenues.

History appears to be repeating itself; in 2000 a market downturn began and continues through mid-2001. In the bull markets of the 1920s and the 1950s–1960s, a period of above-average returns was followed by a period of lower-than-average returns. Such may be the case now in mid-2001. If this occurs when you plan to retire, you could find yourself unable to afford the lifestyle you envisioned.

What can you do to ride out the market's twists and turns? Plan to invest for the long term, because you can't predict stock market gains in advance. They come in sudden clumps—a big month or two, followed by flat or down months. If you try to time the market, selling when a price drop scares you and buying when prices are rising, you won't benefit from the market's successful long-term record. Invest as much as you can now to let compounding work for you. Don't be dazzled by companies with rapid revenue growth but no profits. Finally, diversify you portfolio among asset classes (more on this in Chapter 5).

Sources: Geoffrey Colvin, "From Here to Uncertainty," *Fortune,* October 2, 2000, downloaded from Electric Library, Business Edition, business.elibrary.com; Kathy Kristof, "Bull Run Shouldn't Lead Expectations Astray," *Dallas Morning News,* May 5, 2000, p. 5H; and Jane Bryant Quinn, "Challenging the Gospel of Buy and Hold," *Washington Post,* May 7, 2000, p. H2.

The Time Value of Money*

LG 2   LG 3

time value of money
the fact that as long as an opportunity exists to earn interest, the value of money is affected by the point in time when the money is received.

Imagine that at age 25 you begin making annual cash deposits of $1,000 into a savings account that pays 5% annual interest. After 40 years, at age 65, you will have made deposits totaling $40,000 (40 years × $1,000 per year). Assuming you made no withdrawals, what do you think your account balance will be—$50,000? $75,000? $100,000? The answer is none of the above. Your $40,000 will have grown to nearly $121,000! Why? Because the time value of money allows the deposits to earn interest, and that interest also earns interest over the 40 years. **Time value of money** refers to the fact that as long as an opportunity exists to earn interest, the value of money is affected by the point in time when the money is received.

As a general rule, *the sooner you receive a return on a given investment, the better.* For example, two investments each requiring a $1,000 outlay and each expected to return $100 interest over a 2-year holding period are *not necessarily* equally desirable. If the first investment returns $100 at the end of the first year and the second investment returns the $100 at the end of the second year, the first investment is preferable (assuming that the base value of each remains at $1,000). Investment 1 is preferable because the $100 interest it earns could be *reinvested to earn more interest* while the $100 in interest from investment 2 is still accruing at the end of the first year. You should not fail to consider time-value concepts when making investment decisions.

Interest: The Basic Return to Savers

interest
the "rent" paid by a borrower for use of the lender's money.

A savings account at a bank is one of the most basic forms of investment. The saver receives interest in exchange for placing idle funds in an account. **Interest** can be viewed as the "rent" paid by a borrower for use of the lender's money. The saver will experience neither a capital gain nor a capital loss, because the value of the investment (the initial deposit) will change only by the amount of interest earned. For the saver, the interest earned over a given time frame is that period's current income.

simple interest
interest paid only on the initial deposit for the amount of time it is held.

Simple Interest The income paid on investment vehicles that pay interest (such as CDs and bonds) is most often calculated using **simple interest**: Interest is paid only on the initial deposit for the amount of time it is held. For example, if you held a $100 initial deposit in an account paying 6% interest for 1½ years, you would earn $9 in interest (1½ × 0.06 × $100) over this period. Had you withdrawn $50 at the end of half a year, the total interest earned over the 1½ years would be $6. You would earn $3 interest on $100 for the first half-year (½ × 0.06 × $100) and $3 interest on $50 for the next full year (1 × 0.06 × $50).

true rate of interest (return)
the actual rate of interest earned.

When an investment earns simple interest, the stated rate of interest is the **true rate of interest** (or **return**). This is the actual rate of interest earned. In the foregoing example, the true rate of interest is 6%. Because the interest rate reflects the rate at which current income is earned regardless of the size of the deposit, it is a useful measure of current income.

---

* This section presents the fundamental concepts and techniques of time value of money. Those already familiar with these important ideas may wish to skip this discussion and continue at the heading "Determining a Satisfactory Investment" on page 145.

TABLE 4.4	Savings Account Balance Data (5% interest compounded semiannually)			
Date	(1) Deposit (Withdrawal)	(2) Beginning Account Balance	(3) 0.05 × (2) Interest for Year	(4) (2) + (3) Ending Account Balance
1/1/01	$1,000	$1,000.00	$50.00	$1,050.00
1/1/02	(300)	750.00	37.50	787.50
1/1/03	1,000	1,787.50	89.38	1,876.88

compound interest
interest paid not only on the initial deposit but also on any interest accumulated from one period to the next.

Compound Interest Compound interest is interest paid not only on the initial deposit but also on any interest accumulated from one period to the next. This is the method usually used by savings institutions. When interest is compounded annually over a single year, compound and simple interest calculations provide similar results. In such a case, the stated interest rate and the true interest rate are equal.

The data in Table 4.4 illustrate compound interest. In this case, the interest earned each year is left on deposit rather than withdrawn. The $50 of interest earned on the $1,000 initial deposit during 2001 becomes part of the beginning (initial) balance on which interest is paid in 2002, and so on. *Note that simple interest is used in the compounding process;* that is, interest is paid only on the initial balance held during the given time period.

When an investment earns compound interest, the stated and true interest rates are equal *only* when interest is compounded annually. In general, *the more frequently interest is compounded at a stated rate, the higher the true rate of interest.* The interest calculations for the deposit data in Table 4.4, assuming that interest is compounded semiannually (twice a year), are shown in Table 4.5. The interest for each 6-month period is found by multiplying the beginning (initial) balance for the 6 months by half of the stated 5% interest rate (see column 3 of Table 4.5). You can see that larger returns are associated with more frequent compounding: Compare the end-of-2003 account balance at 5% compounded annually with the end-of-2003 account balance at 5% compounded semiannually. The semiannual compounding results in a higher balance ($1,879.19 versus $1,876.88). Clearly, with semiannual compounding,

TABLE 4.5	Savings Account Balance Data (5% interest compounded semiannually)			
Date	(1) Deposit (Withdrawal)	(2) Beginning Account Balance	(3) 0.05 × 1/2 × (2) Interest for 6 Months	(4) (2) + (3) Ending Account Balance
1/1/01	$1,000	$1,000.00	$25.00	$1,025.00
7/1/01		1,025.00	25.63	1,050.63
1/1/02	(300)	750.63	18.77	769.40
7/1/02		769.40	19.24	788.64
1/1/03	1,000	1,788.64	44.72	1,833.36
7/1/03		1,833.36	45.83	1,879.19

TABLE 4.6	True Rate of Interest for Various Compounding Frequencies (5% stated rate of interest)		
Compounding Frequency	True Rate of Interest	Compounding Frequency	True Rate of Interest
Annually	5.000%	Monthly	5.120%
Semiannually	5.063	Weekly	5.125
Quarterly	5.094	Continuously	5.127

the true rate of interest is greater than the 5% annually compounded rate. The true rates of interest associated with a 5% stated rate and various compounding frequencies are shown in Table 4.6.

continuous compounding
interest calculation in which interest is compounded over the smallest possible interval of time.

Continuous compounding calculates interest by compounding over the smallest possible interval of time. It results in the maximum true rate of interest that can be achieved with a given stated rate of interest. Table 4.6 shows that the more frequently interest is compounded, the higher the true rate of interest. Because of the impact that differences in compounding frequencies have on return, you should evaluate the true rate of interest associated with various alternatives before making a deposit.

Computational Aids for Use in Time Value Calculations

Time-consuming calculations are often involved in adjusting for the time value of money. Although you should understand the concepts and mathematics underlying these calculations, the application of time value techniques can be streamlined. We will demonstrate the use of financial tables and hand-held financial calculators as computational aids. Personal computers can also be used to simplify time value calculations, using spreadsheets.

Financial Tables Financial tables include various interest factors that simplify time value calculations. The values in these tables are easily developed from formulas, with various degrees of rounding. The tables are typically indexed by the interest rate (in columns) and the number of periods (in rows). Figure 4.1 shows this general layout. The interest factor at a 20% interest rate

FIGURE 4.1

Financial Tables

Layout and use of a financial table

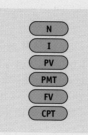

FIGURE 4.2

Calculator Keys

Important financial keys on the typical calculator

N	—	Number of periods
I	—	Interest rate per period
PV	—	Present value
PMT	—	Amount of payment (used only for annuities)
FV	—	Future value
CPT	—	Compute key used to initiate financial calculation once all values are input

for 10 years would be found at the intersection of the 20% column and the 10-period row, as shown by the dark blue box. A full set of the four basic financial tables is included in Appendix A at the end of the book. These tables are described more fully later in this chapter.

Financial Calculators Financial calculators also can be used for time value computations. Generally, *financial calculators* include numerous preprogrammed financial routines. In this and later chapters, we show the keystrokes for various financial computations.

We focus primarily on the keys pictured and defined in Figure 4.2. We typically use four of the five keys in the left column, plus the compute (CPT) key. One of the four keys represents the unknown value being calculated. (Occasionally, all five of the keys are used, with one representing the unknown value.) The keystrokes on some of the more sophisticated calculators are menu-driven: After you select the appropriate routine, the calculator prompts you to input each value; on these calculators, a compute key is not needed to obtain a solution. Regardless, any calculator with the basic time value functions can be used instead of financial tables.

Once you understand the basic underlying concepts, you probably will want to use a calculator to streamline routine financial calculations. With a little practice, you can increase both the speed and accuracy of your financial computations. Note that because of a calculator's greater precision, slight differences are likely to exist between values calculated using financial tables and those found with a financial calculator. Remember that *conceptual understanding of the material is the objective.* An ability to solve problems with a calculator does not necessarily reflect such an understanding, so don't just settle for answers. Work with the material until you are sure you also understand the concepts.

 ## Future Value: An Extension of Compounding

future value
the amount to which a current deposit will grow over a period of time when it is placed in an account paying compound interest.

Future value is the amount to which a current deposit will grow over a period of time when it is placed in an account paying compound interest. Consider a deposit of $1,000 that is earning 8% (0.08 in decimal form) compounded annually. The following calculation yields the future value of this deposit at the end of 1 year.

Equation 4.1

$$\frac{\text{Future value}}{\text{at end of year 1}} = \$1{,}000 \times (1 + 0.08) = \underline{\underline{\$1{,}080}}$$

If the money were left on deposit for another year, 8% interest would be paid on the account balance of $1,080. Thus, at the end of the second year, there would be $1,166.40 in the account. This amount would represent the beginning-of-year balance of $1,080 plus 8% of the $1,080 ($86.40) in interest. The future value at the end of the second year would be calculated as follows.

Equation 4.2

$$\frac{\text{Future value}}{\text{at end of year 2}} = \$1{,}080 \times (1 + 0.08) = \underline{\underline{\$1{,}166.40}}$$

To find the future value of the $1,000 at the end of year n, the procedure illustrated above would be repeated n times. Future values can be determined either mathematically or by using a financial table, financial calculator, or a computer. Here we demonstrate use of a table of future-value interest factors and use of a calculator.

TABLE USE The factors in Appendix A, Table A.1 represent the amount to which an initial $1 deposit would grow for various periods (typically years) and interest rates. For example, a dollar deposited in an account paying 8% interest and left there for 2 years would accumulate to $1.166. Using the future-value interest factor for 8% and 2 years (1.166), we can find the future value of an investment that can earn 8% over 2 years: We would *multiply* the amount invested by the appropriate interest factor. In the case of $1,000 left on deposit for 2 years at 8%, the resulting future value is $1,166 (1.166 × $1,000). This agrees (except for a slight rounding difference) with the value calculated in Equation 4.2.

A few points with respect to Appendix A, Table A.1, Future-Value Interest Factors for One Dollar, should be emphasized.

1. The values in the table represent factors for determining the future value of one dollar at the *end* of the given year.
2. As the interest rate increases for any given year, the future-value interest factor also increases. The higher the interest rate, the greater the future value.
3. For a given interest rate, the future value of a dollar increases with the passage of time.
4. The future-value interest factor is always greater than 1. Only if the interest rate were zero would this factor equal 1, and the future value would therefore equal the initial deposit.

CALCULATOR USE[*] A financial calculator can be used to calculate the future

---

[*]   Many calculators allow the user to set the number of payments per year. Most of these calculators are preset for monthly payments—12 payments per year. Because we work primarily with annual payments—one payment per year—it is important to be sure that your calculator is set for one payment per year. And although most calculators are preset to recognize that all payments occur at the end of the period, it is important to make sure that your calculator is correctly set on the END mode. Consult the reference guide that accompanies your calculator for instructions for setting these values.

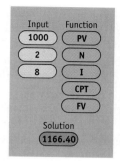

Input	Function
1000	PV
2	N
8	I
	CPT
	FV

Solution
1166.40

value directly.** First punch in $1,000 and depress **PV**; next punch in 2 and depress **N**; then punch in 8 and depress **I**.† Finally, to calculate the future value, depress **CPT** and then **FV**. The future value of $1,166.40 should appear on the calculator display as shown in the art at the left. On many calculators, this value will be preceded by a minus sign (−1166.40). *If a minus sign appears on your calculator, ignore it here as well as in all other "Calculator Use" illustrations in this text.*‡

The calculator is more accurate than the future value factors, which have been rounded to the nearest 0.001. Therefore, a slight difference will frequently exist between the values found by these alternative methods. In this case, there is a $.40 difference. Clearly, the improved accuracy and ease of calculation tend to favor the use of the calculator. (*Note:* In future examples of calculator use, we will use only a display similar to that shown at the left. If you need a reminder of the procedure involved, come back and review the preceding paragraph.)

Future Value of an Annuity

annuity
a stream of equal cash flows that occur at equal intervals over time.

An **annuity** is a stream of equal cash flows that occur at equal intervals over time. Receiving $1,000 per year at the end of each of the next 8 years is an example of an annuity. The cash flows can be *inflows* of returns earned from an investment or *outflows* of funds invested (deposited) to earn future returns.

ordinary annuity
an annuity for which the cash flows occur at the *end* of each period.

Investors are sometimes interested in finding the future value of an annuity. Their concern is typically with what's called an **ordinary annuity**—one for which the cash flows occur at the *end* of each period. Here we can simplify our calculations by using either tables of these factors for an annuity or a financial calculator. (A complete set of these tables is included in Appendix A, Table A.2.)

TABLE USE The factors in Appendix A, Table A.2 represent the amount to which annual end-of-year deposits of $1 would grow for various periods (years) and interest rates. For example, a dollar deposited at the end of each year for 8 years into an account paying 6% interest would accumulate to $9.897. Using the future-value interest factor for an 8-year annuity earning 6% (9.897), we can find the future value of this cash flow: We would *multiply* the annual investment by the appropriate interest factor. In the case of $1,000 deposited at the end of each year for 8 years at 6%, the resulting future value is $9,897 (9.897 × $1,000).

** To avoid including previous data in current calculations, *always* clear all registers of your calculator before inputting values and making each computation.

† The known values *can be punched into the calculator in any order.* The order specified in this as well as other demonstrations of calculator use included in this text merely reflects convenience and personal preference.

‡ The calculator differentiates inflows from outflows with a negative sign. For example, in the problem just demonstrated, the $1,000 present value (PV), because it was keyed as a positive number (1000) is considered an inflow or deposit. Therefore, the calculated future value (FV) of −1166.40 is preceded by a minus sign to show that it is the resulting outflow or withdrawal. Had the $1,000 present value been keyed in as a negative number (−1000), the future value of $1166.40 would have been displayed as a positive number (1166.40). Simply stated, *present value* (PV) and *future value* (FV) *cash flows will have opposite signs.*

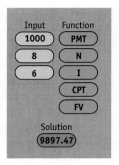

CALCULATOR USE   When a financial calculator is used to find the future value of an annuity, the annual deposit is input using the **PMT** key (rather than the **PV** key, which was used to find the future value of a single deposit). Use of the **PMT** key tells the calculator that a stream of **N** (the number of years input) end-of-year deposits in the amount of **PMT** dollars represents the deposit stream.

Using the calculator inputs shown at the left, we find the future value of the $1,000, 8-year ordinary annuity earning a 6% annual rate of interest to be $9,897.47. This is a slightly more precise answer than that found by using the table.

Present Value: An Extension of Future Value

present value
the *value today* of a sum to be received at some future date; the inverse of future value.

Present value is the inverse of future value. That is, rather than measuring the value of a present amount at some future date, **present value** expresses the *current value of a future sum*. By applying present-value techniques, we can calculate the *value today* of a sum to be received at some future date.

When determining the present value of a future sum, we are answering the basic question "How much would have to be deposited today into an account paying *i*% interest in order to equal a specified sum to be received so many years in the future?" The applicable interest rate when we are finding present value is commonly called the **discount rate** (or *opportunity cost*). It represents the annual rate of return that could be earned currently on a similar investment.

discount rate
the annual rate of return that could be earned currently on a similar investment; used when finding present value; also called *opportunity cost*.

The basic present-value calculation is best illustrated using a simple example. Imagine that you are offered an opportunity that will provide you, 1 year from today, with exactly $1,000. If you could earn 8% on similar types of investments, how much is the most you would pay for this opportunity? In other words, what is the present value of $1,000 to be received 1 year from now, discounted at 8%? Letting *x* equal the present value, we can use Equation 4.3 to describe this situation.

Equation 4.3

$$x \times (1 + 0.08) = \$1,000$$

Solving Equation 4.3 for *x*, we get:

Equation 4.4

$$x = \frac{\$1,000}{(1 + 0.08)} = \underline{\underline{\$925.93}}$$

Thus the present value of $1,000 to be received 1 year from now, discounted at 8%, is $925.93. In other words, $925.93 deposited today into an account paying 8% interest will accumulate to $1,000 in 1 year. To check this conclusion, *multiply* the future-value interest factor for 8% and 1 year, or 1.080 (from Appendix A, Table A.1), by $925.93. The result is a future value of $1,000 (1.080 × $925.93).

The calculations involved in finding the present value of sums to be received in the distant future are more complex than for a 1-year investment. Here we use either tables of present-value interest factors to simplify these calculations or a financial calculator. (A complete set of these tables is included in Appendix A, Table A.3.)

TABLE USE The factors in Appendix A, Table A.3 represent the present value of $1 associated with various combinations of periods (years) and discount (interest) rates. For example, the present value of $1 to be received 1 year from now discounted at 8% is $0.926. Using this factor (0.926), we can find the present value of $1,000 to be received 1 year from now at an 8% discount rate by *multiplying* it by $1,000. The resulting present value of $926 (0.926 × $1,000) agrees (except for a slight rounding difference) with the value calculated in Equation 4.4.

Another example may help clarify the use of present-value tables. The present value of $500 to be received 7 years from now, discounted at 6%, is calculated as follows:

$$\text{Present value} = 0.665 \times \$500 = \underline{\$332.50}$$

The 0.665 represents the present-value interest factor from Appendix A, Table A.3 for 7 years discounted at 6%.

A few points with respect to Appendix A, Table A.3, Present-Value Interest Factors for One Dollar, should be emphasized.

1. The present-value interest factor for a single sum is always less than 1. Only if the discount rate were zero would this factor equal 1.
2. The higher the discount rate for a given year, the smaller the present-value interest factor. In other words, the greater your opportunity cost, the less you have to invest today in order to have a given amount in the future.
3. The further in the future a sum is to be received, the less it is worth at present.
4. At a discount rate of 0%, the present-value interest factor always equals 1. Therefore, in such a case the future value of a sum equals its present value.

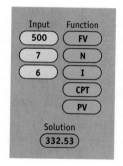

Input	Function
500	FV
7	N
6	I
	CPT
	PV

Solution
332.53

CALCULATOR USE Using the financial calculator inputs shown at the left, we find the present value of $500 to be received 7 years from now, discounted at 6%, to be $332.53. This value is slightly more precise than that found using the table, but for our purposes the difference is insignificant.

The Present Value of a Stream of Returns

mixed stream
a stream of returns that, unlike an annuity, exhibits no special pattern.

In the preceding paragraphs we illustrated the technique for finding the present value of a single sum to be received at some future date. Because the returns from a given investment are likely to be received at various future dates rather than as a single lump sum, we also need to be able to find the present value of a *stream of returns*. A stream of returns can be viewed as a package of single-sum returns; it may be classified as a mixed stream or an annuity. A **mixed stream** of returns is one that exhibits no special pattern. As noted earlier, an *annuity* is a stream of equal periodic returns. Table 4.7 shows the end-of-year returns illustrating each of these types of patterns. To find the present value of each of these streams (measured at the *beginning* of 2002), we must calculate the total of the present values of the individual annual returns. Because shortcuts can be used for an annuity, calculation of the present value of each type of return stream is illustrated separately.

TABLE 4.7	Mixed and Annuity Return Streams	
	Returns	
End of Year	Mixed Stream	Annuity
2002	$30	$50
2003	40	50
2004	50	50
2005	60	50
2006	70	50

TABLE 4.8	Mixed-Stream Present-Value Calculation		
End of Year	(1) Return	(2) 9% Present-Value Interest Factor	(3) (1) × (2) Present Value
2002	$30	.917	$ 27.51
2003	40	.842	33.68
2004	50	.772	38.60
2005	60	.708	42.48
2006	70	.650	45.50
		Present value of stream	$187.77

Note: Column 1 values are from Table 4.7. Column 2 values are from Appendix A, Table A.3, for a 9% discount rate and 1 through 5 periods (years).

Present Value of a Mixed Stream To find the present value of the mixed stream of returns given in Table 4.7, we must find and then total the present values of the individual returns. Assuming a 9% discount rate, we can streamline the calculation of the present value of the mixed stream using either financial tables or a financial calculator.

TABLE USE Table A.3 in Appendix A can be used to find the appropriate present-value interest factors for each of the 5 years of the mixed stream's life at the 9% discount rate. Table 4.8 demonstrates the use of these factors, shown in column 2, with the corresponding year's return, shown in column 1, to calculate the present value of each year's return, shown in column 3. The total of the present values of the returns for each of the 5 years is found by summing column 3. The resulting present value of $187.77 represents the amount today (*beginning* of 2002) that, invested at 9%, would provide the same returns as those shown in column 1 of Table 4.8.

CALCULATOR USE You can use a financial calculator to find the present value of each individual return, as demonstrated on page 143. You then sum the present values to get the present value of the stream. However, most financial calculators have a function that allows you to punch in *all returns* (typically referred to as *cash flows*), specify the discount rate, and then directly calculate the present value of the entire return stream. Because calculators provide solutions more precise than those based on rounded table factors, the present value of the mixed stream of returns in Table 4.7, found using a calculator, will be close to, but not precisely equal to, the $187.77 calculated in Table 4.8.

Present Value of an Annuity The present value of an annuity can be found in the same way as the present value of a mixed stream. Fortunately, however, there are simpler approaches. Here we simplify our calculations by using either tables of these factors for an annuity or a financial calculator. (A complete set of these tables is included in Appendix A, Table A.4.)

TABLE USE The factors in Appendix A, Table A.4 represent the present value of a $1 annuity for various periods (years) and discount (interest) rates. For example, the present value of $1 to be received at the end of each year for the next 5 years discounted at 9% is $3.890. Using the present-value interest factor for a 5-year annuity discounted at 9% (3.890), we can find the present value of the $50, 5-year annuity (given in Table 4.7) at a 9% discount rate: We *multiply* the annual return by the appropriate interest factor. The resulting present value is $194.50 (3.890 × $50).

CALCULATOR USE Using the calculator inputs shown at the left, we find the present value of the $50, 5-year ordinary annuity of returns, discounted at a 9% annual rate, to be $194.48. (*Note:* Because the return stream is an annuity, the annual return is input using the **PMT** key rather than the **FV** key, which was used for finding the present value of a single return.) The value obtained with the calculator is slightly more accurate than the answer found using the table.

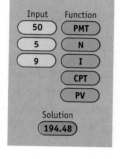

Input	Function
50	PMT
5	N
9	I
	CPT
	PV

Solution
194.48

Determining a Satisfactory Investment

satisfactory investment
an investment whose present value of benefits (discounted at the appropriate rate) *equals* or *exceeds* the present value of its costs.

Time value of money techniques can be used to determine an acceptable investment. Ignoring risk at this point, a **satisfactory investment** would be one for which the present value of benefits (discounted at the appropriate rate) *equals* or *exceeds* the present value of its costs. Because the cost of the investment would be incurred initially (at time zero), the cost and its present value are viewed as one and the same. The three possible benefit–cost relationships and their interpretations follow:

1. If the present value of the benefits *just equals the cost,* you would earn a rate of return equal to the discount rate.
2. If the present value of benefits *exceeds the cost,* you would earn a rate of return greater than the discount rate.
3. If the present value of benefits is *less than the cost,* you would earn a rate of return less than the discount rate.

You would prefer only those investments for which the present value of benefits equals or exceeds its cost—situations 1 and 2. In these cases, the rate of return would be equal to or greater than the discount rate.

The information in Table 4.9 demonstrates the application of present value to investment decision making using a financial table. (*Note:* A financial calculator could have been used, as described earlier, to find the present value of this mixed-stream investment.) Assuming an 8% discount rate, we can see

TABLE 4.9   **Present Value Applied to an Investment**

End of Year	(1) Return	(2) 8% Present-Value Interest Factor*	(3) (1) × (2) Present Value
2002	$ 90	.926	$ 83.34
2003	100	.857	85.70
2004	110	.794	87.34
2005	120	.735	88.20
2006	100	.681	68.10
2007	100	.630	63.00
2008	1,200	.583	699.60
		Present value of income	$1, 175.28

* Column 2 values are from Appendix A, Table A.3, for an 8% discount rate and 1 through 7 periods (years).

that the present value (at the beginning of 2002) of the income (returns) to be received over the assumed 7-year period (year-end 2002 through year-end 2008) is $1,175.28. If the cost of the investment (beginning of 2002) were any amount less than or equal to the $1,175.28 present value, it would be acceptable. At that cost, a rate of return equal to at least 8% would be earned. At a cost above the $1,175.28 present value, the investment would not be acceptable. At that cost, the rate of return would be less than 8%. Clearly, in that case it would be preferable to find an alternative investment with a present value of benefits that equals or exceeds its cost.

IN REVIEW

CONCEPTS

4.4 What is the *time value* of money? Explain why an investor should be able to earn a positive return.

4.5 Define, discuss, and contrast the following terms.
a. Interest   b. Simple interest
c. Compound interest   d. True rate of interest (or return)

4.6 When interest is compounded more frequently than annually at a stated rate, what happens to the *true rate of interest?* Under what condition would the stated and true rates of interest be equal? What is *continuous compounding?*

4.7 Describe, compare, and contrast the concepts of *future value* and *present value.* Explain the role of the *discount rate* in calculating present value.

4.8 What is an *annuity?* How can calculation of the future value of an annuity be simplified? What about the present value of an annuity?

4.9 What is a *mixed stream* of returns? Describe the procedure used to find the present value of such a stream.

4.10 What is a *satisfactory investment?* When the present value of benefits exceeds the cost of an investment, what is true of the rate of return earned by the investor relative to the discount rate?

Measuring Return

LG 4

Thus far, we have discussed the concept of return in terms of its two components (current income and capital gains) and the key factors that affect the level of return (internal characteristics and external forces). These discussions intentionally oversimplified the computations involved in determining the historical or expected return. To compare returns from different investment vehicles, we need to incorporate time value of money concepts that explicitly consider differences in the timing of investment income and capital gains. We must also be able to place a current value on future benefits. Here we will look at several measures that enable us to compare alternative investment vehicles. First, we must define and consider the relationships among various rates of return.

Real, Risk-Free, and Required Returns

Rational investors will choose investments that fully compensate them for the risk involved. The greater the risk, the greater the return required by investors. The return that fully compensates for an investment's risk is called the **required return**. To better understand required returns, it is helpful to consider their makeup. The required return on any investment j consists of three basic components: the real rate of return, an expected inflation premium, and a risk premium, as noted in Equation 4.5.

required return
the rate of return an investor must earn on an investment to be fully compensated for its risk.

Equation 4.5

$$\text{Required return} \atop \text{on investment } j = \text{Real rate} \atop \text{of return} + \text{Expected inflation} \atop \text{premium} + \text{Risk premium} \atop \text{for investment } j$$

Equation 4.5a

$$r_j = r^* + IP + RP_j$$

real rate of return
the rate of return that could be earned in a perfect world where all outcomes are known and certain—where there was no risk.

The **real rate of return** is the rate of return that could be earned in a perfect world where all outcomes were known and certain—where there was no risk. In such a world, the real rate of return would create an equilibrium between the supply of savings and the demand for funds. The real rate of return changes with changing economic conditions, tastes, and preferences. Historically, it has been relatively stable and in the range of 1% to 2%. For convenience, we'll assume a real rate of return of 2%.

expected inflation premium
the average rate of inflation expected in the future.

The **expected inflation premium** represents the average rate of inflation expected in the future. By adding the expected inflation premium to the real rate of return, we get the **risk-free rate**. This is the rate of return that can be earned on a risk-free investment, most commonly a 3-month U.S. Treasury bill. The formula for this rate is shown in Equation 4.6.

risk-free rate
the rate of return that can be earned on a risk-free investment; the sum of the real rate of return and the expected inflation premium.

Equation 4.6

$$\text{Risk-free rate} = \text{Real rate} \atop \text{of return} + \text{Expected inflation} \atop \text{premium}$$

Equation 4.6a

$$R_F = r^* + IP$$

risk premium
a return premium that reflects the issue and issuer characteristics associated with a given investment vehicle.

To demonstrate, a real rate of return of 2% and an expected inflation premium of 4% would result in a risk-free rate of return of 6%.

The required return can be found by adding to the risk-free rate a **risk premium**, which varies depending on specific issue and issuer characteristics.

Issue characteristics are the type of vehicle (stock, bond, etc.), its maturity (2 years, 5 years, infinity, etc.), and its features (voting/nonvoting, callable/non-callable, etc.). *Issuer characteristics* are industry and company factors such as the line of business and financial condition of the issuer. Together, the issue and issuer factors cause investors to require a risk premium above the risk-free rate.

Substituting the risk-free rate, R_F, from Equation 4.6a, into Equation 4.5a for the first two terms to the right of the equal sign ($r^* + IP$), we get Equation 4.7.

Equation 4.7

$$\frac{\text{Required return}}{\text{on investment } j} = \frac{\text{Risk-free}}{\text{rate}} + \frac{\text{Risk premium}}{\text{for investment } j}$$

Equation 4.7a

$$r_j = R_F + RP_j$$

For example, if the required return on IBM common stock is 11% when the risk-free rate is 6%, investors require a 5% risk premium (11% − 6%) as compensation for the risk associated with common stock (the issue) and IBM (the issuer). Later in Chapter 5, we will explore further the relationship between the risk premium and required returns.

Next, we consider the specifics of return measurement.

Holding Period Return

The return to a *saver* is the amount of interest earned on a given deposit. Of course, the amount "invested" in a savings account is not subject to change in value, as is the amount invested in stocks, bonds, and mutual funds. Because we are concerned with a broad range of investment vehicles, we need a measure of return that captures both periodic benefits and changes in value. One such measure is *holding period return.*

holding period
the period of time over which one wishes to measure the return on an investment vehicle.

The **holding period** is the period of time over which one wishes to measure the return on an investment vehicle. When comparing returns, be sure to use holding periods of the same length. For example, comparing the return on a stock over the 6-month period ended December 31, 2001, with the return on a bond over the 1-year period ended June 30, 2001, could result in a poor investment decision. To avoid this problem, be sure you define the holding period. It is often best to annualize the holding period and use that as a standard. And when comparing the returns from alternative investment vehicles, you should use similar periods in time.

Understanding Return Components Earlier in this chapter we identified the two components of investment return: current income and capital gains (or losses). The portion of current income received by the investor during the period is a **realized return.** Most but not all current income is realized. (Accrued interest on taxable zero-coupon bonds is treated as current income for tax purposes but is not a realized return until the bond is sold or matures.) Capital gains returns, on the other hand, are realized only when the investment vehicle is actually sold at the end of the holding period. Until the vehicle is sold, the capital gain is merely a **paper return.**

realized return
current income actually received by an investor during a given period.

paper return
a return that has been achieved but not yet realized by an investor during a given period.

For example, the capital gain return on an investment that increases in market value from $50 to $70 during a year is $20. For that capital gain to be realized, you would have to have sold the investment for $70 at the end of that year. An investor who purchased the same investment but plans to hold it for another 3 years would also have experienced the $20 capital gain return during the year specified, but he or she *would not have realized the gain in terms of cash flow.* However, *even if the capital gains return is not realized during the period over which the total return is measured, it must be included in the return calculation.*

A second point to recognize about returns is that both the current income and the capital gains component can have a negative value. Occasionally, an investment may have negative current income. That is, you may be required to pay out cash to meet certain obligations. This situation is most likely to occur in various types of property investments. For example, assume you have purchased an apartment complex and the rental income is inadequate to meet the payments associated with its operation. In such a case, you would have to pay the deficit in operating costs, and that payment would represent negative current income. A capital loss can occur on *any* investment vehicle: Stocks, bonds, mutual funds, options, futures, real estate, and gold can all decline in market value over a given holding period.

Computing the Holding Period Return (HPR) The **holding period return** (**HPR**) is the total return earned from holding an investment for a specified period of time (the holding period). The HPR is customarily used with holding periods of *1 year or less.* (We'll explain why later.) It represents the sum of current income and capital gains (or losses) achieved over the holding period, divided by the beginning investment value. The equation for HPR is

holding period return (HPR) the total return earned from holding an investment for a specified holding period (*usually 1 year or less*).

Equation 4.8

$$\text{Holding period return} = \frac{\text{Current income during period} + \text{Capital gain (or loss) during period}}{\text{Beginning investment value}}$$

Equation 4.8a

$$\text{HPR} = \frac{C + CG}{V_0}$$

where

Equation 4.9

$$\text{Capital gain (or loss) during period} = \text{Ending investment value} - \text{Beginning investment value}$$

Equation 4.9a

$$CG = V_n - V_0$$

The HPR equation provides a convenient method for either measuring the total return realized or estimating the total return expected. For example, Table 4.10 summarizes the key financial variables for four investment vehicles over the past year. The total current income and capital gain or loss during the holding period are given in the lines labeled (1) and (3), respectively. The total return over the year is calculated, as shown in line (4), by adding these two sources of return. Dividing the total return value [line (4)] by the beginning-of-year investment value [line (2)], we find the holding period return, given in line (5). Over the 1-year holding period the common stock had the highest HPR (12.25%). The savings account had the lowest (6%).

As these calculations show, all we need to find the HPR is beginning- and end-of-period investment values, along with the value of current income

TABLE 4.10   **Key Financial Variables for Four Investment Vehicles**

	Investment Vehicle			
	Savings Account	Common Stock	Bond	Futures Contract
Cash received				
1st quarter	$15	$10	$ 0	$0
2nd quarter	15	10	70	0
3rd quarter	15	10	0	0
4th quarter	15	15	70	0
(1) Total current income	$60	$45	$140	$0
Investment value				
End-of-year	$1,000	$2,200	$ 970	$3,300
(2) Beginning-of-year	1,000	2,000	1,000	3,000
(3) Capital gain (loss)	$ 0	$ 200	($ 30)	$ 300
(4) Total return [(1) + (3)]	$ 60	$ 245	$ 110	$ 300
(5) Holding period return [(4) ÷ (2)]	6.00%	12.25%	11.00%	10.00%

received by the investor during the period. Note that if the current income and capital gain (or loss) values in lines (1) and (3) of Table 4.10 had been drawn from a 6-month rather than a 1-year period, the HPR values calculated in line (5) would have been *the same*.

Holding period return can be negative or positive. HPRs can be calculated with Equation 4.8 using either historical data (as in the preceding example) or forecast data.

Using the HPR in Investment Decisions The holding period return is easy to use in making investment decisions. Because it considers both current income and capital gains relative to the beginning investment value, it tends to overcome any problems that might be associated with comparing investments of different size. If we look only at the total returns calculated for each of the four investments in Table 4.10 [line (4)], the futures contract investment appears best, because it has the highest total return. However, the futures contract investment would require the largest dollar outlay ($3,000). The holding period return offers a *relative comparison,* by dividing the total return by the amount of the investment. Comparing HPRs, we find the investment alternative with the *highest return per invested dollar* to be the common stock's HPR of 12.25%. Because the return per invested dollar reflects the efficiency of the investment, the HPR provides a logical method for evaluating and comparing investment returns, particularly for holding periods of 1 year or less.

 Yield: The Internal Rate of Return

An alternative way to define a satisfactory investment is in terms of the compound annual rate of return it earns. Why do we need an alternative to the HPR? Because *HPR fails to consider the time value of money.* Although the holding period return is useful with investments held for 1 year or less, it is generally inappropriate for longer holding periods. Sophisticated investors typically do not use HPR when the time period is greater than 1 year. Instead,

yield (internal rate of return) the compound annual rate of return earned by a long-term investment; the discount rate that produces a present value of the investment's benefits that just equals its cost.

they use a present-value-based measure, called **yield** (or **internal rate of return**), to determine the compound annual rate of return earned on investments held for longer than one year. Yield can also be defined as the discount rate that produces a present value of benefits just equal to its cost.

Once you know the yield you can decide whether an investment is acceptable. If the yield on an investment *is equal to or greater than the required return,* then the investment is acceptable. An investment with a yield *below the required return* is unacceptable; it will not compensate you adequately for the risk involved.

The yield on an investment providing a single future cash flow is relatively easy to calculate. The yield on an investment providing a stream of future cash flows generally involves more time-consuming calculations. Many hand-held financial calculators as well as computer software programs are available for simplifying these calculations.

Yield for a Single Cash Flow Some investments, such as U.S. savings bonds, stocks paying no dividends, zero-coupon bonds, and futures contracts are purchased by paying a fixed amount up front. The investor expects them to provide *no periodic income,* but to provide a single—and, the investor hopes, a large—future cash flow at maturity or when the investment is sold. The yield on investments expected to provide a single future cash flow can be estimated using either financial tables or a financial calculator.

TABLE USE Assume you wish to find the yield on an investment costing $1,000 today that you expect will be worth $1,400 at the end of a 5-year holding period. We can find the yield on this investment by solving for the discount rate that causes the present value of the $1,400 to be received 5 years from now to equal the initial investment of $1,000.

The first step involves dividing the present value ($1,000) by the future value ($1,400), which results in a value of 0.714. The second step is to find in the table of present-value interest factors the 5-year factor that is closest to 0.714. Referring to the present-value table (Appendix A, Table A.3), we find that for 5 years the factor closest to 0.714 is 0.713, which occurs at a 7% discount rate. Therefore, the yield on this investment is about 7%. If you require a 6% return, this investment is acceptable (7% expected return ≥ 6% required return).

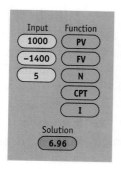

Input	Function
1000	PV
−1400	FV
5	N
	CPT
	I
Solution	
6.96	

CALCULATOR USE Using a financial calculator to find the yield for the investment described above, we can treat the earliest value as a present value, **PV,** and the latest value as a future value, **FV.** (*Note:* Most calculators require *either* the **PV** or the **FV** value to be input as a negative number to calculate an unknown yield.) Using the inputs shown at the left, we find the yield to be 6.96%. This is consistent with, but more precise than, the value found using Appendix A, Table A.3.

Yield for a Stream of Income Investment vehicles such as income-oriented stock and bonds typically provide the investor with a *stream of income.* The yield (or internal rate of return) for a stream of income (returns) is generally more difficult to estimate. The most accurate approach is based on searching for the discount rate that produces a present value of income just equal to the

TABLE 4.11   Yield Calculation for a $1,100 Investment

Year	(1) Income	(2) 9% Present-Value Interest Factor	(3) (1) × (2) Present Value at 9%	(4) 10% Present-Value Interest Factor	(5) (1) × (4) Present Value at 10%
2002	$ 90	.917	$ 82.53	.909	$ 81.81
2003	100	.842	84.20	.826	82.60
2004	110	.772	84.92	.751	82.61
2005	120	.708	84.96	.683	81.96
2006	100	.650	65.00	.621	62.10
2007	100	.596	59.60	.564	56.40
2008	1,200	.547	656.40	.513	615.60
	Present value of income		$1,117.61		$1,063.08

cost of the investment. It can be applied using either financial tables or a financial calculator.

TABLE USE If we use the investment in Table 4.9 and assume that its cost is $1,100, we find that the yield must be greater than 8%. At an 8% discount rate, the present value of income (calculated in column 3 of Table 4.9) is greater than the cost ($1,175.28 vs. $1,100). The present values at 9% and 10% discount rates are calculated in Table 4.11. If we look at the present values of income calculated at the 9% and 10% rates, we see that the yield on the investment must be somewhere between 9% and 10%. At 9% the present value ($1,117.61) is too high. At 10% the present value ($1,063.08) is too low. The discount rate that causes the present value of income to be closer to the $1,100 cost is 9%, because it is only $17.61 away from $1,100. Thus, if you require an 8% return, the investment is clearly acceptable.

CALCULATOR USE A financial calculator can be used to find the yield (or *internal rate of return*) on an investment that will produce a stream of income. This procedure typically involves punching in the cost of the investment (typically referred to as the *cash outflow* at time zero) and all of the income expected each period (typically referred to as the *cash inflow* at in year *x*) and then directly calculating the yield (typically referred to as the *internal rate of return, IRR*). Because calculators provide solutions that are more precise than those based on rounded table factors, the yield of 9.32% found for the investment in Table 4.9 using a financial calculator (keystrokes not shown) is close to, but not equal to, the 9% value estimated above using Table 4.11.

Interest on Interest: The Critical Assumption The critical assumption underlying the use of yield as a return measure is an ability to earn a return equal to the yield on *all income* received during the holding period. This concept can best be illustrated with a simple example. Suppose you buy a $1,000 U.S. Treasury bond that pays 8% annual interest ($80) over its 20-year maturity. Each year you receive $80, and at maturity the $1,000 in principal is repaid. There is no loss in capital, no default; all payments are made right on

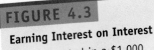

FIGURE 4.3

Earning Interest on Interest

If you invested in a $1,000, 20-year bond with an 8% coupon, you would have only $2,600 at the end of 20 years if you did not reinvest the $80 annual interest receipts—only about a 5% rate of return. If you reinvested the interest at the 8% interest rate, you would have $4,661 at the end of 20 years—an 8% rate of yield of 8%, you must therefore be able to earn interest at the interest at that rate.

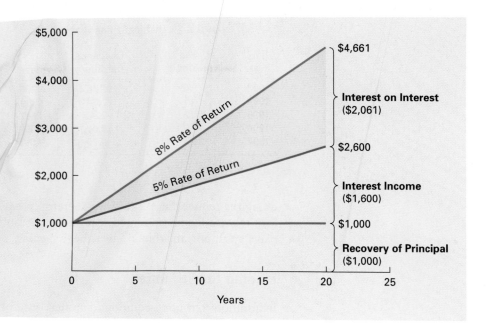

time. But you must be able to *reinvest* the $80 annual interest receipts in order to earn 8% on this investment.

Figure 4.3 shows the elements of return on this investment to demonstrate the point. If you don't *reinvest* the interest income of $80 per year, you'll end up on the 5% line. You'll have $2,600—the $1,000 principal plus $1,600 interest income ($80/year × 20 years)—at the end of 20 years. (The yield on a single cash flow of $1,000 today that will be worth $2,600 in 20 years is about 5%.) To move to the 8% line, you have to earn 8% on the annual interest receipts. If you do, you'll have $4,661—the $1,000 principal plus the $3,661 future value of the 20-year $80 annuity of interest receipts invested at 8% [$80/year × 45.762 (the 8%, 20-year factor from Appendix A, Table A.2)]— at the end of 20 years. (The yield on a single cash flow of $1,000 today that will be worth $4,661 in 20 years is 8%.) The future value of the investment would be $2,061 greater ($4,661 − $2,600) with interest on interest than without reinvestment of the interest receipts.

It should be clear to you that if you start out with an 8% investment, *you have to earn that same rate of return when reinvesting your income.* The rate of return you start with is the required, or minimum, **reinvestment rate**—the rate of return earned on interest or other income received over the relevant investment horizon. By putting your current income to work at this rate, you'll earn the rate of return you set out to. If you fail to do so, your return will decline accordingly. Even though a bond was used in this illustration, the same principle applies to any other type of investment vehicle.

The earning of interest on interest is what the market refers to as a **fully compounded rate of return**. It's an important concept: You can't start reaping the full potential from your investments until you start earning a fully compounded rate of return on them.

Interest on interest is a particularly important element of return for investment programs that involve a lot of current income. You have to reinvest current income. (With capital gains, the investment vehicle itself is automatically

reinvestment rate
the rate of return earned on interest or other income received from an investment over its investment horizon.

fully compounded rate of return
the rate of return that includes interest earned on interest.

TABLE 4.12   Dividends Per Share

Year	Year Number	Dividends per Share	Year	Year Number	Dividends per Share
1993	0	$2.45	1998	5	$3.15
1994	1	2.60	1999	6	3.20
1995	2	2.80	2000	7	3.20
1996	3	3.00	2001	8	3.40
1997	4	3.20	2002	9	3.50

doing the reinvesting.) It follows, therefore, that for investment programs that lean toward income-oriented securities, the continued reinvestment of income plays an important role in investment success.

Finding Growth Rates

rate of growth
the compound annual rate of change in the value of a stream of income.

In addition to finding compound annual rates of return, we frequently find the **rate of growth**. This is the compound annual rate of change in the value of a stream of income, particularly dividends or earnings. Here the an example to demonstrate a simple technique for estimating growth, e using either a financial table or a financial calculator.

TABLE USE Imagine that you wish to find the rate of growth for the dividend given in Table 4.12. The year numbers in the table show that 1993 is viewed as the base year (year 0); the subsequent years, 1994–2002, are considered years 1 through 9, respectively. Although 10 years of data are presented in Table 4.12, they represent only 9 years of growth, because the value for the earliest year must be viewed as the initial value at time zero.

To find the growth rate, we first divide the dividend for the earliest year (1993) by the dividend for the latest year (2002). The resulting quotient is 0.700 ($2.45 ÷ $3.50). It represents the value of the present-value interest factor for 9 years. To estimate the compound annual dividend growth rate, we find the discount rate in Appendix A, Table A.3 associated with the factor closest to 0.700 for 9 years. Looking across year 9 in Table A.3 shows that the factor for 4% is 0.703—very close to the 0.700 value. Therefore, the growth rate of the dividends in Table 4.12 is approximately 4%.

CALCULATOR USE Using a financial calculator to find the growth rate for the dividend stream shown in Table 4.12, we treat the earliest (1993) value as a present value, **PV**, and the latest (2002) value as a future value, **FV**. (*Note:* Most calculators require *either* the **PV** or the **FV** value to be input as a negative number to calculate an unknown growth rate.) As noted above, although 10 years of dividends are shown in Table 4.12, there are only 9 years of growth (**N** = 9) because the earliest year (1993) must be defined as the base year (year 0). Using the inputs shown at the left, we calculate the growth rate to be 4.04%. This rate is consistent with, but more precise than, the value found using the financial tables.

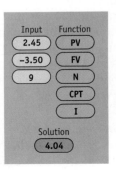

The use of growth rates, which are often an important input to the common stock valuation process, is explored in greater detail in Chapter 8.

TABLE 4.12		Dividends Per Share			
Year	Year Number	Dividends per Share	Year	Year Number	Dividends per Share
1993	0	$2.45	1998	5	$3.15
1994	1	2.60	1999	6	3.20
1995	2	2.80	2000	7	3.20
1996	3	3.00	2001	8	3.40
1997	4	3.20	2002	9	3.50

doing the reinvesting.) It follows, therefore, that for investment programs that lean toward income-oriented securities, the continued reinvestment of income plays an important role in investment success.

Finding Growth Rates

rate of growth
the compound annual rate of change in the value of a stream of income.

In addition to finding compound annual rates of return, we frequently need to find the **rate of growth**. This is the compound annual rate of change in the value of a stream of income, particularly dividends or earnings. Here we use an example to demonstrate a simple technique for estimating growth rates using either a financial table or a financial calculator.

TABLE USE Imagine that you wish to find the rate of growth for the dividends given in Table 4.12. The year numbers in the table show that 1993 is viewed as the base year (year 0); the subsequent years, 1994–2002, are considered years 1 through 9, respectively. Although 10 years of data are presented in Table 4.12, they represent only 9 years of growth, because the value for the earliest year must be viewed as the initial value at time zero.

To find the growth rate, we first divide the dividend for the earliest year (1993) by the dividend for the latest year (2002). The resulting quotient is 0.700 ($2.45 ÷ $3.50). It represents the value of the present-value interest factor for 9 years. To estimate the compound annual dividend growth rate, we find the discount rate in Appendix A, Table A.3 associated with the factor closest to 0.700 for 9 years. Looking across year 9 in Table A.3 shows that the factor for 4% is 0.703—very close to the 0.700 value. Therefore, the growth rate of the dividends in Table 4.12 is approximately 4%.

CALCULATOR USE Using a financial calculator to find the growth rate for the dividend stream shown in Table 4.12, we treat the earliest (1993) value as a present value, **PV**, and the latest (2002) value as a future value, **FV**. (*Note:* Most calculators require *either* the **PV** or the **FV** value to be input as a negative number to calculate an unknown growth rate.) As noted above, although 10 years of dividends are shown in Table 4.12, there are only 9 years of growth ($N = 9$) because the earliest year (1993) must be defined as the base year (year 0). Using the inputs shown at the left, we calculate the growth rate to be 4.04%. This rate is consistent with, but more precise than, the value found using the financial tables.

The use of growth rates, which are often an important input to the common stock valuation process, is explored in greater detail in Chapter 8.

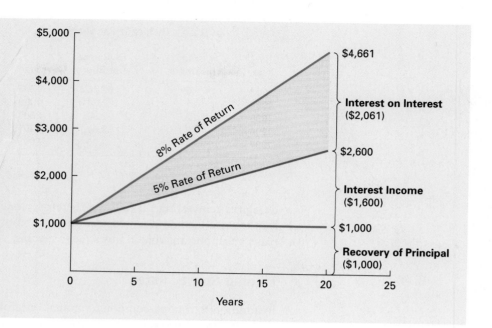

FIGURE 4.3

Earning Interest on Interest

If you invested in a $1,000, 20-year bond with an 8% coupon, you would have only $2,600 at the end of 20 years if you did not reinvest the $80 annual interest receipts—only about a 5% rate of return. If you reinvested the interest at the 8% interest rate, you would have $4,661 at the end of 20 years—an 8% rate of return. To achieve the calculated yield of 8%, you must therefore be able to earn interest on interest at that rate.

reinvestment rate
the rate of return earned on interest or other income received from an investment over its investment horizon.

fully compounded rate of return
the rate of return that includes interest earned on interest.

time. But you must be able to *reinvest* the $80 annual interest receipts in order to earn 8% on this investment.

Figure 4.3 shows the elements of return on this investment to demonstrate the point. If you don't *reinvest* the interest income of $80 per year, you'll end up on the 5% line. You'll have $2,600—the $1,000 principal plus $1,600 interest income ($80/year × 20 years)—at the end of 20 years. (The yield on a single cash flow of $1,000 today that will be worth $2,600 in 20 years is about 5%.) To move to the 8% line, you have to earn 8% on the annual interest receipts. If you do, you'll have $4,661—the $1,000 principal plus the $3,661 future value of the 20-year $80 annuity of interest receipts invested at 8% [$80/year × 45.762 (the 8%, 20-year factor from Appendix A, Table A.2)]— at the end of 20 years. (The yield on a single cash flow of $1,000 today that will be worth $4,661 in 20 years is 8%.) The future value of the investment would be $2,061 greater ($4,661 − $2,600) with interest on interest than without reinvestment of the interest receipts.

It should be clear to you that if you start out with an 8% investment, *you have to earn that same rate of return when reinvesting your income*. The rate of return you start with is the required, or minimum, **reinvestment rate**—the rate of return earned on interest or other income received over the relevant investment horizon. By putting your current income to work at this rate, you'll earn the rate of return you set out to. If you fail to do so, your return will decline accordingly. Even though a bond was used in this illustration, the same principle applies to any other type of investment vehicle.

The earning of interest on interest is what the market refers to as a **fully compounded rate of return.** It's an important concept: You can't start reaping the full potential from your investments until you start earning a fully compounded rate of return on them.

Interest on interest is a particularly important element of return for investment programs that involve a lot of current income. You have to reinvest current income. (With capital gains, the investment vehicle itself is automatically

sources of risk, discussed below, might affect potential investment vehicles. Of course, as discussed in Chapter 2, *currency exchange risk* should also be considered when investing internationally.

business risk
the degree of uncertainty associated with an investment's earnings and the investment's ability to pay the returns owed investors.

Business Risk In general, **business risk** is the degree of uncertainty associated with an investment's earnings and the investment's ability to pay the returns (interest, principal, dividends) owed investors. For example, business owners may receive no return if the firm's earnings are not adequate to meet obligations. Debtholders, on the other hand, are likely to receive some (but not necessarily all) of the amount owed them, because of the preferential treatment legally accorded to debt.

Much of the business risk associated with a given investment vehicle is related to its kind of business. For example, the business risk of a public utility common stock differs from a high-fashion clothing manufacturer's or an Internet start-up's common stock. Generally, investments in similar kinds of firms have similar business risk, although differences in management, costs, and location can cause varying levels of risk.

financial risk
the degree of uncertainty of payment attributable to the mix of debt and equity used to finance a business; the larger the proportion of debt financing, the greater this risk.

Financial Risk The degree of uncertainty of payment attributable to the mix of debt and equity used to finance a business is **financial risk.** The larger the proportion of debt used to finance a firm, the greater its financial risk. Debt financing obligates the firm to make interest payments as well as to repay the debt, thus increasing risk. Inability to meet obligations associated with the use of debt could result in business failure and in losses for bondholders as well as stockholders and owners.

purchasing power risk
the chance that changing price levels (inflation or deflation) will adversely affect investment returns.

Purchasing Power Risk The chance that changing price levels (inflation or deflation) will adversely affect investment returns is **purchasing power risk.** Specifically, this risk is the chance that generally rising prices (inflation) will reduce *purchasing power* (the amount of a given commodity that can be purchased with a dollar). For example, if last year a dollar would buy three candy bars and today it can buy only two because candy bars now cost 50 cents each, the purchasing power of your dollar has decreased. In periods of declining price levels (deflation), the purchasing power of the dollar increases.

In general, investments whose values move with general price levels have low purchasing power risk and are most profitable during periods of rising prices. Those that provide fixed returns have high purchasing power risk, and they are most profitable during periods of low inflation or declining price levels. The returns on stocks of durable-goods manufacturers, for example, tend to move with the general price level, whereas returns from deposit accounts and bonds do not.

interest rate risk
the chance that changes in interest rates will adversely affect a security's value.

Interest Rate Risk Securities are especially affected by interest rate risk. This is particularly true for those securities that offer purchasers a fixed periodic return. **Interest rate risk** is the chance that changes in interest rates will adversely affect a security's value. The interest rate changes themselves result from changes in the general relationship between the supply of and the demand for money.

As interest rates change, the prices of many securities fluctuate: They typically decrease with increasing interest rates, and they increase with decreasing interest rates. As we will see in greater detail in Chapters 9, 10, and 11, the

IN REVIEW

CONCEPTS

4.11 Define the following terms and explain how they are used to find the risk-free rate of return and the required rate of return for a given investment.
a. *Real rate of return.*
b. *Expected inflation premium.*
c. *Risk premium* for a given investment.

4.12 What is meant by the *holding period,* and why it is advisable to use holding periods of equal length when comparing alternative investment vehicles? Define the *holding period return (HPR),* and explain for what length holding periods it is typically used.

4.13 Define yield (or *internal rate of return*). When is it appropriate to use yield rather than the HPR to measure the return on an investment?

4.14 Explain why you must earn 10% on *all* income received from an investment during its holding period in order for its yield actually to equal the 10% value you've calculated.

4.15 Explain how either the present value (of benefits vs. cost) or the yield measure can be used to find a *satisfactory investment.* Given the following data, indicate which, if any, of these investments is acceptable. Explain your findings.

	Investment		
	A	B	C
Cost	$200	$160	$500
Appropriate discount rate	7%	10%	9%
Present value of benefits	—	$150	—
Yield	8%	—	8%

Risk: The Other Side of the Coin

 LG 5 LG 6

risk
the chance that the actual return from an investment may differ from what is expected.

risk-return tradeoff
the relationship between risk and return, in which investments with more risk should provide higher returns, and vice versa.

Thus far, our primary concern in this chapter has been return. However, we cannot consider return without also looking at risk. Expanding a bit on its definition in Chapter 1, **risk** is the chance that the actual return from an investment may differ from what is expected.

The risk associated with a given investment is directly related to its expected return. In general, the broader the range of possible returns, the greater the investment's risk, and vice versa. Put another way, riskier investments should provide higher levels of return. Otherwise, what incentive is there for an investor to risk his or her capital? In general, investors attempt to minimize risk for a given level of return or to maximize return for a given level of risk. This relationship between risk and return is called the **risk-return tradeoff.** It is introduced here and will be discussed in greater detail in Chapter 5. Here we begin by examining the key sources of risk. We then consider the measurement and assessment of risk: the risk of a single asset, the assessment of risk associated with a potential investment, and the steps by which return and risk can be combined in the decision process.

Sources of Risk

The risk associated with a given investment vehicle may result from a combination of possible sources. A prudent investor considers how the major

prices of fixed-income securities (bonds and preferred stock) drop when interest rates rise. They thus provide purchasers with the same rate of return that would be available at prevailing rates. The opposite occurs when interest rates fall: The return on a fixed-income security is adjusted downward to a competitive level by an upward adjustment in its market price.

A second, more subtle aspect of interest rate risk is associated with reinvestment of income. As noted in our earlier discussion of interest on interest, only if you can earn the initial rate of return on income received from an investment can you achieve a *fully compounded rate of return* equal to the initial rate of return. In other words, if a bond pays 8% annual interest, you must be able to earn 8% on the interest received during the bond's holding period in order to earn a fully compounded 8% rate of return over that period. This same aspect of interest rate risk applies to reinvestment of the proceeds received from an investment at its maturity or sale.

A final aspect of interest rate risk is related to investing in short-term securities such as T-bills and certificates of deposit (discussed in Chapter 1). Investors face the risk that when short-term securities mature, their proceeds may have to be invested in lower-yielding, new short-term securities. By initially making a long-term investment, you can lock in a return for a period of years, rather than face the risk of declines in short-term interest rates. Clearly, when interest rates are declining, the returns from a strategy of investing in short-term securities are adversely affected. On the other hand, interest rate increases have a positive impact on such a strategy. The chance that interest rates will decline is therefore the interest rate risk of a short-term security investment strategy.

Most investment vehicles are subject to interest rate risk. Although fixed-income securities are most directly affected by interest rate movements, they also affect other long-term vehicles such as common stock and mutual funds. *Generally, the higher the interest rate, the lower the value of an investment vehicle, and vice versa.*

Liquidity Risk The risk of not being able to liquidate an investment conveniently and at a reasonable price is called **liquidity risk.** The liquidity of a given investment vehicle is an important consideration. In general, investment vehicles traded in *thin markets,* where demand and supply are small, tend to be less liquid than those traded in *broad markets.*

One can generally sell an investment vehicle merely by significantly cutting its price. However, to be liquid, an investment must be easily sold *at a reasonable price.* For example, a security recently purchased for $1,000 would not be viewed as highly liquid if it could be quickly sold only at a greatly reduced price, such as $500. Vehicles such as stocks and bonds of major companies listed on the New York Stock Exchange are generally highly liquid; others, such as the stock of a small company in a declining industry, are not.

Tax Risk The chance that Congress will make unfavorable changes in tax laws is known as **tax risk.** The greater the chance that such changes will drive down the after-tax returns and market values of certain investments, the greater the tax risk. Undesirable changes in tax laws include elimination of tax exemptions, limitation of deductions, and increases in tax rates.

In recent years, Congress has passed numerous changes in tax laws. One of the most significant was the Tax Reform Act of 1986, which contained provisions that reduced the attractiveness of many investment vehicles, particularly real

liquidity risk
the risk of not being able to liquidate an investment conveniently and at a reasonable price.

tax risk
the chance that Congress will make unfavorable changes in tax laws, driving down the after-tax returns and market values of certain investments.

estate and other tax shelters. More recently, the *IRS Restructuring and Reform Act of 1998* reduced the maximum rate applicable to capital gains realized on assets held more than 12 months. Clearly, this change benefits investors and does not represent the unfavorable consequences of tax risk.

Though virtually all investments are vulnerable to increases in tax rates, certain tax-advantaged investments, such as municipal and other bonds, real estate, and natural resources, generally have greater tax risk.

market risk
risk of decline in investment returns because of market factors independent of the given investment.

Market Risk Market risk is the risk that investment returns will decline because of market factors independent of the given investment. Examples include political, economic, and social events, as well as changes in investor tastes and preferences. Market risk actually embodies a number of different risks: purchasing power risk, interest rate risk, and tax risk.

The impact of market factors on investment returns is not uniform. Both the degree and the direction of change in return differ among investment vehicles. For example, legislation placing restrictive import quotas on Japanese goods may result in a significant increase in the value (and therefore the return) of domestic automobile and electronics stocks. Essentially, market risk is reflected in the *price volatility* of a security—the more volatile the price of a security, the greater its perceived market risk.

event risk
risk that comes from an unexpected event that has a significant and usually immediate effect on the underlying value of an investment.

Event Risk Event risk occurs when something happens to a company that has a sudden and substantial impact on its financial condition. Event risk goes beyond business and financial risk. It does not necessarily mean the company or market is doing poorly. Instead, it involves an unexpected event that has a significant and usually immediate effect on the underlying value of an investment. An example of event risk is the August 2000 offer by Bridgestone/Firestone to replace 6.5 million tires, mainly on Ford light trucks and SUVs, based on 46 deaths and more than 300 incidents involving Firestone tires that were alleged to have shredded on the highway. The stock of Bridgestone Corp.—the Japanese parent company of Bridgestone/Firestone—was quickly and negatively affected. It dropped by about 20% on the Tokyo Exchange during the two days immediately following the announcement.

Event risk can take many forms and can affect all types of investment vehicles. Fortunately, its impact tends to be isolated in most cases. For instance, the stocks of only a small number of companies were directly affected by Bridgestone/Firestone's offer to replace tires.

 ## Risk of a Single Asset

Most people have at some time in their lives asked themselves how risky some anticipated course of action is. In such cases, the answer is usually a subjective judgment, such as "not very" or "quite." Such a judgment may or may not help in decision making. In finance, we are able to quantify the measurement of risk, which improves comparisons between investments and enhances decision making.

The risk or variability of both single assets and portfolios of assets can be measured statistically. Here we focus solely on the risk of single assets. We first consider standard deviation, which is an absolute measure of risk. Then we consider the coefficient of variation, a relative measure of risk.

standard deviation, s
a statistic used to measure the dispersion (variation) of returns around an asset's average or expected return.

Standard Deviation: An Absolute Measure of Risk The most common single indicator of an asset's risk is the **standard deviation, s.** It measures the dispersion (variation) of returns around an asset's average or expected return. The formula is

Equation 4.10

$$\text{Standard deviation} = \sqrt{\frac{\sum_{j=1}^{n}\left(\text{Return for outcome } j - \text{Average or expected return}\right)^2}{\text{Total number of outcomes} - 1}}$$

Equation 4.10a

$$s = \sqrt{\frac{\sum_{j=1}^{n}(r_j - \bar{r})^2}{n-1}}$$

Consider two competing investments—A and B—described in Table 4.13. Note that both investments earned an average return of 15% over the 6-year period shown. Reviewing the returns shown for each investment in light of their 15% averages, we can see that the returns for investment B vary more from this average than do the returns for investment A.

The standard deviation provides a quantitative tool for comparing investment risk. Table 4.14 demonstrates the calculation of the standard deviations, s_A and s_B, for investments A and B, respectively. Evaluating the calculations, we can see that the standard deviation of 1.49% for the returns on investment A is, as expected, considerably below the standard deviation of 5.24% for investment B. The greater absolute dispersion of investment B's return, reflected in its larger standard deviation, indicates that B is the more risky investment. Of course, these values are absolute measures based on *historical* data. There is no assurance that the risks of these two investments will remain the same in the future.

coefficient of variation, CV
a statistic used to measure the *relative* dispersion of an asset's returns; it is useful in comparing the risk of assets with differing average or expected returns.

Coefficient of Variation: A Relative Measure of Risk The **coefficient of variation, CV,** is a measure of the *relative* dispersion of an asset's returns. It is useful in comparing the risk of assets with differing average or expected returns. Equation 4.11 gives the formula for the coefficient of variation.

TABLE 4.13 **Returns on Investments A and B**

Year	Rate of Return	
	Investment A	Investment B
1997	15.6%	8.4%
1998	12.7	12.9
1999	15.3	19.6
2000	16.2	17.5
2001	16.5	10.3
2002	13.7	21.3
Average	15.0%	15.0%

TABLE 4.14   Calculation of Standard Deviations of Returns for Investments A and B

Investment A

Year (j)	(1) Return, r_j	(2) Average Return, $\bar{r}$	(3) (1) − (2) $r_j - \bar{r}$	(4) (3)^2 $(r_j - \bar{r})^2$
1997	15.6%	15.0%	.6%	0.36%
1998	12.7	15.0	−2.3	5.29
1999	15.3	15.0	.3	0.09
2000	16.2	15.0	1.2	1.44
2001	16.5	15.0	1.5	2.25
2002	13.7	15.0	−1.3	1.69

$$\sum_{j=1}^{6} (r_j - \bar{r})^2 = 11.12$$

$$s_A = \sqrt{\frac{\sum_{j=1}^{6} (r_j - \bar{r})^2}{n-1}} = \sqrt{\frac{11.12}{6-1}} = \sqrt{2.224} = \underline{1.49\%}$$

Investment B

Year (j)	(1) Return, r_j	(2) Average Return, $\bar{r}$	(3) (1) − (2) $r_j - \bar{r}$	(4) (3)^2 $(r_j - \bar{r})^2$
1997	8.4%	15.0%	−6.6%	43.56%
1998	12.9	15.0	−2.1	4.41
1999	19.6	15.0	4.6	21.16
2000	17.5	15.0	2.5	6.25
2001	10.3	15.0	−4.7	22.09
2002	21.3	15.0	6.3	39.69

$$\sum_{j=1}^{6} (r_j - \bar{r})^2 = 137.16$$

$$s_B = \sqrt{\frac{\sum_{j=1}^{6} (r_j - \bar{r})^2}{n-1}} = \sqrt{\frac{137.16}{6-1}} = \sqrt{27.432} = \underline{5.24\%}$$

INVESTOR FACTS

VOLATILE STOCKS—from 1926 to 2000, the annual standard deviation for large-company stocks was 20.1%. Therefore, the annual return for about 68% of these stocks fell between 20.1% above and 20.1% below the 13.3% average, or between 33.4% and −6.8%. Bonds were less volatile, with a 5.8% standard deviation during the same period.

Source: Walter Updegrave, "The Skeptical Investor," *Money*, June 2000, p. 134.

Equation 4.11

$$\text{Coefficient of variation} = \frac{\text{Standard deviation}}{\text{Average or expected return}}$$

Equation 4.11a

$$CV = \frac{s}{\bar{r}}$$

As was the case for the standard deviation, the higher the coefficient of variation, the greater the risk.

We can substitute into Equation 4.11a the standard deviation values (from Table 4.14) and the average returns (from Table 4.13) for investments A and B. We get a coefficient of variation for A of 0.099 (1.49% ÷ 15%) and for B of 0.349 (5.24% ÷ 15%). Investment B has the higher coefficient of variation and, as expected, has more relative risk than investment A. Because both investments have the same average return, the coefficient of variation in this case has not provided any more information than the standard deviation.

The real utility of the coefficient of variation is in comparing investments that have *different* expected returns. For example, assume you want to select the less risky of two alternative investments—X and Y. The average return, the standard deviation, and the coefficient of variation for each of these investments are as follows.

Statistics	Investment X	Investment Y
(1) Average return	12%	20%
(2) Standard deviation	9%*	10%
(3) Coefficient of variation [(2) ÷ (1)]	0.75	0.50*

* Preferred investment using the given risk measure.

If you compared the investments solely on the basis of their standard deviations, you would prefer investment X. It has a lower standard deviation than investment Y (9% vs. 10%). But by comparing the coefficients of variation, you can see that you would be making a mistake in choosing X over Y. The *relative* dispersion, or risk, of the investments, as reflected in the coefficient of variation, is lower for Y than for X (0.50 vs. 0.75). Clearly, the coefficient of variation considers the relative size, or average return, of each investment.

HOTLINKS

Access Vanguard site's Education, Planning, and Advice section. Then click on [Investing Primer]. Read the sections on [No Reward Without Risk] and [Defining Investment Risks]. Test your knowledge on the Investing Primer.

personal.vanguard.com/educ/inveduc.html

Assessing Risk

Techniques for quantifying the risk of a given investment vehicle are quite useful. However, they will be of little use if you are unaware of your feelings toward risk. The individual investor typically tends to seek answers to these questions: "Is the amount of perceived risk worth taking to get the expected return?" "Can I get a higher return for the same level of risk or a lower risk for the same level of return?" A look at the general risk-return characteristics of alternative investment vehicles and at the question of an acceptable level of risk will help shed light on how to evaluate risk.

Risk-Return Characteristics of Alternative Investment Vehicles A wide variety of risk-return behaviors are associated with each type of investment vehicle. Some common stocks offer low returns and low risk. Others offer high returns and high risk. In general, though, the risk-return characteristics of the major investment vehicles are as shown in Figure 4.4. Of course, a broad range of risk-return behaviors exists for specific investments of each type. In other words, once you have selected the appropriate type of vehicle, you must still decide which specific security to acquire.

An Acceptable Level of Risk The three basic risk preferences (risk-indifferent, risk-averse, and risk-seeking) are depicted graphically in Figure 4.5.

risk-indifferent
describes an investor who does not require a change in return as compensation for greater risk.

risk-averse
describes an investor who requires greater return in exchange for greater risk.

- For the **risk-indifferent** investor, the required return does not change as risk goes from x_1 to x_2. In essence, no change in return would be required for the increase in risk.

- For the **risk-averse** investor, the required return increases for an increase in risk. Because they shy away from risk, these investors require higher expected returns to compensate them for taking greater risk.

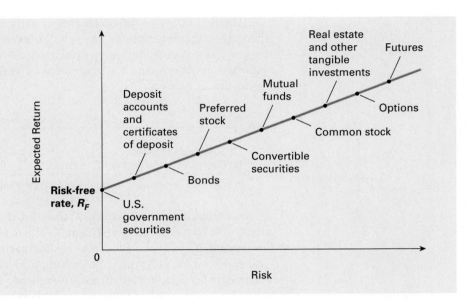

FIGURE 4.4

Risk-Return Tradeoffs for Various Investment Vehicles

A risk-return tradeoff exists such that for a higher risk one expects a higher return, and vice versa. Low-risk-low-return investment vehicles include U.S. government securities and deposit accounts. High-risk-high-return vehicles include real estate and other tangible investments, options, and futures.

risk-seeking
describes an investor who will accept a lower return in exchange for greater risk.

- For the **risk-seeking** investor, the required return decreases for an increase in risk. Theoretically, because they enjoy risk, these investors are willing to give up some return to take more risk.

Most investors are risk-averse: For a given increase in risk, they require an increase in return. This risk-averse behavior is also depicted in Figure 4.5.

Of course, the amount of return required by each investor for a given increase in risk differs depending on the investor's degree of risk aversion (reflected in the slope of the line). Investors generally tend to be conservative when accepting risk. The more aggressive an investor you are (the farther to the right you operate on the risk-averse line), the greater your tolerance for risk, and the greater your required return. To get a feel for your own risk-taking orientation, read the *Investing in Action* box on page 163.

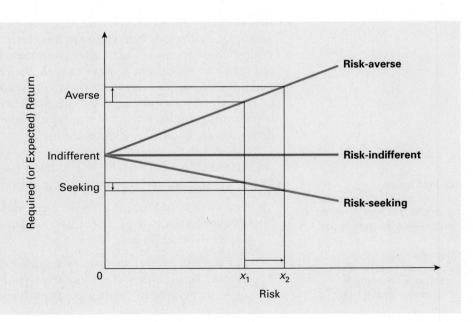

FIGURE 4.5

Risk Preferences

The risk-indifferent investor requires no change in return for a given increase in risk. The risk-averse investor requires an increase in return for a given risk increase. The risk-seeking investor gives up some return for more risk. The majority of investors are risk-averse.

INVESTING in action

How Much Investment Risk Can You Handle?

An effective investment plan is based on a balance between the risks you are willing to take and the returns you need to achieve your goals. The conservative investor saving for retirement or college funding might want to buy only "safe" investments such as U.S. Treasury bills or bank CDs. Historically, though, these fixed-rate investments have barely kept pace with inflation, and taxes lessen returns even further. On the other hand, the stock market—a riskier choice—has far outperformed other investments over the long run. Many financial experts advise having at least 30% to 40% of your portfolio in equities (some suggest even 50% to 75%) if you want to accumulate assets over the long term (more than five to ten years).

The key to risk taking is to determine your personal level of risk tolerance—how comfortable you feel with the volatility of your investments. Understanding your risk tolerance will prevent you from taking more risk than you can handle and will reduce the likelihood that you will panic and abandon your plan midstream.

One way to assess your risk tolerance is to ask yourself how much you could lose on your investments over a 1-year period and still stick to your plan. In general, investors with low risk tolerance can withstand annual losses of no more than 5%, those with moderate tolerance can withstand losses of 6% to 15%, and those with high tolerance will accept losses of 16% to 25%.

The following quiz can help you evaluate your personal capacity for risk. Another, lengthier quiz can be accessed at the book's Web site.

What Is Your Investment Risk Tolerance?

1. Which best describes your feelings about investing?
   a. "Better safe than sorry."
   b. "Moderation in all things."
   c. "Nothing ventured, nothing gained."

2. Which is the most important to you as an investor?
   a. Steady income
   b. Steady income and growth
   c. Rapid price appreciation

3. You won! Which prize would you select?
   a. $4,000 in cash
   b. A 50% chance to win $10,000
   c. A 20% chance to win $100,000

4. The stocks in your retirement account have dropped 20% since last quarter. The market experts are optimistic. What would you do?
   a. Transfer out of stocks to avoid losing more.
   b. Stay in stocks and wait for them to come back.
   c. Shift more money into stocks. If they made sense before, they're a bargain now.

5. The stocks in your retirement account have suddenly gone up 20%. You have no more information. What would you do?
   a. Transfer out of stocks and lock in my gains.
   b. Stay in stocks, hoping for more gains.
   c. Transfer more money into stocks. They might go higher.

6. Would you borrow money to take advantage of a good investment opportunity?
   a. Never
   b. Maybe
   c. Yes

7. How would you characterize yourself as an investor?
   a. Conservative
   b. Moderate risk taker
   c. Aggressive

How to determine your score:

Each (a) answer is worth 1 point. Each (b) is worth 2 points. Each (c) is worth 3 points. Add them up to find your total score.

7–11 points: a conservative investor
12–16 points: a moderate risk taker
17–21 points: an aggressive investor

Sources: Maria Crawford Scott, "Life-Cycle Investing: Investment Decisions and Your Personal Investment Profile," *AAII Journal,* March 1993, pp. 16–19; and Ann Perry, "Putting Stock in the Market," *San Diego Union-Tribune,* July 18, 1993, pp. 11–12.

Steps in the Decision Process: Combining Return and Risk

When you are deciding among alternative investments, you should take the following steps to combine return and risk.

1. Using historical or projected return data, estimate the expected return over a given holding period. Use yield (or present-value) techniques to make sure you give the time value of money adequate consideration.
2. Using historical or projected return data, assess the risk associated with the investment. Subjective risk assessment, use of the standard deviation or coefficient of variation of returns, and use of more sophisticated measures, such as beta (developed in Chapter 5), are the primary approaches available to individual investors.
3. Evaluate the risk-return behavior of each alternative investment to make sure that the return expected is reasonable given the level of risk. If other vehicles with lower levels of risk provide equal or greater returns, the investment is not acceptable.
4. Select the investment vehicles that offer the highest returns associated with the level of risk you are willing to take. As long as you get the highest return for your acceptable level of risk, you have made a "good investment."

Probably the most difficult step in this process is assessing risk. Aside from return and risk considerations, other factors, such as portfolio considerations, taxes, and liquidity, affect the investment decision. We will develop portfolio concepts in Chapter 5 and, in later chapters, will look at all of these factors as they are related to specific investment vehicles.

IN REVIEW

CONCEPTS

4.16 Define *risk*. Explain what we mean by the *risk-return tradeoff*. What happens to the required return as risk increases? Explain.

4.17 Define and briefly discuss each of the following sources of risk.
   a. Business risk   b. Financial risk
   c. Purchasing power risk   d. Interest rate risk
   e. Liquidity risk   f. Tax risk
   g. Market risk   h. Event risk

4.18 Briefly describe each of the following measures of risk or variability, and explain their similarity. Under what circumstances is each preferred when comparing the risk of competing investments?
   a. Standard deviation
   b. Coefficient of variation

4.19 Differentiate among the three basic risk preferences: risk-indifferent, risk-averse, and risk-seeking. Which of these behaviors best describes most investors?

4.20 Judging by the results when you took the quiz in the *Investing in Action* box on page 163, what is your personal tolerance for investment risk? Using the graph in Figure 4.4, determine what investment vehicles might be appropriate for your level of risk tolerance.

4.21 Describe the steps involved in the investment decision process. Be sure to mention how returns and risks can be evaluated together to determine acceptable investments.

Summary

LG 1 **Review the concept of return, its components, and the forces that affect the investor's level of return.** Return is the reward for investing. The total return provided by an investment includes current income and capital gains (or losses). Return is commonly calculated on a historical basis and then used to project expected returns. The level of return depends on internal characteristics and external forces, which include the general level of price changes.

LG 2 **Discuss the time value of money and the calculations involved in finding the future value of various types of cash flows.** Because investors have opportunities to earn interest on their funds, money has a time value. Interest can be applied using either simple interest or compound interest. The more frequently interest is compounded at a stated rate, the higher the true rate of interest. Financial tables and financial calculators can be used to streamline time-value calculations. The future value of a present sum or an annuity can be found using compound interest concepts.

LG 3 **Explain the concept of present value, the procedures for calculating present values, and the use of present value in determining whether an investment is satisfactory.** The present value of a future sum is the amount that would have to be deposited today, into an account earning interest at a given rate, to accumulate the specified future sum. The present value of streams of future returns can be found by adding the present values of the individual returns. When the stream is an annuity, its present value can be more simply calculated. A satisfactory investment is one for which the present value of its benefits equals or exceeds the present value of its costs.

LG 4 **Describe real, risk-free, and required returns and the computation and application of holding period return, yield (internal rate of return), and growth rates.** The required return on an investment is the rate of return an investor must earn to be fully compensated for the investment's risk. It represents the sum of the real rate of return and the expected inflation premium (which together represent the risk-free rate), plus the risk premium for the investment. The risk premium varies depending on issue and issuer characteristics. The holding period return (HPR) is the return earned over a specified period of time. It is frequently used to compare returns earned in periods of 1 year or less.

Yield or internal rate of return is the compound annual rate of return earned on investments held for more than 1 year. If the yield is greater than or equal to the required return, the investment is acceptable. Implicit in the use of yield is an ability to earn a return equal to the calculated yield on all income received from the investment during the holding period. Present-value techniques can be used to find a rate of growth, which is the compound annual rate of change in the value of a stream of income, particularly dividends or earnings.

LG 5 **Discuss the key sources of risk and how they might affect potential investment vehicles.** Risk is the chance that the actual return from an investment will differ from what is expected. The total risk associated with a given investment vehicle may result from a combination of sources: business, financial, purchasing power, interest rate, liquidity, tax, market, and event risk. These risks typically have varying effects on different types of investment vehicles.

LG 6 **Understand the risk of a single asset, risk assessment, and the steps that combine return and risk.** The risk of both single assets and portfolios of assets can be measured statistically on an absolute basis by the standard deviation and on a relative basis by the coefficient of variation. There is a tradeoff between risk and return. Generally, each type of investment vehicle displays certain risk-return characteristics. Most investors are risk-averse: In exchange for a given increase in risk, they require an increase in return. The investment decision involves estimating the return and risk of each alternative and then selecting those investments that offer the highest returns for the level of risk the investor is willing to take.

Discussion Questions

LG 1

Q4.1 Choose a publicly traded company that has been listed on a major exchange or in the over-the-counter market for at least 5 years. Use any data source of your choice to find the annual cash dividend, if any, paid by the company in each of the past 5 calendar years. Also find the closing price of the stock at the end of each of the preceding 6 years.

a. Calculate the return for each of the five 1-year periods.
b. Graph the returns on a set of year (*x*-axis)-return (*y*-axis) axes.
c. On the basis of the graph in part (b), estimate the return for the coming year, and explain your answer.

LG 2 **LG 3**

Q4.2 Estimate the amount of cash you will need each year over the next 20 years to live at the standard you desire. Also estimate the rate of return you can reasonably expect to earn annually, on average, during that 20-year period.

a. How large a single lump sum would you need today to provide the annual cash required to allow you to live at the desired standard over the next 20 years? (*Hint:* Be sure to use the appropriate discount rate.)
b. Would the lump sum calculated in part (a) be larger or smaller if you could earn a higher return during the 20-year period? Explain.
c. If you had the lump sum calculated in part (a) but decided to delay your planned retirement in 20 years for another 3 years, how much extra cash would you have accumulated over the 3-year period if you could invest it to earn a 7% annual rate of return?

LG 4

Q4.3 Access appropriate government and economic data at your public or university library to obtain current estimates of the real rate of return and the expected inflation premium. Use the appropriate data you have gathered to estimate the current risk-free rate.

LG 4 **LG 5** **LG 6**

Q4.4 Choose three NYSE-listed stocks and maintain a record of their dividend payments, if any, and closing prices each week over the next 6 weeks.

a. At the end of the 6-week period, calculate the 1-week holding period returns (HPRs) for each stock for each of the 6 weeks.
b. For each stock, average the six weekly HPRs calculated in part (a) and compare them.
c. Use your finding in part (b) and the six HPRs to calculate each stock's coefficient of variation of return. Discuss the stocks' relative risk-return behaviors over the 6-week period.
d. On the basis of your findings in part (c), did the stock perform as expected (higher risk-higher return) over the 6-week period? What explanations can you suggest for any discrepancies?

Problems

LG 1

P4.1 How much would an investor earn on a stock purchased 1 year ago for $63 if it paid an annual cash dividend of $3.75 and had just been sold for $67.50? Would the investor have experienced a capital gain? Explain.

LG 1

P4.2 Assuming you purchased a share of stock for $50 one year ago, sold it today for $60, and during the year received three dividend payments totaling $2.70, calculate the following.

a. Current income.
b. Capital gain (or loss).
c. Total return
   (1) In dollars.
   (2) As a percentage of the initial investment.

LG 1   P4.3   Consider the historical data given in the accompanying table.
a. Calculate the total return (in dollars) for each year.
b. Indicate the level of return you would expect in 2003 and in 2004.
c. Comment on your forecast.

Year	Income	Market Value (Price)	
		Beginning	Ending
1998	$1.00	$30.00	$32.50
1999	1.20	32.50	35.00
2000	1.30	35.00	33.00
2001	1.60	33.00	40.00
2002	1.75	40.00	45.00

LG 2   P4.4   For each of the savings account transactions in the accompanying table, calculate the following.
a. End-of-year account balance. (Assume that the account balance at December 31, 2001, is zero.)
b. Annual interest, using 6% simple interest and assuming all interest is withdrawn from the account as it is earned.
c. True rate of interest, and compare it to the stated rate of interest. Discuss your finding.

Date	Deposit (Withdrawal)	Date	Deposit (Withdrawal)
1/1/02	$5,000	1/1/04	$2,000
1/1/03	(4,000)	1/1/05	3,000

LG 2   P4.5   Using the appropriate table of interest factors found in Appendix A or a financial calculator, calculate the following.
a. The future value of a $300 deposit left in an account paying 7% annual interest for 12 years.
b. The future value at the end of 6 years of an $800 *annual* end-of-year deposit into an account paying 7% annual interest.

LG 2   P4.6   For each of the following initial investment amounts, calculate the future value at the end of the given investment period if interest is compounded annually at the specified rate of return over the given investment period.

Investment	Investment Amount	Rate of Return	Investment Period
A	$ 200	5%	20 years
B	4,500	8	7
C	10,000	9	10
D	25,000	10	12
E	37,000	11	5

LG 2   P4.7   For each of the following annual deposits into an account paying the stated annual interest rate over the specified deposit period, calculate the future value of the *annuity* at the end of the given deposit period.

Deposit	Amount of Annual Deposit	Interest Rate	Deposit Period
A	$ 2,500	8%	10 years
B	500	12	6
C	1,000	20	5
D	12,000	6	8
E	4,000	14	30

P4.8 If you could earn 9% on similar-risk investments, what is the least you would accept at the end of a 6-year period, given the following amounts and timing of your investment?

    a. Invest $5,000 as a lump sum today.
    b. Invest $2,000 at the end of *each* of the next 5 years.
    c. Invest a lump sum of $3,000 today and $1,000 at the end of *each* of the next 5 years.
    d. Invest $900 at the end of years 1, 3, and 5.

P4.9 For each of the following investments, calculate the present value of the future sum, using the specified discount rate and assuming the sum will be received at the end of the given year.

Investment	Future Sum	Discount Rate	End of Year
A	$ 7,000	12%	4
B	28,000	8	20
C	10,000	14	12
D	150,000	11	6
E	45,000	20	8

P4.10 A Florida state savings bond can be converted to $1,000 at maturity 8 years from purchase. If the state bonds are to be competitive with U.S. savings bonds, which pay 6% interest compounded annually, at what price will the state's bonds sell, assuming they make no cash payments prior to maturity?

P4.11 Find the present value of each of the following streams of income, assuming a 12% discount rate.

A		B		C	
End of Year	Income	End of Year	Income	End of Year	Income
1	$2,200	1	$10,000	1–5	$10,000/yr
2	3,000	2–5	5,000/yr	6–10	8,000/yr
3	4,000	6	7,000		
4	6,000				
5	8,000				

P4.12 Consider the streams of income given in the following table.

    a. Find the present value of each income stream, using a 15% discount rate.
    b. Compare the calculated present values and discuss them in light of the fact that the undiscounted total income amounts to $10,000 in each case.

End of Year	Income Stream A	B
1	$ 4,000	$ 1,000
2	3,000	2,000
3	2,000	3,000
4	1,000	4,000
Total	$10,000	$10,000

P4.13 For each of the investments at the top of page 169, calculate the present value of the *annual* end-of-year returns at the specified discount rate over the given period.

Investment	Annual Returns	Discount Rate	Period
A	$ 1,200	7%	3 years
B	5,500	12	15
C	700	20	9
D	14,000	5	7
E	2,200	10	5

 LG 3 **P4.14** Using the appropriate table of interest factors found in Appendix A or a financial calculator, calculate the following.

a. The present value of $500 to be received 4 years from now, using an 11% discount rate.

b. The present value of the following end-of-year income streams, using a 9% discount rate and assuming it is now the beginning of 2003.

End of Year	Income Stream A	Income Stream B
2003	$80	$140
2004	80	120
2005	80	100
2006	80	80
2007	80	60
2008	80	40
2009	80	20

 LG 2 **LG 3** **P4.15** Terri Allessandro has an opportunity to make any of the following investments. The purchase price, the amount of its lump-sum future value, and its year of receipt are given below for each investment. Terri can earn a 10% rate of return on investments similar to those currently under consideration. Evaluate each investment to determine whether it is satisfactory, and make an investment recommendation to Terri.

Investment	Purchase Price	Future Value	Year of Receipt
A	$18,000	$30,000	5
B	600	3,000	20
C	3,500	10,000	10
D	1,000	15,000	40

 LG 2 **LG 3** **P4.16** Kent Weitz wishes to assess whether the following two investments are satisfactory. Use his required return (discount rate) of 17% to evaluate each investment. Make an investment recommendation to Kent.

	Investment	
	A	B
Purchase price	$13,000	$8,500
End of Year	Income Stream	
1	$ 2,500	$4,000
2	3,500	3,500
3	4,500	3,000
4	5,000	1,000
5	5,500	500

P4.17 Given a real rate of interest of 3%, an expected inflation premium of 5%, and risk premiums for investments A and B of 3% and 5%, respectively, find the following.
    a. The risk-free rate of return, R_F.
    b. The required returns for investments A and B.

P4.18 Calculate the holding period return (HPR) for the following two investment alternatives. Which, if any, of the return components is likely not to be realized if you continue to hold each of the investments beyond 1 year? Which vehicle would you prefer, assuming they are of equal risk? Explain.

	Investment Vehicle	
	X	Y
Cash received		
1st quarter	$ 1.00	$ 0
2nd quarter	1.20	0
3rd quarter	0	0
4th quarter	2.30	2.00
Investment value		
End of year	$29.00	$56.00
Beginning of year	30.00	50.00

P4.19 Assume you invest $5,000 today in an investment vehicle that promises to return $9,000 in exactly 10 years.
    a. Use the present-value technique to estimate the yield on this investment.
    b. If a minimum return of 9% is required, would you recommend this investment?

P4.20 Use the appropriate present-value interest factor table or a financial calculator to estimate the yield for each of the following investments.

Investment	Initial Investment	Future Value	End of Year
A	$ 1,000	$ 1,200	5
B	10,000	20,000	7
C	400	2,000	20
D	3,000	4,000	6
E	5,500	25,000	30

P4.21 Rosemary Santos must earn a return of 10% on an investment that requires an initial outlay of $2,500 and promises to return $6,000 in 8 years.
    a. Use present-value techniques to estimate the yield on this investment.
    b. On the basis of your finding in part (a), should Rosemary make the proposed investment? Explain.

P4.22 Use the appropriate present-value interest factors or a financial calculator to estimate the yield for each of the following two investments.

	Investment	
	A	B
Initial Investment	$8,500	$9,500
End of Year	Income	
1	$2,500	$2,000
2	2,500	2,500
3	2,500	3,000
4	2,500	3,500
5	2,500	4,000

LG 4 **P4.23** Elliott Dumack must earn a minimum rate of return of 11% to be adequately compensated for the risk of the following investment.

Initial Investment	$14,000
End of Year	Income
1	$ 6,000
2	3,000
3	5,000
4	2,000
5	1,000

    a. Use present-value techniques to estimate the yield on this investment.
    b. On the basis of your finding in part (a), should Elliott make the proposed investment? Explain.

 LG 4 **P4.24** Assume the investment that generates income stream B in Problem P4.14 can be purchased at the beginning of 2003 for $1,000 and sold at the end of 2009 for $1,200. Estimate the yield for this investment. If a minimum return of 9% is required, would you recommend this investment? Explain.

 LG 4 **P4.25** For each of the following streams of dividends, estimate the compound annual rate of growth between the earliest year for which a value is given and 2002.

	Dividend Stream		
Year	A	B	C
1993		$1.50	
1994		1.55	
1995		1.61	
1996		1.68	$2.50
1997		1.76	2.60
1998	$5.00	1.85	2.65
1999	5.60	1.95	2.65
2000	6.40	2.06	2.80
2001	7.20	2.17	2.85
2002	8.00	2.28	2.90

 LG 6 **P4.26** The historical returns for two investments—A and B—are summarized in the table below for the period 1998 to 2002. Use the data to answer the questions that follow.

	Investment	
	A	B
Year	Rate of Return	
1998	19%	8%
1999	1	10
2000	10	12
2001	26	14
2002	4	16
Average	12%	12%

    a. On the basis of a review of the return data, which investment appears to be more risky? Why?
    b. Calculate the standard deviation and the coefficient of variation for each investment's returns.
    c. On the basis of your calculations in part (b), which investment is more risky? Compare this conclusion to your observation in part (a).
    d. Does the coefficient of variation provide better risk comparison than the standard deviation in this case? Why or why not?

Case Problem 4.1   *Solomon's Decision*

LG 2   LG 3   LG 4

Dave Solomon, a 23-year-old mathematics teacher at Xavier High School, recently received a tax refund of $1,100. Because Dave doesn't currently need this money for living expenses, he decided to make a long-term investment. After surveying a number of alternative investments costing no more than $1,100, Dave isolated two that seemed most suitable to his needs.

Each of the investments cost $1,050 and was expected to provide income over a 10-year period. Investment A provided a relatively certain stream of income. Dave was a little less certain of the income provided by investment B. From his search for suitable alternatives, Dave found that the appropriate discount rate for a relatively certain investment was 12%. Because he felt a bit uncomfortable with an investment like B, he estimated that such an investment would have to provide a return at least 4% *higher* than investment A. Although Dave planned to reinvest funds returned from the investments in other vehicles providing similar returns, he wished to keep the extra $50 ($1,100 − $1,050) invested for the full 10 years in a savings account paying 5% interest compounded annually.

As he makes his investment decision, Dave has asked for your help in answering the questions that follow the expected return data for these investments.

	Expected Returns			Expected Returns	
Year	A	B	Year	A	B
2003	$150	$100	2008	$ 150	$350
2004	150	150	2009	150	300
2005	150	200	2010	150	250
2006	150	250	2011	150	200
2007	150	300	2012	1,150	150

Questions

a.   Assuming that investments A and B are equally risky and using the 12% discount rate, apply the present-value technique to assess the acceptability of each investment and to determine the preferred investment. Explain your findings.

b.   Recognizing that investment B is more risky than investment A, reassess the two alternatives, applying a 16% discount rate to investment B. Compare your findings relative to acceptability and preference to those found for question (a).

c.   From your findings in questions (a) and (b), indicate whether the yield for investment A is above or below 12% and whether that for investment B is above or below 16%. Explain.

d.   Use the present-value technique to estimate the yield on each investment. Compare your findings and contrast them with your response to question (c).

e.   From the information given, which, if either, of the two investments would you recommend that Dave make? Explain your answer.

f.   Indicate to Dave how much money the extra $50 will have grown to by the end of 2012, assuming he makes no withdrawals from the savings account.

Case Problem 4.2

The Risk-Return Tradeoff: Molly O'Rourke's Stock Purchase Decision

LG 4   LG 5   LG 6

Over the past 10 years, Molly O'Rourke has slowly built a diversified portfolio of common stock. Currently her portfolio includes 20 different common stock issues and has a total market value of $82,500.

Molly is at present considering the addition of 50 shares of one of two common stock issues—X or Y. To assess the return and risk of each of these issues, she has gathered dividend income and share price data for both over each of the last 10 years (1993 through 2002). Molly's investigation of the outlook for these issues suggests that each will, on average, tend to behave in the future just as it has in the past. She therefore believes that the expected return can be estimated by finding the average holding period return (HPR) over the past 10 years for each of the stocks. The historical dividend income and stock price data collected by Molly are given in the accompanying table.

	Stock X			Stock Y		
	Dividend	Share Price		Dividend	Share Price	
Year	Income	Beginning	Ending	Income	Beginning	Ending
1993	$1.00	$20.00	$22.00	$1.50	$20.00	$20.00
1994	1.50	22.00	21.00	1.60	20.00	20.00
1995	1.40	21.00	24.00	1.70	20.00	21.00
1996	1.70	24.00	22.00	1.80	21.00	21.00
1997	1.90	22.00	23.00	1.90	21.00	22.00
1998	1.60	23.00	26.00	2.00	22.00	23.00
1999	1.70	26.00	25.00	2.10	23.00	23.00
2000	2.00	25.00	24.00	2.20	23.00	24.00
2001	2.10	24.00	27.00	2.30	24.00	25.00
2002	2.20	27.00	30.00	2.40	25.00	25.00

Questions

a.   Determine the holding period return (HPR) for each stock in each of the preceding 10 years. Find the expected return for each stock, using the approach specified by Molly.

b.   Use the HPRs and expected return calculated in question (a) to find both the standard deviation and the coefficient of variation of the HPRs for each stock over the 10-year period 1993 to 2002.

c.   Use your findings to evaluate and discuss the return and risk associated with stocks X and Y. Which stock seems preferable? Explain.

d.   What recommendations would you give Molly?

Web Exercises

William F. Sharpe received the 1990 Nobel Prize for Economic Science for his pioneering work in investment theory, particularly in exploring the relationship between risk and return. To learn about investing, he recommends the following:

> The first thing is to get some feel for the lessons history might teach us about what may happen in the future. I like playing around with software that can show you the best and worst years for a diversified portfolio of stocks. Get some history under you, because at the moment the danger is that many people think stocks just always go up. We need to build some reality in. (From an interview at www.vanguard.com/educ/newsstnd/ITV/1997Summer/Sharpesum1997.html; Sharpe's site is www.stanford.edu/~wfsharpe/art/art.htm).

The following sites will help you get some history "under your belt."

W4.1   The Barra site at www.barra.com contains [Summary Returns %] for 3, 5, and 10 years for the S&P 500, S&P/Barra 500 Growth, and S&P/Barra 500 Value indexes. Look at the charts that show these percentage returns. How did growth stocks do relative to value stocks over 3, 5, and 10 years?

W4.2   The research library screen at the Barra site (www.barra.com/research_library) gives you S&P/Barra U.S. Equity indexes. Use [Download monthly returns] and select the [S&P500] index from [January 1985] to [August 2000]. Press the button [Get Returns]. Take a hard look at 1987 and 1998. The upside is very attractive for the long term in equities. But it's important that you see the downside clearly as well.
   a. What were the returns in September, October, and November of 1987?
   b. What was the return in August 1998?
   c. What was the return in November 2000?

W4.3   Data on actual returns on stocks, bonds, and Treasury bills for the United States from 1928 to the most recent year are available at equity.stern.nyu.edu/~adamodar/New_Home_Page/data.html. Click on [Historical Returns on Stocks, Bonds and Bills— United States.]
   a. Compare the Arithmetic Average Annual Returns on Investments for stocks, bonds, and T-bills, for 1928–1999, 1962–1999, and 1990–1999. This will give you some idea of what has happened in the past.
   b. Over the long run, which has done the best—stocks, bonds, or T-bills? Which has done the worst of the three? (A word of caution: These results are for the long run; they do not hold true for every year.)

W4.4   Access www.investools.com/cgi-bin/charts.pl. Print out the two charts showing historical returns for the past year for MSFT and SLE. What similarities or differences do you find between the return patterns of these two firms?

For additional practice with concepts from this chapter, visit
www.awl.com/gitman_joehnk

If you think it's hard to manage a $50,000 investment portfolio, imagine being James Grefenstette. He co-manages $3.4 billion in three mutual funds at Federated Investors. Each fund has different investment strategies.

The first fund, Growth Strategies, invests in companies with total market value over $100 million and above-average growth prospects. In addition to equities, Grefenstette and co-manager Salvatore Esposito may also hold convertible bonds, corporate debt, and ADRs. They diversify by trying to approximate the S&P 500's industry sector weightings. The two also manage the Large Cap Growth Fund, which invests in about 100 large-cap (total market value) companies. Grefenstette and three co-managers also run the specialized Federated Communications Technology Fund, in which at least 65% of the assets are communications technology and service companies.

Federated takes a team approach to fund portfolio management. "If you're ultra-reliant on one person and that person controls the vision and management of the fund, well, if he moves on, the fund may be left without continuity," explains Grefenstette. Federated's team approach protects both the management company and the shareholders. Its managers don't look for star status but focus on providing investors with a fund that follows its stated objectives. "Our goal is to hit a lot of singles, doubles, and the occasional triple, because over time that's what's going to get your customers to enjoy an above-average rate of return with less risk. The people who swing for the fences and hit that occasional home run or grand slam probably strike out a lot."

Federated's strategy provides good lessons for individual investors as well. As we'll see in Chapter 5, understanding your investment objectives and developing appropriate asset allocation strategies are the way to build your own portfolio.

Sources: Jim Grefenstette, "Trimming Technology Close to Market Weight," *Federated Focus*, November 8, 2000, downloaded from www.federatedinvestors.com; Gary Gentile, "This Fund Manager Is a 'Most Valuable Player,'" *Fox Market Wire*, November 1, 1999, downloaded from www.foxmarketwire.com

CHAPTER 5

MODERN PORTFOLIO CONCEPTS

LEARNING GOALS

After studying this chapter, you should be able to:

LG 1 Understanding portfolio management objectives and the procedures to calculate the return and standard deviation of a portfolio.

LG 2 Discuss the concepts of correlation and diversification, and the effectiveness, methods, and benefits of international diversification.

LG 3 Describe the two components of risk, beta, and the capital asset pricing model (CAPM).

LG 4 Review traditional and modern approaches to portfolio management and reconcile them.

LG 5 Describe the role of investor characteristics and objectives and of portfolio objectives and policies in constructing an investment portfolio.

LG 6 Summarize why and how investors use an asset allocation scheme to construct an investment portfolio.

Principles of Portfolio Planning

LG 1   LG 2

growth-oriented portfolio
a portfolio whose primary objective is long-term price appreciation.

income-oriented portfolio
a portfolio that stresses current dividend and interest returns.

efficient portfolio
a portfolio that provides the highest return for a given level of risk or that has the lowest risk for a given level of return.

Investors benefit from holding portfolios of investments rather than single investment vehicles. Without sacrificing returns, investors who hold portfolios can reduce risk, often to a level below that of any of the investments held in isolation. In other words, when it comes to risk, $1 + 1 < 1$.

As defined in Chapter 1, a portfolio is a collection of investment vehicles assembled to meet one or more investment goals. Of course, different investors have different objectives for their portfolios. The primary goal of a **growth-oriented portfolio** is long-term price appreciation. An **income-oriented portfolio** stresses current dividend and interest returns.

Portfolio Objectives

Setting portfolio objectives involves definite tradeoffs: tradeoffs between risk and return, between potential price appreciation and current income, and between varying risk levels in the portfolio. These will depend on your tax bracket, current income needs, and ability to bear risk. The key point is that the portfolio objectives must be established *before* beginning to invest.

The ultimate goal of an investor is an **efficient portfolio,** one that provides the highest return for a given level of risk or that has the lowest risk for a given level of return. Thus, given the choice between two equally risky investments offering different returns, the investor would be expected to choose the one with the higher return. Likewise, given two vehicles offering the same returns but differing in risk, the *risk-averse* investor would prefer the one with the lower risk. Efficient portfolios aren't necessarily obvious: Investors usually must search out investment alternatives to get the best combinations of risk and return.

 ## Portfolio Return and Standard Deviation

The return on a portfolio is calculated as a weighted average of returns on the assets (investment vehicles) from which it is formed. The portfolio return, r_p, can be found by using Equation 5.1:

Equation 5.1

$$\begin{array}{l} \text{Return} \\ \text{on} \\ \text{portfolio} \end{array} = \left(\begin{array}{l} \text{Proportion of} \\ \text{portfolio's total} \\ \text{dollar value} \\ \text{represented by} \\ \text{asset 1} \end{array} \times \begin{array}{l} \text{Return} \\ \text{on asset} \\ 1 \end{array} \right) + \left(\begin{array}{l} \text{Proportion of} \\ \text{portfolio's total} \\ \text{dollar value} \\ \text{represented by} \\ \text{asset 2} \end{array} \times \begin{array}{l} \text{Return} \\ \text{on asset} \\ 2 \end{array} \right) + \cdots +$$

$$\left(\begin{array}{l} \text{Proportion of} \\ \text{portfolio's total} \\ \text{dollar value} \\ \text{represented by} \\ \text{asset } n \end{array} \times \begin{array}{l} \text{Return} \\ \text{on asset} \\ n \end{array} \right) = \sum_{j=1}^{n} \left(\begin{array}{l} \text{Proportion of} \\ \text{portfolio's total} \\ \text{dollar value} \\ \text{represented by} \\ \text{asset } j \end{array} \times \begin{array}{l} \text{Return} \\ \text{on asset} \\ j \end{array} \right)$$

Equation 5.1a

$$r_p = (w_1 \times r_1) + (w_2 \times r_2) + \cdots + (w_n \times r_n) = \sum_{j=1}^{n} (w_j \times r_j)$$

TABLE 5.1   Expected Return, Average Return, and Standard Deviation of Returns for Portfolio XY

A. Expected Portfolio Returns

	(1)	(2)	(3)	(4)
	Expected Return			Expected Portfolio Return, r_p
Year	Asset X	Asset Y	Portfolio Return Calculation*	
2003	8%	16%	$(.50 \times 8\%) + (.50 \times 16\%) =$	12%
2004	10	14	$(.50 \times 10) + (.50 \times 14) =$	12
2005	12	12	$(.50 \times 12) + (.50 \times 12) =$	12
2006	14	10	$(.50 \times 14) + (.50 \times 10) =$	12
2007	16	8	$(.50 \times 16) + (.50 \times 8) =$	12

B. Average Expected Portfolio Return, 2003–2007

$$\bar{r}_p = \frac{12\% + 12\% + 12\% + 12\% + 12\%}{5} = \frac{60\%}{5} = \underline{\underline{12\%}}$$

C. Standard Deviation of Expected Portfolio Returns**

$$s_p = \sqrt{\frac{(12\% - 12\%)^2 + (12\% - 12\%)^2 + (12\% - 12\%)^2 + (12\% - 12\%)^2 + (12\% - 12\%)^2}{5 - 1}}$$

$$= \sqrt{\frac{0\% + 0\% + 0\% + 0\% + 0\%}{4}} = \sqrt{\frac{0\%}{4}} = \underline{\underline{0\%}}$$

*Using Equation 5.1.
**Using Equation 4.10 presented in Chapter 4.

Of course, $\sum_{j=1}^{n} w_j = 1$, which means that 100% of the portfolio's assets must be included in this computation.

The *standard deviation of a portfolio's returns* is found by applying Equation 4.10, the formula we used to find the standard deviation of a single asset. Assume that we wish to determine the return and standard deviation of returns for Portfolio XY, created by combining equal portions (50%) of assets X and Y. The expected returns of assets X and Y for each of the next 5 years (2003–2007) are given in columns 1 and 2, in part A of Table 5.1. In columns 3 and 4, the weights of 50% for both assets X and Y, along with their respective returns from columns 1 and 2, are substituted into Equation 5.1 to get an expected portfolio return of 12% for each year, 2003 to 2007. As shown in part B of Table 5.1, the average expected portfolio return, $\bar{r}_p$, over the 5-year period is also 12%. Substituting into Equation 4.10, we calculate Portfolio XY's standard deviation, s_p, of 0% in part C of Table 5.1. This value should not be surprising. Because the expected return each year is the same (12%), no variability is exhibited in the expected returns from year to year shown in column 4 of part A of the table.

The Correlation Between Series M, N, and P

The perfectly positively correlated series M and P in the graph on the left move exactly together. The perfectly negatively correlated series M and N in the graph on the right move in exactly opposite directions.

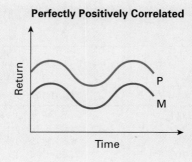

Perfectly Positively Correlated

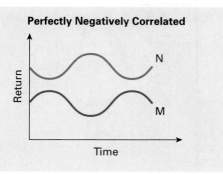

Perfectly Negatively Correlated

Correlation and Diversification

As noted in Chapter 2, *diversification* involves the inclusion of a number of different investment vehicles in a portfolio. It is an important aspect of creating an efficient portfolio. Underlying the intuitive appeal of diversification is the statistical concept of *correlation*. For effective portfolio planning, you need to understand the concepts of correlation and diversification and their relationship to a portfolio's total risk and return.

correlation
a statistical measure of the relationship, if any, between series of numbers representing data of any kind.

positively correlated
describes two series that move in the same direction.

negatively correlated
describes two series that move in opposite directions.

correlation coefficient
a measure of the degree of correlation between two series.

perfectly positively correlated
describes two positively correlated series that have a correlation coefficient of +1.

perfectly negatively correlated
describes two negatively correlated series that have a correlation coefficient of −1.

uncorrelated
describes two series that lack any relationship or interaction and therefore have a correlation coefficient close to zero.

Correlation Correlation is a statistical measure of the relationship, if any, between series of numbers representing data of any kind. If two series move in the same direction, they are **positively correlated.** If the series move in opposite directions, they are **negatively correlated.**

The degree of correlation—whether positive or negative—is measured by the **correlation coefficient.** The coefficient ranges from +1 for **perfectly positively correlated** series to −1 for **perfectly negatively correlated** series. These two extremes are depicted in Figure 5.1 for Series M, N, and P. The perfectly positively correlated series (M and P) move exactly together. The perfectly negatively correlated series (M and N) move in exactly opposite directions.

Diversification To reduce overall risk in a portfolio, it is best to combine assets that have a negative (or a low-positive) correlation. Combining negatively correlated assets can reduce the overall variability of returns, *s,* or risk. Figure 5.2 shows negatively correlated assets F and G, both having the same average expected return, $\bar{r}$. The portfolio that contains those negatively correlated assets also has the same return, $\bar{r}$, but has less risk (variability) than either of the individual assets. Even if assets are not negatively correlated, the lower the positive correlation between them, the lower the resulting risk.

Some assets are **uncorrelated:** They are completely unrelated, with no interaction between their returns. Combining uncorrelated assets can reduce risk—not as effectively as combining negatively correlated assets, but more effectively than combining positively correlated assets. The correlation coefficient for uncorrelated assets is close to zero and acts as the midpoint between perfect positive and perfect negative correlation.

Correlation is important to reducing risk, but it can do only so much. A portfolio of two assets that have perfectly positively correlated returns *cannot* reduce the portfolio's overall risk below the risk of the least risky asset.

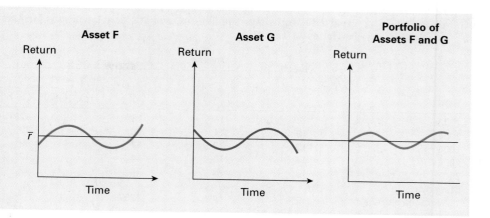

Source: Walter Updegrave, "Investing 101: Why Diversification Pays," *Money*, December 1999, p. 100.

FIGURE 5.2

Combining Negatively Correlated Assets to Diversify Risk

The risk or variability of returns, resulting from combining negatively correlated assets F and G, both having the same expected return, $\bar{r}$, results in a portfolio (shown in the rightmost graph) with the same level of expected return but less risk.

INVESTOR FACTS

"CORRELATIONSHIP" ADVICE—Most assets that individual investors own are positively correlated, although the extent of that correlation varies. Between 1989 and 1999, the S&P 500 index had a correlation of 0.79 with domestic small-caps (total market values). This high correlation would be expected, because both move in step with the U.S. economy. The S&P 500's correlation with foreign stocks is only 0.53 and is even lower (0.36) with intermediate-term government bonds.

However, a portfolio combining two assets with less than perfectly positive correlation *can* reduce total risk to a level below that of either of the components, which in certain situations may be zero.

For example, assume you own the stock of a machine tool manufacturer that is very *cyclical*. This company has high earnings when the economy is expanding and low earnings during a recession. If you bought stock in another machine tool company, which would have earnings positively correlated with those of the stock you already own, the combined earnings would continue to be cyclical. The risk would remain the same.

As an alternative, however, you could buy stock in a sewing machine manufacturer, which is *countercyclical*. It typically has low earnings during economic expansion and high earnings during recession. Combining the machine tool stock and the sewing machine stock should reduce risk: The low machine tool earnings during a recession would be balanced out by high sewing machine earnings, and vice versa.

A numeric example will provide an even better understanding. Table 5.2 presents the expected returns from three different assets—X, Y, and Z—over the next 5 years (2003–2007), along with their average returns and standard deviations. Each of the assets has an expected value of return of 12% and a standard deviation of 3.16%. The assets therefore have equal return and equal risk, although their return patterns are not identical. The returns of assets X and Y are perfectly negatively correlated, because they move in exactly opposite directions over time. The returns of assets X and Z are perfectly positively correlated: They move in precisely the same direction. (The returns for X and Z are identical, although it is not necessary for return streams to be identical in order for them to be perfectly positively correlated.)

Portfolio XY (shown in Table 5.2) combines equal portions of assets X and Y—the perfectly negatively correlated assets. Calculation of portfolio XY's annual expected returns, average expected return, and the standard deviation of expected portfolio returns was demonstrated in Table 5.1. The risk of the portfolio created by this combination, as reflected in the standard deviation, is reduced to 0%, while its average return remains at 12%. Because both assets have the same average return, are combined in the optimum proportions (a 50–50 mix in this case), and are perfectly negatively correlated, the combination results in the complete elimination of risk. Whenever assets are perfectly negatively correlated, an optimum combination (similar to this 50–50

TABLE 5.2   **Expected Returns, Average Returns, and Standard Deviations for Assets X, Y, and Z and Portfolios XY and XZ**

| Year | Assets | | | Portfolios | |
	X	Y	Z	XY* (50%X + 50%Y)	XZ** (50%X + 50%Z)
2003	8%	16%	8%	12%	8%
2004	10	14	10	12	10
2005	12	12	12	12	12
2006	14	10	14	12	14
2007	16	8	16	12	16
Statistics:					
Average return[†]	12%	12%	12%	12%	12%
Standard deviation[‡]	3.16%	3.16%	3.16%	0%	3.16%

*Portfolio XY illustrates *perfect negative correlation,* because these two return streams behave in completely opposite fashion over the 5-year period. The return values shown here were calculated in part A of Table 5.1.

**Portfolio XZ illustrates *perfect positive correlation,* because these two return streams behave identically over the 5-year period. These return values were calculated using the same method demonstrated for Portfolio XY in part A of Table 5.1.

[†]The average return for each asset is calculated as the arithmetic average found by dividing the sum of the returns for the years 2003–2007 by 5, the number of years considered.

[‡]Equation 4.10 was used to calculate the standard deviation. Calculation of the average return and standard deviation for portfolio XY is demonstrated in parts B and C, respectively, of Table 5.1. The portfolio standard deviation can be directly calculated from the standard deviation of the component assets using the following formula:

$$s_p = \sqrt{w_1^2 s_1^2 + w_2^2 s_2^2 + 2w_1 w_2 p_{1,2} s_1 s_2}$$

where w_1 and w_2 are the proportions of the component assets 1 and 2; s_1 and s_2 are the standard deviations of the component assets 1 and 2; and $p_{1,2}$ is the correlation coefficient between the returns of component assets 1 and 2.

mix in assets X and Y) exists for which the resulting standard deviation will equal 0.

Portfolio XZ (shown in Table 5.2) is created by combining equal portions of Assets X and Z—the perfectly positively correlated assets. The risk of this portfolio, reflected by its standard deviation, which remains at 3.16%, is unaffected by this combination. Its average return remains at 12%. Whenever perfectly positively correlated assets such as X and Z are combined, the standard deviation of the resulting portfolio cannot be reduced below that of the least risky asset; the maximum portfolio standard deviation will be that of the riskiest asset. Because assets X and Z have the same standard deviation (3.16%), the minimum and maximum standard deviations are both 3.16%, which is the only value that could be taken on by a combination of these assets.

Impact on Risk and Return   In general, the lower (less positive and more negative) the correlation between asset returns, the greater the potential diversification of risk. For each pair of assets, there is a combination that will result in the lowest risk (standard deviation) possible. *The amount of potential risk reduction for this combination depends on the degree of correlation of the two assets.* Many potential combinations could be made, given the expected return of the two assets, the standard deviation for each, and the correlation coefficient. However, *only one combination* of the infinite number of possibilities will minimize risk.

Three possible correlations—perfect positive, uncorrelated, and perfect negative—illustrate the effect of correlation on the diversification of risk and return. Table 5.3 summarizes the impact of correlation on the range of return and risk. The table shows that as you move from perfect positive correlation to perfect negative correlation, you reduce risk. Note that in no case will a portfolio of assets have risk greater than that of the riskiest asset included in the portfolio.

To demonstrate, assume that a firm has carefully calculated the average return, $\bar{r}$, and risk, s, for each of two assets, A and B, as summarized below.

Asset	Average Return, $\bar{r}$	Risk (Standard Deviation), s
A	6%	3%
B	8%	8%

From these data, we can see that asset A is clearly a lower-risk, lower-return asset than asset B.

To evaluate possible combinations, let's consider three possible correlations: perfect positive, uncorrelated, and perfect negative. The results are shown in Figure 5.3. The ranges of return and risk exhibited are consistent with those in Table 5.3. In all cases, the return will range between the 6% return of A and the 8% return of B. The risk, on the other hand, has a wider variability. That variability depends on the degree of correlation: In the case of perfect positive correlation, the risk ranges between the individual risks of A and B (from 3% to 8%). In the uncorrelated case, the risk ranges from below 3% (the risk of A) but greater than 0%, to 8% (the risk of B). In the case of perfect negative correlation, the risk ranges between 0% and 8%.

Note that *only in the case of perfect negative correlation can the risk be reduced to 0%*. As the correlation becomes less positive and more negative (moving from the top of Figure 5.3 down), the ability to reduce risk improves. Keep in mind that the amount of risk reduction achieved also depends on the proportions in which the assets are combined. Although determining the risk-minimizing combination is beyond the scope of this discussion, you should know that it is an important issue in developing portfolios of assets.

TABLE 5.3 **Correlation, Return, and Risk for Various Two-Asset Portfolio Combinations**

Correlation Coefficient	Range of Return	Range of Risk
+1 (perfect positive)	Between returns of two assets held in isolation	Between risk of two assets held in isolation
0 (uncorrelated)	Between returns of two assets held in isolation	Between risk of most risky asset and less than risk of least risky asset, but greater than 0
−1 (perfect negative)	Between returns of two assets held in isolation	Between risk of most risky asset and 0

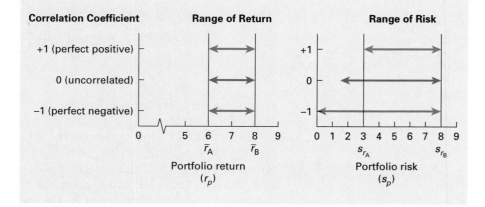

FIGURE 5.3

Range of Portfolio Return and Risk for Combinations of Assets A and B for Various Correlation Coefficients

The range of a portfolio's return (r_p) is between that of the lowest and highest component asset returns and is unaffected by the degree of asset correlation. Portfolio risk (s_p), on the other hand, can be reduced below the risk of the least risky asset as the asset correlation moves from perfectly positive to uncorrelated to perfectly negative, where it can be reduced to zero by combining assets in the proper proportion.

 International Diversification

Diversification is clearly a primary consideration when constructing an investment portfolio. Thus far, our focus and examples have been basically domestic. However, as noted earlier, many opportunities for international diversification are now available. Here we consider three aspects of international diversification: effectiveness, methods, and benefits.

Effectiveness of International Diversification Investing internationally obviously offers greater diversification than investing only domestically. That is true for U.S. investors. It is even truer for investors from countries with capital markets that offer much more limited diversification opportunities than are available in the United States.

However, does international diversification actually reduce risk, particularly the variability of rates of return? Two earlier studies overwhelmingly support the argument that well-structured international diversification does indeed reduce the risk of a portfolio and increase the return on portfolios of comparable risk. One study looked at diversification across 12 European countries in 7 different industries between 1978 and 1992. It demonstrated that an investor could actually reduce the risk of a portfolio much more by diversifying internationally *in the same industry* than by diversifying across industries within one country. If the investor diversified both across countries and across industries, the opportunities for risk reduction would be even greater.

Another study examined the risk-return performance between January 1984 and November 1994 of diversified stock portfolios: the S&P 500 in the United States and Morgan Stanley's Europe/Australia/Far East (EAFE) Index. It found that a 100% EAFE portfolio offered a much greater return than a

100% S&P 500 portfolio did—but at much greater risk. However, a portfolio composed of various combinations of the two indexes would have been better: It would have realized both lower risk and a higher return than for the 100% S&P 500 portfolio, and less risk and a moderately lower return than for the 100% EAFE portfolio. For the U.S. investor, a portfolio consisting of 70% S&P 500 coupled with 30% EAFE would have reduced risk by about 5% and increased return by about 7% (from around 14% to more than 15%). Or, for the same degree of risk, an investor could have increased return by about 18% (from around 14% to more than 16.5%).

Methods of International Diversification In later chapters we will examine a wide range of alternatives for international portfolio diversification. We will see that investments in bonds and other debt instruments can be made abroad in U.S. dollars or in foreign currencies—either directly or via foreign mutual funds. Foreign currency investment, however, brings currency exchange risk. This risk can be hedged using various contracts, most commonly currency forwards, futures, and options.

Investing abroad, even if there is little or no currency exchange risk, is generally less convenient, more expensive, and riskier than investing domestically. When making direct investments abroad, you must know what you're doing: You should have a clear idea of the benefits being sought and should have the time to monitor foreign markets.

International diversification can also be achieved by U.S. domestic investments. Several hundred foreign companies list their stocks on U.S. exchanges or over the counter; most of them are Canadian companies. Also, many foreign issuers, both corporate and government, sell their bonds (called *Yankee bonds*) in the United States. The stocks of about 1,200 foreign companies, from about 40 countries, trade in the United States in the form of American Depositary Receipts. Finally, international mutual funds (such as the Fidelity Japan Fund and the Prudential Global Fund) provide investors with a broad range of foreign investment opportunities. These domestic alternatives offer the advantages of convenience and low cost, often with less risk than investments made directly abroad.

It is important to realize that international diversification typically cannot be achieved by investing in U.S. multinationals. In spite of the fact that U.S.-based firms with major foreign operations may generate sizable revenues and profits abroad, most of their costs and expenses—particularly labor costs—are incurred in the United States. The net result is that the firm's behavior tends to be more U.S.-driven than foreign-driven. The multinational firm's results tend to be positively correlated with those in the domestic market, thereby resulting in low diversification. The strategy of investing in domestic companies that have major foreign operations therefore is generally not as effective as investing directly in foreign companies in the given country.

Benefits of International Diversification Can greater returns be found overseas than in the United States? Yes! Can a portfolio's risk be reduced by including foreign investments? Yes! Is international diversification desirable for you? We don't know! A successful global investment strategy depends on many things, just as a purely domestic strategy does. Included are factors such as your resources, goals, sophistication, and psychology. What percentage of your portfolio you allocate to foreign investments depends on your overall

INVESTING in action

Why Venture Abroad?

Why venture abroad, say many U.S. investors, when stock returns on domestic companies have been so high recently? Overseas investments are risky, involving currency fluctuations and political risk.

Yet returns in U.S. markets may not always be the highest. From 1979 to 1989, for example, average annual returns for the Morgan Stanley Capital International Europe Asia and Far East (EAFE) index were 23%, compared with 17.6% for the (domestic) S&P 500. Despite lackluster gains on international investments in the 1990s, the global economy appears poised for significant growth as foreign economies recover from recessions.

"We [Americans] are the most myopic investors in the world, arguably for a good reason," said John J. Brennan, chairman and chief executive of the Vanguard Group. "We have this huge capital market. You can diversify all sorts of ways. . . . But to think that American companies have a lock on success in the future [and that] the American economy will have a lock on growth in the future is naive."

In fact, investing abroad may be a better long-term strategy now than in past years. In 1970, U.S. stock markets represented about two-thirds of the global $1 trillion stock market. Today the worldwide stock market is about $32 trillion, but the U.S. share is down to about half. In the new, tightly linked, technology-dominated world economy, national borders mean less than ever before.

Investment professionals recommend a different approach to international investing today, however. Diversification used to be the primary reason for making foreign investments: If U.S. markets slipped, foreign markets would provide balance and higher returns. Because the major world stock markets tend to move together now, owning non-U.S. stocks doesn't provide the protection it once did.

There are other compelling reasons to include international stocks in your portfolio, however. You may have to look outside the United States to buy stock in worldwide industry leaders. This is particularly true in heavily global sectors like telecommunications, technology, pharmaceuticals, and energy. For example, Finland's Nokia has a 37% share of the U.S. cellular market.

Rather than diversifying by country or region, investors should diversify across industries. "The best way to make money is to pick the best companies and the best businesses, rather than putting 4% of the portfolio in Europe or 5% in Japan," said William Wilby, a portfolio manager with Oppenheimer Funds Inc.

Some investors believe that they can minimize risk by investing in U.S. multinationals to achieve global diversification. This strategy can be restrictive and eliminates solid foreign companies like BMW, Nokia, Nestle, and Sony. "If you choose to buy those products in your daily life," says David Antonelli, international research director for MFS Investment Management in Boston, "why would you limit your ability to invest in those companies?"

If you are not comfortable buying individual company shares, you can use mutual funds to create a global portfolio. Many mutual fund managers follow a global industry sector strategy, and you will find that foreign companies are well represented in sector funds specializing in technology, health care, and other major industry categories.

Sources: Fred Barbash, "Foreign Funds an Answer to Slide in U.S.," *Washington Post*, October 8, 2000, p. H1; Mara der Hovanesian, "So Who Needs Foreign Investing?" *Business Week*, September 11, 2000, p. 166, E12–14; Christopher Farrell, "The New Global Investor," *Business Week*, September 11, 2000, pp. 160–162; and Erika Gonzalez, "International Investors Optimistic," *Denver Rocky Mountain News*, September 19, 2000, downloaded from Electric Library, Business Edition, business.elibrary.com

investment goals and risk preferences. Commonly cited allocations to foreign investments are around 30%, with about two-thirds of this allocation in established foreign markets and the other one-third in emerging markets.

In general, you should avoid investing directly in foreign-currency-denominated instruments. Unless the magnitude of each foreign investment is in hundreds of thousands of dollars, the transactions costs will tend to be high, not just when you are buying and selling but especially when dividends or interest are paid. Therefore, for most investors looking for international diversification, the optimal vehicles are available in the United States. International mutual funds offer diversified foreign investments, coupled with the professional investment expertise of fund managers. ADRs can be used by those who want to make foreign investments in individual stocks. With either mutual funds or ADRs, you can obtain international diversification along with low cost, convenience, transactions in U.S. dollars, protection under U.S. security laws, and (usually) attractive markets (although some ADRs have thin markets).

We shouldn't leave this topic without saying that some of the benefits of international diversification are diminishing over time. Technological advances in communication have greatly improved the quality of information on foreign companies. In addition, new markets and expanded trading hours have improved access to foreign investments. Participation by a growing number of better-informed investors in the foreign markets continues to reduce the opportunities to earn "excess" returns on the additional risk embodied in foreign investments, thereby leveling the playing field for global investors. Although the opportunities to earn excess returns on foreign investments are shrinking, the relatively low correlation of returns in Asian and emerging markets with U.S. returns continues to make international investments appealing as a way to diversify your portfolio. Foreign investments continue to provide greater risk reduction than domestic investments. Clearly, today an important motive for international investment is portfolio diversification rather than realizing sizable excess returns. The *Investing in Action* box on page 184 presents some strategies for international investing in the new millennium.

IN REVIEW

CONCEPTS

5.1 What is an *efficient portfolio,* and what role should such a portfolio play in investing?

5.2 How can the return and standard deviation of a portfolio be determined? Compare the portfolio standard deviation calculation to that for a single asset.

5.3 What is *correlation,* and why is it important with respect to asset returns? Describe the characteristics of returns that are (a) positively correlated, (b) negatively correlated, and (c) uncorrelated. Differentiate between *perfect positive correlation* and *perfect negative correlation.*

5.4 What is *diversification?* How does the diversification of risk affect the risk of the portfolio compared to the risk of the individual assets it contains?

5.5 Discuss how the correlation between asset returns affects the risk and return behavior of the resulting portfolio. Describe the potential range of risk and return when the correlation between two assets is (a) perfectly positive, (b) uncorrelated, and (c) perfectly negative.

5.6   What benefit, if any, does international diversification offer the individual investor? Compare and contrast the methods of achieving international diversification by investing abroad versus investing domestically.

5.7   According to the *Investing in Action* box on page 184, what are some of the international investment strategies recommended for the new millenium? Which are most appealing to individual investors like you?

The Capital Asset Pricing Model (CAPM)

LG 3

From an investor's perspective, the most important aspect of risk is the *overall risk* of the firm. This overall risk significantly affects the returns earned and the value of the firm in the financial marketplace. Clearly, as we'll learn in Chapter 8, the firm's value is directly determined by its risk and the associated return. The basic theory that links return and risk for all assets is the *capital asset pricing model (CAPM)*.

Components of Risk

The risk of an investment consists of two components: diversifiable and nondiversifiable risk. **Diversifiable risk,** sometimes called **unsystematic risk,** results from uncontrollable or random events that are firm-specific, such as labor strikes, lawsuits, and regulatory actions. It is the portion of an investment's risk that can be eliminated through diversification. **Nondiversifiable risk,** also called **systematic risk,** is attributed to more general forces such as war, inflation, and political events that affect all investments and therefore are not unique to a given vehicle. The sum of nondiversifiable risk and diversifiable risk is called **total risk.**

diversifiable (unsystematic) risk
the portion of an investment's risk that results from uncontrollable or random events that are firm-specific; can be eliminated through diversification.

Equation 5.2

Total risk = Nondiversifiable risk + Diversifiable risk

Any careful investor can reduce or virtually eliminate diversifiable risk by holding a diversified portfolio of securities. Studies have shown that investors can eliminate most diversifiable risk by carefully selecting a portfolio of 8 to 15 securities. Therefore, *the only relevant risk is nondiversifiable risk,* which is inescapable. Each security has its own unique level of nondiversifiable risk, which we can measure, as we'll show in the following section.

nondiversifiable (systematic) risk
the inescapable portion of an investment's risk attributable to forces that affect all investments and therefore are not unique to a given vehicle.

Beta: A Popular Measure of Risk

During the past 35 years much theory has been developed on the measurement of risk and its use in assessing returns. The two key components of this theory are *beta,* which is a measure of risk, and the *capital asset pricing model (CAPM),* which uses beta to estimate return.

First we will look at **beta,** a number that measures *nondiversifiable,* or *market, risk.* Beta indicates how the price of a security responds to market forces. The more responsive the price of a security is to changes in the market,

total risk
the sum of an investment's nondiversifiable risk and diversifiable risk.

beta
a measure of *nondiversifiable,* or *market, risk* that indicates how the price of a security responds to market forces.

market return
the average return on all (or a
large sample of) stocks, such as
those in the *Standard & Poor's
500 Stock Composite Index.*

the higher that security's beta. Beta is found by relating the historical returns
for a security to the market return. **Market return** is the average return for all
(or a large sample of) stocks. The average return on all stocks in the *Standard
& Poor's 500 Stock Composite Index* or some other broad stock index is commonly used to measure market return. You don't have to calculate betas yourself; you can easily obtain them for actively traded securities from a variety of
published and online sources. But you should understand how betas are
derived, how to interpret them, and how to apply them to portfolios.

Deriving Beta The relationship between a security's return and the market
return, and its use in deriving beta, can be demonstrated graphically. Figure
5.4 plots the relationship between the returns of two securities, C and D, and
the market return. Note that the horizontal (*x*) axis measures the market
return, and the vertical (*y*) axis measures the individual security's returns.

The first step in deriving beta is plotting the coordinates for the market
return and the security return at various points in time. Such annual market-
return and security-return coordinates are shown in Figure 5.4 for security D for
the years 1995 through 2002 (the years are noted in parentheses). For example,
in 2002 security D's return was 20% when the market return was 10%.

FIGURE 5.4

**Graphical Derivation of
Beta for Securities C and D***

Betas can be derived graphically
by plotting the coordinates for
the market return and security
return at various points in time
and using statistical techniques
to fit the "characteristic line" to
the data points. The slope of
the characteristic line is beta.
For securities C and D, beta is
found to be 0.80 and 1.30,
respectively.

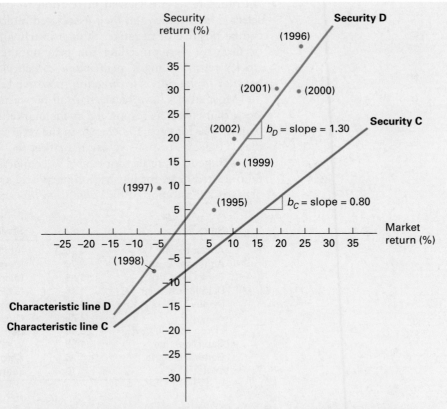

* All data points shown are associated with security D. No data points are shown for
  security C.

TABLE 5.4 Selected Betas and Associated Interpretions

Beta	Comment	Interpretation
2.00 1.00 0.50	Move in same direction as the market	Twice as responsive as the market / Same response as the market / Only half as responsive as the market
0		Unaffected by market movement
−0.50 −1.00 −2.00	Move in opposite direction from the market	Only half as responsive as the market / Same response as the market / Twice as responsive as the market

By use of statistical techniques, the "characteristic line" that best explains the relationship between security-return and market-return coordinates is fit to the data points. *The slope of this line is beta.* The beta for security C is about 0.80; for security D it is about 1.30. Security D's higher beta (steeper characteristic line slope) indicates that its return is more responsive to changing market returns. *Therefore security D is more risky than security C.*

Interpreting Beta The beta for the overall market is considered to be 1.00. All other betas are viewed in relation to this value. Table 5.4 shows some selected beta values and their associated interpretations. As you can see, betas can be positive or negative, though nearly all betas are positive. The positive or negative sign preceding the beta number merely indicates whether the stock's return changes in the *same direction as the general market* (positive beta) or in the *opposite direction* (negative beta).

Most stocks have betas that fall between 0.50 and 1.75. The return of a stock that is half as responsive as the market ($b = 0.50$) is expected to change by ½ of 1% for each 1% change in the return of the market portfolio. A stock that is twice as responsive as the market ($b = 2.0$) is expected to experience a 2% change in its return for each 1% change in the return of the market portfolio. Listed here, for illustration purposes, are the actual betas for some popular stocks, as reported by *Value Line Investment Survey* on May 11, 2001:

Stock	Beta	Stock	Beta
Amazon.com	1.80	Int'l Business Machines	1.00
Anheuser-Busch	0.70	Merrill Lynch & Co.	1.85
Bank One Corp.	1.25	Microsoft	1.10
Daimler Chrysler AG	1.15	NIKE, Inc.	0.90
Disney	0.95	PepsiCo, Inc.	0.80
eBay	2.25	Quaker Oats	0.60
Exxon Mobile Corp.	0.80	Sempra Energy	0.55
Gap (The), Inc.	1.55	Wal-Mart Stores	1.15
General Electric	1.25	Xerox	1.05
Intel	1.10	Yahoo! Inc.	1.80

Many large brokerage firms, as well as subscription services like *Value Line,* publish betas for a broad range of securities. They also can be obtained online through sites such as yahoo.com. The ready availability of security

CHAPTER 5 | MODERN PORTFOLIO CONCEPTS

MUTUAL FUNDS HAVE BETAS, TOO—For mutual funds, beta can be an important factor in an investor's decision to buy. If you had checked *Morningstar.com* on November 15, 2000, you would have found that the Dreyfus Premier Technology Growth Fund A, for example, had a beta of 1.54, as you might expect from a fund investing in technology companies. Its beta of 1.54 means that it is about 50% more volatile than the market—in this case, the S&P 500—which is always assigned a beta of 1.00. Another fund from the same family, Dreyfus Appreciation, is less risky than the market, with a beta of 0.87.

betas has enhanced their use in assessing investment risks. The importance of beta in planning and building portfolios of securities will be discussed later in this chapter.

Applying Beta Individual investors will find beta useful. It can help in assessing market risk and in understanding the impact the market can have on the return expected from a share of stock. In short, beta reveals how a security responds to market forces. For example, if the market is expected to experience a 10% *increase* in its rate of return over the next period, we would expect a stock with a beta of 1.50 to experience an *increase* in return of about 15% ($1.50 \times 10\%$). Because its beta is greater than 1.00, this stock is more volatile than the market as a whole.

For stocks with positive betas, increases in market returns result in increases in security returns. Unfortunately, decreases in market returns are translated into decreasing security returns. In the preceding example, if the market is expected to experience a 10% *decrease*, then a stock with a beta of 1.50 should experience a 15% *decrease* in its return. Because the stock has a beta greater than 1.00, it is more responsive than the market, either up or down.

Stocks that have betas less than 1.00 are, of course, less responsive to changing returns in the market. They are therefore considered less risky. For example, a stock with a beta of 0.50 will increase or decrease its return by about half that of the market as a whole. Thus, if the market went down by 8%, such a stock would probably experience only about a 4% ($0.50 \times 8\%$) decline.

Here are some important points to remember about beta:

- Beta measures the nondiversifiable (or market) risk of a security.
- The beta for the market is 1.00.
- Stocks may have positive or negative betas. Nearly all are positive.
- Stocks with betas greater than 1.00 are more responsive to changes in the market return and therefore are more risky than the market. Stocks with betas less than 1.00 are less risky than the market.
- Because of its greater risk, the higher a stock's beta, the greater should be its level of expected return.

 ## The CAPM: Using Beta to Estimate Return

capital asset pricing model (CAPM)
model that formally links the notions of risk and return; it uses beta, the risk-free rate, and the market return to help investors define the required return on an investment.

About 35 years ago, finance professors William F. Sharpe and John Lintner developed a model that uses beta to formally link the notions of risk and return. Called the **capital asset pricing model (CAPM)**, it explains the behavior of security prices. It also provides a mechanism whereby investors can assess the impact of a proposed security investment on their portfolio's risk and return.

The CAPM can be viewed both as an equation and as a graph.

 The Equation With beta, *b*, as the measure of nondiversifiable risk, the capital asset pricing model defines the required return on an investment as follows.

Equation 5.3

$$\text{Required return on investment } j = \text{Risk-free rate} + \left[\text{Beta for investment } j \times \left(\text{Market return} - \text{Risk-free rate} \right) \right]$$

Equation 5.3a

$$r_j = R_F + [b_j \times (r_m - R_F)]$$

where

r_j = the required return on investment j, given its risk as measured by beta

R_F = the risk-free rate of return; the return that can be earned on a risk-free investment

b_j = beta coefficient, or index of nondiversifiable risk, for investment j

r_m = the market return; the average return on all securities (typically measured by the average return on all securities in the Standard & Poor's 500 Stock Composite Index or some other broad stock market index)

The equation shows that *as beta increases, the required return for a given investment increases.*

Application of the CAPM can be demonstrated with the following example. Assume you are considering security Z with a beta (b_Z) of 1.25. The risk-free rate (R_F) is 6% and the market return (r_m) is 10%. Substituting these data into the CAPM equation, Equation 5.3a, we get:

$$r_z = 6\% + [1.25 \times (10\% - 6\%)] = 6\% + [1.25 \times 4\%]$$

$$= 6\% + 5\% = \underline{11\%}$$

You should therefore expect—indeed, require—an 11% return on this investment as compensation for the risk you have to assume, given the security's beta of 1.25.

If the beta were lower, say 1.00, the required return would be lower:

$$r_z = 6\% + [1.00 \times (10\% - 6\%)] = 6\% + 4\% = \underline{10\%}$$

If the beta were higher, say 1.50, the required return would be higher:

$$r_z = 6\% + [1.50 \times (10\% - 6\%)] = 6\% + 6\% = \underline{12\%}$$

Clearly, the CAPM reflects the positive mathematical relationship between risk and return, because the higher the risk (beta), the higher the required return.

The Graph: The Security Market Line (SML) When the capital asset pricing model is depicted graphically, it is called the **security market line (SML)**. Plotting the CAPM, we would find that the SML is, in fact, a straight line. For each level of nondiversifiable risk (beta), the SML reflects the required return the investor should earn in the marketplace.

The CAPM at a given point in time can be plotted by simply calculating the required return for a variety of betas. For example, as we saw earlier, using a 6%

security market line (SML)
the graphical depiction of the capital asset pricing model; reflects the investor's required return for each level of nondiversifiable risk, measured by beta.

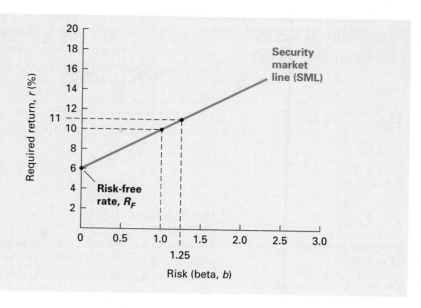

FIGURE 5.5

The Security Market Line (SML)

The security market line clearly depicts the tradeoff between risk and return. At a beta of 0, the required return is the risk-free rate of 6%. At a beta of 1.0, the required return is the market return of 10%. Given these data, the required return on an investment with a beta of 1.25 is 11%.

HOT LINKS

You can find the betas for various companies at the Marketguide site. Under [Search for], click on [Symb] and, in the empty box, type in the stock symbol for a company. You can also calculate the beta of a portfolio of stocks at this site.

www.marketguide.com

risk-free rate and a 10% market return, the required return is 11% when the beta is 1.25. Increase the beta to 2.00, and the required return equals 14% (6% + [2.00 × (10% − 6%)]). Similarly, we can find the required return for a number of betas and end up with the following combinations of risk (beta) and required return.

Risk (beta)	Required Return
0.0	6%
0.5	8
1.0	10
1.5	12
2.0	14
2.5	16

Plotting these values on a graph (with beta on the horizontal axis and required returns on the vertical axis) would yield a straight line like the one in Figure 5.5. It is clear from the SML that as risk (beta) increases, so does the required return, and vice versa.

IN REVIEW

CONCEPTS

5.8 Briefly define and give examples of each of the following components of total risk. Which is the relevant risk, and why?
 a. Diversifiable risk   b. Nondiversifiable risk

5.9 Explain what is meant by *beta*. What is the relevant risk measured by beta? What is the *market return?* How is the interpretation of beta related to the market return?

5.10 What range of values does beta typically exhibit? Are positive or negative betas more common? Explain.

5.11 What is the *capital asset pricing model (CAPM)?* What role does beta play in it? How is the *security market line (SML)* related to the CAPM?

Traditional versus Modern Portfolio

Two approaches are currently used by individual and institutional investors to plan and construct their portfolios. The *traditional approach* refers to the less quantitative methods that investors have been using since the evolution of the public securities markets. *Modern portfolio theory (MPT)* is a more recent, more mathematical development that continues to grow in popularity and acceptance. Some MPT concepts are indirectly used by practitioners of the traditional approach, yet there are major differences between the two.

The Traditional Approach

traditional portfolio management
an approach to portfolio management that emphasizes "balancing" the portfolio by assembling a wide variety of stocks and/or bonds of companies from a broad range of industries.

Traditional portfolio management emphasizes "balancing" the portfolio by assembling a wide variety of stocks and/or bonds. The typical emphasis is *interindustry diversification*. This produces a portfolio with securities of companies from a broad range of industries. Traditional portfolios are constructed using the security analysis techniques discussed in Chapters 7 and 8.

Table 5.5 presents the industry groupings and the percentages invested in them by a typical mutual fund that is managed by professionals using the traditional approach. This fund, the Pilgrim Growth Opportunities Fund, is an open-end mutual fund. The portfolio's value at December 31, 2000, was approximately $728 million. Its objective is to seek long-term growth of capital by investing in the common stock of U.S. companies with above average prospects for growth. The Pilgrim Growth Opportunities Fund holds shares of 97 different stocks from 27 industries, as well as some short-term investments.

Analyzing the stock position of the Pilgrim Growth Opportunities Fund, which accounts for 98% of the fund's total assets, we observe the traditional approach to portfolio management at work. This fund holds numerous stocks from a broad cross section of the total universe of available stocks. The stocks are a mix of large and small companies. By far the largest industry group is telecommunications, with 11.93% of the total portfolio. The fund's largest individual holding is BEA Systems, Inc., a provider of e-commerce infrastructure software, which accounts for only 1.94% of the total portfolio. Bristol-Myers Squibb Co., a major producer and distributor of medicines, ranks second, at 1.90%. The third largest holding—1.83%—is Brocade Communication Systems, Inc., a provider of storage area networking infrastructure solutions. Although most of the fund's 97 stocks are those of small companies, in addition to Bristol-Myers Squibb Co., it does include stocks of some major companies, such as America Online, Inc., Gap, Inc., Genentech Inc., and Starbucks Corp.

Those who manage traditional portfolios want to invest in well-known companies for three reasons. First, because these are known as successful business enterprises, investing in them is perceived as less risky than investing in lesser-known firms. Second, the securities of large firms are more liquid and are available in large quantities. Third, institutional investors prefer successful well-known companies because it is easier to convince clients to invest in them. Called *window dressing*, this practice of loading up a portfolio, particularly at the end of a reporting period, with successful well-known stocks makes it easier for institutional investors to sell their services.

TABLE 5.5	Portfolio of Pilgrim Growth Opportunities Fund, December 31, 2000

The Pilgrim Growth Opportunities Funds appears to adhere to the traditional approach to portfolio management. Its total portfolio value is about $728 million, of which 98% ($713 million) is common stock, including 97 different stocks in 27 industry groupings, plus about 3% ($24 million) in short-term investments, and about −1% (−$9 million) in net liabilities.

Pilgrim Growth Opportunities Fund
Investments by Industry Group
as of December 31, 2000

Industry Group	Percentage	Industry Group	Percentage
Common Stocks	**98.00%**	Internet	0.80%
Apparel	0.94	Leisure time	1.55
Banks	4.72	Machinery—diversified	1.32
Biotechnology	5.61	Media	3.78
Chemicals	0.46	Miscellaneous manufacturing	0.85
Commercial services	0.77	Oil & gas producers	6.48
Computers	5.18	Oil & gas services	1.30
Cosmetics/Personal Care	0.47	Pharmaceuticals	8.53
Diversified financial services	1.41	Pipelines	2.76
Electric	5.24	Retail	4.56
Electronics	1.92	Semiconductors	4.23
Forest products & paper	1.04	Software	8.07
Healthcare—products	1.20	Telecommunications	11.93
Healthcare—services	7.45	**Short-Term Investments**	**3.24**
Insurance	5.43	**Net Liabilities**	**−1.24**

Source: ING Pilgrim U.S. Equity Funds, *2000 Annual Report*, December 31, 2000, pp. 23–24.

Modern Portfolio Theory

modern portfolio theory (MPT) an approach to portfolio management that uses several basic statistical measures to develop a portfolio plan.

During the 1950s, Harry Markowitz, a trained mathematician, first developed the theories that form the basis of modern portfolio theory. Many other scholars and investment experts have contributed to the theory in the intervening years. **Modern portfolio theory (MPT)** utilizes several basic statistical measures to develop a portfolio plan. Included are *expected returns* and *standard deviations* of returns for both securities and portfolios, and the *correlation* between returns. According to MPT, diversification is achieved by combining securities in a portfolio *in such a way that individual securities have negative (or low-positive) correlations between each other's rates of return*. Thus the statistical diversification is the deciding factor in choosing securities for an MPT portfolio.

Two important aspects of MPT are the *efficient frontier* and *beta*.

The Efficient Frontier At any point in time, you are faced with virtually hundreds of investment vehicles from which to choose. You can form any number of possible portfolios. In fact, using only, say, 10 of the vehicles, you could create hundreds of portfolios by changing the proportion of each asset in the portfolio.

FIGURE 5.6

The Feasible or Attainable Set and the Efficient Frontier

The *feasible* or *attainable set* (shaded area) represents the risk-return combinations attainable with all possible portfolios; the *efficient frontier* is the locus of all efficient portfolios. The point 0 where the investor's highest possible indifference curve is tangent to the efficient frontier is the optimal portfolio. It represents the highest level of satisfaction the investor can achieve given the available set of portfolios.

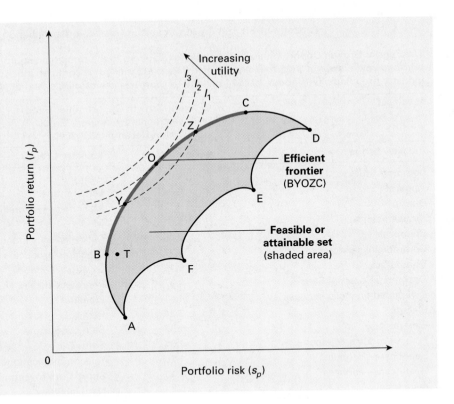

efficient frontier
the leftmost boundary of the *feasible (attainable) set* of portfolios that includes all *efficient portfolios*—those providing the best attainable tradeoff between risk (measured by the standard deviation) and return.

If we were to create all possible portfolios, calculate the return and risk of each, and plot each risk-return combination on a set of risk-return axes, we would have the *feasible* or *attainable set* of all possible portfolios. This set is represented by the shaded area in Figure 5.6. It is the area bounded by ABYOZCDEF. As defined earlier, an *efficient portfolio* is a portfolio that provides the highest return for a given level of risk or provides minimum risk for a given level of return. For example, let's compare portfolio T to portfolios B and Y shown in Figure 5.6. Portfolio Y appears preferable to portfolio T because it has a higher return for the same level of risk. Portfolio B also "dominates" portfolio T because it has lower risk for the same level of return.

The boundary BYOZC of the feasible set of portfolios represents *all efficient portfolios*—those portfolios that provide the best tradeoff between risk and return. This boundary is called the **efficient frontier**. *All portfolios on the efficient frontier are preferable to all other portfolios in the attainable set.* Any portfolios that would fall to the left of the efficient frontier are not available for investment, because they fall outside of the attainable set. Portfolios that fall to the right of the efficient frontier are *not desirable*, because their risk-return tradeoffs are inferior to those of portfolios on the efficient frontier.

The efficient frontier can, in theory, be used to find the highest level of satisfaction the investor can achieve given the available set of portfolios. To do this, we would plot on the risk-return axes an *investor's utility function* or *risk-indifference curves*. These curves indicate, for a given level of utility (satisfaction), the set of risk-return combinations among which an investor would be indifferent. These curves, labeled I_1, I_2, and I_3 in Figure 5.6, reflect increasing satisfaction as we move from I_1 to I_2 to I_3. The optimal portfolio, O, is the point at which indifference curve I_2 meets the efficient frontier. The higher utility provided by I_3 cannot be achieved given the best available portfolios represented by the efficient frontier.

When coupled with a risk-free asset, the efficient frontier can be used to develop the *capital asset pricing model* (introduced earlier) in terms of portfolio risk (measured by the standard deviation, s_p) and return (r_p). Rather than focus further on theory, let's shift our attention to the more practical aspects of the efficient frontier and its extensions. To do so, we consider the use of *beta* in a portfolio.

 Portfolio Betas As we have noted, investors strive to diversify their portfolios by including a variety of noncomplementary investment vehicles in order to reduce risk while meeting return objectives. Remember that investment vehicles embody two basic types of risk: (1) *diversifiable risk*, the risk unique to a particular investment vehicle, and (2) *nondiversifiable risk*, the risk possessed by every investment vehicle.

A great deal of research has been conducted on the topic of risk as it relates to security investments. As we noted earlier, the results show that in general, *to earn more return, one must bear more risk*. More startling, however, are research results showing that only with nondiversifiable risk is there a positive risk-return relationship. High levels of *diversifiable risk* do not result in correspondingly high levels of return. Because there is no reward for bearing diversifiable risk, investors should minimize this form of risk by diversifying the portfolio so that only nondiversifiable risk remains.

Risk Diversification As we've seen, diversification minimizes diversifiable risk by offsetting the poor return on one vehicle with the good return on another. Minimizing diversifiable risk through careful selection of investment vehicles requires that the vehicles chosen for the portfolio come from a wide range of industries.

To understand better the effect of diversification on the basic types of risk, let's consider what happens when we begin with a single asset (security) in a portfolio and then expand the portfolio by randomly selecting additional securities. Using the standard deviation, s_p, to measure the portfolio's *total risk*, we can depict the behavior of the total portfolio risk as more securities are added, as done in Figure 5.7. As securities are added (*x*-axis) the total portfolio risk (*y*-axis) declines because of the effects of diversification (explained earlier), and it tends to approach a limit.

Research has shown that, on average, most of the benefits of diversification, in terms of risk reduction, can be gained by forming portfolios containing 8 to 15 randomly selected securities. Unfortunately, because an investor holds but one of a large number of possible *x*-security portfolios, it is unlikely that he or she will experience the average outcome. As a consequence, some researchers suggest that the individual investor needs to hold about 40 different stocks to achieve efficient diversification. This suggestion tends to support the popularity of investment in mutual funds.

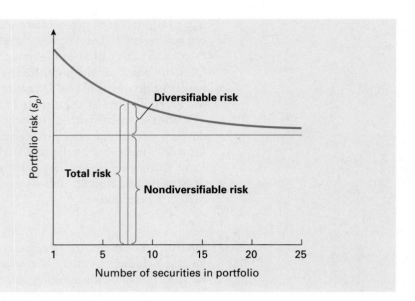

FIGURE 5.7

Portfolio Risk and Diversification

As randomly selected securities are combined to create a portfolio, the total risk of the portfolio (measured by its standard deviation, s_p) declines. The portion of the risk eliminated is the *diversifiable risk;* the remaining portion is the *nondiversifiable* or *relevant risk.* On average, most of the benefits of diversification result from forming portfolios that contain 8 to 15 randomly selected securities.

relevant risk
risk that is nondiversifiable.

Because any investor can create a portfolio of assets that will eliminate virtually all diversifiable risk, the only **relevant risk** is that which is nondiversifiable. You must therefore be concerned solely with nondiversifiable risk. The measurement of nondiversifiable risk is thus of primary importance.

Calculating Portfolio Betas As we saw earlier, the *nondiversifiable* or *relevant risk* of a security can be measured using *beta.* The beta for the market is equal to 1.00. Securities with betas greater than 1.00 are more risky than the market, and those with betas below 1.00 are less risky than the market. The beta for the risk-free asset is 0.

portfolio beta, b_p
the beta of a portfolio; calculated as the weighted average of the betas of the individual assets the portfolio includes.

The **portfolio beta, b_p,** is merely the weighted average of the betas of the individual assets it includes. It can be easily estimated using the betas of the component assets. To find the portfolio beta, b_p, we can use Equation 5.4

Equation 5.4

$$\text{Portfolio beta} = \begin{pmatrix} \text{Proportion of} \\ \text{portfolio's total} \\ \text{dollar value} \times \text{Beta for} \\ \text{represented by} \quad \text{asset 1} \\ \text{asset 1} \end{pmatrix} + \begin{pmatrix} \text{Proportion of} \\ \text{portfolio's total} \\ \text{dollar value} \times \text{Beta for} \\ \text{represented by} \quad \text{asset 2} \\ \text{asset 2} \end{pmatrix} + \cdots +$$

$$\begin{pmatrix} \text{Proportion of} \\ \text{portfolio's total} \\ \text{dollar value} \times \text{Beta for} \\ \text{represented by} \quad \text{asset } n \\ \text{asset } n \end{pmatrix} = \sum_{j=1}^{n} \begin{pmatrix} \text{Proportion of} \\ \text{portfolio's total} \\ \text{dollar value} \times \text{Beta for} \\ \text{represented by} \quad \text{asset } j \\ \text{asset } j \end{pmatrix}$$

Equation 5.4a

$$b_p = (w_1 \times b_1) + (w_2 \times b_2) + \cdots + (w_n \times b_n) = \sum_{j=1}^{n} (w_j \times b_j)$$

Of course, $\sum_{j=1}^{n} w_j = 1$, which means that 100% of the portfolio's assets must be included in this computation.

Portfolio betas are interpreted in exactly the same way as individual asset betas. They indicate the degree of responsiveness of the *portfolio's* return to changes in the market return. For example, when the market return increases by 10%, a portfolio with a beta of 0.75 will experience a 7.5% increase in its return (0.75 × 10%). A portfolio with a beta of 1.25 will experience a 12.5% increase in its return (1.25 × 10%). Low-beta portfolios are less responsive, and therefore less risky, than high-beta portfolios. Clearly, a portfolio containing mostly low-beta assets will have a low beta, and vice versa.

To demonstrate, consider the Austin Fund, a large investment company that wishes to assess the risk of two portfolios, V and W. Both portfolios contain five assets, with the proportions and betas shown in Table 5.6. The betas for portfolios V and W, b_v and b_w, can be calculated by substituting the appropriate data from the table into Equation 5.4, as follows.

$$b_v = (0.10 \times 1.65) + (0.30 \times 1.00) + (0.20 \times 1.30) + (0.20 \times 1.10) + (0.20 \times 1.25)$$
$$= 0.165 + 0.300 + 0.260 + 0.220 + 0.250 = 1.195 \approx \underline{1.20}$$
$$b_w = (0.10 \times 0.80) + (0.10 \times 1.00) + (0.20 \times 0.65) + (0.10 \times 0.75) + (0.50 \times 1.05)$$
$$= 0.080 + 0.100 + 0.130 + 0.075 + 0.525 = \underline{0.91}$$

Portfolio V's beta is 1.20, and portfolio W's is 0.91. These values make sense because portfolio V contains relatively high-beta assets and portfolio W contains relatively low-beta assets. Clearly, portfolio V's returns are more responsive to changes in market returns—and therefore more risky—than portfolio W's.

Using Portfolio Betas The usefulness of beta depends on how well it explains return fluctuations. We can use *the coefficient of determination* (R^2) to evaluate a beta coefficient statistically. This coefficient indicates the percentage of the change in an individual security's return that is explained by its relationship with the market return. R^2 can range from 0 to 1.0. If a regression equation has an R^2 of 0, then none (0%) of the variation in the security's return is explained by its relationship with the market. An R^2 of 1.0 indicates

TABLE 5.6   Austin Fund's Portfolios V and W

Asset	Portfolio V Proportion	Beta	Portfolio W Proportion	Beta
1	0.10	1.65	0.10	0.80
2	0.30	1.00	0.10	1.00
3	0.20	1.30	0.20	0.65
4	0.20	1.10	0.10	0.75
5	0.20	1.25	0.50	1.05
Total	1.00		1.00	

the existence of perfect correlation (100%) between a security and the market.

Beta is much more useful in explaining a portfolio's return fluctuations than a security's return fluctuations. A well-diversified stock portfolio will have a beta equation R^2 of around 0.90. This means that 90% of the stock portfolio's fluctuations are related to changes in the stock market as a whole. Individual security betas have a wide range of R^2s but tend to be in the 0.20 to 0.50 range. Other factors (diversifiable risk, in particular) also cause individual security prices to fluctuate. When securities are combined in a well-diversified portfolio, most of the fluctuation in that portfolio's return is caused by the movement of the entire stock market.

Interpreting Portfolio Betas If a portfolio has a beta of +1.00, the portfolio experiences changes in its rate of return equal to changes in the market's rate of return. The +1.00 beta portfolio would tend to experience a 10% increase in return if the stock market as a whole experienced a 10% increase in return. Conversely, if the market return fell by 6%, the return on the +1.00 beta portfolio would also fall by 6%.

Table 5.7 lists the expected returns for three portfolio betas in two situations: an increase in market return of 10% and a decrease in market return of 10%. The 2.00 beta portfolio is twice as volatile as the market. When the market return increases by 10%, the portfolio return increases by 20%. When the market return declines 10%, the portfolio's return will fall by 20%. This portfolio would be considered a high-risk, high-return portfolio.

The middle, 0.50 beta portfolio is considered a low-risk, low-return portfolio. This would be a conservative portfolio for investors who wish to maintain a low-risk investment posture. The 0.50 beta portfolio is half as volatile as the market.

A portfolio with a beta of −1.00 moves in the opposite direction from the market. A bearish investor would probably want to own a negative-beta portfolio, because this type of investment tends to rise in value when the stock market declines, and vice versa. Finding securities with negative betas is difficult, however. Most securities have positive betas, because they tend to experience return movements in the same direction as changes in the stock market.

The Risk-Return Tradeoff: Some Closing Comments Another valuable outgrowth of modern portfolio theory is the specific link between nondiversifiable risk and investment return. The basic premise is that an investor must have a portfolio of relatively risky investments to earn a relatively high rate of return. That relationship is illustrated in Figure 5.8. The upward-sloping line shows the **risk-return tradeoff**. The point where the risk-return line crosses the return axis is called the **risk-free rate, R_F**. This is the return an investor can earn on a risk-free investment such as a U.S. Treasury bill or an insured money market deposit account.

As we proceed upward along the risk-return tradeoff line, portfolios of risky investments appear. For example, four investment portfolios, A through D, are depicted. Portfolios A and B are investment opportunities that provide a level of return commensurate with their respective risk levels. Portfolio C provides a high return at a relatively low risk level—and therefore would be an excellent investment. Portfolio D, in contrast, offers high risk but low return—an investment to avoid.

risk-return tradeoff
the positive relationship between the risk associated with a given investment and its expected return.

risk-free rate, R_F
the return an investor can earn on a risk-free investment such as a U.S. Treasury bill or an insured money market account.

TABLE 5.7   Portfolio Betas and Associated Changes in Returns

Portfolio Beta	Change in Market Return	Change in Expected Portfolio Return
+2.00	+10.0% −10.0	+20.0% −20.0
+0.50	+10.0 −10.0	+ 5.0 − 5.0
−1.00	+10.0 −10.0	−10.0 +10.0

Reconciling the Traditional Approach and MPT

We have reviewed two fairly different approaches to portfolio management: the traditional approach and MPT. The question that naturally arises is which technique you should use. There is no definite answer; the question must be resolved by the judgment of each investor. However, we can offer a few useful ideas.

The average individual investor does not have the resources, computers, and mathematical acumen to implement a total MPT portfolio strategy. But most individual investors can extract and use ideas from *both* the traditional and MPT approaches. The traditional approach stresses security selection, which is discussed in Chapters 7 and 8. It also emphasizes diversification of the portfolio across industry lines. MPT stresses negative correlations between rates of return for the securities within the portfolio. This approach calls for diversification, to minimize diversifiable risk. Thus diversification must be accomplished to ensure satisfactory performance with either strategy. Also, beta is a useful tool for determining the level of a portfolio's nondiversifiable risk and should be part of the decision-making process.

We recommend the following portfolio management policy, which uses aspects of both approaches:

FIGURE 5.8

The Portfolio risk-Return Tradeoff

As the risk of an investment portfolio increases from zero, the return provided should increase above the risk-free rate, R_F. Portfolios A and B offer returns commensurate with their risk, portfolio C provides a high return at a low-risk level, and portfolio D provides a low return for high risk. Portfolio C is highly desirable; Portfolio D should be avoided.

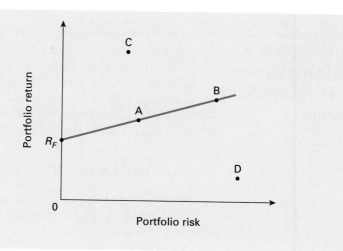

- Determine how much risk you are willing to bear.

- Seek diversification among different types of securities and across industry lines, and pay attention to how the return from one security is related to that from another.

- Consider how a security responds to the market, and use beta in diversifying your portfolio as a way to keep the portfolio in line with your acceptable level of risk.

- Evaluate alternative portfolios to make sure that the portfolio selected provides the highest return for the given level of acceptable risk.

IN REVIEW

CONCEPTS

5.12 Describe *traditional portfolio management*. Give three reasons why traditional portfolio managers like to invest in well-established companies.

5.13 What is *modern portfolio theory (MPT)?* What is the *feasible* or *attainable set* of all possible portfolios? How is it derived for a given group of investment vehicles?

5.14 What is the *efficient frontier?* How is it related to the attainable set of all possible portfolios? How can it be used with an investor's utility function to find the optimal portfolio?

5.15 Define and differentiate among the diversifiable, nondiversifiable, and total risk of a portfolio. Which is considered the *relevant risk*? How is it measured?

5.16 Define *beta*. How can you find the beta of a portfolio when you know the beta for each of the assets included within it?

5.17 What does the *coefficient of determination (R^2)* for the regression equation used to derive a beta coefficient indicate? Would this statistic indicate that beta is more useful in explaining the return fluctuations of individual assets than of portfolios?

5.18 Explain how traditional and modern portfolio approaches can be reconciled.

Constructing a Portfolio Using an Asset Allocation Scheme

LG 5   LG 6

In this section we will examine the criteria for constructing a portfolio and then will use these factors to develop a plan for allocating assets in various investment categories. This plan provides a basic, useful framework for selecting individual investment vehicles for the portfolio. In attempting to weave the concepts of risk and diversification into a solid portfolio policy, we will rely on both traditional and modern approaches.

Investor Characteristics and Objectives

Your financial and family situations are important inputs in determining portfolio policy. Vital determinants include: level and stability of income, family factors, net worth, investor experience and age, and disposition toward risk. The types of investments in your portfolio depend on relative income needs and ability to bear risk.

The size of your income and the certainty of your employment also bear on portfolio strategy. An investor with a secure job can handle more risk than one with a less secure position. And, the higher your income, the more important the tax ramifications of an investment program become. Your investment experience also influences your investment strategy. It normally is best to "get one's feet wet" in the investment market by slipping into it gradually rather than leaping in headfirst. A cautiously developed investment program is likely to provide more favorable long-run results than an impulsive one.

Once you have developed a personal financial profile, the next question is "What do I want from my portfolio?" You must generally choose between earning a high current income or obtaining significant capital appreciation. It is difficult to have both. The price of having high appreciation potential in the portfolio is often low potential for current income.

Your needs may determine which avenue is chosen. A retired investor whose income depends on his or her portfolio will probably choose a lower-risk, current-income-oriented approach. In contrast, a high-income, financially secure investor (such as a physician) may be much more willing to take on risky investments in the hope of improving net worth. Thus it should be clear that a portfolio must be built around the individual's needs, which depend on income, responsibilities, financial resources, age, retirement plans, and ability to bear risk.

Portfolio Objectives and Policies

Constructing a portfolio is a logical activity that is best done after you have analyzed your needs and the available investment vehicles. You should consider these objectives when planning and constructing a portfolio: current income needs, capital preservation, capital growth, tax considerations, and risk.

Any one or more of these factors will play an influential role in defining the desirable type of portfolio. For convenience, these factors can be tied together as follows: The first two items, current income and capital preservation, are portfolio objectives consistent with a low-risk, conservative investment strategy. Normally, a portfolio with this orientation contains low-beta (low-risk) securities. The third item, a capital growth objective, implies increased risk and a reduced level of current income. Higher-risk growth stocks, options, futures, and other more speculative investments may be suitable for this investor. The fourth item, an investor's tax bracket, will influence investment strategy. A high-income investor probably wishes to defer taxes and earn investment returns in the form of capital gains. This implies a strategy of higher-risk investments and a longer holding period. Lower-bracket investors are less concerned with how they earn the income, and they may wish to invest in higher-current-income vehicles. The most important item, finally, is risk. The risk-return tradeoff should be considered *in all investment decisions*.

Developing an Asset Allocation Scheme

asset allocation
a scheme that involves dividing one's portfolio into various asset classes to *preserve capital* by protecting against negative developments while taking advantage of positive ones.

Once you have translated your needs into specific portfolio objectives, you can construct a portfolio designed to achieve these goals. Before buying any investment vehicles, however, you must develop an *asset allocation scheme*. **Asset allocation** involves dividing one's portfolio into various asset classes, such as U.S. stocks, U.S. bonds, foreign securities, short-term securities, and other vehicles like tangibles (especially gold) and real estate. The emphasis of asset allocation is on *preservation of capital*—protecting against negative developments while taking advantage of positive developments. Asset allocation, although similar to diversification in its objective, is a bit different: Its focus is on *investment in various asset classes*. Diversification, in contrast, tends to focus more on **security selection**—selecting the *specific* securities to be held *within* an asset class.

security selection
the procedures used to select the *specific* securities to be held *within* an asset class.

Asset allocation is based on the belief that the total return of a portfolio is influenced more by the division of investments into asset classes than by the actual investments. In fact, studies have shown that as much as 90% or more of a portfolio's *return* comes from asset allocation. Therefore, less than 10% can be attributed to the actual security selection. Furthermore, researchers have found that asset allocation has a much greater impact on reducing *total risk* than does selecting the best investment vehicle in any single asset category. Clearly, asset allocation is a very important aspect of portfolio management.

Approaches to Asset Allocation There are three basic approaches to asset allocation: (1) fixed weightings, (2) flexible weightings, and (3) tactical asset allocation. The first two differ with respect to the proportions of each asset category maintained in the portfolio. The third is a more exotic technique used by institutional portfolio managers.

fixed-weightings approach
asset allocation plan in which a fixed percentage of the portfolio is allocated to each asset category.

Fixed Weightings The **fixed-weightings approach** allocates a fixed percentage of the portfolio to each of the asset categories, of which there typically are three to five. Assuming four categories—common stocks, bonds, foreign securities, and short-term securities—a fixed allocation might be as follows.

Category	Allocation
Common stock	30%
Bonds	50
Foreign securities	15
Short-term securities	5
Total portfolio	100%

Generally, the fixed weightings do not change over time. When market values shift, the portfolio may have to be adjusted annually or after major market moves to maintain the desired fixed-percentage allocations.

HOT LINKS

The *Investing in Action* box at the book's Web site offers some basic portfolio-building tips for the novice investor.

www.awl.com/gitman_joehnk

Fixed weights may or may not represent equal percentage allocations to each category. One could, for example, allocate 25% to each of the four categories above. Research has shown that over a long period (1967–1988) equal (20%) allocations to U.S. stocks, foreign stocks, long-term bonds, cash, and real estate resulted in a portfolio that outperformed the S&P 500 in terms of both return and risk. These findings add further support to the importance of even a somewhat naive "buy and hold" asset allocation strategy.

flexible-weightings approach
asset allocation plan in which weights for each asset category are adjusted periodically based on market analysis.

Flexible Weightings The **flexible-weightings approach** involves periodic adjustment of the weights for each asset category on the basis of market analysis. The use of a flexible weighting scheme is often called *strategic asset allocation*. For example, the initial and new allocation based on a flexible weighting scheme may be as follows.

tactical asset allocation
asset allocation plan that uses
stock-index futures and bond
futures to change a portfolio's
asset allocation based on market
behavior.

Category	Initial Allocation	New Allocation
Common stock	30%	45%
Bonds	40	40
Foreign securities	15	10
Short-term securities	15	5
Total portfolio	100%	100%

A change from the initial to the new allocation would be triggered by shifts in market conditions or expectations. For example, the new allocation shown above may have resulted from an anticipated decline in inflation. That decline would be expected to result in increased domestic stock and bond prices and a decline in foreign and short-term security returns. The weightings were therefore changed to capture greater returns in a changing market.

Tactical Asset Allocation The third approach, **tactical asset allocation,** is a form of market timing that uses stock-index futures and bond futures (see Chapter 15) to change a portfolio's asset allocation. When stocks are forecast to be less attractive than bonds, this strategy involves selling stock-index futures and buying bond futures. Conversely, when bonds are forecast to be less attractive than stocks, the strategy results in buying stock-index futures and selling bond futures. Because this sophisticated technique relies on a large portfolio and the use of quantitative models for market timing, it is generally appropriate only for large institutional investors.

Asset Allocation Alternatives Assuming the use of a fixed-weight asset allocation plan and using, say, four asset categories, we can demonstrate three asset allocations. Table 5.8 shows allocations in each of four categories for conservative (low-return–low-risk), moderate (average-return–average-risk), and aggressive (high-return–high-risk) portfolios. The conservative allocation relies heavily on bonds and short-term securities to provide predictable returns. The moderate allocation consists largely of common stock and bonds and includes more foreign securities and fewer short-term securities than the conservative allocation. Its moderate risk-return behavior reflects a move away from safe, short-term securities to a larger dose of common stock and foreign securities. Finally, in the aggressive allocation, more dollars are invested in common stock, fewer in bonds, and more in foreign securities, thereby generally increasing the expected portfolio return and risk. The *Investing in Action*

TABLE 5.8	**Alternative Asset Allocations**		
	Allocation Alternative		
Category	Conservative (low-return– low-risk)	Moderate (average-return– average-risk)	Aggressive (high-return– high-risk)
Common stock	15%	30%	40%
Bonds	45	40	30
Foreign securities	5	15	25
Short-term securities	35	15	5
Total portfolio	100%	100%	100%

INVESTING in action

University Portfolio Managers Earn an A+

For many portfolio managers, piloting a $6.2-billion portfolio through the ups and down of the current stock market would mean sleepless nights. Laurence Hoagland, chief executive officer for Stanford University's endowment fund, is not worried, however. Although recent market losses may affect the university's financial standing, Stanford's portfolio is diversified to a point where the university will witness little overall effect from any market slide. "The asset allocation that we have is much more diversified than the typical model for the very reason of dampening the impact of fluctuations," said Hoagland. "Around 25% of our assets are allocated towards investments in the U.S. market, while the typical institution will allocate close to 50% of its assets towards the U.S. market."

Stanford resists the temptation to invest heavily in high-technology companies, many of which were founded by Stanford alumni or faculty. The Stanford Management Company, the group that allocates endowment assets, resolves potential conflicts of interest by using outside money managers with little or no connection to the university. "The money managers that we hire have full discretion over which stocks they buy and sell," said Hoagland. "We deliberately select outside money managers who are likely not to invest as heavily in Silicon Valley stocks, so as to achieve a balance in terms of the assets we hold."

Stanford's domestic-market investments are generally conservative and geared toward the long term. However, 18% of the endowment is in alternative investments, usually partnerships with venture-capital firms. "These have been extremely rewarding in recent years [232% in fiscal 1998–1999], and we have witnessed substantial gains from them," said Hoagland. "However, they are very volatile."

Like Hoagland, investment officers at other universities have been enjoying the high returns from the stock market's run up. The *Chronicle of Higher Education* reports that for the fiscal year ended June 30, 2000, returns at the top 10 schools ranged from Northwestern University's 33.7% to the University of Notre Dame's 62%. However, Notre Dame chief investment officer Scott Malpass warns university trustees that returns are likely to be 13% to 14% for 2001. Jack Meyer, head of Harvard Management Co., agrees. "It is important that we not delude ourselves into thinking that double-digit returns will persist indefinitely."

Not all university portfolio managers follow Stanford's diversification policy. Atlanta's Emory University holds about 40% of its $4.5 billion endowment in Coca-Cola stock, the result of a $105 million gift in 1979. Ten years ago, Emory had the fastest-growing endowment, thanks to this stock. Last year it wasn't so lucky, losing over 12% of its endowment's value as Coke's stock price fell. Yet Wayne Coon, Emory's chief investment officer, does not plan to diversify. "I would worry if I didn't know what caused this," he says.

Sources: Scott Dorfman, "Diversified Portfolio Helps Ensure Against Market," *University Wire*, April 18, 2000; David Marcus, "The New College All-Stars," *U.S. News & World Report*, November 13, 2000, p. 49; Bill Scanlon, "Rising Stock Market Benefits Colleges," *Denver Rocky Mountain News*, February 20, 2000, p. 20A.

box above describes the success that Stanford University has had using asset allocation for its endowment fund.

Applying Asset Allocation An asset allocation plan should consider the economic outlook and your investments, savings and spending patterns, tax situation, return expectations, and risk tolerance. Such plans must be formulated for the long run, must stress capital preservation, and must provide for periodic revision to maintain consistency with changing investment goals. Generally, to decide on the appropriate asset mix, you must evaluate each asset category in

asset allocation fund
a mutual fund that seeks to reduce the variability of returns by investing in the right assets at the right time; emphasizes diversification and relatively consistent performance rather than the potential for spectacular gains.

terms of current return, growth potential, safety, liquidity, transaction costs (brokerage fees), and potential tax savings.

Many investors use mutual funds (see Chapter 12) as part of their asset allocation activities, to diversify within each asset category. Or, as an alternative to constructing your own portfolio, you can buy shares in an **asset allocation fund**—a mutual fund that seeks to reduce variability of returns by investing in the right assets at the right time. These funds, like all asset allocation schemes, emphasize diversification. They perform at a relatively consistent level by passing up the potential for spectacular gains in favor of predictability. Some asset allocation funds use fixed weightings, whereas others have flexible weights that change within prescribed limits. As a rule, investors with more than about $100,000 to invest and adequate time can justify do-it-yourself asset allocation. Those with between $25,000 and $100,000 and adequate time can use mutual funds to create a workable asset allocation. Those with less than $25,000 or with limited time may find asset allocation funds most attractive.

Most important, you should recognize that to be effective an asset allocation scheme *must be designed for the long haul.* Develop an asset allocation scheme you can live with for at least 7 to 10 years, and perhaps longer. Once you have it set, stick with it. The key to success is remaining faithful to your asset allocation; that means fighting the temptation to wander.

I N   R E V I E W

CONCEPTS

5.19 What role, if any, do an investor's personal characteristics play in determining portfolio policy? Explain.

5.20 What role do an investor's portfolio objectives play in constructing a portfolio?

5.21 What is *asset allocation?* How does it differ from diversification? What role does asset allocation play in constructing an investment portfolio?

5.22 Briefly describe the three basic approaches to asset allocation: (a) fixed weightings, (b) flexible weightings, and (c) tactical asset allocation.

5.23 What role could an *asset allocation fund* play? What makes an asset allocation scheme effective?

5.24 Based on the *Investing in Action* box on page 204, what is the expected benefit of Stanford University's highly diversified portfolio asset allocation? How would you characterize Stanford's overall investment policy in terms of return and risk?

Summary   LG 1

Understand portfolio management objectives and the procedures to calculate the return and standard deviation of a portfolio. A portfolio is a collection of investment vehicles assembled to achieve one or more investment goals. It involves a tradeoff between risk and return, potential price appreciation and current income, and varying risk levels. The return on a portfolio is calculated as a weighted average of the returns of the assets from which it is formed. The standard deviation of a portfolio's returns is found by applying the same formula that is used to find the standard deviation of a single asset.

LG 2 **Discuss the concepts of correlation and diversification, and the effectiveness, methods, and benefits of international diversification.** Correlation is a statistic used to measure the relationship, if any, between the returns on assets. To diversify, it is best to add assets with negatively correlated returns. In general, the less positive and more negative the correlation between asset returns, the more effectively a portfolio can be diversified to reduce its risk. Through diversification, the risk (standard deviation) of a portfolio can be reduced below the risk of the least risky asset (sometimes to zero); however, the return of the resulting portfolio will be no lower than the smallest return of its component assets. International diversification may allow an investor to reduce portfolio risk without a corresponding reduction in return. It can be achieved by investing abroad or through domestic investment in foreign companies or funds, but it typically cannot be achieved by investing in U.S. multinationals. The preferred method of international diversification for individual investors is the use of ADRs or international mutual funds available in the United States. Although opportunities to earn "excess returns" in international investments are diminishing over time, they continue to be effective diversification vehicles.

LG 3 **Describe the two components of risk, beta, and the capital asset pricing model (CAPM).** The two basic components of total risk are diversifiable (unsystematic) and nondiversifiable (systematic) risk; nondiversifiable risk is the relevant risk. Beta can be used to measure the nondiversible, or market, risk associated with a security investment. It is derived from the historical relationship between a security's return and the market return. The capital asset pricing model (CAPM) relates risk (as measured by beta) to return. It can be depicted graphically as the security market line (SML). The CAPM reflects increasing required returns for increasing risk.

LG 4 **Review traditional and modern approaches to portfolio management and reconcile them.** The traditional approach constructs portfolios by combining a large number of securities issued by companies from a broad cross section of industries. Modern portfolio theory (MPT) uses statistical diversification to develop efficient portfolios. To determine the optimal portfolio, MPT finds the efficient frontier and couples it with an investor's risk-indifference curves. In practice, portfolio betas can be used to develop efficient portfolios consistent with the investor's risk-return preferences. Generally, investors use elements of both the traditional approach and MPT to create portfolios.

LG 5 **Describe the role of investor characteristics and objectives and of portfolio objectives and policies in constructing an investment portfolio.** To construct a portfolio, the investor should consider characteristics such as level and stability of income, family factors, net worth, experience and age, and disposition toward risk. He or she should specify objectives and should plan and construct a portfolio consistent with them. Commonly considered portfolio objectives include current income, capital preservation, capital growth, tax considerations, and level of risk.

LG 6 **Summarize why and how investors use an asset allocation scheme to construct an investment portfolio.** Asset allocation is the key influence on the total return of a portfolio. It involves dividing one's portfolio into various asset classes, whereas diversification tends to focus more on security selection within an asset class. Like diversification, asset allocation aims to protect against negative developments while taking advantage of positive ones. The basic approaches to asset allocation involve the use of fixed weightings, flexible weightings, or tactical asset allocation. Asset allocation can be achieved on a do-it-yourself basis, with the use of mutual funds, or by merely buying shares in an asset allocation fund.

Discussion Questions

LG 1 **Q5.1** State your portfolio objectives. Then construct a 10-stock portfolio that you feel is consistent with your objectives. (Use companies that have been public for at least 5 years.) Obtain annual dividend and price data for each of the past 5 years.

    a. Calculate the historical return for each stock for each year.

    b. Calculate the historical portfolio return for each of the 5 years, using your findings in part (a).

    c. Use your findings in part (b) to calculate the average portfolio return over the 5 years.

    d. Use your findings in parts (b) and (c) to find the standard deviation of the portfolio's returns over the 5-year period.

    e. Use the historical average return from part (c) and the standard deviation from part (d) to evaluate the portfolio's return and risk in light of your stated portfolio objectives.

LG 2 **Q5.2** Using the following guidelines, choose the stocks—A, B, and C—of three firms that have been public for at least 10 years. Stock A should be one you are interested in buying. Stock B should be a stock, possibly in the same line of business or industry, that you feel will have high positive return correlation with stock A. Finally, stock C should be one you feel will have high negative return correlation with stock A.

    a. Calculate the annual rates of return for each of the past 10 years for each stock.

    b. Plot the 10 annual return values for each stock on the same set of axes, where the x-axis is the year and the y-axis is the annual return in percentage terms.

    c. Join the points for the returns for each stock on the graph. Evaluate and describe the returns of stocks A and B in the graph. Do they exhibit the expected positive correlation? Why or why not?

    d. Evaluate and describe the relationship between the returns of stocks A and C in the graph. Do they exhibit the expected negative correlation? Why or why not?

    e. Compare and contrast your findings in parts (c) and (d) to the expected relationships among stocks A, B, and C. Discuss your findings.

LG 3 **Q5.3** Access appropriate government and economic data at your public or university library to obtain current estimates of the risk-free rate (use a 3-month U.S. Treasury bill), the current market return, and the beta (from *Value Line Investment Survey*) for each of the following stocks.

    General Motors (autos)

    Dell (computers)

    Sempra Energy (utilities)

    Kroger (groceries)

    Merrill Lynch (financial services)

    a. Find the required return for each of the five stocks, using the capital asset pricing model (CAPM) and the relevant values gathered earlier.

    b. Discuss, compare, and contrast the relative risks and returns for each of the five stocks.

LG 3 **Q5.4** Find the current risk-free rate and market return. Use *Value Line Investment Survey* to find current betas for each of the companies listed on page 188.

    a. Compare, contrast, and comment on the current betas in light of the May 11, 2001, betas given in the chapter for each of the companies.

    b. Do you think the betas will remain the same over time? What might cause them to change, even in a stable economic environment?

c. Use the current betas and the capital asset pricing model (CAPM) to estimate each stock's required return.

d. Compare and discuss your findings in part (c) with regard to the specific business that each company is in.

LG 2   **LG 4**   Q5.5   Obtain a prospectus and an annual report for a major mutual fund that includes some international securities. Carefully read the prospectus and annual report and study the portfolio's composition in light of the fund's stated objectives.

a. Assess the fund manager's investment approach. Does the fund use a traditional approach, modern portfolio theory (MPT), or a combination of the two?

b. Evaluate the amount of diversification and the types of industries and companies held. Is the portfolio well diversified?

c. Assess the degree of international diversification achieved. Does management consciously include international securities to improve the fund's risk-return outcome?

d. Overall, how well does management seem to be managing the portfolio in light of the fund's stated objectives with regard to diversification?

LG 4   Q5.6   Use *Value Line Investment Survey* or some other source to select six stocks with betas ranging from about 0.50 to 1.50. Record the current market prices of each of these stocks. Assume you wish to create a portfolio that combines all six stocks in such a way that the resulting portfolio beta is about 1.10.

a. Through trial and error, use all six stocks to create a portfolio with the target beta of 1.10.

b. If you have $100,000 to invest in this portfolio, on the basis of the weightings determined in part (a), how much in dollars would you invest in each stock?

c. Approximately how many shares of each of the six stocks would you buy, given the dollar amounts calculated in part (b)?

d. Repeat parts (a), (b), and (c) with a different set of weightings that still result in a portfolio beta of 1.10. Can only one unique portfolio with a given beta be created from a given set of stocks?

e. Why might the use of beta to measure the risk of the portfolios created in parts (a) and (d) not be an accurate measure of risk in this case? Explain.

LG 5   **LG 6**   Q5.7   List your personal characteristics and then state your investment objectives in light of them. Use these objectives as a basis for developing your portfolio objectives and policies. Assume that you plan to create a portfolio aimed at achieving your stated objectives. The portfolio will be constructed by allocating your money to any of the following asset classes: common stock, bonds, foreign securities, and short-term securities.

a. Determine and justify an asset allocation to these four classes in light of your stated portfolio objectives and policies.

b. Describe the types of investments you would choose for each of the asset classes.

c. Assume that after making the asset allocations specified in part (a), you receive a sizable inheritance that causes your portfolio objectives to change to a much more aggressive posture. Describe the changes that you would make in your asset allocations.

d. Describe other asset classes you might consider when developing your asset allocation scheme.

Problems

LG 1

LG 2

P5.1 Assume you are considering a portfolio containing two assets, L and M. Asset L will represent 40% of the dollar value of the portfolio, and asset M will account for the other 60%. The expected returns over the next 6 years, 2003–2008, for each of these assets are summarized in the following table.

	Expected Return (%)	
Year	Asset L	Asset M
2003	14	20
2004	14	18
2005	16	16
2006	17	14
2007	17	12
2008	19	10

a. Calculate the expected portfolio return, r_p, for each of the 6 years.
b. Calculate the average expected portfolio return, $\bar{r}_p$, over the 6-year period.
c. Calculate the standard deviation of expected portfolio returns, s_p, over the 6-year period.
d. How would you characterize the correlation of returns of the two assets L and M?
e. Discuss any benefits of diversification achieved through creation of the portfolio.

LG 1   LG 2

P5.2 You have been given the following return data on three assets—F, G, and H—over the period 2003–2006.

	Expected Return (%)		
Year	Asset F	Asset G	Asset H
2003	16	17	14
2004	17	16	15
2005	18	15	16
2006	19	14	17

Using these assets, you have isolated three investment alternatives:

Alternative	Investment
1	100% of asset F
2	50% of asset F and 50% of asset G
3	50% of asset F and 50% of asset H

a. Calculate the portfolio return over the 4-year period for each of the three alternatives.
b. Calculate the standard deviation of returns over the 4-year period for each of the three alternatives.
c. On the basis of your findings in parts (a) and (b), which of the three investment alternatives would you recommend? Why?

LG 1   LG 2

P5.3 You have been asked for your advice in selecting a portfolio of assets and have been supplied with the following data.

	Expected Return (%)		
Year	Asset A	Asset B	Asset C
2003	12	16	12
2004	14	14	14
2005	16	12	16

You have been told that you can create two portfolios—one consisting of assets A and B and the other consisting of assets A and C—by investing equal proportions (50%) in each of the two component assets.

    a. What is the average expected return, $\bar{r}$, for each asset over the 3-year period?

    b. What is the standard deviation, s, for each asset's expected return?

    c. What is the average expected return, $\bar{r}_p$, for each of the two portfolios?

    d. How would you characterize the correlations of returns of the two assets making up each of the two portfolios identified in part (c)?

    e. What is the standard deviation of expected returns, s_p, for each portfolio?

    f. Which portfolio do you recommend? Why?

LG 1   LG 2   **P5.4** Assume you wish to evaluate the risk and return behaviors associated with various combinations of assets V and W under three assumed degrees of correlation: perfect positive, uncorrelated, and perfect negative. The following average return and risk values were calculated for these assets.

Asset	Average Return, $\bar{r}$ (%)	Risk (Standard Deviation), s (%)
V	8	5
W	13	10

    a. If the returns of assets V and W are *perfectly positively correlated* (correlation coefficient = +1), describe the *range* of (1) return and (2) risk associated with all possible portfolio combinations.

    b. If the returns of assets V and W are *uncorrelated* (correlation coefficient = 0), describe the *approximate range* of (1) return and (2) risk associated with all possible portfolio combinations.

    c. If the returns of assets V and W are *perfectly negatively correlated* (correlation coefficient = −1), describe the *range* of (1) return and (2) risk associated with all possible portfolio combinations.

LG 3   **P5.5** Imagine you wish to estimate the betas for two investments, A and B. You have gathered the following return data for the market and for each of the investments over the past 10 years, 1993–2002.

	Historical Returns		
		Investment	
Year	Market	A	B
1993	6%	11%	16%
1994	2	8	11
1995	−13	− 4	−10
1996	− 4	3	3
1997	− 8	0	− 3
1998	16	19	30
1999	10	14	22
2000	15	18	29
2001	8	12	19
2002	13	17	26

a. On a set of market return (x-axis)–investment return (y-axis) axes, use the data to draw the characteristic lines for investments A and B on the same set of axes.
b. Use the characteristic lines from part (a) to estimate the betas for investments A and B.
c. Use the betas found in part (b) to comment on the relative risks of investments A and B.

 LG 3 **P5.6** A security has a beta of 1.20. Is this security more or less risky than the market? Explain. Assess the impact on the required return of this security in each of the following cases.
a. The market return increases by 15%.
b. The market return decreases by 8%.
c. The market return remains unchanged.

 LG 3 **P5.7** Assume the betas for securities A, B, and C are as shown here.

Security	Beta
A	1.40
B	0.80
C	−0.90

a. Calculate the change in return for each security if the market experiences an increase in its rate of return of 13.2% over the next period.
b. Calculate the change in return for each security if the market experiences a decrease in its rate of return of 10.8% over the next period.
c. Rank and discuss the relative risk of each security on the basis of your findings. Which security might perform best during an economic downturn? Explain.

 LG 3 **P5.8** Use the capital asset pricing model (CAPM) to find the required return for each of the following securities in light of the data given.

Security	Risk-Free Rate	Market Return	Beta
A	5%	8%	1.30
B	8	13	0.90
C	9	12	−0.20
D	10	15	1.00
E	6	10	0.60

 LG 3 **P5.9** The risk-free rate is currently 7%, and the market return is 12%. Assume you are considering the following investment vehicles.

Investment Vehicle	Beta
A	1.50
B	1.00
C	0.75
D	0
E	2.00

a. Which vehicle is most risky? Least risky?
b. Use the capital asset pricing model (CAPM) to find the required return on each of the investment vehicles.
c. Draw the security market line (SML), using your findings in part (b).
d. On the basis of your findings in part (c), what relationship exists between risk and return? Explain.

LG 4

P5.10 Portfolios A through J, which are listed in the following table along with their returns (r_p) and risk (measured by the standard deviation, s_p), represent all currently available portfolios in the feasible or attainable set.

Portfolio	Return (r_p)	Risk (s_p)
A	9%	8%
B	3	3
C	14	10
D	12	14
E	7	11
F	11	6
G	10	12
H	16	16
I	5	7
J	8	4

a. Plot the *feasible* or *attainable set* represented by these data on a set of portfolio risk, s_p (x-axis)–portfolio return, r_p (y-axis) axes.
b. Draw the *efficient frontier* on the graph in part (a).
c. Which portfolios lie on the efficient frontier? Why do these portfolios dominate all others in the feasible or attainable set?
d. How would an investor's *utility function* or *risk-indifference curves* be used with the efficient frontier to find the optimal portfolio?

LG 4

P5.11 For his portfolio, David Finney randomly selected securities from all those listed on the New York Stock Exchange. He began with one security and added securities one by one until a total of 20 securities were held in the portfolio. After each security was added, David calculated the portfolio standard deviation, s_p. The calculated values follow.

Number of Securities	Portfolio Risk, s_p (%)	Number of Securities	Portfolio Risk, s_p (%)
1	14.50	11	7.00
2	13.30	12	6.80
3	12.20	13	6.70
4	11.20	14	6.65
5	10.30	15	6.60
6	9.50	16	6.56
7	8.80	17	6.52
8	8.20	18	6.50
9	7.70	19	6.48
10	7.30	20	6.47

a. On a set of axes showing number of securities in portfolio (x-axis) and portfolio risk, s_p (y-axis), plot the portfolio risk data given in the preceding table.
b. Divide the total portfolio risk in the graph into its *nondiversifiable* and *diversifiable* risk components, and label each of these on the graph.
c. Describe which of the two risk components is the *relevant risk,* and explain why it is relevant. How much of this risk exists in David Finney's portfolio?

LG 4

P5.12 If portfolio A has a beta of +1.50 and portfolio Z has a beta of −1.50, what do the two values indicate? If the return on the market rises by 20%, what impact, if any, would this have on the returns from portfolios A and Z? Explain.

LG 4

P5.13 Stock A has a beta of 0.80, stock B has a beta of 1.40, and stock C has a beta of −0.30.

a. Rank these stocks from the most risky to the least risky.

b. If the return on the market portfolio increases by 12%, what change in the return for each of the stocks would you expect?

c. If the return on the market portfolio declines by 5%, what change in the return for each of the stocks would you expect?

d. If you felt the stock market was about to experience a significant decline, which stock would you be most likely to add to your portfolio? Why?

e. If you anticipated a major stock market rally, which stock would you be most likely to add to your portfolio? Why?

 LG 4

P5.14 Rose Berry is attempting to evaluate two possible portfolios consisting of the same five assets but held in different proportions. She is particularly interested in using beta to compare the risk of the portfolios and, in this regard, has gathered the following data:

| | | Portfolio Weights (%) | |
Asset	Asset Beta	Portfolio A	Portfolio B
1	1.30	10	30
2	0.70	30	10
3	1.25	10	20
4	1.10	10	20
5	0.90	40	20
Total		100	100

a. Calculate the betas for portfolios A and B.

b. Compare the risk of each portfolio to the market as well as to each other. Which portfolio is more risky?

Case Problem 5.1   *Traditional versus Modern Portfolio Theory: Who's Right?*

LG 3   LG 4

Walt Davies and Shane O'Brien are district managers for Lee, Inc. Over the years, as they moved through the firm's sales organization, they became (and still remain) close friends. Walt, who is 33 years old, currently lives in Princeton, New Jersey. Shane, who is 35, lives in Houston, Texas. Recently, at the national sales meeting, they were discussing various company matters, as well as bringing each other up to date on their families, when the subject of investments came up. Each had always been fascinated by the stock market, and now that they had achieved some degree of financial success, they had begun actively investing. As they discussed their investments, Walt said he felt the only way an individual who does not have hundreds of thousands of dollars can invest safely is to buy mutual fund shares. He emphasized that to be safe, a person needs to hold a broadly diversified portfolio and that only those with a lot of money and time can achieve independently the diversification that can be readily obtained by purchasing mutual fund shares.

Shane totally disagreed. He said, "Diversification! Who needs it?" He felt that what one must do is look carefully at stocks possessing desired risk-return characteristics and then invest all one's money in the single best stock. Walt told him he was crazy. He said, "There is no way to measure risk conveniently—you're just gambling." Shane disagreed. He explained how his stockbroker had acquainted him with beta, which is a measure of risk. Shane said that the higher the beta, the more risky the stock, and therefore the higher its return. By looking up the betas for potential stock investments on the Internet, he can pick stocks that have an acceptable risk level for him. Shane explained that with beta, one does not need to diversify; one merely needs to be willing to accept the risk reflected by beta and then hope for the best. The conversation continued, with Walt indicating that although he knew nothing about beta, he didn't believe one could safely invest in a single stock. Shane continued to argue that his broker had explained to him that betas can be calculated not just for a single stock but also for a portfolio of stocks, such as a mutual fund. He said, "What's the difference between a stock with a beta of, say, 1.20 and a mutual fund with a beta of 1.20? They both have the same risk and should therefore provide similar returns."

As Walt and Shane continued to discuss their differing opinions relative to investment strategy, they began to get angry with each other. Neither was able to convince the other that he was right. The level of their voices now raised, they attracted the attention of the company vice-president of finance, Elinor Green, who was standing nearby. She came over and indicated she had overheard their argument about investments and thought that, given her expertise on financial matters, she might be able to resolve their disagreement. She asked them to explain the crux of their disagreement, and each reviewed his own viewpoint. After hearing their views, Elinor responded, "I have some good news and some bad news for each of you. There is some validity to what each of you says, but there also are some errors in each of your explanations. Walt tends to support the traditional approach to portfolio management. Shane's views are more supportive of modern portfolio theory." Just then, the company president interrupted them, needing to talk to Elinor immediately. Elinor apologized for having to leave and offered to continue their discussion later that evening.

Questions

a.   Analyze Walt's argument and explain why a mutual fund investment may be over-diversified. Also explain why one does not necessarily have to have hundreds of thousands of dollars to diversify adequately.

b.   Analyze Shane's argument and explain the major error in his logic relative to the use of beta as a substitute for diversification. Explain the key assumption underlying the use of beta as a risk measure.

c.   Briefly describe the traditional approach to portfolio management, and relate it to the approaches supported by Walt and Shane.

d.   Briefly describe modern portfolio theory (MPT), and relate it to the approaches supported by Walt and Shane. Be sure to mention diversifiable risk, nondiversifiable risk, and total risk, along with the role of beta.

e.   Explain how the traditional approach and modern portfolio theory can be blended into an approach to portfolio management that might prove useful to the individual investor. Relate this to reconciling Walt's and Shane's differing points of view.

Case Problem 5.2   *Susan Lussier's Inherited Portfolio: Does It Meet Her Needs?*

LG 3   LG 4

LG 5   LG 6

Susan Lussier is a 35-year-old divorcée currently employed as a tax attorney for a major oil and gas exploration company. She has no children and earns nearly $125,000 per year from her salary and from participation in the company's drilling activities. Divorced only a year, Susan has found being single quite exciting. An expert on oil and gas taxation, she is not worried about job security—she is content with her income and finds it adequate to allow her to buy and do whatever she wishes. Her current philosophy is to live each day to its fullest, not concerning herself with retirement, which is too far in the future to require her current attention.

A month ago, Susan's only surviving parent, her father, was killed in a sailing accident. He had retired in La Jolla, California, 2 years earlier and had spent most of his time sailing. Prior to retirement, he managed a children's clothing manufacturing firm in South Carolina. Upon retirement he sold his stock in the firm and invested the proceeds in a security portfolio that provided him with retirement income of over $30,000 per year. In his will, which incidentally had been drafted by Susan a number of years earlier, he left his entire estate to her. The estate was structured in such a way that in addition to a few family heirlooms, Susan received a security portfolio having a market value of nearly $350,000 and about $10,000 in cash.

Susan's father's portfolio contained 10 securities: 5 bonds, 2 common stocks, and 3 mutual funds. The accompanying table lists the securities and their key characteristics. The common stocks were issued by large, mature, well-known firms that had exhibited continuing patterns of dividend payment over the past 5 years. The stocks offered only moderate growth potential—probably no more than 2% to 3% appreciation per year.

Case 5.2   The Securities Portfolio That Susan Lussier Inherited

			Bonds			
Par Value	Issue	S&P Rating	Interest Income	Quoted Price	Total Cost	Current Yield
$40,000	Delta Power and Light 10⅛% due 2020	AA	$ 4,050	98	$ 39,200	10.33%
30,000	Mountain Water 9¾% due 2012	A	2,925	102	30,600	9.56
50,000	California Gas 9½% due 2007	AAA	4,750	97	48,500	9.79
20,000	Trans-Pacific Gas 10% due 2018	AAA	2,000	99	19,800	10.10
20,000	Public Service 9⅞% due 2008	AA	1,975	100	20,000	9.88

			Common Stocks				
Number of Shares	Company	Dividend per Share	Dividend Income	Price per Share	Total Cost	Beta	Dividend Yield
2,000	International Supply	$2.40	$ 4,800	$ 22	$ 44,900	0.97	10.91%
3,000	Black Motor	1.50	4,500	17	52,000	0.85	8.82

			Mutual Funds				
Number of Shares	Fund	Dividend per Share	Dividend Income	Price per Share	Total Cost	Beta	Dividend Yield
2,000	International Capital Income A Fund	$ .80	$ 1,600	$ 10	$ 20,000	1.02	8.00%
1,000	Grimner Special Income Fund	2.00	2,000	15	15,000	1.10	7.50
4,000	Ellis Diversified Income Fund	1.20	4,800	12	48,800	0.90	10.00
		Total annual income:	$33,400	Portfolio value:	$338,000	Portfolio current yield:	9.88%

The mutual funds in the portfolio were income funds invested in diversified portfolios of income-oriented stocks and bonds. They provided stable streams of dividend income but offered little opportunity for capital appreciation.

Now that Susan owns the portfolio, she wishes to determine whether it is suitable for her situation. She realizes that the high level of income provided by the portfolio will be taxed at a rate (federal plus state) in excess of 40%. Because she does not currently need it, Susan plans to invest the after-tax income primarily in common stocks offering high capital gain potential. During the coming years she clearly needs to avoid generating taxable income. (Susan is already paying out a sizable portion of her current income in taxes.) She feels fortunate to have received the portfolio and wants to make certain it provides her with the maximum benefits, given her financial situation. The $10,000 cash left to her will be especially useful in paying broker's commissions associated with making portfolio adjustments.

Questions

a.   Briefly assess Susan's financial situation and develop a portfolio objective for her that is consistent with her needs.

b.   Evaluate the portfolio left to Susan by her father. Assess its apparent objective and evaluate how well it may be doing in fulfilling this objective. Use the total cost values to describe the asset allocation scheme reflected in the portfolio. Comment on the risk, return, and tax implications of this portfolio.

c.   If Susan decided to invest in a security portfolio consistent with her needs—indicated in response to question (a)—describe the nature and mix, if any, of securities you would recommend she purchase. What asset allocation scheme would result from your recommendation? Discuss the risk, return, and tax implications of such a portfolio.

d.   Compare the nature of the security portfolio inherited by Susan, from the response to question (b), with what you believe would be an appropriate security portfolio for her, from the response to question (c).

e.   What recommendations would you give Susan about the inherited portfolio? Explain the steps she should take to adjust the portfolio to her needs.

Web Exercises

The Web offers a number of sites that assist individual investors with the topic of asset allocation. Several of these sites are shown here.

Web Address	Primary Investment Focus of the Site
www.efficientfrontier.com	Contains the basics of asset allocation for beginning as well as more advanced investors.
www.columbiafunds.com	An investor-education site. Go to [Planning Tools], [Asset Allocation], [Maximizing Return through Asset Allocation].
www.wellsfargo.com/investment_center	A personal planner and asset allocation guide.

W5.1   Check a simple asset allocation program at www.smartmoney.com/oneasset. Determine the ideal allocation by giving the program your tax bracket and current allocation in cash, bonds, small caps, large caps, international stocks. (Use a hypothetical, but realistic, asset allocation if necessary.) What, if any, revision in your asset allocation was recommended? Comment.

W5.2   Test your knowledge on the basics of asset allocation by taking the quiz at majestic.vanguard.com/EPA/DA/0.2.basics_asset_alloc_quiz. After answering the 10 questions, click on [Get Answers] at the end of the quiz. Review your results.

W5.3   A simple CAPM calculator is available at www-ec.njit.edu/~mathis/ interactive/CAPMFrame.html. Calculate the expected return on asset i by using the following values: risk-free rate = 0.04, expected return on the market = 0.10, and beta = 1.20.

W5.4   Under Class8: Asset Pricing Models, click on the streaming file on [Introduction to the CAPM] at www.duke.edu/~charvey/Classes/ba350_1997/350hyper.htm. What is beta? What is the rationale behind the capital asset pricing model?

For additional practice with concepts from this chapter, visit
www.awl.com/gitman_joehnk

CFA EXAM QUESTIONS

Being certified as a **Chartered Financial Analyst (CFA)** is globally recognized as the highest professional designation you can receive in the field of professional money management. The CFA charter is awarded to those candidates who successfully pass a series of three levels of exams, with each exam lasting 6 hours and covering a full range of investment topics. The CFA program is administered by the Association for Investment Management and Research (AIMR) in Charlottesville, VA, and in 2001, a record 86,421 securities analysts, money managers, investment advisors, and students from all 50 states and 143 countries registered for the 2001 series of CFA exams (for more information about the CFA program, go to: www.aimr.org/cfaprogram/).

Starting with this Part (Two) of the text, and at the end of each part hereafter, you will find a small sample of CFA questions taken from the Level I exam program. These are all questions that have actually appeared on past exams, or are found in the study material put out by AIMR. (When answering the questions, give yourself 1½ minutes for each question.)

The Investment Environment and Conceptual Tools

Following is a sample of 12 Level-I CFA exam questions that deal with many of the topics covered in Parts One and Two of this text, including the time value of money, measures of risk and return, securities markets, asset allocation, and portfolio management.

1. An investment of $231 will increase in value to $268 in 3 years. The annual compound growth rate is closest to:
    a. 3.0%.
    b. 4.0%.
    c. 5.0%.
    d. 6.0%.

2. What quarterly payment is necessary to accumulate $1.5 million over 15 years if the annual interest rate is 6.75% compounded quarterly? Assume payments are made at the end of each quarter.
    a. $10,703.
    b. $14,637.
    c. $24,748.
    d. $25,000.

3. If Stock X's expected return is 30 percent and its expected variance is 25, Stock X's expected coefficient of variation is:
    a. 8.33%.
    b. 16.7%.
    c. 120%.
    d. 600%.

4. An analyst estimates that a stock has the following probabilities of year-end prices:

Stock Price	Probability
$80	0.1
$85	0.3
$90	0.4
$95	0.2

    The stock's expected price at the end of the year is:
    a. $87.50.
    b. $88.50.
    c. $89.00.
    d. $90.00.

CFA EXAM QUESTIONS

5. Direct trading of securities between two parties with no broker intermediary occurs in:
   a. the "third market."
   b. the "fourth market."
   c. over-the-counter trading.
   d. a listed exchange market.

6. An order to buy or sell stock at the best current price is a:
   a. stop order.
   b. limit order.
   c. floor order.
   d. market order

7. Which *one* of the following statements regarding the Dow Jones Industrial Average (DJIA) is *false?*
   a. The DJIA is a price-weighted index.
   b. The DJIA consists of 30 blue chip stocks.
   c. The DJIA is affected equally by changes in low and high priced stocks.
   d. The DJIA divisor needs to be adjusted for stock splits.

8. Which of the following statements *best* reflects the importance of the asset allocation decision to the investment process? The asset allocation decision:
   a. helps the investor decide on realistic investment goals.
   b. identifies the specific securities to include in a portfolio.
   c. determines most of the portfolio's returns and volatility over time.
   d. creates a standard by which to establish an appropriate investment time horizon.

9. For a two-stock portfolio, the most preferred correlation coefficient between the two stocks would be:
   a. −1.00.
   b. 0.
   c. +0.50.
   d. +1.00.

10. Which of the following portfolios *cannot* lie on the efficient frontier as described by Markowitz?

	Portfolio	Expected Return	Standard Deviation
a.	W	9%	21%
b.	X	5%	7%
c.	Y	15%	36%
d.	Z	12%	15%

11. Beta and standard deviation differ as risk measures in that beta measures:
    a. only unsystematic risk, whereas standard deviation measures total risk.
    b. only systematic risk, whereas standard deviation measures total risk.
    c. total risk, whereas standard deviation measures only unsystematic risk.
    d. total risk, whereas standard deviation measures only systematic risk.

12. According to the CAPM, the risk premium an investor expects to receive on any stock or portfolio increases:
    a. directly with alpha.
    b. inversely with alpha.
    c. directly with beta.
    d. inversely with beta.

Answers: 1. c; 2. b; 3. b; 4. b; 5. b; 6. d; 7. c; 8. c; 9. a; 10. a; 11. b; 12. c

CHAPTER 6

COMMON STOCK INVESTMENTS

LEARNING GOALS

After studying this chapter, you should be able to:

LG 1 Explain the investment appeal of common stocks and why individuals like to invest in them.

LG 2 Describe stock returns from a historical perspective and understand how current returns measure up to historical standards of performance.

LG 3 Discuss the basic features of common stocks, including issue characteristics, stock quotations, and transaction costs.

LG 4 Understand the different kinds of common stock values.

LG 5 Discuss common stock dividends, types of dividends, and dividend reinvestment plans.

LG 6 Describe various types of common stocks, including foreign stocks, and note how stocks can be used as investment vehicles.

Investing in common stocks is about taking educated risks. It is also about receiving returns—sometimes spectacular ones. In 1971, a company named Intel sold its stock to the public at $23.50 per share. The company was unprofitable and virtually unknown. That year, though, the company made technological history by introducing the world's first microprocessor, the "brains" that control a computer's central processing of data. Today, of course, Intel is a major supplier to the computing industry of chips, boards, systems, and software. And its original investors have been handsomely rewarded: A purchase of 100 shares at $23.50 per share in 1971 grew to over 100,000 shares, worth more than $8.2 million, by mid-year 2000—a return of more than 3,500 times the initial investment.

In hindsight, it looks so easy. But in fact, investors who put their money at risk need to learn as much as possible about each company they consider and the industry in which it operates. They also need to know how to analyze and interpret the information they gather. This chapter looks at common stocks and introduces some of the key concepts and principles of investing in these complex but potentially rewarding securities.

What Stocks Have to Offer

residual owners
owners/stockholders of a firm, who are entitled to dividend income and a prorated share of the firm's earnings only after all the firm's other obligations have been met.

The basic investment attribute of common stocks is that they enable investors to participate in the profits of the firm. Every shareholder is a part owner of the firm and, as such, is entitled to a piece of the firm's profits. This claim on income is not without limitations, however, because common stockholders are really the **residual owners** of the company. That is, they are entitled to dividend income and a share of the company's earnings only after all other corporate obligations have been met. Equally important, as residual owners, holders of common stock have no guarantee that they will ever receive any return on their investment. The challenge, of course, is to find stocks that will provide the kind of return you're looking for. That's no easy task, for there are literally thousands of actively traded stocks to choose from.

The Appeal of Common Stocks

Common stocks are a popular form of investing, used by millions of individual investors. They are popular, in part, because they offer investors the opportunity to tailor their investment programs to meet individual needs and preferences. Given the size and diversity of the stock market, it's safe to say that no matter what the investment objective, there are common stocks to fit the bill. For people living off their investment holdings, stocks provide a way of earning a steady stream of current income (from the dividends they produce). For investors less concerned about current income, common stocks can serve as the basis for long-run accumulation of wealth. With this strategy, stocks are used very much like a savings account: Investors buy stock for the long haul as a way to earn not only dividends but also a steady flow of capital gains. These investors recognize that stocks have a tendency to go up in price over time, and they simply position themselves to take advantage of that fact. Indeed, it is this potential for capital gains that is the real draw for most investors. Whereas dividends can provide a steady stream of income, the big returns come from capital gains. And few securities can match common stocks when it comes to capital gains.

Putting Stock Price Behavior in Perspective

Given the underlying nature of common stocks, when the market is strong, investors can generally expect to benefit from steady price appreciation. A good example is the performance that took place in 1999, when the market, as measured by the Dow Jones Industrial Average (DJIA), went up by more than 25%. But 1999 was even better for tech stocks and the Nasdaq market, which went up a whopping 85%.

Unfortunately, when the markets falter, so do investor returns. A recent example of such behavior is the 40% drop that occurred in the Nasdaq market in 2000, making it the worst year on record for the Nasdaq. Ironic, isn't it: A year after its best year on record, the Nasdaq recorded its worst year ever! But perhaps, an even more dramatic example of a market gone bad is the hair-raising experience of 1987. In that year, stock prices had shot up almost 30% in the first 6 months, only to experience a terrible crash on October 19. That day was not just another bad day in the market—it was the worst day in the market's history. Stock prices, as measured by the DJIA, fell 508 points on

INVESTOR FACTS

THE SLUMBERING BEAR—Bear markets occur when stock prices are falling. But not all falling markets end up as bears. A drop of *5% or more* in one of the major market indexes, like the Dow Jones Industrial Average (DJIA), is called a **routine decline**. As the name indicates, a routine decline typically occurs several times a year—such as April 14, 2000, when the average dropped 5.6%. A **correction** is a drop of *10% or more* in an index. A correction occurred in mid-summer of 1998, when the DJIA plunged 19.3%. The term **bear market** is reserved for severe market declines of *20% or more*. Bear markets usually occur every 3 to 4 years, but the 1990s were bear-free, although increased market volatility has everyone wondering whether the next bear market isn't just around the corner. (Note: 2000–2001 saw a big-time bear take over the Nasdaq market, as it fell more than 65%, though the Dow, through mid-2001, remained bear-free.)

FIGURE 6.1

**The Great Bull Market
of 1982–2000**

One of the greatest bull markets in history began on August 12, 1982, with the Dow at 777, and has continued for more than 18 years. It was strong enough to survive two market crashes (one in 1987 and another in 1997) and one mild recession (in 1990). Indeed, this bull has had only one down year (1990), as it has charged to a high of over 11,000 on the Dow (so far).

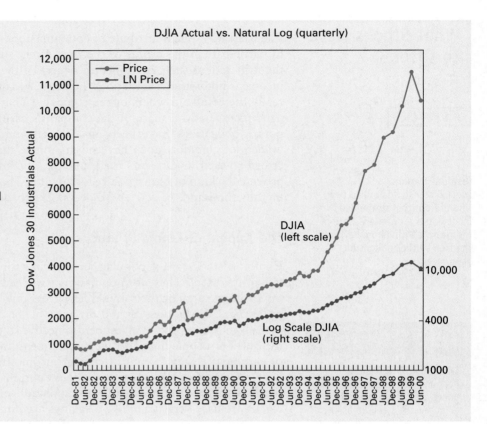

DJIA Actual vs. Natural Log (quarterly)

volume of over 600 million shares. The day set a number of records: the largest point drop, the largest 1-day volume of shares traded, and the largest percentage decline (23%), almost twice the previous single-day record.

Ten years later, almost to the day, it happened again. On October 27, 1997, the DJIA set two new records by dropping 554 points on a volume of 685 million shares. In percentage terms, however, the market ended the day down just over 7%, which wasn't even close to the record. (The 7% decline was the 12th largest in percentage terms.) Unlike the 1987 crash, this one didn't last long. The market recovered all of its losses *within 2 weeks*. In stark contrast, it took over 2½ years for the market to recover from the 1987 crash. Then, as the market entered a new century, *an even bigger drop* occurred; on April 14, 2000, the DJIA plunged an eye-popping 617 points. That decline, however, amounted to a fall of "only" 5.5%. It barely compared to the crash of 1987, which in percentage terms was about four times as bad.

Fortunately, days such as these are the exception rather than the rule. More often than not, the stock market offers attractive returns, rather than just risk and wild price volatility. Take a look at Figure 6.1, which shows the behavior of the market over the 19-year period from 1982 through mid-year 2000. This market run, which began in August 1982, when the Dow stood at 777, has seen the DJIA climb to over 11,000 (more than 14 times higher than where it started), making it the biggest market advance of all time! One thing that makes this market stand out is how far it has moved in a relatively short period of time. That is, the Dow has gone from less than 1,000 points to over 11,000 (through mid-2000)—and about 75% of that advance has occurred in the last 6 to 8 years. Movements of the magnitude seen on October 27, 1997, are hard to comprehend calmly. But 100- or 200-point swings are not the same when the DJIA is at 9,000 or 10,000 as when the market was trading at the 2,000 or 3,000 level—which was happening not all that many years ago.

Look again at Figure 6.1. Note the two lines on the graph. The top one tracks the actual behavior of the Dow; the lower one follows the same performance, on a logarithmic ("log") scale that shows the *rate of change* in the market instead of absolute values. Clearly, rather than showing a market that's going through the roof, the second line shows a strong market that's moving up at a far more stable pace. How long the market can continue to do so remains to be seen. The one thing we know for sure is that the market has been very good to investors for the past 18 years. And so long as earnings remain strong and interest rates remain low, there's no reason the market can't continue to climb.

From Stock Prices to Stock Returns

Our discussion so far has centered on *stock prices*, but what's even more important to investors is *stock returns*, which take into account not only price behavior but also dividend income. Table 6.1 uses the DJIA to show annual market returns over the 50-year period from 1950–2000. In addition to total returns, the table breaks market performance down into the two basic sources of return: dividends and capital gains. These figures, of course, reflect the *general behavior of the*

TABLE 6.1   Annual Returns in the Stock Market, 1950–2000 (returns based on performance of the DJIA)

Year	Rate of Return from Dividends	Rate of Return from Capital Gains	Total Rate of Return	Year	Rate of Return from Dividends	Rate of Return from Capital Gains	Total Rate of Return
2000	1.57%	−9.96%	−7.99%	1974	6.12%	−27.57%	−21.45%
1999	1.47	25.22	26.69	1973	4.15	−16.58	−12.43
1998	1.65	16.10	17.75	1972	3.16	14.58	17.74
1997	1.72	22.64	24.36	1971	3.47	6.11	9.58
1996	2.03	26.01	28.04	1970	3.76	4.82	8.58
1995	2.27	33.45	35.72	1969	4.24	−15.19	−10.95
1994	2.75	2.14	4.89	1968	3.32	4.27	7.59
1993	2.65	13.72	16.37	1967	3.33	15.20	18.53
1992	3.05	4.17	7.22	1966	4.06	−18.94	−14.88
1991	3.00	20.32	23.32	1965	2.95	10.88	13.83
1990	3.90	−4.34	−0.44	1964	3.57	14.57	18.14
1989	3.74	26.96	30.70	1963	3.07	17.00	20.07
1988	3.67	11.85	15.52	1962	3.57	−10.81	−7.24
1987	3.67	2.26	5.93	1961	3.11	18.71	21.82
1986	3.54	22.58	26.12	1960	3.47	−9.34	−5.87
1985	4.01	27.66	31.67	1959	3.05	16.40	19.45
1984	5.00	−3.74	1.26	1958	3.43	33.96	37.39
1983	4.47	20.27	24.74	1957	4.96	−12.77	−7.81
1982	5.17	19.60	24.77	1956	4.60	2.27	6.87
1981	6.42	−9.23	−2.81	1955	4.42	20.77	25.19
1980	5.64	14.93	20.57	1954	4.32	43.96	48.28
1979	6.08	4.19	10.27	1953	5.73	−3.77	1.96
1978	6.03	−3.15	2.88	1952	5.29	8.42	13.71
1977	5.51	−17.27	−11.76	1951	6.07	14.37	20.44
1976	4.12	17.86	21.98	1950	6.85	17.63	24.48
1975	4.39	38.32	42.71				

Note: Total return figures are based on both dividend income *and* capital gains (or losses); all figures are compiled from DJIA performance information, as obtained from *Barron's* and the *Wall Street Journal;* 2000 figures are through the second quarter (June 30) of the year.

market as a whole, not necessarily that of *individual stocks.* Think of them as the return behavior on a well-balanced portfolio of common stocks.

The numbers show a market that, over the past 50 years, has provided annual returns ranging from a low of −21.45% (in 1974) to a high of +48.28% (in 1954). Breaking down the returns into dividends and capital gains reveals that the big returns (or losses) come from capital gains. Overall, as Table 6.2 shows, *stocks provided average annual returns of around 12% over the full 50-year period.* And if you look at just the last 5 to 10 years, you'll find that average returns have been more like 18% to 20%. In fact, over the last 15 years (1985–2000), stocks have produced an average annual return of nearly 18%. Clearly, this market for most of the past 15 years has been anything *but* average.

Keep in mind that the numbers represent market performance; *individual* stocks can and often do perform quite differently. But at least, the averages give us a benchmark against which we can assess current stock returns and our own expectations. For example, if a return of 10% to 12% can be considered a good long-term estimate for stocks, then *sustained* returns of 18% to 20% should definitely be viewed as extraordinary. (These higher returns are possible, of course, but to get them, investors must either take on more risk or hope for a continuation of this incredible market.) Likewise, long-run stock returns of only 6% to 8% should be viewed as substandard performance. If that's the best you think you can do, then you probably should stick with bonds or CDs, where you'll earn almost as much with much less risk.

The Dow, the S&P, and the Nasdaq Most of our discussion in this chapter has been in terms of the DJIA, in large part because the Dow is such a widely followed measure of market performance. However, the DJIA is just one measure of market behavior, and it doesn't always tell the whole story. Two other closely followed market indexes are the S&P (Standard & Poor's) 500 and the Nasdaq Composite.

TABLE 6.2	Holding Period Returns in the Stock Market 1950–2000		
Holding Periods	Average Annual Returns	Cumulative Returns	Amount to Which $10,000 Will Grow
5(+) yrs: 1995–2000	21.8%	196.6%	$ 29,662
5 yrs: 1990–94	10.3	63.0	16,296
10(+) yrs: 1990–00	16.0	376.7	47,663
15 yrs: 1985–99	19.1	1,275.8	137,583
25 yrs: 1975–99	16.3	4,327.7	442,769
50 yrs: 1950–99	12.6	36,855.3	3,695,534
The 1990s: 1990–99	18.3	438.9	53,897
The 1980s: 1980–89	17.2	390.5	49,049
The 1970s: 1970–79	5.3	67.9	16,792
The 1960s: 1960–69	5.2	66.0	16,602
The 1950s: 1950–59	18.0	421.7	52,171

Note: Average annual return figures are fully compounded returns and assume that all dividend income *and* capital gains are automatically reinvested. All figures compiled from DJIA performance information, as obtained from *Barron's* and the *Wall Street Journal;* 2000 data through the second quarter.

The problem with the Dow is that is captures the performance of a small, very select group of (just 30) large-cap stocks. Thus, it does not always reflect what's happening in the broad market. In contrast, the *S&P 500* tracks the performance of 500 of the very biggest and most important firms in the market and as such, is felt to be far more representative of market behavior. The *Nasdaq Composite,* on the other hand, tracks the behavior of many of this country's *tech stocks,* from the very largest, like Microsoft and Intel, to most of the newest (and much smaller) dot-com firms.

To see how these three market measures performed in the 1990s, take a look at Figure 6.2. The upper panel shows the DJIA relative to the S&P 500, and the lower panel shows the Dow relative to the Nasdaq Composite. Starting with the upper panel, we can see very similar performances for the DJIA and S&P 500. Indeed, except for a few minor divergences, the two measures moved in very close unison. So much so, in fact, that if you look in Table 6.3, which shows total returns over various holding periods, you'll see that over the decade of the 1990s (from 1/1/90 to 12/31/99), the two had almost identical returns, 18.35% versus 18.20%. Such uniformity isn't surprising because both the Dow and the S&P track the performance of the same segment of the market: large-cap stocks.

You wouldn't expect the same performance, however, when you match the Dow with the Nasdaq, and you don't get it. But look at the lower panel of Figure 6.2: There's probably more similarity between the two measures than you'd expect—especially in the first 5 or 6 years. Indeed, note in Table 6.3 that in the first half of the decade, the DJIA and the Nasdaq Composite had almost the same average annual returns (10.26% for the Dow vs. 10.58% for the Nasdaq). In fact, these two measures tracked one another fairly closely through 1997. Then, in 1998, they went their separate ways. High-tech stocks and the Nasdaq moved up sharply, while large-cap "old economy" stocks continued up at a far more modest pace. Thus, by the end of the decade, whereas the Dow had a very respectable 10-year return of 18.35%, the Nasdaq registered an incredible 24.50% rate of return (see Table 6.3). In dollar terms, this means that a $10,000 investment in the DJIA at the beginning of the decade

TABLE 6.3   Comparative Returns on the Dow, the S&P, and the Nasdaq

Holding Periods and Return Measures`	DJIA	S&P 500	Nasdaq Composite
The Decade of the '90s: 1990–1999			
• Average annual returns	18.35%	18.20%	24.50%
• Cumulative returns	438.97%	432.33%	794.75%
• Amount to which $10,000 will grow	$53,897	$53,233	$89,475
First Half of the Decade: 1990–1994			
• Average annual returns	10.26%	8.69%	10.58%
• Cumulative returns	62.96%	51.70%	65.34%
• Amount to which $10,000 will grow	$16,296	$15,170	$16,534
Last Half of the Decade: 1995–1999			
• Average annual returns	27.03%	28.54%	40.71%
• Cumulative returns	230.75%	250.91%	441.16%
• Amount to which $10,000 will grow	$33,075	$35,091	$54,116

Note: Average annual return figures are fully compounded and assume that all dividends and capital gains are reinvested.

Source: Morningstar Principia Pro, June 2000.

FIGURE 6.2 **A Decade of the Dow, the S&P, and the Nasdaq (1990 to 1999, *plus the first half of 2000*)**

Here's how the DJIA performed relative to the S&P 500 (top) and the Nasdaq Composite (bottom) in the 1990s. Clearly, the Dow held its own against the S&P but was no match for the tech-heavy Nasdaq.

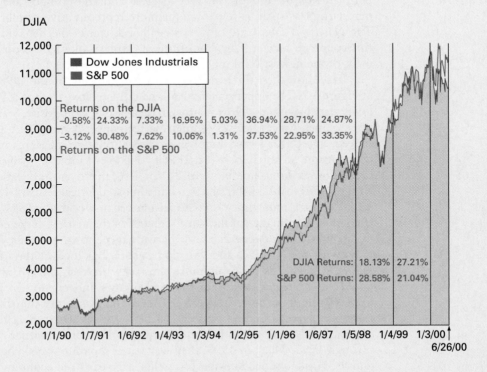

Returns on the DJIA

−0.58%	24.33%	7.33%	16.95%	5.03%	36.94%	28.71%	24.87%
−3.12%	30.48%	7.62%	10.06%	1.31%	37.53%	22.95%	33.35%

Returns on the S&P 500

DJIA Returns: 18.13% 27.21%
S&P 500 Returns: 28.58% 21.04%

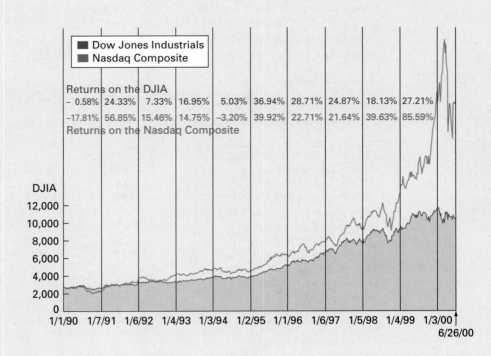

Returns on the DJIA

− 0.58%	24.33%	7.33%	16.95%	5.03%	36.94%	28.71%	24.87%	18.13%	27.21%
−17.81%	56.85%	15.46%	14.75%	−3.20%	39.92%	22.71%	21.64%	39.63%	85.59%

Returns on the Nasdaq Composite

would have been worth more than $50,000 at decade's end, whereas the same amount invested in the Nasdaq would have been worth nearly $90,000.

No matter how you measure it—the Dow, the S&P, or the Nasdaq Composite—the stock market certainly turned in a stellar performance, especially in the last 2 or 3 years of the decade! At least it would appear that way. But what you see isn't always what you get. For as the accompanying *Investing in Action* box reveals, not all stocks participated equally in this market of the nineties.

The types of (overall) market performance turned in, especially in the last half of the decade, has not come without a price: Since 1997, the level of *market volatility* has increased dramatically. There are some important market statistics to back up this claim. For example, in 1997, 1998, and 1999, the market as measured by the DJIA closed at least 1% higher or lower than the preceding day about one-third of the time. That means that with the the Dow at 9,000 or 10,000, moves of 90 to 100 (or more) points a day have been occurring almost every 3 days over the past 3½ years. The S&P 500 has turned in a similar performance, and even more volatility has occurred in the Nasdaq Composite. Although professional stock traders and day traders may love such price volatility, most investors don't. But when you stop to think about it, it's hard to have one result (outsized returns) without the other (outsized risk/price volatility). After all, the big returns are usually produced when there are big swings in the market.

The Pros and Cons of Stock Ownership

One reason why stocks are so appealing to investors is the substantial return opportunities they offer. As we just saw, stocks generally provide attractive, highly competitive returns over the long haul. Indeed, common stock returns compare very favorably to other investment outlets such as long-term corporate bonds and U.S. Treasury securities. For example, over the 50-year period from 1950 through 2000, high-grade corporate bonds averaged annual returns of around 6%—*about half that of common stocks*. Although long-term bonds sometimes outperform stocks on a year-by-year basis (as they did in the mid-1980s, when interest rates were in a free fall), the opposite is true far more often than not; that is, stocks outperform bonds, and usually by a wide margin. Because stocks can be counted on over most periods to provide returns that exceed annual inflation rates, they make ideal inflation hedges. Indeed, since 1982, stocks have done quite well against inflation. As long as inflation rates remain at reasonably low levels of 3% to 4%, stocks are likely to continue to produce attractive inflation-adjusted returns.

Stocks offer other benefits as well: They are easy to buy and sell, and the transaction costs are modest. Moreover, price and market information is widely disseminated in the news and financial media. A final advantage is that the unit cost of a share of common stock is usually within the reach of most individual investors. Unlike bonds, which carry minimum denominations of at least $1,000, and some mutual funds that have fairly hefty minimum investments, common stocks don't have such minimums. Instead, most stocks today are priced at less than $75 a share—and any number of shares, no matter how few, can be bought or sold.

H O T **L I N K S**

Based on broad stock market indexes such as the S&P 500, over long periods of time common stocks have outpaced inflation. Read about outpacing inflation at:

www.putnaminv.com/frames/e101.htm

INVESTING in action

If the Markets Are Doing So Well, Why Don't I Feel Rich?

During the market's boom times from 1997 to 1999, market indexes soared. Nasdaq was the star performer, rising more than 85% in 1999, compared to the very respectable increases of 25% for DJIA and about 20% for the S&P 500. Investors should have been happy with returns like these. To their dismay, however, most investors discovered that their portfolio returns had not tracked any of these market performance measures.

The reason? Since about 1997, the split between a small group of large-cap stocks and the rest of the market widened, creating a very unbalanced two-tier market. A shrinking number of stocks pushed market averages higher, while other companies languished. The technical term for this is *market breadth*, or how broadly the market is moving. If on a particular day, 80% of the issues on the Nasdaq fell in price, you would hear about a "broad decline."

Many money managers label the current (1997–2000) market a "haves versus have-nots" environment, in which a privileged few drive the rest of the market. In such an environment, even though the market might experience a broad decline, the market index continues to rise. Let's look at some statistics that make this point clear.

- In 1999, the prices of 51% of Nasdaq's companies gained. Technology stocks accounted for almost half of the gainers, with 20% at least doubling in price and some reporting 1,000% increases. However, 48% of Nasdaq companies—especially pharmaceuticals, health care, manufacturing, and financial services—fell in price, with an average decline of 32%. The top performers drove the Nasdaq's performance; without them, the Nasdaq composite index was essentially flat. Seldom has a strong market had so many losers.
- The gap between haves and have-nots is even more apparent in the market capitalization of companies on the Wilshire 5000 Total Market Index,. The market value of the 10

largest companies, led by General Electric (GE), Cisco, and Microsoft, represents 20% of the market's total value of $15.3 trillion. The top 10%, about 700 companies, account for 87% of total value; the bottom 700 account for only 0.02 %. GE alone is as big as the smallest 4,940 companies.

With relatively few power-hitters driving the market, an index can keep rising even though more stock prices post declines than advances. This is exactly what happened from about 1997 through mid-2000. Market watchers keep their eyes on the *advance decline (A/D) line*, which represents a cumulative summary of daily price advances, less price declines, for a particular exchange. You can find graphs of the A/D line, the most widely used measure of market breadth for the major exchanges, at www.stockcharts.com These graphs clearly show whether the majority of stocks are following the trend of the market index. If both the market index line and the A/D line are rising, then the market index is fairly representing market performance. When the two move in opposition, it signals that the index is not a good predictor of stock performance.

Another indicator is the *high-low line*, which shows the number of stocks recording their highest or lowest price level in 52 weeks. These are usually shown as moving averages and graphed together to make comparison easy. You'll also find lists of stocks reporting new highs or lows on the stock quotation pages.

Sources: Eric Bjorgen, "A Bull Market? Baloney," *Mutual Funds*, May 2000, p. 28; E. S. Browning, "Nasdaq's Gains Mask a House Divided; Stocks Show Equal Split of Rich and Poor," *Wall Street Journal*, December 20, 1999, pp. C1, C4; E. S. Browning, "Stocks Approach the Stratosphere," *Wall Street Journal*, January 4, 2000, p. R1; Stockcharts.com, www.stockcharts.com; Russ Wiles, "Handful of Companies Dominate Stock Market's Valuation," *Arizona Republic*, April 25, 2000, p. D1.

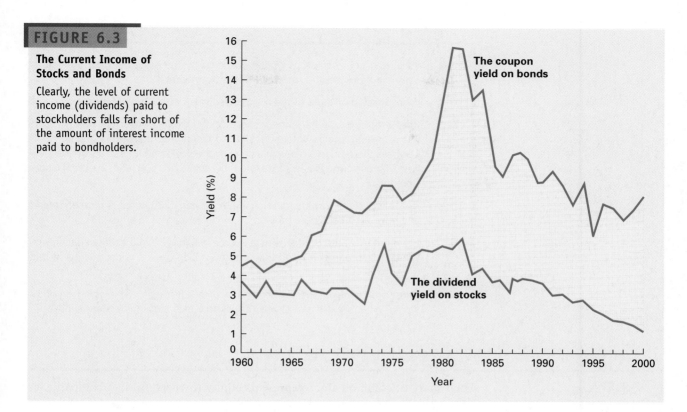

FIGURE 6.3

The Current Income of Stocks and Bonds

Clearly, the level of current income (dividends) paid to stockholders falls far short of the amount of interest income paid to bondholders.

There are also some *disadvantages* to common stock. Risk is perhaps the most significant. Stocks are subject to various types of risk, including business and financial risk, purchasing power risk, market risk, and event risk. All of these can adversely affect a stock's earnings and dividends, its price appreciation, and, of course, the rate of return earned by an investor. Even the best of stocks possess elements of risk that are difficult to overcome, because company earnings are subject to many factors, including government control and regulation, foreign competition, and the state of the economy. Because such factors affect sales and profits, they also affect the price behavior of the stock and possibly even dividends. All of this leads to another disadvantage: The earnings and general performance of stocks are subject to wide swings, so it is difficult to value common stocks and consistently select top performers. The selection process is complex because so many elements go into formulating expectations of stock performance. In other words, not only is the future outcome of the company and its stock uncertain, but the evaluation and selection process itself is far from perfect.

A final disadvantage of stocks is the sacrifice of current income. Several types of investments—bonds, for instance—pay higher levels of current income and do so with much greater certainty. Figure 6.3 compares the dividend yield of common stocks with the coupon yield of bonds. It shows the degree of sacrifice common stock investors make in terms of current income. Clearly, common stocks have a long way to go before they catch up with the *current income levels* available from bonds and most other fixed-income securities.

IN REVIEW

6.1 What is a *common stock?* What is meant by the statement that holders of common stock are the *residual owners* of the firm?

6.2 What are two or three of the major investment attributes of common stocks?

6.3 Briefly describe the behavior of the U.S. stock market over the past 10 to 15 years, paying special attention to the market that started in August 1982. Contrast the market's performance over the 1990s as measured by the DJIA with its performance as measured by the S&P 500 and by the Nasdaq Composite.

6.4 According to the *Investing in Action* box on page 230, what is *market breadth* and how did it become a problem in the latter part of the 1990s?

6.5 How important are dividends as a source of return? What about capital gains? Which is more important to total return? Which causes wider swings in total return?

6.6 What are some of the advantages *and* disadvantages of owning common stock? What are the major types of risk to which stockholders are exposed?

Basic Characteristics of Common Stock

LG 3   LG 4

equity capital
evidence of ownership position in a firm, in the form of shares of common stock.

publicly traded issues
shares of stock that are readily available to the general public and are bought and sold in the open market.

public offering
an offering to sell to the investing public a set number of shares of a firm's stock at a specified price.

rights offering
an offering of a new issue of stock to existing stockholders, who may purchase new shares in proportion to their current ownership position.

Each share of common stock represents equity (ownership) in a company. It's this equity position that explains why common stocks are often referred to as *equity securities* or **equity capital.** Every share entitles the holder to an equal ownership position and participation in the corporation's earnings and dividends, an equal vote, and an equal voice in management. Together, the common stockholders own the company. The more shares an investor owns, the bigger his or her ownership position. Common stock has no maturity date—it remains outstanding indefinitely.

Common Stock as a Corporate Security

All corporations "issue" common stock of one type or another. But the shares of many, if not most, corporations are never traded, because the firms either are too small or are family controlled. The stocks of interest to us in this book are **publicly traded issues**—the shares that are readily available to the general public and which are bought and sold in the open market. The firms issuing such shares range from giants like AT&T and Microsoft to much smaller regional or local firms. The market for publicly traded stocks is enormous: The value of all actively traded listed and OTC stocks in 2000 was over $14 trillion.

Shares of common stock can be issued in several different ways. The most widely used procedure today is the **public offering.** In using this procedure, the corporation offers the investing public a certain number of shares of its stock at a certain price. Figure 6.4 shows an announcement for such an offering. In this case, Arena Pharmaceuticals, a small highly-specialized biopharmaceutical company, sold 6.9 million shares of stock at a price of $18 a share.

New shares of stock can also be issued using what is known as a **rights offering.** In a rights offering, existing stockholders are given the first opportunity

FIGURE 6.4 **An Announcement of a New Stock Issue**

This announcement indicates that Arena Pharmaceuticals (Nasdaq: **ARNA**) is issuing 6.9 million shares of stock at a price of $18 per share. For the company, that will mean nearly $125 million in new capital. Note that even this issue has a global twist to it as the lead banker of this U.S. security offering, ING Barings, is a major multinational investment banking firm headquartered in Amsterdam and London. (*Source: Wall Street Journal,* August 15, 2000.)

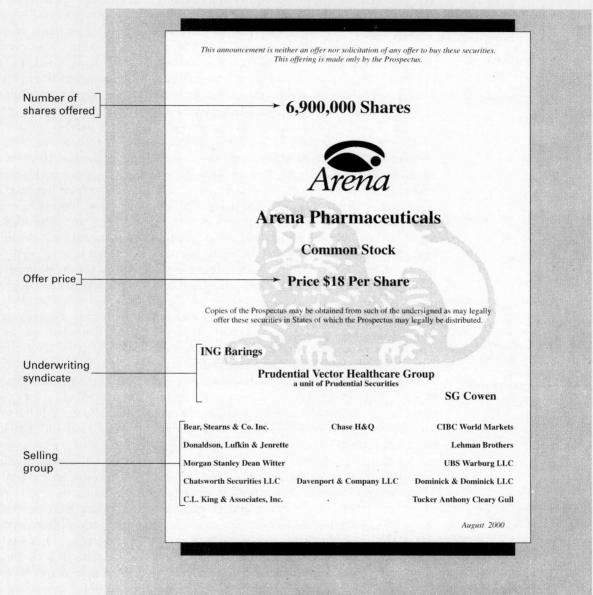

This announcement is neither an offer nor solicitation of any offer to buy these securities.
This offering is made only by the Prospectus.

6,900,000 Shares

Arena

Arena Pharmaceuticals

Common Stock

Price $18 Per Share

Copies of the Prospectus may be obtained from such of the undersigned as may legally
offer these securities in States of which the Prospectus may legally be distributed.

ING Barings

Prudential Vector Healthcare Group
a unit of Prudential Securities

SG Cowen

Bear, Stearns & Co. Inc.	Chase H&Q	CIBC World Markets
Donaldson, Lufkin & Jenrette		Lehman Brothers
Morgan Stanley Dean Witter		UBS Warburg LLC
Chatsworth Securities LLC	Davenport & Company LLC	Dominick & Dominick LLC
C.L. King & Associates, Inc.		Tucker Anthony Cleary Gull

August 2000

ING BARINGS

ING Barings is the organization and trade name used by ING Bank N.V. and certain of its subsidiaries for the conduct of international corporate and investment banking business.
ING Bank N.V. is part of ING Group, one of the largest integrated financial services organizations in the world.

Labels (left margin):
- Number of shares offered
- Offer price
- Underwriting syndicate
- Selling group

to buy the new issue. They can purchase new shares in proportion to their current ownership position. For instance, if a stockholder currently owns 1% of a firm's stock and the firm issues 10,000 additional shares, the rights offering will give that stockholder the opportunity to purchase 1% (100 shares) of the new issue. The net result of a rights offering is the same as that of a public offering: The firm ends up with more equity in its capital structure, and the number of shares outstanding increases.

Perhaps one of the most creative ways of bringing a new issue to the market is through a **stock spin-off**. Basically, a spin-off occurs when a company gets rid of one of its subsidiaries or divisions. For example, Quaker Oats did this when it spun off its Fisher-Price subsidiary. The company doesn't just sell the subsidiary to some other firm. Rather, it creates a new stand-alone company and then distributes stock in that company to its existing stockholders. Thus every Quaker Oats shareholder received a certain (prorated) number of shares in the newly created, and now publicly traded, Fisher-Price company. There have been hundreds of stock spin-offs in the last 10 years or so. Some of the more notable ones were the spin-off of Agilent by Hewlett-Packard, the partial (15%) spin-off of the online travel service Expedia by Microsoft, and the Eckerd Drugstore spin-off by J.C. Penney. Normally, companies execute stock spin-offs if they believe the subsidiary is no longer a good fit, or if they feel they've become too diversified and want to focus on their core products. Not surprisingly, such spin-offs often work very well for investors, too. For more discussion of how stock spin-offs perform compared with their "parents," see this book's homepage, www.awl.com/gitman_joehnk

stock spin-off
conversion of one of a firm's subsidiaries to a stand-alone company by distribution of stock in that new company to existing shareholders.

Stock Splits Companies can also increase the number of shares outstanding by executing a **stock split**. In declaring a split, a firm merely announces that it will increase the number of shares outstanding by exchanging a specified number of new shares for each outstanding share of stock. For example, in a 2-for-1 stock split, two new shares of stock are exchanged for each old share. In a 3-for-2 split, three new shares are exchanged for every two old shares outstanding. A stockholder who owned 200 shares of stock before a 2-for-1 split becomes the owner of 400 shares; the same investor would hold 300 shares if there had been a 3-for-2 split.

stock split
a maneuver in which a company increases the number of shares outstanding by exchanging a specified number of new shares of stock for each outstanding share.

Stock splits are used when a firm wants to enhance its stock's trading appeal by lowering its market price. Normally, the firm gets the desired result: The price of the stock tends to fall in close relation to the terms of the split (unless the stock split is accompanied by a big increase in the level of dividends). For example, using the ratio of the number of old shares to new, we can expect a $100 stock to trade at or close to $50 a share after a 2-for-1 split. Specifically, we divide the original price per share by the ratio of new shares to old. That same $100 stock would trade at about $67 after a 3-for-2 split—that is, $100 \div 3/2 = \$100 \div 1.5 = \$67$. (A variation of the stock split, known as a stock dividend, will be discussed later in this chapter.)

H O T L I N K S

Get the latest information on stock splits at:
biz.yahoo.com/c/s.html

Treasury Stock Instead of increasing the number of outstanding shares, corporations sometimes find it desirable to *reduce* the number of shares in the hands of the investing public by buying back their own stock. Generally speaking, firms repurchase their own stock when they view it as undervalued in the marketplace. When that happens, the company's own stock becomes an attractive investment candidate. Those firms that can afford to do so will purchase their stock in the open market by becoming investors, like any other individual or institution. When these shares are acquired, they become known as **treasury stock**. Technically, treasury stocks are simply shares of stock that have been issued and subsequently repurchased by the issuing firm. Treasury stocks are kept by the corporation and can be used at a later date for various purposes. Such purposes include mergers and acquisitions, to meet employee stock option plans, or as a means of paying stock dividends. Or the shares can simply be held in treasury for an indefinite time.

treasury stock
shares of stock that have been sold and subsequently repurchased by the issuing firm.

The impact of these share repurchases—or *buybacks,* as they're sometimes called—is not clear. Generally, the feeling is that if the buyback is substantial (involving a significant number of shares), the stockholder's equity position and claim on income will increase. This result is likely to benefit stockholders to the extent that such action has a positive effect on the market price of the stock. However, it has also been suggested that buybacks are often used merely as a way to prop up the price of an overvalued stock.

Classified Common Stock For the most part, all the stockholders in a corporation enjoy the same benefits of ownership. Occasionally, a company will issue different classes of common stock, each of which entitles holders to different privileges and benefits. These issues are known as **classified common stock.** Hundreds of publicly traded firms have created such stock classes. Though issued by the same company, each class of common stock is different and has its own value.

classified common stock
common stock issued by a company in different classes, each of which offers different privileges and benefits to its holders.

Classified common stock is customarily used to denote either different voting rights or different dividend obligations. For instance, class A could designate nonvoting shares, and class B would carry normal voting rights. Or the class A stock would receive no dividends, and class B would receive regular cash dividends. Notable for its use of classified stock is Ford Motor Company, which has two classes of stock outstanding. Ford's class A stock is owned by the investing public, and class B stock is owned by the Ford family and their trusts or corporations. The two classes of stock share equally in the dividends. But class A stock has one vote per share, whereas the voting rights of the class B stock are structured to give the Ford family a 40% absolute control of the company. Similar types of classified stock are used at the Washington Post, Dillards Department Stores, Dow Jones & Co., Nike, and Berkshire Hathaway. Regardless of the specifics, whenever there is more than one class of common stock outstanding, investors should take the time to determine the privileges, benefits, and limitations of each class.

Buying and Selling Stocks

Whether buying or selling stocks, you should become familiar with how stocks are quoted and with the costs of executing common stock transactions. Certainly, keeping track of *current prices* is an essential element in the buy-and-sell decisions of investors. They are the link in the decision process that lets investors decide when to buy or sell a stock; they also help investors monitor the market performance of their security holdings. Similarly, *transaction costs* are important because of the impact they can have on investment returns. Indeed, the costs of executing stock transactions can sometimes consume most (or all) of the profits from an investment. These costs should not be taken lightly.

Reading the Quotes Investors in the stock market have come to rely on a highly efficient information system that quickly disseminates market prices to the public. The stock quotes that appear daily in the financial press are a vital part of that information system. To see how price quotations work and what they mean, consider the quotes that appear daily (Monday through Friday) in the *Wall Street Journal*. As we'll see, these quotes give not only the most recent price of each stock but also a great deal of additional information.

Some NYSE stock quotes are presented in Figure 6.5—let's use the Disney quotations for purposes of illustration. These quotes were published in the *Wall Street Journal* on Thursday, May 24, 2001. They describe the trading activity that occurred the day before, which in this case was Wednesday, May 23. A glance at the quotations shows that stocks, like most other securities, are now quoted in dollars and cents. That may not sound like a big deal, but it is. Until the year 2000, stocks had been quoted in fractions, mostly in eighths of a dollar, where each ⅛ of a point was worth 12½ cents. That system, which prevailed for well over 100 years, produced stock quotes like 27¼ and 85⅞, which then had to be translated into dollars prices of $27.25 and $85.875. That all changed in 2000, when stock quotes were switched over to "decimals" (dollars and cents).

In addition to stock prices, a typical stock quote conveys an array of other information, including

- The first column ("YTD % Chg") gives the stock's year-to-date change in price; note that Disney stock has gone up 14.4% since the first of the year. The next two columns, labeled "Hi" and "Lo," show the highest and lowest prices at which the stock sold during the past 52 weeks—you can see that Disney has traded between $43 and $26 a share during the preceding 52-week period.

- Listed to the right of the company's name is its *stock symbol*; Disney goes by the three-letter abbreviation DIS. These symbols are the abbreviations used to identify specific companies; every common stock (and mutual fund) has a unique three- to five-letter symbol that distinguishes it from any other security and is used to execute market trades.

- The figure listed after the stock symbol is the annual cash dividend paid on each share of stock, which for Disney was 21 cents. This is followed by the stock's dividend yield (0.6% for Disney) and its price/earnings (P/E) ratio. Note that the *cc* in the PE column indicates that Disney was trading at more than 100 times its earnings.

- The daily share volume follows the P/E ratio. The sales numbers are listed in lots of 100 shares, so the figure 59521 means that 5,952,100 shares of Disney stock were traded on May 23.

- The next entry, the "Last" column, contains the closing (final) price, $33.11, at which the stock sold on the day in question.

- Finally, as the last ("Net Change") column shows, Disney closed down $1.39. This means the stock closed $1.39 lower than the day before (May 22), when it closed at $34.50.

The same basic quotation system is used for *some* OTC stocks. Actually, for quotation purposes, OTC stocks are divided into two groups: Nasdaq

FIGURE 6.5 Stock Quotations

This figure shows the quotations for a small sample of stocks traded on the NYSE, providing a summary of the transactions that occurred on one day. (*Source: Wall Street Journal,* May 24, 2001.)

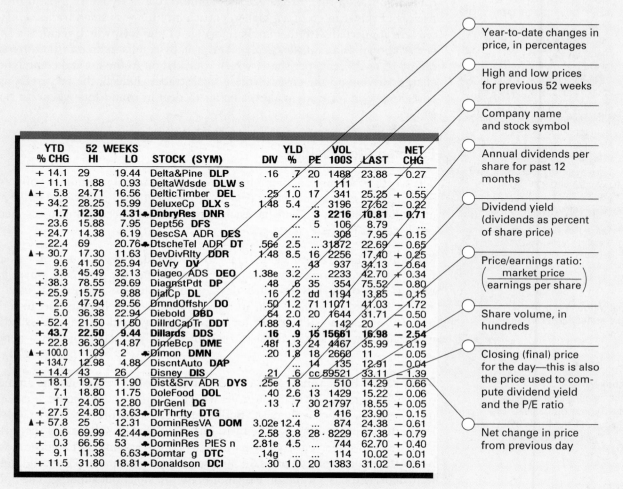

Year-to-date changes in price, in percentages

High and low prices for previous 52 weeks

Company name and stock symbol

Annual dividends per share for past 12 months

Dividend yield (dividends as percent of share price)

Price/earnings ratio:
$$\left(\frac{\text{market price}}{\text{earnings per share}} \right)$$

Share volume, in hundreds

Closing (final) price for the day—this is also the price used to compute dividend yield and the P/E ratio

Net change in price from previous day

YTD % CHG	52 WEEKS HI	LO	STOCK (SYM)	DIV	YLD %	PE	VOL 100S	LAST	NET CHG
+ 14.1	29	19.44	Delta&Pine **DLP**	.16	.7	20	1488	23.88	− 0.27
− 11.1	1.88	0.93	DeltaWdsde **DLW** s		...	1	111	1	...
▲+ 5.8	24.71	16.56	DelticTimber **DEL**	.25	1.0	17	341	25.25	+ 0.55
+ 34.2	28.25	15.99	DeluxeCp **DLX** s	1.48	5.4	...	3196	27.62	− 0.22
− 1.7	12.30	4.31	**DnbryRes DNR**		...	3	2216	10.81	− 0.71
− 23.6	15.88	7.95	Dept56 **DFS**		...	5	106	8.79	...
+ 24.7	14.38	6.19	DescSA ADR **DES**	e	...	...	308	7.95	+ 0.15
− 22.4	69	20.76	♣DtscheTel ADR **DT**	.56e	2.5	...	31872	22.69	− 0.65
▲+ 30.7	17.30	11.63	DevDivRlty **DDR**	1.48	8.5	16	2256	17.40	+ 0.25
− 9.6	41.50	25.94	DeVry **DV**		...	43	937	34.13	− 0.64
− 3.8	45.49	32.13	Diageo ADS **DEO**	1.38e	3.2	...	2233	42.70	+ 0.34
+' 38.3	78.55	29.69	DiagnstPdt **DP**	.48	.6	35	354	75.52	− 0.80
+ 25.9	15.75	9.88	DialCp **DL**	.16	1.2	dd	1194	13.85	− 0.15
+ 2.6	47.94	29.56	DmndOffshr **DO**	.50	1.2	71	11071	41.03	− 1.72
− 5.0	36.38	22.94	Diebold **DBD**	.64	2.0	20	1644	31.71	− 0.50
+ 52.4	21.50	11.50	DillrdCapTr **DDT**	1.88	9.4	...	142	20	+ 0.04
+ 43.7	22.50	9.44	Dillards **DDS**	.16	.9	15	15661	16.98	− 2.54
+ 22.8	36.30	14.87	DimeBcp **DME**	.48f	1.3	24	4467	35.99	− 0.19
▲+ 100.0	11.09	2	♣Dimon **DMN**	.20	1.8	18	2660	11	− 0.05
+ 134.7	12.98	4.88	DiscntAuto **DAP**		...	14	135	12.91	− 0.04
+ 14.4	43	26	Disney **DIS**	.21	.6	cc	69521	33.11	− 1.39
− 18.1	19.75	11.90	Dist&Srv ADR **DYS**	.25e	1.8	...	510	14.29	− 0.66
− 7.1	18.80	11.75	DoleFood **DOL**	.40	2.6	13	1429	15.22	− 0.06
− 1.7	24.05	12.80	DlrGenl **DG**	.13	.7	30	21797	18.55	+ 0.05
+ 27.5	24.80	13.63	♣DlrThrfty **DTG**		...	8	416	23.90	− 0.15
▲+ 57.8	25	12.31	DominResVA **DOM**	3.02e	12.4	...	874	24.38	− 0.61
+ 0.6	69.99	42.44	♣DominRes **D**	2.58	3.8	28	8229	67.38	+ 0.79
+ 0.3	66.56	53	♣DominRes PIES n	2.81e	4.5	...	744	62.70	+ 0.40
+ 9.1	11.38	6.63	♣Domtar g **DTC**	.14g	...	...	114	10.02	+ 0.01
+ 11.5	31.80	18.81	♣Donaldson **DCI**	.30	1.0	20	1383	31.02	− 0.61

National Market issues and other OTC stocks. The National Market stocks are those of major, actively traded companies; *they are quoted just like NYSE issues.* Other OTC stocks (i.e., Nasdaq Small Cap issues) and AMEX stocks are quoted in a highly abbreviated form that includes only stock name, symbol, volume, closing price, and price change.

Transaction Costs As explained in Chapter 3, common stock can be bought and sold in round or odd lots. A *round lot* is 100 shares of stock or multiples thereof. An *odd lot* is a transaction involving less than 100 shares. The sale of 400 shares of stock would be a round-lot transaction; the sale of 75 shares would be an odd-lot transaction. Trading 250 shares of stock would involve a combination of two round lots and an odd lot.

par value
the stated, or face, value of a stock.

book value
the amount of stockholders' equity in a firm; equals the amount of the firm's assets minus the firm's liabilities and preferred stock.

market value
the prevailing market price of a security.

An investor incurs certain transaction costs when buying or selling stock. In addition to some modest transfer fees and taxes paid by the *seller,* the major cost is the brokerage fee paid—by both *buyer and seller*—at the time of the transaction. As a rule, brokerage fees amount to 1% to 5% of most transactions. But they can go much higher, particularly for very small trades. Higher fees are connected with the purchase or sale of odd lots, which requires a specialist known as an *odd-lot dealer.* This usually results in an *odd-lot differential* of 10 to 25 cents per share, which is tacked on to the normal commission charge, driving up the costs of these small trades. Indeed, the relatively high cost of an odd-lot trade makes it better to deal in round lots whenever possible.

Common Stock Values

The worth of a share of common stock can be described in a number of ways. Terms such as *par value, book value, market value,* and *investment value* are all found in the financial media. Each designates some accounting, investment, or monetary attribute of a stock.

Par Value   The term **par value** refers to the stated, or face, value of a stock. Except for accounting purposes, it is relatively useless. In many ways, par value is a throwback to the early days of corporate law, when it was used as a basis for assessing the extent of a stockholder's legal liability. Because the term has little or no significance for investors, many stocks today are issued as no-par or low-par stocks. That is, they may have par values of only a penny or two.

Book Value   **Book value,** another accounting measure, represents the amount of stockholders' equity in the firm. As we will see in the next chapter, it is commonly used in stock valuation. Book value indicates the amount of stockholder funds used to finance the firm. It is calculated by subtracting the firm's liabilities and preferred stock from its assets. Let's assume that a corporation has $10 million in assets, owes $5 million in various forms of short- and long-term debt, and has $1 million worth of preferred stock outstanding. The book value of this firm would be $4 million.

Book value can be converted to a per-share basis—*book value per share*—by dividing it by the number of common shares outstanding. For example, if the firm just described has 100,000 shares of common stock outstanding, then its book value per share is $40. As a rule, most stocks have market prices that are well above their book values.

Market Value   **Market value** is one of the easiest stock values to determine. It is simply the prevailing market price of an issue. In essence, market value indicates how the market participants as a whole have assessed the worth of a share of stock. By multiplying the market price of the stock by the number of shares outstanding, we can also find the market value of the firm itself—or what is known as the firm's *market capitalization.* For example, if a firm has 1 million shares outstanding and its stock trades at $50 per share, the company has a market value (or "market cap") of $50 million. Because investors are always interested in an issue's market price, the market value of a share of stock is generally of considerable importance to stockholders.

investment value
the amount that investors believe
a security should be trading for,
or what they think it's worth.

Investment Value Investment value is probably the most important measure for a stockholder. It indicates the worth investors place on the stock—in effect, what they think the stock *should* be trading for. Determining a security's investment value is a complex process based on expectations of the return and risk behavior of a stock. Any stock has two potential sources of return: annual dividend payments and the capital gains that arise from appreciation in market price. In establishing investment value, investors try to determine how much money they will make from these two sources. They then use that estimate as the basis for formulating the return potential of the stock. At the same time, they try to assess the amount of risk to which they will be exposed by holding the stock. Such return and risk information helps them place an investment value on the stock. This value represents the *maximum* price an investor should be willing to pay for the issue. Investment value is the major topic in Chapter 8.

IN REVIEW

CONCEPTS

6.7 What is a *stock split?* How does a stock split affect the market value of a share of stock? Do you think it would make any difference (in price behavior) if the company also changed the dividend rate on the stock? Explain.

6.8 What is a *stock spin-off?* In very general terms, explain how a stock spin-off works. Are they of any value to investors? Explain.

6.9 Define and differentiate between the following pairs of terms.
a. *Treasury stock* vs. *classified stock*.
b. *Round lot* vs. *odd lot*.
c. *Par value* vs. *market value*.
d. *Book value* vs. *investment value*.

6.10 What is an *odd-lot differential* and what effect does it have on the cost of buying and selling stocks? How can you avoid odd-lot differentials? Which of the following transactions would involve an odd-lot differential?
a. Buy 90 shares of stock.
b. Sell 200 shares of stock.
c. Sell 125 shares of stock.

Common Stock Dividends

LG 5

In 1999, U.S. corporations paid out some $365 billion in dividends. Yet, in spite of these numbers, dividends still don't get much respect. Many investors, particularly younger ones, often put very little value on dividends. That's unfortunate, because dividend income is one of the two basic sources of return to investors. And although dividends are subject to higher taxes than long-term capital gains, they're also far less risky. The stream of annual dividends is far more predictable than the capital gains that may or may not occur. Let's now take a closer look at this important source of income.

The Dividend Decision

By paying out dividends, typically on a quarterly basis, companies share with their stockholders some of the profits they've earned. Actually, the question of how much to pay in dividends is decided by a firm's board of directors. The directors evaluate the firm's operating results and financial condition to determine whether dividends should be paid and, if so, in what amount. If the directors decide to pay dividends, they also establish several important payment dates. In this section we'll look at the corporate and market factors that go into the dividend decision. Then we'll briefly examine some of the key payment dates.

 Corporate Versus Market Factors When the board of directors assembles for its regular dividend meeting, it weighs a variety of factors in making a decision to pay out dividends. First, the board looks at the firm's earnings. Even though a company does not have to show a profit to pay dividends, profits still are considered a vital link in the dividend decision. With common stocks, the annual earnings of a firm are usually measured and reported in terms of **earnings per share** (EPS). Basically, EPS translates total corporate profits into profits on a per-share basis. It provides a convenient measure of the amount of earnings available to stockholders. Earnings per share is found by using the following formula:

earnings per share (EPS)
the amount of annual earnings available to common stockholders, as stated on a per-share basis.

Equation 6.1

$$EPS = \frac{\dfrac{Net\ profit}{after\ taxes} - Preferred\ dividends}{Number\ of\ shares\ of\ common\ stock\ outstanding}$$

For example, if a firm reports a net profit of $1.25 million, pays $250,000 in dividends to preferred stockholders, and has 500,000 shares of common outstanding, it has an EPS of $2—that is, ($1,250,000 − $250,000)/500,000. Note in Equation 6.1 that preferred dividends are subtracted from profits, since they must be paid before any funds can be made available to common stockholders.

While assessing profits, the board also looks at the firm's growth prospects. It is very likely some of the firm's present earnings will be needed for investment purposes and to help finance expected growth. The board also considers how much cash the firm has. Finally, the board will want to make sure that it is meeting all legal and contractual constraints. For example, the firm may be subject to a loan agreement that legally limits the amount of dividends it can pay.

After looking at internal matters, the board will consider certain market effects and responses. Most investors feel that if a company is going to retain earnings rather than pay them out in dividends, it should exhibit proportionately higher growth and profit levels. The market's message is clear: If the firm is investing the money wisely and at a high rate of return, fine; otherwise, pay a larger portion of earnings out in the form of dividends. Moreover, to the extent that different types of investors tend to be attracted to different types of firms, the board must make every effort to meet the dividend expectations of its shareholders. For example, income-oriented investors are attracted to firms that generally pay high dividends. Failure to meet those expectations can lead to disastrous results—a sell-off of the firm's stock—in the marketplace.

Some Important Dates Let's assume the directors decide to declare a dividend. They then must indicate the date of payment and other important dates associated with the dividend. Normally, the directors issue a statement to the

date of record
the date on which an investor must be a registered shareholder of a firm to be entitled to receive a dividend.

payment date
the actual date on which the company will mail dividend checks to shareholders (also known as the *payable date*).

ex-dividend date
three business days before the date of record; determines whether one is an official shareholder of a firm and thus eligible to receive a declared dividend.

press indicating their dividend decision, along with the pertinent dividend payment dates. These statements are widely quoted in the financial media. Typical of such releases are the dividend news captions depicted in Figure 6.6.

Three dates are particularly important to the stockholder: date of record, ex-dividend date, and payment date. The **date of record** is the date on which the investor must be a registered shareholder of the firm to be entitled to a dividend. All investors who are official stockholders as of the close of business on that date will receive the dividends that have just been declared. These stockholders are often referred to as *holders of record*. The **payment date**, also set by the board of directors, generally follows the date of record by a week or two. It is the actual date on which the company will mail dividend checks to holders of record. (Note that in the dividend news reported in Figure 6.6, this date is called the *payable date*.)

Because of the time needed to make bookkeeping entries after a stock is traded, the stock will sell without the dividend (ex-dividend) for three business days prior to the date of record. The **ex-dividend date** will dictate whether you were an official shareholder and therefore eligible to receive the declared dividend. If you sell a stock *on or after* the ex-dividend date, you receive the dividend. If you sell before this date, the new shareholder will receive the recently declared dividend.

To see how this all works, consider the following sequence of events. On June 3, the board of directors of Cash Cow, Inc. declares a quarterly dividend of 50 cents a share to holders of record on June 18. Checks will be mailed on the payment date, June 30. The calendar below shows these various dividend dates. If you owned 200 shares of the stock on June 12, you'd receive a check in the mail sometime after June 30 in the amount of $100.

June

S	M	T	W	T	F	S	
	1	2	3	4	5	6	— Declaration date
7	8	9	10	11	12	13	
14	15	16	17	18	19	20	— Date of record
21	22	23	24	25	26	27	— Ex-dividend date
28	29	30					— Payment date

Unlike long-term capital gains, which are subject to a maximum tax rate of 20%, the IRS views cash dividends as *ordinary income* and therefore subject to normal tax rates (of anywhere from 15% to 39.6%). Thus, unless you hold the stock in some type of tax-sheltered account (such as an IRA or Keogh account), you incur a tax liability with each dividend check you receive.

cash dividend
payment of a dividend in the form of cash.

stock dividend
payment of a dividend in the form of additional shares of stock.

Types of Dividends

Normally, companies pay dividends in the form of cash, though sometimes they do so by issuing additional shares of stock. The first type of distribution is known as a **cash dividend**; the second is called a **stock dividend**. Occasionally, dividends are paid in still other forms, such as a *stock spin-off*

FIGURE 6.6

Important Dates and Data About Dividends

The dividend actions of corporations are big news in the financial community. This news release, taken from the *Wall Street Journal*, provides timely information about cash and stock dividends, as well as stocks that have gone ex-dividend. Note that there's even information about recent stock splits. (*Source: Wall Street Journal*, August 15, 2000.)

CORPORATE DIVIDEND NEWS

DIVIDENDS REPORTED AUG. 14

COMPANY	PERIOD	AMT.	PAYABLE DATE	RECORD DATE
Regular				
Advest Group	Q	.06	10-16-00	9-29
Auto Data Proc	Q	.0875	10-01-00	9-15
Avista Corp	Q	.12	9-15-00	8-22
Bergn Brnswg ClA	Q	.01	9-05-00	8-21
Crane Co.	Q	.10	9-12-00	9-01
Cubic Corp.	S	.19	9-19-00	8-22
Equality Bancorp	Q	.06	9-22-00	9-08
Jefferson-Pilot	Q	.37	12-05-00	11-10
Kelly Svc clA	Q	.25	9-08-00	8-28
Kelly Svc clB	Q	.25	9-08-00	8-28
Redwood Trust pfB	Q	.755	10-23-00	9-29
Santander BanCorp	Q	.11	10-02-00	9-08
Sears Roebuck	Q	.23	10-02-00	c8-30
Sunsource Cap pf	M	.241667	8-31-00	8-24
Symbol Tchnlgs	S	.01	9-18-00	8-24
White MountainsIns	Q	.40	9-27-00	9-18
Irregular				
Medallion Finl	Q	.36	9-05-00	8-25
Ultrapar ParticADS	-	.1845	10-10-00	8-15
Util Holdrs Tr	-	.054	10-02-00	9-08
Util Holdrs Tr	-	.051	10-16-00	9-15
Util Holdrs Tr	-	.0206	10-03-00	9-01
Funds, REITs, Investment Companies, LPs				
EatonVan Balance A	Q	.035	8-31-00	8-14
EatonVan Balance B	Q	.035	8-17-00	8-14
1st Aust PrimeInco	M	.045	9-15-00	8-31
1st Commonwlth Fd	M	.07	9-15-00	8-31
HancockPatPrDivII	M	.065	9-15-00	8-23
Hyperion 2002 Term	M	.02708	8-31-00	8-22
Hyperion 2005 Inv	M	.03542	8-31-00	8-22
Hyperion Total Ret	M	.0725	8-31-00	8-22
NewPlanRlty	Q	.4125	10-17-00	10-04
NewPlanRlty pfA	Q	.53125	10-16-00	10-04
NewPlanRlty pfB	Q	.539062	10-16-00	10-04
Sizeler Property	Q	.23	9-01-00	8-25
USLife Income Fd	Q	.18	9-01-00	c8-18
VK ConvSecsInc	Q	m4.5691	8-17-00	8-14

m-Reflects $0.16 income and $4.4091 capital gains.

COMPANY	AMT.	PAYABLE DATE	RECORD DATE
Stocks			
ACLN Ltd	ss	9-18-00	9-01

s-5-for-4 stock split.

	ss		
ABIOMED Inc	ss	10-01-00	8-14

s-2-for-1 stock split.

Modern Times Grp	ss	8-21-00	8-18

s-s-3.5 shrs of Metro Intl SA Cl B and 1.5 shrs of Metro Intl SA Cl A for each shr held.

Park Electro	ss	–	10-20

s-3-for-2 stock split subj to shrhldr approval 10/10/00.

Pericom Semicond	ss	9-08-00	8-24

s-2-for-1 stock split.

COMPANY	AMT.	PAYABLE DATE	RECORD DATE
Foreign			
Barclays PLC ADR	t1.3155	10-03-00	c8-18
RioTinto PLC ADS	t.8444	9-18-00	c8-18

Increased

		NEW (AMOUNTS)	OLD		
1st Merchants Corp	Q	.23	.22	9-20-00	9-06
Southwest Water Co	Q	.07	.06	10-20-00	9-30

A-Annual. M-Monthly. Q-Quarterly. S-Semi-annual.
b-Payable in Canadian funds. c-Corrected. h-From Income. k-From capital gains. r-Revised. t-Approximate U.S. dollar amount per American Depository Receipt/Share before adjustment for foreign taxes.

STOCKS EX-DIVIDEND AUG. 16

COMPANY	AMOUNT	COMPANY	AMOUNT
AGL Resources Inc	.27	MuniHldgs NJInsd	.059895
Adams Express Co	.12	MuniHldgsNYInsdIV	.068786
All Amer Term Tr	.06	MuniHldgs NY Ins	.067863
Amerco pfd A	.53125	MuniHldgsCAInsdV	.06875
AmerWaterWks5%pref	.3125	MuniInsd Fd	.039545
AmerWaterWrks 5%pf	.3125	MuniVest FdII	.065
Apex Municipal Fd	.048893	MuniVest Fd	.0444
BP Amoco PLC ADS	t.333	MuniYld AZ Fd	.057
Barclays PLC ADR	t1.3155	MuniYld CA Fd	.0659
Beckman Coulter	.16	MuniYld CA Insd	.063672
Black Hills Corp	.27	MuniYld CA InsII	.0673
Brit Telecomm ADR	t2.1559	MuniYld FL Insd	.0626
CarrAmer Rlty pfB	.5356	MuniYld FL Fd	.060975
CarrAmer Rlty pfC	.5344	MuniYld Fd	.0714
CarrAmer Rlty pfD	.5281	MuniYld Insd	.07
CarrAmerica Realty	.4625	MuniYld MI Insd	.064625
Chemed Corp	.10	MuniYld MI Fd	.062299
Chevron Corp	.65	MuniYld NJ Fund	.065691
Circor Int'l Inc	.0375	MuniYld NJ Insd	.0671
Corp HiYldII	.104887	MuniYld NY Insd	.064727
Corp HiYldIII	.123509	MuniYld PAInsdFd	.065922
Corp HiYld	.113917	MuniYld Qlty	.0678
Debt Strat	.066872	MuniYld QltyII	.0665
Debt StratII	.07878	NiSource Inc PIES	.96875
Debt StratIII	.082246	OM Group Inc	.11
Diebold Inc	.155	Oregon Steel Mills	.02
Dun & Bradstreet	.185	ParkerHannifin	.17
Elect Data System	.15	Petroleum & Res	.20
Fedders Corp	.03	Pfizer Inc	.09
Fedders Corp clA	.03	PharmaHoldrsTr	t.0522
Fleming Cos	.02	Phelps Dodge Corp	.50
Gerber Scientific	.08	Placer Dome Inc	.05
Great Lakes Reit A	.609375	Protective Life	.13
HSBC Holdings ADS	t.833	Questar Corp	.17
Hanson PLC ADR	t.404629	RioTinto PLC ADS	t.8444
Harland(John H)Co	.075	Russ Berrie & Co	.22
Honeywell Intl	.1875	ScottishPwrPLC ADS	t.4364
Hudson United Bncp	.25	Sr High Inco Port	.071033
Imperial Chem Ind	t.8333	ShellTransp ADR	t.5738
Inco OppFd2000	.041666	Sherwn-Williams	.135
Insured MuniInco	.064	Smucker (JM) clA	.16
Intl Paper Co	.25	Smucker (JM) clB	.16
Invest GrdMuniInco	.075	Sonoco Products	.20
Liz Claiborne Inc	.1125	StanCorp Finl Grp	.07
Louisiana-Pacific	.14	Target Corp	.055
Macerich Co	.51	v-Increased amount payable on post split shrs.	
Managed HiYldPlus	.11		
MidcoastEnergyRes	.07	Timken Co	.18
Milacron Inc	.12	Tomkins PLC ADR	t.8623
MuniAssets Fund	.068277	Town & Country Tr	.42
Muni Advantage Fd	.06	2002 Target Term	.065
MuniEnhanced Fd	.0531	2002 Target Term	.10
MuniHldgsCAInsII	.064945	USLife Income Fd	.18
MuniHldgsInsFL	.061808	Ultrapar ParticADS	.1845
MuniHldgsFLInsdV	.06761	Walgreen Co	.03375
MuniHldgs Fd	.068937	Worldwd Dollarvest	.052489
MuniHldgsII	.06321	t-Approximate U.S. dollar amount per American Depository Receipt/Share before adjustment for foreign taxes.	
MuniHldgsInsdFd	.060795		
MuniHldgsMIInsdII	.072841		
r-Revised to include amount.			
MuniHldgsNJInsdIV	.06145		

(discussed earlier in this chapter) or perhaps even samples of the company's products. But dividends in the form of either cash or stock remain by far the most popular, so let's take a closer look at them.

Cash or Stock More firms use *cash dividends* than any other type of dividend. A nice by-product of cash dividends is that *they tend to increase over time, as companies' earnings grow*. The average annual increase in dividends is around 3% to 5%. Such a tendency appeals to investors because a steady stream of dividends—even better, a *steadily increasing* stream of dividends—shores up stock returns in soft markets.

A convenient way of assessing the amount of dividends received is to measure the stock's **dividend yield**. Basically, this is a measure of dividends on a relative (percentage) basis, rather than on an absolute (dollar) basis. Dividend yield, in effect, indicates the rate of current income earned on the investment dollar. It is computed as follows:

dividend yield
a measure that relates dividends to share price and puts common stock dividends on a relative (percentage) rather than absolute (dollar) basis.

Equation 6.2

$$\text{Dividend yield} = \frac{\text{Annual dividends received per share}}{\text{Current market price of the stock}}$$

Thus a company that annually pays $2 per share in dividends to its stock-holders, and whose stock is trading at $40, has a dividend yield of 5%.

dividend payout ratio
the portion of earnings per share (EPS) that a firm pays out as dividends.

To put dividend yield into perspective, it is helpful to look at a company's **dividend payout ratio.** The payout ratio describes that portion of earnings per share (EPS) that is paid out as dividends. It is computed as follows:

Equation 6.3

$$\text{Dividend payout ratio} = \frac{\text{Dividends per share}}{\text{Earnings per share}}$$

A company would have a payout ratio of 50% if it had earnings of $4 a share and paid annual dividends of $2 a share. Although stockholders like to receive dividends, they normally do not like to see payout ratios over 60% to 70%. Payout ratios that high are difficult to maintain and may lead the company into trouble.

Occasionally, a firm may declare a *stock dividend.* A stock dividend simply means that the dividend is paid in additional shares of stock. For instance, if the board declares a 10% stock dividend, each shareholder receives 1 new share of stock for each 10 shares currently owned.

Although they seem to satisfy some investors, *stock dividends really have no value,* because they represent the receipt of something already owned. The market responds to such dividends by adjusting share prices according to the terms of the stock dividend. Thus, in the example above, a 10% stock dividend normally leads to a decline of around 10% in the stock's share price. The market value of your shareholdings after a stock dividend is likely to be the same as it was before the stock dividend. There is, however, one bright spot in all this: Unlike cash dividends, stock dividends are not taxed until the stocks are actually sold.

Dividend Reinvestment Plans

dividend reinvestment plans (DRIPs)
plans in which shareholders have cash dividends automatically reinvested into additional shares of the firm's common stock.

Want to have your cake and eat it too? When it comes to dividends, there is a way to do just that. You can participate in a **dividend reinvestment plan (DRIP).** These are corporate-sponsored programs in which shareholders can have their cash dividends automatically reinvested into additional shares of the company's common stock. (Similar reinvestment programs are offered by mutual funds, which we'll discuss in Chapter 12, and by some brokerage houses, such as Merrill Lynch and Fidelity.) The basic investment philosophy is that *if the company is good enough to invest in, it's good enough to reinvest in.* As Table 6.4 demonstrates, such an approach can have a tremendous impact on your investment position over time.

Today more than 1,000 companies (including most major corporations) offer dividend reinvestment plans. Each one provides investors with a convenient and inexpensive way to accumulate capital. Stocks in most DRIPs are acquired free of any brokerage commissions, and most plans allow *partial participation.* That is, participants may specify a portion of their shares for dividend reinvestment and receive cash dividends on the rest. Some plans even sell

TABLE 6.4   **Cash or Reinvested Dividends?**

Situation: You buy 100 shares of stock at $25 a share (total investment $2,500); the stock currently pays $1 a share in annual dividends. The price of the stock increases at 8% per year; dividends grow at 5% per year.

Investment Period	Number of Shares Held	Market Value of Stock Holdings	Total Cash Dividends Received
		Take Dividends in Cash	
5 years	100	$ 3,672	$ 552
10 years	100	5,397	1,258
15 years	100	7,930	2,158
20 years	100	11,652	3,307
		Full Participation in Dividend Reinvestment Plan (100% of cash dividends reinvested)	
5 years	115.59	$ 4,245	$ 0
10 years	135.66	7,322	0
15 years	155.92	12,364	0
20 years	176.00	20,508	0

stocks to their DRIP investors at below-market prices—often at discounts of 3% to 5%. In addition, most plans will credit fractional shares to the investor's account, and many will even allow investors to buy additional shares of the company's stock. For example, once enrolled in the General Mills plan, investors can purchase up to $3,000 worth of the company's stock each quarter, free of commissions.

Shareholders can join dividend reinvestment plans simply by sending a completed authorization form to the company. (Generally, it takes about 30 to 45 days for all the paperwork to be processed.) Once you're in, the number of shares you hold will begin to accumulate with each dividend date. There is a catch, however: Even though these dividends take the form of additional shares of stock, you must pay taxes on them *as though they were cash dividends*. Don't confuse these dividends with stock dividends—*reinvested dividends are taxable as ordinary income in the year they're received*, just as though they had been received in cash.

IN REVIEW

CONCEPTS

6.11 Briefly explain how the dividend decision is made. What corporate and market factors are important in deciding whether, and in what amount, to pay dividends?

6.12 Why is the *ex-dividend date* important to stockholders? If a stock is sold *on* the ex-dividend date, who receives the dividend—the buyer or the seller? Explain.

6.13 What is the difference between a *cash dividend* and a *stock dividend?* Which would be more valuable to you? How does a stock dividend compare to a stock split? Is a 200% stock dividend the same as a 2-for-1 stock split? Explain.

6.14 What are *dividend reinvestment plans*, and what benefits do they offer to investors? Are there any disadvantages?

Types and Uses of Common Stock

LG 6

Common stocks appeal to investors because they offer the potential for everything from current income and stability of capital to attractive capital gains. The market contains a wide range of stock, from the most conservative to the highly speculative. Generally, the kinds of stocks that investors seek will depend on their investment objectives and investment programs. We will examine several of the more popular types of common stocks here, as well as the various ways such securities can be used in different types of investment programs.

Types of Stocks

As an investor, one of the things you'll want to understand is the market system used to classify common stock. That's because a stock's general classification reflects not only its fundamental source of return but also the quality of the company's earnings, the issue's susceptibility to market risks, the nature and stability of its earnings and dividends, and even its susceptibility to adverse economic conditions. Such insight is useful in selecting stocks that will best fit your overall investment objectives. Among the many different types of stocks, the following are the most common: blue chips, income stocks, growth stocks, tech stocks, speculative stocks, cyclical stocks, defensive stocks, mid-cap stocks, and small-cap stocks. We will now look at each of these to see what they are and how they might be used.

HOTLINKS

At this site, you can choose stocks by company size and type, and access growth and return rates. Lists show stock prices, quotes, ratios, and charts. For the Stockscreener, go to:

www.stockscreener.com

blue-chip stocks
financially strong, high-quality stocks with long and stable records of earnings and dividends.

Blue-Chip Stocks Blue chips are the cream of the common stock crop. They are stocks that are unsurpassed in quality and have a long and stable record of earnings and dividends. **Blue-chip stocks** are issued by large, well-established firms that have impeccable financial credentials. These companies hold important, often leading positions in their industries and frequently set the standards by which other firms are measured.

Not all blue chips are alike, however. Some provide consistently high dividend yields; others are more growth oriented. Good examples of blue-chip growth stocks are General Electric, Merck, Wal-Mart, SBC Communications, Citigroup, and Home Depot. (Some basic operating and market information about Home Depot's stock, as obtained from the introductory part of a typical *S&P Stock Report,* is shown in Figure 6.7.) Examples of high-yielding blue chips include such companies as DuPont, Eastman Kodak, International Paper, General Motors, and Philip Morris.

Blue chips are particularly attractive to investors who are looking for quality investment outlets that offer decent dividend yields and respectable growth potential. They're often used for long-term investment purposes and, because of their relatively low risk, as a way of obtaining modest but dependable rates of return. Blue chips are popular with a large segment of the investing public. As a result, they are often relatively high in price, especially when the market is unsettled and investors become more quality-conscious.

income stocks
stocks with long and sustained records of paying higher-than-average dividends.

Income Stocks Some stocks are appealing simply because of the dividends they pay. This is the case with **income stocks.** These are issues that have a long and sustained record of regularly paying higher-than-average dividends. Income stocks are ideal for those who seek a relatively safe and high level of

FIGURE 6.7

A Blue-Chip Stock

(*Source:* Standard & Poor's *Stock Reports,* January 8, 2000.)

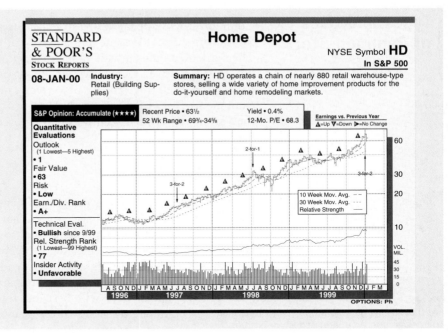

current income from their investment capital. But there's more: Holders of income stocks (unlike bonds and preferred stocks) can expect the dividends they receive to increase regularly over time. Look at Duke Energy, for example. It paid dividends of $1.52 a share in 1989; 10 years later, in 1999, it was paying almost 50% more: $2.20 a share. Percentage-wise, that's a big jump in dividends, and it's something that can have a definite impact on total return.

The major disadvantage of income stocks is that some of them may be paying high dividends because of limited growth potential. Indeed, it's not unusual for income securities to exhibit only low or modest rates of growth in earnings. This does not mean that such firms are unprofitable or lack future prospects. Quite the contrary: Most firms whose shares qualify as income stocks are highly profitable organizations with excellent future prospects. A number of income stocks are among the giants of U.S. industry, and many are also classified as quality blue chips. Many public utilities, such as American Electric Power, Consolidated Edison, DTE Energy, Dominion Resources, and Southern Company, are in this group. Also in this group are phone stocks, such as AT&T and Bell Atlantic, and selected industrial and financial issues, such as Ford, H.J. Heinz, Weyerhaeuser, Bank One, and AmSouth Bancorp. By their very nature, income stocks are not exposed to a great deal of business and market risk. They are, however, subject to a fair amount of interest rate risk.

Growth Stocks Shares that have experienced, and are expected to continue experiencing, consistently high rates of growth in operations and earnings are known as **growth stocks.** A good growth stock might exhibit a *sustained* rate of growth in earnings of 15% to 18% a year over a period when common stocks, on average, are experiencing growth rates of only 6% to 8%. Generally speaking, established growth companies combine steady earnings

growth stocks
stocks that experience high rates of growth in operations and earnings.

FIGURE 6.8

A Growth Stock

(*Source:* Standard & Poor's *Stock Reports,* January 8, 2000.)

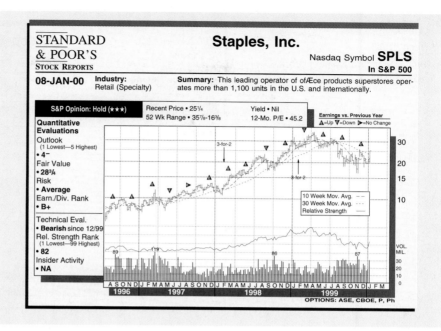

growth with high returns on equity. They also have high operating margins and plenty of cash flow to service their debt. AIG, Enron Corp., General Dynamics, Starbucks, Lowe's, Reliant Energy, and Staples (shown in Figure 6.8) are all prime examples of growth stocks. As this list suggests, some growth stocks also rate as blue chips and provide quality growth, whereas others represent higher levels of speculation.

Growth stocks normally pay little or nothing in the way of dividends, so their payout ratios seldom exceed 10% to 15% of earnings. Instead, all or most of the profits are reinvested in the company and used to help finance rapid growth. Thus the major source of return to investors is price appreciation. Growth shares generally appeal to investors who are looking for attractive capital gains rather than dividends and who are therefore willing to assume a higher element of risk.

Tech Stocks Over the past 10 to 15 years, *tech stocks* have become such a dominant force in the market that they deserve to be put in a class all their own. **Tech stocks** basically represent the technology sector of the market and include companies that produce or provide everything from computers, semiconductors, data storage, computer software, and computer hardware to peripherals, Internet services, content providers, networking, and wireless communications. These are the so-called *new-economy* stocks, issued by the companies that are changing the way things are being done in the world. They provide the high-tech equipment, networking systems, and online services to all lines of businesses, education, health care, communications, governmental agencies, and the home. Some of these stocks are listed on the NYSE and AMEX. The vast majority, though, are traded on the Nasdaq, which explains why the Nasdaq Composite index (discussed earlier) did so well.

HOT LINKS

To read about characteristics of growth and value companies and their performance in recent years, go to:

www.putnaminv.com/frames/e105.htm

tech stocks
stocks that represent the technology, "new-economy" sector of the market.

A Tech Stock

(*Source:* Standard & Poor's *Stock Reports*, January 8, 2000.)

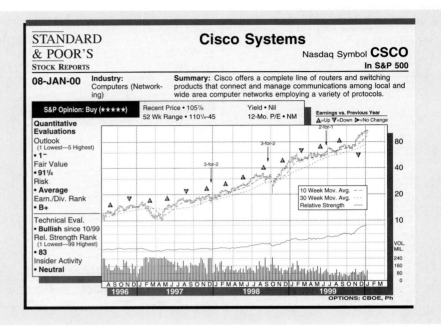

There are literally thousands of companies that fall into the tech-stock category. They include everything from very small firms that provide some service on the Internet to huge multinational companies. In many cases, these stocks have richly rewarded their investors, even though the companies themselves may have never earned a penny in profits. Certainly, this is a category where it's safe to say that not all stocks are equal. Here you find companies that generate lots of revenues and profits, companies that have lots of revenues but little or no profits, and companies that have little in the way of sales or profits (but supposedly lots of potential).

These stocks would probably fall into either the *growth stock* category (see above) or the *speculative stock* class (see below), although some of them are legitimate *blue chips*. Tech stocks may offer the potential for attractive (and, in some cases, phenomenal) returns. But they also involve considerable risk, and are probably most suitable for the more risk-tolerant investor. Included in the tech-stock category you'll find some big names, like Yahoo, Microsoft, Cisco Systems (see Figure 6.9), Adobe Systems, and Amazon.com. You'll also find many not-so-big names, like Intergraph Corp., Synopsys, Abgenix, Exodus, Immuney, and Avid Technology. We'll take another, more detailed look at tech stocks in Chapter 8, including the very difficult job of putting a value on these securities.

Speculative Stocks Shares that lack sustained records of success but still offer the potential for substantial price appreciation are known as **speculative stocks.** Perhaps investors' hopes are spurred by a new management team that has taken over a troubled company or by the introduction of a promising new product. Other times, it's the hint that some new information, discovery, or production technique will favorably affect the growth prospects of the firm. Speculative stocks are a special breed of securities, and they enjoy a wide following, particularly when the market is bullish.

speculative stocks
stocks that offer the potential for substantial price appreciation, usually because of some special situation, such as new management or the introduction of a promising new product.

Generally speaking, the earnings of speculative stocks are uncertain and highly unstable. These stocks are subject to wide swings in price, and they usually pay little or nothing in dividends. On the plus side, speculative stocks such as Cytyc Corp., Krispy Kreme, JAKKS Pacific, Siebel Systems, and Zomax, Inc. offer attractive growth prospects and the chance to "hit it big" in the market. To be successful, however, an investor has to identify the big-money winners before the rest of the market does and the price of the stock is driven up. Speculative stocks are highly risky; they require not only a strong stomach but also a considerable amount of investor know-how. They are used to seek capital gains, and investors will often aggressively trade in and out of these securities as the situation demands.

cyclical stocks
stocks whose earnings and overall market performance are closely linked to the general state of the economy.

Cyclical Stocks Cyclical stocks are issued by companies whose earnings are closely linked to the general level of business activity. They tend to reflect the general state of the economy and to move up and down with the business cycle. Companies that serve markets tied to capital equipment spending by business, or to consumer spending for big-ticket, durable items like houses and cars, typically head the list of cyclical stocks. Examples include Caterpillar, Genuine Parts, Maytag Corp., Rohm & Haas, Harnischfeger, and Timken.

Cyclical stocks generally do well when the economy is moving ahead, but they tend to do *especially well* when the country is in the early stages of economic recovery. They are, however, perhaps best avoided when the economy begins to weaken. Cyclical stocks are probably most suitable for investors who are willing to trade in and out of these issues as the economic outlook dictates and who can tolerate the accompanying exposure to risk.

defensive stocks
stocks that tend to hold their own, and even do well, when the economy starts to falter.

Defensive Stocks Sometimes it is possible to find stocks whose prices remain stable or even increase when general economic activity is tapering off. These securities are known as **defensive stocks**. They tend to be less affected than the average issue by downswings in the business cycle. Defensive stocks include the shares of many public utilities, as well as industrial and consumer goods companies that produce or market such staples as beverages, foods, and drugs. An excellent example of a defensive stock is Bandag. This recession-resistant company is the world's leading manufacturer of rubber used to retread tires. Other examples are Checkpoint Systems, a manufacturer of antitheft clothing security clips, and WD-40, the maker of that famous all-purpose lubricant. Perhaps the best known of all defensive stocks, particularly in inflationary periods, are gold mining shares. These stocks blossom when inflation becomes a serious problem. Defensive shares are commonly used by more aggressive investors. Such investors tend to "park" their funds temporarily in defensive stocks while the economy remains soft, or until the investment atmosphere improves.

Mid-Cap Stocks As explained earlier, a stock's size is based on its market value—or, more commonly, on what is known as its *market capitalization* (the market price of the stock times the number of shares outstanding). Generally speaking, the U.S. stock market can be broken into three segments, as measured by a stock's market "cap":

Small-cap	under $1 billion
Mid-cap	$1 billion to $4 or $5 billion
Large-cap	more than $4 or $5 billion

The large-cap stocks are the real biggies—the AT&Ts, GMs, and Microsofts of the investment world. Although there are far fewer large-cap stocks than any other size, these companies account for about 80% to 90% of the total market value of all U.S. equities. But as the saying goes, bigger isn't necessarily better. Nowhere is that statement more accurate than in the stock market. Indeed, both the small-cap and mid-cap segments of the market tend to hold their own, or even to outperform the large stocks over time.

Mid-cap stocks are a special breed, and offer investors some attractive return opportunities. They provide much of the sizzle of small-stock returns, without as much price volatility. (We'll look at small-cap stocks soon.) At the same time, because mid-caps are fairly good-sized companies and many of them have been around for a long time, they offer some of the safety of the big, established stocks. Among the ranks of the mid-caps are such well-known companies as Wendy's International, Barnes & Noble, Dial Corp. (see Figure 6.10), Hertz, Liz Claiborne, Outback Steakhouse, and Keebler Foods. Although these securities offer a nice alternative to large stocks without the uncertainties of small-caps, they probably are most appropriate for investors who are willing to tolerate a bit more risk and price volatility.

One type of mid-cap stock of particular interest is the so-called *baby blue chip*. Also known as "baby blues," these companies have all the characteristics of a regular blue chip *except size*. Like their larger counterparts, baby blues have rock-solid balance sheets, only modest levels of debt, and long histories of steady profit growth. For the most part, they've been able to secure niches in fast-growing specialty markets. Some of these companies, in fact,

mid-cap stocks
medium-sized stocks, generally with market values of less than $4 or $5 billion but more than $1 billion.

FIGURE 6.10

A Mid-Cap Stock

(*Source:* Standard & Poor's *Stock Reports,* January 8, 2000.)

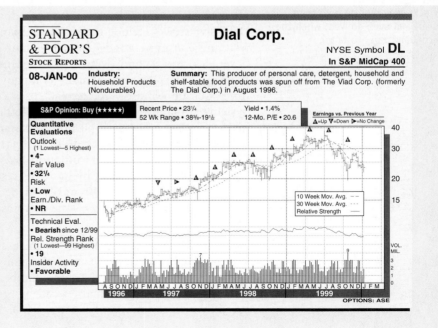

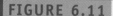

FIGURE 6.11

A Small-Cap Stock

(*Source:* Standard & Poor's *Stock Reports,* January 8, 2000.)

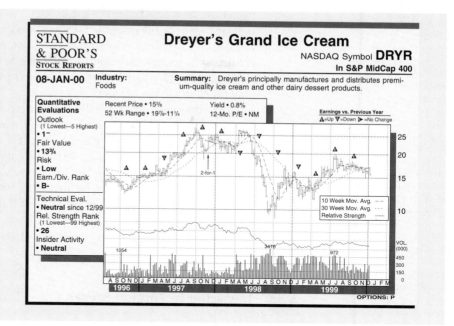

have been posting gains in annual earnings for 30 to 40 years in a row. Baby blues normally pay a modest level of dividends, but like most mid-caps, they tend to emphasize growth. Thus they're considered ideal for investors seeking quality long-term growth. Some well-known baby blues are Tootsie Roll, Reynolds & Reynolds, Hormel, Keane, Inc., and Herman Miller.

Small-Cap Stocks Some investors consider small companies to be in a class by themselves in terms of attractive return opportunities. In many cases, this has turned out to be true. Known as **small-cap stocks,** these companies generally have annual revenues of less than $250 million. Because of their size, spurts of growth can have dramatic effects on their earnings and stock prices. Anchor Financial, Sonic Corp., Papa John's, Sky West, Churchill Downs (where the Kentucky Derby is run), and Dreyer's Ice Cream (see Figure 6.11) are some better-known small-cap stocks.

    Although some small-caps (like Dreyer's Ice Cream) are solid companies with equally solid financials, that's not the case with most of them. Indeed, because many of these companies are so small, they don't have a lot of stock outstanding, and their shares are not widely traded. In addition, small-company stocks have a tendency to be "here today and gone tomorrow." Although some of these stocks may hold the potential for high returns, investors should also be aware of the very high risk exposure that comes with many of them.

    A special category of small-company stock is the so-called *initial public offering (IPO).* Most IPOs are small, relatively new companies that are going public for the first time. (Prior to their public offering, these stocks were privately held and not publicly traded.) Like other small-cap stocks, IPOs are attractive because of the substantial—sometimes phenomenal—capital gains that investors can earn. Of course, there's a catch: In order to stand a chance of buying some of the better, more attractive IPOs, you need to be either a big-time

small-cap stocks
stocks that generally have market values of less than $1 billion but can offer above-average returns.

trader or a preferred client of the broker. Otherwise, the only IPOs you're likely to hear of will be the ones the big guys don't want—which should tell you something about that IPO. More often than not, the small individual investor gets a chance to buy a new issue only after it's been driven way up in price and the initial investors start bailing out, taking their profits with them. Surprisingly, this may take only a few hours or days to occur. If you're not in on the first day, the odds are that your returns will be mediocre, at best. It's an open secret on Wall Street that when it comes to hot IPOs, most individual investors stand little chance of even playing the game, much less winning.

Without a doubt, IPOs are extremely high-risk investments, with the odds stacked against the investor. Because there's no market record to rely on, these stocks should be used only by investors who know what to look for in the company and who can tolerate substantial exposure to risk. IPOs tend to flourish when the market heats up. They very definitely are faddish, their ranks often dominated by trendy retail outlets, food chains, and high-tech firms.

 ## Investing in Foreign Stocks

One of the most dramatic changes to occur in our financial markets in the '80s and '90s was the trend toward globalization. Indeed, globalization became the buzzword of the 1990s, and nowhere was that more evident than in the world equity markets. Consider, for example, that in 1970 the U.S. stock market accounted for fully *two-thirds of the world market*. In essence, our stock market was twice as big as all the rest of the world's stock markets *combined*. That's no longer true: By 1999, the U.S. share of the world equity market had dropped to just over 48%.

Today the world equity markets are dominated by six countries, which together account for about 80% of the total market:

	Market Value (May 2000)
United States	$17.0 trillion
Japan	4.4 trillion
United Kingdom	2.8 trillion
Germany	1.5 trillion
France	1.4 trillion
Canada	820 billion

The United States, still the biggest player, is one of only five countries with trillion-dollar stock markets. In addition to these six, another dozen or so markets are also regarded as major world players. Among the markets in this second tier are Switzerland, Australia, Italy, the Netherlands, Hong Kong, Spain, and Singapore. Finally, some relatively small, emerging markets—South Korea, Mexico, Malaysia, Portugal, Thailand, and Russia—are beginning to make their presence felt. Clearly, the landscape has changed a lot in the last 20 years, and there's every reason to believe that even greater changes lie ahead.

It is clear that the U.S. market dominates in terms of sheer size, as well as in the number of listed companies (over 10,000 of them). But that still leaves unanswered a very important question: How has the U.S. equity market performed in comparison to the rest of the world's major stock markets? The

TABLE 6.5 Comparative Annual Returns in the World's Major Equity Markets, 1980–1999

				Annual Total Returns (in U.S. dollars)					
	Australia	Canada	France	Germany	Japan	Switzerland	United Kingdom	United States	Rank*
1999	18.7%	54.4%	29.7%	20.5%	61.8%	−6.6%	12.4%	26.7%	4th
1998	7.1	−5.7	42.1	29.9	5.2	24.0	17.8	17.8	4th
1997	−9.5	13.3	12.4	25.0	−23.6	44.8	22.6	24.4	3rd
1996	17.7	29.0	21.6	14.0	−15.3	2.8	27.2	28.0	2nd
1995	12.5	19.1	14.8	17.0	0.9	45.0	21.3	35.7	2nd
1994	1.4	−5.1	−7.3	3.1	21.4	30.0	−4.4	4.9	3rd
1993	33.4	17.4	19.6	34.8	23.9	41.7	19.0	16.4	8th
1992	−6.1	−4.6	5.2	−2.1	−26.0	26.0	14.0	7.2	3rd
1991	35.8	12.1	18.6	8.7	9.0	16.8	16.0	23.3	2nd
1990	−16.2	−12.2	−13.3	−8.8	−35.9	−5.1	10.4	−0.4	2nd
1989	10.8	25.2	37.6	48.2	2.3	28.0	23.1	30.7	3rd
1988	38.2	17.9	37.1	19.8	35.4	5.8	4.1	15.5	6th
1987	9.5	14.8	−13.9	−24.6	41.0	−9.2	35.2	5.9	5th
1986	45.0	10.8	79.9	36.4	101.2	34.7	27.7	26.1	7th
1985	21.1	16.2	84.2	138.1	44.0	109.2	53.4	31.7	6th
1984	−12.4	−7.1	4.8	−5.2	17.2	−11.1	5.3	1.2	4th
1983	55.2	32.4	33.2	23.9	24.8	19.9	17.3	24.7	5th
1982	−22.2	2.6	−4.2	10.5	−0.6	2.9	9.0	24.8	1st
1981	−23.8	−10.1	−28.5	−10.3	15.7	−9.5	−10.2	−2.8	2nd
1980	54.7	21.6	−2.0	−10.7	30.4	−7.8	42.0	20.6	5th
			Average Annual Returns Over Extended Holding Periods						
5 years									
1995–99	8.8%	20.5%	23.7%	21.2%	2.1%	20.1%	20.2%	26.4%	
1990–94	7.6	0.9	3.7	6.2	−4.9	20.8	10.7	9.9	
Decades									
1990s	8.6	9.8	13.5	12.8	−0.7	17.4	14.2	17.9	
1980s	13.9	11.6	17.6	16.3	28.6	12.2	19.3	17.2	
20 years									
1980–99	11.2	10.7	15.5	14.5	12.6	14.8	17.3	17.5	

Note: Total return = coupon income + capital gain (or loss) + profit (or loss) from changes in currency exchange rates.

*"Rank" shows how U.S. returns ranked among the listed major markets (e.g., in 1994, the United States ranked third out of the eight markets listed in the table).

Source: International returns obtained from Morgan Stanley Capital International; U.S. returns based on DJIA.

answer: not too well, unfortunately. Table 6.5 summarizes total annual returns (in U.S. dollars) for the 20-year period from 1980 through 1999, for eight of the world's largest equity markets. Note that the United States finished first only once (in 1982). Even so, in the '90s, because the U.S. market consistently finished near the top (every year but 1993), it turned in the best overall performance. Now keep in mind that the returns shown in Table 6.5 *are in U.S. dollars.* As the accompanying *Investing in Action* box reveals, a good deal of the performance of non-U.S. markets is due to the behavior of *currency exchange rates* and not the markets themselves. Indeed, the U.S. stock market is one of the strongest and best performing in the world! Still, the fact remains that when both markets and currencies are combined, some very rewarding opportunities are available to U.S. investors willing to invest in foreign securities.

INVESTING in action

In International Investing, Currencies Can Make or Break You

Investing overseas can pay off in many ways. Capitalism is spreading around the world like wildfire, and economic development in many developing areas outpaces U.S. growth. Accounting practices have improved, because many foreign companies realize that they must make extensive financial disclosure—beyond their normal comfort level—if they want to attract U.S. investors. Finally, investing overseas can help to diversify and strengthen a portfolio. You may have to look overseas to find industry leaders, and foreign markets may rise if the U.S. market stalls.

Even with these global opportunities, it's difficult to believe that an investor in international stocks can consistently outperform one who invests only in U.S. stocks. Take a look at the accompanying graph: Foreign stocks, represented by the EAFE (Europe/Australia/Far East) index, measured in *U.S. dollars*, appear to have outperformed U.S. equities between 1985 and 1995. What the numbers don't show is the impact of a weakening U.S. dollar. To see that, look at the line for the EAFE in *local currency*. From 1990 to 1995, the compound growth is *below* the U.S. stock market line, because the dollar weakened against the local currencies. For the total period 1985 through mid-2000, *if you exclude the currency factor, then U.S. stocks dwarfed the performance of their overseas counterparts.* The average annual return for U.S. equities was

18.45%, compared to 15.43% for the EAFE in U.S. dollars. When you compare U.S. returns to the EAFE in local currencies, the gap widens even further. The average annual return drops to 11.87%—a significant difference.

A favorable currency movement for a U.S. investor in a foreign market is a *weakening* dollar. Money that is invested overseas is typically converted to a local currencies and later converted back to dollars. If the dollar weakens between the time the investor buys and the time she or he sells the stock, the local currency buys more dollars at the time of the sale.

In contrast, a *strengthening* dollar is bad news for U.S. investors buying overseas securities, because the local currency later buys fewer dollars. In the mid-1990s and again at the turn of the century, the U.S. dollar strengthened against most currencies. Over the 3-year period ending November 30, 2000, for example, the U.S. stock market produced average returns of about 12.4%. The German stock market produced an average annual return of about 17.5% in local currency terms. However, in terms of U.S. dollars, the average annual return in Germany was a very poor 8.4%, because the dollar strengthened against the deutsche mark.

continued on next page

Going Global: Direct Investments or ADRs Basically, there are two ways to invest in foreign stocks: through direct investments or through ADRs. (We'll discuss a third way—international mutual funds—in Chapter 12.) Without a doubt, the most adventuresome way is to *buy shares directly in foreign markets.*

Investing directly is *not* for the uninitiated, however. You have to know what you're doing and be prepared to tolerate a good deal of market risk. Although most major U.S. brokerage houses are set up to accommodate investors interested in buying foreign securities, there are still many logistical problems to be faced. To begin with, you have to cope with currency fluctuations and changing foreign exchange rates. These can have a dramatic impact on your returns. But that's just the start: You also have to deal with different regulatory and accounting standards. The fact is that most foreign markets, even the bigger ones, are not so closely regulated as U.S. exchanges. Investors in foreign markets thus have to put up with insider trading and other practices

INVESTING in action

continued from previous page

Indeed, not too many stock markets outperformed the U.S. in dollar terms. The ones that did—among them Bulgaria, Russia, Turkey, and Zimbabwe—were coming from very low base values. And many of these also carried significant risks beyond currency risk, such as concerns about the stability of their governments, that don't worry investors in U.S. stocks.

Sources: Mara der Hovanesian, "So Who Needs Foreign Investing? *Business Week*, September 11, 2000, p. 12-14; Christopher Farrell, "The New Global Investor," *Business Week*, September 11, 2000, pp. 160–162; Craig Karmin, "Comeback Kids Give the World a Jolt," *Wall Street Journal*, January 3, 2000, p. R21.

Source: Data from Morgan Stanley Capital International.

that can cause wild swings in market prices. Furthermore, accounting standards are often much looser, making detailed information about a company's financial condition and operating results a lot harder to come by. Finally, there are the obvious language barriers, tax problems, and general "red tape" that all too often plague international transactions. There's no doubt that the returns from direct foreign investments can be substantial, but so can the obstacles placed in your way.

Fortunately, there is an easier way to invest in foreign stocks, and that is to buy *American Depositary Receipts* (*ADRs*), or *American Depositary Shares* (*ADSs*) as they're sometimes called. As we saw in Chapter 2, ADRs are negotiable instruments. Each ADR represents a specific number of shares in a specific foreign company. (The number of shares can range from a fraction of a share to 20 shares or more.) ADRs are great for investors who want foreign stocks but don't want the hassles that often come with them.

HOT LINKS

Visit the CNN financial network to find out which country's stock market has registered the highest percentage change and which registered the lowest percentage change from the previous trading day. Can you cite the reasons why?

cnnfn.cnn.com/markets/world_markets.html

That's because American Depositary Receipts are bought and sold on U.S. markets just like stocks in U.S. companies. Their prices are quoted in U.S. dollars, not British pounds, Japanese yen, or German marks. Furthermore, dividends are paid in dollars. Although there are about 400 foreign companies *whose shares are directly listed on U.S. exchanges* (over 200 of which are Canadian), most foreign companies are traded in this country as ADRs. Indeed, shares of about 1,000 companies, from more than 40 countries, are traded as ADRs on the NYSE, AMEX, and Nasdaq/OTC markets.

To see how ADRs are structured, we'll look at Cadbury Schweppes, the British food and household products firm. Each Cadbury ADR represents ownership of four shares of Cadbury stock. These shares are held in a custodial account by a U.S. bank (or its foreign correspondent), which receives dividends, pays any foreign withholding taxes, and then converts the net proceeds to U.S. dollars, which it passes on to investors. Other foreign stocks that can be purchased as ADRs include Sony (a Japanese stock), Ericsson Telephone (from Sweden), Nokia (Finland), Vodafone Airtouch (U.K.), Royal Dutch Petroleum (Netherlands), Nestle's (Switzerland), Shanghai Petro-chemicals (China), Elan Corp. (Ireland), and Grupo Televisa (Mexico). You can even buy ADRs on Russian companies, such as Vimpel-Communications, a Moscow-based cellular phone company whose shares trade (as ADRs) on the NYSE.

Putting Returns in a Global Perspective Whether you buy foreign stocks directly or through ADRs, the whole process of global investing is a bit more complex and more risky than domestic investing. When investing globally, *you have to pick both the right stock and the right market.* Basically, foreign stocks are valued much the same way as U.S. stocks. Indeed, the same variables that drive U.S. share prices (earnings, dividends, etc.) also drive stock values in foreign markets. On top of this, each market reacts to its own set of economic forces (inflation, interest rates, level of economic activity), which set the tone of the market. At any given time, therefore, some markets are performing better than others. The challenge facing global investors is to be in the right market at the right time. As with U.S. stocks, foreign shares produce the same two basic sources of returns: dividends and capital gains (or losses).

But with global investing, there is a third variable—*currency exchange rates*—that plays an important role in defining returns to U.S. investors. As the U.S. dollar weakens or strengthens relative to a foreign currency, the returns to U.S. investors from foreign stocks increase or decrease accordingly. In a global context, total return to U.S. investors in foreign securities is defined as follows:

Equation 6.4

$$\begin{array}{c}\text{Total return}\\\text{(in U.S. dollars)}\end{array} = \begin{array}{c}\text{Current income}\\\text{(dividends)}\end{array} + \begin{array}{c}\text{Capital gains}\\\text{(or losses)}\end{array} \pm \begin{array}{c}\text{Changes in currency}\\\text{exchange rates}\end{array}$$

Because current income and capital gains are in the "local currency" (the currency in which the foreign stock is denominated, such as the German mark or the Japanese yen), we can shorten the total return formula to:

Equation 6.5

$$\begin{array}{c}\text{Total return}\\\text{(in U.S. dollars)}\end{array} = \begin{array}{c}\text{Returns from current}\\\text{income and capital gains}\\\text{(in local currency)}\end{array} \pm \begin{array}{c}\text{Returns from}\\\text{changes in currency}\\\text{exchange rates}\end{array}$$

Thus, the two basic components of total return are *those generated by the stocks themselves* (dividends plus change in share prices) and *those derived from movements in currency exchange rates.*

Employing the same two basic components noted above in Equation 6.5, we can compute total return in U.S. dollars by using the following holding period return (HPR) formula, as modified for changes in currency exchange rates.

Equation 6.6

$$\text{Total return (in U.S. dollars)} = \left[\frac{\begin{array}{c}\text{Ending value of} \\ \text{stock in foreign} \\ \text{currency}\end{array} + \begin{array}{c}\text{Amount of dividends} \\ \text{received in} \\ \text{foreign currency}\end{array}}{\begin{array}{c}\text{Beginning value of stock} \\ \text{in foreign currency}\end{array}} \times \frac{\begin{array}{c}\text{Exchange rate} \\ \text{at } \textit{end} \text{ of} \\ \text{holding period}\end{array}}{\begin{array}{c}\text{Exchange rate} \\ \text{at } \textit{beginning} \text{ of} \\ \text{holding period}\end{array}} \right] - 1.00$$

In Equation 6.6, the "exchange rate" represents the *value of the foreign currency in U.S. dollars*—that is, how much one unit of the foreign currency is worth in U.S. money.

This modified HPR formula is best used over investment periods of one year or less. Also, because it is assumed that dividends are received at the same exchange rate as the ending price of the stock, this equation provides only an approximate (though fairly close) measure of return. Essentially, the first component of Equation 6.6 provides returns on the stock in local currency, and the second element accounts for the impact of changes in currency exchange rates.

To see how this formula works, consider a U.S. investor who buys several hundred shares of Petrofina, a large Belgian petroleum and chemical company that trades on the Brussels stock exchange. The investor paid a price *per share* of 9,140 Belgian francs (Bf) for the stock, at a time when the exchange rate between the U.S. dollar and the Belgian franc (U.S.$/Bf) was $0.0307. At that rate, the Bf was worth a little more than 3 cents. Put another way, this exchange rate amounts to 32.55 Bf per U.S. dollar, so 1 U.S.$/32.55 B = $0.0307. The stock paid *annual* dividends of 275 Bf per share. At the end of the year the stock was trading at 9,500 Bf per share, when the U.S.$/Bf exchange rate was $0.0336 (29.75 Bf per U.S. dollar). Clearly, the stock went up in price, so the investor must have done all right. To find out just what kind of return this investment generated (in U.S. dollars), we'll have to use Equation 6.6.

$$\text{Total return (in U.S. dollars)} = \left[\frac{9,500 + 275}{9,140} \times \frac{\$0.0336}{\$0.0307} \right] - 1.00$$

$$= [1.0695 \times 1.0945] - 1.00$$

$$= [1.1705] - 1.00$$

$$= \underline{17.05\%}$$

With a return of 17.05%, the investor seems to have done quite well. However, *most of this return was due to currency movements, not to the behavior of the stock.* Look at just the first part of the equation, which shows the return (in local currency) *earned on the stock* from dividends and capital gains: $1.0695 - 1.00 = 6.95\%$. Thus the stock itself produced a return of less than 7%. All the rest of the return—more than 10% (i.e., 17.05 − 6.95)—came from the change in currency values. In this case, the value of the U.S. dollar went down relative to the Belgian franc and thus added to the return.

As we've just seen, exchange rates can have a dramatic impact on investor returns. They can convert mediocre returns or even losses into very attractive returns—and vice versa. Only one thing determines whether the so-called *currency effect* is going to be positive or negative: the behavior of the U.S. dollar relative to the currency in which the security is denominated. In essence, *a stronger dollar has a negative impact on total returns to U.S. investors, and a weaker dollar has a positive impact.* Thus, other things being equal, the best time to be in foreign securities is when the dollar is *falling*.

Of course, the greater the amount of fluctuation in the currency exchange rate, the greater the impact on total returns. The challenge facing global investors is to find not only the best-performing foreign stock(s) but also the best-performing foreign currencies. You want the *value of both the foreign stock and the foreign currency to go up over your investment horizon.* And note that this rule applies *both* to direct investment in foreign stocks and to the purchase of ADRs. (Even though ADRs are denominated in dollars, their quoted prices vary with ongoing changes in currency exchange rates.)

Alternative Investment Strategies

Basically, common stocks can be used (1) as a "storehouse" of value, (2) as a way to accumulate capital, and (3) as a source of income. Storage of value is important to all investors; nobody likes to lose money. However, some investors are more concerned about it than others, and therefore, rank safety of principal as their most important stock selection criteria. These investors are more quality-conscious and tend to gravitate toward blue chips and other nonspeculative shares. Accumulation of capital, in contrast, is generally an important goal to those with long-term investment horizons. These investors use the capital gains and/or dividends that stocks provide to build up their wealth. Some use growth stocks for this purpose, others do it with income shares, and still others use a little of both. Finally, some investors use stocks as a source of income. To them, a dependable flow of dividends is essential. High-yielding, good-quality income shares are usually the preferred investment vehicle for these people.

Individual investors can use various *investment strategies* to reach their investment goals. These include buy-and-hold, high income, quality long-term growth, aggressive stock management, and speculation and short-term trading. The first three strategies appeal to investors who consider storage of value important. Depending on the temperament of the investor and the time he or she has to devote to an investment program, any of the strategies might be used to accumulate capital. In contrast, the high-income strategy is the logical choice for those using stocks as a source of income.

Buy-and-Hold Buy-and-hold is the most basic of all investment strategies, and is certainly one of the most conservative. The objective is to place money in a secure investment outlet (safety of principal is vital) and watch it grow over time. In this strategy, investors select high-quality stocks that offer attractive current income and/or capital gains and hold them for extended periods—perhaps as long as 10 to 15 years. This strategy is often used to finance future retirement plans, to meet the educational needs of children, or simply to accumulate capital over the long haul. Generally, investors pick out a few good stocks and then invest in them on a regular basis for long periods of time—until either the investment climate or corporate conditions change dramatically.

Buy-and-hold investors regularly add fresh capital to their portfolios (many treat them like savings plans). Most also plow the income from annual dividends back into the portfolio and reinvest in additional shares (often through dividend reinvestment plans). Long popular with so-called *value-oriented investors,* this approach is used by quality-conscious individuals who are looking for competitive returns over the long haul.

High Income Individual investors often use common stocks to seek high levels of current income. Common stocks are desirable for this purpose not so much for their high dividend yields but also because their *dividend levels tend to increase over time.* In this strategy, safety of principal and stability of income are vital, while capital gains are of secondary importance. Quality income shares are the popular medium for this strategy. Some investors adopt it simply as a way of earning high (and relatively safe) returns on their investment capital. More often, however, a high-income strategy is used by those who are trying to supplement their income. Often, they plan to use the added income for consumption purposes, such as a retired couple supplementing their retirement benefits with income from stocks.

Quality Long-Term Growth This strategy is *less conservative* than either of the first two in that it seeks capital gains as the primary source of return. A fair amount of trading takes place with this approach. Most of the trading is confined to quality growth stocks (including tech stocks, as well as baby blues and other mid-caps) that offer attractive growth prospects and the chance for considerable price appreciation. A number of growth stocks also pay dividends, which many growth-oriented investors consider *an added source of return.* But even so, this strategy still emphasizes capital gains as the principal way to earn big returns. The approach involves a greater element of risk, because of its heavy reliance on capital gains. Therefore, a good deal of diversification is often used. Long-term accumulation of capital is the most common reason for using this approach, but compared to the buy-and-hold tactic, the investor aggressively seeks a bigger payoff by doing considerably more trading and assuming more market risk.

A variation of this investment strategy combines quality long-term growth with high income. This is the so-called *total-return approach* to investing. Though solidly anchored in long-term growth, this approach also considers dividend income as a source of return that should be sought after, rather than relegated to an after-thought or treated as merely a pleasant by-product. In essence, with the total return approach, investors seek attractive long-term returns from *both* dividend income *and* capital gains. These investors hold both income stocks and growth stocks in their portfolios. Or they may hold stocks that provide both dividends and capital gains. In the latter case, the investor doesn't necessarily look for high-yielding stocks, but rather for stocks that offer the potential for *high rates of growth in their dividend streams.* Like their counterparts who employ high-income or quality long-term growth strategies, total-return investors are very concerned about quality. Indeed, about the only thing that separates these investors from high-income and quality long-term growth investors is that to them, what matters is not so much the *source of return* as *the amount of return*. For this reason, total-return investors seek the most attractive returns wherever they can find them—be it from a growing stream of dividends or from appreciation in the price of a stock.

Aggressive Stock Management Aggressive stock management also uses quality issues but seeks attractive rates of return through a fully managed portfolio. Such a portfolio would be one in which the investor aggressively trades in and out of stocks in order to achieve eye-catching returns, primarily from capital gains. Blue chips, growth stocks, big-name tech stocks, mid-caps, and cyclical issues are the primary investment vehicles. More aggressive investors might even consider small-cap stocks, including some of the more speculative tech stocks, foreign shares, and ADRs.

This approach is similar to the quality long-term growth strategy. However, it involves considerably more trading, and the investment horizon is generally much shorter. For example, rather than waiting 2 or 3 years for a stock to move, an aggressive stock trader would go after the same investment payoff in 6 months to a year. Timing security transactions and turning investment capital over fairly rapidly are both key elements of this strategy. These investors try to stay fully invested in stocks when the market is bullish. When it weakens, they shift to a more defensive posture by putting a big chunk of their money into defensive stocks or even into cash and other short-term debt instruments. This strategy has substantial risks. It also places real demands on the individual's time and investment skills. But the rewards can be equally substantial.

Speculation and Short-Term Trading Speculation and short-term trading characterize the least conservative of all investment strategies. The sole objective of this strategy is capital gains. The shorter the time in which the objective can be achieved, the better. Although such investors confine most of their attention to speculative or small-cap stocks and tech stocks, they are not averse to using foreign shares (especially those in so-called *emerging markets*) or other forms of common stock if they offer attractive short-term opportunities. Many speculators find that information about the industry or company is much less important than market psychology or the general tone of the market. It is a process of constantly switching from one position to another as new opportunities unfold. Because the strategy involves so much risk, many transactions yield little or no profit, or even substantial losses. The hope is, of course, that when one does hit, it will be in a big way, and returns will be more than sufficient to offset losses. This strategy obviously requires considerable knowledge and time. Perhaps most important, it also requires the psychological and financial fortitude to withstand the shock of financial losses.

Some Popular Investment Styles

We've just seen that investors can choose from a variety of investment *strategies*—buy-and-hold, speculation, and others. They can also employ different investment *styles* when implementing their investment programs. The selection of an investment style depends in large part on one's investment objectives and risk tolerance. Investment style, in effect, defines the *types of securities* you will want to hold in your equity portfolio. It sets the tone for your investment program by determining how aggressive or conservative you'll be in your security selection. Five types of investment styles dominate the market today: income, growth, value, sector rotation, and momentum investing.

Growth investing and *value investing* are based primarily on fundamental analysis. *Sector rotation* and *momentum investing*, in contrast, are based more on perceived market conditions. The premise behind *income investing* is simple: Buy securities that offer a steady stream of income along with some growth. For equity investors, this means common stocks with a history of regular dividend payments. Utility stocks, some blue chips, and preferred stocks are favorites with income investors who, not surprisingly, tend to follow *high income* as well as *buy-and-hold* investment strategies.

growth investing
investing in stocks with above-average forecasts of earnings growth and high price/earnings ratios in expectation of higher returns.

Growth Investing Investors who prefer **growth investing** are willing to pay premium prices for stocks of companies with above-average expectations of earnings growth. They believe that stock prices of companies with high earnings-growth rates—say, over 15% to 20% a year—should ultimately yield higher returns. These companies have high prices, high price-to-book ratios, and high price/earnings ratios. Most growth stocks pay little or nothing in dividends because management reinvests earnings to "grow" the business. Some growth stocks are large companies, but more often they tend to be "glamour" stocks such as high-tech companies and emerging companies in high-growth industries (the Internet, networking, and biotechnology, for example). Microsoft, Intel, and Cisco are classic examples of growth stocks. Growth investing is riskier than some other styles, as growth stocks tend to rise faster, and fall faster, than the S&P 500. Investors who choose growth stocks need to monitor both company performance and industry trends closely, because these stocks are sensitive to change. Waiting too long to buy or sell can wipe out the rewards of the increased risk. Growth investors tend to use investment strategies that focus on capital appreciation: *quality long-term growth, aggressive stock management,* and possibly even *speculation.*

value investing
investing in stocks of companies that are out of favor with the market for some reason, as reflected by low price/earnings ratios and low prices compared to their fundamentals.

Value Investing In contrast to growth investing, **value investing** focuses on companies that are out of favor with the market. Value investors are "contrarians": They buy stocks whose prices are low compared to their fundamentals (strong balance sheets, earnings, book value per share, cash flow, asset values, or similar quantitative measures). These stocks have lower price/earnings ratios, lower price-to-book ratios, and higher dividend yields than the rest of the market. Value investors analyze *why* the company's valuation is low, and they buy if they expect some particular action—new management, corporate takeover, regulatory change, etc.—to drive up the price. Companies whose prices fall on bad news, such as not meeting earnings targets, may be underpriced bargains. Because the market has undervalued these stocks, value investors believe that the stock price will eventually return to a more "correct" price level, which will produce solid returns over time.

Value companies are often in staid, cyclical industries such as automobiles, chemicals, steel, and financial services. They do best when interest rates are low and the economy is recovering. They peak when economic activity slows.

Value investing fell from favor during the strong bull market of the 1990s, when value stocks were harder to find. Patience is definitely a virtue with this style, because it's hard to know just when a company's fortunes will turn. Thus, value investors typically use a *buy-and-hold* strategy.

sector rotation
investing style based on the premise that certain industry sectors perform better during specific stages of the economic cycle.

Sector Rotation With **sector rotation**, investors choose stocks in specific industry sectors that will do best depending on the current and projected stages of the business cycle. The underlying premise is that industries react differently during different stages of the economic cycle—recovery, economic boom, decline, or economic recession. Unlike value and growth investors, who focus on the fundamentals of individual companies, sector rotation investors use a "top-down" approach: They start with the economy as a whole and the forecast for the future. After investors identify industries that should do well in given economic conditions, they select strong companies in those industry sectors. Then, as they anticipate changes in the level of economic activity, they rotate into a different sector.

There are several different ways to define the sectors. One common group divides stocks into four broad sectors: interest-sensitive, consumer durables, capital goods, and defensive. *Interest-sensitive* stocks, like banks, finance companies, and utilities, do well when the economy starts to firm up and interest rates are low. *Consumer durables* are very sensitive to changes in the economy. They tend to do well when the economy is strong, unemployment is low, and consumer disposable income is high. *Capital good manufacturers*, also driven by consumer demand, perform better at a later point in the economic cycle, when economic activity builds greater demand for their products. Finally, *defensive stocks* do well in recessionary periods. Demand for the products that these companies produce remains fairly stable throughout the economic cycle. This sector includes companies that produce staples like food, beverages, and pharmaceuticals, as well as health care providers and utilities.

In sector rotation, investors rotate (move) from one type of stock to the next as the economy moves from one stage of the business cycle to the next. There is obviously a good deal of market timing involved with this approach. Sector rotation investors tend to use investment strategies that focus on *aggressive stock management* and even a bit of *short-term trading*.

momentum investing
investing style that focuses on using relative stock price movement to determine when to buy and sell.

Momentum Investing **Momentum investing** relies heavily on *technical analysis*—an analytical approach that looks at how market forces affect stock prices. (We discuss technical analysis in greater depth in Chapter 8.) Momentum investors focus on relative price movements in the market, rather than on the fundamentals of the underlying companies. They look at stock price, earnings, and other indicators to identify signs that a stock's price is about to soar or fall relative to the market. If the momentum is positive, buying early will produce good returns as more investors jump on the bandwagon and drive the price up even higher.

To select stocks, momentum investors look for stocks in high-growth industries. Momentum stocks tend to have high trading volume and price movements that can be triggered by positive news reports or rumors of high future earnings growth. Basically, momentum investors look for stocks whose prices are rising faster than the S&P 500 (or some other market index or average). They tend to follow either *aggressive stock management* or *speculation and short-term trading* strategies. They typically adopt a relatively short-term approach to investing. Their philosophy is to get in and out fairly quickly—often over no more than a 6- to 12-month period. Some momentum investors are, in fact, very short-term traders, as they will aggressively *day trade* their favorite stock(s), moving in and out on relatively small price changes. Momentum investors have to closely monitor their stocks and watch the direction of the market. This style can be risky if you don't catch the upward movement in time or don't sell before the stock starts to slide.

IN REVIEW

CONCEPTS

6.15 Define and briefly discuss the investment merits of each of the following.
a. *Blue chips.*
b. *Income stocks.*
c. *Mid-cap stocks.*
d. *American Depositary Receipts.*
e. *IPOs.*
f. *Tech stocks.*

6.16 Why do most income stocks offer only limited capital gains potential? Does this mean the outlook for continued profitability is also limited? Explain.

6.17 With all the securities available in this country, why would a U.S. investor want to buy foreign stocks? Briefly describe the two ways in which a U.S. investor can buy stocks in a foreign company. As a U.S. investor, which approach would you prefer? Explain.

6.18 The effects of currency exchange rates on market returns were discussed in the *Investing in Action* box on page 254. Can currency exchange rates have an impact on security returns? Explain. How do returns in the U.S. stock market stack up to returns in foreign markets once currency exchange rates are factored out?

6.19 Which *investment approach (or approaches)* do you feel would be most appropriate for a quality-conscious investor? Explain. What kind of *investment style (or styles)* do you think would be appropriate for a more aggressive investor? Explain.

Summary

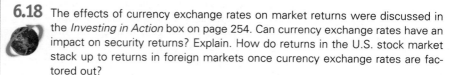

LG 1 **Explain the investment appeal of common stocks and why individuals like to invest in them.** Common stocks have long been a popular investment vehicle, largely because of the attractive return opportunities they provide. From current income to capital gains, there are common stocks available to fit just about any investment need.

LG 2 **Describe stock returns from a historical perspective and understand how current returns measure up to historical standards of performance.** Over the long haul, stocks have provided investors with annual returns of around 10% to 15%. Over the past decade or so, stocks have been especially rewarding, generating returns of anywhere from around 20% (on the Dow and the S&P 500) to nearly 30% in the tech-heavy Nasdaq market. Although these returns consist of both dividends and capital gains, it's clear that capital appreciation has been dominant. Whether such returns will continue remains to be seen, but we can probably expect to see highly attractive returns over relatively short periods of time for those willing to assume a greater amount of risk.

LG 3 **Discuss the basic features of common stocks, including issue characteristics, stock quotations, and transaction costs.** Common stocks are a form of equity capital. Each share represents partial ownership of a company. Publicly traded stock can be issued via public offering or through a rights offering to existing stockholders. Companies can also increase the number of shares outstanding through a stock split. To reduce the number of shares of stock in circulation, companies can buy back shares, which are then held as treasury stock. Occasionally, a company issues different classes of common stock, known as classified common stock.

LG 4   **Understand of the different kinds of common stock values.** There are several ways to calculate the value of a share of stock. Book value represents accounting value. Market and investment values, which are most important to investors, represent what the stock is or should be worth.

LG 5   **Discuss common stock dividends, types of dividends, and dividend reinvestment plans.** Companies often share their profits by paying out cash dividends to stockholders. Such actions are normally taken only after carefully considering a variety of corporate and market factors. Sometimes companies declare stock dividends rather than, or in addition to, cash dividends. Many firms that pay cash dividends have dividend reinvestment plans, through which shareholders can have cash dividends automatically reinvested in the company's stock.

LG 6   **Describe various types of common stocks, including foreign stocks, and note how stocks can be used as investment vehicles.** The type of stock selected depends on an investor's needs and preferences. In today's market, investors can choose blue chips, income stocks, growth stocks, tech stocks, speculative issues, cyclicals, defensive shares, mid-cap stocks, small-cap stocks, and initial public offerings. In addition, U.S. investors can buy the common stocks of foreign companies either directly on foreign exchanges or on U.S. markets as American Depositary Receipts (ADRs). Generally speaking, common stocks can be used as a storehouse of value, as a way to accumulate capital, and as a source of income. Different investment strategies (buy-and-hold, high income, quality long-term growth, aggressive stock management, and speculation and short-term trading) as well as different investment styles (income, growth, value, sector rotation, and momentum investing) can be followed to achieve these objectives.

Discussion Questions

LG 2   **Q6.1** Look at the record of stock returns in Tables 6.1 and 6.2, particularly the return performance during the 1970s, 1980s, and 1990s.
  a. How would you compare the returns during the 1970s with those produced in the 1980s? How would you characterize market returns in the 1990s? Is there anything that stands out about this market?
  b. Now look at Figure 6.2 and Table 6.3. On the basis of the information in these exhibits, how would you describe the market's performance during the 1990s?
  c. Considering the average annual returns that have been generated over holding periods of 5 years or more, what rate of return do you feel is typical for the stock market in general? Is it unreasonable to expect this kind of return, on average, in the future? Explain.

LG 3   **Q6.2** Assume that the following quote for the Alpha Beta Corp. (a NYSE stock) was obtained from the Thursday, April 10, issue of the *Wall Street Journal*.

+6.8   254   150.50   AlphaBet   ALF   6.00   3.1   15   755   189.12   −3.88

Given this information, answer the following questions.

a. On what day did the trading activity occur?

b. At what price did the stock sell at the end of the day on Wednesday, April 9?

c. How much (in percentage terms) has the price of this stock gone up or down since the first of the year?

d. What is the firm's price/earnings ratio? What does that indicate?

e. What is the last price at which the stock traded on the date quoted?

f. How large a dividend is expected in the current year?

g. What are the highest and lowest prices at which the stock traded during the latest 52-week period?

h. How many shares of stock were traded on the day quoted?

i. How much, if any, of a change in stock price took place between the day quoted and the immediately preceding period? At what price did the stock close on the immediately preceding day?

LG 4

Q6.3 Listed below are three pairs of stocks. Look at each pair and select the security you would like to own, given that you want to *select the one that's worth more money*. Then, *after* you make all three of your selections, use the *Wall Street Journal* or some other source to find the latest market value of the two securities in each pair.

a. 50 shares of Berkshire Hathaway (stock symbol BRKA) or 150 shares of Coca-Cola (stock symbol KO). (Both are listed on the NYSE.)

b. 100 shares of WD-40 (symbol WDFC—a Nasdaq National Market issue) or 100 shares of Nike (symbol NKE—a NYSE stock).

c. 150 shares of Wal-Mart (symbol WMT) or 50 shares of Sears (symbol S). (Both are listed on the NYSE.)

How many times did you pick the one that was worth more money? Did the price of any of these stocks surprise you? If so, which one(s)? Does the price of a stock represent its value? Explain.

LG 6

Q6.4 Assume that a wealthy individual comes to you looking for some investment advice. She is in her early forties and has $250,000 to put into stocks. She wants to build up as much capital as she can over a 15-year period and is willing to tolerate a "fair amount" of risk.

a. What types of stocks do you think would be most suitable for this investor? Come up with at least three different types of stocks, and briefly explain the rationale for each.

b. Would your recommendations change if you were dealing with a smaller amount of money—say, $50,000? What if the investor were more risk-averse? Explain.

LG 6

Q6.5 Identify and briefly describe the three sources of return to U.S. investors in foreign stocks. How important are currency exchange rates? With regard to currency exchange rates, when is the best time to be in foreign securities?

a. Listed below are exchange rates (for the beginning and end of a hypothetical 1-year investment horizon) for three currencies: the British pound (B£), Australian dollar (A$), and Mexican peso (Mp).

	Currency Exchange Rates at	
Currency	Beginning of Investment Horizon	End of One-Year Investment Horizon
British pound (B£)	1.55 U.S.$ per B£	1.75 U.S.$ per B£
Australian dollar (A$)	1.35 A$ per U.S.$	1.25 A$ per U.S.$
Mexican peso (Mp)	0.10 U.S.$ per Mp	0.08 U.S.$ per Mp

From the perspective of a U.S. investor holding a foreign (British, Australian, or Mexican) stock, which of the above changes in currency exchange rates would have a positive effect on returns (in U.S. dollars)? Which would have a negative effect?

b. ADRs are denominated in U.S. dollars. Are their returns affected by currency exchange rates? Explain.

LG 6   Q6.6   Briefly define each of the following types of investment programs, and note the kinds of stock (blue chips, speculative stocks, etc.) that would best fit with each.
a. A buy-and-hold strategy.   b. A high-income portfolio.
c. Long-term total return.   d. Aggressive stock management.
e. Value style of investing.   f. Sector rotation.

Problems

LG 3   P6.1   An investor owns some stock in General Refrigeration & Cooling. The stock recently underwent a 5-for-2 stock split. If the stock was trading at $50 per share just before the split, how much is each share most likely selling for after the split? If the investor owned 200 shares of the stock before the split, how many shares would she own afterward?

 LG 4   P6.2   The Kracked Pottery Company has total assets of $2.5 million, total short- and long-term debt of $1.8 million, and $200,000 worth of 8% preferred stock outstanding. What is the firm's total book value? What would its book value per share be if the firm had 50,000 shares of common stock outstanding?

 LG 5   P6.3   The MedTech Company recently reported net profits after taxes of $15.8 million. It has 2.5 million shares of common stock outstanding and pays preferred dividends of $1 million per year.
a. Compute the firm's earnings per share (EPS).
b. Assuming that the stock currently trades at $60 per share, determine what the firm's dividend yield would be if it paid $2 per share to common stockholders.
c. What would the firm's dividend payout ratio be if it paid $2 a share in dividends?

 LG 4   LG 5   P6.4   Consider the following information about Truly Good Coffee, Inc.

Total assets	$240 million
Total debt	$115 million
Preferred stock	$25 million
Common stockholders' equity	$100 million
Net profits after taxes	$22.5 million
Number of preferred stock outstanding	1 million shares
Number of common stock outstanding	10 million shares
Preferred dividends paid	$2/share
Common dividends paid	$0.75/share
Market price of the preferred stock	$30.75/share
Market price of the common stock	$25.00/share

Use the given information to find the following.
a. The company's book value.
b. Its book value per share.
c. The stock's earnings per share (EPS).
d. The dividend payout ratio.
e. The dividend yield on the common stock.
f. The dividend yield on the preferred stock.

LG 5   **P6.5** Collin Smythies owns 200 shares of Consolidated Glue. The company's board of directors recently declared a cash dividend of 50 cents a share payable April 18 (a Wednesday) to shareholders of record on March 22 (a Thursday).

     a. How much in dividends, if any, will Collin receive if he *sells* his stock on March 20?

     b. Assume Collin decides to hold on to the stock rather than sell it. If he belongs to the company's dividend reinvestment plan, how many new shares of stock will he receive if the stock is currently trading at 40 and the plan offers a 5% discount on the share price of the stock? (Assume that all of Collin's dividends are diverted to the plan.) Will Collin have to pay any taxes on these dividends, given that he is taking them in stock rather than cash?

LG 5   **P6.6** Southern Cities Trucking Co. has the following 5-year record of earnings per share.

Year	EPS
1997	$1.40
1998	2.10
1999	1.00
2000	3.25
2001	0.80

Which of the following procedures would produce the greater amount of dividends to stockholders over this 5-year period?

     a. Paying out dividends at a fixed ratio of 40% of EPS.

     b. Paying out dividends at the fixed rate of $1 per share.

 LG 4   LG 5   **P6.7** Using the resources available at your campus or public library, or on the Internet, select any three common stocks you like, and determine the latest book value per share, earnings per share, dividend payout ratio, and dividend yield for each. (Show all your calculations.)

LG 4   LG 5   **P6.8** In January 1996, an investor purchased 800 shares of Engulf & Devour, a rapidly growing high-tech conglomerate. Over the 5-year period from 1996 through 2000, the stock turned in the following dividend and share price performance.

Year	Share Price at Beginning of Year	Dividends Paid During Year	Share Price at End of Year
1996	$42.50*	$0.82	$ 54.00
1997	54.00	1.28	74.25
1998	74.25	1.64	81.00
1999	81.00	1.91	91.25
2000	91.25	2.30	128.75

*Investor purchased stock in 1996 at this price.

     a. On the basis of this information, find the *annual* holding period returns for 1996 through 2000. (*Hint:* See Chapter 4 for the HPR formula.)

     b. Use the return information in Table 6.1 to evaluate the investment performance of this stock. How do you think Engulf & Devour stacks up against the market? Would you consider this a good investment? Explain.

 LG 6   **P6.9** George Robbins considers himself to be an aggressive investor. At the present time, he's thinking about investing in some foreign securities. In particular, he's looking at two stocks: (1) Löwenbräu, the famous German beer maker, and (2) Ciba-Geigy, the big Swiss pharmaceutical firm.

Löwenbräu, which trades on the Frankfurt Exchange, is currently priced at 2,400 German marks (Dm) per share. It pays annual dividends of 25 Dm per share. Robbins expects the stock to climb to 2,700 Dm within a period of 12 months. The current exchange rate is 1.58 Dm/U.S.$, but that's expected to rise to 1.75 Dm/U.S.$.

The other company, Ciba-Geigy, trades on the Zurich Exchange and is currently priced at 715 Swiss francs (Sf) per share. The stock pays annual dividends of 15 Sf per share. Its share price is expected to go up to 760 Sf within a year. At current exchange rates, one Sf is worth $0.75 U.S., but that's expected to go to $0.85 by the end of the 1-year holding period.

    a. *Ignoring the currency effect,* which of the two stocks promises the higher total return (in its local currency)? Based on this information, which of the two stocks looks like the better investment?

    b. Now, which of the two stocks has the better total return *in U.S. dollars?* Did currency exchange rates affect their returns in any way? Do you still want to stick with the same stock you selected in part (a)? Explain.

Case Problem 6.1

LG 1   LG 6

Sara Decides to Take the Plunge

Sara Thomas is a child psychologist who has built up a thriving practice in her hometown of Boise, Idaho. Over the past several years she has been able to accumulate a substantial sum of money. She has worked long and hard to be successful, but she never imagined anything like this. Success has not spoiled Sara. Still single, she keeps to her old circle of friends. One of her closest friends is Terry Jenkins, who happens to be a stockbroker, and who acts as Sara's financial adviser.

Not long ago, Sara attended a seminar on investing in the stock market and since then she's been doing some reading about the market. She has concluded that keeping all of her money in low-yielding savings accounts doesn't make any sense. As a result, Sara has decided to move part of her money to stocks. One evening, Sara told Terry about her decision and explained that she had found several stocks that she thought looked "sort of interesting." She described them as follows:

- *North Atlantic Swim Suit Company.* This highly speculative stock pays no dividends. Although the earnings of NASS have been a bit erratic, Sara feels that its growth prospects have never been brighter—"what with more people than ever going to the beaches the way they are these days," she says.

- *Town and Country Computer.* This is a long-established computer firm that pays a modest dividend yield (of about 1½%). It is considered a quality growth stock. From one of the stock reports she read, Sara understands that T&C offers excellent long-term growth and capital gains potential.

- *Southeastern Public Utility Company.* This income stock pays a dividend yield of around 5%. Although it's a solid company, it has limited growth prospects because of its location.

- *International Gold Mines, Inc.* This stock has performed quite well in the past, especially when inflation has become a problem. Sara feels that if it can do so well in inflationary times, it will do even better in a strong economy. Unfortunately, the stock has experienced wide price swings in the past. It pays almost no dividends.

Questions

a. What do you think of the idea of Sara keeping "substantial sums" of money in savings accounts? Would common stocks make better investments than savings accounts? Explain.

b.   What is your opinion of the four stocks Sara has described? Do you think they are suitable for her investment needs? Explain.

c.   What kind of common stock investment program would you recommend for Sara? What investment objectives do you think she should set for herself, and how can common stocks help her achieve her goals?

Case Problem 6.2 — Wally Wonders Whether There's a Place for Dividends

LG 5   LG 6

Wally Wilson is a commercial artist who makes a good living by doing freelance work—mostly layouts and illustrations for local ad agencies and major institutional clients (such as large department stores). Wally has been investing in the stock market for some time, buying mostly high-quality growth stocks. He has been seeking long-term growth and capital appreciation. He feels that with the limited time he has to devote to his security holdings, high-quality issues are his best bet. He has become a bit perplexed lately with the market, disturbed that some of his growth stocks aren't doing even as well as many good-grade income shares. He therefore decides to have a chat with his broker, Al Fried.

During the course of their conversation, it becomes clear that both Al and Wally are thinking along the same lines. Al points out that dividend yields on income shares are indeed way up and that, because of the state of the economy, the outlook for growth stocks is not particularly bright. He suggests that Wally seriously consider putting some of his money into income shares to capture the high dividend yields that are available. After all, as Al says, "the bottom line is not so much where the payoff comes from as how much it amounts to!" They then talk about a high-yield public utility stock, Hydro-Electric Light and Power. Al digs up some forecast information about Hydro-Electric and presents it to Wally for his consideration:

Year	Expected EPS	Expected Dividend Payout Ratio
2001	$3.25	40%
2002	3.40	40
2003	3.90	45
2004	4.40	45
2005	5.00	45

The stock currently trades at $60 per share. Al thinks that within 5 years it should be trading at a level of $75 to $80. Wally realizes that in order to buy the Hydro-Electric stock, he will have to sell his holdings of CapCo Industries—a highly regarded growth stock that Wally is disenchanted with because of recent substandard performance.

Questions

a.   How would you describe Wally's present investment program? How do you think it fits him and his investment objectives?

b.   Consider the Hydro-Electric stock.
   1. Determine the amount of annual dividends Hydro-Electric can be expected to pay over the years 2001 to 2005.
   2. Compute the total dollar return that Wally will make from Hydro-Electric if he invests $6,000 in the stock and all the dividend and price expectations are realized.

3. If Wally participates in the company's dividend reinvestment plan, how many shares of stock will he have by the end of 2005? What will they be worth if the stock trades at $80 on December 31, 2005? Assume that the stock can be purchased through the dividend reinvestment plan at a net price of $50 a share in 2001, $55 in 2002, $60 in 2003, $65 in 2004, and $70 in 2005. Use fractional shares, to two decimals, in your computations. Also, assume that, as in part (b), Wally starts with 100 shares of stock and all dividend expectations are realized.

c. Would Wally be going to a different investment strategy if he decided to buy shares in Hydro-Electric? If the switch is made, how would you describe his new investment program? What do you think of this new approach? Is it likely to lead to more trading on Wally's behalf? If so, can you reconcile that with the limited amount of time he has to devote to his portfolio?

Web Exercises

W6.1   Go to www.yahoo.com, click on [Finance/Quotes]. Under Investing, Today's markets, click on [Indices], then click on ^DJI for Dow Jones Industrial Average. Underneath the chart, click on [big 1y] (which stands for "big 1-year" chart). Put check marks in S&P and Nasdaq, and click on the compare button. You will get a comparison of the Dow, S&P, and Nasdaq. Comment on this comparison of the three indexes for 1 year.

Now click on [Moving Average]. This graph will show you the Dow versus a 200-day moving average and a 50-day moving average. Discuss the trend of the Dow versus the two moving averages.

W6.2   Visit Barra at www.Barra.com/research. Click on [S&P/Barra U.S. Equity Indexes], and then on [Fundamentals] (which is under [Research + Indexes] on the left).
a. Select a date. For that date, which index has the largest capitalization? Which has the highest mean capitalization? Which has the lowest median capitalization? Which has the highest price/book ratio?
b. Go back one screen and click on [Summary Returns]. Compare the 3-, 5-, and 10-year rates of return for the S&P 500 Index to those for the S&P/BARRA 500 Growth and the S&P/BARRA 500 Value indexes. What conclusions can you draw about the returns on these various indexes?

W6.3   Visit www.iimagazine.com/premium/rr/. Register as a new user. Go to the section Equity Rankings. You can search through Institutional Investors' benchmark rankings of equity research analysts in the United States, Europe, Asia, and Latin America. Choose [All America Research Team], and click on year 2000. Which three firms' research teams led the rankings?

W6.4   Go to MoneyCentral's site (moneycentral.msn.com). Click on [Investor], then [Stocks], then [Stock Screener].
a. Among the large-, mid-, and small-cap stock lists, which has the highest percentage price change? Which has the lowest?
b. Which predefined basic search list shows stocks with the highest dividend yield, the lowest price-earnings ratio, and the lowest price?

W6.5   Global Investing. Check the following sites: (1) Ernst & Young Int'l at www.ey.com offers guidance for investing in foreign countries. (2) Fortune at www.fortune.com/global500 provides a list of top 500 international companies, along with information on each company. (3) Global Investor at www.global-investor.com has a good directory of global investing sites and a listing of international ADRs issued in United States. Also, www.zdii.com offers a glimpse of global market activity with its ZDII Global Index that tracks the performance of 30 Asian, 30 European, and 40 North American companies. There are also separate indexes for Asia, Europe, and North America.

W6.6
a. *Business Week* Online (www.businessweek.com/index/html) overflows with investment ideas. Click on [Investing], then [Stocks], and then surf down the page and click on [The BW50] under Indexes for fastest-growing companies in the S&P 500. Which are the top five companies on that list?
b. For lists of stock picks by *Individual Investor,* see www.individualinvestor.com/ Look at the [Magic25] list. Do any of the five fastest-growing companies appear on this list? Explain why or why not.

For additional practice with concepts from this chapter, visit

www.awl.com/gitman_joehnk

CHAPTER 7

ANALYTICAL DIMENSIONS OF STOCK SELECTION

LEARNING GOALS

After studying this chapter, you should be able to:

LG 1 Discuss the security analysis process, including its goals and functions.

LG 2 Appreciate the purpose and contributions of economic analysis.

LG 3 Describe industry analysis and note how it is used.

LG 4 Demonstrate a basic understanding of fundamental analysis and why it is used.

LG 5 Calculate a variety of financial ratios and describe how financial statement analysis is used to gauge the financial vitality of a company.

LG 6 Use various financial measures to assess a company's performance, and explain how the insights derived form the basic input for the valuation process.

With over 7,000 companies listed on the NYSE and the Nasdaq National Market, how do you decide which ones are good investment candidates? You could start with companies whose goods and services you know. Dell Computer, Disney, Ford, General Electric, McDonald's, and Wal-Mart are just a few companies that come to mind. Familiarity with a company's products is certainly helpful. But it shouldn't be the only criterion for buying securities. You would eliminate many attractive investment opportunities that way.

Take, for example, Medtronic, Inc., a leading medical instrumentation company. Founded in 1949 in a garage in Minneapolis, the company developed the first implantable pacemaker for cardiac-rhythm disorders. In addition to devices that control irregular heartbeats, Medtronic's product line now includes a wide array of implantable and intervention devices for cardiac, neurological, and other disorders.

In addition to the product lineup, you'd also want to know more about its market share, patents on its products, and new products under development. Evaluating this company's products tells you only part of the story, however. After researching the company's stock price history, you'd learn that in the 10 years from January 1, 1991, to December 31, 2000, Medtronic's stock price grew at a compound annual rate of about 33%, compared to the 15.2% annual growth rate of the S&P 500 index over the same period. To put it another way, if you had invested $1,000 in Medtronic stock a decade ago, you have over $17,700; in comparison, $1,000 invested in the stock market as a whole would only be worth about $3,250.

Why did Medtronic's stock perform so much better than the market in general? The answers may lie in analyses of the economy, the medical-device industry, or the company's fundamentals (its financial and operating statistics). This chapter, the first of two on security analysis, introduces some of the techniques and procedures you can use to evaluate the future of the economy, of industries, and of specific companies, such as Medtronics.

Security Analysis

LG 1

The obvious motivation for investing in stocks is to watch your money grow. Consider, for example, the case of the computer software company Oracle Corp. If you had purchased $5,000 worth of Oracle stock in January 1990, that investment would have grown to over $235,000 by the end of the decade (December 1999). That works out to an average annual rate of return of nearly 47%, compared to the 18% or 19% return generated over the same period by the average large-cap stock, as measured by the S&P 500. Unfortunately, for every story of great success in the market, there are dozens more that don't end so well. Most of the disasters can be traced to bad timing, greed, poor planning, or failure to use common sense in making investment decisions. Although these chapters on stock investments cannot offer the keys to sudden wealth, they do provide sound principles for formulating a successful long-range investment program. The techniques described are quite traditional; they are the same proven methods that have been used by millions of investors to achieve attractive rates of return on their capital.

Principles of Security Analysis

security analysis
the process of gathering and organizing information and then using it to determine the intrinsic value of a share of common stock.

intrinsic value
the underlying or inherent value of a stock, as determined through fundamental analysis.

Security analysis consists of gathering information, organizing it into a logical framework, and then using the information to determine the intrinsic value of a common stock. That is, given a rate of return that's compatible to the amount of risk involved in a proposed transaction, **intrinsic value** provides a measure of the underlying worth of a share of stock. It provides a standard for helping you judge whether a particular stock is undervalued, fairly priced, or overvalued. The entire concept of stock valuation is based on the belief that all securities possess an intrinsic value that their market value must approach over time.

In investments, the question of value centers on return. In particular, a satisfactory investment candidate is one *that offers a level of expected return commensurate with the amount of risk involved.* That is, the *minimum rate of return* that you should be able to earn on an investment varies with the amount of risk you have to assume. As a result, not only must an investment candidate be profitable, it must be *sufficiently* profitable—in the sense that you'd expect it to generate a return that's high enough to offset the perceived exposure to risk.

If you could have your way, you'd probably like to invest in something that offers complete preservation of capital, along with sizable helpings of current income and capital gains. The problem, of course, is finding such a security. One approach is to buy whatever strikes your fancy. A more rational approach is to use security analysis to look for promising investment candidates. Security analysis addresses the question of *what to buy* by determining what a stock *ought to be worth.* Presumably, an investor will buy a stock *only if its prevailing market price does not exceed its worth*—its intrinsic value. Ultimately, intrinsic value depends on several factors:

1. Estimates of the stock's future cash flows (the amount of dividends you expect to receive over the holding period and the estimated price of the stock at time of sale).
2. The discount rate used to translate these future cash flows into a present value.
3. The amount of risk embedded in achieving the forecasted level of performance.

Traditional security analysis usually takes a "top-down" approach: It begins with economic analysis and then moves to industry analysis and finally to fundamental analysis. *Economic analysis* assesses the general state of the economy and its potential effects on security returns. *Industry analysis* deals with the industry within which a particular company operates. It looks at how the company stacks up against the major competitors in the industry, and the general outlook for that industry. *Fundamental analysis* looks in depth at the financial condition and operating results of a specific company and the underlying behavior of its common stock. In essence, it looks at the "fundamentals of the company." These fundamentals include the company's investment decisions, the liquidity of its assets, its use of debt, its profit margins and earnings growth, and ultimately the future prospects of the company and its stock.

Fundamental analysis is closely linked to the notion of intrinsic value, because it *provides the basis for projecting a stock's future cash flows.* A key part of this analytical process is *company analysis,* which takes a close look at the actual financial performance of the company. Such analysis is not meant simply to provide interesting tidbits of information about how the company has performed in the past. Rather, company analysis is done to *help investors formulate expectations about the future performance of the company and its stock.* Make no mistake about it: In investments, it's the future that matters. But in order to understand the future prospects of the firm, an investor should have a good handle on the company's current condition and its ability to produce earnings. That's just what company analysis does: It helps investors predict the future by looking at the past and determining how well the company is situated to meet the challenges that lie ahead.

Who Needs Security Analysis in an Efficient Market?

The concept of security analysis in general and fundamental analysis in particular is based on the assumption that investors are capable of formulating reliable estimates of a stock's future behavior. Fundamental analysis operates on the broad premise that some securities may be mispriced in the marketplace at any given point in time. Further, fundamental analysis assumes that, by undertaking a careful analysis of the inherent characteristics of each of the firms in question, it is possible to distinguish those securities that are correctly priced from those that are not.

To many, those two assumptions of fundamental analysis seem reasonable. However, there are others who just don't accept the assumptions of fundamental analysis. These are the so-called *efficient market* advocates. They believe that the market is so efficient in processing new information that securities trade very close to or at their correct values at all times. Thus, they argue, it is virtually impossible to outperform the market on a consistent basis. In its strongest form, the *efficient market hypothesis* asserts the following: (1) Securities are rarely, if ever, substantially mispriced in the marketplace. (2) No security analysis, however detailed, is capable of identifying mispriced securities with a frequency greater than that which might be expected by random chance alone. Is the efficient market hypothesis correct? Is there a place for fundamental analysis in modern investment theory? Interestingly, most financial theorists and practitioners would answer yes to both questions.

The solution to this apparent paradox is quite simple. Basically, fundamental analysis is of value in the selection of alternative investment vehicles for two important reasons. First, financial markets are as efficient as they are because a large number of people and powerful financial institutions invest a great deal of time and money in analyzing the fundamentals of most widely held investments. In other words, markets tend to be efficient, and securities tend to trade at or near their intrinsic values, simply because a great many people have done the research to determine just what their intrinsic values should be. Second, although the financial markets are generally quite efficient, they are by no means perfectly efficient. Pricing errors are inevitable. Those individuals who have conducted the most thorough studies of the fundamentals of a given security are the most likely to profit when errors do occur. We will study the ideas and implications of efficient markets in some detail in Chapter 8. For now, however, we will assume that traditional security analysis is useful in identifying attractive equity investments.

I N   R E V I E W

CONCEPTS

7.1 Identify the three major parts of security analysis, and explain why security analysis is important to the stock selection process.

7.2 What is *intrinsic value?* How does it fit into the security analysis process?

7.3 How would you describe a satisfactory investment vehicle? How does security analysis help in identifying investment candidates?

7.4 Would there be any need for security analysis if we operated in an efficient market environment? Explain.

Economic Analysis

LG 2

economic analysis
a study of general economic conditions that is used in the valuation of common stock.

If we lived in a world where economic activity had absolutely no effect on the stock market or on security prices, we would not need to study the economy. The fact is, of course, that we do not live in such a world. Rather, stock prices are heavily influenced by the state of the economy and by economic events. As a rule, stock prices tend to move up when the economy is strong, and they retreat when the economy starts to soften. It's not a perfect relationship, but it is a powerful one.

The reason why the economy is so important to the market is simple: The overall performance of the economy has a significant bearing on the performance and profitability of the companies that issue common stock. As the fortunes of the issuing firms change with economic conditions, so do the prices of their stocks. Of course, not all stocks are affected in the same way or to the same extent. Some sectors of the economy, like food retailing, may be only mildly affected by the economy. Others, like the construction and auto industries, are often hard hit when times get rough. The nearby *Investing in Action* box looks at some of the key factors that drive our economy and at the effects those factors have had on the economic environment.

Economic analysis—a general study of the economy—should not only give an investor a grasp of the *underlying nature of the economic environment* but also enable him or her to assess the *current state of the economy* and formulate expectations about its *future course*. Economic analysis can go so far as

INVESTING in action

Seven Engines That Drive the Economy

As the bull market roared through the 1990s, market watchers sought explanations for its continued growth. Jay Mueller, economist at Strong Investments, identified the following seven positive forces as the primary drivers of the strong U.S. economy.

1. **Positive demographics.** The largest age group in the United States today are those who are 40 to 44 years old (those born at the end of postwar baby boom); it is followed by the 35 to 39 age group. These seasoned, experienced workers account for about 17% of the U.S. population. They are major contributors to the increase in U.S. labor productivity, a trend that is expected to continue for 5 to 10 more years.

2. **Deregulation.** As deregulation hit various industries (airlines, oil, trucking, telecommunications, financial services, and competition increased. Consumers enjoyed the benefits of lower prices and more choices, which in turn encouraged higher spending.

3. **Strategic tax rate cuts.** Reductions in the marginal tax rates in the 1980s played a major role in initiating the economic expansion that continued through at least early 2001. Long-term capital gains taxes also fell, the top rate dropping to 20% in 2000. Lower capital gains taxes promote investment. In addition, the elimination of some deductions and tax loopholes shifted the focus to business and investment decisions based on economic fundamentals rather than tax avoidance.

4. **Trade liberalization.** Goods and services flow more freely across national borders since the 1993 passage of the North American Free Trade Agreement (NAFTA) and recent decisions under the General Agreement on Tariffs and Trade (GATT). Other developments in this area include the move toward market-oriented economies in Eastern Europe and Asia. Like deregulation, trade liberalization encourages competition in markets that were formerly closed to new players. The result is higher-quality products and more efficient production, leading to lower prices and economic growth.

5. **The technology revolution.** Technological advances have changed the way we work, play, communicate, and invest. The Internet is a prime mover in this trend, offering not just faster communication and data transfer but even new ways to shop. Computer hardware prices have fallen drastically, making technology affordable to more people than ever. Corporate investments in information technology equipment are now paying off in terms of increased output per worker. Annual U.S. productivity growth, which averaged about 1.8% from 1991 to 1995, jumped to 2.6% between 1996 and 1999.

6. **Welfare reform.** More states now have welfare-to-work programs to help welfare recipients become self-sufficient, productive members of the work force. The percentage of the U.S. population now on welfare is about 2.4%—half of the 1989 figure. The technology revolution has also helped workers with low or no skills enter the labor pool by making it easier to perform certain tasks (such as working at supermarket and other checkout counters) and then upgrade their skills to move up into better paying jobs.

7. **Monetary policy.** The Federal Reserve now takes a more proactive role in using monetary policy to control inflation. Strategic interest rate increases and cuts have stabilized the business cycle and allowed growth to continue.

Keeping an eye on these seven trends will provide you with a sense of what's to come. A weakening of several trends could signal a downshift that will negatively affect the stock market.

Sources: Gene Koretz, "A Test for the New Economy," *Business Week*, December 11, 2000, p. 36; Rich Miller et al., "How Prosperity Is Reshaping the American Economy," *Business Week*, February 14, 2000, pp. 100–110; and Jay N. Mueller, "Seven Engines of the Economy," *Mutual Funds*, August 2000, pp. 38–39.

Check out Economics Network, U.S. business cycle dates, at

www.yardeni.com

to include a detailed examination of each sector of the economy, or it may be done on a very informal basis. However, from a security analysis perspective, its purpose is always the same: to establish a sound foundation for the valuation of common stock.

Economic Analysis and the Business Cycle

Economic analysis sets the tone for security analysis. If the economic future looks bleak, you can probably expect most stock returns to be equally dismal. If the economy looks strong, stocks should do well. As we saw in Chapter 2, the behavior of the economy is captured in the **business cycle,** which reflects changes in total economic activity over time. Two widely followed measures of the business cycle are gross domestic product and industrial production. *Gross domestic product* (GDP) represents the market value of all goods and services produced in a country over the period of a year. *Industrial production* is a measure (it's really an index) of the activity/output in the industrial or pro-ductive segment of the economy. Normally, GDP and the index of industrial production move up and down with the business cycle.

business cycle
an indication of the current state of the economy, reflecting changes in total economic activity over time.

Key Economic Factors

Financial and market decisions are made by economic units at all levels, from individual consumers and households to business firms and governments. These various decisions together have an impact on the direction of economic activity. Particularly important in this regard are the following:

> *Government fiscal policy*
> Taxes
> Government spending
> Debt management
>
> *Monetary policy*
> Money supply
> Interest rates
>
> *Other factors*
> Inflation
> Consumer spending
> Business investments
> Foreign trade and foreign exchange rates

Government fiscal policy tends to be expansive when it encourages spending—when the government reduces taxes and/or increases the size of the budget. Similarly, monetary policy is said to be expansive when money is readily available and interest rates are relatively low. An expansive economy also depends on a generous level of spending by consumers and business concerns. These same variables moving in a reverse direction can have a con-tractionary (recessionary) impact on the economy, as for example, when taxes and interest rates increase or when spending by consumers and businesses falls off.

The impact of these major forces filters through the system and affects several key dimensions of the economy. The most important of these are industrial production, corporate profits, retail sales, personal income, the unemployment rate, and inflation. For example, a strong economy exists when industrial production, corporate profits, retail sales, and personal income are moving up and unemployment is down. Thus, when conducting an economic analysis, an investor should keep an eye on fiscal and monetary policies, consumer and business spending, and foreign trade *for the potential impact they have on the economy.* At the same time, he or she must stay abreast of the level of industrial production, corporate profits, retail sales, personal income, unemployment, and inflation *in order to assess the state of the business cycle.*

To help you keep track of the economy, Table 7.1 provides a brief description of some key economic measures. These economic statistics are compiled by various government agencies and are widely reported in the financial media. (Most of the reports are released monthly.) Take the time to carefully read about the various economic measures and reports cited in Table 7.1. When you understand the behavior of these statistics, you can make your own educated guess as to the current state of the economy and where it's headed.

HOT LINKS

To keep up with the status of the economy, you can view the monthly leading index of economic indicators computed by the Conference Board in New York.

At the White House site, you can visit the economic statistics briefing room. *The Economist* also provides data useful for keeping track of the economy. See the following sites:

www.conference-board.org/
www.whitehouse.gov/fsbr/esbr.html
www.economist.com

Developing an Economic Outlook

Conducting an economic analysis involves studying fiscal and monetary policies, inflationary expectations, consumer and business spending, and the state of the business cycle. Often investors do this on a fairly informal basis. As they form their economic judgments, many rely on one or more of the popular published sources (e.g., the *Wall Street Journal, Barron's, Fortune,* and *Business Week*) as well as on periodic reports from major brokerage houses. These sources provide a convenient summary of economic activity and give investors a general feel for the condition of the economy.

Once you have developed a general economic outlook, you can use the information in one of two ways. One approach is to construct an economic outlook and then consider where it leads in terms of possible areas for further analysis. For example, suppose you uncover information that strongly suggests the outlook for business spending is very positive. On the basis of such an analysis, you might want to look more closely at capital goods producers, such as office equipment manufacturers. Similarly, if you feel that because of sweeping changes in world politics, U.S. government defense spending is likely to drop off, you might want to avoid the stocks of major defense contractors.

A second way to use information about the economy is to consider specific industries or companies and ask, "How will they be affected by expected developments in the economy?" Take an investor with an interest in *business equipment stocks.* This industry category includes companies involved in the production of everything from business machines and electronic systems to work lockers and high-fashion office furnishings. In this industry you'll find

HOT LINKS

At this site, choose from the left side of the box Today's Economy, and from the categories, select [Especially for Students]. Read an article that interests you.

www.dismal.com

TABLE 7.1   Keeping Track of the Economy

To help you sort out the confusing array of figures that flow almost daily from Washington, D.C., and keep track of what's happening in the economy, here are some of the most important economic measures and reports to watch.

- **Gross domestic product (GDP).** This is the broadest measure of the economy's performance. Issued every 3 months by the Commerce Department, it is an estimate of the total dollar value of all the goods and services produced in this country. Movements in many areas of the economy are closely related to changes in GDP, so it is a good analytic tool. In particular, watch the annual rate of growth or decline in "real" or "constant" dollars. This number eliminates the effects of inflation and thus measures the actual volume of production. Remember, though, that frequent revisions of GDP figures sometimes change the picture of the economy.

- **Industrial production.** Issued monthly by the Federal Reserve Board, this index shows changes in the physical output of U.S. factories, mines, and electric and gas utilities. The index tends to move in the same direction as the economy; it is thus a good guide to business conditions between reports on GDP. Detailed breakdowns of the index give a reading on how individual industries are faring.

- **The index of leading indicators.** This boils down to one number, which summarizes the movement of a dozen statistics that tend to predict—or "lead"—changes in the GDP. This monthly index, issued by the Commerce Department, includes such things as layoffs of workers, new orders placed by manufacturers, changes in the money supply, and the prices of raw materials. If the index moves in the same direction for several months, it's a fairly good sign that total output will move the same way in the near future.

- **Personal income.** A monthly report from the Commerce Department, this shows the before-tax income received in the form of wages and salaries, interest and dividends, rents, and other payments, such as Social Security, unemployment compensation, and pensions. As a measure of individuals' spending power, the report helps explain trends in consumer buying habits, a major part of total GDP. When personal income rises, people often increase their buying. But note a big loophole: Excluded are the billions of dollars that change hands in the so-called underground economy—cash transactions that are never reported to tax or other officials.

- **Retail sales.** The Commerce Department's monthly estimate of total sales at the retail level includes everything from cars to groceries. Based on a sample of retail establishments, the figure gives a rough clue to consumer attitudes. It can also indicate future conditions: A long slowdown in sales can lead to cuts in production.

- **Money supply.** The Federal Reserve reports weekly this measure of the amount of money in circulation. Actually, there are three measures of the money supply: *M1* is basically currency, demand deposits, and NOW accounts. *M2*, the most widely followed measure, equals M1 plus savings deposits, money market deposit accounts, and money market mutual funds. *M3* is M2 plus large CDs and a few other less significant types of deposits/transactions. Reasonable growth in the money supply, as measured by M2, is thought to be necessary for an expanding economy. However, too rapid a rate of growth in money is considered inflationary; in contrast, a sharp slowdown in the growth rate is viewed as recessionary.

- **Consumer prices.** Issued monthly by the Labor Department, this index shows changes in prices for a fixed market basket of goods and services. The most widely publicized figure is for all urban consumers. A second, used in labor contracts and some government programs, covers urban wage earners and clerical workers. Both are watched as a measure of inflation, but many economists believe that flaws cause them to be inaccurate.

- **Producer prices.** This monthly indicator from the Labor Department shows price changes of goods at various stages of production, from crude materials such as raw cotton to finished goods like clothing and furniture. An upward surge may mean higher consumer prices later. However, the index can miss discounts and may exaggerate rising price trends. Watch particularly changes in the prices of finished goods. These do not fluctuate as widely as the prices of crude materials and thus are a better measure of inflationary pressures.

- **Employment.** The percentage of the work force that is involuntarily out of work is a broad indicator of economic health. But another monthly figure issued by the Labor Department—the number of payroll jobs—may be better for spotting changes in business. A decreasing number of jobs is a sign that firms are cutting production.

- **Housing starts.** A pickup in the pace of housing starts usually follows an easing in the availability and cost of money and is an indicator of improving in economic health. This monthly report from the Commerce Department also includes the number of new building permits issued across the country, an even earlier indicator of the pace of future construction.

TABLE 7.2	Economic Variables and the Stock Market
Economic Variable	Potential Effect on the Stock Market
Real growth in GDP	Positive impact—it's good for the market.
Industrial production	Continued increases are a sign of strength, which is good for the market.
Inflation	Detrimental to stock prices. Higher inflation leads to higher interest rates and lower price/earnings multiples, and generally makes equity securities less attractive.
Corporate profits	Strong corporate earnings are good for the market.
Unemployment	A downer—an increase in unemployment means business is starting to slow down.
Federal budget surplus or deficit	Budget surpluses have replaced budget deficits (at least for now), which is great news for interest rates and stock prices. Budget deficits, in contrast, may be positive for a depressed economy but can lead to inflation in a stronger economic environment and therefore have a negative impact.
Weak dollar	Often the result of big trade imbalances, a weak dollar has a negative effect on the market. It makes our markets less attractive to foreign investors. However, it also makes our products more affordable in overseas markets and therefore can have a positive impact on our economy.
Interest rates	Another downer—rising rates tend to have a negative effect on the market for stocks.
Money supply	Moderate growth can have a positive impact on the economy and the market. Rapid growth, however, is inflationary and therefore detrimental to the stock market.

companies like Bell & Howell, Diebold, Herman Miller, Smith Corona, and Steelcase. These stocks are highly susceptible to changing economic conditions. When the economy starts slowing down, companies can put off purchases of durable equipment and fixtures. Especially important to this industry is the outlook for corporate profits and business investments. So long as these economic factors look good, the prospects for business equipment stocks should be positive.

In this instance, our imaginary investor would first want to assess the current state of the business cycle. Using that insight, he would then formulate some expectations about the future of the economy and the potential impact it holds for the stock market in general and business equipment stocks in particular. (Table 7.2 shows how some of the more important economic variables can affect the behavior of the stock market.) To see how this might be done, let's assume that the economy has just gone through a brief (9-month) recession and is now in the recovery stage of the business cycle: Employment is starting to pick up. Inflation and interest rates have come back down. Both GDP and industrial production have experienced sharp increases in the past two quarters. And Congress is putting the finishing touches on a major piece of legislation that would lead to reduced taxes. More important, although the economy is now in the early stages of a recovery, things are expected to get even better in the future. The economy is definitely starting to build steam, and all indications are that both corporate profits and business spending should undergo a sharp increase. All of these predictions should be good news for the producers of business equipment and office furnishings, as a good deal of their sales and an even larger portion of their profits depend on the level of corporate profits and business spending. In short, our investor sees an economy in good shape and set to become even stronger, the consequences of which are favorable not only for the market but for business equipment stocks as well.

Note that these conclusions could have been reached by relying on sources no more sophisticated than *Barron's* or *Business Week*. In fact, about the only "special thing" this investor would have to do is pay careful attention to those economic forces that are particularly important to the business equipment industry (e.g., corporate profits). The economic portion of the analysis, in effect, has set the stage for further evaluation by indicating what type of economic environment to expect in the near future. The next step is to narrow the focus a bit and conduct the industry phase of the analysis.

However, before we continue our analysis, it is vital to clarify a bit the relationship that normally exists between the stock market and the economy. In particular, as we just saw, the economic outlook is used to get a handle on the market and to direct investors to developing industry sectors. Yet it is important to note that changes in stock prices normally occur *before* the actual forecasted changes become apparent in the economy. Indeed, the current trend of stock prices is frequently used to help *predict* the course of the economy itself. The apparent conflict here can be resolved somewhat by noting that because of this relationship, it is even more important to derive a reliable economic outlook and to be sensitive to underlying economic changes that may mean the current outlook is becoming dated. Investors in the stock market tend to look into the future to justify the purchase or sale of stock. If their perception of the future is changing, stock prices are also likely to be changing. Therefore, watching the course of stock prices as well as the course of the general economy can make for more accurate investment forecasting.

IN REVIEW

CONCEPTS

7.5 Describe the general concept of *economic analysis*. Is this type of analysis necessary, and can it really help the individual investor make a decision about a stock? Explain.

7.6 According to the *Investing in Action* box on page 276, what are the seven economic factors (or "engines") that are driving our economy today?

7.7 Why is the business cycle so important to economic analysis? Does the business cycle have any bearing on the stock market?

7.8 Briefly describe each of the following:
a. Gross domestic product.   b. Leading indicators.
c. Money supply.   d. Producer prices.

7.9 What effect, if any, does inflation have on common stocks?

Industry Analysis

Have you ever thought about buying oil stocks, or autos, or chemicals? How about computer stocks or electric utility stocks? Looking at securities in terms of industry groupings is widely used by both individual and institutional investors. This is a sensible approach because stock prices are influenced by industry conditions. The level of demand in an industry and other industry forces set the tone for individual companies. Clearly, if the outlook is good for an industry, then the prospects are likely to be strong for many of the companies that make up that industry.

Key Issues

industry analysis
study of industry groupings that looks at the competitive position of a particular industry in relation to others and identifies companies that show particular promise within an industry.

The first step in **industry analysis** is to establish the competitive position of a particular industry *in relation to others,* for, as Table 7.3 indicates, not all industries perform alike. The next step is to identify companies *within the industry* that hold particular promise. This sets the stage for a more thorough analysis of individual companies and securities. Analyzing an industry means looking at such things as its makeup and basic characteristics, the key economic and operating variables that drive industry performance, and the outlook for the industry. The investor will also want to keep an eye out for specific companies that appear well situated to take advantage of industry conditions. Companies with strong market positions should be favored over those with less secure positions. Such dominance is indicative of an ability to maintain pricing leadership and suggests that the firm will be in a position to enjoy economies of scale and low-cost production. Market dominance also enables a company to support a strong research and development effort, thereby helping it secure its leadership position for the future.

Normally, an investor can gain valuable insight about an industry by seeking answers to the following questions:

1. *What is the nature of the industry?* Is it monopolistic, or are there many competitors? Do a few set the trend for the rest, and if so, who are those few?
2. *To what extent is the industry regulated?* Is it regulated (e.g., public utilities)? If so, how "friendly" are the regulatory bodies?
3. *What role, if any, does labor play in the industry?* How important are labor unions? Are there good labor relations within the industry? When is the next round of contract talks?
4. *How important are technological developments?* Are any new developments taking place? What impact are potential breakthroughs likely to have?
5. *Which economic forces are especially important to the industry?* Is demand for the industry's goods and services related to key economic variables? If so, what is the outlook for those variables? How important is foreign competition to the health of the industry?
6. *What are the important financial and operating considerations?* Is there an adequate supply of labor, material, and capital? What are the capital spending plans and needs of the industry?

growth cycle
a reflection of the amount of business vitality that occurs within an industry (or company) over time.

These questions can sometimes be answered in terms of an industry's **growth cycle**, which reflects the vitality of the industry over time. In the first phase—*initial development*—investment opportunities are usually not

| TABLE 7.3 | A Look at the Stock Performance of Key Industry Groups |

In searching for value, an early step is to look at the big picture: *industry-group trends.* One source for such information is Standard & Poor's, which tracks the performance of 115 industries that it breaks into 11 major industrial groups. Shown here is the performance of all 11 of those major industrial groups, plus a wide-ranging sample of 30 separate industries. Each of these groups or industries, in effect, has its own market index (much like, say, the S&P 500) that measures the performance of stocks within that group or industry. As is apparent in the numbers below, some industries simply do much better than others, at least over certain time periods. (*Source: S&P Index Services*, as reported on its Web site, www.spglobal.com, release date, September 29, 2001.)

	Industry Performance (% Price Change)		
	Year to date (through 3rd Qtr. 2000)	1999	5 years
Major Industry Groups			
Basic Material (1)	−28.7%	18.2%	−1.7%
Capital Goods (2)	7.8	25.5	20.1
Communication Services (3)	−24.7	18.2	13.7
Consumer Cyclicals (4)	−19.7	15.0	13.1
Consumer Staples (5)	−3.4	−7.7	12.0
Energy (6)	15.0	17.8	16.3
Financial (7)	20.6	0.8	22.2
Health Care (8)	25.0	−7.8	23.5
Technology (9)	−9.4	75.9	36.6
Transportation (10)	−2.3	−8.3	5.8
Utilities (11)	47.7	−12.9	12.7
Individual Industries			
Aluminum (1)	−36.4%	90.4%	6.9%
Paper Containers & Packaging (1)	−20.1	−6.6	−3.3
Iron & Steel (1)	−42.0	2.7	−13.6
Metal & Glass Containers (2)	−52.6	−21.0	−18.5
Electrical Equipment (2)	11.4	47.8	33.7
Manufacturing (Diversified) (2)	1.0	18.6	17.8
Telecommunications—Wireless (3)	−19.6	208.4	37.9
Telephone (3)	−10.9	5.5	14.3
Building Materials (4)	−36.1	−18.6	−4.8
Publishing (4)	7.3	6.3	16.2
Retail—Speciality Apparel (4)	−36.0	13.5	24.7
Textiles—Speciality (4)	−28.4	−33.6	−19.2
Broadcasting—Radio/TV (5)	−25.6	79.5	23.2
Entertainment (5)	15.3	16.3	21.3
Housewares (5)	−20.9	−16.6	−5.6
Retail Drug Stores (5)	19.2	−25.1	27.8
Oil & Gas Drilling & Equipment (6)	49.7	48.7	23.0
International Oil (6)	5.4	14.6	16.7
Diversified Financial (7)	23.1	29.1	33.6
Multiline Insurance (7)	33.6	26.8	30.4
Investment Banking & Brokerage (7)	45.5	33.1	38.1
Biotechnology (8)	33.5	104.6	36.7
Long-term Health Care (8)	7.2	−56.5	−20.3
Communication Equipment (9)	−28.8	128.9	27.6
Computers—Networking (9)	11.1	129.9	51.5
Electronics—Semiconductors (9)	14.6	66.0	33.0
Railroads (10)	−11.7	−15.6	−1.0
Trucking (10)	−19.4	−6.6	−1.4
Electric Utility Companies (11)	34.5	−22.1	7.0
Independent Power Producers (11)	111.8	50.6	62.0

Note: The parenthetical number behind the industry name represents the industry group to which it belongs. For example, the first three industries are identified with a (1), meaning they belong to the "Basic Materials" industry group, which is also identified with a (1).

available to most investors. The industry is new and untried, and the risks are very high. The second stage is *rapid expansion,* during which product acceptance is spreading and investors can foresee the industry's future more clearly. At this stage, economic and financial variables have little to do with the industry's overall performance (sound a bit like some Internet stocks?). Investors will be interested in investing almost regardless of the economic climate. This is the phase that is of substantial interest to investors, and a good deal of work is done to find such opportunities.

Unfortunately, most industries do not experience rapid growth for long. Instead, they eventually slip into the next category in the growth cycle, *mature growth,* which is the third stage and the one most influenced by economic developments. In this stage, expansion comes from growth of the economy. It is a slower source of overall growth than that experienced in stage 2. In stage 3, the long-term nature of the industry becomes apparent. Industries in this category include defensive ones, like food and apparel, and cyclical industries, like autos and heavy equipment.

The last phase is either *stability* or *decline*. In the decline phase, demand for the industry's products is diminishing, and companies are leaving the industry. Investment opportunities at this stage are almost nonexistent, unless you are seeking only dividend income. Investors want to avoid this stage. However, few really good companies ever reach this final stage because they continually bring new products to the market and, in so doing, remain at least in the mature growth phase.

Developing an Industry Outlook

Industry analysis can be conducted by individual investors themselves. Or, as is more often the case, it can be done with the help of published industry reports such as the popular *S&P Industry Surveys*. These surveys cover all the important economic, market, and financial aspects of an industry, providing commentary as well as vital statistics. Other widely used sources of industry information include brokerage house reports and articles in the popular financial media.

Let's resume our example of the imaginary investor who is thinking about buying business equipment stocks. Recall from our prior discussion that the economic phase of the analysis suggested a strong economy for the foreseeable future—one in which corporate profits and business spending will be expanding. Now the investor is ready to focus on the industry. A logical starting point is to assess the expected industry response to forecasted economic developments. Demand for the product and industry sales would be especially important. The industry is made up of many large and small competitors, and although it is labor-intensive, labor unions are not an important force. Thus, our investor may want to look closely at the potential effect of these factors on the industry's cost structure. Also worth a look is the work being done in research and development (R&D), and in industrial design within the industry. You would want to know which firms are coming out with the new products and fresh ideas, because these firms are likely to be the industry leaders (or potential industry leaders).

Industry analysis yields an understanding of the nature and operating characteristics of an industry, which can then be used to form judgments about the prospects for industry growth. Let's assume that our investor, by using various types of published reports, has examined the key elements of the office equipment industry and has concluded that the industry, *particularly the office furnishings segment,* is well positioned to take advantage of the rapidly improving economy. Many new and exciting products have come out in the last couple of years, and more are on the drawing board or in the R&D stage. Even more compelling is the current emphasis on new products that will contribute to the long-term productivity of businesses and other institutions. Thus the demand for office furniture and fixtures should increase, and although profit margins may tighten a bit, the level of profits should move up smartly, providing a healthy outlook for growth.

In the course of researching the industry, our investor has noticed several companies that stand out, but one looks particularly attractive: Universal Office Furnishings. Long regarded as one of the top design firms in the industry, Universal designs, manufactures, and sells to commercial and institutional users a full line of high-end office furniture and fixtures (desks, chairs, credenzas, modular work stations, filing systems, etc.). In addition, the company produces and distributes state-of-the-art computer furniture and a specialized line of institutional furniture for the hospitality, health care, and educational markets. The company was founded over 50 years ago, and its stock (which trades under the symbol UVRS) has been listed on the NYSE since the late 1960s. Universal would be considered a *mid-cap stock,* with total market capitalization of around $2 or $3 billion. The company experienced rapid growth in the '90s, as it expanded its product line, and is expected to benefit from the strong economic environment now under way. Everything about the economy and the industry looks good for the stock, so our investor decides to take a close look at Universal Office Furnishings.

H O T L I N K S

From the main page of the MSN site, go to [Investor], [Markets], [Top 10 Lists], [Industries] to find the 10 best-performing and 10 worst-performing industries. Go to:

moneycentral.msn.com

I N   R E V I E W

CONCEPTS

7.10 What is *industry analysis,* and why is it important?

7.11 Identify and briefly discuss several aspects of an industry that are important to its behavior and operating characteristics. Note especially how economic issues fit into industry analysis.

7.12 What are the four stages of an industry's growth cycle? Which of these stages offers the biggest payoff to investors? Which stage is most influenced by forces in the economy?

Fundamental Analysis

LG 4   LG 5   LG 6

fundamental analysis
the in-depth study of the financial condition and operating results of a firm.

Fundamental analysis is the study of the financial affairs of a business for the purpose of better understanding the nature and operating characteristics of the company that issued the common stock. In this part of the chapter, we will deal with several aspects of fundamental analysis. We will examine the general concept of fundamental analysis, and introduce several types of financial statements that provide the raw material for this analysis. We will then describe the key financial ratios widely used in company analysis, and will conclude with an interpretation of those financial ratios. It's important to understand that this represents the more traditional approach to security analysis. It's commonly used to evaluate both growth and value oriented stocks, as well as income shares, turn-arounds, and other situations where investors can rely on financial statements and other data bases to at least partially form a decision. This approach really has very little, if any, place in the valuation of highly speculative stocks, including many tech stocks, and most IPO's. For now, however, our attention will center on the traditional approach to security analysis; in the latter part of the next chapter (Chapter 8), we'll look at some popular valuation concepts that are being used to evaluate tech stocks.

The Concept

Fundamental analysis rests on the belief that *the value of a stock is influenced by the performance of the company that issued the stock*. If a company's prospects look strong, the market price of its stock is likely to reflect that and be bid up.

However, the value of a security depends not only on the return it promises but also on the amount of its risk exposure. Fundamental analysis captures these dimensions (risk and return) and conveniently incorporates them into the valuation process. It begins with a historical analysis of the financial strength of a firm: the so-called c*ompany analysis* phase. Using the insights obtained, along with economic and industry analyses, an investor can then formulate expectations about the future growth and profitability of a company.

In the historical (or company analysis) phase, the investor studies the financial statements of the firm to learn its strengths and weaknesses, identify any underlying trends and developments, evaluate operating efficiencies, and gain a general understanding of the nature and operating characteristics of the firm. The following points are of particular interest:

1. The competitive position of the company.
2. Its composition and growth in sales.
3. Profit margins and the dynamics of company earnings.
4. The composition and liquidity of corporate resources (the company's asset mix).
5. The company's capital structure (its financing mix).

The historical phase is in many respects the most demanding and the most time-consuming. Most investors, however, have neither the time nor the inclination to conduct such an extensive study, so they rely on published reports for the background material. Fortunately, individual investors have a variety of sources to choose from. These include the reports and recommendations of major brokerage houses, the popular financial media, and financial subscrip-

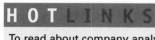

tion services like S&P and *Value Line,* not to mention a whole array of computer-based software and online financial sources, such as CNBC.com, Morningstar Net, MSN Money Central, Quicken.com, Smart Money Interactive, Wall Street City, and Stock Selector.com. These are all valuable sources of information, and the paragraphs that follow are not intended to replace them. Yet to be an intelligent investor, you should understand fully the content and implications of such financial reports. Ultimately, you will be making your own judgment about the company and its stock.

Financial Statements

Financial statements are a vital part of company analysis, because they enable investors to develop an opinion about the operating results and financial con-

balance sheet
a financial summary of a firm's assets, liabilities, and shareholders' equity at a single point in time.

income statement
a financial summary of the operating results of a firm covering a specified period of time, usually 1 year.

statement of cash flows
a financial summary of a firm's cash flow and other events that caused changes in the company's cash position.

dition of a firm. Three types of financial statements are used in company analysis: the balance sheet, the income statement, and the statement of cash flows. The first two statements are essential to carrying out basic financial analysis. (In particular, they contain data needed to compute many of the financial ratios.) The third statement—the cash flow statement—is used primarily to assess the cash/liquidity position of the firm. Company statements are prepared on a quarterly basis (these are *abbreviated* statements, compiled for each 3-month period of operation) and again at the end of each calendar year or *fiscal year* (a 12-month period the company has defined as its operating year, which may or may not end on December 31). Annual financial statements must be fully verified by independent certified public accountants (CPAs). They then must be filed with the U.S. Securities and Exchange Commission, and distributed on a timely basis to all stockholders in the form of annual reports. By themselves, corporate financial statements are a most important source of information to the investor. When used with financial ratios and in conjunction with fundamental analysis, they become even more powerful.

The Balance Sheet The **balance sheet** is a statement of the company's assets, liabilities, and stockholders' equity. The *assets* represent the resources of the company (the things the company owns). The *liabilities* are its debts. *Equity* is the amount capital the stockholders have invested in the firm. A balance sheet may be thought of as a summary of the firm's assets balanced against its debt and ownership positions *at a single point in time* (on the last day of the calendar or fiscal year, or at the end of the quarter). To balance, the total assets must equal the total amount of liabilities and equity.

A typical balance sheet is illustrated in Table 7.4. It shows the comparative 2000–2001 figures for Universal Office Furnishings, the firm our investor is analyzing. Note that although the Universal name is fictitious, the financial statements are not. *They are the actual financial statements of a real company.* Some of the entries have been slightly modified for pedagogical purposes, but these tables accurately depict what real financial statements look like and how they're used in financial statement analysis.

The Income Statement The **income statement** provides a financial summary of the operating results of the firm. It shows the amount of revenues generated over a period of time, the cost and expenses incurred over the same period, and the company's profits. (Profits are calculated by subtracting all costs and expenses, including taxes, from revenues.) Unlike the balance sheet, the income statement covers activities that have occurred over the course of time, or for a given operating period. Typically, this period extends no longer than a fiscal or calendar year. Table 7.5 shows the income statements for Universal Office Furnishings for 2000 and 2001. Note that these annual statements cover operations for the 12-month period ending on December 31, which corresponds to the date of the balance sheet. The income statement indicates how successful the firm has been in using the assets listed on the balance sheet. That is, management's success in operating the firm is reflected in the profit or loss the company generates during the year.

The Statement of Cash Flows The **statement of cash flows** provides a summary of the firm's cash flow and other events that caused changes in its cash position. A relatively new report, first required in 1988, it is also one of the

TABLE 7.4	Corporate Balance Sheet

Universal Office Furnishings, Inc.
Comparative Balance Sheet
December 31
($ in millions)

	2001	2000
Assets		
Current assets		
Cash and equivalents	$ 95.8	$ 80.0
Receivables	227.2	192.4
Inventories	103.7	107.5
Other current assets	73.6	45.2
Total current assets	500.3	425.1
Noncurrent Assets		
Property, plant, & equipment, gross	771.2	646.6
Accumulated depreciation & depletion	(372.5)	(379.9)
Property, plant, & equipment, net	398.7	316.7
Other noncurrent assets	42.2	19.7
Total current liabilities	440.9	336.4
Total assets	**$941.2**	**$761.5**
Liabilities and Stockholders' Equity		
Current liabilities		
Accounts payable	$ 114.2	$ 82.4
Short-term debt	174.3	79.3
Other current liabilities	85.5	89.6
Total current liabilities	374.0	251.3
Noncurrent liabilities		
Long-term debt	177.8	190.9
Other noncurrent liabilities	94.9	110.2
Total noncurrent liabilities	272.7	301.1
Total Liabilities	**$646.7**	**$552.4**
Stockholders' Equity		
Common shares	92.6	137.6
Retained earnings	201.9	71.5
Total equity	294.5	209.1
Total Liabilities and Stockholders' Equity	**$941.2**	**$761.5**

most useful, because it shows how the company is doing in generating cash. The fact is, a company's reported earnings may bear little resemblance to its cash flow. Whereas profits are simply the difference between revenues and the accounting costs that have been charged against them, *cash flow is the amount of money a company actually takes in as a result of doing business.*

Table 7.6 presents the 2000–2001 statement of cash flows for Universal Office Furnishings. This report brings together items from *both* the balance sheet and the income statement to show how the company obtained its cash and how it used this valuable liquid resource. The statement is broken into three parts. The most important part is the first one, labeled "Cash from Operations." It captures the *net cash flow from operations*—the line highlighted on the statement. This is what is often meant by the term *cash flow,* as

TABLE 7.5	Corporate Income Statement

Universal Office Furnishings, Inc.
Income Statements
Fiscal Year Ended December 31
($ in millions)

	2001	2000
Net sales	$1,938.0	$1,766.2
Cost of goods sold	1,128.5	1,034.5
Gross operating profit	$ 809.5	$ 731.7
Selling, administrative, and other operating expenses	497.7	445.3
Depreciation & authorization	77.1	62.1
Other income, net	0.5	12.9
Earnings before interest & taxes	$235.2	$237.2
Interest expense	13.4	7.3
Earnings before taxes	$221.8	$229.9
Income taxes	82.1	88.1
Net profit after taxes	**$139.7**	**$141.8**
Dividends paid per share	$0.15	$0.13
Earnings per share (EPS)	$2.26	$2.17
Number of common shares outstanding (in millions)	61.8	65.3

it represents the amount of cash generated by the company and available for investment and financing activities.

Note that Universal's 2001 cash flow from operations was over $200 million, down a bit from the year before. As it turned out, this gave the company more than enough for its investing activities ($150.9 million) and its financing activities ($35.4 million), so it's actual cash position (see the line near the bottom of the statement, labeled "Net increase (decrease) in cash") increased by some $15.8 million. That result was a big improvement over the year before, when the firm's cash position fell by more than $35 million. A high (and preferably increasing) cash flow means the company has enough money to pay dividends, service debt, and finance growth. In addition, you'd like to see the firm's cash position increase over time because of the positive impact that has on the company's liquidity and its ability to meet operating needs in a prompt and timely fashion.

Key Financial Ratios

To see what accounting statements really have to say about the financial condition and operating results of a firm, it is necessary to turn to *financial ratios*. Such ratios are useful because they provide a different perspective on the financial affairs of the firm—particularly with regard to the balance sheet and income statement—and thus *expand the information content of the company's financial statements*. Ratios lie at the very heart of company analysis. Indeed, company analysis as a system of information would be incomplete without this key ingredient.

Ratio analysis is the study of the relationships between various financial statement accounts. Each measure relates one item on the balance sheet (or income statement) to another, or, as is more often the case, a balance sheet

ratio analysis
the study of the relationships between financial statement accounts.

TABLE 7.6	Statement of Cash Flows

Universal Office Furnishings, Inc.
Statements of Cash Flows
Fiscal Year Ended December 31
($ in millions)

	2001	2000
Cash from Operations		
Net earnings	$139.7	$141.8
Depreciation and amortization	77.1	62.1
Other noncash charges	5.2	16.7
Increase (decrease) in current assets	(41.7)	14.1
Increase (decrease) in current liabilities	21.8	(29.1)
Net cash flow from operations	$202.1	$205.6
Cash from Investing Activities		
Acquisitions of property, plant, and equipment—net	(150.9)	(90.6)
Net cash flow from investing activities	($150.9)	($90.6)
Cash from Financing Activities		
Proceeds from long-term borrowing	749.8	79.1
Reduction in long-term debt, including current maturities and early retirements	(728.7)	(211.1)
Net repurchase of capital stock	(47.2)	(9.8)
Payment of dividends on common stock	(9.3)	(8.5)
Net cash flow from financing activities	($35.4)	($150.3)
Net increase (decrease) in cash	$15.8	($35.3)
Cash and equivalents at beginning of period	$80.0	$115.3
Cash and equivalents at end of period	$95.8	$80.0

account to an operating (income statement) element. In this way, the investor looks not so much at the absolute size of the financial statement accounts as at what it indicates about the liquidity, activity, or profitability of the firm. However, as the accompanying *Investing in Action* box suggests, to get the most from ratio analysis, you must have a good understanding of the uses and limitations of the financial statements themselves.

The most significant contribution of financial ratios is that they enable an investor to assess the firm's past and present financial condition and operating results. The mechanics of ratio analysis are actually quite simple: Selected information is obtained from annual financial statements and used to compute a set of ratios, which are then compared to historical and/or industry standards to evaluate the financial condition and operating results of the company. When historical standards are used, the company's ratios are compared and studied from one year to the next. Industry standards, in contrast, involve comparison of a particular company's ratios to those of other companies in the same line of business.

Remember, the reason we're doing all this is *to develop information about the past that can be used to get a handle on the future.* It's only from an understanding of a company's past performance that you can forecast its future with some degree of accuracy. For example, even if sales have been expanding rapidly over the past few years, you must carefully assess the reasons for the growth before naively assuming that past growth-rate trends will continue into

INVESTING in action

The Ten Commandments of Financial Statement Analysis

Individuals must pass a test before obtaining a driver's license, but investors don't need to pass any type of test before trying to use financial statements as part of their investment analyses. Yet analyzing financial statements requires at least as much knowledge and skill as driving an automobile. Perhaps each financial statement should contain a warning to potential users, similar to those found on many products. As a starter, the warning might include these ten commandments:

1. **Thou shalt not use financial statements in isolation.** Instead, use them with other available information, such as data on economy-wide conditions and industry-wide conditions.

2. **Thou shalt not use financial statements as the only source of firm-specific information.** There are many other sources of information about the company. Consider, for example, financial periodicals, analysts' reports, and of course the Internet.

3. **Thou shalt not avoid reading footnotes, which are an integral part of financial statements.** Financial statements cannot be reasonably analyzed without reading and understanding the footnotes.

4. **Thou shalt not focus on a single number. Financial statements are not designed to be reduced to a single number.** Net income is not intended to be the number that summarizes all the information relevant to an investment decision. A user must analyze growth and leverage, among other factors, as well as profitability.

5. **Thou shalt not overlook the implications of what is read.** It is not sufficient simply to know that a company is a high-growth or

highly leveraged firm; one must also know that such characteristics typically imply higher risk as well.

6. **Thou shalt not ignore events subsequent to the financial statements.** Financial statements are not forecasts of the future; rather, they report the financial condition of the company as of year-end. They do not capture the effects of events that occur after year-end. They thus become increasingly out of date as the year progresses.

7. **Thou shalt not overlook the limitations of financial statements.** Financial statements report only a specified set of events, not all events or all possible financial effects of a single event. Financial statements do not generally represent estimates of the market values of the reported assets and liabilities, nor do they reflect changes in the market values of those assets and liabilities.

8. **Thou shalt not use financial statements without adequate knowledge.** Investors should be sufficiently competent to read, understand, and analyze financial statements.

9. **Thou shalt not shun professional help.** If unwilling or unable to attain adequate knowledge, the investor should defer to someone who does have this ability, such as a financial analyst or a professional money manager.

10. **Thou shalt not take unnecessary risks.** If unwilling or unable to obtain professional help, the investor should undertake investments where investment risk is minimal or where analysis of financial statements is not an issue.

the future. Such insights are obtained from financial ratios and financial statement analysis.

Financial ratios can be divided into five groups: (1) liquidity, (2) activity, (3) leverage, (4) profitability, and (5) common stock, or market, measures. Using the 2001 figures from the Universal financial statements (Tables 7.4 and 7.5), we will now identify and briefly discuss some of the widely used measures in each of these five categories.

liquidity measures
financial ratios concerned with a firm's ability to meet its day-to-day operating expenses and satisfy its short-term obligations as they come due.

Measuring Liquidity **Liquidity** is concerned with the firm's ability to meet its day-to-day operating expenses and satisfy its short-term obligations as they come due. Of major concern is whether a company has adequate cash and other liquid assets on hand to service its debt and operating needs in a prompt and timely fashion. A general overview of a company's liquidity can often be obtained from two simple measures: current ratio and net working capital.

Current Ratio One of the most commonly cited of all financial ratios, the current ratio is computed as follows:

Equation 7.1

$$\text{Current ratio} = \frac{\text{Current assets}}{\text{Current liabilities}}$$

In 2001, Universal Office Furnishings (UVRS) had a current ratio of

$$\text{Current ratio for Universal} = \frac{\$500.3}{\$374.0} = \underline{\underline{1.34}}$$

This figure indicates that UVRS had $1.34 in short-term resources to service every dollar of current debt. That's a fairly good number and, by most standards today, would suggest that the company has more than enough current liability.

Net Working Capital Though technically not a ratio, net working capital is often viewed as such. Actually, net working capital is an absolute measure of liquidity and indicates the dollar amount of equity in the working capital position of the firm. It is the difference between current assets and current liabilities. For 2001, the net working capital position for UVRS amounted to

Equation 7.2

Net working capital = current assets − current liabilities

For Universal = $500.3 − $374.0 = $126.3 million

A net working capital figure that exceeds $125,000,000 is indeed substantial A net working capital figure that exceeds $125,000,000 is indeed substantial (especially for a firm this size) and serves to reinforce our contention that the liquidity position of this firm is very solid—so long as it is not made up of slow-moving, obsolete inventories and/or past-due accounts receivable.

activity ratios
financial ratios that are used to measure how well a firm is managing its assets.

Activity Ratios Measuring general liquidity is only the beginning of the analysis. We must also assess the composition and underlying liquidity of key current assets, and evaluate how effectively the company is managing these assets. **Activity ratios** compare company sales to various asset categories in order to measure how well the company is utilizing its assets. Three of the most widely used activity ratios deal with accounts receivable, inventory, and total assets.

Accounts Receivable Turnover A glance at most financial statements will reveal that the asset side of the balance sheet is dominated by just a few accounts that make up 80% to 90%, or even more, of total resources. Certainly, this is the case with Universal Office Furnishings, where, as you can see in Table 7.4, three entries (accounts receivable, inventory, and net long-term assets) accounted for nearly 80% of total assets in 2001. Like Universal, most firms invest a significant amount of capital in accounts receivable, and for this reason they are viewed as a crucial corporate resource. Accounts receivable turnover is a measure of how these resources are being managed. It is computed as follows:

Equation 7.3

$$\text{Accounts receivable turnover} = \frac{\text{Annual sales}}{\text{Accounts receivable}}$$

$$\text{For Universal} = \frac{\$1,938.0}{\$227.2} = \underline{\underline{8.53}}$$

In essence, this turnover figure indicates the kind of return the company is getting from its investment in accounts receivable. Other things being equal, the higher the turnover figure, the more favorable it is. In 2001, UVRS was turning its receivables about 8½ times a year. That excellent turnover rate suggests a very strong credit and collection policy. It also means that each dollar invested in receivables was supporting, or generating, $8.53 in sales.

Inventory Turnover Another important corporate resource—and one that requires a considerable amount of management attention—is inventory. Control of inventory is important to the well-being of a company and is commonly assessed with the inventory turnover measure:

Equation 7.4

$$\text{Inventory turnover} = \frac{\text{Annual sales}}{\text{Inventory}}$$

$$\text{For Universal} = \frac{\$1,938.0}{\$103.7} = \underline{\underline{18.69}}$$

Again, the more sales the company can get out of its inventory, the better the return on this vital resource. In 2001, Universal was doing an outstanding job of getting the most from its inventory. A turnover of almost 19 times a year means that the firm is holding inventory for less than a month—actually, for about 20 days (365/18.69 = 19.5). That's the kind of performance you like to see. The higher the turnover figure, the less time an item spends in inventory and the better the return the company is able to earn from funds tied up in inventory.

Total Asset Turnover Total asset turnover indicates how efficiently assets are being used to support sales. It is calculated as follows:

Equation 7.5

$$\text{Total asset turnover} = \frac{\text{Annual sales}}{\text{Total assets}}$$

$$\text{For Universal} = \frac{\$1,938.0}{\$941.2} = \underline{\underline{2.06}}$$

Note in this case that UVRS is generating more than $2.00 in revenues from every dollar invested in assets. This is a fairly high number and is important because it has a direct bearing on corporate profitability. The principle at work here is much like the return to an individual investor: Earning $100 from a $1,000 investment is far more desirable than earning the same amount from a $2,000 investment. A high total asset turnover figure suggests that corporate resources are being well managed and that the firm is able to realize a high level of sales (and, ultimately, profits) from its asset investments.

Leverage Measures **Leverage** looks at the firm's different types of financing, and indicates the amount of debt being used to support the resources and operations of the company. The amount of indebtedness within the financial structure and the ability of the firm to service its debt are major concerns in leverage analysis. There are two widely used leverage ratios. The first, the debt-equity ratio, measures the *amount of debt* being used by the company. The second, times interest earned, assesses how well the company can *service its debt*.

leverage measures
financial ratios that measure the amount of debt being used to support operations and the ability of the firm to service its debt.

Debt-Equity Ratio The *debt-equity ratio* measures leverage, or the relative amount of funds provided by lenders and owners. It is computed as follows:

Equation 7.6

$$\text{Debt-equity ratio} = \frac{\text{Long-term debt}}{\text{Stockholders' equity}}$$

$$\text{For Universal} = \frac{\$177.8}{\$294.5} = \underline{\underline{0.60}}$$

Because highly leveraged firms (those that use large amounts of debt) run an increased risk of defaulting on their loans, this ratio is particularly helpful in assessing a stock's risk exposure. The 2001 debt-equity ratio for UVRS is reasonably low (at 60%) and shows that most of the company's capital comes from its owners. Stated another way, there was only 60 cents worth of debt in the capital structure for every dollar of equity.

Times Interest Earned *Times interest earned* is a so-called coverage ratio. It measures the ability of the firm to meet its fixed interest payments and is calculated as follows:

Equation 7.7

$$\text{Times interest earned} = \frac{\text{Earnings before interest and taxes}}{\text{Interest expense}}$$

$$\text{For Universal} = \frac{\$235.2}{\$13.4} = \underline{\underline{17.55}}$$

The ability of the company to meet its interest payments (which, with bonds, are fixed contractual obligations) in a timely and orderly fashion is an important consideration in evaluating risk exposure. Universal's times interest earned ratio indicates that the firm has about $17.50 available to cover every dollar of interest expense. That's an outstanding coverage ratio—way above average! As a rule, a ratio 8 to 9 times earnings is considered very strong, so a ratio that exceeds 17 is definitely up there. To put this number in perspective, there's usually little concern until times interest earned drops to something less than 2 or 3 times earnings.

profitability measures
financial ratios that measure a firm's returns by relating profits to sales, assets, or equity.

Measuring Profitability **Profitability** is a relative measure of success. Each of the various profitability measures relates the returns (profits) of a company to its sales, assets, or equity. There are three widely used profitability measures: net profit margin, return on assets, and return on equity.

Net Profit Margin This is the "bottom line" of operations. Net profit margin indicates the rate of profit being earned from sales and other revenues. It is computed as follows:

Equation 7.8

$$\text{Net profit margin} = \frac{\text{Net profit after taxes}}{\text{Total revenues}}$$

$$\text{For Universal} = \frac{\$139.7}{\$1,938.0} = \underline{7.2\%}$$

The net profit margin looks at profits as a percent of sales (and other revenues). Because it moves with costs, it also reveals the type of control management has over the cost structure of the firm. Note that UVRS had a net profit margin of 7.2% in 2001. That is, the company's return on sales was better than 7 cents on the dollar. That may be about average for the large U.S. companies, but as we shall see, that's well above average for firms in the business equipment industry.

Return on Assets As a profitability measure, *return on assets (ROA)* looks at the amount of resources needed to support operations. Return on assets reveals management's effectiveness in generating profits from the assets it has available, and is perhaps *the single most important measure of return*. ROA is computed as follows:

Equation 7.9

$$\text{ROA} = \frac{\text{Net profit after taxes}}{\text{Total assets}}$$

$$\text{For Universal} = \frac{\$139.7}{\$941.2} = \underline{14.8\%}$$

In the case of Universal Office Furnishings, the company earned almost 15% on its asset investments in 2001. That is a very healthy return, and, indeed, is well above average. As a rule, you'd like to see a company maintain as high an ROA as possible. The higher the ROA, the more profitable the company.

Return on Equity A measure of the overall profitability of the firm, *return on equity (ROE)* is closely followed by investors because of its direct link to the profits, growth, and dividends of the company. Return on equity—or return on investment (ROI), as it's sometimes called—measures the return to the firm's stockholders by relating profits to shareholder equity:

Equation 7.10

$$\text{ROE} = \frac{\text{Net profit after taxes}}{\text{Stockholders' equity}}$$

$$\text{For Universal} = \frac{\$139.7}{\$294.5} = \underline{47.4\%}$$

ROE shows the annual payoff to investors, which in the case of UVRS amounts to nearly 48 cents for every dollar of equity. That, too, is an outstanding measure of performance and suggests that the company is doing what it has to do to keep its shareholders happy. Generally speaking, look for a high or increasing ROE. In contrast, watch out for a falling ROE, which could mean trouble later on.

Breaking Down ROA and ROE Both ROA and ROE are important measures of corporate profitability. But to get the most from these two measures, we have to break them down into their component parts. ROA, for example, is made up of two key components: the firm's net profit margin and its total asset turnover. Thus, rather than using Equation 7.9 to find ROA, we can use the following expanded format:

Equation 7.11

$$\text{ROA} = \text{Net profit margin} \times \text{Total asset turnover}$$

Using the net profit margin and total asset turnover figures that we computed (Equations 7.8 and 7.5, respectively), we can find Universal's 2001 ROA.

$$\text{ROA} = 7.2\% \times 2.06 = \underline{14.0\%}$$

Note that we end up with the same figure as that found with equation 7.9. So why would you want to use the expanded version of ROA? *The major reason is that it shows you what's driving company profits.* As an investor, you want to know if ROA is moving up (or down) because of improvement (or deterioration) in the company's profit margin and/or its total asset turnover. Ideally, you'd like to see ROA moving up (or staying high) because the company does a good job of managing *both* its profits and its assets.

Just as ROA can be broken into its component parts, so too can the return on equity (ROE) measure. Actually, ROE is nothing more than an extension of ROA. It introduces the company's financing decisions into the assessment of profitability. That is, the expanded ROE measure indicates the extent to which financial leverage (or "trading on the equity") can increase return to stockholders. The use of debt in the capital structure, in effect, means that *ROE will always be greater than ROA.* The question is how much greater. Rather than using the abbreviated version of ROE in Equation 7.10, we can compute ROE as follows:

Equation 7.12

$$\text{ROE} = \text{ROA} \times \text{Equity multiplier}$$

where

$$\text{Equity multiplier} = \frac{\text{Total assets}}{\text{Total stockholders' equity}}$$

To find ROE according to Equation 7.12, we first have to find the equity multiplier.

$$\text{Equity multiplier for Universal} = \frac{\$941.2}{\$294.5} = 3.20$$

Now we can find the 2001 ROE for Universal as follows:

$$ROE = 14.8 \times 3.20 = \underline{47.3\%}$$

Here we can see that the use of debt (the equity multiplier) has magnified—in this case, tripled—returns to stockholders. (Note that small rounding errors account for the difference between the number computed here, 47.3%, and the one computed earlier, 47.4%, when we used Equation 7.10.)

Alternatively, we can expand Equation 7.12 still further by breaking ROA in the equation *into its component parts*. In this case, we could compute ROE as

Equation 7.13

$$ROE = ROA \times Equity\ multiplier$$

$$= (Net\ profit\ margin \times Total\ asset\ turnover) \times Equity\ multiplier$$

For Universal $= 7.2\% \times 2.06 \times 3.20 = \underline{47.4\%}$

This expanded version of ROE is especially helpful, because it enables investors to assess the company's profitability in terms of three key components: net profit margin, total asset turnover, and financial leverage. In this way, you can determine whether ROE is moving up simply because the firm is employing more debt, which isn't necessarily beneficial, or because of the way the firm is managing its assets and operations, which certainly does have positive long-term implications. To stockholders, ROE is a critical measure of performance (and thus merits careful attention) because of the impact it has on growth and earnings—both of which, as we'll see in Chapter 8, play vital roles in the stock valuation process.

common stock (market) ratios
financial ratios that convert key information about a firm to a per-share basis.

Common Stock Ratios Finally, there are a number of **common stock,** or so-called **market ratios,** that convert key bits of information about the company to a per-share basis. They tell the investor exactly what portion of total profits, dividends, and equity is allocated to each share of stock. Popular common stock ratios include earnings per share, price/earnings ratio, dividends per share, dividend yield, payout ratio, and book value per share. We examined two of these measures (earnings per share and dividend yield) in Chapter 6. Let's look now at the other four.

Price/Earnings Ratio This measure, an extension of the earnings per share ratio, is used to determine how the market is pricing the company's common stock. The price/earnings (P/E) ratio relates the company's earnings per share (EPS) to the market price of its stock.

Equation 7.14

$$P/E = \frac{Market\ price\ of\ common\ stock}{EPS}$$

To compute the P/E ratio, it is necessary first to know the stock's EPS. Using the earnings per share equation from the previous chapter, we see that the EPS for UVRS in 2001 was

INVESTOR FACTS

RATIOS ON THE RISE—Should you buy a stock priced at $30 a share or one in the same industry selling for $75 a share? Knowing price alone isn't enough. You'd also want information on P/E ratios, which can provide an indication of how the marketplace values the firm's shares. Recently the average P/E rose to about 23 times based on 2000 earnings, compared to the historical large-company U.S. stock average of about 15. The reason? Many high-tech firms are making little or no profits, and this gives them high P/Es. For example, in early January 2001, Compaq Computer, Nokia, Qualcomm, and Sun Micro-systems all had P/E ratios above 80. Even nontechnology companies had high P/Es: Disney was at 67, Coca-Cola, 59, Home Depot 56, and Wal-Mart 44.

Source: Amy Baldwin, "Price-Earnings Ratio a Tricky Stock Gauge," *The Washington Times,* October 13, 2000, p. B10; Eric Tyson, "Stock Price Alone Doesn't Reflect Value," *The Washington Times,* November 3, 2000, p. B11; and Quicken.com Stock Search, www.quicken.com/investments/stocks/search, January 11, 2001.

$$\text{EPS} = \frac{\text{Net profit after taxes} - \text{Preferred dividends}}{\text{Number of common shares outstanding}}$$

$$\text{For Universal} = \frac{\$139.7 - \$0}{61.8} = \underline{\$2.26}$$

In this case, the company's profits of $139.7 million translate into earnings of $2.26 for *each share* of outstanding common stock. Given this EPS figure and the stock's current market price (assume it is currently trading at $41.50), we can use Equation 7.14 to determine the P/E ratio for Universal.

$$\text{P/E} = \frac{\$41.50}{\$2.26} = \underline{18.4}$$

In effect, the stock is currently selling at a multiple of about 18 times its 2001 earnings.

Price/earnings multiples are widely quoted in the financial press and are an essential part of many stock valuation models. Other things being equal, you'd like to find stocks with *rising P/E ratios,* because higher P/E multiples usually translate into higher future stock prices and better returns to stock-holders. But even though you'd like to see them going up, you also want to *watch out for P/E ratios that become too high* (relative either to the market or to what the stock has done in the past). When this multiple gets too high, it may be a signal that the stock is becoming overvalued (and may be due for a fall).

One way to assess the P/E ratio is to compare it to the company's rate of growth in earnings. The market has developed a measure of this comparison called the **PEG ratio.** Basically, it looks at the latest P/E relative to the 3- to 5-year rate of growth in earnings. (The earnings growth rate can be all histor-ical—the last 3 to 5 years—or perhaps part historical and part forecasted.) The PEG ratio is computed as

Equation 7.15

$$\text{PEG ratio} = \frac{\text{Stock's P/E ratio}}{\text{3- to 5-year growth rate in earnings}}$$

PEG ratio
a financial ratio that relates a stock's price/earnings multiple to the company's rate of growth in earnings.

Universal Office Furnishings had a P/E ratio of 18.4 times earnings in 2001. If corporate earnings for the past 5 years had been growing at an average annual rate of, say, 15%, then its PEG ratio would be

$$\text{For Universal} = \frac{18.4}{15.0} = \underline{1.21}$$

A PEG ratio this close to 1.0 is certainly reasonable. It suggests that the com-pany's P/E is not out of line with the earnings growth of the firm. In fact, the idea is to *look for stocks that have PEG ratios that are equal to or less than one.* In contrast, a high PEG means the stock's P/E has outpaced its growth in earnings and, if anything, the stock is probably "fully valued." Some investors, in fact, won't even look at stocks if their PEGs are too high—say, more than 1.5 or 2.0. At the minimum, PEG is probably something you would want to look at, because it is certainly not unreasonable to expect some correlation between a stock's P/E and its rate of growth in earnings.

Dividends per Share The principle here is the same as for EPS: to translate total common dividends paid by the company into a per-share figure. (*Note:* If it is not on the income statement, the amount of dividends paid to common stockholders can usually be found on the statement of cash flows—Table 7.6.) Dividends per share is measured as follows:

Equation 7.16

$$\text{Dividends per share} = \frac{\text{Annual dividends paid to common stock}}{\text{Number of common shares outstanding}}$$

$$\text{For Universal} = \frac{\$9.3}{61.8} = \underline{\$0.15}$$

For fiscal 2001, Universal paid out dividends of $0.15 per share—at a quarterly rate of about 3¾ cents per share.

As we saw in the preceding chapter, we can also relate dividends per share to the market price of the stock to determine its dividend yield: i.e., $0.15 ÷ $41.50 = 0.4%. Clearly, you won't find Universal Office Furnishings within the income sector of the market. It pays very little in annual dividends, and thus, has a dividend yield of less than ½ of 1%.

Payout Ratio Another important dividend measure is the dividend payout ratio. It indicates how much of its earnings a company pays out to stockholders in the form of dividends. Well-managed companies try to maintain target payout ratios. If earnings are going up over time, so will its dividends. The payout ratio is calculated as follows:

Equation 7.17

$$\text{Payout ratio} = \frac{\text{Dividends per share}}{\text{Earnings per share}}$$

$$\text{For Universal} = \frac{\$0.15}{\$2.26} = \underline{0.07}$$

For Universal in 2001, dividends accounted for about 7% of earnings. Traditionally, most companies that paid dividends tended to pay out somewhere between 40% and 60% of earnings. By that standard, Universal's payout, like its dividend yield, is quite low. However, it is becoming increasingly common for companies, particularly growth-oriented firms, to have low payouts and dividend yields. The fact is that payout ratios have been on the decline in recent years, as companies have become more tax-efficient by retaining more of their earnings or using them for other purposes. (One such purpose is buying back shares of their stock—which UVRS has been doing.) Viewed in this light, Universal's relatively low payout seems perfectly acceptable.

Although low dividend payout ratios are certainly not a cause for concern, high payout ratios may be. In particular, once the payout ratio reaches 70% to 80% of earnings, extra care should be taken. A payout ratio that high is often an indication that the company may not be able to maintain its current level of dividends. That generally means that dividends will have to be cut back to more reasonable levels. And if there's one thing the market doesn't like, it's cuts in dividends.

Book Value per Share   The last common stock ratio is book value per share, a measure that deals with stockholders' equity. Actually, book value is simply another term for equity (or net worth). It represents the difference between total assets and total liabilities. And note that in this case we're defining equity as *common stockholders' equity,* which would *exclude* preferred stock. That is, *common stockholders' equity = total equity less preferred stocks.* (Universal has no preferred outstanding, so its total equity equals its common stockholders' equity.) Book value per share is computed as follows:

Equation 7.18

$$\text{Book value per share} = \frac{\text{Common stockholders' equity}}{\text{Number of common shares outstanding}}$$

$$\text{For Universal} = \frac{\$294.5}{61.8} = \underline{\$4.76}$$

Presumably, a stock should sell for *more* than its book value (as Universal does). If not, it could be an indication that something is seriously wrong with the company's outlook and profitability.

A convenient way to relate the book value of a company to the market price of its stock is to compute the price-to-book-value ratio.

Equation 7.19

$$\text{Price-to-book-value} = \frac{\text{Market price of common stock}}{\text{Book value per share}}$$

$$\text{For Universal} = \frac{\$41.50}{\$4.76} = \underline{8.72}$$

Widely used by investors, this ratio shows how aggressively the stock is being priced. Most stocks have a price-to-book-value ratio of more than 1.0—which simply indicates that the stock is selling for more than its book value. In fact, in strong bull markets, it's not uncommon to find stocks trading at four or five times their book values, or even more. Universal's price-to-book ratio of 8.7 times is definitely on the high side. That is something that you'll want to closely evaluate. It may indicate that the stock is already fully priced, or perhaps even overpriced. Or it could result from nothing more than a relatively low owners' equity ratio.

Interpreting the Numbers

Rather than compute all the financial ratios themselves, most investors rely on published reports for such information. Many large brokerage houses and a variety of financial services firms publish such reports. An example is given in Figure 7.1. These reports provide a good deal of vital information in a convenient and easy-to-read format. Best of all, they relieve investors of the chore of computing the financial ratios themselves. (Similar information is also available from a number of online services, as well as from various software providers.) Even so, you, as an investor, must be able to evaluate this published information. To do that, you need not only a basic understanding of financial ratios but also some standard of performance, or benchmark, against which you can assess trends in company performance.

Basically, two types of performance standards are used in financial statement analysis: historical and industry. With *historical standards,* various financial ratios and measures are run on the company for a period of 3 to 5

FIGURE 7.1 An Example of a Published Report with Financial Statistics

This and similar reports are widely available to investors and play an important part in the security analysis process. (*Source:* Standard & Poor's *Stock Reports,* January 8, 2000.)

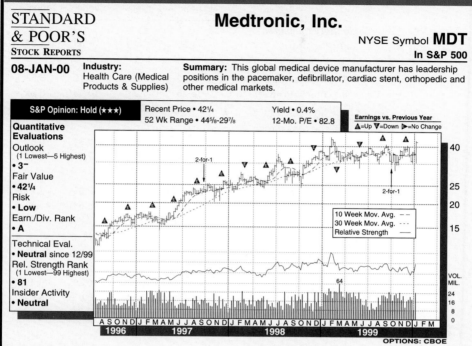

STANDARD & POOR'S
STOCK REPORTS

Medtronic, Inc.

NYSE Symbol **MDT**
In S&P 500

08-JAN-00

Industry: Health Care (Medical Products & Supplies)

Summary: This global medical device manufacturer has leadership positions in the pacemaker, defibrillator, cardiac stent, orthopedic and other medical markets.

S&P Opinion: Hold (★★★)

Recent Price • 42¼
52 Wk Range • 44⅝-29⅞

Yield • 0.4%
12-Mo. P/E • 82.8

Earnings vs. Previous Year
▲=Up ▼=Down ▶=No Change

Quantitative Evaluations

Outlook (1 Lowest—5 Highest)
• **3⁻**

Fair Value
• **42¼**

Risk
• **Low**

Earn./Div. Rank
• **A**

Technical Eval.
• **Neutral** since 12/99

Rel. Strength Rank (1 Lowest—99 Highest)
• **81**

Insider Activity
• **Neutral**

10 Week Mov. Avg. – –
30 Week Mov. Avg. – – –
Relative Strength ——

OPTIONS: CBOE

Overview - 23-DEC-99

Revenue growth of 16% is projected for FY 00 (Apr.), reØecting strong growth across the cardiac rhythm management, surgical and spinal/neurological areas. Although the vascular business suffered from difficult comparisons during the first half of the year, we expect strong growth in coming quarters, following the launch of the S670 cardiac stent both in the U.S. and in Japan. Industrywide stent pricing in the U.S. remains generally firm. Revenues in the second half of FY 00 and into FY 01 should also benefit from new product launches in the miniaturized defibrillator and abdominal aortic aneurysm markets. A favorable sales mix should push gross margins toward 74%, although SG&A line improvements could be hindered by the cost of product launches. With R&D costs equal to about 10% of sales, and assuming taxes at 33.0%, we see FY 00 operating EPS growth of about 20%, to $0.92, and look for FY 01 EPS of $1.10.

Valuation - 23-DEC-99

The shares have significantly underperformed the S&P 500 thus far in 1999, falling about 6%, versus a gain of nearly 17% for the S&P 500. Although MDT is one of the more compelling names in the medical technology sector, the health care sector is likely to remain under pressure until signs of a slowdown in earnings growth within the S&P 500, a development that could improve relative valuation measures and result in some sector rotation by investors. In addition, MDT carries an extreme valuation of 38X our FY 00 EPS estimate, nearly 7X projected sales, and 26X operating profits, all of which are far in excess of the company's projected growth rates, medical device group averages, and the P/E for the S&P 500. At recent levels, we would not add to existing positions.

Key Stock Statistics

S&P EPS Est. 2000	0.92	Tang. Bk. Value/Share	1.99
P/E on S&P Est. 2000	45.9	Beta	1.14
S&P EPS Est. 2001	1.10	Shareholders	38,000
Dividend Rate/Share	0.16	Market cap. (B)	$ 50.5
Shs. outstg. (M)	1194.4	Inst. holdings	63%
Avg. daily vol. (M)	3.804		

Value of $10,000 invested 5 years ago: $ 62,064

Fiscal Year Ending Apr. 30

	2000	1999	1998	1997	1996	1995
Revenues (Million $)						
1Q	1,105	991.7	646.3	600.9	523.8	403.8
2Q	1,161	984.5	642.1	598.1	518.5	408.1
3Q	–	1,039	631.4	598.8	529.2	413.7
4Q	–	1,119	685.0	640.5	596.1	516.7
Yr.	–	4,134	2,605	2,438	2,169	1,742
Earnings Per Share ($)						
1Q	0.21	0.20	0.15	0.13	0.11	0.07
2Q	0.22	0.10	0.15	0.13	0.11	0.08
3Q	E0.24	-0.03	0.01	0.13	0.12	0.08
4Q	E0.25	0.13	0.17	0.15	0.14	0.10
Yr.	E0.92	0.40	0.48	0.55	0.45	0.32

Next earnings report expected: late February
Dividend Data (Dividends have been paid since 1977.)

Amount ($)	Date Decl.	Ex-Div. Date	Stock of Record	Payment Date
0.065	Mar. 04	Apr. 07	Apr. 09	Apr. 30 '99
0.080	Jun. 24	Jun. 30	Jul. 02	Jul. 30 '99
2-for-1	Aug. 25	Sep. 27	Sep. 10	Sep. 24 '99
0.040	Oct. 28	Jan. 05	Jan. 07	Jan. 28 '00

A Division of The **McGraw·Hill** Companies

TABLE 7.7 Comparative Historical and Industry Ratios

	Historical Figures for Universal Office Furnishings				Industry Averages for the Office Equipment Industry in 2001
	1998	1999	2000	2001	
Liquidity measures					
Current ratio	1.55	1.29	1.69	1.34	1.45
Activity measures					
Receivables turnover	9.22	8.87	9.18	8.53	5.70
Inventory turnover	15.25	17.17	16.43	18.69	7.80
Total asset turnover	1.96	2.12	2.32	2.06	0.85
Leverage measures					
Debt-equity ratio	0.70	0.79	0.91	0.60	1.58
Times interest earned	15.37	26.22	32.49	17.55	5.60
Profitability measures					
Net profit margin	6.6%	7.5%	8.0%	7.2%	4.6%
Return on assets	9.8%	16.4%	18.6%	14.8%	3.9%
Return on equity	25.9%	55.5%	67.8%	47.4%	17.3%
Common stock measures					
Earnings per share	$1.92	$2.00	$2.17	$2.26	N/A
Price/earnings ratio	16.2	13.9	15.8	18.4	16.2
Dividend yield	0.3%	0.4%	0.4%	0.4%	1.1%
Payout ratio	5.2%	5.5%	6.0%	6.6%	24.8%
Price-to-book-value ratio	7.73	10.73	9.34	8.72	3.54

years (or longer). You would use these to assess developing trends in the company's operations and financial condition. That is, are they improving or deteriorating, and where do the company's strengths and weaknesses lie? In contrast, *industry standards* enable you to compare the financial ratios of the company with comparable firms or with the average results for the industry as a whole. Here, we focus on determining the relative strength of the firm with respect to its competitors. Using Universal Office Furnishings, we'll see how to use both of these standards of performance to evaluate and interpret financial ratios.

Using Historical and Industry Standards Look at Table 7.7. It provides a summary of historical data and average industry figures (for the latest year) for most of the ratios we have discussed. By carefully evaluating these ratios, we should be able to draw some basic conclusions about the financial condition, operating results, and general financial health of the company. By comparing the financial ratios contained in Table 7.7, we can make the following observations about UVRS:

1. Universal's *liquidity position* is a bit below average. But this doesn't seem to be a source of major concern, especially when you consider its receivables and inventory positions. That is, based on its respective turnover ratios (see item 2 below), both of these current assets seem to be very well controlled, which could explain the relatively low current ratio of this company. The current ratio is a bit below average, not because the firm has a lot of current liabilities, but because it is doing such a good job in controlling current assets.

TABLE 7.8	Comparative Financial Statistics: Universal Office Furnishings and Its Major Competitors (All Figures are for year-end 2001 or for the 5-year period ended in 2001; $ in millions)			
Financial Measure	Universal Office Industries	Cascade Industries	Colwyn Furniture	High Design, Inc.
Total assets	$ 941.2	$ 906.7	$342.7	$3,037.6
Long-term debt	$ 177.8	$ 124.2	$ 73.9	$ 257.8
Stockholders' equity	$ 294.5	$ 501.3	$183.9	$1,562.2
Stockholders' equity as a % of total assets	31.3%	55.3%	53.7%	51.4%
Total revenues	$1,938.0	$1,789.3	$642.2	$3,316.1
Net earnings	$ 139.7	$ 87.4	$ 38.5	$ 184.2
Net profit margin	7.2%	4.9%	6.0%	5.5%
5-year growth rates in:				
Total assets	14.36%	19.44%	17.25%	17.73%
Total revenues	18.84%	17.76%	15.91%	15.84%
EPS	56.75%	38.90%	21.10%	24.66%
Dividends	1.48%	11.12%	N/A	12.02%
Total asset turnover	2.06×	1.97×	1.88×	1.09×
Debt-equity ratio	0.60	0.43	1.46	0.17
Times interest earned	17.55×	13.38×	8.35×	14.36×
ROA	14.8%	9.5%	6.7%	6.7%
ROE	47.4%	18.8%	21.8%	13.0%
P/E ratio	18.4×	14.4×	13.3×	12.4×
PEG ratio	1.21	2.42	1.98	1.09
Payout ratio	6.6%	26.2%	N/A	32.4%
Dividend yield	0.4%	1.8%	N/A	2.6%
Price-to-book-value ratio	8.72	2.71	2.93	1.59

2. Universal's *activity measures* are all way above average. This company consistently has very high turnover measures, which in turn make significant contributions not only to the firm's liquidity position but also to its profitability! Clearly, the company has been able to get a lot more from its assets than the industry as a whole.

3. The *leverage position* of Universal Office Furnishings seems well controlled. The company tends to use a lot less debt in its financial structure than the average firm in the office equipment industry. The payoff for this judicious use of debt comes in the form of a coverage ratio that's well above average.

4. The *profitability picture* for Universal is equally attractive. The profit margin, return on assets, and ROE all remain well above the industry norm. Clearly, the company is doing an outstanding job in managing its profits and is getting as much as it can from its sales, assets, and equity.

In summary, our analysis above shows that this firm is very well managed and highly profitable. The results of this are reflected in *common stock ratios* that are consistently equal or superior to industry averages. Universal does not pay out a lot in dividends, but that's only because it's using those valuable resources to finance its growth and to reward its investors with consistently high ROEs.

Looking at the Competition In addition to analyzing a company historically and relative to the average performance of the industry, it's also useful to evaluate the firm relative to two or three of its major competitors. A lot can be gained from seeing how a company stacks up against its competitors and by determining whether it is, in fact, well positioned to take advantage of unfolding developments. Table 7.8 offers an array of comparative financial statistics for Universal and three of its major competitors. One is about the same size (Cascade Industries), one is much smaller (Colwyn Furniture), and one is much larger (High Design, Inc.). (This type of firm-specific data can generally be obtained from industry surveys similar to those put out by S&P and others—or, again, from the Internet or from various software providers.)

As the data in Table 7.8 show, Universal can hold its own against other leading producers in the industry. Indeed, in virtually every category, Universal's numbers are about equal or superior to those of its three major competitors. It may not be the biggest (or the smallest), but it outperforms them all in profit margins and growth rates (in revenues and earnings). Equally important, it has the highest asset turnover, ROE, and price/earnings ratio. Tables 7.7 and 7.8 clearly show that Universal Office Furnishings is a solid, up-and-coming business that's been able to make a name for itself in a highly competitive industry. The company has done well in the past and appears to be well managed today. Our major concern at this point (and the topic of the first part of Chapter 8) is whether Universal can continue to produce above-average returns to investors.

IN REVIEW

CONCEPTS

7.13 What is *fundamental analysis?* Does the performance of a company have any bearing on the value of its stock? Explain.

7.14 Why do investors bother to look at the historical performance of a company when future behavior is what really counts? Explain.

7.15 What is *ratio analysis?* Describe the contribution of ratio analysis to the study of a company's financial condition and operating results.

7.16 In the *Investing in Action* box on page 291, which of the "Ten Commandments" listed there do you feel is most important? Explain. Why is it important to review footnotes carefully when analyzing a company's financial statements?

7.17 Contrast historical standards of performance with industry standards. Briefly note the role of each in analyzing the financial condition and operating results of a company.

Summary

LG 1 **Discuss the security analysis process, including its goals and functions.** Success in buying common stocks is largely a matter of careful security selection and investment timing. Security analysis helps the investor make the selection decision by gauging the intrinsic value (underlying worth) of a stock.

LG 2 **Appreciate the purpose and contributions of economic analysis.** Economic analysis evaluates the general state of the economy and its potential effects on security returns. Its purpose is to characterize the future economic environment the investor is likely to face, and is used to set the tone for the security analysis process.

LG 3 **Describe industry analysis and note how it is used.** In industry analysis, the investor focuses on the activities of one or more industries. Especially important are how the competitive position of a particular industry stacks up against others and which companies within an industry hold special promise.

LG 4 **Demonstrate a basic understanding of fundamental analysis and why it is used.** Fundamental analysis looks closely at the financial and operating characteristics of the company—at its competitive position, its sales and profit margins, its asset mix, its capital structure, and, eventually, its future prospects. A key aspect of this analytical process is company analysis, which involves an in-depth study of the financial conditions and operating results of the company.

LG 5 **Calculate a variety of financial ratios and describe how financial statement analysis is used to gauge the financial vitality of a company.** The company's balance sheet, income statement, and statement of cash flows are all used in company analysis. An essential part of this analysis is financial ratios, which expand the perspective and information content of financial statements. There are five broad categories of financial ratios—liquidity, activity, leverage, profitability, and market (common stock) ratios. All involve the study of relationships between financial statement accounts.

LG 6 **Use various financial measures to assess a company's performance, and explain how the insights derived form the basic input for the valuation process.** In order to evaluate financial ratios properly, it is necessary to base the analysis on historical and industry standards of performance. Historical standards are used to assess developing trends in the company. Industry benchmarks enable the investor to see how the firm stacks up against competitors.

Discussion Questions

LG 2 Q7.1 Economic analysis is generally viewed as an integral part of the "top-down" approach to security analysis. In this context, identify each of the following and note how each would probably behave in a strong economy.
 a. Fiscal policy.
 b. Interest rates.
 c. Industrial production.
 d. Retail sales.
 e. Producer prices.

LG 1 **LG 2** Q7.2 As an investor, what kind(s) of economic information would you look for if you were thinking about investing in the following?
 a. An airline stock.
 b. A cyclical stock.
 c. An electrical utility stock.
 d. A building materials stock.
 e. An aerospace firm, with heavy exposure in the defense industry.

LG 5   Q7.3   Match the specific ratios in the left-hand column with the category in the right-hand column to which it belongs.

a. Inventory turnover
b. Debt-equity ratio
c. Current ratio
d. Net profit margin
e. Return on assets
f. Total asset turnover
g. Price/earnings ratio
h. Times interest earned
i. Price-to-book-value ratio
j. Payout ratio

1. Profitability ratios
2. Activity ratios
3. Liquidity ratios
4. Leverage ratios
5. Common stock ratios

Problems

 LG 5   P7.1   Assume you are given the following abbreviated financial statements.

	($ in millions)
Current assets	$150.0
Fixed and other assets	200.0
Total assets	$350.0
Current liabilities	$100.0
Long-term debt	50.0
Stockholders' equity	200.0
	$350.0
Common shares outstanding	10 million shares
Total revenues	$500.0
Total operating costs and expenses	435.0
Interest expense	10.0
Income taxes	$ 20.0
Net profits	$ 35.0
Dividends paid to common stockholders	$ 10.0

On the basis of this information, calculate as many liquidity, activity, leverage, profitability, and common stock measures as you can. (*Note:* Assume the current market price of the common stock is $75/share.)

 LG 6   P7.2   The Amherst Company has net profits of $10 million, sales of $150 million, and 2.5 million shares of common stock outstanding. The company has total assets of $75 million and total stockholders' equity of $45 million. It pays $1 per share in common dividends, and the stock trades at $20 per share. Given this information, determine the following:

a. Amherst's EPS.
b. Amherst's book value per share and price-to-book-value ratio.
c. The firm's P/E ratio.
d. The company's net profit margin.
e. The stock's dividend payout ratio and its dividend yield.
f. The stock's PEG ratio, given that the company's earnings have been growing at an average annual rate of 7.5%.

 LG 5   P7.3   Highgate Computer Co. produces $2 million in profits from $28 million in sales. It had total assets of $15 million.

a. Calculate Highgate's total asset turnover and its net profit margin.
b. Find the company's ROA, ROE, and book value per share, given that it has a total net worth of $6 million and 500,000 shares of common stock outstanding.

 LG 5 LG 6

P7.4 Financial Learning Systems has 2.5 million shares of common stock outstanding and 100,000 shares of preferred stock. (The preferred pays annual cash dividends of $5 a share, and the common pays annual cash dividends of 25 cents a share.) Last year, the company generated net profits (after taxes) of $6,850,000. The company's balance sheet shows total assets of $78 million, total liabilities of $32 million, and $5 million in preferred stock. The firm's common stock is currently trading in the market at $45 a share.

a. Given the preceding information, find the EPS, P/E ratio, and book value per share.
b. What will happen to the price of the stock if EPS rises to $3.75 and the P/E ratio stays where it is? What will happen if EPS *drops* to $1.50 and the P/E ratio doesn't change?
c. What will happen to the price of the stock if EPS rises to $3.75 and the P/E ratio jumps to 25 times earnings?
d. What will happen if *both* EPS and the P/E ratio *drop*—to $1.50 and 10 times earnings, respectively?
e. Comment on the effect that EPS and the P/E ratio have on the market price of the stock.

 LG 5

P7.5 The Buffalo Manufacturing Company has total assets of $10 million, an asset turnover of 2.0 times, and a net profit margin of 15%.

a. What is Buffalo's return on assets?
b. Find Buffalo's ROE, given that 40% of the assets are financed with stockholders' equity.

 LG 5

P7.6 Find the EPS, P/E ratio, and dividend yield of a company that has 5 million shares of common stock outstanding (the shares trade in the market at $25), earns 10% after taxes on annual sales of $150 million, and has a dividend payout ratio of 35%. At what rate would the company's net earnings be growing if the stock had a PEG ratio of 2.0?

 LG 5

P7.7 Using the resources available at your campus or public library (or on the Internet), select any common stock you like and determine as many of the profitability, activity, liquidity, leverage, and market ratios as you can. Compute the ratios for the latest available fiscal year. (*Note:* Show your work for all calculations.)

 LG 4 LG 5 LG 6

P7.8 Listed below are six pairs of stocks. Pick *one of these pairs* and then, using the resources available at your campus or public library (or on the Internet), comparatively analyze the two stocks. Which is fundamentally stronger and holds more promise for the future? Compute (or obtain) as many ratios as you see fit. As part of your analysis, obtain the latest S&P and/or *Value Line* reports on both stocks, and use them for added insights about the firms and their stocks.

a. Wal-Mart vs. Kmart.
b. Sara Lee vs. Campbell Soup.
c. IBM vs. Intel.
d. Tupperware vs. Crown Cork & Seal.
e. Liz Claiborne vs. Hartmarx.
f. General Dynamics vs. Boeing.

LG 4 LG 5 LG 6

P7.9 Listed here are the 2000 and 2001 financial statements for Otago Bay Marine Motors, a major manufacturer of top-of-the-line outboard motors.

Otago Bay Marine Motors
Balance Sheets ($ in thousands)

	As of December 31,	
	2001	2000
Assets		
Current assets		
Cash and cash equivalents	$ 56,203	$ 88,942
Accounts receivable, net of allowances	20,656	12,889
Inventories	29,294	24,845
Prepaid expenses	5,761	6,536
Total current assets	111,914	133,212
Property, plant, and equipment, at cost	137,273	85,024
Less: Accumulated depreciation and amortization	(50,574)	(44,767)
Net fixed assets	86,699	40,257
Other assets	105,327	51,001
Total assets	$303,940	$224,470
Liabilities and Shareholders' Equity		
Current liabilities		
Notes and accounts payable	$ 28,860	$ 4,927
Dividends payable	1,026	791
Accrued liabilities	20,976	16,780
Total current liabilities	50,862	22,498
Noncurrent liabilities		
Long-term debt	40,735	20,268
Shareholders' equity		
Common stock	7,315	7,103
Capital in excess of par value	111,108	86,162
Retained earnings	93,920	88,439
Total shareholders' equity	212,343	181,704
Total liabilities and equity	$303,940	$224,470
Average number of common shares outstanding	10,848,000	10,848,000

Otago Bay Marine Motors Income Statements ($ in thousands)

	For the Year Ended December 31,	
	2001	2000
Net sales	$259,593	$245,424
Cost of goods sold	133,978	127,123
Gross profit margin	125,615	118,301
Operating expenses:	72,098	70,368
Earnings from operations	53,517	47,933
Other income (expense), net	4,193	3,989
Earnings before income taxes	57,710	51,922
Provision for income taxes	22,268	19,890
Net earnings	$ 35,442	$ 32,032
Cash dividends ($0.35 and $0.27 per share)	$ 3,769	$ 2,947
Average price per share of common stock (in the fourth quarter of the year)	$74.25	$80.75

a. On the basis of the information provided, calculate the following financial ratios for 2000 and 2001.

	Otago Bay Marine Motors		Industry Averages (for 2001)
	2000	2001	
Current ratio			2.36
Total asset turnover			1.27
Debt-equity ratio			10.00
Net profit margin			9.30
ROA			15.87
ROE			19.21
EPS			1.59
P/E ratio			19.87
Dividend yield			.44
Payout ratio			.26
Price-to-book-value			6.65

b. Considering the financial ratios you computed, along with the industry averages, how would you characterize the financial condition of Otago Bay Marine Motors? Explain.

  P7.10 The following summary financial statistics were obtained from the 1997 Otago Bay Marine Motors (OBMM) annual report.

	1997 ($ in millions)
Net sales	$179.3
Total assets	$136.3
Net earnings	$ 20.2
Shareholders' equity	$109.6

a. Use the profit margin and asset turnover to compute the 1997 ROA for OBMM. Now introduce the equity multiplier to find ROE.
b. Use the summary financial information from the 2001 OBMM financial statements (see Problem 7.9) to compute the 2001 ROA and ROE. Use the same procedures to calculate these measures as you did in part (a).
c. On the basis of your calculations, describe how *each* of the three components (profit margin, asset turnover, and leverage) contributed to the change in OBMM's ROA and ROE between 1997 and 2001. Which component(s) contributed the most to the change in ROA? Which contributed the most to the change in ROE?
d. Generally speaking, do you think that these changes are fundamentally healthy for the company?

Case Problem 7.1   *Some Financial Ratios Are Real Eye-Openers*

LG 5   LG 6

Jack Arnold is a resident of Lubbock, Texas, where he is a prosperous rancher and businessman. He has also built up a sizable portfolio of common stock, which, he believes, is due to the fact that he thoroughly evaluates each stock he invests in. As Jack says, "Y'all can't be too careful about these things! Anytime I'm fixin' to invest in a stock, you can bet I'm gonna learn as much as I can about the company." Jack prefers to compute his own ratios even though he could easily obtain analytical reports from his broker at no cost. (In fact, Billy Bob Smith, his broker, has been volunteering such services for years.)

Recently, Jack has been keeping an eye on a small chemical stock. This firm, South Plains Chemical Company, is big in the fertilizer business—which is something Jack knows a lot about. Not long ago, he received a copy of the firm's latest financial statements (summarized here) and decided to take a closer look at the company.

South Plains Chemical Company
Balance Sheet
($ Thousands)

Cash	$ 1,250		
Accounts receivable	8,000	Current liabilities	$10,000
Inventory	12,000	Long-term debt	8,000
Current assets	21,250	Stockholders' equity	12,000
Fixed and other assets	8,750	Total liabilities and	
Total assets	$30,000	stockholders' equity	$30,000

Income Statement
($ Thousands)

Sales	$50,000
Cost of goods sold	25,000
Operating expenses	15,000
Operating profit	10,000
Interest expense	2,500
Taxes	2,500
Net profit	$ 5,000
Dividends paid to common stockholders ($ in thousands)	$1,250
Number of common shares outstanding	5 million
Recent market price of the common stock	$25

Questions

a. Compute the following ratios, using the South Plains Chemical Company figures.

	Latest Industry Averages			Latest Industry Averages
Liquidity			*Common Stock Ratios*	
a. Net working capital	N/A		k. Earnings per share	$2.00
b. Current ratio	1.95		l. Price/earnings ratio	20.0
			m. Dividends per share	$1.00
Activity			n. Dividend yield	2.5%
c. Receivables turnover	5.95		o. Payout ratio	50.0%
d. Inventory turnover	4.50		p. Book value per share	$6.25
e. Total asset turnover	2.65		q. Price-to-book-value	
			ratio	6.4
Leverage				
f. Debt-equity ratio	0.45			
g. Times interest earned	6.75			
Profitability				
h. Net profit margin	8.5%			
i. Return on assets	22.5%			
j. ROE	32.2%			

b. Compare the company ratios you prepared to the industry figures given in part (a). What are the company's strengths? What are its weaknesses?

c. What is your overall assessment of South Plains Chemical? Do you think Jack should continue with his evaluation of the stock? Explain.

Case Problem 7.2   *Doris Looks at an Auto Issue*

LG 2   LG 3   LG 5

Doris Wise is a young career woman. She lives in Phoenix, Arizona, where she owns and operates a highly successful modeling agency. Doris manages her modest but rapidly growing investment portfolio, made up mostly of high-grade common stocks. Because she's young and single and has no pressing family requirements, Doris has invested primarily in stocks that offer the potential for attractive capital gains. Her broker recently recommended an auto company stock and sent her some literature and analytical reports to study. One report, prepared by the brokerage house she deals with, provided an up-to-date look at the economy, an extensive study of the auto industry, and an equally extensive review of several auto companies (including the one her broker recommended). She feels strongly about the merits of security analysis and believes it is important to spend time studying a stock before making an investment decision.

Questions

a. Doris tries to stay informed about the economy on a regular basis. At the present time, most economists agree that the economy, now well into the third year of a recovery, is healthy, with industrial activity remaining strong. What other information about the economy do you think Doris would find helpful in evaluating an auto stock? Prepare a list—and be specific. Which three items of economic information (from your list) do you feel are most important? Explain.

b. In relation to a study of the auto industry, briefly note the importance of each of the following.
1. Auto imports.
2. The United Auto Workers union.
3. Interest rates.
4. The price of a gallon of gas.

c. A variety of financial ratios and measures are provided about one of the auto companies and its stock. These are incomplete, however, so some additional information will have to be computed. Specifically, we know the following:

Net profit margin	15%
Total assets	$25 billion
Earnings per share	$3.00
Total asset turnover	1.5
Net working capital	$3.4 billion
Payout ratio	40%
Current liabilities	$5 billion
Price/earnings ratio	12.5

Given this information, calculate the following:
1. Sales.
2. Net profits after taxes.
3. Current ratio.
4. Market price of the stock.
5. Dividend yield.

Web Exercises

W7.1   Visit dismal.com/, choose [Economy] from the list box at the top left, and look at [U.S. Economic Releases]. Click on the definition of one of the releases, such as Retail Sales.
  a. What are the strengths and weaknesses of this release?
  b. What impact would you expect it to have on financial markets?
    Also check out the following sites: www.moodys.com, click on [Economic Commentary]; and www.vanguard.com, click on [Personal Investors], [Economic Week in Review]. Describe in your own words the prevailing economic conditions.

W7.2   Go to www.smartmoney.com. Select [Stocks], Maps, Sector Maps, [Sector Tracker]. Browser should be Java enabled. You can track 120 industry groups in 10 broad market sectors using Dow Jones indexes and see instantly which sectors are leading or lagging the broader market.
  a. Use the drop-down menus to select the sector and time period. Which sector has the largest 1-day gain? Which has the largest 1-day loss?
  b. Select [Time Period: Year to Date, Category: Consumer, Cyclical]. Which sector had the largest gain? Which has the largest loss?

At www.bigchart.com, the section on [Industries] is quite useful in evaluating industry performance ranging from 1 week to 5 years (select the time span from the list box). The default setting on this page gives you the 10 best- and worst-performing industries for the past 3 months. Click on one of the best-performing industries to see the best- and worst-performing stocks in that industry over the selected time span.

  c. How did the following industries fare: technology; semiconductors; computers; wireless communications; home construction; heavy machinery; tobacco; forest products?
  d. Now click on [Show All Industries] from the left side menu. Which industries come under the Consumer, Non-cyclical sector?

W7.3   Calculate the stock market's fair value at dismal.com/dismal/dsp/tools/calculator/stocks.asp by choosing an estimate for corporate profit growth (say, 5%) and a long-term interest rate (say, 5.5%). Click on [Methodology] for an explanation of the methodology behind the Stock Price Valuation Model. How does the author consider whether an asset or stock is appropriately valued?

W7.4   At marketguide.com/MGI/home.asp, type IBM in the symbol box on the left-hand side of the main page, and click on [Go]. Study the snapshot report. Now click on [Click here to learn how to use the Snapshot report].
  a. How do you interpret the report for IBM?
    Next, from the left menu, under Analysis, click on [Comparison] to get the report.
  b. How does IBM compare to the industry, the sector, and the S&P 500? If you need help, click on [Click here to learn how to use the Comparison report].

For additional practice with concepts from this chapter, visit

www.awl.com/gitman_joehnk

CHAPTER 8

STOCK VALUATION AND INVESTMENT DECISIONS

LEARNING GOALS

After studying this chapter, you should be able to:

LG 1 Explain the role that a company's future plays in the stock valuation process and develop a forecast of a stock's expected cash flow.

LG 2 Discuss the concepts of intrinsic value and required rates of return, and note how they are used.

LG 3 Determine the underlying value of a stock using the dividend valuation model, as well as other present value– and price/earnings–based stock valuation models.

LG 4 Gain a basic appreciation of the procedures used to value different types of stocks, from traditional dividend-paying shares to new-economy stocks with their extreme price/earnings ratios.

LG 5 Describe the key attributes of technical analysis, including some popular measures and procedures used to assess the market.

LG 6 Discuss the idea of random walks and efficient markets and note the challenges these theories hold for the stock valuation process.

Tech stocks have been at the forefront of stock market news the past few years. Often this sector, rather than blue-chip industrials, drives the market—both up and down. Take Qualcomm, for example; a company that is a leading developer and supplier of digital wireless communications products and services. It pioneered Code Division Multiple Access (CDMA) technology, a standard for the wireless communications industry. Investors in Qualcomm stock have experienced a roller coaster ride recently. The firm's 1999 stock price started at $6.48 and soared steadily upward to end the year when it hits $176.13—*after* splitting 2-for-1 in May and 4-for-1 in December. This represents an annual return of over 2,600%, the year's best. The following year was another matter, however. Fears of slowing growth sent the stock price into free-fall: It plummeted from $163.25 to $51.50, before rebounding to $82.19 at year end, for a −53% return. Even after the decline, the stock was still trading at a price/earnings ratio of about 85 in early January 2001, a substantial premium over the average P/E of 29 for the S&P 500.

Despite Qualcomm's fluctuating stock price, investors looked with favor on the company's earnings growth—94% from 1997 through 2000, which far outstripped the S&P 500's 14%. The company consistently met or exceeded quarterly earnings estimates, and analysts project continued earning growth to $1.26 per share in 2001, an increase of 48% over 2000.

What do all these numbers mean in terms of the value of Qualcomm's stock? This chapter explains how to determine a stock's intrinsic value by using dividend valuation, dividend-and-earnings, price/earnings, and other models. We also look at how to value technology stocks. Finally, we'll review the use of technical analysis as a way to assess the state of the market in general.

Sources: Adrienne Carter, "The Big Score," *Money Technology 2000*, October 15, 2000, p.60; "Morningstar Quicktake Report—Qualcomm" *Morningstar.com*, downloaded from www.morningstar.com, January 15, 2001; and Qualcomm Web site, www.qualcomm.com

Valuation: Obtaining a Standard of Performance

LG 1   LG 2

stock valuation
the process by which the underlying value of a stock is established on the basis of its forecasted risk and return performance.

Obtaining a standard of performance that can be used to judge the investment merits of a share of stock is the underlying purpose of **stock valuation.** A stock's intrinsic value provides such a standard because it indicates the future risk and return performance of a security. The question of whether and to what extent a stock is under- or overvalued is resolved by comparing its current market price to its intrinsic value. At any given point in time, the price of a share of common stock depends on investor expectations about the future behavior of the security. If the outlook for the company and its stock is good, the price will probably be bid up. If conditions deteriorate, the price of the stock will probably go down. Let's look now at the single most important issue in the stock valuation process: *the future.*

Valuing a Company and Its Future

Thus far, we have examined several aspects of security analysis: economic and industry analysis, and the historical (company) phase of fundamental analysis. It should be clear, however, that it's *not the past* that's important but *the future.* The primary reason for looking at past performance is to gain insight about the future direction of the firm and its profitability. Granted, past performance provides no guarantees about future returns, but it can give us a good idea of a company's strengths and weaknesses. For example, it can tell us how well the company's products have done in the marketplace, how the company's fiscal health shapes up, and how management tends to respond to difficult situations. In short, the past can reveal how well the company is positioned to take advantage of the things that may occur in the future.

Because *the value of a stock is a function of its future returns,* the investor's task is to use available historical data to project key financial variables into the future. In this way, you can assess the future prospects of the company and the expected returns from its stock. We are especially interested in dividends and price behavior.

Forecasted Sales and Profits The key to our forecast is, of course, the future behavior of the *company* and the most important aspects to consider in this regard are the outlook for sales and the trend in the net profit margin. One way to develop a sales forecast is to assume that the company will continue to perform as it has in the past and simply extend the historical trend. For example, if a firm's sales have been growing at the rate of 10% per year, then assume they will continue at that rate. Of course, if there is some evidence about the economy, industry, or company that suggests a faster or slower rate of growth, the forecast should be adjusted accordingly. More often than not, this "naive" approach will be about as effective as more complex techniques.

Once the sales forecast has been generated, we can shift our attention to the net profit margin. We want to know what kind of return on sales to expect. A naive estimate can be obtained by simply using the average profit margin that has prevailed for the past few years. Again, it should be adjusted to account for any unusual industry or company developments. For most individual investors, valuable insight about future revenues and earnings can be obtained from industry or company reports put out by brokerage houses, advisory services (e.g., *Value Line*), the financial media (e.g., *Forbes*), and from

various investor Web sites. Or, as the accompanying *Investing in Action* box explains, you might even want to take a look at so-called "whisper forecasts" as a way to get a handle on earnings estimates.

Given a satisfactory sales forecast and estimate of the future net profit margin, we can combine these two pieces of information to arrive at future earnings.

Equation 8.1

$$\begin{array}{c}\text{Future after-tax} \\ \text{earnings in year } t\end{array} = \begin{array}{c}\text{Estimated sales} \\ \text{for year } t\end{array} \times \begin{array}{c}\text{Net profit margin} \\ \text{expected in year } t\end{array}$$

The "year *t*" notation in this equation simply denotes a given calendar or fiscal year in the future. It can be next year, the year after that, or any other year in which we are interested. Let's say that in the year just completed, a company reported sales of $100 million, we estimate that revenues will grow at an 8% annual rate, and the net profit margin should be about 6%. Thus estimated sales next year will equal $108 million ($100 million × 1.08). And, with a 6% profit margin, we should expect to see earnings next year of

$$\begin{array}{c}\text{Future after-tax} \\ \text{earnings next year}\end{array} = \$108 \text{ million} \times 0.06 = \underline{\$6.5 \text{ million}}$$

Using this same process, we would then estimate sales and earnings *for all other years* in our forecast period.

Forecasted Dividends and Prices At this point we have an idea of the future earnings performance of the company. We are now ready to evaluate the effects of this performance on returns to common stock investors. Given a corporate earnings forecast, we need three additional pieces of information:

- An estimate of future dividend payout ratios.
- The number of common shares that will be outstanding over the forecast period.
- A future price/earnings (P/E) ratio.

For the first two, unless we have evidence to the contrary, we can simply project the firm's recent experience into the future. Payout ratios are usually fairly stable, so there is little risk in using a recent average figure. (Or, if a company follows a fixed-dividend policy, we could use the latest dividend rate in our forecast.) It is also generally safe to assume that the number of common shares outstanding will hold at the latest level or perhaps change at some moderate rate of increase (or decrease) that's reflective of the past.

Getting a Handle on the P/E Ratio The only really thorny issue in this whole process is coming up with an estimate of the future P/E ratio—a figure that has considerable bearing on the stock's future price behavior. Generally speaking, the P/E ratio is a function of several variables, including:

1. The growth rate in earnings.
2. The general state of the market.
3. The amount of debt in a company's capital structure.

INVESTING in action

I've Got a Secret: Whisper Forecasts

As a fiscal quarter ends, investors rush to compare companies' actual reported earnings with consensus (average) security analysts' estimates published by firms such as First Call, Zacks, and I/B/E/S. If a company falls below the analysts' figure by even a penny or two, its stock price can tumble 30% or more in one day. In fact, *Kiplinger's* magazine considers this comparison perhaps the most important factor driving share price performance over the short term, and it affects longer-term performance as well.

Now investors have another set of earnings forecasts to follow. "Whisper forecasts" are unofficial earnings estimates that circulate among traders and investors. They are rumors rather than "official" (analysts') estimates. Whisper numbers tend to be higher than analysts' forecasts, and some market watchers believe they are the analysts' *real* earnings estimates.

Until recently, only the wealthiest individual and institutional investors had access to the super-secret analysts' forecasts. Now whisper numbers are widely available on the Internet. Data come from varied sources: from discussions with stockbrokers, from financial analysts, from investor relations departments, and from investors themselves. For example, Whisper Number (www.whispernumber.com), founded in 1998, combines information from investor forums with polling and daily computer searches of hundreds of thousands of sources, including message boards on Yahoo!, Silicon Investor, Motley Fool, Raging Bull, and America Online. Other Web sites dedicated to these unofficial earnings reports include Earnings Whispers (www.earningswhispers.com), Just Whispers (www.justwhispers.com), and The Whisper Number (www.thewhispernumbers.com). Each site claims to have the "real" whisper numbers. (The "Frequently Asked Questions" pages at these sites describe how each compiles its whisper earnings.)

How valid are whisper earnings? Whisper Numbers claims that about 74% of the time, a company that beats the whisper number will see its stock rise within 5 days of its earnings announcement, and those that fail to reach their whisper numbers will see their stock values decline.

A formal study by professors at Purdue and Indiana Universities compared average whisper forecasts and consensus analysts' estimates (from First Call) for 127 mostly high-tech firms from January 1995 to May 1997. The study treated all whispers equally, making no judgments of the poster's credibility. In addition, they used whisper forecasts in several trading strategies. The results showed that whisper forecasts tended to be more accurate than analysts' estimates and also provided information not included in analysts' forecasts. Because whisper forecasts are distributed widely, part of this information is reflected in stock prices before the actual earnings reports. Proponents of whisper forecasts claim that these forecasts also counteract the pessimistic bias of analysts, which derives from corporate pressure to keep estimates low so that positive earnings surprises will be more common than disappointments.

Not everyone believes in whisper forecasts. Some in the industry criticize whisper numbers as rumors, unsubstantiated speculation, or idle gossip from unknown sources that lack accountability. Many observers question the ethics of the practice. Company insiders or short sellers, for example, could plant high numbers to manipulate prices. For this reason, you should use whisper forecasts only in combination with other securities analysis techniques and tools.

Sources: Mark Bagnoli, Messod Daniel Beneish, and Susan G. Watts, "Earnings Expectations: How Important Are the Whispers?" *AAII Journal,* June 2000, pp. 11–14; Just Whispers Web site, www.justwhispers.com; Lynnette Khalfani, "Psst! Get the Scoop on Whisper Numbers," *Wall Street Journal,* January 12, 2001, p. C1; Manual Schiffros, "The Earnings Game," *Kiplinger's,* April 2000, pp. 60–62; and Whisper Numbers Web site, www.whispernumbers.com

4. The current and projected rate of inflation.
5. The level of dividends.

As a rule, higher P/E ratios can be expected with higher rates of growth in earnings, an optimistic market outlook, and lower debt levels (less debt means less financial risk).

The link between the inflation rate and P/E multiples is a bit more complex. Generally speaking, as inflation rates rise, so do bond interest rates. This, in turn, causes required returns on stocks to rise (in order for stock returns to remain competitive with bond returns) and higher required returns on stocks mean lower stock prices and lower P/E multiples. On the other hand, declining inflation (and interest) rates normally translate into higher P/E ratios and stock prices. We can also argue that a high P/E ratio should be expected with high dividend payouts. In practice, however, most companies with high P/E ratios have *low dividend payouts*. The reason: Earnings growth tends to be more valuable than dividends, especially in companies with high rates of return on equity.

A useful starting point for evaluating the P/E ratio is the *average market multiple*, which is simply the average P/E ratio of stocks in the marketplace. The average market multiple indicates the general state of the market. It gives us an idea of how aggressively the market, in general, is pricing stocks. Other things being equal, the higher the P/E ratio, the more optimistic the market. Table 8.1 lists S&P price/earnings multiples for the past 30 years. It shows that market multiples tend to move over a fairly wide range.

relative P/E multiple
a measure of how a stock's P/E behaves relative to the average market multiple.

With the market multiple as a benchmark, you can evaluate a stock's P/E performance relative to the market. That is, you can calculate a **relative P/E multiple** by dividing a stock's P/E by the market multiple. For example, if a stock currently has a P/E of 35 and the market multiple is 25, the stock's relative P/E is 35/25 = 1.40. Looking at the relative P/E, you can quickly get a feel for how aggressively the stock has been priced in the market and what kind of relative P/E is normal for the stock. Other things being equal, a high relative P/E is desirable. The higher this measure, the higher the stock will be priced in the market. But watch out for the downside: High relative P/E multiples can also mean lots of price volatility. (Similarly, we can use average *industry* multiples to get a feel for the kind of P/E multiples that are standard for a given industry. We can then use that information, along with market multiples, to assess or project the P/E for a particular stock.)

Now we can generate a forecast of what the stock's *future* P/E will be over the anticipated *investment horizon* (the period of time over which we expect to hold the stock). For example, with the existing P/E multiple as a base, an *increase* might be justified if you believe the *market multiple* will increase (as the market tone becomes more bullish), and the *relative P/E* is likely to increase also.

Estimating Earnings per Share So far we've been able to come up with an estimate for the dividend payout ratio, the number of shares outstanding, and the price/earnings multiple. We're now ready to forecast the stock's future earnings per share (EPS), which can be done as follows:

Equation 8.2

$$\text{Estimated EPS in year } t = \frac{\text{Future after-tax earnings in year } t}{\text{Number of shares of common stock outstanding in year } t}$$

TABLE 8.1 Average Market P/E Multiples 1971–2000

Year	Market Multiples (Average S&P P/E Ratio)	Year	Market Multiples (Average S&P P/E Ratio)
1971	18.3	1986	16.3
1972	19.1	1987	15.1
1973	12.2	1988	12.2
1974	7.3	1989	15.1
1975	11.7	1990	15.5
1976	11.0	1991	26.2
1977	8.8	1992	22.8
1978	8.3	1993	21.3
1979	7.4	1994	17.0
1980	9.1	1995	17.4
1981	8.1	1996	20.7
1982	10.2	1997	23.9
1983	12.4	1998	32.3
1984	10.0	1999	33.4
1985	13.7	2000	28.5*

Note: By May 2001, the average P/E ratio on the S&P 500 was down to about 23 times earnings.

Source: Average year-end multiples derived from various sources, including Standard & Poor's *Index of 500 Stocks* and its *Statistical Service—Security Price Index Record*. Listed P/Es are all year-end (December) figures, except 2000, which is as of end of the third quarter.

Equation 8.2 simply converts aggregate or total corporate earnings to a per-share basis, by relating company (forecasted) profits to the expected number of shares outstanding. Though this approach works quite effectively, some investors would rather bypass the projection of aggregate sales and earnings and instead, *concentrate on earnings from a per-share basis right from the start*. That can be done by looking at the major forces that drive earnings per share: ROE and book value. Quite simply, by employing these two variables, we can define earnings per share as follows:

Equation 8.3   EPS = ROE × Book value per share

This formula will produce the same results as the standard EPS equation shown first in Chapter 6 (Equation 6.1) and then again in Chapter 7. The major advantage of this form of the equation is that it allows you to assess the extent to which EPS is influenced by the company's book value and (especially) its ROE. As we saw in the previous chapter, ROE is a key financial measure, because it captures the amount of success the firm is having in managing its assets, operations, and capital structure. And as we see here, ROE not only is important in defining overall corporate profitability but it also plays a crucial role in defining a stock's EPS.

To produce an estimated EPS using Equation 8.3, you would go directly to the two basic components of the formula and try to get a handle on their future behavior. In particular, what kind of growth is expected in the firm's book value per share, *and* what's likely to happen to the company's ROE? In the vast majority of cases, ROE is really the driving force, so it's important to produce a good estimate of that variable. Investors often do that by breaking ROE into its component parts—margin, turnover, and the equity multiplier (see Equation 7.13 in Chapter 7).

Once you have projected ROE and book value per share, you can plug these figures into Equation 8.3 to produce estimated EPS. The bottom line is that, one way or another (using the approach reflected in Equation 8.2 or that in Equation 8.3), you have to arrive at a forecasted EPS number that you are comfortable with. When that's been done, it's a pretty simple matter to use the forecasted payout ratio to estimate dividends per share:

Equation 8.4

$$\frac{\text{Estimated dividends}}{\text{per share in year } t} = \frac{\text{Estimated EPS}}{\text{in year } t} \times \frac{\text{Estimated}}{\text{payout ratio}}$$

The last item is the future price of the stock, which can be determined as

Equation 8.5

$$\frac{\text{Estimated share price}}{\text{at end of year } t} = \frac{\text{Estimated EPS}}{\text{in year } t} \times \frac{\text{Estimated P/E}}{\text{ratio}}$$

Pulling It All Together We've seen the various components that go into our estimates of future dividends and share prices. Now, to see how they all fit together, let's continue with the example we started above. Using the aggregate sales and earnings approach, if the company had 2 million shares of common stock outstanding and that number was expected to hold in the future, then given the estimated earnings of $6.5 million that we computed earlier, the firm should generate earnings per share (EPS) next year of

$$\frac{\text{Estimated EPS}}{\text{next year}} = \frac{\$6.5 \text{ million}}{2 \text{ million}} = \underline{\$3.25}$$

This result, of course, would be equivalent to the firm having a projected ROE of, say, 15% and an estimated book value per share of $21.67. According to Equation 8.3, those conditions would also produce an estimated EPS of $3.25 (i.e., 0.15 × $21.67). Using this EPS figure, along with an estimated payout ratio of 40%, we see that dividends per share next year should equal

$$\frac{\text{Estimated dividends}}{\text{per share next year}} = \$3.25 \times .40 = \underline{\$1.30}$$

If the firm adheres to a *fixed-dividend policy*, this estimate may have to be adjusted to reflect the level of dividends being paid. For example, if the company has been paying annual dividends at the rate of $1.25 per share *and is expected to continue doing so for the near future*, then you would adjust estimated dividends accordingly (i.e., use $1.25/share). Finally, if it has been estimated that the stock should sell at 17.5 times earnings, then a share of stock in this company should be trading at a price of about $56.90 by the *end* of next year.

$$\frac{\text{Estimated share price}}{\text{at the end of next year}} = \$3.25 \times 17.5 = \underline{\$56.88}$$

Actually, we are interested in the price of the stock at the end of our anticipated investment horizon. Thus the $56.90 figure would be appropriate if we had a 1-year horizon. However, if we had a 3-year holding period, we would have to extend the EPS figure for 2 more years and repeat our calculations with the new data. As we shall see, *the estimated share price is important because it has embedded in it the capital gains portion of the stock's total return.*

Developing an Estimate of Future Behavior

Using information obtained from Universal Office Furnishings (**UVRS**), we can illustrate the forecasting procedures we discussed above. Recall from Chapter 7 that an assessment of the economy and the office equipment industry was positive and that the company's operating results and financial condition looked strong, both historically and relative to industry standards. Because everything looks favorable for Universal, we decide to take a look at the future prospects of the company and its stock. Assume we have chosen a 3-year investment horizon, because we believe (from earlier studies of economic and industry factors) that the economy and the market for office equipment stocks will start running out of steam near the end of 2004 or early 2005.

Table 8.2 provides selected historical financial data for the company. They cover a 5-year period (ending with the latest fiscal year) and will provide the basis for much of our forecast. The data reveal that, with one or two exceptions, the company has performed at a fairly steady pace and has been able to maintain a very attractive rate of growth. Our economic analysis suggests that the economy is about to pick up, and our research (from Chapter 7) indicates that the industry and company are well situated to take advantage of the upswing. Therefore, we conclude that the rate of growth in sales should pick up dramatically from the abnormally low level of 2001, attaining a growth rate of over 20% in 2002—more in line with the firm's 5-year average. After a modest amount of pent-up demand is worked off, the rate of growth in sales should drop to about 19% in 2003 and to 15% in 2004.

The essential elements of the financial forecast for 2002–2004 are provided in Table 8.3. Highlights of the key assumptions and the reasoning behind them follow.

- *Net profit margin.* Various published industry and company reports suggest a comfortable improvement in earnings, so we decide to use a profit margin of 8.0% in 2002 (up a bit from the latest margin of 7.2% recorded in 2001). We're projecting even better profit margins (8.5%) in 2003 and 2004, as some cost improvements start to take hold.

TABLE 8.2   **Selected Historical Financial Data, Universal Office Furnishings**

	1997	1998	1999	2000	2001
Total assets (millions)	$554.2	$694.9	$755.6	$761.5	$941.2
Total asset turnover	1.72×	1.85×	1.98×	2.32×	2.06×
Net sales (millions)	$953.2	$1,283.9	$1,495.9	$1,766.2	$1,938.0
Annual rate of growth in sales*	11.5%	34.7%	16.5%	18.1%	9.7%
Net profit margin	4.2%	3.6%	5.0%	8.0%	7.2%
Payout ratio	6.8%	5.6%	5.8%	6.0%	6.6%
Price/earnings ratio	13.5×	21.7×	14.9×	15.7×	18.4×
Number of common shares outstanding (millions)	77.7	78.0	72.8	65.3	61.8

*Annual rate of growth in sales = Change in sales from one year to the next ÷ Level of sales in the base (or earliest) years. For 1998, the annual rate of growth in sales equaled 34.7% = (1998 sales − 1997 sales)/1997 sales = ($1,283.9 − $953.2)/$953.2 = 0.3467.

| TABLE 8.3 | Summary Forecast Statistics, Universal Office Furnishings |

	Latest Actual Figures (Fiscal 2001)	Average for the Past 5 Years (1997–2001)	Forecasted Figures		
			2002	2003	2004
Annual rate of growth in sales	9.7%	18.1%	22%	19%	15%
Net sales (millions)	$1,938.0	N/A*	$2,364.4**	$2,813.6**	$3,235.6**
× Net profit margin	7.2%	5.6%	8.0%	8.5%	8.5%
= Net after-tax earnings (millions)	$139.7	N/A	$189.2	$239.2	$275.0
÷ Common shares outstanding (millions)	61.8	71.1	61.5	60.5	59.0
= Earnings per share	$ 2.26	N/A	$ 3.08	$ 3.95	$ 4.66
× Payout ratio	6.6%	6.2%	6.0%	6.0%	6.0%
= Dividends per share	$ 0.15	$0.08	$ 0.18	$ 0.24	$ 0.28
Earnings per share	$ 2.26	N/A	$ 3.08	$ 3.95	$ 4.66
× P/E ratio	18.4	16.8	20	19	20
= Share price at year end	$ 41.58	N/A	$ 61.60	$ 75.00	$ 93.20

*N/A: Not applicable.
**Forecasted sales figures: Sales from *preceding* year × Growth rate in sales = Growth in sales; then Growth in sales + Sales from preceding year = Forecast sales for the year. For example, for 2002: $1,938.0 × 0.22 = $426.4 + $1938.0 = $2,364.4.

- *Common shares outstanding.* We believe the company will continue to pursue its share buyback program, but at a substantially lower pace than in the 1998–2001 period. From a current level of 61.8 million shares, we project that the number of shares outstanding will drop to 61.5 million in 2002, to 60.5 million in 2003, and to 59.5 million in 2004.

- *Payout ratio.* We assume that the dividend payout ratio will hold at a steady 6% of earnings, as it has for most of the recent past.

- *P/E ratio.* Primarily on the basis of expectations for improved growth in revenues and earnings, we are projecting a P/E multiple that will rise from its present level of 18½ times earnings to roughly 20 times earnings in 2002. Although this is a fairly conservative increase in the P/E, when it is coupled with the hefty growth in EPS, the net effect will be a big jump in the projected price of Universal stock.

Table 8.3 also shows the sequence involved in arriving at forecasted dividends and price behavior:

1. The company dimensions of the forecast are handled first. These include sales and revenue estimates, net profit margins, net earnings, and the number of shares of common stock outstanding. Note that after-tax earnings are derived according to the procedure described earlier in this chapter.

2. Next we estimate earnings per share, following the procedures established earlier.

3. The bottom line of the forecast is, of course, the returns in the form of dividends and capital gains expected from a share of Universal stock, given that the assumptions about net sales, profit margins, earnings per

share, and so forth hold up. We see in Table 8.3 that dividends should go up to 28 cents a share, which is a big jump. Even so, with annual dividends of a little over a quarter a share, it's clear that dividends still won't account for much of the stock's return. In fact, the dividend yield in 2004 is projected to *fall* to just 3/10 of 1%. The returns from this stock are going to come from capital gains, not dividends. That's clear when you look at year-end share prices, which are expected to more than double over the next 3 years. That is, if our projections are valid, the price of a share of stock should rise from around $41.50 to over $93.00 by year-end 2004.

We now have an idea of what the future cash flows of the investment are likely to be. We now can establish an intrinsic value for Universal Office Furnishings stock.

The Valuation Process

valuation
process by which an investor uses risk and return concepts to determine the worth of a security.

Valuation is a process by which an investor determines the worth of a security using the risk and return concepts introduced in Chapter 5. This process can be applied to any asset that produces a stream of cash flow—a share of stock, a bond, a piece of real estate, or an oil well. To establish the value of an asset, the investor must determine certain key inputs, including the amount of future cash flows, the timing of these cash flows, and the rate of return required on the investment.

In terms of common stock, the essence of valuation is to determine what the stock *ought to be worth,* given estimated returns to stockholders (future dividends and price behavior) and the amount of potential risk exposure. Toward this end, we employ various types of stock valuation models, the end product of which represents the elusive intrinsic value we have been seeking. That is, the stock valuation models determine either an *expected rate of return* or the *intrinsic worth of a share of stock,* which in effect represents the stock's "justified price." In this way, we obtain a standard of performance, based on future stock behavior, that can be used to judge the investment merits of a particular security.

Either of two conditions would make us consider a stock a worthwhile investment candidate: (1) if the computed rate of return equals or exceeds the yield we feel is warranted, or (2) if the justified price (intrinsic worth) is equal to or greater than the current market price. Note especially that a security is considered acceptable even if its yield simply *equals* the required rate of return or if its intrinsic value simply *equals* the current market price of the stock. There is nothing irrational about such behavior. In either case, the security meets your minimum standards to the extent that it is giving you the rate of return you wanted.

HOT LINKS

For a valuation example, see
www.stocksense.com/valuation.html

However, remember this about the valuation process: Even though valuation plays an important part in the investment process, there is *absolutely no assurance* that the actual outcome will be even remotely similar to the forecasted behavior. The stock is still subject to economic, industry, company, and market risks, any one of which could negate *all* your assumptions about the future. Security analysis and stock valuation models are used not to guarantee success but to help you better understand the return and risk dimensions of a proposed transaction.

required rate of return
the return necessary to
compensate an investor for the
risk involved in an investment.

Required Rate of Return One of the key elements in the stock valuation process is the **required rate of return.** Generally speaking, the amount of return required by an investor should be related to the level of risk that must be assumed in order to generate that return. In essence, the required return establishes a level of compensation compatible with the amount of risk involved. Such a standard helps you determine whether the expected return on a stock (or any other security) is satisfactory. Because you don't know for sure what the cash flow of an investment will be, you should expect to earn a rate of return that reflects this uncertainty. Thus the greater the perceived risk, the more you should expect to earn. As we saw in Chapter 5, this is basically the notion behind the *capital asset pricing model* (CAPM).

Recall that using the CAPM, we define a stock's required return as

Equation 8.6

$$\text{Required rate of return} = \text{Risk-free rate} + \left[\text{Stock's beta} \times \left(\text{Market return} - \text{Risk-free rate} \right) \right]$$

The required inputs for this equation are readily available: You can obtain a stock's beta from *Value Line* or S&P's *Stock Reports* (or from just about any of the many Internet sites, such **as Quicken.com, MSN MoneyCentral,** or **Morningstar.com**). The risk-free rate is basically the average return on Treasury bills for the past year or so. And a good proxy for the market return is the average stock returns over the past 10 to 15 years (like the data reported in Table 6.1).

In the CAPM, the risk of a stock is captured by its beta. For that reason, the required return on a stock increases (or decreases) with increases (or decreases) in its beta. As an illustration of the CAPM at work, consider Universal's stock, which has a beta of 1.30. Given that the risk-free rate is 5.5% and the expected market return is, say, 15%, this stock would have a required return of

$$\text{Required return} = 5.5\% + [1.30 \times (15.0\% - 5.5\%)] = \underline{17.85\%}$$

This return—let's round it to 18%—can now be used in a stock valuation model to assess the investment merits of a share of stock.

As an alternative, or perhaps even in conjunction with the CAPM, you could take a more subjective approach to finding required return. For example, if your assessment of the historical performance of the company had uncovered some volatility in sales and earnings, you could conclude that the stock is subject to a good deal of business risk. Also important is market risk, as measured by a stock's beta. A valuable reference point in arriving at a measure of risk is the rate of return available on less risky but competitive investment vehicles. For example, you could use the rate of return on long-term Treasury bonds or high-grade corporate issues as a starting point in defining your desired rate of return. That is, starting with yields on long-term bonds, you could adjust such returns for the levels of business and market risk to which you believe the common stock is exposed.

To see how these elements make up the desired rate of return, let's go back to Universal Office Furnishings. Assume that it is now early 2002 and rates on high-grade corporate bonds are hovering around 9%. Given that our analysis thus far has indicated that the office equipment industry in general and Universal in particular are subject to a "fair" amount of business risk, we would want to adjust that figure upward—probably by around 2 or 3 points. In addition, with its beta of 1.30, we can conclude that the stock carries a good deal of market risk. Thus we should increase our base rate of return even more—say, by another 4 or 5 points. That is, starting from a base (high-grade corporate bond) rate of 9%, we tack on, say, 3% for the company's added business risk and another 4½ or 5% for the stock's market risk. Adding these up, we find that an appropriate required rate of return for Universal's common stock is around 17% or 17½%. This figure is reasonably close to what we would obtain with CAPM using a beta of 1.30, a risk-free rate of 5.5%, and an expected market return of 15% (as in Equation 8.6). The fact that the two numbers are close shouldn't be surprising. If they're carefully (and honestly) done, the CAPM and the subjective approach should yield similar results. Whichever procedure you use, the required rate of return stipulates the minimum return you should expect to receive from an investment. To accept anything less means you'll fail to be fully compensated for the risk you must assume.

IN REVIEW

CONCEPTS

8.1 What is the purpose of stock valuation? What role does *intrinsic value* play in the stock valuation process?

8.2 Are the expected future earnings of the firm important in determining a stock's investment suitability? Discuss how these and other future estimates fit into the stock valuation framework.

8.3 Can the growth prospects of a company affect its price/earnings multiple? Explain. How about the amount of debt a firm uses? Are there any other variables that affect the level of a firm's P/E ratio?

8.4 What is the *market multiple,* and how can it help in evaluating a stock's P/E? Is a stock's *relative P/E* the same thing as the market multiple? Explain.

8.5 In the stock valuation framework, how can you tell whether a particular security is a worthwhile investment candidate? What roles does the required rate of return play in this process? Would you invest in a stock if all you could earn was a rate of return that equaled your required return? Explain.

8.6 According to the *Investing in Action* box on page 317, what are *whisper forecasts* and how can investors use them? How accurate are whisper forecasts? Explain.

Stock Valuation Models

LG 3   LG 4

Take a look at the market and you'll discover that investors employ a number of different types of stock valuation models. Though they all may be aimed at a security's future cash benefits, their approaches to valuation are nonetheless considerably different. Take, for example, those investors who search for value in a company's financials—by keying in on such factors as book value, debt load, return on equity, and cash flow. These are the so-called *value investors,* who rely as much on historical performance as on earnings projections to identify undervalued stock. Then there are the *growth investors,* who concentrate solely on growth in earnings. To them, though past growth is important, the real key lies in projected earnings—that is, in finding companies that are going to produce big earnings, along with big price/earnings multiples, in the future.

There are still other stock valuation models being used in
this market—models that employ variables such as dividend
yield, price-to-sales ratios, abnormally low P/E multiples, relative price performance over time, and even company size or
market caps as key elements in the decision-making process. For
purposes of our discussion here, we'll focus on several stock valuation models that are both theoretically sound and widely
used. In one form or another, these models use the required rate of return,
along with expected cash flows from dividends and/or the future price of the
stock, to derive the intrinsic value of an investment. We'll look first at stocks
that pay dividends and at a procedure known as the dividend valuation model.
From there, we'll look at several valuation procedures that can be used with
companies that pay little or nothing in dividends (the more growth-oriented
companies). Then we'll move on to tech stocks, many of which not only don't
pay dividends but may not even generate earnings (at least for now), or if they
do produce earnings, they trade at astronomical P/E multiples.

The Dividend Valuation Model

In the valuation process, the intrinsic value of any investment equals the *present
value of the expected cash benefits.* For common stock, this amounts to the
cash dividends received each year plus the future sale price of the stock. One
way to view the cash flow benefits from common stock is to assume that the
dividends will be received over an infinite time horizon—an assumption that is
appropriate so long as the firm is considered a "going concern." Seen from this
perspective, *the value of a share of stock is equal to the present value of all the
future dividends it is expected to provide over an infinite time horizon.*

Although a stockholder can earn capital gains in addition to dividends by
selling a stock for more than he or she paid for it, from a strictly theoretical
point of view, what is really being sold is the right to all remaining future dividends. Thus, just as the *current* value of a share of stock is a function of future
dividends, the *future* price of the stock is also a function of future dividends.
In this framework, the *future* price of the stock will rise or fall as the outlook
for dividends (and the required rate of return) changes. This approach, which
holds that the value of a share of stock is a function of its future dividends, is
known as the **dividend valuation model (DVM)**.

There are three versions of the dividend valuation model, each based on
different assumptions about the future rate of growth in dividends: (1) *The
zero-growth model,* which assumes that dividends will not grow over time. (2)
The constant-growth model, which is the basic version of the dividend valuation model, and assumes that dividends will grow by a fixed/constant rate over
time. (3) *The variable-growth model,* which assumes that the rate of growth
in dividends varies over time.

Zero Growth The simplest way to picture the dividend valuation model is to
assume the stock has a fixed stream of dividends. In other words, dividends stay
the same year in and year out, and they're expected to do so in the
future. Under such conditions, the value of a zero-growth stock is
simply *the capitalized value of its annual dividends.* To find the
capitalized value, just divide annual dividends by the required rate
of return, which in effect acts as the capitalization rate. That is,

dividend valuation model (DVM)
a model that values a share of
stock on the basis of the future
dividend stream it is expected to
produce; its three versions are
zero-growth, constant-growth,
and variable-growth.

Equation 8.7

$$\frac{\text{Value of a}}{\text{share of stock}} = \frac{\text{Annual dividends}}{\text{required rate of return}}$$

For example, if a stock paid a (constant) dividend of $3 a share and you wanted to earn 10% on your investment, the value of the stock would be $30 a share ($3/0.10 = $30).

As you can see, the only cash flow variable that's used in this model is the fixed annual dividend. Given that the annual dividend on this stock never changes, does that mean the price of the stock never changes? Absolutely not! For as the capitalization rate—that is, the required rate of return—changes, so will the price of the stock. Thus, if the capitalization rate goes up to, say, 15%, the price of the stock will fall to $20 ($3/0.15). Although this may be a very simplified view of the valuation model, it's actually not as far-fetched as it may appear. As we'll see in Chapter 11, this is basically the procedure used to price *preferred stocks* in the marketplace.

Constant Growth The zero-growth model is a good beginning, but it does not take into account a growing stream of dividends, which is more likely to be the case in the real world. The standard and more widely recognized version of the dividend valuation model assumes that dividends will grow over time at a specified rate. In this version, the value of a share of stock is still considered to be a function of its future dividends, but such dividends are expected to grow forever (to infinity) at a constant rate of growth, g. Accordingly, the value of a share of stock can be found as follows:

Equation 8.8

$$\frac{\text{Value of a}}{\text{share of stock}} = \frac{\text{Next year's dividends}}{\text{Required rate} - \text{Constant rate of}}_{\text{of return} \quad \text{growth in dividends}}$$

Equation 8.8a

$$V = \frac{D_1}{k - g}$$

where

$D_1 =$ annual dividends expected to be paid *next* year (the first year in the forecast period)

$k =$ the capitalization rate, or discount rate (which defines the required rate of return on the investment)

$g =$ the annual rate of growth in dividends, which is expected to hold constant to infinity

This model succinctly captures the essence of stock valuation: *Increase* the cash flow (through D or g) and/or *decrease* the required rate of return (k), and the value of the stock will *increase*. Also note that in the DVM, k defines the total return to the stockholder and g represents the expected capital gains on the investments. We know that, in practice, there are potentially two components that make up the total return to a stockholder: dividends and capital gains. As it turns out, the returns from both dividends and capital gains are captured in the DVM. That is, because k represents total returns and g defines the amount of capital gains embedded in k, it follows that if you subtract g from k ($k - g$), you'll have the expected dividend yield on the stock. Thus the expected total return on a stock (k) equals the returns from capital gains (g) plus the returns from dividends ($k - g$).

The constant-growth DVM should not be used with just any stock. Rather, *it is best suited to the valuation of mature companies* that hold established market positions. These are companies with strong track records that have reached the "mature" stage of growth. This means that you're probably dealing with large-cap (or perhaps even some mature mid-cap) companies that have demonstrated an ability to generate steady—though perhaps not spectacular—rates of growth year in and year out. The growth rates *may not be identical* from year to year, but they tend to move within such a small range that they are seldom far off the average rate. These are companies that have established dividend policies, particularly with regard to the payout ratio, and fairly predictable growth rates in earnings and dividends. Thus, to use the constant-growth DVM on such companies, all that's required is some basic information about the stock's *current* level of dividends and the expected rate of growth in dividends, *g*.

One popular and fairly simple way to find the dividend growth rate is to look at the *historical* behavior of dividends. If they are growing at a relatively constant rate, you could assume that they'll continue to grow at (or near) that average rate in the future. You can get historical dividend data in a company's annual report, from various online Internet sources, or from publications like *Value Line*. Given this stream of dividends, you can use basic present-value arithmetic to find the average rate of growth. Here's how: Take the level of dividends, say, 10 years ago and the level that's being paid today. Presumably, dividends today will be (much) higher than they were 10 years ago, so, using your calculator, find the present value discount rate that equates the (higher) dividend today to the level paid 10 years earlier. When you find that, you've found the growth rate, because in this case, the *discount rate is the average rate of growth in dividends*. (See Chapter 5 for a detailed discussion of how to use present value to find growth rates.)

Once you've determined the dividend growth rate, *g*, you can find next year's dividend, D_1, as $D_0 \times (1 + g)$, where D_0 equals the actual (current) level of dividends. Let's say that in the latest year Amalgamated Anything paid \$2.50 a share in dividends. If you expect these dividends to grow at the rate of 6% a year, you can find next year's dividends as follows: $D_1 = D_0 (1 + g) = \$2.50 (1 + .06) = \$2.50 (1.06) = \$2.65$. The only other information you need is the capitalization rate, or required rate of return, *k*. (Note that *k* must be greater than *g* for the constant-growth model to be mathematically operative.)

To see this dividend valuation model at work, consider a stock that currently pays an annual dividend of \$1.75 a share. Let's say that by using the present-value approach described above, you find that dividends are growing at a rate of 8% a year, and you expect they will continue to do so into the future. In addition, you feel that because of the risks involved, the investment should carry a required rate of return of 12%. Given this information, you can use Equation 8.8 to price the stock. That is, given $D_0 = \$1.75$, $g = 0.08$, and $k = 0.12$, it follows that

$$\text{Value of a share of stock} = \frac{D_0 (1 + g)}{k - g} = \frac{\$1.75 (1.08)}{0.12 - 0.08} = \frac{\$1.89}{0.04} = \underline{\$47.25}$$

Thus, if you want to earn a 12% return on this investment—made up of 8% in capital gains (*g*), plus 4% in dividend yield (i.e., \$1.89/\$47.25 = 0.04)—

then according to the constant-growth dividend valuation model, you should pay no more than $47.25 a share for this stock.

With this version of the DVM, *the price of the stock will increase over time* so long as k and g don't change. This occurs because the cash flow from the investment will increase as dividends grow. To see how this happens, let's carry our example further. Recall that $D_0 = \$1.75$, $g = 8\%$, and $k = 12\%$. On the basis of this information, we found the current value of the stock to be $47.25. Now look what happens to the price of this stock if k and g don't change:

Year	Dividend	Stock Price*
(Current year) 0	$1.75	$47.25
1	1.89	51.00
2	2.04	55.00
3	2.20	59.50
4	2.38	64.25
5	2.57	69.50

*As determined by the dividend valuation model, given $g = 0.08$, $k = 0.12$, and D_0 = dividend level for any given year.

As the table shows, we can also find the expected price of the stock *in the future* by using the standard dividend valuation model. To do this, we simply redefine the appropriate level of dividends. For example, to find the price of the stock in year 3, we use the expected dividend in the third year, $2.20, and increase it by the factor $(1 + g)$. Thus the stock price in year $3 = D_3 \times (1 + g)/(k - g) = \$2.20 \times (1 + 0.08)/(0.12 - 0.08) = \$2.38/0.04 = \$59.50$. Of course, if future expectations about k or g do change, the *future price* of the stock will change accordingly. Should that occur, an investor could use the new information to decide whether to continue to hold the stock.

Variable Growth Although the constant-growth dividend valuation model is an improvement over the zero-growth model, it still has some shortcomings. The most obvious of these is the fact that it does not allow for changes in expected growth rates. To overcome this problem, we can use a form of the DVM that allows for *variable rates of growth* over time. Essentially, the *variable-growth dividend valuation model* derives, in two stages, a value based on future dividends and the future price of the stock (which price is a function of all future dividends to infinity). The variable-growth version of the model finds the value of a share of stock as follows:

Equation 8.9

$$\text{Value of a share of stock} = \text{Present value of future dividends during the initial variable-growth period} + \text{Present value of the price of the stock at the end of the variable-growth period}$$

Equation 8.9a

$$V = (D_1 \times PVIF_1) + (D_2 \times PVIF_2) + \cdots + (D_v \times PVIF_v) + \left(\frac{D_v(1 + g)}{k - g} \times PVIF_v\right)$$

where

D_1, D_2, etc. = future annual dividends

$PVIF_t$ = present value interest factor, as specified by the required rate of return for a given year t (Table A.3 in the Appendix)

v = number of years in the initial variable-growth period

Note that the last element in this equation is the standard constant-growth dividend valuation model, which is used to find the price of the stock at the end of the initial variable-growth period.

This form of the DVM is appropriate for companies that are expected to experience rapid or variable rates of growth for a period of time—perhaps for the first 3 to 5 years—and then settle down to a constant (average) growth rate thereafter. This, in fact, is the growth pattern of many companies, so the model has considerable application in practice. (It also overcomes one of the operational shortcomings of the constant-growth DVM in that k does not always have to be greater than g. That is, *during the variable-growth period,* the rate of growth, g, can be greater than the required rate of return, k, and the model will still be fully operational.)

Finding the value of a stock using Equation 8.9 is actually a lot easier than it looks. All you need do is follow these steps:

1. Estimate annual dividends during the initial variable-growth period and then specify the constant rate, g, at which dividends will grow after the initial period.
2. Find the present value of the dividends expected during the initial variable-growth period.
3. Using the constant-growth DVM, find the price of the stock at the end of the initial growth period.
4. Find the present value of the price of the stock (as determined in step 3). Note that the price of the stock is discounted at the same PVIF as the last dividend payment in the initial growth period, because the stock is being priced (per step 3) at the end of this initial period.
5. Add the two present-value components (from steps 2 and 4) to find the value of a stock.

To see how this works, let's apply the variable-growth model to one of our favorite companies: Sweatmore Industries. Let's assume that dividends will grow at a variable rate for the first 3 years (2001, 2002, and 2003). After that, the annual rate of growth in dividends is expected to settle down to 8% and stay there for the foreseeable future. Starting with the latest (2000) annual dividend of $2.21 a share, we estimate that Sweatmore's dividends should grow by 20% next year (in 2001), by 16% in 2002, and then by 13% in 2003 before dropping to an 8% rate. Using these (initial) growth rates, we therefore project that dividends in 2001 will amount to $2.65 a share ($2.21 × 1.20), and will rise to $3.08 ($2.65 × 1.16) in 2002 and to $3.48 ($3.08 × 1.13) in 2003. In addition, given Sweatmore's risk profile, we feel that the investment should produce a minimum (required) rate of return (k) of at least 14%. We now have all the input we need and are ready to put a value on Sweatmore Industries. Table 8.4 shows the variable-growth DVM in action. The value of Sweatmore stock, according to the variable-growth DVM, is just under $49.25 a share. In essence, that's the maximum price you should be willing to pay for the stock if you want to earn a 14% rate of return.

TABLE 8.4	Using the Variable-Growth DVM to Value Sweatmore Stock

Step

1. Projected annual dividends:

	2001	$2.65
	2002	$3.08
	2003	$3.48

   Estimated annual rate of growth in dividends, g, for 2004 and beyond: 8%

2. Present value of dividends, using a required rate of return, k, of 14%, during the initial variable-growth period:

Year	Dividends	$\times$	PVIF ($k = 14\%$)	$=$	Present Value
2001	$2.65		0.877		$2.32
2002	3.08		0.769		2.37
2003	3.48		0.675		2.35
				Total	$7.04 (to step 5)

3. Price of the stock at the end of the initial growth period:

$$P_{2003} = \frac{D_{2004}}{k-g} = \frac{D_{2003} \times (1+g)}{k-g} = \frac{\$3.48 \times (1.08)}{0.14 - 0.08} = \frac{\$3.75}{0.06} = \underline{\$62.50}$$

4. Discount the price of the stock (as computed above) back to its present value, at $k = 14\%$:

$$PV(P_{2003}) = \$62.50 \times PVIF_{14\%, \, 3 \, yr} = \$62.50 \times 0.675 = \underline{\$42.19} \text{ (to step 5)}$$

5. Add the present value of the initial dividend stream (step 2) to the present value of the price of the stock at the end of the initial growth period (step 4):

   Value of Sweatmore stock = $7.04 + $42.19 = $49.23

Defining the Expected Growth Rate Mechanically, application of the DVM is really quite simple. It relies on just three key pieces of information: future dividends, future growth in dividends, and a required rate of return. But this model is not without its difficulties, and certainly one of the most difficult (and most important) aspects of the DVM is *specifying the appropriate growth rate, g, over an extended period of time.* Whether you are using the constant-growth or the variable-growth version of the dividend valuation model, the growth rate, *g*, is a crucial element in the DVM and has an enormous impact on the value derived from the model. Indeed, the DVM is *very sensitive* to the growth rate being used, because that rate affects both the model's numerator and its denominator.

As we saw earlier in this chapter, we can choose the growth rate from a strictly historical perspective (by using present value to find the past rate of growth) and then use it (or something close) in the DVM. That technique might work fine with the constant-growth model, but it has some obvious shortcomings with the variable-growth DVM. One procedure widely used in practice is to define the growth rate, *g*, as follows:

Equation 8.10 $g = \text{ROE} \times \text{The firm's retention rate, } rr$

where

   $rr = 1 - \text{dividend payout ratio}$

Both variables in Equation 8.10 (ROE and *rr*) are *directly related to the firm's rate of growth,* and both play key roles in defining a firm's future growth. The *retention rate* represents the percentage of the firm's profits that are plowed back into the company. Thus, if the firm pays out 35% of its earnings in dividends (i.e., it has a dividend payout ratio of 35%), then it has a retention rate of 65%: *rr* = 1 − 0.35 = 0.65. The retention rate, in effect, indicates the amount of capital that is flowing into the company to finance its growth. Other things being equal, the more money that's being retained in the company, the higher the rate of growth. The other component of Equation 8.10 is the familiar return on equity. Clearly, the more the company can earn on its retained capital, the higher the growth rate.

Let's look at some numbers to see how this actually works. For example, if a company retained, on average, about 80% of its earnings and generated an ROE of around 15%, you'd expect it to have a growth rate of around:

$$g = \text{ROE} \times rr = 0.15 \times 0.80 = \underline{12\%}$$

Actually, the growth rate will probably be a bit more than 12%, because Equation 8.10 ignores financial leverage, which in itself will magnify growth. But at least the equation gives you a good idea what to expect. Or it can serve as a starting point in assessing past and future growth. That is, you can use Equation 8.10 to compute expected growth and then assess the two key components of the formula (ROE and *rr*) to see whether they're likely to undergo major changes in the future. If so, then what impact is the change in ROE and/or *rr* likely to have on the growth rate, *g*? The idea is to take the time to study the forces (ROE and *rr*) that drive the growth rate, because the DVM itself is so sensitive to the rate of growth being used. Employ a growth rate that's too high and you'll end up with an intrinsic value that's way too high also. The downside to that, of course, is that you may end up buying a stock that you really shouldn't.

 ## Some Alternatives to the DVM

The variable-growth approach to stock valuation is fairly compatible with the way most people invest. That is, unlike the underlying assumptions in the standard dividend valuation model (which employs an infinite investment horizon), most investors have a holding period that seldom exceeds 5 to 7 years. Under such circumstances, *the relevant cash flows are future dividends and the future selling price of the stock.*

There are some alternatives to the DVM that use such cash flow streams to value stock. One is the so-called *dividends-and-earnings approach,* which in many respects is similar to the variable-growth DVM. Another is the *P/E approach,* which builds the stock valuation process around the stock's price/earnings ratio. One of the major advantages of these procedures is that *they don't rely on dividends as the key input.* Accordingly, they can be used with stocks that are more growth-oriented and pay little or nothing in dividends. It is very difficult, if not impossible, to apply the DVM to stocks that pay little or nothing in dividends. That's not a problem with the dividend-and-earnings approach or the P/E approach. Let's now take a closer look at both of these, as well as a technique that arrives at the expected return on the stock (in percentage terms) rather than a (dollar-based) "justified price."

A Dividends-and-Earnings Approach As we saw earlier the value of a share of stock is a function of the amount and timing of future cash flows and the level of risk that must be taken on to generate that return. A stock valuation model has been developed that conveniently captures the essential elements of expected risk and return and does so in a present-value context. The model is as follows:

Equation 8.11

$$\text{Present value of a share of stock} = \text{Present value of future dividends} + \text{Present value of the price of the stock at date of sale}$$

Equation 8.11a

$$V = (D_1 \times PVIF_1) + (D_2 \times PVIF_2) + \cdots$$
$$+ (D_N \times PVIF_N) + (SP_N \times PVIF_N)$$

where

$D_t =$ future annual dividend in year t

$PVIF_t =$ present-value interest factor, specified at the required rate of return (Table A.3 in the Appendix near the end of the book)

$SP_N =$ estimated share price of the stock at date of sale, year N

$N =$ number of years in the investment horizon

dividends-and-earnings (D&E) approach
stock valuation approach that uses projected dividends, EPS, and P/E multiples to value a share of stock.

This is the so-called **dividends-and-earnings (D&E) approach** to stock valuation. Note its similarities to the variable-growth DVM: It's also present-value-based, and its value is also derived from future dividends and the expected future price of the stock. The big difference between the two procedures revolves around the role that dividends play in determining the future price of the stock. That is, the D&E approach doesn't rely on dividends as the principal player in the valuation process. Therefore, it works just as well with companies that pay little or nothing in dividends as with stocks that pay out a lot in dividends. And along that line, whereas the variable-growth DVM relies on future dividends to price the stock, the D&E approach employs projected earnings per share and estimated P/E multiples. These are the same two variables that drive the price of the stock in the market. Thus, the D&E approach is far more flexible than the DVM and is easier to understand and apply. Using the D&E valuation approach, we focus on projecting future dividends and share price behavior over a defined, finite investment horizon, much as we did for Universal Office Furnishings in Table 8.3.

Especially important in the D&E approach is finding a viable P/E multiple that can be used to project the future price of the stock. This is a critical part of this valuation process, because of the major role that capital gains (and therefore the estimated price of the stock at its date of sale) play in defining the level of security returns. Using market or industry P/Es as benchmarks, you should try to establish a multiple that you feel the stock will trade at in the future. Like the growth rate, *g*, in the DVM, the P/E multiple is the single most important (and most difficult) variable to project in the D&E approach. Using this input, along with estimated future dividends, this present-value-based model generates a *justified price* based on estimated returns. This intrinsic value represents the price you should be willing to pay for the stock, given its expected dividend and price behavior, and assuming you want to generate a return that is equal to or greater than your required rate of return.

To see how this procedure works, consider once again the case of Universal Office Furnishings. Let's return to our original 3-year investment horizon. Given the forecasted annual dividends and share price from Table 8.3, along with a required rate of return of 18% (as computed earlier using Equation 8.6), we can see that the value of Universal's stock is

$$
\begin{aligned}
\text{Present value of a share} &= \frac{(\$0.18 \times 0.847) + (\$0.24 \times 0.718) + (\$0.28 \times 0.609)}{+ (\$93.20 \times 0.609)} \\
\text{of Universal stock} \\
&= \$0.15 + \$0.17 + \$0.17 + \$56.76 \\
&= \underline{\underline{\$57.25}}
\end{aligned}
$$

According to the D&E approach, Universal's stock should be valued at about $57 a share. That assumes, of course, that our projections hold up—particularly with regard to our forecasted EPS and P/E multiple in 2004. For example, if the P/E drops from 20 to 17 times earnings, then the value of a share of stock will drop to less than $50 (to around $48.75/share). Given that we have confidence in our projections, the present-value figure computed here means that we would realize our (18%) desired rate of return so long as we can buy the stock at no more than $57 a share. Because UVRS is currently trading at (around) $41.50, we can conclude that the stock at present is an *attractive investment vehicle*. That is, because we can buy the stock at *less* than its computed intrinsic value, we'll be able to earn our required rate of return, *and then some*. By most standards, Universal would be considered a highly risky investment, if for no other reason than the fact that *nearly all the return is derived from capital gains*. Indeed, dividends alone account for less than 1% of the value of the stock. That is, only 49 cents of the $57.25 comes from dividends! Clearly, if we're wrong about EPS or the P/E multiple, the future price of the stock (in 2004) could be way off the mark, and so, too, would our projected return.

Determining Expected Return

Sometimes investors find it more convenient to deal in terms of expected return rather than a dollar-based justified price. This is no problem, nor is it necessary to sacrifice the present-value dimension of the stock valuation model to achieve such an end. That's because expected return can be found by using the (present-value-based) *internal rate of return (IRR)* procedure first introduced in Chapter 5. This approach to stock valuation uses forecasted dividend and price behavior, along with the *current market price*, to arrive at the fully compounded rate of return you can expect from a given investment.

To see how a stock's expected return is computed, let's look once again at Universal Office Furnishings. Using 2002–2004 data from Table 8.3, along with the stock's current price of $41.58, we can determine Universal's expected return. To do so, we find the discount rate that equates the future stream of benefits (i.e., the future annual dividends and future price of the stock) to the stock's current market price. In other words, find the discount rate that produces a present value of future benefits equal to the price of the stock, and you have the IRR, or expected return on that stock.

Here's how it works: Using the Universal example, we know that the stock is expected to pay per-share dividends of $0.18, $0.24, and $0.28 over the next 3 years. At the end of that time, we hope to sell the stock for $93.20. Given that the stock is currently trading at $41.58, we're looking for the discount rate that will produce a present value (of the future annual dividends and stock price) equal to $41.58. That is,

$$(\$0.18 \times PVIF_1) + (\$0.24 \times PVIF_2) \\ + (\$0.28 \times PVIF_3) + (\$93.20 \times PVIF_3) = \$41.58$$

We need to solve for the discount rate (the present-value interest factors) in this equation. Through a process of "hit and miss" (and with the help of a personal computer or hand-held calculator), you'll find that with an interest factor of 31.3%, the present value of the future cash benefits from this investment will equal exactly $41.58. That, of course, is our expected return. Thus Universal can be expected to earn a fully compounded annual return of about 31%, assuming that the stock can be bought at $41.58, is held for 3 years (during which time investors receive indicated annual dividends), and then is sold for $93.20 at the end of the 3-year period. When compared to its 18% *required rate of return,* the 31.3% *expected return* makes Universal look like a very attractive investment candidate.

The Price/Earnings (P/E) Approach

price/earnings (P/E) approach
stock valuation approach that tries to find the P/E ratio that's most appropriate for the stock; this ratio along with estimated EPS, is used to determine a reasonable stock price.

One of the problems with the stock valuation procedures we've looked at above is that they are fairly mechanical. They involve a good deal of "number crunching." Although such an approach is fine with some stocks, it doesn't work well with others. Fortunately, there is a more intuitive approach. That alternative is the **price/earnings** (or **P/E**) **approach** to stock valuation.

The P/E approach is a favorite of professional security analysts and is widely used in practice. It's relatively simple to use, because it's based on the standard P/E formula first introduced in Chapter 7 (Equation 7.14). There we showed that a stock's P/E is equal to its market price divided by the stock's EPS. Using this equation and solving for the market price of the stock, we have

Equation 8.12

Stock price = EPS × P/E ratio

Equation 8.12 basically captures the P/E approach to stock valuation. That is, given an estimated EPS figure, *you decide on a P/E ratio that you feel is appropriate for the stock. Then you use it in Equation 8.12 to see what kind of price you come up with and how that compares to the stock's current price.*

Actually, this approach is no different from what's used in the market every day. Look at the stock quotes in the *Wall Street Journal.* They include the stock's P/E and show what investors are willing to pay for one dollar of earnings. The higher the multiple, the better investors feel about the company and its future prospects. Essentially, the *Journal* relates the company's earnings per share for the *last* 12 months (known as *trailing earnings*) to the latest price of the stock. In practice, however, investors buy stocks not for their past earnings but for their *expected future earnings.* Thus, in Equation 8.12, it's customary to *use forecasted EPS for next year.*

To implement the P/E approach, the first thing you have to do is come up with forecasted EPS one year out. In the early part of this chapter, we saw how this might be done (see, for instance, Equation 8.3). Given the forecasted EPS, the next task is to evaluate the variables that drive the P/E ratio. Most of that assessment is intuitive. For example, you might want to look at the stock's expected rate of growth in earnings, any potential major changes in the firm's capital structure or dividends, and any other factors such as relative market or industry P/Es that might affect the stock's multiple. You could use such inputs to come up with a base P/E, and then adjust that base, as necessary, to account for the perceived state of the market and/or anticipated changes in the rate of inflation.

Along with estimated EPS, we now have the P/E we need to compute (via Equation 8.12) the price at which the stock should be trading. By comparing that targeted price to the current market price of the stock, we can decide whether the stock is a good buy. For example, we would consider the stock undervalued and therefore a good buy if the computed price of the stock were more than its market price.

Putting a Value on Tech Stocks

Tech stocks have become a major force both in the United States and in equity markets around the world. As a result, they're playing a more important role in a growing number of individual as well as institutional portfolios. As an example of just how important they've become, consider the *Fidelity Blue Chip Growth* fund. According to recent information, 39.4% of the fund was invested in the technology sector, and six of the fund's top ten holdings were tech stocks: Cisco Systems, Intel, EMC Corporation, Microsoft, Sun Microsystems, and IBM. Now, keep in mind, Fidelity Blue Chip Growth is not even considered a tech-stock fund!

Broadly speaking, most investors would define a tech stock as *the stock of a firm whose core business contains a significant technology component.* Admittedly, this definition could include almost any firm, because technology now plays a key role in the development and production of even the most basic

HOT LINKS

See the Internet stock valuation technique at
www.stocksontheweb.com/overview.htm

products. What separates tech stocks from the rest is that these are the companies that are *providing the technology,* not just using it. Table 8.5 presents an overview of selected tech-stock groups as they are categorized on the Yahoo! Finance Web site (finance.yahoo.com). Some groupings, such as *Computer software,* quickly come to mind—this is, after all, a very large group made up of some 227 firms. We also see some fairly specialized groups, such as *Optical character recognition* (6 firms). Of course, we cannot discuss tech stocks without referring to those firms that specialize in the Internet. Interestingly, Yahoo! has three Internet stock groups: *Internet content, Internet services,* and *Internet software.* In addition, Yahoo! has a closely related group called *Electronic commerce.* Many high-tech firms are fairly young and not exactly household names, while others (like Microsoft and Oracle) are big-name companies with market caps in the hundreds of billions of dollars.

Tiers of Tech Stocks For valuation purposes, it is often convenient to put tech stocks into three broad categories, or tiers. *Top-tier* tech stocks include firms like Microsoft, Intel, and Cisco Systems. These firms are well-established

TABLE 8.5	Some Tech-Stock Groups	
Group Name	Numbers of Firms	Selected Firms
Business information services	22	Gartner Group, Keynote Systems
Computer networks	87	Cisco Systems, Juniper Networks
Computer software	227	Microsoft, Oracle
Defense electronics	27	REMEC, Teledyne
Electrical components—semiconductors	114	Intel, Xilinx
Electronic commerce	59	Amazon.com, eBay
Fiber optics	18	Corning, JDS Uniphase
Industrial automation/robotics	5	Gerber Scientific, Rockwell
Instrumentation—control	10	Datum, Eaton
Internet content	62	CNET, Travelocity.com
Internet services	102	America Online, CMGI
Internet software	94	Ariba, Synquest
Medical—biomedical/gene	145	Amgen, Biogen
Optical character recognition	6	PSC, Scansource
Telecommunications—wireless	57	AT&T Wireless, Vodafone
Telecommunications equipment	139	Lucent, Motorola
Telecommunications services	21	Global Crossing, RCN

Source: Yahoo! finance Web site (finance.yahoo.com).

market leaders with solid track records. There are probably no more than a hundred or so firms that would fall into this category. Most of them have normal financial and market ratios and are valued pretty much like any other growth stock, as described earlier in this chapter.

Next are the *mid-tier* stocks; there are literally hundreds of these firms, such as NVIDIA, Transwitch, and Black Box Corporation. Though many of them may not be household names, they have been around for some time and have demonstrated an ability to not only generate substantial revenues but also to earn solid profits year after year. NVIDIA, for example, had sales of nearly $650 million in 1999 and profits of over $80 million. Many of these tech stocks have very high P/E ratios and therefore may not be compatible with standard stock valuation models. A potential problem in valuing some of these mid-tier firms is that they may not have highly diversified product offerings and customer bases. Thus, a shift in industry fundamentals or technology could change their fortunes (i.e., earnings and growth rates) dramatically.

Lower-tier tech stocks include firms like bingo.com and Laser Corporation. Firms at this level typically have yet to generate any earnings. In many cases, they have very little in revenues. Valuation of these firms is extremely difficult and often amounts to little more than hunches. Indeed, these stocks are often bought by investors who pay little attention to fundamentals but instead rely on little more than "stories," such as some media report that's related to the firm's products, an unsubstantiated comment on the Internet, or the advice of a friend who has suddenly become an "expert" at investing.

Tech-Stock Valuation Methods Generally speaking, the methods used to value tech stocks are pretty much the same as those used to value any other type of stock. However, *tech-stock valuation definitely presents some unique* *challenges*. We'll look at the two primary techniques used to value tech stocks: discounted cash flow analysis and the use of price multiples. After describing each of these methods, we will discuss a concept known as the "burn rate," and then conclude with an example of a tech-stock valuation.

Discounted Cash Flow (DCF) Analysis Earlier in this chapter, we noted that the intrinsic value of any investment is the present value of its expected cash benefits. Actually, that's the principle behind the dividend valuation model (DVM). Recall that in the DVM the value of a share of stock is the present value of its future stream of dividends. The same can be said of the dividends-and-earnings (D&E) approach, except that it relies not only on dividends but also on expected future earnings, P/E multiples, and the future price of the stock. Both the DVM and D&E approaches are examples of discounted cash flow (DCF) models. DCF analysis involves the projection of future cash flows, such as dividends, which are then discounted back to the present at a rate that reflects the investor's required return.

There's an obvious problem in trying to apply the DVM to the valuation of tech stocks: *Very few of them pay dividends.* We could, of course, assume that the companies will *eventually* pay dividends and then discount these dividends back to the present to obtain an estimated value. But far more often than not, such computed values are *highly unreliable!* A viable alternative to the DVM would be to use a variation of the dividends-and-earnings approach. In this version, all of the dividends would be set to zero, so the computed value of the stock would come solely from our future projection of the firm's earnings and P/E ratio—in other words, the future price of the stock. That may work in some cases. But for many tech firms, earnings growth rates are so uncertain that techniques such as the D&E approach are not feasible. In an attempt to get around some of the problems that arise forecasting earnings, some investors use other measures of cash flow, such as *free cash flow*. But even here, it is difficult to forecast cash flow figures for rapidly growing high-tech firms. In fact, it may be *more difficult* to forecast cash flows for these firms because of all the assumptions that have to be made regarding growth rates, capital expenditures, and working-capital requirements. Thus, although DCF may be useful in valuing some of the larger, more established high-tech companies, most market observers regard it as impractical in the valuation of smaller and newer firms.

Price-Multiple Methods Instead of using DCF, a lot of tech-stock investors base their valuations on *stock price multiples*. To do so, investors identify firms that are comparable to the one being valued, determine the average (or typical) multiples being applied to those comparable firms, and then use it/them to put a value on the firm under consideration. Commonly used multiples include those based on *earnings* (price/earnings), *book value* (price/book value), and *sales* (price/sales). The use of these multiples follows the same steps that we outlined earlier in our discussion of the price/earnings (P/E) approach. That is, given the appropriate P/E multiple, we simply multiply EPS by the P/E ratio, and we have our estimate of the stock price. Similarly, we could *multiply book value per share by the appropriate price/book ratio*, or *sales per share by the appropriate price/sales ratio*, to estimate the value of the stock.

Although price/earnings multiples are widely used in valuation, they can be difficult or even impossible to apply to many tech stocks, because these companies often have earnings that are either highly erratic or even negative. Moreover, the use of price/book ratios may work well when valuing banks or other firms *whose assets are easily measured,* but it can be problematic when valuing tech stocks. The reason is that the book value of the firm as reported on the balance sheet may bear little resemblance to the value of the firm in the marketplace. Much of the marketplace value may stem from *intangible assets* such as the firm's growth potential or technological capabilities. The potential shortcomings of price/earnings and price/book ratios have led many investors to use the price/sales (P/S) ratio as the "multiple of choice" when valuing tech stocks. An advantage of the P/S ratio is that even when earnings are negative, sales are positive.

As is the case with P/E ratios, the P/S multiple can be calculated two ways: on a *trailing* basis or on a *forward* basis. The trailing price/sales ratio is computed simply by dividing share price by the sales per share for the most recent year. Alternatively, the forward price/sales ratio is computed by dividing share price by the *estimated* or *forecasted* sales per share for the *coming year.* This estimate can be obtained from analysts' reports (or, if you are adventurous, you could generate your own forecast). Because it's common for sales to grow over time, the forward price/sales ratio will tend to be lower than the trailing ratio.

Although price/sales ratios are popular in the valuation of tech stocks with little or no earnings, they do have shortcomings. First, although sales will be positive even when earnings are negative, many analysts would argue that our focus should ultimately be on the "bottom line" (earnings and profitability) rather than on the "top line" (sales). A second potential shortcoming of using any price multiple with tech stocks is that the multiple itself is highly volatile because of wide fluctuations in both share price and the characteristic (such as sales) in the denominator. Earlier in this chapter, we showed that there was considerable variation in marketwide P/E multiples over time. For tech stocks, the variation in P/S multiples can be even greater. The problem is this: An investor may determine that a set of comparable firms currently has an average P/S ratio of say, 6½ and then finds that this average has dropped to 3½ only a short time later. Such wide swings introduce into the valuation process the potential for considerable error. In addition, the question arises as to whether the firm being valued should receive the average multiple for the industry, that for a group of comparable firms, or some higher or lower value. Although this is a very difficult question to answer, all else being equal, price multiples do tend to increase with a firm's growth rate and to decrease with higher risk. We noted this earlier for P/E multiples, and the same concept applies to price/sales (P/S) multiples.

The "Burn Rate" in Tech Stocks Before proceeding to an example of valuation, we should define one other term that is often used in discussing tech stocks: the **burn rate,** or the **cash burn rate.** The burn rate refers to the *rate at which the firm is using up* ("burning up") *its supply of cash over time.* Because it usually takes a while for many start-up firms to generate cash from operations, their survival depends on their having an adequate supply of cash on hand to meet expenses. The burn rate is determined by examining a firm's statement of cash flows. As we saw in Chapter 7, the statement of cash flows

burn rate
the rate at which the firm is using up its supply of cash over time.

reports the change in the firm's cash position from one period to the next by accounting for the cash flows from operations, investment activities, and financing activities. Other things being equal, a higher burn rate is viewed more negatively, and is likely to result in a lower valuation for the firm.

To illustrate the concept of the "burn rate" refer to Table 8.6, which presents a highly abbreviated statement of cash flows for U.S. Internetworking, Inc. (USIX). This firm implements, operates, and supports packaged software applications over the Internet. The statement of cash flows in Table 8.6 covers the first 9 months of 2000 and the corresponding period for 1999. Let's focus on a few of the key cash flow items relevant to USIX's burn rate. First, the net cash from operations was a *negative* $93 million for the first 9 months of 2000. This result implies that the core business operations of the firm consumed (burned) cash at the rate of about $10 million per month, largely because of the firm's substantial—and growing—operating loss. Second, USIX made significant capital investment in new assets. As a result, the net cash flow from investing also was *negative,* to the tune of $63 million. That represents another significant use of cash. Indeed, the net cash burned by operations and investing together amounted to over $150 million—or a burn rate of nearly $17 million a month! Some would argue that a more appropriate (and more liberal) way to estimate a firm's burn rate would be to ignore the cash used for investing and simply focus on the cash from operations. But that doesn't seem to be very realistic, because most firms do, in fact, have to make some capital expenditures in order to continue operations. As a compromise, we won't even consider the cash used to meet payments on the firm's long-term debt and lease obligations, as that would just *add* another $2.5 million to the monthly burn rate.

Examination of the firm's financing activities gives us some idea of how USIX met these substantial cashs outflows. In particular, the firm raised nearly $150 million by issuing additional common stock and long-term debt. Because USIX had approximately $81 million in cash at the end of the period, it is likely to run out of cash in about 6 to 8 months, depending on which burn rate you use. USIX can avoid that fate if it (1) significantly decreases its burn rate or perhaps even begins to *generate* cash from operations, or (2) continues to issue significant amounts of debt or equity. Of course, the continued ability to raise additional capital is not guaranteed for any firm and is particularly questionable for risky tech firms.

Tech-Stock Valuation Example As an exercise in tech-stock valuation, let's consider the hypothetical firm Global Applications Software Products (GASP). Actually, although the name is fictitious, the financial statements and values are for a real company operating in roughly the same line of business. GASP is an application software provider, which means that it essentially "hosts" software on its computers and rents this software to other firms. GASP's income statement (see Table 8.7) indicates that revenues for the most recent year were $56.5 million, yet net income was a negative $92.2 million. In other words, the firm had a loss of almost $100 million on sales of some $56 million.

Constructing a set of comparable firms is probably the most challenging part of this valuation process. Investors face a difficult tradeoff: On one hand, the larger the set of comparable firms, the more confident we might be in our estimate of the appropriate multiple. On the other hand, a larger set of com-

TABLE 8.6	Statement of Cash Flows

U.S. Internetworking, Inc.
Statement of Cash Flows
($ in millions)

	For the 9 Months Ended Sept. 30	
	2000	1999
Net loss	($129.4)	($ 69.1)
Other operating activities	36.1	12.6
Net cash flow from operations	**($ 93.3)**	**($ 56.5)**
Net cash flow from investing	**($ 63.0)**	**($ 98.9)**
Payments on long-term debt & capital leases	($ 22.9)	($ 4.5)
Other financing activities	148.0	144.7
Net cash flow from financing	**$125.1**	**$140.2**
Net cash flow	($ 31.2)	($ 15.2)
Cash & equivalents, at beginning of period	$ 112.3	$ 43.8
Cash & equivalents, at end of period	$ 81.1	$ 28.6

parable firms may include some that are not truly similar to the firm being valued. Let's assume that we have collected data on the price/sales ratios and other financial characteristics for five publicly traded companies in roughly the same line of business as GASP, as shown in Table 8.8.

The sales levels of the comparable firms range from $32.2 million for Corio to $128.8 million for Interliant. *Net losses* range from $164 million for U.S. Internetworking to $44 million for Breakaway Solutions. The levels of sales and net losses for GASP are within those ranges, although GASP had lower sales than average ($56.5 million vs. $79.4 million) and generated less of a loss than the average firm ($92.2 million vs. $110.4 million).

TABLE 8.7	Income Statement for a Tech Firm

Global Applications Software Products
Income Statement
Fiscal Year Ended December 31, 2000
($ in thousands)

Sales	$56,500
Expenses	
Direct cost of services	$64,700
Network and infrastructure costs	35,900
General and administrative	22,400
Sales and marketing	59,300
Depreciation and amortization	31,400
Total costs and expenses	$133,700
Operating loss	($77,200)
Interest expense	15,000
Net loss	**($92,200)**

(No taxes are shown because of the operating loss.)

TABLE 8.8	Financial Data on Five Firms Comparable to GASP			
Company Name	Market Cap ($ millions)	Sales ($ millions)	Losses ($ millions)	Price/Sales Ratio
U.S. Internetworking	$532	$ 87	$ -164	5.2
Corio	174	32	-161	2.9
Interliant	313	129	-125	2.3
Navisite	311	50	-58	5.7
Breakaway Solutions	76	99	-44	0.6
Averages	$281.2	$79.4	$ -110.4	3.34

Using the price/sales multiple, the simplest approach is to use the average multiple of the comparable firms to find the value of our GASP shares. But first we have to find sales per share for GASP. Using trailing sales, that can be done by taking the firm's total sales for last year and dividing it by the number of shares outstanding. Assuming 30 million shares outstanding, GASP had trailing sales per share of

$$\$56.5 \text{ million}/30 \text{ million} = \underline{\$1.88/\text{share}}$$

Now, to find the value of a share of GASP stock, we simply multiply the firm's sales per share by the average price to sales ratio (of 3.34 times):

$$\$1.88 \times 3.34 = \underline{\$6.28/\text{share}}$$

Thus we end up with an estimated share price of $6.28.

How does that stack up to our set of comparable firms? To find out, we can convert the GASP share price to a market cap by multiplying price per share by the number of shares outstanding. That results in a market cap of some $188.4 million ($6.28 × 30 million shares). This result is within the range of our five comparable firms, but still below average, so we're probably about where we want to be.

For illustrative purposes, we've greatly simplified the tech-stock valuation process. In practice, you might want to discard one or more of the firms from the comparable analysis, or you might subjectively adjust the average multiple to a higher or lower value on the basis of differences between GASP and the comparables. Or you might want to make some other adjustment based on, say, perceived exposure to risk or perhaps some other variable. The idea is to continue to modify (or "tweak") the P/S ratio until you come up with a multiple that you're comfortable with and that you feel is a proper basis for valuation. Once that's done, the procedure becomes purely mechanical. Simply multiply the ratio you've come up with by the firm's trailing or forward *annual* sales figure. In the case of GASP, if we conclude that a price/sales ratio of around 3.3 to 3.4 is appropriate, then on the basis of trailing annual sales, the stock should be trading for around $6.25 to $6.30 a share. If we can buy it for that price or less, the stock might make a good investment. If not, we'll have to keep looking.

IN REVIEW

8.7 Briefly describe the *dividend valuation model* and the three versions of this model. Explain how CAPM fits into the *variable-growth DVM*.

8.8 What is the difference between the variable-growth dividend valuation model and the *dividends-and-earnings approach* to stock valuation? Which procedure would work better if you were trying to value a growth stock that pays little or no dividends? Explain.

8.9 How would you go about finding the *expected return* on a stock? Note how such information would be used in the stock selection process.

8.10 Briefly describe the *P/E approach* to stock valuation and note how this approach differs from the variable-growth DVM.

8.11 Explain how risk fits into the stock valuation process. Note especially its relationship to the investment return of a security.

8.12 Why are (some) tech stocks difficult to value? What are some of the problems you're likely to encounter in using the DVM or D&E approach to value tech stocks?

8.13 Briefly describe the *price/sales* ratio (multiple), and explain how it is used to value tech stocks. Why not just use the P/E or price-to-book-value multiple?

Technical Analysis

LG 5

technical analysis
the study of the various forces at work in the marketplace and their effect on stock prices.

How many times have you turned on the TV or radio and in the course of the day's news heard a reporter say, "The market was up 47 points today" or "The market remained sluggish in a day of light trading"? Such comments reflect the importance of the stock market itself in determining the price behavior of common stocks. In fact, some experts believe that studying the market should be the major, if not the only, ingredient in the stock selection process. These experts argue that much of what is done in security analysis is useless because it is the *market* that matters, not individual companies. Others argue that studying the stock market is only one element in the security analysis process and is useful in helping the investor time decisions.

Analyzing the various forces at work in the stock market is known as **technical analysis.** For some investors, it's another piece of information to use when deciding whether to buy, hold, or sell a stock. For others, it's the *only* input they use in their investment decisions. And for still others, technical analysis, like fundamental analysis, is regarded as a big waste of time. Here we will assume that technical analysis does have some role to play in the investment decision process. We will examine the major principles of market analysis, as well as some of the techniques used to assess market behavior.

Principles of Market Analysis

Analyzing market behavior dates back to the 1800s, when there was no such thing as industry or company analysis. Detailed financial information simply was not made available to stockholders, let alone the general public. There were no industry figures, balance sheets, or income statements to study, no sales forecasts to make, and no EPS data or P/E multiples. About the only thing investors could study was the market itself. Some investors used detailed charts in an attempt to monitor what large market operators were doing. These charts were intended to show when major buyers were moving into or out of particular stocks and to provide information that could be used to make profitable buy-and-sell decisions. The charts centered on stock price movements. It was believed that these movements produced certain "formations" that indicated when the time was right to buy or sell a particular stock. The same principle is still applied today: Technical analysts argue that internal market factors, such as trading volume and price movements, often reveal the market's future direction long before it is evident in financial statistics.

If the behavior of stock prices were completely independent of market movements, market studies and technical analysis would be useless. But we have ample evidence that stock prices do, in fact, tend to move with the market. Studies of stock betas have shown that as a rule, anywhere from 20% to 50% of the price behavior of a stock can be traced to market forces. When the market is bullish, stock prices in general can be expected to behave accordingly. When the market turns bearish, you can safely expect most issues to be affected by the "downdraft."

Stock prices, in essence, react to various forces of supply and demand that are at work in the market. After all, it's the *demand* for securities and the *supply* of funds in the market that determine whether we're in a bull or a bear market. So long as a given supply-and-demand relationship holds, the market will remain strong (or weak). When the balance begins to shift, however, future prices can be expected to change as the market itself changes. Thus, more than anything else, technical analysis is intended to monitor the pulse of the supply-and-demand forces in the market and to detect any shifts in this important relationship.

Measuring the Market

If assessing the market is a worthwhile endeavor, then we need some sort of tool or measure to do it. Charts are popular with many investors because they provide a visual summary of the behavior of the market and the price movements of individual stocks. As an alternative or supplement to *charting,* some investors prefer to study various *market statistics.* These statistics include the volume of trading, the amount of short selling, and the buying and selling patterns of small investors (odd-lot transactions). This approach is based on the idea that by assessing some of the key elements of market behavior, investors can gain valuable insights into the general condition of the market and, perhaps, where it's headed over the next few months. Normally, several of these measures are used together, either in an informal way or more formally as a series of complex ratios and measures. Although there are many market measures—or *technical indicators,* as they are called—we will confine our discussion here to several of the more widely followed technical measures: (1) market volume, (2) breadth of the market, (3) short interest, and (4) odd-lot trading. In addition to these, the accompanying *Investing in Action* box describes another popular market measure, the *relative strength index* (RSI for short).

INVESTING in action

Relative Strength Weighs In on Buy and Sell Decisions

One of the most widely used technical indicators is the *relative strength index (RSI)*. It is an internal index measuring a security's price relative to itself over time. The RSI indicates a security's momentum, and it gives the best results when used by active investors for short trading periods. It also helps to identify market extremes and points of divergence, signaling that a security is approaching its price top or bottom and may reverse its price trend. (Another type of RSI shows how a security's price movement performs *against a broad market measure* such as the DJIA or S&P 500.)

The RSI is the ratio of the average price change on up days to the average price change on down days during the same period. The index formula is

$$RSI = 100 - \left[100 \bigg/ \left(1 + \frac{\text{Average price change on up days}}{\text{Average price change on down days}} \right) \right]$$

The RSI can cover various periods of time (days, weeks, or months). The most common RSIs at the popular technical-analysis Web sites are 9-, 14-, and 25-period RSIs.

The RSI ranges between 0 and 100. Most RSIs range between 30 and 70. Generally, RSI values above 70–80 indicate an *overbought* condition (more and stronger buying than the fundamentals justify), which may signal that a reversal of the upward price trend is possible. RSI values below 30 indicate a possible *oversold* condition (more selling than fundamentals might indicate) and a possible reversal of the downward trend. When the RSI crosses these points, it signals a possible trend reversal. The wider 80–20 range is often used with the 9-day RSI, which tends to be more volatile than longer-period RSIs. In bull markets, 80 may be a better upper indicator than 70, whereas in bear markets, 20 is a more accurate lower level. Different sectors and industries have varying RSI threshold levels. By watching the RSI over the long

term (one year or more), you can determine the historical RSI trading level and the turning points for a particular stock. Also, the entrance of the RSI into the extreme levels does not mean you should buy or sell, but it does tell you to watch for that possibility.

How can you use the RSI in your own trading? Here are three possible strategies using extremes:

- Buy when the RSI moves above 70 and sell when it falls below 30. However, the trend may have further to run, and you may trade too soon.
- Sell when the RSI crosses below 70 and buy when it moves above 30. This is a popular strategy using 9-day RSIs. However, this strategy has the opposite drawback to the strategy above: You could enter a trade after the trend reversal occurs.
- Sell when an above-70 RSI begins to turn down or buy when a below-30 RSI turns upward. This also has some pitfalls, because the RSI tends to move to extremes during periods of strong price trends and may give false signals.

Another way to use RSIs is to compare price charts and RSIs. Most of the time, both move in the same direction. Hence a divergence between RSI and a price chart can be a strong signal of a changing trend.

Like other technical indicators, the RSI has limitations. It should not be used alone but, rather, works best in combination with other tools such as charting, moving averages, and trendlines. Among the Web sites that offer RSI as a charting option are BigCharts (www.big charts.com) and MetaStock Online (www.metastock.com).

Sources: "Using the Relative Strength Index," *Investopedia.com*, www.investopedia.com; Geoffrey N. Smith, "Riding the Wave," *Fidelity Outlook*, Fall 1999, pp. 8–9; and Wayne A. Thorp, "Measuring Internal Strength: Wilder's Indicator," *AAII Journal*, May 2000, pp. 28–32.

FIGURE 8.1

Some Market Statistics

Individual investors can obtain all sorts of technical information at little or no cost from brokerage houses, investment services, the popular financial media, or the Internet. Here, for example, is a sample of information from the *Wall Street Journal*. Note that a variety of information about market volume, new highs and lows, number of advancing and declining stocks, and market averages is available from this one source. (*Source: Wall Street Journal,* October 10, 2000, p. C2.)

STOCK MARKET DATA BANK   10/9/00

MAJOR INDEXES

†12-MO HIGH	LOW		DAILY HIGH	LOW	CLOSE	NET CHG	% CHG	†12-MO CHG	% CHG	FROM 12/31	% CHG
DOW JONES AVERAGES											
11722.98	9796.03	30 Industrials	10641.31	10546.23	10568.43	− 28.11	− 0.27	− 79.75	− 0.75	− 928.69	− 8.08
3099.67	2263.59	20 Transportation	2543.65	2483.75	2490.63	− 53.02	− 2.08	− 535.39	− 17.69	− 486.57	− 16.34
401.47	269.20	15 Utilities	384.72	378.92	381.50	+ 2.52	+ 0.66	+ 85.78	+ 29.01	+ 98.14	+ 34.63
3305.46	2751.55	65 Composite	3143.80	3113.62	3120.64	− 11.52	− 0.37	+ 31.57	+ 1.02	− 93.74	− 2.92
364.71	285.95	DJ US Total Mkt	330.10	324.80	328.51	− 1.13	− 0.34	+ 22.79	+ 7.46	− 13.06	− 3.82
NEW YORK STOCK EXCHANGE											
677.58	576.17	Composite	656.73	651.55	653.55	− 2.57	− 0.39	+ 40.22	+ 6.56	+ 3.25	+ 0.50
851.94	728.87	Industrials	815.84	809.44	812.68	− 1.08	− 0.13	+ 37.75	+ 4.87	− 15.53	− 1.88
519.96	443.98	Utilities	467.25	462.83	463.74	− 2.90	− 0.62	− 25.86	− 5.28	− 47.41	− 9.28
493.03	353.51	Transportation	412.96	405.09	406.04	− 5.82	− 1.41	− 53.23	− 11.59	− 60.66	− 13.00
634.16	442.71	Finance	606.34	598.22	599.44	− 6.41	− 1.06	+ 104.11	+ 21.02	+ 82.83	+ 16.03
STANDARD & POOR'S INDEXES											
1527.46	1247.41	500 Index	1409.69	1392.48	1402.03	− 6.96	− 0.49	+ 66.82	+ 5.00	− 67.22	− 4.58
1917.64	1544.13	Industrials	1687.16	1664.50	1677.99	− 7.04	− 0.42	+ 29.03	+ 1.76	− 163.93	− 8.90
341.15	215.62	Utilities	326.33	321.87	325.77	+ 3.90	+ 1.21	+ 87.51	+ 36.73	+ 98.55	+ 43.37
548.60	369.50	400 MidCap	513.31	502.85	513.04	+ 0.12	+ 0.02	+ 121.48	+ 31.02	+ 68.37	+ 15.38
225.12	168.96	600 SmallCap	206.57	203.02	206.14	− 0.43	− 0.21	+ 29.36	+ 16.61	+ 8.35	+ 4.22
324.40	262.26	1500 Index	300.76	296.96	299.32	− 1.36	− 0.45	+ 19.36	+ 6.92	− 9.57	− 3.10
NASDAQ STOCK MARKET											
5048.62	2688.18	Composite	3376.92	3233.19	3355.56	− 5.45	− 0.16	+ 439.61	+ 15.08	− 713.75	− 17.54
4704.73	2362.11	Nasdaq 100	3359.93	3185.28	3318.90	+ 6.96	+ 0.21	+ 740.02	+ 28.70	− 388.93	− 10.49
2841.00	1549.93	Industrials	1886.69	1806.19	1879.09	− 3.45	− 0.18	+ 194.58	+ 11.55	− 359.88	− 16.07
2075.12	1602.08	Insurance	1840.73	1818.94	1840.73	− 24.09	− 1.29	− 167.08	− 8.32	− 55.55	− 2.93
1837.10	1340.36	Banks	1749.17	1721.52	1735.59	− 13.50	− 0.77	+ 1.98	+ 0.11	+ 44.30	+ 2.62
2964.66	1448.32	Computer	1946.91	1855.05	1927.72	− 6.74	− 0.35	+ 346.39	+ 21.90	− 397.68	− 17.10
1230.06	639.02	Telecommunications	678.53	645.71	673.67	+ 6.42	+ 0.96	− 33.24	− 4.70	− 341.73	− 33.65
OTHERS											
1036.40	774.49	Amex Composite	923.34	914.11	921.90	+ 1.19	+ 0.13	+ 131.88	+ 16.69	+ 44.93	+ 5.12
813.71	646.79	Russell 1000	752.37	740.87	748.51	− 3.07	− 0.41	+ 57.05	+ 8.25	− 19.46	− 2.53
606.12	408.90	Russell 2000	491.02	481.64	489.53	− 1.49	− 0.30	+ 59.34	+ 13.79	− 15.22	− 3.02
844.78	667.03	Russell 3000	776.72	764.94	773.13	− 3.12	− 0.40	+ 61.54	+ 8.65	− 20.18	− 2.54
439.78	394.35	Value-Line (geom.)	405.45	401.08	405.16	− 0.15	− 0.04	− 15.49	− 3.68	− 25.88	− 6.00
14751.64	11446.60	Wilshire 5000	....	....	13099.79	− 42.37	− 0.32	+ 902.69	+ 7.40	− 712.88	− 5.16

†-Based on comparable trading day in preceding year.

MOST ACTIVE ISSUES

NYSE	VOLUME	CLOSE	CHANGE
Motorola	15,679,200	27.00	− 0.75
Nokia	11,569,900	37.00	− 0.69
NortelNtwks	11,531,400	63.25	+ 0.94
EMC Cp	11,522,500	89.75	+ 0.56
LucentTch	11,443,800	32.31	− 0.94
AT&T	10,183,000	26.56	− 0.69
TX Instr	9,756,500	45.38	− 1.50
GenElec	9,687,200	58.50	− 0.94
SBC Comm	9,384,900	52.44	− 0.88
AmOnline	8,565,400	57.10	− 2.03
AdvMicro	7,879,500	22.38	+ 0.38
MicronTch	7,038,800	39.75	− 1.06
OwenCorn	6,749,100	1.06	+ 0.31
Firstar	6,550,900	17.94	− 1.06
Compaq	6,509,500	25.48	+ 0.47
NASDAQ			
Intel	55,627,000	39.06	− 0.88
CiscoSys	45,487,400	53.69	− 2.50
DellCptr	37,031,700	25.63	+ 0.31
Microsoft	28,166,400	54.19	− 1.38
WorldCom	23,456,400	25.94	+ 0.75
BroadVisn	20,481,800	21.94	+ 3.69
OracleCp	20,037,000	66.75	− 0.88
Connetics	20,027,900	5.31	− 20.19
SunMicrsys	19,674,100	106.81	− 0.69
JDS Uniphs	17,489,000	93.56	+ 2.19
AlteraCp	14,390,100	40.88	− 3.44
AppldMatl	13,702,100	55.75	+ 1.56
Yahoo	12,844,800	85.75	+ 4.50
AMEX			
NASDAQ100	28,825,000	82.63	− 0.38
SPDR	4,499,800	140.00	− 1.06
SPDR Engy	1,375,800	32.75	+ 0.50
Biotch HLDRs	1,028,400	174.50	+ 1.31
S&P Midcap	768,900	94.25	+ 0.25

DIARIES

NYSE	MON	FRI	WK 10/6
Issues traded	3,241	3,284	3,353
Advances	1,194	816	1,265
Declines	1,562	2,009	1,646
Unchanged	485	459	442
New highs	18	47	109
New lows	88	119	75
zAdv vol (000)	302,482	256,079	527,508
zDecl vol (000)	379,166	833,336	438,532
zTotal vol (000)	714,147	1,139,205	1,023,912
Closing tick[1]	− 204	− 747	− 304
Closing Arms[2] (trin)	.96	1.32	.64
zBlock trades	14,794	24,596	21,083
NASDAQ			
Issues traded	4,548	4,596	4,726
Advances	1,497	1,076	1,422
Declines	2,378	2,902	2,731
Unchanged	673	618	573
New highs	16	21	85
New lows	300	313	168
Adv vol (000)	656,400	347,249	445,623
Decl vol (000)	715,415	1,413,816	1,223,868
Total vol (000)	1,401,613	1,801,431	1,721,643
Block trades	n.a.	22,543	20,552
AMEX			
Issues traded	713	742	779
Advances	211	155	225
Declines	346	427	383
Unchanged	156	160	171
New highs	2	3	13
New lows	50	45	32
zAdv vol (000)	8,391	4,400	11,380
zDecl vol (000)	31,759	50,771	30,912
zTotal vol (000)	41,868	57,393	44,746
Comp vol (000)	58,223	78,577	63,237
zBlock trades	n.a.	1,399	954

short interest
the number of stocks sold short in the market at any given time; a technical indicator believed to indicate future market demand.

Market Volume Market volume is an obvious reflection of the amount of investor interest. Volume is a function of the supply of and demand for stock, and it indicates underlying market strengths and weaknesses. The market is considered *strong* when volume goes up in a rising market or drops off during market declines. It is considered *weak* when volume rises during a decline or drops during rallies. For instance, the market would be considered strong if the Dow Jones Industrial Average went up by, say, 108 points while market volume was heavy. Investor eagerness to buy or sell is felt to be captured by market volume figures. The financial press regularly publishes volume data, and investors can conveniently watch this important technical indicator. An example of this and other vital market information is shown in Figure 8.1.

Breadth of the Market Each trading day, some stocks go up in price and others go down. In market terminology, some stocks *advance* and others *decline*. The breadth-of-the-market indicator deals with these advances and declines. The idea is actually quite simple: So long as the number of stocks that advance in price on a given day exceeds the number that decline, the market is considered strong. The extent of that strength depends on the spread between the number of advances and declines. For example, if the spread narrows so that the number of declines starts to approach the number of advances, market strength is said to be deteriorating. Similarly, the market is considered weak when the number of declines repeatedly exceeds the number of advances. The principle behind this indicator is that the number of advances and declines reflects the underlying sentiment of investors. When the mood is optimistic, for example, look for advances to outnumber declines. Again, data on advances and declines are published daily in the financial press.

Short Interest When investors anticipate a market decline, they sometimes sell a stock short. That is, they sell borrowed stock. The number of stocks sold short in the market at any given point in time is known as the **short interest.** The more stocks that are sold short, the higher the short interest. Because all short sales must eventually be "covered" (the borrowed shares must be returned), a short sale in effect ensures *future demand for the stock.* Thus, the market is viewed optimistically when the level of short interest becomes relatively high by historical standards. The logic is that as shares are bought back to cover outstanding short sales, the additional demand will push stock prices up. The amount of short interest on the NYSE, the AMEX, and Nasdaq's National Market is published monthly in the *Wall Street Journal* and *Barron's.* Figure 8.2 shows the type of information that's available.

Keeping track of the level of short interest can indicate future market demand, but it can also reveal *present* market optimism or pessimism. Short selling is usually done by knowledgeable investors, and a significant buildup or decline in the level of short interest is thought to reveal the sentiment of sophisticated investors about the current state of the market or a company. For example, a significant shift upward in short interest is believed to indicate pessimism concerning the *current* state of the market, even though it may signal optimism with regard to *future* levels of demand.

Odd-Lot Trading A rather cynical saying on Wall Street suggests that the best thing to do is just the opposite of whatever the small investor is doing. The reasoning behind this is that as a group, small investors are notoriously wrong in their timing of investment decisions: The investing public usually does not

The amount of short selling in the market is closely watched by many investment professionals and individual investors. The summary report shown here provides an overview of the extent to which stocks are being shorted in the NYSE and the AMEX. In addition to summary statistics, this monthly report lists all stocks that have been sold short and the number of shares shorted. (*Source: Wall Street Journal,* October 20, 2000.)

NYSE AND AMEX SHORT-SELLING HIGHLIGHTS

LARGEST SHORT POSITIONS

RANK	Oct. 13	Sep. 15	CHANGE
NYSE			
1 Sprint Corp PCS	66,415,612	74,456,483	−8,040,871
2 Citigroup Inc	59,637,216	49,068,672	10,568,544
3 Conseco Inc	59,353,764	66,583,520	−7,229,756
4 Disney (Walt)	58,335,995	56,281,733	2,054,262
5 Nortel Networks	53,909,149	49,342,343	4,566,806
6 VodafoneGroPlcAd	51,661,895	47,106,170	4,555,725
7 America Online Inc	49,938,130	56,219,225	−6,281,095
8 Motorola Inc	43,513,358	37,351,171	6,162,187
9 Rite Aid Corp	41,647,092	37,854,017	3,793,075
10 Lucent Techs	39,733,955	30,721,305	9,012,650
11 AT&T Corp	39,382,017	45,378,252	−5,996,235
12 Deutsche Telkom AG	38,821,574	27,056,296	11,765,278
13 Dow Chemical	35,187,991	33,674,653	1,513,338
14 HCA-Healthcare Co.	34,518,092	32,378,947	2,139,145
15 Wal-Mart Stores	33,995,355	35,030,387	−1,035,032
16 Chase Manhattan	30,865,889	7,336,920	23,528,969
17 Adv Micro Dev Inc.	30,368,955	25,631,649	4,737,306
18 General Electric	27,419,114	27,622,049	−202,935
19 Telefonos Mex Serl	27,175,400	28,008,846	−833,446
20 Wells Fargo Co	26,907,461	23,438,098	3,469,363
AMEX			
1 Nasdaq-100 Trust	43,061,899	51,574,112	−8,512,213
2 SPDR	15,145,106	14,877,818	267,288
3 Nabor Indus Inc	10,054,415	9,649,077	405,338
4 Trans World Airlin	9,233,693	9,673,034	−439,341
5 Ivax Corp	6,758,079	7,387,020	−628,941

LARGEST CHANGES

RANK	Oct. 13	Sep. 15	CHANGE
NYSE			
POSITIVE			
1 Chase Manhattan	30,865,889	7,336,920	23,528,969
2 Federal-Mogul	18,858,451	4,338,848	14,519,603
3 Deutsche Telkom AG	38,821,574	27,056,296	11,765,278
4 Citigroup Inc	59,637,216	49,068,672	10,568,544
5 Lucent Techs	39,733,955	30,721,305	9,012,650
6 Tyco Intl	25,881,088	17,064,934	8,816,154
7 NiSource Inc	18,143,636	11,517,539	6,626,097
8 Motorola Inc	43,513,358	37,351,171	6,162,187
NEGATIVE			
1 Sprint Corp PCS	66,415,612	74,456,483	−8,040,871
2 Conseco Inc	59,353,764	66,583,520	−7,229,756
3 America Online Inc	49,938,130	56,219,225	−6,281,095
4 AT&T Corp	39,382,017	45,378,252	−5,996,235
5 Compaq Computer	20,483,166	26,301,585	−5,818,419
6 ClearChannelCommun	14,613,705	20,108,201	−5,494,496
7 Micron Technology	12,028,233	16,242,673	−4,214,440
8 Limited Inc	7,468,738	11,520,926	−4,052,188
AMEX			
POSITIVE			
1 SPDR Enrgy Sel XLE	4,328,985	1,511,584	2,817,401
2 SPDR Fin Selct XLF	3,269,081	720,753	2,548,328
3 SPDR Cycl/Trans	1,643,780	232,040	1,411,740
4 Biotech Holdrs Tru	3,194,219	2,195,468	998,751
5 iShares S&P500	1,815,197	1,138,255	676,942
NEGATIVE			
1 Nasdaq-100 Trust	43,061,899	51,574,112	−8,512,213
2 S&P MidCap	2,428,659	3,661,636	−1,232,977
3 U.S. Cellular Corp	3,693,788	4,688,187	−994,399
4 iShares MSCI UK	71,920	793,733	−721,813
5 Ivax Corp	6,758,079	7,387,020	−628,941

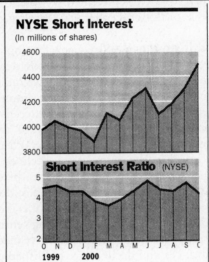

NYSE Short Interest (In millions of shares)

Short Interest Ratio (NYSE)

O N D J F M A M J J A S O
1999 2000

LARGEST SHORT INTEREST RATIOS

The short interest ratio is the number of days it would take to cover the short interest if trading continued at the average daily volume for the month.

RANK	Oct. 13 SHORT INT.	AVG DLY VOL-a	DAYS TO COVER
NYSE			
1 Philippine LdTel-G	1,839,900	1,605	1,146
2 Madeco Adr	4,170,300	15,335	272
3 Quebecor World Inc	1,181,093	5,715	207
4 Comp Cerv Unidas	4,161,100	29,225	142
5 Co Siderurgica ADS	4,034,006	31,815	127
6 Royal Group Techno	3,081,090	26,165	118
7 Compnha Vle DoRioD	14,830,873	151,035	98
8 FltchrChlBlgADS	2,000,900	24,150	83
9 Advocat Inc	1,945,200	29,375	66
10 Vector Group LTD	1,577,345	25,530	62
11 TelecomNZ ADR	4,108,655	65,915	62
12 Revlon Inc. Cl A	3,400,272	58,330	58
13 Total Sys Svcs	1,735,756	29,905	58
14 Nova Chemicals	1,225,518	21,895	56
15 Penn Treaty Americ	954,091	18,175	52
16 Chiquita Brands	3,827,179	78,880	49
17 Aviation Sales	2,563,891	54,405	47
18 Coachmen Indus	1,133,375	24,055	47
AMEX			
1 Blackrock 1999 Ter	1,500,061	6,225	241
2 BioTime Inc	1,441,606	22,630	64
3 iShares MSCI Mexico	2,005,032	33,160	60
4 Hemispherx Biophar	3,584,269	64,320	56
5 Alterra Healthcare	2,493,147	73,055	34

a-Includes securities with average daily volume of 20,000 shares or more. n-New. r-Revised.
Issues that split in the latest month are excluded.
The largest percentage increase and decrease sections are limited to issues with previously established short provisions in both months.

LARGEST % INCREASES

RANK	Oct. 13	Sep. 15	%
NYSE			
1 Conectiv	2,802,595	264,949	957.8
2 Gulf Canada Resour	3,368,086	341,607	886.0
3 GPU Inc	1,808,172	381,978	373.4
4 Federal-Mogul	18,858,451	4,338,848	334.6
5 Chase Manhattan	30,865,889	7,336,920	320.7
6 Alliant Energy	1,306,216	364,477	258.4
7 Gabelli Eqty Tr	964,100	284,662	238.7
8 AmbacFinlGrp	984,589	299,174	229.1
9 Vivendi	4,806,932	1,559,812	208.2
10 JohnsonControls	1,081,475	379,814	184.7
11 Analog Devices Inc	5,289,947	1,893,027	179.4
12 Scana Corp	1,629,705	625,838	160.4
13 Intl Game Tech	2,519,920	1,032,534	144.1
14 Korea Telecom	1,121,799	459,884	143.9
15 Paine Webber Grp	1,957,592	841,000	132.8
16 Rockwell Intl	3,774,401	1,663,914	126.8
17 SunGard Data Systm	3,930,772	1,762,217	123.1
18 Pitney Bowes	4,653,647	2,090,339	122.6
19 United Technolgies	4,558,864	2,051,191	122.3
20 Furniture Brands	1,208,087	545,090	121.6
AMEX			
1 SPDR Cycl/Trans	1,643,780	232,040	608.4
2 SPDR Fin Selct XLF	3,269,081	720,753	353.6
3 SPDR Enrgy Sel XLE	4,328,985	1,511,584	186.4
4 iShares S&P500	1,815,197	1,138,255	59.5
5 Biotech Holdrs Tru	3,194,219	2,195,468	45.5

LARGEST % DECREASES

RANK	Oct. 13	Sep. 15	%
NYSE			
1 Pearson PLC	146,001	1,240,855	−88.2
2 Energy East Cp-Hld	114,351	936,646	−87.8
3 Repsol YPE S.A.Ads	379,705	2,136,419	−82.2
4 Homestake Mining	939,550	4,797,345	−80.4
5 Northeast Util	250,892	1,263,620	−80.1
6 UltramarDiamondShm	353,513	1,408,915	−74.9
7 Unicom Corp	775,030	2,564,199	−69.8
8 Ahold NV ADS	474,805	1,483,099	−68.0
9 Nabisco Grp Hldgs	489,992	1,483,293	−67.0
10 Praxair Inc	700,894	1,877,167	−62.7
11 Scientific-Atlanta	732,349	1,914,601	−61.7
12 TXU Corp	2,328,336	6,079,240	−61.7
13 Lincoln Natl Corp	1,079,785	2,799,976	−61.4
14 Stora Enso Oyj	1,066,432	2,764,438	−61.4
15 OGE Energy Corp	1,180,221	2,946,598	−59.9
16 Taiwan Semi	2,525,063	6,088,230	−58.5
17 Fox Entertainment	1,214,996	2,899,208	−58.1
18 Intrstate Bakeries	537,136	1,263,873	−57.5
19 Sherwn-Williams	729,687	1,694,424	−56.9
20 Hillenbrand Indus	657,187	1,453,999	−54.8
AMEX			
1 iShares MSCI UK	71,920	793,733	−90.9
2 S&P MidCap	2,428,659	3,661,636	−33.7
3 U.S. Cellular Corp	3,693,788	4,688,187	−21.2
4 Diamonds Trust	1,981,893	2,375,294	−16.6
5 Nasdaq-100 Trust	43,061,899	51,574,112	−16.5

come into the market in force until after a bull market has pretty much run its course, and it does not get out until late in a bear market. Although its validity is debatable, this is the premise behind a widely followed technical indicator and is the basis for the **theory of contrary opinion.** This theory uses the amount and type of odd-lot trading as an indicator of the current state of the market and pending changes.

theory of contrary opinion
a technical indicator that uses the amount and type of odd-lot trading as an indicator of the current state of the market and pending changes.

Because many individual investors deal in transactions of less than 100 shares, their combined sentiments are supposedly captured in odd-lot figures. The idea is to see what odd-lot investors are doing "on balance." So long as there is little or no difference in the spread between the volume of odd-lot purchases and sales, the theory of contrary opinion holds that the market will probably continue pretty much along its current line (either up or down). When the balance of odd-lot purchases and sales begins to change dramatically, it may be a signal that a bull or bear market is about to end. For example, if the amount of odd-lot purchases starts to exceed odd-lot sales by an ever widening margin, it may suggest that speculation on the part of small investors is starting to get out of control—an ominous signal that the final stages of a bull market may be at hand.

Using Technical Analysis

Investors have a wide range of choices with respect to technical analysis. They can use the charts and complex ratios of the technical analysts. Or they can, more informally, use technical analysis just to get a general sense of the market. In the latter case, market behavior itself is not as important as the implications such behavior can have on the price performance of a particular stock. Thus technical analysis might be used in conjunction with fundamental analysis to determine when to add a particular stock to one's portfolio. Some investors and professional money managers, in fact, look at the technical side of a stock *before* doing any fundamental analysis. If the stock is found to be technically sound, then they'll look at its fundamentals; if not, they'll look for another stock. For these investors, the concerns of technical analysis are still the same: *Do the technical factors indicate that this might be a good stock to buy?*

Most investors rely on published sources, such as those put out by brokerage firms—or, now, widely available on the Internet—to obtain necessary technical insights. They often find it helpful to use several different approaches. For example, an investor might follow market P/Es and dividend yields and also keep track of market volume and breadth of the market. Such information provides the investor with a convenient and low-cost way of staying abreast of the market. Certainly, trying to determine the right (or best) time to get into the market is a principal objective of technical analysis—and one of the major pastimes of many investors.

Charting

charting
the activity of charting price behavior and other market information and then using the patterns these charts form to make investment decisions.

Charting is perhaps the best-known activity of the technical analyst. Technicians—analysts who believe it is chiefly (or solely) supply and demand that drives stock prices—use various types of charts to plot the behavior of everything from the Dow Jones Industrial Average to the share price movements of individual listed and OTC stocks. Just about every kind of technical

FIGURE 8.3   A Stock Chart

This chart for Medtronics, Inc. contains information about the daily price behavior of the stock, along with the stock's relative strength, its moving average, its trading volume, and several other pieces of supplementary data. (*Source:* Chart courtesy of Stockcharts.com *Note:* Visit this Web site's glossary for expanded definitions.)

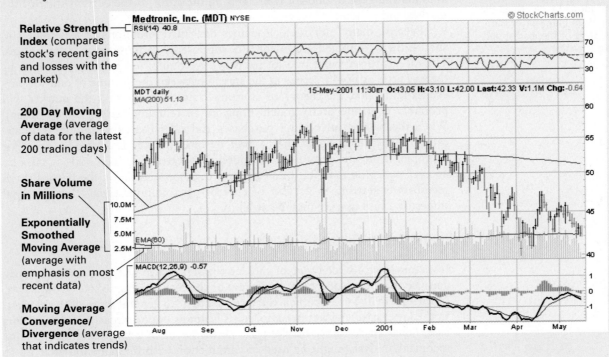

Relative Strength Index (compares stock's recent gains and losses with the market)

200 Day Moving Average (average of data for the latest 200 trading days)

Share Volume in Millions

Exponentially Smoothed Moving Average (average with emphasis on most recent data)

Moving Average Convergence/ Divergence (average that indicates trends)

---

indicator is charted in one form or another. Figure 8.3 shows a typical stock chart. In this case, the price behavior of Medtronic, Inc. has been plotted, along with a variety of supplementary technical information about the stock.

Charts are popular because they provide a visual summary of activity over time. Perhaps more important (in the eyes of technicians, at least), they contain valuable information about developing trends and the future behavior of the market and/or individual stocks. Chartists believe price patterns evolve into *chart formations* that provide signals about the future course of the market or a stock. We will now briefly review the practice of charting, including popular types of charts, chart formations, and investor uses of charts.

Bar Charts The simplest and probably most widely used type of chart is the **bar chart**. Market or share prices are plotted on the vertical axis, and time is plotted on the horizontal axis. This type of chart derives its name from the fact that prices are recorded as vertical bars that depict high, low, and closing prices. A typical bar chart is shown in Figure 8.4. Note that on December 31, this particular stock had a high price of 29 a low of 27, and closed at 27.50. Because these charts contain a time element, technicians frequently plot a variety of other pertinent information on them. For example, volume is often put at the base of bar charts (see the Medtronic chart in Figure 8.3).

Point-and-Figure Charts **Point-and-figure charts** are used strictly to keep track of emerging price patterns. Because there is no time dimension on them, they are *not* used for plotting technical measures. Point-and-figure charts are unique in

bar chart
the simplest kind of chart, on which share price is plotted on the vertical axis and time on the horizontal axis; stock prices are recorded as vertical bars showing high, low, and closing prices.

point-and-figure charts
charts used to keep track of emerging price patterns by plotting significant price changes with *X*s and *O*s but with no time dimension used.

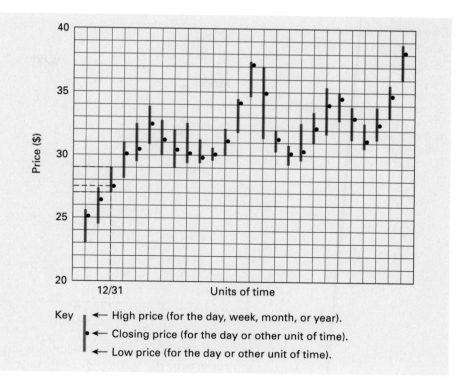

FIGURE 8.4

A Bar Chart

Bar charts are widely used to track stock prices, market averages, and numerous other technical measures.

Key
← High price (for the day, week, month, or year).
← Closing price (for the day or other unit of time).
← Low price (for the day or other unit of time).

two other ways: First, only *significant* price changes are recorded on these charts. That is, prices have to move by a certain minimum amount—usually at least a point or two—before a new price level is recognized. Second, price *reversals* show up only after a predetermined change in direction occurs. Normally, only closing prices are charted, though some point-and-figure charts use all price changes during the day. An *X* is used to denote an increase in price, an *O* a decrease.

Figure 8.5 shows a common point-and-figure chart. In this case, the chart employs a 2-point box: The stock must move by a minimum of 2 points before any changes are recorded. The chart can cover a span of one year or less if the stock is highly active. Or it can cover a number of years if the stock is not very active. As a rule, low-priced stocks are charted with 1-point boxes, moderately priced shares with increments of 2 to 3 points, and high-priced securities with 3- to 5-point boxes.

Here is how point-and-figure charts work: Suppose we are at point A on the chart in Figure 8.5. The stock has been hovering around this $40–$41 mark for some time. Assume, however, that it just closed at $42.25. Now, because the minimum 2-point movement has been met, the chartist would place an X in the box immediately *above* point A. The chartist would remain with this new box as long as the price moved (up or down) within the 2-point range of 42 to 44. Although the chartist follows *daily* prices, a new entry is made on the chart only after the price has changed by a certain minimum amount and moved into a new 2-point box. We see that from point A, the price generally moved up over time to nearly $50 a share. At that point (indicated as point B on the chart), things began to change as a reversal set in. That is, the price of the stock began to drift downward and in time moved out of the $48–$50 box. This reversal prompts the chartist to change columns and symbols, by moving one column to the right and recording the new price level with an O in the $46–$48 box. The chartist will continue to use Os as long as the stock continues to close on a generally lower note.

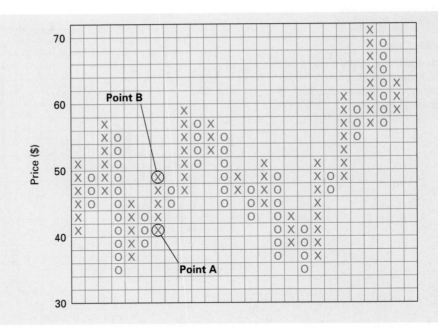

Chart Formations The information that charts supposedly contain about the future course of the market (or a stock) is thought by some to be revealed in chart *formations*. That is, chartists believe that in response to certain supply and demand forces, emerging price patterns result in various formations that historically have indicated that certain types of market behavior are imminent. If you know how to interpret charts (which is no easy task), you can see formations building and recognize buy and sell signals. These chart formations are often given some pretty exotic names, such as *head and shoulders, falling wedge, scallop and saucer, ascending triangle,* and *island reversal,* to name just a few.

Figure 8.6 shows four formations. The patterns form "support levels" and "resistance lines" that, when combined with the basic formations, yield buy and sell signals. Panel A is an example of a *buy* signal that occurs when prices break out above a resistance line in a particular pattern. In contrast, when prices break out below a support level, as they do at the end of the formation in panel B, a *sell* signal is said to occur. Supposedly, a sell signal means everything is in place for a major drop in the market (or in the price of a share of stock). A buy signal indicates that the opposite is about to occur. Unfortunately, one of the major problems with charting is that the formations rarely appear as neatly and cleanly as those in Figure 8.6. Rather, identifying and interpreting them often demands considerable imagination.

Investor Uses Charts are merely tools used by market analysts and technicians to assess conditions in the market and/or the price behavior of individual stocks. Unlike other types of technical measures, charting is seldom done on an informal basis. Either you chart because you believe in its value, or you don't chart at all. A chart by itself tells you little more than where the market or a stock has been. But to chartists, those price patterns yield formations that, along with things like resistance lines, support levels, and breakouts, tell them what to expect in the future. Chartists believe that history repeats itself, so they study the historical reactions of stocks (or the market) to various formations, and they devise trading rules based on these observations. It makes no

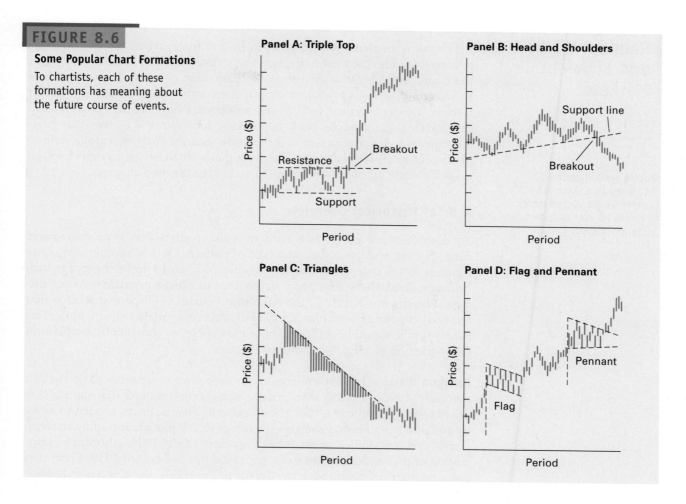

FIGURE 8.6

Some Popular Chart Formations

To chartists, each of these formations has meaning about the future course of events.

difference to chartists whether they are following the market or an individual stock. *It is the formation that matters,* not the issue being plotted. The value of charts lies in knowing how to "read" them and how to respond to the signals they are said to give about the future. A long-standing debate (some would call it a feud) still rages on Wall Street regarding the merits of charting. Although a large segment of investors and investment professionals may scoff at it, to avid chartists, charting is no laughing matter.

IN REVIEW

CONCEPTS

8.14 What is the purpose of *technical analysis?* Explain how and why it is used by technicians; note how it can be helpful in timing investment decisions.

8.15 Can the market really have a measurable effect on the price behavior of individual securities? Explain.

8.16 What is the *relative strength index* (as described in the *Investing in Action* box on page 345)?

8.17 What is a stock chart? What kind of information can be put on charts, and what is the purpose of charting?
   a. What is the difference between a bar chart and a point-and-figure chart?
   b. What are chart formations, and why are they important?

Random Walks and Efficient Markets

LG 6

random walk hypothesis
the theory that stock price movements are unpredictable, so there's no way to know where prices are headed.

If a drunk were abandoned in an open field at night, where would you begin to search for him the next morning? The answer, of course, is the spot where the drunk was left the night before, because there's no way to predict where he will go. To some analysts, stock prices seem to wander about in a similar fashion. Observations of such erratic movements have led to a body of evidence called the **random walk hypothesis**. Its followers believe that price movements are unpredictable and therefore security analysis will not help to predict future market behavior. This hypothesis obviously has serious implications for much of what we have discussed in the last two chapters.

A Brief Historical Overview

To describe stock prices as a random walk suggests that price movements cannot be expected to follow any type of pattern. Or, put another way, price movements are independent of one another. In order to find a theory for such behavior, researchers developed the concept of efficient markets. As we discussed briefly in Chapter 7, the basic idea behind an efficient market is that the market price of securities always fully reflects available information. This means that it would be difficult, if not impossible, to consistently outperform the market by picking "undervalued" stocks.

Random Walks The first evidence of random price movements dates back to the early 1900s. During that period, statisticians noticed that commodity prices seemed to follow a "fair game" pattern. That is, prices seemed to move up and down randomly, giving no advantage to any particular trading strategy. Although a few studies on the subject appeared in the 1930s, thorough examination of the randomness in stock prices did not begin until 1959. From that point on, particularly through the decade of the 1960s, the random walk issue was one of the most keenly debated topics in stock market literature. The development of high-speed computers has helped researchers compile convincing evidence that stock prices do, in fact, come very close to a random walk.

Efficient Markets Given the extensive random walk evidence, market researchers were faced with another question: What sort of market would produce prices that seem to fluctuate randomly? Such behavior could be the result of investors who are irrational and make investment decisions on whim. However, it has been argued much more convincingly that investors are not irrational. Rather, random price movements are evidence of highly efficient markets.

efficient market
a market in which securities reflect all possible information quickly and accurately.

An **efficient market** is one in which securities fully reflect all possible information quickly and accurately. The concept holds that investors incorporate all available information into their decisions about the price at which they are willing to buy or sell. At any point in time, then, the current price of a security incorporates all information. Additionally, the current price reflects not only past information, such as might be found in company reports and financial publications, but also information about events that have been announced but haven't yet occurred, like a forthcoming dividend payment. Furthermore, the current price reflects *predictions* about future information: Investors actively forecast important events and incorporate those forecasts into their estimates. Obviously, because of keen competition among investors, when new information becomes known, the price of the security adjusts quickly. This adjustment is not always perfect. Sometimes it is too large and at other times too small. But on average it balances out and is correct. The new price, in effect, is set after investors have fully assessed the new information.

Why Should Markets Be Efficient?

Active markets, such as the New York Stock Exchange, are efficient because they are made up of many rational, highly competitive investors who react quickly and objectively to new information. Investors, searching for market profits, compete vigorously for new information and do extremely thorough analyses. The **efficient markets hypothesis (EMH)**, which is the basic theory describing the behavior of such a market, has several tenets:

1. There are many knowledgeable investors actively analyzing, valuing, and trading any particular security. No one of these individual traders alone can affect the price of any security.
2. Information is widely available to all investors at approximately the same time, and this information is practically "free," or nearly so.
3. Information on events, such as labor strikes, industrial accidents, and changes in product demand, tends to occur randomly.
4. Investors react quickly and accurately to new information, causing prices to adjust quickly and, on average, accurately.

For the most part, the securities markets do, in fact, exhibit these characteristics.

efficient markets hypothesis (EMH)
basic theory of the behavior of efficient markets, in which there are a large number of knowledgeable investors who react quickly to new information, causing securities prices to adjust quickly and accurately.

Levels of Market Efficiency

The efficient markets hypothesis is concerned with *information*—not only the type and source of information, but also the quality and speed with which it is disseminated among investors. It is convenient to discuss the EMH in three cumulative categories or forms: past prices only; past prices *plus* all other public data, and, finally, past prices and public data *plus* private information. Together, these three ways of looking at information flows in the market represent three forms of the EMH: the weak, semi-strong, and strong forms.

weak form (EMH)
form of the EMH holding that past data on stock prices are of no use in predicting future prices.

Weak Form The **weak form of the EMH** holds that past data on stock prices are of no use in predicting future price changes. If prices follow a random walk, price changes over time are random. Today's price change is unrelated to yesterday's or to that of any other day, just as each step by a drunk is unrelated to previous steps. If new information arrives randomly, then prices will change randomly.

A number of people have asserted that it is possible to profit from "runs" in a stock's price. They contend that when a stock's price starts moving up, it will continue to move up for a period of time, developing momentum. If you can spot a run, then, on the basis of past prices alone, you can develop a trading strategy that will produce a profit. The results from much careful research suggest that momentum in stock prices does exist, and if investors quickly trade at the beginning of the run, large profits can be made. But there's a problem: In addition to spotting a run (no easy task), an investor would have to make numerous trades; when commissions are factored in, the person most likely to make a profit is the broker. Many other trading rules have been tested to determine whether profits can be made by examining past price movements, and there is very little, if any, evidence that a trading rule *based solely on past price data* can outperform a simple buy-and-hold strategy.

Semi-Strong Form   The **semi-strong form of the EMH** holds that abnormally large profits cannot be consistently earned using publicly available information. This information includes not only past price and volume data but also data such as corporate earnings, dividends, inflation, and stock splits. The semi-strong information set includes all of the information publicly considered in the weak form, *as well as all other information publicly available*. Tests of the semi-strong form of the EMH are basically concerned with the speed at which information is disseminated to investors. The research conclusions of research tests support the position that stock prices adjust very rapidly to new information and therefore support the semi-strong form of the EMH.

Most tests of semi-strong efficiency have examined how a stock price changes in response to an economic or financial event. A famous study involved stock splits. A stock split does not change the value of a company, so the value of the stock should not be affected by a stock split. The research indicated that there are sharp increases in the price of a stock *before* a stock split, but the changes after the split are random. Investors, therefore, cannot gain by purchasing stocks on or after the announcement of a split. To earn abnormal profits they would have to purchase before the split is announced. By the time of the announcement, the market has already incorporated into the price any favorable information associated with the split.

Other studies have examined the impact of major events on stock prices. The overwhelming evidence indicates that stock prices react within minutes, if not seconds, to any important new information. Certainly, by the time an investor reads about the event in the newspaper, the stock price has almost completely adjusted to the news. Even hearing about the event on the radio or television usually allows too little time to complete the transaction in time to make an abnormal profit.

Strong Form   The **strong form of the EMH** holds that there is no information, public or private, that allows investors to consistently earn abnormal profits. It states that stock prices immediately adjust to any information, even if it isn't available to every investor. This extreme form of the EMH has not received universal support.

One type of private information is the kind obtained by corporate insiders, such as officers or directors of a corporation. They have access to valuable information about major strategic and tactical decisions the company makes. They also have detailed information about the financial state of the firm that may not be available to other shareholders. Corporate insiders may legally trade shares of stock in their company, if they report the transactions to the Securities and Exchange Commission (SEC) each month. This information is then made public, usually within several weeks. It should not be surprising to learn that most studies of corporate insiders find that they consistently earn abnormally large profits when they sell their company stock. They are able to sell stock holdings before major announcements are made to the public and can thereby profit from the stock price adjustment that comes quickly after important news is released.

---

semi-strong form (EMH)
form of the EMH holding that abnormally large profits cannot be consistently earned using publicly available information.

strong form (EMH)
form of the EMH that holds that there is no information, public or private, that allows investors to earn abnormal profits consistently.

Other market participants occasionally have inside—nonpublic—information that they obtained *illegally*. With this information, they can gain an unfair advantage that permits them to earn an excess return. Clearly, those who trade securities on the basis of illegal inside information have an unfair advantage. Empirical research has confirmed that those with such inside information do indeed have an opportunity to earn an excess return—but there might be an awfully high price attached, such as spending time in prison, if they're caught.

Possible Implications

The concept of an efficient market holds serious implications for investors. In particular, it could have considerable bearing on traditional security analysis and stock valuation procedures. Some, in fact, contend that investors should spend less time analyzing securities and more time on such matters as reducing taxes and transaction costs, eliminating unnecessary risk, and constructing a widely diversified portfolio. Make no mistake about it: *Even in an efficient market, all sorts of return opportunities are available.* But to proponents of efficient markets, the only way to increase returns is to invest in a portfolio of higher-risk securities.

Implications for Technical Analysis The most serious challenge the random walk evidence presents is to technical analysis. If price fluctuations are purely random, charts of past prices are unlikely to produce significant trading profits. In a highly efficient market, shifts in supply and demand occur so rapidly that technical indicators simply measure after-the-fact events, with no implications for the future. But if markets are less than perfectly efficient, information may be absorbed slowly, producing gradual shifts in supply and demand conditions—and profit opportunities for those who recognize the shifts early. Although the great bulk of evidence supports a random walk, many investors follow a technical approach because they believe it improves their investment results.

Implications for Fundamental Analysis Many strict fundamental analysts were at first pleased by the random walk attack on technical analysis. Further development of the efficient markets concept, however, was not so well received: In an efficient market, it's argued, prices react so quickly to new information that not even security analysis will enable investors to realize consistently superior returns. Because of the extreme competition among investors, security prices are seldom far above or below their justified levels, and fundamental analysis thus loses much of its value. The problem is not that fundamental analysis is poorly done. On the contrary, it is done all too well! So many investors, competing so vigorously for profit opportunities, simply eliminate the opportunities before other investors can capitalize on them.

So Who Is Right?

Some type of fundamental analysis probably has a role in the stock selection process, for even in an efficient market, there is no question that stock prices reflect a company's profit performance. Some companies are fundamentally strong and others fundamentally weak, and investors must be able to distinguish between the two. Thus some time can profitably be spent in evaluating a company and its stock to determine, not if it is undervalued, but whether it is fundamentally strong.

The level of investor return, however, is more than a function of the fundamental condition of the company; it is also related to risk exposure. Fundamental analysis can help assess risk exposure and identify securities that possess risk commensurate with the return they offer.

The extent to which the markets are efficient is still subject to considerable debate. At present, there seems to be a growing consensus that although the markets may not be *perfectly* efficient, evidence suggests that they are at least *reasonably* efficient.

In the final analysis, the individual investor must decide on the merits of fundamental and technical analysis. Certainly, a large segment of the investing public believes in security analysis, even in a market that may be efficient. What is more, the principles of stock valuation—that promised return should be commensurate with exposure to risk—are valid in any type of market setting.

IN REVIEW

CONCEPTS

8.18 What is the *random walk hypothesis,* and how does it apply to stocks? What is an *efficient market?* How can a market be efficient if its prices behave in a random fashion?

8.19 Explain why it is difficult, if not impossible, to consistently outperform an efficient market.
a. Does this mean that high rates of return are not available in the stock market?
b. How can an investor earn a high rate of return in an efficient market?

8.20 What are the implications of random walks and efficient markets for technical analysis? For fundamental analysis? Do random walks and efficient markets mean that technical analysis and fundamental analysis are useless? Explain.

Summary

LG 1 **Explain the role a company's future plays in the stock valuation process and develop a forecast of a stock's expected cash flow.** The final phase of security analysis involves an assessment of the investment merits of a specific company and its stock. The focus here is on formulating expectations about the company's prospects and the risk and return behavior of the stock. In particular, we would want some idea of the stock's future earnings, dividends, and share prices, because that's ultimately the basis of our return.

LG 2 **Discuss the concepts of intrinsic value and required rates of return, and note how they are used.** Information such as projected sales, forecasted earnings, and estimated dividends are important in establishing intrinsic value. This is a measure, based on expected return and on risk exposure, of what the stock ought to be worth. A key element is the investor's required rate of return, which is used to define the amount of return that should be earned given the stock's perceived exposure to risk. The more risk in the investment, the more return one should require.

LG 3   Determine the underlying value of a stock using the dividend valuation model, as well as other present value– and price/earnings–based stock valuation models. The dividend valuation model derives the value of a share of stock from the stock's future growth in dividends. Another popular valuation procedure is the dividends-and-earnings approach, which uses a finite investment horizon to derive a present value–based "justified price." There's also the price/earnings approach to stock valuation, which uses projected EPS and the stock's P/E ratio to determine whether a stock is fairly valued. At times, investors find it more convenient to deal in terms of expected returns than in dollar-based justified prices. To do so, one would find the fully compounded rate of return by solving for the discount rate in the present value–based stock valuation model.

LG 4   Gain a basic appreciation of the procedures used to value different types of stock, from traditional dividend-paying shares to new-economy stocks with their extreme price/earnings ratios. Various forms of the dividend valuation model work fine for companies that pay dividends. For those that pay little or nothing in dividends, the dividend-and-earnings and P/E approaches are used. But even these procedures often don't work well with many of the new-economy tech stocks, which may not have dividends, may not even have profits, and may sell at astronomical P/E ratios. To value these stocks, we use the discounted cash flow approach (which is like the D&E approach except that value is based solely on the estimated future price of the stock) or some type of price multiple (usually, the price/sales multiple). Though far from perfect, these procedures at least enable investors to get a rough idea of the value of these high-flying tech stocks.

LG 5   Describe the key attributes of technical analysis, including some popular measures and procedures used to assess the market. Technical analysis is another phase of the analytical process. It deals with the behavior of the stock market itself and the various economic forces at work in the marketplace. A number of tools can be used to assess the state of the market, including market measures like volume of trading, breadth of the market, short-interest positions, odd-lot trading, and relative strength. Some investors use charting to assess the condition of everything from the overall market to specific stocks.

LG 6   Discuss the idea of random walks and efficient markets, and note the challenges these theories hold for the stock valuation process. In recent years, both technical and fundamental analysis have been seriously challenged by the random walk and efficient market hypotheses. Indeed, considerable evidence indicates that stock prices do move in a random fashion. The efficient market hypothesis is an attempt to explain *why* prices behave randomly. The idea behind an efficient market is that available information is always fully reflected in the price of securities, so investors should *not* expect to outperform the market consistently.

Discussion Questions

LG 1

LG 2

 LG 3

Q8.1   Using the resources available at your campus or public library, select a company from *Value Line* that would be of interest to you. (*Hint:* Pick a company that's been publicly traded for at least 10 to 15 years, and avoid public utilities, banks, and other financial institutions.) Obtain a copy of the latest *Value Line* report on your chosen company. Using the historical and forecasted data reported in *Value Line,* along with one of the valuation techniques described in this chapter, calculate the maximum (i.e., justified) price you'd be willing to pay for this stock. Use the CAPM to find the required rate of return on your stock. (For this problem, use a market rate of return of 12%, and for the risk-free rate, use the latest 3-month Treasury bill rate.)

  a. How does the justified price you computed above compare to the latest market price of the stock?

  b. Would you consider this stock a worthwhile investment candidate? Explain.

LG 5 **Q8.2** Briefly define each of the following, and note the conditions that would suggest the market is technically strong.
  a. Breadth of the market.
  b. Short interest.
  c. The relative strength index (RSI).
  d. Theory of contrary opinion.
  e. Head and shoulders.

LG 6 **Q8.3** A lot has been written and said about the concept of an *efficient market*. It's probably safe to say that some of your classmates believe the markets are efficient and others believe they are not. Have a debate to see whether you can resolve this issue (at least among yourselves). Pick a side, either for or against efficient markets, and then develop your "ammunition." Be prepared to discuss these three aspects:
  a. Exactly what is an efficient market? Do such markets really exist?
  b. Are stock prices always (or nearly always) correctly set in the market? If so, does that mean there's little opportunity to find undervalued stocks?
  c. Can you find any reason(s) to use fundamental and/or technical analysis in your stock selection process? If not, how would you go about selecting stocks?

LG 4 **Q8.4** The *burn rate* is a concept that is often employed to help investors gain insights about performance of tech stocks, especially relatively new high-tech firms (those that have recently gone public). Define the burn rate, and explain how it is used in the valuation of tech stocks. Is it used to actually put a value on tech stocks. Explain.
  a. Take another look at Table 8.6. Using the 1999 statement of cash flows, find the *monthly* burn rate based on *net cash flows from operations*. (Remember that the statements cover only 9 months.) What is the *monthly* burn rate if you include the net cash flows from *both* operations and investing? If the firm had $150 million cash on hand, how long would it take to run out of cash at these burn rates? What can the firm do to avoid running out of cash?

Problems

LG 1   **P8.1** An investor estimates that next year's sales for New World Products should amount to about $75 million. The company has 2.5 million shares outstanding, generates a net profit margin of about 5%, and has a payout ratio of 50%. All figures are expected to hold for next year. Given this information, compute the following.
  a. Estimated net earnings for next year.
  b. Next year's dividends per share.
  c. The expected price of the stock (assuming the P/E ratio is 24.5 times earnings).
  d. The expected holding period return (latest stock price: $25/share).

  LG 2 **P8.2** Charlene Lewis is thinking about buying some shares of Education, Inc. at $50 per share. She expects the price of the stock to rise to $75 over the next 3 years. During that time she also expects to receive annual dividends of $5 per share.
  a. What is the intrinsic worth of this stock, given a 10% required rate of return?
  b. What is its expected return?

  LG 1 **P8.3** Amalgamated Aircraft Parts, Inc. is expected to pay a dividend of $1.50 in the coming year. The required rate of return is 16%, and dividends are expected to grow at 7% per year. Using the dividend valuation model, find the intrinsic value of the company's common shares.

  LG 3 **P8.4** Assume you've generated the following information about the stock of Bufford's Burger Barns: The company's latest dividends of $4 a share are expected to

grow to $4.32 next year, to $4.67 the year after that, and to $5.04 in year 3. In addition, the price of the stock is expected to rise to $77.75 in 3 years.

a. Use the dividends-and-earnings model and a required rate of return of 15% to find the value of the stock.
b. Use the IRR procedure to find the stock's expected return.
c. Given that dividends are expected to grow indefinitely at 8%, use a 15% required rate of return and the dividend valuation model to find the value of the stock.
d. Assume dividends in year 3 actually amount to $5.04, the dividend growth rate stays at 8%, and the required rate of return stays at 15%. Use the dividend valuation model to find the price of the stock at the end of year 3. [*Hint:* In this case, the value of the stock will depend on dividends in year 4, which equal $D_3 \times (1 + g)$.] Do you note any similarity between your answer here and the forecasted price of the stock ($77.75) given in the problem? Explain.

 LG 3 | **P8.5** Let's assume that you're thinking about buying stock in West Coast Electronics. So far in your analysis, you've uncovered the following information: The stock pays annual dividends of $2.50 a share (and that's not expected to change within the next few years—*nor are any of the other variables*). It trades at a P/E of 18 times earnings and has a beta of 1.15. In addition, you plan on using a risk-free rate of 7% in the CAPM, along with a market return of 14%. You would like to hold the stock for 3 years, at the end of which time you think EPS will peak out at about $7 a share. Given that the stock currently trades at $70, use the IRR approach to find this security's expected return. Now use the present-value (dividends-and-earnings) model to put a price on this stock. Does this look like a good investment to you? Explain.

 LG 3 | **P8.6** The price of Consolidated Everything is now $75. The company pays no dividends. Ms. Bossard expects the price 3 years from now to be $100 per share. Should Ms. B. buy Consolidated E. if she desires a 10% rate of return? Explain.

 LG 3 | **P8.7** This year, Shoreline Light and Gas (SLL&G) paid its stockholders an annual dividend of $3 a share. A major brokerage firm recently put out a report on SLL&G stating that, in its opinion, the company's annual dividends should grow at the rate of 10% per year for each of the next 5 years and then level off and grow at the rate of 6% a year thereafter.

a. Use the variable-growth DVM and a required rate of return of 12% to find the maximum price you should be willing to pay for this stock.
b. Redo the SLL&G problem in part (a), this time assuming that after year 5, dividends stop growing altogether (for year 6 and beyond, $g = 0$). Use all the other information given to find the stock's intrinsic value.
c. Contrast your two answers and comment on your findings. How important is growth to this valuation model?

 LG 3 | **P8.8** Assume there are three companies that in the past year paid exactly the same annual dividend of $2.25 a share. In addition, the future annual rate of growth in dividends for each of the three companies has been estimated as follows:

Buggies-Are-Us	Steady Freddie, Inc.	Gang Buster Group	
$g = 0\%$ (i.e., dividends are expected to remain at $2.25/share)	$g = 6\%$ (for the foreseeable future)	Year 1	$2.53
		2	$2.85
		3	$3.20
		4	$3.60
		Year 5 and beyond: $g = 6\%$	

Assume also that as the result of a strange set of circumstances, these three companies all have the same required rate of return ($k = 10\%$).

a. Use the appropriate DVM to value each of these companies.
b. Comment briefly on the comparative values of these three companies. What is the major cause of the differences among these three valuations?

 LG 3 **P8.9** New Millenium Company's stock sells at a P/E ratio of 21 times earnings. It is expected to pay dividends of $2 per share in each of the next 5 years and to generate an EPS of $5 in year 5. Using the dividends-and-earnings model and a 12% discount rate, compute the stock's justified price.

 LG 3 **P8.10** A particular company currently has sales of $250 million; these are expected to grow by 20% next year (year 1). For the year after next (year 2), the growth rate in sales is expected to equal 10%. Over each of the next 2 years, the company is expected to have a net profit margin of 8% and a payout ratio of 50%, and to maintain the number of shares of common stock outstanding at 15 million shares. The stock always trades at a P/E ratio of 15 times earnings, and the investor has a required rate of return of 20%. Given this information:

a. Find the stock's intrinsic value (its justified price).
b. Use the IRR approach to determine the stock's expected return, given that it is currently trading at $15 per share.
c. Find the holding period returns for this stock for year 1 and for year 2.

 LG 2 **LG 3** **P8.11** Assume a major investment service has just given Oasis Electronics its highest investment rating, along with a strong buy recommendation. As a result, you decide to take a look for yourself and to place a value on the company's stock. Here's what you find: This year, Oasis paid its stockholders an annual dividend of $3 a share, but because of its high rate of growth in earnings, its dividends are expected to grow at the rate of 12% a year for the next 4 years and then to level out at 9% a year. So far, you've learned that the stock has a beta of 1.80, the risk-free rate of return is 6%, and the expected return on the market is 11%. Using the CAPM to find the required rate of return, put a value on this stock.

 LG 3 **P8.12** Consolidated Software doesn't currently pay any dividends but is expected to start doing so in 4 years. That is, Consolidated will go 3 more years without paying any dividends, and then is expected to pay its first dividend (of $3 per share) in the fourth year. Once the company starts paying dividends, it's expected to continue to do so. The company is expected to have a dividend payout ratio of 40% and to maintain a return on equity of 20%. Based on the DVM, and given a required rate of return of 15%, what is the maximum price you should be willing to pay for this stock today?

 LG 3 **P8.13** Assume you obtain the following information about a certain company:

Total assets	$50,000,000
Total equity	$25,000,000
Net income	$ 3,750,000
EPS	$5.00 per share
Dividend payout ratio	40%
Required return	12%

Use the constant-growth DVM to place a value on this company's stock.

 LG 3 **P8.14** You're thinking about buying some stock in Affiliated Computer Corporation and want to use the P/E approach to value the shares. You've estimated that next year's

earnings should come in at about $4.00 a share. In addition, although the stock normally trades at a relative P/E of 1.15 times the market, you believe that the relative P/E will rise to 1.25, whereas the market P/E should be around 18½ times earnings. Given this information, what is the maximum price you should be willing to pay for this stock? If you buy this stock today at $87.50, what rate of return will you earn over the next 12 months if the price of the stock rises to $110.00 by the end of the year? (Assume that the stock doesn't pay any dividends.)

 LG 3 **P8.15** AviBank Plastics generated an EPS of $2.75 over the last 12 months. The company's earnings are expected to grow by 25% next year, and because there will be no significant change in the number of shares outstanding, EPS should grow at about the same rate. You feel the stock should trade at a P/E of around 30 times earnings. Use the P/E approach to set a value on this stock.

 LG 4 **P8.16** World Wide Web Wares (4W, for short) is an online retailer of small kitchen appliances and utensils. The firm has been around for a few years and has created a nice market niche for itself. In fact, it actually turned a profit last year, though a fairly small one. After doing some basic research on the company, you've decided to take a closer look. You plan to use the price/sales ratio to value the stock, and you have collected P/S multiples on the following Internet retailer stocks:

Company	P/S Multiples
Amazing.com	4.5
PotsAnPans Online	12.2
Furnishings.com	1.3
ReallyCooking.com	4.1
Fixtures & Appliances Online	3.8

Pick *three* of these firms to use as your set of comparables, and compute the *average P/S ratio* of those three firms. Given that 4W had sales last year of $40 million and has 10 million shares of stock outstanding, use the average P/S ratio you computed above to put a value on 4W's stock.

Now repeat the valuation process, but this time use all five of the companies to compute the average P/S ratio. Then use the P/S ratio to value 4W's stock. If you had to put a value on 4W stock, what would it be? Explain. If the stock were trading at $15 a share right now, would you buy it? Explain.

Case Problem 8.1   *Chris Looks for a Way to Invest His Newfound Wealth*

LG 1 Chris Norton is a young Hollywood writer who is well on his way to television superstardom. After writing several successful television specials, he was recently named the head writer for one of TV's top-rated sitcoms. Chris fully realizes that his business is a fickle one and, on the advice of his dad and manager, has decided to set up an investment program. Chris will earn about a half-million dollars this year. Because of his age, income level, and desire to get as big a bang as possible from his investment dollars, he has decided to invest in speculative, high-growth stocks.

Chris is currently working with a respected Beverly Hills broker and is in the process of building up a diversified portfolio of speculative stocks. The broker recently sent him information on a hot new issue. She advised Chris to study the numbers and, if he likes them, to buy as many as 1,000 shares of the stock. Among other things, corporate sales for the next 3 years have been forecasted as follows:

Year	Sales (in millions)
1	$22.5
2	35.0
3	50.0

The firm has 2.5 million shares of common stock outstanding. They are currently being traded at $70 a share and pay no dividends. The company has a net profit rate of 20%, and its stock has been trading at a P/E of around 40 times earnings. All these operating characteristics are expected to hold in the future.

 Questions

a. Looking first at the stock:
   1. Compute the company's net profits and EPS for each of the next 3 years.
   2. Compute the price of the stock 3 years from now.
   3. Assuming that all expectations hold up and that Chris buys the stock at $70, determine his expected return on this investment.
   4. What risks is he facing by buying this stock? Be specific.
   5. Should he consider the stock a worthwhile investment candidate? Explain.

b. Now, looking at Chris's investment program in general:
   1. What do you think of his investment program? What do you see as its strengths and weaknesses?
   2. Are there any suggestions you would make?
   3. Do you think Chris should consider adding foreign stocks to his portfolio? Explain.

Case Problem 8.2   *An Analysis of a High-Flying Stock*

LG 3   LG 5

Glenn Wilt is a recent university graduate and a security analyst with the Kansas City brokerage firm of Lippman, Brickbats, and Shaft. Wilt has been following one of the hottest issues on Wall Street, C&I Medical Supplies, a company that has turned in an outstanding performance lately and, even more important, has exhibited excellent growth potential. It has 5 million shares outstanding and pays a nominal annual dividend of 5 cents per share. Wilt has decided to take a closer look at C&I to see whether it still has any investment play left. Assume the company's sales for the past 5 years have been as follows:

Year	Sales (in millions)
1997	$10.0
1998	12.5
1999	16.2
2000	22.0
2001	28.5

Wilt is concerned with the future prospects of the company, not its past. As a result, he pores over the numbers and generates the following estimates of future performance:

Expected net profit margin	12%
Estimated annual dividends per share	5¢
Number of common shares outstanding	No change
P/E ratio at the end of 2002	35
P/E ratio at the end of 2003	50

Questions

a. Determine the average annual rate of growth in sales over the past 5 years. (Assume sales in 1996 amounted to $7.5 million.)
  1. Use this average growth rate to forecast revenues for next year (2002) and the year after that (2003).
  2. Now determine the company's net earnings and EPS for each of the next 2 years (2002 and 2003).
  3. Finally, determine the expected future price of the stock at the end of this 2-year period.

b. Because of several intrinsic and market factors, Wilt feels that 25% is a viable figure to use for a desired rate of return.
  1. Using the 25% rate of return and the forecasted figures you came up with in question (a), compute the stock's justified price.
  2. If C&I is currently trading at $32.50 per share, should Wilt consider the stock a worthwhile investment candidate? Explain.

c. The stock is actively traded on the Nasdaq National Market and enjoys considerable market interest. Recent closing prices are shown in the accompanying table.
  1. Prepare a point-and-figure chart of these prices (use a 1-point system—that is, make each box worth $1).
  2. Discuss how these and similar charts are used by technical analysts.
  3. Cite several other types of technical measures, and note how they might be used in the analysis of this stock.

Recent Price Behavior: C&I Medical Supplies

14 (8/15/01)	18.55	20	17.50
14.25	17.50	20.21	18.55
14.79	17.50	20.25	19.80
15.50	17.25	20.16	19.50
16	17	20	19.25
16	16.75	20.25	20
16.50	16.50	20.50	20.90
17	16.55	20.80	21
17.25	16.15	20	21.75
17.20	16.80	20	22.50
18	17.15	20.25	23.25
18 (9/30/01)	17.22	20	24
18.55	17.31 (10/31/01)	19.45	24.25
18.65	17.77	19.20	24.15
18.80	18.23	18.25 (11/30/01)	24.75
19	19.22	17.50	25
19.10	20.51	16.75	25.50
18.92	20.15	17	25.55 (12/31/01)

Web Exercises

W8.1   Check out the dividend valuation model (zero growth, constant growth, and non-constant growth) at www.bluebloodcells.com/fun/cs4262/div.html. Using the constant-growth model, a dividend D_0 of 2, an expected growth rate, G, of 15%, a number of years t of 4, and a required equity return, K_e, of 18%, calculate the market price of the stock.

W8.2   ASK Research at www.askresearch.com has one of the best and fastest charting tools. It will provide you with several technical indicators, company news, and portfolio tracking. The pages will automatically refresh themselves with latest quotes and charts. Assume that you are a day trader, and follow the market activity. For example, click on [Nasdaq Composite Index] and compare the Intraday Chart with the On-Balance Volume. Is there a correlation between the movements of the two lines?

W8.3   10K Wizard at www.10kwizard.com provides real-time online access and full text search of EDGAR, thus providing a link to SEC filings. You can view the latest SEC filings of more than 68,000 companies and search historical filings, from the start date of each company's existence, by keywords, phrases, and names. For example, select [Computer/Office Equipment] in the [Industry] box, and type ORCL in the [Ticker] box. This will retrieve a list of recently filed forms for Oracle. Click on the first [10-Q Quarterly report] form. What were Oracle's reported earnings per share? What was its comprehensive income?

W8.4

a. NAIC Investor's Tool Kit at www.better-investing.org/computer/toolkit.html provides what you need to analyze and evaluate common stocks for your portfolio. Investor's Toolkit PRO adds the portfolio management tools you will want later to optimize the performance of your portfolio.

b. Validea at www.validea.com allows you to analyze an individual stock. Check the "buzz" on your stock by entering ticker symbol ORCL, and click on the [Go] button. Check [Guru Analysis] on this stock by clicking on it. Analyze the report cards from the All Star Gurus. What factors do they consider? How might these opinions influence your estimate of the stock? Check the [Media Buzz] for the stock. What does it report?

W8.5   Find the stock analyzer at www.decisionpoint.com. Click on [Chart Spotlite] for quick technical analysis of the selected stock, market index, and market indicator charts. New charts are featured weekly. Select the article [VXN:New Volatility Index] for the Nasdaq 100 Index for the latest available date. What does the index measure? How does volatility correlate with performance?

W8.6   If you are interested in socially responsible investing, see www.environmental investors.com, www.socialinvest.org, and www.goodmoney.com. Examine a couple of stocks (or mutual funds) at these sites. Can you determine how they qualify as socially responsible investments? How does their performance compare with that of other stocks?

W8.7

a. See how to value stocks at www.fool.com/school/howtovaluestocks.htm

b. See Internet stock valuation techniques at the following sites:
www.acusd.edu/~mpraum/internetvalue.html
www.timeinc.net/fortune/year.in.review/1998/internetstock.html
www.techweek.com/articles/5-3-99/stockwat.htm

For additional practice with concepts from this chapter, visit
www.awl.com/gitman_joehnk

CFA EXAM QUESTIONS

Investing in Common Stocks

Following is a sample of 12 Level-I CFA exam questions that deal with many of the topics covered in Chapters 6, 7, and 8 of this text, including the use of financial ratios, various stock valuation models, technical analysis, and efficient market concepts. (*Note:* You will find the term, "dividend discount model" used in many of the questions below; read that as "dividend valuation model," as these two terms have the same meaning).

1. Assume that at the end of the next year, Company A will pay a $2.00 dividend per share, an increase from the current dividend of $1.50 per share. After that, the dividend is expected to increase at a constant rate of 5%. If you require a 12% return on the stock, what is the value of the stock?
   a. $28.57.
   b. $28.79.
   c. $30.00.
   d. $31.78.

2. The constant-growth dividend discount model will *not* produce a finite value for a stock if the dividend growth rate is:
   a. above its historical average.
   b. below its historical average.
   c. above the required rate of return on the stock.
   d. below the required rate of return on the stock.

3. Which of the following assumptions is **NOT** required by the constant-growth dividend discount model?
   a. Dividends grow at a constant rate.
   b. The stock is sold at some future date.
   c. The dividend growth rate continues indefinitely.
   d. The required rate of return is greater than the dividend growth rate.

4. The constant-growth dividend discount model would typically be most appropriate in valuing the stock of a:
   a. new venture expected to retain all earnings for several years.
   b. rapidly growing company.
   c. moderate growth, "mature" company.
   d. company with valuable assets not yet generating profits.

5. In applying the constant-growth dividend discount model, lowering the market capitalization rate will cause a stock's intrinsic value to:
   a. decrease.
   b. increase.
   c. remain unchanged.
   d. decrease or increase, depending upon other factors.

6. A company's current ratio is 2.0. If the company uses cash to retire notes payable that are due within one year, would this transaction *most likely* increase or decrease the current ratio and total asset turnover ratio, respectively?

	Current Ratio	Asset Turnover Ratio
a.	Increase	Increase
b.	Increase	Decrease
c.	Decrease	Increase
d.	Decrease	Decrease

CFA EXAM QUESTIONS

7. Two companies are identical except for substantially different dividend payout ratios. After several years, the company with the lower dividend payout ratio is *most likely* to have:
a. lower stock price.
b. higher debt/equity ratio.
c. less rapid growth of earnings per share.
d. more rapid growth of earnings per share.

8. A share of stock is expected to pay a dividend of $1.00 one year from now, with growth at 5 percent thereafter. In the context of a dividend discount model, the stock is correctly priced today at $10. According to the single stage, constant growth dividend discount model, if the required return is 15 percent, the value of the stock two years from now should be:
a. $11.03.
b. $12.10.
c. $13.23.
d. $14.40.

9. Company B paid a $1.00 dividend per share last year and is expected to continue to pay out 40% of its earnings as dividends for the foreseeable future. If the firm is expected to generate a 10% return on equity in the future, and if you require a 12% return on the stock, what is the value of the stock?
a. $12.50.
b. $13.00.
c. $16.67.
d. $17.67.

10. A stock is not expected to pay dividends until three years from now. The dividend is then expected to be $2.00 per share, the dividend payout ratio is expected to be 40 percent, and the return on equity is expected to be 15 percent. If the required rate of return is 12 percent, the value of the stock today is *closest to:*
a. $27.
b. $33.
c. $53.
d. $67.

11. A basic assumption of technical analysis in contrast to fundamental analysis is that:
a. financial statements provide information crucial in valuing a stock.
b. a stock's market price will approach its intrinsic value over time.
c. aggregate supply of and demand for goods and services are key determinants of stock value.
d. security prices move in patterns, which repeat over long periods.

12. The semi-strong form of the efficient market hypothesis asserts that stock prices:
a. fully reflect all historical security market information.
b. fully reflect all public information.
c. fully reflect all relevant information from public and private sources.
d. may be predictable.

Answers: 1. a; 2. c; 3. b; 4. c; 5. b; 6. a; 7. d; 8. a; 9. d; 10. c; 11. d; 12. b

INVESTING IN FIXED-INCOME SECURITIES

BOND INVESTMENTS

We've all seen ads for telecommunications companies like Sprint, promising to integrate into one neat package all our communications needs: wire-line long-distance and local phone and data services, wireless communications, and Internet services. Sprint is in a good position to deliver on its promises. The company built and operates the first nationwide all-digital, fiber-optic network and is a leader in advanced data communications services. Through its Sprint Integrated ON-Demand Network (Sprint ION), the company delivers simultaneous voice, video, and data services over a single existing connection.

Maintaining Sprint's telecommunications edge is expensive. The company spends from $5 billion to $7 billion a year to upgrade to fiber-optic networks and implement other advanced technologies. Making these and future expenditures for technology and also for acquisitions is essential to the company's survival in today's competitive telecommunications industry. With deregulation, any company that doesn't keep up with cutting-edge technology will lose customers to eager competitors.

Like other companies in capital-intensive businesses, Sprint uses debt as well as equity to finance its growth. Its September 2000 quarterly balance sheet showed $17 billion in long-term debt. Sprint issues bonds through its Sprint Capital Corp. subsidiary. Current debt offerings have maturities ranging from 1 to 20 years. Because its debt obligations are rated Baa1/BBB+ by Moody's and Standard & Poor's, Sprint will have to offer higher interest rates than competitors such as WorldCom (rated A3/A−), AT&T (rated A2/A or better), and Southwestern Bell (rated AA2/AA). As you will see in this chapter, investors in bonds like Sprint's have to consider credit quality, interest rates, maturity, and other factors to decide whether to invest in these securities.

Source: Sprint Web page, www.sprint.com; CNNfn Bond Center, cnnfn.cnn.com/markets/bondcenter

Why Invest in Bonds

LG 1

bonds
negotiable, publicly traded long-term debt securities, whereby the issuer agrees to pay a fixed amount of interest over a specified period of time and to repay a fixed amount of principal at maturity.

In contrast to stocks, *bonds are liabilities*—they are nothing more than publicly traded IOUs where the bondholders are actually *lending money* to the issuer. Technically, **bonds** can be described as negotiable, publicly traded, long-term debt securities. They are issued in various denominations, by a variety of borrowing organizations, including the U.S. Treasury, agencies of the U.S. government, state and local governments, and corporations. Bonds are often referred to as *fixed-income securities* because the debt-service obligations of the issuers are fixed. That is, the issuing organization agrees to pay a fixed amount of interest periodically and to repay a fixed amount of principal at maturity.

Like any other type of investment vehicle, bonds provide investors with two kinds of income: (1) They provide a generous amount of current income, and (2) given the right market environment, they can also be used to generate substantial amounts of capital gains. The current income, of course, is derived from the interest payments received over the life of the issue. Capital gains, in contrast, are earned whenever market interest rates fall. A basic trading rule in the bond market is that *interest rates and bond prices move in opposite directions*. When interest rates rise, bond prices fall. When rates drop, bond prices move up. Thus, it is possible to buy bonds at one price and to sell them later at a higher price. Of course, it is also possible to incur a capital loss, should market rates move against you. Taken together, the current income and capital gains earned from bonds can lead to attractive returns.

Bonds are also a versatile investment outlet. They can be used conservatively by those who seek high current income, or they can be used aggressively by those who go after capital gains. Although bonds have long been considered attractive investments for those seeking current income, it wasn't until the late-'60s and the advent of volatile interest rates that they also become recognized for their capital gains potential and as trading vehicles. Investors found that, given the relation of bond prices to interest rates, the number of profitable trading opportunities increased substantially as wider and more frequent swings in interest rates began to occur.

In addition, certain types of bonds can be used for tax shelter: Municipal obligations are perhaps the best known in this regard. But as we'll see later in this chapter, Treasury and certain federal agency issues also offer some tax advantages. Finally, because of the general high quality of many bond issues, they can also be used for the preservation and long-term accumulation of capital. For with quality issues, not only do investors have a high degree of assurance that they'll get their money back at maturity, but the stream of interest income is also highly dependable.

Putting Bond Market Performance in Perspective

The bond market is driven by interest rates. In fact, *the behavior of interest rates is the single most important force in the bond market*. Interest rates determine not only the amount of current income investors will receive but also the amount of capital gains (or losses) bondholders will incur. It's not surprising, therefore, that bond market participants follow interest rates closely and that bond market performance is often portrayed in terms of market interest rates.

Figure 9.1 provides a look at bond interest rates over the 40-year period from 1961 through 2000. It shows that from a state of relative stability, interest rates rose steadily in the latter half of the 1960s. Over the course of the next 15 years, the rates paid on high-grade bonds almost tripled. Indeed, interest rates rose from the 4% to 5% range in the early 1960s to over 16% by 1982. But then rates dropped sharply. By 1986 they were back to the single-digit range once again. Thus, after a protracted bear market, bonds abruptly reversed course, and the strongest bull market on record occurred from 1982 to early 1987. (The bond market is considered *bearish* when market interest rates are high or rising, *bullish* when rates are low or falling.) Even though interest rates did move back up for a short time in 1987–1988, they quickly retreated and by 1998–1999, had fallen to levels not seen in over 30 years. Indeed, by early 1999, long-term Treasury bonds were yielding *less then* 5%.

Historical Returns As with stocks, *total returns* in the bond market are made up of both current income and capital gains (or losses). Tables 9.1 and 9.2 provide an overview of (total) returns in the bond market—on an annual basis and for various investment horizons—over the 40-year period from 1961 through the second quarter of the year 2000. Take a look at Table 9.1, which lists *year-end market yields* and total *annual returns* for high-grade corporate bonds. Note how bond returns started to slip in 1965, as market yields began to climb. In fact, from 1965 to 1981, there were no fewer than 8 years when average returns were negative. In contrast, look what happened over the 16-year period from 1982 through 1998, when rates were in a general state of decline: There were only 2 years of negative returns (in 1987 and 1994), whereas double-digit returns (of 10.7% to 43.8%) occurred in no fewer than 10 of the 16 years.

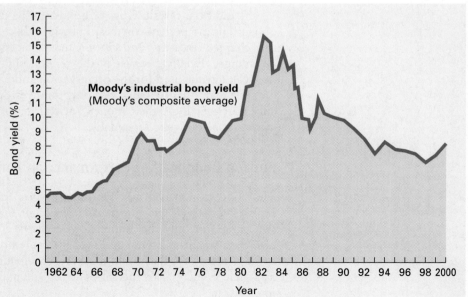

FIGURE 9.1

The Behavior of Interest Rates Over Time—1961–2000

From an era of relative stability, bond interest rates rose dramatically and became highly volatile. The net result was that bond yields not only became competitive with the returns offered by other securities but also provided investors with attractive capital gains opportunities. (2000 yields through the second quarter, June 2000.)

TABLE 9.1 Historical Annual Yields and Returns in the Bond Market, 1961–2000*
(Yields and returns based on performance of high-grade corporate bonds)

Year	Year-End Bond Yields*	Total Rates of Return**	Year	Year-End Bond Yields*	Total Rates of Return**
2000*	7.15%	2.62%	1980	3.15%	−2.62%
1999	7.05	−5.76	1979	10.87	−4.18
1998	6.53	9.16	1978	9.32	−0.07
1997	7.16	13.46	1977	8.50	1.71
1996	7.43	2.20	1976	8.14	18.65
1995	6.86	27.94	1975	8.97	14.64
1994	8.64	−5.76	1974	8.89	−3.06
1993	7.31	13.64	1973	7.79	1.14
1992	8.34	9.34	1972	7.41	7.26
1991	8.58	20.98	1971	6.48	11.01
1990	9.61	6.48	1970	6.85	18.37
1989	9.18	15.29	1969	7.83	−8.09
1988	9.81	10.49	1968	6.62	2.57
1987	10.33	1.47	1967	6.30	−4.95
1986	9.02	18.71	1966	5.55	0.20
1985	10.63	30.90	1965	4.79	−0.46
1984	12.05	16.39	1964	4.46	4.77
1983	12.76	4.70	1963	4.46	2.19
1982	11.55	43.80	1962	4.34	7.95
1981	14.98	−0.96	1961	4.56	4.82

*Year-end bond yields are for (S&P) AA-rated corporate (industrial and utility) bonds; 2000 yields and returns through the second quarter (June) 2000.

**Total return figures are based on interest income as well as capital gains (or losses).

Sources: Annual yields derived from Standard & Poor's *S&P Trade and Security Statistics.* Total return figures (for 1961–1985) from Ibbotson and Sinquefield, *Stocks, Bonds, Bills, and Inflation: Historical Returns.* Total returns for 1986 through the second quarter of 2000 obtained from the *Lehman Bros. Long-Term Corporate Bond* database.

Table 9.2 contains return performance over various holding periods of 5 to 40 years. These figures demonstrate the type of long-term returns possible from bonds and show that *average annual returns of around 8% to 10% on high-grade issues are not out of the question.* Although such performance may lag behind that of stocks (which it should, in light of the reduced exposure to risk), it really isn't that bad, especially from the the perspective of risk-adjusted rate of return. The big question facing bond investors, however, is what kind of returns will they be able to produce over the next 10 to 12 years? The 1980s and early 1990s were very good for bond investors. *But that market was driven by falling interest rates, which in turn produced hefty capital gains and outsize returns.* Whether market interest rates will (or even can) continue on that path is doubtful. Most market observers, in fact, caution against expecting abnormally high rates of return over the next decade or so.

Bonds Versus Stocks Although bonds definitely have their good points (low risk, high levels of current income, and desirable diversification properties), they also have a significant downside: their *comparative* returns. The fact is, *relative to stocks,* the long-run returns on bonds just don't hold up too well. Look at Figure 9.2. It tracks the comparative returns of stocks (via the S&P 500) and bonds (using the Lehman Bros. Long-Term Corporate Bond Index) over the 1990s. As can be seen, for the first half of the period, bonds held up very well,

TABLE 9.2	Holding Period Returns in the Bond Market: 1961–2000*		
	Average Annual Returns*	Cumulative Total Returns	Amount to Which a $10,000 Investment Will Grow Over the Holding Period
5(+) years: 1995–2000*	8.50%	56.61%	$ 15,661
5 years: 1990–94	8.57	50.85	15,085
10(+) years: 1990–2000*	8.53	136.24	23,624
15 years: 1985–99	10.58	352.06	45,206
25 years: 1975–99	9.77	929.37	102,937
40 years: 1961–99	7.08	1,440.13	154,013
The 1960s: 1960–69	1.7%	18.1%	$11,809
The 1970s: 1970–79	6.2	83.1	18,305
The 1980s: 1980–89	13.0	240.2	34,022
The 1990s: 1990–99	8.7	130.2	23,020

*Average annual return figures are fully compounded returns and are based on interest income as well as capital gains (or losses). 2000 data through the second quarter (June).
Sources: Annual yields derived from Standard & Poor's *S&P Trade and Security Statistics.* Total return figures (1961–85) from Ibbotson and Sinquefield, *Stocks, Bonds, and Inflation: Historical Returns.* Total return data for 1986 through the second quarter of 2000 from *Lehman Bros. Long-Term Corporate Bond* series.

pretty much matching the returns in the stock market. But things started to change in 1995, as stock returns shot up, while bond returns began to level off. The net result was that for the decade as a whole, bonds produced average annual returns of 8.7%, whereas stocks turned in average returns of 18.2%. That difference meant that a $10,000 investment in bonds would have led to a terminal value of some $23,000, compared to more than $53,000 for stocks.

That's a high opportunity cost to pay for holding bonds, and it prompted some market observers to question whether bonds should have *any place at all* in an investment portfolio. They reason that if interest rates have, in fact, bottomed out, then bonds won't have much to offer, other than relatively low returns. But that view ignores one of the key aspects of bonds: *the element of stability they add to a portfolio.* The fact is, bonds possess excellent portfolio diversification properties and, except for the most aggressive of investors, have a lot to contribute from a portfolio perspective. Indeed, as a general rule, adding bonds to a portfolio will, *up to a point,* have a much greater impact on lowering risk than on return. Face it: you don't buy bonds for their high returns (except when you think interest rates are heading down). Rather, you buy them for their current income and/or for the stability they bring to your portfolio. And that's still true, even today. What's more, it's important to keep in mind that most of the comparative return performance in the '90s was due to a phenomenal 5-year run (from 1995–1999) for stocks. Thus, when stock returns come back down to earth and return to more normal levels (which has to happen, sooner or later), bond returns will once again become more competitive.

For information on bond investment considerations, go to the Bond Market Association's site whose address is shown below. Click on [Bond Basics]: Key bond investment considerations.

www.investinginbonds.com

Exposure to Risk

Like any other type of investment vehicle, fixed-income securities should be viewed in terms of their risk and return. Generally speaking, bonds are

FIGURE 9.2 **Comparative Performance of Stocks and Bonds in the 1990s—January 1990–December 1999**

This graph shows what happened to $10,000 invested in bonds over the decade of the '90s, versus the same amount invested in stocks. Obviously, while the beginning amount was the same, the ending (or "terminal") amounts were not. And, we should point out, the difference would have been even bigger had we used the Nasdaq Composite Index instead of the S&P 500— indeed, a $10,000 investment in the Nasdaq Composite would have grown to nearly $89,500, due in part to the phenomenal year in 1999, when the Nasdaq shot up more than 85%. (*Source: Morningstar Principia Pro for Mutual Funds,* release date March 31, 2000.)

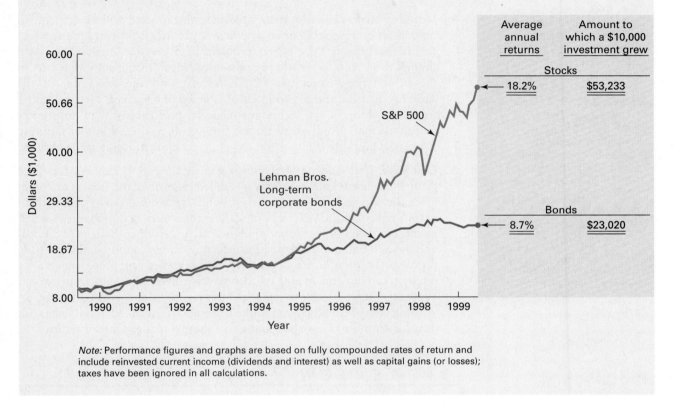

Note: Performance figures and graphs are based on fully compounded rates of return and include reinvested current income (dividends and interest) as well as capital gains (or losses); taxes have been ignored in all calculations.

exposed to five major types of risks: interest rate risk, purchasing power risk, business/financial risk, liquidity risk, and call risk.

- **Interest Rate Risk.** Interest rate risk is the number one source of risk to fixed-income investors, *because it's the major cause of price volatility in the bond market.* For bonds, interest rate risk translates into market risk: The behavior of interest rates, in general, affects *all* bonds and cuts across *all* sectors of the market, even the U.S. Treasury market. When market interest rates rise, bond prices fall, and vice versa. And as interest rates become more volatile, so do bond prices.

- **Purchasing Power Risk.** Purchasing power risk accompanies inflation. During periods of mild inflation, bonds do pretty well, because their returns tend to outstrip inflation rates. Purchasing power risk really heats up when inflation takes off, as it did in the late 1970s; when that happens, bond yields start to lag behind inflation rates. The reason: Even though market yields are rising with inflation, your return is locked in by the fixed coupon rate on your bond.

- **Business/Financial Risk.** This is basically the risk that the *issuer will default on interest and/or principal payments.* Also known as *credit risk,* business/financial risk has to do with the quality and financial integrity of the issuer. The stronger the issuer, the less business/financial risk there is to worry about. This risk doesn't even exist for some securities (e.g., U.S. Treasuries). For others, such as corporate and municipal bonds, it's a very important consideration.

- **Liquidity Risk.** Liquidity risk is the risk that a bond will be difficult to unload, at a reasonable price, if you want to sell it. In certain sectors of the market, this is a far bigger problem than investors realize. For even though the U.S. bond market is enormous, much of the activity occurs in the primary/new-issue market. Therefore, with the exception of the Treasury market and a good deal of the agency market, relatively little trading is done in the secondary markets, particularly with corporates and municipals. And where there's little trading, there's lots of liquidity risk. So, if liquidity is important to you, steer clear of thinly traded bonds.

- **Call Risk.** Call risk, or *prepayment risk,* is the risk that a bond will be "called" (retired) long before its scheduled maturity date. Issuers are often given the opportunity to prepay their bonds, and they do so by calling them in for prepayment. (We'll examine call features later in this chapter.) When issuers call their bonds, the bondholders end up getting cashed out of the deal and have to find another place for their investment funds—and there's the problem. Because bonds are nearly always called for prepayment after interest rates have taken a big fall, comparable investment vehicles just aren't available. Thus you have to replace a high-yielding bond with a much lower-yielding issue. From the bondholder's perspective, a called bond means not only a disruption in cash flow but also a sharply reduced rate of return.

IN REVIEW

CONCEPTS

9.1 What appeal do bonds hold for individual investors? Give several reasons why bonds make attractive investment outlets.

9.2 How would you describe the behavior of market interest rates and bond returns over the last 30–40 years? Do swings in market interest rates have any bearing on bond returns? Explain.

9.3 Identify and briefly describe the five types of risk to which bonds are exposed. What is the most important source of risk for bonds in general? Explain.

Essential Features of a Bond

LG 2   LG 3

A *bond* is a negotiable, long-term debt instrument that carries certain obligations (including the payment of interest and the repayment of principal) on the part of the issuer. Because bondholders are only lending money to the issuer, they are not entitled to any of the rights and privileges that go along with an ownership position. But bondholders, as well as bond issuers, do have a number of well-defined rights and privileges that together help define the essential features of a bond. We'll now take a look at some of these features. As you will see, when it comes to bonds, it's especially important to know what you're getting into, *for many seemingly insignificant features (like a bond's coupon or maturity) can have dramatic effects on its price behavior and investment return.* This is especially true in periods of low interest rates, because knowing what to buy and when to buy can mean the difference between earning a mediocre return and earning a highly competitive one.

Bond Interest and Principal

In the absence of any trading, a bond investor's return is limited to fixed interest and principal payments. That's because bonds involve a fixed claim on the issuer's income (as defined by the size of the periodic interest payments) and a fixed claim on the assets of the issuer (equal to the repayment of principal at maturity). As a rule, bonds pay interest every 6 months. There are exceptions, however; some issues carry interest payment intervals as short as a month, and a few as long as a year. The amount of interest due is a function of the **coupon,** which defines the annual interest income that will be paid by the issuer to the bondholder. For instance, a $1,000 bond with an 8% coupon pays $80 in interest annually—generally in the form of two $40 semiannual payments. The **principal** amount of a bond, also known as an issue's *par value,* specifies the amount of capital that must be repaid at maturity. For example, there is $1,000 of principal in a $1,000 bond.

Of course, debt securities regularly trade at market prices that differ from their principal (par) values. This occurs whenever an issue's coupon differs from the prevailing market rate of interest. That is, the price of the issue changes inversely with interest rates until its yield is compatible with the prevailing market yield. Such behavior explains why a 7% issue will carry a market price of only $825 in a 9% market. The drop in price from its par value of $1,000 is necessary to raise the yield on this bond from 7% to 9%. In essence, the new, higher yield is produced in part from annual coupons and in part from capital gains, as the price of the issue moves from $825 back to $1,000 at maturity.

Maturity Date

Unlike common stock, all debt securities have limited lives and will expire on a given date in the future, the issue's **maturity date.** Although a bond carries a series of specific interest payment dates, the principal is repaid only once: on or before maturity. The maturity date is fixed (and never changes). It not only defines the life of a new issue but also denotes the amount of time remaining for older, outstanding bonds. Such a life span is known as an issue's *term to maturity.* For example, a new issue may come out as a 25-year bond, but 5 years later, it will have only 20 years remaining to maturity.

Two types of bonds can be distinguished on the basis of maturity: term and serial issues. A **term bond** has a single, fairly lengthy maturity date and is the most common type of issue. A **serial bond,** in contrast, has a series of different maturity dates, perhaps as many as 15 or 20, within a single issue. For example, a 20-year term bond issued in 1999 has a single maturity date of 2019, but that same issue as a serial bond might have 20 annual maturity dates that extend from 1999 through 2019. At each of these annual maturity dates,

coupon
feature on a bond that defines the amount of annual interest income.

principal
on a bond, the amount of capital that must be paid at maturity.

maturity date
the date on which a bond matures and the principal must be repaid.

term bond
a bond that has a single, fairly lengthy maturity date.

serial bond
a bond that has a series of different maturity dates.

note
a debt security originally issued with a maturity of from 2 to 10 years.

a certain portion of the issue would come due and be paid off. Maturity is also used to distinguish a *note* from a *bond*. That is, a debt security that's originally issued with a maturity of 2 to 10 years is known as a **note,** whereas a *bond* technically has an initial term to maturity of more than 10 years. In practice, notes are often issued with maturities of 5 to 7 years, whereas bonds normally carry maturities of 20 to 30 years or more.

Call Features—Let the Buyer Beware!

Consider the following situation: You've just made an investment in a high-yielding, 25-year bond. Now all you have to do is sit back and let the cash flow in, right? Well, perhaps. Certainly, that will happen for the first several years. But, if market interest rates drop, it's also likely that you'll receive a notice from the issuer that the bond is being *called*. This means that the issue is being retired before its maturity date. There's really nothing you can do but turn in the bond and invest your money elsewhere. It's all perfectly legal because every bond is issued with a **call feature,** which stipulates whether and under what conditions a bond can be called in for retirement prior to maturity.

call feature
feature that specifies whether and under what conditions the issuer can retire a bond prior to maturity.

Basically, there are three types of call features:

1. A bond can be *freely callable,* which means the issuer can prematurely retire the bond at any time.
2. A bond can be *noncallable,* which means the issuer is prohibited from retiring the bond prior to maturity.
3. The issue could carry a *deferred call,* which means the issue cannot be called until after a certain length of time has passed from the date of issue. In essence, the issue is noncallable during the deferment period and then becomes freely callable thereafter.

Obviously, in our illustration above, either the high-yielding bond was issued as freely callable or it became freely callable with the end of its call deferment period.

Call features are placed on bonds *for the benefit of the issuers.* They're used most often to replace an issue with one that carries a lower coupon, and the issuer benefits by the reduction in annual interest cost. Thus, when market interest rates undergo a sharp decline, as they did in 1982–1987 and again in 1991–1993, bond issuers retire their high-yielding bonds (by calling them in) and replace them with lower-yielding obligations. *The net result is that the investor is left with a much lower rate of return than anticipated.*

call premium
the amount added to a bond's par value and paid to investors when a bond is retired prematurely.

call price
the price the issuer must pay to retire a bond prematurely; equal to par value plus the call premium.

In a halfhearted attempt to compensate investors who find their bonds called out from under them, a **call premium** is tacked onto a bond and paid to investors, along with the issue's par value, when the bond is called. The sum of the par value plus call premium represents the issue's **call price.** This is the amount the issuer must pay to retire the bond prematurely. As a general rule, call premiums usually equal about 8 to 12 months' interest at the earliest date of call and then become progressively smaller as the issue nears maturity. Using this rule, the initial call price of a 9% bond could be as high as $1,090, where $90 represents the call premium.

refunding provisions
provisions that prohibit the premature retirement of an issue from the proceeds of a lower-coupon refunding bond.

In addition to call features, some bonds may also carry **refunding provisions.** These are much like call features except that they prohibit just one thing: the premature retirement of an issue from the proceeds of a lower-coupon bond. For example, a bond could come out as freely callable but *non-refundable* for 5 years. In this case, the bond would probably be sold by brokers as a *deferred refunding issue,* with little or nothing said about its call feature. The distinction is important, however. It means that a nonrefunding or deferred refunding issue *can still be called and prematurely retired for any reason other than refunding*. Thus, an investor could face a call on a high-yielding nonrefundable issue if the issuer has the cash to retire the bond prematurely.

Sinking Funds

sinking fund
a provision that stipulates the amount of principal that will be retired annually over the life of a bond.

Another provision that's important to investors is the **sinking fund,** which stipulates how a bond will be paid off over time. This provision applies only to term bonds, of course, because serial issues already have a predetermined method of repayment. Not all (term) bonds have sinking-fund requirements, but for those that do, a sinking fund specifies the annual repayment schedule that will be used to pay off the issue. It indicates how much principal will be retired each year. Sinking-fund requirements generally begin 1 to 5 years after the date of issue and continue annually thereafter until all or most of the issue is paid off. Any amount not repaid (which might equal 10% to 25% of the issue) would then be retired with a single "balloon" payment at maturity. Unlike a call or refunding provision, the issuer generally does not have to pay a call premium with sinking-fund calls. Instead, the bonds are normally called at par for sinking-fund purposes.

There's another difference between sinking-fund provisions and call or refunding features. That is, whereas a call or refunding provision gives the issuer the *right* to retire a bond prematurely, a sinking-fund provision *obligates* the issuer to pay off the bond systematically over time. The issuer has no choice. It must make sinking-fund payments in a prompt and timely fashion or run the risk of being in default.

Secured or Unsecured Debt

senior bonds
secured debt obligations, backed by a legal claim on specific property of the issuer.

mortgage bonds
senior bonds secured by real estate.

collateral trust bonds
senior bonds backed by securities owned by the issuer but held in trust by a third party.

equipment trust certificates
senior bonds secured by specific pieces of equipment; popular with transportation companies such as airlines.

first and refunding bonds
bonds secured in part with both first and second mortgages.

junior bonds
debt obligations backed only by the promise of the issuer to pay interest and principal on a timely basis.

A single issuer may have a number of different bonds outstanding at any given point in time. In addition to coupon and maturity, one bond can be differentiated from another by the type of collateral behind the issue. Issues can be either junior or senior. **Senior bonds** are secured obligations, which are backed by a legal claim on some specific property of the issuer. Such issues would include **mortgage bonds,** which are secured by real estate; **collateral trust bonds,** which are backed by financial assets owned by the issuer but held in trust by a third party; **equipment trust certificates,** which are secured by specific pieces of equipment (e.g., boxcars and airplanes) and are popular with railroads and airlines; and **first and refunding bonds,** which are basically a combination of first mortgage and junior lien bonds (i.e., the bonds are secured in part by a first mortgage on some of the issuer's property and in part by second or third mortgages on other properties). (Note that first and refunding bonds are *less secure* than, and should *not* be confused with, straight first-mortgage bonds.)

Junior bonds, on the other hand, are backed only by the promise of the issuer to pay interest and principal on a timely basis. There are several classes

FIGURE 9.3

Announcement of a New Corporate Debt Issue

This $1.5 billion global note was issued by Hewlett-Packard in 2000 and is secured by nothing more than the good name of the company. Raising this kind of money without having to put up any collateral may be hard to imagine, but for big, financially secure companies like HP, it's done all the time. And note that the price was right: The coupon on this unsecured debt is only 7.15%, which at the time was considerably less than what the average homeowner would have had to pay to get a $150,000 mortgage. Even so, over the short, 5-year life of this note, HP will be paying more than $100,000,000 in interest! (*Source: Wall Street Journal,* July 12, 2000.)

This announcement is neither an offer to sell nor a solicitation of offers to buy any of these securities. The offering is made only by the Prospectus and the related Prospectus Supplement, copies of which may be obtained in any State or jurisdiction in which this announcement is circulated only from such of the underwriters as may legally offer these securities in such State or jurisdiction.

NEW ISSUE   June 6, 2000

$1,500,000,000

7.15% Global Notes due June 15, 2005

Price 99.666%

plus accrued interest, if any, from June 9, 2000

Credit Suisse First Boston   Salomon Smith Barney

Bear, Stearns & Co. Inc.

Chase Securities Inc.

Goldman, Sachs & Co.

Morgan Stanley Dean Witter

The Williams Capital Group, L.P.

debenture
an unsecured (junior) bond.

subordinated debentures
unsecured bonds whose claim is secondary to other debentures.

income bonds
unsecured bonds requiring that interest be paid only after a specified amount of income is earned.

premium bond
a bond with a market value in excess of par; occurs when interest rates drop below the coupon rate.

discount bond
a bond with a market value lower than par; occurs when market rates are greater than the coupon rate.

of unsecured bonds, the most popular of which is known as a **debenture.** Figure 9.3 shows the announcement for a very large issue that came out in June 2000. This particular issue happens to be a *note,* but just like a debenture, it too is unsecured (essentially, this note is nothing more than a short-term debenture). Even though there was no collateral backing up this obligation, the issuer, Hewlett-Packard, was able to sell $1.5 *billion* worth of these securities at an interest rate of just 7.15%.

Subordinated debentures can also be found in the market. These issues have a claim on income secondary to other debenture bonds. **Income bonds,** the most junior of all bonds, are unsecured debts requiring that interest be paid only after a certain amount of income is earned. With these bonds, there is no legally binding requirement to meet interest payments on a timely or regular basis so long as a specified amount of income has not been earned. These issues are similar in many respects to *revenue bonds* found in the municipal market.

Principles of Bond Price Behavior

The price of a bond is a function of its coupon, its maturity, and the movement of market interest rates. The relationship of bond prices to market interest rates is captured in Figure 9.4. Basically, the graph reinforces the *inverse relationship* that exists between bond prices and market rates: *Lower* rates lead to *higher* bond prices.

Figure 9.4 also shows the difference between premium and discount bonds. A **premium bond** is one that sells for more than its par value. A premium results whenever market interest rates drop below the bond's coupon rate. A **discount bond,** in contrast, sells for less than par. The discount is the result of market rates being greater than the issue's coupon rate. Thus, the 10% bond in Figure 9.4 trades at a premium when market rates are at 8%, but at a discount when rates are at 12%.

When a bond is first issued, it is usually sold to the public at a price that equals or is very close to its par value. Likewise, when the bond matures—some 15, 20, or 30 years later—it will once again be priced at its par value. What happens to the price of the bond in between is of considerable interest to most bond investors. We know that the extent to which bond prices move depends not only on the *direction* of change in interest rates but also on the *magnitude* of such change: The greater the moves in interest rates, the greater the swings in bond prices.

However, bond price volatility also varies according to an issue's coupon and maturity. That is, bonds with *lower coupons* and/or *longer maturities* respond more vigorously to changes in market rates and therefore undergo sharper price swings. (Note in Figure 9.4 that for a given change in interest rates—e.g., from 10% to 8%—the largest change in price occurs when the bond has the greatest number of years to maturity.) Therefore, if a *decline* in interest rates is anticipated, you should seek lower coupons and longer maturities (to maximize capital gains). When interest rates move *up,* you should do just the opposite: seek high coupons with short maturities. This choice will minimize price variation and act to preserve as much capital as possible.

Actually, of the two variables, the *maturity* of an issue has the greater impact on price volatility. For example, look what happens to the price of an 8% bond when market interest rates rise by 1, 2, or 3 percentage points:

| | Change in the Price of an 8% Bond When Interest Rates Rise by: | | |
Bond Maturity	1 Percentage Point	2 Percentage Points	3 Percentage Points
5 years	−4.0%	−7.7%	−11.2%
25 years	−9.9%	−18.2%	−25.3%

For purposes of this illustration, we assume the changes in interest rate occur "instantaneously," so the maturities remain fixed, at 5 or 25 years. Given the computed price changes, it's clear that the shorter (5-year) bond offers a lot more price stability. Such behavior is universal with all fixed-income securities, and is very important. It means that if you want to reduce your exposure to capital loss or, more to the point, to lower the price volatility in your bond holdings, then just *shorten your maturities*.

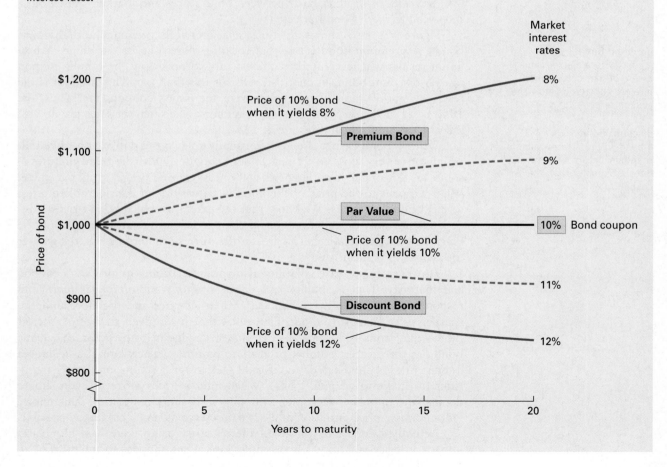

FIGURE 9.4 **The Price Behavior of a Bond**

A bond will sell at its par value so long as the prevailing market interest rate remains the same as the bond's coupon—in this case, 10%. However, when market rates drop, bond prices move up. When rates rise, bond prices move down. As a bond approaches its maturity, the price of the issue moves toward its par value regardless of the level of prevailing interest rates.

IN REVIEW

C O N C E P T S

9.4 Can issue characteristics (such as coupon and call features) affect the yield and price behavior of bonds? Explain.

9.5 What is the difference between a *call feature* and a *sinking-fund provision?* Briefly describe the three different types of call features. Can a bond be freely callable but nonrefundable?

9.6 What is the difference between a *premium bond* and a *discount bond?* What three attributes are most important in determining an issue's price volatility?

The Market for Debt Securities

Thus far, our discussion has dealt with basic bond features. We now shift attention to a review of the market in which these securities are traded. To begin with, the bond market is chiefly over-the counter in nature, as listed bonds represent only a small portion of total outstanding obligations. In addition, this market is far more stable than the stock market. Indeed, although interest rates—and therefore bond prices—do move up and down over time, when bond price activity is measured on a daily basis, it is *remarkably stable.* There are two other things that stand out about the bond market: It's big, and it has been growing rapidly. From a $250 billion market in 1950, it has grown to the point where, in early 2000, the amount of bonds outstanding in this country reached nearly *$15 trillion!* That makes the bond market even bigger than the U.S. stock market, although the gap is definitely narrowing.

Here's what the U.S. bond market looked like at the beginning of the new millenium (January 2000):

	Amount Outstanding ($ in trillions)
U.S. Treasury securities	$ 2.46
Agency securities	1.62
Municipal bonds	1.35
Corporate bonds	4.13
Mortgage-backed securities	2.29
Foreign issues and Eurodollar bonds	2.74
Total	$14.59

Source: "Size & Structure of the World Bond Market: 2000," Merrill Lynch, April 2000.

The growth in this market has been remarkable. It has doubled in size since 1992, which translates into a compound rate of growth of more than 10% per year. Domestic issues alone (*excluding* foreign issues and Eurodollar bonds) account for $11.9 trillion, or 81% of the total U.S. market. Let's now take a look at each of these various segments.

Major Market Segments

There are bonds available in today's market to meet almost any investment objective and to suit just about any type of investor. As a matter of convenience, the bond market is normally separated into four major segments, according to type of issuer: Treasury, agency, municipal, and corporate. As we shall see, each sector has developed its own features, as well as its own trading characteristics.

Treasury Bonds "Treasuries" (or "governments," as they are sometimes called) are a dominant force in the fixed-income market. If not the most popular type of bond, they certainly are the best known. In addition to T-bills (a popular short-term debt security), the U.S. Treasury issues notes and bonds. It also issues *inflation-indexed securities,* which are the newest type of Treasury debt, introduced in January 1997. All Treasury obligations are of the highest quality because they are all backed by the "full faith and credit" of the U.S. government. This backing, along with their liquidity, makes them very popular with individual and institutional investors both here and abroad. Indeed, Treasury securities are traded in all the major markets of the world, from New York to London to Sydney and Tokyo.

Treasury notes are issued with maturities of 2, 5, and 10 years, whereas **Treasury bonds** carry 30-year maturities. (The Treasury last issued 20-year bonds in 1986.) The Treasury issues its notes and bonds at regularly scheduled auctions, the results of which are widely reported by the financial media (see Figure 9.5). In this auction process, the Treasury establishes the initial yields and coupons on the securities it issues.

Actually, because of the ever-widening federal budget *surplus,* the Treasury has announced that it will be sharply reducing the issuance of new notes and bonds. Indeed, the supply of these securities is to be reduced across the board as the Treasury eliminates the auctions of some maturities all together and reduces the size or frequency of others. Even so, a full array of Treasury notes and bonds is still available in the aftermarket. But many of those may soon become extinct, as the Treasury uses part of the budget surplus to pay down the national debt by buying back outstanding securities.

All Treasury notes and bonds are sold in $1,000 denominations. Interest income from these securities is subject to normal federal income tax but *is exempt from state and local taxes.* The Treasury today issues only *noncallable* securities. The last time the U.S. Treasury issued callable debt was in 1984. Until then, most Treasury bonds carried long-term call deferments, under which the bonds became freely callable during the last 5 years of the issue's life. There are still some deferred-call Treasuries outstanding; they're easy to identify because the deferred-call features are a specific part of the bond listing system. For example, a 10% issue of 2005–10 signifies that this Treasury bond has a maturity date of 2010 and a deferred-call feature that extends through 2005.

As noted above, the newest form of Treasury security is the **Treasury inflation-indexed obligation.** Also known as **TIPS,** which stands for "Treasury inflation-protection securities," they are issued as notes (with 10-year maturities) and bonds (with 30-year maturities). They offer investors the opportunity to stay ahead of inflation by periodically adjusting their returns for any inflation that has occurred. That is, if inflation is running at an annual rate of, say, 3%, then at the end of the year, the par (maturity) value of the bond will increase by 3%. (Actually, the adjustments to par value are done every 6

Treasury notes
U.S. Treasury debt securities that are issued with maturities of 2 to 10 years or less.

Treasury bonds
U.S. Treasury debt securities that are issued with 30-year maturities.

Treasury inflation-indexed obligations (TIPS)
a type of Treasury security that provides protection against inflation by adjusting investor returns for the annual rate of inflation.

FIGURE 9.5 **The Reported Results of a Treasury Note Auction**

Treasury auctions are closely followed by the financial media; here, the results of a 10-year Treasury note auction are reported. These auctions are highly competitive. The number of bids submitted generally far exceeds the size of the issue, so the spread between the highest and lowest bids is quite small—sometimes as small as 2 basis points, or 2/100 of 1%. (*Source:* Department of the Treasury—Bureau of Public Debt, and *Wall Street Journal*.)

Here are details of yesterday's 10-year note auction:

All bids are awarded at a single price at the market-clearing yield. Rates are determined by the difference between that price and the face value.

10-YEAR NOTES

Applications	$20,940,987,000
Accepted bids	$ 8,005,987,000
Bids at market-clearing yield accepted ...	38%
Accepted noncompetitively	$108,592,000
Auction price (rate)	100.153 (6.475%)
Interest rate	6 1/2%
CUSIP number	912827521

   The notes are dated February 15, 2000, will be issued May 15, 2000, and mature February 15, 2010.

- The amount of bids submitted
- Size of the issue—the number of bids accepted
- The number of noncompetitive bids submitted (and accepted)
- The average price and yield (rate) on the issue
- The coupon that the issue will carry, which is set after the auction

months.) Thus the $1,000 par value will grow to $1,030 at the end of the first year. If the 3% inflation rate continues for the second year, the par value will once again increase, this time from $1,030 to $1,061 ($1,030 × 1.03). Unfortunately, the coupons on these securities are set very low, because they're meant to provide investors with so-called *real (inflation-adjusted) returns*. Thus one of these bonds might carry a coupon of only 3.5% at a time when regular T-bonds are paying, say, 6.5% or 7%. But there's an advantage even to this: *The actual size of the coupon payment will increase over time as the par value on the bond goes up.* For investors who are concerned about inflation protection, these securities may be just the ticket. But as the accompanying *Investing in Action* box suggests, TIPS are a lot more complex than the traditional Treasury bond.

agency bonds
debt securities issued by various agencies and organizations of the U.S. government.

Agency Bonds **Agency bonds** are debt securities issued by various agencies and organizations of the U.S. government, such as the Federal Home Loan Bank, the Federal Farm Credit Systems, the Small Business Administration, the Student Loan Marketing Association, and the Federal National Mortgage Association. Though these securities are the closest things to Treasuries, they are not obligations of the U.S. Treasury and technically should not be considered the same as a Treasury bond. Even so, *they are very high-quality securities that have almost no risk of default.* In spite of the similar default risk exposure, these securities usually provide yields that are comfortably

INVESTING in action

Some Hints on TIPS

Bondholders look at inflation like Superman looks at kryptonite. Superman weakens when faced with the dreaded substance and would die if exposed to it for long. Bondholders weaken when inflation heats up because it causes bond prices to buckle and fixed payments to lose their purchasing power. Some people have the mistaken impression that they can't lose money investing in Treasury bonds. But they can because bond prices fall in an inflationary environment. So that investors can buy its bonds without fearing inflation, in 1997 Uncle Sam created TIPS, Treasury inflation-protected securities.

Here's how TIPS work: The government issues a 10-year bond with a $1,000 face value that pays, say, 3% interest—and that rate stays fixed for the life of the issue. But if the consumer price index rises, so does the face amount of the bond. For example, because the CPI rose 3.4% in 2000, the new face amount was adjusted up to $1,000 × 1.034 = $1,034. Therefore, in 2001, the annual interest payment would be $31.02 (3% of $1,034). When the TIPS mature in 10 years, the investor gets the inflation-adjusted face value at that time, which could be as much as $2,000 if inflation really takes off. A lot can change over a decade, but inflation looks pretty tame these days. As one professional investor puts it, buying TIPS now is like buying flood insurance during a drought. TIPS also protect you if deflation occurs. The bond's value will not fall below its initial face value (of $1,000).

Are TIPS a good deal or not? They certainly are for the government, which is able to pay 3% interest instead of an inflation-adjusted premium like 6% or 7%. Taxpayers should like that too, because it helps keep government interest payments down. And, unlike the case with conventional fixed-income securities, the investor doesn't have to worry about the Treasury bond's value plummeting if inflation heats up.

Take a look at what happens to a conventional bond if inflation is rekindled beyond the implied inflation premium (in this case, 3%). Investors get 6% per year, or $60, no matter what happens to the level of prices. In 10 years, that $1,000 principal will certainly have less purchasing power than it does today. It might be able to buy just $700 worth of goods. In addition, rising inflation generally means rising interest rates. In the marketplace, conventional bond prices fall when interest rates rise. Therefore, an investor who wishes to sell a conventional bond prior to maturity is likely to take a loss if interest rates are higher than when the bond was purchased.

TIPS protect investors from such erosion in bond prices. TIPS are not so great, however, if inflation stays dormant, because the investors are getting only 3% on their money. You could get that kind of interest at your local bank, and you don't need to lock up your money nearly as long as you do with TIPS.

There's one other downside to TIPS: taxes. Investors have to pay a tax on the increasing face value of their bonds—$34 in the first year in the foregoing example. That may not seem like much, but the government doesn't actually pay out the increase in the bond's face value until maturity. Thus you end up paying taxes on income you've earned but don't have in hand. For that reason, TIPS probably make the most sense for individual retirement accounts (IRAs) and other tax-deferred retirement accounts.

TIPS are also a good idea for investors who want to allocate a portion of their assets to income-generating securities and don't want to worry that inflation will erode their value. But the tradeoff for that protection is significant: loss of about half the income.

Sources: Robert Barker, "A Bond Anybody Can Love," *Business Week,* June 19, 2000, p.260; and James Grant, "An Inflation Tip," *Forbes,* October 30, 2000, p. 402.

above the market rates for Treasuries. Thus they offer investors a way to increase returns with little or no real difference in risk.

There are basically two types of agency issues: government-sponsored and federal agencies. Although there are only six government-sponsored organizations, the number of federal agencies exceeds two dozen. To over-

TABLE 9.3	Characteristics of Some Popular Agency Issues				
Type of Issue	Minimum Denomination	Initial Maturity	Tax Status*		
			Federal	State	Local
Federal Farm Credit System	$ 1,000	13 months to 15 years	T	E	E
Federal Home Loan Bank	10,000	1 to 20 years	T	E	E
Federal Land Banks	1,000	1 to 10 years	T	E	E
Farmers Home Administration	25,000	1 to 25 years	T	T	T
Federal Housing Administration	50,000	1 to 40 years	T	T	T
Federal Home Loan Mortgage Corp.** ("Freddie Mac")	25,000	18 to 30 years	T	T	T
Federal National Mortgage Association** ("Fannie Mae")	25,000	1 to 30 years	T	T	T
Government National Mortgage Association** (GNMA—"Ginnie Mae")	25,000	12 to 40 years	T	T	T
Student Loan Marketing Association	10,000	3 to 10 years	T	E	E
Tennessee Valley Authority (TVA)	1,000	5 to 50 years	T	E	E
U.S. Postal Service	10,000	25 years	T	E	E
Federal Financing Corp.	1,000	1 to 20 years	T	E	E

*T = taxable; E = tax-exempt
**Mortgage-backed securities.

come some of the problems in the marketing of many relatively small federal agency securities, Congress established the Federal Financing Bank to consolidate the financing activities of all federal agencies. (As a rule, the generic term *agency* is used to denote both government-sponsored and federal agency obligations.)

Selected characteristics of some of the more popular agency bonds are presented in Table 9.3. As the list of issuers shows, most of the government agencies that exist today were created to support either agriculture or housing. Although agency issues are not direct liabilities of the U.S. government, a few of them actually do carry government guarantees and therefore represent the full faith and credit of the U.S. Treasury. But even those issues that do not carry such guarantees are highly regarded in the marketplace. They are all viewed as *moral obligations* of the U.S. government, as it's highly unlikely that Congress would ever allow one of them to default. Also, like Treasury securities, agency issues are normally noncallable or carry lengthy call deferment features. One final point: Since 1986 *all new agency (and Treasury) securities* have been issued in *book entry form*. This means that no certificate of ownership is issued to the buyer of the bonds. Rather, the buyer receives a "confirmation" of the transaction, and his or her name is entered in a computerized logbook, where it remains as long as the security is owned.

HOTLINKS

To access a database of corporate, agency, and municipal bond offerings, go to

www.bondtrac.com/info/infoServices.html

municipal bonds
debt securities issued by states, counties, cities, and other political subdivisions; most of these bonds are tax-exempt (free of federal income tax on interest income).

Municipal Bonds Municipal bonds are the issues of states, counties, cities, and other political subdivisions (such as school districts and water and sewer districts). This is a trillion-dollar market today, and it's the only segment of the bond market that's dominated by individual investors: About two-thirds of all municipal bonds are held by individuals. (There are few tax incentives for institutional investors to hold these securities.) These bonds are often issued as *serial obligations*, which means that the issue is broken into a series of smaller bonds, each with its own maturity date and coupon.

general obligation bonds
municipal bonds backed by the full faith, credit, and taxing power of the issuer.

revenue bonds
municipal bonds that require payment of principal and interest only if sufficient revenue is generated by the issuer.

municipal bond guarantees
guarantees from a party other than the issuer that principal and interest payments will be made in a prompt and timely manner.

Municipal bonds ("munis") are brought to the market as either general obligation or revenue bonds. **General obligation bonds** are backed by the full faith, credit, and taxing power of the issuer. **Revenue bonds,** in contrast, are serviced by the income generated from specific income-producing projects (e.g., toll roads). Although general obligations used to dominate the municipal market, the vast majority of munis today come out as revenue bonds (accounting for about 70% to 75% of the new-issue volume).

The distinction between a general obligation bond and a revenue bond is important for a bondholder, because the issuer of a revenue bond is obligated to pay principal and interest *only if a sufficient level of revenue is generated.* If the funds aren't there, the issuer does not have to make payment on the bond. General obligation bonds, however, are required to be serviced in a prompt and timely fashion irrespective of the level of tax income generated by the municipality. Obviously, revenue bonds involve a lot more risk than general obligations, and because of that, they provide higher yields. Regardless of the type, municipal bonds are customarily issued in $5,000 denominations.

A somewhat unusual aspect of municipal bonds is the widespread use of **municipal bond guarantees.** With these guarantees, a party other than the issuer assures the bondholder that principal and interest payments will be made in a prompt and timely manner. The third party, in essence, provides an additional source of collateral in the form of insurance, placed on the bond at the date of issue, that is nonrevocable over the life of the obligation. As a result of the guarantee, bond quality is improved. The three principal insurers are the Municipal Bond Investors Assurance Corporation (MBIA), the American Municipal Bond Assurance Corporation (AMBAC), and the Financial Guaranty Insurance Co. (FGIC). These guarantors will normally insure any general obligation or revenue bond as long as it carries an S&P rating of triple-B or better. (We'll explore bond ratings later in this chapter.) Municipal bond insurance results in higher ratings (usually triple-A) and improved liquidity for these bonds, which are generally more actively traded in the secondary markets. Insured bonds are especially common in the revenue market, and insurance markedly boosts their attractiveness. Whereas an uninsured revenue bond lacks certainty of payment, a guaranteed issue is very much like a general obligation bond because the investor knows that principal and interest payments will be made on time.

 Tax Advantages Without a doubt, the thing that makes municipal securities unique is the fact that, in most cases, their interest income is exempt from federal income taxes. That's why these issues are known as *tax-free,* or *tax-exempt,* bonds. Normally, the obligations are also exempt from state and local taxes *in the state in which they were issued.* For example, a California issue is free of California tax if the bondholder lives in California, but its interest income is subject to state tax if the investor resides in Arizona. Note that *capital gains on municipal bonds are not exempt from taxes.*

Individual investors are the biggest buyers of municipal bonds, and tax-free yield is certainly a major draw. Table 9.4 shows what a taxable bond would have to yield to equal the net yield of a tax-free bond. *It demonstrates how the yield attractiveness of municipals varies with an investor's income level.* Clearly, the higher the individual's tax bracket, the more attractive municipal bonds become. Generally speaking, an investor has to be in one of

TABLE 9.4	Taxable Equivalent Yields for Various Tax-Exempt Returns										
Taxable Income*			Tax-Free Yield								
Joint Returns ($000)	Individual Returns ($000)	Federal Tax Bracket	5%	6%	7%	8%	9%	10%	12%	14%
$0–$43.8	$0–$26.2	15%	5.88	7.06	8.24	9.41	10.59	11.76	14.12	16.47
$43.8–$105.9	$26.2–$63.5	28	6.94	8.33	9.72	11.11	12.50	13.89	16.67	19.44
$105.9–$161.4	$63.5–$132.6	31	7.25	8.70	10.15	11.59	13.04	14.49	17.39	20.29
$161.4–$288.3	$132.6–$288.3	36	7.81	9.38	10.94	12.50	14.06	15.63	18.75	21.88
$288.3 and above	$288.3 and above	39.6	8.28	9.93	11.59	13.25	14.90	16.56	19.87	23.18

*Taxable income and federal tax rates effective January 1, 2000.

the higher federal tax brackets (31% to 39.6%) before municipal bonds offer yields that are competitive with fully taxable issues. This is so because municipal yields are lower than those available from fully taxable issues (such as corporates); and unless the tax effect is sufficient to raise the yield on a municipal to a figure that equals or surpasses taxable rates, it doesn't make much sense to buy municipal bonds.

taxable equivalent yield
the return a fully taxable bond would have to provide to match the after-tax return of a lower-yielding, tax-free municipal bond.

We can determine the level of return a fully taxable bond would have to provide in order to match the after-tax return of a lower-yielding, tax-free issue by computing what is known as a municipal's **taxable equivalent yield**. This measure can be calculated according to the following simple formula:

Equation 9.1

$$\text{Taxable equivalent yield} = \frac{\text{Yield of municipal bond}}{1 - \text{Federal tax rate}}$$

For example, if a municipal offered a yield of 6.5%, then an individual in the 39.6% tax bracket would have to find a fully taxable bond with a yield of 10.76% (i.e., 6.5%/0.604 = 10.76%) to reap the same after-tax returns as the municipal.

Note, however, that Equation 9.1 considers *federal taxes only*. As a result, the computed taxable equivalent yield applies only to certain situations: (1) to states that have no state income tax, (2) to situations where the investor is looking at an out-of-state bond (which would be taxable by the investor's state of residence), or (3) where the investor is comparing a municipal bond to a Treasury (or agency) bond—in which case *both* the Treasury and the municipal bonds are free from state income tax. Under any of these conditions, the only tax that's relevant is federal income tax, so using Equation 9.1 is appropriate. But what if the investor is comparing an in-state bond to, say, a corporate bond? In this case, the in-state bond would be free from both federal and state taxes, but the corporate bond would not. As a result, Equation 9.1 could not be used. Instead, the investor should use a form of the equivalent yield formula that considers *both* federal and state income taxes:

Equation 9.2

$$\frac{\text{Taxable equivalent yield for}}{\text{both federal and state taxes}} = \frac{\text{Municipal bond yield}}{1 - \left[\dfrac{\text{Federal}}{\text{tax rate}} + \dfrac{\text{State}}{\text{tax rate}} \left(1 - \dfrac{\text{Federal}}{\text{tax rate}} \right) \right]}$$

When both federal and state taxes are included in the calculations, the net effect is to *increase* the taxable equivalent yield. Of course, the size of the increase depends on the level of state income taxes. In a high-tax state like California, for example, the impact can be substantial. Return to the 6.5% municipal bond introduced above: If a California resident in the maximum federal and state tax brackets (39.6% and 11%, respectively) were considering a corporate issue, she would have to get a yield of 12.09% on the corporate to match the 6.5% yield on the California bond:

$$\text{Taxable equivalent yield for both federal and state taxes} = \frac{6.5}{1 - [.396 + .11(1 - .3960)]}$$

$$= \frac{6.5}{1 - [.396 + .066]}$$

$$= \underline{12.09\%}$$

This yield compares to a taxable equivalent yield of 10.76% when only federal taxes were included in the calculation. That's a difference of more than one full percentage point—certainly *not* an insignificant amount.

Corporate Bonds Corporations are the major nongovernmental issuers of bonds. The market for corporate bonds is customarily subdivided into four segments: *industrials* (the most diverse of the groups), *public utilities* (the dominant group in terms of volume of new issues), *rail and transportation bonds,* and *financial issues* (banks, finance companies, etc.). Not only is there a full range of bond quality available in the corporate market, but there is also a wide assortment of different types of bonds. These range from first-mortgage obligations to convertible bonds (which we'll examine in Chapter 11), debentures, subordinated debentures, senior subordinated issues, capital notes (a type of unsecured debt issued by banks and other financial institutions), and income bonds. Interest on corporate bonds is paid semiannually, and sinking funds are fairly common. The bonds usually come in $1,000 denominations and are issued on a term basis with a single maturity date. Maturities usually range from 25 to 40 years or more. Many corporates, especially the longer ones, carry call deferment provisions that prohibit prepayment for the first 5 to 10 years. Corporate issues are popular with individuals because of their relatively attractive yields.

Most corporates fit the general description above. One that does not is the *equipment trust certificate,* a security issued by railroads, airlines, and other transportation concerns. The proceeds from equipment trust certificates are used to purchase equipment (e.g., jumbo jets and railroad engines) that serves as the collateral for the issue. These bonds are usually issued in serial form and carry uniform annual installments throughout. They normally carry maturities that range from 1 year to a maximum of 15 to 17 years. An attractive feature of equipment trust certificates is that despite a near-perfect payment record that dates back to pre-Depression days, these issues generally offer above-average yields to investors.

Specialty Issues

In addition to the basic bond vehicles described above, investors can also choose from a number of *specialty issues*—bonds that possess unusual issue characteristics. For the most part, these bonds have coupon or repayment provisions that are out of the ordinary. Most are issued by corporations, although they are being used increasingly by other issuers as well. Four of the most actively traded specialty issues today are zero-coupon bonds, mortgage-backed securities, asset-backed securities, and high-yield junk bonds. All four of these rank as some of the more popular bonds on Wall Street. Let's now take a closer look at each of these specialty issues.

zero-coupon bonds
bonds with no coupons that are sold at a deep discount from par value.

Zero-Coupon Bonds As the name implies, **zero-coupon bonds** have no coupons. Rather, these securities are sold at a deep discount from their par values and then increase in value over time at a compound rate of return so that at maturity, they are worth much more than their initial investment. Other things being equal, the cheaper the zero-coupon bond, the greater the return an investor can earn: For example, a 6% might cost $420, but one with a 10% yield might cost only $240.

Because they don't have coupons, these bonds do not pay interest semiannually. In fact, they pay *nothing* to the investor until the issue matures. As strange as it might seem, this feature is the main attraction of zero-coupon bonds. Because there are no interest payments, investors do not have to worry about reinvesting coupon income twice a year. Instead, the fully compounded rate of return on a zero-coupon bond is virtually guaranteed at the rate stated when the issue was purchased. For example, in mid-2000, U.S. Treasury zero-coupon bonds with 20-year maturities were available at yields of around 6.25%. Thus, for less than $300, you could buy a bond that would be worth more than three times that amount, or $1,000, at maturity in 20 years. Best of all, you would be *locking in* a 6.25% compound rate of return on your investment for the full 20-year life of the issue.

The foregoing advantages notwithstanding, zeros do have some serious disadvantages. One is that if rates do move up over time, you won't be able to participate in the higher return (you'll have no coupon income to reinvest). In

HOT LINKS

To read about Treasury strips, go to:
www.bondsonline.com/asp/treas/zeros.asp

addition, zero-coupon bonds are subject to tremendous price volatility: If market rates climb, you'll experience a sizable capital loss as the prices of zero-coupons plunge. (Of course, if interest rates *drop,* you'll reap enormous capital gains if you hold long-term zeros. Indeed, such issues are unsurpassed in capital gains potential.) A final disadvantage is that the IRS has ruled that zero-coupon bondholders must report *interest as it is accrued,* even though no interest is actually received. For this reason, most fully taxable zero-coupon bonds should either be used in tax-sheltered investments, such as IRAs, or be held by minor children who are likely to be taxed at the lowest rate, if at all.

Treasury strips (Strip-Ts)
zero-coupon bonds created from U.S. Treasury securities.

Zeros are issued by corporations, municipalities, and federal agencies. You can even buy U.S. Treasury notes and bonds in the form of zero-coupon securities. They're known as **Treasury strips,** or **strip-Ts,** for short. Actually, the Treasury does *not* issue zero-coupon bonds. Instead, it *allows government securities dealers to sell regular coupon-bearing notes and bonds in the form of zero-coupon securities.* Essentially, the coupons are stripped from the bond, repackaged, and then sold separately as zero-coupon bonds. For example, a 20-year Treasury bond has 40 semiannual coupon payments, plus one principal payment. These 41 cash flows can be repackaged and sold as 41 different zero-coupon securities, with maturities that range from 6 months to 20 years. Because they sell at such large discounts, Treasury strips are often sold

INVESTING in action

Life Without Treasuries

As the federal government enjoys its first budget surplus since 1969, the U.S. Treasury is using the excess funds to buy back longer-term Treasury notes and bonds. The level of federal debt is dropping quickly. At the current rate of tax revenue inflow, all $3.3 trillion of Treasury debt will disappear by 2012. The Treasury is also issuing fewer securities and not rolling over maturing issues. Especially hard-hit are 30-year bonds, because the Treasury buybacks are heavier at the long end of the yield curve. The decreased supply and demand from the traditional buyers of long-term Treasuries (pension funds, banks, and insurance companies) put upward pressure on bond prices, resulting in a corresponding drop in yields. In mid-2000 an inverted yield curve (where longer-term issues yield less than shorter maturities) replaced the more typical upward-sloping curve.

Despite the benefits of an almost debt-free government (such as less pressure on credit markets and lower interest rates), watchers of the financial markets are concerned about the long-term implications of a possible lack of Treasury securities. The Treasury yield curve is the principal benchmark in valuing non-Treasury bonds. As we learned in Chapter 4, the yield on a corporate bond is based on the interest rate for a similar-maturity Treasury bond plus a risk premium related to the issuer's credit quality. With wider and more volatile yield spreads between Treasuries and other debt instruments, as well as the distorted yield pattern due to supply, financial managers are finding it difficult to price private-sector bonds.

What will replace the disappearing Treasury bond as the new yardstick? The best bet is federal agency debt from Fannie Mae and Freddie Mac. These government-sponsored organizations regularly issue notes and bonds ranging from 3 months to 30 years. Although they do not carry the full faith and credit of the U.S. government, the default risk is extremely low.

Without U.S. government debt, individual and institutional investors for whom safety is paramount will lose a valuable investment vehicle: a risk-free security exempt from state income taxes. In addition, most Treasury securities are not callable, whereas most corporate bonds are. Buying a Treasury locks in that rate for the life of the investment. Possible replacements that offer respectable, relatively safe yields include investment-grade corporate bonds and 5- to 7-year bond certificates of deposit. There are some noncallable corporates. Look for banks to fill the gap with new types of CDs with longer maturities and less restrictive withdrawal rules. Savings bonds are another alternative; they offer some inflation protection through indexing.

Sources: Ronald E. Desautels and Mary Jo English, "Are U.S. Treasuries Headed for the Endangered Species List?" *AAII Journal*, July 2000, pp. 12–15; "From Debt We Do Part," *Kiplinger's*, September 2000, pp. 23–24; and Robert Lenzner and Michael Maiello, "Treasuries, the Endangered Species," *Forbes*, July 24, 2000, pp. 362–363.

in minimum denominations (par values) of $10,000. But with their big discounts, that means you probably will pay only $2,800 or $2,900 for $10,000 worth of 20-year strip-Ts. Because there's an active secondary market for Treasury strips, investors can get in and out of these securities with ease just about any time they want. Strip-Ts offer the maximum in issue quality, a full array of different maturities, and an active secondary market—all of which explains why they are so popular.

mortgage-backed bond
a debt issue secured by a pool of home mortgages; issued primarily by federal agencies.

Mortgage-Backed Securities Simply put, a **mortgage-backed bond** is a debt issue that is secured by a pool of residential mortgages. An issuer, such as the Government National Mortgage Association (GNMA), puts together a pool of home mortgages and then issues securities in the amount of the total mortgage pool. These securities, also known as *pass-through securities* or *participation certificates,* are usually sold in minimum denominations of $25,000. Though their maturities can go out as far as 30 years, the average life is generally much shorter (perhaps as short as 8 to 10 years) because many of the mortgages are paid off early.

As an investor in one of these securities, you hold an undivided interest in the pool of mortgages. When a homeowner makes a monthly mortgage payment, that payment is essentially passed through to you, the bondholder, to pay off the mortgage-backed bond you hold. Although these securities come with normal coupons, *the interest is paid monthly rather than semiannually.* Actually, the monthly payments received by bondholders are, like mortgage payments, made up of both principal and interest. Because the principal portion of the payment represents return of capital, it is considered tax-free. The interest portion, however, is subject to ordinary state and federal income taxes.

HOTLINKS

For an index of agency issues and mortgage-backed bonds, see:

stocks.about.com/money/stocks/cs/
bonds_mortgage/index.htm

Mortgage-backed securities are issued primarily by three federal agencies. Although there are some state and private issuers (mainly big banks and S&Ls), agency issues dominate the market and account for 90% to 95% of the activity. The major agency issuers of mortgage-backed securities (MBSs) are:

- *Government National Mortgage Association (GNMA).* Known as Ginnie Mae, it is the oldest and largest issuer of MBSs.

- *Federal Home Loan Mortgage Corporation (FHLMC).* Known as Freddie Mac, it was the first to issue pools containing conventional mortgages. Stock in FHLMC is publicly owned and traded on the NYSE.

- *Federal National Mortgage Association (FNMA).* Known as Fannie Mae, it's the newest agency player and the leader in marketing seasoned/older mortgages. Its stock is also publicly owned and traded on the NYSE.

Together, these securities represent an important and rapidly growing segment of the U.S. bond market. Indeed, it has been estimated that by 2002 or 2003 *the mortgage-backed market will actually be bigger than the U.S. Treasury market.* And as the accompanying Investing in Action box explains, as the supply of Treasury securities dwindle, MBSs may soon replace U.S. Treasury securities as the benchmark yield.

One problem with mortgage-backed securities is that they *are self-liquidating investments;* a portion of the monthly cash flow to the investor is repayment of principal. Thus the investor is always receiving back part of the original investment capital; at maturity there is *no* big principal payment. To counter this problem, a number of *mutual funds* were formed that invest in mortgage-backed securities *but* automatically and continually reinvest the capital/principal portion of the cash flows. Mutual fund investors therefore receive only the interest from their investments and are thus able to preserve their capital.

collateralized mortgage obligation (CMO)
mortgage-backed bond whose holders are divided into classes based on the length of investment desired; principal is channeled to investors in order of maturity, with short-term classes first.

Collateralized Mortgage Obligations Loan prepayments are another problem with mortgage-backed securities. In fact, it was in part an effort to defuse some of the prepayment uncertainty in standard mortgage-backed securities that led to the creation of **collateralized mortgage obligations (CMOs).**

Normally, as pooled mortgages are prepaid, all bondholders receive a pro-rated share of the prepayments. The net effect is to sharply reduce the life of the bond. A CMO, in contrast, divides investors into classes (called "tranches," which is French for "slice"), depending on whether they want a short, intermediate, or long-term investment. Although interest is paid to all bondholders, all principal payments go first to the shortest tranche until it is fully retired. Then the next class in the sequence becomes the sole recipient of principal, and so on until the last tranche is retired.

Basically, CMOs are *derivative securities* created from traditional mortgage-backed bonds, which are placed in a trust. Participation in this trust is then sold to the investing public in the form of CMOs. The net effect of this transformation is that CMOs look and behave very much like any other bond: They offer predictable interest payments and have (relatively) predictable maturities. However, although they carry the same triple-A ratings and implicit U.S. government backing as the mortgage-backed bonds that underlie them, CMOs represent a quantum leap in complexity. Some types of CMOs can be as simple and safe as Treasury bonds. But others can be far more volatile—and risky—than the standard MBSs they're made from. That's because when putting CMOs together, Wall Street performs the financial equivalent of gene splicing: Investment bankers isolate the interest and principal payments from the underlying MBSs and rechannel them to the different tranches. It's not issue quality or risk of default that's the problem here, but rather prepayment, or call, risk. All the bonds will be paid off; it's just a matter of when. Different types of CMO tranches have different levels of prepayment risk. The overall risk in a CMO cannot, of course, exceed that of the underlying mortgage-backed bonds, so in order for there to be some tranches with very little (or no) prepayment risk, others have to endure a lot more. The net effect is that while some CMO tranches are low in risk, others are extremely volatile.

Unfortunately, CMOs became so complex and so exotic that nobody, not even professional money managers, knew exactly what they were getting into. When market interest rates shot way up in 1994, CMO investors took huge losses. In the process, they lost much of their appetite for these securities. Of course, the mortgage market still exists today, but investors are no longer so interested in the "exotics." Instead, their attention has shifted back to "plain vanilla" MBSs or to simpler, less exotic (i.e., less risky) CMOs.

Asset-Backed Securities The creation of mortgage-backed securities and CMOs quickly led to the development of a new market technology—the process of **securitization**, whereby various lending vehicles are transformed into marketable securities, much like a mortgage-backed security. Investment bankers are now selling billions of dollars worth of pass-through securities, known as **asset-backed securities** (**ABS**), which are backed by pools of auto loans and credit card bills (two of the principal types of collateral), as well as computer leases, hospital receivables, small business loans, truck rentals, and even royalty fees. These securities, first introduced in the mid-1980s, are created when an investment banker bundles together some type of debt-linked asset (such as loans or receivables), and then sells investors—via asset-backed securities—the right to receive all or part of the future payments made on that debt. For example, GMAC, the financing arm of General Motors, is a regular issuer of collateralized *auto loan* securities. When it wants to get some of its car loans off its books, GMAC takes the monthly cash flow from a pool of

securitization
the process of transforming lending vehicles such as mortgages into marketable securities.

asset-backed securities (ABS)
securities similar to mortgage-backed securities that are backed by a pool of bank loans, leases, and other assets.

THE DREAM FACTORY—Which would you rather own— mundane financial assets like home mortgages and credit card receivables, or a piece of a rock star or best-selling author? Wall Street financier David Pullman made it possible to own part of a rock star in 1997 with "Bowie bonds," asset backed securities based on royalties of David Bowie songs. Since then his firm has offered more than $200 million of bonds secured by works of stars such as James Brown, Marvin Gaye, and the Isley Brothers. What's next for Pullman? He believes any form of intellectual property is a good securitization candidate: authors' earnings, patents, and screenplays.

Source: Daniel Kadlec, "Creative Bonds: Banking on the Stars," *Time*, October 16, 2000, p. 82.

junk bonds
high-risk securities that have low ratings but produce high yields.

PIK-bond
a payment-in-kind junk bond that gives the issuer the right to make annual interest payments in new bonds rather than in cash.

auto loans and pledges them to a new issue of bonds, which are then sold to investors. In similar fashion, *credit card receivables* are regularly used as collateral for these bonds (indeed, they represent the biggest segment of the ABS market), as are *home equity loans,* the second-biggest type of ABS.

Investors are drawn to ABSs for a number of reasons. One is the relatively *high yields* they offer. Another is their *short maturities,* which often extend out no more than 3 to 5 years. A third is the *monthly, rather than semiannual, principal/interest payments* that accompany many of these securities. Also important to investors is their *high credit quality.* That's due to the fact that most of these deals are backed by generous credit protection. For example, the securities are often overcollateralized, which means that the pool of assets backing the bonds may be 25% to 50% larger than the bond issue itself. For whatever reason, the vast majority of ABS receive the highest credit rating possible (triple-A) from the leading agencies.

Most of the ABS market is centered on the three major forms of collateral—credit card receivables, home equity loans, and auto loans. The rest of the market is anything but traditional, though. Indeed, it seems that just about anything can be securitized, from trade receivables and aircraft loans to taxi medallions and lottery winnings.

Junk Bonds Junk bonds or (*high-yield bonds,* as they're also called) are highly speculative securities that have received low, sub-investment-grade ratings (typically Ba or B). These bonds are issued primarily by corporations and, also, by municipalities. Junk bonds generally take the form *of subordinated debentures,* which means the debt is unsecured and has a low claim on assets. These bonds are called "junk" because of their high risk of loss. The companies that issue them generally have excessive amounts of debt in their capital structures, and their ability to service that debt is subject to considerable doubt. Probably the most unusual type of junk bond is something called a **PIK-bond.** PIK stands for *payment in kind* and means that rather than paying the bond's coupon in cash, the issuer can make annual interest payments in the form of additional debt. This "financial printing press" usually goes on for 5 or 6 years, after which time the issuer is supposed to start making interest payments in real money.

Traditionally, the term *junk bond* was applied to the issues of troubled companies, which might have been well rated when first issued but slid to low ratings through corporate mismanagement, heavy competition, or other factors. That all changed during the 1980s, when the vast majority of junk bonds originated not with troubled companies but with a growing number of mature (fairly well-known) firms that used enormous amounts of debt to finance takeovers and buyouts. These companies would change overnight from investment-grade firms to junk as they piled on debt to finance a takeover—or the threat of one. (Wall Street refers to these firms as "fallen angels.")

Why would any rational investor be drawn to junk bonds? The answer is simple: They offer very high yields. Indeed, in a typical market, relative to investment-grade bonds, you can expect to pick up anywhere from 2.5 to 5 percentage points in added yield. In mid-2000, for example, investors were getting 11% or 12% yields on junk bonds, compared to 7% or 8% on investment-grade corporates. Obviously, *such yields are available only because of the correspondingly higher exposure to risk.* However, as we saw earlier in this chapter, there's more to bond returns than yield alone: The *returns* you end up with don't always correspond to the *yields* you went in with. Junk bonds are subject to a good deal of risk, and their prices are unstable. Indeed, unlike investment-grade bonds, whose prices are closely linked to the behavior of market interest rates, junk bonds tend to behave more like stocks. As a result, the returns you actually end up with are highly unpredictable. Accordingly, only investors who are thoroughly familiar with the risks involved, and who are comfortable with such risk exposure, should use these securities.

 ## A Global View of the Bond Market

Globalization has hit the bond market, just as it has the stock market. Foreign bonds have caught on with U.S. investors because of their high yields and attractive returns. There are risks with foreign bonds, of course, but high risk of default is *not* one of them. Instead, the big risk with foreign bonds has to do with the impact that currency fluctuations can have on returns in U.S. dollars.

By year-end 1999, the total value of the world bond market reached some $31 trillion. The United States has the biggest debt market, accounting for about 47% of the total. Far behind the Unites States is Japan, with about 18% of the world market, followed by Germany (at 8%), then Italy, the U.K., France, and Canada. Together, these seven countries account for nearly 85% of the world bond market. Worldwide, various forms of government bonds (e.g., Treasuries, agencies, and munis) dominate the market, accounting for about 55% of the total.

Although the United States today accounts for about half of the available fixed-income securities, that percentage is sure to decline in the future as foreign markets continue to expand. Therefore, by investing solely in U.S. fixed-income securities, an investor is excluding not only half of the investment possibilities worldwide but, more important, the faster growing half. Also, as Table 9.5 reveals, investors in U.S. bonds are missing out on some pretty attractive returns. (The results reported in the table *are total returns in U.S. dollars* and include coupon income, capital gains or losses, and the effects of changes in currency exchange rates.) In fact, over the 20-year period from 1980 through 1999, the U.S. market provided the highest annual return just once (in 1982). A lot of the difference between U.S. and foreign returns in the bond market is due, of course, to the impact of currency exchange rates. Still, the fact remains that from an international perspective, better returns to U.S. investors are usually available to those willing to go offshore.

U.S.-Pay Versus Foreign-Pay Bonds There are several different ways to invest in foreign bonds (*excluding* foreign bond mutual funds, which we'll examine in Chapter 12). From the perspective of a U.S. investor, foreign bonds can be divided into two broad categories on the basis of the currency in which the bond is denominated: *U.S.-pay* (or dollar-denominated) bonds and *foreign-pay* (or non-dollar-denominated) bonds. All the cash flows—including purchase price, maturity value, and coupon income—from dollar-denominated foreign bonds are in U.S. dollars, whereas the cash flows from nondollar bonds are designated in a foreign currency or in a basket of foreign currencies, such as the European Currency Unit (ECU).

TABLE 9.5   Comparative Annual Returns in the World's Major Bond Markets

Annual Total Returns (in U.S. dollars)

	Australia	Canada	France	Germany	Italy	Japan	U.K.	U.S.
1980	−19.0%	−1.6%	−11.0%	−10.3%	−11.8%	24.0%	31.2%	−2.6%
1981	−7.1	−4.7	−18.8	−8.8	−25.0	8.4	−18.8	−0.9
1982	15.0	1.4	5.3	16.5	11.5	3.6	28.8	43.8
1983	0.5	1.9	−0.4	−7.7	15.1	12.3	8.1	4.7
1984	4.9	1.1	6.6	1.4	21.9	2.3	−12.4	16.4
1985	−13.2	34.0	34.4	41.8	37.5	36.8	38.6	30.9
1986	17.1	19.5	27.6	38.4	88.6	36.4	36.4	19.8
1987	29.1	10.4	2.2	28.6	14.2	41.4	41.4	−0.3
1988	29.8	18.9	2.2	−6.6	−1.0	2.6	2.5	6.8
1989	5.1	16.1	8.9	5.6	15.5	−14.5	−3.7	14.0
1990	16.3	7.2	22.4	14.8	28.8	7.2	31.3	8.6
1991	24.3	21.5	13.4	9.8	15.1	23.4	12.8	14.8
1992	−0.1	−0.5	4.6	6.2	−14.4	11.3	−3.9	7.2
1993	16.2	11.4	13.1	7.3	14.0	27.1	19.5	10.1
1994	6.2	−9.9	4.6	9.1	2.1	8.5	−1.7	−2.9
1995	14.9	23.2	27.8	26.5	20.7	10.4	15.8	17.3
1996	19.8	11.3	4.8	−0.3	29.6	−5.9	18.3	2.9
1997	−7.3	4.8	−7.0	−8.9	−1.6	−4.3	10.4	10.0
1998	3.8	2.1	21.2	20.3	20.8	15.9	21.1	10.3
1999	4.1	4.3	−17.2	−16.5	−17.0	15.7	−4.4	−2.9

Average Annual Returns Over Extended Holding Periods

	Australia	Canada	France	Germany	Italy	Japan	U.K.	U.S.
5 years:								
1995–99	7.1%	9.1%	5.9%	4.2%	10.5%	6.4%	12.2%	7.5%
1990–94	12.6	6.0	11.6	9.4	9.1	15.5	11.6	7.6
10 years:								
1990–99 (the '90s)	9.8%	7.5%	8.8%	6.8%	9.8%	10.9%	11.9%	7.5%
1980–89 (the '80s)	5.0	9.1	4.6	8.3	13.4	14.0	13.1	12.4
15 years:								
1985–99	11.1%	11.6%	10.9%	11.7%	16.9%	14.1%	15.6%	9.8%
20 years:								
1980–99	8.0%	8.6%	7.2%	8.4%	13.2%	13.1%	13.6%	10.4%

Note: Total return = Coupon income + Capital gain (or loss) + Profit (or loss) from changes in currency exchange rates.
The returns shown here are *government bond returns* and as such, *the U.S. returns* will differ a bit from those shown in Tables 9.1 and 9.2 (which are yields and returns for *corporate bonds*).
Source: Datastream

Yankee bonds
bonds issued by foreign governments or corporations but denominated in dollars and registered with the SEC.

Dollar-Denominated Bonds Dollar-denominated foreign bonds are of two types: Yankee bonds and Eurodollar bonds. **Yankee bonds** are issued by foreign governments or corporations or by so-called supernational agencies, like the World Bank and the InterAmerican Bank. These bonds are issued and traded in the United States; they're registered with the SEC, and all transactions are in U.S. dollars. Buying a Yankee bond is really no different from buying any other U.S. bond: These bonds are traded on U.S. exchanges and

Eurodollar bonds
foreign bonds denominated in
dollars but not registered with
the SEC, thus restricting sales of
new issues.

the OTC market, and *because everything is in dollars, there's no currency exchange risk to deal with.* The bonds are generally very high in quality (which is not surprising, given the quality of the issuers) and offer highly competitive yields to investors.

Eurodollar bonds, in contrast, are issued and traded outside the United States. They are denominated in U.S. dollars, but they are not registered with the SEC, which means underwriters are legally prohibited from selling new issues to the U.S. public. (Only "seasoned" Eurodollar issues can be sold in this country.) The Eurodollar market today is dominated by foreign-based investors (though that is changing) and is primarily aimed at institutional investors.

Foreign-Pay Bonds From the standpoint of U.S. investors, foreign-pay international bonds encompass all those issues denominated in a currency other than dollars. These bonds are issued and traded overseas and are not registered with the SEC. Examples are German government bonds, which are payable in deutsche marks; Japanese bonds, issued in yen; and so forth. When investors speak of *foreign bonds,* it's this segment of the market that most of them are thinking of.

Foreign-pay bonds are subject to changes in currency exchange rates, which can dramatically affect total returns to U.S. investors. The returns on foreign-pay bonds are a function of three things: (1) the level of coupon (interest) income earned on the bonds; (2) the change in market interest rates, which determine the level of capital gains (or losses); and (3) the behavior of currency exchange rates. The first two variables are the same as those that drive bond returns in this country and are, of course, just as important to foreign bonds as they are to domestic bonds. Thus, if you're investing overseas, you still want to know what the yields are today and where they're headed. *It's really the third variable that separates the return behavior of dollar-denominated from foreign-pay bonds.*

We can assess returns from foreign-pay bonds by employing the same (modified) holding period return formula first introduced in our discussion of foreign stock returns. (See Equation 6.6 in Chapter 6.) For example, assume a U.S. investor purchased a German government bond, in large part because of the attractive 10% coupon it carried. If the bond was bought at par and market rates fell over the course of the year, the security itself would have provided a return in excess of 10% (because the decline in rates would provide some capital gains). However, if the deutsche mark (DM) fell relative to the dollar, the total return (in U.S. dollars) could have actually ended up at a lot less than 10%, depending on what happened to the U.S. $/DM exchange rate. To find out exactly how this investment turned out, you could use Equation 6.6, and make a few (very minor) modifications to it (e.g., use interest income in place of dividends received). Like foreign stocks, *foreign-pay bonds can pay off from both the behavior of the security and the behavior of the currency.* As Table 9.5 shows, that combination, in many cases, means superior returns to U.S. investors. Knowledgeable investors find these bonds attractive not only because of their competitive returns but also because of *the positive diversification effects they have on bond portfolios.*

IN REVIEW

CONCEPTS

9.7 Briefly describe each of the following types of bonds: (a) *Treasury bonds,* (b) *agency issues,* (c) *municipal securities,* and (d) *corporate bonds.* Note some of the major advantages and disadvantages of each.

9.8 Briefly define each of the following and note how they might be used by fixed-income investors: (a) *zero-coupon bonds,* (b) *CMOs,* (c) *junk bonds,* and (d) *Yankee bonds.*

9.9 According to the *Investing in Action* box on page 386, why would investors be interested in TIPS? Why would the U.S. Treasury issue such a security? What are the advantages and disadvantages of this security from the investor's point of view?

9.10 According to the *Investing in Action* box on page 392, what might be some effects of a debt-free U.S. government? What might replace T-bonds as the risk-free yardstick?

9.11 What are the special tax features of (a) *Treasury securities,* (b) *agency issues,* and (c) *municipal bonds?*

9.12 Describe an *asset-backed security* (ABS) and identify some of the different forms of collateral used with these issues. Briefly note how an ABS differs from a MBS. What is the central idea behind securitization?

9.13 Identify the six or seven biggest bond markets in the world. How important is the U.S. bond market relative to the rest of the world?

9.14 What's the difference between dollar-denominated and non-dollar-denominated (foreign-pay) bonds? Briefly describe the two major types of U.S.-pay bonds. Can currency exchange rates affect the total return of U.S.-pay bonds? Of foreign-pay bonds? Explain.

Trading Bonds

LG 6

In large part as a result of the perceived safety and stability of bonds, many individual investors view bond investing as a relatively simple process. Such thinking, however, can often lead to unsatisfactory results, even losses. The fact is that not all bonds are alike, and picking the right security for the time is just as important for bond investors as it is for stock investors. Indeed, success in the bond market demands a thorough understanding not only of the different types of bonds but also of the many technical factors that drive bond yields, prices, and returns—things like call features, refunding provisions, and the impact that coupon and maturity can have on bond price volatility. Also, because bond ratings are so important to a smooth-running bond market, investors should become thoroughly familiar with them. Let's now take a look at these ratings and at the quotation system used for bonds.

Bond Ratings

bond ratings
letter grades that designate investment quality and are assigned to a bond issue by rating agencies.

Bond ratings are like grades: A letter grade that designates investment quality is assigned to an issue on the basis of extensive, professionally conducted financial analysis. Ratings are widely used and are an important part of the municipal and corporate bond markets, where issues are regularly evaluated and rated by one or more of the rating agencies. Even some agency issues, like the Tennessee Valley Authority (TVA), are rated, though they always receive ratings that confirm the obvious—that the issues are prime grade. The two largest and best-known rating agencies are Moody's and Standard & Poor's; another lesser known but still important bond-rating agency is Fitch Investors Service.

How Ratings Work Every time a large new issue comes to the market, it is analyzed by a staff of professional bond analysts to determine default risk exposure and investment quality. (A fee, usually ranging from $1,000 to $15,000 and paid by the issuer or the underwriter of the securities, is charged for rating each bond.) The rating agency thoroughly studies the financial records of the issuing organization and assesses its future prospects. Although the specifics of the actual credit analysis conducted by the rating agencies change with each issue, several major factors enter into most bond ratings. With a corporate issue, for example, these factors include an analysis of the issue's indenture provisions, an in-depth study of the firm's earning power (including the stability of its earnings), a look at the company's liquidity and how it is managed, a study of the company's relative debt burden, and an in-depth exploration of its coverage ratios to determine how well it can service both existing debt and any new bonds that are being contemplated or proposed. As you might expect, the firm's financial strength and stability are very important in determining the appropriate bond rating. Indeed, although there is far more to setting a rating than cranking out a few financial ratios, a strong relationship exists between the operating results and financial condition of the firm and the rating its bonds receive. Generally, the higher ratings are associated with more profitable companies that rely *less* on debt as a form of financing, are more liquid, have stronger cash flows, and have no trouble servicing their debt in a prompt and timely fashion.

Table 9.6 lists the various ratings assigned to bonds by the two major services. In addition to the standard rating categories noted in the table, Moody's uses numerical modifiers (1, 2, or 3) on bonds rated double-A to B, while S&P uses plus (+) or minus (−) signs on the same rating classes to show relative standing within a major rating category. For example, A+ (or A1) means a strong, high A rating, whereas A− (or A3) indicates that the issue is on the low end of the A rating scale. Except for slight variations in designations (Aaa vs. AAA), the meanings and interpretations are basically the same.

Note that the top four ratings (Aaa through Baa, or AAA through BBB) designate *investment-grade* bonds. Such ratings are highly coveted by issuers, as they indicate financially strong, well-run companies. The next two ratings (Ba/B or BB/B) are reserved for junk bonds. These ratings mean that although *the principal and interest payments on the bonds are still being met in a timely fashion,* the risk of default is relatively high. The issuers of these bonds generally lack the financial strength that backs investment-grade issues. (Sometimes the Caa1/CCC+ category is counted as part of the junk category, although technically the C rating class is meant to designate bonds that are already in default or getting very close to it.) Most of the time, Moody's and S&P assign identical ratings. Sometimes, however, an issue carries two different ratings. These **split ratings** are viewed simply as "shading" the quality of an issue one way or another. For example, an issue might be rated Aa by Moody's but A or A+ by S&P.

split ratings
different ratings given to a bond issue by the two major rating agencies.

TABLE 9.6   **Bond Ratings**

Moody's	S&P	Definition
Aaa	AAA	*High-grade investment bonds.* The highest rating assigned, denoting extremely strong capacity to pay principal and interest. Often called "gilt-edge" securities.
Aa	AA	*High-grade investment bonds.* High quality by all standards but rated lower primarily because the margins of protection are not quite as strong.
A	A	*Medium-grade investment bonds.* Many favorable investment attributes, but elements may be present that suggest susceptibility to adverse economic changes.
Baa	BBB	*Medium-grade investment bonds.* Adequate capacity to pay principal and interest but possibly lacking certain protective elements against adverse economic conditions.
Ba	BB	*Speculative issues.* Only moderate protection of principal and interest in varied economic times. (This is one of the ratings carried by junk bonds.)
B	B	*Speculative issues.* Generally lacking desirable characteristics of investment bonds. Assurance of principal and interest may be small; this is another junk-bond rating.
Caa	CCC	*Default.* Poor-quality issues that may be in default or in danger of default.
Ca	CC	*Default.* Highly speculative issues, often in default or possessing other market shortcomings.
C		*Default.* These issues may be regarded as extremely poor in investment quality.
	C	*Default.* Rating given to income bonds on which no interest is paid.
	D	*Default.* Issues actually in default, with principal or interest in arrears.

Source: Moody's *Bond Record* and Standard & Poor's *Bond Guide.*

Also, just because a bond is given a certain rating at the time of issue doesn't mean it will keep that rating for the rest of its life. Ratings change as the financial condition of the issuer changes. In fact, all rated issues are reviewed on a regular basis to ensure that the assigned rating is still valid. Many issues do carry a single rating to maturity, but it is not uncommon for ratings to be revised up or down. As you might expect, the market responds to rating revisions by adjusting bond yields accordingly. For example, an upward revision (e.g., from A to AA) causes the market yield on the bond to drop, as a reflection of the bond's improved quality. One final point: Although it may appear that the firm is receiving the rating, it is actually the *issue* that receives it. As a result, a firm's different issues can have different ratings. The senior securities, for example, might carry one rating and the junior issues another, lower rating.

HOT LINKS

For further explanation of Moody's bond ratings, go to:

www.moneypages.com/syndicate/
bonds/index.html

What Ratings Mean Most bond investors pay close attention to agency ratings, because ratings can affect not only potential market behavior but comparative market yields as well. Specifically, the higher the rating, the lower the yield, other things being equal. For example, whereas an A-rated bond might offer a 7.5% yield, a comparable triple-A issue would probably yield something like 7%. Furthermore, investment-grade securities are far more interest-sensitive and tend to exhibit more uniform price behavior than junk bonds and other lower-rated issues. Perhaps most important, *bond ratings serve to relieve individual investors of the drudgery of evaluating the investment quality of an issue on their own.* Large institutional investors often have their own staff of credit analysts who independently assess the creditworthiness of various corporate and municipal issuers; individual investors, in contrast, have little if anything to gain from conducting their own credit analysis. After all, credit analysis is time-consuming and costly, and it demands a good deal more expertise than the average individual investor possesses. Most important, the ratings are closely adhered to by a large segment of the bond investment community, in large part because it has been shown that *the rating agencies do a remarkably good job of assessing bond quality*. Thus individual investors can depend on assigned agency ratings as a viable measure of the creditworthiness of the issuer and an issue's risk of default. A word of caution is in order, however: Bear in mind that bond ratings are intended to measure only an issue's *default risk*, which has no bearing whatsoever on an issue's exposure to *market risk*. Thus if interest rates increase, even the highest-quality issues go down in price, subjecting investors to capital loss and market risk.

Reading the Quotes

One thing you quickly learn in the bond market is that transactions are not always as easy to conduct as they may seem. In the first place, many bonds have relatively "thin" markets. Indeed, some issues may trade only five or ten bonds a week, and many have no secondary market at all. There are, of course, numerous high-volume issues, but even so, you should pay particularly close attention to an issue's trading volume—especially if you're looking for lots of price action and need prompt order executions. In addition, it's not always easy to obtain current information on bond prices. That's because most bonds trade in over-the-counter markets, which are somewhat specialized, rather than on centralized exchanges; and except for Treasury securities, the financial pages provide little information on general market activity and even less on particular securities. Indeed, daily price quotes are widely available on only a few of the thousands of publicly traded corporate and municipal bonds. Finally, investors often have to look to both brokers and bankers to complete transactions. Most brokerage houses tend to confine their activities to new issues and to secondary market transactions of listed Treasury obligations, agency issues, and corporate bonds. Commercial banks, in contrast, are still the major dealers in municipal bonds and are active in Treasury and agency securities as well.

Except for municipal issues (which are usually quoted in terms of the yield they offer), bonds are quoted on the basis of their dollar prices. Such quotes are always interpreted as a *percent of par*. Thus, a quote of 97½ does not mean $97.50 but, instead, means that the issue is trading at 97.5% of the par value of the obligation. In the bond market, it's assumed that we're dealing with bonds that have par values of $1,000—or some multiple thereof. Accordingly, a quote of 97½ translates into a dollar price of $975. (With bond quotes, 1 point = $10, and ⅛ of a point = $1.25.) As you can see in the bond quotes in Figure 9.6, one quotation system is used for corporate bonds and another for governments. (Treasuries and agencies are quoted the same.)

Corporate Bond Quotes   To understand the system used with corporate bonds, look at the Duke Energy issue highlighted in Figure 9.6. The group of numbers immediately following the company name (which is often highly abbreviated) gives the coupon and the year in which the bond matures. Thus,

FIGURE 9.6 Price Quotations for Corporate and Government Bonds

Both corporate and Treasury bonds are quoted as a percent of their par value. But note that corporate bonds are quoted in eighths of a point, whereas Treasuries are quoted in thirty-seconds. Also observe that both coupon and maturity play vital roles in the quotation system. (*Source: Wall Street Journal,* July 7, 2000.)

CORPORATES

Bonds	Cur Yld.	Vol	Close	Net Chg
ChespkE 9¹/₈06	9.6	20	95	...
ChespkE 8¹/₂12	9.9	17	86	+ 2
ChiqBr 10s09	12.7	15	78¹/₂	+ ³/₈
vjClardg 11³/₄02f	...	10	49³/₄	− 1¹/₄
ClrkOil 9¹/₂04	10.3	51	91⁷/₈	+ 1⁷/₈
Coastl 9³/₄03	9.4	25	103¹/₂	− 1⁷/₈
Consec 8¹/₈03	9.7	109	83¹/₂	− 1
Conseco 10¹/₂04	12.5	22	83⁷/₈	− ¹/₈
Conseco 10¹/₂02	14.1	472	72³/₄	+ ¹/₄
ConPort 11s06	15.6	21	70¹/₂	+ ¹/₂
DR Hrtn 10s06	10.2	10	98	− 1³/₄
DevonE 4.9s08	cv	10	96¹/₄	+ ³/₄
Dole 7s03	7.5	10	93⁵/₈	+ ¹/₄
DukeEn 6³/₄25	7.9	10	85	+ 1¹/₄
DukeEn 7¹/₂25	7.9	25	94¹/₂	+ 1³/₄
Exxon 6s05	6.2	6	96¹/₄	...
Florsh 12³/₄02	13.7	2	93	+ 1
GEICap 7⁷/₈06	7.6	25	104	− ³/₄
GMA 5¹/₂01	5.6	14	97³/₈	− ¹/₈
GMA 9⁵/₈01	9.3	35	103¹/₂	+ 1⁵/₈
GMA 6⁷/₈01	7.0	5	98⁷/₈	...
GMA 7s02	7.0	15	99⁵/₈	...
GMA 8¹/₂03	8.3	35	102⁵/₈	...
GMA 8³/₄05	8.3	16	105	...
GMA zr12	...	12	37¹/₂	− 2
vjGenesH 9³/₄05f	...	105	12¹/₂	+ 1
HRPT 7¹/₂03	cv	5	90	+ 1
Hallwd 10s05	11.0	5	91	− ⁷/₈
HlthcrR 6.55s02	cv	40	86	− 4
Hilton 5s06	cv	589	80	+ 1¹/₈
Hollngr 9¹/₄06	9.3	10	99⁷/₈	+ 1³/₄
Honywll zr2000	...	45	98⁵/₃₂	...
Honywll zr03	...	40	79³/₄	+ ³/₄
HousF 9⁵/₈00	9.7	9	99⁵/₈	− ¹/₄
IBM 7¹/₄02	7.2	10	100³/₈	− ¹/₈
IBM 6.45s07	6.7	50	96⁷/₈	+ ⁵/₈
IBM 7¹/₂13	7.5	5	100³/₈	− 1⁷/₈
IntShip 9s03	9.0	33	99¹/₂	...
JCPL 6³/₈03	6.6	1	96¹/₂	+ ³/₈
KaufB 9³/₈03	9.5	80	99	− ¹/₄
KaufB 7³/₄04	8.4	10	92¹/₄	+ ⁵/₈
KaufB 9⁵/₈06	9.8	68	98	+ ⁵/₈
KerrM 7¹/₂14	cv	1	97	+ 1³/₄
Leucadia 8¹/₄05	8.6	20	96	...
Leucadia 7³/₄13	8.9	29	87¹/₄	...
LibPrp 8s01	cv	19	134	+ 2
Loews 3¹/₈07	cv	78	81¹/₂	− ¹/₂
Lucent 7¹/₄06	7.4	20	98¹/₈	− 1⁷/₈
MBNA 8.28s26	9.8	101	84³/₄	− 2³/₈
MSC Sf 7⁷/₈04	cv	50	87	...
MailWell 5s02	cv	18	83	+ 3

← Duke Energy bond

10³/₄% Treasury bond (noncallable)

GMAC zero-coupon bond

Stripped (zero-coupon) Treasuries

U.S. TREASURY STRIPS

Mat.	Type	Bid	Asked	Chg.	Ask Yld.
Feb 13	ci	45:23	45:29	−7	6.28
May 13	ci	45:01	45:06	−7	6.28
Aug 13	ci	44:10	44:15	−8	6.28
Nov 13	ci	43:20	43:25	−7	6.28
Feb 14	ci	42:29	43:02	−8	6.29
May 14	ci	42:08	42:13	−8	6.29
Aug 14	ci	41:19	41:24	−8	6.29
Nov 14	ci	40:30	41:04	−8	6.29
Feb 15	ci	40:09	40:14	−8	6.30
Feb 15	bp	40:09	40:15	−8	6.30
May 15	ci	39:21	39:26	−7	6.30
Aug 15	ci	39:01	39:07	−7	6.30
Aug 15	bp	39:04	39:10	−8	6.28
Nov 15	ci	38:14	38:19	−7	6.30
Nov 15	bp	38:19	38:24	−8	6.27
Feb 16	ci	37:27	38:01	−7	6.30
Feb 16	bp	38:02	38:07	−8	6.26
May 16	ci	37:09	37:15	−7	6.29
May 16	bp	37:22	37:27	−8	6.23
Aug 16	ci	36:23	36:29	−7	6.29
Nov 16	ci	36:06	36:11	−7	6.29
Nov 16	bp	36:15	36:21	−8	6.24
Feb 17	ci	35:20	35:26	−3	6.29
May 17	ci	35:03	35:09	−4	6.28
May 17	bp	35:07	35:13	−6	6.26
Aug 17	ci	34:19	34:24	−6	6.28
Aug 17	bp	34:23	34:28	−6	6.26
Nov 17	ci	33:30	34:03	−6	6.30
Feb 18	ci	33:16	33:22	−6	6.28
May 18	ci	33:00	33:06	−6	6.28
May 18	bp	33:02	33:08	−6	6.27

TREASURIES

Rate	Maturity Mo/Yr	Bid	Asked	Chg.	Ask Yld.
11¹/₈	Aug 03	113:03	113:07	−7	6.36
4¹/₄	Nov 03n	93:27	93:29	−6	6.29
11⁷/₈	Nov 03	116:09	116:13	−7	6.36
4³/₄	Feb 04n	95:02	95:04	−7	6.28
5⁷/₈	Feb 04n	98:22	98:24	−7	6.27
5¹/₄	May 04n	96:16	96:18	−7	6.26
7¹/₄	May 04n	103:06	103:08	−6	6.28
12³/₈	May 04	120:07	120:13	−8	6.32
6	Aug 04n	99:03	99:05	−7	6.23
7¹/₄	Aug 04n	103:14	103:16	−6	6.27
13³/₄	Aug 04	126:11	126:17	−8	6.32
5⁷/₈	Nov 04n	98:18	98:19	−7	6.25
7⁷/₈	Nov 04n	105:30	106:00	−7	6.28
11⁵/₈	Nov 04	119:31	120:05	−8	6.26
7¹/₂	Feb 05n	104:27	104:29	−8	6.26
6¹/₂	May 05n	101:05	101:07	−6	6.20
6³/₄	May 05n	102:14	102:15	−7	6.15
12	May 05	123:17	123:23	−8	6.26
6¹/₂	Aug 05n	101:03	101:05	−7	6.23
10³/₄	Aug 05	119:08	119:12	−9	6.26
5⁷/₈	Nov 05n	98:11	98:13	−8	6.23
5⁵/₈	Feb 06n	97:04	97:06	−6	6.22
9³/₈	Feb 06	114:15	114:19	−8	6.25
6⁷/₈	May 06n	103:01	103:03	−7	6.23
7	Jul 06n	103:24	103:26	−7	6.23
6¹/₂	Oct 06n	101:10	101:12	−7	6.23
3³/₈	Jan 07i	96:03	96:04	....	4.06
6¹/₄	Feb 07n	100:06	100:08	−7	6.24
7⁵/₈	Feb 02-07	101:18	101:20	−3	6.54
6⁵/₈	May 07n	102:07	102:09	−7	6.21
6¹/₈	Aug 07n	99:15	99:17	−7	6.21
7⁷/₈	Nov 02-07	102:25	102:27	−4	6.55
3⁵/₈	Jan 08i	97:04	97:05	....	4.07
5¹/₂	Feb 08n	95:26	95:28	−8	6.19
5⁵/₈	May 08n	96:18	96:20	−8	6.17
8³/₈	Aug 03-08	104:31	105:01	−7	6.56
4³/₄	Nov 08n	90:28	90:30	−8	6.15
8³/₄	Nov 03-08	106:17	106:19	−6	6.53
3⁷/₈	Jan 09i	98:20	98:21	....	4.06
5¹/₂	May 09n	95:21	95:23	−11	6.13
9¹/₈	May 04-09	108:22	108:24	−6	6.52
6	Aug 09n	99:01	99:02	−17	6.13
10³/₈	Nov 04-09	114:14	114:18	−6	6.48
4¹/₄	Jan 10i	101:22	101:23	....	4.03
6¹/₂	Feb 10n	103:09	103:10	−15	6.04
11³/₄	Feb 05-10	120:18	120:24	−9	6.47
10	May 05-10	114:11	114:15	−9	6.48
12³/₄	Nov 05-10	127:29	128:03	−10	6.46
13⁷/₈	May 06-11	135:18	135:24	−12	6.44
14	Nov 06-11	138:25	138:31	−12	6.43
10³/₈	Nov 07-12	122:26	123:00	−13	6.40
12	Aug 08-13	134:26	135:00	−16	6.40
13¹/₄	May 09-14	145:20	145:26	−17	6.39

13⁷/₈% Treasury bond (deferred call)

current yield
measure of the annual interest income a bond provides relative to its current market price.

the 7½ means that this particular bond carries a 7½% annual coupon and will mature in the year 2025.

The next column, labeled "Cur Yld," provides the *current yield*—in this case, 7.9%—being offered by the issue at its *current market price.* **Current yield** is a measure of the amount of annual interest income a bond provides relative to its prevailing market price. It is found by dividing annual coupon income by the closing price of the issue. In many respects, it is equivalent to the dividend yield measure used with stocks. We'll look at this bond valuation measure in more detail in Chapter 10.

The next entry in the Duke Energy quote in Figure 9.6 is the "Vol" column, which shows the actual number of bonds traded. In this case, 25 bonds were traded on the day of the quotes. The last two columns provide the bond's closing price for the day and the net change in the closing price. Thus the bond's closing (or last) price was 94½, up a point and three-quarters (+1¾) from its last close. In dollars, that means the bond traded at $945, which was $17.50 higher than its previous close. Note that corporate bonds are usually quoted in eighths of a point (as are munis) although, as we'll see, that's not the case with Treasury and agency bonds.

Government Bond Quotes In contrast to corporates (and munis), U.S. government bonds (Treasuries as well as agency issues) are listed in thirty-secondths of a point. With government bonds, the figures to the right of the colon (:) indicate the number of thirty-seconds in the fractional bid or ask price. For example, look at the ask price of the highlighted 10¾% Treasury issue in Figure 9.6: It is being quoted at 119:12 (ask). Translated, that means the bond is being quoted at 119¹²⁄₃₂, or 119.375% of par. Thus if you wanted to buy, say, $15,000 worth of this issue, you would have to pay $17,906.25 ($15,000 × 1.19375). Actually, the amount would be more than that after transaction costs were tacked on. Here's an example of a bond that is trading at a big premium (some 19 percent *above* its par value), in large part because market interest rates have fallen well below the bond's coupon.

Treasury (and agency) bond quotes include not only the coupon (see the "Rate" column) but also the year and *month* of maturity. Note also that when there's more than one date in the maturity column (e.g., see the 13⅞% Treasury bond, which shows a maturity of May 06–11), it's the *second* figure that indicates the issue's maturity date; the first one shows when the bond becomes freely callable. Thus the 13⅞% bond matures in May 2011, and it carries a call deferment provision that extends through May 2006. In contrast, a Treasury note or bond with a single maturity date, such as the 10¾% bond of August 2005, indicates that the issue is *noncallable.*

Unlike corporates, government bonds are quoted in bid/ask terms. The bid price signifies what the bond dealers are willing to pay for the securities (which is how much you can sell them for). The ask price is what the dealers will sell the bonds for (what you have to pay to buy them). Again, keep in mind that these bid/ask prices ignore transaction costs. When transaction costs are factored in, you'll end up getting *less* than the quoted price when you sell and paying *more* than the quoted price when you buy. This is especially true in the Treasury, agency, and municipal markets, where secondary market trades of, say, $25,000 or less can involve transactions costs of as much as *1% to 5%* of the amount traded. Finally, note that the "Yld" column with Treasuries is not the current yield of the issue but rather the bond's *promised yield-to-maturity.*

Promised yield-to-maturity is basically a fully compounded measure of return that captures both current income and capital gains or losses. (We'll examine yield-to-maturity in Chapter 10.)

Quotes on Zero-Coupon Bonds Also highlighted in both the corporate and Treasury quotes are some zero-coupon bonds. Look at the GMAC ("GMA") bonds highlighted in the corporate column; these are zero-coupon bonds. Such bonds are easy to pick out because they're identified by the letters *zr* in place of their coupons. For example, with the highlighted GMAC bonds, the *zr12* tells you the issue is a zero-coupon bond that matures in 2012.

Zeros are even easier to pick out in the Treasury quotes, because they're all listed under the heading "U.S. Treasury Strips." As we discussed earlier in this chapter, these securities are created by "stripping" the coupons from their bond issues and selling them separately from the principal. Thus the principal and interest *cash flows* can be sold on their own. (Look at the Strips quotes: A *ci* behind the maturity date means the issue is made up of coupon/interest cash flow, whereas a *bp* means it is made up of bond principal.) Regardless of whether they're corporates or stripped Treasuries, the prices of most zeros are quite low compared to regular coupon bonds. This is particularly true for longer maturities. Thus the quoted price of 37½ for the highlighted GMAC issue is *not* a misprint. Rather, it means that you could have purchased this bond for $375 (or 37.5% of par) and in the year 2012, receive $1,000 in return. Likewise, you could have purchased the (highlighted) February 15 stripped Treasury for just $400 (and change) and in 2015, receive a payment of $1,000 (which, by the way, would provide you with a fully compounded return of 6.30%).

IN REVIEW

CONCEPTS

9.15 What are *bond ratings,* and how can they affect investor returns? What are *split ratings?*

9.16 From the perspective of an individual investor, what good are bond ratings? Do bond ratings indicate the amount of market risk embedded in a bond? Explain.

9.17 Bonds are said to be quoted "as a percent of par." What does that mean? What is 1 point worth in the bond market?

9.18 Why should an aggressive bond trader be concerned with the trading volume of a particular issue?

Summary

LG 1 **Explain the basic investment attributes of bonds and their use as investment vehicles.** Bonds are publicly traded debt securities that provide investors with two basic sources of return: (1) current income and (2) capital gains. Current income is derived from the coupon (interest) payments received over the life of the issue. Capital gains can be earned whenever market interest rates fall. In addition to their yields and returns, bonds can also be used to shelter income from taxes and for the preservation and long-term accumulation of capital. Just as important, the diversification properties of bonds are such that they can greatly enhance portfolio stability.

LG 2 | **Describe the essential features of a bond and distinguish among different types of call, refunding, and sinking-fund provisions.** All bonds carry some type of coupon, which specifies the annual rate of interest to be paid by the issuer. Bonds also have predetermined maturity dates: Term bonds carry a single maturity date, and serial bonds have a series of maturity dates. Every bond is issued with some type of call feature, be it freely callable, noncallable, or deferred callable. Call features spell out whether an issue can be prematurely retired and, if so, when. Some bonds (temporarily) prohibit the issuer from paying off one bond with the proceeds from another by including a refunding provision. Others are issued with sinking-fund provisions, which specify how a bond is to be paid off over time.

LG 3 | **Describe the relationship between bond prices and yields, and explain why some bonds are more volatile than others.** The price behavior of a bond depends on the issue's coupon and maturity and on the movement in market interest rates. When interest rates go down, bond prices go up, and vice versa. However, the extent to which bond prices move up or down depends on the coupon and maturity of an issue. Bonds with lower coupons and/or longer maturities generate larger price swings.

LG 4 | **Identify the different types of bonds and the kinds of investment objectives these securities can fulfill.** The bond market is divided into four major segments: Treasuries, agencies, municipals, and corporates. Treasury bonds are issued by the U.S. Treasury and are virtually default-free. Agency bonds are issued by various political subdivisions of the U.S. government and make up an increasingly important segment of the bond market. Municipal bonds are issued by state and local governments in the form of either general obligation or revenue bonds. Corporate bonds make up the major non-government sector of the market and are backed by the assets and profitability of the issuing companies. Generally speaking, Treasuries are attractive because of their high quality, agencies and corporates because of the added returns they provide, and munis because of the tax shelter they offer.

LG 5 | **Discuss the global nature of the bond market and the difference between dollar-denominated and non-dollar-denominated foreign bonds.** There's growing investor interest in foreign bonds, particularly foreign-pay securities, because of their highly competitive yields and returns. Foreign-pay bonds cover all those issues that are denominated in some currency other than U.S. dollars. These bonds have an added source of return: currency exchange rates. In addition, there are dollar-denominated foreign bonds— Yankee bonds and Eurodollar bonds. These have no currency exchange risk because they are issued in U.S. dollars.

LG 6 | **Describe the role that bond ratings play in the market and the quotation system used with various types of bonds.** Municipal and corporate issues are regularly rated for bond quality by independent rating agencies. A rating of Aaa indicates an impeccable record. Lower ratings, such as A or Baa, indicate more risk. As with all investments, the returns required of lower-quality instruments generally are higher than those required of high-quality bonds. The bond market also has its own quotation system, wherein bonds are quoted as a percent of par. Thus, 1 point in the bond market represents $10 (not $1 as in the stock market).

Discussion Questions

LG 1 | Q9.1 Using the bond returns in Tables 9.1 and 9.2 as a basis of discussion:
   a. Compare the returns during the 1970s to those produced in the 1980s. How do you explain the differences?
   b. How did the bond market do in the 1990s? How does the performance in this decade compare to that in the 1980s and 1970s? Explain.

   c. What do you think would be a fair rate of return to expect from bonds in the future? Explain.

LG 1 Q9.2 Use the data in Tables 6.1 and 6.2 (for stocks) and Tables 9.1 and 9.2 (for bonds) to compare returns for stocks and bonds during the '70s, '80s, and '90s.

   a. Using both annual and holding-period returns, how would you describe the comparative performance of these two markets over each of three decades? Which market was more volatile?

   b. In view of these comparative returns, develop an argument for why investors *should* hold bonds. Can you think of any reason(s) why investors should *not* hold bonds? What are they?

   c. Assume that you're out of school and hold a promising, well-paying job. How much of your portfolio (in percentage terms) would you, personally, want to hold in bonds? Explain. What role do you see bonds playing in your own portfolio, particularly as you go farther and farther into the future.

LG 4 Q9.3 Identify and briefly describe each of the following types of bonds.

   a. Agency bonds.   b. Municipal bonds.
   c. Zero-coupon bonds.   d. Junk bonds.
   e. Foreign bonds.   f. Collateralized mortgage obligations (CMOs).
What type of investor do you think would be most attracted to each?

LG 1   LG 4 Q9.4 "Treasury securities are guaranteed by the U.S. government. Therefore, there is no risk in the ownership of such bonds." Briefly discuss the wisdom (or folly) of this statement.

LG 4   LG 5 Q9.5 Select the security in the left-hand column that best fits the investor desire described in the right-hand column.

   a. 5-year Treasury note.   1. Lock in a high coupon yield.
   b. A bond with a low coupon   2. Accumulate capital over a long period
      and a long maturity.   of time.
   c. Yankee bond.   3. Generate a monthly income.
   d. Insured revenue bond.   4. Avoid a lot of price volatility.
   e. Long-term Treasury strips.   5. Generate tax-free income.
   f. Noncallable bond.   6. Invest in a foreign bond.
   g. CMO.   7. Go for the highest yield available.
   h. Junk bond.   8. Invest in a pool of credit-card receivables.
   i. ABS.   9. Go for maximum price appreciation.

LG 6 Q9.6 Using the quotes in Figure 9.6, answer the following questions.

   a. What's the dollar (bid) price of the February 17 Treasury strip bond, and when does it mature?

   b. What's the current yield on the February 17 Treasury strip issue?

   c. Which is higher priced: the IBM 7½13 or the 7½% U.S. Treasury of Feb 05? (Use the ask price with the Treasury issue.) Both bonds carry roughly the same coupons; why don't they sell for about the same price?

   d. What's the dollar (ask) price of the 14% U.S. Treasury of Nov 06–11? Why is that issue priced so high? When does it mature?

   e. Contrast the call feature on the 12% Aug 08–13 Treasury bond with the 12% May 05 Treasury issue.

   f. Which bond was more actively traded, the GMAC 6⅞01 or the Conseco 10½–02?

   g. Which of the following bonds has the highest current yield, Conseco 8⅛03, the U.S. Treasury 13¾% of Aug–04, or the U.S. Treasury strip of Nov–17? Which one has the lowest current yield? Which one would produce the most dollar amount of annual interest income (per $1,000 par bond)?

Problems

LG 6

P9.1   A 6%, 15-year bond has 3 years remaining on a deferred call feature (the call premium is equal to 1 year's interest). The bond is currently priced in the market at $850. What is the issue's current yield?

LG 4

P9.2   An investor is in the 28% tax bracket and lives in a state with no income tax. He is trying to decide which of two bonds to purchase. One is a 7½% corporate bond that is selling at par. The other is a municipal bond with a 5¼% coupon that is also selling at par. If all other features of these two bonds are comparable, which should the investor select? Why? Would your answer change if this were an *in-state* municipal bond and the investor lived in a place with high state income taxes? Explain.

LG 4

P9.3   Sara Thomas is a wealthy investor who's looking for a tax shelter. Sara is in the maximum (39.6%) federal tax bracket and lives in a state with a very high state income tax. (She pays the maximum of 11½% in state income tax.) Sara is currently looking at two municipal bonds, both of which are selling at par. One is a double-A-rated *in-state* bond that carries a coupon of 6⅜%. The other is a double-A-rated *out-of-state* bond that carries a 7⅛% coupon. Her broker has informed her that comparable fully taxable corporate bonds are currently available with yields of 9¾%. Alternatively, long Treasuries are now available at yields of 9%. She has $100,000 to invest, and because all the bonds are high-quality issues, she wants to select the one that will give her maximum after-tax returns.
   a. Which one of the four bonds should she buy?
   b. Rank the four bonds (from best to worst) in terms of their taxable equivalent yields.

LG 6

P9.4   Which of the following three bonds offers the highest current yield?
   a. A 9½%, 20-year bond quoted at 97¾.
   b. A 16%, 15-year bond quoted at 164⅝.
   c. A 5¼%, 18-year bond quoted at 54.

LG 6

P9.5   Assume that an investor pays $850 for a long-term bond that carries a 7½% coupon. Over the course of the next 12 months, interest rates drop sharply. As a result, the investor sells the bond at a price of $962.50.
   a. Find the current yield that existed on this bond at the beginning of the year. What was it by the end of the 1-year holding period?
   b. Determine the holding period return on this investment. (See Chapter 5 for the HPR formula.)

LG 1

P9.6   In early January 1996, an investor purchased $30,000 worth of some single-A-rated corporate bonds. The bonds carried a coupon of 8⅞% and mature in 2013. The investor paid 94⅛ when she bought the bonds. Over the 5-year period from 1996 through 2000, the bonds were priced in the market as follows:

Year	Quoted Prices		Year-End Bond Yields
	Beginning of the Year	End of the Year	
1996	94⅛	100⅝	8.82%
1997	100⅝	102	8.70
1998	102	104⅝	8.48
1999	104⅝	110¼	8.05
2000	110¼	121⅛	7.33

Coupon payments were made on schedule throughout the 5-year period.

a. Find the annual holding period returns for 1996 through 2000. (See Chapter 5 for the HPR formula.)

b. Use the return information in Table 9.1 to evaluate the investment performance of this bond. How do you think it stacks up against the market? Explain.

P9.7 Letticia Garcia, an aggressive bond investor, is currently thinking about investing in a foreign (non-dollar-denominated) government bond. In particular, she's looking at a German government bond that matures in 15 years and carries a 9½% coupon. The bond has a par value of 10,000 DM and is currently trading at 110 (i.e., at 110% of par).

Letticia plans to hold the bond for a period of 1 year, at which time she thinks it will be trading at 117½—she's anticipating a sharp decline in German interest rates, which explains why she expects bond prices to move up. The current exchange rate is 1.58 DM/U.S. $, but she expects that to fall to 1.25 DM/U.S. $. Use the foreign investment return formula introduced in Chapter 6 (Equation 6.6) to answer the questions below.

a. *Ignoring the currency effect,* find the bond's total return (in its local currency).

b. Now find the total return on this bond *in U.S. dollars.* Did currency exchange rates affect the return in any way? Do you think this bond would make a good investment? Explain.

Case Problem 9.1 | *Max and Heather Develop a Bond Investment Program*

Max and Heather Peters, along with their two teenage sons, Terry and Thomas, live in Portland, Oregon. Max is a sales rep for a major medical firm, and Heather is a personnel officer at a local bank. Together, they earn an annual income of around $100,000. Max has just learned that his recently departed rich uncle has named him in his will to the tune of some $250,000 after taxes. Needless to say, the family is elated. Max intends to spend $50,000 of his inheritance on a number of long-overdue family items (e.g., some badly needed remodeling of their kitchen and family room, the down payment on a new Porsche Boxster, and braces to correct Tom's overbite). Max wants to invest the remaining $200,000 in various types of fixed-income securities.

Max and Heather have no unusual income requirements or health problems. Their only investment objectives are that they want to achieve some capital appreciation and they want to keep their funds fully invested for a period of at least 20 years. They would rather not have to rely on their investments as a source of current income but want to maintain some liquidity in their portfolio just in case.

Questions

a. Describe the type of *bond investment program* you think the Peters family should follow. In answering this question, give appropriate consideration to both return and risk factors.

b. List several different types of bonds that you would recommend for their portfolio, and briefly indicate why you would recommend each.

c. Using a recent issue of the *Wall Street Journal* or *Barron's,* construct a $200,000 bond portfolio for the Peters family. *Use real securities* and select any bonds (or notes) you like, given the following ground rules:

1. The portfolio must include at least one Treasury, one agency, and one corporate bond; also, in total, the portfolio must hold at least 5, but no more than 8 bonds or notes.

2. No more than 5% of the portfolio can be in short-term U.S. Treasury bills (but note that if you hold a T-bill, that limits your selections to just 7 other notes/bonds).

3. Ignore all transaction costs (i.e., invest the full $200,000) and assume all securities have par values of $1,000 (though they can be trading in the market at something other than par).

4. Use the latest available quotes to determine how many bonds/notes/bills you can buy.

d.   Prepare a schedule listing all the securities in your recommended portfolio. *Use a form like the one shown here,* and include the information it calls for on each security in the portfolio.

Security Issuer-Coupon-Maturity	Latest Quoted Price	Number of Bonds Purchased	Amount Invested	Annual Coupon Income	Current Yield
Example: U.S. Treas - 8½%-'05	96⁸⁄₃₂	25	$ 24,062	$ 2,125	8.83%
1.					
2.					
3.					
4.					
5.					
6.					
7.					
8.					
Totals	—	_____	$200,000	$_____	_____%

e.   *In one brief paragraph,* note the key investment attributes of your recommended portfolio and the investment objectives you hope to achieve with it.

Case Problem 9.2   *The Case of the Missing Bond Ratings*

LG 6

A lot goes into a bond rating, but it's probably safe to say that there's nothing more important in determining a bond's rating than the underlying financial condition and operating results of the company issuing the bond. Generally speaking, a variety of financial ratios are used to assess the financial health of a firm, and just as financial ratios can be used in the analysis of common stocks, they can also be used in the analysis of bonds—a process we refer to as *credit analysis*. In credit analysis, attention is directed toward the basic liquidity and profitability of the firm, the extent to which the firm employs debt, and the ability of the firm to service its debt.

The following financial ratios are often helpful in carrying out such analysis: (1) current ratio, (2) quick ratio, (3) net profit margin, (4) return on total capital, (5) long-term debt to total capital, (6) owners' equity ratio, (7) pretax interest coverage, and (8) cash flow to total debt. The first two ratios measure the liquidity of the firm, the next two its profitability, the following two the debt load, and the final two the ability of the firm to service its debt load. (For ratio 5, the *lower* the ratio, the better. For all the others, the *higher* the ratio, the better.) The following table lists each of these ratios for six different companies.

A Table of Financial Ratios
(All ratios are real and pertain to real companies)

Financial Ratio	Company 1	Company 2	Company 3	Company 4	Company 5	Company 6
1. Current ratio	1.13 ×	1.39 ×	1.78 ×	1.32 ×	1.03 ×	1.41 ×
2. Quick ratio	0.48 ×	0.84 ×	0.93 ×	0.33 ×	0.50 ×	0.75 ×
3. Net profit margin	4.6%	12.9%	14.5%	2.8%	5.9%	10.0%
4. Return on total capital	15.0%	25.9%	29.4%	11.5%	16.8%	28.4%
5. Long-term debt to total capital	63.3%	52.7%	23.9%	97.0%	88.6%	42.1%
6. Owners' equity ratio	18.6%	18.9%	44.1%	1.5%	5.1%	21.2%
7. Pretax interest coverage	2.3 ×	4.5 ×	8.9 ×	1.7 ×	2.4 ×	6.4 ×
8. Cash flow to total debt	34.7%	48.8%	71.2%	20.4%	30.2%	42.7%

Notes: Ratio (2)—Whereas the current ratio relates current assets to current liabilities, the quick ratio considers only the most liquid current assets (cash, short-term securities, and accounts receivable) and relates them to current liabilities.
Ratio (4)—Relates pretax profit to the total capital structure (long-term debt + equity) of the firm.
Ratio (6)—Shows the amount of stockholders' equity used to finance the firm (stockholders' equity ÷ total assets).
Ratio (8)—Looks at the amount of corporate cash flow (from net profits + depreciation) relative to the total (current + long-term) debt of the firm.
The other four ratios are as described in Chapter 6.

Questions

a. Three of these companies have bonds that carry investment-grade ratings. The other three companies carry junk-bond ratings. Judging by the information in the table, which three companies have the investment-grade bonds and which three the junk bonds? Briefly explain your selections.

b. One of these six companies is a AAA-rated firm and one is B-rated. Identify those two companies. Briefly explain your selection.

c. Of the remaining four companies, one carries a AA rating, one carries an A rating, and two are BB-rated. Which companies are they?

Web Exercises

The following table shows Web sites on various topics related to bonds.

Web Address	Primary Investment Focus
www.publicdebt.treas.gov/servlet /bpdindex	Public debt site index. Excellent source of information on U.S. Treasury debt.
www.investinginbonds.com	Investing in Bonds is a great starting place.
www.bonds-online.com	Get prices on over 15,000 bond offerings.
www.moneyline.com	Bond glossary.
www.bradynet.com/	Bond prices—globals and Euro.
www.fitchibca.com/	Duff and Phelps is a leading global rating agency.
www.wallstreetcity.com/planning /planning_main.asp	Use the personal investment planner for planning and asset management. The planner will determine your risk level and calculate how long your current investments will last after your retirement.

W 9.1   Go to www.financenter.com/products/analyzers/bond.fcs. Click on [Bond Calculators] and [What is my yield to maturity?]. Use the following inputs: 98% for price paid, 7.0% coupon, 180 months to maturity, 15% federal tax, 8% state tax, 4% coupon investment rate, and corporate bond. Click on [Results]. What is your return before and after taxes on a taxable investment?

W 9.2   Return to the opening screen for the site in Exercise W 9.1. Click on [Bond Calculators] and [How will rate changes affect my bond's current value?]. Change the market rate to 9% and note the results. What is your bond's value (a) if rates drop to 7%, and (b) if rates rise to 11%?

W 9.3   Refer to www.smartmoney.com/onebond/index.cfm?story=bondcalculator. Begin by entering the bond's coupon rate % (7) and maturity (October 2025). If you then enter a price (89.38), the calculator will display the bond's yield-to-maturity as 8%. If you enter a yield % (8), the calculator will show you the corresponding price, 89.38. Now do a calculation of your own. What is the yield (%) when the price is 105? What is the price when the yield is 7%?

You can also use the sliders to see the effects of price and yield changes. Watch prices and yields literally move in opposite directions. Note that prices are written in the standard bond format, where 100 means face value, 90 means 90% of face value, and so on.

W 9.4   Knowledge of the probability of default is very important in choosing a bond. Visit Moody's at www.moodys.com and click on [Rating Actions]. Choose any two firms or banks whose ratings are placed on review

for possible downgrade. What bond ratings were changed, and why?

For additional practice with concepts from this chapter, visit

www.awl.com/gitman_joehnk

Black & Decker Corp. is one of the nation's largest and most diversified manufacturers, ranking 356 on the Fortune 500 and ninth in its industry group. Over the years, Black & Decker has used acquisitions of smaller companies to expand into many different areas beyond its original line of power tools and accessories. Black & Decker's product line today also includes residential security hardware, household appliances, and metal and plastic fasteners/fastening systems for commercial applications.

To finance its growth, Black & Decker often used long-term bonds. In 1991 the company had $2.6 billion of long-term debt on its books, giving it a debt-to-equity ratio of 2.56—well above industry averages. Although the company reduced its debt load steadily, it still had $1.6 billion as of 1997. Its six issues, with maturities from 2000 to 2028, carried interest rates ranging from 6.55% to 7.5%. Because of the relatively large amount of debt on Black & Decker's balance sheet, Standard & Poor's Corporation rated its bonds BBB–, the lowest investment grade rating. As a result, the company had to pay more interest on its debt than a higher-rated company. Had the company's financial position weakened further, S&P might have downgraded the bonds to BB or lower—the high-yield, or "junk," bond category. The market price of Black & Decker bonds would have declined in reaction to such a move. However, in April 1999, S&P upgraded Black & Decker's bonds to BBB as the company continued to make significant strides in reducing its debt. By December 31, 2000, long-term debt was just under $800 million, and the debt-to-equity ratio, though still above industry standards, was 1.15.

As we'll see in this chapter, a bond's price is affected by many factors, including credit quality and the general level of interest rates. Investors must evaluate these factors when deciding whether the market value of a bond will provide the return they need.

CHAPTER 10

BOND VALUATION AND ANALYSIS

LEARNING GOALS

After studying this chapter, you should be able to:

LG 1 Explain the behavior of market interest rates, and identify the forces that cause interest rates to move.

LG 2 Describe the term structure of interest rates, and note how these so-called yield curves can be used by investors.

LG 3 Understand how bonds are valued in the marketplace.

LG 4 Describe the various measures of yield and return, and explain how these standards of performance are used in bond valuation.

LG 5 Understand the basic concept of duration, how it can be measured, and its use in the management of bond portfolios.

LG 6 Discuss various bond investment strategies and the different ways these securities can be used by investors.

The Behavior of Market Interest Rates

LG 1 LG 2

You will recall from Chapter 4 that rational investors try to earn a return that fully compensates them for risk. In the case of bondholders, that required return (r_i) has three components: the real rate of return (r^*), an expected inflation premium (IP), and a risk premium (RP). Thus the required return on a bond can be expressed by the following equation:

Equation 10.1

$$r_i = r^* + IP + RP$$

The real rate of return and inflation premium are external economic factors, and together they equal the risk-free rate (R_F). Now, to find the required return, we need to consider the unique features and properties of the bond issue itself; we can do this by adding the bond's risk premium to the risk-free rate. A bond's risk premium (RP) will take into account key issue and issuer characteristics, including such variables as the type of bond, the issue's term-to-maturity, its call features, and bond rating. Together, the three components in Equation 10.1 (r^*, IP, and RP) determine the level of interest rates at any given point in time.

Because interest rates have a significant bearing on bond prices and yields, both conservative and aggressive investors closely monitor them. Conservative investors watch interest rates because one of their major objectives is to lock in high yields. Aggressive traders also have a stake in interest rates because their investment programs are often built on the capital gains opportunities that accompany major swings in rates.

Keeping Tabs on Market Interest Rates

Just as there is no single bond market but a series of different market sectors, so too there is no single interest rate that applies to all segments of the market. Rather, each segment has its own, unique level of interest rates. Granted, the various rates tend to drift in the same direction over time and follow the same general pattern of behavior. But it's also common for **yield spreads** (interest rate differentials) to exist among the various market sectors. We can summarize the more important market yields and yield spreads as follows:

yield spreads
differences in interest rates that exist among various sectors of the market.

- Municipal bonds usually carry the lowest market rates because of their tax-exempt feature. As a rule, their market yields are about 20% to 30% lower than corporates. In the taxable sector, Treasuries have the lowest yields (because they have the least risk), followed by agencies and then corporates, which provide the highest returns.
- Issues that normally carry bond ratings (e.g., municipals or corporates) generally display the same behavior: the lower the rating, the higher the yield.
- There is generally a direct relationship between the coupon an issue carries and its yield. Discount (low-coupon) bonds yield the least, and premium (high-coupon) bonds yield the most.
- In the municipal sector, revenue bonds yield more than general obligation bonds.
- Bonds that are freely callable generally provide the highest returns, at least at date of issue. These are followed by deferred call obligations and then by noncallable bonds, which yield the least.

- As a rule, bonds with long maturities tend to yield more than short issues. However, this rule does not hold; sometimes, as in mid-2000, short-term yields equal or exceed the yields on long-term bonds.

The preceding list can be used as a general guide to the higher-yielding segments of the market. For example, income-oriented municipal bond investors might do well to consider certain high-quality revenue bonds as a way to increase yields; and investors who like to stick to high-quality issues might select agency bonds, rather than Treasuries, for the same reason.

As an investor, you should pay close attention to interest rates and yield spreads, and try to stay abreast not only of the current state of the market but also of the *future direction in market rates*. For example, if you are a conservative (income-oriented) investor and think that rates have just about peaked, that should be a clue to try to lock in the prevailing high yields with some form of call protection. (For example, buy bonds, like Treasuries or double-A-rated utilities, that are noncallable or still have lengthy call deferments.) In contrast, if you're an aggressive bond trader who thinks rates have peaked (and are about to drop), that should be a signal to buy bonds that offer maximum price appreciation potential (low-coupon bonds that still have a long time before they mature.) Clearly, in either case, *the future direction of interest rates is important!*

But how do you formulate such expectations? Unless you have considerable training in economics, you will probably have to rely on various published sources. Fortunately, a wealth of such information is available. Your broker is an excellent source for such reports, as are investor services like Moody's and Standard & Poor's; and, of course, there are numerous online sources. Finally, there are widely circulated business and financial publications (the *Wall Street Journal, Forbes, Business Week,* and *Fortune,* to name a few) that regularly address the current state and future direction of market interest rates. One of the best sources is illustrated in Figure 10.1. Predicting the direction of interest rates is not easy. However, by taking the time to read some of these publications and reports regularly and carefully, you, too, can keep track of the behavior of interest rates and at least get a handle on what experts predict is likely to occur in the near future—say, over the next 6 to 12 months, perhaps even longer.

What Causes Rates to Move?

Although interest rates are a complex economic issue, we do know that certain forces are especially important in influencing their general behavior. Serious bond investors should make it a point to become familiar with the major determinants of interest rates and try to monitor those variables, at least informally.

And in that regard, perhaps no variable is more important than *inflation*. Changes in the inflation rate (or even expectations about its future course) have a direct and pronounced effect on market interest rates. Clearly, if inflation is expected to slow down, then market interest rates should fall as well. To gain an appreciation of the extent to which interest rates are linked to inflation, take a look at Figure 10.2. Note that as inflation drifts up, so do interest rates. On the other hand, a drop in inflation is matched by a similar decline in interest rates.

CREDIT MARKETS

Bond Prices Finish Lower After a Thin Session, Depressed by Expected Heavy New-Issue Slate

By MICHAEL S. DERBY
And GREGORY ZUCKERMAN
Staff Reporters of THE WALL STREET JOURNAL

NEW YORK—The afterglow of Friday's noninflationary employment report died out quickly yesterday, as bonds slipped in weak trading, weighed down by what is expected to be a heavy calendar of corporate-bond sales this week.

At 4 p.m., the price of the 10-year Treasury note was down 5/32, or $1.5625 per $1,000 face amount, at 103 14/32. Its yield rose to 6.022% from 6.001% Friday, as yields move inversely to prices.

Meanwhile, the price of the 30-year Treasury bond was down 9/32 at 105 5/32, as its yield rose to 5.881% from 5.861%.

Treasury prices spent most of the day losing ground. But Treasurys were able to stage a small rally late in the day, aided by a little bit of bargain-hunting buying that came amid thin overall levels of trade, traders said.

"We've done quite a bit better toward the close, but we're sort of in a hangover mode from Friday" and its overly optimistic price increases, said Richard Hollocher, vice president with broker-dealer A.G. Edwards in St. Louis.

Traders said that while Friday's employment figures were reassuring, they weren't good enough to help the bond market break out of its recent range. But if inflation data in coming weeks prove benign, a rally could begin. "We're laying the building blocks now to a rally," said one long-bond trader.

On Friday, Treasurys posted robust gains after the June jobs report showed a nonfarm payroll gain of 11,000 jobs, far below expectations and the smallest monthly increase in the past four years. The report comforted some bond traders worried that the Federal Reserve in August will feel a need to raise interest rates, to ward off inflation.

Treasury Yield Curve

Yields as of 4:30 p.m. Eastern time

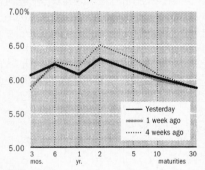

— Yesterday
••••••• 1 week ago
- - - 4 weeks ago

Source: Reuters

YIELD COMPARISONS

Based on Merrill Lynch Bond Indexes, priced as of midafternoon Eastern time.

			—52 Week—	
	7/10	7/7	High	Low
Corp.-Govt. Master	6.91%	6.89%	7.43%	6.16%
Treasury 1-10yr	6.32	6.29	6.90	5.52
10+ yr	6.21	6.20	6.93	6.02
Agencies 1-10yr	7.06	7.02	7.65	6.17
10+ yr	6.91	6.89	7.35	6.50
Corporate				
1-10 yr High Qlty	7.33	7.32	7.89	6.30
Med Qlty	7.91	7.88	8.43	6.79
10+yr High Qlty	7.84	7.83	8.24	7.05
Med Qlty	8.33	8.32	8.76	7.50
Yankee bonds(1)	7.60	7.58	8.10	7.01
Current-coupon mortgages (2)				
GNMA 7.50%	7.66	7.64	8.15	7.22
FNMA 8.00%	7.91	7.89	8.39	7.16
FHLMC8.00%	7.92	7.91	8.41	7.19
High-yield corporates	12.11	12.12	12.50	10.18
Tax-Exempt Bonds				
7-12-yr G.O. (AA)	4.98	4.98	5.50	4.71
12-22-yr G.O. (AA)	5.61	5.62	6.14	5.14
22+yr revenue (A)	5.86	5.87	6.35	5.38

Note: High quality rated AAA-AA; medium quality A-BBB/Baa; high yield, BB/Ba-C.
(1) Dollar-denominated, SEC-registered bonds of foreign issuers sold in the U.S. (2) Reflects the 52-week high and low of mortgage-backed securities indexes rather than the individual securities shown.

"failed to stage a breakout" from their recent trading range, and may head lower as a result.

A number of market participants also tied some of the market's weakness to nervousness ahead of two scheduled speeches by Federal Reserve Chairman Alan Greenspan, and key wholesale and inflation data to be released on Friday. Mr. Greenspan will speak on the "New Economy" today and global economic challenges tomorrow.

Mark Sauvigne, a government-bond trader at Chase Securities in New York, said that "everyone's going to wait for the news this week" before they'll be willing to shift into bonds.

Richard Hinderlie, who manages fixed-income funds for Invesco in Denver, said: "We think the economy is going to slow down a little bit. But is that enough to get the Fed off of our backs?"

Treasurys showed little reaction to a Fed coupon-pass action, in which it purchased securities maturing between August 2003 and May 2005.

Corporate & Junk Bonds

Electric utility **Dominion Resources** sold $1.1 billion of notes in two parts, the first of several jumbo corporate-bond offerings expected this week.

The Richmond, Va., utility's $400 million of three-year notes were priced at a yield margin of 1.30 percentage points over Treasurys, while the $700 million five-year notes came at 1.55 points over Treasurys.

Both issues came at yield margins that were narrower than early indications, a sign of strong demand for the credit as well as an improved market tone following the recent benign economic data, said Jim Probert, managing director and head of U.S. syndicate at Banc of America Securities, which was a joint lead manager on the deal with Chase Securities and Lehman Brothers.

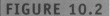

FIGURE 10.2

The Impact of Inflation on the Behavior of Interest Rates

The behavior of interest rates has always been closely tied to the movements in the rate of inflation. What changed in the early 1980s, however, was the spread between inflation and interest rates. Whereas a spread of roughly 3 points was common in the past, it has held at about 5 to 6 percentage points 1982.

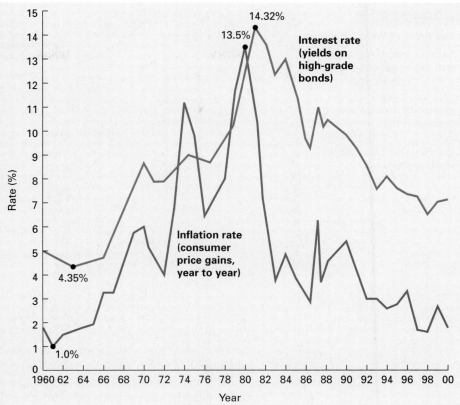

In addition to inflation, there are at least five other important economic variables that can significantly affect the level of interest rates:

- *Changes in the money supply.* An increase in the money supply pushes rates down (as it makes more funds available for loans), and vice versa. This is true only up to a point, however. If the growth in the money supply becomes excessive, it can lead to inflation, which, of course, means higher interest rates.

- *The size of the federal budget surplus.* What arguably was one of the biggest problems facing the U.S. economy at the beginning of the '90s had completely reversed course by the end of the decade, as 30 years of growing budget deficits gave way to a new era of *budget surpluses.* Because the U.S Treasury no longer needs to borrow money to cover deficits, the decreased demand for funds will reduce pressure on interest rates which, in turn, will promote lower rates. That's why bond market participants view a budget surplus so favorably. That is, as the federal budget deficit declines/disappears, so too will a lot of the pressure on bond interest rates (which brings with it the potential for falling market rates).

- *The level of economic activity.* Businesses need more capital when the economy expands. This need increases the demand for funds, and rates tend to rise. During a recession, economic activity contracts, and rates typically fall.

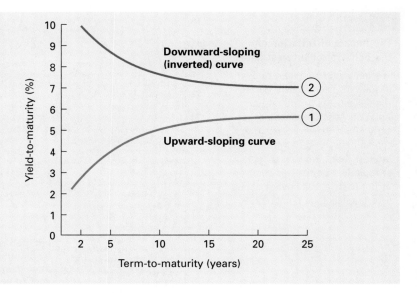

FIGURE 10.3

Two Types of Yield Curves

A yield curve relates term-to-maturity to yield-to-maturity at a given point in time. Although yield curves come in many shapes and forms, the most common is the *upward-sloping curve*. It shows that investor returns (yields) increase with longer maturities.

• *Policies of the Federal Reserve.* Actions of the Federal Reserve to control inflation also have a major effect on market interest rates. For example, when the Fed wants to slow real (or perceived) inflation, it usually does so by driving up interest rates, as it did several times in 1999–2000. Unfortunately, such actions can also have the nasty side effect of slowing down business activity as well.

• *The level of interest rates in major foreign markets.* Today, investors look beyond national borders for investment opportunities. If rates in major foreign markets rise, that puts pressure on rates in the United States to rise as well; if they don't rise, foreign investors may be tempted to dump their dollars to buy higher-yielding foreign securities.

The Term Structure of Interest Rates and Yield Curves

term structure of interest rates
the relationship between the interest rate or rate of return (yield) on a bond and its time to maturity.

yield curve
a graph that represents the relationship between a bond's term to maturity and its yield at a given point in time.

Although many factors affect the behavior of market interest rates, one of the most popular and widely studied is *bond maturity.* The relationship between interest rates (yield) and time to maturity for any class of similar-risk securities is called the **term structure of interest rates.** This relationship can be depicted graphically by a **yield curve,** which relates a bond's *term* to maturity to its *yield* to maturity at a given point in time. A particular yield curve exists for only a short period of time. As market conditions change, so do the yield curve's shape and location.

Types of Yield Curves Two different types of yield curves are illustrated in Figure 10.3. By far, the most common type is curve 1, the *upward-sloping* curve. It indicates that yields tend to increase with longer maturities. The longer a bond has to go until maturity, the greater the potential for price volatility and the risk of loss. Investors, therefore, require higher risk premiums to induce them to buy the longer, riskier bonds. Occasionally, the yield curve becomes *inverted,* or downward-sloping, as shown in curve 2, which occurs when short-term rates are higher than long-term rates. This curve generally results from actions by the Federal Reserve to curtail inflation by driving short-term interest rates way up. In addition to these, there are two other types of yield curves that appear from time to time: the *flat* yield curve, when rates for short- and long-term debt are essentially the same, and the *humped* yield curve, when intermediate-term rates are the highest.

Plotting Your Own Curves Yield curves are constructed by plotting the yields for a group of bonds that are similar in all respects but maturity. Treasury securities (bills, notes, and bonds) are typically used to construct yield curves. There are several reasons for this: Their yields are easily found in financial publications, they have no risk of default, and they are homogeneous with regard to quality and other issue characteristics. Investors can also construct yield curves for other classes of debt securities, such as A-rated municipal bonds, Aa-rated corporate bonds, or even certificates of deposit.

Figure 10.4 shows the yield curves for Treasury securities on two dates, November 18, 1997, and July 10, 2000. To draw these curves, you need Treasury quotes from the *Wall Street Journal*. (Note that actual quoted yields for curve 2 are provided in the boxed information right below the graph.) Given the required quotes, select the yields for the Treasury bills, notes, and bonds maturing in approximately 3 months, 6 months, and 1, 2, 5, 10, 20, and 30 years. The yields used for this curve are highlighted. (You could include more points, but they would not have much effect on the general shape of the curve.) Next, plot the points on a graph whose horizontal (*x*) axis represents time to maturity in years and whose vertical (*y*) axis represents yield to maturity. Connect the points to create the curves shown in Figure 10.4. You'll notice that because curve 2 is downward-sloping (i.e., the 30-year yield is less than T-bills rates), it ended with a lower yield than curve 1, even though it started at a substantially higher level.

Explanations of the Term Structure of Interest Rates As we noted earlier, the shape of the yield curve can change over time. Three commonly cited theories—the expectations hypothesis, the liquidity preference theory, and the market segmentation theory—explain more fully the reasons for the general shape of the yield curve.

Expectations Hypothesis The **expectations hypothesis** suggests that the yield curve reflects investor expectations about the future behavior of interest rates. This theory argues that the relationship between rates today and rates expected in the future is due primarily to investor expectations about inflation. If investors anticipate higher rates of inflation in the future, they will require higher long-term interest rates today, and vice versa. To see how this explanation can be applied in practice, consider the behavior of U.S. Treasury securities.

Because Treasury securities are considered essentially risk-free, only two components determine their yield: the real rate of interest and inflation expectations. Because the real interest rate is the same for all maturities, variations in yields are caused by differing inflation expectations associated with different maturities. This hypothesis can be illustrated using the July 10, 2000, yields for four of the Treasury maturities in Figure 10.4. If we assume that the

---

HOT LINKS

For the latest information on the U.S. economy and bonds, go to the SmartMoney Web site at:

www.smartmoney.com/bonds

expectations hypothesis
theory that the shape of the yield curve reflects investor expectations of future interest rates.

FIGURE 10.4

Yield Curves on U.S. Treasury Issues

Here we see two yield curves constructed from actual market data (quotes). Note the different shapes of the two curves: Curve 1 has a normal upward slope, and curve 2 is actually downward sloping. As a result, Curve 2 started well above curve 1, but ended well below it. (*Source: Wall Street Journal,* July 11, 2000.)

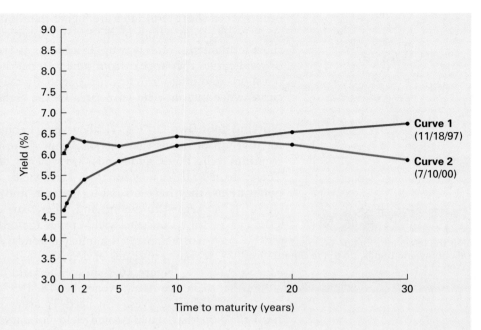

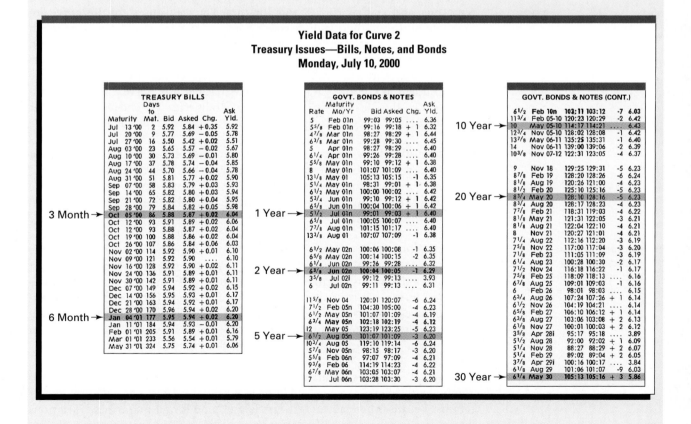

Yield Data for Curve 2
Treasury Issues—Bills, Notes, and Bonds
Monday, July 10, 2000

real rate of interest is 3%, then the inflation expectation during the period to maturity is as shown in column 3 of the following table.

Maturity	(1) November 18, 1997 Yield	(2) Real Rate of Interest	(3) Inflation Expectation [(1) − (2)]
3 months	6.04%	3.00%	3.04%
1 year	6.40	3.00	3.40
5 years	6.20	3.00	3.20
10 years	6.43	3.00	3.43

According to the expectations hypothesis, the numbers in column 3 would suggest that in early July 2000, investors didn't foresee much of a problem with inflation. As a result, the yield curve (in Figure 10.4) was a lot flatter in 2000 than it was in 1997.

Generally, under the expectations hypothesis, an increasing inflation expectation results in an upward-sloping yield curve, a decreasing inflation expectation results in a downward-sloping yield curve, and a stable inflation expectation results in a relatively flat yield curve. Although, as we'll see below, other theories do exist, the observed strong relationship between inflation and interest rates lends considerable credence to this widely accepted theory.

Liquidity Preference Theory More often than not, yield curves have at least a mild upward slope, as in 1997. One explanation for the frequency of upward-sloping yield curves is the **liquidity preference theory.** This theory states that, intuitively, long-term bond rates should be higher than short-term rates because of the added risks involved with the longer maturities. In other words, because of the risk differential (real or perceived) between long- and short-term debt securities, rational investors will prefer the less risky, short-term obligations *unless they can be motivated, via higher interest rates, to invest in the longer bonds.*

Actually, there are a number of reasons why rational investors should prefer short-term securities. To begin with, they are more liquid (more easily converted to cash) and less sensitive to changing market rates, which means there is less risk of loss of principal. For a given change in market rates, the prices of longer-term bonds will show considerably more movement than the prices of short-term bonds. Simply put, uncertainty increases over time, and investors therefore require a premium to invest in long maturities. In addition, just as investors tend to require a premium for tying up funds for longer periods, borrowers will also pay a premium in order to obtain long-term funds. Borrowers thus assure themselves that funds will be available, and they avoid having to roll over short-term debt at unknown and possibly unfavorable rates. All of these preferences and market forces explain why higher rates of interest should be associated with longer maturities and why it's perfectly rational to expect upward-sloping yield curves.

Market Segmentation Theory Another often-cited theory, the **market segmentation theory,** suggests that the market for debt is segmented on the basis of maturity preferences of different types of financial institutions and

liquidity preference theory
theory that investors tend to prefer the greater liquidity of short-term securities and therefore require a premium to invest in long-term securities.

market segmentation theory
theory that the market for debt is segmented on the basis of maturity, that supply and demand within each segment determines the prevailing interest rate, and that the slope of the yield curve depends on the relationship between the prevailing rates in each segment.

investors. According to this theory, the yield curve changes as the supply and demand for funds within each maturity segment determines its prevailing interest rate. The equilibrium between the financial institutions that supply the funds for short-term maturities (e.g., banks) and the borrowers of those short-term funds (e.g., businesses with seasonal loan requirements) establishes interest rates in the short-term markets. Similarly, the equilibrium between suppliers and demanders in such long-term markets as life insurance and real estate determines the prevailing long-term interest rates.

The shape of the yield curve can be either upward- or downward-sloping, as determined by the general relationship between rates in each market segment. When supply outstrips demand for short-term loans, short-term rates are relatively low. If, at the same time, the demand for long-term loans is higher than the available supply of funds, then long-term rates will move up. Thus, low rates in the short-term segment and high rates in the long-term segment cause an upward-sloping yield curve, and vice versa.

Which Theory Is Right? It is clear *that all three theories* of the term structure have merit in explaining the shape of the yield curve. From them, we can conclude that at any time, the slope of the yield curve is affected by (1) inflationary expectations, (2) liquidity preferences, and (3) the supply and demand conditions in the short- and long-term market segments. Upward-sloping yield curves result from higher inflation expectations, lender preferences for shorter-maturity loans, and greater supply of short- rather than of long-term loans relative to the respective demand in each market segment. The opposite behavior, of course, results in a flat or downward-sloping yield curve. At any point in time, the interaction of these forces determines the prevailing slope of the yield curve.

Using the Yield Curve in Investment Decisions Bond investors often use yield curves in making investment decisions. As noted earlier, yield curves change in accordance with market conditions. Analyzing the changes in yield curves over time provides investors with information about future interest rate movements and how they can affect price behavior and comparative returns. For example, if the yield curve begins to rise sharply, it usually means that inflation is starting to heat up or is expected to do so in the near future. In that case, investors can expect that interest rates, too, will rise. Under these conditions, most seasoned bond investors turn to short or intermediate (3 to 5 years) maturities, which provide reasonable returns and at the same time minimize exposure to capital loss when interest rates go up (and bond prices fall). A downward-sloping yield curve, though unusual, generally results from actions of the Federal Reserve to reduce inflation. As suggested by the expectations hypothesis, this would signal that rates have peaked and are about to fall.

Another factor to consider is the difference in yields on different maturities—the "steepness" of the curve. For example, a steep yield curve is one where long rates are *much higher* than short rates. This shape is often seen as an indication that long-term rates may be near their peak and are about to fall, thereby narrowing the spread between long and short rates. Steep yield curves are generally viewed as a bullish sign. For aggressive bond investors, they could be the signal to start moving into long-term securities. Flatter yield curves, on the other hand, sharply reduce the incentive for going long-term. For example, look at yield curve 2 in Figure 10.4. Note that the difference in yield between the 5- and 20-year maturities is quite small. (In fact, it's almost nonexistent. It amount to *only 3 basis points,* or ³⁄₁₀₀ of 1%.) As a result, there's not much incentive to go long-term. Under these conditions, investors would be well advised to just stick with the 5- to 10-year maturities, which will generate about the same yield as long bonds but without the risks. You'll also notice that in July 2000, the 30-year bonds had even lower yields. A lot of this was due to a "scarcity effect" as the Treasury began to sharply curtail the supply of long bonds. In other words, because there was more demand than supply, rates fell.

IN REVIEW

CONCEPTS

10.1 Is there a single market rate of interest applicable to all segments of the bond market, or are there a series of market yields? Explain and note the investment implication of such a market environment.

10.2 Explain why interest rates are important to both conservative and aggressive bond investors. What causes interest rates to move, and how can you monitor such movements?

10.3 What is the *term structure of interest rates,* and how is it related to the *yield curve?* What information is required to plot a yield curve? Describe an upward-sloping yield curve and explain what it has to say about the behavior of interest rates. Do the same for a flat yield curve.

10.4 How might you, as a bond investor, use information about the term structure of interest rates and yield curves when making investment decisions?

The Pricing of Bonds

LG 3

If there's one common denominator in the bond market, it's the way bonds are priced. No matter who the issuer is, what kind of bond it is, or whether it's fully taxable or tax-free, all bonds are priced pretty much the same. In particular, all bonds (including *notes* with maturities of more than a year) are priced according to the *present value of their future cash flow* streams. Indeed, once the prevailing or expected market yield is known, the whole process becomes rather mechanical.

Bond prices are driven by market yields. That's because in the marketplace, the *appropriate yield at which the bond should sell is determined first,* and then that yield is used to find the price (or market value) of the bond. The appropriate yield on a bond is a function of certain market and economic forces (e.g., the risk-free rate of return and inflation), as well as key issue and issuer characteristics (e.g., years to maturity and the bond rating). Together, these forces combine to form the *required rate of return,* which is the rate of return the investor would like to earn in order to justify an investment in a given fixed-income security. In the bond market, required return is market driven and is generally considered to be the issue's market yield. That is, the required return defines the yield at which the bond should be trading and serves as the *discount rate* in the bond valuation process.

Basically, bond investors are entitled to two distinct types of cash flows: (1) the periodic receipt of coupon income over the life of the bond, and (2) the recovery of principal (or par value) at the end of the bond's life. Thus, in valuing a bond, you're dealing with an *annuity* of coupon payments plus a large *single cash flow,* as represented by the recovery of principal at maturity. These cash flows, along with the required rate of return on the investment, are then used in a present-value-based bond valuation model to find the dollar price of a bond. We'll demonstrate the bond valuation process in two ways. First, we'll use *annual compounding*—that is, because of its computational simplicity, we'll assume we're dealing with coupons that are paid once a year. Second, we'll examine bond valuation under conditions of *semiannual compounding,* which is more like the way most bonds actually pay their coupons.

We'll use present-value interest factors to define and illustrate the various bond price and yield measures. But all these calculations can be done just as easily (in fact, more easily) on a good hand-held calculator. Even so, before you revert to the regular use of one of these calculators (see the *Calculator Use* sections for keystroke guidelines), we strongly encourage you to work through the bond valuation model at least once or twice, using the procedures outlined below. Doing so will help you gain a thorough understanding of what's embedded in a bond price or yield measure.

Annual Compounding

Along with a table of present-value interest factors (see Appendix A, Tables A.3 and A.4), the following information is needed to value a bond: (1) the size of the annual coupon payment, (2) the bond's par value, and (3) the number of years remaining to maturity. The prevailing market yield (or an estimate of future market rates) is then used as the discount rate to compute the price of a bond, as follows:

Equation 10.2
$$\text{Bond price} = \frac{\text{Present value of the annuity}}{\text{of annual interest income}} + \frac{\text{Present value of the}}{\text{bond's par value}}$$

Equation 10.2a
$$BP = (I \times PVIFA) + (PV \times PVIF)$$

where

I = amount of annual interest income

$PVIFA$ = present-value interest factor for an *annuity* (Appendix A, Table A.4)

PV = par value of the bond, which is assumed to be $1,000

$PVIF$ = present-value interest factor for a *single cash flow* (Appendix A, Table A.3)

To illustrate the bond price formula in action, consider a 20-year, 9½% bond that is being priced to yield 10%. From this we know the bond pays an annual coupon of 9½% (or $95), has 20 years left to maturity, and should be priced to provide a market yield of 10%. As we saw in Chapter 4, the maturity and market yield information is used to find the appropriate present-value interest factors (in Appendix A, Tables A.3 and A.4). Given these interest factors, we can now use Equation 10.2 to find the price of our bond.

Bond price = ($95 × *PVIFA* for 10% and 20 years) +
($1,000 × *PVIF* for 10% and 20 years)

= ($95 × 8.514) + ($1,000 × .149) = $957.83

Note that because this is a coupon-bearing bond, we have an annuity of coupon payments of $95 a year for 20 years, plus a single cash flow of $1,000 that occurs at the end of year 20. Thus, in bond valuation, we find the present value of the coupon annuity and then add that amount to the present value of the recovery of principal at maturity. In this particular case, you should be willing to pay about $958 for this bond, so long as you're satisfied with earning 10% on your money.

CALCULATOR USE For *annual compounding,* to price a 20-year, 9½% bond to yield 10%, use the keystrokes shown in the margin, where:

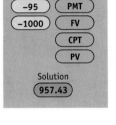

N	=	number of years to maturity,
I	=	yield on the bond (what the bond is being priced to yield),
PMT	=	stream of annual coupon payments,
FV	=	par value of the bond, and
PV	=	computed price of the bond.

Semiannual Compounding

Although using annual compounding, as we did above, simplifies the valuation process a bit, it's not the way bonds are actually valued in the marketplace. In practice, most (domestic) bonds pay interest every 6 months, so semiannual compounding is used in the valuation of bonds. Fortunately, it's relatively easy to go from annual to semiannual compounding: All you need do is cut the annual coupon payment in half, and make two minor modifications to the present-value interest factors. Given these changes, finding the price of a bond under conditions of semiannual compounding is much like pricing a bond using annual compounding. That is,

Equation 10.3

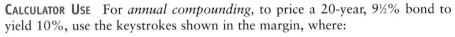

Bond price (with semi-
annual compounding) = Present value of an annuity of *semiannual* coupon payments + Present value of the bond's par value

Equation 10.3a

$$BP = (I/2 × PVIFA^*) + (PV × PVIF^*)$$

where

PVIFA * = present-value interest factor for an annuity, with required return and years-to-maturity adjusted for *semiannual compounding* (Appendix A, Table A.4)

PVIF * = present-value interest factor for a single cash flow, with required return and years-to-maturity adjusted for *semiannual compounding* (Appendix A, Table A.3)

I, PV = as described above

Note that in Equation 10.3, we adjusted the present-value interest factors (both *PVIFA* and *PVIF*) to accommodate semiannual compounding. By simply cutting the required return in half and doubling the number of years to maturity, we are, in effect, dealing with a semiannual measure of return and using the number of 6-month periods to maturity (rather than *years*). For example, in our bond illustration above, we wanted to price a 20-year bond to yield 10%. With semiannual compounding, we would be dealing with a semiannual return of 10%/2 = 5%, and with 20 × 2 = 40 semiannual periods to maturity. Thus we'd find the present-value interest factors for 5% and 40 periods from Table A.4 (for *PVIFA**) and from Table A.3 (for *PVIF**). Note that we adjust the present-value interest factor for the $1,000 par value, because that too will be subject to semiannual compounding, even though the cash flow will still be received in one lump sum.

To see how this all fits together, consider once again the 20-year, 9½% bond. This time assume it's being priced to yield 10%, *compounded semiannually*. Using Equation 10.3, you'd have:

$$
\begin{aligned}
\text{Bond price (with semi-annual compounding)} &= (\$95/2 \times PVIFA^* \text{ for } 5\% \text{ and } 40 \text{ periods}) \\
&\quad + (\$1,000 \times PVIF^* \text{ for } 5\% \text{ and } 40 \text{ periods}) \\
&= (\$47.50 \times 17.159) + (\$1,000 \times .142) = \underline{\$957.02}
\end{aligned}
$$

The price of the bond in this case ($957.02) is slightly less than the price we obtained with annual compounding ($957.83). Clearly, it doesn't make much difference whether we use annual or semiannual compounding, though the differences do tend to increase a bit with lower coupons and shorter maturities.

CALCULATOR USE For *semiannual compounding,* to price a 20-year, 9½% bond to yield 10%, use the keystrokes shown in the margin, where:

N = number of 6-month periods to maturity (20 × 2 = 40),

I = yield on the bond, adjusted for semiannual compounding (10/2 = 5.0),

PMT = stream of semiannual coupon payments (95.00/2 = 47.50),

FV and PV = remain the same.

Note that the price of the bond is a bit higher here due to rounding (i.e., we get $957.10 with the calculator vs. $957.02 with the tables.

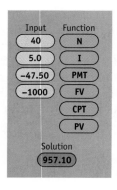

Input	Function
40	N
5.0	I
-47.50	PMT
-1000	FV
	CPT
	PV

Solution
957.10

IN REVIEW

10.5 Explain how market yield affects the price of a bond. Could you price a bond without knowing its market yield? Explain.

10.6 Why are bonds generally priced using semiannual compounding? Does it make much difference if you use annual compounding?

CONCEPTS

Measures of Yield and Return

As surprising as it may seem, in the bond market, investment decisions are made more on the basis of a bond's yield than its dollar price. Not only does yield affect the price at which a bond trades, it also serves as an important measure of return. To use yield as a measure of return, we *simply reverse the bond valuation process* described above and solve for yield rather than price. Actually, there are three widely used measures of yield: current yield, yield-to-maturity, and yield-to-call. We'll look at all three of them here, along with a concept known as *expected return,* which measures the expected (or actual) rate of return earned over a specific holding period.

Current Yield

current yield
return measure that indicates the amount of current income a bond provides relative to its market price.

Current yield is the simplest of all return measures, but it also has the most limited application. This measure looks at just one source of return: *a bond's interest income.* In particular, it indicates the amount of current income a bond provides relative to its prevailing market price. It is calculated as follows:

Equation 10.4

$$\text{Current yield} = \frac{\text{Annual interest}}{\text{Current market price of the bond}}$$

For example, an 8% bond would pay $80 per year in interest for every $1,000 of principal. However, if the bond were currently priced at $800, it would have a current yield of 10% ($80/$800 = 0.10). Current yield is a measure of a bond's annual coupon income, so it would be of interest primarily to investors seeking high levels of current income.

Yield-to-Maturity

yield-to-maturity (YTM)
the fully compounded rate of return earned by an investor over the life of a bond, including interest income and price appreciation.

promised yield
same as yield-to-maturity.

Yield-to-maturity (YTM) is the most important and widely used bond valuation measure. It evaluates both interest income and price appreciation and considers total cash flow received over the life of an issue. Also known as **promised yield,** YTM shows the fully compounded rate of return earned by an investor, *given that the bond is held to maturity and all principal and interest payments are made in a prompt and timely fashion.* This measure of yield is used not only to gauge the return on a single issue but also to track the behavior of the market in general. In other words, market interest rates are basically a reflection of the average promised yields that exist in a given segment of the market. Promised yield provides valuable insight about an issue's investment merits and is used to assess the attractiveness of alternative investment vehicles. Other things being equal, the higher the promised yield of an issue, the more attractive it is.

Although there are a couple of ways to compute promised yield, the best and most accurate procedure is one that is derived directly from the bond valuation model described above. That is, assuming annual compounding, you can use Equation 10.2 to measure the YTM on a bond. The difference is that now, rather than trying to determine the price of the bond, *we know its price and are trying to find the discount rate that will equate the present value of the bond's cash flow (coupon and principal payments) to its current market price.* This procedure may sound familiar: It's just like the *internal rate of return* measure described in Chapter 4. Indeed, we're basically looking for the internal rate of return on a bond. When we find that, we have the bond's yield-to-maturity.

Unfortunately, unless you have a hand-held calculator or computer software that will do the calculations for you, finding yield-to-maturity is a matter of trial and error. Let's say we want to find the yield-to-maturity on a 7½% ($1,000 par value) bond that has 15 years remaining to maturity and is currently trading in the market at $809.50. From Equation 10.2, we know that

$$\text{Bond price} = (I \times PVIFA) + (PV \times PVIF)$$

As it now stands, we know the current market price of the bond ($809.50), the amount of annual interest/coupon income (7½% = $75), the par value of the bond ($1,000), and the number of years to maturity (15). To compute yield-to-maturity, we need to find the discount rate (in the present-value interest factors) that produces a bond price of $809.50.

Here's what we have so far:

$$\text{Bond price} = (I \times PVIFA) + (PV \times PVIF)$$

$$\$809.50 = (\$75 \times PVIFA \text{ for 15 years and a discount rate of ?\%})$$
$$+ (\$1,000 \times PVIF \text{ for 15 years and a discount rate of ?\%})$$

Right now we know only one thing about the yield on this bond—it has to be more than 7½%. (Why? Because this is a discount bond, so the yield-to-maturity must exceed the coupon rate.) Through trial and error, we might start with a discount rate of, say, 8% or 9% (or any number above the bond's coupon). Sooner or later, we'll move to a discount rate of 10%. And look what happens at that point: Using Equation 10.2 to price this bond at a discount rate of 10%, we see that

$$\text{Bond price} = (\$75 \times PVIFA \text{ for 15 years and 10\%})$$
$$+ (\$1,000 \times PVIFA \text{ for 15 years and 10\%})$$

$$= (\$75 \times 7.606) + (\$1,000 \times 0.239)$$

$$= \underline{\$809.45}$$

The computed price of $809.45 is reasonably close to the bond's current market price of $809.50. As a result, the 10% rate represents the yield-to-maturity on this bond. That is, 10% is the discount rate that leads to a *computed bond price* equal (or very close) to the bond's *current market price*. In this case, if you were to pay $809.50 for the bond and hold it to maturity, you would expect to earn a yield of 10.0%. Now there's no doubt that promised yield is an important measure of performance. However, as discussed in the accompanying *Investing in Action* box, this measure tells only part of the story.

Input	Function
15	N
809.50	PV
−75	PMT
−1000	FV
	CPT
	I

Solution
10.00

CALCULATOR USE For *annual compounding,* to find the YTM of a 15-year, 7½% bond that is currently priced in the market at $809.50, use the keystrokes shown in the margin. The present value (*PV*) key represents the current market price of the bond, and all other keystrokes are as defined earlier.

INVESTING in action

There's More to Bond Returns Than Yield Alone

When individuals choose bond investments, they usually focus on yields, in the belief that higher yields generate better returns. But yields and returns are two different things, and investors who blindly chase higher yields can end up regretting it.

The fact is that yield is only part of the story: It tells you what you can expect going into an investment, not what you'll actually end up earning on the deal. Indeed, yield is often a poor proxy for return, and confusing the two can be damaging to your wealth!

Total return for fixed-income investments is made up of not only the initial yield but also (1) interest on reinvested interest and (2) price change. Only in the case of short-term investments, such as 1-year CDs or Treasury bills, is yield a good gauge of return. For long-term bonds and bonds purchased at prices far above or below face value, other factors often dwarf yield in determining returns. That's true even when the bonds are of triple-A quality.

For instance, interest on interest easily becomes the biggest factor in returns for buy-and-hold investors in long-term bonds, especially if interest rates rise during the life of the bond. If you bought a 30-year Treasury bond yielding 6.0% today and interest rates subsequently rose so that your average reinvestment rate was 8.0% over the life of the bond, more than 75% of your total return at maturity would come from income on reinvested interest. On the other hand, although interest on interest dominates bond returns for long holding periods, price change dominates return for short-term investors. In either case, *future interest rate changes are the major concern for investors who want to safeguard their total returns.*

The starting yield on a bond becomes a bigger boon or burden to investors the longer the bond's maturity—which makes total returns on longer-term bonds much more sensitive to interest rate swings. For instance, from 1950 to 1980, long-term Treasury bonds actually had lower total returns than money market funds, despite their persistently higher yields. Unfortunately, steadily rising interest rates erased an average of 2.5% a year from the value of long-term bond portfolios during that period, more than wiping

out the bonds' yield advantage over T-bills. In the 1980s and 1990s, by contrast, a steady decline in interest rates meant long-term bonds put on a much better showing than yields would have indicated. Rising bond prices, caused by falling market rates, pushed total returns on Treasury bonds up to an average of 12.6% a year, beating T-bill returns by 3.7 percentage points.

In the year 2000, rising prices were again the biggest component of bond returns. Yields on all types of high-grade long-term bonds dropped as the economy slowed. By year-end, yields on 10-year Treasury notes fell to 5.11% and on 30-year Treasury bonds to 5.46%. Thus principal values (prices) rose so that total returns for the 10- and 30-year securities were 14.8% and 21.0%, respectively.

Of course, no one really knows where interest rates will go—and trying to predict them can prove to be a fruitless exercise. But investors can get a handle on the risks they face in the short run by considering how total returns on different investments might react to interest rate changes over, say, the next 12 months. For example, if interest rates were to fall 1 percentage point over the next 12 months, a typical portfolio of long-term bonds (with lives of more than 10 years) would generate an estimated total return of about 13%. But if interest rates were to rise by 1 percentage point, the total return would shrink to about 1%, making a money fund return look good by comparison. Looking at the problem this way tells the investor how much rates would have to rise before the returns on long-term bonds were reduced to the level of, say, bank CDs or some other short-term benchmark. Clearly, the farther rates have to rise, the more cushion you have and the more secure your investments.

The old adage "You can't judge a book by its cover" certainly does apply to the bond market: Just because a bond promises a yield of *x* percent doesn't mean that's the return you'll actually end up with.

Sources: Tom Petruno, "Quality Bond Funds Had a Good Year," *Newsday,* December 16, 2000, p. F4; Gregory Zuckerman and Michael Derby, "Government Bonds Provide a Safe Haven as High-Yield Market Delivers a Bruising," *Wall Street Journal,* January 2, 2001, p. R8.

Using Semiannual Compounding Given some fairly simple modifications, it's also possible to find yield-to-maturity using semiannual compounding. To do so, we cut the annual coupon in half, double the number of years (periods) to maturity, and use the bond valuation model in Equation 10.3. Returning to our 7½%, 15-year bond, let's see what happens when we try a discount rate of 10%. In this case, with semiannual compounding, we'd use a discount rate of 5% (10% ÷ 2); using this discount rate and 30 six-month periods to maturity (15 × 2) to specify the present-value interest factor, we have

$$\text{Bond price} = (\$75/2 \times PVIFA^* \text{ for } 5\% \text{ and } 30 \text{ periods})$$
$$+ (\$1{,}000 \times PVIFA \text{ for } 5\% \text{ and } 30 \text{ periods})$$

$$= (\$37.50 \times 15.373) + (\$1{,}000 \times 0.231) = \underline{\$807.49}$$

As you can see, a semiannual discount rate of 5% results in a computed bond value that's a bit short of our target price of $809.50. Given the inverse relationship between price and yield, it follows that if we need a higher price, we'll have to try a lower yield (discount rate). Therefore, we know the semiannual yield on this bond has to be something less than 5%. Through interpolation, we find that a semiannual discount rate of (around) 4.97% gives us a computed bond value that's very close to $809.50.

At this point, because we're dealing with semiannual cash flows, to be technically accurate we should find the bond's "effective" annual yield. However, that's not the way it's done in practice. Rather, *market convention is to simply state the annual yield as twice the semiannual yield.* This practice produces what the market refers to as the **bond-equivalent yield**. Returning to the bond-yield problem we started above, we know that the issue has a semiannual yield of 4.97%. According to the bond-equivalent yield convention, all we have to do now is *double the solving rate in order to obtain the annual rate of return on this bond.* Doing this gives us a yield-to-maturity (or promised yield) of 4.97% × 2 = 9.94%. This is the annual rate of return we'll earn on the bond if we hold it to maturity.

bond-equivalent yield
the annual yield on a bond, calculated as twice the semiannual yield.

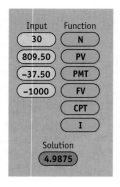

CALCULATOR USE For *semiannual compounding,* to find the YTM of a 15-year, 7½% bond that is currently priced in the market at $809.50, use the keystrokes shown here. As before, the *PV* key is the current market price of the bond, and all other keystrokes are as defined earlier. Remember that to find the bond-equivalent yield, you have to double the computed value of *I.* That is, 4.9875% × 2 = 9.975%.

Yield Properties Actually, in addition to holding the bond to maturity, there are a couple of other critical assumptions embedded in any yield-to-maturity figure. The promised yield measure—whether computed with annual or semiannual compounding—is based on present-value concepts and therefore contains important reinvestment assumptions. That is, the yield-to-maturity figure itself is the *minimum required reinvestment rate the investor must subsequently earn on each of the interim coupon receipts* in order to generate a return equal to or greater than the promised yield. In essence, the calculated yield-to-maturity figure is the return "promised" only so long as the issuer meets all interest and principal obligations on a timely basis and the investor reinvests all coupon income (from the date of receipt to maturity) at an average rate equal to or greater than the computed promised yield. In our example above, the investor would have to reinvest (to maturity) each of the coupons received over the next 15 years at a rate of about 10%. *Failure to do so would result in a realized yield of less than the 10% promised.* In fact, if the worst did occur and the investor made no attempt to reinvest any of the coupons, he or she would earn a realized yield over the 15-year investment horizon of just over 6½%—far short of the 10% promised return. Clearly, unless it's a zero-coupon bond, a significant portion of a bond's total return over time is derived from the *reinvestment of coupons.*

Finding the Yield on a Zero The same promised-yield procedures described above (Equation 10.2 with annual compounding or Equation 10.3 with semi-annual compounding) can also be used to find the yield-to-maturity on a zero-coupon bond. The only difference is that the coupon portion of the equation can be ignored because it will, of course, equal zero. All you have to do to find the promised yield on a zero is to divide the current market price of the bond by $1,000 (the bond's par value) and then look for the computed interest factor in the present-value Table A.3 (in Appendix A).

To illustrate, consider a 15-year zero-coupon issue that can be purchased today for $315. Dividing this amount by the bond's par value of $1,000, we obtain an interest factor of $315/$1,000 = 0.315. Now, using annual compounding, look in Table A.3 (the table of present-value interest factors for single cash flows). Go down the first column to year 15 and then look across that row until you find an interest factor that equals (or is very close to) 0.315. Once you've found the factor, look up the column to the "Interest Rate" heading and you've got the promised yield of the issue. Using this approach, we see that the bond in our example has a promised yield of 8%. Had we been using semiannual compounding, we'd do exactly the same thing, except we'd go down to "year 30" and start the process there.

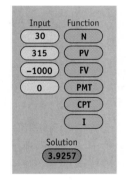

Input	Function
30	N
315	PV
−1000	FV
0	PMT
	CPT
	I

Solution
3.9257

CALCULATOR USE For *semiannual compounding,* to find the YTM of a 15-year, 7½% bond that is currently priced in the market at $315, use the keystrokes shown in the margin. *PV* is the current market price of the bond, and all other keystrokes are as defined earlier. To find the bond-equivalent yield, double the computed value of *I.* That is, 3.9257% × 2 = 7.85%.

Yield-to-Call

Bonds can be either noncallable or callable. Recall from Chapter 9 that a *noncallable bond* prohibits the issuer from calling the bond in for retirement prior to maturity. Because such issues will remain outstanding to maturity, they can all be valued by using the standard *yield-to-maturity* measure. In contrast, a *callable bond* gives the issuer the right to retire the bond prematurely, so the issue may or may not remain outstanding to maturity. As a result, YTM may not always be the appropriate measure of value. Instead, we must consider the impact of the bond being called. A common way to do that is to use a measure known as **yield-to-call (YTC),** which shows the yield on a bond if the issue remains outstanding *not* to maturity but, rather, until its first (or some other specified) call date.

Yield-to-call is commonly used with bonds that carry *deferred-call provisions.* Remember that such issues start out as noncallable bonds and then,

yield-to-call (YTC)
the yield on a bond if it remains outstanding only until a specified call date.

after a call deferment period (of 5 to 10 years), become freely callable. Under these conditions, *YTC would measure the expected yield on a deferred-call bond assuming that the issue is retired at the end of the call deferment period* (that is, when the bond first becomes freely callable). We can find YTC by making two simple modifications to the standard YTM equation (Equation 10.2 or 10.3). First, we define the length of the investment horizon (N) as *the number of years to the first call date,* not the number of years to maturity. Second, instead of using the bond's par value ($1,000), we *use the bond's call price* (which is stipulated in the indenture and is nearly always greater than the bond's par value).

For example, assume you want to find yield-to-call on a 20-year, 10½% deferred-call bond that is currently trading in the market at $1,204, but has 5 years to go to first call (that is, before it becomes freely callable), at which time it can be called in at a price of $1,085. Thus, rather than using the bond's maturity of 20 years in the valuation equation (Equation 10.2 or 10.3), we use the number of years to first call (5 years), and rather than the bond's par value, $1,000, we use the issue's call price, $1,085. Note, however, we still use the bond's coupon (10½%) and its current market price ($1,204). Thus, for annual compounding, here's what we'd have:

Equation 10.5

$$\text{Bond price} = (I \times PVIFA) + (CP \times PVIF)$$

$$\$1,204.00 = (\$105 \times PVIFA \text{ for 5 years and a discount rate of ?\%}) \\ + (\$1,085 \times PVIF \text{ for 5 years and a discount rate of ?\%})$$

In Equation 10.5, *CP* equals the call price on the issue, and the present-value interest factors (for both *PVIFA* and *PVIF*) are for the number of years to first call date, not the term to maturity.

Through trial and error, we finally hit upon a discount rate of 7%. At that point, the present value of the future cash flows (coupons over the next 5 years, plus call price) will exactly (or very nearly) equal the bond's current market price of $1,204. That is,

$$\text{Bond price} = (\$105 \times PVIFA_{5 \text{ years, 7\%}}) + (\$1,085 \times PVIF_{5 \text{ years, 7\%}})$$

$$= (\$105 \times 4.100) + (\$1,085 \times 0.713)$$

$$= \$430.50 + \$773.61 = \underline{\$1,204.11}$$

Thus *the YTC on this bond is 7%.* In contrast, the bond's YTM is 8.36%. In practice, bond investors normally compute *both* YTM and YTC for deferred-call bonds that are *trading at a premium.* They do this to find which of the two yields is lower; market convention is to *use the lower, more conservative measure of yield (YTM or YTC) as the appropriate indicator of value.* As a result, the premium bond in our example would be valued relative to its yield-to-call. The assumption is that because interest rates have dropped so much (the bond is trading 2 percentage points below its coupon), it will be called in the first chance the issuer gets. However, the situation is totally different when this or any bond trades at a discount. Why? Because YTM on any *discount bond,* whether callable or not, *will always be less* than YTC. Thus YTC is a totally irrelevant measure for discount bonds—it's used only with premium bonds.

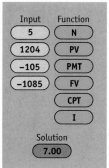

Input	Function
5	N
1204	PV
–105	PMT
–1085	FV
	CPT
	I

Solution

7.00

CALCULATOR USE For *annual compounding,* to find the YTC of a 20-year, 10½% bond that is currently trading at $1,204 but can be called in 5 years at a call price of $1,085, use the keystrokes shown in the margin. In this computation, N is the number of years to first call date, and FV represents the bond's call price. All other keystrokes are as defined earlier.

Expected Return

expected return
the rate of return an investor can expect to earn by holding a bond over a period of time that's less than the life of the issue.

realized yield
same as expected return.

Rather than just buying and holding bonds, some investors prefer to actively trade in and out of these securities over fairly short investment horizons. As a result, yield-to-maturity and yield-to-call have relatively little meaning, other than as indicators of the rate of return used to price the bond. These investors obviously need an alternative measure of return that can be used to assess the investment appeal of those bonds they intend to trade in and out of. Such an alternative measure is **expected return.** It indicates the rate of return an investor can expect to earn by holding a bond over a period of time that's less than the life of the issue. (Expected return is also known as **realized yield,** because it shows the return an investor would realize by trading in and out of bonds over short holding periods.)

Expected return lacks the precision of yield-to-maturity (and YTC), because the major cash flow variables are largely the product of investor estimates. In particular, going into the investment, both the length of the holding period and the future selling price of the bond are pure estimates and therefore subject to uncertainty. Even so, we can use pretty much the same procedure to find realized yield as we did to find promised yield. That is, with some simple modifications to the standard bond-pricing formula, we can use the following equation to find the expected return on a bond.

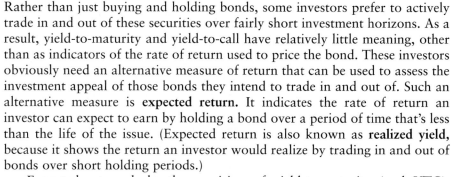

Equation 10.6

$$\text{Bond price} = \begin{array}{c} \text{Present value of the bond's} \\ \text{annual interest income} \\ \text{over the holding period} \end{array} + \begin{array}{c} \text{Present value of the bond's} \\ \text{future price at the} \\ \text{end of the holding period} \end{array}$$

Equation 10.6a

$$BP = (I \times PVIFA) + (FV \times PVIF)$$

where the present-value interest factors (for both *PVIFA* and *PVIF*) are for the length of the expected holding period only, not for the term to maturity, and *FV* is the expected future price of the bond.

Note that in this case, the *expected future price* of the bond is used in place of par value ($1,000), and *the length of the holding period* is used in place of term to maturity. As indicated above, we must determine the *future price* of the bond when computing expected realized yield; this is done by using the standard bond price formula, as described earlier. The most difficult part of deriving a reliable future price is, of course, coming up with future market interest rates that you feel will exist when the bond is sold. By evaluating current and expected market interest rate conditions, *the investor estimates a promised yield that the issue is expected to carry at the date of sale and then uses that yield to calculate the bond's future price.*

To illustrate, take one more look at our 7½%, 15-year bond. This time, let's assume that you feel the price of the bond, which is now trading at a discount, will rise sharply as interest rates fall over the next few years. In particular, assume the bond is currently priced at $810 (to yield 10%) and that you anticipate holding the bond for 3 years. Over that time, you expect market rates to drop, so the price of the bond should rise to around $960 by the end of the 3-year holding period. (Actually, we found the future price of the bond—$960—by assuming interest rates would fall to 8% in 3 year. We then used the standard bond price formula—in this case Equation 10.2—to find the value of a 7½%, 12-year obligation, which is how many years to maturity a 15-year bond will have at the end of a 3-year holding period.) Thus, we are assuming that you will buy the bond today at a market price of $810 and sell it 3 years later—after interest rates have declined to 8%—at a price of $960. Given these assumptions, the expected return (realized yield) on this bond is 14.6%, which is the discount rate in the following equation that will produce a current market price of $810.

$$\text{Bond price} = (\$75 \times PVIFA \text{ for 3 years and } 14.6\%)$$
$$+ (\$960 \times PVIF \text{ for 3 years and } 14.6\%)$$
$$= (\$75 \times 2.301) + (\$960 \times 0.664) = \underline{\$810.02}$$

The better-than-14½% return on this investment is fairly substantial, but keep in mind that this is only a measure of *expected return*. It is, of course, subject to variation if things do not turn out as anticipated, particularly with regard to the market yield expected at the end of the holding period. (*Note:* This illustration uses annual compounding, but you could just as easily have used *semiannual compounding*, which, everything else being the same, would have resulted in an expected yield of 14.4% rather than the 14.6% found with annual compounding. Also, if the anticipated horizon is 1 year or less, you would want to use the simple *holding-period return (HPR)* measure described in Chapter 4.)

Input	Function
6	N
810	PV
−37.50	PMT
−960	FV
	CPT
	I

Solution
7.205

CALCULATOR USE For *semiannual compounding*, to find the expected return on a 7½% bond that is currently priced in the market at $810 but is expected to rise to $960 within a 3-year holding period, use the keystrokes shown in the margin. In this computation, *PV* is the current price of the bond, and *FV* is the expected price of the bond at the end of the (3-year) holding period. All other keystrokes are as defined earlier. To find the bond-equivalent yield, double the computed value of *I*: 7.205% × 2 = 14.41%.

Valuing a Bond

Depending on investor objectives, the value of a bond can be determined by either its promised yield or its expected return. Conservative, income-oriented investors employ *promised yield* (YTM or YTC) to value bonds. Coupon income over extended periods of time is their principal objective, and promised yield provides a viable measure of return—assuming, of course, the reinvestment assumptions embedded in the yield measure are reasonable. More aggressive bond traders, on the other hand, use *expected return* to value bonds. The capital gains that can be earned by buying and selling bonds over relatively short holding periods is their chief concern, and expected return is more important to them than the promised yield at the time the bond is purchased.

In either case, promised or expected yield provides a *measure of return* that can be used to determine the relative attractiveness of fixed-income securities. But to do so, we must evaluate the measure of return in light of the *risk* involved in the investment. Bonds are no different from stocks in that the amount of return (promised or expected) should be sufficient to cover the investor's exposure to risk. Thus, the greater the amount of perceived risk, the greater the amount of return the bond should generate. If the bond meets this hurdle, it could then be compared to other potential investments outlets. If you find it difficult to do better in a risk–return sense, then the bond under evaluation should be given serious consideration as an investment outlet.

IN REVIEW

CONCEPTS

10.7   What's the difference between *current yield* and *yield-to-maturity?* Between *promised yield* and *realized yield?* How does *YTC* differ from *YTM?*

10.8   Briefly describe the term *bond-equivalent yield.* Is there any difference between promised yield and bond-equivalent yield? Explain.

10.9   Why is the reinvestment of interest income so important to bond investors?

10.10 According to the *Investing in Action* box on page 429, is there any difference between a bond's yield and its return? If so, which of these measures is more important? Explain.

Duration and Immunization

LG 5

One of the problems with yield-to-maturity (YTM) is that it assumes you can reinvest the bond's periodic coupon payments at the same rate over time. But if you reinvest this interest income at a lower rate (or if you spend it), your real return will be much lower than that indicated by YTM. The assumption that interest rates will remain constant is a key weakness of YTM. Another flaw is that YTM assumes the issuer will make all payments on time and won't call the bonds before maturity, as often happens when interest rates drop. For bonds that are not held to maturity, prices will reflect prevailing interest rates, which are likely to differ from YTM. If rates have moved up since a bond was purchased, the bond will sell at a discount. If interest rates have dropped, it will sell at a premium. The sales price will obviously have a major impact on the total return earned.

The problem with yield-to-maturity, then, is that it fails to take into account the effects of reinvestment risk and price (or market) risk. To see how reinvestment and price risks behave relative to one another, consider a situation in which market interest rates have undergone a sharp decline. Under such conditions, you might be tempted to cash out your holdings and take some gains (i.e., do a little "profit taking"). Indeed, selling before maturity is the only way to take advantage of falling interest rates, because a bond will pay its par value at maturity, regardless of prevailing interest rates. But there's a downside to falling rates: When interest rates fall, so do the opportunities to invest at high rates. Therefore, although you gain on the price side, you lose on the reinvestment side. Even if you don't sell out, you are faced with increased reinvestment risk, because in order to earn the YTM promised on your bonds, you have to be able to reinvest each coupon payment at the same YTM rate. Obviously, as rates fall, you'll find it increasingly difficult to reinvest the stream of coupon payments at or above the YTM rate. When market rates rise, just the opposite happens: The price of the bond falls, but your reinvestment opportunities improve.

What is needed is a measure of performance that overcomes these deficiencies and takes into account both price and reinvestment risks. Such a yardstick is provided by something called **duration**. It captures in a single measure the extent to which the price of a bond will react to different interest rate environments. Because duration gauges the price volatility of a bond, it gives you an idea of how likely you are to earn the YTM you expect. That in turn will help you tailor your holdings to your expectations of interest rate movements.

duration
a measure of bond price volatility, which captures both price and reinvestment risks and which is used to indicate how a bond will react in different interest rate environments.

The Concept of Duration

The concept of duration was first developed in 1938 by actuary Frederick Macaulay to help insurance companies match their cash inflows with payments. When applied to bonds, duration recognizes that the amount and frequency of interest payments, yield-to-maturity, and time to maturity all affect the "time dimension" of a bond. Time to maturity is important because it influences how much a bond's price rises or falls as interest rates change. In general, when rates move, bonds with longer maturities fluctuate more than shorter-term issues. However, maturity alone isn't a sufficient measure of the time dimension of bonds. Maturity tells you only when the last payment will be made; it doesn't say anything about interim payments. The amount of reinvestment risk is also directly related to the size of a bond's coupons: Bonds that pay high coupons have greater reinvestment risk simply because there's more to reinvest.

Any change in interest rates will cause price risk and reinvestment risk to push and pull bonds in opposite directions. An increase in rates will produce a drop in price but will lessen reinvestment risk by making it easier to reinvest coupon payments at or above the YTM rate. Declining rates, in contrast, will boost prices but increase reinvestment risk. At some point in time, these two forces should exactly offset each other. *That point in time is the bond's duration.*

In general, bond duration possesses the following properties:

- Higher coupons result in shorter durations.
- Longer maturities mean longer durations.
- Higher yields (YTMs) lead to shorter durations.

A bond's coupon, maturity, and yield interact to produce the issue's measure of duration. Knowing a bond's duration is helpful because it captures the underlying price *volatility* of a bond. That is, since *a bond's duration and volatility are directly related, it follows that the shorter the duration, the less volatility there is in bond prices—and vice versa, of course.*

Measuring Duration

Duration is a measure of the effective, as opposed to actual, maturity of a fixed-income security. As we will see, only those bonds promising a single payment to be received at maturity (zero-coupon bonds) have durations equal to their actual years to maturity. For all other bonds, *duration measures are always less than their actual maturities.*

Although a bond's term to maturity is a useful concept, it falls short of being a reliable measure of a bond's effective life, because it does not consider all of the bond's cash flows or the time value of money. Duration is a far superior measure of the effective timing of a bond's cash flows, as it explicitly considers both the time value of money and the bond's coupon and principal payments. Duration may be thought of as the *weighted-average life of a bond,* where the weights are the relative future cash flows of the bond, all of which are discounted to their present values. Mathematically, we can find the duration of a bond as follows:

Equation 10.7

$$\text{Duration} = \sum_{t=1}^{T} \left[\frac{PV(C_t)}{P_{\text{bond}}} \times t \right]$$

where

$PV(C_t)$ = present value of a future coupon or principal payment

P_{bond} = current market price of the bond

t = year in which the cash flow (coupon or principal) payment is received

T = remaining life of the bond, in years

The duration measure obtained from Equation 10.7 is commonly referred to as *Macaulay duration*—named after the actuary who developed the concept.

Although duration often is computed using semiannual compounding, Equation 10.7 uses *annual coupons and annual compounding* in order to keep the ensuing discussion and calculations as simple as possible. But even so, the formula looks more formidable than it really is. If you follow the basic steps noted below, you'll find that duration is not tough to calculate. Here are the steps involved:

Step 1. Find the present value of each annual coupon or principal payment [$PV(C_t)$]. *Use the prevailing YTM on the bond as the discount rate.*

Step 2. Divide this present value by the current market price of the bond (P_{bond}).

Step 3. Multiply this relative value by the year in which the cash flow is to be received (*t*).

Step 4. Repeat steps 1 through 3 for each year in the life of the bond, and then *add up* the values computed in step 3.

Duration for a Single Bond Table 10.1 illustrates the four-step procedure for calculating the duration of a 7½%, 15-year bond priced (at $957) to yield 8%. Note that this particular 15-year bond has a duration of less than 9½ years (9.36 years, to be exact). Here's how we found that value: Along with the

TABLE 10.1 Duration Calculation for a 7½%, 15-year Bond Priced to Yield 8%

(1)	(2)	(3)	(4)	(5)	(6)
Year (t)	Annual Cash Flow (C_t)	PVIF (at 8%)	Present Value of Annual Cash Flows [$PV(C_t)$] (2) × (3)	$PV(C_t)$ Divided by Current Market Price of the Bond* (4) ÷ $957	Time-Weighted Relative Cash Flow (1) × (5)
1	$ 75	.926	$ 69.45	.0726	.0726
2	75	.857	64.27	.0672	.1343
3	75	.794	59.55	.0622	.1867
4	75	.735	55.12	.0576	.2304
5	75	.681	51.08	.0534	.2668
6	75	.630	47.25	.0494	.2962
7	75	.583	43.72	.0457	.3198
8	75	.540	40.50	.0423	.3386
9	75	.500	37.50	.0392	.3527
10	75	.463	34.72	.0363	.3628
11	75	.429	32.18	.0336	.3698
12	75	.397	29.78	.0311	.3734
13	75	.368	27.60	.0288	.3749
14	75	.340	25.50	.0266	.3730
15	1,075	.315	338.62	.3538	5.3076
					Duration: 9.36 yrs.

*If this bond is priced to yield 8%, it will be quoted in the market at $957.

current market price of the bond ($957), the first three columns of Table 10.1 provide the basic input data: Column (1) is the year (t) of the cash flow. Column (2) is the amount of the annual cash flows (from coupons and principal). And column (3) lists the appropriate present-value interest factors, given an 8% discount rate (which is equal to the prevailing YTM on the bond).

The first thing we do (step 1) is find the present value of each of the annual cash flows (column 4). Then (step 2) we divide each of these present values by the current market price of the bond (column 5). Multiplying the relative cash flows from column (5) by the year (t) in which the cash flow occurs (step 3) results in a time-weighted value for each of the annual cash flow streams (column 6). Adding up all the values in column (6) (step 4) yields the duration of the bond. As you can see, the duration of this bond is a lot less than its maturity—a condition that would exist with any coupon-bearing bond. In addition, keep in mind *that the duration on any bond will change over time* as YTM and term to maturity change. For example, the duration on this 7½%, 15-year bond will fall as the bond nears maturity and/or as the market yield (YTM) on the bond increases.

Duration for a Portfolio of Bonds The concept of duration is not applied merely to single securities. It can also be applied to whole portfolios of fixed-income securities. The duration of an entire portfolio is fairly easy to calculate. All we need are the durations of the individual securities in the portfolio and their weights (i.e., the proportion that each security contributes to the overall value of the portfolio). Given this, *the duration of a portfolio is simply the weighted average of the durations of the individual securities in the portfolio.* For example, consider the following five-bond portfolio:

INVESTOR FACTS

DIFFERENT BONDS, SAME DURATIONS—Sometimes, you really can't judge a book—or a bond, for that matter—by its cover. Here are three bonds that, on the surface, appear to be totally different:

- An 8-year, zero-coupon bond priced to yield 6%.
- A 12-year, 8¾% bond that trades at a yield of 8%.
- An 18-year, 10½% bond priced to yield 13%.

Although these three bonds have different coupons and different maturities, they have one thing in common: They all have *identical durations* of 8 years. Thus if interest rates went up or down by 50 to 100 basis points, the market prices of these bonds would all behave pretty much the same!

Bond	Amount Invested*	Weight	×	Bond Duration	=	Portfolio Duration
Government bonds	$ 270,000	0.15		6.25		0.9375
Aaa corporates	180,000	0.10		8.90		0.8900
Aa utilities	450,000	0.25		10.61		2.6525
Agency issues	360,000	0.20		11.03		2.2060
Baa industrials	540,000	0.30		12.55		3.7650
	$1,800,000	1.00				10.4510

*Amount invested = Current market price × Par value of the bonds. That is, if the government bonds are quoted at 90 and the investor holds $300,000 in these bonds, then 0.90 × $300,000 = $270,000.

In this case, the $1.8 million bond *portfolio* has an average duration of approximately 10.5 years. Obviously, if you want to change the duration of the portfolio, you can do so by either (1) changing the asset mix of the portfolio (shift the weight of the portfolio to longer- or shorter-duration bonds, as desired) and/or (2) adding new bonds to the portfolio with the desired duration characteristics. As we will see below, this approach is often used in a bond portfolio strategy known as *bond immunization*.

Bond Duration and Price Volatility

A bond's price volatility is, in part, a function of its term to maturity and, in part, a function of its coupon yield. Unfortunately, there is no exact relationship between bond maturities and bond price volatilities with respect to interest rate changes. There is, however, a fairly close relationship between bond duration and price volatility—at least, so long as the market doesn't experience wide swings in yield. Duration can be used as a viable predictor of price volatility *only so long as the yield swings are relatively small* (no more than 50 to 100 basis points, or so). That's because whereas duration is a straight-line relationship, the price-yield relationship of a bond is convex in nature. That is, when bond yields change, bond prices actually move in a curved (convex) manner rather than in a straight line, as depicted by duration. Thus, when the market (or bond) undergoes a *big change* in yield, duration will *understate* the appreciation in price when rates fall and *overstate* the price decline when rates rise. Assuming that's not the case (i.e., that we're dealing with relatively small changes in market yield), then multiplying a bond's duration value by −1 results in its price elasticity with respect to interest rate changes. Thus, by calculating a bond's duration, we can obtain a fairly accurate measure of how much its price will change relative to a given (reasonably small) change in market interest rates.

The mathematical link between bond price and interest rate changes involves the concept of *modified duration*. To find modified duration, we simply take the (Macaulay) duration for a bond (as found from Equation 10.7) and adjust it for the bond's yield to maturity.

Equation 10.8

$$\text{Modified duration} = \frac{(\text{Macaulay}) \text{ Duration in years}}{1 + \text{Yield to maturity}}$$

Thus the modified duration for the 15-year bond discussed above is

$$\text{Modified duration} = \frac{9.36}{1 + 0.08} = \underline{\underline{8.67}}$$

Note that here we use the bond's computed (Macaulay) duration of 9.36 years and the same YTM we used to compute duration in Equation 10.7; in this case, the bond was priced to yield 8%, so we use a yield-to-maturity of 8%.

To determine, in percentage terms, how much the price of this bond would change as market interest rates increased from, say, 8% to 8½%, we multiply the modified duration value calculated above first by −1 (because of the inverse relationship between bond prices and interest rates) and then by the change in the level of the market interest rates. That is,

Equation 10.9

$$\frac{\text{Percent change}}{\text{in bond price}} = -1 \times \text{Modified duration} \times \text{Change in interest rates}$$

$$= -1 \times 8.67 \times 0.5\% = \underline{-4.33\%}$$

Thus a 50-basis-point (or ½ of 1%) increase in market interest rates will lead to an almost 4½% drop in the price of this 15-year bond. Such information is useful to bond investors seeking—or trying to avoid—price volatility.

Uses of Bond Duration Measures

Bond investors have learned to use duration analysis in many ways. For example, as we saw above, you can use modified duration to measure the potential price volatility of a particular issue. Another, perhaps more important use of duration is in the *structuring of bond portfolios*. That is, if you thought that interest rates were about to increase, you could calculate the expected percentage decrease in the value of the portfolio, given a certain change in market interest rates, and then reduce the overall duration of the portfolio by selling higher-duration bonds and buying those of shorter duration bonds. Such a strategy would prove profitable, because short-duration bonds do not decline in value to the same degree as longer bonds. On the other hand, if you felt that interest rates were about to decline, the opposite strategy would be appropriate.

Although active, short-term investors frequently use duration analysis in their day-to-day operations, longer-term investors also employ it in planning their investment decisions. Indeed, a strategy known as *bond portfolio immunization* represents one of the most important uses of duration.

Bond Immunization   Some investors hold portfolios of bonds not for the purpose of "beating the market" but, rather, to *accumulate a specified level of wealth by the end of a given investment horizon*. For these investors, bond portfolio immunization often proves to be of great value. Immunization allows you to derive a specified rate of return from bond investments over a given investment interval *regardless of what happens to market interest rates over the course of the holding period*. In essence, you are able to "immunize" your portfolio from the effects of changes in market interest rates over a given investment horizon.

To understand how and why bond portfolio immunization is possible, you need to understand that changes in market interest rates lead to two distinct and opposite changes in bond valuation: The first effect is known as the *price effect*. It results in portfolio valuation changes when interest rates change before the end of the desired investment horizon. This is true because interest rate decreases lead to bond price increases, and vice versa. The second effect is known as the *reinvestment effect*. It arises because the YTM calculation assumes that all coupon payments will be reinvested at the YTM rate that existed when the bond was purchased. If interest rates increase, however, the coupons may be reinvested at a higher rate, leading to increases in investor wealth. Of course, the opposite is true when interest rates decrease. Thus, whereas an increase in rates has a negative effect on a bond's price, it has a positive effect on the reinvestment of coupons. Therefore, when interest rate changes do occur, the price and reinvestment effects work against each other from the standpoint of the investor's wealth.

When do these counteracting effects offset each other and leave the investor's position unchanged? You guessed it: when the average duration of the portfolio just equals the investment horizon. This should not come as much of a surprise, because such a property is already embedded in the duration measure itself. And, if it applies to a single bond, it should also apply to the *weighted-average duration of a bond portfolio*. When such a condition (of offsetting price and reinvestment effects) exists, *a bond portfolio is said to be immunized*. More specifically, your wealth position is immunized from the effects of interest rate changes *when the weighted-average duration of the bond portfolio exactly equals your desired investment horizon*. Table 10.2 provides an example of bond immunization using a 10-year, 8% coupon bond with a duration of 8 years. Here, we assume the investor's desired investment horizon is also 8 years in length.

The example in Table 10.2 assumes that you originally purchased the 8% coupon bond at par. It further assumes that market interest rates for bonds of this quality drop from 8% to 6% at the end of the fifth year. Because you had an investment horizon of exactly 8 years and desire to lock in an interest rate return of exactly 8%, it follows that you expect to have a terminal value of $1,850.90 [i.e., $1,000 invested at 8% for 8 years = $1,000 \times (1.08)^8 = $1,850.90], regardless of interest rate changes in the interim. As can be seen from the results in Table 10.2, the immunization strategy netted you a total of $1,850.31—just 59 cents short of your desired goal. Note that in this case, although reinvestment opportunities declined in years 5, 6, and 7 (when market interest rates dropped to 6%), that same lower rate led to a higher market price for the bond. That higher price, in turn, provided enough capital gains to offset the loss in reinvested income. This remarkable result clearly demonstrates the power of bond immunization and the versatility of bond duration. And note that even though the table uses a single bond for purposes of illustration, the same results can be obtained from a bond *portfolio* that is maintained at the *proper weighted-average duration*.

Although bond immunization is a powerful investment tool, it is clearly not a passive investment strategy. Maintaining a fully immunized portfolio (of more than one bond) requires *continual portfolio rebalancing*. Indeed, every time interest rates change, the duration of a portfolio changes. Because effective immunization requires that the portfolio have a duration value equal in length to the *remaining investment horizon*, the composition of the portfolio must be rebalanced each time interest rates change. Further, even in the absence of interest rate changes, a bond's duration declines more slowly than its term to maturity. This, of course, means that the mere passage of time will dictate changes in portfolio composition.

TABLE 10.2   **Bond Immunization**

Year	Cash Flow from Bond							Terminal Value of Reinvested Cash Flow
1	$80	$\times$	$(1.08)^4$	$\times$	$(1.06)^3$		=	$ 129.63
2	80	$\times$	$(1.08)^3$	$\times$	$(1.06)^3$		=	120.03
3	80	$\times$	$(1.08)^2$	$\times$	$(1.06)^3$		=	111.14
4	80	$\times$	(1.08)	$\times$	$(1.06)^3$		=	102.90
5	80	$\times$	$(1.06)^3$				=	95.28
6	80	$\times$	$(1.06)^2$				=	89.89
7	80	$\times$	(1.06)				=	84.80
8	80						=	80.00
8	$1,036.64*						=	1,036.64
					Total			$1,850.31
					Investor's required wealth at 8%			$1,850.90
					Difference			$ .59

*The bond could be sold at a market price of $1,036.64, which is the value of an 8% bond with 2 years to maturity that is priced to yield 6%.

Note: Bond interest coupons are assumed to be paid at year-end. Therefore, there are 4 years of reinvestment at 8% and 3 years at 6% for the first year's $80 coupon.

Such changes will ensure that the duration of the portfolio continues to match the remaining time in the investment horizon. In summary, portfolio immunization strategies can be extremely effective, but it is important to realize that immunization is not a passive strategy and is not without potential problems, the most notable of which are associated with portfolio rebalancing.

IN REVIEW

CONCEPTS

10.11 What does the term *duration* mean to bond investors, and how does the duration of a bond differ from its maturity? What is *modified duration,* and how is it used?

10.12 Describe the process of *bond portfolio immunization,* and explain why an investor would want to immunize a portfolio. Would you consider portfolio immunization a passive investment strategy comparable to, say, a buy-and-hold approach? Explain.

Bond Investment Strategies

LG 6

Generally, bond investors tend to follow one of three kinds of investment programs. First, there are those who live off the income: the conservative, quality-conscious, income-oriented investors who seek to maximize current income. Then there are the speculators (bond traders), who have a considerably different investment objective: to maximize capital gains, often within a short time span. This investment approach requires considerable expertise, because it is based almost entirely on estimates of the future course of interest rates.

INVESTING in action

Getting Starting in Bond Investing

After the stock market's wild ride in the late 1990s and the even wilder ride in 2000 and 2001, you may be beginning to think that perhaps bonds may make a good addition to your portfolio. Perhaps you want to preserve capital or think that bonds would exert a stabilizing influence on your portfolio. You'll need to answer some basic questions before you start. Do you want a taxable or a tax-exempt security? The answer depends on your tax bracket and on whether you are buying the securities for a tax-advantaged account such as your 401(k) retirement account. The next question is a bit harder: *Should you buy individual bonds or a bond mutual fund* (an investment company that invests shareholders' money in bonds)?

Individual bonds offer certain advantages. You know the interest rate you will earn and how much you will get back when the bond matures. Individual bonds may suit your needs if you have a specific goal in mind or a specific date on which you will need funds. In this case, zero-coupon bonds are a good choice, because you buy them at a discount and get the par value at maturity. The returns are modest, but the risk is correspondingly low. Finally, individual bonds are less costly to purchase than bond mutual funds, which have ongoing fees. However, investing in bonds is not always simple. For one thing, it can be hard to find information. Credit research is more difficult on corporate and municipal bonds than on stocks. You also need to understand a bond's features, such as call options. One way around a lot of these problems is to invest in bond funds, rather than individual issues.

With a bond mutual fund, a professional manager deals with these and other problems. Unlike individual bonds, however, you have no guarantee of a fixed interest rate. Bond fund returns are governed by the fund's portfolio and market interest rate trends, so you can't predict the value of your fund shares in the future. They are also more subject to market fluctuations, because the manager is buying and selling securities. Investors in a bond fund could lose their principal, which is not likely with individual bonds of good credit quality held to maturity. And of course you should factor in expenses. (Chapter 12 discusses mutual fund costs.)

Some factors are important whether you choose individual bonds or bond funds. Both react to interest rate changes, and the duration of the bond or the fund tells you just how sensitive it is to interest rates. The duration of a bond mutual fund is the average of the durations of the bonds in its portfolio. The duration of money market funds is close to zero. For short-term funds it is 1–3 years; for medium-term funds, 4–6 years; and for long-term funds, 7–10 years. If interest rates increase 1 point, a long-term fund with a duration of 12 will fall about 12%. As you'd expect, longer-term bonds or bond funds are most sensitive to interest rate fluctuations. At the Morningstar Web site (**www.morningstar.com**), you can find taxable and tax-exempt bond funds categorized by their potential interest rate sensitivity, as measured by average portfolio durations.

Sources: Sarah C. Bush, "Five Tips for Choosing a Bond Fund," *Morningstar.com,* June 8, 2000, and "Why Bond Funds Can Get So Wild," *Morningstar.com,* October 4, 1999, both downloaded from news.morningstar.com/news; Chris Kelsch, "How Risky IS Your Bond Fund?" *Morningstar.com,* March 24, 2000, downloaded from news.morningstar.com/news; Peter Di Teresa, "Should You Buy Bonds or Bond Funds?" *Morningstar.com,* August 24, 2000, downloaded from news.morningstar.com/news; and Tom Petruno, "Quality Bond Funds Had a Good Year," *Newsday,* December 16, 2000, p. F4.

Finally, there are the serious long-term investors, whose objective is to maximize *total return*—from both current income and capital gains—over fairly long holding periods.

In order to achieve the objectives of any one of these three programs, you need to adopt a strategy that is compatible with your goals. Professional money managers use a variety of techniques to manage the multi-million (or

Another bond portfolio strategy is called a *barbell*. For information on that approach, see the Investing in Action box at:

www.awl.com/gitman_joehnk

multi-billion) dollar bond portfolios under their direction. These range from passive approaches, to semiactive strategies, to active, fully managed strategies using interest rate forecasting and yield spread analysis. Most of these strategies are fairly complex and require substantial computer support. Even so, we can look briefly at some of the more basic strategies to gain an appreciation of the different ways in which fixed-income securities can be used to reach different investment objectives. Before doing that, however, you might want to take a look at the nearby *Investing in Action* box, which offers some guidelines for getting started in bonds and introduces another way to invest in bonds—via mutual funds (a topic we discuss in detail in Chapter 12).

Passive Strategies

Prudential Securities has an informative article about laddering at:

www.prusec.com/financial_concerns/ladder.htm

The bond immunization strategies we have discussed are considered to be primarily *passive* in nature, to the extent that investors using these tools typically are *not* attempting to beat the market. Rather, these investors immunize their portfolios in an effort to lock in specified rates of return (or terminal values) that they deem acceptable, given the risks involved. Generally speaking, passive investment strategies are characterized by a lack of input regarding investor expectations of changes in interest rate and/or bond price. Further, these strategies typically do not generate significant transaction costs. A *buy-and-hold* strategy is perhaps the most passive of all investment strategies: All that is required is that the investor replace bonds that have deteriorating credit ratings, have matured, or have been called. Although buy-and-hold investors restrict their ability to earn above-average returns, they also minimize the losses that transaction costs represent.

bond ladders
an investment strategy wherein equal amounts of money are invested in a series of bonds with staggered maturities.

One popular approach that is a bit more active than buy-and-hold is the use of so-called **bond ladders.** In this strategy, equal amounts are invested in a *series* of bonds with staggered maturities. Here's how a bond ladder works: Suppose you want to confine your investing to fixed-income securities with maturities of 10 years or less. Given that maturity constraint, you could set up a ladder by investing in (roughly) equal amounts of, say, 3-, 5-, 7-, and 10-year issues. When the 3-year issue matures, the money from it (along with any new capital) would be put into a new 10-year note. The process would continue rolling over like this so that eventually you would hold a full ladder of staggered 10-year notes. By rolling into new 10-year issues every 2 or 3 years, you can do a kind of dollar-cost averaging and thereby lessen the impact of swings in market rates. Actually, the laddered approach is a safe, simple, and almost automatic way of investing for the long haul. Indeed, once the ladder is set up, it should be followed in a fairly routine manner. A key ingredient of this or any other passive strategy is, of course, the use of high-quality investment vehicles that possess attractive features, maturities, and yields.

Trading on Forecasted Interest Rate Behavior

In contrast, a highly risky approach to bond investing is the *forecasted interest rate* approach. It seeks attractive capital gains when interest rates are expected to decline and preservation of capital when an increase in interest rates is antic-

KEY QUESTIONS TO ASK ABOUT A BOND INVESTMENT—There are several key variables to consider before investing in bonds. The following factors help to determine the value of the investment and how well it meets your financial goals:
- What is the bond's maturity?
- Can it be redeemed early through call features?
- What is the credit quality? What is the bond rating? Is it insured?
- What is the price?
- What is the yield to maturity? What is the yield to call?
- Is it taxable or tax-exempt?

Source: Investing in Bonds, www.investinginbonds.com/info/checklist.htm

bond swap
an investment strategy wherein an investor liquidates one bond holding and simultaneously buys a different issue in its place.

yield pickup swap
replacement of a low-coupon bond for a comparable higher-coupon bond in order to realize an increase in current yield and yield-to-maturity.

tax swap
replacement of a bond that has a capital loss for a similar security; used to offset a gain generated in another part of an investor's portfolio.

ipated. It's risky because it relies on the imperfect forecast of future interest rates. The idea is to increase the return on a bond portfolio by making strategic moves in anticipation of interest rate changes. Such a strategy is essentially *market timing.* An unusual feature of this tactic is that most of the trading is done with *investment-grade securities,* because a high degree of interest rate sensitivity is required to capture the maximum amount of price behavior.

Once interest rate expectations have been specified, this strategy rests largely on technical matters. For example, when a decline in rates is anticipated, aggressive bond investors often seek to lengthen the maturity (or duration) of their bonds (or bond portfolios). The reason: Longer-term bonds rise more in price than shorter-term issues. At the same time, investors look for low-coupon and/or moderately discounted bonds, which will add to duration and increase the amount of potential price volatility. These interest swings are usually short-lived, so bond traders try to earn as much as possible in as short a time as possible. (Margin trading—the use of borrowed money to buy bonds—is also used as a way of magnifying returns when rate declines are expected.) When rates start to level off and move up, these investors begin to shift their money out of long, discounted bonds and into high-yielding issues with short maturities. In other words, they do a complete reversal. During those periods when bond prices are dropping, investors are more concerned about preservation of capital, so they take steps to protect their money from capital losses. Thus, they tend to use such short-term obligations as Treasury bills, money funds, short-term (2–5 year) notes, or even variable-rate notes.

Bond Swaps

In a **bond swap,** an investor simply liquidates one position and at the same time buys a different issue in its place. Swaps can be executed to increase current yield or yield-to-maturity, to take advantage of shifts in interest rates, to improve the quality of a portfolio, or for tax purposes. Although some swaps are highly sophisticated, most are fairly simple transactions. They go by a variety of colorful names, such as "profit takeout," "substitution swap," and "tax swap," but they are all used for one basic reason: *to seek portfolio improvement.* We will briefly review two types of bond swaps that are fairly simple and hold considerable appeal: the yield pickup swap and the tax swap.

In a **yield pickup swap,** an investor switches out of a low-coupon bond into a comparable higher-coupon issue in order to realize an instantaneous pickup of current yield and yield-to-maturity. For example, you would be executing a yield pickup swap if you sold 20-year, A-rated, 6½% bonds (which were yielding 8% at the time) and replaced them with an equal amount of 20-year, A-rated, 7% bonds that were priced to yield 8½%. By executing the swap, you would improve your current yield (your coupon income would increase from $65 a year to $70 a year) as well as your yield-to-maturity (from 8 to 8½%). Basically, such swap opportunities arise because of the *yield spreads* that normally exist between, say, industrial and public utility bonds. The mechanics are fairly simple, and you can execute such swaps simply by watching for swap candidates and/or asking your broker to do so. In fact, the only thing you have to be careful of is that transaction costs do not eat up all the profits.

The other type of swap that's popular with many investors is the **tax swap,** which is also relatively simple and involves few risks. The technique can be used whenever an investor has a substantial tax liability that has come about as a result of selling some security holdings at a profit. The objective is to execute a swap so that the tax liability accompanying the capital gains can be *eliminated or substantially reduced*. This is done by selling an issue that has undergone capital *loss* and replacing it with a comparable obligation. For example, assume that you had $10,000 worth of corporate bonds that you sold (in the current year) for $15,000, resulting in a capital gain of $5,000.

You can eliminate the tax liability accompanying the capital gain by selling securities that have *capital losses of $5,000*. Let's assume you find you hold a 20-year, 4¾% municipal bond that (strictly by coincidence, of course) has undergone a $5,000 drop in value. Thus you have the required tax shield in your portfolio. All you have to do is find a viable swap candidate. Suppose you find a comparable 20-year, 5% municipal issue currently trading at about the same price as the issue being sold. By selling the 4¾s and simultaneously buying a comparable amount of the 5s, you will not only increase your tax-free yields (from 4¾% to 5%) but also eliminate the capital gains tax liability. The only precaution is that *identical issues cannot be used* in such swap transactions. The IRS would consider that a "wash sale" and disallow the loss. Moreover, the capital loss must occur in the same taxable year as the capital gain. This limitation explains why the technique is so popular with knowledgeable investors, particularly at year-end, when tax loss sales and tax swaps multiply as investors hurry to establish capital losses.

HOTLINKS

For details on IRS regulations regarding wash sales, go to the book's Web site and click on Chapter 17. Go to the section on Strategies that Trade Current Income for Capital Gains and then on Tax Swaps.

www.awl.com/gitman_joehnk

IN REVIEW

CONCEPTS

10.13 Briefly describe a *bond ladder*, and note how and why an investor would use this investment strategy. What is a *tax swap*, and why would it be used?

10.14 What strategy would you expect an aggressive bond investor (someone who's looking for capital gains) to employ?

10.15 Why is interest sensitivity important to bond speculators? Does the need for interest sensitivity explain why active bond traders tend to use high-grade issues? Explain.

Summary

LG 1 **Explain the behavior of market interest rates, and identify the forces that cause interest rates to move.** The behavior of interest rates is the single most important force in the bond market. It determines not only the amount of current income an investor will receive but also the investor's capital gains (or losses). Changes in market interest rates can have a dramatic impact on the total returns obtained from bonds over time.

LG 2 **Describe the term structure of interest rates, and note how these yield curves can be used by investors.** Many forces drive the behavior of interest rates over time, including inflation, the cost and availability of funds, and the level of interest rates in major foreign markets. One particularly important force is the term structure of interest rates, which relates yield-to-maturity to term-to-maturity.

LG 3 | **Understand how bonds are valued in the marketplace.** Bonds are valued (priced) in the marketplace on the basis of their required rates of return (or market yields). The whole process of pricing a bond begins with the yield it should provide. Once that piece of information is known (or estimated), a standard, present-value-based model is used to find the dollar price of a bond.

LG 4 | **Describe the various measures of yield and return, and explain how these standards of performance are used in bond valuation.** Four types of yields are important to investors: current yield, promised yield, yield-to-call, and expected yield (or return). Promised yield (yield-to-maturity) is the most widely used bond valuation measure. It captures both the current income and the price appreciation of an issue. The same can be said of yield-to-call, which assumes the bond will be outstanding only until its first call date. Expected return, in contrast, is a valuation measure that's used by aggressive bond traders to show the total return that can be earned from trading in and out of a bond long before it matures.

LG 5 | **Understand the basic concept of duration, how it can be measured, and its use in the management of bond portfolios.** Bond duration is an important concept in bond valuation. Duration takes into account the effects of both reinvestment and price (or market) risks. It captures, in a single measure, the extent to which the price of a bond will react to different interest rate environments. Equally important, duration can be used to immunize whole bond portfolios from the often devastating forces of changing market interest rates.

LG 6 | **Discuss various bond investment strategies and the different ways these securities can be used by investors.** As investment vehicles, bonds can be used as a source of income, as a way to seek capital gains by speculating on the movement in interest rates, or as a way to earn attractive long-term returns. To achieve these objectives, investors often employ one or more of the following strategies: passive strategies such as buy-and-hold, bond ladders, and portfolio immunization; bond trading based on forecasted interest rate behavior; and bond swaps.

Discussion Questions

LG 2 | Q10.1 Briefly describe each of the following theories of the term structure of interest rates.
  a. Expectations hypothesis
  b. Liquidity preference theory
  c. Market segmentation theory

According to these theories, what conditions would result in a downward-sloping yield curve? What conditions would result in an upward-sloping yield curve? Which theory do *you* think is most valid, and why?

LG 2 | Q10.2 Using a recent copy of the *Wall Street Journal* or *Barron's*, find the bond yields for Treasury securities with the following maturities: 3 months, 6 months, 1 year, 3 years, 5 years, 10 years, 15 years, and 20 years. Construct a yield curve based on these reported yields, putting term-to-maturity on the horizontal (x) axis and yield-to-maturity on the vertical (y) axis. Briefly discuss the general shape of your yield curve. What conclusions might you draw about future interest rate movements from this yield curve?

LG 5 | Q10.3 Briefly explain what will happen to a bond's duration measure if each of the following events occur.

a. The yield-to-maturity on the bond falls from 8½% to 8%.
b. The bond gets 1 year closer to its maturity.
c. Market interest rates go from 8% to 9%.
d. The bond's *modified* duration falls by half a year.

LG 6

Q10.4 Assume that an investor comes to you looking for advice. She has $200,000 to invest and wants to put it all into bonds.
 a. If she considers herself a fairly aggressive investor who is willing to take the risks necessary to generate the big returns, what kind of investment strategy (or strategies) would you suggest? Be specific.
 b. What kind of investment strategies would you recommend if your client were a very conservative investor who could not tolerate market losses?
 c. What kind of investor do you think is most likely to use:
  (1) An immunized bond portfolio?
  (2) A yield pickup swap?
  (3) A bond ladder?
  (4) A long-term zero-coupon bond when interest rates fall?

 LG 4 **LG 5**

Q10.5 Using the resources available at your campus or public library (or on the Internet), select any six bonds you like, consisting of *two* Treasury bonds, *two* corporate bonds, and *two* agency issues. Determine the latest current yield and promised yield for each. (For promised yield, use annual compounding.) In addition, find the duration and modified duration for each bond.
 a. Now, assuming that you put an equal amount of money into each of the six bonds you selected, find the duration for this six-bond portfolio.
 b. What would happen to your bond portfolio if market interest rates fell by 100 basis points?
 c. Assuming that you have $100,000 to invest, use at least four of these bonds to develop a bond portfolio that emphasizes either the potential for capital gains or the preservation of capital. Briefly explain your logic.

Problems **LG 3**

P10.1 Two bonds have par values of $1,000. One is a 5%, 15-year bond priced to yield 8%. The other is a 7½%, 20-year bond priced to yield 6%. Which of these two has the lower price? (Assume annual compounding in both cases.)

 LG 3

P10.2 Using semiannual compounding, find the prices of the following bonds:
 a. A 10½%, 15-year bond priced to yield 8%.
 b. A 7%, 10-year bond priced to yield 8%.
 c. A 12%, 20-year bond priced at 10%.

Repeat the problem using annual compounding. Then comment on the differences you found in the prices of the bonds.

 LG 3

P10.3 An investor is considering the purchase of an 8%, 18-year corporate bond that's being priced to yield 10%. She thinks that in a year, this same bond will be priced in the market to yield 9%. Using annual compounding, find the price of the bond today and in 1 year. Next, find the holding period return on this investment, assuming that the investor's expectations are borne out. (If necessary, see Chapter 4 for the holding period return formula.)

 LG 4

P10.4 Compute the current yield of a 10%, 25-year bond that is currently priced in the market at $1,200. Use annual compounding to find the promised yield on this bond. Repeat the promised yield calculation, but this time use semiannual compounding to find yield-to-maturity.

LG 4 **P10.5** A 10%, 25-year bond has a par value of $1,000 and a call price of $1,075. (The bond's first call date is in 5 years.) Coupon payments are made semiannually (so use semiannual compounding where appropriate).

a. Find the current yield, YTM, and YTC on this issue, given that it is currently being priced in the market at $1,200. Which of these three yields is the highest? Which is the lowest? Which yield would you use to value this bond? Explain.

b. Repeat the three calculations above, given that the bond is being priced at $850. Now which yield is the highest? Which is the lowest? Which yield would you use to value this bond? Explain.

 LG 4 **P10.6** Assume that an investor is looking at two bonds: Bond A is a 20-year, 9% (semiannual pay) bond that is priced to yield 10½%. Bond B is a 20-year, 8% (annual pay) bond that is priced to yield 7½%. Both bonds carry a 5-year call deferments and call prices (in 5 years) of $1,050.

a. Which bond has the higher current yield?

b. Which bond has the higher YTM?

c. Which bond has the higher YTC?

 LG 4 **P10.7** A 25-year, zero-coupon bond was recently being quoted at 11⅛. Find the current yield *and* the promised yield of this issue, given that the bond has a par value of $1,000. Using semiannual compounding, determine how much an investor would have to pay for this bond if it were priced to yield 12%.

 LG 4 **P10.8** Assume that an investor pays $800 for a long-term bond that carries an 8% coupon. In 3 years, he hopes to sell the issue for $950. If his expectations come true, what realized yield will this investor earn? (Use annual compounding.) What would the holding period return be if he were able to sell the bond (at $950) after only 9 months?

 LG 4 **P10.9** Using annual compounding, find the yield-to-maturity for each of the following bonds.

a. A 9½%, 20-year bond priced at $957.43.

b. A 16%, 15-year bond priced at $1,684.76.

c. A 5½%, 18-year bond priced at $510.65.

Now assume that each of the above three bonds is callable as follows: Bond *a* is callable in 7 years at a call price of $1,095; bond *b* is callable in 5 years at $1,250; and bond *c* is callable in 3 years at $1,050. Use annual compounding to find the yield-to-call for each bond.

LG 5 **P10.10** Find the Macaulay duration and the modified duration of a 20-year, 10% corporate bond priced to yield 8%. According to the modified duration of this bond, how much of a price change would this bond incur if market yields rose to 9%? Using annual compounding, calculate the price of this bond in 1 year if rates do rise to 9%. How does this price change compare to that predicted by the modified duration? Explain the difference.

 LG 5 **P10.11** Which *one* of the following bonds would you select if you thought market interest rates were going to fall by 50 basis points over the next 6 months?

a. A bond with a Macaulay duration of 8.46 years that's currently being priced to yield 7½%.

b. A bond with a Macaulay duration of 9.30 years that's priced to yield 10%.

c. A bond with a Macaulay duration of 8.75 years that's priced to yield 5¾%.

 LG 5 **LG 6** **P10.12** Mary Richards is an aggressive bond trader who likes to speculate on interest rate swings. Market interest rates are currently at 9%, but she expects them to fall to 7% within a year. As a result, Mary is thinking about buying either a 25-year, zero-coupon

bond or a 20-year, 7½% bond. (Both bonds have $1,000 par values and carry the same agency rating.) Assuming that Mary wants to maximize capital gains, which of the two issues should she select? What if she wants to maximize the total return (interest income and capital gains) from her investment? Why did one issue provide better capital gains than the other? Based on the duration of each bond, which one should be more price volatile?

 LG 5 **LG 6**

P10.13 Elliot Karlin is a 35-year-old bank executive who has just inherited a large sum of money. Having spent several years in the bank's investments department, he's well aware of the concept of duration and decides to apply it to his bond portfolio. In particular, Elliot intends to use $1 million of his inheritance to purchase four U.S. Treasury bonds:

- An 8½%, 13-year bond that's priced at $1,045 to yield 7.47%.
- A 7⅞%, 15-year bond that's priced at $1,020 to yield 7.60%.
- A 20-year stripped Treasury that's priced at $202 to yield 8.22%.
- A 24-year, 7½% bond that's priced at $955 to yield 7.90%.

a. Find the duration and the modified duration of each bond.
b. Find the duration of the whole bond portfolio if Elliot puts $250,000 into each of the four U.S. Treasury bonds.
c. Find the duration of the portfolio if Elliot puts $360,000 each into bonds 1 and 3 and $140,000 each into bonds 2 and 4.
d. Which portfolio—(b) or (c)—should Elliot select if he thinks rates are about to head up and he wants to avoid as much price volatility as possible? Explain. From which portfolio does he stand to make more in annual interest income? Which portfolio would you recommend, and why?

Case Problem 10.1   *The Bond Investment Decisions of Kelley and Erin Coates*

LG 4   **LG 6**

Kelley and Erin Coates live in the Boston area, where Kelley has a successful orthodontics practice. Kelley and Erin have built up a sizable investment portfolio and have always had a major portion of their investments in fixed-income securities. They adhere to a fairly aggressive investment posture and actively go after both attractive current income and substantial capital gains. Assume that it is now 2001 and Erin is currently evaluating two investment decisions: One involves an addition to their portfolio, the other a revision to it.

The Coates' first investment decision involves a short-term trading opportunity. In particular, Erin has a chance to buy a 7½%, 25-year bond that is currently priced at $852 to yield 9%; she feels that in 2 years the promised yield of the issue should drop to 8%.

The second is a bond swap. The Coates hold some Beta Corporation 7%, 2016 bonds that are currently priced at $785. They want to improve both current income and yield-to-maturity, and they are considering one of three issues as a possible swap candidate: (a) Dental Floss, Inc., 7½%, 2016, currently priced at $780; (b) Root Canal Products of America, 6½%, 2014, selling at $885; and (c) Kansas City Dental Insurance, 8%, 2018, priced at $950. All of the swap candidates are of comparable quality and have comparable issue characteristics.

 Questions

a. Regarding the short-term trading opportunity:
   1. What basic trading principle is involved in this situation?
   2. If Erin's expectations are correct, what will the price of this bond be in 2 years?
   3. What is the expected return on this investment?
   4. Should this investment be made? Why?

b. Regarding the bond swap opportunity:
1. Compute the current yield and the promised yield (use semiannual compounding) for the bond the Coates currently hold and for each of the three swap candidates.
2. Do any of the three swap candidates provide better current income and/or current yield than the Beta Corporation bonds the Coates now hold? If so, which one(s)?
3. Do you see any reason why Erin should switch from her present bond holding into one of the other three issues? If so, which swap candidate would be the best choice? Why?

Case Problem 10.2 *Emily Decides to Immunize Her Portfolio*

LG 4 LG 5 LG 6

Emily Hartley is the owner of an extremely successful dress boutique in downtown Chicago. Although high fashion is Emily's first love, she's also interested in investments, particularly bonds and other fixed-income securities. She actively manages her own investments and over time has built up a substantial portfolio of securities. She's well versed on the latest investment techniques and is not afraid to apply those procedures to her own investments.

Emily has been playing with the idea of trying to immunize a big chunk of her bond portfolio. She'd like to cash out this part of her portfolio in 7 years and use the proceeds to buy a vacation home on the South Carolina seashore. To do this, she intends to use the $200,000 she now has invested in the following four corporate bonds (she currently has $50,000 invested in each one).

1. A 12-year, 7½% bond that's currently priced at $895.
2. A 10-year, zero-coupon bond priced at $405.
3. A 10-year, 10% bond priced at $1,080.
4. A 15-year, 9¼% bond priced at $980.
   (*Note:* These are all noncallable, investment-grade, nonconvertible/straight bonds.)

 Questions

a. Given the information provided, find the current yield and the promised yield for each bond in the portfolio. (Use annual compounding.)

b. Calculate the Macaulay and modified durations of each bond in the portfolio, and indicate how the price of each bond would change if interest rates were to rise by 75 basis points. How would the price change if interest rates were to fall by 75 basis points?

c. Find the duration of the current four-bond portfolio. Given the 7-year target that Emily has, would you consider this to be an immunized portfolio? Explain.

d. How could you lengthen or shorten the duration of this portfolio? What's the shortest portfolio duration you can achieve? What's the longest?

e. Using one or more of the four bonds described above, is it possible to come up with a $200,000 bond portfolio that will exhibit the duration characteristics Emily is looking for? Explain.

f. Using one or more of the four bonds, put together a $200,000 immunized portfolio for Emily. Because this portfolio will now be immunized, will Emily be able to treat it as a buy-and-hold portfolio—one she can put away and forget about? Explain.

Web Exercises

The following table shows Web sites on various topics related to bonds.

Web Address	Primary Investment Focus
www.bondsonline.com	Fixed-income securities
www.smartmoney.com/onebond/index.cfm?story=yieldcurve	Living yield curve, and other tools such as calculators and charts.
www.moneypages.com/syndicate/bonds/	Municipal, corporate, and government debt.
www.aaii.org/fxdincme/	Good articles about fixed-income securities.
www.etrade.com	For buying and selling bonds, the Bond Center at E*Trade offers munis, corporates, zero-coupons, and Treasuries, among others. E*Trade's searchable database organizes bonds according to the price, yield, credit rating, and maturity.

W10.1   Bond Market Association's "Investing in Bonds" at www.investinginbonds.com is a great starting place. The site not only explains how bonds work but also gives advice on identifying investing objectives and finding the right mix of stocks, bonds, and cash.

Under the Features section, choose [Investor's Checklist]. Read two sections: [What are the key questions you should ask about an investment in bonds?] and [What types of bonds are available in the market?]

a. An investment in bonds, like any other investment you make, should be tailored to your investment goals, your tolerance for risk, and other individual circumstances. Describe your investment objectives, how much risk you are willing to take, and what impact taxes will have on your investment.

b. Find out what types of bonds are available in the market. Which types are of particular interest to you?

c. Should you invest in individual bonds or bond funds? Why?

W10.2   Visit Smart Money's site at www.smartmoney.com/bonds/. Choose from the left-hand menu under Bond Tools Living Yield Curve.

a. What is the shape of the latest yield curve? What does it say about the future of the economy?

b. Compare the latest yield curve with the average, normal, steep, inverted, and flat yield curves. What are your conclusions?

c. Move the pointer underneath the Play button back and forth to see the changes in the yield curve over the period 1978–2000. In what period(s) do you observe an inverted yield curve?

W10.3   Bond calculators are available at www.aaii.com/otherinv/calc/. Click on [What is my yield-to-maturity?]. By inserting the following data, calculate your yield-to-maturity and your return before and after taxes.

Price you paid (% of face value): 98
Face value: $1,000
Coupon rate: 7.75%
Months to maturity: 120
Federal tax rate: 15%
State tax rate: 8%
Rate of investment of coupon income: 4%
Type of bond: Treasury security.

Now click on [Results] at the bottom of the page.

For additional practice with concepts from this chapter, visit

www.awl.com/gitman_joehnk

In 2000, when neither equity nor debt seemed to interest investors, companies often found it easier to sell convertible bonds—a type of security that combines the features of both debt and equity. With convertibles, the cost of borrowing is lower, and the conversion premium that allows bondholders to convert to a stated number of common shares creates less dilution (reduction) in earnings per share than a regular issue of common stock. For example, in January 2000, advertising agency Young & Rubicam Inc. (Y&R) issued $287.5 million of convertible bonds with a 3% coupon and a 30% conversion premium. CFO Jay Kushner was pleased with the issue because it added diversity to Y&R's investor base and enabled the company to retire more expensive debt. Investors were happy, too. In March 2000, Y&R stock was trading down about 20%, but these convertibles were off by only 8%.

Zero-coupon convertible bonds were also popular in 2000, representing about one-third the year's issues. Like nonconvertible zeros, these bonds pay no interest until maturity, are issued below par, and mature at face value. Investment-grade companies such as Solectron Corp., an electronics contact manufacturer, found them a cheap way to raise debt when interest rates were rising. The company issued $2 billion of convertible zeros at a yield of 2.75% and a 24% conversion premium. The issue was such a success that Solectron returned to the market in November with another $1.5 billion issue.

In this chapter, you will learn about the advantages that preferred stock and convertible securities offer both investor and issuer.

Sources: Steve Bergsman, "Hopping in the Convertible," *CFO,* April, 2000; Avital Louria Hahn, "Convertibles, Led by Zeros, Hit $59 Billion Record as Equities, Debt Lost Their Appeal," *Investment Dealers' Digest*, January 8, 2001; and Avital Louria Hahn, "Soaring Convert Market Falls to Earth with a Thud," *Investment Dealers' Digest*, March 27, 2000, all downloaded from www.findarticles.com

CHAPTER 11

PREFERRED STOCKS AND CONVERTIBLE SECURITIES

Learning Goals

After studying this chapter, you should be able to:

LG 1 Describe the basic features of preferred stock, including sources of value and exposure to risk.

LG 2 Discuss the rights and claims of preferred stockholders, and note some of the popular issue characteristics that are often found with these securities.

LG 3 Understand the various measures of investment worth, and identify several investment strategies that can be used with preferred stocks.

LG 4 Identify the fundamental characteristics of convertible securities, and explain the nature of the underlying conversion privilege.

LG 5 Describe the advantages and disadvantages of investing in convertible securities, including their risk and return attributes.

LG 6 Measure the value of a convertible security, and explain how these securities can be used to meet different investment objectives.

Preferred Stocks

LG 1   LG 2

HOTLINKS

To learn more about preferred stocks, click on [20 Investments You Should Know] at:

www.investopedia.com

preferred stock
a stock that has a prior claim (ahead of common) on the income and assets of the issuing firm.

What would you think of a stock that promised to pay you a fixed annual dividend for life—nothing more, nothing less? If you're an income-oriented investor, the offer might sound pretty good. But where would you find such an investment? Right on the NYSE or AMEX, where hundreds of these securities trade every day, in the form of *preferred stock*—a type of security that looks like a stock but doesn't behave like one. In the first two sections of this chapter we will look at preferred stock as an investment vehicle. In the third and fourth sections we will turn our attention to *convertible debentures*. These are securities originally issued as bonds that later can be converted into shares of the issuing firm's common stock. Both of these investment vehicles—preferred stock and convertibles—are forms of *fixed-income* corporate securities. As you'll see in the chapter, both are also *hybrid securities*, meaning they contain elements of both debt and equity.

Preferred stocks carry fixed dividends that are paid quarterly and are expressed either in dollar terms or as a percentage of the stock's par (or stated) value. They are used by companies that need money but don't want to raise debt to get it; in effect, they are widely viewed by issuers as an alternative to debt. Companies like to issue preferreds because they don't count as common stock (and, therefore, don't affect EPS). However, being a form of equity, they don't count as debt, either—and therefore don't add to the company's debt load. There are today perhaps a thousand OTC and listed preferred stocks outstanding. Many of them are issued by public utilities, although the number of industrial, financial, and insurance issues is rapidly increasing.

Preferred Stocks as Investment Vehicles

Preferred stocks are available in a wide range of quality ratings, from investment-grade to highly speculative. Table 11.1 provides a representative sample

TABLE 11.1	A Sample of Some High-Yielding Preferred Stock			
Moody's Pfd. Stock Rating	Issuer	Annual Dividend	Market Price	Dividend Yield
a	American Express	$1.75	$22.94	7.63%
aa	Bank One	2.00	24.75	8.08
a	Bear Sterns	1.88	22.75	8.26
baa	Con Edison	5.00	65.00	7.69
ba	Finova	2.75	17.12	16.06
a	Ford Motor Credit	2.25	26.19	8.59
a	IBM	1.88	25.38	7.41
aa	Merrill Lynch	2.00	25.19	7.94
baa	Public Storage	2.07	19.25	10.75
b	Tesoro	1.16	10.25	11.32
a	Virginia Elec. Power	5.00	67.25	7.43
baa	Wendy's	2.50	47.00	5.31

Note: All of these issues are straight (nonconvertible) preferred stocks traded on the NYSE. All the information that appears in this table was obtained in August 2000.

Source: Investor's Business Daily, August 25, 2000.

FIGURE 11.1

Average High-Grade Preferred Stock Yields Versus Average Market Yields on AA-Rated Corporate Bonds

Note that preferred stock yields tend to move in concert with the market behavior of bond returns—and that they tend to stay below bond yields. (*Source: Most recent data from Mergent (Moody's) Bond Record,* August 2000 and earlier issues.)

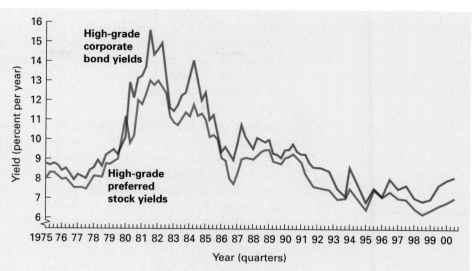

of some actively traded preferred stocks. It shows the types of annual dividends and dividend yields that these securities were providing in August 2000. Note especially the variety of different types of issuers and how the market price of a preferred tends to vary with agency ratings and the size of the annual dividend.

Advantages and Disadvantages Investors are attracted to preferred stocks because of the current income they provide. Moreover, such dividend income is highly predictable, even though it can, under certain circumstances, be temporarily discontinued. Figure 11.1 illustrates the average yields on preferred stocks, from 1975 through 2000, and shows how they compare to high-grade bond returns. Note that preferreds tend to generate yields that are slightly *less* than those of high-grade bonds. This is due to the fact that 70 percent of the preferred dividends *received by a corporation* are exempt from federal income taxes; and since corporations are big investors in preferred stock, the net effect of this favorable tax treatment is reduced preferred dividend yields. Another reason for investing in preferreds is the level of safety they offer investors. That is, despite a few well-publicized incidents, *high-grade* preferred stocks have an excellent record of meeting dividend payments in a timely manner. A final advantage of preferred stocks is the low unit cost ($25 to $50 per share) of many of the issues. These low unit costs give even small investors the opportunity to actively participate in preferreds.

A major disadvantage of preferred stocks is their susceptibility to inflation and high interest rates. Like many other fixed-income securities, preferred stocks simply have not proved to be satisfactory long-term hedges against inflation. Another disadvantage is that preferred dividends may be suspended, or "passed," if the earnings of the corporate issuer drop off. Thus, unlike coupon payments on a bond, dividends on preferreds have no legal backing, and failure to pay them does not lead to default. Still another drawback is that most preferreds lack substantial capital gains potential. Although it is possible to enjoy fairly attractive capital gains from preferred stocks when interest rates decline dramatically, these amounts generally do not match the price performance of common stocks. Finally, perhaps the biggest disadvantage of preferreds is the *yield give-up* they incur relative to bonds. In essence, there is virtually nothing a preferred has to offer that can't be obtained from a comparably rated corporate bond—and *at less risk and more return than can be earned from a preferred.*

 Sources of Value With the exception of convertible preferreds, the value of high-grade preferred stocks is a function of the dividend yields they provide. More specifically, the value (or market price) of a preferred stock is closely related to prevailing market rates: As the general level of interest rates moves up, so do the yields on preferreds, and their prices decline accordingly. When interest rates drift downward, so do the yields on preferreds, as their prices rise. Just like bond prices, therefore, *the price behavior of a high-grade preferred stock is inversely related to market interest rates.* Moreover, its price is directly linked to the issue's level of income. That is, other things being equal, the higher the dividend payment, the higher the market price of an issue. Thus, the price of a preferred stock can be defined as follows:

Equation 11.1

$$\text{Price of a preferred stock} = \frac{\text{Annual dividend income}}{\text{Prevailing market yield}}$$

This equation is simply a variation of the standard dividend yield formula, but here we solve for the price of the issue. (You might also detect a similarity between this formula and the zero-growth dividend valuation model introduced in Chapter 8.) Equation 11.1 is used to price preferred stocks and to compute the future price of a preferred, given an estimate of expected market interest yields. For example, a $2.50 preferred stock (meaning the stock pays a dividend of $2.50 per year) would be priced at $20.83 if the prevailing market yield were 12%:

$$\text{Price} = \frac{\$2.50}{0.12} = \underline{\$20.83}$$

Note that as market yield decreases, you get higher preferred stock prices, thus giving you the inverse relationship between price and yield.

The yield that a preferred stock offers (and therefore its market value) is a function not only of market interest rates but also the issue's credit quality: *The lower the quality of a preferred, the higher its yield.* Such behavior is, of course, compatible with the risk-return tradeoffs that usually exist in the marketplace. Fortunately, preferred stocks are rated, much like bonds, by Moody's and Standard & Poor's. Finally, the value of a preferred is also affected by issue characteristics such as call features and sinking-fund provisions. For example, freely callable preferreds normally provide higher yields than noncallable issues because of their greater call risk. Quality and issue features, however, have only slight effects on price behavior over time, and they certainly do not compare in importance with the movement of market yields.

Risk Exposure Preferred stock investors are exposed to both business and interest rate risks. *Business risk* is important with preferreds, because these

Published Quotes for Preferred Stock

In publications like the *Wall Street Journal,* preferred stock quotes are listed separately from common stocks. Many companies have more than one issue of preferred outstanding, in which case, each issue is identified alphabetically, such as pfD, pfR, etc. (*Source: Wall Street Journal,* May 24, 2001.)

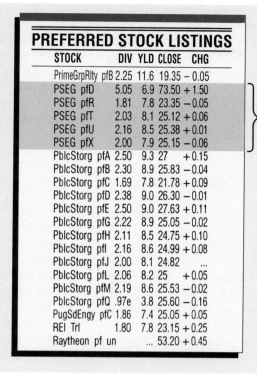

PREFERRED STOCK LISTINGS

STOCK	DIV	YLD	CLOSE	CHG
PrimeGrpRlty pfB	2.25	11.6	19.35	− 0.05
PSEG pfD	5.05	6.9	73.50	+ 1.50
PSEG pfR	1.81	7.8	23.35	− 0.05
PSEG pfT	2.03	8.1	25.12	+ 0.06
PSEG pfU	2.16	8.5	25.38	+ 0.01
PSEG pfX	2.00	7.9	25.15	− 0.06
PblcStorg pfA	2.50	9.3	27	+ 0.15
PblcStorg pfB	2.30	8.9	25.83	− 0.04
PblcStorg pfC	1.69	7.8	21.78	+ 0.09
PblcStorg pfD	2.38	9.0	26.30	− 0.01
PblcStorg pfE	2.50	9.0	27.63	+ 0.11
PblcStorg pfG	2.22	8.9	25.05	− 0.02
PblcStorg pfH	2.11	8.5	24.75	+ 0.10
PblcStorg pfI	2.16	8.6	24.99	+ 0.08
PblcStorg pfJ	2.00	8.1	24.82	...
PblcStorg pfL	2.06	8.2	25	+ 0.05
PblcStorg pfM	2.19	8.6	25.53	− 0.02
PblcStorg pfQ	.97e	3.8	25.60	− 0.16
PugSdEngy pfC	1.86	7.4	25.05	+ 0.05
REI Trl	1.80	7.8	23.15	+ 0.25
Raytheon pf un		...	53.20	+ 0.45

Public Service Enterprise Group's preferred stocks

securities are a form of equity ownership and, as such, lack many of the legal protections of bonds. Annual operating costs and corporate financial strength, therefore, are of concern to preferred stockholders. Preferred stock ratings (discussed later in the chapter) can be used to assess the amount of business risk embedded in an issue. Higher-quality/higher-rated issues are believed to possess less business risk.

Because of the fixed-income nature of these securities and the way they're valued in the market, *interest rate risk* is also important to preferred stockholders. That is, when market interest rates move up, the value of these securities (like that of bonds) falls. Indeed, such risk exposure can be very damaging if interest rates move against you in a big way.

Market Transactions Preferred stocks are subject to the same transaction costs (brokerage fees and transfer taxes) as shares of common stock. In addition, preferred stock investors use the same types of orders (market, limit, and stop-loss) and operate under the same margin requirements. And in some newspapers, even the quotes for preferred stocks ar commingled with those of common. However, as can be seen in Figure 11.2, the *Wall Street Journal* has a separate listing for preferred stock quotes, which includes the name of the stock, the amount of annual dividends, the dividend yield, closing price, and change in price.

Also, note that a single company can have any number of preferred stock issues outstanding, each with its own annual dividend. Certainly, that's the case with the Public Service Enterprise Group (PSEG) and Public Storage (PblcStorg) preferreds. The quotes in Figure 11.2 show, for example, that there are five issues of preferred stock listed for Public Service Enterprise Group. Actually, the company may have even more preferred issues outstanding, but if those issues did not trade on the day of the quotes, they would not be listed. PSEG's preferreds pay annual dividends of anywhere from $1.81 to $5.05 per share. (Note that, generally speaking, the higher the annual dividend, the higher the price of the stock.) At quoted market prices, these preferreds were providing current yields of 6.9% to 8.5%. Observe also the relatively low unit cost of the stock. With very few exceptions, preferred stocks usually trade at around $20 to $25 a share.

Issue Characteristics

Preferred stocks possess features that not only distinguish them from other types of securities but also help differentiate one preferred from another. For example, preferred stocks may be issued as convertible or nonconvertible, although the majority fall into the nonconvertible category. A convertible preferred has a **conversion feature** that allows the holder to convert the preferred stock into a specified number of shares of the issuing company's common stock. Because convertible preferreds are, for all intents and purposes, very much like convertible bonds, we will discuss them later in the chapter. At this point, we'll concentrate on *nonconvertible issues*, although many of the features we are about to discuss apply equally to convertible preferreds. In addition to convertibility, investors should be aware of several other important features of preferred stocks; they include the rights of preferred stockholders and the special provisions (such as those pertaining to passed dividends or call features) that are built into preferred stock issues.

conversion feature
allows the holder of a convertible preferred to convert to a specified number of shares of the issuing company's common stock.

Rights of Preferred Stockholders The contractual agreement of a preferred stock specifies the rights and privileges of preferred stockholders. The most important of these deal with the level of annual dividends, the claim on income, voting rights, and the claim on assets. The issuing company agrees that it will pay preferred stockholders a (minimum) fixed level of quarterly dividends and that such payments *will take priority over common stock dividends*. The only condition is that the firm generate income sufficient to meet the preferred dividend requirements. However, the firm is not legally bound to pay dividends. Of course, it cannot pass dividends on preferred stock and then pay dividends on common stock. To do so would violate the preferreds' prior claim on income.

Although most preferred stocks are issued with dividend rates that remain fixed for the life of the issue, in the early 1980s some preferreds began to appear with floating dividend rates. Known as **adjustable-rate** (or **floating-rate**) **preferreds**, these issues adjust their dividends periodically in line with yields on specific Treasury issues, although minimum and maximum dividend rates are usually established as a safeguard for investors and issuers.

Even though they hold an ownership position in the firm, preferred stockholders normally have no voting rights. However, if conditions deteriorate to the point where the firm needs to pass one or more consecutive quarterly dividends, preferred shareholders are usually given the right to elect a certain number of corporate directors so that their views can be represented. And if

HOT LINKS
Read about variable-rate preferred stock at:
askmerrill.ml.com/product_details/0,,146,00.html

adjustable-rate (floating-rate) preferreds
preferred stock whose dividends are adjusted periodically in line with yields on certain Treasury issues.

liquidation becomes necessary, the holders of preferreds are given a prior claim on assets. These preferred claims, limited to the par or stated value of the stock, must be satisfied before the claims of the common stockholders. Of course, this obligation does not always mean that the full par or stated value of the preferred will be recovered, because the claims of senior securities (like bonds) must be met first. That is, all bonds (including convertible bonds) have a higher claim on assets (and income) than preferred stock, whereas preferreds have a higher claim than common stock. Thus preferred shareholders have a claim that's somewhere between that of bondholders and common stockholders.

Finally, when a company has more than one issue of preferred stock outstanding, it sometimes issues **preference** (or **prior preferred**) **stock.** Essentially, this stock has seniority over other preferred stock in its right to receive dividends and in its claim on assets in the event of liquidation. Therefore, preference stocks should be viewed as *senior preferreds.* They're usually easy to pick out in the financial pages because they use the letters *pr* instead of *pf* in their quotes.

Preferred Stock Provisions There are three preferred stock provisions that investors should be well aware of *before* making an investment in a preferred security. Especially important is the obligation of the issuer in case any dividends are missed. In addition, you should determine whether the stock has a call feature and/or a sinking fund provision. Let's start by looking at how passed dividends are handled, which depends on whether the preferred stock is issued on a cumulative or a noncumulative basis.

Fortunately for investors, most preferred stocks are issued on a **cumulative** basis. This means that any preferred dividends that have been passed *must be made up in full* before dividends can be paid to common stockholders. Any outstanding unfulfilled preferred dividend obligations are said to be in arrears, and so long as dividends on preferred stock remain in arrears, a corporation may not make dividend payments on common shares. Assume, for example, that a firm normally pays a $1 quarterly dividend on its preferred stock but has missed the dividend for three quarters in a row. In this case, the firm has preferred dividends in arrears of $3 a share. It must meet these past dividends, along with the next quarterly dividend before it can pay dividends to common shareholders. The firm could fulfill this obligation by paying, say, $2 per share to the preferred stockholders at the next quarterly dividend date and $3 per share at the following one (with the $3 covering the remaining $2 in arrears and the current $1 quarterly payment). If the preferred stock had carried a **noncumulative provision,** the issuing company would have been under no obligation to make up any of the passed dividends. Of course, the firm could not make dividend payments on common stock either. But it could resume such payments simply by meeting the next quarterly preferred dividend. Other things being equal, a cumulative preferred stock should be more highly valued than an issue without such a provision. That is, the cumulative feature should increase the price (and in so doing, lower the yield) of these issues.

Since the early 1970s, it has become increasingly popular to issue preferred stocks with call features. Today, a large number of preferreds carry this provision, which gives the firm the right to call the preferred for retirement. Callable preferreds are usually issued on a *deferred-call basis,* which means they cannot be retired for a certain number of years after the date of issue.

preference (prior preferred) stock
a type of preferred stock that has seniority over other preferred stock in its right to receive dividends and in its claim on assets.

cumulative provision
a provision requiring that any preferred dividends that have been passed must be paid in full before dividends can be restored to common stockholders.

in arrears
having outstanding unfulfilled preferred dividend obligations.

noncumulative provision
a provision found on some preferred stocks excusing the issuing firm from having to make up any passed dividends.

INVESTOR FACTS

HOW TO HIDE FROM RISING RATES—One of the biggest fears of fixed-income investors (including preferred stock investors) is rising interest rates. To hedge against rising rates, investors often turn to *adjustable-rate preferreds,* whose cash dividends are adjusted quarterly to reflect market conditions. The dividends on adjustable preferreds usually have a floor and a ceiling, but that still leaves plenty of room to move up or down with market rates. When rates move up, rather than the price of the issue going down, the dividend payment goes up instead. Bottom line: There's far less price volatility with adjustables than with fixed-rate preferreds.

After the deferral period, usually 5 to 7 years, the preferreds become freely callable. Of course, such issues are then susceptible to call if the market rate for preferreds declines dramatically. This explains why the yields on freely callable preferreds should be higher than those on noncallable issues. As with bonds, the call price of a preferred is made up of the par value of the issue and a call premium that may amount to as much as one year's dividends.

Another preferred stock feature that has become popular is the *sinking-fund provision*. This provision specifies how all or a part of an issue will be paid off—amortized—over time. Sinking-fund preferreds actually have *implied* maturity dates. They are used by firms to reduce the cost of financing, because sinking-fund issues generally have *lower* yields than nonsinking-fund preferreds. A typical sinking-fund preferred might require the firm to retire half the issue over a 10-year period by retiring, say, 5% of the issue each year. Unfortunately, the investor has no control over which shares are called for sinking-fund purposes.

IN REVIEW

CONCEPTS

11.1 Define a *preferred stock*. What types of prior claims do preferred shareholders enjoy?

11.2 In what ways is a preferred stock like equity? In what ways is it like a bond?

11.3 What are the advantages and the disadvantages of investing in preferreds?

11.4 Distinguish a *cumulative* preferred from a *callable* preferred. Do cumulative dividend provisions and call features affect the investment merits of preferred issues? Explain.

Valuing and Investing in Preferreds

LG 3

As we just saw, although preferred stocks may be a form of equity, they behave in the market more like a bond than a stock. Therefore, it seems logical that *preferreds should be valued much like bonds,* with market interest rates and investment quality playing key roles. Similarly, when it comes to investing in preferreds, you would expect interest rates (either the level of market interest rates or the movements therein) to play key roles in preferred stock investment strategies. In fact, that's exactly what you find: The two most widely used preferred stock strategies involve either going after high levels of current income or seeking capital gains when market rates are falling.

 ## Putting a Value on Preferreds

Evaluating the investment suitability of preferreds involves assessing comparative return opportunities. Let's look now at some of the return measures that are important to preferred stockholders, and then at the role that agency ratings play in the valuation process.

Dividend Yield: A Key Measure of Value Dividend yield is critical to determining the price and return behavior of most preferred stocks. It is computed according to the following simple formula:

Equation 11.2

$$\text{Dividend yield} = \frac{\text{Annual dividend income}}{\text{Current market price of the preferred stock}}$$

dividend yield
a measure of the amount of return earned on annual dividends.

Dividend yield is a measure of the amount of return earned on annual dividends, and is the basis upon which comparative preferred investment opportunities are evaluated. (It is basically the same as the *dividend yield* used in Chapter 7 with common stocks and is comparable to the *current yield* measure used with bonds, as described in Chapter 10.)

Here's how dividend yield works: Suppose an 8% preferred stock has a par value of $25 and is currently trading at a price of $27.50 per share. For preferreds whose dividends are denoted as a percent of par (or stated) value, the dollar value of the annual dividend is found by multiplying the dividend rate (in this case, 8%) by the par value ($25). Thus, the annual dividend on this stock is: $.08 \times \$25 = \$2$. Therefore, the dividend yield in this example is

$$\text{Dividend yield} = \frac{\$2}{\$27.50} = \underline{\underline{7.27\%}}$$

As you can see, at $27.50 a share, this preferred is yielding about 7.3% to investors. If the price of this preferred moves down (to say, $21 a share), the dividend yield increases (in this case, to about 9½%). In practice, we would expect investors to compute or have available a current dividend yield measure for each preferred under consideration and then to make a choice by comparing the yields on the alternative preferreds—along with, of course, the risk and issue characteristics of each.

Whereas long-term investors may consider dividend yield a key factor, that's not necessarily the case with the short-term traders. Instead, these traders generally focus on anticipated price behavior and the expected return from buying and selling an issue over a short period of time. Thus *the expected future price of a preferred* is important to short-term traders. Expected price can be found by first forecasting future market interest rates and then using that information to determine expected future price. To illustrate, suppose a preferred stock pays $3 in dividends and its yield is expected to decline to 6% within the next 3 years. If such market rates prevail, then 3 years from now, the issue will have a market price of $50 (using Equation 11.1, annual dividend ÷ yield = $3 ÷ 0.06 = $50). This forecasted price, along with the current market price and level of annual dividends, would then be used in either the expected return or the holding period return formula to assess the return potential of the investment.

To continue with our example, if the stock were currently priced at $28 a share, it would have an *expected return* (over the 3-year investment horizon) of a very attractive 30.3%. This can be found by using *the IRR approach* we first introduced in Chapter 4 and then applied (as a measure of expected return) to common stocks in Chapter 8 and to bonds in Chapter 10. Basically, you'd want to find the discount rate, in the present-value-based yield formula, that equates the expected future cash flows from this preferred to its current market price of $28 a share. (The preferred's cash flows are the $50 price in 3 years, plus the annual dividends of $3 a share over each of the next 3 years.) As it turns out, that discount rate equals 30.3%; at that rate, the present value of the future cash flows amounts to $28 a share. (As an aside, *this problem can readily be solved with a financial calculator* by letting $N = 3$, $PV = -28$, $PMT = 3$, and $FV = 50$ and then solve for I. Try it. You should end up with a value (return) of 30.34.)

You now have a measure of the relative attractiveness of this preferred stock. Of course, other things (like risk) being equal, the higher the expected return, the more appealing the investment. (Note that if the above performance had occurred over a period of 6 months, rather than 3 years, you would use the *holding-period return* measure to assess the potential return of this preferred. See Chapter 4 for details.)

book value (net asset value)
a measure of the amount of debt-free assets supporting each share of preferred stock.

Book Value The **book value** (or **net asset value**) of a preferred stock is a measure of the amount of debt-free assets supporting each share of preferred stock. Book value per share is found by subtracting all the liabilities of the firm from its total assets and dividing the difference by the number of preferred shares outstanding. It reflects the quality of an issue with regard to the preferred's *claim on assets*. Obviously, a preferred with a book value of $150 per share enjoys generous asset support and more than adequately secures a par value of, say, $25 a share. Net asset value is most relevant when it is used relative to an issue's par (or stated) value. Other things being equal, *the quality of an issue improves as the margin by which book value exceeds par value increases.*

fixed charge coverage
a measure of how well a firm is able to cover its preferred stock dividends.

Fixed Charge Coverage **Fixed charge coverage** is a measure of how well a firm is able to cover its preferred dividends. Here attention is centered on the firm's ability to service preferred dividends and live up to the preferred's preferential *claim on income*. As such, fixed charge coverage is important in determining the quality of a preferred stock. Fixed charge coverage is computed as follows:

Equation 11.3

$$\text{Fixed charge coverage} = \frac{\text{Earnings before interest and taxes (EBIT)}}{\text{Interest expense} + \dfrac{\text{Preferred dividends}}{0.65}}$$

Note in this equation that preferred dividends are adjusted by a factor of 0.65. This adjustment takes into account the fact that *a company pays dividends from the earnings that are left after taxes.* The adjustment factor (0.65) implies a corporate tax rate of 35%, which is a reasonable rate to use for our purposes here. By making the indicated adjustment, you essentially place preferred dividends on the same basis as interest paid on bonds, which is a tax-deductible expense. *Normally, the higher the fixed charge coverage, the greater the margin of safety.* A ratio of 1.0 means the company is generating just enough earnings to meet its preferred dividend payments—not a very healthy situation. A coverage ratio of 0.7 suggests the potential for some real problems, whereas a coverage of, say, 7.0 indicates that preferred dividends are fairly secure.

Agency Ratings Standard & Poor's has long rated the investment quality of preferred stocks, and since 1973, so has Moody's. S&P uses basically the same rating system as it does for bonds; Moody's uses a slightly different system. For both agencies, the greater the likelihood that the issuer will be able to pay dividends promptly, the higher the rating. Much like bonds, the top four ratings

H O T L I N K S

Moody's Preferred stock ratings definitions are at:

www.bondtalk.com/rules/ratings/moodys.htm

Or, to learn about the approach to the rating of debt and preferred stock go to:

www.ambest.com/ratings/debtrating/

designate *investment-grade* (high-quality) preferreds. Although preferreds come in a full range of agency ratings, most tend to fall in the medium-grade categories (a and baa) or lower. Generally speaking, higher agency ratings reduce the market yield of an issue and increase its interest sensitivity. Agency ratings not only eliminate much of the need for fundamental analysis, but also help investors get a handle on the yield and potential price behavior of an issue.

Investment Strategies

There are several investment strategies that preferred stockholders can follow. Each is useful in meeting a different investment objective, and each offers a different level of return and exposure to risk.

Looking for Yields This strategy represents perhaps the most popular use of preferred stocks and is ideally suited for serious long-term investors. *High current income* is the objective, and the procedure basically involves seeking out those preferreds with the most attractive yields. Of course, consideration must also be given to such features as the quality of the issue, whether the dividends are cumulative, and the existence of any call or sinking-fund provisions.

Certainty of income and safety are important in this strategy, because yields are attractive only as long as dividends are paid. Some investors never buy anything but the highest-quality preferreds. Others sacrifice quality in return for higher yields when the economy is strong and use higher-quality issues only during periods of economic distress. Whenever you leave one of the top four agency ratings, you should recognize the speculative position you are assuming. This is especially so with preferreds; after all, their dividends lack legal enforcement. You should also keep in mind that this investment strategy is *likely to involve giving up some yield relative to what could be obtained from comparably rated corporate bonds,* for as noted earlier, preferreds usually generate somewhat lower yields than bonds, even though they are less secure and may be subject to a bit more risk.

There is, however, a way to get around that yield give-up and earn *monthly income* to boot. That is to consider investing in a type of hybrid security known as **monthly income preferred stock** (**MIPS,** for short). But as the accompanying *Investing in Action* box explains, although these securities do offer attractive yields, they are a very unusual type of investment vehicle. As such, you should learn as much as you can about MIPS before investing in them.

monthly income preferred stock (MIPS)
a type of preferred stock that offers attractive tax provisions to the issuers, and attractive monthly returns to investors.

Trading on Interest Rate Swings Rather than assuming a "safe" buy-and-hold position, the investor who trades on movements in interest rates adopts an aggressive short-term trading posture. This is done for one major reason: *capital gains*. Of course, although a high level of return is possible with this approach, it comes with higher risk exposure. Because preferreds are fixed-income securities, the market behavior of *investment-grade issues* is closely linked to movements in interest rates. If market interest rates are expected to decline substantially, attractive capital gains opportunities may be realized from preferred stocks. Indeed, this is precisely what happened in the mid-1980s, and

INVESTING in action

MIPS: There's More to Them Than Higher Yields and Monthly Income

In 1993 Goldman Sachs & Co., a leading investment banking firm, invented *monthly income preferred stock,* or *MIPS,* which looks like a win–win arrangement: Everyone seems to benefit. The issuer gets a tax deduction. The investor gets high *monthly* income, as well as the upside potential inherent in a stock. Here's how they work: XYZ Corporation creates a new entity called a limited-life company (LLC) that sells MIPS to the public and lends the proceeds to the parent corporation. The parent pays interest to the LLC on the loan, which in turn is paid to MIPS holders in the form of monthly dividends.

From the issuer's point of view, MIPS are attractive because the payments are tax deductible, even though MIPS are not considered straight debt and thus do not raise the corporation's debt ratio. That's good, because credit rating agencies don't like to see debt ratios rise. MIPS are typically listed on the New York Stock Exchange, like many preferred stocks. Issuers have included such household names as Aetna, GTE, and Corning. From the investor's point of view, MIPS offer higher yields than certificates of deposit and money market funds. They also provide higher yields than corporate bonds and conventional preferred stock. And the payments are made monthly, whereas bonds pay interest every 6 months and stocks pay dividends quarterly.

The yield on conventional preferred stock tends to be driven down by corporate investors, who can deduct up to 70% of the dividend payments from their corporate income tax. Individual investors don't get that tax break, so conventional preferreds haven't been marketed heavily to individuals. But MIPS have gotten their attention.

Not everyone thinks MIPS are great. The first drawback is that despite the term *preferred* in their name, MIPS are quite low on the issuing corporation's list of obligations. If an issuer gets into financial trouble, MIPS holders have to stand toward the end of the repayment line. The second drawback is lack of call protection. If interest rates fall, the issuer can redeem the securities at par without paying a penalty. That leaves the investor stuck with cash to reinvest at lower rates. The third drawback has to do with your taxes. Corporations set up partnerships to issue these securities, which means that you get a K-1 instead of a Form 1099 at the end of the year. In contrast to 1099s, which are sent out at the end of January, most K-1s aren't sent out until mid-March. And they're a more complicated document. That means you'll spend more time on your taxes—or your accountant will, which means a higher bill to you. Indeed, a high accounting fee could even wipe out the higher yields that MIPS offer.

again in the early '90s (1991 through 1993), when market interest rates dropped sharply. During such periods, it's not uncommon to find preferreds generating *annual* returns of 20% to 30%, or more.

As is probably clear by now, this strategy is identical to that used by bond investors. In fact, many of the same principles used with bonds apply to preferred stocks. For example, it is important to select high-grade preferred stocks, because interest sensitivity is a key ingredient of this strategy. Moreover, margin trading is often used to magnify short-term holding period returns. A basic difference is that the very high leverage rates of bonds are not available with preferreds, because they fall under the same, less generous margin requirements as common stocks. The investment selection process is simplified somewhat as well, because neither maturity nor the size of the annual preferred dividend (which is equivalent to a bond's coupon) has any effect on the *rate of*

Price Pattern of a Hypothetical Preferred Turnaround Candidate

Although a turnaround issue seeks the price level of other preferreds of comparable quality and dividend payout, this level also acts as a type of price cap and clearly limits capital.

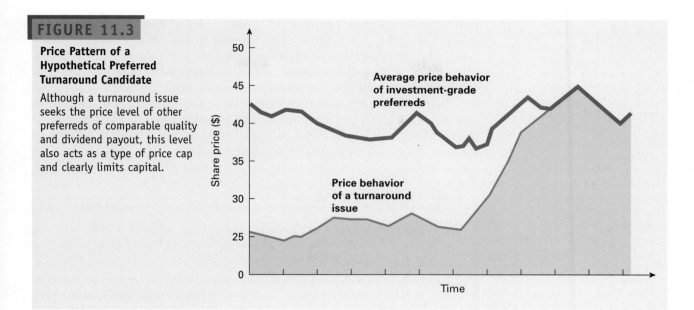

price volatility. That is, a $2 preferred will appreciate just as much (in percentage terms) as an $8 preferred for a given change in market yields.

Speculating on Turnarounds This speculative investment strategy can prove profitable if you're nimble enough to catch a trading opportunity before everyone else does. The idea is to find preferred stocks whose dividends have gone into arrears and whose rating has tumbled to one of the speculative categories. The price of the issue, of course, would be depressed to reflect the corporate problems of the issuer. There is more to this strategy, however, than simply finding a speculative-grade preferred stock. The difficult part is to uncover a speculative issue whose fortunes, for one reason or another, *are about to undergo a substantial turnaround.* This strategy requires a good deal of fundamental analysis and is, in many respects, akin to investing in speculative common stock.

In essence, the investor is betting that the firm will undergo a turnaround and will once again be able to service its preferred dividend obligations in a timely fashion. Such a bet obviously involves a fair amount of risk. Unfortunately, although the rewards from this kind of high-risk investing can be substantial, they are somewhat limited. For example, if the turnaround candidate is expected to recover to a single-a rating, we would expect its capital gains potential to be limited by the price level of other a-rated preferreds. This condition is depicted in Figure 11.3. As the figure shows, although price performance may be somewhat limited, it is still substantial and can readily amount to holding period returns of 50% or more. But in view of the substantial risks involved, such returns are certainly not out of line.

Investing in Convertible Preferreds The investor following this strategy uses the conversion feature to go after speculative opportunities and the chance for attractive returns. The use of *convertible preferreds* is based on their link to the company's common stock and on the belief that they will provide generous price appreciation. Convertibles will be reviewed in detail below, but at this point, suffice it to say that as the price of the underlying common stock appreciates, so does the market price of a convertible preferred. This strategy can offer handsome returns, but remember that investors who employ it are actually speculating on the common stock dimension of the security. Therefore, it is the equity position of the issue that should be subjected to scrutiny. The idea is to look for equity situations that hold considerable promise for appreciation, and then, rather than buying the common stock of the firm, purchase its convertible preferred instead.

I N   R E V I E W

C O N C E P T S

11.5 Describe how high-grade preferred stocks are priced in the market. What role does dividend yield play in the valuation of preferred stocks? Could you use the zero-growth dividend valuation model to value a preferred stock? Explain.

11.6 Discuss why dividend yield is critical in evaluating the investment merits of high-grade preferred stocks during periods when market yields are expected to decline.

11.7 The *Investing in Action* box on page 464 discussed *monthly income preferred stock*. Briefly describe these securities, and note why investors might be interested in buying them. Do these securities have any noteworthy features? Are there any unusual risks associated with them? Explain.

11.8 Identify several investment uses of preferred stocks. Would preferreds be suitable for both conservative and aggressive investors? Explain.

Convertible Securities

 LG 4   LG 5

convertible securities
fixed-income obligations that have a feature permitting the holder to convert the security into a specified number of shares of the issuing company's common stock.

equity kicker
another name for the conversion feature, giving the holder of a convertible security a deferred claim on the issuer's common stock.

Convertible securities, more commonly known simply as *convertibles,* represent still another type of fixed-income security. Usually issued as debenture notes or bonds, these securities are subsequently convertible into shares of the issuing firm's common stock. Although they possess the features and performance characteristics of both fixed-income and equity securities, convertibles should be viewed primarily *as a form of equity.* That's because most investors commit their capital to such obligations not for the attractive yields they provide but, rather, for the potential price performance of the stock side of the issue. In fact, it is always a good idea *to determine whether a corporation has convertible issues outstanding whenever you are considering a common stock investment.* In some circumstances, the convertible may be a better investment than the firm's common stock.

Convertibles as Investment Outlets

Convertible securities are popular with investors because of their **equity kicker**—that is, the right of the investor to convert his or her bonds into the company's common stock. Because of this feature, the market price of the convertible has a tendency to behave very much like the price of the underlying common stock. Convertibles are used by all types of companies and are issued either as convertible *bonds* (by far the most common type) or as convertible *preferreds.* Companies like to issue convertibles principally because *they*

deferred equity
securities issued in one form and later redeemed or converted into shares of common stock.

enable firms to raise equity capital at fairly attractive prices. That is, when a company issues stock in the normal way (by simply selling more shares in the company), it does so by setting a price on the stock that's *below* prevailing market prices. For example, it might be able to get $25 for a stock that's currently priced in the market at, say, $30 a share. In contrast, when it issues the stock indirectly through a convertible issue, a firm can set a price that's *above* the prevailing market—for example, it might be able to get $35 for the same stock. As a result, the company can raise the *same amount of money* by issuing a lot less stock through a convertible than by selling it directly in the market. Thus, companies issue convertibles *not* as a way of raising debt capital but as a way of raising equity. Because they are supposed to be converted eventually into shares of the issuing company's common stock, convertibles are usually viewed as a form of **deferred equity**.

Not surprisingly, whenever the stock market is strong, convertibles tend to perform well. When the market softens, so does interest in convertibles. Convertible bonds and convertible preferreds are both linked to the equity position of the firm, so they are usually considered interchangeable for investment purposes. Except for a few peculiarities (e.g., the fact that preferreds pay dividends rather than interest and do so on a quarterly basis rather than semiannually), convertible bonds and convertible preferreds are evaluated in much the same way. Because of their similarities, the discussion that follows will be couched largely in terms of bonds, but the information and implications apply equally well to convertible preferreds.

Convertible Notes and Bonds Convertible bonds are usually issued as debentures (long-term, unsecured corporate debt), but they carry the provision that within a stipulated time period, *the bond may be converted into a certain number of shares of the issuing company's common stock.* (Convertible *notes* are just like convertible bonds except that the debt portion of the security carries a shorter maturity—usually of 5 to 10 years. Other than the life of the debt, there is no real difference between the two types of issues: They're both unsecured debt obligations, and they're usually subordinated to other forms of debt. Most important, they're both convertible into common stock on pretty much the same terms. Thus, for our purposes here, we'll use the terms interchangeably.)

Generally speaking, there is little or no cash involved at the time of conversion. You merely trade in the convertible bond (or note) for a stipulated number of shares of common stock. Figure 11.4 provides some details about a convertible note recently issued by Cypress Semiconductor Corporation. Notice that this obligation was originally issued as a 3¾% subordinated (unsecured) note. The reason why the issue carries such a low coupon (compared to prevailing market rates of more like 7% or 8%) is the fact that it offers an attractive conversion feature. In particular, each $1,000 note can be converted into Cypress stock at roughly $62.55 a share. Thus, *regardless of what happens to the market price of the stock,* the convertible investor can redeem each note for 15.98 shares of the company's stock ($1,000 ÷ $62.55 = 15.98 shares). If Cypress stock is trading in the market at, say, $125 a share at the time of conversion, then the investor would have just converted a $1,000 debt obligation into $1,997.50 worth of stock (15.98 × $125 = $1,997.50).

FIGURE 11.4

A New Convertible Comes to the Market

Holders of this Cypress Semiconductor note can convert it into the company's common stock at the stated conversion price of $62.548 per share. As a result, they would receive 15.988 shares of stock for each $1,000 convertible bond owned. Prior to conversion, the bondholder will receive annual interest income of $37.50 for each bond—which, in the context of market interest rates in the year 2000, clearly makes this *a very low-yielding* corporate debt security. (*Source: Wall Street Journal,* August 3, 2000.)

This announcement is neither an offer to sell nor a solicitation of offers to buy any of these securities. The offering is made only by the Prospectus and the related Prospectus Supplement, copies of which may be obtained in any State or jurisdiction in which this announcement is circulated only from such of the underwriters as may legally offer these securities in such State or jurisdiction.

NEW ISSUE

June 20, 2000

$287,500,000

CYPRESS

3¾% Convertible Subordinated Notes
Due July 1, 2005

Price 100%

plus accrued interest, if any, from June 26, 2000

The Notes are convertible at any time prior to maturity into shares of Cypress Semiconductor Corporation common stock at a conversion price of $62.548 per share, subject to certain adjustments.

Credit Suisse First Boston

Bear, Stearns & Co. Inc.

Lehman Brothers

Prudential Volpe Technology Group
a unit of Prudential Securities

forced conversion
the calling in of convertible bonds by the issuing firm.

HOT LINKS

For information on how to hedge your bets with convertible bonds, see:

moneycentral.msn.com/articles/
invest/strat/3295.asp

Actually, while it's the *bondholder* who has the right to convert the bond at any time, more often than not, the issuing firm initiates conversion by calling the bonds—a practice known as **forced conversion**. To provide the corporation with the flexibility to retire the debt and force conversion, most convertibles come out as freely callable issues, or they carry very short call deferment periods. To force conversion, the corporation would call for the retirement of the bond and give the bondholder one of two options: Either convert the bond into common stock, or redeem it for cash at the stipulated call price (which, in the case of convertibles, contains very little call premium).

So long as the convertible is called when the market value of the stock exceeds the call price of the bond (which is almost always the case), seasoned investors would never choose the second option. Instead, they would opt to convert the bond, as the firm wants them to. Then they can hold the stocks if they want to, or they can sell their new shares in the market (and end up with more cash than they would have received by taking the call price). After the conversion is complete, the bonds no longer exist; instead, there is additional common stock in their place.

conversion privilege
the conditions and specific nature of the conversion feature on convertible securities.

conversion period
the time period during which a convertible issue can be converted.

conversion ratio
the number of shares of common stock into which a convertible issue can be converted.

conversion price
the stated price per share at which common stock will be delivered to the investor in exchange for a convertible issue.

Conversion Privilege The key element of any convertible is its **conversion privilege,** which stipulates the conditions and specific nature of the conversion feature. To begin with, it states exactly when the debenture can be converted. With some issues, there may be an initial waiting period of 6 months to perhaps 2 years after the date of issue, during which time the security cannot be converted. The **conversion period** then begins, and the issue can be converted at any time. The conversion period typically extends for the remaining life of the debenture, but in some instances, it may exist for only a certain number of years. This is done to give the issuing firm more control over its capital structure. If the issue has not been converted by the end of its conversion period, it reverts to a straight-debt issue with no conversion privileges.

From the investor's point of view, the most important piece of information is the *conversion price* or the *conversion ratio.* These terms are used interchangeably and specify, either directly or indirectly, the number of shares of stock into which the bond can be converted. **Conversion ratio** denotes the number of common shares into which the bond can be converted. **Conversion price** indicates the stated value per share at which the common stock will be delivered to the investor in exchange for the bond. When you stop to think about these two measures, it becomes clear that a given conversion ratio implies a certain conversion price, and vice versa. For example, a $1,000 convertible bond might stipulate a conversion ratio of 20, which means that the bond can be converted into 20 shares of common stock. This same privilege could also be stated in terms of a conversion price: The $1,000 bond may be used to acquire the stock at a "price" of $50 per share. Here, the conversion ratio of 20 signifies a conversion price of $50. Note that the Cypress convertible depicted in Figure 11.4 uses just the conversion price ($62.548 a share) to describe its conversion feature. Even so, that stated conversion price still carries an implied conversion ratio—in this case, 15.988 shares of stock. (One basic difference between a convertible debenture and a convertible preferred relates to conversion ratio: The conversion ratio of a debenture generally deals with large multiples of common stock, such as 15, 20, or 30 shares. The conversion ratio of a preferred is generally very small, often less than 1 share of common and seldom more than 3 or 4 shares.)

HOT LINKS

A good glossary of convertibles can be found at:
www.convertbond.com/tutor/Glossary.asp

The conversion ratio is generally fixed over the conversion period, although some convertibles are issued with variable ratios/prices. In such cases, the conversion ratio decreases (while the conversion price increases) over the life of the conversion period, to reflect the supposedly higher value of the equity. The conversion ratio is also normally adjusted for stock splits and significant stock dividends, to maintain the conversion rights of the investor. As a result, if a firm declares, say, a 2-for-1 stock split, the conversion ratio of any of its outstanding convertible issues also doubles. And when the conversion ratio includes a fraction, such as 33½ shares of common, the conversion privilege specifies how any fractional shares are to be handled. Usually, the investor can either put up the additional funds necessary to purchase another full share of stock at the conversion price or receive the cash equivalent of the fractional share (at the conversion price). Table 11.2 lists some basic features for a number of actively traded convertible bonds and preferreds, and reveals a

TABLE 11.2   Convertible Preferred Stocks and Bonds

Convertible Preferreds	S&P Rating	Mkt.Price/ Convertibles	Yield*	Conversion Ratio	Conversion Value	Conversion Premium	Payback Period
Citizens Utilities $2.50 pfd	A−	$63.56	3.93%	3.76	$62.04	2.50%	0.6 yrs
Crown Castle $3.125 pfd	CCC+	54.38	5.75	1.36	46.24	17.9	2.6
El Paso Energy $2.375 pfd	BBB−	61.88	3.84	1.20	58.05	6.4	2.7
Finova Group $2.75 pfd	BBB−	24.31	11.31	1.28	13.36	82.3	6.0
Host Marriott $3.375 pfd	BB−	38.06	8.87	3.25	36.16	5.2	3.0
International Paper $2.625 pfd	BBB−	41.50	6.33	0.93	31.62	31.8	6.0
Lehman Brothers $1.955 pfd	BBB+	40.38	4.84	0.32	36.08	12.7	2.5
St. Paul Companies $3.00 pfd	A−	76.00	3.95	1.70	75.65	0.8	0.5
USX Corp. $3.25 pfd	BB+	40.00	8.13	1.08	19.38	105.7	9.5
Wendy's International $2.50 pfd	BBB	43.94	5.69	1.89	32.02	37.0	5.8

Convertible Bonds/Notes							
Checkpoint Systems 5.25%—2005	NR	$686.25	14.34%	54.41	$496.49	38.2%	3.6 yrs
Clear Channel 2.625%—2003	BBB−	1,312.50	Neg**	16.14	1,229.67	6.7	3.1
E*Trade 6.00%—2007	B+	865.00	8.96	42.37	635.55	36.1	3.8
Hilton Hotels 5.00%—2006	BB+	813.75	9.44	45.11	462.38	76.0	7.6
Imax Corp. 5.75%—2003	B	1,245.00	Neg**	46.71	1,167.75	6.6	1.3
Inco Ltd. 7.75%—2016	BB+	857.50	9.75	26.14	383.94	123.3	6.1
Kerr-McGee 5.25%—2010	BBB−	1,105.00	3.96	16.37	898.30	23.0	9.0
LSI Logic 4.25%—2004	B	1,412.50	Neg**	63.79	1,262.40	11.9	3.3
Potomac Electric 5.00%—2002	A−	975.00	6.40	33.43	825.32	18.1	NM†
Telxon Corp. 5.75%—2003	CCC+	905.00	10.55	36.36	663.57	36.4	4.2

*Yield-to-maturity for convertible bonds; current yield for convertible preferreds; all prices and yields as of July 2000
**Yield is negligible—that is, less than 1%.
†Not meaningful.

Source: Morgan Stanley Dean Witter, *ConvertBond.com.*

variety of conversion privileges and issue characteristics. And note the appearance of high tech and Internet companies (like LSI Logic and E*Trade) on the list of convertible bond issuers—indeed, as the accompanying *Investing in Action* box explains, no market segment has taken a bigger liking to convertibles than the net.

PERC
preferred equity redemption cumulative stock; preferred securities that carry potentially restrictive conversion privileges in exchange for attractive dividend returns.

PERCs and LYONs Wall Street is notorious for taking a basic investment product and turning it into a new investment vehicle. Certainly that's the case with two very special types of convertible securities, known as PERCs and LYONs. These securities have certain features and characteristics that separate them from the rest of the pack of convertibles. The acronym **PERC** stands for **preferred equity redemption cumulative stock.** It is a type of convertible preferred that offers not only an equity kicker but an attractive dividend yield to boot. There is a catch, however: A cap is placed on the capital appreciation potential of these securities. A regular convertible stipulates (or implies) a certain number of shares of stock into which the security can be converted, regardless of the market value of the stock. A PERC, on the other hand, stipulates a certain *dollar amount of the underlying common stock that will be received on the stipulated maturity date of the PERC.* Such a conversion privilege sets a cap on the amount of capital gains you can earn. For example, a conversion price of $50 a share defines

INVESTING in action

The Net Turns to Debt—Convertible, That Is

Amazon.com is a pioneer not only in Internet commerce but also in Net financing. In January 1999, Amazon became the first e-commerce company to tap the convertible bond market. It raised $1.25 billion through an offer of 10-year subordinated bonds with a 4.75% coupon, convertible into common stock at $156.05 a share—a 27% conversion premium over the share price on the issue date. Despite a below-investment grade rating of Caa3, the issue sold out. Amazon.com returned to the debt market in 2000 to sell another $690 million in 6.875% convertible bonds—a high coupon rate for a convertible, but low compared to other below- investment-grade credits.

Other Internet companies followed Amazon's lead. By late 2000, Internet-related companies had raised more than $13 billion in 34 different convertible bond issues. Convertible debt offers these capital-hungry companies another financing option besides selling stock or issuing high-yield debt. The 20% to 30% conversion premium over the current stock price allows e-businesses to raise more funds than they could by selling straight debt—and to get a relatively low interest rate, with considerable flexibility in terms. Even though plunging Internet stock prices delayed conversion of the bonds into stock, issuers locked in interest rates 4% to 7% lower than straight bonds (which they might not have been able to sell anyway). Because of the conversion feature, high-tech companies are paying lower rates than "old-economy" companies with higher bond ratings. And there is still time for stock prices to rebound before the bonds mature.

Investors continue to like Internet convertibles, as well as those in the biotech and telecom industries. "It's a risk-controlled way of investing in the growth sector of the economy—while being paid to wait," says Anand Iyer, head of global convertible research at Morgan Stanley Dean Witter. For example, an investor who purchased an E*Trade convertible bond for $1,000 when it was issued in February 2000 received an attractive fixed-price option to buy the equivalent of about 42 shares in the online securities brokerage in future years. In the meantime, in return for paying an 18% premium above the cost of the straight stock, the investor gets steady income from the bond's 6% annual coupon. The ongoing interest payments provide some protection from market volatility.

A new twist on convertible financing appeared in fall 2000 when young fiber-optics companies turned to convertible bonds rather than venture capital to finance growth. Kestrel Solutions Inc. issued $125 million of 5.5% convertible bonds, and Cyras Systems Inc. raised $150 million at 4.5%. *Yet neither company is public!* These pre-IPO issues carry conversion premiums of 100% to 150% of the initial public offering price—with no guarantee that the companies will in fact ever issue stock. Why would investors take this risk? It may be hard for them "to get a big stake in [an exciting] IPO," said Brooks Harris, head of convertibles at Morgan Stanley Dean Witter & Co. "So they may be willing to buy this security at a premium rather than not have the ability to invest at all."

Sources: Suzanne Koudsi, "Switch Hitters," *Fortune,* March 6, 2000, p. 442; Michael Lewis, "Tech Startups Break Venture Capital Habit," *Los Angeles Business Journal,* October 16, 2000, downloaded from www.findarticles.com; Hilary Rosenberg, "Steep Climb for Convertibles," *CFO,* December 2000, downloaded from www.findarticles.com; and Allan Sloan, "Between Net and Debt," *Newsweek,* March 20, 2000, p. 74H.

the most you can receive. If the underlying stock is trading at $50 or less on the maturity date of the PERC, you'll receive one share of stock. But if it's trading at more than $50 a share, you'll receive less than a full share of stock. Thus, if the stock is at $75, you'll receive 2/3 of a share, or $50 worth of stock. This is the price you pay to have both the equity kicker and an attractive dividend yield. In essence, in return for the relatively high dividend yield, you have to be willing to accept limits on the equity kicker. As an investor, you

LYON
liquid yield option note; a zero-coupon bond that carries both a conversion feature and a put option.

have to decide which is more important to you: full participation in the equity kicker or an attractive dividend yield.

The term **LYON** stands for **liquid yield option note.** Basically, a LYON is a *zero-coupon bond* that carries both *a conversion feature* and *a put option.* These bonds are convertible, at a fixed conversion ratio, for the life of the issue. Thus, they offer you the built-in increase in value over time that accompanies any zero-coupon bond (as it moves toward its par value at maturity), plus full participation in the equity side of the issue via the equity kicker. Unlike a PERC, there's no current income with a LYON (because it is a zero-coupon bond), but there's no limit on capital gains either. In addition, the option feature enables you to "put" the bonds back to the issuer (at specified values). That is, *the put option gives bondholders the right to redeem their bonds periodically at prespecified prices.* Thus you know you can get out of these securities, at set prices, if things move against you. Although LYONs may appear to provide the best of all worlds, they do have some negatives. True, LYONs provide downside protection (via the put option feature) and full participation in the equity kicker. But being zero-coupon bonds, they don't generate current income. And you have to watch out for the put option: Depending on the type of put option, the payout doesn't have to be in cash—it can be in stocks or bonds/notes. One other thing: Because the conversion ratio on the LYON is fixed while the underlying value of the zero-coupon bond keeps increasing (as it moves to maturity), *the conversion price on the stock increases over time.* Thus the market price of the stock had better go up by more than the bond's rate of appreciation or you'll never be able to convert your LYON.

Sources of Value

Because convertibles—even PERCs and LYONs—are fixed-income securities linked to the equity position of the firm, they are normally valued in terms of *both the stock and the bond dimensions* of the issue. In fact, it is ultimately both of these dimensions that give the convertible its value. This, of course, explains why it is so important to analyze the underlying common stock *and* to formulate interest rate expectations when considering convertibles as an investment outlet. Let's look first at the stock dimension.

Convertible securities trade much like common stock whenever the market price of the stock starts getting close to (or exceeds) the stated conversion price. (In effect, they will derive their value from the underlying common stock.) This means that whenever a convertible trades near its par value ($1,000) or above, it will exhibit price behavior that closely matches that of the underlying common stock: If the stock goes up in price, so does the convertible, and vice versa. In fact, the absolute price change of the convertible will exceed that of the common because of the conversion ratio, which will define the convertible's rate of change in price. For example, if a convertible carries a conversion ratio of, say, 20, then for every point the common stock goes up (or down) in price, the price of the convertible moves *in the same direction* by roughly that same multiple (in this case, 20). In essence, whenever a convertible trades as a stock, its market price will approximate a multiple of the share price of the common, with the size of the multiple being defined by the conversion ratio. Indeed, convertibles have a tendency to behave so much like their underlying common stocks that it is often difficult to detect any real differences in their comparative returns.

When the price of the common is depressed, so that its trading price is well below the conversion price, the convertible loses its tie to the underlying common stock and begins to trade as a bond. When that happens, the convertible becomes linked to prevailing bond yields, and investors should focus their attention on *market rates of interest.* However, because of the equity kicker and their relatively low agency ratings, *convertibles generally do not possess high interest rate sensitivity.* Gaining more than a rough idea of what the prevailing yield of a convertible obligation ought to be is often difficult. For example, if the issue is rated Baa and the market rate for this quality range is 9%, then the convertible should be priced to yield *something around 9%,* plus or minus perhaps half a percentage point. The bond feature will also establish a *price floor* for the convertible, which tends to parallel interest rates and is independent of the behavior of common share prices.

Advantages and Disadvantages of Investing in Convertibles

The major advantage of a convertible issue is that it reduces downside risk (via the issue's bond value or price floor) and at the same time provides upward price potential comparable to that of the firm's common stock. This two-sided feature is critical with convertibles and is impossible to match with straight common stock or straight debt. Another benefit is that the current income from bond interest normally exceeds the income from the dividends that would be paid with a *comparable investment* in the underlying common stock. For example, let's say you had the choice of investing $1,000 in a new 8% convertible or investing the same amount in the company's common stock, currently trading at $42.50 a share. (As is customary with new convertibles, the stock price will be a bit *below* the bond's conversion price—of $50 a share.) Under these circumstances, you could buy *one* convertible or *23½ shares* of common stock ($1,000/$42.50 = 23.5). If the stock paid $2 a share in annual dividends, a $1,000 investment in the stocks would yield $47 a year in dividends. In contrast, you could collect substantially more by putting the same amount into the company's convertible bond, where you would receive $80 a year in interest income. Thus it is possible with convertibles to reap the advantages of common stock (in the form of potential upward price appreciation) and yet generate improved current income.

H O T **L I N K S**

Find three basic ways to invest with convertibles at:

moneycentral.msn.com/articles/
invest/strat/3295.asp

On the negative side, buying the convertible instead of directly owning the underlying common stock means you have to give up some potential profits. Consider the example in the preceding paragraph: Put $1,000 directly into the common stock and you can buy 23½ shares; put the same $1,000 into the company's convertible bond and you end up with a claim on only 20 shares of stock. Thus the convertible bond investor is left with a *shortfall* of 3½ shares of stock—which represents potential price appreciation you will never enjoy. In effect, it's a *give-up* you have to absorb in exchange for the convertible's higher current income and safety. Looked at from another angle, this is basically what **conversion premium** is all about. That is, unless the market price of the stock exceeds the conversion price by a wide margin, a convertible almost always trades at a price that is above its true value. The amount of this excess price is conversion premium, which has the unfortunate side effect of diluting the price appreciation potential of a convertible. One

conversion premium
the amount by which the market price of a convertible exceeds its conversion value.

FIGURE 11.5

Listed Quotes for Convertible Bonds

Convertible bonds (of which there are three in this figure) are listed right along with other corporate issues and are identified by the letters *cv* in the "Cur Yld" column. Except for this distinguishing feature, they are quoted like any other corporate bond. (*Source: Wall Street Journal,* August 30, 2000.)

Bonds	Cur yld.	Vol.	Close	Net Chg.
vjClardg $11^3/_4$02f	...	40	$69^1/_2$	$+ 2^3/_4$
ClrkOil $9^1/_2$04	10.3	25	$91^7/_8$	$- ^1/_8$
Coastl $10^1/_4$04	9.4	20	109	$+ 2^1/_2$
CmclFd 7.95s06	8.4	10	95	$- 1$
Consec $8^1/_8$03	11.5	159	71	$+ ^1/_2$
Conseco $10^1/_2$04	14.5	375	$72^1/_2$	$- ^1/_2$
Conseco $10^1/_4$02	15.8	309	65	$- ^3/_4$
ConPort 11s06	13.9	45	79	$+ 4$
CypSemi 4s05	cv	2	$123^1/_2$	$- ^1/_2$
DR Hrtn 10s06	9.9	35	$101^1/_8$	$- ^3/_8$
DelcoR $8^5/_8$07	9.5	25	$90^5/_8$	$+ ^1/_8$
DevonE 4.9s08	cv	6	96	$+ ^1/_8$
DukeEn $6^1/_4$04	6.4	5	98	$+ 1^5/_8$
DukeEn $7^1/_2$25	7.9	61	$95^3/_8$	$- ^3/_8$
FnclFed $4^1/_2$05	cv	2	84	$+ 2$
Florsh $12^3/_4$02	28.3	38	45	$+ 3$
FordCr $6^3/_8$08	6.9	26	$91^7/_8$	$- 1^1/_4$

} Cypress Semiconductor Convertible Notes

other disadvantage of owning convertibles is that any investor who truly wants to hold bonds can almost certainly find better current and promised yields from straight-debt obligations.

So then, if improved returns are normally available from the direct investment in either straight debt and/or straight equity, why buy convertibles? The answer is simple: Convertibles provide a great way to achieve attractive risk-return tradeoffs. In particular, by combining the characteristics of both stocks and bonds into one security, convertibles offer some risk protection and at the same time, considerable—though perhaps not maximum—upward price potential. Thus, although the return may not be the most in absolute terms, neither is the risk.

Executing Trades

Convertible bonds are subject to the same brokerage fees and transfer taxes as straight corporate debt, while convertible preferreds trade at the same costs as straight preferreds and common stock. Any market or limit order that can be used with bonds or stocks can also be used with convertibles.

Convertible notes and bonds are listed along with other corporate bonds. They are distinguished from straight-debt issues by the letters *cv* in the "Cur Yld" column of the bond quotes, as illustrated in Figure 11.5. Note that it's not unusual for some convertibles to trade at fairly high prices (e.g., the Cypress Semiconductor 4% issue of 2005). These situations are justified by the high values of the underlying common stock.

Convertible preferreds, in contrast, normally are listed with other preferreds in the common stock listings. They are indicated with a *pf* annotation, but carry no other distinguishing symbols. As a result, you must turn to some other source to find out whether a preferred is convertible. One national business newspaper, *Investor's Business Daily,* provides a separate list of preferred stocks traded on the NYSE, AMEX, and Nasdaq and uses boldface type to highlight the convertible issues.

IN REVIEW

CONCEPTS

11.9 What is a *convertible debenture*? How does a *convertible bond* differ from a *convertible preferred*?

11.10 According to the *Investing in Action* box on page 471, why are convertible bonds so appealing to e-businesses? How have investors responded to these issues, and why?

11.11 Identify the *equity kicker* of a convertible security and explain how it affects the value and price behavior of convertibles.

11.12 Explain why it is necessary to examine both the bond and the stock properties of a convertible debenture when determining its investment appeal.

11.13 What are the investment attributes of convertible debentures? What are the disadvantages of such investment vehicles?

Valuing and Investing in Convertibles

LG 6

Basically, investing in convertibles can take two different forms: Either you use convertibles as a type of deferred equity investment, in which case you're looking at the stock side of the security. Or you use convertibles as a high-yield, fixed-income investment, where it's the bond value that's important. Regardless of which approach you follow, to get the most from your investment program, you need a good understanding of the normal price and investment behavioral characteristics of convertibles. Of course, you also have to know how to value a convertible. Let's take a look at the valuation concepts used with convertible bonds, and then we'll look at a couple of convertible bond investment strategies.

Measuring the Value of a Convertible

In order to evaluate the investment merits of convertible securities, you must consider both the bond and the stock dimensions of the issue. Fundamental security analysis of the equity position is, of course, especially important in light of the key role the equity kicker plays in defining the price behavior of a convertible. In contrast, market yields and agency ratings are widely used in evaluating the bond side of the issue. But there's more: In addition to analyzing the bond and stock dimensions of the issue, it is also essential to evaluate the conversion feature itself. The two critical areas in this regard are conversion value and investment value. These measures have a vital bearing on a convertible's price behavior and therefore can have a dramatic effect on an issue's holding period return.

conversion value
an indication of what a convertible issue would trade for if it were priced to sell on the basis of its stock value.

Conversion Value In essence, **conversion value** indicates what a convertible issue would trade for if it were priced to sell on the basis of its stock value. Conversion value is easy to find:

Equation 11.4

Conversion value = Conversion ratio × Current market price of the stock

conversion equivalent (conversion parity)
the price at which the common stock would have to sell in order to make the convertible security worth its present market price.

For example, a convertible that carries a conversion ratio of 20 would have a conversion value of $1,200 if the firm's stock traded at a current market price of $60 per share (20 × $60 = $1,200).

Sometimes an alternative measure is used, and the **conversion equivalent,** or what is also known as **conversion parity,** may be computed. The conversion equivalent indicates the price at which the common stock would have to sell in order to make the convertible security worth its present market price. Conversion equivalent is calculated as follows:

Equation 11.5

$$\text{Conversion equivalent} = \frac{\text{Current market price of the convertible bond}}{\text{Conversion ratio}}$$

Thus, if a convertible were trading at $1,400 and had a conversion ratio of 20, the conversion equivalent of the common stock would be $70 per share ($1,400 ÷ 20 = $70). In effect, you would expect the current market price of the common stock in this example to be at or near $70 per share in order to support a convertible trading at $1,400.

Conversion Premium Unfortunately, convertible issues *seldom* trade precisely at their conversion values. Rather, as noted earlier, they usually trade at a conversion premium. The absolute size of an issue's conversion premium is found by taking the difference between the convertible's market price and its conversion value (per Equation 11.4). To place the premium on a relative basis, simply divide the dollar amount of the conversion premium by the issue's conversion value. That is,

Equation 11.6

$$\text{Conversion premium (in \$)} = \frac{\text{Current market price}}{\text{of the convertible bond}} - \frac{\text{Conversion}}{\text{value}}$$

where conversion value is found according to Equation 11.4. Then

Equation 11.7

$$\text{Conversion premium (in \%)} = \frac{\text{Conversion premium (in \$)}}{\text{Conversion value}}$$

To illustrate, if a convertible trades at $1,400 and its conversion value equals $1,200, it has a conversion premium of $200 ($1,400 − $1,200 = $200). In relation to what the convertible should be trading at, this $200 differential would amount to a conversion premium of 16.7% ($200/$1,200 = 0.167). Conversion premiums are common in the market and can often amount to as much as 30% to 40% (or more) of an issue's true conversion value.

Investors are willing to pay a premium primarily because of the added current income a convertible provides relative to the underlying common stock. An investor can recover this premium through the added current income the convertible provides, or by selling the issue at a premium equal to or greater than that which existed at the time of purchase. Unfortunately, the latter source of recovery is tough to come by, because conversion premiums tend to fade away as the price of the convertible goes up. That means that if a convertible is purchased for its potential price appreciation (which most are), then the investor must accept the fact that all or a major portion of the price premium is very likely to disappear as the convertible appreciates over time and moves closer to its true conversion value. Thus, if an investor hopes to recover any conversion premium, it will probably have to come from the added current income that the convertible provides.

payback period
the length of time it takes for the buyer of a convertible to recover the conversion premium from the extra current income earned on the convertible.

Payback Period The size of the conversion premium can obviously have a major impact on investor return. So, when picking convertibles, one of the major questions you should ask is whether the premium is justified. One way to assess conversion premium is to compute the issue's **payback period,** a measure of the length of time it takes for the buyer to recover the conversion premium from the *extra* interest income earned on the convertible. Because this added income is a principal reason for the conversion premium, it makes sense to use it to assess the premium. The payback period can be found as follows:

Equation 11.8

$$\text{Payback period} = \frac{\text{Conversion premium (in \$)}}{\begin{array}{c}\text{Annual interest} \\ \text{income from the} \\ \text{convertible bond}\end{array} - \begin{array}{c}\text{Annual dividend} \\ \text{income from the} \\ \text{underlying common stocks}\end{array}}$$

In this equation, annual dividends are found by multiplying the stock's latest annual dividends per share by the bond's conversion ratio.

For example, in the foregoing illustration, the bond had a conversion premium of $200. Now let's say this bond (which carries a conversion ratio of 20) has an 8½% coupon, and the underlying stock paid dividends this past year of 50 cents a share. Given this information, we can use Equation 11.8 to find the payback period.

$$\text{Payback period} = \frac{\$200}{\$85 - (20 \times \$0.50)}$$

$$= \frac{\$200}{\$85 - (\$10.00)} = \underline{2.7 \text{ years}}$$

In essence, the investor in this case will recover the premium in 2.7 years (a fairly decent payback period). As a rule, everything else being equal, *the shorter the payback period, the better.* Also, watch out for excessively high premiums (of 50% or more); you may have real difficulty ever recovering such astronomical premiums. Indeed, to avoid such premiums, most experts recommend that you look for convertibles that have payback periods of around 5 years or less. Take another look at Table 11.2. You'll notice that in addition to basic issue characteristics, this table also shows the conversion value, conversion premium, and payback period for each convertible issue listed. In order to get the most from these investments, you would be well advised to take the time to fully evaluate a bond's conversion premium (and its payback period) before investing.

investment value
the price at which a convertible would trade if it were nonconvertible and priced at or near the prevailing market yields of comparable nonconvertible issues.

Investment Value The price floor of a convertible is defined by its bond properties and is the object of the investment value measure. It's the point within the valuation process where attention focuses on current and expected market interest rates. **Investment value** is the price at which the bond would trade if it were nonconvertible and if it were priced at or near the prevailing market yields of comparable nonconvertible bonds.

The same bond price formula given in Chapter 10 is used to compute investment value. See, for example, Equation 10.2 (page 424). (As with any other type of bond, yield-to-maturity and current yield are also used with convertible issues.) Because the coupon and maturity are known, the only additional piece of information needed is the market yield-to-maturity of comparably rated issues. For example, if comparable nonconvertible bonds were trading at 9% yields and if a particular 20-year convertible carried a 6% coupon, its investment value would be roughly $725. This figure indicates how far the convertible will have to fall before it hits its price floor and begins trading as a straight-debt instrument. Other things being equal, the greater the distance between the current market price of a convertible and its investment value, the farther the issue can fall in price and as a result, the greater the downside risk exposure.

An Overview of Price and Investment Behavior

The price behavior of a convertible security is influenced by both the equity and the fixed-income elements of the obligation. The variables that play key roles in defining the market value of a typical convertible therefore include: (1) the potential price behavior of the underlying common stock and (2) expectations regarding the pattern of future market yields and interest rates.

The typical price behavior of a convertible issue is depicted in Figure 11.6. In the top panel are the three market elements of a convertible bond: the bond value (or price floor), the stock (conversion) value, and the actual market price of the convertible. The figure reveals the customary relationship among these three elements and shows that conversion premium is a common occurrence. Note especially that the conversion premium tends to diminish as the price of the stock increases.

The top panel of Figure 11.6 is somewhat simplified because of the steady price floor (which unrealistically assumes no variation in market interest rates) and the steady upswing in the stock's value. The lower panel of the figure relaxes these conditions, although for simplicity we ignore conversion premium. The figure illustrates that the market value of a convertible approximates the price behavior of the underlying stock *so long as stock value is greater than bond value.* When the stock value drops below the bond value floor, as it does in the shaded area of the lower panel, the market value of the convertible becomes linked to the bond portion of the obligation, and it continues to move as a debt security until the price of the underlying stock picks up again and approaches or equals this price floor.

Investment Strategies

Investors can use convertibles to generate attractive returns from either the stock or the bond side of the issue. For stock investors, convertibles can serve as a form of deferred equity, where the investor is more focused on capital gains than on current income. This, of course, represents a fairly aggressive use of convertibles. But for the more conservative investor, who is looking for current income as a key source of return, convertibles can also serve as a form of high-yielding fixed-income security. Let's now take a look at both of these investment strategies.

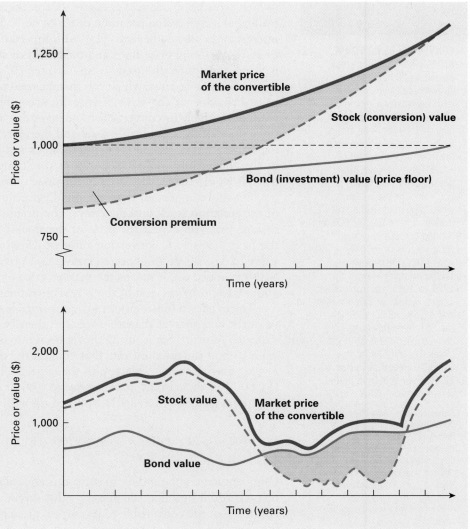

FIGURE 11.6

Typical Price Behavior of a Convertible Bond

The price behavior of a convertible security is tied to either the stock or the bond dimension of the issue. When the price of the underlying stock is up, the convertible trades much like the stock; when the price of the stock falls, the bond value acts as a price floor for the convertible.

 Convertibles as Deferred Equity Investments Convertible securities (even zero-coupon convertibles) are purchased most often because of their equity attributes. Using convertibles as an alternative to common stock, you may be able to match (or even exceed) the return from the common, but with less exposure to risk. Also, convertibles generally offer better current income than stocks. Convertibles can be profitably used as alternative equity investments whenever you feel that *the underlying stock offers desired capital gains opportunities.* In order to achieve maximum price appreciation, you would want assurance that the convertible is trading in concert with its stock value and that it does not have an inordinate amount of conversion premium. If these necessary conditions exist, then you can begin to focus on the potential market behavior of the underlying stock. To assess such behavior you need to evaluate both the current and expected conversion values.

For example, assume a 7% convertible bond carries a conversion ratio of 25 and is currently trading in the market at $900. In addition, assume the stock

CONVERTIBLES GO FOR A RIDE—The turbulent stock market in 2000 made convertible bonds popular with investors. A record 146 new issues that year raised over $61 billion. The Froley, Revy Convertible Bond Index reported a total return of −1.6% for the year. That doesn't look very good, until you compare these results to what happened in the stock market, where the S&P500 and Nasdaq Composite turned in total returns of roughly −10% and −40%, respectively. Taking a longer view, from 1973 to 1999, the compound annual return for convertibles was 12.6% versus 13.9% for the S&P 500. However, convertibles demonstrated lower volatility, with an annual standard deviation of 12.4% over this time period, versus the S&P 500's 16.7%.

Sources: "Froley, Revy Convertible Bond Index Reports 2000 Total Return of Negative 1.61%," Business Wire, January 9, 2001, downloaded from www.news .morningstar.com; and "Investment News," Froley, Revy Investment Company, Third Quarter 2000, downloaded from www.froleyrevy .com, p. 1.

(which pays no dividends) is currently trading at $32, and the convertible is trading at a conversion premium of $100, or 12.5%. The formulation of future interest rates also comes into play with this trading strategy, as you will want to assess the bond price floor and the extent of downward risk exposure. That is, using the approach discussed in Chapter 10, you would try to get a handle on future interest rates, which can then be used to determine the possible bond price behavior of the issue. Generally speaking, a drop in interest rates is viewed positively by convertible bond investors, as behavior signals a rise in the price floor of the convertible issue and therefore a reduction in downside risk exposure. That is, should the common stock not perform as expected, the price of the convertible could still go up as the (bond) price floor rises—or at the least, it would reduce any drop in the price of the convertible issue.

But more important than the bond price floor is the anticipated behavior of the common stock and the conversion premium. To continue our example, assume that you expect the price of the stock to rise to $60 per share within the next 2 years. A conversion ratio of 25 would yield a future conversion value of $1,500. If an expected conversion premium of 6% to 7% (or about $100) is added on, it means the market price of the convertible should rise to about $1,600 by the end of the 2-year investment horizon.

The expected future price of the convertible, along with its annual coupon payment and current market price, can then be used to determine the issue's expected return. That is, using the internal rate of return (IRR) procedure, you want to find the discount rate that equates the annual coupon payments ($70 a year) over the next 2 years, plus the expected future price of the convertible ($1,600), to the current market price ($900) of the issue. Putting all this into a formula (see Equation 10.2), you end up with something like this:

$$\$900 = (\$70 \times PVIFA_{2\text{yr},?\%}) + (\$1,600 \times PVIF_{2\text{yr},?\%})$$

Using annual compounding to solve this equation (see the calculator solutions below), you'll find that the present-value discount rate that equates the future cash flow of the convertible to its current price is 40.2%—which is, of course, the expected return on this investment.

Although this 40.2% rate of return may indeed appear attractive, you should be sure of several points before committing capital to this security. In particular, you should be certain that this approach is in fact superior to a direct investment in the issuer's common stock (at least from a risk-return point of view). You also should determine that there is no better rate of return (with commensurate risk exposure) available from some other investment vehicle. To the extent that these conditions are met, investing in a convertible may be a suitable course of action, especially if (1) The price of the underlying common stock is under strong upward pressure, (2) bond interest rates are falling off sharply, and (3) there is little or no conversion premium in the price of the convertible. The first condition means that conversion value should move up, leading to appreciation in the price of the convertible. The second means that the bond value (price floor) should also move up, thereby reducing exposure to risk. And the third means that you should be able to capture all or most of the price appreciation of the underlying common stock rather than losing a chunk of it to the inevitable drop in conversion premium. Although it would be nice if all three of these attributes were available from a single security, very rarely is that the case. Thus investors normally have to settle for only one or two of these features and then assess the effect of the missing condition(s) on potential returns.

Input	Function
2	N
900	PV
−70	PMT
−1600	FV
	CPT
	I

Solution
| 40.16 |

CALCULATOR USE For *annual compounding,* to find the expected return on a 7% convertible bond that is currently trading at $900 but is expected to be trading at $1,600 in 2 years, use the keystrokes shown in the margin where N = length of the holding period (2 years), PV = current market price of the convertible, PMT = annual coupon payments, and FV = expected (future) price of the convertible in 2 years.

Convertibles as High-Yield Fixed-Income Investments Another common use of convertibles is to buy them for the attractive fixed-income returns they offer. The key element in this strategy is the issue's bond dimension. Many convertible securities provide current yields and yields-to-maturity that are safe and highly competitive with straight debt obligations. Investors should make certain, however, that the high yields are not a function of low (speculative) ratings. Normally, investors using this strategy would seek discount issues, particularly those trading close to their bond price floor. Otherwise, the issue would be trading at a premium price, which would certainly involve a yield give-up, and perhaps a substantial one. Most investors who use this strategy view convertibles as ideal for locking in high rates of return. They are not widely used for speculating on interest rates, however, because even investment-grade convertibles often lack the needed interest sensitivity (because of the equity kicker). Yet for those who use convertibles to seek high, safe yields, the equity kicker can provide an added source of return if the underlying stock does indeed take off. You then have a bond that offers a handsome rate of return and an equity kicker to boot.

IN REVIEW

CONCEPTS

11.14 What is the difference between *conversion parity* and *conversion value?* How would you describe the *payback period* on a convertible? What is the *investment value* of a convertible, and what does it reveal?

11.15 Discuss the alternative investment uses of convertible debentures. What are the three major attributes that investors should look for when using convertibles as deferred equity investments?

Summary

| LG 1 |

Describe the basic features of preferred stock, including sources of value and exposure to risk. Preferred stocks are hybrid securities that combine features of both debt and equity. Preferred stocks are considered senior to common: They have a higher claim on the income and assets of the issuing company. Among other things, this means that preferred dividends have to be paid before the company can pay dividends to its common stockholders. As investment vehicles, preferreds provide attractive dividend yields. When interest rates decline, they can produce capital gains as well.

LG 2   **Discuss the rights and claims of preferred stockholders, and note some of the popular issue characteristics that are often found with these securities.** Preferreds are considered less risky than common stock because their shareholders enjoy a senior position with regard to dividend payments and asset claims. The most important feature of a preferred stock is its preferential claim on dividends. Investors should also be aware of several other preferred stock provisions: the obligations of the issuer in case any dividends are missed (whether the stock is cumulative or noncumulative), whether it is callable, and whether it carries sinking-fund provisions.

LG 3   **Understand the various measures of investment worth, and identify several investment strategies that can be used with preferred stocks.** Except for convertible preferreds, the value of a preferred is generally linked to the dividend yield it provides to investors. Indeed, the price behavior of a preferred stock is inversely related to market interest rates. The principal reason for holding preferreds is their yield. But they can also be held for capital gains purposes by investors willing to trade on interest rates or on turnaround situations.

LG 4   **Identify the fundamental characteristics of convertible securities, and explain the nature of the underlying conversion privilege.** Convertible securities are initially issued as bonds (or preferreds), but can subsequently be converted into shares of common stock. These securities offer investors a stream of fixed income (in the form of annual coupon payments), plus an equity kicker.

LG 5   **Describe the advantages and disadvantages of investing in convertible securities, including their risk and return attributes.** Convertibles provide a combination of both good upside potential (from the equity feature) and good downside protection (through the fixed-income characteristics). This risk-return tradeoff, combined with the relatively high current income of convertibles, is unmatched by any other type of security.

LG 6   **Measure the value of a convertible security, and explain how these securities can be used to meet different investment objectives.** The value of a convertible depends largely on the price behavior of the underlying common stock. This is captured in the security's conversion value, which represents the convertible's worth if it were converted into common stock. Investors use convertible securities primarily as a form of deferred equity, where the investment is a way to capture the capital gains potential of the underlying common stock. Convertibles can also be used as high-yielding fixed-income investments. In this case, the investor principally goes after the higher current income of the bond (and the equity kicker is viewed as little more than a pleasant by-product).

Discussion Questions

LG 2 LG 3   Q11.1 Briefly describe each of the following, and note how each differs from a conventional preferred stock.
 a. Convertible preferreds.
 b. Floating-rate preferreds.
 c. Prior preferred stocks.
 d. MIPS.

As an investor, why would you choose a *convertible preferred* over a straight preferred? Why would you choose a *floating-rate preferred* over a (fixed rate) preferred? Finally, instead of investing in a conventional preferred, why not just invest in a common stock?

LG 2   Q11.2 Is it possible for a firm to pass (miss) dividends on preferred stocks, even if it earns enough to pay them? Explain. What usually happens when a company passes a dividend on a cumulative preferred stock? Are common stock dividends affected in any way?

LG 1 **LG 4** **Q11.3** Why do companies like to issue convertible securities—what's in it for them? What about preferred stocks—why do companies like to issue them?

LG 4 **Q11.4** Describe *PERCs* and *LYONs,* noting especially the unusual features and characteristics of each. How does each differ from conventional convertibles? Are there any similarities between these securities and conventional convertibles? Explain. What kind of investor might be attracted to a PERC? To a LYON?

 LG 6 **Q11.5** Using the resources available at your campus or public library or on the Internet, find the information requested below.

    a. Select any two *convertible debentures* (notes or bonds) and determine the conversion ratio, conversion parity, conversion value, conversion premium, and payback period for each.

    b. Select any two *convertible preferreds* and determine the conversion ratio, conversion parity, conversion value, conversion premium, and payback period for each.

    c. In what way(s) are the two convertible bonds and the two convertible preferreds you selected similar to one another? Are there any differences? Explain.

Problems

 LG 3 **P11.1** An adjustable-rate preferred is currently selling at a dividend yield of 9%. Assume that the dividend rate on the stock is adjusted once a year and that it is currently paying an annual dividend of $5.40 a share. Because of major changes that have occurred in the market, it's anticipated that annual dividends will drop to $4.50 a share on the next dividend adjustment date, which is just around the corner. What will the new dividend yield on this issue be if its market price does not change? What will the new market price on the issue be if the stock's dividend yield holds at 9%? What will it be if the yield drops to 7%?

 LG 3 **P11.2** The Bullorbear Company has 500,000 shares of $2 preferred stock outstanding. It generates an EBIT of $40 million and has annual interest payments of $2 million. Given this information, determine the fixed charge coverage of the preferred stock.

 LG 3 **P11.3** Select one of the preferred stocks listed in Table 11.1. Using the resources available at your campus or public library, or on the Internet, determine the following.

    a The stock's latest market price.   b. Its dividend yield.

    c. Its fixed charge coverage.   d. Its book value per share.

    e. Its stated par value.

Now comment briefly on the issue's yield and the quality of its claim on income and assets.

 LG 1 **P11.4** Fabozzi Co. has a preferred stock outstanding that pays annual dividends of $3.50 a share. At what price would this stock be trading if market yields were 7½%? Use one of the dividend valuation models (from Chapter 8) to price this stock, assuming you have a 7½% required rate of return. Are there any similarities between the two prices? Explain.

 LG 3 **P11.5** Charlene Weaver likes to speculate with preferred stock by trading on movements in market interest rates. Right now, she believes the market is poised for a big drop in rates. Accordingly, she is thinking seriously about investing in a certain preferred stock that pays $7 in annual dividends and is currently trading at $75 a share. What rate of return will she realize on this investment if the market yield on the preferred drops to 6½% within 2 years? What if the drop in rates takes place in 1 year?

LG 6

P11.6 A certain 6% annual pay convertible bond (maturing in 20 years) is convertible at the holder's option into 20 shares of common stock. The bond is currently trading at $800. The stock (which pays 75¢ a share in annual dividends) is currently priced in the market at $35 a share.

a. What is the current yield of the convertible bond?
b. What is the conversion price?
c. What is the conversion ratio?
d. What is the conversion value of this issue? What is its conversion parity?
e. What is the conversion premium, in dollars and as a percentage?
f. What is the bond's payback period?
g. What is the yield-to-maturity of the convertible bond?
h. If comparably rated nonconvertible bonds sell to yield 8%, what is the investment value of the convertible?

 LG 6

P11.7 An 8% convertible bond carries a par value of $1,000 and a conversion ratio of 20. Assume that an investor has $5,000 to invest and that the convertible sells at a price of $1,000 (which includes a 25% conversion premium). How much total income (coupon plus capital gains) will this investment offer if, over the course of the next 12 months, the price of the stock moves to $75 per share and the convertible trades at a price that includes a conversion premium of 10%? What is the holding period return on this investment? Finally, given the information in the problem, determine what the underlying common stock is currently selling for.

 LG 6

P11.8 Assume you just paid $1,200 for a convertible bond that carries a 7½% coupon and has 15 years to maturity. The bond can be converted into 24 shares of stock, which are now trading at $50 a share. Find the bond investment value of this issue, given that comparable nonconvertible bonds are currently selling to yield 9%.

 LG 6

P11.9 Find the conversion value of a *convertible preferred stock* that carries a conversion ratio of 1.8, given that the market price of the underlying common stock is $40 a share. Would there be any conversion premium if the convertible preferred were selling at $90 a share? If so, how much (in dollar and percentage terms)? Also, explain the concept of conversion parity, and then find the conversion parity of this issue, given that the preferred trades at $90 per share.

Case Problem 11.1   *Penni Shows a Preference for Preferreds*

LG 1   **LG 2**

Kathleen "Penni" Jock is a young career woman who has built up a substantial investment portfolio. Most of her holdings are preferred stocks—a situation she does not want to change. Penni is now considering the purchase of $4,800 worth of LaRamie Corporation's $5 preferred, which is currently trading at $48 a share. Penni's stockbroker, Mr. Michaels, has told her that he feels the market yield on preferreds like LaRamie should drop to 7% within the next 3 years and that these preferreds would make a sound investment. Instead of buying the LaRamie preferred, Penni could choose an alternative investment (with comparable risk exposure) that she is confident can produce earnings of about 10% over each of the next 3 years.

Questions

a. If preferred yields behave as Penni's stockbroker thinks they will, what will be the price of the LaRamie $5 preferred in 3 years?

b.   What return will this investment offer over the 3-year holding period if all the expectations about it come true (particularly with regard to the price it is supposed to reach)? How much profit (in dollars) will Penni make from her investment?

c.   Would you recommend that she buy the LaRamie preferred? Why?

d.   What are the investment merits of this transaction? What are its risks?

Case Problem 11.2   *Dave and Marlene Consider Convertibles*

LG 5   LG 6

Dave and Marlene Jenkins live in Hayward, California, where she manages a bridal shop and he runs an industrial supply firm. Their annual income is usually in the middle to upper nineties; they have no children and maintain a "comfortable" lifestyle. Recently, they came into some money and are eager to invest it in a high-yielding fixed-income security. Though they are not aggressive investors, they like to maximize the return on every investment dollar they have. For this reason, they like the high yields and added equity kicker of convertible bonds and are now looking at such an issue as a way to invest their recent windfall. In particular, Dave and Marlene have their eye on the convertible debentures of MedTech, Inc. They have heard that the price of the stock is on the way up, and after some in-depth analysis of their own, feel the company's prospects are indeed bright. They've also looked at market interest rates, and on the basis of economic reports obtained from their broker, they expect interest rates to decline sharply.

The details on the convertible they're looking at are as follows: It's a 20-year, $1,000 par value issue that carries a 7½% annual-pay coupon and is at present trading at $800. The issue is convertible into 15 shares of stock. The stock, which pays no dividends, was recently quoted at $49.50 per share.

Questions

a.   Ignoring conversion premium, find the price of the convertible if the stock goes up to $66.67 per share in 2 years. What if it goes up to $75 per share? To $100 per share? Repeat the computations, assuming that the convertible will trade at a 5% conversion premium.

b.   Find the promised yield of the convertible. (*Hint:* Use annual compounding and the same approach that we used with straight bonds in Chapter 10.)

   1. Now find the bond value of the convertible if, within 2 years, interest rates drop to 8%. (*Remember:* In 2 years, the security will have only 18 years remaining to maturity.) What if interest rates drop to 6%?
   2. What implication does the drop in interest rates hold as far as the investment appeal of the convertible is concerned?

c.   Given expected future stock prices and interest rate levels (as stated above), find the minimum and maximum expected yield that this investment offers over the 2-year holding period. (Assume a zero conversion premium in both cases.)

   1. What is the worst return Dave and Marlene can expect over their 2-year holding period if the price of the stock drops to $40 per share and interest rates drop to 9%?
   2. What if the price of the stock drops to $40 and interest rates rise to 11%?

d.   Should Dave and Marlene invest in the MedTech convertibles? Discuss the pros and cons of the investment.

Web Exercises

W11.1   Read about hedge hassle at www.businessweek.com/1998/46/b3604179.htm. Identify one listed convertible bond that would currently be appropriate for a convertible hedge. You can find convertible bond quotes in newspapers, on the Web (one source is www.convertbond .com), or in Value Line's Convertibles Survey, which is available at most public libraries.

W11.2   If your goal is to remain exposed to stocks, but you're afraid of the market's gyrations, convertibles may be an acceptable middle ground. To help crunch the numbers, you can find a good convertible bond calculator on the Web at www.numa.com/derivs/ref/calculat/ cb/calc-cba.htm). Change the convertible bond inputs, including maturity 15, conversion ratio 50, coupon 5.5 semi, par value 1000, stock price 30, dividend yield 3.2, share volatility 23, dividend growth 5, convertible bond price $1,600, straight bond yield 6.6, and risk-free rate 4.7. You'll see an income comparison between shares and the convertible bond given in the output. Look at the downside risk by comparing conversion value and the straight value of the bond.

W11.3   Assume purchase of one convertible bond and the short sale of the equivalent number of common shares, rounded to the nearest whole share at the beginning of the year, thus creating a convertible hedge. Ignoring commission costs and taxes and assuming interest payment on the bond for one year, you can calculate the holding-period (assuming one year) return for the hedge. Contrast this return with what it would have been if you had taken only a long position in the convertible bond or only a short position in the common stock. Would these investment alternatives have been more or less risky than the hedge? Check your answers against those given below:

LISTED CONVERTIBLE BOND (as of the beginning of the year)

Company	Bond		Convertible into		Mkt. Price, Bond	Mkt. Price, Stock	Conversion Value of Bond	% Premium on Bond	Yield Advantage**
ABC	6.88%	07	94.25 shares	$10.61 price	$65	$6.63	$62	4%*	10.6%

* % premium on bond = 94.25 × 6.63 = $624.87 sold for $650; (650 − 624.87)/624.87 = 0.0402
** Yield advantage = 6.88/650 = 10.6%

PRICE AND DIVIDEND INFORMATION (as of the end of the year)

Company	Bond Price	Stock Price	Annual DPS, $	Stock Dividend %
ABC	$93	$8.13	—	—

Holding-period return for the convertible hedge:
ABC: Beginning investment = $650
Cash dividend   = $0
Interest   = $68.80
Gain/Loss on bond   = $280
Gain/Loss on stock   = 94.25 × ($6.63 − $8.13) = −$141.37
Holding period return = [($650 − $0 + $68.8 + $280 − $141)/$650] − 1 = 0.3197
Holding period return for only convertible bonds:
                        = [$650 + $68.8 + $280)/$650] − 1 = 0.54
Holding period return for only common stock:
                        = [$623 + $0 − $141]/$623 − 1 = −0.2263

For additional practice with concepts from this chapter, visit
www.awl.com/gitman_joehnk

CFA EXAM QUESTIONS

Investing in Fixed-Income Securities

Following is a sample of 12 Level-1 CFA exam questions that deal with many of the topics covered in Chapters 9, 10, and 11 of this text, including bond prices and yields, interest rates and risks, bond price volatility, and bond redemption provisions.

1. The interest rate risk of a noncallable bond is *most likely* to be positively related to the:
   a. risk free rate.
   b. bond's coupon rate.
   c. bond's time to maturity.
   d. bond's yield to maturity.

2. The following are quotes for a U.S. Treasury bond:

Bid	Asked
102:2	102:5

   If the face value of the bond is $1,000, the price an investor should pay for the bond is closest to:
   a. $1,020.63.
   b. $1,021.56.
   c. $1,025.00.
   d. $1,026.25.

3. Which of the following statements about call features is (are) true?
   I. A deferred call provision allows the issuer to call the bond during the call deferment period.
   II. A bond can be retired early even if it is non-refundable.
   III. Call price and call premium are the same thing.
   IV. To exercise the call feature, the issuer must retire the bond in its entirety.
   a. I and II only.
   b. II only.
   c. III only.
   d. III and IV only.

4. A municipal bond carries a coupon of 6¾% and is trading at par. To a taxpayer in the 34% tax bracket, this bond would provide a taxable equivalent yield of:
   a. 4.5%.
   b. 10.2%.
   c. 13.4%.
   d. 19.9%.

5. Zello Corporation's $1,000 par value bond sells for $960, matures in five years, and has a 7% coupon rate paid semiannually. What is the bond's yield to maturity?
   a. 7.0%.
   b. 7.3%.
   c. 8.0%.
   d. 8.1%.

6. If a bond is selling at a premium:
   a. it is an attractive investment.
   b. its realized compound yield will be less than yield-to-maturity.
   c. its coupon is below market.
   d. its current yield is lower than its coupon.

7. An investment in a coupon bond will provide the investor with a return equal to the bond's yield to maturity at the time of purchase if:
   I. the bond is not called for redemption at a price that exceeds its par value.
   II. all sinking fund payments are made in a prompt and timely fashion during the life of the issue.
   III. the reinvestment rate is the same as the bond's yield-to-maturity.
   a. I only.
   b. III only.
   c. I and II only.
   d. II and III only.

8. A newly issued ten-year option-free bond is valued at par on June 1, 2000. The bond bas an annual coupon of 8.0 percent. On June 1, 2003, the bond has a yield-to-maturity of 7.1 percent. The first coupon is reinvested at 8.0 percent and the second coupon is reinvested at 7.0 percent. The future price of the bond on June 1, 2003 is *closest* to:
   a. 100.0% of par.
   b. 102.5% of par.
   c. 104.8% of par.
   d. 105.4% of par.

9. Which of the following statements about duration characteristics are **true**?
   I. The duration of a coupon bond will always be less than its term to maturity.
   II. There is generally an inverse relationship between term to maturity and duration.
   III.. There is a positive relationship between coupon and duration.
   IV. There is an inverse relationship between yield-to-maturity and duration.
   a. I and II only
   b. I and IV only.
   c. II and III only.
   d. III and IV only.

10. An 8%, 20-year corporate semi-annual bond is priced to yield 9%. The Macaulay duration for this bond is 8.85 years. Given this information, the bond's modified duration is:
    a. 8.12.
    b. 8.47.
    c. 8.51.
    d. 9.25.

11. A 9-year bond has a yield-to-maturity of 10% and a modified duration of 6.54 years. If the market yield changes by 50 basis points, the bond's expected price change is:
    a. 3.27%.
    b. 3.66%.
    c. 5.00%.
    d. 6.54%.

12. A firm's preferred stock often sells at yields below its bonds because:
    a. preferred stock generally carries a higher agency rating.
    b. owners of preferred stock have a prior claim on the firm's earnings.
    c. owners of preferred stock have a prior claim on a firm's assets in the event of liquidation.
    d. corporations owning stock may exclude from income taxes most of the dividend income they receive.

Answers: 1. c; 2. b; 3. b; 4. b; 5. c; 6. d; 7. b; 8. c; 9. b; 10. b; 11. a; 12. d

CHAPTER 12

MUTUAL FUNDS: PROFESSIONALLY MANAGED INVESTMENT PORTFOLIOS

LEARNING GOALS

After studying this chapter, you should be able to:

LG 1 Describe the basic features of mutual funds, and note what they have to offer as investment vehicles.

LG 2 Distinguish between open- and closed-end funds, as well as other types of professionally managed investment companies, and discuss the various types of fund loads, fees, and charges.

LG 3 Discuss the types of funds available and the variety of investment objectives these funds seek to fulfill.

LG 4 Discuss the investor services offered by mutual funds and how these services can fit into an investment program.

LG 5 Gain an appreciation of the investor uses of mutual funds, along with the variables to consider when assessing and selecting funds for investment purposes.

LG 6 Identify the sources of return and compute the rate of return earned on a mutual fund investment.

Imagine learning that the Dow Jones Industrial Average had dropped 600 points and the Nasdaq, 300 points, and thinking, "Cool!" That was Blaine Rollins's reaction on April 14, 2000. Rollins, a manager for Janus Funds, had previously moved significant fund assets into cash and was ready to buy heavily for the fund. "I basically bought my 10 worst-performing names of the day, which were all down 15%, 25%, and 30%," Rollins said. "I thought, 'Hey, cheap stock.' "

Not many individual investors would have had the courage to follow Rollins into the market at a time when stocks were tumbling. And that's exactly why mutual funds are so appealing: They offer the expertise of professional money managers who study market trends and invest in a portfolio of securities. Buying shares in one of the nearly 8,000 mutual funds gives an investor shares in a diversified portfolio.

Janus's investment philosophy centers on bottom-up, company-focused fundamental research rather than on more "macro" trends in the economy or markets. Its analysis emphasizes sustainable future earnings growth, cash flow, return on invested capital, dominant franchises, and shareholder-focused management. Unlike funds that diversify broadly, Janus's various funds own about 550 different stocks (compared to almost 2,000 at Putnam Funds and 3,370 at Fidelity). Its concentration strategy—buying relatively few high-priced growth stocks—paid off in the late 1990s when the bull market was at its peak. However, when the market dipped in 2000, the value of Janus Funds' holdings did also.

If Janus's investment strategy doesn't appeal to you, you can find a different approach at another mutual fund. Approaches range from funds that track the movement of a particular market index to emerging-markets funds that invest in stocks in developing economies. As you'll learn in this chapter, mutual funds can help you reach your investment goals.

Sources: Lisa Gibbs, "Glory Days at Janus," Money, June 2000, pp. 122–130; "About Janus," Janus Funds Web site, www.janus.com

The Mutual Fund Phenomenon

LG 1   LG 2

mutual fund
an investment company that invests its shareholders' money in a diversified portfolio of securities.

Questions of which stock or bond to select, when to buy, and when to sell have plagued investors for as long as there have been organized securities markets. Such concerns lie at the very heart of the mutual fund concept and in large part explain the growth that mutual funds have experienced. Many investors lack the time, know-how, or commitment to manage their own portfolios, so they turn to professional money managers and simply let them decide which securities to buy and when to sell. More often than not, when investors look for professional help, they look to mutual funds.

Basically, a **mutual fund** is a type of financial services organization that receives money from its shareholders and then invests those funds on their behalf in a diversified portfolio of securities. Thus, when investors buy shares in a mutual fund, they actually become *part owners of a widely diversified portfolio of securities*. In an abstract sense, a mutual fund can be thought of as the *financial product* sold to the public by an investment company. That is, the investment company builds and manages a portfolio of securities and sells ownership interests—shares of stock—in that portfolio through a vehicle known as a mutual fund.

Recall from Chapter 5 that portfolio management deals with both asset allocation and security selection decisions. By investing in mutual funds, investors delegate some, if not all, of the *security selection decision*s to professional money managers. As a result, they can concentrate on key asset allocation decisions—which, of course, play a vital role in determining long-term portfolio returns. Indeed, it's for this reason that *many investors consider mutual funds to be the ultimate asset allocation vehicle*. For with mutual funds, all investors have to do is decide where they want to invest—in large-cap stocks, for example, or in technology stocks, high-yield bonds, the S&P 500 index, or international securities—and then let the professional money managers at the mutual funds do the rest, that is, decide which securities to buy and sell, and when.

Mutual funds have been a part of the investment landscape for over 75 years. The first one (MFS) was started in Boston in 1924 and is still in business today. By 1940 the number of mutual funds had grown to 68, and by 1980 there were 564 of them. But that was only the beginning: The next 20 years saw unprecedented growth in the mutual fund industry, as assets under management grew from less than $100 billion in 1980 to over $7 trillion in 2000. Indeed, by *2000 there were nearly 8,000 publicly traded mutual funds*. (Actually, counting duplicate and multiple fund offerings from the same portfolio, there are more like *12,000 funds available*.) To put that number in perspective, *there are more mutual funds in existence today than there are stocks listed on the New York and American exchanges combined*. The mutual fund industry has grown so much, in fact, that it is now *the largest financial intermediary* in this country—even ahead of banks. Obviously, the funds must be doing something right!

An Overview of Mutual Funds

Mutual funds are big business in the United States and, indeed, all over the world. As the year 2000 began, an estimated 83 million individuals in 48 million U.S. households owned mutual funds. That's nearly half of all U.S. households! Table 12.1 provides some additional statistics about mutual funds in this country and abroad. Clearly, mutual funds appeal to a lot of investors—

TABLE 12.1   Some Mutual Fund Statistics

I. Total Number of U.S. Shareholder Accounts (in millions)

	1990*	1999*
Stock funds	22.2	149.0
Bond funds	13.6	20.7
Money market funds	23.0	43.6
Other funds	3.2	14.4
Total	62.0	227.7

II. Total Number of Funds

	1990*	1999*
Stock funds	1,100	3,952
Bond funds	1,046	2,261
Money market funds	741	1,045
Other funds	194	533
Total—U.S. funds	3,081	7,791
Number of funds in other countries**	N/A	35,979
Total—worldwide	N/A	43,770

III. Total Net Assets Under Management (in billions of dollars)

	1990*	1999*
Stock funds	$239.5	$4,041.9
Bond funds	291.3	808.1
Money market funds	498.3	1,613.1
Other funds	36.1	383.2
Total—U.S. funds	$1,065.2	$ 6,846.3
Net assets under mgmt. in other countries**	N/A	$ 3,687.5
Total—worldwide	N/A	$10,533.8

IV. Composition of Mutual Fund Ownership in U.S. (relative to total mutual fund assets)

Owned by U.S. households	1990*	1999*
in dollars	$790 billion	$5.5 trillion
% of total	74.0%	81.0%
Owned by institutions		
in dollars	$275 billion	$1.3 trillion
% of total	26.0%	19.0%

Notes: *All data are for year-end 1990 and 1999.
**Totals for 30 countries, the major ones being Canada, France, Germany, U.K., Japan, Hong Kong, Italy, Korea, and Spain.

Source: 2000 Mutual Fund Fact Book, Investment Company Institute, 2000; obtained from www.ici.org

investors from all walks of life and all income levels. They range from inexperienced to highly experienced investors who all share a common view: Each has decided, for one reason or another, to turn over at least a part of his or her investment management activities to professionals.

Pooled Diversification As noted above, an investment in a mutual fund really represents *an ownership position in a professionally managed portfolio*

FIGURE 12.1   A Partial List of Portfolio Holdings

This exhibit represents just *two pages* of security holdings for this particular fund. The total list of holdings goes on for 28 pages and includes stocks in hundreds of different companies. Certainly, this is far more diversification than most individual investors could ever hope to achieve. (*Source: Fidelity Low-Priced Stock Fund,* January 2000.)

Common Stocks – continued

	Shares	Value (Note 1) (000s)
SERVICES – continued		
Services – continued		
The Go-Ahead Group PLC	225,000	$ 2,170
Thomas Group (a)	170,900	1,987
Velcro Industries NV	114,500	1,489
Viad Corp.	2,000,000	52,625
Wesco, Inc.	200,000	745
		202,600
TOTAL SERVICES		408,763
TECHNOLOGY – 17.9%		
Communications Equipment – 0.6%		
Champion Technology Holdings Ltd.	100,000	7
KTK Telecommunications Engineering Co. Ltd.	100,000	493
Kyosan Electric Manufacturing Co. Ltd.	500,000	1,173
LoJack Corp. (a)	110,500	856
Perceptron, Inc. (a)	233,500	934
Tollgrade Communications, Inc. (a)(d)	509,000	29,586
Turnstone Systems, Inc.	1,200	35
		33,084
Computer Services & Software – 5.4%		
Affiliated Computer Services, Inc. Class A (a)	1,000,000	39,750
Aladdin Knowledge Systems Ltd. (a)	315,000	5,906
Analysts International Corp.	100,000	1,256
Avant! Corp. (a)	1,227,600	21,867
Black Box Corp. (a)(d)	1,400,000	82,775
Computer Learning Centers, Inc. (a)(d)	1,161,200	2,177
Condor Technology Solutions, Inc. (a)	134,000	184
Cotelligent, Inc. (a)	352,800	1,852
Daitec Co. Ltd.	425,200	6,215
Directrix, Inc. (a)	90,000	529
Fair, Isaac & Co., Inc.	520,000	23,790
GSE Systems, Inc. (a)(d)	353,800	1,548
Infinium Software, Inc. (a)	152,500	867
Informa Group PLC	875,000	8,312
JDA Software Group, Inc. (a)	1,000,000	20,000
Mapics, Inc. (a)	676,000	10,140
Meta Group, Inc. (a)	75,000	1,697
National Data Corp.	5,000	160

Common Stocks – continued

	Shares	Value (Note 1) (000s)
TECHNOLOGY – continued		
Computer Services & Software – continued		
Ontrack Data International, Inc. (a)	244,000	$ 1,800
Phoenix Technologies Ltd. (a)	1,000,000	20,625
Project Software & Development, Inc. (a)	700,000	33,075
Prophet 21, Inc. (a)	115,500	1,444
Remedy Corp. (a)	100,000	4,044
RWD Technologies, Inc. (a)	62,000	605
SPSS, Inc. (a)(d)	861,100	22,227
Symantec Corp. (a)	100,000	5,006
Timberline Software Corp.	353,600	4,177
Unigraphics Solutions, Inc. Class A (a)(d)	520,000	12,253
		334,281
Computers & Office Equipment – 4.3%		
Adaptec, Inc. (a)	375,000	19,641
Advanced Digital Information Corp. (a)	1,250,000	61,250
Amplicon, Inc.	523,400	5,757
Caere Corp. (a)	25,000	219
Cybex Corp. (a)(d)	674,000	35,385
Equinox Systems, Inc. (a)(d)	535,000	5,083
Kronos, Inc. (a)(d)	935,000	56,100
Maezawa Kasei Industries Co. Ltd.	200,000	3,203
Nam Tai Electronics, Inc.	431,500	5,825
Nam Tai Electronics, Inc. warrants 11/24/00 (a)	140,000	144
Pomeroy Computer Resources, Inc. (a)(d)	1,179,800	19,172
PSC, Inc. (a)	60,000	480
Quantum Corp. – DLT & Storage Systems (a)	550,010	5,294
SBS Technologies, Inc. (a)(d)	495,000	17,696
SED International Holdings, Inc. (a)(d)	960,000	1,830
Tech Data Corp. (a)	20,000	446
Zebra Technologies Corp.	500,000	29,594
		267,119
Electronic Instruments – 1.0%		
BTU International, Inc. (a)(d)	603,300	4,148
Cohu, Inc.	300,000	12,375
Halma PLC	750,000	1,393
Hurco Companies, Inc. (a)(d)	379,028	1,469
Intest Corp. (a)(d)	650,000	13,366
Mesa Laboratories, Inc. (a)	125,400	494
MOCON, Inc.	119,600	673

of securities. To appreciate the extent of such diversification, look at Figure 12.1. It provides a partial list of the securities held in the portfolio of a major mutual fund. (The exhibit shows just two pages out of a 28-page list of security holdings.) Note that in January 2000, this fund owned anywhere from 1,200 shares of Turnstone Systems to 2 *million* shares of Viad Corporation. Furthermore, note that within each industry segment, the fund diversified its holdings across a number of different stocks. Clearly, this is far more diversification than most investors could ever attain. Yet each investor who owns shares in this fund is, in effect, a part owner of this diversified portfolio.

Of course, not all funds are as big or as widely diversified as the one depicted in Figure 12.1. But whatever the size of the fund, as the securities held by it move up and down in price, the market value of the mutual fund shares moves accordingly. And when dividend and interest payments are received by the fund, they too are passed on to the mutual fund shareholders and distributed on the basis of prorated ownership. For example, if you own 1,000 shares in a mutual fund and that represents 1% of all shares outstanding, you will

WHO OWNS THE FUNDS, AND WHY?—The average mutual fund shareholder is 45 years old, married, college-educated, and employed, with $69,000 of household income, $74,400 of mutual fund assets, and $199,000 of total financial assets. Almost 90% own equity mutual funds, and about half own money market funds. Nearly all mutual fund investors consider their holdings as long-term savings. The top four reasons why they select mutual funds are professional management, investment diversification, potential for high returns, and ease of making investments.

Source: 2000 Mutual Fund Fact Book (Washington, DC: Investment Company Institute, May 2000), downloaded from www.ici.org

pooled diversification
a process whereby investors buy into a diversified portfolio of securities for the collective benefit of the individual investors.

management fee
a fee levied annually for professional mutual fund services provided; paid regardless of the performance of the portfolio.

receive 1% of the dividends paid by the fund. When a security held by the fund is sold for a profit, the capital gain is also passed on to fund shareholders. The whole mutual fund idea, in fact, rests on the concept of **pooled diversification**. This process works very much like health insurance, whereby individuals pool their resources for the collective benefit of all the contributors.

Attractions and Drawbacks of Mutual Fund Ownership The attractions of mutual fund ownership are numerous. One of the most important is *diversification*. It benefits fund shareholders by spreading out holdings over a wide variety of industries and companies, thus reducing risk. Another appeal of mutual funds is *full-time professional management,* which relieves investors of many day-to-day management and record-keeping chores. What's more, the fund is probably able to offer better investment expertise than individual investors can provide. Still another advantage is that most mutual fund investments can be started with a *modest capital outlay.* Sometimes no minimum investment is required, and after the initial investment additional shares can usually be purchased in small amounts. The *services that mutual funds offer* also make them appealing to many investors: These include automatic reinvestment of dividends, withdrawal plans, and exchange privileges. Finally, mutual funds offer *convenience.* They are relatively easy to acquire; the funds handle the paperwork and record keeping; their prices are widely quoted; and it is possible to deal in fractional shares.

There are, of course, some major drawbacks to mutual fund ownership. One of the biggest disadvantages is that mutual funds in general can be costly and involve *substantial transaction costs.* Many funds carry sizable commission fees ("load charges"). In addition, a **management fee** is levied annually for the professional services provided. It is deducted right off the top, regardless of whether the fund has had a good or a bad year. And, even in spite of all the professional management and advice, it seems that *mutual fund performance* over the long haul is at best about equal to what you would expect from the market as a whole. There are some notable exceptions, of course, but most funds do little more than keep up with the market. In many cases, they don't even do that.

Figure 12.2 shows the investment performance for 12 different types of equity (or equity-oriented) funds over the 10½-year period from January 1990 through mid-2000. The reported returns are average, fully compounded annual rates of return. They assume that all dividends and capital gains distributions are reinvested into additional shares of stock. Note that when compared to the S&P 500, only three fund categories outperformed the market, whereas several fell far short. The message is clear: *Consistently beating the market is no easy task,* even for professional money managers. Although a handful of funds have given investors above-average and even spectacular rates of return, most mutual funds simply do not meet those levels of performance. This is not to say that the long-term returns from mutual funds are substandard or that they fail to equal what you could achieve by putting your money in, say, a savings account or some other risk-free investment outlet. Quite the contrary: The long-term returns from mutual funds have been substantial (and perhaps even better than what a lot of individual investors could have achieved on their own), but most of these returns can be traced to strong market conditions and/or to the reinvestment of dividends and capital gains.

FIGURE 12.2 **The Comparative Performance of Mutual Funds Versus the Market**

Even with the services of professional money managers, it's tough to outperform the market. In this case, the average performance of 9 out of the 12 fund categories failed to meet the market's standard of return (for the period from January 1990 to mid-2000). (*Source: Morningstar,* June 2000.)

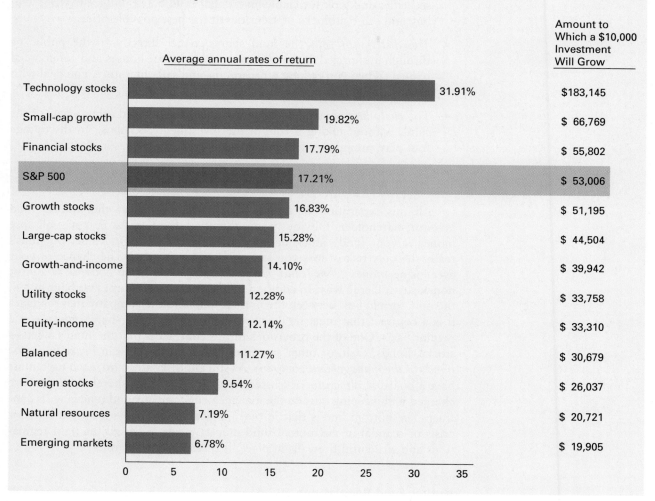

How Mutual Funds Are Organized and Run Although it's tempting to think of a mutual fund as a single large entity, that view is not really accurate. Various functions—investing, record keeping, safekeeping, and others—are split among two or more companies. To begin with, there's the fund itself, which is organized as a separate corporation or trust and is owned by the shareholders, not by the firm that runs it. In addition, there are several other main players:

- The *management company* runs the fund's daily operations. Management companies are the firms we know as Fidelity, Vanguard, T. Rowe Price, American Century, and Dreyfus. They are the ones that create the funds in the first place. Usually, the management firm also serves as investment adviser.

- The *investment adviser* buys and sells stocks or bonds and otherwise oversees the portfolio. Usually, three parties participate in this phase of the operation: (1) *The money manager,* who actually runs the portfolio and makes the buy and sell decisions; (2) *Securities analysts,* who analyze securities and look for viable investment candidates; and (3) *traders,* who buy and sell big blocks of securities at the best possible price.

- The *distributor* sells the fund shares, either directly to the public or through authorized dealers (like major brokerage houses and commercial banks). When you request a prospectus and sales literature, you deal with the distributor.

- The *custodian* physically safeguards the securities and other assets of the fund, without taking a role in the investment decisions. To discourage foul play, an independent party (usually a bank) serves in this capacity.

- The *transfer agent* keeps track of purchase and redemption requests from shareholders and maintains other shareholder records.

All this separation of duties is designed to protect the mutual fund investor/shareholder. Obviously, as a mutual fund investor, you will lose money if your fund's stock or bond holdings go down in value. But that's really the only risk of loss you face with a mutual fund. The chance of your ever losing *money from fraud, scandal, or a mutual fund collapse* is almost nonexistent. Here's why: In addition to the separation of duties we have noted, the only formal link between the mutual fund and the company that manages it is a contract that must be renewed—and approved by shareholders—on a regular basis. One of the provisions of this contract is that the fund's assets—stocks, bonds, cash, or other securities in the portfolio—can *never be in the hands of the management company.* As still another safeguard, each fund must have a board of directors, or trustees, who are elected by shareholders and are charged with keeping tabs on the management company and renewing its contract. The bottom line is that in over 70 years there has never been a major crisis or scandal in the mutual fund industry. Nor, given all the tight regulations and structural firewalls in place, is there likely to be one.

Mutual Fund Regulations We discussed securities regulations in Chapter 2, but it might be helpful to review some of the major regulatory provisions that apply to mutual funds. To begin with, the *Securities Act of 1933* requires the filing of full information about a mutual fund with the SEC. This act also requires the fund to provide potential investors with a fund profile or current prospectus. This document discloses the fund's management, its investment policies and objectives, and other essential data. In addition, the purchase and sale of mutual fund shares are subject to the antifraud provisions of the *Securities Exchange Act of 1934,* while the *Investment Advisers Act of 1940* regulates the activities of the investment advisers that work for mutual funds. Most important, in order to qualify for investment company status, a fund must comply with the provisions of the *Investment Company Act of 1940.* That comprehensive piece of legislation provides the foundation for the regulation of the mutual fund industry and, among other things, establishes standards of income distribution, fee structures, and diversification of assets.

From a tax perspective, a mutual fund can be treated as an essentially tax-exempt organization (and thereby avoid the double taxation of dividends and income) so long as it qualifies under *Subchapter M* of the Internal Revenue Code of 1954. Briefly, to operate as a regulated investment company and enjoy the attendant tax benefits, a fund must annually distribute to its shareholders all of its realized capital gains and at least 90% of its interest and dividend income. That way, the fund will pay *no* taxes on any of its earnings, whether they're derived from current income or capital gains.

Open- or Closed-End Funds

Although investing in mutual funds has been made as simple as possible, investors nevertheless should have a clear understanding of what they're getting into. For starters, it's essential that you be aware of the different organizational structures, particularly with regard to open- and closed-end funds, as well as a type of fund that combines the characteristics of open- and closed-end funds, the so-called "exchange-traded funds."

Open-End Investment Companies The term *mutual fund* is commonly used to describe an open-end investment company. In an **open-end investment company,** investors buy their shares from, and sell them back to, the mutual fund itself. When an investor buys shares in an open-end fund, the fund issues new shares of stock and fills the purchase order with those new shares. There is no limit, other than investor demand, to the number of shares the fund can issue. (Occasionally, funds *temporarily* close themselves to new investors—they won't open any new accounts—in an attempt to keep fund growth in check.) All open-end mutual funds stand behind their shares and buy them back when investors decide to sell. There is never any trading between individuals.

Open-end mutual funds are the dominant type of investment company and account for well over 95% of the assets under management. All the statistics cited above, including those in Table 12.1, pertain to these types of funds. Many of these funds are very large and hold *billions* of dollars' worth of securities. Indeed, in 2000, the typical stock or bond fund held an average portfolio of some $750 million, and there were more than 800 billion-dollar funds.

Both buy and sell transactions in (open-end) mutual funds are carried out at prices based on the current market value of all the securities held in the fund's portfolio. (Technically, this would also include the book value of any other assets, such as cash and receivables from securities transactions, that the fund might hold at the time, though for all practical purposes, these other assets generally account for only a tiny fraction of the fund's total portfolio.) Known as the fund's **net asset value** (**NAV**), this current market value is calculated at least once a day and represents the underlying value of a share of stock in a particular mutual fund. NAV is found by taking the total market value of all assets held by the fund, less any liabilities, and dividing this amount by the number of fund shares outstanding. For example, if the market value of all the

open-end investment company a type of investment company in which investors buy shares from, and sell them back to, the mutual fund itself, with no limit on the number of shares the fund can issue.

HOTLINKS
Vanguard's mututal fund investor education glossary is at:
www.vanguard.com/educ/glossary/glossintro.html

net asset value (NAV) the underlying value of a share of stock in a particular mutual fund.

assets held by the XYZ mutual fund on a given day equaled $10 million, and if XYZ on that particular day had 500,000 shares outstanding, the fund's net asset value per share would be $20 ($10,000,000 ÷ 500,000). This figure, as we will see, is then used to derive the price at which the fund shares are bought and sold.

Closed-End Investment Companies Although the term *mutual fund* is supposed to be used only with open-end funds, it is also commonly used to refer to closed-end investment companies. **Closed-end investment companies** operate with a fixed number of shares outstanding, and do not regularly issue new shares of stock. In effect, they have a capital structure like that of any other corporation, except that the corporation's business happens to be investing in marketable securities. Shares in closed-end investment companies, like those of any other common stock, are actively traded in the secondary market. But unlike open-end funds, *all trading in closed-end funds is done between investors in the open market.* The fund itself plays no role in either buy or sell transactions. Once the shares are issued, the fund is out of the picture. By far, most closed-end investment companies are traded on the New York Stock Exchange, a few are traded on the American Exchange, and occasionally some are traded in the OTC market or on some other exchange. Even so, while these shares are traded (on the NYSE, AMEX, or Nasdaq) like any other stock, their quotes are listed separately—in the *Wall Street Journal* at least. Figure 12.3 shows the quotes for a small sample of closed-end funds listed on the NYSE, including Gabelli Equity Trust (one of the bigger closed-end investment companies). These quotes are grouped by the exchange on which the funds are traded, and are just like any other NYSE or Nasdaq National Market quotes, except they don't show the P/E ratio.

A closed-end fund is, in many respects, both a common stock and an investment company. As the original form of investment company, closed-end funds have enjoyed a long history that dates back to nineteenth-century England and Scotland. In the United States, closed-end funds were actively traded during the 1920s bull market, when they far outnumbered their open-end relatives. During that freewheeling era, however, they were highly leveraged and consequently were hit hard during the Crash of 1929, earning a bad reputation with investors. They remained something of an oddity for decades afterward. It wasn't until the bull market that began in the early 1980s that closed-end funds came back into fashion.

Many of the investment advisers that today run closed-end funds (like Putnam, Kemper, Nuveen, MFS, and Franklin-Templeton) also manage open-end funds, often with similar investment objectives. They offer both closed- and open-end funds because they are really *two different investment products.* For although it may not appear so at first glance, there are some major differences between these two types of funds. To begin with, closed-end funds have a fixed amount of capital to work with. Therefore, they don't have to be concerned about keeping cash on hand (or readily available) to meet redemptions. Equally important, because there is no pressure on portfolio managers to cash in these securities at inopportune times, they can be more aggressive in their investment styles by investing in obscure yet attractive securities that may not be actively traded. And, of course, because they don't have new money flowing in all the

closed-end investment companies
a type of investment company that operates with a fixed number of shares outstanding.

FIGURE 12.3

Stock Quotations for Closed-End Investment Companies

The quotes for closed-end investment companies are listed separately from other common stocks. Nonetheless, except for the lack of a P/E ratio, their quotes are pretty much the same as any other NYSE or Nasdaq National Market stock. (*Source: Wall Street Journal,* May 24, 2001.)

Gabelli →
Equity
Trust

CLOSED-END FUNDS

YTD % CHG	52 WEEKS HI	LO	STOCK (SYM)	DIV	YLD %	VOL 100S	CLOSE	NET CHG
+ 7.0	8.48	6.88	Fortis Sec **FOR** x	.67	8.5	99	7.89	− 0.02
− 14.8	15.75	8	FraGrthFd **FRF**	3.18e	35.5	98	8.95	− 0.07
+ 6.5	9.05	7.25	FrnklnMulti **FMI**	.67a	7.5	118	8.92	− 0.07
+ 8.1	8.74	6.75	FrnklnUnvlTr **FT**	.80a	10.0	213	8.04	+ 0.01
+ 17.9	11.60	8.63	GabelliConv **GCV**	.80a	7.4	72	10.76	− 0.13
+ 3.1	12.69	10	GabelliTr **GAB**	1.08a	9.2	1173	11.79	− 0.06
+ 10.3	15.69	9.32	GabelliMlti **GGT**	1.56e	13.7	115	11.37	− 0.47
+ 1.7	9.38	7.63	GabelliUt **GUT**	.60a	6.7	102	8.90	− 0.02
+ 6.6	39.70	31.49♣	GenAmInv **GAM**	4.05e	10.6	371	38.37	− 0.15
− 9.5	12.98	7.75♣	GermanyFd **GER**	2.39	27.8	604	8.60	+ 0.01
− 13.7	13.02	6.75♣	NewGrmnyFd **GF**	.08	1.0	565	7.66	− 0.14
+ 6.4	14.20	11.69	GlblHilnco **GHI**	1.61	11.7	439	13.76	− 0.09
+ 13.0	12.30	9.88	GlblIncFd **GDF**	1.42	12.2	223	11.65	+ 0.14
+ 31.9	11.10	7.44♣	GtChina **GCH**	.03	.3	115	10.80	− 0.02
+ 6.2	37.81	18.08♣	H&Q Hlth **HQH**	4.97e	19.1	258	26.03	− 0.42
+ 4.9	32.56	15	H&Q LifeSci **HQL**	4.08e	17.9	131	22.75	− 0.35
− 0.6	9.31	6.63♣	HnckJ BkOpp **BTO**	.77	8.7	1387	8.82	− 0.12
+ 1.8	15.25	12.63♣	HnckJ IncSec **JHS**	1.03m	7.0	65	14.70	...
+ 1.6	20.10	16.56♣	HnckJ Invst **JHI**	1.37m	7.0	134	19.56	− 0.08
+ 4.2	12.65	10.25♣	HnckJ PtGlb **PGD**	.97	7.8	37	12.50	+ 0.10
+ 6.4	12.20	10	HnckJ PtPfd	.86	7.4	25	11.70	+ 0.10
+ 2.9	9.90	7.88♣	HnckJ PtPrem **PDF**	.65	7.2	87	9	+ 0.09
+ 2.3	11	9.06♣	HnckJ PtPremll **PDT**	.78	7.2	121	10.81	+ 0.05
+ 12.1	14.80	11.81♣	HnckJ PtSel **DIV**	1.08	7.4	70	14.64	+ 0.16
+ 2.6	14.19	11.88	HatterasSec **HAT**	1.02	7.5	5	13.66	− 0.05
+ 5.2	9.75	7.63♣	HilncoFd **HIO**	.97	10.7	770	9.07	+ 0.07
+ 5.4	6.34	4.44	HiYldFd **HYI**	.60	10.5	76.	5.73	− 0.02
− 0.5	7	4.76	HiYldPlsFd **HYP**	.87	14.9	1174	5.85	− 0.26
+ 4.4	9.22	7.94	Hyperion02 **HTB**	.10	1.1	151	9.20	...
+ 5.8	9.20	7.63	Hyperion05 **HTO**	.55f	6.0	276	9.19	+ 0.08
+ 2.1	9.50	7.38	HyperionFd **HTR**	.87	9.9	625	8.81	+ 0.01
− 12.0	15.13	9.29	IndiaFd **IFN**	j	...	2180	10.61	+ 0.16

time, portfolio managers don't have to worry about finding new investments. Instead, they can concentrate on a set portfolio of securities.

Of course, this also puts added pressures on the money managers, since their investment styles and fund portfolios are closely monitored and judged by the market. That is, the share prices of closed-end companies are determined not only by their net asset values but also by general supply and demand conditions in the stock market. As a result, depending on the market outlook and investor expectations, closed-end companies generally trade at a discount or premium to NAV. (They almost never trade at net asset value.) Share price discounts and premiums can at times become quite large. In fact, it's not unusual for such spreads to amount to as much as 25% to 30% of net asset value (occasionally more) depending on market judgments and expectations. And while these funds can trade at either premiums or discounts, price discounts are, in fact, far more common.

Exchange-Traded Funds

Combine some of the operating characteristics of an open-end fund with some of the trading characteristics of a closed-end fund, and what you'll end up with is something called an *exchange-traded fund*. These securities are being promoted as the newest product to hit the fund world, but they're really a recreation of a product that's been around since the early 1990s. Technically, an **exchange-traded fund (ETF)** is a type of open-end mutual fund that trades as a listed security on one of the stock exchanges (mostly the AMEX). Actually, all EFTs thus far (mid-year 2000) have been structured as *index funds* set up to match the performance of a certain segment of the market. They do this by owning all, or a representative sample, of the stocks in a targeted market segment or index. (We'll examine traditional index funds in more detail later in this chapter.) Thus, ETFs offer the professional money management of traditional mutual funds *and* the liquidity of an exchange-traded stock.

Even though these securities are like closed-end funds in that ETFs are traded on listed exchanges, *they are in reality open-end mutual funds,* where the number of shares outstanding can be increased or decreased in response to market demand. That is, although ETFs can be bought or sold like any stock on a listed exchange, *the ETF distributor can also create new shares or redeem old shares.* This is done through a special type of security known as a *payment-in-kind creation unit.* This is done to prevent the fund from trading at (much of) a premium or discount and thereby avoid one of the pitfalls of closed-end funds. For the most part, individual investors are *not* involved in the creation or redemption of shares (that's done with the big institutional investors). Instead, individual investors will buy and sell ETFs in the secondary market by placing orders with their brokers, as they would normally do with any stock.

By mid-2000, there were more than 60 ETFs listed on the American Stock Exchange, and every one of them was based on some domestic or international stock market index. The biggest and oldest (started in 1993) are based on the S&P 500 and are known as *spiders*. In addition to spiders, there are *diamonds* (which are based on the DJIA) and *qubes* (based on the Nasdaq 100 and so-named because of their QQQ ticker symbol). There also are ETFs based on 19 international markets (from Australia and Canada to Germany, Japan, and the U.K.). Just about every major U.S. index, in fact, has its own ETF. So do a lot of minor indexes (some of which were created by the distributors) that cover very specialized (and sometimes fairly small) segments of the market. The net asset values of ETFs are set at a fraction of the underlying index value at any given time. For example, if the S&P 500 index stands at, say, 1464.46, the EFT on that index will trade at around 146.50 (that is, at about 1/10 of the index). Likewise, the ETF on the Dow is set at 1/100 of the DJIA. (Thus, when the DJIA is at say, 10449.30, the EFT will trade at around 104.50).

ETFs combine many of the advantages of closed-end funds with those of traditional (open-end) index funds. As with closed-end funds, you can buy and sell ETFs at *any time of the day* by placing an order through your broker (and paying a standard commission, just as you would with any other stock). In contrast, you *cannot* trade a traditional open-end fund on an intraday basis;

---

exchange-traded fund (ETF)
an open-end mutual fund that trades as a listed security on a stock exchange.

HOT LINKS

Which are the most active index shares—
Nasdaq 100 index shares, SPDRs, Midcap
SPDRs, or Diamonds? To find out, visit:

amex.com

all buy and sell orders for those funds are filled at the end of the trading day, at closing prices. What's more, because ETFs are passively managed, they offer all the advantages of any index fund: low cost, low portfolio turnover, and low taxes. In fact, the fund's tax liability is kept very low, because ETFs rarely distribute any capital gains to shareholders. Thus, you could hold one of these things for decades and never pay a dime in capital gains taxes (at least not until you sell the shares). The accompanying *Investing in Action* box provides some additional information about ETFs—information that might help you decide whether they are right for you.

Some Important Considerations

When you buy or sell shares in a *closed-end* investment company (or in *ETFs,* for that matter), you pay a commission, just as you would with any other listed or OTC stock. This is not the case with open-end mutual funds, however. The cost of investing in an open-end fund depends on the types of fees and load charges that the fund levies on its investors.

load fund
a mutual fund that charges a commission when shares are bought; also known as a *front-end load fund.*

no-load fund
a mutual fund that does not charge a commission when shares are bought.

low-load fund
a mutual fund that charges a small commission (2% to 3%) when shares are bought.

back-end load
a commission charged on the *sale* of shares in a mutual fund.

12(b)-1 fee
a fee levied annually by some mutual funds to cover management and other operating costs; amounts to as much as 1% of the average net assets.

Load and No-Load Funds The *load charge* on an open-end fund is the commission the investor pays when buying shares in a fund. Generally speaking, the term **load fund** is used to describe a mutual fund that charges a commission when shares are bought. (Such charges are also known as *front-end loads.*) In a **no-load fund** no sales charges are levied. Load charges can be fairly substantial and can amount to as much as 8½% of the *purchase price* of the shares. However, very few funds charge the maximum. Instead, many funds charge commissions of only 2% or 3%. Such funds are known as **low-load funds.**

Although there may be little or no difference in the performance of load and no-load funds, *the cost savings with no-load funds tend to give investors a head start in achieving superior rates of return.* Unfortunately, the true no-load fund is becoming harder to find, as more and more no-loads are becoming *12(b)-1 funds.* While these funds do not directly charge commissions at the time of purchase, they *annually* assess what are known as 12(b)-1 charges to make up for any lost commissions. (These charges are more fully described below.) Overall, less than 40% of the funds sold today are pure no-loads; the rest charge some type of load or fee.

Occasionally, a fund will have a **back-end load,** which means commissions are levied when shares are sold. These loads may amount to as much as 7¼% of the value of the shares sold, although back-end loads tend to decline over time and usually disappear altogether after 5 or 6 years from date of purchase. The stated purpose of back-end loads is to enhance fund stability by discouraging investors from trading in and out of the funds over short investment horizons. In addition, a substantial (and growing) number of funds charge something called a **12(b)-1 fee** that's assessed annually for as long as you own the fund. Known appropriately as *hidden loads,* these fees are designed to help funds (particularly the no-loads) cover their distribution and marketing costs. They can amount to as much as 1% per year of assets under management. In good markets and bad, these fees are paid right off the top, and that can take its toll. Consider, for instance, $10,000 invested in a fund that charges a 1% 12(b)-1

INVESTING in action

Adding ETFs to Your Investment Portfolio

Exchange-traded funds (ETFs), which are one of the fastest-growing investment vehicles today, are similar to index mutual funds but trade like stocks. Each share represents a basket of securities that closely tracks one specific index. New types of ETFs are being introduced regularly, such as bond ETFs that track the Lehman Brothers and other bond indexes. Some fund companies are even proposing actively managed ETFs that don't track an index.

Because ETFs trade on the stock market, it's easy to buy and sell them through a brokerage account throughout the day—not just after the markets close, as with mutual funds. ETFs also have extremely low costs because they have no research or management fees and minimal back-office costs. For example, annual expenses for SPDRS (S&P 500 Depositary Receipts) are just 0.12%—$12 per $10,000 investment; Barclays iShares S&P 500 charges just 0.0945%. Another benefit is their tax advantage. Because they are not actively managed, ETFs have little or no taxable income and capital gains distributions.

ETFs do have some drawbacks, though. Although fees are low, investors incur brokerage commissions any time they trade ETFs, as well as a small bid/ask spread. Frequent trades can quickly wipe out any profits. ETFs do not offer dividend reinvestment or monthly purchase programs. Traditional mutual funds can reinvest dividends and capital gains immediately to continuously compound their gains, whereas ETFs can reinvest the cash only monthly or quarterly. And some ETFs have highly concentrated portfolios: for example, 43% of QQQs' holdings are in just 10 stocks, with Cisco and Intel accounting for about 15% of the portfolio.

Despite the downside, ETFs offer investors a quick way to get exposure to a market segment. They provide diversification and precise market tracking, and they appeal to both active traders and long-term investors. It's easy to add a specific equity component on the basis of one of the following:

- **Style:** Choose an ETF that tracks a growth or value index such as the S&P 400 Mid Cap Barra Growth or the S&P 600 Small Cap Value.

- **Size:** Market capitalization is another ETF segmentation strategy. You will find ETFs that track small-, mid-, and large-caps, using the S&P, Dow, Nasdaq, and Russell indexes.
- **Sector:** Many ETFs, including Barclays' iShares and Merrill Lynch HOLDRS, target specific industries or sectors, such as biotechnology, real estate investment trusts, pharmaceuticals, telecommunications, health care, energy, noncyclical companies, and subsectors of the Internet industry. They offer exposure to a small part of an industry that mutual funds may not cover and give broader coverage than one could obtain buying several individual stocks.
- **Region:** ETFs make it easy to achieve geographical diversification—whether to just one country or to an entire region—without the high loads and fees of most foreign stock funds. Barclays' iShares include Webs (World Equity Benchmark shares) that track the Morgan Stanley Capital International (MSCI) indexes for 20 countries as well as regional ETFs that track the S&P Europe 350 and Global 100 and MSCI European Monetary Union. However, international index funds are a less costly way to get broad exposure.

The bottom line on any investment is how well it performs over time. Investors can track ETF total returns and compare them to traditional mutual funds in similar sectors at Morningstar.com (www.morningstar.com/Cover/ETF.html) and with the *Wall Street Journal's* monthly Mutual Fund Report.

Sources: "About iShares," Barclays iShares Web site, www.ishares.com; "Better Than Index Funds," *Forbes*, August 21, 2000, p. 268; Diane Forrest, "Weighing the Risks," *Maclean's*, January 29, 2001; Odette Galli, "Not Just for Day Traders," *Smart Money*, September 2000, p. 124; Eric Jacobson, "Barclays to Roll Out Exchange-Traded Bond Funds, *Morningstar.com*, January 8, 2001, downloaded from www.morningstar.com; Mark Mclaughlin, "Xtreme Indexing," *Kiplinger's Personal Finance Magazine*, June, 2000; and Anne Tergesen, "All Aboard for Exchange-Traded Funds," *Business Week*, September 11, 2000, p. 166; and Chet Currier, "Understanding Prospectuses Leads to Informed Investing," *Dallas Morning News*, June 18, 2000, p. 11H.

fee. That translates into a charge of $100 a year—certainly not an insignificant amount of money.

The latest trend in mutual fund fees is the so-called *multiple-class sales charge*. You'll find such arrangements at firms like American Capital, Dreyfus, Merrill Lynch, MFS, Keystone, Smith Barney, and Prudential. The mutual fund simply issues different classes of stocks on the same portfolio of securities, with each class having a different fee structure. For example, class A shares might have normal (relatively high) front-end loads; class B shares might have no front-end loads but substantial back-end loads along with a modest annual 12(b)-1 fee; and class C shares might carry only maximum 12(b)-1 fees. In other words, you "choose your own poison."

To try to bring some semblance of order to fund charges and fees, in 1992 the SEC instituted a series of caps on mutual fund fees. Under the 1992 rules, a mutual fund cannot charge more than 8½% in *total sales charges and fees*, including front- and back-end loads as well as 12(b)-1 fees. Thus, if a fund charges a 5% front-end load and a 1% 12(b)-1 fee, it can charge a maximum of only 2½% in back-end load charges without violating the 8½% cap. In addition, the SEC set a 1% cap on annual 12(b)-1 fees and, perhaps more significantly, stated that true no-load funds cannot charge more than 0.25% in annual 12(b)-1 fees. If they do, they have to drop the no-load label in their sales and promotional material.

Other Fees and Costs Another cost of owning mutual funds is the *management fee*. This is the compensation paid to the professional managers who administer the fund's portfolio. It must be paid regardless of whether a fund is load or no-load, and whether it is an open- or closed-end fund, or an exchange-traded fund. Unlike load charges, which are one-time costs, management fees and 12(b)-1 charges, if imposed, are levied annually. They are paid regardless of the fund's performance. In addition, there are the administrative costs of operating the fund. These are fairly modest and represent the normal cost of doing business (e.g., the commissions paid when the fund buys and sells securities). The various fees that funds charge generally range from less than 0.5% to as much as 3% or 4% of average assets under management. Total expense ratios bear watching, because high expenses take their toll on performance. As a point of reference, in 2000, domestic stock funds had average expense ratios of around 1.45%, foreign stock funds of around 1.90%, stock index funds of around 0.65%, and domestic bond funds of around 1.10%.

A final cost of mutual funds is the taxes paid on securities transactions. To avoid double taxation, nearly all mutual funds operate as *regulated investment companies*. This means that all (or nearly all) of the dividend and interest income is passed on to the investor, as are any capital gains realized when securities are sold. The mutual fund therefore passes the tax liability on to its shareholders. This holds true whether such distributions are reinvested in the company (in the form of additional mutual fund shares) or paid out in cash. Mutual funds annually provide each stockholder with a summary report on the amount of dividends and capital gains received and the amount of taxable income earned by the fund shareholder.

Keeping Track of Fund Fees and Loads Critics of the mutual fund industry have come down hard on the proliferation of fund fees and charges. Some argue that the different charges and fees are meant to do one thing: confuse the investor. A lot of funds were going to great lengths (lowering a cost here, tacking on a fee there, hiding a charge somewhere else) to make themselves look like something they weren't. The funds were following the letter of the law, and were fully disclosing all their expenses and fees. The trouble was that the funds were able to hide all but the most conspicuous charges in "legalese." Fortunately, steps have been taken to bring fund fees and loads out into the open.

For one thing, fund charges are more widely reported now than they were in past. Most notably, today you can find detailed information about the types and amounts of fees and charges on just about any mutual fund by accessing a variety of Web sites, such as www.quicken.com/investments/mutualfunds, www.kiplinger.com/investing/funds/, or www.morningstar.com/Cover/Funds.html.

Figure 12.4 provides excerpts from one of these sites and shows the kind of information that's readily available, at no charge, on the Web.

Alternatively, you can use the mutual fund quotes that appear daily in most major, large-city newspapers or in the *Wall Street Journal*. For example, look at the *Wall Street Journal* quotations in Figure 12.5. Note the use of the letters *r, p,* and *t* behind the name of the fund. An *r* behind a fund's name means that the fund charges some type of redemption fee, or back-end load, when you sell your shares. This is the case, for example, with the Dreyfus Aggressive Value Fund. A *p* in the quotes means that the fund levies a 12(b)-1 fee, which you'll have to pay, for example, if you invest in the Dreyfus Global Growth Fund. Finally, a *t* indicates funds that charge both redemption fees and 12(b)-1 fees. Note, for example, that the FBR Financial Services Fund is one such fund.

The quotations, of course, tell you only the *kinds* of fees charged by the funds. They do not tell you *how much* is charged. To get the specifics on the amount charged, you'll have to turn to other sources. Furthermore, these published quotes (which are fairly representative of what you'd find in other major newspapers) *tell you nothing about the front-end loads,* if any, charged by the funds. Refer once again to the quotes in Figure 12.5, and compare the Dodge & Cox Balanced and FPA Paramount Funds. They look alike, don't they? But they're not. For even though neither of them charges redemption or 12(b)-1 fees, only one of them is a no-load fund. Dodge & Cox does not charge a front-end load, and is in fact a no-load fund. The FPA fund, in contrast, comes with a hefty 6½% front-end load. As a point of interest, the other three funds highlighted in Figure 12.5—Dreyfus Aggressive Value, Global Growth, and FBR Financial Services—don't charge front-end loads either, but you'd never know that from the quotes. (It should be noted that the *Wall Street Journal* also publishes a *Monthly Mutual Fund Review* on the first or second Monday of each month. Among other things, it provides some specifics on front-end loads and annual expense charges, including 12(b)-1 fees.

In addition to the public sources noted above, the mutual funds themselves are required by the SEC to disclose all of their fees and expenses fully in a standardized, easy-to-understand format. Every fund profile or prospectus must contain, up front, a fairly detailed *fee table,* much like the one illustrated in Table 12.2. This table has three parts. The first specifies *all shareholder*

FIGURE 12.4   Fund Fees and Charges on the Web

The Internet has become the motherlode of information on just about any topic imaginable, including mutual fund fees and charges. Here's an example of information taken from the Kiplinger Web site. These excerpts show, among other things, all the fees and expenses levied by each fund. The two funds in the exhibit provide a stark contrast in fees and expenses. The Smith Barney fund carries both a high front-end load and a 12(b)-1 fee, plus a substantial management fee/expense ratio. The Vanguard fund, on the other hand, provides a vivid example of a truly low-cost fund: no loads or fees and a *very low* management fee/expense ratio. (*Source:* www.kiplinger.com/investing/funds/, August 2, 2000.)

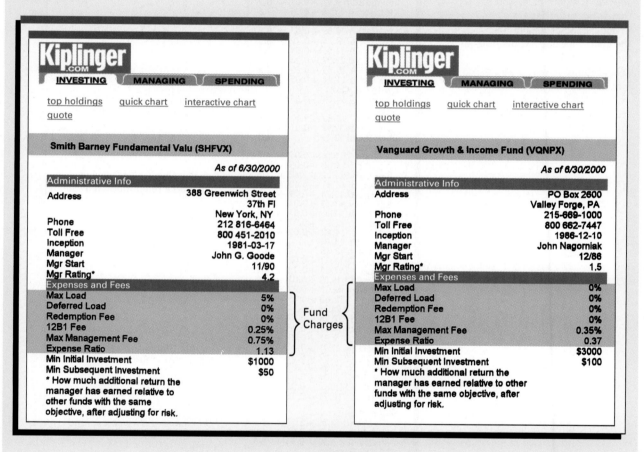

transaction costs. In effect, this tells you what it's going to cost to buy and sell shares in the mutual fund. The next section lists the *annual operating expenses* of the fund. Showing these expenses as a percentage of average net assets, the fund must break out management fees, 12(b)-1 fees, and any other expenses. The third section provides a rundown of *the total cost over time* of buying, selling, and owning the fund. This part of the table contains both transaction and operating expenses and shows what the total costs would be over hypothetical 1-, 3-, 5-, and 10-year holding periods. To ensure consistency and comparability, the funds must follow a rigid set of guidelines when constructing the illustrative costs.

FIGURE 12.5

Mutual Fund Quotes

Open-end mutual funds are listed separately from other securities. They have their own quotation system, an example of which, from the *Wall Street Journal,* is shown here. Note that these securities are quoted in dollars and cents and that the quotes include not only the fund's NAV but year-to-date (YTD) returns as well. Also included is an indication of whether the fund charges redemption and/or 12(b)-1 fees. (*Source: Wall Street Journal,* August 2, 2000.)

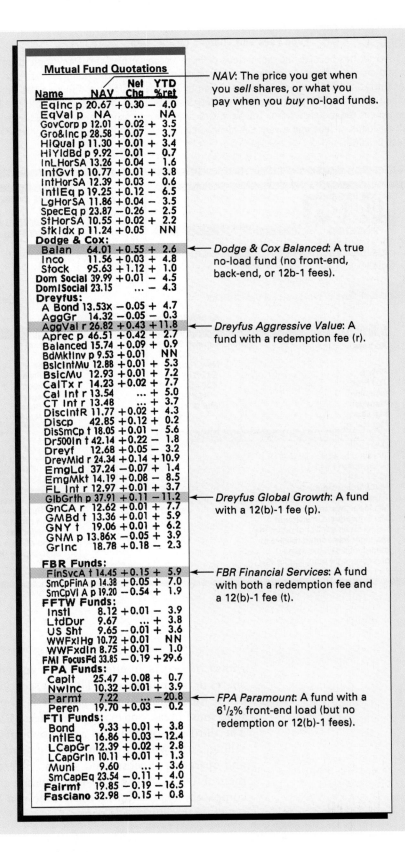

Mutual Fund Quotations

Name	NAV	Net Chg	YTD %ret
EqInc p	20.67	+0.30	− 4.0
EqVal p	NA	...	NA
GovCorp p	12.01	+0.02	+ 3.5
Gro&Inc p	28.58	+0.07	− 3.7
HiQual p	11.30	+0.01	+ 3.4
HiYldBd p	9.92	−0.01	− 0.7
InLHorSA	13.26	+0.04	− 1.6
IntGvt p	10.77	+0.01	+ 3.8
IntHorSA	12.39	+0.03	− 0.6
IntlEq p	19.25	+0.12	− 6.5
LgHorSA	11.86	+0.04	− 3.5
SpecEq p	23.87	−0.26	− 2.5
StHorSA	10.55	+0.02	+ 2.2
StkIdx p	11.24	+0.05	NN
Dodge & Cox:			
Balan	64.01	+0.55	+ 2.6
Inco	11.56	+0.03	+ 4.8
Stock	95.63	+1.12	+ 1.0
Dom Social	39.99	+0.01	− 4.5
DomISocial	23.15	...	− 4.3
Dreyfus:			
A Bond	13.53x	−0.05	+ 4.7
AggGr	14.32	−0.05	− 0.3
AggVal r	26.82	+0.43	+11.8
Aprec p	46.51	+0.42	− 2.7
Balanced	15.74	+0.09	+ 0.9
BdMktInv p	9.53	+0.01	NN
BsicIntMu	12.88	+0.01	+ 5.3
BsicMu	12.93	+0.01	+ 7.2
CalTx r	14.23	+0.02	+ 7.7
Cal Int r	13.54	...	+ 5.0
CT Int r	13.48	...	+ 3.7
DiscIntR	11.77	+0.02	+ 4.3
Discp	42.85	+0.12	− 0.2
DisSmCp t	18.05	+0.01	− 5.6
Dr500In t	42.14	+0.22	− 1.8
Dreyf	12.68	+0.05	− 3.2
DreyMid r	24.34	+0.14	+10.9
EmgLd	37.24	−0.07	+ 1.4
EmgMkt	14.19	+0.08	− 8.5
FL Int r	12.97	+0.01	+ 3.7
GlbGrth p	37.91	+0.11	−11.2
GnCA r	12.62	+0.01	+ 7.7
GMBd t	13.36	+0.01	+ 5.9
GNY t	19.06	+0.01	+ 6.2
GNM p	13.86x	−0.05	+ 3.9
GrInc	18.78	+0.18	− 2.3
FBR Funds:			
FinSvcA t	14.45	+0.15	+ 5.9
SmCpFinA p	14.38	+0.05	+ 7.0
SmCpVl A p	19.20	−0.54	+ 1.9
FFTW Funds:			
Instl	8.12	+0.01	− 3.9
LtdDur	9.67	...	+ 3.8
US Sht	9.65	−0.01	+ 3.6
WWFxlHg	10.72	+0.01	NN
WWFxdIn	8.75	+0.01	− 1.0
FMI FocusFd	33.85	−0.19	+29.6
FPA Funds:			
Capit	25.47	+0.08	+ 0.7
NwInc	10.32	+0.01	+ 3.9
Parmt	7.22	...	−20.8
Peren	19.70	+0.03	− 0.2
FTI Funds:			
Bond	9.33	+0.01	+ 3.8
IntlEq	16.86	+0.03	−12.4
LCapGr	12.39	+0.02	− 2.8
LCapGrIn	10.11	+0.01	+ 1.3
Muni	9.60	...	+ 3.6
SmCapEq	23.54	−0.11	+ 4.0
Fairmt	19.85	−0.19	−16.5
Fasciano	32.98	−0.15	+ 0.8

NAV: The price you get when you *sell* shares, or what you pay when you *buy* no-load funds.

Dodge & Cox Balanced: A true no-load fund (no front-end, back-end, or 12b-1 fees).

Dreyfus Aggressive Value: A fund with a redemption fee (r).

Dreyfus Global Growth: A fund with a 12(b)-1 fee (p).

FBR Financial Services: A fund with both a redemption fee and a 12(b)-1 fee (t).

FPA Paramount: A fund with a 6½% front-end load (but no redemption or 12(b)-1 fees).

TABLE 12.2 Mutual Fund Fee Table (Required by Federal Law)

The following table describes the fees and expenses that are incurred when you buy, hold, or sell shares of the fund.

Shareholder Fees (paid by the investor directly)

Maximum sales charge (load) on purchases (as a % of offering price)	3%
Sales charge (load) on reinvested distributions	None
Deferred sales charge (load) on redemptions	None
Exchange fees	None
Annual account maintenance fee (for accounts under $2,500)	$12.00

Annual fund operating expenses (paid from fund assets}

Management fee	0.45%
Distribution and Service (12b-1) fee	None
Other expenses	0.20%
Total annual fund operating expenses	0.65%

Example

This example is intended to help an investor compare the cost of investing in different funds. The example assumes a $10,000 investment in the fund for one, three, five, and ten years and then a redemption of all fund shares at the end of those periods. The example also assumes that an investment returns 5 percent each year and that the fund's operating expenses remain the same. Although actual costs may be higher or lower, based on these assumptions an investor's costs would be:

1 year	$364
3 years	$502
5 years	$651
10 years	$1,086

HOTLINKS

For a detailed discussion of two other types of investment companies—real estate investment trusts and annuities—see our Web site, at:

www.awl.com/gitman_joehnk

unit investment trust (UIT)
a type of investment vehicle whereby the trust sponsors put together a fixed/unmanaged portfolio of securities and then sell ownership units in the portfolio to individual investors.

Other Types of Investment Companies

In addition to open-end, closed-end, and exchange-traded funds, there are three other types of investment companies: (1) unit investment trusts, (2) real estate investment trusts, and (3) annuities. Unit investment trusts and annuities are similar to mutual funds to the extent that they, too, invest primarily in marketable securities, such as stocks and bonds. Real estate investment trusts, in contrast, invest primarily in various types of real estate–related investments, like mortgages. We'll look at unit investment trusts in this section. The other two types of investment companies are discussed in detail at the book's Web site.

Unit Investment Trusts A **unit investment trust** (UIT) represents little more than an interest in an *unmanaged* pool of investments. UITs are like mutual funds to the extent that they involve a portfolio of securities. But that's where the similarity ends. Once a portfolio of securities is put together, it is simply held in safekeeping for investors under conditions set down in a trust agreement. Traditionally, these portfolios were made up of various types of *fixed-income securities,* with long-term municipal bonds being the most popular type of investment vehicle. There is no trading in the portfolios, so the returns, or yields, are fixed and fairly predictable—at least for the short term. Not surprisingly, these unit investment trusts appeal mainly to income-oriented investors looking for a safe, steady stream of income.

In the early 1990s, brokerage firms began aggressively marketing a new type of investment product, the *stock-oriented UIT*. These new equity trusts caught on quickly with investors seeking capital gains and attractive returns. By year-end 1999, these products accounted for nearly 70% of this $95 billion market. A popular theme among equity trusts is the "dogs of the Dow" strategy (selecting and holding the five or ten companies in the DJIA that pay the highest dividend yields), although growth stock, high dividend yield, and market index trusts also do well. Stock trusts are normally offered with terms that range from 1-year (typical of the Dow-dogs products) to 5 years or more (found on many stock index trusts). Except for the shorter terms (1 to 5 years for equity trusts vs. 15 to 30 years for fixed-income products), these trusts are no different from the traditional bond-oriented UITs: Once the portfolios are put together, they usually remain untouched for the life of the trust.

Various sponsoring brokerage houses put together these pools of securities and then sell units of the pool to investors. (Each unit is like a share in a mutual fund.) For example, a brokerage house might put together a pool of corporate securities that amounts to, say, $100 million. The sponsoring firm would then sell units in this pool to the investing public at anywhere from $250 (for many equity trusts) to $1,000 per unit (common for fixed-income products). The sponsoring organization does little more than routine record-keeping. It services the investments by collecting coupons or dividends and distributing the income (often on a monthly basis) to the holders of the trust units.

There is a dark side to UITs, however. *They tend to be very costly.* These products can have not only substantial up-front transaction costs but also hefty annual fees. For example, many equity UITs assess load charges of 1% to 3% and then another 1½% to 2½% in annual fees. Both of these amounts are well above what you'd pay for a typical equity mutual fund. Brokers argue that they earn those fat fees by removing fear and greed from the investment process and by enabling investors to build a well-diversified portfolio at a reasonable cost.

IN REVIEW

CONCEPTS

12.1 What is a *mutual fund?* Discuss the mutual fund concept, including the importance of diversification and professional management.

12.2 What are the attractions and drawbacks of mutual fund ownership?

12.3 Briefly describe how a mutual fund is organized. Who are the key players in a typical mutual fund organization?

12.4 Define each of the following:
   a. Open-end investment companies
   b. Closed-end investment companies
   c. Exchange-traded funds
   d. Unit investment trusts

12.5 According to the *Investing in Action* box on page 502, what are four ways of structuring exchange-traded funds? What investment advantages do ETFs offer?

12.6 What is the difference between a *load fund* and a *no-load fund*? What are the advantages of each type? What is a 12(b)-1 fund? Can such a fund operate as a no-load fund?

12.7 Describe a *back-end load,* a *low load,* and a *hidden load.* How can you tell what kind of fees and charges a fund has?

Types of Funds and Services

LG 3   LG 4

Some mutual funds specialize in stocks, others in bonds. Some have maximum capital gains as an investment objective, and some high current income. Some funds appeal to speculators, while others are of interest primarily to income-oriented investors. Every fund has a particular investment objective, and each fund is expected to do its best to conform to its stated investment policy and objective. Categorizing funds according to their investment policies and objectives is a common practice in the mutual fund industry. The categories indicate similarities in how the funds manage their money, and also their risk and return characteristics. Some of the more popular types of mutual funds are growth, aggressive growth, value, equity-income, balanced, growth-and-income, bond, money market, index, sector, socially responsible, asset allocation, and international funds. Let's look now at these various types of mutual funds to see what they are and how they operate.

Types of Mutual Funds

growth fund
a mutual fund whose primary goals are capital gains and long-term growth.

Growth Funds The objective of a **growth fund** is simple: capital appreciation. Long-term growth and capital gains are the primary goals. Growth funds invest principally in well-established, large- or mid-cap companies that have above-average growth potential. They may offer little (if anything) in the way of dividends and current income. Because of the uncertain nature of their investment income, growth funds may involve a fair amount of risk exposure. They are usually viewed as long-term investment vehicles most suitable for the more aggressive investor who wants to build up capital and has little interest in current income.

aggressive growth fund
a highly speculative mutual fund that seeks large profits from capital gains.

Aggressive Growth Funds Aggressive growth funds are the so-called performance funds that tend to increase in popularity when markets heat up. **Aggressive growth funds** are highly speculative investment vehicles that seek large profits from capital gains. Also known as *capital appreciation* or *small-cap* funds, many are fairly small, and their portfolios consist mainly of "high-flying" common stocks. These funds often buy stocks of small, unseasoned companies, stocks with relatively high price/earnings multiples, and common stocks whose prices are highly volatile. They seem to be especially fond of turnaround situations and may even use leverage in their portfolios (i.e., buy stocks on margin); they also use options fairly aggressively, various hedging techniques, and perhaps even short selling. These

HOTLINKS

For more information on fund objectives, go to the site listed below. Click on [education] and then [mfs], [How to Read a Prospectus]. Read the objectives ("Investment Style") section.

www.individualinvestor.com

techniques are designed, of course, to yield big returns. But aggressive funds are also highly speculative and are among the most volatile of all mutual funds. When the markets are good, aggressive growth funds do well; but when the markets are bad, these funds often experience substantial losses.

Value Funds Value funds confine their investing to stocks considered to be *undervalued* by the market. That is, the funds look for stocks that are fundamentally sound but have yet to be discovered. These funds hold stocks as much for their underlying intrinsic value as for their *growth potential*. In stark contrast to growth funds, value funds look for stocks with relatively low price/earnings ratios, high dividend yields, and moderate amounts of financial leverage. They prefer undiscovered companies that offer the potential for growth, rather than those that are already experiencing rapid growth.

Value investing is not easy. It involves extensive evaluation of corporate financial statements and any other documents that will help fund managers uncover value (investment opportunities) *before the rest of the market does* (that's the key to the low P/Es). And the approach seems to work. For even though value investing is generally regarded as *less risky* than growth investing (lower P/Es, higher dividend yields, and fundamentally stronger companies all translate into reduced risk exposure), the long-term return to investors in value funds is competitive with that from growth funds and even aggressive growth funds. Thus, value funds are often viewed as a viable investment alternative for relatively conservative investors who are looking for the attractive returns that common stocks have to offer, yet want to keep share price volatility and investment risk in check.

Equity-Income Funds Equity-income funds emphasize current income by investing primarily in high-yielding common stocks. Capital preservation is also important, and so are capital gains, although capital appreciation is not a primary objective of equity-income funds. These funds invest heavily in high-grade common stocks, some convertible securities and preferred stocks, and occasionally even junk bonds or certain types of high-grade foreign bonds. As far as their stock holdings are concerned, they lean heavily toward blue chips (including perhaps even "baby blues"), public utilities, and financial shares. They like securities that generate hefty dividend yields but also consider potential price appreciation over the longer haul. In general, because of their emphasis on dividends and current income, these funds tend to hold higher-quality securities that are subject to less price volatility than the market as a whole. They're generally viewed as a fairly low-risk way of investing in stocks.

Balanced Funds Balanced funds tend to hold a balanced portfolio of both stocks and bonds for the purpose of generating a well-balanced return of both current income and long-term capital gains. In many respects, they're much like equity-income funds, but balanced funds usually put more into fixed-income securities; generally, they keep at least 25% to 50% of their portfolios in bonds. The bonds are used principally to provide current income, and stocks are selected mainly for their long-term growth potential.

The funds can, of course, shift the emphasis in their security holdings one way or the other. Clearly, the more the fund leans toward fixed-income securities, the more income-oriented it will be. For the most part, balanced funds

value fund
a mutual fund that seeks stocks that are undervalued in the market by investing in shares that have low P/E multiples, high dividend yields, and promising futures.

equity-income fund
a mutual fund that emphasizes current income and capital preservation and invests primarily in high-yielding common stocks.

balanced fund
a mutual fund whose objective is to generate a balanced return of both current income and long-term capital gains.

tend to confine their investing to high-grade securities, including growth-oriented blue-chip stocks, high-quality income shares, and high-yielding investment-grade bonds. Balanced funds are usually considered a relatively safe form of investing, in which you can earn a competitive rate of return without having to endure a lot of price volatility.

growth-and-income fund
a mutual fund that seeks both long-term growth and current income, with primary emphasis on capital gains.

Growth-and-Income Funds Growth-and-income funds also seek a balanced return made up of both current income and long-term capital gains, but they place a greater emphasis on growth of capital. Unlike balanced funds, growth-and-income funds put most of their money into equities. In fact, it's not unusual for these funds to have 80% to 90% of their capital in common stocks. They tend to confine most of their investing to quality issues, so growth-oriented blue-chip stocks appear in their portfolios, along with a fair amount of high-quality income stocks. Part of the appeal of these funds is the fairly substantial returns many have generated over the long haul. Of course, these funds involve a fair amount of risk, if for no other reason than the emphasis they place on stocks and capital gains. Thus growth-and-income funds are most suitable for those investors who can tolerate the risk and price volatility.

bond fund
a mutual fund that invests in various kinds and grades of bonds, with income as the primary objective.

Bond Funds As the name implies, **bond funds** invest exclusively in various types and grades of bonds—from Treasury and agency bonds to corporates and municipals. Income is the primary investment objective, although capital gains are not ignored. There are three important advantages of buying shares in bond funds rather than investing directly in bonds. First, the bond funds are generally more liquid than direct investments in bonds. Second, they offer a cost-effective way of achieving a high degree of diversification in an otherwise expensive investment vehicle. (Most bonds carry minimum denominations of $1,000 to $5,000.) Third, bond funds will automatically reinvest interest and other income, thereby allowing the investor to earn fully compounded rates of return.

Bond funds are generally considered to be a fairly conservative form of investment. But they are not without risk; that's because *the prices of the bonds held in the fund's portfolio fluctuate with changing interest rates.* Many bond funds are managed pretty conservatively, but a growing number are becoming increasingly aggressive. In fact, much of the growth that bond funds have experienced recently can be attributed to a more aggressive investment attitude. In today's market, investors can find everything from high-grade government bond funds to highly speculative funds that invest in nothing but junk bonds or even in highly volatile derivative securities. Indeed, exotic derivative securities became a real problem in 1993–1994, when many of the bond funds that had large positions in derivatives experienced eye-popping losses. These losses taught investors a valuable lesson: Watch out for funds with heavy exposure to exotic derivative securities, or at least recognize that if the fund is heavily invested in such securities, you may be in for a very bumpy ride.

Bond funds today remain a sound investment and continue to be popular with investors who seek a relatively conservative investment outlet. Here's a list of the different types of domestic bond funds available to investors:

- *Government bond funds,* which invest in U.S. Treasury and agency securities.

- *Mortgage-backed bond funds,* which put their money into various types of mortgage-backed securities of the U.S. government (e.g., GNMA issues). These funds appeal to investors for several reasons: (1) They provide diversification. (2) They are an affordable way to get into mortgage-backed securities. (3) They allow investors (if they so choose) to reinvest the principal portion of the monthly cash flow, thereby enabling them to preserve rather than consume their capital.

- *High-grade corporate bond funds,* which invest chiefly in investment-grade securities rated triple-B or better.

- *High-yield corporate bond funds,* which are risky investments that buy junk bonds for the yields they offer.

- *Convertible bond funds,* which invest primarily in securities (domestic and possibly foreign) that can be converted or exchanged into common stocks. These funds offer investors some of the price stability of bonds, along with the capital appreciation potential of stocks.

- *Municipal bond funds,* which invest in tax-exempt securities and are suitable for investors who seek tax-free income. Like their corporate counterparts, municipal funds can be packaged as either high-grade or high-yield funds. A special type of municipal bond fund is the so-called *single-state fund*, which invests in the municipal issues of only one state, thus producing (for residents of that state) interest income that is *fully exempt* from both federal and state taxes (and possibly even local/city taxes as well).

- *Intermediate-term bond funds,* which invest in bonds with maturities of 7 to 10 years or less and offer not only attractive yields but relatively low price volatility as well. Shorter (2- to 5-year) funds are also available; these shorter-term funds are often used as substitutes for money market investments by investors looking for higher returns on their money, especially when short-term rates are way down.

Clearly, no matter what you're looking for in a fixed-income security, you're likely to find a bond fund that fits the bill. The number and variety of such funds have skyrocketed in the past 15 years or so, and by mid-2000, there were nearly 3,000 publicly traded bond funds that together had almost *$1 trillion* worth of bonds under management.

money market mutual fund (money fund)
a mutual fund that pools the capital of investors and uses it to invest in short-term money market instruments.

Money Market Funds The first **money market mutual fund,** or **money fund** for short, was set up in November 1972 with just $100,000 in total assets. It was a new idea that applied the mutual fund concept to the buying and selling of short-term money market instruments—bank certificates of deposit, U.S. Treasury bills, and the like. For the first time, investors with modest amounts of capital were given access to the high-yielding money market, where many instruments require minimum investments of $100,000 or more. The idea caught on quickly, and the growth in money funds was nothing short of phenomenal. That growth temporarily peaked in 1982, when the introduction of money market deposit accounts by banks and S&Ls caused money fund assets to level off and eventually decline. It didn't take long for the industry to recover, however, and by mid-2000, there were some 1,200 money funds that together held nearly $1.7 *trillion* in assets.

There are several different kinds of money market mutual funds:

- *General-purpose money funds,* which invest in any and all types of money market investment vehicles, from Treasury bills and bank CDs to corporate commercial paper. The vast majority of money funds are of this type. They invest their money wherever they can find attractive short-term yields.

- *Government securities money funds,* which were established as a way to meet investor concerns for safety. They effectively eliminate any risk of default by confining their investments to Treasury bills and other short-term securities of the U.S. government, or its agencies.

- *Tax-exempt money funds,* which limit their investing to very short (30- to 90-day) tax-exempt municipal securities. Because their income is free from federal income taxes, they appeal predominantly to investors in high tax brackets. The yields on these funds are about 30% to 35% below the returns on other types of money funds, so you need to be in a high enough tax bracket to produce a competitive after-tax return. Some tax-exempt funds confine their investing to the securities of a single state so that residents of high-tax states can enjoy income that's free from both federal and state taxes.

Just about every major brokerage firm has at least four or five money funds of its own, and hundreds more are sold by independent fund distributors. Most require minimum investments of $1,000 (although $2,500 to $5,000 minimums are not uncommon). Because the maximum average maturity of their holdings cannot exceed 90 days, money funds are highly liquid investment vehicles. They're also very low in risk and virtually immune to capital loss, because at least 95% of the fund's assets must be invested in top-rated/prime-grade securities. Since the fund's interest income tends to follow general interest rate conditions, the returns to shareholders are subject to the ups and downs of market interest rates. Even so, the yields on money funds are highly competitive with those of other short-term securities. And with the check-writing privileges they offer, money funds are just as liquid as checking or savings accounts. They are viewed by many investors as a convenient, safe, and profitable way to accumulate capital and temporarily store idle funds.

index fund
a mutual fund that buys and holds a portfolio of stocks (or bonds) equivalent to those in a specific market index.

Index Funds "If you can't beat 'em, join 'em." That saying pretty much describes the idea behind index funds. Essentially, an **index fund** is a type of mutual fund that buys and holds a portfolio of stocks (or bonds) equivalent to those in a market index like the S&P 500. An index fund that's trying to match the S&P 500, for example, would hold the same 500 stocks that are held in that index, in exactly (or very nearly) the same proportions. Rather than trying to beat the market, as most actively managed funds do, *index funds simply try to match the market.* That is, they seek to match the performance of the index on which the fund is based. They do this through low-cost investment management. In fact, in most cases, the whole portfolio is run almost entirely by a computer that matches the fund's holdings with those of the targeted index.

The approach of index funds is strictly buy-and-hold. Indeed, about the only time an index-fund portfolio changes is when the targeted market index alters its "market basket" of securities. (Occasionally an index will drop a few securities and replace them with new ones.) A pleasant by-product of this buy-and-hold approach is that the funds have extremely low portfolio turnover rates and, therefore, very little in *realized* capital gains. As a result, aside from a modest amount of dividend income, these funds produce very little taxable income from year to year, which leads many high-income investors to view them as a type of tax-sheltered investment.

In addition to their tax shelter, these funds provide something else: By simply trying to match the market, index funds actually produce *highly competitive returns.* It's very tough to outperform the market, whether you are a professional money manager or a seasoned individual investor. Index funds readily acknowledge this fact and don't even try to outperform the market; instead, all they try to do is match market returns. Surprisingly, the net result of this strategy, combined with *a very low cost structure,* is that most index funds outperform the vast majority of all other types of stock funds. Historical data show that only about 20% to 25% of stock funds outperform the market. Because an index fund pretty much matches the market, these funds tend to produce better returns than 75% to 80% of competing stock funds. Granted, every now and then the fully managed stock funds will have a year when they outperform index funds. But this is the exception rather than the rule, especially when you look at multi-year returns, covering periods of 3 to 5 years or more—indeed, over most multi-year periods, the vast majority of fully managed stock funds just can't keep up with index funds.

Besides the S&P 500, which is the most popular index, a number of other market indexes are used, including the S&P Midcap 400, the Russell 2000 Small Stock, and the Wilshire 5000 indexes, as well as value-stock indexes, growth-stock indexes, international-stock indexes, and even bond indexes. When picking index funds, be sure to avoid high-cost funds, as such fees significantly *reduce* the chance that the fund will be able to match the market. Also, avoid index funds that use gimmicks as a way to "enhance" yields: That is, rather than follow the index, these funds will "tilt" their portfolios in an attempt to outperform the market. Your best bet is to buy a *true* index fund (one that has no added "bells and whistles"), and a low-cost one at that.

sector fund
a mutual fund that restricts its investments to a particular segment of the market.

Sector Funds One of the hottest products on Wall Street is the so-called **sector fund,** a mutual fund that restricts its investments to a particular sector (or segment) of the market. These funds concentrate their investment holdings in one or more industries that make up the sector being aimed at. For example, a health care sector fund would focus on such industries as drug companies, hospital management firms, medical suppliers, and biotech concerns. The portfolio of a sector fund would consist of promising growth stocks from these particular industries. Among the more popular sector funds are those that concentrate their investments in technology, financial services, leisure and entertainment, natural resources, electronics, chemicals, computers, telecommunications, utilities, and, of course, health care—all the "glamour" industries.

The overriding investment objective of a sector fund is *capital gains.* A sector fund is similar to a growth fund in many respects and should be considered speculative. The sector fund concept is based on the belief that the really attractive returns come from small segments of the market. So rather than diversifying your portfolio across the market, put your money where the action is! It's an interesting notion that may warrant consideration by investors willing to take on the added risks that often accompany these funds.

Socially Responsible Funds For some, investing is far more than just cranking out financial ratios and calculating investment results. To these investors, the security selection process doesn't end with bottom lines, P/E ratios, growth rates, and betas. Rather, it also includes the *active, explicit consideration of moral, ethical, and environmental issues.* The idea is that social concerns should play just as big a role in investment decisions as do profits and other financial matters. Not surprisingly, a number of funds cater to such investors: Known as **socially responsible funds,** they actively and directly incorporate ethics and morality into the investment decision. Their investment decisions revolve around *both* morality and profitability.

socially responsible fund
a mutual fund that actively and directly incorporates ethics and morality into the investment decision.

Socially responsible funds consider only certain companies for inclusion in their portfolios. If a company doesn't meet the fund's moral, ethical, or environmental tests, fund managers simply won't consider buying the stock, no matter how good the bottom line looks. Generally speaking, these funds refrain from investing in companies that derive revenues from tobacco, alcohol, gambling, or weapons, or that operate nuclear power plants. In addition, the funds tend to favor firms that produce "responsible" products or services, that have strong employee relations and positive environmental records, and that are socially responsive to the communities in which they operate. Although these screens might seem to eliminate a lot of stocks from consideration, these funds (most of which are fairly small) still find plenty of securities to choose from. As far as performance is concerned, the general perception is that there's a price to pay, in the form of lower average returns, for socially responsible investing. That's not too surprising, however, for whenever you add more investment hurdles, you're likely to reduce return potential. But to those who truly believe in socially responsible investing, the sacrifice apparently is worth it.

Asset Allocation Funds Studies have shown that the most important decision an investor can make is where to allocate his or her investment assets. As we saw in Chapter 5, *asset allocation* involves deciding how you're going to divide up your investments among different types of securities. For example, what portion of your money do you want to devote to money market securities, what portion to stocks, and what portion to bonds? Asset allocation deals in broad terms (types of securities) and does not address individual security selection. Strange as it may seem, asset allocation has been found to be a far more important determinant of total portfolio returns than individual security selection.

asset allocation fund
a mutual fund that spreads investors' money across stocks, bonds, and money market securities.

Because many individual investors have a tough time making asset allocation decisions, the mutual fund industry has created a product to do the job for them. Known as **asset allocation funds,** these funds spread investors' money across different types of markets. That is, whereas most mutual funds concentrate on one type of investment—whether stocks, bonds, or money market securities—asset allocation funds put money into all these markets. Many of them also include foreign securities in the asset allocation scheme. Some even include inflation-resistant investments, such as gold or real estate. By mid-year 2000, there were nearly 300 asset allocation funds in existence. All were designed for people who want to hire fund managers not only to select individual securities but also to allocate money among the various markets.

Here's how a typical asset allocation fund works. The money manager establishes a desired allocation mix, which might look something like this: 50% of the portfolio goes to U.S. stocks, 30% to bonds, 10% to foreign securities, and 10% to money market securities. Securities are then purchased for the fund in these proportions, and the overall portfolio maintains the desired mix. Actually, each segment of the fund is managed almost as a separate port-folio. Thus securities within, say, the stock portion are bought, sold, and held as the market dictates.

What really separates asset allocation funds from the rest of the pack is that *as market conditions change over time, the asset allocation mix changes as well.* For example, if the U.S. stock market starts to soften, funds will be moved out of stocks to some other area. As a result, the stock portion of the portfolio might drop to, say, 35%, and the foreign securities portion might increase to 25%. Of course, there's no assurance that the money manager will make the right moves at the right time, but the expectation is that he or she will. (It's interesting to note that *balanced funds* are really a form of asset allocation fund, except that they tend to follow a *fixed-mix* approach to asset allocation. That is, the fund may put, say, 60% of the portfolio into stocks and 40% into bonds, and then pretty much stick to that mix, no matter what the markets are doing.)

Asset allocation funds are supposed to provide investors with one-stop shopping. That is, you find an asset allocation fund that fits your needs and invest in it, rather than buying a couple of stock funds, a couple of bond funds, and so on. The success of these funds rests not only on how well the money manager picks securities but also on how well he or she times the market and moves capital among different segments of the market.

International Funds In their search for higher yields and better returns, U.S. investors have shown a growing interest in foreign securities. Sensing an opportunity, the mutual fund industry was quick to respond with a prolifera-tion of so-called **international funds**—a type of mutual fund does all or most of its investing in foreign securities. Just compare the number of international funds that are around today with those in existence a few years ago: In 1985 there were only about 40 of these funds; by 2000, the number had grown to nearly 1,900. The fact is that a lot of people would like to invest in foreign securities but simply don't have the experience or know-how to do so. International funds may be just the vehicle such investors, *provided they have at least a basic appreciation of international economics.* Because these funds deal with the international economy, balance-of-trade positions, and currency valuations, investors should have a fundamental understanding of what these issues are and how they can affect fund returns.

Technically, the term *international fund* describes a type of fund that invests *exclusively in foreign securities.* Such funds often confine their activi-ties to specific geographic regions (e.g., Mexico, Australia, Europe, or the Pacific Rim). In contrast, *global funds* invest not only in foreign securities but also in U.S. companies—usually multinational firms. As a rule, global funds provide more diversity and, with access to both foreign and domestic markets, can go wherever the action is.

Regardless of whether they're global or international (we'll use the term *international* to apply to both), you'll find just about any type of fund you could possibly want in the international sector. There are international stock funds, international bond funds, even international money market funds. There are aggressive growth funds, balanced funds, long-term growth funds, high-grade bond funds, and so forth. There are funds that confine their investing to large, established markets (like Japan, Germany, and Australia) and others that stick to the more exotic (and risky) emerging markets (such as Thailand, Mexico, Chile, and even former Communist countries like Poland).

international fund
a mutual fund that does all or most of its investing in foreign securities.

No matter what your investment philosophy or objective, you're likely to find what you're looking for in the international area.

Basically, these funds attempt to take advantage of international economic developments in two ways: (1) by capitalizing on changing market conditions and (2) by positioning themselves to benefit from devaluation of the dollar. They can make money either from rising share prices in a foreign market or, perhaps just as important, from a falling dollar (which in itself produces capital gains for U.S. investors in international funds). Many of these funds, however, attempt to protect their investors from currency exchange risks by using various types of *hedging strategies*. That is, by using foreign currency options and futures, or some other type of derivative product (all of which are discussed in Chapters 14 and 15), the fund tries to eliminate (or reduce) the effects of fluctuating currency exchange rates. Some funds, in fact, do this on a permanent basis: In essence, these funds hedge away exchange risk so that they can concentrate on the higher returns offered by the foreign securities themselves. Others use currency hedges only occasionally, when they feel there's a real chance of a substantial swing in currency values. But even with currency hedging, international funds are still considered fairly high-risk investments and should be used only by investors who understand and are able to tolerate such risks.

Investor Services

Ask most investors why they buy a particular mutual fund and they'll probably tell you that the fund provides the kind of income and return they're looking for. Now, no one would question the importance of return in the investment decision, but there are some other important reasons for investing in mutual funds, not the least of which are the valuable services they provide. Some of the most sought-after *mutual fund services* are automatic investment and reinvestment plans, regular income programs, conversion and phone-switching privileges, and retirement programs.

Automatic Investment Plans It takes money to make money. For an investor, that means being able to accumulate the capital to put into the market. Unfortunately, that's not always easy. But mutual funds have come up with a program that makes savings and capital accumulation as painless as possible. The program is the **automatic investment plan.** This service allows fund shareholders to automatically funnel fixed amounts of money *from their paychecks or bank accounts* into a mutual fund. It's much like a payroll deduction plan.

This fund service has become very popular, because it enables shareholders to invest on a regular basis without having to think about it. Just about every fund group offers some kind of automatic investment plan for virtually all of its stock and bond funds. To enroll, you simply fill out a form authorizing the fund to siphon a set amount (usually a minimum of $25 to $100 per period) from your bank account or paycheck at regular intervals, such as monthly or quarterly. Once enrolled, you'll be buying more shares every month or quarter (most funds deal in fractional shares). Of course, if it's a load fund, you'll still have to pay normal sales charges on your periodic investments. To remain diversified, you can divide your money among as

automatic investment plan
a mutual fund service that allows shareholders to automatically send fixed amounts of money from their paychecks or bank accounts into the fund.

many funds (within a given fund family) as you like. Finally, you can get out of the program any time, without penalty, by simply calling the fund. Although convenience is perhaps the chief advantage of automatic investment plans, they also make solid investment sense: One of the best ways of building up a sizable amount of capital is to *add funds to your investment program systematically over time*. The importance of making regular contributions to your investment portfolio cannot be overstated; it ranks right up there with compound interest.

Automatic Reinvestment Plans An automatic reinvestment plan is another of the real draws of mutual funds and is offered by just about every open-ended fund. Whereas automatic investment plans deal with money the shareholder is putting into a fund, automatic *re*investment plans deal with the dividends the funds pay to their shareholders. Much like the dividend reinvestment plans we looked at with stocks (in Chapter 6), the **automatic reinvestment plans** of mutual funds enable you to keep your capital fully employed. Through this service, dividend and/or capital gains income is automatically used to buy additional shares in the fund (most funds deal in fractional shares). Such purchases are often commission-free. Keep in mind, however, that even though you may reinvest all dividends and capital gains distributions, the IRS still treats them as cash receipts and taxes them as investment income in the year in which they were received.

> **automatic reinvestment plan**
> a mutual fund service that enables shareholders to automatically buy additional shares in the fund through the reinvestment of dividends and capital gains income.

Automatic reinvestment plans are especially attractive because they enable you to earn fully compounded rates of return. That is, by plowing back profits, you can essentially put them to work in generating even more earnings. Indeed, the effects of these plans on total accumulated capital over the long run can be substantial. Figure 12.6 shows the long-term impact of one such plan. (These are the actual performance numbers for a *real* mutual fund, Fidelity Growth Company.) In the illustration, we assume the investor starts out with $10,000 and, except for the reinvestment of dividends and capital gains, *adds no new capital over time*. Even so, note that the initial investment of $10,000 grew to nearly $191,000 over a 15-year period (which amounts to a compounded rate of return of almost 21%). Of course, not all periods will match this performance, nor will all mutual funds be able to perform as well, even in strong markets. The point is that as long as care is taken in selecting an appropriate fund, *attractive benefits can be derived from the systematic accumulation of capital offered by automatic reinvestment plans*.

Regular Income Although automatic investment and reinvestment plans are great for the long-term investor, what about the investor who's looking for a steady stream of income? Once again, mutual funds have a service to meet this need. Called a **systematic withdrawal plan**, it's offered by most open-ended funds. Once enrolled in one of these plans, an investor automatically receives a predetermined amount of money every month or quarter. Most funds require a minimum investment of $5,000 or more in order to participate. The size of the minimum payment must normally be $50 or more per period (with no limit on the maximum). The funds will pay out the monthly or quarterly income first from dividends and realized capital gains. If this source proves to be inadequate and the shareholder so authorizes, the fund can then tap the principal or original paid-in capital to meet the required periodic payments.

> **systematic withdrawal plan**
> a mutual fund service that enables shareholders to automatically receive a predetermined amount of money every month or quarter.

The Effects of Reinvesting Income

Reinvesting dividends or capital gains can have a tremendous impact on one's investment position. This graph shows the results of a hypothetical investor who initially invested $10,000 and, for a period of 15 years, reinvested all dividends and capital gains distributions in additional fund shares. (No adjustment has been made for any income taxes payable by the shareholder, which is appropriate so long as the fund was held in an IRA or Keogh account.) (*Source: Morningstar Principia.*)

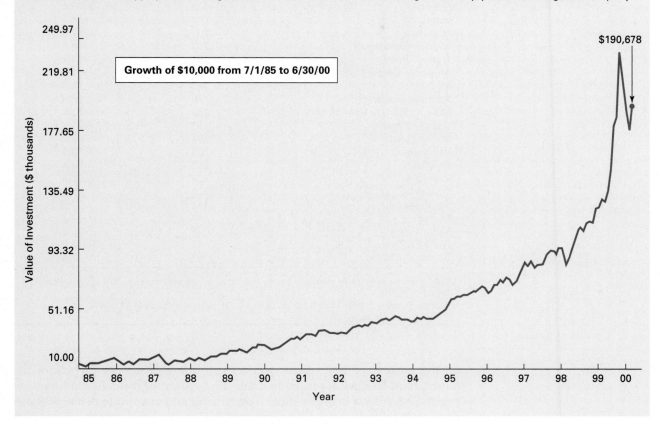

Conversion Privileges and Phone Switching Sometimes investors find it necessary to switch out of one fund and into another. For example, an investor's objectives or the investment climate itself may have changed. **Conversion** (or **exchange**) **privileges** were devised to meet such needs conveniently and economically. Investment management companies that offer a number of different funds—known as **fund families**—often provide conversion privileges. These enable shareholders to move easily from one fund to another. With *phone switching* you simply pick up the phone to move money among funds. The only constraint is that the switches must be confined to the same *family* of funds. For example, you can switch from a Dreyfus growth fund to a Dreyfus money fund, or any other fund managed by Dreyfus.

With some fund families, the alternatives open to investors seem almost without limit. Indeed, some of the larger families offer literally hundreds of funds. Fidelity has over 300 different funds in its family: from high-performance stock funds to bond funds, tax-exempt funds, a couple of dozen sector funds, and a couple of dozen money funds. More than 400 fund families are in operation today. They all provide low-cost conversion/phone-switching privileges. Some even provide these privileges free, although most have limits

conversion (exchange) privilege
feature of a mutual fund that allows shareholders to move money from one fund to another, within the same family of funds.

fund families
different kinds of mutual funds offered by a single investment management company.

TABLE 12.3	Twenty of the Biggest Fund Families	
Fund Families	Total Number of Funds Available	Total Amount of Assets Under Management ($ billions)
Fidelity	326	$628.8
Vanguard	90	508.4
Putnam	201	237.4
Franklin-Templeton	207	156.8
T. Rowe Price	81	154.7
American Century	95	93.2
MFS	168	92.8
American Express	108	91.4
Morgan Stanley Dean Witter	263	83.9
Oppenheimer	151	75.5
Merrill Lynch	284	67.2
Van Kampen	135	59.6
Dreyfus	261	54.4
Evergreen	204	37.6
Prudential	200	36.3
Smith Barney	144	34.5
Kemper	144	34.2
Eaton Vance	142	25.8
Wells Fargo	97	17.8
Goldman Sachs	167	17.5

Note: Number of funds in existence at mid-year 2000; assets under management for stock-and-bond funds only.
Source: Principia Pro for Mutual Funds, Morningstar, Release date, June 30, 2000.

on the number of times such switches can occur each year. Twenty of the largest fund families are listed in Table 12.3. Together these 20 families have nearly $2.5 *trillion* in assets under management and offer more than 3,400 different mutual funds to the investing public. (Many of these funds are actually duplicates of the same portfolio, because fund distributors often use multiple distribution channels or have multiple load/commission structures. As a result, several "different" mutual funds are sold from the same portfolio of securities.)

Conversion privileges are usually considered beneficial for shareholders. They allow investors to meet their ever-changing long-term goals. They also permit investors to manage their mutual fund holdings more aggressively by allowing them to move in and out of funds as the investment environment changes. Unfortunately, there is one major drawback: For tax purposes, the exchange of shares from one fund to another is regarded as a sale transaction followed by a subsequent purchase of a new security. As a result, if any capital gains exist at the time of the exchange, the investor is liable for the taxes on that profit, even though the holdings were not truly liquidated.

Retirement Programs As a result of government legislation, self-employed individuals are permitted to divert a portion of their pretax income into self-directed retirement plans. And all working Americans, whether or not they are

HOT **LINKS**

You can obtain details on the various IRA programs, as well as other tax-sheltered retirement plans at the book's Web site. Click on the Web-chapter titled Tax-Advantaged Investments and then on Tax Deferred Retirement Programs. To access our Web site, go to:

www.awl.com/gitman_joehnk

self-employed, are allowed to establish individual retirement arrangements (IRAs). Indeed, with legislation passed in 1997, *qualified investors* can now choose between deductible and nondeductible (Roth) IRAs. Even those who make too much to qualify for one of these programs can set up special non-deductible IRAs. Today all mutual funds provide a special service that allows individuals to set up tax-deferred retirement programs as either IRA or Keogh accounts—or, through their place of employment, to participate in a tax-shel-tered retirement plan, such as a 401(k). The funds set up the plans and handle all the administrative details so that the shareholder can easily take full advantage of available tax savings.

IN REVIEW

CONCEPTS

12.8 Briefly describe each of the following types of mutual funds:
a. Aggressive growth funds.   b. Equity-income funds.
c. Growth-and-income funds.   d. Bond funds.
e. Sector funds.   f. Socially responsible funds.

12.9 What is an *asset allocation fund,* and how does it differ from other types of mutual funds?

12.10 If growth, income, and capital preservation are the primary objectives of mutual funds, why do we bother to categorize funds by type? Do you think such classifications are helpful in the fund selection process? Explain.

12.11 What are *fund families?* What advantages do fund families offer investors? Are there any disadvantages?

12.12 Briefly describe some of the investor services provided by mutual funds. What are *automatic reinvestment plans,* and how do they differ from *automatic investment plans?* What is phone switching, and why would an investor want to use this service?

Investing in Mutual Funds

LG 5   LG 6

Suppose you are confronted with the following situation: You have money to invest and are trying to select the right place to put it. You obviously want to pick a security that meets your idea of acceptable risk and will generate an attractive rate of return. The problem is that you have to make the selection from a list of nearly 8,000 securities. Sound like a "mission impossible"? Well that's basically what you're up against when trying to select a suitable mutual fund. However, if you approach the problem systematically, it may not be so formidable a task. First, it might be helpful to examine more closely the various investor uses of mutual funds. With this background, we can then look at the selection process and at several measures of return that can be used to assess performance. As we will see, it is possible to whittle down the list of alternatives by matching your investment needs with the investment objectives of the funds.

Investor Uses of Mutual Funds

Mutual funds can be used in a variety of ways. For instance, performance funds can serve as a vehicle for capital appreciation, whereas bond funds can provide current income. Regardless of the kind of income a mutual fund provides, investors tend to use these securities for one of three reasons: (1) as a way to accumulate wealth, (2) as a storehouse of value, or (3) as a speculative vehicle for achieving high rates of return.

Accumulation of Wealth Accumulation of wealth is probably the most common reason for using mutual funds. Basically, the investor uses mutual funds over the long haul to build up investment capital. Depending on investor goals, a modest amount of risk may be acceptable, but usually preservation of capital and capital stability are considered important. The whole idea is to form a "partnership" with the mutual fund in building up as big a capital pool as possible: *You provide the capital by systematically investing and reinvesting in the fund, and the fund provides the return by doing its best to invest your resources wisely.*

Storehouse of Value Investors also use mutual funds as a storehouse of value. The idea is to find a place where investment capital can be fairly secure and relatively free from deterioration yet still generate a relatively attractive rate of return. Short- and intermediate-term bond funds are logical choices for such purposes, and so are money funds. Capital preservation and income over the long term are very important to some investors. Others might seek storage of value only for the short term, using, for example, money funds as a place to "sit it out" until a more attractive opportunity comes along.

Speculation and Short-Term Trading Although speculation is becoming more common, it is still not widely used by mutual fund investors. The reason, of course, is that most mutual funds are long-term in nature and thus not meant to be used as aggressive trading vehicles. However, a growing number of funds (e.g., sector funds) now cater to speculators. Some investors find that mutual funds are, in fact, attractive outlets for speculation and short-term trading.

One way to do this is to trade in and out of funds aggressively as the investment climate changes. Load charges can be avoided (or reduced) by dealing in families of funds offering low-cost conversion privileges and/or by dealing only in no-load funds. Other investors might choose to invest in funds for the long run but still seek high rates of return by investing in aggressive mutual funds. A number of funds follow very aggressive trading strategies, which may appeal to investors willing to accept substantial risk exposure. These are usually the fairly specialized, smaller funds. Examples are sophisticated enhanced-yield funds, leverage funds, option funds, emerging-market funds, small-cap aggressive growth funds, and sector funds. In essence, investors in such funds are simply applying the basic mutual fund concept to their investment needs by letting professional money managers handle their accounts in a way they would like to see them handled: *aggressively.*

The Selection Process

When it comes to mutual funds, there is one question every investor has to answer: Why invest in a mutual fund to begin with—why not just go it alone by buying individual stocks and bonds directly? For beginning investors and investors with little capital, the answer is simple: With mutual funds, investors are able to achieve far more diversification than they could ever get on their own, and they get the help of professional money managers at a very reasonable cost. For more seasoned investors, the answers are probably a bit more involved. Certainly, diversification and professional money management come into play, but there are other reasons as well. The competitive returns offered by mutual funds are a factor with many investors, as are the services they provide. Many seasoned investors simply have decided they can get better returns over the long haul by carefully selecting mutual funds than by investing on their own. As a result, they put all or a big chunk of their money into funds. Some of these investors use part of their capital to buy and sell individual securities on their own and use the rest *to buy mutual funds that invest in areas they don't fully understand or don't feel well informed about.* For example, they'll use mutual funds to get into foreign markets, to buy mortgage-backed securities, to buy junk bonds (where diversification is so very important), or to buy value funds (because that's such a tricky and time-consuming way to invest).

Once you have decided to use mutual funds, you have to decide which fund(s) to buy. In many respects, the selection process is critical in determining how much success you will have with mutual funds. It means putting into action all you know about funds, in order to gain as much return as possible from an acceptable level of risk. The selection process begins with an assessment of your own investment needs, which sets the tone of the investment program. Obviously, what you want to do is select from those 8,000 or so funds the one or two (or three or four) that will best meet your total investment needs.

Objectives and Motives for Using Funds Selecting the right investment means finding those funds that are most suitable to your investment needs. The place to start is with your own investment objectives. In other words, why do you want to invest in a mutual fund, and what are you looking for in a fund? Obviously, an attractive rate of return would be desirable, but there is also the matter of a tolerable amount of risk exposure. Probably, when you look at your own risk temperament in relation to the various types of mutual funds available, you will discover that certain types of funds are more appealing to you than others. For instance, aggressive growth or sector funds are usually *not* attractive to individuals who wish to avoid high exposure to risk.

Another important factor in the selection process is the intended use of the mutual fund. That is, do you want to invest in mutual funds as a means of accumulating wealth, as a storehouse of value, or to speculate for high rates of return? This information puts into clearer focus the question of exactly what you are trying to do with your investment dollars. Finally, there is the matter of the types of services provided by the fund. If you are particularly interested in certain services, you should be sure to look for them in the funds you select. Having assessed what you are looking for in a fund, you are ready to look at what the funds have to offer.

What the Funds Offer Just as each individual has a set of investment needs, each fund has its own *investment objective,* its own *manner of operation,* and its own *range of services.* These three parameters are useful in helping you to assess investment alternatives. But where do you find such information? One obvious place is the fund's *profile,* or its prospectus ("Statement of Additional Information"), which supplies information on investment objectives, portfolio

FIGURE 12.7   Some Relevant Information About Specific Mutual Funds

Investors who want in-depth information about the operating characteristics, investment holdings, and market behavior of specific mutual funds, such as the Fidelity Growth Company profiled here, can usually find what they're looking for in publications like *Morningstar Mutual Funds* or, as shown here, from computer-based information sources like *Morningstar's Principia*. (*Source:* Morningstar, Inc., *Principia Pro Plus*, release date: March 22, 2000.)

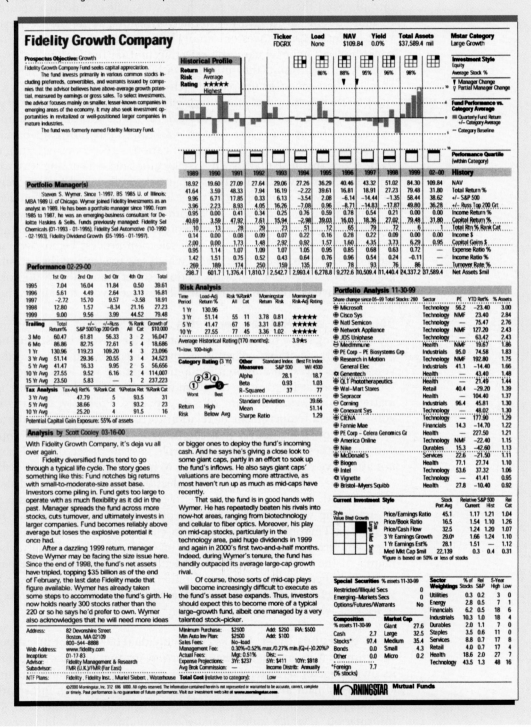

composition, management, and past performance. Publications such as the *Wall Street Journal, Barron's, Money, Fortune,* and *Forbes* also offer useful information about mutual funds. These sources provide a wealth of operating and performance statistics in a convenient and easy-to-read format. For instance, each year *Forbes* rates a couple thousand mutual funds, and every quarter *Barron's* publishes an extensive mutual fund performance report.

A number of reporting services also provide background information and assessments on funds. Among the best in this category are *Morningstar Mutual Funds* (a sample of which is shown in Figure 12.7), Wiesenberger's *Investment Companies* (an annual publication with quarterly updates), Standard & Poor's/Lipper Analytical's *Mutual Fund ProFiles* (a publication that comes out quarterly), and *Value Line Mutual Fund Survey* (which produces a mutual fund report similar to its stock report). In addition, all sorts of performance statistics are available on disks and on the Internet for easy use on home computers. For example, quarterly or annually updated software is available, at very low cost, from Morningstar or from the American Association of Individual Investors (AAII).

Using sources like these, investors can obtain information on such things as investment objectives, load charges and annual expense rates, summary portfolio analyses, services offered, historical statistics, and reviews of past performance. Or, you can look to the publications put out by the funds themselves, as explained in the nearby *Investing in Action* box.

Whittling Down the Alternatives At this point, the fund selection becomes a process of elimination. A large number of funds can be eliminated from consideration simply because they fail to meet stated needs. Some funds may be too risky; others may be unsuitable as a storehouse of value. Thus, rather than trying to evaluate 8,000 different funds, you can narrow down the list to two or three *types* of funds that best match your investment needs. From here, you can whittle down the list a bit more by introducing other constraints. For example, because of cost considerations, you may want to deal only in no-load or low-load funds (more on this topic below). Or you may be seeking certain services that are important to your investment goals.

Now we introduce the final (but certainly not the least important) element in the selection process: the *fund's investment performance*. Useful information includes (1) how the fund has performed over the past 5 to 7 years, (2) the type of return it has generated in good markets as well as bad, (3) the level and stability of dividend and capital gains distributions, and (4) the amount of volatility/risk in the fund's return. Note that the dividend and capital gains distribution is an important indication not only of how much current income the fund distributes annually but also of the fund's *tax efficiency.* As a rule, funds that have low dividends and low asset turnover expose their shareholders to less taxes and therefore have higher tax-efficiency ratings. And while you're looking at performance, it probably wouldn't hurt to check out the fund's *fee structure.* Be on guard for funds that charge abnormally high management fees; they can really hurt returns over time.

Note that in this decision process, considerable weight is given to *past performance.* Now as a rule, the past is given little or no attention in the investment decision. After all, it's the future that matters. Although the *future performance* of a mutual fund is still the variable that holds the key to success, investors should look carefully at past investment results to see how successful

INVESTING in action

Knowing Where to Look Is Half the Battle

Only a lawyer could love a mutual fund prospectus. So many words, so little meaning. No wonder half of the investing public ignores the admonition to "read the prospectus before you invest." But the prospectus really does contain a wealth of information if you know how to separate the wheat from the chaff. Among the most important data are the mutual fund's *expenses.* The Expenses section explains whether the fund has a sales load and how much it is; it also breaks out management and marketing fees for your approval or disapproval.

The Investment Objective section will tell you about the fund's *investment style*—whether it seeks value, growth, income, or whatever. You might get some real detail here, such as the information that the fund buys small stocks with market values between $100 million and $500 million. Then there's the discussion of *risk.* A good prospectus alerts you to specific risks that pertain to your portfolio. For example, the prospectus could tell you that the fund's bias toward high-dividend stocks could limit its potential for capital appreciation. In contrast, a poorly prepared prospectus provides general risk information that applies to all mutual funds. Such general information can go on for pages, and it probably protects the mutual fund company in the event of a lawsuit. Unfortunately, it doesn't help the investor make a prudent investment decision.

Most funds list long-term *total returns* in the prospectus. You might discover that the fund's returns are very volatile and not to your liking. If the prospectus does not list total returns, it may be because the results aren't very good.

A prospectus also gives you a biography of the *portfolio manager.* Why is this important information? If the manager is brand new, then the total return is irrelevant because the current manager didn't compile it.

Still, reading a prospectus has not always been something that most people like to do. But now, rules adopted by the SEC give investors the choice of buying into a mutual fund on the basis of a brief (2 to 6 pages), concise, readable document called a fund profile, or requesting a more detailed prospectus from the fund company. The *fund profile* is designed to tell you (in plain English and in a standardized format) the most important things you need to know about a fund (e.g., its investment objectives, principle risks, fees and expenses, etc.) without overwhelming you in a bunch of unnecessary legalese. Likewise, the fund prospectuses are now far more user-friendly, as they too must be simplified and downsized (by removing all the irrelevant "boilerplate"); and they must be written in plain English, as well.

Should you want even more information than provided in either the profile or prospectus, you can always ask for a copy of the fund's *Statement of Additional Information,* which provides detailed information on the fund's investment objectives, portfolio composition, management, and past performance. Or, ask to see the fund company's last annual or semiannual report. That document usually has a lot to say about a fund's performance, what the portfolio includes, and the portfolio managers' outlook for the future.

the fund's investment managers have been. In essence, the success of a mutual fund rests in large part on the *investment skills of the fund managers.* Therefore, look for consistently good performance, in up as well as down markets, over *extended* periods of time (5 years or more). Most important, check whether the same key people are still running the fund. Although past success is certainly no guarantee of future performance, a strong team of money managers can have a significant bearing on the level of fund returns.

Stick with No-Loads or Low-Loads There's a long-standing "debate" in the mutual fund industry regarding load funds and no-load funds. Do load funds add value? If not, then why pay the load charges? As it turns out, empirical results generally do not support the idea that load funds provide added value. Load fund returns, in general, don't seem to be any better than the returns from no-load funds. In fact, in many cases, the funds with abnormally high loads and 12(b)-1 charges often produce returns that are far less than what you can get from no-load funds. In addition, because of compounding, the differential returns tend to widen with longer holding periods. But that should come as no surprise, because big load charges and/or 12(b)-1 fees reduce your investable capital—and therefore the amount of money you have working for you. In fact, the only way a load fund can overcome this handicap is to produce *superior returns,* which is no easy thing to do, year in and year out. Granted, a handful of load funds have produced very attractive returns over extended periods of time, but they are the exception rather than the rule.

Obviously, it's in your best interest to pay close attention to load charges (and other fees). As a rule, to maximize returns, you should *seriously consider sticking to no-load funds or to low-loads* (funds that have total load charges, including 12(b)-1 fees, of 3% or less). At the very minimum, you should consider a more expensive load fund *only* if it has a much better performance record (and offers more return potential) than a less expensive fund. There may well be times when the higher costs are justified. But far more often than not, you're better off trying to minimize load charges. That shouldn't be difficult to do, however, because there are literally thousands of no-load and low-load funds to choose from. And they come in all types and sizes. What's more, most of the top-performing funds are found in the universe of no-loads or low-loads. So why would you even want to look anywhere else?

Investing in Closed-End Funds

The assets of closed-end funds (CEFs) represent only a fraction of the more than $7 trillion invested in open-end funds. Indeed, in early 2000 there were over 500 CEFs, which together held total assets of "only" $158 billion (about 2% of the amount held by open-end funds). Like open-end funds, CEFs come in a variety of different types and styles, including funds that specialize in municipal bonds, taxable bonds, various types of equity securities, and international securities, as well as regional and single-country funds. Both taxable and tax-free bonds dominate the CEF universe. In fact, municipal bonds alone account for about 46% of CEF assets. In addition to bonds and the domestic equity market, many closed-end funds target foreign stock markets. For example, regional funds focus on a group of countries within a broad geographic area, such as Europe or Latin America. In contrast, *single-country funds* target either *emerging markets* (such as Brazil, China, the Czech Republic, India, Indonesia, Mexico, the Philippines, and Turkey) or *developed markets* (such as France, Germany, Japan, and the United Kingdom).

Some Key Differences Between Closed-End and Open-End Funds Because closed-end funds trade like stocks, you must deal with a broker to buy or sell shares, and the usual brokerage commissions apply. Open-end funds, in contrast, are bought from and sold to the fund operators themselves. Another important difference between open- and closed-end funds is their liquidity. You can buy and sell relatively large dollar amounts of an open-end mutual fund at its NAV without worrying about affecting the price. However, a relatively large buy or sell order for a CEF could easily bump its price up or down. Thus, the greater liquidity of open-end funds gives them a distinct advantage. Like open-end funds, most CEFs offer dividend reinvestment plans, but in many cases, that's about it. CEFs simply don't provide the full range of services that mutual fund investors are accustomed to.

All things considered, probably the most important difference is the way these funds are priced in the marketplace. This is important because it *directly affects* investor costs and returns. Whereas open-end funds can be bought and sold at NAV (plus any front-end load or minus any redemption charge), CEFs *have two values*—a market value (or stock price) and net asset value (NAV). The two are rarely the same, because CEFs typically trade at either a premium or a discount. A *premium* occurs when a fund trades for more than its NAV; a *discount* occurs when it trades for less. As a rule, CEFs trade at discounts. Indeed, at mid-year 2000, the typical CEF traded at an average *discount of around 10%*. Premiums and discounts are reported weekly in *Barron's,* the *Wall Street Journal,* and other newspapers.

The premium or discount is calculated as follows:

Equation 12. 1   Premium (or discount) = (Share price − NAV) / NAV

Suppose Fund A has a NAV of $10. If its share price is $8, it will sell at a 20% discount. That is,

Premium (or discount) = ($8 − $10)/$10

= −$2/$10 = −.20 = <u>−20%</u>

Because this value is negative, the fund is trading at a *discount* (or below its NAV). On the other hand, if this same fund were priced at $12 per share, it would be trading at a *premium* of 20%—that is, ($12 − $10)/$10 = $2/$10 = 0.20. Because the value is positive, the fund is trading at a premium (above its NAV).

What to Look for in a Closed-End Fund If you know what to look for and your timing and selection are good, you may find that some *deeply discounted CEFs* provide a great way to earn attractive returns. For example, if a fund trades at a 20% discount, you pay only 80 cents for each dollar's worth of assets. At certain times, the market offers the opportunity to pick up funds at attractive prices. (This could well be the case when double-digit discounts exist.) At other times, discounts may be too narrow to represent any special value. If you can buy a fund at an abnormally wide discount and sell it when the discount narrows or turns to a premium, you can enhance your overall return. In fact, even if the discount does not narrow, your return will be improved, because the yield on your investment is higher than it would be with an otherwise equivalent open-end fund. The reason: You're investing less money. Here's a simple example. Suppose a CEF trades at $8, a 20% discount from its NAV of $10. If the fund distributed $1 in dividends for the year, it would yield 12.5% ($1 divided by its $8 price). However, if it was a no-load, open-end fund, it would be trading at its higher NAV and therefore would yield only 10% ($1 divided by its $10 NAV). Thus, when investing in CEFs, pay close attention to the size of the premium and discount. In particular, keep your eyes open for funds trading at deep discounts, because that feature alone can enhance potential returns.

For the most part, except for the premium or discount, a CEF should be analyzed just like any other mutual fund. That is, pay attention to the expense ratio, portfolio turnover rate, past performance, cash position, and so on. In addition, study the history of the discount. Information on closed-end funds can be found in such publications as *Morningstar Closed-End Funds,* Standard & Poor's *Stock Reports,* and *Value Line Investment Survey.* Also, keep in mind that with CEFs, you probably won't get a prospectus (as you might with an open-end fund), because they do not continuously offer new shares to investors.

One final point to keep in mind when developing a closed-end fund investment program: Stay clear of new issues (IPOs) of closed-end funds and funds that sell at steep *premiums.* Never buy new CEFs when they are brought to the market as IPOs. Why? Because IPOs are always brought to the market at *hefty premiums.* You therefore face the almost inevitable risk of losing money as the shares fall to a discount within a month or two. This drop in price occurs because the IPO funds have to be offered at a premium just to cover the amount of the underwriting spread. You also want to avoid funds that are trading at premiums—especially at steep premiums—such as volatile single-country portfolios. That too can lead to built-in losses when, if sentiment sours, these premiums quickly turn to discounts.

Measuring Performance

As in any investment decision, return performance is a major dimension in the mutual fund selection process. The level of dividends paid by the fund, its capital gains, and its growth in capital are all important aspects of return. Such return information enables you to judge the investment behavior of a fund and to appraise its performance in relation to other funds and investment vehicles. Here, we will look at different measures that mutual fund investors use to assess return. Also, because risk is so important in defining the investment behavior of a fund, we will examine mutual fund risk as well.

Sources of Return An open-end mutual fund has three potential sources of return: (1) dividend income, (2) capital gains distribution, and (3) change in the price (or net asset value) of the fund. Depending on the type of fund, some mutual funds derive more income from one source than another. For example, we would normally expect income-oriented funds to have much higher dividend income than capital gains distributions.

Open-end mutual funds regularly publish reports that recap investment performance. One such report is the *Summary of Income and Capital Changes,* an example of which is provided in Table 12.4. This statement is found in the fund's profile or prospectus. It gives a brief overview of the fund's investment activity, including expense ratios and portfolio turnover rates. Of interest to us here is the top part of the report (which runs from "net asset value, beginning of period" to "net asset value, end of period"—lines 1 to 10). This part reveals the amount of dividend income and capital gains distributed to the shareholders, along with any change in the fund's net asset value.

TABLE 12.4	A Report of Mutual Fund Income and Capital Changes (For a share outstanding throughout the year)		
	2001	**2000**	**1999**
1. Net asset value, beginning of period	$24.47	$27.03	$24.26
2. Income from investment operations:			
3. Net investment income	$0.60	$0.66	$0.50
4. Net gains on securities (realized and unrealized)	6.37	(1.74)	3.79
5. Total from investment operations	6.97	(1.08)	4.29
6. Less distributions:			
7. Dividends from net investment income	($0.55)	($0.64)	($0.50)
8. Distributions from realized gains	(1.75)	(.84)	(1.02)
9. Total distributions	(2.30)	(1.48)	(1.52)
10. Net asset value, end of period	$29.14	$24.47	$27.03
11. Total return	28.48%	(4.00%)	17.68%
12. Ratios/supplemental data			
13. Net assets, end of period ($000)	$307,951	$153,378	$108,904
14. Ratio of expenses to average net assets	1.04%	0.85%	0.94%
15. Ratio of net investment income to average net assets	1.47%	2.56%	2.39%
16. Portfolio turnover rate*	85%	144%	74%

*Portfolio turnover rate relates the number of shares bought and sold by the fund to the total number of shares held in the fund's portfolio. A high turnover rate (in excess of 100%) means the fund has been doing a lot of trading.

dividend income
income derived from the dividend and interest income earned on the security holdings of a mutual fund.

capital gains distributions
payments made to mutual fund shareholders that come from the profits that a fund makes from the sale of its securities.

unrealized capital gains (paper profits)
a capital gain made only "on paper"-that is, not realized until the fund's holdings are sold.

Dividend income (see line 7 of Table 12.4) is derived from the dividend and interest income earned on the security holdings of the mutual fund. It is paid out of the *net investment income* that's left after all operating expenses have been met. When the fund receives dividend or interest payments, it passes these on to shareholders in the form of dividend payments. The fund accumulates all of the current income it has received for the period and then pays it out on a prorated basis. If a fund earned, say, $2 million in dividends and interest in a given year and if that fund had 1 million shares outstanding, each share would receive an annual dividend payment of $2.

Capital gains distributions (see line 8) work on the same principle, except that these payments are derived from the capital gains earned by the fund. It works like this: Suppose the fund bought some stock a year ago for $50 and sold that stock in the current period for $75 per share. Clearly, the fund has achieved capital gains of $25 per share. If it held 50,000 shares of this stock, it would have realized a total capital gain of $1,250,000 ($25 × 50,000 = $1,250,000). Given that the fund has 1 million shares outstanding, each share is entitled to $1.25 in the form of a capital gains distribution. Note that this capital gains distribution applies only to *realized* capital gains (that is, the security holdings were actually sold and the capital gains actually earned).

Unrealized capital gains (or **paper profits**) are what make up the third and final element of a mutual fund's return. When the fund's holdings go up or down in price, the net asset value of the fund moves accordingly. Suppose an investor buys into a fund at $10 per share and sometime later the fund is quoted at $12.50. The difference of $2.50 per share is the unrealized capital gains. It represents the profit that shareholders would receive (and are entitled to) if the fund were to sell its holdings. (Actually, as Table 12.4 shows, some of the change in net asset value can also be made up of undistributed income.)

The return on *closed-end* investment companies is derived from the same three sources as that of open-end funds and from a *fourth source* as well:

changes in price discounts or premiums. But because discount or premium is already embedded in the share price of a fund, it follows that, for a closed-end fund, the third element of return—change in share price—is made up not only of change in net asset value but also of change in price discount or premium.

What About Future Performance? There's no doubt that a statement like the one in Table 12.4 provides a convenient recap of a fund's past behavior. Looking at past performance is useful, but it doesn't tell you what the future will be. Ideally, you want an indication of what the same three elements of return—dividend income, capital gains distribution, and change in NAV—*will be*. But it's extremely difficult—if not impossible—to get a firm grip on what the future holds in dividends, capital gains, and NAV. This is because a mutual fund's future performance is directly linked to the *future make-up of the securities in its portfolio,* something that is next to impossible to get a clear reading on. It's not like evaluating the expected performance of a share of stock, in which case you're keying in on one company. With mutual funds, investment performance depends on the behavior of many different stocks and bonds.

Where, then, do you look for insight on future performance? Most market observers suggest that the first place to look is the market itself. In particular, try to get a fix on the future direction of *the market as a whole*. This is important because the behavior of a well-diversified mutual fund tends to reflect the general tone of the market. Thus, if the feeling is that the market is going to be drifting up, so should the investment performance of mutual funds. Also spend some time evaluating the *track records* of mutual funds in which you are interested. Past performance has a lot to say about the investment skills of the fund's money managers. In essence, look for funds that you think will be able to capture the best of what the future market environment holds.

Measures of Return A simple but effective measure of performance is to describe mutual fund return in terms of the three major sources noted above: dividends earned, capital gains distributions received, and change in price. When dealing with investment horizons of 1 year or less, we can easily convert these fund payoffs into a return figure by using the standard holding period return (HPR) formula. The computations necessary are illustrated below using the 2001 figures from Table 12.4. Referring to the exhibit, we can see that in 2001, this hypothetical no-load, open-end fund paid 55 cents per share in dividends and another $1.75 in capital gains distributions. It had a price at the beginning of the year of $24.47 that rose to $29.14 by the end of the year. Thus, summarizing this investment performance, we have

Price (NAV) at the *beginning* of the year	$24.47
Price (NAV) at the *end* of the year	29.14
Net increase	$ 4.67
Return for the year:	
Dividends received	$ .55
Capital gains distributions	1.75
Net increase in price (NAV)	4.67
Total return	$ 6.97
Holding period return (HPR)	28.5%
(Total return/beginning price)	

This HPR measure (which is shown in Table 12.4 as "Total Return" on line 11) not only captures all the important elements of mutual fund return but also provides a handy indication of yield. Note that the fund had a total dollar return of $6.97. On the basis of a beginning investment of $24.47 (the initial share price of the fund), the fund produced an annual return of 28.5%.

HPR with Reinvested Dividends and Capital Gains   Many mutual fund investors have their dividends and/or capital gains distributions reinvested in the fund. How, then, do you obtain a measure of return when you receive your (dividend/capital gains) payout in additional shares of stock rather than cash? With slight modifications, you can continue to use holding period return. The only difference is that you have to keep track of the number of shares acquired through reinvestment. To illustrate, let's continue with the example above and assume that you initially bought 200 shares in the mutual fund. Assume also that you were able to acquire shares through the fund's reinvestment program at an average price of $26.50 a share. Thus, the $460 in dividends and capital gains distributions [($.55 + $1.75) × 200] provided you with another 17.36 shares in the fund ($460/$26.50). Holding period return under these circumstances would relate the market value of the stock holdings at the beginning of the period with holdings at the end:

Equation 12. 2

$$\text{Holding period return} = \frac{\left(\begin{array}{c}\text{Number of} \\ \text{shares at } end \\ \text{of period}\end{array} \times \begin{array}{c}\text{ending} \\ \text{price}\end{array}\right) - \left(\begin{array}{c}\text{Number of} \\ \text{shares at } beginning \\ \text{of period}\end{array} \times \begin{array}{c}\text{Initial} \\ \text{price}\end{array}\right)}{\begin{array}{c}\text{Number of shares} \\ \text{at } beginning \text{ of period}\end{array} \times \begin{array}{c}\text{Initial} \\ \text{price}\end{array}}$$

Thus the holding period would be

$$\text{Holding period return} = \frac{(217.36 \times \$29.14) - (200 \times \$24.47)}{(200 \times \$24.47)}$$

$$= \frac{(\$6,333.87) - (\$4,894.00)}{\$4,894.00} = \underline{29.4\%}$$

This holding period return, like the preceding one, provides a rate-of-return measure that can now be used to compare the performance of this fund to those of other funds and investment vehicles.

Measuring Long-Term Returns   Rather than using 1-year holding periods, it is sometimes necessary to assess the performance of mutual funds over extended periods of time. In these cases, it would be inappropriate to employ holding period return as a measure of performance. When faced with multiple-year investment horizons, we can use the present-value-based *internal rate of return* (IRR) procedure to determine the fund's average annual compound rate of return. To illustrate, refer once again to Table 12.4. Assume that this time we want to find the annual rate of return over the full 3-year period (1999 through 2001). In this case, we see that the mutual fund had the following annual dividends and capital gains distribution.

	2001	2000	1999
Annual dividends paid	$ .55	$ .64	$ .50
Annual capital gains distributed	$1.75	$ .84	$1.02
Total distributions	$2.30	$1.48	$1.52

Now, given that the fund had a price of $24.26 at the beginning of the period (1/1/99) and was trading at $29.14 at the end of 2001 (3 years later), we have the following time line of cash flows:

Initial Cash Flow	Subsequent Cash Flows		
	Year 1	Year 2	Year 3
$24.26 (Beginning Price)	$1.52 (Distributions)	$1.48 (Distributions)	$2.30 + $29.14 (Distributions + Ending Price)

The idea is to find the discount rate that will equate the annual dividends/capital gains distributions *and* the ending price in year 3 to the beginning (1999) price of the fund ($24.26).

Using standard present-value calculations, we find that the mutual fund in Table 12.4 provided its investors with an annual rate of return of 13.1% over the 3-year period from 1999 through 2001. That is, at 13.1%, the present values of the cash flows in years 1, 2, and 3 equal the beginning price of the fund ($24.26). Such information helps us assess fund performance and compare the return performance of one fund to other funds and investment vehicles. According to SEC regulations, if mutual funds report historical return behavior, they must do so in a standardized format that employs fully compounded, total-return figures similar to those obtained from the above present value-based measure of return. The funds are not required to report such information. But, if they do cite performance in their promotional material, they must follow a full-disclosure manner of presentation that takes into account not only dividends and capital gains distributions but also any increases or decreases in the fund's NAV that have occurred over the past 1-, 3-, 5-, and 10-year periods.

Returns on Closed-End Funds The returns of CEFs are customarily reported on the basis of their NAVs. That is, *price premiums and discounts are ignored when computing various return measures*. At the same time, it's becoming increasingly common to see return performance expressed in terms of actual market prices, a practice that captures the impact of changing market premiums or discounts on holding period returns. As you might expect, the greater the premiums or discounts and the greater the changes in these values over time, the greater their impact on reported returns. It's not at all uncommon for CEFs to have different market-based and NAV-based holding period returns. When NAVs are used, you find the returns on CEFs in exactly the same way as you do the returns on open-end funds. In contrast, when market values are used to measure return, all you need do *is substitute the market price of the fund* (with its embedded premium or discount) *for the corresponding NAV in the holding period or internal rate of return* measure. Some CEF investors like to run *both* NAV-based and market-based measures of return to see how changing premiums (or discounts) have added to or hurt the returns on their mutual fund holdings. Even so, as a rule, NAV-based return numbers are generally viewed as the preferred measures of performance. Because fund managers often have little or no control over changes in premium or discounts, NAV-based measures are felt to give a truer picture of the performance of the fund itself.

The Matter of Risk Because most mutual funds are so diversified, their investors are largely immune to the business and financial risks normally present with individual securities. Even with extensive diversification, however, the investment behavior of most funds is still exposed to a considerable amount of *market risk*. In fact, because mutual fund portfolios are so well diversified, they often tend to perform very much like the market—or some segment of the market that's being targeted by the fund. Although a few funds, like gold funds, tend to be defensive (countercyclical), market risk is an important behavioral ingredient in a large number of mutual funds, both open- and closed-end. Investors should be aware of the effect the general market has on the investment performance of a mutual fund. For example, if the market is trending downward and you anticipate that trend to continue, it might be best to place any new investment capital into something like a money fund until the market reverses itself. At that time, you can make a more long-term commitment.

Another important risk consideration revolves around the management practices of the fund itself. If the portfolio is managed conservatively, the risk of a loss in capital is likely to be much less than for aggressively managed funds. Obviously, the more speculative the investment goals of the fund, the greater the risk of instability in the net asset value. But, a conservatively managed portfolio does not necessarily eliminate all price volatility. The securities in the portfolio are still subject to inflation, interest rate, and general market risks. However, these risks are generally reduced or minimized as the investment objectives and portfolio management practices of the funds become more conservative.

IN REVIEW

CONCEPTS

12.13 How important is the general behavior of the market in affecting the price performance of mutual funds? Explain. Why is a fund's past performance important to the mutual fund selection process? Does the future behavior of the market matter in the selection process? Explain.

12.14 The *Investing in Action* box on the use of a *fund prospectus* (page 526) suggested five or six things you should do to get the most from these fund documents. List and briefly discuss each of these points.

12.15 What is the major/dominant type of closed-end fund? What is the difference between regional funds and single-country funds? How do CEFs differ from open-end funds?

12.16 Identify three potential sources of return to mutual fund investors and briefly discuss how each could affect total return to shareholders. Explain how the discount or premium of a closed-end fund can also be treated as a return to investors.

12.17 Discuss the various types of risk to which mutual fund shareholders are exposed. What is the major risk exposure of mutual funds? Are all funds subject to the same level of risk? Explain.

Summary

LG 1 **Describe the basic features of mutual funds, and note what they have to offer as investment vehicles.** Mutual fund shares represent ownership in a diversified, professionally managed portfolio of securities. Many investors who lack the time, know-how, or commitment to manage their own money turn to mutual funds. Mutual funds shareholders benefit from a level of diversification and investment performance they might otherwise find difficult to achieve. In addition, they can establish an investment program with a limited amount of capital and obtain a variety of investor services not available elsewhere.

LG 2 **Distinguish between open- and closed-end mutual funds, as well as other types of professionally managed investment companies, and discuss the various types of fund loads, fees, and charges.** Open-end funds have no limit on the number of shares they may issue. Closed-end funds have a fixed number of shares outstanding and trade in the secondary markets like any other share of common stock. Exchange-traded funds possess characteristics of both open-end and closed-end funds. Other types of investment companies are unit investment trusts, REITs (which invest primarily in various types of real estate products), and variable annuities. Mutual fund investors face an array of loads, fees, and charges, including front-end loads, back-end loads, annual 12(b)-1 charges, and annual management fees. Some of these costs are one-time charges (e.g., front-end loads). Others are paid annually [e.g., 12(b)-1 and management fees]. Investors should understand fund costs, which can be a real drag on fund performance and return.

LG 3 **Discuss the types of funds available and the variety of investment objectives these funds seek to fulfill.** Each fund has an established investment objective that determines its investment policy and identifies it as a certain type of fund. Some of the more popular types of funds are growth funds, aggressive growth funds, value funds, equity-income funds, balanced funds, growth-and-income funds, asset allocation funds, index funds, bond funds, money funds, sector funds, socially responsible funds, and international funds. The different categories of funds have different risk-return characteristics.

LG 4 **Discuss the investor services offered by mutual funds and how these services can fit into an investment program.** Mutual funds also offer special services, such as automatic investment and reinvestment plans, systematic withdrawal programs, low-cost conversion and phone-switching privileges, and retirement programs.

LG 5 **Gain an appreciation of the investor uses of mutual funds, along with the variables to consider when assessing and selecting funds for investment purposes.** Mutual funds can be used to accumulate wealth, as a storehouse of value, or as a vehicle for speculation and short-term trading. The fund selection process generally starts by assessing the investor's needs and wants. The next step is to consider what the funds have to offer, particularly with regard to investment objectives, risk exposure, and investor services. The investor then narrows down the alternatives by aligning his or her needs with the types of funds available and, from this short list of funds, applies the final selection tests: fund performance and cost.

LG 6 **Identify the sources of return and compute the rate of return earned on a mutual fund investment.** The payoff from investing in a mutual fund includes dividend income, distribution of realized capital gains, growth in capital (unrealized capital gains), and—for closed-end funds—the change in premium or discount. Various measures of return recognize these elements and provide simple yet effective ways of gauging the annual rate of return from a mutual fund. Risk is also important to mutual fund investors. A fund's extensive diversification may protect investors from business and financial risks. But considerable market risk still remains because most funds tend to perform much like the market, or like that segment of the market in which they specialize.

Discussion Questions

LG 1

LG 2

Q12.1 Contrast *mutual fund ownership* with *direct investment in stocks and bonds*. Assume your class is going to debate the merits of investing through mutual funds versus investing directly in stocks and bonds. Develop some arguments on each side of this debate and be prepared to discuss them in class. If you had to choose one side to be on, which would it be? Why?

LG 2

Q12.2 Using the mutual fund quotes in Figure 12.5, answer the questions listed below for each of the following 5 funds:
   (1) Fairmont Fund (Fairmt).
   (2) FPA Capital Fund (Capit).
   (3) Dreyfus Aggressive Growth Fund (AggGr).
   (4) Dreyfus GNMA Bond Fund (GNBd).
   (5) FMI Focus Fund (FMI Focusfd).
Based on the information reported in Figure 12.5:
   a. How much would you receive for each fund if you were selling them?
   b. Which of the five listed funds have 12(b)-1 fees?
   c. Which funds have redemption fees?
   d. Do any of the funds have both 12(b)-1 and redemption fees?
   e. Can you tell whether any of the funds are no-loads?
   f. Which fund has the highest front-end load?
   g. Which fund has the highest year-to-date return? Which has the lowest?

LG 3

Q12.3 For each pair of funds listed below, select the one that is likely to be the *less* risky. Briefly explain your answer.
   a. Growth versus growth-and-income funds.
   b. Equity-income versus high-grade corporate bond funds.
   c. Balanced versus sector funds.
   d. Global versus aggressive growth funds.
   e. Intermediate-term bonds versus high-yield municipal bond funds.

LG 2   LG 3

Q12.4 Describe an ETF and explain how these funds combine the characteristics of both open-end and close-end funds. Consider the Vanguard family of funds. Which of their funds most closely resembles a "spider" (SPDR)? In what respects are the Vanguard fund (that you selected) and spiders the same? How are they different? If you could invest in only one of them, which would it be? Explain.

LG 3   LG 5

Q12.5 Imagine that you've just inherited $20,000. Now you're faced with the "problem" of how to spend it. You could make a down payment on a condo, or you could buy that sports car you've always wanted. Or you could build a mutual fund portfolio. After some soul-searching, you decide to build a $20,000 mutual fund portfolio. Using actual mutual funds and actual quoted prices, come up with a plan to invest as much of the $20,000 as you can in a portfolio of mutual funds. (In addition to one or more open-end funds, include at least one CEF *or* one ETF.) Be specific! Briefly describe your planned portfolio, including the investment objectives you are trying to achieve.

Problems

LG 6

P12.1 A year ago, an investor bought 200 shares of a mutual fund at $8.50 per share. Over the past year, the fund has paid dividends of 90 cents per share and had a capital gains distribution of 75 cents per share.
   a. Find the investor's holding period return, given that this no-load fund now has a net asset value of $9.10.

b. Find the holding period return, assuming all the dividends and capital gains distributions are reinvested into additional shares of the fund at an average price of $8.75 per share.

 LG 6   P12.2 A year ago, the Really Big Growth Fund was being quoted at a NAV of $21.50 and an offer price of $23.35. Today it's being quoted at $23.04 (NAV) and $25.04 (offer). What is the holding period return on this load fund, given that it was purchased a year ago and that its dividends and capital gains distributions over the year have totaled $1.05 per share? (*Hint:* You, as an investor, buy fund shares at the offer price and sell at the NAV.)

 LG 6   P12.3 The All-State Mutual Fund has the following 5-year record of performance.

	2000	1999	1998	1997	1996
Net investment income	$ .98	$ .85	$ .84	$ .75	$ .64
Dividends from net investment income	(.95)	(.85)	(.85)	(.75)	(.60)
Net realized and unrealized gains (or losses) on security transactions	4.22	5.08	(2.18)	2.65	(1.05)
Distributions from realized gains	(1.05)	(1.00)	—	(1.00)	—
Net increase (decrease) in NAV	$ 3.20	$ 4.08	($ 2.19)	$ 1.65	($ 1.01)
NAV at beginning of year	12.53	8.45	10.64	.99	10.00
NAV at end of year	$15.73	$12.53	$ 8.45	$10.64	$ 8.99

Find this no-load fund's 5-year (1996–2000) average annual compound rate of return. Also find its 3-year (1998–2000) average annual compound rate of return. If an investor bought the fund in 1996 at $10.00 a share and sold it 5 years later (in 2000) at $15.73, how much total profit per share would she have made over the 5-year holding period?

 LG 6   P12.4 You've uncovered the following per-share information about a certain mutual fund.

	1999	2000	2001
Ending share prices:			
Offer	$46.20	$64.68	$61.78
NAV	43.20	60.47	57.75
Dividend income	2.10	2.84	2.61
Capital gains distribution	1.83	6.26	4.32
Beginning share prices:			
Offer	55.00	46.20	64.68
NAV	51.42	43.20	60.47

On the basis of this information, find the fund's holding period return for 1999, 2000, and 2001. (In all three cases, assume you buy the fund at the beginning of the year and sell it at the end of each year.) In addition, find the fund's average annual compound rate of return over the 3-year period, 1999–2001. What would the 2000 holding period return have been if the investor had initially bought 500 shares of stock and reinvested both dividends and capital gains distributions into additional shares of the fund at an average price of $52.50 per share?

P12.5 Listed is the 10-year, per-share performance record of Larry, Moe, & Curly's Growth Fund, as obtained from the fund's May 30, 2001, prospectus.

	Years Ended March 31									
	2001	**2000**	**1999**	**1998**	**1997**	**1996**	**1995**	**1994**	**1993**	**1992**
1. **Net asset value, beginning of period**	$58.60	$52.92	$44.10	$59.85	$55.34	$37.69	$35.21	$34.25	$19.68	$29.82
2. **Income from investment operations:**										
3. Net investment income	$1.39	$1.35	$1.09	$0.63	$0.42	$ 0.49	$ 0.79	$0.37	$ 0.33	$0.38
4. Net gains on securities (realized and unrealized)	8.10	9.39	8.63	(6.64)	11.39	19.59	5.75	2.73	15.80	(0.02)
5. Total from investment operations	9.49	10.74	9.72	(6.01)	11.81	20.08	6.54	3.10	16.13	0.36
6. **Less distributions:**										
7. Dividends from net investment income	($0.83)	($1.24)	($0.90)	($0.72)	($0.46)	($0.65)	($0.37)	($0.26)	($0.33)	($0.58)
8. Distributions from realized gains	(2.42)	(3.82)	—	(9.02)	(6.84)	(1.78)	(3.69)	(1.88)	(1.23)	(9.92)
9. Total distributions	(3.25)	(5.06)	(0.90)	(9.74)	(7.30)	(2.43)	(4.06)	(2.14)	(1.56)	(10.50)
10. **Net asset value, end of period**	$64.84	$58.60	$52.92	$44.10	$59.85	$55.34	$37.69	$35.21	$34.25	$19.68

Use this information to find LM&C's holding period return in 2001 and 1998. Also find the fund's rate of return over the 5-year period 1997–2001, and the 10-year period 1992–2001. Finally, rework the four return figures assuming the LM&C fund has a front-end load charge of 3% (of NAV). Comment on the impact of load charges on the return behavior of mutual funds.

P12.6 Using the resources available at your campus or public library (or those available on the Internet), select five mutual funds—a growth fund, an equity-income fund, an international (stock) fund, an index fund, and a high-yield corporate bond fund—that you feel would make good investments. Briefly explain why you selected these funds. List the funds' holding period returns for the past year and their annual compound rates of return for the past 3 years. (Use a schedule like the one in Table 12.4 to show relevant performance figures.)

P12.7 One year ago, Super Star Closed-End Fund had a NAV of $10.40 and was selling at an 18% discount. Today its NAV is $11.69 and it is priced at a 4% premium. During the year, Super Star paid dividends of 40 cents and had a capital gains distribution of 95 cents. On the basis of the above information, calculate each of the following.

a. Super Star's NAV-based holding period return for the year.

b. Super Star's market-based holding period return for the year. Did the market premium/discount hurt or add value to the investor's return? Explain.

c. Repeat the market-based holding period return calculation, except this time assume the fund started the year at an 18% *premium* and ended it at a 4% *discount*. (Assume the beginning and ending NAVs remain at $10.40 and $11.69, respectively.) Is there any change in this measure of return? Why?

LG 6

P12.8 The Well Managed Closed-End Fund turned in the following performance for the year 2000.

	Beginning of the Year	End of the Year
NAV	$7.50	$9.25
Market price of the fund shares	$7.75	$9.00
Dividends paid over the year	—	$1.20
Capital gains distributed over the year	—	$0.90

a. Based on this information, what was the NAV-based HPR for the WMCEF in 2000?

b. Find the percentage (%) premium or discount at which the fund was trading at the beginning of the year and at the end of the year.

c. What was the market-based HPR for the fund in 2000? Did the market premium or discount add to or hurt the holding period return on this CEF? Explain.

Case Problem 12.1 *Reverend Robin Ponders Mutual Funds*

LG 3   LG 5

Reverend Robin is the minister of a church in the San Antonio area. He is married, has one young child, and earns a "modest income." Because religious organizations are not notorious for their generous retirement programs, the reverend has decided he should do some investing on his own. He would like to set up a program that enables him to supplement the church's retirement program and at the same time provide some funds for his child's college education (which is still some 12 years away). He is not out to break any investment records but wants some backup in order to provide for the long-run needs of his family.

Although he has a modest income, Reverend Robin believes that with careful planning, he can probably invest about $250 a quarter (and, with luck, increase this amount over time). He currently has about $15,000 in a passbook savings account that he would be willing to use to begin this program. In view of his investment objectives, he is not interested in taking a lot of risk. Because his knowledge of investments extends to savings accounts, Series EE savings bonds, and a little bit about mutual funds, he approaches you for some investment advice.

Questions

a. In light of Reverend Robin's long-term investment goals, do you think mutual funds are an appropriate investment vehicle for him?

b. Do you think he should use his $15,000 savings to start a mutual fund investment program?

c. What type of mutual fund investment program would you set up for the reverend? Include in your answer some discussion of the types of funds you would consider, the investment objectives you would set, and any investment services (e.g., withdrawal plans) you would seek. Would taxes be an important consideration in your investment advice? Explain.

Case Problem 12.2   *Tom Yee Seeks the Good Life*

LG 3   LG 4

LG 5   LG 6

Tom Yee is a widower who recently retired after a long career with a major midwestern manufacturer. Beginning as a skilled craftsman, he worked his way up to the level of shop supervisor over a period of more than 30 years with the firm. Tom receives Social Security benefits and a generous company pension. Together, these two sources amount to over $3,500 per month (part of which is tax-free). The Yees had no children, so he lives alone. Tom owns a two-bedroom rental house that is next to his home, and the rental income from it covers the mortgage payments for both the rental house and his house.

Over the years, Tom and his late wife, Camille, always tried to put a little money aside each month. The results have been nothing short of phenomenal. The value of Tom's liquid investments (all held in bank CDs and passbook savings accounts) runs well into the six figures. Up to now, Tom has just let his money grow and has not used any of his savings to supplement his Social Security, pension, and rental income. But things are about to change. Tom has decided, "What the heck, it's time I start living the good life!" Tom wants to travel and, in effect, start reaping the benefits of his labors. He has therefore decided to move $100,000 from one of his savings accounts to one or two high-yielding mutual funds. He would like to receive $1,000–$1,500 a month from the fund(s) for as long as possible, because he plans to be around for a long time.

Questions

a. Given Tom's financial resources and investment objectives, what kinds of mutual funds do you think he should consider?

b. What factors in Tom's situation should be taken into consideration in the fund selection process? How might these affect Tom's course of action?

c. What types of services do you think he should look for in a mutual fund?

d. Assume Tom invests in a mutual fund that earns about 12% annually from dividend income and capital gains. Given that Tom wants to receive $1,000 to $1,500 a month from his mutual fund, what would be the size of his investment account 5 years from now? How large would the account be if the fund earned 16% on average and everything else remained the same? How important is the fund's rate of return to Tom's investment situation? Explain.

Web Exercises

W12.1   Spiders and diamonds are striking fear into the heart of the mutual funds industry. The good news is that exchange-traded funds (ETFs) can be bought and sold any time the market is open. The downside is that you might be tempted to do so. If you buy and sell ETFs too much, you eradicate the much-touted benefits of lower cost and greater tax efficiency. Visit amex.com and list the symbols and share volume of the top five most active index shares (in terms of share volume).

W12.2   Go to www.individualinvestor.com. Click [Education], and then, in the right-side menu under "How to Read" click on [A Prospectus]. Summarize the important points.

Now click on the [Funds] link at the bottom of the page. In the Company Research list box at the top of the left corner of the page, type VFINX (for Vanguard Index Trust 500 Index Fund), and click on Go. See the "Quote and Analysis" and "Profile and Financials" on the left-side menu.

From [Quote and Analysis], answer the following questions:
a. What is the last (that is, the closing) price?
b. Is this a small-cap (less than $1 billion), a mid-cap (between $1 and $5 billion), or a large-cap (over $5 billion) fund?
c. Compare the present volume (000) of trading with the historical volume. What does this indicate to you?

Investors pore through vast amounts of information to arrive at investment decisions.
d. Click on [Profile and Financials], and identify the information needed for making an investment decision.

W12.3   Use Fund screener at screen.yahoo.com/funds.html. From the <u>Category</u> list box, select Large Value funds. From <u>Morningstar rating,</u> select any; from <u>Min. initial investment,</u> $5,001–10,000; from <u>Total expense ratio,</u> up to 1%; from <u>Net assets,</u> any; from <u>Turnover,</u> any; from <u>1-year performance,</u> any; and from <u>Rank in category,</u> any. In Search Results, Sort Net Assets by clicking the column footer to sort in descending order. How does the largest-size fund perform in terms of Morningstar's rating?

W12.4   Visit www.stanford.edu/~wfsharpe/art/sa/sa.htm and read two articles:
• William F. Sharpe, "Asset Allocation: Management Style and Performance Measurement," *The Journal of Portfolio Management,* Winter 1992, pp. 7–19. (www.stanford.edu/~wfsharpe/art/ls100/ls100.htm)
• The Styles and Performance of Large Seasoned U.S. Mutual Funds, published on the World Wide Web, March 1995. A study of the style and performance of 100 large, seasoned U.S. mutual funds. Tests the hypothesis that "winners repeat."

What are the important conclusions of these two articles?

For additional practice with concepts from this chapter, visit

www.awl.com/gitman_joehnk

CHAPTER 13

ADMINISTERING YOUR OWN PORTFOLIO

LEARNING GOALS

After studying this chapter, you should be able to:

LG 1 Construct portfolios with asset allocations and risk-return profiles consistent with the investor's objectives.

LG 2 Discuss the data and indexes needed to measure and compare investment performance.

LG 3 Understand the techniques used to measure income, capital gains, and total portfolio return.

LG 4 Use the Sharpe, Treynor, and Jensen measures to compare a portfolio's return with a risk-adjusted, market-adjusted rate of return, and discuss portfolio revision.

LG 5 Describe the role and logic of dollar-cost averaging, constant-dollar plans, constant-ratio plans, and variable-ratio plans.

LG 6 Explain the role of limit and stop-loss orders in investment timing, warehousing liquidity, and timing investment sales.

He's known as the "Oracle of Omaha" for his stock-picking common sense. As chairman of Berkshire Hathaway Inc., Warren Buffet has multiplied his investors' money by a factor of 1,000 over the past three decades. The Omaha-based company is really a publicly held investment firm, with major holdings in over 500 companies, including American Express, Coca-Cola, Disney, the Federal Home Mortgage Corporation, GEICO insurance, Gillette, McDonald's, Shaw Industries, The Washington Post, Wells Fargo, and others. Berkshire Hathaway stock doesn't come cheap: In February 2001, it was selling for roughly $69,300 per share. From 1965 through 2000, the company's per share book value has grown from $19 to over $44,000. Buffet's claim to fame has been his ability to buy businesses at prices far below what he calls their "intrinsic" value, which includes such intangibles as quality of management and the power of superior brand names. He's also known for his "aw-shucks" demeanor, displayed in his annual letter to shareholders—which you can find at www.berkshirehathaway.com on the Internet.

As you'll see in this chapter, which describes administration of your securities portfolio, investing is a process of analysis, followed by action, followed by still more analysis. What has made Buffet so successful is his long-term horizon and his patience—a trait that is often in short supply on Wall Street. You may not be the next Warren Buffet (or maybe you will!), but understanding the techniques for evalating portfolio performances will put you on the right track.

Portfolio Planning in Action

LG 1

We begin this chapter by analyzing four portfolios that have been developed by individual investors to meet four different investment objectives. The principles and ideas discussed throughout this book are applied to these four situations.

In each of these analyses, the objectives and the portfolios are real, although the investors' and securities' names are fictitious. When possible, asset allocation weights are given. The specific reasons why a stock or bond is included in the portfolio are also given. As a useful exercise, you might want to consider each situation and develop your own recommendations using current investment information. The *Investing in Action* box on page 544 emphasizes the importance of keeping good records of transactions as your portfolio grows over time.

The four cases have different risk-return profiles because the investors for whom the portfolios are designed have different incomes and lifestyles. Each portfolio relies heavily on the *traditional approach* (see Chapter 5), with the following exceptions: First, the number of securities in each portfolio is *below the normal number* the traditional portfolio manager would be likely to recommend. In line with *modern portfolio theory (MPT)* (see Chapter 5), it is assumed that the proper interindustry diversification can be achieved with the careful selection of 8 to 12 securities in a $100,000 portfolio. A traditionalist might recommend more. Second, beta (see Chapter 5) is utilized to quantify risk in the all-equity portfolios. Thus these examples blend elements of MPT with the traditional approach to portfolio management.

Dara Yasakawa: Woman Wonder

At age 28, Dara Yasakawa has done well for herself. She has built a $300,000 investment portfolio. It consists of investment real estate in Honolulu, Hawaii, with a current market value of $240,000, and $60,000 in short-term securities. Her current asset allocation is therefore 80% real estate ($240,000 ÷ $300,000) and 20% short-term securities ($60,000 ÷ $300,000). Dara is currently employed as the controller of Kamehameha Management, a real estate management firm in Honolulu. She is a CPA, and her income from salary and property rentals is $75,000 per year. This puts her in a 35% marginal income tax bracket (federal and Hawaii state income tax combined). Dara is single and relatively debt-free.

Dara Yasakawa has decided to diversify her portfolio, to reduce her risk exposure and increase her overall investment return. Most of her net worth consists of rental condominiums in Honolulu. The Hawaii real estate market is somewhat unpredictable, and Dara wishes to lessen her risk exposure in that market. She asked her investment adviser, Marjorie Wong, to help her diversify into common stock. Marjorie recommended selling one of Dara's properties for $60,000 and selling $15,000 of her short-term securities to obtain $75,000 to invest in common stock. The resulting asset allocation would be 60% real estate ($180,000 ÷ $300,000), 25% common stock ($75,000 ÷ $300,000), and 15% short-term securities ($45,000 ÷ $300,000). Because of her relatively young age and her strong future earning capacity, Dara can bear the risks of a speculative investment program. Her portfolio of stocks will emphasize issues that have a strong price appreciation potential.

INVESTOR FACTS

A LITTLE GOES A LONG WAY—Too much diversification can be as bad as too little. According to a recent study by Dow Theory Forecasts analyst David Wright, five to nine funds investing in domestic and international stocks and bonds are all you need. Putting together five conservative stock funds—one each of large-cap, mid-cap, and small-cap U.S. stocks, international stocks, and intermediate-term bonds—he created a portfolio with a 15% standard deviation. Adding a high-yield bond fund shaved it to 14 percent, a municipal bond fund to 12. Adding another large-stock fund pushed the standard deviation up to 13. "More is not always better, " he said.

Source: Chet Currie, "Temper Diversification to Avoid Diminishing Returns," *The Dallas Morning News,* July 9, 2000, p. 11H.

INVESTING in action

Taming the Portfolio Monster

As your portfolio grows in number and type of investments, it's easy to become overwhelmed and confused by the paperwork you accumulate. Before long, you might lose control of your investments or lose track of important details, such as why you bought that stock in the first place. "People tend to build portfolios the way they pick up seashells on the beach," says Roger Gibson, author of *Asset Allocation: Balancing Financial Risk*. As a result, many investors don't know whether the parts of their portfolio make sense when taken together.

How do you get an overall view of your portfolio? A good place to start is by doing a thorough housecleaning of your financial assets. That means sorting through stacks of paper: mutual fund "welcome" kits, prospectuses, annual and quarterly reports, brokerage firm and mutual fund statements. Take all the paperwork from each brokerage firm and mutual fund and put it in one pile, organized by date, with the most recent mailing on top. You can throw out items you no longer need, such as welcome kits, old annual reports, and monthly or quarterly statements whose information is included in the annual statement. Then file each set of documents in an individual file folder.

Next, list all of your assets categorized by asset categories. Across the top, make columns for cash, domestic bonds, international bonds, domestic stocks, international stocks, real estate, and so on. Use the rows for the source, such as ABC mutual fund or XYZ brokerage firm. If one investment falls into two or more categories, such as a 401(k) retirement plan with both bond and stock investments, then divide it accordingly. Add up all of your assets by category, and calculate the percentage of your portfolio for each asset category.

You may discover that you have many small, similar investments that can be consolidated to simplify your portfolio while still achieving your objectives. For example, do you really need three stockbrokers, or can you combine your accounts at one firm? The same goes for mutual funds. You may want to concentrate on one or two large fund families with many fund choices. Consolidating brokerage firms and mutual funds will certainly cut down on the blizzard of paperwork.

Having organized records also will be a major benefit at tax time. Your records will provide you with the necessary details about securities you sold during the year—such as the purchase and sale dates, the number of shares you bought or sold, and the purchase and sale prices. But most important, having neat files and summary tables will make it easy for you to make informed investment decisions that fit your life circumstances.

Dara Yasakawa's common stock portfolio is presented in Table 13.1. It consists of eight stocks, all of which have above-average risk-return potential. The betas of the issues range from 1.13 to 2.31. The portfolio's beta (calculated using Equation 5.4 from Chapter 5) is approximately 1.59, indicating an above-average risk exposure. The portfolio is diversified across industry lines, with a fairly wide mix of securities. All are selected for their above-average price appreciation potential. Altuna Airlines, an interisland carrier in Hawaii, was chosen because of the expected increase in the number of visitors to Hawaii. Betta Computer is a fast-growing personal computer manufacturer. Easy Work Inc. is a growing retailer that services the do-it-yourself home improvement market. Gomez Industries is a rapidly expanding glass manufacturer and photo processor. Hercules is a growing brewer. Jama Motor, based in Japan, provides a measure of international diversification for the portfolio. eChowNow is an expanding Internet-based home grocery operation based in California. Ranch Petroleum is a small oil company with refining and oil-production interests.

TABLE 13.1 **Dara Yasakawa's Common Stock Portfolio**

Objective: Speculative Growth (High Risk, Potential for High Return)

Number of Shares	Company	Dividend per Share	Dividend Income	Price per Share	Total Cost (including commission)	Beta	Dividend Yield
1,200	Altuna Airlines	$ —	$ —	$ 7	$ 8,480	1.75	—%
300	Betta Computer	—	—	30	9,090	1.87	—
400	Easy Work Inc.	—	—	25	10,090	1.59	—
300	Gomez Industries	0.36	108	30	9,090	1.19	1.2
300	Hercules Brewing	0.80	240	32	9,700	1.27	2.5
300	Jama Motor ADR	0.35	105	33	10,000	1.13	1.1
500	eChowNow	—	—	20	10,100	1.79	—
1,300	Ranch Petroleum	—	—	6	7,880	2.31	—
	Total		$453		$74,430		0.6%

Portfolio beta = 1.59

Most of these securities are not "household names." Rather, they are firms with exciting growth potential. Given the portfolio's beta, Dara's holdings should fluctuate in value at a rate approximately 1.6 times greater than the stock market as a whole. The dividend yield on the portfolio is a relatively low 0.6%. Most of the return Dara anticipates from this portfolio is in the form of price appreciation. She plans to hold the stocks for at least 3 to 5 years to realize this anticipated appreciation. Given Dara Yasakawa's relatively high marginal income tax bracket, it seems preferable for her to defer taxes and earn returns in the form of capital gains.

Bob and Gail Weiss: Lottery Winners

Bob Weiss, a professor of political science at the University of West Bay City in Michigan, and his wife, Gail, are lucky people. Professor Weiss bought a $1 Michigan State Lottery ticket and won $300,000! After paying income taxes on the prize and spending a small amount for personal needs, Bob and Gail had $210,000 left. Because of their philosophy of saving any windfalls and not spending accumulated capital on day-to-day living expenses, they chose to invest these funds. (In contrast, many lottery winners simply blow their winnings on fast living.)

Bob Weiss is 37 years of age and has a secure teaching position. His salary is approximately $70,000 per year. In addition, he earns approximately $20,000 per year from book publishing royalties and some consulting work. Bob Weiss's tax bracket (federal and state) is approximately 33%. His life insurance protection of approximately $90,000 is provided by the university. Gail Weiss is a librarian. She currently is at home with their two young children and is not expected to be a source of steady income for another several years.

The Weiss family owns (free and clear) their home in Bay City. In addition, they have about $40,000 in a money market mutual fund. Therefore, their asset allocation prior to the lottery windfall was 100% money funds ($40,000 ÷ $40,000). They have no outstanding debts.

TABLE 13.2	Bob and Gail Weiss's Common Stock Portfolio

Objective: Long-term Growth (Average Risk, Moderate Dividends)

Number of Shares	Company	Dividend per Share	Dividend Income	Price per Share	Total Cost (including commission)	Beta	Dividend Yield
1,000	Bancorp West, Inc.	$1.20	$ 1,200	$22	$ 22,200	0.86	5.4%
600	BST Inc.	2.80	1,680	40	24,200	1.00	6.9
1,000	Florida Southcoast Banks	1.20	1,200	23	23,200	0.84	5.2
1,000	Kings	1.60	1,600	25	25,300	0.88	6.3
500	Light Newspapers	0.92	460	46	23,200	1.12	2.0
600	Miller Foods	1.88	1,128	37	22,400	1.07	5.0
800	State Oil of California	1.00	800	27	21,800	1.30	3.7
600	Vornox	2.28	1,368	40	24,200	1.04	5.7
600	Woodstock	1.30	780	36	21,800	1.32	3.6
	Total		$10,216		$208,300		4.9%

Portfolio beta = 1.04

The Weisses asked their investment adviser, Gene Bowles, to develop an investment portfolio for them. Together, they decided on the following strategy: First, Bob and Gail tend to be somewhat risk-averse; they do not wish to bear inordinate amounts of risk of loss. In addition, the Weisses indicated they would welcome some increase in spendable income. Given these facts, Gene Bowles suggested the portfolio presented in Table 13.2. With this portfolio their asset allocation would become about 84% common stock ($210,000 ÷ $250,000) and 16% money funds ($40,000 ÷ $250,000).

The emphasis in the portfolio is long-term growth at an average risk level, with a moderate dividend return. The portfolio consists of nine issues. This appears to be sufficient diversification. The portfolio's beta is 1.04, indicating a level of nondiversifiable risk about equal to the stock market as a whole. The portfolio's dividend yield is about 4.9%, which approximates the average dividend return for the entire stock market. The betas of individual securities in the portfolio vary somewhat. However, the portfolio's overall risk is moderate.

The Weiss portfolio consists of stocks from a wide range of U.S. businesses. All the companies have above-average growth potential. None is engaged in high-risk businesses that could face technological obsolescence or heavy foreign competition. Two banking stocks are included: Bancorp West, Inc., and Florida Southcoast Banks. The former is a well-managed bank holding company that owns the largest bank in California. The latter is a growing bank holding company located on the south coast of Florida. Both regions are experiencing rapid economic growth and population increases. BST Inc. appears to be well positioned in the growing communications industry. Kings is a food processor with a solid future. Light Newspapers is a large chain with many Sunbelt papers. Miller Foods is expanding as well, helped by its 2001 acquisition of Denton Companies, a superbly managed supermarket chain. The portfolio has two natural resource stocks, State Oil of California and Woodstock. These companies are well positioned in their respective industries. Vornox is a major drug firm that should benefit from America's aging demographic mix. All of the stocks in the Weisses' portfolio are securities of well-managed companies. With this portfolio, the Weisses will have potential price appreciation coupled with a steady dividend income.

Julio and Gina Vitello: Retirees

Having just sold their family business and liquidated their real estate investment property, Julio and Gina Vitello are eager to begin their retirement. At age 60, both have worked hard for 35 years building the successful business they recently sold. In addition, they have made some successful real estate investments over the years. The sale of their business and real estate holdings has netted them $600,000 after taxes. They wish to invest these funds and have asked their investment adviser, Jane Tuttle, to develop a portfolio for them.

Relevant financial information about the Vitellos is as follows: They own their home free and clear and have a $300,000 bond portfolio that yields yearly income of $30,000. In addition, they have $100,000 in short-term securities that they wish to hold as a ready cash reserve. Their most recent asset allocation is therefore 60% business and real estate investments ($600,000 ÷ $1,000,000), 30% bonds ($300,000 ÷ $1,000,000), and 10% short-term securities ($100,000 ÷ $1,000,000). Julio has a $200,000 whole-life insurance policy on his life, with Gina the designated beneficiary.

Now that they are retired, neither of the Vitellos plans to seek employment. They do have a small pension plan that will begin paying an income of $6,000 per year in 5 years. However, their main source of income will be their investment portfolio. During their last few working years, their combined yearly income was approximately $85,000. Their standard of living is comfortable, and they do not wish to change their lifestyle significantly. They do not plan to spend any of their investment capital on living expenses, because they want to keep their estate intact for their two children. Thus the Vitellos' basic investment objective is current income with some capital appreciation potential.

The Vitellos do not wish to reinvest in real estate but, rather, have asked Jane Tuttle to develop a $600,000 securities portfolio for them. (They will leave their $300,000 bond portfolio and $100,000 in short-term securities undisturbed.) Their resulting asset allocation would shift to 60% common stock, 30% bonds, and 10% short-term securities. The portfolio Jane developed for the Vitellos is shown in Table 13.3.

The Vitello's portfolio contains nine stocks with approximately $65,000 invested in each issue. The emphasis is on quality, with low-risk–high-yield issues, and diversification. The portfolio's beta is approximately 0.80—a risk level that is below that of the general stock market. It is expected that a large portion of the portfolio's total return (dividends plus price appreciation) will be in the form of dividend income. The portfolio has a current dividend yield of approximately 8.7%, an above-average dividend yield. Dividend income totals over $52,000. That amount, added to the bond income and the short-term securities' interest, will provide the Vitellos with a gross income of about $85,000. The Vitellos' after-tax income will equal their working years' income, so they will not have to alter their lifestyle.

Four public utility stocks are included in the Vitellos' portfolio. Utility stocks are often suitable for low-risk, current-income-oriented portfolios. High-quality electric and natural gas concerns tend to have moderate growth in earnings and dividends. The four issues in the portfolio—Findly Power and Light, Gulf Gas and Electric, Public Power Company, and Southwest Utilities—have growing service areas and records of increases in profits and dividends. The stocks of two large U.S. companies, Energon and Smith,

TABLE 13.3	Julio and Gina Vitello's Common Stock Portfolio

Objective: Current Income (Low Risk, High Yield)

Number of Shares	Company	Dividend per Share	Dividend Income	Price per Share	Total Cost (including commission)	Beta	Dividend Yield
3,000	Alaska Bancorp, Inc.	$1.20	$ 3,600	$22	$ 66,600	0.86	5.4%
2,000	Dallas National Corporation	2.40	4,800	30	60,600	0.81	7.9
2,500	Energon	3.00	7,500	27	68,100	1.01	11.0
2,000	Findly Power and Light	3.36	6,720	32	64,600	0.63	10.4
2,000	Geoco	2.80	5,600	35	70,700	1.13	7.9
2,500	Gulf Gas and Electric	3.00	7,500	28	70,700	0.53	10.6
4,000	Public Power Company	1.76	7,040	16	64,600	0.72	10.9
2,500	Smith, Roberts & Company	1.36	3,400	27	68,100	0.92	5.0
3,000	Southwest Utilities	2.04	6,120	21	63,600	0.60	9.6
	Total		$52,280		$597,600		8.7%

Portfolio beta = 0.80

Roberts & Company, are included in the portfolio. Energon is a large U.S. energy company that offers a high dividend yield. Smith, Roberts is one of the largest retailers, and the company is now diversifying into information services. Two bank holding company stocks were also selected: Alaska Bancorp and Dallas National. Alaska Bancorp offers a top-quality vehicle to participate in Alaska's growth. Dallas National was selected because of its above-average dividend yield and because the firm is well positioned in the strong Dallas market. Additionally, the company has raised its dividend several times in recent years, and future dividend increases are expected. Geoco is a large company with chemical and other diversified operations. All the issues in the Vitellos' portfolio are well-known, relatively large corporations. Stability, low risk, and a relatively high dividend yield with some potential for increased share values characterize the stocks in this portfolio.

Lucille Hatch: Widow

Most retirees have less money to invest than the Vitellos in the preceding example. Lucille Hatch, age 70, was recently widowed. Between the estate of her late husband, her personal assets, and their jointly owned assets, she has approximately $485,000 in liquid assets. All of it is in savings and money market accounts (short-term investments). Her current asset allocation is therefore 100% short-term investments. Lucille owns her home free and clear. Other than the interest on her savings, her income consists of $900 per month from Social Security. Unfortunately, her husband's employer did not have a pension plan. She has turned to her investment adviser, Charles Puckett, to discuss strategy and develop an investment policy.

Between Social Security and interest earned on her short-term investments, Lucille Hatch's current income is approximately $35,000 annually. She wishes to increase that income, if possible, while only minimally raising her risk exposure. Charles Puckett recommended the investment portfolio presented in

TABLE 13.4	Lucille Hatch's Bond Portfolio							
		Objective: Maximize Current Income (Minimal Risk)						
Par Value	Issue	Standard & Poor's Bond Rating	Interest Income	Quoted Price	Total Cost	Yield to Maturity	Current Yield
$70,000	Boise Northern 8⅞% due 2023	A	$ 6,212.50	100	$ 70,000	8.875%	8.875%
70,000	Dalston Company 7½% due 2007	A	5,250.00	98	68,600	8.000	7.650
70,000	Maryland-Pacific 6.70% due 2005	A	4,690.00	97	67,900	7.860	6.900
70,000	Pacific Utilities 8⅞% due 2031	AA	6,212.50	100	70,000	8.875	8.875
70,000	Trans-States Telephone 8.70% due 2037	A	6,090.00	97	67,900	8.980	8.970
70,000	Urban Life 8½% due 2008	AA	5,950.00	100	70,000	8.500	8.500
	Total		$34,405.00		$414,400	8.340%	8.300%

Table 13.4. The portfolio's objective is to maximize current income while keeping risk at a low level. All of the money is invested in fixed-income securities. Approximately $415,000 goes to high-quality corporate bonds, and the balance ($70,000) is retained in short-term investments to provide a substantial contingency reserve. The resulting asset allocation is about 86% bonds ($415,000 ÷ $485,000) and 14% short-term investments ($70,000 ÷ $485,000). Investing in the bond portfolio will increase Lucille Hatch's yearly income from approximately $35,000 to about $48,700 ($10,800 Social Security, $3,500 earnings on short-term investments, and $34,400 bond interest). This puts her in a 30% marginal tax bracket (federal and state tax combined). Taxable corporate bonds were recommended over tax-free municipal bonds because her after-tax rate of return would be greater with the former.

Turning to the portfolio, we see that there are six corporate bond issues that cost about $70,000 each. Each issuer is a high-quality company with a low risk of default. Lucille's portfolio is diversified in several ways: First, it contains a mix of utility, industrial, railroad, and financial issues. The two utility bond issues are Pacific Utilities and Trans-States Telephone. Both companies are large and financially secure. The two industrial concerns, Dalston and Maryland-Pacific, are large as well. Boise Northern is a financially solid railroad, and Urban Life is a large, secure insurance company. A second added measure of diversification is attained by staggering the bonds' maturities. They mature in six different years: 2005, 2007, 2008, 2023, 2031, and 2037. The shorter-term bonds will provide ready cash when they mature, and they generally will fluctuate less in price than the longer-term bonds. The portfolio has been diversified to keep the risk of loss low. By switching funds out of her short-term investments into bonds, Lucille Hatch was able to increase her current income substantially while experiencing only a small increase in risk.

IN REVIEW

CONCEPTS

13.1 Evaluate the effective system for keeping track of your portfolio records that was described in the *Investing in Action* box on page 544. How might this system help you consolidate your portfolio?

13.2 Describe and contrast the expected portfolios for each of the following investors:
a. A retired investor in need of income.
b. A high-income, financially secure investor.
c. A young investor with a secure job and no dependents.

Evaluating the Performance of Individual Investments

LG 2

Imagine that one of your most important personal goals is to have accumulated $20,000 of savings 3 years from now in order to make the down payment on your first house. You project that the desired house will cost $100,000 and that the $20,000 will be sufficient to make a 15% down payment and pay the associated closing costs. Your calculations indicate that this goal can be achieved by investing existing savings plus an additional $200 per month over the next 3 years in a vehicle earning 12% per year. Projections of your earnings over the 3-year period indicate that you should just be able to set aside the needed $200 per month. You consult with an investment adviser, Cliff Orbit, who leads you to believe that under his management, the 12% return can be achieved.

It seems simple: Give Cliff your existing savings, send him $200 each month over the next 36 months, and at the end of that period, you will have the $20,000 needed to purchase the house. Unfortunately, there are many uncertainties involved. What if you don't set aside $200 each month? What if Cliff fails to earn the needed 12% annual return? What if in 3 years the desired house costs more than $100,000? Clearly, you must do more than simply devise what appears to be a feasible plan for achieving a future goal. Rarely is an investor guaranteed that planned investment and portfolio outcomes will actually occur. Although the four portfolios developed in the prior section are consistent with the investors' goals, there is no guarantee that their actual outcomes will be as forecast. Therefore, it is important to assess periodically your progress toward achieving your investment goals.

As actual outcomes occur, you must compare them to the *planned* outcomes and make any necessary alterations in your plans—or in your goals. Knowing how to measure investment performance is therefore crucial. Here we will emphasize measures suitable for analyzing investment performance. We begin with sources of data.

Obtaining Needed Data

The first step in analyzing investment returns is gathering data that reflect the actual performance of each investment. As pointed out in Chapter 3, many sources of investment information are available, both online and in print. The *Wall Street Journal* and *Yahoo.com,* for example, contain numerous items of information useful in assessing the performance of securities. The same type of information that is used to *make* an investment decision is used to *evaluate* the performance of investments. Two key areas to stay informed about are (1) returns on owned investments and (2) economic and market activity.

Return Data The basic ingredient in analyzing investment returns is current market information, such as daily price quotations for stocks and bonds. Investors often maintain logs that contain the cost of each investment, as well as dividends, interest, and other sources of income received. By regularly recording price and return data, you can create an ongoing record of price fluctuations and cumulative returns. You should also monitor corporate earnings and dividends, which will affect a company's stock price. The two sources of investment return—current income and capital gains—must of course be combined to determine total return. Combining return components using the techniques presented in Chapter 4 will be illustrated for some popular investment vehicles later in this chapter.

Economic and Market Activity Changes in the economy and market will affect returns—both the level of current income and the market value of an investment vehicle. The astute investor keeps abreast of international, national, and local economic and market developments. By following economic and market changes, you should be able to assess their potential impact on returns. As economic and market conditions change, you must be prepared to make revisions in the portfolio. In essence, being a knowledgeable investor will improve your chances of generating a profit (or avoiding a loss).

Indexes of Investment Performance

In measuring investment performance, it is often worthwhile to compare your returns with broad-based market measures. Indexes useful for the analysis of common stock include the Dow Jones Industrial Average (DJIA), the Standard & Poor's 500 Stock Composite Index (S&P 500), and the Nasdaq Composite Index. (Detailed discussions of these averages and indexes can be found in Chapter 3.) Although the DJIA is widely cited by the news media, it is *not* considered the most appropriate comparative gauge of stock price movement, because of its narrow coverage. If your portfolio is composed of a broad range of common stocks, the S&P 500 index is probably a more appropriate tool.

A number of indicators are also available for assessing the general behavior of the bond markets. These indicators consider either bond price behavior or bond yield. The Dow Jones composite bond average, based on the closing prices of 10 utility and 10 industrial bonds, is a popular measure of bond price behavior. Like bond quotations, it reflects the average percentage of face value at which the 20 bonds sell. Also available are bond yield data. These reflect the rate of return one would earn on a bond purchased today and held to maturity. Popular sources of these data include the *Wall Street Journal*, *Barron's*, Standard & Poor's, Moody's Investor Services, Yahoo.com, and the Federal Reserve. Indexes of bond price and bond yield performance can be obtained for specific types of bonds (industrial, utility, and municipal), as well as on a composite basis. In addition, indexes reported in terms of *total returns* are available for both stocks and bonds. They combine dividend/interest income with price behavior (capital gain or loss) to reflect total return.

The Lipper indexes are frequently used to assess the general behavior of mutual funds. They are available for various types of equity and bond funds. Unfortunately, for most other types of funds, no widely published index or average is available. A few other indexes cover listed options and futures.

Measuring the Performance of Investment Vehicles

Reliable techniques for consistently measuring the performance of each investment vehicle are needed to monitor an investment portfolio. In particular, the holding period return (HPR) measure, first presented in Chapter 4, can be used to determine *actual* return performance. Investment holdings need to be evaluated periodically over time—at least once a year. HPR is an excellent way to assess actual return behavior, because it captures *total return* performance. It is most appropriate for holding or assessment periods of 1 year or less. Total return, in this context, includes the periodic cash income from the investment as well as price appreciation (or loss), whether realized or unrealized. The calculation of returns for periods of more than a year should be made using yield (internal rate of return), because it recognizes the time value of money. Yield can be calculated using the techniques described in Chapter 4 (pages 150–152). Because the following discussions center on the annual assessment of return, HPR will be used as the measure of return.

The formula for HPR, presented in Chapter 4 (Equation 4.8) and applied throughout this chapter, is restated in Equation 13.1:

Equation 13.1
$$\text{Holding period return} = \frac{\text{Current income during period} + \text{Capital gain (or loss) during period}}{\text{Beginning investment value}}$$

Equation 13.1a
$$\text{HPR} = \frac{C + CG}{V_0}$$

where

Equation 13.2
$$\text{Capital gain (or loss) during period} = \text{Ending investment value} - \text{Beginning investment value}$$

Equation 13.2a
$$CG = V_n - V_0$$

Stocks and Bonds   There are several measures of investment return for stocks and bonds. *Dividend yield,* discussed in Chapter 6, measures the current yearly dividend return earned from a stock investment. It is calculated by dividing a stock's yearly cash dividend by its price. The *current yield* and *promised yield* (yield-to-maturity) for bonds, analyzed in Chapter 10, capture various components of return but do not reflect actual total return. The *holding period return* method *measures the total return (income plus change in value) actually earned on an investment over a given investment period.* We will use HPR, with a holding period of approximately 1 year, in the illustrations that follow.

Stocks   The HPR for common and preferred stocks includes both cash dividends received and any price change in the security during the period of ownership. Table 13.5 illustrates the HPR calculation as applied to the actual performance of a common stock. Assume you purchased 1,000 shares of Dallas National Corporation in May 2001 at a cost of $27,312 (including commissions). After holding the stock for just over 1 year, you sold the stock, reaping proceeds of $32,040. You also received $2,000 in cash dividends during the period of ownership and realized a $4,728 capital gain on the sale. Thus the calculated HPR is 24.63%.

TABLE 13.5   Calculation of Pretax HPR on a Common Stock

Security: Dallas National Corporation common stock
Date of purchase: May 1, 2001
Purchase cost: $27,312
Date of sale: May 7, 2002
Sale proceeds: $32,040
Dividends received (May 2001 to May 2002): $2,000

$$\text{Holding period return} = \frac{\$2,000 + (\$32,040 - \$27,312)}{\$27,312}$$

$$= +\underline{\$24.63\%}$$

This HPR was calculated without consideration for income taxes paid on the dividends and capital gain. Because many investors are concerned with both pretax and after-tax rates of return, it is useful to calculate an after-tax HPR. We assume, for simplicity in this example, that you are in the 30% ordinary tax bracket (federal and state combined). We also assume that, for federal and state tax purposes, capital gains for holding periods of more than 12 months are taxed at a 20% rate. Thus your dividend income is taxed at a 30% rate and your capital gain income is taxed at a 20% rate. Income taxes reduce the after-tax dividend income to $1,400 [(1 − 0.30) × $2,000] and the after-tax capital gain to $3,782 [(1 − 0.20) × ($32,040 − $27,312)]. The after-tax HPR is therefore 18.97% [($1,400 + $3,782) ÷ $27,312], a reduction of 5.66 percentage points. It should be clear that both pretax HPR and after-tax HPR are useful gauges of return.

Bonds The HPR for a bond investment is similar to that for stocks. The calculation holds for both straight debt and convertible issues. It includes the two components of a bond investor's return: interest income and capital gain or loss. Calculation of the HPR on a bond investment is illustrated in Table 13.6. Assume you purchased Phoenix Brewing Company bonds for $10,000, held them for just over 1 year, and then realized $9,704 at sale. In addition, you earned $1,000 in interest during the period of ownership. The HPR of this investment is 7.04%. The HPR is lower than the bond's current yield of 10% ($1,000 interest ÷ $10,000 purchase price) because the bonds were sold at a capital loss. Assuming a 30% ordinary tax bracket and a 20% capital gains rate (because the bond has been held more than 12 months), the after-tax HPR is 4.63%: {[(1 − 0.30) × $1,000] + [(1 − 0.20) × ($9,704 − $10,000)]} ÷ $10,000. This is about 2.4% less than the pretax HPR.

TABLE 13.6   Calculation of Pretax HPR on a Bond

Security: Phoenix Brewing Company 10% bonds
Date of purchase: June 2, 2001
Purchase cost: $10,000
Date of sale: June 5, 2002
Sale proceeds: $9,704
Interest earned (June 2001 to June 2002): $1,000

$$\text{Holding period return} = \frac{\$1,000 + (\$9,704 - \$10,000)}{\$10,000}$$

$$= +\underline{7.04\%}$$

TABLE 13.7   Calculation of Pretax HPR on a Mutual Fund

Security: Pebble Falls Mutual Fund
Date of purchase: July 1, 2001
Purchase cost: $10,400
Date of redemption: July 3, 2002
Sale proceeds: $10,790
Distributions received (July 2001 to July 2002)
  Investment income dividends: $270
  Capital gains dividends: $320

$$\text{Holding period return} = \frac{(\$270 + \$320) + (\$10{,}790 - \$10{,}400)}{\$10{,}400}$$

$$= +\underline{9.42\%}$$

Mutual Funds The two basic components of return from a mutual fund investment are dividend income (including any capital gains distribution) and change in value. The basic HPR equation for mutual funds is identical to that for stocks. Table 13.7 presents a holding period return calculation for a no-load mutual fund. Assume you purchased 1,000 shares of the fund in July 2001 at a NAV of $10.40 per share. Because it is a no-load fund, no commission was charged, so your cost was $10,400. During the 1-year period of ownership, the Pebble Falls Mutual Fund distributed investment income dividends totaling $270 and capital gains dividends of $320. You redeemed (sold) this fund at a NAV of $10.79 per share, thereby realizing $10,790. As seen in Table 13.7, the pretax holding period return on this investment is 9.42%. Assuming a 30% ordinary tax bracket and a 20% capital gains rate (because the fund has been held for more than 12 months), the after-tax HPR for the fund is 6.97%: {[(1 − 0.30) × ($270 + $320)] + [(1 − 0.20) × ($10,790 − $10,400)]} ÷ $10,400. This is about 2.5% below the pretax return.

Options and Futures The only source of return on options and futures is capital gains. To calculate a holding period return for an investment in a call option, for instance, the basic HPR formula is used, but current income is set equal to zero. If you purchased a call on 100 shares of ecommerce.com for $325 and sold the contract for $385 after holding it for just over 12 months, the pretax holding period return would be 18.46%. This is simply sales proceeds ($385) minus cost ($325) divided by cost. Assuming the 20% capital gains tax rate applies, the after-tax HPR would be 14.77%, which is the after-tax gain of $48 [(1 − 0.20) × $60] divided by cost ($325). The HPRs of futures are calculated in a similar fashion. Because the return is in the form of capital gains only, the HPR analysis can be applied to any investment on a pretax or an after-tax basis. (The same basic procedure is used for securities that are sold short.)

Comparing Performance to Investment Goals

After computing an HPR (or yield) on an investment, you should compare it to your investment goal. Keeping track of an investment's performance will help you decide which investments you should continue to hold and which you might want to sell. Clearly, an investment would be a candidate for sale under the following conditions: (1) The investment failed to perform up to expectations and no real change in performance is anticipated. (2) It has met the original investment objective. Or (3) better investment outlets are currently available.

Balancing Risk and Return In this book, we have frequently discussed the basic tradeoff between investment risk and return. The relationship is fundamentally as follows: To earn more return, you must take more risk. In analyzing an investment, the key question is, "Am I getting the proper return for the amount of investment risk I am taking?"

Nongovernment security investments are by nature riskier than U.S. government bonds or insured money market deposit accounts. This implies that *a rational investor should invest in these riskier vehicles only when the expected rate of return is well in excess of what could have been earned from a low-risk investment.* Thus one benchmark against which to compare investment returns is the rate of return on low-risk investments. If one's risky investments are outperforming low-risk investments, they are obtaining extra return for taking extra risk. If they are not outperforming low-risk investments, you should carefully reexamine your investment strategy.

Isolating Problem Investments A *problem investment* is one that has not lived up to expectations. It may be a loss situation or an investment that has provided a return less than you expected. Many investors try to forget about problem investments, hoping the problem will go away or the investment will turn itself around. This is obviously a mistake. Problem investments require immediate attention, not neglect. In studying a problem investment, the key question is, "Should I take my loss and get out, or should I hang on and hope it turns around?"

It is best to analyze each investment in a portfolio periodically. For each, two questions should be considered. First, has it performed in a manner that could reasonably be expected? Second, if you didn't currently own it, would you buy it today? If the answers to both are negative, then the investment probably should be sold. A negative answer to one of the questions qualifies the investment for the "problem list." It should then be watched closely. In general, maintaining a portfolio of investments requires constant attention and analysis to ensure the best chance of satisfactory returns. Problem investments need special attention and work.

IN REVIEW

CONCEPTS

13.3 Why is it important to continuously manage and control your portfolio?

13.4 What role does current market information play in analyzing investment returns? How do changes in economic and market activity affect investment returns? Explain.

13.5 Which indexes can you use to compare your investment performance to general market returns? Briefly explain each of these indexes.

13.6 What are indicators of bond market behavior, and how are they different from stock market indicators? Name three sources of bond yield data.

13.7 Briefly discuss *holding period return (HPR)* and *yield* as measures of investment return. Are they equivalent? Explain.

13.8   Distinguish between the types of dividend distributions that mutual funds make. Are these dividends the only source of return for a mutual fund investor? Explain.

13.9   Under what three conditions would an investment holding be a candidate for sale? What must be true about the expected return on a risky investment, when compared with the return on a low-risk investment, to cause a rational investor to acquire the risky investment? Explain.

13.10   What is a *problem investment?* What two questions should one consider when analyzing an investment portfolio?

Assessing Portfolio Performance

LG 3   LG 4

active portfolio management
building a portfolio using traditional and modern approaches and managing and controlling it to achieve its objectives; a worthwhile activity that can result in superior returns.

A portfolio can be either passively or actively built and managed. A *passive portfolio* results from buying and holding a well-diversified portfolio over the given investment horizon. An *active portfolio* is built using the traditional and modern approaches presented in Chapter 5 and is managed and controlled to achieve its stated objectives. Passive portfolios may at times outperform equally risky active portfolios. But evidence suggests that **active portfolio management** can result in superior returns. Many of the ideas presented in this text are consistent with the belief that active portfolio management will improve your chance of earning superior returns.

Once a portfolio is built, the first step in active portfolio management is to assess performance on a regular basis and use that information to revise the portfolio. Calculating the portfolio return can be tricky, as discussed in the *Investing in Action* box on page 559. The procedures used to assess portfolio performance are based on many of the concepts presented earlier in this chapter. Here we will demonstrate how to assess portfolio performance, using a hypothetical securities portfolio over a 1-year holding period. We will examine each of three measures that can be used to compare a portfolio's return with a risk-adjusted, market-adjusted rate of return.

Measuring Portfolio Return

Table 13.8 presents the investment portfolio, as of January 1, 2002, of Bob Hathaway. He is a 50-year-old widower, whose children are married. His income is $60,000 per year. His primary investment objective is long-term growth with a moderate dividend return. He selects stocks with two criteria in mind: quality and growth potential. On January 1, 2002, his portfolio consisted of 10 issues, all of good quality. Hathaway has been fortunate in his selection process: He has approximately $74,000 in unrealized price appreciation in his portfolio. During 2002, he decided to make a change in the portfolio. On May 7 he sold 1,000 shares of Dallas National Corporation for $32,040. Hathaway's holding period return for that issue was discussed earlier in this chapter (see Table 13.5). Using funds from the Dallas National sale, he acquired an additional 1,000 shares of Florida Southcoast Banks on May 10, because he liked the prospects for the Florida bank. Florida Southcoast is based in one of the fastest-growing counties in the country.

TABLE 13.8	Bob Hathaway's Portfolio (January 1, 2002)					
Number of Shares	Company	Date Acquired	Total Cost (including commission)	Cost per Share	Current Price per Share	Current Value
1,000	Bancorp West, Inc.	1/16/00	$ 21,610	$21.61	$30	$ 30,000
1,000	Dallas National Corporation	5/01/01	27,312	27.31	29	29,000
1,000	Dator Companies, Inc.	4/13/96	13,704	13.70	27	27,000
500	Excelsior Industries	8/16/99	40,571	81.14	54	27,000
1,000	Florida Southcoast Banks	12/16/99	17,460	17.46	30	30,000
1,000	Maryland-Pacific	9/27/99	22,540	22.54	26	26,000
1,000	Moronson	2/27/99	19,100	19.10	47	47,000
500	Northwest Mining and Mfg.	4/17/00	25,504	51.00	62	31,000
1,000	Rawland Petroleum	3/12/00	24,903	24.90	30	30,000
1,000	Vornox	4/16/00	37,120	37.12	47	47,000
	Total		$249,824			$324,000

Measuring the Amount Invested Every investor would be well advised to list his or her holdings periodically, as is done in Table 13.8. The table shows number of shares, acquisition date, cost, and current value for each issue. These data aid in continually formulating strategy decisions. The cost data, for example, are used to determine the amount invested. Hathaway's portfolio does not utilize the leverage of a margin account. Were leverage present, all return calculations would be based on the investor's *equity* in the account. (Recall from Chapter 2 that an investor's equity in a margin account equals the total value of all the securities in the account minus any margin debt.)

To measure Hathaway's return on his invested capital, we need to calculate the 1-year holding period return. His invested capital as of January 1, 2002, is $324,000. No new additions of capital were made in the portfolio during 2002, although he sold one stock, Dallas National, and used the proceeds to buy another, Florida Southcoast Banks.

Measuring Income There are two sources of return from a portfolio of common stocks: income and capital gains. Current income is realized from dividends or, for bonds, is earned in the form of interest. Investors must report taxable dividends and interest on federal and state income tax returns. Companies are required to furnish income reports (Form 1099-DIV for dividends and Form 1099-INT for interest) to stockholders and bondholders. Many investors maintain logs to keep track of dividend and interest income as it is received.

Table 13.9 lists Hathaway's dividends for 2002. He received two quarterly dividends of 45 cents per share before he sold the Dallas National stock. He also received two 32-cent-per-share quarterly dividends on the additional Florida Southcoast Banks shares he acquired. His total dividend income for 2002 was $10,935.

Measuring Capital Gains Table 13.10 shows the unrealized gains in value for each of the issues in the Hathaway portfolio. The January 1, 2002, and December 31, 2002, values are listed for each issue except the additional shares of Florida Southcoast Banks. The amounts listed for Florida Southcoast

| TABLE 13.9 | Dividend Income on Hathaway's Portfolio (Calendar year 2002) |

Number of Shares	Company	Annual Dividend per Share	Dividends Received
1,000	Bancorp West, Inc.	$1.20	$ 1,200
1,000	Dallas National Corporation*	1.80	900
1,000	Dator Companies, Inc.	1.12	1,120
500	Excelsior Industries	2.00	1,000
2,000	Florida Southcoast Banks**	1.28	1,920
1,000	Maryland-Pacific	1.10	1,100
1,000	Moronson	—	—
500	Northwest Mining and Mfg.	2.05	1,025
1,000	Rawland Petroleum	1.20	1,200
1,000	Vornox	1.47	1,470
	Total		$10,935

*Sold May 7, 2002.
**1,000 shares acquired on May 10, 2002.

Banks reflect the fact that 1,000 additional shares of the stock were acquired on May 10, 2002, at a cost of $32,040. Hathaway's current holdings had beginning-of-the-year values of $327,040 (including the additional Florida Southcoast Banks shares at the date of purchase) and are worth $356,000 at year-end.

During 2002, the portfolio increased in value by 8.9%, or $28,960, in unrealized capital gains. In addition, Hathaway realized a capital gain in 2002 by selling his Dallas National holding. From January 1, 2002, until its sale on

| TABLE 13.10 | Unrealized Gains in Value of Hathaway's Portfolio (January 1, 2002, to December 31, 2002) |

Number of Shares	Company	Market Value (1/1/02)	Market Price (12/31/02)	Market Value (12/31/02)	Unrealized Gain (Loss)	Percentage Change
1,000	Bancorp West, Inc.	$ 30,000	$27	$ 27,000	($ 3,000)	−10.0%
1,000	Dator Companies, Inc.	27,000	36	36,000	9,000	+33.3
500	Excelsior Industries	27,000	66	33,000	6,000	+22.2
2,000	Florida Southcoast Banks*	62,040	35	70,000	7,960	+12.8
1,000	Maryland-Pacific	26,000	26	26,000	—	—
1,000	Moronson	47,000	55	55,000	8,000	+17.0
500	Northwest Mining and Mfg.	31,000	60	30,000	(1,000)	− 3.2
1,000	Rawland Petroleum	30,000	36	36,000	6,000	+20.0
1,000	Vornox	47,000	43	43,000	(4,000)	− 8.5
	Total	$327,040**		$356,000	$28,960	+ 8.9%

*1,000 additional shares acquired on May 10, 2002, at a cost of $32,040. The value listed is the cost plus the market value of the previously owned shares as of January 1, 2002.
**This total includes the $324,000 market value of the portfolio on January 1, 2002 (from Table 13.8) plus the $3,040 *realized* gain on the sale of the Dallas National Corporation stock on May 7, 2002. The inclusion of the realized gain in this total is necessary to calculate the *unrealized* gain on the portfolio during 2002.

INVESTING in action

Portfolio Return Is Tough to Calculate

Portfolio return is not an easy number to calculate, as the Beardstown Ladies Investment Club learned to their chagrin. The Ladies wrote a best-selling book that touted an average annual return of 23.4% on their investment portfolio for the decade ending 1993, a return above that of most hot-shot Wall Street investors. But in 1998 the club was forced to concede that it had made a mistake in its performance calculations. Indeed, an audit by the accounting firm of Price Waterhouse showed an average annual return of just 9.1% during that period.

Most investors have a pretty good idea of how major market benchmarks like the S&P 500 Stock Composite Index did during the year, because the results are published in newspapers. But when it comes to their own performance, most people have only a rough idea. And there aren't many easy answers in year-end brokerage and mutual fund statements. Why don't they provide this information? For one thing, it would be a lot of work and a lot of computer programming effort. Another reason could be that if the results are poor, it might reflect badly on the broker.

True, if all you have is one brokerage account with a $50,000 balance, if you don't add any funds during the year, and if you don't withdraw any funds, it's pretty easy to calculate your total return. Let's say your ending balance is $60,000; that means your total return is $10,000, or $10,000/$50,000 = 20%.

Now, to make the calculation a little bit more complicated, let's say you begin the year with a $100,000 portfolio and end it with $125,000. During the year, your additions to the portfolio less your withdrawals totaled $5,000. You began the year with $100,000 and ended it with $125,000, so you can make the assumption that your average balance during the year was $112,500. Your total gain during the year would be your ending balance minus your beginning balance minus your additions to the portfolio, or $20,000 ($125,000 − $100,000 − $5,000). Your total return percentage is $20,000 divided by $112,500, or roughly 18% before taxes.

The next step would be to compare your results against the appropriate benchmark: the S&P 500 Stock Composite Index for large domestic stocks, the Morgan Stanley EAFE (Europe, Australia, and Far East) Index for international stocks, or the Russell 2000 Index for small U.S. stocks. If it's a bond portfolio, then you might compare your results against the Lehman Brothers Government/Corporate Bond Index.

If you want to compute your precise rate of return, you will need software like Quicken Deluxe or the portfolio tracker available free on *Money* magazine's Web site (www.money.com). You would also need to know the exact timing of any additions or withdrawals you made during the year. It's a lot of work to come up with these numbers, and it may not be worth the effort to be that precise, unless, like the Beardstown Ladies, you plan to advertise your results in the media.

May 7, 2002, the Dallas National holding rose in value from $29,000 to $32,040. This was the only sale in 2002, so the total *realized* gain was $3,040. During 2002, the portfolio had both a realized gain of $3,040 and an unrealized gain of $28,960. The total gain in value equals the sum of the two: $32,000. Put another way, no capital was added to or withdrawn from the portfolio over the year. Therefore, the total capital gain is simply the difference between the year-end market value (of $356,000, from Table 13.10) and the value on January 1 (of $324,000, from Table 13.8). This, of course, amounts to $32,000. Of that amount, for tax purposes, only $3,040 is considered realized.

Measuring the Portfolio's Holding-Period Return We use the holding period return (HPR) to measure the total return on the Hathaway portfolio during 2002. The basic 1-year HPR formula for portfolios is

Equation 13.3

$$
\begin{array}{l}
\text{Holding}\\
\text{period}\\
\text{return for}\\
\text{a portfolio}
\end{array}
=
\dfrac{
\begin{array}{c}
\text{Dividends and}\\
\text{interest} \\
\text{received}
\end{array}
+
\begin{array}{c}
\text{Realized}\\
\text{gain}
\end{array}
+
\begin{array}{c}
\text{Unrealized}\\
\text{gain}
\end{array}
}{
\begin{array}{c}
\text{Initial}\\
\text{equity}\\
\text{investment}
\end{array}
+
\left(
\begin{array}{c}
\text{New}\\
\text{funds}
\end{array}
\times
\dfrac{
\begin{array}{c}
\text{Number of}\\
\text{months in}\\
\text{portfolio}
\end{array}
}{12}
\right)
-
\left(
\begin{array}{c}
\text{Withdrawn}\\
\text{funds}
\end{array}
\times
\dfrac{
\begin{array}{c}
\text{Number of months}\\
\text{withdrawn}\\
\text{from portfolio}
\end{array}
}{12}
\right)
}
$$

Equation 13.3a

$$
\text{HPR}_p = \dfrac{C + RG + UG}{E_0 + \left(NF \times \dfrac{ip}{12}\right) - \left(WF \times \dfrac{wp}{12}\right)}
$$

This formula includes both the realized gains (income plus capital gains) and the unrealized yearly gains of the portfolio. Portfolio additions and deletions are time-weighted for the number of months they are in the portfolio.

Table 13.10 lays out in detail the portfolio's change in value: All the issues that are in the portfolio as of December 31, 2002, are listed, and the unrealized gain during the year is calculated. The beginning and year-end values are included for comparison purposes. The crux of the analysis is the HPR calculation for the year, presented in Table 13.11. All the elements of a portfolio's return are included. Dividends total $10,935 (from Table 13.9). The realized gain of $3,040 represents the increment in value of the Dallas National holding from January 1, 2002, until its sale. During 2002 the portfolio had a $28,960 unrealized gain (from Table 13.10). There were no additions of new funds, and no funds were withdrawn. Utilizing Equation 13.3 for HPR, we find that the portfolio had a total return of 13.25% in 2002.

Comparison of Return with Overall Market Measures

Bob Hathaway can compare the HPR figure for his portfolio with market measures such as stock indexes. This comparison will show how Hathaway's portfolio is doing in relation to the stock market as a whole. The S&P 500 Stock Composite Index and the Nasdaq Composite Index are acceptable indexes for this type of analysis. They are broadly based and so can be said to represent the stock market as a whole. Assume that during 2002, the return on the S&P 500 index was +10.75% (including both dividends and capital gains). The return from Hathaway's portfolio was +13.25%, which compares very favorably with the broadly based index. The Hathaway portfolio performed about 23% better than the broad indicator of stock market return.

Such a comparison factors out general market movements, but *it fails to consider risk*. Clearly, a raw return figure, such as this +13.25%, requires further analysis. A number of risk-adjusted, market-adjusted rate-of-return measures are available for use in assessing portfolio performance. Here we'll discuss three of the most popular—Sharpe's measure, Treynor's measure, and Jensen's measure—and demonstrate their application to Hathaway's portfolio.

TABLE 13.11 Holding Period Return Calculation on Hathaway's Portfolio (January 1, 2002, to December 31, 2002, holding period)

Data

Portfolio value (1/1/02):	$324,000
Portfolio value (12/31/02):	$356,000
Realized appreciation (1/1/02 to 5/7/02 when Dallas National was sold):	$ 3,040
Unrealized appreciation (1/1/02 to 12/31/02):	$ 28,960
Dividends received:	$ 10,935
New funds invested or withdrawn:	None

Portfolio HPR Calculation

$$HPR_p = \frac{\$10,935 + \$3,040 + \$28,960}{\$324,000}$$

$$= +\underline{13.25\%}$$

Sharpe's measure
a measure of portfolio performance that measures the *risk premium per unit of total risk,* which is measured by the portfolio standard deviation of return.

Sharpe's Measure **Sharpe's measure** of portfolio performance, developed by William F. Sharpe, compares the risk premium on a portfolio to the portfolio's standard deviation of return. The risk premium on a portfolio is the total portfolio return minus the risk-free rate. Sharpe's measure can be expressed as the following formula:

Equation 13.4

$$\text{Sharpe's measure} = \frac{\text{Total portfolio return} - \text{Risk-free rate}}{\text{Portfolio standard deviation of return}}$$

Equation 13.4a

$$SM = \frac{r_p - R_F}{s_p}$$

This measure allows the investor to assess the *risk premium per unit of total risk,* which is measured by the portfolio standard deviation of return.

Assume the risk-free rate, R_F, is 7.50% and the standard deviation of return on Hathaway's portfolio, s_p, is 16%. The total portfolio return, r_p, which is the HPR for Hathaway's portfolio calculated in Table 13.11, is 13.25%. Substituting those values into Equation 13.4, we get Sharpe's measure, *SM*.

$$SM = \frac{13.25\% - 7.50\%}{16\%} = \frac{5.75\%}{16\%} = \underline{0.36}$$

Sharpe's measure is meaningful when compared either to other portfolios or to the market. In general, the higher Sharpe's measure, the better—the higher the risk premium per unit of risk. If we assume that the market return, r_m, is currently 10.75% and the standard deviation of return for the market portfolio, s_{p_m}, is 11.25%, Sharpe's measure for the market, SM_m, is

$$SM_m = \frac{10.75\% - 7.50\%}{11.25\%} = \frac{3.25\%}{11.25\%} = \underline{0.29}$$

Because Sharpe's measure of 0.36 for Hathaway's portfolio is greater than the measure of 0.29 for the market portfolio, Hathaway's portfolio exhibits superior performance. Its risk premium per unit of risk is above that of the market. Had Sharpe's measure for Hathaway's portfolio been below that of the market (below 0.29), the portfolio's performance would be considered inferior to the market performance.

Treynor's Measure Jack L. Treynor developed a portfolio performance measure similar to Sharpe's measure. **Treynor's measure** uses the portfolio beta to measure the portfolio's risk. Treynor therefore focuses only on *nondiversifiable risk,* assuming that the portfolio has been built in a manner that diversifies away all diversifiable risk. (In contrast, Sharpe focuses on *total risk.*) Treynor's measure is calculated as shown in Equation 13.5.

Treynor's measure
a measure of portfolio performance that measures the *risk premium per unit of nondiversifiable risk,* which is measured by the portfolio's beta.

Equation 13.5

$$\text{Treynor's measure} = \frac{\text{Total portfolio return} - \text{Risk-free rate}}{\text{Portfolio beta}}$$

Equation 13.5a

$$TM = \frac{r_p - R_F}{b_p}$$

This measure gives *the risk premium per unit of nondiversifiable risk,* which is measured by the portfolio beta.

Using the data for the Hathaway portfolio presented earlier and assuming that the beta for Hathaway's portfolio, b_p, is 1.20, we can substitute into Equation 13.5 to get Treynor's measure, TM, for Hathaway's portfolio.

$$TM = \frac{13.25\% - 7.50\%}{1.20} = \frac{5.75\%}{1.20} = \underline{\underline{4.79\%}}$$

HOTLINKS

A good discussion of the Sharpe, Treynor, and Jenson measures of performance can be found at:

**www.duke.edu/~charvey/
Classes/ba350_1997/perf/perf.htm**

Treynor's measure, like Sharpe's, is useful when compared either to other portfolios or to the market. Generally, the higher the value of Treynor's measure, the better—the greater the risk premium per unit of nondiversifiable risk. Again assuming that the market return, r_m, is 10.75%, and recognizing that, by definition, the beta for the market portfolio, b_{p_m}, is 1.00, we can use Equation 13.5 to find Treynor's measure for the market, TM_m.

$$TM_m = \frac{10.75\% - 7.50\%}{1.00} = \frac{3.25\%}{1.00} = \underline{\underline{3.25\%}}$$

The fact that Treynor's measure of 4.79% for Hathaway's portfolio is greater than the market portfolio measure of 3.25% indicates that Hathaway's portfolio exhibits superior performance. Its risk premium per unit of nondiversifiable risk is above that of the market. Conversely, had Treynor's measure for Hathaway's portfolio been below that of the market (below 3.25%), the portfolio's performance would be viewed as inferior to that of the market.

Jensen's Measure (Jensen's Alpha) Michael C. Jensen developed a portfolio performance measure that seems quite different from the measures of

Jensen's measure (Jensen's alpha)
a measure of portfolio performance that uses the portfolio's beta and CAPM to calculate its *excess return,* which may be positive, zero, or negative.

Sharpe and Treynor yet is theoretically consistent with Treynor's measure. **Jensen's measure,** also called **Jensen's alpha,** is based on the *capital asset pricing model (CAPM),* which was developed in Chapter 5 (see Equation 5.3). It calculates the portfolio's *excess return.* Excess return is the amount by which the portfolio's actual return deviates from its required return, which is determined using its beta and CAPM. The value of the excess return may be positive, zero, or negative. Like Treynor's measure, Jensen's measure focuses only on the *nondiversifiable,* or *relevant, risk* by using beta and CAPM. It assumes that the portfolio has been adequately diversified. Jensen's measure is calculated as shown in Equation 13.6.

Equation 13.6

$$\text{Jensen's measure} = (\text{Total portfolio return} - \text{Risk-free rate}) - [\text{Portfolio beta} \times (\text{Market return} - \text{Risk-free rate})]$$

Equation 13.6a

$$JM = (r_p - R_F) - [b_p \times (r_m - R_F)]$$

Jensen's measure indicates the difference between the portfolio's actual return and its required return. Positive values are preferred. They indicate that the portfolio earned a return in excess of its risk-adjusted, market-adjusted required return. A value of zero indicates that the portfolio earned *exactly* its required return. Negative values indicate the portfolio failed to earn its required return.

Using the data for Hathaway's portfolio presented earlier, we can substitute into Equation 13.6 to get Jensen's measure, *JM,* for Hathaway's portfolio.

$$JM = (13.25\% - 7.50\%) - [1.20 \times (10.75\% - 7.50\%)]$$
$$= 5.75\% - (1.20 \times 3.25\%) = 5.75\% - 3.90\% = \underline{1.85\%}$$

TIME TO REVISE YOUR PORTFOLIO?—Over time, you will need to review your portfolio to ensure that it reflects the right risk-return characteristics for your goals and needs. Here are four good reasons to perform this task:
• A major life event—marriage, birth of a child, job loss, illness, loss of a spouse, a child's finishing college—changes your investment objectives.
• The proportion of one asset class increases or decreases substantially.
• You expect to reach a specific goal within 2 years.
• The percentage in an asset class varies from your original allocation by 10% or more.

The 1.85% value for Jensen's measure indicates that Hathaway's portfolio earned an *excess return* 1.85 percentage points above its required return, given its nondiversifiable risk as measured by beta. Clearly, Hathaway's portfolio has outperformed the market on a risk-adjusted basis.

Note that unlike the Sharpe and Treynor measures, Jensen's measure, through its use of CAPM, automatically adjusts for the market return. Therefore, there is no need to make a separate market comparison. In general, the higher Jensen's measure, the better the portfolio has performed. Only those portfolios with positive Jensen measures have outperformed the market on a risk-adjusted basis. Because of its computational simplicity, its reliance only on nondiversifiable risk, and its inclusion of both risk and market adjustments, Jensen's measure (alpha) tends to be preferred over those of Sharpe and Treynor for assessing portfolio performance.

Portfolio Revision

In the Hathaway portfolio we have been discussing, one transaction occurred during 2002. The reason for this transaction was that Hathaway believed the Florida Southcoast Banks stock had more return potential than the Dallas National stock. You should periodically analyze your portfolio with one basic question in mind: "Does this portfolio continue to meet my needs?" In other words, does the portfolio contain those issues that are best suited to your

portfolio revision
the process of selling certain issues in a portfolio and purchasing new ones to replace them.

risk-return needs? Investors who systematically study the issues in their portfolios will occasionally find a need to sell certain issues and purchase new securities to replace them. This process is commonly called **portfolio revision.** As the economy evolves, certain industries and stocks become either less or more attractive as investments. In today's stock market, timeliness is the essence of profitability.

Given the dynamics of the investment world, periodic reallocation and rebalancing of the portfolio are a necessity. Many circumstances require such changes. As we demonstrated earlier in this chapter, as an investor nears retirement, the portfolio's emphasis normally evolves from a strategy that stresses growth/capital appreciation to one that seeks to preserve capital. Changing a portfolio's emphasis normally occurs as an evolutionary process rather than an overnight switch. Individual issues in the portfolio often change in risk-return characteristics. As this occurs, you would be wise to eliminate those issues that do not meet your objectives. In addition, the need for diversification is constant. As issues rise or fall in value, their diversification effect may be lessened. Thus portfolio revision may be needed to maintain diversification in the portfolio.

IN REVIEW

CONCEPTS

13.11 What is *active portfolio management?* Will it result in superior returns? Explain.

13.12 Describe the steps involved in measuring portfolio return. Explain the role of the portfolio's HPR in this process, and explain why one must differentiate between realized and unrealized gains.

13.13 According to the *Investing in Action* box on page 559, why don't year-end brokerage and mutual fund statements provide performance data? How should you calculate your portfolio's return, and against what benchmarks should you compare it?

13.14 Why is comparing a portfolio's return to the return on a broad market index generally inadequate? Explain.

13.15 Briefly describe each of the following return measures available for assessing portfolio performance, and explain how they are used.
a. Sharpe's measure.
b. Treynor's measure.
c. Jensen's measure (Jensen's alpha).

13.16 Why is Jensen's measure (alpha) generally preferred over the measures of Sharpe and Treynor for assessing portfolio performance? Explain.

13.17 Explain the role of *portfolio revision* in the process of managing a portfolio.

Timing Transactions

LG 5   LG 6

The essence of timing is to "buy low and sell high." This is the dream of all investors. Although there is no tried-and-true way to achieve such a goal, there are several methods you can utilize to time purchases and sales. First, there are formula plans, which we discuss next. Investors can also use limit and stop-loss orders as a timing aid, can follow procedures for warehousing liquidity, and can take into consideration other aspects of timing when selling their investments.

Formula Plans

Formula plans are mechanical methods of portfolio management that try to take advantage of price changes that result from cyclical price movements. Formula plans are not set up to provide unusually high returns. Rather, they are conservative strategies employed by investors who do not wish to bear a high level of risk. Four popular formula plans are discussed here: dollar-cost averaging, the constant-dollar plan, the constant-ratio plan, and the variable-ratio plan.

Dollar-Cost Averaging **Dollar-cost averaging** is a formula plan in which a fixed dollar amount is invested in a security at fixed intervals. In this passive buy-and-hold strategy, the periodic dollar investment is held constant. To make the plan work, you must have the discipline to invest on a regular basis. The goal of a dollar-cost averaging program is growth in the value of the security to which the funds are allocated. The price of the investment security will probably fluctuate over time. If the price declines, more shares are purchased per period. Conversely, if the price rises, fewer shares are purchased per period.

Look at the example of dollar-cost averaging in Table 13.12. The table shows investment of $500 per month in the Wolverine Mutual Fund, a growth-oriented, no-load mutual fund. Assume that during 1 year's time, you have placed $6,000 in the mutual fund shares. (Because this is a no-load fund, shares are purchased at net asset value, NAV.) You made purchases at NAVs ranging from a low of $24.16 to a high of $30.19. At year-end, the value of your holdings in the fund was slightly less than $6,900. Dollar-cost averaging is a passive strategy; other formula plans are more active.

Constant-Dollar Plan A **constant-dollar plan** consists of a portfolio that is divided into two parts, speculative and conservative. The speculative portion consists of securities that have high promise of capital gains. The conservative portion consists of low-risk investments such as bonds or a money market account. The target dollar amount for the speculative portion is constant. The investor establishes trigger points (upward or downward movement in the speculative portion) at which funds are removed from or added to that portion. The constant-dollar plan basically skims off profits from the speculative portion of the portfolio if it rises a certain percentage or amount in value and adds these funds to the conservative portion of the portfolio. If the speculative portion of the portfolio declines by a specific percentage or amount, funds are added to it from the conservative portion.

Assume that you have established the constant-dollar plan shown in Table 13.13. The beginning $20,000 portfolio consists of $10,000 invested in a high-beta, no-load mutual fund and $10,000 deposited in a money market account. You have decided to rebalance the portfolio every time the speculative portion is worth $2,000 more or $2,000 less than its initial value of $10,000. If the speculative portion of the portfolio equals or exceeds $12,000, you sell sufficient shares of the fund to bring its value down to $10,000. The proceeds from the sale are added to the conservative portion. If the speculative portion declines in value to $8,000 or less, you use funds from the conservative portion to purchase sufficient shares to raise the value of the speculative portion to $10,000.

TABLE 13.12 **Dollar-Cost Averaging ($500 per month, Wolverine Mutual Fund shares)**

Transactions

Month	Net Asset Value (NAV) Month-End	Number of Shares Purchased
January	$26.00	19.23
February	27.46	18.21
March	27.02	18.50
April	24.19	20.67
May	26.99	18.53
June	25.63	19.51
July	24.70	20.24
August	24.16	20.70
September	25.27	19.79
October	26.15	19.12
November	29.60	16.89
December	30.19	16.56

Annual Summary

Total investment: $6,000.00
Total number of shares purchased: 227.95
Average cost per share: $26.32
Year-end portfolio value: $6,881.81

Two portfolio-rebalancing actions are taken in the time sequence illustrated in Table 13.13. Initially, $10,000 was allocated to each portion of the portfolio. When the mutual fund's net asset value (NAV) rose to $12.00, the speculative portion was worth $12,000. At that point you sold 166.67 shares valued at $2,000, and added the proceeds to the money market account. Later, the mutual fund's NAV declined to $9.50 per share, causing the value of the speculative portion to drop below $8,000. This change triggered the purchase of sufficient shares to raise the value of the speculative portion to $10,000. Over the long run, if the speculative investment of the constant-dollar plan rises in value, the conservative component of the portfolio will increase in dollar value as profits are transferred into it.

Constant-Ratio Plan   The **constant-ratio plan** is similar to the constant-dollar plan except that it establishes a desired fixed *ratio* of the speculative portion to the conservative portion of the portfolio. When the actual ratio of the two differs by a predetermined amount from the desired ratio, rebalancing occurs. At that point, transactions are made to bring the actual ratio back to the desired ratio. If you use the constant-ratio plan, you must decide on the appropriate apportionment of the portfolio between speculative and conservative investments. You must also choose the ratio trigger point at which transactions occur.

To see how this works, assume that the constant-ratio plan illustrated in Table 13.14 is yours. The initial portfolio value is $20,000. You have decided to allocate 50% of the portfolio to the speculative, high-beta mutual fund and 50% to a money market account. You will rebalance the portfolio when the ratio of the speculative portion to the conservative portion is greater than or

constant-ratio plan
a formula plan for timing investment transactions, in which a desired fixed *ratio* of the speculative portion to the conservative portion of the portfolio is established; when the actual ratio differs by a predetermined amount from the desired ratio, transactions are made to rebalance the portfolio to achieve the desired ratio.

TABLE 13.13 Constant-Dollar Plan

Mutual Fund NAV	Value of Speculative Portion	Value of Conservative Portion	Total Portfolio Value	Transactions	Number of Shares in Speculative Portion
$10.00	$10,000.00	$10,000.00	$20,000.00		1,000
11.00	11,000.00	10,000.00	21,000.00		1,000
12.00	12,000.00	10,000.00	22,000.00		1,000
→ 12.00	10,000.00	12,000.00	22,000.00	Sold 166.67 shares	833.33
11.00	9,166.63	12,000.00	21,166.63		833.33
9.50	7,916.64	12,000.00	19,916.64		833.33
→ 9.50	10,000.00	9,916.64	19,916.64	Purchased 219.30 shares	1,052.63
10.00	10,526.30	9,916.64	20,442.94		1,052.63

equal to 1.20 or less than or equal to 0.80. A sequence of changes in net asset value (NAV) is listed in Table 13.14. Initially, $10,000 is allocated to each portion of the portfolio. When the fund NAV reaches $12, the 1.20 ratio triggers the sale of 83.33 shares. Then the portfolio is back to its desired 50–50 ratio. Later, the fund NAV declines to $9, lowering the value of the speculative portion to $8,250. The ratio of the speculative portion to the conservative portion is then 0.75, which is below the 0.80 trigger point. You purchase 152.78 shares to bring the desired ratio back up to the 50–50 level.

The long-run expectation under a constant-ratio plan is that the speculative securities will rise in value. When this occurs, the investor will sell securities to reapportion the portfolio and increase the value of the conservative portion. This philosophy is similar to the constant-dollar plan, except that a ratio is utilized as a trigger point.

variable-ratio plan
a formula plan for timing investment transactions, in which the ratio of the speculative portion to the total portfolio varies depending on the movement in value of the speculative securities; when the ratio rises or falls by a predetermined amount, the amount committed to the speculative portion of the portfolio is reduced or increased, respectively.

Variable-Ratio Plan The **variable-ratio plan** is the most aggressive of these four fairly passive formula plans. It attempts to turn stock market movements to the investor's advantage by timing the market. That is, it tries to "buy low and sell high." The ratio of the speculative portion to the total portfolio value varies depending on the movement in value of the speculative securities. When the ratio rises a certain predetermined amount, the amount committed to the

TABLE 13.14 Constant-Ratio Plan

Mutual Fund NAV	Value of Speculative Portion	Value of Conservative Portion	Total Portfolio Value	Ratio of Speculative Portion to Conservative Portion	Transactions	Number of Shares in Speculative Portion
$10.00	$10,000.00	$10,000.00	$20,000.00	1.000		1,000
11.00	11,000.00	10,000.00	21,000.00	1.100		1,000
12.00	12,000.00	10,000.00	22,000.00	1.200		1,000
→ 12.00	11,000.00	11,000.00	22,000.00	1.000	Sold 83.33 shares	916.67
11.00	10,083.00	11,000.00	21,083.00	0.917		916.67
10.00	9,166.70	11,000.00	20,166.70	0.833		916.67
9.00	8,250.00	11,000.00	19,250.00	0.750		916.67
→ 9.00	9,625.00	9,625.00	19,250.00	1.000	Purchased 152.78 shares	1,069.44
10.00	10,694.40	9,625.00	20,319.40	1.110		1,069.44

speculative portion of the portfolio is reduced. Conversely, if the value of the speculative portion declines so that it drops significantly in proportion to the total portfolio value, the amount committed to the speculative portion of the portfolio is increased.

When implementing the variable-ratio plan, you have several decisions to make. First, you must determine the initial allocation between the speculative and conservative portions of the portfolio. Next, you must choose trigger points to initiate buy or sell activity. These points are a function of the ratio between the value of the speculative portion and the value of the total portfolio. Finally, you must set adjustments in that ratio at each trigger point.

Assume that you use the variable-ratio plan shown in Table 13.15. Initially, you divide the portfolio equally between the speculative and the conservative portions. The speculative portion consists of a high-beta (around 2.0) mutual fund. The conservative portion is a money market account. You decide that when the speculative portion reaches 60% of the total portfolio, you will reduce its proportion to 45%. If the speculative portion of the portfolio drops to 40% of the total portfolio, then you will raise its proportion to 55%. The logic behind this strategy is an attempt to time the cyclical movements in the mutual fund's value. When the fund moves up in value, profits are taken, and the proportion invested in the no-risk money market account is increased. When the fund declines markedly in value, the proportion of capital committed to it is increased.

A sequence of transactions is depicted in Table 13.15. When the fund net asset value (NAV) climbs to $15, the 60% ratio trigger point is reached, and you sell 250 shares of the fund. The proceeds are placed in the money market account, which causes the speculative portion then to represent 45% of the value of the portfolio. Later the fund NAV declines to $10, causing the speculative portion of the portfolio to drop to 35%. This triggers a portfolio rebalancing, and you purchase 418.75 shares, moving the speculative portion to 55%. When the fund NAV then moves to $12, the total portfolio is worth in excess of $23,500. In comparison, had the initial investment of $20,000 been allocated equally and had no rebalancing been done between the mutual fund and the money market account, the total portfolio value at this time would have been only $22,000 ($12 × 1,000 = $12,000 in the speculative portion plus $10,000 in the money market account).

| TABLE 13.15 | Variable-Ratio Plan |

Mutual Fund NAV	Value of Speculative Portion	Value of Conservative Portion	Total Portfolio Value	Ratio of Speculative Portion to Total Portfolio Value	Transactions	Number of Shares in Speculative Portion
$10.00	$10,000.00	$10,000.00	$20,000.00	0.50		1,000
15.00	15,000.00	10,000.00	25,000.00	0.60		1,000
→ 15.00	11,250.00	13,750.00	25,000.00	0.45	Sold 250 shares	750
10.00	7,500.00	13,750.00	21,250.00	0.35		750
→ 10.00	11,687.50	9,562.50	21,250.00	0.55	Purchased 418.75 shares	1,168.75
12.00	14,025.00	9,562.50	23,587.50	0.59		1,168.75

Using Limit and Stop-Loss Orders

In Chapter 3 we discussed the market order, the limit order, and the stop-loss order. (See pages 106–108 to review these types of orders.) Here we will see how the limit and stop-loss orders can be employed to rebalance a portfolio. These types of security orders, if properly used, can increase return by lowering transaction costs.

Limit Orders There are many ways investors can use limit orders when securities are bought or sold. For instance, if you have decided to add a stock to the portfolio, a limit order to buy will ensure that you buy only at the desired purchase price or below. A limit *good-'til-canceled (GTC)* order to buy instructs the broker to buy stock until the entire order is filled. The primary risk in using limit instead of market orders is that the order may not be executed. For example, if you placed a GTC order to buy 100 shares of State Oil of California at $27 per share and the stock never traded at $27 per share or less, the order would never be executed. Thus you must weigh the need for immediate execution (market order) against the possibility of a better price with a limit order.

Limit orders, of course, can increase your return if they enable you to buy a security at a lower cost or sell it at a higher price. During a typical trading day, a stock will fluctuate up and down over a normal trading range. For example, suppose the common shares of Jama Motor traded ten times in the following sequence: 36.00, 35.88, 35.75, 35.94, 35.50, 35.63, 35.82, 36.00, 36.13, 36.00. A market order to sell could have been executed at somewhere between 35.50 (the low) and 36.13 (the high). A limit order to sell at 36.00 would have been executed at 36.00. Thus a half-point per share (50 cents) might have been gained by using a limit order.

Stop-Loss Orders Stop-loss orders can be used to limit the downside loss exposure of an investment. For example, assume you purchase 500 shares of Easy Work at 26.00 and have set a specific goal to sell the stock if it reaches 32.00 or drops to 23.00. To implement this goal, you would enter a GTC stop order to sell with a price limit of 32.00 and another stop order at a price of 23.00. If the issue trades at 23.00 or less, the stop-loss order becomes a market order, and the broker sells the stock at the best price available. Or, if the issue trades at 32.00 or higher, the broker will sell the stock. In the first situation, you are trying to reduce your losses, in the second, to protect a profit.

whipsawing
the situation where a stock temporarily drops in price and then bounces back upward.

The principal risk in using stop-loss orders is **whipsawing**—a situation where a stock temporarily drops in price and then bounces back upward. If Easy Work dropped to 23.00, then 22.57, and then rallied back to 26.00, you would have been sold out at a price between 23.00 and 22.57. For this reason, limit orders, including stop-loss orders, require careful analysis before they are placed. You must consider the stock's probable fluctuations as well as the need to purchase or sell the stock when choosing among market, limit, and stop-loss orders.

Warehousing Liquidity

Investing in risky stocks or in options or futures offers probable returns in excess of money market deposit accounts or bonds. However, stocks and options and futures are risky investments. One recommendation for an efficient portfolio is to keep a portion of it in a low-risk, highly liquid investment to protect against total loss. The low-risk asset acts as a buffer against possible investment adversity. A second reason for maintaining funds in a low-risk asset is the possibility of future opportunities. When opportunity strikes, an investor who has extra cash available will be able to take advantage of the situation. If you have set aside funds in a highly liquid investment, you need not disturb the existing portfolio.

There are two primary media for warehousing liquidity: money market deposit accounts at financial institutions and money market mutual funds. The money market accounts at savings institutions provide relatively easy access to funds and furnish returns competitive with (but somewhat lower than) money market mutual funds. Over time, the products offered by financial institutions are expected to become more competitive with those offered by mutual funds and stock brokerage firms.

Timing Investment Sales

Knowing when to sell a stock is as important as deciding which stock to buy. Periodically, you should review your portfolio and consider possible sales and new purchases. Here we discuss two issues relevant to the sale decision: tax consequences and achieving investment goals.

Tax Consequences Taxes affect nearly all investment actions. All investors can and should understand certain basics. The treatment of capital losses is important: *A maximum of $3,000 of losses in excess of capital gains can be written off against other income in any one year.* If you have a loss position in an investment and have concluded that it would be wise to sell it, the best time to sell is when a capital gain is available against which the loss can be applied. Clearly, one should carefully consider the tax consequences of investment sales prior to taking action.

Achieving Investment Goals Every investor would enjoy buying an investment at its lowest price and selling it at its top price. At a more realistic level, an investment should be sold when it no longer meets the needs of the portfolio's owner. In particular, if an investment has become either more or less risky than is desired, or if it has not met its return objective, it should be sold. The tax consequences mentioned above help to determine the appropriate time to sell. However, *taxes are not the foremost consideration in a sale decision.* The dual concepts of risk and return should be the overriding concerns.

Each investment should be examined periodically in light of its return performance and relative risk. You should sell any investment that no longer belongs in the portfolio and should buy vehicles that are more suitable. Finally, you should not hold out for every nickel of profit. Very often, those who hold out for the top price watch the value of their holdings plummet. If an investment looks ripe to sell, sell it, take the profit, reinvest it in an appropriate vehicle, and enjoy your good fortune.

HOTLINKS

For some tips on knowing when and what to sell, see the *Investing in Action* box on our Web site:

www.awl.com/gitman_joehnk

CONCEPTS

13.18 Explain the role that *formula plans* can play in the timing of security transactions. Describe the logic underlying the use of these plans.

13.19 Briefly describe each of the following plans and differentiate among them.
a. Dollar-cost averaging.   b. Constant-dollar plan.
c. Constant-ratio plan.   d. Variable-ratio plan.

13.20 Describe how a limit order can be used when securities are bought or sold. How can a stop-loss order be used to reduce losses? To protect profit?

13.21 Give two reasons why an investor might want to maintain funds in a low-risk, highly liquid investment.

13.22 Describe the two items an investor should consider before reaching a decision to sell an investment vehicle.

Summary

LG 1 **Construct portfolios with asset allocations and risk-return profiles consistent with the investor's objectives.** An investor's objectives determine the asset allocations and risk-return profile for his or her portfolio. A single investor who wants to build wealth quickly will tend to allocate funds to more risky assets that have high growth potential. A retired couple who needs income to meet their living expenses will allocate funds to conservative, low-risk investment vehicles that provide periodic income in the form of dividends or interest.

LG 2 **Discuss the data and indexes needed to measure and compare investment performance.** To analyze the performance of individual investments, the investor must gather current market information and stay abreast of international, national, and local economic and market developments. Indexes of investment performance such as the Dow Jones Industrial Average (DJIA) and bond market indicators are available for use in assessing market behavior. The performance of individual investment vehicles can be measured on both a pretax and an after-tax basis by using the holding period return. HPR measures the total return (income plus change in value) actually earned on the investment during the investment period. HPR can be compared to investment goals to assess whether the proper return is being earned for the risk involved and to isolate any problem investments.

LG 3 **Understand the techniques used to measure income, capital gains, and total portfolio return.** To measure portfolio return, the investor must estimate the amount invested, the income earned, and any capital gains (both realized and unrealized) over the relevant current time period. Using these values, the investor can calculate the portfolio's holding period return (HPR) by dividing the total returns by the amount of investment during the period. Comparison of the portfolio's HPR to overall market measures can provide some insight with regard to the portfolio's performance relative to the market.

LG 4 **Use the Sharpe, Treynor, and Jensen measures to compare a portfolio's return with a risk-adjusted, market-adjusted rate of return, and discuss portfolio revision.** A risk-adjusted, market-adjusted evaluation of a portfolio's return can be made using Sharpe's measure, Treynor's measure, or Jensen's measure. Sharpe's and Treynor's measures find the risk premium per unit of risk, which can be compared with similar market measures to assess the portfolio's performance. Jensen's measure, which is theoretically consistent with Treynor's, calculates the portfolio's excess return using beta and CAPM. Because it is relatively easy to calculate and directly makes both risk and market adjustments, Jensen's measure tends to be preferred. Portfolio revision—selling certain issues and purchasing new ones to replace them—should take place when returns are unacceptable or when the portfolio fails to meet the investor's objectives.

LG 5   **Describe the role and logic of dollar-cost averaging, constant-dollar plans, constant-ratio plans, and variable-ratio plans.** Formula plans are used to time purchase and sale decisions to take advantage of price changes that result from cyclical price movements. The four commonly used formula plans are dollar-cost averaging, the constant-dollar plan, the constant-ratio plan, and the variable-ratio plan. All of them have certain decision rules or triggers that signal a purchase and/or sale action.

LG 6   **Explain the role of limit and stop-loss orders in investment timing, warehousing liquidity, and timing investment sales.** Limit and stop-loss orders can be used to trigger the rebalancing of a portfolio to contribute to improved portfolio returns. Low-risk, highly liquid investment vehicles such as money market deposit accounts and money market mutual funds can warehouse liquidity. Such liquidity can protect against total loss and allow the investor to seize quickly any attractive opportunities that occur. Investment sales should be timed to obtain maximum tax benefits (or minimum tax consequences) and to contribute to the achievement of the investor's goals.

Discussion Questions

LG 2   **Q13.1** Choose an established local (or nearby) company whose stock is listed and actively traded on a major exchange. Find the stock's closing price at the end of each of the preceding 6 years and the amount of dividends paid in each of the preceding 5 years. Also, obtain the value of the Dow Jones Industrial Average (DJIA) at the end of each of the preceding 6 years.
   a. Use Equation 13.1 to calculate the pretax holding period return (HPR) on the stock for each of the preceding 5 years.
   b. Study the international, national, and local economic and market developments that occurred during the preceding 5 years.
   c. Compare the stock's returns to the DJIA for each year over the 5-year period of concern.
   d. Discuss the stock's returns in light of the economic and market developments noted in part (b) and the behavior of the DJIA as noted in part (c) over the 5 preceding years. How well did the stock perform in light of these factors?

LG 2   **Q13.2** Assume that you are in the 35% tax bracket (federal and state combined). Select a major stock, bond, and mutual fund in which you are interested in investing. For each of them, gather data for each of the past 3 years on the annual dividends or interest paid and the capital gain (or loss) that would have resulted had they been purchased at the start of each year and sold at the end of each year. For the mutual fund, be sure to separate any dividends paid into investment income dividends and capital gains dividends.
   a. For each of the three investment vehicles, calculate the pretax and after-tax HPR for each of the 3 years.
   b. Use your annual HPR findings in part (a) to calculate the average after-tax HPR for each of the investment vehicles over the 3-year period.
   c. Compare the average returns found in part (b) for each of the investment vehicles. Discuss the relative risks in view of these returns and the characteristics of each vehicle.

LG 3   Q13.3 Choose six actively traded stocks for inclusion in your investment portfolio. Assume the portfolio was created 3 years earlier by purchasing 200 shares of each of the six stocks. Find the acquisition price of each stock, the annual dividend paid by each stock, and the year-end prices for the 3 calendar years. Record for each stock its total cost, cost per share, current price per share, and total current value at the end of each of the 3 calendar years.

    a. For each of the 3 years, find the amount invested in the portfolio.

    b. For each of the 3 years, measure the annual income from the portfolio.

    c. For each of the 3 years, determine the unrealized capital gains from the portfolio.

    d. For each of the 3 years, calculate the portfolio's HPR, using the values in parts (a), (b), and (c).

    e. Use your findings in part (d) to calculate the average HPR for the portfolio over the 3-year period. Discuss your finding.

LG 4   Q13.4 Find five actively traded stocks and record their prices at the start and the end of the most recent calendar year. Also, find the amount of dividends paid on each stock during that year and each stock's beta at the end of the year. Assume that the five stocks were held during the year in an equal-dollar-weighted portfolio (20% in each stock) created at the start of the year. Also find the current risk-free rate, R_F, and the market return, r_m, for the given year. Assume that the standard deviation for the portfolio of the five stocks is 14.25% and that the standard deviation for the market portfolio is 10.80%.

    a. Use the formula presented in Chapter 5 (Equation 5.1) to find the portfolio return, r_p, for the year under consideration.

    b. Calculate Sharpe's measure for both the portfolio and the market. Compare and discuss these values. On the basis of this measure, is the portfolio's performance inferior or superior? Explain.

    c. Calculate Treynor's measure for both the portfolio and the market. Compare and discuss these values. On the basis of this measure, is the portfolio's performance inferior or superior? Explain.

    d. Calculate Jensen's measure (Jensen's alpha) for the portfolio. Discuss its value. On the basis of this measure, is the portfolio's performance inferior or superior? Explain.

    e. Compare, contrast, and discuss your analysis using the three measures in parts (b), (c), and (d). Evaluate the portfolio.

LG 5   Q13.5 Choose a high-growth mutual fund and a money market mutual fund. Find and record their closing net asset values (NAVs) at the end of each *week* for the immediate past year. Assume that you wish to invest $10,400.

    a. Assume you use dollar-cost averaging to buy shares in both the high-growth and the money market funds by purchasing $100 of each of them at the end of each week—a total investment of $10,400 (52 weeks × $200/week). How many shares would you have purchased in each fund by year-end? What are the total number of shares, the average cost per share, and the year-end portfolio value of each fund? Total the year-end fund values and compare them to the total that would have resulted from investing $5,200 in each fund at the end of the first week.

    b. Assume you use a constant-dollar plan with 50% invested in the high-growth fund (speculative portion) and 50% invested in the money market fund (conservative portion). If the portfolio is rebalanced every time the speculative portion is worth $500 more or $500 less than its initial value of $5,200, what would be the total portfolio value and the number of shares in the speculative portion at year-end?

    c. Assume that, as in part (b), you initially invest 50% in the speculative portion and 50% in the conservative portion. But in this case you use a constant-ratio plan under which rebalancing to the 50–50 mix occurs whenever the ratio of the speculative to the conservative portion is greater than or equal to 1.25 or less than or equal to 0.75. What would be the total portfolio value and the number of shares in the speculative portion at year-end?

d. Compare and contrast the year-end values of the total portfolio under each of the plans in parts (a), (b), and (c). Which plan would have been best in light of these findings? Explain.

Problems

LG 2

P13.1 Mark Smith purchased 100 shares of Tomco Corporation in December 2001, at a total cost of $1,762. He held the shares for 15 months and then sold them, netting $2,500. During the period he held the stock, the company paid him $200 in cash dividends. How much, if any, was the capital gain realized upon the sale of stock? Calculate Mark's pretax HPR.

 LG 2

P13.2 Jill Clark invested $25,000 in the bonds of Industrial Aromatics, Inc. She held them for 13 months, at the end of which she sold them for $26,746. During the period of ownership she earned $2,000 interest. Calculate the pretax and after-tax HPR on Jill's investment. Assume that she is in the 31% ordinary tax bracket (federal and state combined) and pays a 20% capital gains rate for holding periods longer than 12 months.

LG 2

P13.3 Charlotte Smidt bought 2,000 shares of the balanced no-load LaJolla Fund exactly 1 year and 2 days ago for a NAV of $8.60 per share. During the year, the fund distributed investment income dividends of 32 cents per share and capital gains dividends of 38 cents per share. At the end of the year, Charlotte, who is in the 35% ordinary tax bracket (federal and state combined) and pays a 20% capital gains rate for holding periods longer than 12 months, realized $8.75 per share on the sale of all 2,000 shares. Calculate Charlotte's pretax and after-tax HPR on this transaction.

LG 2

P13.4 Marilyn Gore, who is in a 33% ordinary tax bracket (federal and state combined) and pays a 20% capital gains rate for holding periods longer than 12 months, purchased 10 options contracts for a total cost of $4,000 just over 1 year ago. Marilyn netted $4,700 upon the sale of the 10 contracts today. What are Marilyn's pretax and after-tax HPRs on this transaction?

LG 3

P13.5 On January 1, 2002, Simon Love's portfolio of 15 common stocks, completely equity-financed, had a market value of $264,000. At the end of May 2002, Simon sold one of the stocks, which had a beginning-of-year value of $26,300, for $31,500. He did not reinvest those or any other funds in the portfolio during the year. He received total dividends from stocks in his portfolio of $12,500 during the year. On December 31, 2002, Simon's portfolio had a market value of $250,000. Find the HPR on Simon's portfolio during the year ended December 31, 2002. (Measure the amount of withdrawn funds at their beginning-of-year value.)

LG 4

P13.6 Niki Malone's portfolio earned a return of 11.8% during the year just ended. The portfolio's standard deviation of return was 14.1%. The risk-free rate is currently 6.2%. During the year, the return on the market portfolio was 9.0% and its standard deviation was 9.4%.

a. Calculate Sharpe's measure for Niki Malone's portfolio for the year just ended.

    b. Compare the performance of Niki's portfolio found in part (a) to that of Hector Smith's portfolio, which has a Sharpe's measure of 0.43. Which portfolio performed better? Why?

    c. Calculate Sharpe's measure for the market portfolio for the year just ended.

    d. Use your findings in parts (a) and (c) to discuss the performance of Niki's portfolio relative to the market during the year just ended.

LG 4

P13.7 During the year just ended, Anna Schultz's portfolio, which has a beta of 0.90, earned a return of 8.6%. The risk-free rate is currently 7.3%, and the return on the market portfolio during the year just ended was 9.2%.

    a. Calculate Treynor's measure for Anna's portfolio for the year just ended.

    b. Compare the performance of Anna's portfolio found in part (a) to that of Stacey Quant's portfolio, which has a Treynor's measure of 1.25%. Which portfolio performed better? Explain.

    c. Calculate Treynor's measure for the market portfolio for the year just ended.

    d. Use your findings in parts (a) and (c) to discuss the performance of Anna's portfolio relative to the market during the year just ended.

LG 4

P13.8 Chee Chew's portfolio has a beta of 1.3 and earned a return of 12.9% during the year just ended. The risk-free rate is currently 7.8%. The return on the market portfolio during the year just ended was 11.0%.

    a. Calculate Jensen's measure (Jensen's alpha) for Chee's portfolio for the year just ended.

    b. Compare the performance of Chee's portfolio found in part (a) to that of Carri Uhl's portfolio, which has a Jensen's measure of -0.24. Which portfolio performed better? Explain.

    c. Use your findings in part (a) to discuss the performance of Chee's portfolio during the period just ended.

LG 4

P13.9 The risk-free rate is currently 8.1%. Use the data in the accompanying table for the Fio family's portfolio and the market portfolio during the year just ended to answer the questions that follow.

Data Item	Fios' Portfolio	Market Portfolio
Rate of return	12.8%	11.2%
Standard deviation of return	13.5%	9.6%
Beta	1.10	1.00

    a. Calculate Sharpe's measure for the portfolio and the market. Compare the two measures, and assess the performance of the Fios' portfolio during the year just ended.

    b. Calculate Treynor's measure for the portfolio and the market. Compare the two, and assess the performance of the Fios' portfolio during the year just ended.

    c. Calculate Jensen's measure (Jensen's alpha). Use it to assess the performance of the Fios' portfolio during the year just ended.

    d. On the basis of your findings in parts (a), (b), and (c), assess the performance of the Fios' portfolio during the year just ended.

LG 5

P13.10 Over the past 2 years, Jonas Cone has used a dollar-cost averaging formula to purchase $300 worth of FCI common stock each month. The price per share paid each month over the 2 years is given in the following table. Assume that Jonas paid no brokerage commissions on these transactions.

| | Price per Share of FCI | |
Month	Year 1	Year 2
January	11.63	11.38
February	11.50	11.75
March	11.50	12.00
April	11.00	12.00
May	11.75	12.13
June	12.00	12.50
July	12.38	12.75
August	12.50	13.00
September	12.25	13.25
October	12.50	13.00
November	11.85	13.38
December	11.50	13.50

a. How much was Jonas's total investment over the 2-year period?
b. How many shares did Jonas purchase over the 2-year period?
c. Use your findings in parts (a) and (b) to calculate Jonas's average cost per share of FCI.
d. What was the value of Jonas's holdings in FCI at the end of the second year?

Case Problem 13.1   *Assessing the Stalchecks' Portfolio Performance*

LG 2   LG 3   LG 4

Mary and Nick Stalcheck have an investment portfolio containing four vehicles. It was developed to provide them with a balance between current income and capital appreciation. Rather than acquire mutual fund shares or diversify within a given class of investment vehicle, they developed their portfolio with the idea of diversifying across various types of vehicles. The portfolio currently contains common stock, industrial bonds, mutual fund shares, and options. They acquired each of these vehicles during the past 3 years, and they plan to invest in other vehicles sometime in the future.

Currently, the Stalchecks are interested in measuring the return on their investment and assessing how well they have done relative to the market. They hope that the return earned over the past calendar year is in excess of what they would have earned by investing in a portfolio consisting of the S&P 500 Stock Composite Index. Their research has indicated that the risk-free rate was 7.2% and that the (before-tax) return on the S&P stock portfolio was 10.1% during the past year. With the aid of a friend, they have been able to estimate the beta of their portfolio, which was 1.20. In their analysis, they have planned to ignore taxes, because they feel their earnings have been adequately sheltered. Because they did not make any portfolio transactions during the past year, all of the Stalchecks' investments have been held more than 12 months and they would have to consider only unrealized capital gains, if any. To make the necessary calculations, the Stalchecks have gathered the following information on each of the four vehicles in their portfolio.

> *Common stock.* They own 400 shares of KJ Enterprises common stock. KJ is a diversified manufacturer of metal pipe and is known for its unbroken stream of dividends. Over the past few years, it has entered new markets and, as a result, has offered moderate capital appreciation potential. Its share price has risen from 17.25 at the start of the last calendar year to 18.75 at the end of the year. During the year, quarterly cash dividends of 20, 20, 25, and 25 cents were paid.

Industrial bonds. The Stalchecks own eight Cal Industries bonds. The bonds have a $1,000 par value, have a 9¼% coupon, and are due in 2012. They are A-rated by Moody's. The bond was quoted at 97 at the beginning of the year and ended the calendar year at 96⅜.

Mutual fund. The Stalchecks hold 500 shares in the Holt Fund, a balanced, no-load mutual fund. The dividend distributions on the fund during the year consisted of 60 cents in investment income and 50 cents in capital gains. The fund's NAV at the beginning of the calendar year was $19.45, and it ended the year at $20.02.

Options. The Stalchecks own 100 options contracts on the stock of a company they follow. The value of these contracts totaled $26,000 at the beginning of the calendar year. At year-end the total value of the options contracts was $29,000.

Questions

 a. Calculate the holding period return on a before-tax basis for each of these four investment vehicles.

 b. Assuming that the Stalchecks' ordinary income is currently being taxed at a combined (federal and state) tax rate of 38%, and that they would pay a 20% capital gains tax for holding periods longer than 12 months, determine the after-tax HPR for each of their four investment vehicles.

 c. Recognizing that all gains on the Stalchecks' investments were unrealized, calculate the before-tax portfolio HPR for their four-vehicle portfolio during the past calendar year. Evaluate this return relative to its current income and capital gain components.

 d. Use the HPR calculated in question (c) to compute Jensen's measure (Jensen's alpha). Use that measure to analyze the performance of the Stalchecks' portfolio on a risk-adjusted, market-adjusted basis. Comment on your finding. Is it reasonable to use Jensen's measure to evaluate a four-vehicle portfolio? Why or why not?

e. On the basis of your analysis in questions (a), (c), and (d), what, if any, recommendations might you offer the Stalchecks relative to the revision of their portfolio? Explain your recommendations.

Case Problem 13.2 *Evaluating Formula Plans: Charles Spurge's Approach*

LG 5

Charles Spurge, a mathematician with Ansco Petroleum Company, wishes to develop a rational basis for timing his portfolio transactions. He currently holds a security portfolio with a market value of nearly $100,000, divided equally between a very conservative, low-beta common stock, ConCam United, and a highly speculative, high-beta stock, Fleck Enterprises. On the basis of his reading of the investments literature, Charles does not believe it is necessary to diversify one's portfolio across 8 to 15 securities. His own feeling, based on his independent mathematical analysis, is that one can achieve the same results by holding a two-security portfolio in which one security is very conservative and the other is highly speculative. His feelings on this point will not be altered. He plans to continue to hold such a two-security portfolio until he finds that his theory does not work. During the past couple of years, he has earned a rate of return in excess of the risk-adjusted, market-adjusted rate expected on such a portfolio.

Charles's current interest centers on possibly developing his own formula plan for timing portfolio transactions. The current stage of his analysis focuses on the evaluation of four commonly used formula plans in order to isolate the desirable features of each. The four plans being considered are (1) dollar-cost averaging, (2) the constant-dollar plan, (3) the constant-ratio plan, and (4) the variable-ratio plan. Charles's analysis of the plans will involve the use of two types of data. Dollar-cost averaging is a passive buy-and-hold strategy in which the periodic investment is held constant. The other plans are more active in that they involve periodic purchases and sales within the portfolio. Thus, differing data are needed to evaluate the plans.

For evaluating the dollar-cost averaging plan, Charles decided he would assume an investment of $500 at the end of each 45-day period. He chose to use 45-day time intervals to achieve certain brokerage fee savings that would be available by making larger transactions. The $500 per 45 days totaled $4,000 for the year and equaled the total amount Charles invested during the past year. (*Note:* For convenience, the returns earned on the portions of the $4,000 that remain uninvested during the year are ignored.) In evaluating this plan, he would assume that half ($250) was invested in the conservative stock (ConCam United) and the other half in the speculative stock (Fleck Enterprises). The share prices for each of the stocks at the end of the eight 45-day periods when purchases were to be made are given in the accompanying table.

| | Price per Share | |
Period	ConCam	Fleck
1	22.13	22.13
2	21.88	24.50
3	21.88	25.38
4	22.00	28.50
5	22.25	21.88
6	22.13	19.25
7	22.00	21.50
8	22.25	23.63

To evaluate the three other plans, Charles decided to begin with a $4,000 portfolio evenly split between the two stocks. He chose to use $4,000, because that amount would correspond to the total amount invested in the two stocks over one year using dollar-cost averaging. He planned to use the same eight points in time given earlier to assess the portfolio and make transfers within it if required. For each of the three plans evaluated using these data, he established the following triggering points.

Constant-dollar plan. Each time the speculative portion of the portfolio is worth 13% more or less than its initial value of $2,000, the portfolio is rebalanced to bring the speculative portion back to its initial $2,000 value.

Constant-ratio plan. Each time the ratio of the value of the speculative portion of the portfolio to the value of the conservative portion is (1) greater than or equal to 1.15 or (2) less than or equal to 0.84, the portfolio is rebalanced through sale or purchase, respectively, to bring the ratio back to its initial value of 1.0.

Variable-ratio plan. Each time the value of the speculative portion of the portfolio rises above 54% of the total value of the portfolio, its proportion is reduced to 46%. Each time the value of the speculative portion of the portfolio drops below 38% of the total value of the portfolio, its proportion is raised to 50%.

Questions

a.   Under the dollar-cost averaging plan, determine the total number of shares purchased, the average cost per share, and the year-end portfolio value expressed both in dollars and as a percentage of the amount invested for (1) the conservative stock, (2) the speculative stock, and (3) the total portfolio.

b.   Using the constant-dollar plan, determine the year-end portfolio value expressed both in dollars and as a percentage of the amount initially invested for (1) the conservative portion, (2) the speculative portion, and (3) the total portfolio.

c.   Repeat question (b) for the constant-ratio plan. Be sure to answer all parts.

d.   Repeat question (b) for the variable-ratio plan. Be sure to answer all parts.

e.   Compare and contrast your results from questions (a) through (d). You may want to summarize them in tabular form. Which plan would appear to have been most beneficial in timing Charles's portfolio activities during the past year? Explain.

Web Exercises

W13.1   Visit www.morningstar.com. Free membership allows you to create, save, and monitor portfolios. Become a member. Click on [Quicktake Reports], and then enter the appropriate ticker symbols to obtain the individual company reports for WMT, MSFT, and F. Each Quicktake includes more than 25 detailed reports, including price quotes, earnings estimates, and analysis of balance sheets, performance, and earnings. Under stock performance, total returns % are provided.
   a. Which of these three stocks had the highest year-to-date performance?
   b. How did the stock in (a) perform relative to the industry and relative to the S&P 500?

W13.2   The Portfolio Manager at the site www.morningstar.com tracks and analyzes your portfolio (Cost basis per share $, Cost basis $, Gain/loss since purchase $, Gain/loss since purchase %, Year-to-date returns of every security in the portfolio, and Portfolio weight %), to determine whether the portfolio is still balanced and meeting your goals. "Portfolio X-Rays" helps in fundamental analysis; identifies small-cap to large-cap, value to growth, and industry-sector classification; determines your portfolio's true asset allocation and stock overlap; compares sector allocations with those of the S&P 500 Index; and offers advice about how to improve diversification.
   a. Create a portfolio of ten stocks: ADM, CSCO, F, IBM, INTC, MCD, MRK, MSFT, SLE, WMT. Give it the name **Watchlist 1.**
   b. In the Portfolio Tracking tab, select Fundamental View, and see the stock industry category, EPS, P/E, P/B, and yield % for each stock. Print the results.
   c. Select Performance View and see the Total Return Year to date % for each stock. Print the results.
   d. Click on Portfolio X-Rays tab and look at asset allocation, style box diversification, stock sector, and stock type for your portfolio. Again print your results.
   e. Evaluate the stocks in your portfolio.

For additional practice with concepts from this chapter, visit

www.awl.com/gitman_joehnk

CFA EXAM QUESTIONS

Portfolio Management

Following is a sample of 10 Level-l CFA exam questions that deal with many of the topics covered in Chapters 12 and 13 of this text, including the structure of mutual funds, portfolio diversification, portfolio returns, and the administration of personal portfolios.

1. Which of the following statements *typically* does **NOT** characterize the structure of an investment company ?
   a. an investment company adopts a corporate form of organization.
   b. an investment company invests a pool of funds belonging to many investors in a portfolio of individual investments.
   c. an investment company receives an annual management fee ranging from 5 to 10 percent of the total value of the fund.
   d. the board of directors of an investment company hires a separate investment management company to manage the portfolio of securities and to handle other administrative duties.

2. An investor has a portfolio with a market value of $50,000 at the end of May. The market value of the portfolio is $48,700 at the end of June. The holding-period return the investor's portfolio for June is closest to:
   a. −1.30%.
   b. −2.60%.
   c. −2.63%.
   d. −2.67%.

3. Which of the following is **NOT** an implication of risk aversion for the investment process?
   a. The security market line is upward sloping.
   b. The promised yield on AAA-rated bonds is higher than on A-rated bonds.
   c. Investors expect a positive relationship between expected return and expected risk.
   d. Investors prefer portfolios that lie on the efficient frontier to other portfolios with equal rates of return.

4. An investor is considering adding another investment to a portfolio. To achieve the maximum diversification benefits, the investor should add an investment that has a correlation coefficient with the existing portfolio *closest* to:
   a. −1.0.
   b. −0.5.
   c. 0.0.
   d. +1.0.

5. The annual rate of return for JSI's common stock has been:

	1993	1994	1995	1996
Return	14%	19%	−10%	14%

   What is the mean rate of return for JSI's common stock over the four years?
   a. 8.62%.
   b. 9.25%.
   c. 14.00%.
   d. 14.25%.

CFA EXAM QUESTIONS

6. A three-asset portfolio has the following characteristics:

Asset	Expected Return	Expected Standard Deviation	Weight
X	0.15	0.22	0.50
Y	0.10	0.08	0.40
Z	0.06	0.03	0.10

The expected return on this three-asset portfolio is:
a. 10.3%.
b. 11.0%.
c. 12.1%.
d. 14.8%.

7. According to the capital asset pricing model, the rate of return of a portfolio with a beta of 1.2 and a risk premium of 6.5 percent while the risk-free rate is 5 percent is:
a. 7.0%.
b. 11.5%.
c. 12.5%.
d. 12.8%.

8. Both Portfolio X and Portfolio Y are well-diversified. The risk-free rate is 8 percent, and the return for the market is 16 percent, that is:

Portfolio	Expected Return	Beta
X	16%	1.00
Y	12%	0.25

In this situation, which of the following about Portfolio X and Portfolio Y is **true**?

	Portfolio X	Portfolio Y
a.	overvalued	properly valued
b.	properly valued	undervalued
c.	undervalued	properly valued
d.	properly valued	overvalued

9. The expected return of a zero-beta security is
a. the market rate of return.
b. a zero rate of return.
c. a negative rate of return.
d. the risk-free rate of return.

10. An investor has a $10,000 portfolio consisting of $9,000 in Stock X with an expected return of 20% and $1,000 in Stock Y with an expected return of 10%. What is the investor's expected return on the portfolio?
a. 18%.
b. 19%.
c. 20%.
d. 23%.

Answers: 1. c; 2. b; 3. b; 4. a; 5. b; 6. c; 7. d; 8. b; 9. d; 10. b

PART SIX

DERIVATIVE SECURITIES

CHAPTER 14

OPTIONS: PUTS, CALLS, AND WARRANTS

Put, call, strike price, naked option, in-the-money option, market index option—these terms are all part of the confusing, mysterious world of options. From what you have heard about options, you may wonder why you even need to know about them. Options can indeed be speculative instruments that can lead to losses for even the most experienced investor. Many options investors use them to gamble on near-term price changes. But options also can play a role in the conservative investor's portfolio. They are versatile investments—a form of insurance that enables you to hedge risk. With them, you can protect stock holdings from a decline in market price, position yourself for a big market move even when you don't know which way prices will go, or benefit from a rising stock price without actually buying the stock.

When might options work to your advantage? Suppose you are going to buy a car in two months and plan to sell stock to pay for it. You could sell your stock now and hold the proceeds. But if the stock price is currently down and you think it will come back by the time you need the funds, you can use options to lock in the current price and still have an opportunity to participate in the upside. Assume that you own 200 shares of Eli Lilly. The stock is currently trading at about $75 but has been as high as 109 in the past 52 weeks. You can buy a put option at $75 that expires in 3 months, at a cost of $5 a share. If the stock drops in price, the put locks in your right to sell the stock at $75 a share, no matter how far the price falls. "It puts a floor under your wealth," says Lee Reid, head of retail options at A.G. Edwards.

This is just one example of how you can use options with stocks in your portfolio. In this chapter you will learn about the essential characteristics of options and how they can be used effectively in your investment program.

Sources: Chicago Board Options Exchange Web site, www.cboe.com/education/learningcenter, and Daniel Kadlec, "Know Your Options," *Time*, June 26, 2000, p. 80.

Put and Call Options

LG 1   LG 2

option
a security that gives the holder the right to buy or sell a certain amount of an underlying financial asset at a specified price for a specified period of time.

When investors buy shares of common or preferred stock, they become the registered owners of these securities and are entitled to all the rights and privileges of ownership. Investors who acquire bonds or convertible issues are also entitled to the benefits of ownership. Stocks, bonds, and convertibles are all examples of *financial assets*. They represent financial claims on the issuing organization. In contrast, investors who buy options acquire nothing more than the right to subsequently buy or sell other, related securities. That is, an **option** gives the holder the right to buy or sell a certain amount of an underlying security at a specified price over a specified period of time. Options are *contractual instruments,* whereby two parties enter into a contract to give something of value to the other. The option *buyer* has the right to buy or sell an underlying asset for a given period of time, at a price that was fixed at the time of the contract. The option *seller* stands ready to buy or sell the underlying asset according to the terms of the contract, for which the seller has been paid a certain amount of money.

We'll look at two basic kinds of options in this chapter: (1) puts and calls and (2) warrants. Another kind of option that can be found in the market, but is not covered in this text, is the *stock right*. Rights are like short-term call options that originate when corporations raise money by issuing new shares of common stocks. Essentially, the rights enable stockholders to buy shares of the new issue at a specified price for a specified, fairly short period of time. Because their life span is so short—usually no more than a few weeks—stock rights hold very little investment appeal for the average individual investor. Puts and calls, on the other hand, enjoy considerable popularity as attractive trading vehicles, and so, to a lesser extent, do warrants. These securities are a bit unusual, however, and their use requires special investor know-how.

HOTLINKS

For a more extensive discussion of rights, including their basic characteristics and investment attributes, see this textbook's Web site at

www.awl.com/gitman_joehnk

Basic Features and Behavioral Characteristics

One of the market phenomena of the 1970s was the remarkable performance and investment popularity of stock options, particularly puts and calls on common stock. By the early 1980s, the interest in options spilled over to other kinds of financial assets. Today, investors can trade puts and calls on:

- Common stock
- Stock indexes
- Debt instruments
- Foreign currencies
- Commodities and financial futures

As we will see, although the underlying financial assets may vary, the basic features and behavioral characteristics of these securities are pretty much the same. Regardless of the type, much of the popularity of options stems from the fact that *investors can buy a lot of price action with a limited amount of capital, while nearly always enjoying limited exposure to risk.*

A Negotiable Contract Puts and calls are negotiable instruments, issued in bearer form, that allow the holder to buy or sell a specified amount of a specified security at a specified price. For example, a put or a call on common stock covers 100 shares of stock in a specific company. A **put** enables the holder to sell the underlying security at the specified price (known as the *exercise* or *strike* price) over a set period of time. A **call,** in contrast, gives the holder the right to buy the securities at the stated (strike) price within a certain time period. As with any option, there are no voting rights, no privileges of ownership, and no interest or dividend income. Instead, *puts and calls possess value to the extent that they allow the holder to participate in the price behavior of the underlying financial asset.*

Because puts and calls derive their value from the price behavior of some other real or financial asset, they are known as **derivative securities.** Rights and warrants, as well as futures contracts (which we'll study in Chapter 15), are also derivative securities. The fact is that many different types of derivative securities are available. Although certain segments of this market are for big institutional investors only, there's still ample room for the individual investor. Many of these securities—especially those on listed exchanges—are readily available to, and are actively traded by, individuals as well as institutions.

One of the key features of puts and calls (and of many other types of derivative securities) is the very attractive **leverage** opportunities they offer investors. Such opportunities exist because of the low prices these options carry relative to the market prices of the underlying financial assets. And what's more, the lower cost in no way affects the payoff or capital appreciation potential of your investment! To illustrate, consider a call on a common stock that gives the holder the right to buy 100 shares of a $50 stock at a (strike) price of $45 a share. The stock, of course, would be priced at $50. But the call would trade at an effective price of only $5 a share (or the difference between the market price of the common and the price at which it can be purchased, as specified on the call). Because a single stock option always involves 100 shares of stock, the actual cost of our $5 call would be $500. Even so, for $500 you get (just about) all the capital gains potential of a $5,000 investment—or at least that part of the capital gains that occurs over the life of the call option.

Maker Versus Buyer Puts and calls are a unique type of security because they are *not* issued by the organizations that issue the underlying stock or financial asset. Instead, puts and calls *are created by investors.* It works like this: Suppose you want to sell to another investor the right to buy 100 shares of common stock. You could do this by "writing a call." The individual (or institution) writing the option is known as the **option maker** or **writer.** As the option writer, you sell the option in the market and so are entitled to receive the price paid for the put or call (less modest commissions and other transaction costs). The put or call option is now a full-fledged financial asset and trades in the open market much like any other security.

Puts and calls are both written (sold) and purchased through securities brokers and dealers. In fact, they're just as easy to buy and sell as common stocks; a simple phone call is all it takes. The writer stands behind the option, because it is the *writer* who must buy or deliver the stocks or other financial assets according to the terms of the option. (*Note:* The writers of puts and calls *have a legally binding obligation* to stand behind the terms of the contracts they have written. The buyer can just walk away from the deal if it turns sour; the writer cannot.) Puts and calls are written for a variety of reasons, most of which we will explore below. At this point, suffice it to say that writing options can be a viable investment strategy and can be a profitable course of action because, more often than not, *options expire worthless.*

How Puts and Calls Work   Taking the *buyer's* point of view, let's now briefly examine how puts and calls work and how they derive their value. To understand the mechanics of puts and calls, it is best to look at their profit-making potential. For example, using stock options as a basis of discussion, consider a stock currently priced at $50 a share. Assume you can buy a call on the stock for $500, which enables you to purchase 100 shares of the stock at a fixed price of $50 each. A rise in the price of the underlying security (in this case, common stock) is what you, as an investor, hope for. What is the profit potential from this transaction if the price of the stock does indeed move up to, say, $75 by the expiration date on the call?

The answer is that you will earn $25 ($75 − $50) on each of the 100 shares of stock in the call. You'll earn a total gross profit of $2,500 from your $500 investment. This is so because you have the right to buy 100 shares of the stock, from the option writer, at a price of $50 each, and you can immediately turn around and sell them in the market for $75 a share. You could have made the same ($2,500) profit by investing directly in the common stock. But because you would have had to invest $5,000 (100 shares × $50 per share), your rate of return would have been much lower. Obviously, there is considerable difference between the return potential of common stocks and calls. It is this difference that attracts investors and speculators to calls whenever the price outlook for the underlying financial asset is positive. Such differential returns, of course, are the direct result of *leverage*, which rests on the principle of reducing the level of capital required in a given investment position *without materially affecting the dollar amount of the payoff or capital appreciation from that investment.* (Note that although our illustration is couched in terms of common stock, this same valuation principle applies to any of the other financial assets that may underlie call options, such as market indexes, foreign currencies, and futures contracts.)

A similar situation can be worked out for puts. Assume that for the same $50 stock you could pay $500 and buy a put to *sell* 100 shares of the stock at a strike price of $50 each. As the buyer of a put, you want the price of the stock to *drop*. Assume that your expectations are correct and the price of the stock does indeed drop, to $25 a share. Here again, you realize a gross profit of $25 for each of the 100 shares in the put. Such profit is available by going to the market and buying 100 shares of the stock at a price of $25 a share and then immediately selling them to the writer of the put at a price of $50 per share.

Fortunately, put and call investors do *not* have to exercise their options and make simultaneous buy and sell transactions in order to receive their profit. That's because *the options themselves have value and therefore can be traded in the secondary market.* In fact, the value of both puts and calls is directly linked to the market price of the underlying financial asset. That is, the *value of a call* increases as the market price of the underlying security *rises*. The *value of a put* increases as the price of the security *declines*. Thus *investors can get their money out of options by selling them in the open market,* just as with any other security.

Advantages and Disadvantages The major advantage of investing in puts and calls is the leverage they offer. This feature also carries the advantage of limiting the investor's exposure to risk, because only a set amount of money (the purchase price of the option) can be lost. Also appealing is the fact that puts and calls can be used profitably when the price of the underlying security goes up *or* down.

A major disadvantage of puts and calls is that the holder enjoys neither interest or dividend income nor any other ownership benefit. Moreover, because the instruments have limited lives, the investor has a limited time frame in which to capture desired price behavior. Another disadvantage is that puts and calls themselves are a bit unusual, and many of their trading strategies are complex. Thus investors must possess special knowledge and must fully understand the subtleties of this trading vehicle.

Options Markets

Although the concept of options can be traced back to the writings of Aristotle, options trading in the United States did not begin until the late 1700s. And even then, up to the early 1970s, this market remained fairly small, largely unorganized, and the almost private domain of a handful of specialists and traders. All of this changed, however, on April 26, 1973, when a new securities market was created with the opening of the Chicago Board Options Exchange (CBOE).

Conventional Options Prior to the creation of the CBOE, put and call options trading was conducted in the over-the-counter market through a handful of specialized dealers. Investors who wished to purchase puts and calls contacted their own brokers, who contacted the options dealers. The dealers would find individuals (or institutions) willing to write the options. If the buyer wished to exercise an option, he or she did so with the writer and no one else—a system that largely prohibited any secondary trading. On the other hand, there were virtually no limits to what could be written, so long as the buyer was willing to pay the price. Put and call options were written on New York and American exchange stocks, as well as on regional and over-the-counter securities, for as short a time as 30 days and for as long as a year. Over-the-counter options, known today as **conventional options**, were initially hit hard by the CBOE. However, the conventional (OTC) market has bounced back and is today every bit as big as the listed market, though it is used almost exclusively by institutional investors. Accordingly, our attention in this chapter will focus on listed markets, like the CBOE, where individual investors do most of their options trading.

H O T L I N K S

Some questions and answers by investors regarding options, along with a good glossary on options, are available at:

www.schaeffersresearch.com/option/

conventional options
put and call options sold over the counter.

listed options
put and call options listed and traded on organized securities exchanges, such as the CBOE.

Listed Options The creation of the CBOE signaled the birth of so-called **listed options**, a term that describes put and call options traded on organized exchanges rather than over the counter. The CBOE launched trading in calls on just 16 firms. From these rather humble beginnings, there evolved in a relatively short time a large and active market for listed options. Today, trading in listed options is done in both puts and calls and takes place on four exchanges, the largest of which is the CBOE. Options are also traded on the

AMEX, the Philadelphia Exchange, and the Pacific Stock Exchange. In total, *put and call options are now traded on over 2,600 different stocks.* (Actually, around 4,000 options were listed on all four exchanges in early 2000, as many of the more actively traded options are listed on more than one exchange.) Although many of the options are written on large, well-known NYSE companies, the list also includes a number of AMEX and OTC/Nasdaq stocks, both large and small, and in both the "old-economy" and the "new-economy" (high-tech) sectors of the market. Indeed, many of the most actively traded options today are those written on high-tech stocks. In addition to stocks, listed options are available on stock indexes, debt securities, foreign currencies, and even commodities and financial futures.

Listed options not only provided a convenient market for the trading of puts and calls, but also standardized expiration dates and exercise prices. The listed options exchanges created a clearinghouse organization that eliminated direct ties between buyers and writers of options and reduced the cost of executing put and call transactions. They also developed an active secondary market, with wide distribution of price information. As a result, it is now as easy to trade a listed option as a listed stock.

Stock Options

The advent of the CBOE and other listed option exchanges had a quick and dramatic impact on the trading volume of puts and calls. In fact, the level of activity in listed stock options grew so rapidly that it took only 8 years for the annual volume of contracts traded to pass the 100 million mark. Today well over 500 million listed options contracts are traded each year. Indeed, of the nearly 508 million contracts traded in 1999, *almost 88%* (or 448.8 million) *were stock options.* During that year, the volume of contracts traded was divided among the four options exchanges as follows:

	Total Number of Contracts Traded (in millions)	% of the Total
CBOE	254.3	50.1%
AMEX	129.7	25.5%
Pacific Exchange	75.8	14.9%
Philadelphia Exchange	48.1	9.5%
Total	507.9	100.0%

Today, the CBOE and AMEX account for about *75% of all stock options trading,* while the CBOE alone handles about *90% of all index options trading.*

The continued expansion of listed options exchanges has unquestionably added a new dimension to investing. In order to avoid serious (and possibly expensive) mistakes with these securities, however, you must fully understand their basic features. In the sections that follow, we will look closely at the investment attributes of stock options and trading strategies that can be used with them. Later, we'll explore stock-index options and then briefly look at other types of puts and calls, including interest rate and currency options, and long-term options. (Futures options will be taken up in Chapter 15, after we study futures contracts.)

Stock Option Provisions Because of their low unit cost, stock options (or *equity options*, as they're also called) are very popular with individual investors. Except for the underlying financial asset, they are like any other type of put or call, subject to the same kinds of contract provisions and market forces. As far as stock options are concerned, there are two provisions that are especially important: (1) the price—known as the *strike price*—at which the stock can be bought or sold, and (2) the amount of time remaining until expiration. As we'll see below, both the strike price and the time remaining to expiration have a significant bearing on the valuation and pricing of options.

strike price
the price contract between the buyer of an option and the writer; the stated price at which you can buy a security with a call or sell a security with a put.

Strike Price The **strike price** represents the price contract between the buyer of the option and the writer. For a call, the strike price specifies the price at which each of the 100 shares of stock can be bought. For a put, it represents the price at which the stock can be sold to the writer. With conventional (OTC) options, there are no constraints on the strike price. It is usually specified at or near the prevailing market price of the stock at the time the option is written (but does not have to be). With listed options, however, strike prices are *standardized*: Stocks selling for less than $25 per share carry strike prices that are set in 2½ dollar increments ($7.50, $10.00, $12.50, $15, etc.). The increment jumps to $5 for stocks selling between $25 and $200 per share. For stocks that trade at more than $200 a share, the strike price is set in $10 increments. Of course, the strike price is adjusted for substantial stock dividends and stock splits.

expiration date
the date at which an option expires.

Expiration Date The **expiration date** is also an important provision, because it specifies the life of the option, just as the maturity date indicates the life of a bond. The expiration date, in effect, specifies the length of the contract between the holder and the writer of the option. Thus, if you hold a 6-month call on Sears with a strike price of, say, $40, that option gives you the right to buy 100 shares of Sears common stock at $40 per share at any time over the next 6 months. *No matter what happens to the market price of the stock*, you can use your call option to buy 100 shares of Sears at $40 a share. If the price of the stock moves up, you stand to make money. If it goes down, you'll be out the cost of the option.

Expiration dates for options in the conventional market can fall on any working day of the month. In contrast, expiration dates are standardized in the *listed* options market. The exchanges initially created three expiration cycles for all listed options. Each issue is assigned to one of these three cycles. One cycle is January, April, July, and October. Another is February, May, August, and November. The third is March, June, September, and December. The exchanges still use the same three expiration cycles, but they've been altered so that investors are always able to trade in the two nearest (current and following) months, plus the next two closest months in the option's regular expiration cycle. For reasons that are pretty obvious, this is sometimes referred to as a *two-plus-two* schedule.

Take, for example, the January cycle. The following options are available in January: January, February, April, and July. These represent the two current months (January and February) and the next two months in the cycle (April and July). In February, the available contracts would be February, March, April, and July. The expiration dates continue rolling over in this way during

FIGURE 14.1 Quotations for Listed Stock Options

The quotes for puts and calls are listed side by side. In addition to the closing price of the option, the latest price of the underlying security is shown, along with the strike price on the option. (*Source: Wall Street Journal,* August 29, 2000.)

Call option quotes —

Put option quotes —

OPTION/STRIKE		EXP.	CALL VOL.	CALL LAST	PUT VOL.	PUT LAST
Inktomi	115	Sep	56	9^{50}	318	6
118	120	Sep	363	7^{38}	84	8
118	125	Sep	48	4^{50}	271	12^{50}
118	130	Sep	100	3^{25}	3005	15^{38}
118	135	Sep	251	2^{13}	...	...
Intel	50	Jan	440	25^{88}	84	0^{81}
73^{88}	60	Jan	259	18	200	1^{94}
73^{88}	65	Sep	230	9^{25}	221	0^{31}
73^{88}	65	Oct	271	11^{63}	2466	1^{31}
73^{88}	65	Apr	...	...	2520	4^{63}
73^{88}	70	Sep	10855	5^{25}	3286	1^{06}
73^{88}	70	Oct	2630	7^{75}	1225	2^{63}
73^{88}	75	Sep	13474	2	2456	2^{06}
73^{88}	75	Oct	5373	4^{25}	689	4^{13}
73^{88}	75	Jan	650	8^{25}	333	7^{38}
73^{88}	77^{50}	Sep	1548	1	195	4
73^{88}	77^{50}	Oct	288	3^{25}	36	6
73^{88}	80	Sep	2013	0^{44}	344	6^{50}
73^{88}	80	Jan	517	6^{13}	70	10
73^{88}	82^{50}	Oct	628	1^{75}	...	...
73^{88}	85	Oct	701	1^{13}	...	...
73^{88}	85	Jan	547	4^{13}	...	...
73^{88}	87^{50}	Oct	328	0^{75}	...	...
73^{88}	90	Oct	628	0^{50}	...	...
73^{88}	90	Jan	645	3^{13}	10	16
73^{88}	100	Jan	311	1^{50}	...	...
I B M	40	Jan	733	8^{88}	14	14^{38}
130	95	Jan	83	40^{50}	256	1
130	105	Jan	16	31^{88}	762	2^{13}
130	110	Sep	44	22^{50}	336	0^{13}
130	110	Jan	909	27^{25}	963	3^{25}
130	115	Oct	68	18^{75}	891	1^{44}
130	115	Jan	130	24	805	4
130	120	Sep	818	11^{13}	562	0^{50}
130	120	Oct	155	14^{88}	366	2^{50}
130	120	Jan	270	19^{50}	281	5^{63}

Name of company — Intel

Price of a January call (that carries a strike price of 50)

Month of expiration (October 2000)

Strike price on the option — 75

Number of January 2001 puts traded (with a strike price of 75)

Number of September calls traded (with a strike price of 80)

Latest market price of the underlying common stock — 73^{88}

Price of a January 2001 put (that carries a strike price of 90)

the course of the year. Given the month of expiration, the actual day of expiration is always the same: the Saturday following the third Friday of each expiration month. Thus, for all practical purposes, *listed options always expire on the third Friday of the month of expiration.*

Put and Call Transactions Option traders are subject to commission and transaction costs whenever they buy or sell an option or whenever an option is written. The writing of puts and calls is subject to normal transaction costs because these costs effectively represent remuneration to the broker or dealer for *selling* the option.

Listed options have their own marketplace and quotation system. Finding the price (or *premium,* as it's called) of a listed stock option is fairly easy, as the options quotations in Figure 14.1 indicate. Note that quotes are provided for calls and puts separately. For each option, quotes are listed for various combinations of strike prices and expiration dates. Because there are so many options and a substantial number of them are rarely traded, financial publications like the *Wall Street Journal* list quotes only for the most actively traded options. Also, the quotes listed are only for the options that actually traded on the day in question. For example, in Figure 14.1, there may be many other options available on Intel, but only the ones that actually traded (on Monday, August 28, 2000) are listed.

The quotes are standardized: The name of the company and the closing price of the underlying stock are listed first; note that Intel stock closed at 73.88. The strike price is listed next, followed by the expiration date (or month in which the option expires). Then the closing prices of the call (and/or put) options are quoted relative to their strike prices and expiration dates. For example, an Intel January *call* with a strike price of $60 is quoted at 18 (which translates into a dollar price of $1,800 because stock options trade in 100-share lots). In contrast, an Intel *put* with an $75 strike price and a January expiration date is trading at 7.38 (or $738).

IN REVIEW

CONCEPTS

14.1 Describe *put* and *call* options. Are they issued like other corporate securities? Explain.

14.2 What are *listed options,* and how do they differ from *conventional options?*

14.3 What are the main investment attractions of put and call options? What are the risks?

14.4 What is a *stock option?* What is the difference between a stock option and a *derivative security?* Describe a derivative security and give several examples.

14.5 What is a *strike price?* How does it differ from the market price of the stock? Do both puts and calls have strike prices? Explain.

14.6 Why do put and call options have expiration dates? Is there a market for options that have passed their expiration dates? Explain.

Options Pricing and Trading

LG 3   LG 4

The value of a put or call depends to a large extent on the market behavior of the financial asset that underlies the option. Getting a firm grip on the current and expected future value of a put or call is extremely important to options traders and investors. Similarly, to get the most from any options trading program, it is imperative that you understand how options are priced in the market. *Continuing to use stock options as a basis of discussion*, let's look now at the basic principles of options valuation and pricing. We'll start with a brief review of how profits are derived from puts and calls. Then we'll take a look at several ways in which investors can use these options.

The Profit Potential from Puts and Calls

Although the quoted market price of a put or call is affected by such factors as time to expiration, stock volatility, and market interest rates, by far the most important variable is the *price behavior of the underlying common stock*. This is the variable that drives any significant moves in the price of the option and that determines the option's profit (return) potential. Thus, when the underlying stock *moves up in price, calls do well*. When the price of the underlying stock *drops, puts do well*. Such performance also explains why it's important to get a good handle on the expected future price behavior of a stock *before* buying or selling (writing) an option.

The typical price behavior of an option is illustrated graphically in Figure 14.2. The diagram on the left depicts a call, the one on the right a put. The *call* diagram is constructed assuming you pay $500 for a call that carries a strike price of $50. With the call, the diagram shows what happens to the value of the option when the price of the stock increases. Observe that a call does not gain in value until the price of the stock *advances past the stated exercise price* ($50). Also, because it costs $500 to buy the call, the stock has to move up another 5 points (from $50 to $55) in order for you to recover the premium and thereby reach a break-even point. So long as the stock continues to rise in price, everything from there on out is profit. Once the premium is recouped, the profit from the call position is limited only by the extent to which the stock price increases over the remaining life of the contract.

The value of a put is also derived from the price of the underlying stock, except that their respective market prices move in opposite directions. The *put* diagram in Figure 14.2 assumes you can buy a put for $500 and obtain the right to sell the underlying stock at $50 a share. It shows that the value of the put remains constant until the market price of the corresponding stock *drops to the exercise price* ($50) on the put. Then, as the price of the stock continues to fall, the value of the option increases. Again, note that because the put cost $500, you don't start making money on the investment until the price of the stock drops below the break-even point of $45 a share. Beyond that point, the profit from the put is defined by the extent to which the price of the underlying stock continues to fall over the remaining life of the option.

 ## Fundamental Value

As we have seen, the fundamental value of a put or call depends ultimately on the exercise price stated on the option, as well as on the prevailing market

FIGURE 14.2 **The Valuation Properties of Put and Call Options**

The value of a put or call reflects the price behavior of its underlying common stock (or other financial asset). The cost of the option has been recovered when the option passes its break-even point. After that, the profit potential of a put or call is limited only by the price behavior of the underlying asset and by the length of time to the expiration of the option.

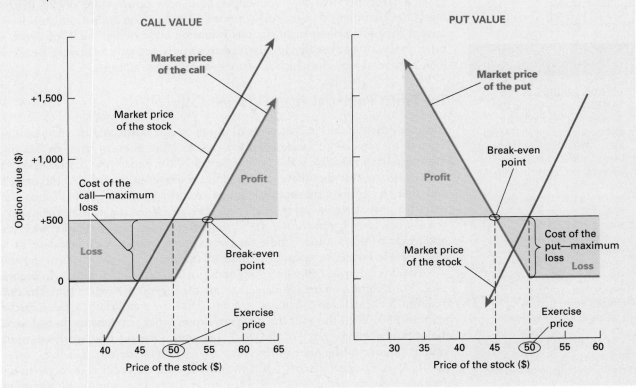

price of the underlying common stock. More specifically, the *value of a call* is determined according to the following simple formula:

Equation 14.1

$$\text{Fundamental value of a call} = \begin{pmatrix} \text{Market price of} \\ \text{underlying} \\ \text{common stock,} \\ \text{or other} \\ \text{financial asset} \end{pmatrix} - \begin{matrix} \text{Strike price} \\ \text{on} \\ \text{the call} \end{matrix} \end{pmatrix} \times 100$$

$$V = (MP - SPC) \times 100$$

In other words, the fundamental value of a call is nothing more than the difference between market price and strike price. As implied in Equation 14.1, a call has an intrinsic value whenever the market price of the underlying financial asset exceeds the strike price stipulated on the call. A simple illustration will show that a call carrying a strike price of $50 on a stock currently trading at $60 has an intrinsic value of $1,000: ($60 − $50) × 100 = $10 × 100 = $1,000.

A put, on the other hand, cannot be valued in the same way, because puts and calls allow the holder to do different things. To find the *value of a put*, we must change the order of the equation a bit:

Equation 14.2

$$\text{Fundamental value of a put} = \left(\begin{array}{ccc} \text{Strike price} & & \text{Market price of} \\ \text{on} & - & \text{underlying} \\ \text{the put} & & \text{common stock,} \\ & & \text{or other} \\ & & \text{financial asset} \end{array} \right) \times 100$$

$$V = (SPP - MP) \times 100$$

In this case, a put has value so long as the market price of the underlying stock (or financial asset) *is less than* the strike price stipulated on the put.

HOTLINKS

Options calculators are available at:

www.cboe.com/tradtool/optioncalculator.asp
(Java calculator)

in-the-money
a call option with a strike price less than the market price of the underlying security; a put option whose strike price is greater than the market price of the underlying security.

out-of-the-money
a call option with no real value because the strike price exceeds the market price of the stock; a put option whose market price exceeds the strike price.

In-the-Money/Out-of-the-Money When written, options do not necessarily have to carry strike prices at the prevailing market prices of the underlying common stocks. Also, as an option subsequently trades on listed exchanges, the price of the option will move in response to moves in the price of the underlying common stock. When a call has a strike price that is less than the market price of the underlying common stock, it has a positive intrinsic value and is known as an **in-the-money** option. A major portion of the option price in this case is based on (or derived from) the fundamental value of the call. When the strike price exceeds the market price of the stock, the call has no "real" value, in which case it is known as an **out-of-the-money** option. Because the option has no intrinsic value, its price is made up solely of investment premium.

As you might expect, the situation is reversed for put options. That is, a put is considered in-the-money when its strike price is greater than the market price of the stock. It's considered out-of-the-money when the market price of the stock exceeds the strike price. These terms are much more than exotic names given to options. As we will see, they characterize the investment behavior of options and can affect return and risk.

HOTLINKS

Visit this site to find the top five calls and the top five puts by volume:

www.quote.com/quotecom/options/market.asp

option premium
the quoted price the investor pays to buy a listed put or call option.

Option Prices and Premiums Put and call values, as found according to Equations 14.1 and 14.2, denote what the options *should* be valued and trading at. This rarely occurs, however. These securities almost always trade at prices that exceed their intrinsic values, especially for options that still have a long time to run. That is, puts and calls nearly always trade at premium prices. The term **option premium** is used to describe the market price of listed put and call options. Technically, the option premium is the (quoted) price the buyer pays for the *right* to buy or sell a certain amount of the underlying financial asset at a specified price for a specified period of time. The option seller, on the other hand, receives the premium and gets to keep it whether or not the option is exercised. To the seller, the option premium represents compensation for agreeing to fulfill certain *obligations* of the contract.

As we'll see below, the term *premium* is also used to denote the extent to which the market price of an option exceeds its fundamental or intrinsic value. Thus, to avoid confusion and keep matters as simple as possible, we'll use the word *price* in the usual way: to describe the amount it takes to buy an option in the market.

What Drives Options Prices?

time premium
the amount by which the option price exceeds the option's fundamental value.

Option prices can be reduced to two separate components. The first is the *fundamental (intrinsic)* value of the option, which is driven by the current market price of the underlying financial asset. As we saw in Equations 14.1 and 14.2, the greater the difference between the market price of the underlying asset and the strike price on the option, the greater the value of the put or call. The second component of an option price is customarily referred to as the **time premium**. It represents, in effect, the excess value embedded in the option price. That is, time premium is *the amount by which the option price exceeds the option's fundamental value.* Table 14.1 lists some quoted prices for an actively traded call option. These quoted prices (panel A) are then separated into fundamental value (panel B) and time premium (panel C). Note that three strike prices are used—$65, $70, and $75. Relative to the market price of the stock ($71.75), one strike price ($65) is well below market; this is an in-the-money call. One ($70) is fairly near the market. The third ($75) is well above the market; this is an out-of-the-money call. Note the considerable difference in the makeup of the options prices as we move from an in-the-money call to an out-of-the-money call.

Panel B in the table lists the fundamental values of the call options, as determined by Equation 14.1. For example, note that although the March 65 call (the call with the March expiration date and $65 strike price) is trading at 7.75, its intrinsic value is only 6.75. The intrinsic value (of 6.75) represents, in effect, the extent to which the option is trading in-the-money. But observe that although most of the price of the March 65 call is made up of fundamental value, not all of it is. Look at the calls with the $75 strike price. None of these has any fundamental value; they're all out-of-the-money and as such, their prices are made up solely of time premium. Basically, the value of these options is determined entirely by the *belief* that the price of the underlying stock could rise to over $75 a share before the options expire.

TABLE 14.1	Option Price Components for an Actively Traded Call Option		

Stock Price	Strike Price	Expiration Months		
		February	March	June
Panel A: Quoted Options Prices				
71.75	65	—	7.75	9.75
71.75	70	2.25	3.88	6.75
71.75	75	0.19	1.50	3.88
Panel B: Underlying Fundamental Values				
71.75	65	—	6.75	6.75
71.75	70	1.75	1.75	1.75
71.75	75	neg.	neg.	neg.
Panel C: Time Premiums				
71.75	65	—	1.00	3.00
71.75	70	0.50	2.12	5.00
71.75	75	0.19	1.50	3.88

Note: neg. indicates that options have negative fundamental values.

Panel C shows the amount of *time premium* embedded in the call prices. Such a premium represents the difference between the *quoted call price* (panel A) and the call's *fundamental value* (panel B). It shows that the price of (just about) every traded option contains at least some premium. Indeed, unless the options are about to expire, you'd expect them to be trading at a premium. Also, note that with all three strike prices, *the longer the time to expiration, the greater the size of the premium.*

As you might expect, *time to expiration* is an important element in explaining the size of the price premium in panel C. However, a couple of other variables also have a bearing on the behavior of this premium. One is the *price volatility of the underlying common stock.* Other things being equal, the more volatile the stock, the more it enhances the speculative appeal of the option—and therefore the bigger the time premium. In addition, the size of the premium is *directly related to the level of interest rates.* That is, the amount of premium imbedded in a call option generally increases along with interest rates. Less important variables include the dividend yield on the underlying common stock, the trading volume of the option, and the exchange on which the option is listed. For the most part, therefore, four major forces drive the price of an option. They are, in descending order of importance, (1) the price behavior of the underlying financial asset, (2) the amount of time remaining to expiration, (3) the amount of price volatility in the underlying financial asset, and (4) the general level of interest rates.

HOTLINKS

A more detailed discussion of the Black-Scholes option-pricing model, including the basic equations used in the model, can be found on the book's Web site, at

www.awl.com/gitman_joehnk

Option-Pricing Models Some fairly sophisticated option-pricing models have been developed, notably by Myron Scholes and the late Fisher Black, to value options. Many active options traders use these formulas to identify and trade over- and under-valued options. Not surprisingly, these models are based on the same variables we identified above. For example, the five parameters used in the Black-Scholes option-pricing model are (1) the risk-free rate of interest, (2) the price volatility of the underlying stock, (3) the current price of the underlying stock, (4) the strike price of the option, and (5) the option's time to expiration.

Trading Strategies

For the most part, stock options can be used in three different kinds of trading strategies: (1) buying puts and calls for speculation, (2) hedging with puts and calls, and (3) option writing and spreading.

Buying for Speculation Buying for speculation is the simplest and most straightforward use of puts and calls. Basically, it is just like buying stock ("buy low, sell high") and, in fact, represents an alternative to investing in stock. For example, if you feel the market price of a particular stock is going to move up, one way to capture that price appreciation is to buy a call on the stock. In contrast, if you feel the stock is about to drop in price, a put could convert that price decline into a profitable situation. In essence, investors buy options rather than stock whenever the options are likely to yield a greater return. The principle here, of course, is to get the biggest return from your investment dollar. Puts and calls often meet this objective because of the added leverage they offer. Furthermore, options offer downside protection: The most you can lose is the cost of the option, which is always less than the cost of the underlying stock. Thus, by using options as a vehicle for speculation, you can put a cap on losses and still get almost as much profit potential as with the underlying stock.

Speculating with Calls To illustrate the essentials of speculating with options, imagine that you have uncovered a stock you feel will move up in price over the next 6 months. What would happen if you were to buy a call on this stock rather than investing directly in the firm's common? To find out, let's see what the numbers show. The price of the stock is now $49, and you anticipate that within 6 months, it will rise to about $65. You need to determine the expected return associated with each of your investment alternatives. Because (most) options have relatively short lives, and because we're dealing in this case with an investment horizon of only 6 months, holding period return can be used to measure yield (see Chapter 4). Thus, if your expectations about the stock are correct, it should go up by $16 a share and, in so doing, provide you with a 33% holding period return [($65 − $49)/$49 = $16 / $49 = 0.33].

But there are also some listed options available on this stock. Let's see how they would do. For illustrative purposes, we will use two 6-month calls that carry a $40 and a $50 strike price, respectively. Table 14.2 compares the behavior of these two calls, with the behavior of the underlying common stock. Clearly, from a holding period return perspective, either call option represents a superior investment to buying the stock itself. The dollar amount of profit may be a bit more with the stock. But note that the size of the required investment ($4,900) is a lot more too, so that alternative has the lowest HPR.

Observe that one of the calls is an in-the-money option (the one with the $40 strike price). The other is out-of-the-money. The difference in returns generated by these calls is rather typical. That is, investors are usually able to generate much better rates of return with lower-priced (out-of-the-money) options

TABLE 14.2	Speculating with Call Options		
	100 Shares of Underlying Common Stock	6-Month Call Options on the Stock	
		$40 Strike Price	$50 Strike Price
Today			
Market value of stock (at $49/share)	$4,900		
Market price of calls*		$1,100	$ 400
6 Months Later			
Expected value of stock (at $65/share)	$6,500		
Expected price of calls*		$2,500	$1,500
Profit	$1,600	$1,400	$1,100
Holding period return**	**33%**	**127%**	**275%**

*The price of the calls was computed according to Equation 14.1. It includes some investment premium in the purchase price but none in the expected sales price.

**Holding period return (HPR) = (Ending price of the stock or option − Beginning price of the stock or option)/Beginning price of the stock or option.

and also enjoy less exposure to loss. Of course, the major drawback of out-of-the-money options is that their price is made up solely of investment premium—a sunk cost that will be lost if the stock does not move in price.

Speculating with Puts To see how you can speculate in puts, consider the following situation. The price of your stock is now $51, but you anticipate a drop in price to about $35 per share within the next 6 months. If that occurs, you could sell the stock short and make a profit of $16 per share. (See Chapter 2 for a discussion of short selling.) Alternatively, you can purchase an out-of-the-money put (with a strike price of $50) for, say, $300. Again, if the price of the underlying stock does indeed drop, you will make money with the put. The profit and rate of return on the put are summarized below, along with the comparative returns from short selling the stock.

Comparative Performance Given Price of Stock Moves from $51 to $35/Share Over a 6-Month Period:	Buy 1 Put ($50 strike price)	Sell Short 100 Shares of Stock
Purchase price (today)	$ 300	
Selling price (6 months later)	1,500*	
Short sell (today)		$5,100
Cover (6 months later)		3,500
Profit	$1,200	$1,600
Holding period return	400%	63%**

*The price of the put was computed according to Equation 14.2 and does not include any investment premium.

**Assumes the short sale was made with a required margin deposit of 50%.

Once again, in terms of holding period return, the stock option is the superior investment vehicle by a wide margin.

Of course, not all option investments perform as well as the ones in our examples. Success with this strategy rests on picking the right underlying common stock. Thus *security analysis and proper stock selection are critical dimensions of this technique*. It is a highly risky investment strategy, but it may be well suited for the more speculatively inclined investor.

hedge
a combination of two or more securities into a single investment position for the purpose of reducing or eliminating risk.

Hedging A **hedge** is simply a combination of two or more securities into a single investment position for the purpose of reducing risk. This strategy might involve buying stock and simultaneously buying a put on that same stock. Or it might consist of selling some stock short and then buying a call. There are many types of hedges, some of which are very simple and others very sophisticated. They are all used for the same basic reason: to earn or protect a profit without exposing the investor to excessive loss.

An options hedge may be appropriate if you have generated a profit from an earlier common stock investment and wish to protect that profit. Or it may be appropriate if you are about to enter into a common stock investment and wish to protect your money by limiting potential capital loss. If you hold a stock that has gone up in price, the purchase of a put would provide the type of downside protection you need; the purchase of a call, in contrast, would provide protection to a short seller of common stock. Thus option hedging always involves two transactions: (1) the initial common stock position (long or short) and (2) the simultaneous or subsequent purchase of the option.

Let's examine a simple options hedge in which a put is used to limit capital loss or protect profit. Assume that you want to buy 100 shares of stock. Being a bit apprehensive about the stock's outlook, you decide to use an option hedge to protect your capital against loss. Therefore, you simultaneously (1) buy the stock and (2) buy a put on the stock (which fully covers the 100 shares owned). This type of hedge is known as a *protective put*. Preferably, the put would be a low-priced option with a strike price at or near the current market price of the stock. Suppose you purchase the common at $25 and pay $150 for a put with a $25 strike price. Now, no matter what happens to the price of the stock over the life of the put, *you can lose no more than $150*. At the same time, *there's no limit on the gains*. If the stock does not move, you will be out the cost of a put. If it drops in price, then whatever is lost on the stock will be made up with the put. The bottom line? The most you can lose is the cost of the put ($150, in this case). However, if the price of the stock goes up (as hoped), the put becomes useless, and you will earn the capital gains on the stock (less the cost of the put, of course).

The essentials of this option hedge are shown in Table 14.3. The $150 paid for the put is sunk cost. That's lost no matter what happens to the price of the stock. In effect, it is the price paid for the hedge. Moreover, this hedge is good only for the life of the put. When this put expires, you will have to replace it with another put or forget about hedging your capital.

The other basic use of an option hedge involves entering into the options position *after* a profit has been made on the underlying stock. This could be done because of investment uncertainty or for tax purposes (to carry over a profit to the next taxable year). For example, if you bought 100 shares of a stock at $35 and it moved to $75, there would be a profit of $40 per share

TABLE 14.3   Limiting Capital Loss with a Put Hedge

		Stock	Put*
Today			
Purchase price of the stock		$25	
Purchase price of the put			$1.50
Sometime Later			
A. **Price of common goes *up* to:**		$50	
Value of put			$ 0
Profit:			
100 shares of stock ($50 − $25)	$2,500		
Less: Cost of put	− 150		
Profit:	**$2,350**		
B. **Price of common goes *down* to:**		$10	
Value of put**			$15
Profit:			
100 shares of stock (loss: $10 − $25)	−$1,500		
Value of put (profit)	+ 1,500		
Less: Cost of put	− 150		
Loss:	**$ 150**		

*The put is purchased simultaneously and carries a strike price of $25.
**See Equation 14.2.

TABLE 14.4	Protecting Profits with a Put Hedge		
		Stock	3-Month Put with a $75 Strike Price
Purchase price of the stock		$ 35	
Today			
Market price of the stock		$ 75	
Market price of the put			$2.50
3 Months Later			
A. **Price of common goes *up* to:**		$100	
Value of put			$ 0
Profit:			
100 shares of stock ($500 − $35)	$6,500		
Less: Cost of put	− 250		
Profit:	$6,250		
B. **Price of common goes *down* to:**		$ 50	
Value of put*			$25
Profit:			
100 shares of stock ($50 − $35)	$1,500		
Value of put (profit)	2,500		
Less: Cost of put	− 250		
Profit:	$3,750		

*See Equation 14.2.

to protect. You could protect the profit with an option hedge by buying a put. Assume you buy a 3-month put with a $75 strike price at a cost of $250. Now, regardless of what happens to the stock over the life of the put, you are guaranteed a minimum profit of $3,750 (the $4,000 profit in the stock made so far, less the $250 cost of the put). This can be seen in Table 14.4. Note that if the price of the stock should fall, the worst that can happen is a guaranteed minimum profit of $3,750. And there is still *no limit on how much profit can be made.* As long as the stock continues to go up, you will reap the benefits.

Although this discussion pertained to put hedges, it should be clear that call hedges can also be set up to limit the loss or protect a profit on a short sale. For example, when a stock is sold short, a call can be purchased to protect the short seller against a rise in the price of the stock—with the same basic results as outlined above.

HOTLINKS

To find some good articles on strategies using options, go to:

www.888options.com/learning/strategy.jsp

Option Writing and Spreading The advent of listed options has led to many intriguing options-trading strategies. Yet, despite the appeal of these techniques, there is one important point that all the experts agree on: *Such specialized trading strategies should be left to experienced investors who fully understand their subtleties.* Our goal at this point is not to master these specialized strategies but to explain in general terms what they are and how they operate. There are two types of specialized options strategies: (1) writing options and (2) spreading options.

Writing Options Generally, investors write options because they believe the price of the underlying stock is going to move in their favor. That is, it is not going to rise as much as the buyer of a call expects, nor will it fall as much as the buyer of a put hopes. *More often than not, the option writer is right;* he or she makes money far more often than the buyer of the put or call. Such favorable odds explain, in part, the underlying economic motivation for writing put and call options. Options writing represents an investment transaction to the writers: They receive the full option premium (less normal transaction costs) in exchange for agreeing to live up to the terms of the option.

naked options
options written on securities not owned by the writer.

Investors can write options in one of two ways. One is to write **naked options,** which involves writing options on stock not owned by the writer. You simply write the put or call, collect the option premium, and hope the price of the underlying stock does not move against you. If successful, naked writing can be highly profitable because of the modest amount of capital required. Remember, though: The amount of return to the writer is always limited to the amount of option premium received. On the other hand, there is really *no limit to loss exposure.* That's the catch: The price of the underlying stock can rise or fall by just about any amount over the life of the option and can deal a real blow to the writer of the naked put or call.

covered options
options written against stock owned (or short sold) by the writer.

Such risk exposure can be partially offset by writing **covered options.** In this case the options are written against stocks the investor (writer) already owns or has a position in. For example, you could write a call against stock you own or write a put against stock you have short sold. In this way, you can use the long or short position to meet the terms of the option. Such a strategy is a fairly conservative way to generate attractive rates of return. The object is to write a slightly *out-of-the-money* option, pocket the option premium, and hope the price of the underlying stock will move up or down to (but not exceed) the option's strike price. In effect, you are adding option premium to the other usual sources of return (dividends and/or capital gains). But there's more: While the option premium adds to the return, it also reduces risk. It can be used to cushion a loss if the price of the stock moves against the investor.

There is a hitch to all this, of course: *The amount of return the covered option investor can realize is limited.* For once the price of the underlying common stock exceeds the strike price on the option, the option becomes valuable. When that happens, you start *to lose* money on the options. From this point on, for every dollar you make on the stock position, you lose an equal amount on the option position. That's a major risk of writing covered call options—if the price of the underlying stock takes off, you'll miss out on the added profits.

To illustrate the ins and outs of covered call writing, let's assume you own 100 shares of PFP, Inc.—an actively traded, high-yielding common stock. The stock is currently trading at $73.50 and pays *quarterly* dividends of $1 a share. You decide to write a 3-month call on PFP, giving the buyer the right to take the stock off your hands at $80 a share. Such options are trading in the market at 2.50, so you receive $250 for writing the call. You fully intend to hold on to the stock, so you'd like to see the price of PFP stock rise to no more than 80 by the expiration date on the call. If that happens, the call option will expire worthless. As a result, not only will you earn the dividends and capital gains on the stock, but you also get to pocket the $250 you received when you wrote the call. Basically, you've just *added* $250 to the quarterly return on your stock.

TABLE 14.5   Covered Call Writing

	Stock	3-Month Call with an $80 Strike Price
Current market price of the stock	$73.50	
Current market price of the put		$ 2.50

3 Months Later

A. Price of the stock is *unchanged*: $73.50

Value of the call		$ 0
Profit:		
Quarterly dividends received	$ 100	
Proceeds from sale of call	250	
Total profit:	$ 350	

B. Price of the stock goes *up* to: $80 ⟵   Price Where Maximum Profit Occurs

Value of the call		$ 0
Profit:		
Quarterly dividends received	$ 100	
Proceeds from sale of call	250	
Capital gains on stock ($80 − $73.50)	650	
Total profit:	$1,000	

C. Price of the stock goes *up* to: $90

Value of the call*		$10
Profit:		
Quarterly dividends received	$ 100	
Proceeds from sale of call	250	
Capital gains on stock ($90 − $73.50)	$1,650	
Less: Loss on call	($1,000)	
Net profit:	$1,000	

D. Price of the stock *drops* to: $71 ⟵   Break-even Price

Value of the call*		$ 0
Profit:		
Capital loss on stock ($71 − $73.50)	($ 250)	
Proceeds from sale of call	250	} $0 profit or loss
Quarterly dividends	100	
Net profit:	$ 100	

*See Equation 14.1.

Table 14.5 summarizes the profit and loss characteristics of this covered call position. Note that the maximum profit on this transaction occurs *when the market price of the stock equals the strike price on the call*. If the price of the stock keeps going up, you miss out on the added profits. Even so, the $1,000 profit that's earned at a stock price of 80 or above translates into a (3-month) holding period return of a very respectable 13.6% ($1,000/$7,350). That represents an *annualized* return of nearly 55%! With this kind of return potential, it's not difficult to see why covered call writing is so popular. Moreover, as *situation D* in the table illustrates, covered call writing adds a

CREATE YOUR OWN CONVERTIBLES—What can you do when you want to buy a company's convertible bond but it doesn't offer one? You can design your own (synthetic) convertible by combining interest-bearing securities and call options. One popular method is the 90/10 strategy. You place 10% of your money into call options, and the 90% goes in an interest-bearing security such as a money market instrument that is held until the option expires. The options provide leverage and give you the right to buy shares in the company (just like a convertible); the money market security limits risk. Your downside loss exposure is the amount of the call premium less the interest you earn on the money market investments.

Source: Witold Sames, "Up, Down, or Sideways," *Bloomberg Personal,* October 1997, p. 30; and Avital Louria Hahn, "Market Laps Up Synthetic Convert; MSDW, AIG Cleanup," *Investment Dealers' Digest,* May 15, 2000, downloaded from www.findarticles.com

option spreading
combining two or more options with different strike prices and/or expiration dates into a single transaction.

option straddle
the simultaneous purchase (or sale) of a put and a call on the same underlying common stock (or financial asset).

little cushion to losses: The price of the stock has to drop more than 2½ points (which is what you received when you wrote/sold the call) before you start losing money.

Besides covered calls and protective puts, there are many different ways of combining options with other types of securities to achieve a given investment objective. Probably none is more unusual than the creation of so-called *synthetic securities*. A case in point: Say you want to buy a convertible bond on a certain company, but that company doesn't have any convertibles outstanding. That's really not a big problem. You can create your own customized convertible by combining a straight (nonconvertible) bond with a listed call option on your targeted company.

Spreading Options Option spreading is nothing more than the combination of two or more options into a single transaction. You could create an options spread, for example, by simultaneously buying and writing options on the same underlying stock. These would not be identical options. They would differ with respect to strike price and/or expiration date. Spreads are a very popular use of listed options, and they account for a substantial amount of the trading activity on the listed options exchanges. These spreads go by a variety of exotic names, such as *bull spreads, bear spreads, money spreads, vertical spreads,* and *butterfly spreads.* Each spread is different and each is constructed to meet a certain type of investment goal.

Consider, for example, a *vertical spread.* It would be set up by *buying* a call at one strike price and then *writing* a call (on the same stock and for the same expiration date) at a higher strike price. For instance, you could buy a February call on XYZ at a strike price of, say, 30 and simultaneously sell (write) a February call on XYZ at a strike price of 35. Strange as it may sound, such a position would generate a hefty return if the price of the underlying stock went up by just a few points. Other spreads are used to profit from a falling market. Still others try to make money when the price of the underlying stock moves either way up *or* down.

Whatever the objective, most spreads are created to take advantage of differences in prevailing option prices and premiums. The payoff from spreading is usually substantial, but *so is the risk*. In fact, some spreads that seem to involve almost no risk may end up with devastating results if the market and the difference between option premiums move against the investor.

A variation on this theme involves an **option straddle**. This is the simultaneous purchase (or sale) of *both* a put *and* a call on the same underlying common stock. Unlike spreads, straddles normally involve the same strike price and expiration date. Here, the object is to earn a profit from *either* a big or a small swing in the price of the underlying common stock. For example, in a *long straddle*, you *buy* an equal number of puts and calls. You make money in the long straddle when the underlying stock undergoes a big change in price—either up or down. If the price of the stock shoots way up, you make money on the call side of the straddle but are out the cost of the puts. If the price of the stock plummets, you make money on the puts, but the calls are useless. In either case, so long as you make more money on one side than the cost of the options for the other side, you're ahead of the game. In a similar fashion, in a *short straddle,* you *sell/write* an equal number of puts and calls. You make money in this position when the price of the underlying stock goes nowhere. In effect, you get to keep all or most of the option premiums you collected when you wrote the options.

Except for obvious structural differences, the principles that underlie the creation of straddles are much like those for spreads. The object is to combine options that will enable you to capture the benefits of certain types of stock price behavior. But keep in mind that if the prices of the underlying stock and/or the option premiums do not behave in the anticipated manner, you lose. *Spreads and straddles are extremely tricky and should be used only by knowledgeable investors.*

IN REVIEW

CONCEPTS

14.7 Briefly explain how you would make money on (a) a call option and (b) a put option. Do you have to exercise the option to capture the profit? Explain.

14.8 How do you find the intrinsic value of a call? Of a put? Does an *out-of-the-money option* have intrinsic value? Explain.

14.9 Name at least four variables that affect the price behavior of listed options, and briefly explain how each affects prices. How important are fundamental (intrinsic) value and time value to in-the-money options? To out-of-the-money options?

14.10 Describe at least three different ways in which investors can use stock options.

14.11 What's the most that can be made from writing calls? Why would an investor want to write *covered calls?* Can you reduce the risk on the underlying common stock by writing covered calls? Explain.

14.12 What is a *synthetic security?* Give an example of a synthetic security.

Stock-Index and Other Types of Options

LG 5

Imagine being able to buy or sell a major stock market index like the S&P 500—and at a reasonable cost. Think of what you could do: If you felt the market was heading up, you could invest in a security that tracks the price behavior of the S&P 500 index and make money when the market goes up. No longer would you have to go through the process of selecting specific stocks that you hope will capture the market's performance. Rather, you could play the *market as a whole.* That's exactly what you can do *with stock-index options*—puts and calls that are written on major stock market indexes. Index options have been around since 1983 and have become immensely popular with both individual and institutional investors. Let's now take a closer look at these popular and often highly profitable investment vehicles.

Stock-Index Options: Contract Provisions

stock-index option
a put or call option written on a specific stock market index, such as the S&P 500.

Basically, a **stock-index option** is a put or call written on a specific stock market index. The underlying security in this case is the specific market index. Thus, when the market index moves in one direction or another, the value of the index option moves accordingly. Because there are no stocks or other financial assets backing these options, settlement is defined in terms of cash. Specifically, the cash value of an *index option* is equal to 100 times the published market index that underlies the option. For example, if the S&P 500 is at 1,500, then the cash value of an S&P 500 index option will be $100 \times 1,500 = \$150,000$. If the underlying index moves up or down in the market, so will the cash value of the option.

In mid-2000, put and call options were available on more than 75 market measures of performance. These included options on just about every major U.S. stock market index or average (such as the Dow Jones Industrial Average, the S&P 500, the Russell 2000, and the Nasdaq 100), options on a handful of foreign markets (e.g., Mexico and Japan), and options on different segments of the market (pharmaceuticals, oil services, semiconductors, bank, and utility indexes). Many of these options, however, are very thinly traded and really don't amount to much of a market. The following five indexes actually dominate the stock-index options market and account for the vast majority of trading activity:

- The S&P 500 Index (traded on the CBOE)
- The S&P 100 Index (CBOE)
- The Dow Jones Industrial Average (CBOE)
- The Nasdaq 100 Index (CBOE)
- The Russell 2000 Index (CBOE)

The S&P 500 Index is a widely used index that captures the market behavior of large-cap stocks. The S&P 100 Index is another large-cap index composed of 100 stocks, drawn from the S&P 500, that have actively traded stock options. The most popular index of all is the DJIA. Trading in this measure of the blue-chip segment of the market began in October 1997. Within a matter of weeks, it became one of the most actively traded index options. The Nasdaq 100 index tracks the behavior of the 100 largest (nonfinancial) stocks on the Nasdaq and is composed of mostly large, high-tech companies (such as Intel and Cisco). The Russell 2000 Index tracks the behavior of small-cap stocks. Of these five index options, the S&P 500, the S&P 100, and the DJIA are by far the most popular. In fact, there's more trading in these three contracts than in all the other index options combined. Indeed, these are three of *the most actively traded of all listed options, regardless of type.* Though all four of the options exchanges deal in index options, the CBOE dominates the market. It alone accounts for nearly 90% of all trades and, as the foregoing list shows, is home to all five of the most actively traded index options.

Both puts and calls are available on index options. They are valued and have issue characteristics like any other put or call. That is, a put lets a holder profit from a drop in the market. (When the underlying market index goes down, the value of a put goes up.) A call enables the holder to profit from a market that's going up. As seen in Figure 14.3, these options even have a quotation system that is very similar to that used for puts and calls on stocks. (Actually, there is one small difference between the *Wall Street Journal* quotes for stock options and those for index options: The closing value for the underlying index is not listed with the rest of the quote. Instead, these values are listed separately in a table that accompanies the quotes.)

FIGURE 14.3 Quotations on Index Options

The quotation system used with index options is a lot like that used with stock options: Strike prices and expiration dates are shown along with closing option prices. The biggest differences are that put (p) and call (c) quotes are mixed together, and the closing values for the underlying indexes are shown separately. (*Source: Wall Street Journal,* August 30, 2000.)

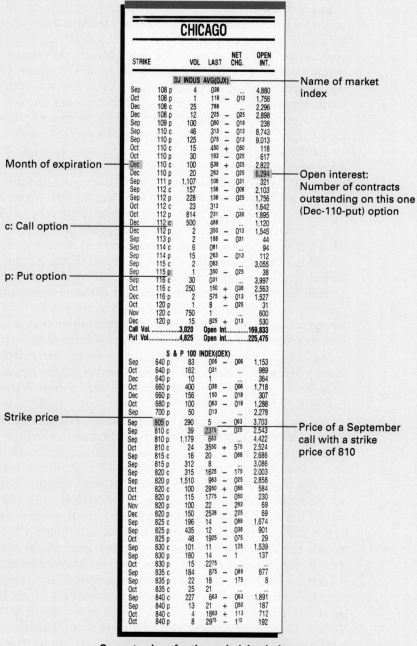

Name of market index

Month of expiration

c: Call option

p: Put option

Strike price

Open interest: Number of contracts outstanding on this one (Dec-110-put) option

Price of a September call with a strike price of 810

Current values for the underlying indexes

DJIA:	111.93
S&P 100:	823.55

Putting a Value on Stock-Index Options As is true of equity options, the market price of index options is a function of the difference between the strike price on the option (stated in terms of the underlying index) and the latest published stock market index. To illustrate, consider the highly popular S&P 100 Index traded on the CBOE. As the index option quotes in Figure 14.3 reveal, this index recently closed at 823.55. (See the highlighted "Current values for the underlying indexes" at the bottom of the exhibit.) At the same time, there was a September call on this index that carried a strike price of 820. A stock-index *call* will have a value so long as the underlying index exceeds the index strike price (just the opposite for puts). Hence, the intrinsic value of this call would be 823.55 − 820 = 3.55. As the quotes in Figure 14.3 show, this call was actually trading at 16.25—nearly 13 points *above* the call's underlying fundamental value. This difference, of course, was the *time premium*. Just as in stock options, the amount of premium in an index option tends to *increase with longer options* and with *more volatile market conditions*.

If the S&P 100 Index in our example were to go up to, say, 850 by late September (the expiration date on the call), this option would be quoted at 850 − 820 = 30. Because index options (like equity options) are valued in multiples of $100, this contract would be worth $3,000. If you had purchased this option when it was trading at 16.25, it would have cost you $1,625 and, in less than 2 months, would have generated a profit of $3,000 − $1,625 = $1,375. That translates into a holding period return of more than 80%.

This example illustrates several points. First, it's not the value of the underlying index that drives the market price of the option but, rather, the difference between the prevailing value of the underlying index and the strike price on the option. Second, because index options are valued just like equity options, Equations 14.1 and 14.2 are used to value calls and puts, respectively, on index options. Finally, because they're a form of derivative security, stock-index options are valued according to how the market (that is, the market index) performs. Thus *calls should be more highly valued if the market is expected to go up in the future. Puts should be more highly valued in falling markets.*

Most broad-based index options use the full market value of the underlying index for purposes of options trading and valuation. But that's not the case with two of the Dow Jones measures. In particular, the option on the *Dow Jones Industrial Average is based on 1% (1/100) of the actual Industrial Average, and the Dow Transportation Average option is based on 10% (1/10) of the actual average.* For example, if the DJIA is at 11,193, the index option would use 1% of that amount, or 111.93. Thus the cash value of this option is not $100 times the underlying DJIA but $100 times 1% of the DJIA, which equals the Dow Jones Industrial Average itself: $100 × 111.93 = $11,193. Fortunately, the option strike prices are also based on the same 1% of the Dow, so there is really no effect on option valuation: What matters is still the difference between the strike price on the option and (1% of) the DJIA. For instance, note in Figure 14.3 that the DJIA option index closed at 111.93 (the actual Dow was at 11,193). Note also that there was a December call option available on this index with a strike price of 108: it was trading at 7.88—that is, it was trading at 7.88 × $100 = $788. Using Equation 14.1, you can see that this in-the-money option had an intrinsic value of 111.93 − 108.00 = 3.93 (or $393). The rest was time premium.

Except for this little twist, Dow Jones index options are valued like any other. Indeed, the greatest impact of this pricing mechanism is the *number of options necessary to establish a given position*. For example, look once more at Figure 14.3. Note that whereas the S&P 100 index option has a cash value of $82,355, the DJIA option is worth considerably less than that—$11,193. Thus it would take a bit more than seven Dow options to give you the same $82,355 position as one S&P 100 index option. Hence the lower Dow index option prices are a bit misleading when you consider that it would take a lot more of them to give you approximately the same coverage/position as one S&P 100 index option.

Investment Uses

Although index options, like equity options, can be used in spreads, straddles, or even covered calls, they are perhaps used most often for speculating or for hedging. When used as a speculative vehicle, index options give investors an opportunity to play the market as a whole, with a relatively small amount of capital. Like any other put or call, *index options provide attractive leverage opportunities and at the same time limit exposure to loss to the price paid for the option.*

Index options are equally effective as *hedging vehicles*. In fact, hedging is a major use of index options and accounts for a good deal of the trading in these securities. To see how these options can be used for hedging, consider an investor who holds a diversified portfolio of common stocks. One way to protect the portfolio against an adverse market is to buy puts on one of the market indexes. If you hold a portfolio of, say, a dozen different stocks and you think the market is heading down, you can protect your capital by selling all of your stocks. However, that could become expensive, especially if you plan to get back into the market after it drops, and it could lead to a good deal of unnecessary taxes. Fortunately, there is a way to "have your cake and eat it too," and that is to hedge your stock portfolio with a stock index put. In this way, if the market does go down, you'll make money on your puts, which can then be used to buy more stocks at the lower, "bargain" prices. On the other hand, if the market continues to go up, you'll be out *only the cost of the puts*. That amount could well be recovered from the increased value of your stock holdings. The principles of hedging with stock-index options are exactly the same as those for hedging with equity options. The only difference is that with stock-index options, you're trying to protect a *whole portfolio* of stocks rather than *individual* stocks.

There is one important consideration to keep in mind: The amount of profit you make or the protection you obtain depends in large part on how closely the behavior of your stock portfolio is matched by the behavior of the stock-index option you employ. *There is no guarantee that the two will behave in the same way.* You should therefore select an index option that closely reflects the nature of the stocks in your portfolio. If, for example, you hold a number of small-cap stocks, you might be well advised to select something like the Russell 2000 index option as the hedging vehicle. If you hold mostly blue chips, you might choose the DJIA index option. You probably can't get dollar-for-dollar portfolio protection, but you should try to get as close a match as possible. Another factor that's important is the cost of the underlying hedge vehicle itself. This and

INVESTING in action

Using Index Options to Protect a Whole Portfolio

When the stock market heads down, investors begin to worry about protecting the value of their portfolios. But simply liquidating their stock holdings and putting the proceeds into a money market fund is too drastic a step for most people. Not only would they incur substantial brokerage commissions and capital gains taxes, but they would also lose out if the market rallies. A far less drastic—and less costly—way for investors to shield their portfolios from the possibility of a sustained sell-off is to buy "insurance" in the form of stock-index put options.

These options offer a simple method of insuring the value of an entire portfolio with a single trade. That can be especially helpful because many issues in an investor's portfolio may not have individual put options traded on them. Such portfolio protection is similar to any other kind of insurance. The more protection investors want and the less risk they are willing to bear, the more the insurance costs. For example, suppose an investor wants to hedge a $125,000 stock portfolio and, after examining the characteristics of the major stock indexes, concludes that the S&P 100 best matches the portfolio. With the S&P 100 Index standing at, say, 675 in February, the market value of the S&P 100 Index would be $67,500. So the investor would buy two puts to approximate the $125,000 portfolio value.

The investor might buy two May 660 puts that expire in 3 months (i.e., in June) with a strike price of 660 and a price of about 23. To turn that into dollars, an investor multiplies by 100; the puts would cost $2,300 each—$4,600 for both—or 3.7% of the $125,000 portfolio. If the market retreats about 15% from current levels, bringing the S&P 100 down to about 574, each May 660 put would be worth a minimum of 86 points (660 − 574), or $8,600. After paying their cost, the investor would have a profit on the puts of $12,600 ($8,600 − $2,300 = $6,300 × 2),

offsetting a substantial portion of the $18,750 the portfolio would have lost in a 15% decline.

By purchasing puts with strike prices that are 15 points below the current level of the S&P Index, the investor effectively insures the portfolio against any losses that occur *after* the market has fallen 15 points, or 2.2%, to 660. An investor willing to bear more market risk could reduce the insurance cost even further by purchasing puts with even lower strike prices. On the other hand, to be fully insured, an investor might have bought puts with a higher strike price, but that would have raised the cost of the insurance. May 670 puts, for instance, would have cost about 27, or $2,700 each. Harrison Roth, an options strategist, says the basic question for investors is "Do you want to hedge against any and all declines, or do you simply want protection against catastrophic moves?" He believes most investors are in the second camp.

Even with relatively low-cost puts such as the May 660s, the cost of put option hedges can add up if the insurance goes unused. Buying 3-month puts like these four times a year would cost the equivalent of almost 15% of a $125,000 portfolio. One way to reduce the cost is to sell the put options before they expire. Put options lose most of their value in the final few weeks before their expiration if they have strike prices below the current price of the underlying securities. For this reason, some market advisers recommend that investors hold their options for only a month, sell them, and then buy the next month out. This strategy recovers most of the options' value, significantly reducing the cost to hedge, even after the higher commissions.

Source: Donald J. Korn, "The Price Is Right," *Black Enterprise,* December 2000, downloaded from FindArticles.com, **www.findarticles.com**

other considerations are discussed in the accompanying *Investing in Action* box, which deals with the use of index options in portfolio hedging.

Given their effectiveness for either speculating or hedging the entire market, it's little wonder that index options have become so popular with investors. But a word of caution is in order: Although trading index options appears simple and seems to provide high rates of return, these vehicles involve *high risk* and are subject to considerable price volatility. They should not be used by amateurs. True, there's only so much you can lose with these options. The trouble is that it's very easy to lose that amount. Attractive profits are indeed available from these securities. But they're not investments you can buy and then forget about until just before they expire. With the wide market swings that are so common today, *these securities must be closely monitored on a daily basis.*

Other Types of Options

Options on stocks and stock indexes account for most (over 95%) of the market activity in listed options. But put and call options can also be obtained on debt instruments and foreign currencies. You can also buy puts and calls with extended expiration dates; these options are known as *LEAPS*. Let's now take a brief look at these other kinds of options, starting with interest rate options.

interest rate options
put and call options written on fixed-income (debt) securities.

Interest Rate Options Puts and calls on fixed-income (debt) securities are known as **interest rate options**. At the present time, interest rate options are written only on U.S. Treasury securities. There are four maturities used: 30-year T-bonds, 10-year and 5-year T-notes, and short-term (13-week) T-bills. These options are a bit unusual because they are *yield-based* rather than price-based. This means they track the yield behavior (rather than the price behavior) of the underlying Treasury security. Other types of options (equity and index options) are set up so that they react to movements in the price (or value) of the underlying asset. Interest rate options, in contrast, are set up to react to *the yield of the underlying Treasury security*. Thus, when yields rise, the value of a call goes up. When yields fall, puts go up in value. In effect, because bond prices and yields move in opposite directions, the value of an interest rate call option goes up at the very time that the price (or value) of the underlying debt security is going down. (The opposite is true for puts.) This unusual behavioral characteristic may help explain why the market for interest rate options remains very small. Most professional investors simply don't care for interest rate options. Instead, they prefer to use interest rate futures contracts or options on these futures contracts (both of which will be examined in Chapter 15).

currency options
put and call options written on foreign currencies.

Currency Options Foreign exchange options, or just **currency options** as they're more commonly called, provide a way for investors to speculate on foreign exchange rates or to hedge foreign currency or foreign security holdings. Currency options are available on the currencies of most of the countries with which the U.S. has strong trading ties. These options are traded on the Philadelphia Exchange and include the following currencies:

- British pound
- Swiss franc
- German mark
- Euro
- Canadian dollar
- Japanese yen
- Australian dollar
- French franc

Note that in addition to pounds, marks, francs, and yen, there are also options available on the *euro,* the currency unit used within the European Economic Community. To learn more about the *euro,* look at the accompanying *Investing in Action* box. Puts and calls on euros and other foreign currencies give the holders the right to sell or buy large amounts of the specified currency. However, in contrast to the standardized contracts used with stock and stock-index options, the specific unit of trading in this market varies with the particular underlying currency. The details are spelled out in Table 14.6. Currency options are traded in full or fractional cents per unit of the underlying currency, relative to the amount of foreign currency involved. Thus, if a put or call on the British pound were quoted at, say, 6.40 (which is read as "6.4 cents"), it would be valued at $2,000, because 31,250 British pounds underlie this option (that is, $31,250 \times .064 = \$2,000$).

The value of a currency option is linked to the exchange rate between the U.S. dollar and the underlying foreign currency. For example, if the Canadian dollar becomes stronger *relative to the U.S. dollar,* causing the exchange rate to go up, the price of a *call* option on the Canadian dollar will increase, and the price of a *put* will decline. [*Note:* Some cross-currency options are available in the market, but such options/trading techniques are beyond the scope of this book. We will focus solely on foreign currency options (or futures) linked to U.S. dollars.]

To understand how you can make money with currency options, consider a situation in which an investor wants to speculate on exchange rates. The strike price of a currency option is stated in terms of *exchange rates.* Thus a strike price of 150 implies that each unit of the foreign currency (such as one British pound) is worth 150 cents, or $1.50, in U.S. money. If you held a 150 call on this foreign currency, you would make money if *the foreign currency strengthened relative to the U.S. dollar* so that the exchange rate rose—say, to 155. In contrast, if you held a 150 put, you would profit from a decline in the exchange rate—say, to 145. Success in forecasting movements in foreign exchange rates is obviously essential to a profitable foreign currency options program.

LEAPS They look like regular puts and calls, and they behave pretty much like regular puts and calls, but they're not regular puts and calls. They're different. We're talking about **LEAPS,** which are puts and calls with lengthy expiration dates. Basically, LEAPS are long-term options. Whereas standard options have

LEAPS
long-term options.

TABLE 14.6	Foreign Currency Option Contracts on the Philadelphia Exchange		
Underlying Currency*	Size of Contracts	Underlying Currency*	Size of Contracts
British pound	31,250 pounds	Canadian dollar	50,000 dollars
Swiss franc	62,500 francs	Japanese yen	6,250,000 yen
German mark	62,500 marks	Australian dollar	50,000 dollars
Euro	62,500 Euros	French franc	250,000 francs

*The British pound, Swiss franc, German mark, Canadian dollar, and Australian dollar are all quoted in full cents. The French franc is quoted in tenths of a cent. The Japanese yen is quoted in hundredths of a cent.

INVESTING in action

Euro-kay, I'm Okay

On January 1, 1999, a new currency arrived on the world financial scene. The euro became the common currency for members of the European Monetary Union (EMU). The member countries met economic criteria with regard to levels of inflation, budget deficits, government debt, long-term interest rates, and exchange rates. The original 11 participants—Germany, France, Ireland, Finland, Italy, Spain, Portugal, Belgium, Luxembourg, Holland, and Austria—were joined in 2001 by Greece, which did not qualify for membership in 1999. (Great Britain, Denmark, and Sweden, the other European Union nations, qualified but chose not to join the EMU.) During a 3-year transition period, the euro was used only for noncash transactions. Once the new euro coins and bills come into circulation in 2002, national currencies such as marks, francs, lira, and pesetas [will pass] into history.

In accepting the euro, EMU nations turned over control of monetary policy to a new European Central Bank (ECB) located in Frankfurt. Like the U.S. Federal Reserve Bank, the ECB's mission is to maintain solid growth among the member nations. It sets interest rates, handles foreign exchange operations, manages reserves, and performs other activities to make the payment systems work smoothly. At the same time, it has the difficult task of setting policies that benefit the region as a whole without favoring any one country more than another.

By eliminating most monetary borders in Western Europe, the euro creates one of the world's largest trading blocs—and one that rivals the United States in terms of population, percent of GDP, and percent of world trade. The unified economic environment will foster stability, growth, and investment. Intra-European and global trade should increase because goods, services, and people can flow freely across national borders, and currency exchange transaction costs are eliminated within the EMU. The unified financial market is more efficient and provides easier access to the European capital markets. As a result of the euro's introduction, investors began to view Europe as a single stock market, even though each country retained its national stock exchange. The euro also simplifies currency risk management and reduces hedging costs.

The euro's value fluctuates daily against other leading currencies such as the dollar, pound, and yen. These changes in its value will create risks and opportunities for investors. A weak euro erodes the value of profits earned in Europe and makes U.S. goods more expensive in Europe. When the euro is strong, the reverse is true.

The euro was worth $1.17 when it debuted in January 1999 and was expected to rise as capital flowed into the EMU. As the euro struggled for acceptance, however, the U.S. economy continued to boom. The euro sank steadily against the dollar, going as low as 85¢ during 2000.

In September 2000, many U.S. corporations—especially consumer products and service multinationals such as Colgate-Palmolive, Gillette, and McDonald's—warned that the weak euro would negatively affect earnings. At the same time, the technology and capital goods sectors saw higher prices on American goods reduce their sales.

On the other hand, the weak euro benefited U.S. investors who took advantage of low prices on European blue-chip stocks. If the euro regains some of its value by the time the investor sells, the investor's return will be higher because of the favorable currency exchange when euros are converted back to dollars.

Sources: Helene Cooper, "The Euro: What You Need to Know," *Wall Street Journal*, January 4, 1999, pp. A5, A6; Michael Sivy, "Euro Play," *Money.com*, April 28, 2000; Michael Sivy, "How Now Mad Cow," *Money.com*, December 13, 2000; and Michael Sivy, "Foreign Entanglements," *Money.com*, September 18, 2000; all downloaded from www.money.com

maturities of 8 months or less, LEAPS have expiration dates that extend out as far as 3 years. Known formally as *Long-term Equity AnticiPation Securities*, they are listed on all four of the major options exchanges. LEAPS are available on over 300 different stocks and more than a dozen stock indexes, including the S&P 100, the S&P 500, and the DJIA.

Aside from their time frame, LEAPS work like any other equity or index option. For example, a single (equity) LEAPS contract gives the holder the right to buy or sell 100 shares of stock at a predetermined price on or before the specified expiration date. LEAPS give investors more time to be right about their bets on the direction of a stock or stock index, and they give hedgers more time to protect their positions. But there's a price for this extra time: You can expect to pay a lot more for a LEAPS than you would for a regular (short-term) option. For example, in mid-2000, a 6-month, out-of-the-money call on Lucent (with a strike price of 55) was trading at 6.25. The same call with a 1½-year expiration date was trading at 12.75. The difference should come as no surprise. LEAPS, being nothing more than long-term options, are loaded with *time premium*. And as we saw earlier in this chapter, other things being equal, *the more time an option has to expiration, the higher the quoted price.*

IN REVIEW

CONCEPTS

14.13 Briefly describe the differences and similarities between *stock-index options* and *stock options*. Do the same for *foreign currency options* and stock options.

14.14 Identify and briefly discuss two different ways to use stock-index options. Do the same for foreign currency options. Explain how index options can be used by investors to hedge or protect a whole portfolio of stocks, as discussed in the *Investing in Action* box on page 610.

14.15 Why would an investor want to use index options to hedge a portfolio of common stock? If the investor thinks the market is in for a fall, why not just sell the stock?

14.16 What benefits did the members of the EMU expect from the euro? What effect would a weak euro have on U.S. investors?

14.17 What are *LEAPS?* Why would an investor want to use a LEAPS option rather than a regular listed option?

Warrants

LG 6

warrant
a long-lived option that gives the holder the right to buy stock in a company at a price specified on the warrant.

A **warrant** is a long-term option that gives the holder the right to buy a certain number of shares of stock in a certain company for a given period of time. Like most options, warrants are found in the corporate sector of the market. Occasionally, warrants can be used to purchase preferred stock or even bonds, but common stock is the leading redemption vehicle.

General Attributes

Of the various types of options, warrants normally have the longest lives, with maturities that extend to 5, 10, or even 20 years or more. Some warrants have no maturity date at all. Warrants have no voting rights, pay no dividends, and have no claim on the assets of the company. What they do offer is a chance to participate indirectly in the market behavior of the issuing firm's common stock and, in so doing, to generate capital gains. Warrants are perhaps most closely related to *call LEAPS* (long-term *call* options), although there are some important differences. First, whereas call LEAPS cover 100 shares of stock, a warrant usually covers just one or two shares of the underlying stock (or some fraction thereof). The second big difference involves the issuer of the instruments: Whereas warrants are issued by the same company that issues the underlying stock, LEAPS can be written by anybody or any institution.

Warrants are usually created as "sweeteners" to bond issues. To make a bond more attractive, the issuing company sometimes attaches warrants. These give the holder *the right to purchase a stipulated number of stock at a stipulated price anytime within a stipulated period*. A single warrant usually allows the holder to buy one full share of stock. (Some involve more than one share per warrant and a few involve fractional shares.) The life of a warrant is specified by its *expiration date*. The stock purchase price stipulated on the warrant is known as the *exercise price*. Because warrants are a type of equity issue, they can be margined at the same rate as common stock. They are purchased through brokers and are subject to transaction costs similar to those for common stock.

Advantages and Disadvantages

Warrants offer investors several advantages. One is their tendency to exhibit price behavior much like the common stock to which they are linked—just what you'd expect from a call option. Warrants, therefore, provide the investor with an alternative way of achieving capital gains from an equity issue. That is, instead of buying the stock, you can purchase warrants on the stock. Indeed, such a tactic may even be more rewarding than investing directly in the stock. Another advantage is the relatively low unit cost and the attractive leverage potential that accompanies it. That is, you can use warrants to obtain a given equity position at a substantially reduced capital investment. And in so doing, you can *magnify returns*, because the warrant provides roughly the same capital appreciation potential as the more costly common stock. A final advantage of warrants is that their low unit cost leads to reduced downside risk exposure. In essence, the lower unit cost simply means there is less to lose if the investment goes sour. For example, a $50 stock can drop to $25 if the market falls. But there is no way that the same company's $10 warrants can drop by the same amount.

However, warrants do have some *disadvantages*. For one thing, warrants pay no dividends. This means that investors sacrifice current income. Second, because these issues usually carry an expiration date, there is only a certain period of time during which you can capture the price behavior sought. Although this may not be much of a problem with long-term warrants, it can be a burden for those issues with fairly short lives (of 1 to 2 years, or less).

 ## Putting a Value on Warrants

A warrant, like any option, is a type of *derivative security*—i.e., the value of a warrant is directly linked to the price behavior of teh underlying common stock. Thus, under the right conditions, when the stock goes up (or down) in price, the warrants will too. Actually, warrants possess value whenever the market price of the underlying common exceeds the exercise price on the warrant. This so-called *fundamental value* is determined as follows:

Equation 14.3

Fundamental value of a warrant $= (M - E) \times N$

where

M = prevailing market price of the common stock

E = exercise price stipulated on the warrant

N = number of shares of stock that can be acquired with one warrant
(If one warrant entitles the holder to buy one share of stock, $N = 1$. If two warrants are necessary to buy one share of stock, $N = 0.5$, etc.)

The fundamental value calculated by the formula represents what the market value of a warrant *should be,* given the input data. As an example, consider a warrant that carries an exercise price of $40 per share and enables the holder to purchase one share of stock per warrant. If the common stock has a current market price of $50 a share, then the warrants should be valued at $10 each:

Fundamental value of a warrant = ($50 − $40) × 1 = ($10) × 1 = $\underline{\$10}$

Obviously, the greater the spread between the market and exercise prices, the greater the fundamental value of a warrant. *So long as the market price of the stock equals or exceeds the exercise price of the warrant,* and the redemption provision carries a 1-to-1 ratio (one share of common can be bought with each warrant), the value of a warrant will be closely linked to the price behavior of the common stock.

Premium Prices Equation 14.3 indicates how warrants should be valued, but they seldom are priced exactly that way in the marketplace. Instead, the market price of a warrant usually *exceeds* its fundamental value. This happens when warrants with negative values trade at prices greater than zero. It also occurs when warrants with positive fundamental values trade at even higher market prices (e.g., when a warrant that's valued at $10 trades at $15). This discrepancy is known as **warrant premium.** As a rule, the amount of premium embedded in the market price of a warrant is directly related to the option's time to expiration and the volatility of the underlying common stock. On the other hand, the amount of premium does tend to diminish as the underlying (fundamental) value of a warrant increases. This can be seen in Figure 14.4, which shows the typical behavior of warrant premiums.

The premium on a warrant is easy to measure: Just take the difference between the value of a warrant (as computed with Equation 14.3) and its market price. For instance, a warrant has $5 in premium if it has a value of $10 but is trading at $15. The amount of premium can also be expressed on a relative (percentage) basis by dividing the dollar premium by the warrant's fundamental value. For example, there is a 50% premium embedded in the price of that $15

warrant premium
the difference between the true value of a warrant and its market price.

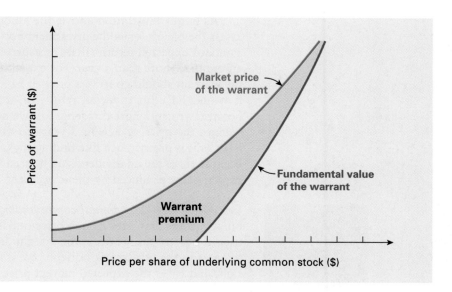

FIGURE 14.4

The Normal Price Behavior of Warrant Premiums

Observe that as the price of the underlying common stock increases, the amount of premium in the market price of the warrant tends to decrease—though it never totally disappears.

warrant (the dollar premium ÷ the fundamental value of the warrant = $5 ÷ $10 = 0.50). Premiums on warrants can at times become fairly substantial. Indeed, premiums of 20% to 30% or more are not at all uncommon.

Trading Strategies

Because their attraction to investors rests primarily with the capital gains opportunities they provide, warrants are used chiefly as alternatives to common stock investments. Let's now look at some warrant-trading strategies and the basic ways in which these securities can be profitably employed by investors.

The Basic Price Behavior of Warrants Because warrants carry relatively low unit costs, they possess much greater *price volatility* and the potential for generating substantially higher *rates of return* than a direct investment in the underlying common stock. Consider the following illustration, which involves the common shares and warrants of the same company. Assume the price of the common is now $50 per share. The warrant, which carries a one-to-one redemption provision, has a $40 exercise price. (We will ignore premium in this illustration.) Observe what happens when the price of the stock increases by $10.

	Common Stock	Warrant
Issue price *before* increase	$50	$10
Increase in price of common	$10	—
Issue price *after* increase	$60	$20
Increase in market value	$10	$10
Holding period return	**20%**	**100%**
(increase in value/beginning issue price)		

The warrant provides a rate of return five times greater than the common stock. The reason is, of course, that the two issues move parallel to one another, though the warrant carries a much lower unit cost.

As in our illustration above, the holding period return formula is used to assess the payoff when the investment horizon is 1 year or less. In contrast, the standard expected return (IRR) measure is used when the investment horizon amounts to more than a year. For example, in the illustration above, if we felt the warrant should go from a price of $10 to $20 over a 3-year period of time, it would have an expected return of around 26%. Note that in this case, because we can ignore dividends, all we need do is find the discount rate that equates the price of $20 in 3 years to the warrant's current market price of $10. This is pretty much like finding the yield on a zero-coupon bond. That is, because there are no dividends on warrants, the returns are based solely on the capital gains produced by the investment.

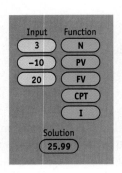

CALCULATOR USE For *annual compounding,* to find the expected return (IRR) on a warrant that goes from a price of $10 to $20 in a 3-year period of time, use the keystrokes shown in the margin. In this computation, N is the number of years in the investment horizon, PV is the current market price of the warrant, and FV is the expected market price of the warrant (in 3 years).

Trading with Warrants Warrant trading generally follows one of two approaches: (1) The leverage embedded in warrants is used to magnify dollar returns. Or (2) their low unit cost is used to reduce the amount of invested capital and limit losses. The first approach is the more aggressive. The second has considerable merit as a conservative strategy.

Our comparative illustration above (where the price of the stock goes from $50 to $60 a share) can be used to demonstrate the first technique, which seeks to magnify returns. If you want to make a $5,000 equity investment and if price appreciation is the main objective, you would be better off committing such a sum to the warrants. The reason is that a $5,000 investment in the common stock will buy 100 shares of stock ($5,000 ÷ $50 = 100 shares), which will generate only $1,000 in capital gains ($10 profits per share × 100 shares). That same $5,000 invested in the lower-priced warrants will buy 500 warrants ($5,000 ÷ $10 = 500 warrants). This will result in $5,000 in profits ($10 in profits per warrant × 500 warrants). The common stock provides a 20% HPR, whereas the warrants yield 100%. The biggest risk in this investment is the potential loss exposure. If the price of the stock decreases by $10, the warrant investment is virtually wiped out. (Actually, the warrant will probably retain some value greater than zero, but not much.) In contrast, the price of the stock drops to "only" $40, and as a stockholder, you will still have $4,000 in capital left.

One way to limit this exposure to loss is to follow the second, more conservative trading approach: You buy only enough warrants to realize the level of capital gains available from the common stock. Again, in our illustration above, because we are dealing with options that carry one-to-one redemption provisions, you would need to acquire only 100 warrants to obtain the same price behavior as that of 100 shares of stock. Thus, rather than buying $5,000 worth of stock, you would purchase only $1,000 worth of the warrants to realize the same capital gains. If the stock performs as expected, you will realize a 100% return by generating the same amount of capital gains as the stock ($1,000). But this will be done with substantially less capital, so the yield with the warrants will be greater *and* the loss exposure will be less. In this case, if the price of the stock drops by 10 points, the most the warrant holder can lose is $1,000. If the price of the stock drops by *more* than $10 a share, the warrant holder still will lose no more than $1,000, whereas the stockholder can lose a lot more.

IN REVIEW

CONCEPTS

14.18 What is a *warrant* and what is its chief attraction? Describe the leverage features of a warrant and note why leverage is so attractive to investors.

14.19 What factors are important in determining the investment appeal of warrants? Why is the price of the warrant itself so important in the investment decision?

Summary

LG 1 **Discuss the basic nature of options in general and puts and calls in particular, and understand how these investment vehicles work.** An option gives the holder the right to buy or sell a certain amount of some real or financial asset at a set price for a set period of time. Puts and calls are by far the most widely used type of option. These derivative securities offer attractive value and considerable leverage potential. A put enables the holder to *sell* a certain amount of a specified security at a specified price over a specified time period. A call gives the holder the right to *buy* the security at a specified price over a specified period of time.

LG 2 **Describe the options market and note key options provisions, including strike prices and expiration dates.** The options market is made up of conventional (OTC) options and listed options. OTC options are used predominantly by institutional investors. Listed options are traded on organized exchanges such as the CBOE and the AMEX. The creation of listed options exchanges led to the use of standardized options features and opened the way for widespread use of options by individual investors. Among the provisions stipulated on options are the strike price (the stipulated price at which the underlying asset can be bought or sold) and the expiration date (the date when the contract expires).

LG 3 **Explain how put and call options are valued and the forces that drive options prices in the marketplace.** The value of a call is measured as the market price of the underlying security less the strike price designated on the call. The value of a put is its strike price less the market price of the security. The value of an option is driven by the current market price of the underlying asset. Most puts and calls sell at premium prices. The size of the premium depends on the length of the option contract (the so-called time premium), the speculative appeal and amount of price volatility in the underlying financial asset, and the general level of interest rates.

LG 4 **Describe the profit potential of puts and calls, and note some popular put and call investment strategies.** Investors who hold puts make money when the value of the underlying asset goes down over time. In contrast, call investors make money when the underlying asset moves up in price. Aggressive investors will use puts and calls either for speculation or in highly specialized writing and spreading programs. Conservative investors are attracted to puts and calls because of their low unit costs and the limited risk they offer in absolute dollar terms. Conservative investors often use options in covered call writing programs or to form hedge positions in combination with other securities.

LG 5 **Describe market index options, puts and calls on foreign currencies, and LEAPS, and show how these securities can be used by investors.** Standardized put and call options are available on stock-market indexes, like the S&P 500 (index options), and on a number of foreign currencies (currency options). Also available are LEAPS, which are listed options that carry lengthy expiration dates. Although these securities can be used just like stock options, the index and currency options tend to be used primarily for speculation or to develop hedge positions.

LG 6 **Discuss the investment characteristics of stock warrants, and describe the trading strategies that can be used to gain maximum benefits from this investment vehicle.** A warrant is similar to a call option, but its maturity is much longer. Usually attached to bond issues as "sweeteners," warrants allow the holder to purchase common stock at a set exercise price on or before a stipulated expiration date. Trading in warrants is done primarily as a substitute for common stock investing and is based on the magnified capital gains that warrants offer. The value of a warrant changes directly with, and by approximately the same amount as, the underlying common stock. Because a warrant's unit cost is often much lower than that of the common stock, the same dollar change in price represents a considerably larger percentage yield.

Discussion Questions

LG 2 Q14.1 Using the stock or index option quotations in Figures 14.1 and 14.3, respectively, find the option premium, the time premium, and the stock or index break-even point for the following puts and calls.
  a. The October Intel *call* with the $65 strike price.
  b. The October IBM *put* with the $120 strike price.
  c. The January Intel *call* with the strike price of 50.
  d. The October S&P 100 *call* with the strike price of 810.
  e. The December DJIA *put* with the strike price of 108.

LG 3 Q14.2 Prepare a schedule similar to the one in Table 14.1 for the September and October S&P 100 *calls* listed in Figure 14.3 (Use the ones with strike prices of 810 and 840.) Do the same for the September and October *puts* (using the same two strike prices). Briefly explain your findings.

LG 5 Q14.3 Assume you hold a well-balanced portfolio of common stocks. Under what conditions might you want to use a stock-index option to hedge the portfolio?
  a. Briefly explain how such options could be used to hedge a portfolio against a drop in the market.
  b. Discuss what happens if the market does, in fact, go down.
  c. What happens if the market goes up instead?

LG 3 **LG 4** Q14.4 Using the resources available at your campus or public library (or on the Internet), complete each of the following tasks. (*Note:* Show your work for all calculations.)
  a. Find an *in-the-money call* that has 2 or 3 months to expiration. (Select an *equity option* that is at least $5 in the money.) What's the fundamental value of this option, and how much premium is it carrying? Using the current market price of the underlying stock (the one listed with the option), determine what kind of dollar and percentage return the option would gen-

erate if the underlying stock goes up 10%. How about if the stock goes down 10%?

b. Repeat part (a), but this time use an *in-the-money put*. (Choose an equity option that's at least $5 in the money and has 2 or 3 months to expiration.) Answer the same questions as above.

c. Repeat once more the exercise in part (a), but this time use an *out-of-the-money call*. (Select an equity option, at least $5 out of the money, 2 or 3 months to expiration.) Answer the same questions.

d. Compare the valuation properties and performance characteristics of in-the-money calls and out-of-the-money calls [from parts (a) and (c)]. Note some of the advantages and disadvantages of each.

Problems

LG 3

P.14.1 A 6-month call on a certain common stock carries a strike price of $60. It can be purchased at a cost of $600. Assume that the underlying stock rises to $75 per share by the expiration date of the option. How much profit would this option generate over the 6-month holding period? Using HPR, what is its rate of return?

LG 5

P.14.2 Dorothy Lasnicka does a lot of investing in the stock market and is a frequent user of stock-index options. She is convinced that the market is about to undergo a broad retreat and has decided to buy a put on the S&P 100 Index. The put carries a strike price of 890 and is quoted in the financial press at 4.50. Although the S&P Index of 100 stocks is currently at 886.45, Dorothy thinks it will drop to 865 by the expiration date on the option. How much profit will she make, and what will be her holding period return if she is right? How much will she lose if the S&P 100 goes up (rather than down) by 25 points and reaches 915 by the date of expiration?

LG 3   LG 4

P.14.3 Bill Weeks holds 600 shares of Lubbock Gas and Light. He bought the stock several years ago at 48.50, and the shares are now trading at 75. Bill is concerned that the market is beginning to soften. He doesn't want to sell the stock, but he would like to be able to protect the profit he's made. He decides to hedge his position by buying 6 puts on Lubbock G&L. The 3-month puts carry a strike price of 75 and are currently trading at 2.50.

a. How much profit or loss will Bill make on this deal if the price of Lubbock G&L does indeed drop, to $60 a share, by the expiration date on the puts?

b. How would he do if the stock kept going up in price and reached $90 a share by the expiration date?

c. What do you see as the major advantages of using puts as hedge vehicles?

d. Would Bill have been better off using in-the-money puts—that is, puts with an $85 strike price that are trading at 10.50? How about using out-of-the-money puts—say, those with a $70 strike price, trading at 1.00? Explain.

LG 4   LG 5

P.14.4 P. F. Chang holds a well-diversified portfolio of high-quality, large-cap stocks. The current value of Chang's portfolio is $775,000, but he is concerned that the market is heading for a big fall (perhaps as much as 20%) over the next 3 to 6 months. He doesn't want to sell all his stocks because he feels they all have good long-term potential and should perform nicely once stock prices have bottomed out. As a result, he decides to look into the possibility of using index options to hedge his portfolio. Assume that the S&P 500 currently stands at 1570 and among the many put options available on this index are two that have caught his eye: (1) a 6-month put with a strike price of 1550 that's trading at 26, and (2) a 6-month put with a strike price of 1490 that's quoted at 4.50.

a. How many S&P 500 puts would Chang have to buy to protect his $775,000 stock portfolio? How much would it cost him to buy the necessary number of 1550 puts? How much would it cost to buy the 1490 puts?

b. Now, considering the performance of both the put options and the Chang portfolio, determine how much *net* profit (or loss) Chang will earn from each of these put hedges if both the market (as measured by the S&P 500) and the Chang portfolio fall by 15% over the next 6 months? What if the market and the Chang portfolio fall by only 5%? What if they go up by 10%?

c. Do you think Chang should set up the put hedge and, if so, using which put option? Explain.

d. Finally, assume that the DJIA is currently at 10,950 and that a 6-month put option on the Dow is available with a strike price of 108, and is currently trading at 2.50. How many of these puts would Chang have to buy to protect his portfolio, and what would they cost? Would Chang be better off with the Dow options or the S&P 1550 puts? Briefly explain.

LG 3 **LG 4** P.14.5 Angelo Martino just purchased 500 shares of AT&E at 61.50, and he has decided to write covered calls against these stocks. Accordingly, he sells 5 AT&E calls at their current market price of 5.75. The calls have 3 months to expiration and carry a strike price of 65. The stock pays a quarterly dividend of 80 cents a share.

a. Determine the total profit and holding period return Angelo will generate if the stock rises to $65 a share by the expiration date on the calls.

b. What happens to Angelo's profit (and return) if the price of the stock rises to more than $65 a share?

c. Does this covered call position offer any protection (or cushion) against a drop in the price of the stock? Explain.

LG 4 **LG 5** P.14.6 Here's your chance to try your hand at setting up an index-option *straddle*. Use the quotes for the DJIA index options listed in Figure 14.3. Assume that the market, as measured by the DJIA, stands at 11,000 and you decide to set up a *long straddle* on the Dow by buying 100 Dec. 110 calls and an equal number of Dec. 110 puts. (Ignore transaction costs.)

a. What will it cost you to set up the straddle, and how much profit (or loss) do you stand to make if the market falls by 750 points by the expiration dates on the options? What if it goes up by 750 points by expiration? What if it stays at 11,000?

b. Repeat part (a), but this time assume that you set up a *short straddle* by selling/writing 100 Dec. 110 puts and calls.

c. What do you think of the use of option straddles as an investment strategy? What are the risks, and what are the rewards?

LG 6 P.14.7 Assume that 1 warrant gives the holder the right to buy 2½ shares of stock at an exercise price of $40.

a. What is the value of this warrant if the current market price of the stock is $44? At what premium (in dollars and as a percentage) would the warrants be trading if they were quoted in the market at a price of $12.50?

b. Rework this problem given that 1 warrant gives the holder the right to buy just 1 share of stock at the stipulated exercise price. In this case, assume that the warrants are currently trading in the market at a price of $5 each.

LG 6

P.14.8 A particular warrant carries an exercise price of $20. Assume it takes 3 of these warrants to buy 1 share of stock. At what price would the warrant be trading if it sold at a 20% premium and the market price of the stock was $35 per share? What holding period return will an investor make if he or she buys these warrants (at a 20% premium) when the stock is trading at $35 and sells them sometime later, when the stock is at $48.50 and the premium on the warrants has dropped to 15%?

Case Problem 14.1   *The Franciscos' Investment Options*

LG 3   LG 4

LG 6

Hector Francisco is a successful businessman in Atlanta. The box-manufacturing firm he and his wife, Judy, founded several years ago has prospered. Because he is self-employed, Hector is building his own retirement fund. So far, he has accumulated a substantial sum in his investment account, mostly by following an aggressive investment posture. He does this because, as he puts it, "In this business, you never know when the bottom's gonna fall out." Hector has been following the stock of Rembrandt Paper Products (RPP), and after conducting extensive analysis, he feels the stock is about ready to move. Specifically, he believes that within the next 6 months, RPP could go to about $80 per share, from its current level of $57.50. The stock pays annual dividends of $2.40 per share. Hector figures he would receive two quarterly dividend payments over his 6-month investment horizon.

In studying the company, Hector has learned that it has some warrants outstanding. They mature in 8 years and carry an exercise price of $45. Also, it has 6-month call options (with $50 and $60 strike prices) listed on the CBOE. Each warrant is good for 1 share of stock, and they are currently trading at $15. The CBOE calls are quoted at $8 for the options with $50 strike prices and at $5 for the $60 options.

Questions

a. How many alternative investment vehicles does Hector have if he wants to invest in RPP for no more than 6 months? What if he has a 2-year investment horizon?

b. Using a 6-month holding period and assuming the stock does indeed rise to $80 over this time frame:

- Find the market price of the warrants at the end of the holding period, given that they then trade at a premium of 10%.

- Find the value of both calls, given that at the end of the holding period neither contains any investment premium.

- Determine the holding period return for each of the four investment alternatives open to Hector Francisco.

c. Which course of action would you recommend if Hector simply wants to maximize profit? Would your answer change if other factors (e.g., comparative risk exposure) were considered along with return? Explain.

Case Problem 14.2   *Fred's Quandary: To Hedge or Not to Hedge*

LG 3   LG 4

A little more than 10 months ago, Fred Weaver, a mortgage banker in Phoenix, bought 300 shares of stock at $40 per share. Since then, the price of the stock has risen to $75 per share. It is now near the end of the year, and the market is starting to weaken. Fred feels there is still plenty of play left in the stock but is afraid the tone of the market will be detrimental to his position. His wife, Denise, is taking an adult education course on the stock market and has just learned about put and call hedges. She suggests that he use puts to hedge his position. Fred is intrigued by the idea, which he discusses with his broker, who advises him that the needed puts are indeed available on his stock. Specifically, he can buy 3-month puts, with $75 strike prices, at a cost of $550 each (quoted at 5.50).

Questions

a.   Given the circumstances surrounding Fred's current investment position, what benefits could be derived from using the puts as a hedge device? What would be the major drawback?

b.   What will Fred's minimum profit be if he buys three puts at the indicated option price? How much would he make if he did not hedge but instead sold his stock immediately at a price of $75 per share?

c.   Assuming Fred uses three puts to hedge his position, indicate the amount of profit he will generate if the stock moves to $100 by the expiration date of the puts. What if the stock drops to $50 per share?

d.   Should Fred use the puts as a hedge? Explain. Under what conditions would you urge him *not* to use the puts as a hedge?

Web Exercises

W14.1 Visit the CBOE at www.cboe.com/tradtool/optioncalculator.asp. This program provides access to index and equity option evaluation models, which enables you to test and understand the dynamic relationships between the value of an option and the factors that affect this value. Once you have input all the factors of the option evaluation model, the Option Calculator will provide a theoretical value for the call and put you are valuing, as well as other important values (delta, gamma, etc.) Click on the tab [Equity Options]. Suppose the current date is 3/10/01. Change to equity price 100, strike price 90, volatility (% per year) 20, annual interest rate 5, quarterly dividend amount 3, first dividend date 03/12/01, and expiration month/year Oct01. You'll see the theoretical price of the call and put change before your eyes. Change the expiration month/year to May01. What are the new call and put prices? Explain the changes in prices.

W14.2 Again, visit the CBOE at www.cboe.com. Click on S&P 500 (SPX). How many calls and puts are traded on SPX? Assume that someone believes the S&P 500 index will rise over the next few weeks. Describe some option trades that would take advantage of this anticipated rise in prices. Which would be the most risky? Which would be the least risky?

W14.3 From the same site as in Exercise W14.2, describe some option trades that would take advantage of a probable decline in the S&P 500 index over the next few weeks. Which would be the most risky? Which would be the least risky?

For additional practice with concepts from this chapter, visit

www.awl.com/gitman_joehnk

CHAPTER 15

COMMODITIES AND FINANCIAL FUTURES

LEARNING GOALS

After studying this chapter, you should be able to:

LG 1 Describe the essential features of a futures contract and explain how the futures market operates.

LG 2 Explain the role that hedgers and speculators play in the futures market, including how profits are made and lost.

LG 3 Describe the commodities segment of the futures market and the basic characteristics of these investment vehicles.

LG 4 Discuss the trading strategies investors can use with commodities, and explain how investment returns are measured.

LG 5 Explain the difference between a physical commodity and a financial future, and discuss the growing role of financial futures in the market today.

LG 6 Discuss the trading techniques that can be used with financial futures, and note how these securities can be used in conjunction with other investment vehicles.

I t's not the biggest. It's not the most "buttoned-down." But in terms of sheer profitability, few Wall Street firms can match Bear Stearns. In 2000 the company earned $773 million on $5.5 billion in revenues. Like most Wall Street investment banks, Bear Stearns conducts futures and options activity. Its Futures Department advises clients on the use of exchange-traded futures and options in their global trading and hedging strategies. The firm's emphasis is on financial futures, principally interest rates, stock indexes, and foreign currencies. Specialists within the department also actively trade in the energy and tropical commodities (cocoa, coffee, and sugar) markets. Bear Stearns's Derivatives Department is an active trader of various derivative securities, such as interest rate swaps, equity swaps, and equity options, which can be combined with fixed-income securities, stocks, foreign exchange, and entire portfolios to create a wide array of risk management solutions.

The use of futures contracts for commodities and financial instruments is a very important tool to control risk. You'll see in this chapter how these investment vehicles work and how individual investors can use them.

Sources: Bear Sterns *1999 Annual Report* and "The Bear Stearns Companies Inc. Reports Fiscal Year and Fourth Quarter Results," January 4, 2001, downloaded from Bear Stearns's Web site, www.bearstearns.com

The Futures Market

LG 1   LG 2

"Psst, hey buddy. Wanna buy some copper? How about some coffee, or pork bellies, or propane? Maybe the Japanese yen or Swiss franc strikes your fancy?" Sound a bit unusual? Perhaps, but these items have one thing in common: They all represent real investment vehicles. This is the more exotic side of investing—the market for commodities and financial futures—and it often involves a considerable amount of speculation. In fact, the risks are enormous. But with a little luck, the payoffs can be phenomenal, too. Even more important than luck is the need for patience and know-how. Indeed, *these are specialized investment products that require specialized investor skills.*

The amount of futures trading in the United States has mushroomed over the past two or three decades. An increasing number of investors have turned to futures trading as a way to earn attractive, highly competitive rates of return. But it's *not* the traditional commodities contracts that have drawn many of these investors; rather, it's the new investment vehicles that are being offered. Indeed, a major reason behind the growth in the volume of futures trading has been the *number and variety of futures contracts now available for trading.* Today, markets exist for the traditional primary commodities, such as grains and metals, as well as for live animals, processed commodities, crude oil and gasoline, electricity, foreign currencies, money market securities, U.S. and foreign debt securities, Eurodollar securities, and common stocks (via stock market indexes). You can even buy listed put and call *options* on just about any actively traded futures contract. All these commodities and financial assets are traded in what is known as the *futures market.*

cash market
a market where a product or commodity changes hands in exchange for a cash price paid when the transaction is completed.

futures market
the organized market for the trading of futures contracts.

Market Structure

When a bushel of wheat is sold, the transaction takes place in the **cash market.** The bushel changes hands in exchange for the cash price paid to the seller. The transaction occurs at that point in time and for all practical purposes is completed then and there. Most traditional securities are traded in this type of market. However, a bushel of wheat could also be sold in the **futures market,** the organized market for the trading of futures contracts. In this market, the seller would not actually deliver the wheat until some mutually agreed-upon date in the future. As a result, the transaction would not be completed for some time: The seller would receive partial payment for the bushel of wheat at the time the agreement was entered into and the balance on delivery. The buyer, in turn, would own a highly liquid futures contract that could be held (and presented for delivery of the bushel of wheat) or traded in the futures market. No matter what the buyer does with the contract, as long as it is outstanding, the seller has a *legally binding obligation to make delivery* of the stated quantity of wheat on a specified date in the future. The buyer/holder has a similar *obligation to take delivery* of the underlying commodity.

HOT LINKS

For information on more than 70 exchanges around the world and details on the futures and options contracts they trade, see:

www.numa.com/ref/exchange.htm

futures contract
a commitment to deliver a certain amount of some specified item at some specified date in the future.

delivery month
the time when a commodity must be delivered; defines the life of a futures contract.

Futures Contracts A **futures contract** is a commitment to deliver a certain amount of a specified item at a specified date at an agreed-upon price. Each market establishes its own contract specifications. These include not only the quantity and quality of the item but also the delivery procedure and delivery month. The **delivery month** on a futures contract is much like the expiration

TABLE 15.1	Futures Contract Dimensions	
Contract	Size of a Contract*	Recent Market Value of a Single Contract**
Corn	5,000 bu	$ 8,750
Wheat	5,000 bu	12,000
Live cattle	40,000 lb	26,400
Pork bellies	40,000 lb	30,000
Coffee	37,500 lb	30,000
Cotton	50,000 lb	32,500
Gold	100 troy oz	27,450
Copper	25,000 lb	21,750
Japanese yen	12.5 million yen	115,000
Treasury bills	$1 million	935,000
Treasury bonds	$100,000	101,500
S&P 500 Stock Index	$250 times the index	374,500

*The size of some contracts may vary by exchange.
**Contract values are representative of those that existed at mid-year 2000.

date on put and call options. It specifies when the commodity or item must be delivered and thus defines the life of the contract. For example, the Chicago Board of Trade specifies that each of its soybean contracts will involve 5,000 bushels of USDA No. 2 yellow soybeans; delivery months are January, March, May, July, August, September, and November. In addition, futures contracts have *their own trading hours.* Unlike listed stocks and bonds, which begin and end trading at the same time, normal trading hours for commodities and financial futures vary widely. For example, oats trade from 9:30 a.m. to 1:15 p.m. (Central); silver, from 7:25 a.m. to 1:25 p.m.; live cattle, from 9:05 a.m. to 1:00 p.m.; U.S. Treasury bonds, from 7:20 a.m. to 2:00 p.m.; and S&P 500 stock-index contracts, from 8:30 a.m. to 3:15 p.m. It sounds a bit confusing, but it seems to work.

Table 15.1 lists a cross section of 12 different commodities and financial futures. As you can see, the typical futures contract covers a large quantity of the underlying product or financial instrument. However, although the value of a single contract is normally quite large, the actual amount of investor capital required to deal in these vehicles is relatively small, because *all trading in this market is done on a margin basis.*

Options Versus Futures Contracts In many respects, futures contracts are closely related to the call options we studied in Chapter 14. Both involve the future delivery of an item at an agreed-upon price. But there is a *significant difference* between a futures contract and an options contract. To begin with, a futures contract *obligates* a person to buy or sell a specified amount of a given commodity on or before a stated date—unless the contract is canceled or liquidated before it expires. In contrast, an option gives the holder the *right* to buy or sell a specific amount of a real or financial asset at a specific price over a specified period of time. In addition, whereas *price* (strike price) is one of the specified variables on a call option, it is *not* stated anywhere on a futures contract. Instead, the price on a futures contract is established through trading on the floor of a commodities exchange. This means that the delivery price is set by supply and demand at whatever price the contract sells for. Equally important, the risk of loss with an option is limited to the price paid for it. A futures contract has *no such limit on exposure to loss.*

Major Exchanges Futures contracts in this country got their start in the agricultural segment of the economy over 150 years ago, when individuals who produced, owned, and/or processed foodstuffs sought a way to protect themselves against adverse price movements. Later, futures contracts came to be traded by individuals who were not necessarily connected with agriculture, but who wanted to make money with commodities by speculating on their price swings.

The first organized commodities exchange in this country was the Chicago Board of Trade, which opened its doors in 1848. Over time, additional markets opened. At one time there were more than a dozen U.S. exchanges that dealt in listed futures contracts. Since then, this market has gone through a period of consolidation and as a result, there are now just eight commodities exchanges left in operation in this country. The Chicago Board of Trade (CBT) is the largest and most active U.S. exchange. (In fact, it's the largest commodities exchange in the world.) The CBT is followed in size by the Chicago Mercantile Exchange (CME), and the New York Mercantile Exchange (NYMerc). Together, these three exchanges account for about 80 to 90 percent of all the trading conducted on American futures exchanges.

Most exchanges deal in a number of different commodities or financial assets, and many commodities and financial futures are traded on more than one exchange. Although the exchanges are highly efficient and annual volume has surpassed the trillion-dollar mark, futures trading is still conducted by **open outcry auction:** Actual trading on the floors of these exchanges is conducted through a series of shouts, body motions, and hand signals, as shown in Figure 15.1. As the *Investing in Action* box on page 631 discusses, changes taking place on the futures exchanges may soon bring electronic trading.

Trading in the Futures Market

Basically, the futures market contains two types of traders: hedgers and speculators. The market could not exist and operate efficiently without either one. The **hedgers** are commodities producers and processors who use futures contracts as a way to protect their interests in the underlying commodity or financial instrument. For example, if a rancher thinks the price of cattle will drop in the near future, he will hedge his position by selling a futures contract on cattle in the hope of locking in as high a price as possible for his herd. In effect, the hedgers provide the underlying strength of the futures market and represent the very reason for its existence. (Today, hedgers also include financial institutions and corporate money managers.) *Speculators,* in contrast, give the market liquidity. They are the ones who trade futures contracts simply to earn a profit on expected swings in the price of a futures contract. They are the investors who have no inherent interest in any aspect of the commodity or financial future other than the price action and potential capital gains it can produce.

Trading Mechanics Once futures contracts are created, they can readily be traded in the market. Like common stocks, futures contracts are bought and sold through local brokerage offices. Most firms have at least one or two

open outcry auction
in futures trading, an auction in which trading is done through a series of shouts, body motions, and hand signals.

hedgers
producers and processors who use futures contracts to protect their interest in an underlying commodity or financial instrument.

FIGURE 15.1

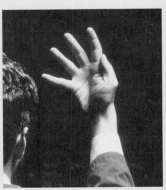

The Auction Market at Work on the Floor of the Chicago Board of Trade

Traders employ a system of open outcry and hand signals to indicate whether they wish to buy or sell and the price at which they wish to do so. Fingers held *vertically* indicate the number of contracts a trader wants to buy or sell. Fingers held *horizontally* indicate the fraction of a cent above or below the last traded full-cent price at which the trader will buy or sell. (*Source:* Chicago Board of Trade.)

people in each office who specialize in futures contracts. In addition, a number of commodity firms that deal only in futures contracts stand ready to help individuals trade futures. Except for setting up a special commodities trading account, there is really no difference between trading futures and dealing in stocks or bonds. The same types of orders are used, and the use of margin is the standard way of trading futures. Any investor can buy or sell any contract, with any delivery month, at any time, so long as it is currently being traded on one of the exchanges.

Buying a contract is referred to as taking a *long position*. Selling one is termed taking a *short position*. It is exactly like going long or short with stocks and has the same connotation: The investor who is long wants the price to rise, and the short seller wants it to drop. Both long and short positions can be liquidated simply by executing an offsetting transaction. The short seller, for

INVESTING in action

What's Ahead for Futures?

Will futures trading pits at venerable exchanges like the Chicago Board of Trade soon be history? The end of the open-outcry auction may be in sight as competition, technology, and global trading bring sweeping changes to the futures industry both in the United States and overseas.

The European exchanges have pulled ahead of their U.S. counterparts in organizational restructuring, consolidation of customers and exchanges, and the shift from floor trading to electronic systems. They have already restructured from member-owned exchanges to for-profit business entities and have installed advanced electronic trading systems. Exchanges such as Eurex AG (the world's largest futures exchange), the London International Financial Futures and Options Exchange (Liffe), and Euronext are first to market with new products and services. Many target individual investors, who have the potential to become bigger players in the futures markets thanks to electronic trading.

Liffe, which almost collapsed in 1998, reorganized as a for-profit company and implemented Connect, a state-of-the-art trading and clearing system. In October 2000, it introduced the Mini-FTSE 100 Futures, which is electronically traded. It appeals to individual investors because it is one-fifth the size of the regular FTSE 100 futures contract. In February 2001, Liffe launched Universal Stock Futures (USFs), futures on the stocks of 15 individual companies in the banking, oil, pharmaceutical, technology, and telecommunications sectors. Eurex and Euronext also offer USFs, but under current (February 2001) securities regulations, U.S. exchanges cannot do so.

The major U.S. futures exchanges have moved to regain lost ground. In August 2000, the Chicago Board of Trade (CBOT) and Eurex formed a/c/e (Alliance/CBOT/Eurex), an electronic joint venture that expands trading time after the close of the traditional public auction hours. The Chicago Mercantile Exchange and the New York Mercantile Exchange converted from member-owned organizations to for-profit, shareholder-owned corporations in November 2000.

However, many U.S. futures traders still prefer the exchange floor, with its system of trading pits, open outcry, and hand signals, to the computer screen. As one floor trader of S&P 500 options commented, "Down here you use your five senses. It's going to be tough to get used to staring at a screen. You're going to lose the feeling of the marketplace." Large traders also prefer the higher liquidity of the trading floor.

Small, independent traders whose floor volume dropped favor electronic trading. They have salvaged their careers by moving into nearby arcades with electronic trading systems. Although many miss the hectic activity of the trading floor, the arcades have some advantages. "On the floor you make decisions based on emotions and paper flow," says Paul Sherman, who now trades for York Business Associates from an arcade instead of the pit. "Here your decisions are more concrete, based on charts and news." Electronic trading also is less tied to an "old-boy" network and does not rely on personal relationships. Traders have access to more information and can trade more markets. There is also less chance of lost orders and clerical errors.

At the CBOT, floor trading and electronic trading occur simultaneously for 7 hours a day in some listed futures. Floor trading still dominates. For example, electronic trading in 10-year Treasury futures is only 20% of the total. "Clients who trade on U.S. exchanges have not embraced electronic trade," said Alan Zavarro, head of the U.S. Futures Division of ABN Amro. But it clearly is the way of the future.

Sources: Silvia Ascarelli, "Universal Stock Futures Provide a New Instrument for Investors," *Wall Street Journal,* February 9, 2001, downloaded from interactive.wsj.com; Zahida Hafeez, "Locals Forsake Floor for Arcades," Dow Jones Commodities Service, November 8, 2000, downloaded from interactive.wsj.com; Christine Marie Nielsen, "Electronic Trading System for Treasury Futures Isn't Luring Many Players from Exchange Floor," *Wall Street Journal,* January 22, 2001, p. C16; and Henry E. Teitelbaum, "Futures Exchanges Race to Restructure," *Wall Street Journal,* November 14, 2000, p. C17.

example, would cover his or her position by buying an equal amount of the contract. In general, only about 1% of all futures contracts are settled by delivery. The rest are offset prior to the delivery month. All trades are subject to normal transaction costs, which include **round-trip commissions** of about $60 to $90 for each contract traded. (A round-trip commission includes the commission costs on both ends of the transaction—to buy and to sell a contract.) The exact size of the commission depends on the number and type of contracts being traded.

Margin Trading Buying on margin means putting up only a fraction of the total price in cash. Margin, in effect, is the *amount of equity* that goes into the deal. Margin trading plays a crucial role in futures transactions because *all futures contracts are traded on a margin basis*. The margin required usually ranges from about 2% to 10% of the value of the contract. This is very low when compared to the margin required for stocks and most other types of securities. Furthermore, there is *no borrowing* required on the part of the investor to finance the balance of the contract. The margin, or **margin deposit**, as it is called with futures, represents security to cover any loss in the market value of the contract that may result from adverse price movements. It exists simply as a way to guarantee fulfillment of the contract. The margin deposit is not a partial payment for the commodity or financial instrument, nor is it in any way related to the value of the product or item underlying the contract.

The size of the required margin deposit is specified as a dollar amount. It varies according to the type of contract (i.e., the amount of price volatility in the underlying commodity or financial asset). In some cases, it also varies according to the exchange on which the commodity is traded. Table 15.2 gives the margin requirements for the same 12 commodities and financial instruments listed in Table 15.1 on page 628. Compared to the size and value of futures contracts, margin requirements are very low. The **initial deposit** noted in Table 15.2 is the amount of investor capital that must be deposited with the broker when the transaction is initiated and represents the amount of money required to make a given investment.

After the investment is made, the market value of a contract will, of course, rise and fall as the quoted price of the underlying commodity or financial instrument goes up or down. Such market behavior will cause the amount of margin on deposit to change. To be sure that an adequate margin is always on hand, investors are required to meet a second type of margin requirement, the **maintenance deposit**. This deposit, which is slightly less than the initial deposit, establishes the minimum amount of margin that must be kept in the account at all times. For instance, if the initial deposit on a commodity is $1,000 per contract, its maintenance margin might be $750. So long as the market value of the contract does not fall by more than $250 (the difference between the contract's initial and maintenance margins), the investor has no problem. But if the market moves against the investor and the value of the contract drops by more than the allowed amount, the investor will receive a *margin call*. He or she must then immediately deposit enough cash to bring the position back to the initial margin level.

An investor's margin position is checked daily via a procedure known as **mark-to-the-market**. That is, the gain or loss in a contract's value is determined at the end of each session. At that time the broker debits or credits the trader's account accordingly. In a falling market, an investor may receive a number of margin calls and be required to make additional margin payments. Failure to do so will mean that the broker has no choice but to close out the position—that is, to sell the contract.

round-trip commissions
the commission costs on both ends (buying and selling) of a futures transaction.

margin deposit
amount deposited with a broker to cover any loss in the market value of a futures contract that may result from adverse price movements.

initial deposit
the amount of investor capital that must be deposited with a broker at the time of a commodity transaction.

maintenance deposit
the minimum amount of margin that must be kept in a margin account at all times.

mark-to-the-market
a daily check of an investor's margin position, determined at the end of each session, at which time the broker debits or credits the account as needed.

TABLE 15.2	Margin Requirements for a Sample of Commodities and Financial Futures	
	Initial Margin Deposit	Maintenance Margin Deposit
Corn	$ 750	$ 500
Wheat	1,000	750
Live cattle	750	500
Pork bellies	1,750	1,200
Coffee	4,900	3,500
Cotton	1,000	750
Gold	1,350	1,000
Copper	1,350	1,000
Japanese yen	3,750	2,700
Treasury bills	1,000	750
Treasury bonds	2,700	2,000
S&P 500 Stock Index	23,500	18,750

Note: These margin requirements were specified by a major full-service brokerage firm in mid-2000. They may equal or exceed the minimums established by the various exchanges. They are meant to be typical of the ongoing requirements that customers are expected to live up to. Depending on the volatility of the market, exchange-minimum margin requirements are changed frequently. Thus the requirements in this table are also subject to change on short notice.

IN REVIEW

CONCEPTS

15.1 What is a *futures contract?* Briefly explain how it is used as an investment vehicle.

15.2 Discuss the difference between a *cash market* and a *futures market.*

15.3 What is the major source of return to commodities speculators? How important is current income from dividends and interest?

15.4 Why are both hedgers and speculators important to the efficient operation of a futures market?

15.5 What are the pros and cons of electronic futures trading, as noted in the *Investing in Action* box on page 631.

15.6 Explain how margin trading is conducted in the futures market.
 a. What is the difference between an *initial deposit* and a *maintenance deposit?*
 b. Are investors ever required to put up additional margin? If so, when?

Commodities

Physical commodities like grains, metals, wood, and meat make up a major portion of the futures market. They have been actively traded in this country for well over a century. The material that follows focuses on *commodities trading.* We begin with a review of the basic characteristics and investment merits of these vehicles.

LG 3   LG 4

Basic Characteristics

Various types of physical commodities are found on nearly all of the U.S. futures exchanges. (In fact, several of them deal only in commodities.) The

TABLE 15.3	Major Classes of Commodities
Grains and Oilseeds	*Metals and Petroleum*
Corn	Electricity
Oats	Copper
Soybeans	Gold
Soybean meal	Platinum
Soybean oil	Silver
Wheat	Palladium
Barley	Gasoline
Canola	Heating oil
Flaxseed	Crude oil
Rice	Gas oil
	Propane
	Natural gas
Livestock and Meat	*Food and Fiber*
Cattle—live	Cocoa
Cattle—feeder	Coffee
Hogs	Cotton
Pork bellies	Orange juice
	Sugar

market for commodity contracts is divided into four major segments: grains and oilseeds, livestock and meat, metals and petroleum, and food and fiber. Such segmentation does not affect trading mechanics and procedures. It merely provides a convenient way of categorizing commodities into groups based on similar underlying characteristics. Table 15.3 shows the diversity of the commodities market and the variety of contracts available. Although the list changes yearly, the table indicates that investors had nearly three dozen different commodities to choose from in 2000. A number of these (e.g., soybeans, wheat, and sugar) are available in several different forms or grades. Actually, Table 15.3 lists only some of the more actively traded commodities. *Not included* are dozens of commodities (such as butter, milk, cheese, boneless beef, and others) that are not widely traded but still make up a part of this market.

A Commodities Contract Every commodity (whether actively or thinly traded) has certain specifications that spell out in detail the amounts and quality of the product being traded. Figure 15.2 (on page 636) is an excerpt from the "Futures Prices" section of the *Wall Street Journal* and shows the contract and quotation system used with commodities. Each commodity quote is made up of the same five parts, and all prices are quoted in an identical fashion. In particular, every commodities contract or quote specifies: (1) the product; (2) the exchange on which the contract is traded; (3) the size of the contract (in bushels, pounds, tons, etc.); (4) the method of valuing the contract, or pricing unit (e.g., cents per pound or dollars per ton); and (5) the delivery month. Using a corn contract as an illustration, we can see each of these parts in the following illustration:

KEY
1 the product
2 the exchange
3 the size of the contract
4 the pricing unit
5 the delivery months

	Open	High	Low	Settle	Change	Lifetime High	Low	Open Interest
1 **2** **3** **4**								
Corn (CBT)—5,000 bu.; cents per bu.								
May	253½	253¾	252¼	252½	−1¾	286½	230½	42,796
July	258	258	256½	256¾	−1¾	288	233	60,477
Sept.	260	260½	259	259	−1½	263	236	7,760
Dec.	263½	264	262½	263	−1¼	267¼	244	41,638
Mar. 99	271¾	272	270½	271	−1¼	276	254¾	11,098
May	277¼	278	276¼	277	−1	281	273¼	1,326

(**5** denotes the delivery months column group)

settle price
the closing price (last price of the day) for commodities and financial futures.

open interest
the number of contracts currently outstanding on a commodity or financial future.

The quotation system used for commodities is based on the size of the contract and the pricing unit. The financial media generally report the open, high, low, and closing prices for each delivery month. With commodities, the last price of the day, or the closing price, is known as the **settle price.** Also reported, at least by the *Wall Street Journal,* is the amount of **open interest** in each contract—that is, the number of contracts currently outstanding. Note in the above illustration that the settle price for May corn was 252½. Since the pricing system is cents per bushel, this means that the contract was being traded at $2.52½ per bushel and the market value of the contract was $12,625. (Each contract involves 5,000 bushels of corn and each bushel is worth $2.52½; thus 5,000 × $2.525 = $12,625.)

Price Behavior Commodity prices react to a unique set of economic, political, and international pressures—as well as to the weather. The explanation of *why* commodity prices change is beyond the scope of this book. But it should be clear that they do move up and down just like any other investment vehicle, which is precisely what speculators want. Because we are dealing in such large trading units (5,000 bushels of this or 40,000 pounds of that), even a modest price change can have an enormous impact on the market value of a contract, and therefore on investor returns or losses. For example, if the price of corn goes up or down by just 20 cents per bushel, the value of a *single contract* will change by $1,000. A corn contract can be bought with a $750 initial margin deposit, so it is easy to see the effect this kind of price behavior can have on investor return.

But do commodity prices really move all that much? Judge for yourself: The price change columns in Figure 15.2 show some excellent examples of sizable price changes that occur from one day to the next. Note, for example, that September corn fell $125 (5,000 bu. × $.025 = $125), August soybeans rose $312.50, September crude oil fell $320, and September gasoline went down a whopping $609. Keep in mind that these are *daily* price swings that occurred on *single* contracts. These are sizable changes, even by themselves. But when you look at them relative to the (very small) original investment required (sometimes as low as $750), they quickly add up to serious returns (or losses)! And they occur not because of the volatility of the underlying prices but because of the sheer magnitude of the commodities contracts themselves.

Clearly, this kind of price behavior is one of the magnets that draws investors to commodities. The exchanges recognize the volatile nature of commodities contracts and try to put lids on price fluctuations by imposing daily

FIGURE 15.2 **Quotations on Actively Traded Commodity Futures Contracts**

These quotes reveal at a glance key information about the various commodities, including the latest high, low, and closing ("settle") prices, as well as the lifetime high and low prices for each contract. (*Source: Wall Street Journal,* August 14, 2000.)

Friday, August 11, 2000

Open Interest Reflects Previous Trading Day.

GRAINS AND OILSEEDS

CORN (CBT) 5,000 bu.; cents per bu.

	Open	High	Low	Settle	Change	Lifetime High	Lifetime Low	Open Interest
Sept	177	177½	174	174¾	– 2½	265½	174	104,879
Nov	185	185	182	182¾	– 2½	268½	182	1,447
Dec	189¼	189½	185½	187¼	– 2¼	279½	185½	191,448
Ja01	....	....	....	190½	– 2¼	271	192¾	284
Mar	201½	201½	198½	199¼	– 2½	279¾	198½	45,525
May	209¼	209¼	206½	207	– 2½	282½	206½	12,002
July	216¾	216¾	214	214½	– 2½	287½	214	17,248
Sept	220½	222	220½	220¾	– 2¼	276½	220½	1,888
Dec	231	231¾	230½	231	– 1½	275	230½	11,523
Dc02	....	....	....	249½	– 1	272	245	334

Est vol 85,000; vol Thu 54,194; open int 386,940, +795.

OATS (CBT) 5,000 bu.; cents per bu.

	Open	High	Low	Settle	Change	Lifetime High	Lifetime Low	Open Interest
Sept	98	98¾	97	98½	– ¾	132½	96½	6,198
Dec	108¼	108¾	107½	108½	– ½	137	107	8,227
Mr01	116¾	118	116¾	118	– ½	142	116	1,122

Est vol 1,300; vol Thu 618; open int 15,643, –227.

SOYBEANS (CBT) 5,000 bu.; cents per bu.

	Open	High	Low	Settle	Change	Lifetime High	Lifetime Low	Open Interest
Aug	443	455½	443	452	+ 6¼	584½	433½	1,256
Sept	445½	457	444	452½	+ 5	587½	436¾	17,099
Nov	456½	467	453	462	+ 5¼	631	445½	73,386
Ja01	466¾	477½	464½	472¼	+ 5	600	456	9,364
Mar	473½	487½	473½	482¾	+ 6¼	604½	467	8,652
May	484	495½	483½	493	+ 6	604	474½	6,836
July	493	504½	493	501½	+ 5½	609	484	5,909
Nov	506	515½	506	510	+ 4½	605	493	1,903

Est vol 48,000; vol Thu 28,385; open int 124,562, –2,046.

SOYBEAN MEAL (CBT) 100 tons; $ per ton.

	Open	High	Low	Settle	Change	Lifetime High	Lifetime Low	Open Interest
Aug	149.00	152.50	148.50	150.60	+ .30	188.40	131.00	2,493
Sept	149.80	152.80	148.00	151.20	+ 1.50	188.00	132.00	17,036
Oct	147.50	152.50	147.50	151.20	+ 2.10	187.80	135.00	14,196
Dec	150.60	154.80	149.00	153.20	+ 2.50	189.60	135.50	39,851
Ja01	151.50	155.00	151.00	154.00	+ 2.80	189.50	146.70	8,262
Mar	152.00	157.50	152.00	155.70	+ 2.40	189.50	148.10	6,996
May	156.00	159.00	156.00	158.00	+ 2.80	189.50	149.80	4,135
July	160.00	161.00	159.70	160.00	+ 2.80	190.00	152.00	1,899
Aug	159.00	159.50	159.00	159.50	+ 2.40	190.40	152.00	271

Est vol 22,000; vol Thu 19,060; open int 95,486, +333.

SOYBEAN OIL (CBT) 60,000 lbs.; cents per lb.

	Open	High	Low	Settle	Change	Lifetime High	Lifetime Low	Open Interest
Aug	15.05	15.25	15.05	15.15	+ .01	21.00	15.01	491
Sept	15.16	15.37	15.13	15.24	....	21.70	15.13	24,410
Oct	15.35	15.55	15.35	15.44	+ .01	22.25	15.35	15,928
Dec	15.77	15.93	15.73	15.82	....	20.62	15.67	57,725
Ja01	16.11	16.22	16.09	16.13	– .01	20.10	16.09	15,691
Mar	16.50	16.62	16.45	16.45	– .01	20.38	16.45	7,285
May	16.82	16.99	16.82	16.82	....	20.68	16.82	6,036
July	17.25	17.40	17.17	17.17	– .02	20.95	17.17	4,479
Aug	17.50	17.60	17.31	17.31	+ .01	20.98	17.30	578
Sept	17.80	17.80	17.52	17.52	....	21.15	17.51	472
Oct	18.00	18.00	17.72	17.72	....	20.35	17.61	602
Dec	18.30	18.30	18.02	18.02	....	21.25	18.02	952

Est vol 13,000; vol Thu 10,867; open int 134,649, +1,377.

WHEAT (CBT) 5,000 bu.; cents per bu.

	Open	High	Low	Settle	Change	Lifetime High	Lifetime Low	Open Interest
Sept	236	238	232½	236¾	+ 1	335	232½	43,254
Dec	254½	256	251	255¼	+ ¾	345	251	70,754
Mr01	268½	272¾	268	272½	+ ¾	327	268	20,791
May	279¼	283½	279¼	283	+ 1	326	279¼	1,367
July	288	292	288	291½	+ 1½	350	288	9,057
Dec	308½	310½	308½	310½	+ 2	343	307	477

Est vol 21,000; vol Thu 26,537; open int 146,120, +1,200.

WHEAT (KC) 5,000 bu.; cents per bu.

	Open	High	Low	Settle	Change	Lifetime High	Lifetime Low	Open Interest
Sept	271½	275	271	274	+ ¾	346	271	22,916
Dec	286½	296¾	280¼	290¾	+ ¾	354	280¼	44,602
Mr01	301½	305½	301¼	305	+ 1½	349	301	9,149
May	311	313	311	312¾	+ ¾	352½	310	1,144
July	318	320	318	319½	+ 1	355	317	753

Est vol 9,462; vol Thu 13,364; open int 78,569, –259.

WHEAT (MPLS) 5,000 bu.; cents per bu.

	Open	High	Low	Settle	Change	Lifetime High	Lifetime Low	Open Interest
Sept	286½	289¼	286½	287½	– 1¼	385	286½	10,260
Dec	302½	305¼	302½	303¼	– 1¾	390	302½	10,455
Mr01	318	320	317¾	318¼	– 2¼	375½	317¾	2,981
May	327¼	328½	327	327¼	– 1¾	379	327	354

Est vol 2,990; vol Thu 3,713; open int 24,259, +292.

CANOLA (WPG) 20 metric tons; Can. $ per ton

	Open	High	Low	Settle	Change	Lifetime High	Lifetime Low	Open Interest
Aug	....	....	....	244.10	....	311.00	241.90	215
Sept	246.70	248.20	246.60	246.80	+ 0.30	295.90	244.50	3,511
Nov	251.50	254.30	251.50	252.70	+ 0.20	315.90	250.70	37,739
Ja01	258.20	260.00	258.00	259.00	+ 0.10	303.20	256.50	6,192
Mar	264.80	264.80	264.60	264.70	– 0.10	305.50	263.00	1,130

Est vol n.a.; vol Thur 3,017; open int 48,805, +545.

	Open	High	Low	Settle	Change	Lifetime High	Lifetime Low	Open Interest
Dec	....	....	....	521.4	+ 2.1	613.0	495.0	1,504
Dc03	....	....	....	526.7	+ 2.1	565.0	510.0	443
Dc04	540.0	540.0	540.0	531.0	+ 2.1	560.0	529.0	527

Est vol 9,000; vol Thu 9,653; open int 92,317, +1,199.

CRUDE OIL, Light Sweet (NYM) 1,000 bbls.; $ per bbl.

	Open	High	Low	Settle	Change	Lifetime High	Lifetime Low	Open Interest
Sept	31.23	31.85	30.90	31.02	– 0.32	31.85	14.40	83,915
Oct	30.84	31.35	30.50	30.58	– 0.29	31.35	14.22	81,972
Nov	30.00	30.65	29.90	29.98	– 0.27	30.65	15.60	36,171
Dec	29.31	30.10	29.25	29.42	– 0.28	30.10	13.85	41,762
Ja01	29.07	29.50	28.95	28.89	– 0.28	29.50	14.25	21,261
Feb	28.45	29.00	28.45	28.38	– 0.29	29.00	14.30	10,509
Mar	28.05	28.50	28.05	27.92	– 0.30	28.50	14.44	9,993
Apr	....	....	....	27.49	– 0.31	27.88	15.80	6,913
May	27.18	27.49	27.18	27.09	– 0.33	27.49	15.80	5,695
June	26.80	27.29	26.80	26.74	– 0.35	27.29	14.56	17,180
July	26.49	26.90	26.49	26.43	– 0.36	26.90	19.05	7,682
Aug	....	....	....	26.13	– 0.37	26.50	18.40	3,793
Sept	....	....	....	25.84	– 0.38	26.00	17.96	8,573
Oct	....	....	....	25.56	– 0.39	25.20	19.80	4,719
Nov	....	....	....	25.28	– 0.40	25.08	18.20	5,033
Dec	25.30	25.55	24.90	25.00	– 0.41	25.55	14.90	24,921
Ja02	25.15	25.15	25.15	24.74	– 0.42	25.15	18.90	5,052
Feb	....	....	....	24.50	– 0.43	24.25	19.94	3,840
Mar	....	....	....	24.27	– 0.44	22.10	18.45	2,858
Apr	....	....	....	24.04	– 0.45	23.75	20.95	358
May	....	....	....	23.82	– 0.46	20.84	20.84	157
June	....	....	....	23.62	– 0.47	23.85	17.35	7,450
July	23.81	23.81	23.81	23.43	– 0.48	23.81	19.85	321
Aug	....	....	....	23.26	– 0.48	21.70	20.53	114
Sept	....	....	....	23.10	– 0.48	21.23	20.43	193
Dec	23.00	23.00	23.00	22.65	– 0.48	23.11	15.50	18,020
Ju03	....	....	....	21.72	– 0.49	22.30	19.82	1,285
Dec	21.32	21.32	21.32	20.90	– 0.52	22.00	15.92	12,214
Dc04	20.60	20.60	20.60	20.18	– 0.52	20.85	16.35	4,839
Dc05	20.08	20.08	20.08	19.66	– 0.52	20.45	17.00	2,809
Dc06	....	....	....	19.29	– 0.52	20.20	19.12	165

Est vol 188,956; vol Thu 189,437; open int 429,871, +12,412.

HEATING OIL NO. 2 (NYM) 42,000 gal; $ per gal.

	Open	High	Low	Settle	Change	Lifetime High	Lifetime Low	Open Interest
Sept	.8635	.8800	.8525	.8582	– .0046	.8800	.4260	31,975
Oct	.8600	.8770	.8525	.8571	– .0048	.8770	.4717	30,614
Nov	.8530	.8735	.8510	.8551	– .0048	.8735	.4792	20,138
Dec	.8460	.8700	.8460	.8516	– .0048	.8700	.5110	28,725
Ja01	.8410	.8620	.8400	.8431	– .0048	.8620	.5254	17,782
Feb	.8220	.8400	.8210	.8236	– .0058	.8400	.5360	12,755
Mar	.7820	.7995	.7820	.7811	– .0083	.7995	.5250	9,145
Apr	.7490	.7625	.7490	.7431	– .0093	.7625	.5140	4,673
May	.7220	.7305	.7220	.7131	– .0123	.7305	.5075	2,164
June	.7010	.7060	.7010	.6941	– .0133	.7060	.5590	2,779
July	.6960	.6960	.6960	.6881	– .0133	.6960	.5800	482
Aug	....	....	....	.6901	– .0133	.6870	.5740	439
Sept	....	....	....	.6931	– .0133	.6825	.5850	406
Oct	....	....	....	.6961	– .0133	.6870	.5920	468
Nov	....	....	....	.6991	– .0133	.6950	.6325	433
Dec	....	....	....	.7011	– .0133	.6975	.6400	927
Ja02	....	....	....	.7001	– .0133	.6950	.6800	161

Est vol 39,805; vol Thu 50,243; open int 164,066, +1,892.

GASOLINE-NY Unleaded (NYM) 42,000; $ per gal.

	Open	High	Low	Settle	Change	Lifetime High	Lifetime Low	Open Interest
Sept	.9230	.9285	.9090	.9119	– .0145	.9690	.5980	29,552
Oct	.8525	.8660	.8480	.8500	– .0078	.8880	.6300	16,355
Nov	.8205	.8330	.8205	.8195	– .0078	.8340	.6395	5,266
Dec	.8070	.8160	.8040	.8025	– .0083	.8160	.6275	5,835
Ja01	.8010	.8040	.8010	.7945	– .0088	.8040	.6600	1,809
Feb	....	....	....	.7940	– .0090	.7925	.6580	2,956
Mar	....	....	....	.7955	– .0095	.7950	.6600	1,021
Apr	....	....	....	.8425	– .0110	.8300	.6825	1,254
May	....	....	....	.8340	– .0110	.8160	.7850	404
June	....	....	....	.8215	– .0110	.8270	.7520	286

Est vol 32,964; vol Thu 42,244; open int 64,740, +3,141.

NATURAL GAS, (NYM) 10,000 MMBtu.; $ per MMBtu's

	Open	High	Low	Settle	Change	Lifetime High	Lifetime Low	Open Interest
Sept	4.475	4.520	4.395	4.475	+ .007	4.620	2.100	43,415
Oct	4.470	4.470	4.390	4.461	+ .008	4.590	2.100	32,983
Nov	4.500	4.510	4.420	4.495	+ .007	4.640	2.240	18,606
Dec	4.515	4.555	4.490	4.550	+ .012	4.710	2.380	27,418
Ja01	4.510	4.525	4.480	4.522	+ .012	4.720	2.400	27,700
Feb	4.235	4.250	4.210	4.258	+ .013	4.490	2.305	16,467
Mar	3.980	3.995	3.970	4.001	+ .015	4.270	2.210	19,922
Apr	3.725	3.750	3.725	3.748	+ .015	4.050	2.120	11,631
May	3.630	3.650	3.630	3.651	+ .013	3.900	2.119	8,793
June	3.610	3.630	3.610	3.632	+ .014	3.880	2.095	12,948
July	3.610	3.625	3.610	3.614	+ .014	3.900	2.095	10,252
Aug	3.580	3.620	3.580	3.610	+ .015	3.900	2.102	11,058
Sept	....	....	....	3.587	+ .015	3.900	2.137	7,105
Oct	3.580	3.580	3.580	3.570	+ .015	3.910	2.133	8,075
Nov	....	....	....	3.663	+ .017	4.010	2.275	5,741
Dec	3.740	3.740	3.730	3.740	+ .017	4.110	2.415	8,052
Ja02	3.740	3.740	3.740	3.735	+ .017	4.123	2.450	7,054

daily price limit
restriction on the day-to-day change in the price of an underlying commodity.

maximum daily price range
the amount a commodity price can change during the day; usually equal to twice the daily price limit.

price limits and maximum daily price ranges. (Similar limits are also put on some financial futures.) The **daily price limit** restricts the interday change in the price of the underlying commodity. For example, the price of corn can change by no more than 10 cents per bushel from one day to the next. The daily limit on copper is 3 cents per pound. Such limits, however, still leave plenty of room to turn a quick profit. For example, the daily limits on corn and copper translate into per-day changes of $500 for one corn contract and $750 for a copper contract. The **maximum daily price range,** in contrast, limits the amount the price can change *during* the day and is usually equal to twice the daily limit restrictions. For example, the daily price limit on corn is 10 cents per bushel and its maximum daily range is 20 cents per bushel.

Return on Invested Capital Futures contracts have only one source of return: the capital gains that can be earned when prices move in a favorable direction. There is no current income of any kind. The volatile price behavior of futures contracts is one reason why high returns are possible; the other is leverage. That is, because all futures trading is done on margin, it takes only a small amount of money to control a large investment position—and to participate in the price swings that accompany many futures contracts. Of course, the use of leverage also means that it is possible for an investment to be wiped out with just one or two bad days.

return on invested capital
return to investors based on the amount of money actually invested in a security, rather than the value of the contract itself.

Investment return on a commodities contract can be measured by calculating **return on invested capital.** This is simply a variation of the standard holding period return formula, where return is based on the *amount of money actually invested in the contract,* rather than on the value of the contract itself. It is used because of the generous amount of leverage (margin) used in commodities trading. The return on invested capital for a commodities position can be determined according to the following simple formula:

Equation 15.1

$$\text{Return on invested capital} = \frac{\text{Selling price of commodity contract} - \text{Purchase price of commodity contract}}{\text{Amount of margin deposit}}$$

Equation 15.1 can be used for both long and short transactions. To see how it works, assume you just bought two September corn contracts at 280 ($2.80 per bushel) by depositing the required initial margin of $1,500 ($750 for each contract). Your investment amounts to only $1,500, but you control 10,000 bushels of corn worth $28,000 at the time of purchase. Now, assume that September corn has just closed at 294, so you decide to sell out and take your profit. Your return on invested capital is

$$\text{Return on invested capital} = \frac{\$29,400 - \$28,000}{\$1,500}$$

$$= \frac{\$1,400}{\$1,500} = \underline{\underline{93\%}}$$

Clearly, this high rate of return was due not only to an increase in the price of the commodity but also (and perhaps more crucially) to the fact that you were using very low margin. (The initial margin in this particular transaction equaled just 5% of the underlying value of the contract.)

Trading Commodities

Investing in commodities takes one of three forms. The first, *speculating*, involves using commodities as a way to generate capital gains. In essence, speculators try to capitalize on the wide price swings that are characteristic of so many commodities. Figure 15.3 graphically illustrates the volatile behavior of commodity prices. It provides daily futures prices (in cents per bushel) for wheat contracts over the 7½-month period from January through mid-August 2000. Although such volatile price movements appeal to speculators, they frighten many other investors. As a result, some of these more cautious investors turn to *spreading*, the second form of commodities investing. Futures investors use this trading technique, much like the spreading that's done with put and call options, as a way to capture some of the benefits of volatile commodities prices but without all the exposure to loss.

HOTLINKS
You can study the behavior of commodity prices in a chart at:
www.barchart.com/

Finally, commodities futures can be used as *hedging* vehicles. A hedge in the commodities market is more of a technical strategy that is used almost exclusively by producers and processors to protect a position in a product or commodity. For example, a producer or grower would use a commodity hedge to obtain as *high a price* as possible for the goods he or she sells. On the other hand, the processor or manufacturer who uses the commodity would use a hedge for the opposite reason: to obtain the goods at as *low a price* as possible. A successful hedge, in effect, means added income to producers or lower costs to processors.

Let's now look briefly at the two trading strategies that are most used by individual investors—speculating and spreading—to gain a better understanding of how commodities can be used as investment vehicles.

Speculating   Speculators are in the market for one reason: They expect the price of a commodity to go up or down, and they hope to capitalize on it by going long or short. To see why a speculator would go long when prices are expected to rise, assume you buy a March silver contract at 595½ (i.e., $5.95½ an ounce) by depositing the required initial margin of $1,250. One silver contract involves 5,000 troy ounces, so it has a market value of $29,775. If silver goes up, you make money. Assume that it does and that by February (1 month before the contract expires), the price of the contract rises to 614. You then liquidate the contract and make a profit of 18½ cents per ounce (614 − 595½). That means a $925 profit from an investment of just $1,250—which translates into a return on invested capital of 74.0%.

HOTLINKS
At the Chicago Board of Trade Web site, go to [Knowledge Center], [FAQ], and answer the question "What is hedging and speculating?"
www.cbot.com

Of course, instead of rising, the price of silver could have dropped by 18½ cents per ounce. In this case, you would have lost most of your original investment ($1,250 − $925 leaves only $325, out of which would have to come a round-trip commission of $60 or $70). But the drop in price would be just what a *short seller* is after. Here's why: You sell "short" the March silver at 595½ and buy it back sometime later at 577. Clearly, the difference between the selling price and the purchase price is the same 18½ cents. But in this case it is *profit*, because the selling price exceeds the purchase price. (See Chapter 2 for a review of short selling.)

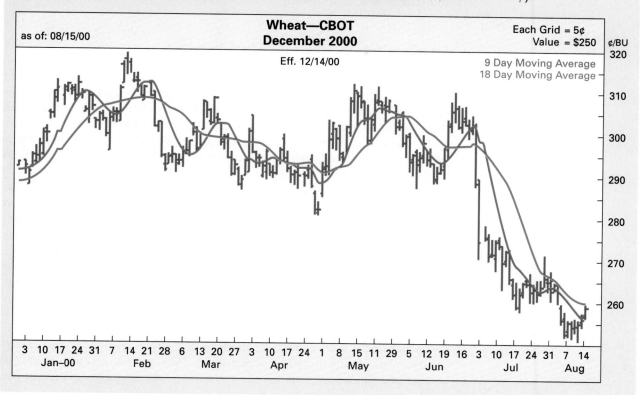

FIGURE 15.3 The Behavior of Commodity Prices over Time

This graph shows the volatile nature of commodity prices and underscores the investor's need for know-how when dealing in commodities. (*Source:* "Charts & Studies section of the Chicago Board of Trade Web site, www.cbot.com/)

Spreading Instead of attempting to speculate on the price behavior of a futures contract, you might choose to follow the more conservative tactic of *spreading*. Much like spreading with put and call options, the idea is to combine two or more different contracts into one position that offers the potential for a modest amount of profit but restricts your exposure to loss. One very important reason for spreading in the commodities market is that, unlike options, *there is no limit to the amount of loss that can occur with a futures contract*. You set up a spread by buying one contract and simultaneously selling another. Although one side of the transaction will lead to a loss, you hope that the profit earned from the other side will more than offset the loss, and that the net result will be at least a modest amount of profit. And if you're wrong, the spread will serve to limit (but not eliminate) any losses.

Here is a simple example of how a spread might work: Suppose you buy contract A at 533½ and at the same time short sell contract B for 575½. Sometime later, you close out your interest in contract A by selling it at 542, and you simultaneously cover your short position in B by purchasing a contract at 579. Although you made a profit of 8½ points (542 − 533½) on the long position, contract A, you lost 3½ points (575½ − 579) on the contract you shorted, B. The net effect, however, is a profit of 5 points. If you were dealing in cents per pound, those 5 points would mean a profit of $250 on a 5,000-pound contract. All sorts of commodity spreads can be set up for almost any type of investment situation. Most of them, however, are highly sophisticated and require specialized skills.

Commodities and the Individual Investor

Commodities appeal to investors because of the high rates of return they offer and their ability to act as inflation hedges during periods of rapidly rising consumer prices. More often than not, in periods of high inflation, investors stand to lose more in purchasing power than they gain from after-tax returns. Under such conditions, investors can be expected to seek outlets that provide better protection against inflation, which explains why the interest in commodities tends to pick up with inflation.

Commodities can play an important role in your portfolio so long *as you understand the risks involved and are well versed in the principles and mechanics of commodities trading.* Making money in the commodities market is extremely difficult. It may look easy—perhaps too easy—but very few investors (even the most experienced) are able to earn big returns consistently by trading futures. Indeed, for most people, the quickest way to lose money in commodities is to jump in without knowing what they are doing. Because there is the potential for a lot of price volatility and because commodity trading is done on a very low margin, the potential for loss is enormous.

Accordingly, most experts recommend that only a portion of your investment capital be committed to commodities. The specific amount would, of course, be a function of your aversion to risk and the amount of resources you have available. You have to be prepared mentally and should be in a position financially to absorb losses—perhaps a number of them. An adequate cash reserve should be kept on hand (to absorb losses or to meet margin calls). It's also a good idea to maintain a diversified holding of commodities in order to spread your risks.

HOTLINKS

For information on commodity pools and commodity trading advisers, see:

www.fiafii.org/tutorial/professionals6.htm

If you decide to try your hand at commodities, keep in mind there are several different ways to do so. You can invest directly in the commodities market by trading futures contracts on your own. Or, to reduce your risk exposure a bit, you might want to trade put and call options on some of the more actively traded futures contracts. Alternatively, you can invest in limited partnership *commodity pools.* These pools are a lot like mutual funds. You might use them if you wanted to invest in the commodities market but lacked the time or expertise to manage your own investments. Still another alternative is to consider investing in *commodities-oriented futures funds.* These are essentially mutual funds that pool investors' money and actively trade futures contracts. Most of these funds invest only about 20% to 25% of their money in margined futures contracts and keep the rest in interest-earning assets such as T-bills or bonds. They may offer a way to gain some exposure to the commodities market, but they do have a downside: Not only can their performance be highly volatile, but their costs can also be quite high, sometimes running to as much as 20% of assets under management. All of which should come as no surprise, because in this market, there's no easy way to make money!

IN REVIEW

CONCEPTS

15.7 List and briefly define the five essential parts of a commodity contract. Which parts have a direct bearing on the price behavior of the contract?

15.8 Briefly define each of the following:
a. Settle price.
b. Daily price limit.
c. Open interest.
d. Maximum daily price range.
e. Delivery month.

15.9 What is the one source of return on futures contracts? What measure is used to calculate the return on a commodity contract?

15.10 Note several approaches to investing in commodities and explain the investment objectives of each.

15.11 Explain why you should be well versed in the behavior and investment characteristics of commodities futures when investing in this market. Why should futures holdings be well diversified?

Financial Futures

LG 5 LG 6

financial futures
a type of futures contract in which the underlying "commodity" is a financial asset, such as debt securities, foreign currencies, or market baskets of common stocks.

Another dimension of the futures market is **financial futures,** a segment of the market in which futures contracts are traded on a variety of financial instruments. Actually, financial futures are an extension of the commodities concept. They were created for much the same reason as commodity futures, they are traded in the same market, their prices behave a lot like commodities, and they have similar investment merits. But financial futures are unique because of the underlying assets. Let's now look more closely at financial futures and see how investors can use them.

The Financial Futures Market

Though relatively young, the financial futures market is a dominant force in the whole futures market. Indeed, the level of trading in financial futures far surpasses that of traditional commodities. Much of the interest in financial futures is due to hedgers and big institutional investors who use these contracts as portfolio- and debt-management tools. But individual investors can also find plenty of opportunities here. For example, financial futures offer yet another way to speculate on the behavior of interest rates. And they can also be used to speculate in the stock market. They even offer a convenient way to speculate in the highly specialized foreign currency markets.

The financial futures market was established in response to the economic turmoil the United States experienced during the 1970s. The dollar had become unstable on the world market and was causing serious problems for multinational firms. Closer to home, interest rates had become highly volatile, which caused severe difficulties for corporate treasurers, financial institutions, and money managers in general. All of these parties needed a way to protect themselves from the wide fluctuations in the value of the dollar and interest rates. Thus a market for financial futures was born. Hedging provided the economic rationale for the market in financial futures. But speculators were quick to join in, as they found the price volatility of these instruments attractive and at times highly profitable.

At present, most of the financial futures trading in this country occurs on just two exchanges—the Chicago Board of Trade and the Chicago Mercantile Exchange. Financial futures also are traded on several foreign exchanges, the most noteworthy of which is the London International Financial Futures Exchange. The three basic types of financial futures include foreign currencies, debt securities, and stock indexes.

Foreign Currencies, Interest Rates, and Stock Indexes The financial futures market started rather inconspicuously in May 1972, with the listing of a handful of foreign currency contracts. Known as **currency futures,** they have become a major hedging vehicle as international trade has mushroomed. Most of the currency trading today is conducted in the following eight foreign currencies:

- British pound
- German mark
- Swiss franc
- Mexican peso
- Canadian dollar
- Japanese yen
- Australian dollar
- Euro

currency futures
futures contracts on foreign currencies, traded much like commodities.

All of these currencies are issued by countries with which the United States has strong international trade and exchange ties.

In October 1975, the first futures contract on debt securities, or **interest rate futures,** as they are more commonly known, was established when trading started in GNMA pass-through certificates (a special type of mortgage-backed bond issued by an agency of the U.S. government). In time, other issues were added and today, trading is carried out in a variety of U.S. and foreign debt securities and interest rates, including:

interest rate futures
futures contracts on debt securities.

- U.S. Treasury bills
- U.S. Treasury notes
- U.S. Treasury bonds
- U.S. agency notes
- Municipal bonds (via a muni bond index)
- Various 30-day interest rate contracts (e.g., 30-day Federal Funds)
- 90-day Euromarket deposits (e.g., Eurodollar deposits, Euromark deposits, etc.)
- Various foreign government bonds (e.g., bonds issued by the British, German, and Canadian governments)

Interest rate futures were immediately successful, and their popularity continues to grow.

In February 1982, a new trading vehicle was introduced: the stock-index futures contract. **Stock-index futures,** as they are called, are contracts pegged to broad-based measures of stock market performance. Today, trading is done in most of the (major) U.S. stock indexes, including:

stock-index futures
futures contracts written on broad-based measures of stock market performance (e.g., the S&P 500 Stock Index), allowing investors to participate in the general movements of the stock market.

- The Dow Jones Industrial Average
- The S&P 500 Index
- The S&P MidCap 400 Index

- The NYSE Composite Index
- The Nasdaq 100 Index
- The Russell 2000 Index

In addition to these (and other) U.S. indexes, investors can also trade stock-index futures contracts based on the London, Tokyo, Paris, Sydney, Berlin, Zurich, and Toronto stock exchanges. Stock-index futures, which are similar to the stock-index options we discussed in Chapter 14, allow investors to participate in the general movements of the entire stock market.

Stock index futures (and other futures contracts) represent a type of *derivative security*. Like options, they derive their value from the price behavior of the assets that underlie them. In the case of stock-index futures, they are supposed to reflect the general performance of the stock market as a whole, as measured by a particular index. Thus, when the market, as measured by the S&P 500, goes up, the value of an S&P 500 futures contract should go up as well. Accordingly, investors can use stock-index futures as a way to buy the market—or a reasonable proxy thereof—and thereby participate in broad market moves.

Contract Specifications In principle, financial futures contracts are like commodities contracts. They control large sums of the underlying financial instrument and are issued with a variety of delivery months. All this can be seen in Figure 15.4, which lists quotes for several foreign currency, interest rate, and stock-index futures contracts. Looking first at currency futures, we see that the contracts entitle the holders to a certain position in a specified foreign currency. In effect, the owner of a currency future holds a claim on a certain amount of foreign money. The precise amount ranges from 62,500 British pounds to 12.5 million Japanese yen. Similarly, holders of interest rate futures have a claim on a certain amount of the underlying debt security. This claim is also quite large. It amounts to $100,000 worth of Treasury notes and bonds, $1 million worth of Treasury bills, and $5 million in 30-day Federal Funds contracts.

Stock-index futures, however, are a bit different because the seller of one of these contracts is *not* obligated to deliver the *underlying stocks* at the expiration date. Instead, ultimate delivery is in the form of *cash*. (This is fortunate, as it would indeed be a task to make delivery of the 2,000 small-cap stocks that are in the Russell 2000 Index or the 500 issues in the S&P Index.) Basically, the amount of underlying cash is set at a certain multiple of the value of the underlying stock index. In particular,

Index	Multiple
DJIA	$10 × index
S&P 500	$250 × index
Nasdaq 100	$100 × index
S&P 400	$500 × index
NYSE Composite	$500 × index
Russell 2000	$500 × index

Thus, if the S&P 500 stood at 1550, then the amount of cash underlying a single S&P 500 stock-index futures contract would be $250 × 1550 = $387,500. Again, the amount is substantial. In terms of delivery months, the

FIGURE 15.4

Quotations on Selected Actively Traded Financial Futures

The trading exchange, size of the trading unit, pricing unit, and delivery months are all vital pieces of information included as part of the quotation system used with financial futures. (*Source: Wall Street Journal,* August 15, 2000.)

CURRENCY

	Open	High	Low	Settle	Change	Lifetime High	Low	Open Interest
JAPAN YEN (CME)-12.5 million yen; $ per yen (.00)								
Sept	.9268	.9268	.9179	.9187	− .0069	1.0272	.9179	75,432
Dec	.9350	.9350	.9329	.9337	− .0070	1.0434	.9225	3,099
Mr01	....	....	....	.9490	− .0071	1.0300	.9490	136

Est vol 7,344; vol Fri 7,257; open int 78,668, +450.

DEUTSCHEMARK (CME)-125,000 marks; $ per mark								
Sept	.4616	.4638	.4616	.4637	+ .0009	.5250	.4576	706

Est vol 2; vol Fri 0; open int 718, +4.

CANADIAN DOLLAR (CME)-100,000 dlrs.; $ per Can $								
Sept	.6747	.6755	.6737	.6738	− .0014	.7017	.6623	61,454
Dec	.6768	.6768	.6750	.6755	− .0014	.7025	.6640	4,832
Mr01	....	....	....	.6772	− .0014	.7040	.6672	637
June	....	....	....	.6789	− .0014	.6990	.6695	142

Est vol 3,008; vol Fri 4,359; open int 67,077, −182.

BRITISH POUND (CME)-62,500 pds.; $ per pound								
Sept	1.5032	1.5120	1.5014	1.5048	+ .0010	1.6780	1.4700	30,653
Dec	1.5100	1.5150	1.5030	1.5070	+ .0010	1.6500	1.4730	432

Est vol 4,034; vol Fri 5,107; open int 31,098, −328.

INTEREST RATE

TREASURY BONDS (CBT)-$100,000; pts. 32nds of 100%

	Open	High	Low	Settle	Change	Lifetime High	Low	Open Interest
Sept	99-21	100-01	99-12	100-00	+ 11	100-12	88-19	419,853
Dec	99-18	100-00	99-13	99-31	+ 11	100-11	88-31	17,451
Mr01	99-24	100-00	99-24	100-00	+ 11	100-03	88-06	1,501

Est vol 83,000; vol Fri 219,958; open int 438,880, −1,131.

TREASURY BONDS (MCE)-$50,000; pts. 32nds of 100%

Sept	99-18	100-01	99-12	100-00	+ 9	100-12	92-23	4,776

Est vol 900; vol Fri 1,045; open int 4,793, −58.

TREASURY NOTES (CBT)-$100,000; pts. 32nds of 100%

Sept	99-18	99-24	99-115	99-235	+ 4.5	100-07	94-22	570,928
Dec	99-15	99-215	99-095	99-21	+ 4.5	100-04	96-075	56,337

Est vol 91,000; vol Fri 236,609; open int 627,290, +14,061.

10 YR AGENCY NOTES (CBT)-$100,000; pts. 32nds of 100%

Sept	93-20	93-26	93-155	93-255	+ 3.5	94-06	88-045	43,197

Est vol 1,200; vol Fri 3,598; open int 4,344, +256.

5 YR TREAS NOTES (CBT)-$100,000; pts. 32nds of 100%

Sept	99-185	99-205	99-15	99-20	+ 1.0	100-00	96-14	392,629
Dec	99-19	99-225	99-175	99-22	....	100-02	98-13	15,543

Est vol 40,000; vol Fri 81,386; open int 408,172, −6,763.

2 YR TREAS NOTES (CBT)-$200,000; pts. 32nds of 100%

Sept	99-152	99-162	99-145	99-16	+ .2	99-225	98-025	51,144

Est vol 500; vol Fri 3,615; open int 51,144, −750.

30-DAY FEDERAL FUNDS (CBT)-$5 million; pts. of 100%

Aug	93.495	93.505	93.495	93.500	....	93.730	93.120	12,444
Sept	93.46	93.47	93.46	93.47	....	93.64	92.98	15,134
Oct	93.45	93.46	93.45	93.46	....	93.52	92.93	7,444
Nov	93.42	93.43	93.42	93.43	....	93.45	92.90	4,126
Dec	93.40	93.41	93.38	93.41	....	93.44	93.11	2,730

Est vol 1,500; vol Fri 3,552; open int 42,247, +1,275.

MUNI BOND INDEX (CBT)-$1,000; times Bond Buyer MBI

Sept	98-23	99-03	98-20	99-03	+ 9	99-13	90-03	22,225

Est vol 340; vol Fri 1,058; open int 22,644, +65.
Index: Close 98-27; Yield 5.76.

TREASURY BILLS (CME)-$1 mil.; pts. of 100%

	Open	High	Low	Settle	Discount Chg	Settle	Open Chg	Interest
Sept	93.89	93.89	93.88	93.88	+ .01	6.12	− .01	1,135

Est vol 11; vol Fri 76; open int 1,135, +75.

INDEX

DJ INDUSTRIAL AVERAGE (CBOT)-$10 times average

	Open	High	Low	Settle	Change	Lifetime High	Low	Open Interest
Sept	11095	11235	11050	11220	+ 135	12126	9995	13,516
Dec	11240	11380	11205	11369	+ 136	12180	8100	2,110

Est vol 8,500; vol Fri 11,829; open int 15,634, +912.
Idx prl: Hi 11177.61; Lo 11006.19; Close 11176.14, +148.34.

S&P 500 INDEX (CME)-$250 times index

Sept	147930	149980	147600	149810	+ 1960	159500	99000	377,978
Dec	150300	152200	149860	152060	+ 2000	161860	126650	10,364
Mr01	153030	154470	152170	154390	+ 2020	164260	132430	1,298
June	155810	156790	154490	156760	+ 2070	166660	134280	1,286
Sept	....	....	....	159260	+ 2070	169060	136130	152

Est vol 43,063; vol Fri 52,019; open int 391,091, +1,848.
Idx prl: Hi 1491.64; Lo 1468.56; Close 1491.56, +19.72.

lives of financial futures contracts run from about 12 months or less for most stock-index and currency futures to about 6 years or less for interest rate instruments.

Prices and Profits There are three basic types of financial futures. Not surprisingly, the price of each type of contract is quoted somewhat differently.

- *Foreign currency futures.* All currency futures are quoted in dollars or cents per unit of the underlying foreign currency (e.g., dollars per British pound or cents per Japanese yen). Thus, according to the closing ("settle") prices in Figure 15.4, one September British pound contract was worth $94,050 (62,500 pounds × 1.5048). A December Japanese yen contract was valued at $116,712.50 (because a quote of 0.9337 cent per yen equals less than a penny a yen, we have 12,500,000 yen × $0.009337).

- *Interest rate futures.* Except for the quotes on Treasury bills and other short-term securities (which we'll examine in the next section), interest rate futures contracts are priced as a percentage of the par value of the underlying debt instrument (e.g., Treasury notes or Treasury bonds). Because these instruments are quoted in increments of 1/32 of 1%, a quote of 99-20 for the settle price of the September 5-year Treasury notes (in Figure 15.4) translates into 99-20/32, which converts to a quote of 99⅝, or 99.625% of par. Applying this rate to the par value of the underlying security, we see that this September Treasury note contract is worth $99,625 (i.e., $100,000 × 0.99625).

- *Stock-index futures.* Stock-index futures are quoted in terms of the actual underlying index. But, as noted above, they carry a face value of anywhere from $10 to $500 times the index. Thus, according to the settle price in Figure 15.4, the March 2001 S&P 500 contract would be worth $385,975, because the value of this particular contract is equal to $250 times the (settle) price of the index (1543.90 × $250). The September DJIA contract is worth $112,200 (11220 × $10).

The value of an interest rate futures contract responds to interest rates exactly as the debt instrument that underlies the contract. That is, when interest rates go up, the value of an interest rate futures contract goes down, and vice versa. However, the quote system for interest rate as well as currency and stock-index futures is set up to reflect the *market value of the contract* itself. Thus, when the price or quote of a financial futures contract increases, the investor who is long makes money. In contrast, when the price decreases, the short seller makes money.

Price behavior is the only source of return to speculators. Even though stocks and debt securities are involved in some financial futures, such contracts have no claim on the dividend and interest income of the underlying issues. Even so, huge profits (or losses) are possible with financial futures because of the equally large size of the contracts. For instance, if the price of Swiss francs goes up by just 2 cents against the dollar, the investor is ahead $2,500. Likewise, a 3-point drop in the NYSE Composite Index means a $1,500 loss to an investor (3 × $500). When related to the relatively small initial margin deposit required to make transactions in the financial futures markets, such price activity can mean very high rates of return—or very high risk of a total wipeout.

Pricing Futures on Treasury Bills and Other Short-Term Securities

index price
technique used to price T-bill and other short-term securities futures contracts, by subtracting current yield from an index of 100.

Because Treasury bills and other short-term securities are normally traded in the money market on a discount basis, it was necessary to devise a special pricing system that would reflect the actual price movements of these futures contracts. To accomplish this, an **index price** system was developed whereby the yield is subtracted from an index of 100. Thus, when the yield on an underlying security, such as a Treasury bill or Eurodollar deposit, is 5.25%, the contract would be quoted at an index of 94.75 (100.00 − 5.25). Under such a system, when you buy, say, a T-bill future and the index goes up, you have made money. When the index price goes down, a short seller has made money. Note also that 30-day interest rate futures, as well as 90-day T-bill and Eurodollar/Euromarket contracts, are quoted in basis points. One basis point equals 1/100 of 1%. Thus, a quote of 95.07 translates into a T-bill yield of 4.93% (i.e., 100.000 − 95.07).

The index price system traces only the price behavior of the futures contract. To find the *actual price or value* of a 90-day T-bill or Eurodollar contract, we use the formula

Equation 15.2

$$\text{Price of a 90-day futures contract} = \$1{,}000{,}000 - \left(\frac{\text{Security's yield} \times 90 \times \$10{,}000}{360} \right)$$

A similar formula would be used to find the price of a 30-day interest rate contract, except a value of 30 would be used in place of the 90 in the formula's numerator.

Note that this price formula is based not on the quoted price index but on the *yield of the security itself*. That yield can be determined by subtracting the price index quote from 100. To see how it works, consider the 90-day T-bill futures contract quoted at 95.07. Subtract that amount from 100.00, and we find that this T-bill futures contract is priced to yield 4.93%—i.e., 100.00 − 95.07 = 4.93. Now, using Equation 15.2, we can see that the price (or value) of this futures contract is

$$\text{Price of a 90-day futures contract} = \$1{,}000{,}000 - \left(\frac{4.93 \times 90 \times \$10{,}000}{360} \right)$$

$$= \$1{,}000{,}000 - \$12{,}325$$

$$= \underline{\$987{,}675}$$

There's a handy shortcut for *tracking the price behavior* of T-bill or Eurodollar/Euromarket futures contracts: Remember that the price of a *90-day contract* will change by $25 for every basis point change in yield. Thus, when the yield on the underlying 90-day security moves from 4.93% to 5.08% (a change of 15 basis points), the price of the futures contract drops by 15 × $25 = $375.

Trading Techniques

Like commodities, financial futures can be used for hedging, spreading, and speculating. Multinational companies and firms that are active in international trade might consider *hedging* with currency or Euromarket futures. Various financial institutions and corporate money managers often use interest rate futures for hedging purposes. In either case, the objective is the same: to lock in the best monetary exchange or interest rate possible. In addition, individual investors and portfolio managers hedge with stock-index to protect their security holdings against temporary market declines. Financial futures can also be used for *spreading*. This tactic is popular with investors who simultaneously buy and sell combinations of two or more contracts to form a desired investment position. Finally, financial futures are widely used for *speculation*.

Although investors can employ any one of the three trading strategies noted above, we will focus primarily on the use of financial futures by speculators and hedgers. We will first examine speculating in currency and interest rate futures. Then we'll look at how these contracts can be used to hedge investments in stocks, bonds, and foreign securities.

Speculating in Financial Futures Speculators are especially interested in financial futures because of the size of the contracts. For instance, in mid-2000, Canadian dollar contracts were worth over $67,000, Treasury notes and bonds were going for around $100,000, and 30-day federal funds contracts were being quoted at close to $4.7 million each. With contracts of this size, it obviously doesn't take much movement in the underlying asset to produce big price swings—and therefore big profits.

Currency and interest rate futures are popular with investors, and can be used for just about any speculative purpose. For example, if you expect the dollar to be devalued relative to the German mark, you could buy mark currency futures, because the contracts should go up in value. Or, if you anticipate a rise in interest rates, you might "go short" (sell) interest rate futures, because they should go down in value. Because margin is used and financial futures have the same source of return as commodities (price appreciation), return on invested capital (Equation 15.1) is used to measure their profitability of financial futures.

 Going Long a Foreign Currency Contract Suppose you believe that the Swiss franc is about to appreciate in value relative to the dollar. You decide to go long (buy) three September S-franc contracts at 0.7055—i.e., at a quote of just over 70 cents a franc. Each contract would be worth $88,187.50 (125,000 S-francs × 0.7055). The total underlying value of the three contracts would be $264,562.50. Even so, given an initial margin requirement of, say, $2,500 per contract, you would have to deposit only $7,500 to acquire this position. Now, if Swiss francs move up just a few pennies, say, from 0.7055 to 0.75 (75 cents a franc), the value of the three contracts will rise to $281,250, and in a matter of months, you will have made a profit of $16,687.50. Using Equation 15.1 for return on invested capital, we find that such a profit translates into an unbelievable 222% rate of return. Of course, an even smaller fractional change in the other direction would have wiped out this investment, so it should be clear that these *high returns are not without equally high risk*.

Going Short an Interest Rate Contract Let's assume that you're anticipating a sharp rise in long-term rates. A rise in rates means that interest rate futures will drop in value. So you decide to short sell two June T-bond contracts at 115-00, which means that the contracts are trading at 115% of par. Thus the two contracts are worth $230,000 ($100,000 × 1.15 × 2). The amount of money required to make the investment is only $5,400 (the initial margin deposit is $2,700 per contract). Assume that interest rates do, in fact, move up. As a result, the price on Treasury bond contracts drops to 106-16 (or 106½). Under such circumstances, you would buy back the two June T-bond contracts (in order to cover the short position) and in the process make a profit of $17,000. (You originally sold the two contracts at $230,000 and bought them back sometime later at $213,000. As with any investment, such a difference between what you pay for a security and what you sell it for is profit.) In this case, the return on invested capital amounts to 315%. Again, however, this kind of return is due in no small part to the *enormous risk of loss* you assumed.

Trading Stock-Index Futures Most investors use stock-index futures for speculation or hedging. (Stock-index futures are similar to the *index options* introduced in Chapter 14. Therefore, much of the discussion that follows also applies to index options.) Whether speculating or hedging, the key to success is *predicting the future course of the stock market.* Because you are "buying the market" with stock-index futures, it is important to get a handle on the future direction of the market via technical analysis (as discussed in Chapter 8) or some other technique. Once you have a feel for the market's direction, you can formulate a stock-index futures trading or hedging strategy. For example, if you feel that the market is headed up, you would want to go long (buy stock-index futures). In contrast, if your analysis suggests a sharp drop in equity values, you could make money by going short (selling stock-index futures).

Assume, for instance, that you believe the market is undervalued and a move up is imminent. You can try to identify one or a handful of stocks that should go up with the market (and assume the stock selection risks that go along with this approach). Or you can buy an S&P 500 stock-index futures contract currently trading at, say, 1574.45. To execute this speculative transaction, you would need to deposit an initial margin of only $23,500. Now, if the market does rise so that the S&P 500 Index moves to, say, 1622.85 by the expiration of the futures contract, you earn a profit of $12,100—that is, $(1622.85 - 1574.45) \times \$250 = \$12,100$. Given the $23,500 investment, your return on invested capital would amount to a hefty 51.5%. Of course, keep in mind that if the market drops by some 90 points (or less than 6 percent), the investment will be a *total loss*.

Hedging with Stock-Index Futures Stock-index futures also make excellent hedging vehicles. They provide investors with a highly effective way of protecting stock holdings in a declining market. Although this tactic is not perfect, it does enable investors to obtain desired protection against a decline in market value without disturbing their equity holdings. Here's how a so-called *short hedge* would work: Assume that you hold a total of 2,000 shares of stock in a dozen different companies and that the market value of this portfolio is around $235,000. If you think the market is about to undergo a temporary sharp decline, you can do one of two things: sell all of your shares or buy puts on each of the stocks. Clearly, these alternatives are cumbersome and/or costly and therefore undesirable for protecting a widely diversified portfolio. The desired results could also be achieved, however, by *short selling stock-index futures*. (Or, basically the same protection can be obtained in this hedging situation by turning to options and buying a *stock-index put*.)

Suppose for purposes of illustration that you short sell one NYSE stock-index futures contract at 468.75. Such a contract would provide a close match to the current value of your portfolio (it would be valued at 468.75 × $500 = $234,375), and yet the stock-index futures contract would require an initial margin deposit of only $3,500. (Margin deposits are lower for hedgers than for speculators.) Now, if the NYSE Composite Index drops to 448.00, you will make a profit from the short-sale of some $10,000. That is, because the index fell 20.75 points (468.75 − 448.00), the total profit will be $10,375 (20.75 × $500). Ignoring taxes, this profit can then be added to the portfolio (additional shares of stock can be purchased at their new lower prices). The net result will be a new portfolio position that will approximate the one that existed prior to the decline in the market.

How well the "before" and "after" portfolio positions match will depend on how far the portfolio dropped in value. If the average price dropped about $5 per share in our example, the positions will closely match. But this does not always happen. The price of some stocks will change more than others, so the amount of protection provided by this type of short hedge depends on how sensitive the stock portfolio is to movements in the market. Thus, the types of stocks that are held in the portfolio is an important consideration in structuring a stock-index short hedge.

A key to success with this kind of hedging is to make sure that the characteristics of the hedging vehicle (the futures contract) closely match those of the portfolio (or security position) being protected. Thus, if the portfolio is made up mostly (or exclusively) of large-cap stocks, use something like the S&P 500 Stock Index futures contract as the hedging vehicle. If the portfolio is mostly blue-chip stocks, use the DJIA contract. And if the portfolio holds mostly tech stocks, consider the Nasdaq 100 Index contract. Again, the point is to pick a hedging vehicle that closely reflects the types of securities you want to protect. For the investor who keeps that caveat in mind, hedging with stock-index futures can be a low-cost yet effective way of obtaining protection against loss in a declining stock market. (For an unusual aspect relating to the timing of investments in stock-index futures, see the nearby *Investing in Action* box.)

Hedging Other Securities Just as stock-index futures can be used to hedge stock portfolios, *interest rate futures* can be used to hedge bond portfolios. Or, *foreign currency futures* can be used with foreign securities as a way to protect against foreign exchange risk. *Let's consider an interest rate hedge:* If you held a substantial portfolio of bonds, the last thing you would want to see is a big jump in interest rates, which could cause a sharp decline in the value of your portfolio. Assume you hold around $300,000 worth of Treasury and agency issues, with an average (approximate) maturity of about 18 years. If you believe that market rates are headed up, you can hedge your bond portfolio by short selling three U.S. Treasury bond futures contracts. (Each T-bond futures contract is worth about $100,000, so it would take three of them to cover a $300,000 portfolio.) Now, if rates do head up, the portfolio will be protected against loss. As we noted with stocks above, the exact amount of protection will depend on how well the T-bond futures contracts parallel the price behavior of your particular bond portfolio.

INVESTING in action

Triple Witching Day

There's an unusually volatile day on Wall Street on the third Friday in March, June, September, and December, and the volatility has nothing to do with the U.S. economy, corporate profits, interest rates, inflation, or other factors that are normally associated with stock market performance. It's the *Triple Witching Day,* when stock options, stock-index options, and stock-index futures all expire more or less simultaneously.

Here's why the volatility occurs: Let's say you manage an index fund for individual investors, who merely expect you to keep up with the Standard & Poor's 500 Index. Suddenly, there's pessimism in the marketplace, and the S&P 500 Index futures contract is trading at a 2% discount to its fair value. So you sell the 500 stocks and buy the futures contract, thereby guaranteeing that you will beat the S&P 500 by 2% (less transaction costs) between the date of the transaction and the expiration of the futures contract. By making this trade, you will beat the market by 2%, whether the market goes up or down. On the contract's expiration day, however, you must go out and buy the exact stocks that are in the index; otherwise you're not performing the job you were hired to do. If enough people attempt to make this trade at the same time, then there will be an order imbalance: Buyers won't care what price they pay because it's the same exact price at which the futures contracts are settled.

The other side of the trade could occur when market sentiment is "frothy" and the futures contract is overvalued. In this situation, as the index fund manager you would sell the futures contract and buy the stocks, again locking in the difference. On expiration day, you must sell the stocks to have the cash to settle the futures contract. Again, this can cause an order imbalance, pushing stock prices downward.

All this may seem like a free lunch, and it was for a number of years. When stock-index futures contracts were in their infancy, they were much more inefficiently priced than they are today. For example, during the stock market crash of 1987, General Motors sold billions of dollars worth of stocks in its pension plan and bought futures contracts. On the day of the crash, the Dow Jones Industrial Average fell from about 2,200 to 1,700, and at the end of the day, the futures contract was priced at the equivalent of 1,200, indicating the extreme bearishness that gripped the market that day. GM pension managers reasoned that if the market stayed at 1,700, then they would profit by 500 DJIA points merely by switching from stocks to futures.

However, the ability to make money in this transaction has diminished over the years, and so the triple witching volatility has decreased some in recent years. Today, there are many more players in the market, making the available profits much thinner, and that is one reason the volatility has diminished. Another reason for the diminished volatility is that the exchanges have spread the expirations over a longer period. Although options on individual stocks and on the S&P 100 Index still expire at the close on Friday, S&P 500 Index options and futures now settle at the beginning of that business day. (They used to expire within a single hour.) By spreading out the expiration times, the exchanges have diluted the impact of the Triple Witching Day. But it's still enough to cause extra volatility in the stock market—and nervousness on Wall Street four times a year.

There is, of course, a downside: *If market interest rates go down, rather than up, you will miss out on potential profits as long as the short hedge position remains in place.* This is so because the profits being made in the portfolio will be offset by losses from the futures contracts. Actually, this will occur with any type of portfolio (stocks, bonds, or anything else) that's tied to an offsetting short hedge, because when you create the short hedge you essentially lock in a position at that point. Although you don't lose anything when the market falls, you also don't make anything when the market goes up. In either case, the profits you make from one position are offset by losses from the other.

 Hedging Foreign Currency Exposure Now let's see how futures contracts can be used to hedge foreign exchange risk. Let's assume that you have just purchased $150,000 worth of German government 1-year notes. (You did this because higher yields were available on the German notes than on comparable U.S. Treasury securities.) Because these notes are denominated in *marks*, this investment is subject to loss if currency exchange rates move against you (i.e., if the value of the dollar rises relative to the mark). If all you wanted was the higher yield offered by the German note, you could eliminate most of the currency exchange risk by setting up a currency hedge. Here's how: Let's say that at the current exchange rate, one U.S. dollar will "buy" 1.65 marks. This means that marks are worth about 60 cents ($1/1.65 marks = $0.60). If currency contracts on German marks were trading at around $0.60 a mark, you would have to *sell* two contracts in order to protect the $150,000 investment. Each mark contract covers 125,000 marks, so if they're being quoted at 0.6000, then each contract is worth $0.60 × 125,000 = $75,000.

Assume that 1 year later, the value of the dollar has increased, relative to the mark. One U.S. dollar will now "buy" 1.725 marks. Under such conditions, a German mark futures contract would be quoted at around 0.5800 (i.e., $1/1.72 = $0.58). At this price, each futures contract would be worth $72,500 (125,000 × $0.58). Each contract, in effect, would be worth $2,500 less than it was a year ago. But because the contract was sold short when the hedge was set up, you will make a profit of $2,500 per contract—for a total profit of $5,000 on the two contracts. Unfortunately, that's not *net profit*, because this profit will offset the loss you will incur on the German note investment. In very simple terms, when you sent $150,000 overseas to buy the German notes, the money was worth 250,000 marks. However, when you brought the money back a year later, those 250,000 marks purchased only 145,000 U.S. dollars. Thus, you are is out $5,000 on your original investment. Were it not for the currency hedge, you would be out the full $5,000, and the return on this investment would be a lot lower. But the hedge covered the loss, and the net effect was that you were able to enjoy the added yield of the German note without having to worry about any potential loss from currency exchange rates.

Financial Futures and the Individual Investor

Financial futures can play an important role in your portfolio so long as three factors apply: (1) You must thoroughly understand these investment vehicles. (2) You must clearly recognize the tremendous risk exposure of these vehicles. And (3) you must be fully prepared (financially and emotionally) to absorb some losses. Financial futures are highly volatile securities that have enormous potential for profit and for loss. For instance, in the year 2000, during a 6-month period of time, the December S&P 500 futures contract fluctuated in price from a low of 1266.50 to a high of 1618.60. This range of over 350 points for a single contract translates into a *potential* profit—or loss—of some $88,000, and all from an initial investment of only $23,500. Investment diversification is obviously essential as a means of reducing the potentially devastating impact of price volatility. Financial futures are exotic investment vehicles, but if properly used, they can provide generous returns.

Options on Futures

futures options
options that give the holders the right to buy or sell a single standardized futures contract for a specified period of time at a specified strike price.

The evolution that began with listed stock options and financial futures spread, over time, to interest rate options and stock-index futures. Eventually, it led to the merger of options and futures and to the creation of the ultimate leverage vehicle: *options on futures contracts*. **Futures options,** as they are called, represent listed puts and calls on actively traded futures contracts. In essence, they give the holders the right to buy (with calls) or sell (with puts) a single standardized futures contract for a specific period of time at a specified strike price. Table 15.4 lists many of the actively traded futures options available in 2000. Such options are available on both commodities and financial futures. For the most part, these puts and calls cover the same amount of assets as the underlying futures contracts—for example, 112,000 pounds of sugar, 100 ounces of gold, 62,500 British pounds, or $100,000 in Treasury bonds. Thus, they also involve the same amount of price activity as is normally found with commodities and financial futures.

Futures options have the same standardized strike prices, expiration dates, and quotation system as other listed options. Depending on the strike price on the option and the market value of the underlying futures contract, these options can also be in-the-money or out-of-the-money. Futures options are valued like other puts and calls—by the difference between the option's strike price and the market price of the underlying futures contract (see Chapter 14). Moreover, they can also be used like any other listed option—

TABLE 15.4	Futures Options: Puts and Calls on Futures Contracts		
	Commodities		
Corn	Pork bellies	Coffee	Gold
Soybeans	Live hogs	Sugar	Silver
Soybean meal	Lean hogs	Wheat	Crude oil
Soybean oil	Feeder cattle	Oats	Natural gas
Cotton	Lumber	Rice	Heating oil
Live cattle	Orange juice	Platinum	Gas oil
	Cocoa	Copper	Gasoline
	Financial Futures		
British pound	U.S. dollar index	Muni bond index	
German mark	Eurodollar deposits	British government bonds	
Swiss franc	Euromark deposits	German government bonds	
Japanese yen	Treasury bills	NYSE Composite Index	
Canadian dollar	Treasury notes	S&P 500 Stock Index	
Russian ruble	Treasury bonds	Dow Jones Industrial Average	
Mexican peso	Agency notes	Nasdaq 100 Index	

that is, for speculating or hedging, in options writing programs, or for spreading. The biggest difference between a futures option and a futures contract is that *the option limits the loss exposure* to the price of the option. The most you can lose is the price paid for the put or call option. With the futures contract, there is no real limit to the amount of loss an investor can incur.

To see how futures options work, assume that you want to trade some gold contracts. You believe that the price of gold will increase over the next 4 or 5 months, from its present level of $285 an ounce to around $330 an ounce. You can buy a futures contract at 288.10 by depositing the required initial margin of $1,350. Or you can buy a futures call option with a $280 strike price that is currently being quoted at 10.90. (Because the underlying futures contract covers 100 ounces of gold, the total cost of this option would be $10.90 × 100 = $1,090.) The call is an in-the-money option, because the market price of gold exceeds the exercise price on the option. The figures below summarize what happens to both investments if the price of gold increase by $45 an ounce by the expiration date and also what happens if the price of gold drops by $45 an ounce.

	Futures Contract		Futures Option	
	Dollar Profit (or Loss)	Return on Invested Capital	Dollar Profit (or Loss)	Return on Invested Capital
If price of gold *increases* by $45 an ounce	$4,190	310.4%	$3,910	358.7%
If price of gold *decreases* by $45 an ounce	($4,810)	—	($1,090)	—

Clearly, the futures option provides not only a competitive rate of return (in this case, it's even a bit higher), but also a reduced exposure to loss. Futures options offer interesting investment opportunities. As always, *they should be used only by knowledgeable commodities and financial futures investors.*

IN REVIEW

CONCEPTS

15.12 What is the difference between physical *commodities* and *financial futures?* What are their similarities?

15.13 Describe a *currency future* and contrast it with an *interest rate future*. What is a *stock-index future,* and how can it be used by investors?

15.14 Discuss how stock-index futures can be used for speculation and for hedging. What advantages are there to speculating with stock-index futures rather than specific issues of common stock?

15.15 What are *futures options?* Explain how they can be used by speculators. Why would an investor want to use an option on an interest rate futures contract rather than the futures contract itself?

15.16 The *Investing in Action* box on page 650 describes a market phenomenon known as the "triple witching day." Why is it called that, and what are its implications for investors?

Summary

LG 1 **Describe the essential features of a futures contract, and explain how the futures market operates.** Commodities and financial futures are traded in futures markets. Today, there are eight U.S. exchanges that deal in futures contracts, which are commitments to make (or take) delivery of a certain amount of some real or financial asset at a specified date in the future.

LG 2 **Explain the role that hedgers and speculators play in the futures market, including how profits are made and lost.** Futures contracts control large amounts of the underlying commodity or financial instrument. They can produce wide price swings and very attractive rates of return (or very unattractive losses). Such returns (or losses) are further magnified because all trading in the futures market is done on margin. A speculator's profit is derived directly from the wide price fluctuations that occur in the market. Hedgers derive their profit from the protection they gain against adverse price movements.

LG 3 **Describe the commodities segment of the futures market and the basic characteristics of these investment vehicles.** Commodities such as grains, metals, and meat make up the traditional (commodities) segment of the futures market. A large portion of this market is concentrated in the agricultural segment of our economy. There's also a very active market for various metals and petroleum products. As the prices of commodities go up and down in the market, the respective futures contracts behave in much the same way. Thus, if the price of corn goes up, the value of corn futures contracts rises as well.

LG 4 **Discuss the trading strategies that investors can use with commodities, and explain how investment returns are measured.** The trading strategies used with commodities contracts are speculating, spreading, and hedging. Regardless of whether investors are in a long or a short position, they have only one source of return from commodities and financial futures: appreciation (or depreciation) in the price of the contract. Rate of return on invested capital is used to assess the actual or potential profitability of a futures transaction.

LG 5 **Explain the difference between a physical commodity and a financial future, and discuss the growing role of financial futures in the market today.** Whereas commodities deal with physical assets, financial futures deal with financial assets, such as stocks, bonds, and currencies. Though the nature of the underlying assets differs, both are traded in the same place: the futures market. Financial futures are the newcomers, but the volume of trading in financial futures now far exceeds that of commodities.

LG 6 **Discuss the trading techniques that can be used with financial futures, and note how these securities can be used in conjunction with other investment vehicles.** There are three types of financial futures: currency futures, interest rate futures, and stock-index futures. The first type deals in different kinds of foreign currencies. Interest rate futures involve various types of short- and long-term debt instruments. Stock-index futures are pegged to broad movements in the stock market, as measured by such indexes as the S&P 500 and the NYSE Composite Index. These securities can be used for speculating, spreading, or hedging. They hold a special appeal to investors who use them to hedge other security positions. For example, interest rate futures contracts are used to protect bond portfolios against a big jump in market interest rates. Likewise, currency futures are used to hedge the foreign currency exposure that accompanies investments in foreign securities.

Discussion Questions

LG 1

Q15.1 Three of the biggest U.S. commodities exchanges—the CBT, CME, and NYMerc—were identified in this chapter. Other U.S. exchanges and several foreign commodities exchanges are also closely followed in the United States. Obtain a recent copy of the *Wall Street Journal* and look in the "Futures Prices" section of the paper for the futures quotes. As noted in this chapter, futures quotes include the name of the exchange on which a particular contract is traded.

  a. Using these quotes, how many more U.S. *commodities exchanges* can you identify? List them.
  b. Are quotes from *foreign exchanges* listed in the *Wall Street Journal?* If so, list them, too.
  c. For each U.S. and foreign exchange you found in parts (a) and (b), give an example of one or two contracts traded on that exchange. For example: CBT—Chicago Board of Trade: oats and Treasury bonds.

LG 3 **LG 5**

Q15.2 Using settle prices from Figures 15.2 and 15.4, find the value of the following commodity and financial futures contracts.

  a. July soybean oil.
  b. May 2001 corn.
  c. September heating oil.
  d. December British pounds.
  e. September 10-year agency notes.
  f. June S&P 500 Index.

LG 4 **LG 6**

Q15.3 Listed below are a variety of futures transactions. On the basis of the information provided, indicate how much profit or loss you would make in each of the transactions. (*Hint:* You might want to refer to Figures 15.2 and 15.4 for the size of the contract, pricing unit, etc.)

  a. You buy three yen contracts at a quote of 1.0180 and sell them a few months later at 1.0365.
  b. The price of wheat goes up 60 cents a bushel, and you hold three contracts.
  c. You short sell two crude oil contracts at $28.75 a barrel, and the price of crude oil drops to $24.10 a barrel.
  d. You recently purchased a 90-day Treasury bill contract at 94.15, and T-bill interest rates rise to 6.60%.
  e. You short sell S&P 500 contracts when the index is at 1996.55 and cover when the index moves to 1971.95.
  f. You short three corn contracts at $2.34 a bushel, and the price of corn goes to $2.49½ a bushel.

Problems

LG 3

LG 4

P15.1 Jeff Rink considers himself a shrewd commodities investor. Not long ago he bought one July cotton contract at 54 cents a pound, and he recently sold it at 58 cents a pound. How much profit did he make? What was his return on invested capital if he had to put up a $1,500 initial deposit?

LG 4

P15.2 Shirley McCain is a regular commodities speculator. She is currently considering a short position in July oats, which are now trading at 148. Her analysis suggests that July oats should be trading at about 140 in a couple of months. Assuming that her expectations hold up, what kind of return on invested capital will she make if she shorts three July oats contracts (each contract covers 5,000 bushels of oats) by depositing an initial margin of $500 per contract?

LG 5   **LG 6**   P15.3   Mark Seby is thinking about doing some speculating in interest rates. He thinks rates will fall and, in response, the price of Treasury bond futures should move from 92–15, their present quote, to a level of about 98. Given a required margin deposit of $2,700 per contract, what would Mark's return on invested capital be if prices behave as he expects?

 LG 5   **LG 6**   P15.4   Annie Ryan has been an avid stock market investor for years. She manages her portfolio fairly aggressively and likes to short sell whenever the opportunity presents itself. Recently, she has become fascinated with stock-index futures, especially the idea of being able to play the market as a whole. Annie thinks the market is headed down, and she decides to short sell some NYSE Composite stock-index futures. Assume she shorts three contracts at 787.95 and has to make a margin deposit of $16,000 for each contract. How much profit will she make, and what will her return on invested capital be if the market does indeed drop so that the NYSE contracts are trading at 765.00 by the time they expire?

LG 6   P15.5   A wealthy investor holds $500,000 worth of U.S. Treasury bonds. These bonds are currently being quoted at 105% of par. The investor is concerned, however, that rates are headed up over the next 6 months, and he would like to do something to protect this bond portfolio. His broker advises him to set up a hedge using T-bond futures contracts. Assume these contracts are now trading at 111–06.

 a. Briefly describe how the investor would set up this hedge. Would he go long or short? How many contracts would he need?
 b. It's now 6 months later, and rates have indeed gone up. The investor's Treasury bonds are now being quoted at 93½, and the T-bond futures contracts used in the hedge are now trading at 98–00. Show what has happened to the value of the bond portfolio and the profit (or loss) made on the futures hedge.
 c. Was this a successful hedge? Explain.

LG 6   P15.6   Not long ago, Vanessa Woods sold her company for several million dollars (after taxes). She took some of that money and put it into the stock market. Today, Vanessa's portfolio of blue-chip stocks is worth $3.8 million. Vanessa wants to keep her portfolio intact, but she's concerned about a developing weakness in the market for blue chips. She decides, therefore, to hedge her position with 6-month futures contracts on the Dow Jones Industrial Average (DJIA), which are currently trading at 12960.

 a. Why would she choose to hedge her portfolio with the DJIA rather than the S&P 500?
 b. Given that Vanessa wants to cover the full $3.8 million in her portfolio, describe how she would go about setting up this hedge.
 c. If each contract required a margin deposit of $5,000, how much money would she need to set up this hedge?
 d. Assume that over the next 6 months stock prices do fall, and the value of Vanessa's portfolio drops to $3.3 million. If DJIA futures contracts are trading at 11400, how much will she make (or lose) on the futures hedge? Is it enough to offset the loss in her portfolio? That is, what is her net profit or loss on the hedge?
 e. Will she now get her margin deposit back, or is that a "sunk cost"—gone forever?

 LG 6   P15.7   An American currency speculator feels strongly that the value of the Canadian dollar is going to fall relative to the U.S. dollar over the short run. If he wants to profit from these expectations, what kind of position (long or short) should he take in Canadian dollar futures contracts? How much money would he make from each contract if Canadian dollar futures contracts moved from an initial quote of 0.6775 to an ending quote of 0.6250?

LG 6

P15.8 With regard to futures options, how much profit would an investor make if she bought a call option on gold at 7.20 when gold was trading at $482 an ounce, given that the price of gold went up to $525 an ounce by the expiration date on the call? (*Note:* Assume the call carried a strike price of 480.)

Case Problem 15.1   *T.J.'s Fast Track Investments: Interest Rate Futures*

LG 5   LG 6

T.J. Patrick is a young, successful industrial designer in Portland, Oregon, who enjoys the excitement of commodities speculation. T.J. has been dabbling in commodities since he was a teenager—he was introduced to this market by his dad, who is a grain buyer for one of the leading food processors. T.J. recognizes the enormous risks involved in commodities speculating but feels that because he's young, he can afford to take a few chances. As a principal in a thriving industrial design firm, T.J. earns more than $100,000 a year. He follows a well-disciplined investment program and annually adds $15,000 to $20,000 to his portfolio.

Recently, T.J. has started playing with financial futures—interest rate futures, to be exact. He admits he is no expert in interest rates, but he likes the price action these investment vehicles offer. This all started several months ago, when T.J. met Vinnie Banano, a broker who specializes in financial futures, at a party. T.J. liked what Vinnie had to say (mostly how you couldn't go wrong with interest-rate futures) and soon set up a trading account with Vinnie's firm, Banano's of Portland.

The other day, Vinnie called T.J. and suggested he get into T-bill futures. As Vinnie saw it, interest rates were going to continue to head up at a brisk pace, and T.J. should short sell some 90-day T-bill futures. In particular, Vinnie thinks that rates on T-bills should go up by another half-point (moving from about 5½% up to 6%), and he recommends that T.J. short four contracts. This would be a $4,000 investment, because each contract requires an initial margin deposit of $1,000.

Questions

a. Assume 90-day T-bill futures are now being quoted at 94.35.
1. Determine the current price (underlying value) of this T-bill futures contract.
2. What would this futures contract be quoted at if Vinnie is right and the yield goes up by ½ of 1%?

b. How much profit will T.J. make if he shorts four contracts at 94.35 and T-bill yields do go up by ½ of 1% (that is, if T.J. covers his short position when T-bill futures contracts are quoted at 93.85)? Also, calculate the return on invested capital from this transaction.

c. What happens if rates go down? For example, how much will T. J. make if the yield on T-bill futures goes down by just ¾ of 1%?

d. What risks do you see in the recommended short-sale transaction? What is your assessment of T. J.'s new interest in financial futures? How do you think it compares to his established commodities investment program?

Case Problem 15.2   *Jim and Polly Pernelli Try Hedging with Stock-Index Futures*

LG 5   LG 6

Jim Pernelli and his wife, Polly, live in Augusta, Georgia. Like many young couples, the Pernellis are a two-income family. Jim and Polly are both college graduates and hold well-paying jobs. Jim has been an avid investor in the stock market for a number of years and over time has built up a portfolio that is currently worth nearly $275,000.

The Pernellis' portfolio is well diversified, although it is heavily weighted in high-quality, mid-cap growth stocks. The Pernellis reinvest all dividends and regularly add investment capital to their portfolio. Up to now, they have avoided short selling and do only a modest amount of margin trading.

Their portfolio has undergone a substantial amount of capital appreciation in the last 18 months or so, and Jim is eager to protect the profit they have earned. And that's the problem: Jim feels the market has pretty much run its course and is about to enter a period of decline. He has studied the market and economic news very carefully and does not believe the retreat will be of a major magnitude or cover an especially long period of time. He feels fairly certain, however, that most, if not all, of the stocks in his portfolio will be adversely affected by these market conditions—though some will drop more in price than others.

Jim has been following stock-index futures for some time and believes he knows the ins and outs of these securities pretty well. After careful deliberation, Jim and Polly decide to use stock-index futures—in particular, the S&P MidCap 400 futures contract—as a way to protect (hedge) their portfolio of common stocks.

Questions

a.   Explain why the Pernellis would want to use stock-index futures to hedge their stock portfolio, and how they would go about setting up such a hedge. Be specific.

    1. What alternatives do Jim and Polly have to protect the capital value of their portfolio?

    2. What are the benefits and risks of using stock-index futures as hedging vehicles?

 b.   Assume that S&P MidCap 400 futures contracts are currently being quoted at 525.60. How many contracts would the Pernellis have to buy (or sell) to set up the hedge?

    1. Say the value of the Pernelli portfolio dropped 12% over the course of the market retreat. To what price must the stock-index futures contract move in order to cover that loss?

    2. Given that a $12,500 margin deposit is required to buy or sell a single S&P 400 futures contract, what would be the Pernellis' return on invested capital if the price of the futures contract changed by the amount computed in part (b1)?

c.   Assume that the value of the Pernelli portfolio declined by $52,000, while the price of an S&P 400 futures contract moved from 525.60 to 447.60. (Assume that Jim and Polly short sold one futures contract to set up the hedge.)

    1. Add the profit from the hedge transaction to the new (depreciated) value of the stock portfolio. How does this amount compare to the $275,000 portfolio that existed just before the market started its retreat?

    2. Why did the stock-index futures hedge fail to give complete protection to the Pernelli portfolio? Is it possible to obtain *perfect* (dollar-for-dollar) protection from these types of hedges? Explain.

d.   What if, instead of hedging with futures contracts, the Pernellis decide to set up the hedge by using *futures options?* Unfortunately, no futures options are currently available on the S&P MidCap 400 Index, but let's say there are. (Assume that these future options, like their underlying futures contracts, are valued/priced at $500 times the premiums.) Now, suppose a put on the S&P MidCap 400 futures contract (with a strike price of 525) is currently quoted at 5.80, and a comparable call is quoted at 2.35. Use the same portfolio and futures price conditions as set out in part (c) to determine how well the portfolio would be protected. (*Hint:* Add the net profit from the hedge to the new depreciated value of the stock portfolio.) What are the advantages and disadvantages of using futures options, rather than the stock-index futures contract itself, to hedge a stock portfolio?

Web Exercises

W15.1   Visit the Chicago Board of Trade at www.cbot.com. Go to [Knowledge Center], [Contract Specs].
a. What agricultural, financial, and miscellaneous contracts are traded on the CBOT?
b. What deliverable grades, contract months, and delivery methods are specified for gold 100-ounce futures contracts?

W15.2   Visit the Chicago Board of Trade at www.cbot.com. Check out [Knowledge Center], [FAQ]. Answer the following questions:
a. What is the difference between a stock exchange and a futures exchange?
b. Why do we need futures markets?
c. What are hedging and speculating?
d. What kind of economic indicators do traders watch in the agriculture (Ag.) and the financial markets?
e. How many other futures exchanges are there worldwide?

W15.3   Agricultural commodity futures, foreign currency futures, interest rate futures, and index futures are traded on the Chicago Mercantile Exchange (CME). Visit http://www.cme.com/education/courses/interactive_features/education_courses_interactivefeatures_webinstantlessons.cfm and click on [Contracts Traded].
a. From information you find there, describe which index futures are traded on the CME.
b. Why are stock index futures very popular and highly traded contracts?

W15.4   Visit www.cbot.com and go to [Knowledge Center], [Contract Specs]. Look at the futures and options that are available for the Dow Jones Industrial Average. Describe the DJIA Futures Contract in terms of trading unit, contract months, last delivery day, and settlement.

W15.5   Assume that a trader is long in 30-year U.S. T-bonds in the cash market.
a. What is this person concerned about in the near term?
b. Visit the futures market at www.cbot.com. Click on [Quotes and Data], [Financial Futures], [30-Year U.S. Treasury Bonds]. What position should this person establish in the futures market?

For additional practice with concepts from this chapter, visit

www.awl.com/gitman_joehnk

CFA EXAM QUESTIONS

Derivative Securities

Following is a sample of 12 Level-I CFA exam questions that deal with many of the topics covered in Chapters 14 and 15 of this text, including basic properties of options and futures, pricing characteristics, return behavior, and various option strategies.

1. The open interest on a futures contract at any given time is the total number of outstanding:
   a. contracts.
   b. unhedged positions.
   c. clearinghouse positions.
   d. long and short positions.

2. A silver futures contract requires the seller to deliver 5,000 Troy ounces of silver. An investor sells one July silver futures contract at a price of $8 per ounce, posting a $2,025 initial margin. If the required maintenance margin is $1,500, the price per ounce at which the investor would first receive a maintenance margin call is *closest to*:
   a. $5.92.
   b. $7.89.
   c. $8.11.
   d. $10.80.

3. Most futures contracts are closed through:
   a. delivery.
   b. arbitrage.
   c. reversing trades.
   d. exchange-for-physicals.

4. A call is "in-the-money" when:
   a. the stock price is above the exercise price.
   b. the stock price is below the exercise price.
   c. the stock price and the exercise price are equal.
   d. not enough information to tell.

5. The following price quotations are for exchange-listed options on Primo Corporation common stock.

Company	Strike	Expiration	Call	Put
65⅛	60	Feb	7¼	⁷⁄₁₆

Ignoring transaction costs , how much would a buyer have to pay for one call option contract?
   a. $7.25.
   b. $72.50.
   c. $398.75.
   d. $725.00.

6. The following diagram shows the value of a put option at expiration:

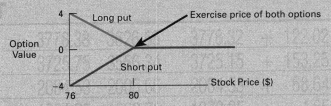

Ignoring transaction costs, which of the following statements about the value of the put option at expiration is **TRUE?**
   a. The value of the short position in the put is $4 if the stock price is $76.
   b. The value of the long position in the put is −$4 if the stock price is $76.
   c. The long put has value when the stock price is below the $80 exercise price.
   d. The value of the short position in the put is zero for stock prices equaling or exceeding $76.

7. Which of the following statements describing options is false?
a. A put option gives its holder the right to sell an asset for a specified price on or before the option's expiration date.
b. A call option will be exercised only if the market value of the underlying asset is more than the exercise price.
c. A put option's profit increases when the value of the underlying asset increases.
d. A put option will be exercised only if the market value of the underlying asset is less than the exercise price.

8. A put on Stock X with a strike price of $40 is priced at $2.00 per share, while a call with a strike price of $40 is priced at $3.50. What is the maximum per share *loss* to the *writer* of the uncovered put and the maximum per share *gain* to the *writer* of the uncovered call?

	Maximum Loss to Put Writer	Maximum Gain to Call Writer
a.	$38.00	$ 3.50
b.	$38.00	$36.50
c.	$40.00	$ 3.50
d.	$40.00	$40.00

9. An investor buys a call option with a $25 exercise price priced at $4 and writes a call option with a $40 exercise price priced at $2.50. If the price of the stock increases to $50 at expiration and the options are exercised on the expiration date, the net profit at expiration (ignoring transaction costs) is:
a. $ 8.50.
b. $13.50.
c. $16.50.
d. $23.50.

10. An investor purchases stock for $38/share and sells call options on that stock with an exercise price of $40 for a premium of $3/share. Ignoring dividends and transactions, what *maximum* profit can the investor earn if the position is held to expiration?
a. $2.
b. $3.
c. $5.
d. None of the above.

11. The current price of an asset is 75. A three-month, at-the-money call option on the asset has a current value of 5. At what value of the asset will a covered call writer break even at expiration?
a. $70.
b. $75.
c. $80.
d. $85.

12. An at-the-money protective put position (comprising owning the stock and buying a put):
a. protects against loss at any stock price below the strike price of the put.
b. has limited profit potential when the stock price rises.
c. returns any increase in the stock's value, dollar for dollar, less the cost of the put.
d. provides a pattern of returns similar to a stop loss order at the current stock price.

Congratulations!

As a student purchasing Fundamentals of Investing, Eighth Edition, *you are entitled to pre-paid access to the downloadable student study software on the text's Companion Web Site!*

FUNDAMENTALS OF INVESTING
GITMAN · JOEHNK

The software includes:

- Interactive calculations of virtually all the formulas, ratios, and valuation procedures presented in the book.
- A new animated calculator tutorial, which mimics the HP 12c, HP 10b, and TI BA II Plus financial calculators.
- Graphing for key modules so you can see a visual representation of the problem.

The duration of your subscription is 6 months.

To activate your prepaid subscription:
1. Point your Web browser to www.aw.com/gitman_joehnk
2. Click on "Student Software"
3. Select the "Register Here" link
4. Enter your preassigned Access Code, exactly as it appears below

5. Select "Submit"
6. Complete the online registration form to establish your personal User ID and Password
7. Once your personal User ID and Password are confirmed, you can begin downloading and using the Gitman/Joehnk student software!

This Access Code can only be used once to establish a subscription. This subscription to the Gitman/Joehnk software portion of the Companion Web Site is valid for six months upon activation and is not transferable.

If you did not purchase this product new and in a shrink-wrapped package, this Access Code may not be valid!

Is something missing?

If the tear-out card is missing from this book, then you're missing out on an important part of your learning package. Choose to buy a new text book.

Play the
STUDENT INVESTMENT
MANAGEMENT GAME.
Ask your professor how.

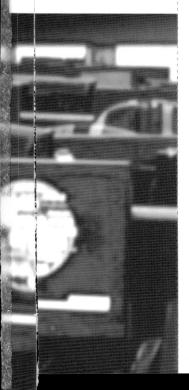

Play the Stock Market with SIMGame!

The Student Investment Management Game allows you to learn about investing in the Stock Market without risking your own money.

Ask your professor how you can play SIMGame!

FINANCIAL TABLES

TABLE A.1   Future-Value Interest Factors for One Dollar, *FVIF*

Period	1%	2%	3%	4%	5%	6%	7%	8%	9%	10%	11%	12%	13%	14%	15%	16%	17%	18%	19%	20%
1	1.010	1.020	1.030	1.040	1.050	1.060	1.070	1.080	1.090	1.100	1.110	1.120	1.130	1.140	1.150	1.160	1.170	1.180	1.190	1.200
2	1.020	1.040	1.061	1.082	1.102	1.124	1.145	1.166	1.188	1.210	1.232	1.254	1.277	1.300	1.322	1.346	1.369	1.392	1.416	1.440
3	1.030	1.061	1.093	1.125	1.158	1.191	1.225	1.260	1.295	1.331	1.368	1.405	1.443	1.482	1.521	1.561	1.602	1.643	1.685	1.728
4	1.041	1.082	1.126	1.170	1.216	1.262	1.311	1.360	1.412	1.464	1.518	1.574	1.630	1.689	1.749	1.811	1.874	1.939	2.005	2.074
5	1.051	1.104	1.159	1.217	1.276	1.338	1.403	1.469	1.539	1.611	1.685	1.762	1.842	1.925	2.011	2.100	2.192	2.288	2.386	2.488
6	1.062	1.126	1.194	1.265	1.340	1.419	1.501	1.587	1.677	1.772	1.870	1.974	2.082	2.195	2.313	2.436	2.565	2.700	2.840	2.986
7	1.072	1.149	1.230	1.316	1.407	1.504	1.606	1.714	1.828	1.949	2.076	2.211	2.353	2.502	2.660	2.826	3.001	3.185	3.379	3.583
8	1.083	1.172	1.267	1.369	1.477	1.594	1.718	1.851	1.993	2.144	2.305	2.476	2.658	2.853	3.059	3.278	3.511	3.759	4.021	4.300
9	1.094	1.195	1.305	1.423	1.551	1.689	1.838	1.999	2.172	2.358	2.558	2.773	3.004	3.252	3.518	3.803	4.108	4.435	4.785	5.160
10	1.105	1.219	1.344	1.480	1.629	1.791	1.967	2.159	2.367	2.594	2.839	3.106	3.395	3.707	4.046	4.411	4.807	5.234	5.695	6.192
11	1.116	1.243	1.384	1.539	1.710	1.898	2.105	2.332	2.580	2.853	3.152	3.479	3.836	4.226	4.652	5.117	5.624	6.176	6.777	7.430
12	1.127	1.268	1.426	1.601	1.796	2.012	2.252	2.518	2.813	3.138	3.498	3.896	4.334	4.818	5.350	5.936	6.580	7.288	8.064	8.916
13	1.138	1.294	1.469	1.665	1.886	2.133	2.410	2.720	3.066	3.452	3.883	4.363	4.898	5.492	6.153	6.886	7.699	8.599	9.596	10.699
14	1.149	1.319	1.513	1.732	1.980	2.261	2.579	2.937	3.342	3.797	4.310	4.887	5.535	6.261	7.076	7.987	9.007	10.147	11.420	12.839
15	1.161	1.346	1.558	1.801	2.079	2.397	2.759	3.172	3.642	4.177	4.785	5.474	6.254	7.138	8.137	9.265	10.539	11.974	13.589	15.407
16	1.173	1.373	1.605	1.873	2.183	2.540	2.952	3.426	3.970	4.595	5.311	6.130	7.067	8.137	9.358	10.748	12.330	14.129	16.171	18.488
17	1.184	1.400	1.653	1.948	2.292	2.693	3.159	3.700	4.328	5.054	5.895	6.866	7.986	9.276	10.761	12.468	14.426	16.672	19.244	22.186
18	1.196	1.428	1.702	2.026	2.407	2.854	3.380	3.996	4.717	5.560	6.543	7.690	9.024	10.575	12.375	14.462	16.879	19.673	22.900	26.623
19	1.208	1.457	1.753	2.107	2.527	3.026	3.616	4.316	5.142	6.116	7.263	8.613	10.197	12.055	14.232	16.776	19.748	23.214	27.251	31.948
20	1.220	1.486	1.806	2.191	2.653	3.207	3.870	4.661	5.604	6.727	8.062	9.646	11.523	13.743	16.366	19.461	23.105	27.393	32.429	38.337
21	1.232	1.516	1.860	2.279	2.786	3.399	4.140	5.034	6.109	7.400	8.949	10.804	13.021	15.667	18.821	22.574	27.033	32.323	38.591	46.005
22	1.245	1.546	1.916	2.370	2.925	3.603	4.430	5.436	6.658	8.140	9.933	12.100	14.713	17.861	21.644	26.186	31.629	38.141	45.923	55.205
23	1.257	1.577	1.974	2.465	3.071	3.820	4.740	5.871	7.258	8.954	11.026	13.552	16.626	20.361	24.891	30.376	37.005	45.007	54.648	66.247
24	1.270	1.608	2.033	2.563	3.225	4.049	5.072	6.341	7.911	9.850	12.239	15.178	18.788	23.212	28.625	35.236	43.296	53.108	65.031	79.496
25	1.282	1.641	2.094	2.666	3.386	4.292	5.427	6.848	8.623	10.834	13.585	17.000	21.230	26.461	32.918	40.874	50.656	62.667	77.387	95.395
30	1.348	1.811	2.427	3.243	4.322	5.743	7.612	10.062	13.267	17.449	22.892	29.960	39.115	50.949	66.210	85.849	111.061	143.367	184.672	237.373
35	1.417	2.000	2.814	3.946	5.516	7.686	10.676	14.785	20.413	28.102	38.574	52.799	72.066	98.097	133.172	180.311	243.495	327.988	440.691	590.657
40	1.489	2.208	3.262	4.801	7.040	10.285	14.974	21.724	31.408	45.258	64.999	93.049	132.776	188.876	267.856	378.715	533.846	750.353	1051.642	1469.740
45	1.565	2.438	3.781	5.841	8.985	13.764	21.002	31.920	48.325	72.888	109.527	163.985	244.629	363.662	538.752	795.429	1170.425	1716.619	2509.583	3657.176
50	1.645	2.691	4.384	7.106	11.467	18.419	29.456	46.900	74.354	117.386	184.559	288.996	450.711	700.197	1083.619	1670.669	2566.080	3927.189	5988.730	9100.191

Using the Calculator to Compute the Future Value of a Single Amount

Before you begin, clear the memory, ensure that you are in the *end mode* and that your calculator is set for *one payment per year*, and set the number of decimal places that you want (usually two for dollar-related accuracy).

Sample Problem

You place $800 in a savings account at 6% compounded annually. What is your account balance at the end of 5 years?

Hewlett-Packard HP 12C, 17 BII, and 19 BII[a]

Input	Function
800	PV
5	N
6	I%YR
	FV

Solution
(1070.58)[b]

---

[a] For the 12C, you would use the n key instead of the N key, and the i key instead of the I%YR key.

[b] The minus sign that precedes the output should be ignored.

TABLE A.1 *(Continued)*

Period	21%	22%	23%	24%	25%	26%	27%	28%	29%	30%	31%	32%	33%	34%	35%	40%	45%	50%
1	1.210	1.220	1.230	1.240	1.250	1.260	1.270	1.280	1.290	1.300	1.310	1.320	1.330	1.340	1.350	1.400	1.450	1.500
2	1.464	1.488	1.513	1.538	1.562	1.588	1.613	1.638	1.664	1.690	1.716	1.742	1.769	1.796	1.822	1.960	2.102	2.250
3	1.772	1.816	1.861	1.907	1.953	2.000	2.048	2.097	2.147	2.197	2.248	2.300	2.353	2.406	2.460	2.744	3.049	3.375
4	2.144	2.215	2.289	2.364	2.441	2.520	2.601	2.684	2.769	2.856	2.945	3.036	3.129	3.224	3.321	3.842	4.421	5.063
5	2.594	2.703	2.815	2.932	3.052	3.176	3.304	3.436	3.572	3.713	3.858	4.007	4.162	4.320	4.484	5.378	6.410	7.594
6	3.138	3.297	3.463	3.635	3.815	4.001	4.196	4.398	4.608	4.827	5.054	5.290	5.535	5.789	6.053	7.530	9.294	11.391
7	3.797	4.023	4.259	4.508	4.768	5.042	5.329	5.629	5.945	6.275	6.621	6.983	7.361	7.758	8.172	10.541	13.476	17.086
8	4.595	4.908	5.239	5.589	5.960	6.353	6.767	7.206	7.669	8.157	8.673	9.217	9.791	10.395	11.032	14.758	19.541	25.629
9	5.560	5.987	6.444	6.931	7.451	8.004	8.595	9.223	9.893	10.604	11.362	12.166	13.022	13.930	14.894	20.661	28.334	38.443
10	6.727	7.305	7.926	8.594	9.313	10.086	10.915	11.806	12.761	13.786	14.884	16.060	17.319	18.666	20.106	28.925	41.085	57.665
11	8.140	8.912	9.749	10.657	11.642	12.708	13.862	15.112	16.462	17.921	19.498	21.199	23.034	25.012	27.144	40.495	59.573	86.498
12	9.850	10.872	11.991	13.215	14.552	16.012	17.605	19.343	21.236	23.298	25.542	27.982	30.635	33.516	36.644	56.694	86.380	129.746
13	11.918	13.264	14.749	16.386	18.190	20.175	22.359	24.759	27.395	30.287	33.460	36.937	40.745	44.912	49.469	79.371	125.251	194.620
14	14.421	16.182	18.141	20.319	22.737	25.420	28.395	31.691	35.339	39.373	43.832	48.756	54.190	60.181	66.784	111.119	181.614	291.929
15	17.449	19.742	22.314	25.195	28.422	32.030	36.062	40.565	45.587	51.185	57.420	64.358	72.073	80.643	90.158	155.567	263.341	437.894
16	21.113	24.085	27.446	31.242	35.527	40.357	45.799	51.923	58.808	66.541	75.220	84.953	95.857	108.061	121.713	217.793	381.844	656.841
17	25.547	29.384	33.758	38.740	44.409	50.850	58.165	66.461	75.862	86.503	98.539	112.138	127.490	144.802	164.312	304.911	553.674	985.261
18	30.912	35.848	41.523	48.038	55.511	64.071	73.869	85.070	97.862	112.454	129.086	148.022	169.561	194.035	221.822	426.875	802.826	1477.892
19	37.404	43.735	51.073	59.567	69.389	80.730	93.813	108.890	126.242	146.190	169.102	195.389	225.517	260.006	299.459	597.625	1164.098	2216.838
20	45.258	53.357	62.820	73.863	86.736	101.720	119.143	139.379	162.852	190.047	221.523	257.913	299.937	348.408	404.270	836.674	1687.942	3325.257
21	54.762	65.095	77.268	91.591	108.420	128.167	151.312	178.405	210.079	247.061	290.196	340.446	398.916	466.867	545.764	1171.343	2447.515	4987.883
22	66.262	79.416	95.040	113.572	135.525	161.490	192.165	228.358	271.002	321.178	380.156	449.388	530.558	625.601	736.781	1639.878	3548.896	7481.824
23	80.178	96.887	116.899	140.829	169.407	203.477	244.050	292.298	349.592	417.531	498.004	593.192	705.642	838.305	994.653	2295.829	5145.898	11222.738
24	97.015	118.203	143.786	174.628	211.758	256.381	309.943	374.141	450.974	542.791	652.385	783.013	938.504	1123.328	1342.781	3214.158	7461.547	16834.109
25	117.388	144.207	176.857	216.539	264.698	323.040	393.628	478.901	581.756	705.627	854.623	1033.577	1248.210	1505.258	1812.754	4499.816	10819.242	25251.164
30	304.471	389.748	497.904	634.810	807.793	1025.904	1300.477	1645.488	2078.208	2619.936	3297.081	4142.008	5194.516	6503.285	8128.426	24201.043	69348.375	191751.000
35	789.716	1053.370	1401.749	1861.020	2465.189	3258.053	4296.547	5653.840	7423.988	9727.598	12719.918	16598.906	21617.363	28096.695	36448.051	130158.687	*	*
40	2048.309	2846.941	3946.340	5455.797	7523.156	10346.879	14195.051	19426.418	26520.723	36117.754	49072.621	66519.313	89962.188	121388.437	163433.875	700022.688	*	*
45	5312.758	7694.418	11110.121	15994.316	22958.844	32859.457	46897.973	66748.500	94739.937	134102.187	*	*	*	*	*	*	*	*
50	13779.844	20795.680	31278.301	46889.207	70064.812	104354.562	154942.687	229345.875	338440.000	497910.125	*	*	*	*	*	*	*	*

*Not shown because of space limitations.

Texas Instruments BA-35, BAII, BAII Plus[c]

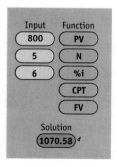

Input	Function
800	PV
5	N
6	%i
	CPT
	FV

Solution
(1070.58)[d]

---

[c] For the Texas Instruments BAII, you would use the **2nd** key instead of the **CPT** key; for the Texas Instruments BAII Plus, you would use the **I/Y** key instead of the **%i** key.
[d] If a minus sign precedes the output, it should be ignored.

TABLE A.2   Future-Value Interest Factors for a One-Dollar Annuity, *FVIFA*

Period	1%	2%	3%	4%	5%	6%	7%	8%	9%	10%	11%	12%	13%	14%	15%	16%	17%	18%	19%	20%
1	1.000	1.000	1.000	1.000	1.000	1.000	1.000	1.000	1.000	1.000	1.000	1.000	1.000	1.000	1.000	1.000	1.000	1.000	1.000	1.000
2	2.010	2.020	2.030	2.040	2.050	2.060	2.070	2.080	2.090	2.100	2.110	2.120	2.130	2.140	2.150	2.160	2.170	2.180	2.190	2.200
3	3.030	3.060	3.091	3.122	3.152	3.184	3.215	3.246	3.278	3.310	3.342	3.374	3.407	3.440	3.472	3.506	3.539	3.572	3.606	3.640
4	4.060	4.122	4.184	4.246	4.310	4.375	4.440	4.506	4.573	4.641	4.710	4.779	4.850	4.921	4.993	5.066	5.141	5.215	5.291	5.368
5	5.101	5.204	5.309	5.416	5.526	5.637	5.751	5.867	5.985	6.105	6.228	6.353	6.480	6.610	6.742	6.877	7.014	7.154	7.297	7.442
6	6.152	6.308	6.468	6.633	6.802	6.975	7.153	7.336	7.523	7.716	7.913	8.115	8.323	8.535	8.754	8.977	9.207	9.442	9.683	9.930
7	7.214	7.434	7.662	7.898	8.142	8.394	8.654	8.923	9.200	9.487	9.783	10.089	10.405	10.730	11.067	11.414	11.772	12.141	12.523	12.916
8	8.286	8.583	8.892	9.214	9.549	9.897	10.260	10.637	11.028	11.436	11.859	12.300	12.757	13.233	13.727	14.240	14.773	15.327	15.902	16.499
9	9.368	9.755	10.159	10.583	11.027	11.491	11.978	12.488	13.021	13.579	14.164	14.776	15.416	16.085	16.786	17.518	18.285	19.086	19.923	20.799
10	10.462	10.950	11.464	12.006	12.578	13.181	13.816	14.487	15.193	15.937	16.722	17.549	18.420	19.337	20.304	21.321	22.393	23.521	24.709	25.959
11	11.567	12.169	12.808	13.486	14.207	14.972	15.784	16.645	17.560	18.531	19.561	20.655	21.814	23.044	24.349	25.733	27.200	28.755	30.403	32.150
12	12.682	13.412	14.192	15.026	15.917	16.870	17.888	18.977	20.141	21.384	22.713	24.133	25.650	27.271	29.001	30.850	32.824	34.931	37.180	39.580
13	13.809	14.680	15.618	16.627	17.713	18.882	20.141	21.495	22.953	24.523	26.211	28.029	29.984	32.088	34.352	36.786	39.404	42.218	45.244	48.496
14	14.947	15.974	17.086	18.292	19.598	21.015	22.550	24.215	26.019	27.975	30.095	32.392	34.882	37.581	40.504	43.672	47.102	50.818	54.841	59.196
15	16.097	17.293	18.599	20.023	21.578	23.276	25.129	27.152	29.361	31.772	34.405	37.280	40.417	43.842	47.580	51.659	56.109	60.965	66.260	72.035
16	17.258	18.639	20.157	21.824	23.657	25.672	27.888	30.324	33.003	35.949	39.190	42.753	46.671	50.980	55.717	60.925	66.648	72.938	79.850	87.442
17	18.430	20.012	21.761	23.697	25.840	28.213	30.840	33.750	36.973	40.544	44.500	48.883	53.738	59.117	65.075	71.673	78.978	87.067	96.021	105.930
18	19.614	21.412	23.414	25.645	28.132	30.905	33.999	37.450	41.301	45.599	50.396	55.749	61.724	68.393	75.836	84.140	93.404	103.739	115.265	128.116
19	20.811	22.840	25.117	27.671	30.539	33.760	37.379	41.446	46.018	51.158	56.939	63.439	70.748	78.968	88.211	98.603	110.283	123.412	138.165	154.739
20	22.019	24.297	26.870	29.778	33.066	36.785	40.995	45.762	51.159	57.274	64.202	72.052	80.946	91.024	102.443	115.379	130.031	146.626	165.417	186.687
21	23.239	25.783	28.676	31.969	35.719	39.992	44.865	50.422	56.764	64.002	72.264	81.698	92.468	104.767	118.809	134.840	153.136	174.019	197.846	225.024
22	24.471	27.299	30.536	34.248	38.505	43.392	49.005	55.456	62.872	71.402	81.213	92.502	105.489	120.434	137.630	157.414	180.169	206.342	236.436	271.028
23	25.716	28.845	32.452	36.618	41.430	46.995	53.435	60.893	69.531	79.542	91.147	104.602	120.203	138.295	159.274	183.600	211.798	244.483	282.359	326.234
24	26.973	30.421	34.426	39.082	44.501	50.815	58.176	66.764	76.789	88.496	102.173	118.154	136.829	158.656	184.166	213.976	248.803	289.490	337.007	392.480
25	28.243	32.030	36.459	41.645	47.726	54.864	63.248	73.105	84.699	98.346	114.412	133.333	155.616	181.867	212.790	249.212	292.099	342.598	402.038	471.976
30	34.784	40.567	47.575	56.084	66.438	79.057	94.459	113.282	136.305	164.491	199.018	241.330	293.192	356.778	434.738	530.306	647.423	790.932	966.698	1181.865
35	41.659	49.994	60.461	73.651	90.318	111.432	138.234	172.314	215.705	271.018	341.583	431.658	546.663	693.552	881.152	1120.699	1426.448	1816.607	2314.173	2948.294
40	48.885	60.401	75.400	95.024	120.797	154.758	199.630	259.052	337.872	442.580	581.812	767.080	1013.667	1341.979	1779.048	2360.724	3134.412	4163.094	5529.711	7343.715
45	56.479	71.891	92.718	121.027	159.695	212.737	285.741	386.497	525.840	718.881	986.613	1358.208	1874.086	2590.464	3585.031	4965.191	6879.008	9531.258	13203.105	18280.914
50	64.461	84.577	112.794	152.664	209.341	290.325	406.516	573.756	815.051	1163.865	1668.723	2399.975	3459.344	4994.301	7217.488	10435.449	15088.805	21812.273	31514.492	45496.094

Using the Calculator to Compute the Future Value of an Annuity

Before you begin, clear the memory, ensure that you are in the *end mode* and that your calculator is set for *one payment per year*, and set the number of decimal places that you want (usually two for dollar-related accuracy).

Sample Problem

You want to know what the future value will be at the end of 5 years if you place five end-of-year deposits of $1,000 in an account paying 7% annually. What is your account balance at the end of 5 years?

Hewlett-Packard HP 12C, 17 BII, and 19 BII[a]

Input	Function
1000	PMT
5	N
7	I%YR
	FV

Solution
(5750.74)[b]

---

[a] For the 12C, you would use the n key instead of the N key, and the i key instead of the I%YR key.

[b] The minus sign that precedes the output should be ignored.

TABLE A.2 (Continued)

Period	21%	22%	23%	24%	25%	26%	27%	28%	29%	30%	31%	32%	33%	34%	35%	40%	45%	50%
1	1.000	1.000	1.000	1.000	1.000	1.000	1.000	1.000	1.000	1.000	1.000	1.000	1.000	1.000	1.000	1.000	1.000	1.000
2	2.210	2.220	2.230	2.240	2.250	2.260	2.270	2.280	2.290	2.300	2.310	2.320	2.330	2.340	2.350	2.400	2.450	2.500
3	3.674	3.708	3.743	3.778	3.813	3.848	3.883	3.918	3.954	3.990	4.026	4.062	4.099	4.136	4.172	4.360	4.552	4.750
4	5.446	5.524	5.604	5.684	5.766	5.848	5.931	6.016	6.101	6.187	6.274	6.362	6.452	6.542	6.633	7.104	7.601	8.125
5	7.589	7.740	7.893	8.048	8.207	8.368	8.533	8.700	8.870	9.043	9.219	9.398	9.581	9.766	9.954	10.946	12.022	13.188
6	10.183	10.442	10.708	10.980	11.259	11.544	11.837	12.136	12.442	12.756	13.077	13.406	13.742	14.086	14.438	16.324	18.431	20.781
7	13.321	13.740	14.171	14.615	15.073	15.546	16.032	16.534	17.051	17.583	18.131	18.696	19.277	19.876	20.492	23.853	27.725	32.172
8	17.119	17.762	18.430	19.123	19.842	20.588	21.361	22.163	22.995	23.858	24.752	25.678	26.638	27.633	28.664	34.395	41.202	49.258
9	21.714	22.670	23.669	24.712	25.802	26.940	28.129	29.369	30.664	32.015	33.425	34.895	36.429	38.028	39.696	49.152	60.743	74.887
10	27.274	28.657	30.113	31.643	33.253	34.945	36.723	38.592	40.556	42.619	44.786	47.062	49.451	51.958	54.590	69.813	89.077	113.330
11	34.001	35.962	38.039	40.238	42.566	45.030	47.639	50.398	53.318	56.405	59.670	63.121	66.769	70.624	74.696	98.739	130.161	170.995
12	42.141	44.873	47.787	50.895	54.208	57.738	61.501	65.510	69.780	74.326	79.167	84.320	89.803	95.636	101.840	139.234	189.734	257.493
13	51.991	55.745	59.778	64.109	68.760	73.750	79.106	84.853	91.016	97.624	104.709	112.302	120.438	129.152	138.484	195.928	276.114	387.239
14	63.909	69.009	74.528	80.496	86.949	93.925	101.465	109.611	118.411	127.912	138.169	149.239	161.183	174.063	187.953	275.299	401.365	581.858
15	78.330	85.191	92.669	100.815	109.687	119.346	129.860	141.302	153.750	167.285	182.001	197.996	215.373	234.245	254.737	386.418	582.980	873.788
16	95.779	104.933	114.983	126.010	138.109	151.375	165.922	181.867	199.337	218.470	239.421	262.354	287.446	314.888	344.895	541.985	846.321	1311.681
17	116.892	129.019	142.428	157.252	173.636	191.733	211.721	233.790	258.145	285.011	314.642	347.307	383.303	422.949	466.608	759.778	1228.165	1968.522
18	142.439	158.403	176.187	195.993	218.045	242.583	269.885	300.250	334.006	371.514	413.180	459.445	510.792	567.751	630.920	1064.689	1781.838	2953.783
19	173.351	194.251	217.710	244.031	273.556	306.654	343.754	385.321	431.868	483.968	542.266	607.467	680.354	761.786	852.741	1491.563	2584.665	4431.672
20	210.755	237.986	268.783	303.598	342.945	387.384	437.568	494.210	558.110	630.157	711.368	802.856	905.870	1021.792	1152.200	2089.188	3748.763	6648.508
21	256.013	291.343	331.603	377.461	429.681	489.104	556.710	633.589	720.962	820.204	932.891	1060.769	1205.807	1370.201	1556.470	2925.862	5436.703	9973.762
22	310.775	356.438	408.871	469.052	538.101	617.270	708.022	811.993	931.040	1067.265	1223.087	1401.215	1604.724	1837.068	2102.234	4097.203	7884.215	14961.645
23	377.038	435.854	503.911	582.624	673.626	778.760	900.187	1040.351	1202.042	1388.443	1603.243	1850.603	2135.282	2462.669	2839.014	5737.078	11433.109	22443.469
24	457.215	532.741	620.810	723.453	843.032	982.237	1144.237	1332.649	1551.634	1805.975	2101.247	2443.795	2840.924	3300.974	3833.667	8032.906	16579.008	33666.207
25	554.230	650.944	764.596	898.082	1054.791	1238.617	1454.180	1706.790	2002.608	2348.765	2753.631	3226.808	3779.428	4424.301	5176.445	11247.062	24040.555	50500.316
30	1445.111	1767.044	2160.459	2640.881	3227.172	3941.953	4812.891	5873.172	7162.785	8729.805	10632.543	12940.672	15737.945	19124.434	23221.258	60500.207	154105.313	383500.000
35	3755.814	4783.520	6090.227	7750.094	9856.746	12527.160	15909.480	20188.742	25596.512	32422.090	41028.887	51868.563	65504.199	82634.625	104134.500	325394.688	*	*
40	9749.141	12936.141	17153.691	22728.367	30088.621	39791.957	52570.707	69376.562	91447.375	120389.375	*	*	*	*	*	*	*	*
45	25294.223	34970.230	48300.660	66638.937	91831.312	126378.937	173692.875	238384.312	326686.375	447005.062	*	*	*	*	*	*	*	*

*Not shown because of space limitations.

Texas Instruments BA-35, BAII, BAII Plus[c]

Input	Function
1000	PMT
5	N
7	%i
	CPT
	FV

Solution
5750.74[d]

---

[c] For the Texas Instruments BAII, you would use the 2nd key instead of the CPT key; for the Texas Instruments BAII Plus, you would use the I/Y key instead of the %i key.

[d] If a minus sign precedes the output, it should be ignored.

TABLE A.3 Present-Value Interest Factors for One Dollar, *PVIF*

Period	1%	2%	3%	4%	5%	6%	7%	8%	9%	10%	11%	12%	13%	14%	15%	16%	17%	18%	19%	20%
1	.990	.980	.971	.962	.952	.943	.935	.926	.917	.909	.901	.893	.885	.877	.870	.862	.855	.847	.840	.833
2	.980	.961	.943	.925	.907	.890	.873	.857	.842	.826	.812	.797	.783	.769	.756	.743	.731	.718	.706	.694
3	.971	.942	.915	.889	.864	.840	.816	.794	.772	.751	.731	.712	.693	.675	.658	.641	.624	.609	.593	.579
4	.961	.924	.888	.855	.823	.792	.763	.735	.708	.683	.659	.636	.613	.592	.572	.552	.534	.516	.499	.482
5	.951	.906	.863	.822	.784	.747	.713	.681	.650	.621	.593	.567	.543	.519	.497	.476	.456	.437	.419	.402
6	.942	.888	.837	.790	.746	.705	.666	.630	.596	.564	.535	.507	.480	.456	.432	.410	.390	.370	.352	.335
7	.933	.871	.813	.760	.711	.665	.623	.583	.547	.513	.482	.452	.425	.400	.376	.354	.333	.314	.296	.279
8	.923	.853	.789	.731	.677	.627	.582	.540	.502	.467	.434	.404	.376	.351	.327	.305	.285	.266	.249	.233
9	.914	.837	.766	.703	.645	.592	.544	.500	.460	.424	.391	.361	.333	.308	.284	.263	.243	.225	.209	.194
10	.905	.820	.744	.676	.614	.558	.508	.463	.422	.386	.352	.322	.295	.270	.247	.227	.208	.191	.176	.162
11	.896	.804	.722	.650	.585	.527	.475	.429	.388	.350	.317	.287	.261	.237	.215	.195	.178	.162	.148	.135
12	.887	.789	.701	.625	.557	.497	.444	.397	.356	.319	.286	.257	.231	.208	.187	.168	.152	.137	.124	.112
13	.879	.773	.681	.601	.530	.469	.415	.368	.326	.290	.258	.229	.204	.182	.163	.145	.130	.116	.104	.093
14	.870	.758	.661	.577	.505	.442	.388	.340	.299	.263	.232	.205	.181	.160	.141	.125	.111	.099	.088	.078
15	.861	.743	.642	.555	.481	.417	.362	.315	.275	.239	.209	.183	.160	.140	.123	.108	.095	.084	.074	.065
16	.853	.728	.623	.534	.458	.394	.339	.292	.252	.218	.188	.163	.141	.123	.107	.093	.081	.071	.062	.054
17	.844	.714	.605	.513	.436	.371	.317	.270	.231	.198	.170	.146	.125	.108	.093	.080	.069	.060	.052	.045
18	.836	.700	.587	.494	.416	.350	.296	.250	.212	.180	.153	.130	.111	.095	.081	.069	.059	.051	.044	.038
19	.828	.686	.570	.475	.396	.331	.277	.232	.194	.164	.138	.116	.098	.083	.070	.060	.051	.043	.037	.031
20	.820	.673	.554	.456	.377	.312	.258	.215	.178	.149	.124	.104	.087	.073	.061	.051	.043	.037	.031	.026
21	.811	.660	.538	.439	.359	.294	.242	.199	.164	.135	.112	.093	.077	.064	.053	.044	.037	.031	.026	.022
22	.803	.647	.522	.422	.342	.278	.226	.184	.150	.123	.101	.083	.068	.056	.046	.038	.032	.026	.022	.018
23	.795	.634	.507	.406	.326	.262	.211	.170	.138	.112	.091	.074	.060	.049	.040	.033	.027	.022	.018	.015
24	.788	.622	.492	.390	.310	.247	.197	.158	.126	.102	.082	.066	.053	.043	.035	.028	.023	.019	.015	.013
25	.780	.610	.478	.375	.295	.233	.184	.146	.116	.092	.074	.059	.047	.038	.030	.024	.020	.016	.013	.010
30	.742	.552	.412	.308	.231	.174	.131	.099	.075	.057	.044	.033	.026	.020	.015	.012	.009	.007	.005	.004
35	.706	.500	.355	.253	.181	.130	.094	.068	.049	.036	.026	.019	.014	.010	.008	.006	.004	.003	.002	.002
40	.672	.453	.307	.208	.142	.097	.067	.046	.032	.022	.015	.011	.008	.005	.004	.003	.002	.001	.001	.001
45	.639	.410	.264	.171	.111	.073	.048	.031	.021	.014	.009	.006	.004	.003	.002	.001	.001	.001	*	*
50	.608	.372	.228	.141	.087	.054	.034	.021	.013	.009	.005	.003	.002	.001	.001	.001	*	*	*	*

PVIF is zero to three decimal places.

Using the Calculator to Compute the Present Value of a Single Amount

Before you begin, clear the memory, ensure that you are in the *end mode* and that your calculator is set for *one payment per year*, and set the number of decimal places that you want (usually two for dollar-related accuracy).

Sample Problem

You want to know the present value of $1,700 to be received at the end of 8 years, assuming an 8% discount rate.

Hewlett-Packard HP 12C, 17 BII, and 19 BII[a]

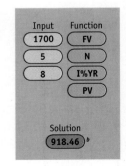

Input	Function
1700	FV
5	N
8	I%YR
	PV

Solution
918.46[b]

---

[a] For the 12C, you would use the `n` key instead of the `N` key, and the `i` key instead of the `I%YR` key.

[b] The minus sign that precedes the output should be ignored.

TABLE A.3 (Continued)

Period	21%	22%	23%	24%	25%	26%	27%	28%	29%	30%	31%	32%	33%	34%	35%	40%	45%	50%
1	.826	.820	.813	.806	.800	.794	.787	.781	.775	.769	.763	.758	.752	.746	.741	.714	.690	.667
2	.683	.672	.661	.650	.640	.630	.620	.610	.601	.592	.583	.574	.565	.557	.549	.510	.476	.444
3	.564	.551	.537	.524	.512	.500	.488	.477	.466	.455	.445	.435	.425	.416	.406	.364	.328	.296
4	.467	.451	.437	.423	.410	.397	.384	.373	.361	.350	.340	.329	.320	.310	.301	.260	.226	.198
5	.386	.370	.355	.341	.328	.315	.303	.291	.280	.269	.259	.250	.240	.231	.223	.186	.156	.132
6	.319	.303	.289	.275	.262	.250	.238	.227	.217	.207	.198	.189	.181	.173	.165	.133	.108	.088
7	.263	.249	.235	.222	.210	.198	.188	.178	.168	.159	.151	.143	.136	.129	.122	.095	.074	.059
8	.218	.204	.191	.179	.168	.157	.148	.139	.130	.123	.115	.108	.102	.096	.091	.068	.051	.039
9	.180	.167	.155	.144	.134	.125	.116	.108	.101	.094	.088	.082	.077	.072	.067	.048	.035	.026
10	.149	.137	.126	.116	.107	.099	.092	.085	.078	.073	.067	.062	.058	.054	.050	.035	.024	.017
11	.123	.112	.103	.094	.086	.079	.072	.066	.061	.056	.051	.047	.043	.040	.037	.025	.017	.012
12	.102	.092	.083	.076	.069	.062	.057	.052	.047	.043	.039	.036	.033	.030	.027	.018	.012	.008
13	.084	.075	.068	.061	.055	.050	.045	.040	.037	.033	.030	.027	.025	.022	.020	.013	.008	.005
14	.069	.062	.055	.049	.044	.039	.035	.032	.028	.025	.023	.021	.018	.017	.015	.009	.006	.003
15	.057	.051	.045	.040	.035	.031	.028	.025	.022	.020	.017	.016	.014	.012	.011	.006	.004	.002
16	.047	.042	.036	.032	.028	.025	.022	.019	.017	.015	.013	.012	.010	.009	.008	.005	.003	.002
17	.039	.034	.030	.026	.023	.020	.017	.015	.013	.012	.010	.009	.008	.007	.006	.003	.002	.001
18	.032	.028	.024	.021	.018	.016	.014	.012	.010	.009	.008	.007	.006	.005	.005	.002	.001	.001
19	.027	.023	.020	.017	.014	.012	.011	.009	.008	.007	.006	.005	.004	.004	.003	.002	.001	*
20	.022	.019	.016	.014	.012	.010	.008	.007	.006	.005	.005	.004	.003	.003	.002	.001	.001	*
21	.018	.015	.013	.011	.009	.008	.007	.006	.005	.004	.003	.003	.003	.002	.002	.001	*	*
22	.015	.013	.011	.009	.007	.006	.005	.004	.004	.003	.003	.002	.002	.002	.001	.001	*	*
23	.012	.010	.009	.007	.006	.005	.004	.003	.003	.002	.002	.002	.001	.001	.001	*	*	*
24	.010	.008	.007	.006	.005	.004	.003	.003	.002	.002	.002	.001	.001	.001	.001	*	*	*
25	.009	.007	.006	.005	.004	.003	.003	.002	.002	.001	.001	.001	.001	.001	.001	*	*	*
30	.003	.003	.002	.002	.001	.001	.001	.001	*	*	*	*	*	*	*	*	*	*
35	.001	.001	.001	.001	*	*	*	*	*	*	*	*	*	*	*	*	*	*
40	*	*	*	*	*	*	*	*	*	*	*	*	*	*	*	*	*	*
45	*	*	*	*	*	*	*	*	*	*	*	*	*	*	*	*	*	*
50	*	*	*	*	*	*	*	*	*	*	*	*	*	*	*	*	*	*

*PVIF is zero to three decimal places.

Texas Instruments BA-35, BAII, BAII Plus[c]

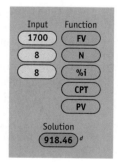

Input	Function
1700	FV
8	N
8	%i
	CPT
	PV
Solution	
918.46 [d]	

---

[c] For the Texas Instruments BAII, you would use the **2nd** key instead of the **CPT** key; for the Texas Instruments BAII Plus, you would use the **I/Y** key instead of the **%i** key.
[d] If a minus sign precedes the output, it should be ignored.

TABLE A.4 — Present-Value Interest Factors for a One-Dollar Annuity, *PVIFA*

Period	1%	2%	3%	4%	5%	6%	7%	8%	9%	10%	11%	12%	13%	14%	15%	16%	17%	18%	19%	20%
1	.990	.980	.971	.962	.952	.943	.935	.926	.917	.909	.901	.893	.885	.877	.870	.862	.855	.847	.840	.833
2	1.970	1.942	1.913	1.886	1.859	1.833	1.808	1.783	1.759	1.736	1.713	1.690	1.668	1.647	1.626	1.605	1.585	1.566	1.547	1.528
3	2.941	2.884	2.829	2.775	2.723	2.673	2.624	2.577	2.531	2.487	2.444	2.402	2.361	2.322	2.283	2.246	2.210	2.174	2.140	2.106
4	3.902	3.808	3.717	3.630	3.546	3.465	3.387	3.312	3.240	3.170	3.102	3.037	2.974	2.914	2.855	2.798	2.743	2.690	2.639	2.589
5	4.853	4.713	4.580	4.452	4.329	4.212	4.100	3.993	3.890	3.791	3.696	3.605	3.517	3.433	3.352	3.274	3.199	3.127	3.058	2.991
6	5.795	5.601	5.417	5.242	5.076	4.917	4.767	4.623	4.486	4.355	4.231	4.111	3.998	3.889	3.784	3.685	3.589	3.498	3.410	3.326
7	6.728	6.472	6.230	6.002	5.786	5.582	5.389	5.206	5.033	4.868	4.712	4.564	4.423	4.288	4.160	4.039	3.922	3.812	3.706	3.605
8	7.652	7.326	7.020	6.733	6.463	6.210	5.971	5.747	5.535	5.335	5.146	4.968	4.799	4.639	4.487	4.344	4.207	4.078	3.954	3.837
9	8.566	8.162	7.786	7.435	7.108	6.802	6.515	6.247	5.995	5.759	5.537	5.328	5.132	4.946	4.772	4.607	4.451	4.303	4.163	4.031
10	9.471	8.983	8.530	8.111	7.722	7.360	7.024	6.710	6.418	6.145	5.889	5.650	5.426	5.216	5.019	4.833	4.659	4.494	4.339	4.192
11	10.368	9.787	9.253	8.760	8.306	7.887	7.499	7.139	6.805	6.495	6.207	5.938	5.687	5.453	5.234	5.029	4.836	4.656	4.486	4.327
12	11.255	10.575	9.954	9.385	8.863	8.384	7.943	7.536	7.161	6.814	6.492	6.194	5.918	5.660	5.421	5.197	4.988	4.793	4.611	4.439
13	12.134	11.348	10.635	9.986	9.394	8.853	8.358	7.904	7.487	7.013	6.750	6.424	6.122	5.842	5.583	5.342	5.118	4.910	4.715	4.533
14	13.004	12.106	11.296	10.563	9.899	9.295	8.745	8.244	7.786	7.367	6.982	6.628	6.302	6.002	5.724	5.468	5.229	5.008	4.802	4.611
15	13.865	12.849	11.938	11.118	10.380	9.712	9.108	8.560	8.061	7.606	7.191	6.811	6.462	6.142	5.847	5.575	5.324	5.092	4.876	4.675
16	14.718	13.578	12.561	11.652	10.838	10.106	9.447	8.851	8.313	7.824	7.379	6.974	6.604	6.265	5.954	5.668	5.405	5.162	4.938	4.730
17	15.562	14.292	13.166	12.166	11.274	10.477	9.763	9.122	8.544	8.022	7.549	7.120	6.729	6.373	6.047	5.749	5.475	5.222	4.990	4.775
18	16.398	14.992	13.754	12.659	11.690	10.828	10.059	9.372	8.756	8.201	7.702	7.250	6.840	6.467	6.128	5.818	5.534	5.273	5.033	4.812
19	17.226	15.679	14.324	13.134	12.085	11.158	10.336	9.604	8.950	8.365	7.839	7.366	6.938	6.550	6.198	5.877	5.584	5.316	5.070	4.843
20	18.046	16.352	14.878	13.590	12.462	11.470	10.594	9.818	9.129	8.514	7.963	7.469	7.025	6.623	6.259	5.929	5.628	5.353	5.101	4.870
21	18.857	17.011	15.415	14.029	12.821	11.764	10.836	10.017	9.292	8.649	8.075	7.562	7.102	6.687	6.312	5.973	5.665	5.384	5.127	4.891
22	19.661	17.658	15.937	14.451	13.163	12.042	11.061	10.201	9.442	8.772	8.176	7.645	7.170	6.743	6.359	6.011	5.696	5.410	5.149	4.909
23	20.456	18.292	16.444	14.857	13.489	12.303	11.272	10.371	9.580	8.883	8.266	7.718	7.230	6.792	6.399	6.044	5.723	5.432	5.167	4.925
24	21.244	18.914	16.936	15.247	13.799	12.550	11.469	10.529	9.707	8.985	8.348	7.784	7.283	6.835	6.434	6.073	5.746	5.451	5.182	4.937
25	22.023	19.524	17.413	15.622	14.094	12.783	11.654	10.675	9.823	9.077	8.422	7.843	7.330	6.873	6.464	6.097	5.766	5.467	5.195	4.948
30	25.808	22.396	19.601	17.292	15.373	13.765	12.409	11.258	10.274	9.427	8.694	8.055	7.496	7.003	6.566	6.177	5.829	5.517	5.235	4.979
35	29.409	24.999	21.487	18.665	16.374	14.498	12.948	11.655	10.567	9.644	8.855	8.176	7.586	7.070	6.617	6.215	5.858	5.539	5.251	4.992
40	32.835	27.356	23.115	19.793	17.159	15.046	13.332	11.925	10.757	9.779	8.951	8.244	7.634	7.105	6.642	6.233	5.871	5.548	5.258	4.997
45	36.095	29.490	24.519	20.720	17.774	15.456	13.606	12.108	10.881	9.863	9.008	8.283	7.661	7.123	6.654	6.242	5.877	5.552	5.261	4.999
50	39.196	31.424	25.730	21.482	18.256	15.762	13.801	12.233	10.962	9.915	9.042	8.304	7.675	7.133	6.661	6.246	5.880	5.554	5.262	4.999

Using the Calculator to Compute the Present Value of an Annuity

Before you begin, clear the memory, ensure that you are in the *end mode* and that your calculator is set for *one payment per year*, and set the number of decimal places that you want (usually two for dollar-related accuracy).

Sample Problem

You want to know what the present value of an annuity of $700 per year received at the end of each year for 5 years will be, given a discount rate of 8%.

Hewlett-Packard HP 12C, 17 BII, and 19 BII[a]

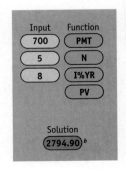

Input	Function
700	PMT
5	N
8	I%YR
	PV

Solution
2794.90[b]

---

[a] For the 12C, you would use the **n** key instead of the **N** key, and the **i** key instead of the **I%YR** key.

[b] The minus sign that precedes the output should be ignored.

TABLE A.4 (Continued)

Period	21%	22%	23%	24%	25%	26%	27%	28%	29%	30%	31%	32%	33%	34%	35%	40%	45%	50%
1	.826	.820	.813	.806	.800	.794	.787	.781	.775	.769	.763	.758	.752	.746	.741	.714	.690	.667
2	1.509	1.492	1.474	1.457	1.440	1.424	1.407	1.392	1.376	1.361	1.346	1.331	1.317	1.303	1.289	1.224	1.165	1.111
3	2.074	2.042	2.011	1.981	1.952	1.923	1.896	1.868	1.842	1.816	1.791	1.766	1.742	1.719	1.696	1.589	1.493	1.407
4	2.540	2.494	2.448	2.404	2.362	2.320	2.280	2.241	2.203	2.166	2.130	2.096	2.062	2.029	1.997	1.849	1.720	1.605
5	2.926	2.864	2.803	2.745	2.689	2.635	2.583	2.532	2.483	2.436	2.390	2.345	2.302	2.260	2.220	2.035	1.876	1.737
6	3.245	3.167	3.092	3.020	2.951	2.885	2.821	2.759	2.700	2.643	2.588	2.534	2.483	2.433	2.385	2.168	1.983	1.824
7	3.508	3.416	3.327	3.242	3.161	3.083	3.009	2.937	2.868	2.802	2.739	2.677	2.619	2.562	2.508	2.263	2.057	1.883
8	3.726	3.619	3.518	3.421	3.329	3.241	3.156	3.076	2.999	2.925	2.854	2.786	2.721	2.658	2.598	2.331	2.109	1.922
9	3.905	3.786	3.673	3.566	3.463	3.366	3.273	3.184	3.100	3.019	2.942	2.868	2.798	2.730	2.665	2.379	2.144	1.948
10	4.054	3.923	3.799	3.682	3.570	3.465	3.364	3.269	3.178	3.092	3.009	2.930	2.855	2.784	2.715	2.414	2.168	1.965
11	4.177	4.035	3.902	3.776	3.656	3.544	3.437	3.335	3.239	3.147	3.060	2.978	2.899	2.824	2.752	2.438	2.185	1.977
12	4.278	4.127	3.985	3.851	3.725	3.606	3.493	3.387	3.286	3.190	3.100	3.013	2.931	2.853	2.779	2.456	2.196	1.985
13	4.362	4.203	4.053	3.912	3.780	3.656	3.538	3.427	3.322	3.223	3.129	3.040	2.956	2.876	2.799	2.469	2.204	1.990
14	4.432	4.265	4.108	3.962	3.824	3.695	3.573	3.459	3.351	3.249	3.152	3.061	2.974	2.892	2.814	2.478	2.210	1.993
15	4.489	4.315	4.153	4.001	3.859	3.726	3.601	3.483	3.373	3.268	3.170	3.076	2.988	2.905	2.825	2.484	2.214	1.995
16	4.536	4.357	4.189	4.033	3.887	3.751	3.623	3.503	3.390	3.283	3.183	3.088	2.999	2.914	2.834	2.489	2.216	1.997
17	4.576	4.391	4.219	4.059	3.910	3.771	3.640	3.518	3.403	3.295	3.193	3.097	3.007	2.921	2.840	2.492	2.218	1.998
18	4.608	4.419	4.243	4.080	3.928	3.786	3.654	3.529	3.413	3.304	3.201	3.104	3.012	2.926	2.844	2.494	2.219	1.999
19	4.635	4.442	4.263	4.097	3.942	3.799	3.664	3.539	3.421	3.311	3.207	3.109	3.017	2.930	2.848	2.496	2.220	1.999
20	4.657	4.460	4.279	4.110	3.954	3.808	3.673	3.546	3.427	3.316	3.211	3.113	3.020	2.933	2.850	2.497	2.221	1.999
21	4.675	4.476	4.292	4.121	3.963	3.816	3.679	3.551	3.432	3.320	3.215	3.116	3.023	2.935	2.852	2.498	2.221	2.000
22	4.690	4.488	4.302	4.130	3.970	3.822	3.684	3.556	3.436	3.323	3.217	3.118	3.025	2.936	2.853	2.498	2.222	2.000
23	4.703	4.499	4.311	4.137	3.976	3.827	3.689	3.559	3.438	3.325	3.219	3.120	3.026	2.938	2.854	2.499	2.222	2.000
24	4.713	4.507	4.318	4.143	3.981	3.831	3.692	3.562	3.441	3.327	3.221	3.121	3.027	2.939	2.855	2.499	2.222	2.000
25	4.721	4.514	4.323	4.147	3.985	3.834	3.694	3.564	3.442	3.329	3.222	3.122	3.028	2.939	2.856	2.499	2.222	2.000
30	4.746	4.534	4.339	4.160	3.995	3.842	3.701	3.569	3.447	3.332	3.225	3.124	3.030	2.941	2.857	2.500	2.222	2.000
35	4.756	4.541	4.345	4.164	3.998	3.845	3.703	3.571	3.448	3.333	3.226	3.125	3.030	2.941	2.857	2.500	2.222	2.000
40	4.760	4.544	4.347	4.166	3.999	3.846	3.703	3.571	3.448	3.333	3.226	3.125	3.030	2.941	2.857	2.500	2.222	2.000
45	4.761	4.545	4.347	4.166	4.000	3.846	3.704	3.571	3.448	3.333	3.226	3.125	3.030	2.941	2.857	2.500	2.222	2.000
50	4.762	4.545	4.348	4.167	4.000	3.846	3.704	3.571	3.448	3.333	3.226	3.125	3.030	2.941	2.857	2.500	2.222	2.000

Texas Instruments BA-35, BAII, BAII Plus[c]

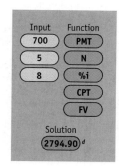

[c] For the Texas Instruments BAII, you would use the 2nd key instead of the CPT key; for the Texas Instruments BAII Plus, you would use the I/Y key instead of the %i key.

[d] If a minus sign precedes the output, it should be ignored.

CREDITS

INDEX